The O'Leary Series

Microsoft®
Office XP

Volume I

The O'Leary Series

Microsoft® Office XP

Volume I

Timothy J. O'Leary

Arizona State University

Linda I. O'Leary

InformationTechnology

Boston Burr Ridge, IL Dubuque, IA Madison, WI New York
San Francisco St. Louis Bangkok Bogotá Caracas Kuala Lumpur
Lisbon London Madrid Mexico City Milan Montreal New Delhi
Santiago Seoul Singapore Sydney Taipei Toronto

McGraw-Hill Higher Education

*A Division of The **McGraw-Hill** Companies*

THE O'LEARY SERIES: MICROSOFT® OFFICE XP, VOLUME I
Published by McGraw-Hill/Irwin, an imprint of the McGraw-Hill Companies, Inc. 1221 Avenue of the Americas, New York, NY, 10020. Copyright © 2002 by the McGraw-Hill Companies, Inc. All rights reserved. No part of this publication may be reproduced or distributed in any form or by any means, or stored in a database or retrieval system, without the prior written consent of The McGraw-Hill Companies, Inc., including, but not limited to, in any network or other electronic storage or transmission, or broadcast for distance learning.

Some ancillaries, including electronic and print components, may not be available to customers outside the United States.

This book is printed on acid-free paper.

domestic   4 5 6 7 8 9 0 QPD/QPD 0 9 8 7 6 5 4 3 2
international   1 2 3 4 5 6 7 8 9 0 QPD/QPD 0 9 8 7 6 5 4 3 2 1

ISBN 0-07-247247-2

Publisher: *George Werthman*
Developmental editor: *Alexandra Arnold*
Senior marketing manager: *Jeffrey Parr*
Project manager: *James Labeots*
Manager, new book production: *Melonie Salvati*
Media producer: *David Barrick*
Freelance design coordinator: *Gino Cieslik*
Lead supplement coordinator: *Marc Mattson*
Photo research coordinator: *David A. Tietz*
Cover & interior design: *Maureen McCutcheon*
Cover image: *Digitalvision*
Typeface: *10.5/13 New Aster*
Compositor: *Rogondino & Associates*
Printer: *Quebecor World Dubuque Inc.*

Library of Congress Control Number 2001092430

INTERNATIONAL EDITION ISBN 0-07-112475-6

www.mhhe.com

InformationTechnology

Information Technology at McGraw-Hill/Irwin

At McGraw-Hill Higher Education, we publish instructional materials targeted at the higher education market. In an effort to expand the tools of higher learning, we publish texts, lab manuals, study guides, testing materials, software, and multimedia products.

At McGraw-Hill/Irwin (a division of McGraw-Hill Higher Education), we realize that technology has created and will continue to create new mediums for professors and students to use in managing resources and communicating information to one another. We strive to provide the most flexible and complete teaching and learning tools available as well as offer solutions to the changing world of teaching and learning.

McGraw-Hill/Irwin is dedicated to providing the tools for today's instructors and students to successfully navigate the world of Information Technology.

- **Seminar Series** McGraw-Hill/Irwin's Technology Connection seminar series offered across the country every year demonstrates the latest technology products and encourages collaboration among teaching professionals.

- **McGraw-Hill/Osborne** This division of The McGraw-Hill Companies is known for its best-selling Internet titles, *Internet & Web Yellow Pages* and the *Internet Complete Reference*. For more information, visit Osborne at **www.osborne.com**.

- **Digital Solutions** McGraw-Hill/Irwin is committed to publishing digital solutions. Taking your course online doesn't have to be a solitary adventure, nor does it have to be a difficult one. We offer several solutions that will allow you to enjoy all the benefits of having your course material online.

- **Packaging Options** For more information about our discount options, contact your McGraw-Hill/Irwin Sales representative at 1-800-338-3987 or visit our web site at **www.mhhe.com/it**.

Brief Contents

Detailed Contents

WORD

Lab 3 Creating Reports and Tables WD3.1

EXCEL

Lab 2 — Charting Worksheet Data EX2.1

Lab 3 — Managing and Analyzing a Workbook EX3.1

ACCESS

Overview to Access 2002 — ACO.1

Lab 1 — Creating a Database — AC1.1

Acknowledgments

The new edition of The O'Leary Series has been made possible only through the enthusiasm and dedication of a great team of people. Because the team spans the country, literally from coast to coast, we have utilized every means of working together including conference calls, FAX, e-mail, and document collaboration. We have truly tested the team approach and it works!

Leading the team from McGraw-Hill/Irwin are George Werthman, Publisher and Alexandra Arnold, Developmental Editor. Their renewed commitment, direction, and support have infused the team with the excitement of a new project.

The production staff is headed by James Labeots, Project Manager, whose planning and attention to detail has made it possible for us to successfully meet a very challenging schedule. Members of the production team include: Gino Cieslik, Designer; Pat Rogondino, Compositor; Susan Defosset, Copy Editor; Melonie Salvati, Production Supervisor; Marc Mattson, Supplement Coordinator; and David Barrick, Media Producer. We would particularly like to thank Pat and Susan—team members for many past editions whom we can always depend on to do a great job.

Finally, we are particularly grateful to a small but very dedicated group of people who helped us develop the manuscript. Colleen Hayes, Susan Demar, and Kathy Duggan have helped on the last several editions and continue to provide excellent developmental and technical support. To Steve Willis and Carol Cooper who provide technical expertise, youthful perspective, and enthusiasm, my thanks for helping get the manuscripts out the door and meeting the deadlines.

Preface

Introduction

The 20th century not only brought the dawn of the Information Age, but also rapid changes in information technology. There is no indication that this rapid rate of change will be slowing— it may even be increasing. As we begin the 21st century, computer literacy will undoubtedly become prerequisite for whatever career a student chooses. The goal of the O'Leary Series is to assist students in attaining the necessary skills to efficiently use these applications. Equally important is the goal to provide a foundation for students to readily and easily learn to use future versions of this software. This series does this by providing detailed step-by step instructions combined with careful selection and presentation of essential concepts.

About the Authors

Tim and Linda O'Leary live in the American Southwest and spend much of their time engaging instructors and students in conversation about learning. In fact, they have been talking about learning for more than 25 years. Something in those early conversations convinced them to write a book, to bring their interest in the learning process to the printed page. Today, they are as concerned as ever about learning, about technology, and about the challenges of presenting material in new ways, both in terms of content and the method of delivery.

A powerful and creative team, Tim combines his years of classroom teaching experience with Linda's background as a consultant and corporate trainer. Tim has taught courses at Stark Technical College in Canton, Ohio, Rochester Institute of Technology in upper New York state, and is currently a professor at Arizona State University in Tempe, Arizona. Tim and Linda have talked to and taught students from ages 8 to 80, all of them with a desire to learn something about computers and the applications that make their lives easier, more interesting, and more productive.

About the Book

Times are changing, technology is changing, and this text is changing, too. Do you think the students of today are different from yesterday? There is no doubt about it—they are. On the positive side, it is amazing how much effort students will put toward things they are convinced are relevant to them. Their effort directed at learning application programs and exploring the Web seems at times limitless. On the other hand, students can often be shortsighted, thinking that learning the skills to use the application is the only objective. The mission of the series is to build upon and extend this interest by not only teaching the specific application skills but by introducing the concepts that are common to all applications, providing students with the confidence, knowledge, and ability to easily learn the next generation of applications.

What's New in This Edition?

- **Introduction to Computer Essentials**—A brief introduction to the basics of computer hardware and software (Appears in Office XP, Volume I only).

- **Introduction to Windows 2000**—Two hands-on labs devoted to Windows 2000 basics (Appears in Office XP, Volume I only).

- **Introduction to the WWW: Internet Explorer and E-mail**—Hands-on introductions for using Internet Explorer to browse the WWW and using e-mail (Appears in Office XP, Volume I only).

- **Topic Reorganization**—The text has been reorganized to include main and subtopic heads by grouping related tasks. For example, tasks such as changing fonts and applying character effects appear under the "Formatting" topic head. This results in a slightly more reference-like approach, making it easier for students to refer back to the text to review. This has been done without losing the logical and realistic development of the case.

- **Clarified Marginal Notes**—Marginal notes have been enhanced by more clearly identifying the note content with box heads and the use of different colors.

    Additional Information—Brief asides with expanded discussion of features.

    Having Trouble?—Procedural tips advising students of possible problems and how to overcome.

    Another Method—Alternative methods of performing a procedure.

- **Larger Screen Figures**—Make it easier to identify elements and read screen content.

- All **Numbered Steps** and bullets appear in left margin space making it easy not to miss a step.

- A **MOUS (*Microsoft Office User Specialist*) Skills** table, appearing at the end of each lab, contains page references to MOUS skills learned in the lab.

- **Two New References** are included at the end of each text.

    Data File List—Helps organize all data and solution files.

    MOUS (*Microsoft Office User Specialist*) Skills—Links all MOUS objectives to text content and end-of-chapter exercises.

Same Great Features as the Office 2000 Series

- **Relevant Cases**—Four separate running cases demonstrate the features in each application. Topics are of interest to students—At Arizona State University, over 600 students were surveyed to find out what topics are of interest to them.

- **Focus on Concepts**—Each chapter focuses on the concepts behind the application. Students learn the essentials, so they can succeed regardless of the software package they might be using.

- **Steps**—Numbered procedural steps clearly identify each hands-on task needed to complete the step.

- **Screens**—Plentiful screen illustrations illustrate the completion of each numbered step to help students stay on track.

- **Callouts**—Meaningful screen callouts identify the results of the steps as well as reinforce the associated concept.

- **End-of-Chapter Material**

    Terminology—Questions and exercises test recall of the basic information and terminology in the lab.

    - Screen Identification
    - Matching
    - Multiple Choice

    Concepts—Questions and exercises review students' understanding of concepts and ability to integrate ideas presented in different parts of the lab.

    - Fill-In
    - Discussion Questions

    Hands-On Practice Exercises—Students apply the skills and concepts they learned to solve case-based exercises. Many cases in the practice exercises tie to a running case used in another application lab. This helps to demonstrate the use of the four applications across a common case setting. For example, the Adventure Travel Tours case used in the Word labs is continued in practice exercises in Excel, Access, and PowerPoint.

    - Step-by-Step
    - On Your Own
    - On The Web

- **Rating System**—The 3-star rating system identifies the difficulty level of each practice exercise in the end-of-chapter materials.

- **Working Together Labs**—At the completion of the brief and introductory texts, a final lab demonstrates the integration of the MS Office applications and the WWW.

Instructor's Guide

We understand that, in today's teaching environment, offering a textbook alone is not sufficient to meet the needs of the many instructors who use our books. To teach effectively, instructors must have a full complement of supplemental resources to assist them in every facet of teaching from preparing for class, to conducting a lecture, to assessing students' comprehension. *The O'Leary Series* offers a fully-integrated supplements package and Web site, as described below.

Instructor's Resource Kit

The **Instructor's Resource Kit** contains a computerized Test Bank, an Instructor's Manual, and PowerPoint Presentation Slides. Features of the Instructor's Resource Kit are described below.

- **Instructor's Manual** The Instructor's Manual contains lab objectives, concepts, outlines, lecture notes, and command summaries. Also included are answers to all end-of chapter material, tips for covering difficult materials, additional exercises, and a schedule showing how much time is required to cover text material.

- **Computerized Test Bank** The test bank contains over 1,300 multiple choice, true/false, and discussion questions. Each question will be accompanied by the correct answer, the level of learning difficulty, and corresponding page references. Our flexible Diploma software allows you to easily generate custom exams.

- **PowerPoint Presentation Slides** The presentation slides will include lab objectives, concepts, outlines, text figures, and speaker's notes. Also included are bullets to illustrate key terms and FAQs.

Online Learning Center/Web Site

Found at **www.mhhe.com/oleary**, this site provides additional learning and instructional tools to enhance the comprehension of the text. The OLC/Web Site is divided into these three areas:

- **Information Center** Contains core information about the text, supplements, and the authors.

- **Instructor Center** Offers instructional materials, downloads, additional exercises, and other relevant links for professors.

- **Student Center** Contains data files, chapter competencies, chapter concepts, self-quizzes, flashcards, projects, animations, additional Web links, and more.

Skills Assessment

SimNet (Simulated Network Assessment Product) provides a way for you to test students' software skills in a simulated environment. SimNet is available for Microsoft Office 97, Microsoft Office 2000, and Microsoft Office XP. SimNet provides flexibility for you in your course by offering:

- Pre-testing options
- Post-testing options
- Course placement testing
- Diagnostic capabilities to reinforce skills
- Proficiency testing to measure skills
- Web or LAN delivery of tests.
- Computer-based training tutorials (new for Office XP)
- MOUS preparation exams

For more information on skills assessment software, please contact your local sales representative, or visit us at **www.mhhe.com/it**.

Digital Solutions to Help You Manage Your Course

PageOut is our Course Web Site Development Center that offers a syllabus page, URL, McGraw-Hill Online Learning Center content, online exercises and quizzes, gradebook, discussion board, and an area for student Web pages.

Available free with any McGraw-Hill/Irwin product, PageOut requires no prior knowledge of HTML, no long hours of coding, and a way for course coordinators and professors to provide a full-course web site. PageOut offers a series of templates—simply fill them with your course information and click on one of 16 designs. The process takes under an hour and leaves you with a professionally designed Web site. We'll even get you started with sample web sites, or enter your syllabus for you! PageOut is so straightforward and intuitive, it's little wonder why over 12,000 college professors are using it. For more information, visit the PageOut Web site at **www.pageout.net**.

Online courses are also available. Online Learning Centers (OLCs) are your perfect solutions for Internet-based content. Simply put, these Centers are "digital cartridges" that contain a book's pedagogy and supplements. As students read the book, they can go online and take self-grading quizzes or work through interactive exercises. These also provide students appropriate access to lecture materials and other key supplements.

Online Learning Centers can be delivered through any of these platforms:

McGraw-Hill Learning Architecture (TopClass)

Blackboard.com

Ecollege.com (formerly Real Education)

WebCT (a product of Universal Learning Technology)

McGraw-Hill has partnerships with WebCT and Blackboard to make it even easier to take your course online. Now you can have McGraw-Hill content delivered through the leading Internet-based learning tool for higher education. At McGraw-Hill, we have the following service agreements with WebCT and Blackboard:

Instructor Advantage Instructor Advantage is a special level of service McGraw-Hill offers in conjuction with WebCT designed to help you get up and running with your new course. A team of specialists will be immediately available to ensure everything runs smoothly through the life of your adoption.

Instructor Advantage Plus Qualified McGraw-Hill adopters will be eligible for an even higher level of service. A certified WebCT or Blackboard specialist will provide a full day of on-site training for you and your staff. You will then have unlimited e-mail and phone support through the life of your adoption. Please contact your local McGraw-Hill representative for more details.

Technology Connection Seminar Series

McGraw-Hill/Irwin's Technology Connection seminar series offered across the country every year demonstrates the latest technology products and encourages collaboration among teaching professionals.

Computing Essentials

Available alone, or packaged with the O'Leary Series, *Computing Essentials* offers a unique, visual orientation that gives students a basic understanding of computing concepts. *Computing Essentials* is one of the few books on the market that is written by a professor who still teaches the course every semester and loves it! While combining current topics and technology into a highly illustrated design geared to catch students' interest and motivate them in their learning, this text provides an accurate snapshot of computing today. When bundled with software application lab manuals, students are given a complete representation of the fundamental issues surrounding the personal computing environment.

The text includes the following features:

- **A "Learn By Doing" approach** encourages students to engage in activity that is more interactive than the traditional learning pattern students typically follow in a concepts course. The exercises, explorations, visual orientation, inclusion of screen shots and numbered steps, and integrated internet references combine several methods to achieve an interactive learning environment for optimum reinforcement.

- **Making IT Work For You** sections visually demonstrate how technology is used in everyday life. Topics covered include how find a job online and how to protect a computer against viruses. These "gallery" style boxes combine text and art to take students step-by-step through technological processes that are both interesting and useful. As an added bonus, the *CE 2001-2002 Making IT Work Video Series* has been created to compliment the topics presented throughout the text.

- **On the Web Explorations** appear throughout the margins of the text and encourage students to go to the Web to visit several informative and established sites in order to learn more about the chapter's featured topic.

- **On the Web Exercises** present thought-provoking questions that allow students to construct articles and summaries for additional practice on topics relevant to that chapter while utilizing Web resources for further research. These exercises serve as additional reinforcement of the chapter's pertinent material while also allowing students to gain more familiarity with the Web.

- **A Look to the Future** sections provide insightful information about the future impact of technology and forecasts of how upcoming enhancements in the world of computing will play an important and powerful role in society.

- **Colorful Visual Summaries**, appearing at the end of every chapter, provide dynamic, graphical reviews of the important lessons featured in each chapter for additional reinforcement.

- **End-of-Chapter Review** material follows a three-level format and includes exercises that encourage students to review terms, concepts, and applications of concepts. Through matching, true/false, multiple choice, short answer completion, concept matching, and critical thinking questions, students have multiple review opportunities.

PowerWeb

PowerWeb is an exciting new online product available from McGraw-Hill. A nominally priced token grants students access through our web site to a wealth of resources—all corresponding to computer literacy. Features include an interactive glossary; current events with quizzing, assessment, and measurement options; Web survey; links to related text content; and WWW searching capability via Northern Lights, an academic search engine. Visit the PowerWeb site at **www.dushkin.com/powerweb**.

Interactive Companion CD-ROM

This free student CD-ROM, designed for use in class, in the lab, or at home by students and professors alike, includes a collection of interactive tutorial labs on some of the most popular and difficult topics in information technology. By combining video, interactive exercises, animation, additional content, and actual "lab" tutorials, we expand the reach and scope of the textbook. The lab titles are listed below.

- Binary Numbers
- Basic Programming
- Computer Anatomy
- Disk Fragmentation
- E-mail Essentials
- Multimedia Tools
- Workplace Issues (ergonomics/privacy/security)
- Introduction to Databases
- Programming II
- Network Communications
- Purchasing Decisions
- User Interfaces
- File Organization
- Word Processing and Spreadsheets
- Internet Overview
- Photo Editing
- Presentation Techniques
- Computer Troubleshooting
- Programming Overview
- SQL Queries

Student's Guide

As you begin each lab, take a few moments to read the **Case Study** and the **Concept Overview**. The case study introduces a real-life setting that is interwoven throughout the entire lab, providing the basis for understanding the use of the application. Also, notice the **Additional Information**, **Having Trouble?**, and **Another Method** boxes scattered throughout the book. These tips provide more information about related topics, help to get you out of trouble if you are having problems and offer suggestions on other ways to perform the same task. Finally, read the text between the steps. You will find the few minutes more it takes you is well worth the time when you are completing the practice exercises.

Many learning aids are built into the text to ensure your success with the material and to make the process of learning rewarding. The pages that follow call your attention to the key features in the text.

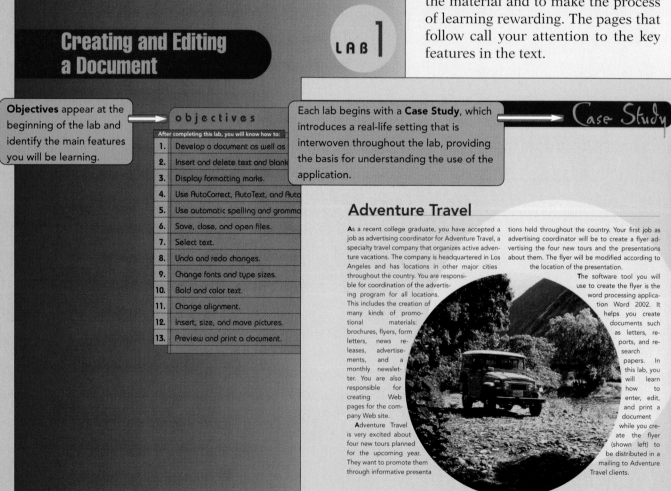

Creating and Editing a Document

LAB 1

Objectives appear at the beginning of the lab and identify the main features you will be learning.

objectives

After completing this lab, you will know how to:

1.	Develop a document as well as
2.	Insert and delete text and blank
3.	Display formatting marks.
4.	Use AutoCorrect, AutoText, and Auto
5.	Use automatic spelling and gramma
6.	Save, close, and open files.
7.	Select text.
8.	Undo and redo changes.
9.	Change fonts and type sizes.
10.	Bold and color text.
11.	Change alignment.
12.	Insert, size, and move pictures.
13.	Preview and print a document.

Each lab begins with a **Case Study**, which introduces a real-life setting that is interwoven throughout the lab, providing the basis for understanding the use of the application.

Case Study

Adventure Travel

As a recent college graduate, you have accepted a job as advertising coordinator for Adventure Travel, a specialty travel company that organizes active adventure vacations. The company is headquartered in Los Angeles and has locations in other major cities throughout the country. You are responsible for coordination of the advertising program for all locations. This includes the creation of many kinds of promotional materials: brochures, flyers, form letters, news releases, advertisements, and a monthly newsletter. You are also responsible for creating Web pages for the company Web site.

Adventure Travel is very excited about four new tours planned for the upcoming year. They want to promote them through informative presenta

tions held throughout the country. Your first job as advertising coordinator will be to create a flyer advertising the four new tours and the presentations about them. The flyer will be modified according to the location of the presentation.

The software tool you will use to create the flyer is the word processing application Word 2002. It helps you create documents such as letters, reports, and research papers. In this lab, you will learn how to enter, edit, and print a document while you create the flyer (shown left) to be distributed in a mailing to Adventure Travel clients.

Using Word Wrap

Now you will continue entering more of the paragraph. As you type, when the text gets close to the right margin, do not press ↵Enter to move to the next line. Word will automatically wrap words to the next line as needed.

> The **Concepts** that are common to all applications are emphasized— providing you with the confidence, knowledge, and ability to easily learn the next generation of applications.

① ● Press →.

● Type: about some of the earth's greatest unspoiled habitats and to find out how you can experience the adventure of a lifetime.

Your screen should be similar to Figure 1.22

HAVING TROUBLE?
Do not worry about typing errors as you enter this text. You will correct them shortly.

> **Having Trouble?** notes help resolve potential problems as you work through each lab.

The program has wrapped the text that would overlap the beginning of the next line. You will continue the par a second sentence.

① ● Click ☒ Close Window in the menu bar.

Another Method
The menu equivalent is File/Close and the keyboard shortcut is Ctrl + F4.

Your screen should be similar to Figure 1.28

> **Another Method** notes offer additional ways to perform a procedure.

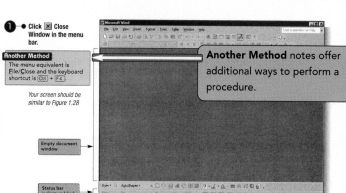

Figure 1.28

Because you did not make any changes to the document since saving it, the document window is closed immediately. If you had made additional changes, Word would ask if you wanted to save the file before closing it. This prevents the accidental closing of a file that has not been saved first. Now the Word window displays an empty document window, and the status bar indicators are blank because there are no open documents.

Opening a File

You asked your assistant to enter the remaining information in the flyer for you while you attended the meeting. Upon your return, you find a note from your assistant on your desk. The note explains that he had a little trouble entering the information and tells you that he saved the revised file as Flyer2. You want to open the file and continue working on the flyer.

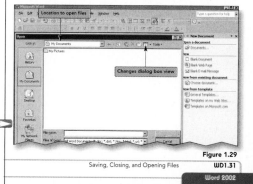

Figure 1.29

① ● Move to Z (second line of paragraph below tour list).

● Drag to the right until all the text including the space before the word "locations" is highlighted.

HAVING TROUBLE?
Hold down the left mouse button while moving the mouse to drag.

Additional Information
When you start dragging over a word, the entire word including the space after it is automatically selected.

Your screen should be similar to Figure 1.41

> Clear **Step-by-Step Instructions** detail how to complete a task, or series of tasks.

> **Additional Information** notes offer brief asides with expanded coverage of content.

Figure 1.41

The ch be mo remov

② ● Press Delete.

> **Screen captures** and **callouts** to features show how your screen should look at the completion of a step.

You also decide to delete the entire last sentence of the paragraph. You can quickly select a standard block of text. Standard blocks include a sentence, paragraph, page, tabular column, rectangular portion of text, or the entire document. The following table summarizes the techniques used to select standard blocks.

To Select	Procedure
Word	Double-click in the word.
Sentence	Press Ctrl and click within the sentence.
Line	Click to the left of a line when the mouse pointer is ↗.
Multiple lines	Drag up or down to the left of a line when the mouse pointer is ↗.
Paragraph	Triple-click on the paragraph or double-click to the left of the paragraph when the mouse pointer is a ↗.
Multiple paragraphs	Drag to the left of the paragraphs when the mouse pointer is ↗.
Document	Triple-click or press Ctrl and click to the left of the text when the mouse pointer is ↗.
	Use Edit/Select All or the keyboard shortcut Ctrl + Alt.

> **Tables** provide quick summaries of toolbar buttons, key terms, and procedures for specific tasks.

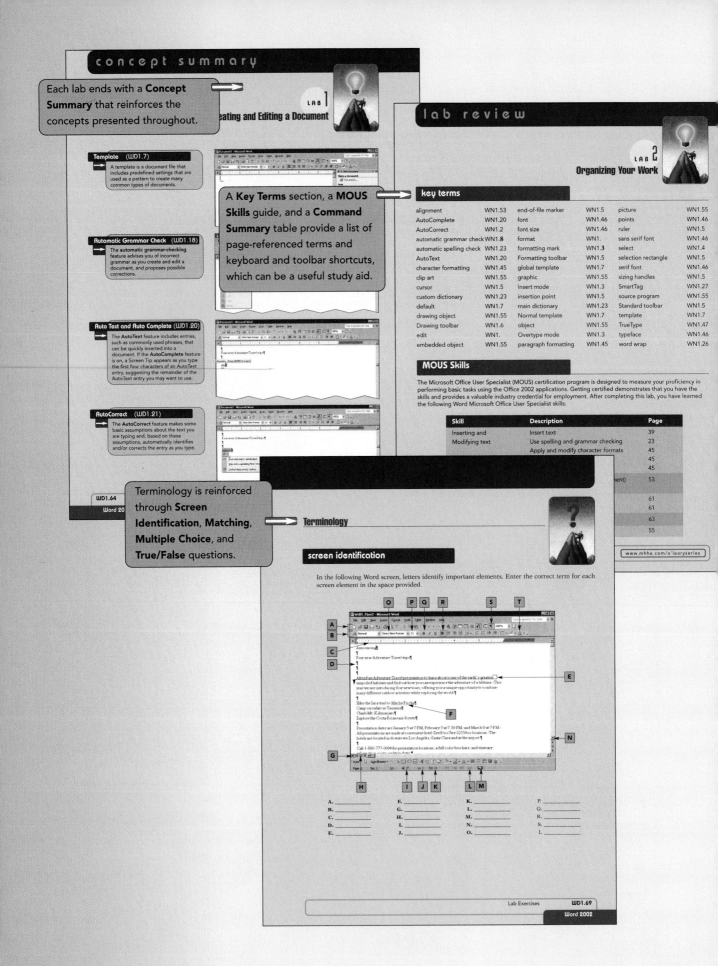

Each lab ends with a **Concept Summary** that reinforces the concepts presented throughout.

LAB 1

Creating and Editing a Document

Template (WD1.7)

A template is a document file that includes predefined settings that are used as a pattern to create many common types of documents.

A **Key Terms** section, a **MOUS Skills** guide, and a **Command Summary** table provide a list of page-referenced terms and keyboard and toolbar shortcuts, which can be a useful study aid.

Automatic Grammar Check (WD1.18)

The automatic grammar-checking feature advises you of incorrect grammar as you create and edit a document, and proposes possible corrections.

Auto Text and Auto Complete (WD1.20)

The AutoText feature includes entries, such as commonly used phrases, that can be quickly inserted into a document. If the **AutoComplete** feature is on, a Screen Tip appears as you type the first four characters of an AutoText entry, suggesting the remainder of the AutoText entry you may want to use.

AutoCorrect (WD1.21)

The AutoCorrect feature makes some basic assumptions about the text you are typing and, based on these assumptions, automatically identifies and/or corrects the entry as you type.

WD1.64

Word 20

Terminology is reinforced through **Screen Identification**, **Matching**, **Multiple Choice**, and **True/False** questions.

LAB 2

Organizing Your Work

alignment	WN1.53	end-of-file marker	WN1.5	picture	WN1.55
AutoComplete	WN1.20	font	WN1.46	points	WN1.46
AutoCorrect	WN1.2	font size	WN1.46	ruler	WN1.5
automatic grammar check	WN1.8	format	WN1.	sans serif font	WN1.46
automatic spelling check	WN1.23	formatting mark	WN1.3	select	WN1.4
AutoText	WN1.20	Formatting toolbar	WN1.5	selection rectangle	WN1.5
character formatting	WN1.45	global template	WN1.7	serif font	WN1.46
clip art	WN1.55	graphic	WN1.55	sizing handles	WN1.5
cursor	WN1.5	Insert mode	WN1.3	SmartTag	WN1.27
custom dictionary	WN1.23	insertion point	WN1.5	source program	WN1.55
default	WN1.7	main dictionary	WN1.23	Standard toolbar	WN1.5
drawing object	WN1.55	Normal template	WN1.7	template	WN1.7
Drawing toolbar	WN1.6	object	WN1.55	TrueType	WN1.47
edit	WN1.	Overtype mode	WN1.3	typeface	WN1.46
embedded object	WN1.55	paragraph formatting	WN1.45	word wrap	WN1.26

The Microsoft Office User Specialist (MOUS) certification program is designed to measure your proficiency in performing basic tasks using the Office 2002 applications. Getting certified demonstrates that you have the skills and provides a valuable industry credential for employment. After completing this lab, you have learned the following Word Microsoft Office User Specialist skills:

Skill	Description	Page
Inserting and	Insert text	39
Modifying text	Use spelling and grammar checking	23
	Apply and modify character formats	45
		45
		45
(ment)		53
		61
		61
		63
		55

www.mhhe.com/o'learyseries

In the following Word screen, letters identify important elements. Enter the correct term for each screen element in the space provided.

A.	F.	K.	P.
B.	G.	L.	Q.
C.	H.	M.	R.
D.	I.	N.	S.
E.	J.	O.	t.

lab exercises

Concepts

Fill-in questions

1. A small blue box appearing under a word or character indicates that the _____ feature was applied.

2. If a word is underlined with purple dots, this indicates a(n) _____.

3. The _____ feature displays each page of your document in a reduced size so you can see the page layout.

4. To size a graphic evenly, click and drag the _____ in one corner of the graphic.

5. It is good practice to use only _____ types of fonts in a document.

6. When you use _____, new text replaces existing text as you type.

7. The _____ sits on the right side of the window and contains buttons and icons to help you perform common tasks, such as opening a blank document.

8. Use _____ when you want to keep your existing document with the original name and make a copy with a new name.

9. The _____ window displays a reduced view of how the current page will appear when printed.

10. The _____ feature includes entries, such as commonly used phrases, that can be quickly inserted into a document.

discussion questions

1. Discuss several uses you may have for a word processor. Then e2002lain the steps you would follow to create a document.

2. Discuss how the AutoCorrect and Spelling and Grammar Checker features help you as you type. [...] s of corrections does the AutoCorrect feature make?

[...] ow word wrap works. What happens when text is added? What happens when text is [...]

[...] ree ways you can select text. Discuss when it would be appropriate to use the different [...]

[...] how the Undo and Redo features work. What are some advantages of these features?

[...] ow graphics can be used in a document. What should you consider when adding graphics [...] nt? Can the use of a graphic change the reader's response to a document?

Hands-On Exercises

rating system
★ Easy
★★ Moderate
★★★ Difficult

step-by-step

★ Writing a Memo

1. Universal Industries is starting a casual Friday policy. Ms. Jones, the Vice President of Human Resources, has sent a memo informing employees of this new policy. Your completed memo is shown here.

   a. Open a blank Word document and create the memo with the following text. Press [Tab⇥] twice ater you type colons (:) in the To, From, Date, and RE lines. This will make the information following the colons line up evenly. Enter a blank line below the RE line and between paragraphs.

   To: [Your Name]
   From: Ms. Jones
   Date: [Current date]
   RE: Business Casual Dress Code

   Effective next Friday, business casual will be allowed in the corporate facility on Fridays and the day before a holiday break. Business casual is sometimes difficult to interpret. For men, it is a collared shirt and tailored trousers. For women, it is a pantsuit or tailored trousers or skirt. Business casual is not jeans, t-shirts, or exercise clothes. A detailed dress code will be available on the company intranet.

   Thank you for your cooperation in this matter.

   CSJ/xxx

   b. Correct any spelling and grammar errors that are identified.
   c. Change the font for the entire memo to14 pt.
   d. Change the alignment of the memo body to justified.
   e. Insert a blank line under the Date line and insert the AutoText reference line "RE:".
   f. Press [Tab⇥] and type "Business Casual Dress Code".
   g. Save the document as **Dress Code** on your data disk.
   h. Preview and print the document.

The O'Leary Series

Microsoft®
Office XP

Volume I

Introduction to Computer Essentials

objectives

After completing this lab, you will know how to:

1. Explain the five parts of an information system: people, procedures, software, hardware, and data.

2. Distinguish application software from system software.

3. Distinguish four kinds of computers—microcomputer, mini-computer, mainframe, and supercomputer—and describe hardware devices for input, processing, storage, output, and communications.

4. Describe document, worksheet, database, and presentation files.

5. Explain computer connectivity, the Internet, and the Web.

Computer competency: This notion may not be familiar to you, but it's easy to understand. The purpose of this book is to help you become competent in computer-related skills. Specifically, we want to help you walk into a job and immediately be valuable to an employer. In this chapter, we first present the five parts of an information system: people, procedures, software, hardware, and data. Competent end users need to understand these basic parts and how connectivity through the Internet and the Web expands the role of information technology (IT) in our lives.

Fifteen years ago, most people had little to do with computers, at least directly. Of course, they filled out computerized forms, took computerized tests, and paid computerized bills. But the real work with computers was handled by specialists—programmers, data-entry clerks, and computer operators.

Then microcomputers came along and changed everything. Now it is easy for nearly everybody to use a computer. People who use microcomputers are called end users. Today:

- Microcomputers are common tools in all areas of life. Writers write, artists draw, engineers and scientists calculate—all on microcomputers. Students and businesspeople do all this, and more.

- New forms of learning have developed. People who are homebound, who work odd hours, or who travel frequently may take courses on the Web. A college course need not fit within the usual time of a quarter or a semester.

- New ways to communicate, to find people with similar interests, and to buy goods are available. All kinds of people are using electronic mail, electronic commerce, and the Internet to meet and to share ideas and products.

 Many interesting and practical uses of information technology have recently surfaced to make our personal lives richer and more entertaining. These applications range from virus protection programs to instant messaging. (See Making IT Work for You below.) What about you? How can information technology and microcomputers enhance your life?

Competent end users need to know the five parts of an information system made up of people, procedures, software, hardware, and data. Additionally, they need to understand connectivity through the Internet and the Web and to recognize the role of information technology in their professional and personal lives.

MAKING IT WORK FOR YOU

Virus Protection
Ever been attacked by a computer virus? If not, chances are that you will in the near future. Fortunately, special software is available to protect you against computer viruses.

Personal Web Site
Do you have anything to share with the world? Would you like a personal Web site, but don't want to deal with learning HTML and paying for server time? Many services are available to get you started for FREE!

TV Tuner Cards and Video Clips
Want to watch your favorite television program while you work? Perhaps you would like to include a video clip from television in a class presentation. It's easy using a TV tuner card.

CD-R Drives and Music from the Internet
Did you know that you could use the Internet to locate music, download it to your computer, and create your own compact discs? All it takes is the right software, hardware, and a connection to the Internet.

Instant Messaging
Do you enjoy chatting with your friends? Are you working on a project and need to collaborate with others in your group? Perhaps instant messaging is just what you're looking for.

Information Systems

An information system has five parts: people, procedures, software, hardware, and data.

When you think of a microcomputer, perhaps you think of just the equipment itself. That is, you think of the monitor or the keyboard. There is more to it than that. The way to think about a microcomputer is as part of an information system. An **information system** has five parts: *people, procedures, software, hardware,* and *data.* (See Figure 1.)

- **People:** It is easy to overlook people as one of the five parts of a microcomputer system. Yet that is what microcomputers are all about—making **people**, end users like yourself, more productive.

- **Procedures: Procedures** are rules or guidelines for people to follow when using software, hardware, and data. Typically, these procedures are documented in manuals written by computer specialists. Software and hardware manufacturers often provide manuals with their products.

- **Software: Software** is another name for a program or programs. A **program** consists of the step-by-step instructions that tell the computer how to do its work. The purpose of software is to convert *data* (unprocessed facts) into *information* (processed facts).

- **Hardware:** The **hardware** consists of the equipment: keyboard, mouse, monitor, system unit, and other devices. Hardware is controlled by software. It actually processes the data to create information.

- **Data: Data** consists of the raw, unprocessed facts, including text, numbers, images, and sounds. Examples of raw facts are hours you worked and your pay rate. After data is processed through the computer, it is usually called **information**. An example of such information is the total wages owed you for a week's work.

Figure 1

The five parts of an information system

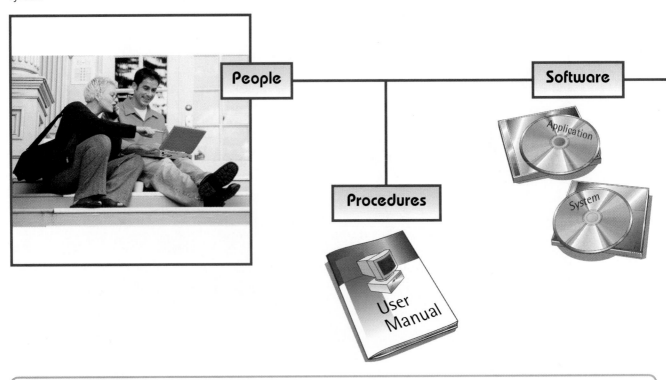

In large computer systems, there are specialists who deal with writing procedures, developing software, and capturing data. In microcomputer systems, however, end users often perform these operations. To be a competent end user, you must understand the essentials of **information technology (IT)**, including software, hardware, and data.

Concept Check

✔ What are the five parts of an information system?

✔ To be a competent end user, you must understand the essentials of information technology, including _____, _____, and _____.

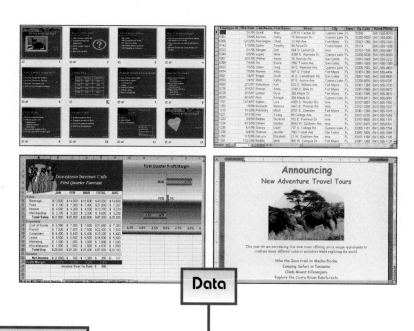

Data

Hardware

People

People are the most important part of an information system. Examples include people in entertainment, medicine, education, and business.

Although easy to overlook, people are surely the most important part of any information system. Our lives are touched every day by computers and information systems. Many times the contact is direct and obvious such as when we create documents using a word processing program or when we connect to the Internet.

Other times, the contact is not as obvious. Nonetheless, computers and information systems touch our lives hundreds of times every day. Consider just the following four examples. (See Figure 2.)

People just like you are making information technology work for them every day. In this chapter you will find several features designed to make technology work for you. Three specific features are Making IT Work for You topics, Tips, and On the Web Exercises.

Entertainment

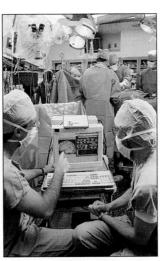
Medicine

Business

Education

Figure 2
Computers in entertainment, medicine, business, and education

Figure 3
Windows 2000 operating system

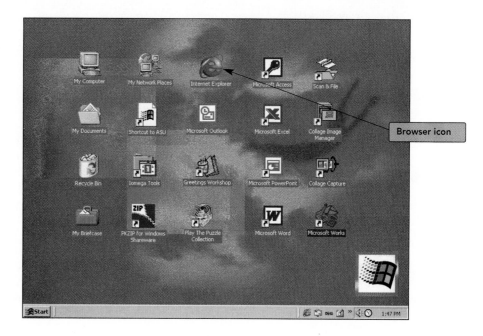

Browser icon

Software

Software is of two kinds: system software and application software.

Software or programs are the instructions that tell the computer how to process data into the form you want. There are two major kinds of software—*system software* and *application software*.

System Software

The user interacts with application software. **System software** enables the application software to interact with the computer hardware. System software is "background" software that helps the computer manage its own internal resources.

The most important system software program is the **operating system**, which interacts with the application software and the computer. Windows 2000 is one of the best-known operating systems for today's microcomputer users. (See Figure 3.) **Utilities** are specialized programs designed to make computing easier. One of the most important utilities is for virus protection. (See Making IT Work for You: Virus Protection on pages 8 and 9.)

Application Software

Application software might be described as "end-user" software. Application software performs useful work on general-purpose tasks such as word processing and data analysis.

There are certain general-purpose programs or basic applications. These programs are widely used in nearly all career areas. They are the kind of programs you *have* to know to be considered computer competent. One of these basic applications is a browser to navigate, explore, and find information on the Internet. (See Figure 4.) The

continued on CE.10

TIPS

Have you used the Internet? If so, then you probably already know how to use a browser. For those of you who do not, here are a few tips to get you started.

1. *Start browser.* Typically, all you need to do is double-click the browser's icon on the desktop.
2. *Enter URL.* In the browser's location box, type the URL (uniform resource locator, or address) of the Internet or Web location (site) that you want to visit.
3. *Press ENTER.* On your keyboard, press the ENTER key to connect to the site.
4. *Read and explore.* Once connected to the site, read the information displayed on your monitor. Click on underlined text to explore other locations.
5. *Close browser.* Once you are done exploring, click on your browser's CLOSE button.

Virus Protection

Worried about computer viruses? Did you know that others could be intercepting your private e-mail? It is even possible for them to gain access and control over your computer system. Fortunately, Internet security suites are available to help ensure your safety while you are on the Internet.

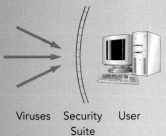

Viruses Security User
Suite

How It Works

Internet security suites are collections of programs that create a protective barrier around your computer system. These suites, such as Norton AntiVirus and eSafe, are designed to protect against computer viruses and to ensure security and privacy of computer system resources.

Getting Started

The first step is to install an Internet security suite. Once installed, the software will continually work to ensure security and privacy. One such suite, eSafe, has a version available free from the Internet. To install this suite, follow the instructions below.

1. Connect to ealaddin.com/esafe and click *Downloads*.
2. Click *Home Users*.

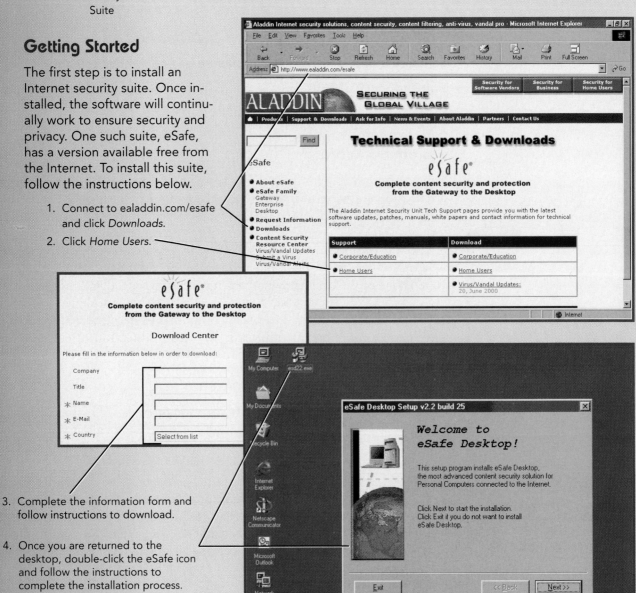

3. Complete the information form and follow instructions to download.

4. Once you are returned to the desktop, double-click the eSafe icon and follow the instructions to complete the installation process.

eSafe

Numerous security files have been installed. One of these, Desktop Watch, runs continually to search for privacy and security violations to the computer system. Another program, Desktop Configuration, provides a menu to access some of eSafe's most powerful applications including Sandbox, Personal Firewall, and Anti-Virus.

Sandbox

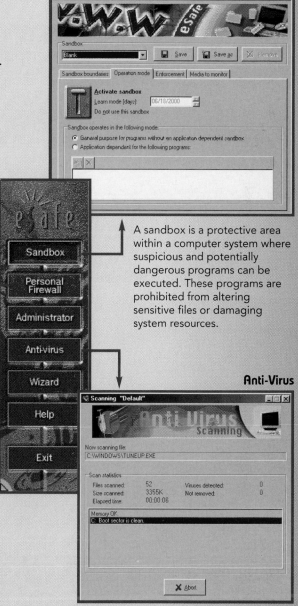

A sandbox is a protective area within a computer system where suspicious and potentially dangerous programs can be executed. These programs are prohibited from altering sensitive files or damaging system resources.

Personal Firewall

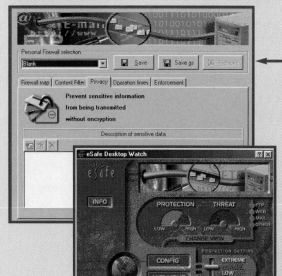

Personal Firewalls are programs that monitor all inbound and outbound traffic to a computer system. They limit access to only authorized users, automatically check files for viruses, and filter out unwanted content.

Anti-Virus

Anti-virus controls how frequently the computer system is searched for computer viruses. When a file is checked, it is compared to the profile of over 6,000 known viruses. Once a virus is detected, it is typically either eliminated from the file or the entire file is deleted.

The Web is continually changing and some of the specifics presented in this Making IT Work for You may have changed. See our Web site at http://www.mhhe.com/it/oleary/IT.mhtml for possible changes and to learn more about this application of technology.

two most widely used browsers are Microsoft's Internet Explorer and Netscape's Navigator. For a summary of the basic applications, see Figure 5.

There are many other applications that are more specialized. One of the most exciting is Web publishers, which allows users to create interactive multimedia Web pages. (See Making IT Work for You: Personal Web Sites on pages 12 and 13.) For a summary of these specialized applications, see Figure 6.

Concept Check

✔ Name the two major kinds of software.
✔ The most important system software program is the _____ _____.

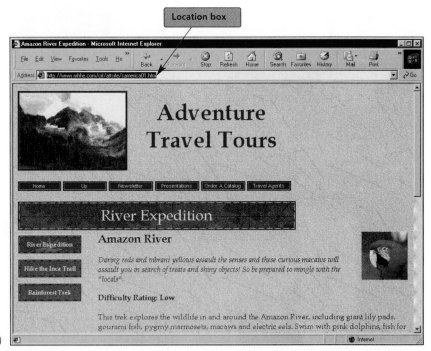

Figure 4
Browser (Internet Explorer)

Type	Description
Word processor	Prepare written documents
Spreadsheet	Analyze and summarize numerical data
Database management system	Organize and manage data and information
Presentation graphics	Communicate a message or persuade other people
Browser	Navigate, explore, and find information on the Internet
Information managers	Maintain electronic calendars, address books, and to-do lists

Figure 5
Basic applications

Type	Description
Multimedia	Integrate video, music, voice, and graphics to create interactive presentations
Web publishers	Create interactive multimedia Web pages
Graphics programs	Create professional publications: draw, edit, and modify images
Virtual reality	Create realistic three-dimensional virtual or simulated environments
Artificial intelligence	Simulate human thought processes and actions
Project managers	Plan projects, schedule people, and control resources

Figure 6
Specialized applications

Hardware

Four types of computers are supercomputer, mainframe computer, minicomputer, and microcomputer. Microcomputer hardware consists of the system unit, input/output, secondary storage, and communications devices.

Computers are electronic devices that can follow instructions to accept input, process that input, and produce information. This chapter focuses principally on microcomputers. However, it is almost certain that you will come in contact, at least indirectly, with other types of computers.

Types of Computers

There are four types of computers: supercomputers, mainframe computers, minicomputers, and microcomputers.

- **Supercomputers:** The most powerful type of computer is the **supercomputer**. These machines are special, high-capacity computers used by very large organizations. For example, NASA uses supercomputers to track and control space explorations.

- **Mainframe computers:** These large computers occupy specially wired, air-conditioned rooms. Although not nearly as powerful as supercomputers, **mainframe computers** are capable of great processing speeds and data storage. (See Figure 7.) For example, insurance companies use mainframes to process information about millions of policyholders.

continued on CE.14

Figure 7
Mainframe computer
(IBM ES/9000)

Personal Web Sites

Do you have anything to share with the world? Would you like a personal Web site, but don't want to deal with learning HTML and paying for server time? Many services are available to get you started—for FREE!

How It Works

A service site on the Web provides access to tools to create personal Web pages. After registering with the site, you create your Web pages. Once completed, the service site acts as a host for your personal Web site and others are free to visit it from anywhere on the Web.

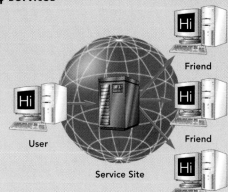

Getting Started

The first step to creating your own Web site is to register with a service site. One of the most popular Personal Web site services is Homestead. To connect to and register for your Web site, follow the instructions below.

1. Connect to www.homestead.com.

2. Click *SIGN UP*, complete the registration procedure, and LOG in.

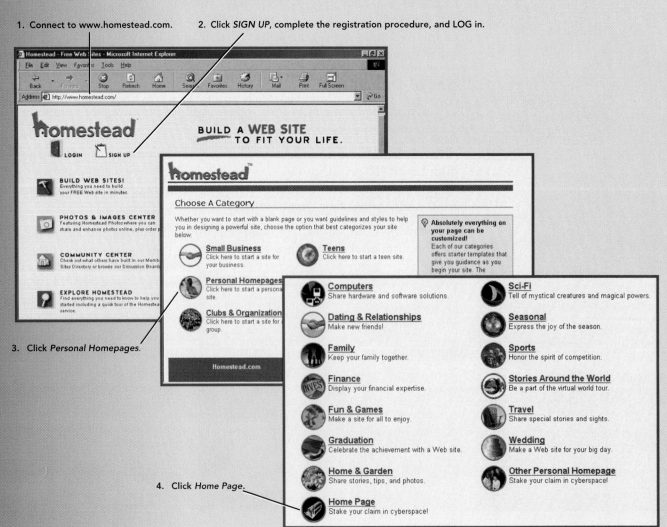

3. Click *Personal Homepages*.

4. Click *Home Page.*

Selecting a Template

Once you have registered with a Personal Web service site, you are ready to create your Web pages. Homestead offers a variety of templates to assist in the development of Web pages. For example:

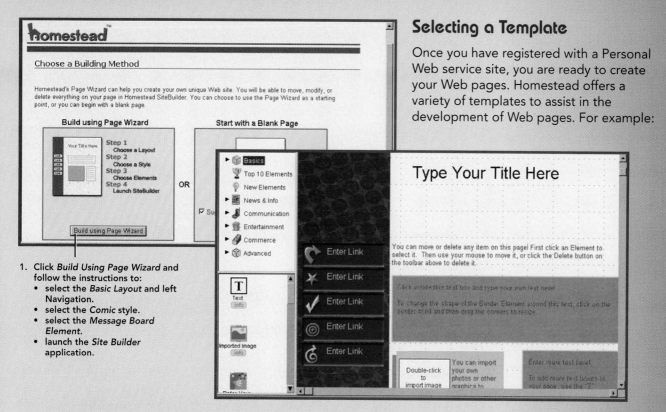

1. Click *Build Using Page Wizard* and follow the instructions to:
   - select the *Basic Layout* and left Navigation.
   - select the *Comic* style.
   - select the *Message Board Element*.
   - launch the *Site Builder* application.

Creating Your Web Pages

Once you have selected the template, you are ready to customize it by adding elements, photos, text and/or links to your Web page. After completing the page(s), save it to make it available to anyone over the Internet.

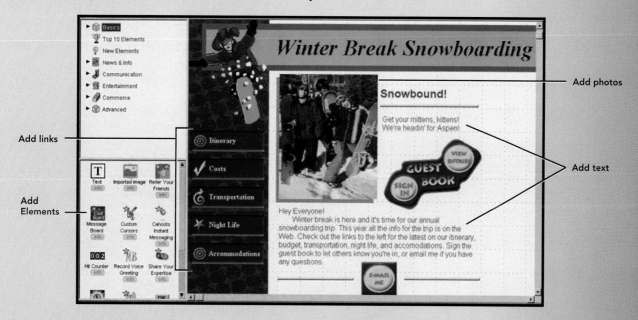

Add photos

Add links

Add text

Add Elements

The Web is continually changing and some of the specifics presented in this Making IT Work for You may have changed. See our Web site at http://www.mhhe.com/it/oleary/IT.mhtml for possible changes and to learn more about this application of technology.

- **Minicomputers:** Also known as **midrange computers**, **minicomputers** are desk-sized machines. Medium-sized companies or departments of large companies typically use them for specific purposes. For example, production departments use minicomputers to monitor certain manufacturing processes and assembly-line operations.

- **Microcomputers:** Although the least powerful, **microcomputers** are the most widely used and fastest-growing type of computer. Apple recently introduced their iMac computers. (See Figure 8.) Categories of microcomputer include *desktop, notebook,* and *personal digital assistants*. **Desktop computers** are small enough to fit on top of or alongside a desk, yet are too big to carry around. **Notebook computers** are portable, weigh between 4 and 10 pounds, and fit into most briefcases. (See Figure 9.) **Personal digital assistants (PDAs)** are also known as **palmtop computers** or **handheld computers**. They combine pen input, writing recognition, personal organizational tools, and communications capabilities in a very small package. (See Figure 10.)

Microcomputer Hardware

Hardware for a microcomputer system consists of a variety of different devices. See Figure 11 for a typical system. This physical equipment falls into four basic categories: system unit, input/output, secondary storage, and communication devices.

- **System unit:** The **system unit** is electronic circuitry housed within the computer cabinet. (See Figure 12.) Two important components of the system unit are the *microprocessor* and *memory*. The **microprocessor** controls and manipulates data to produce information. **Memory**, also known as **primary storage** or **random access memory (RAM)**, holds data and program instructions for processing the data. It also holds the processed information before it is output. The system unit's capabilities can be expanded by inserting an expansion card such as a TV tuner card. (See Making It Work for You: TV Tuner Cards and Video Clips on pages 16 and 17.)

- **Input/output devices: Input devices** translate data and programs that humans can understand into a form that the computer can process.

continued on CE.18

Figure 8

Colorful desktop computers from Apple (iMac)

Figure 9

Notebook computer

Figure 10

Personal digital assistant

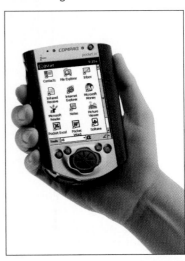

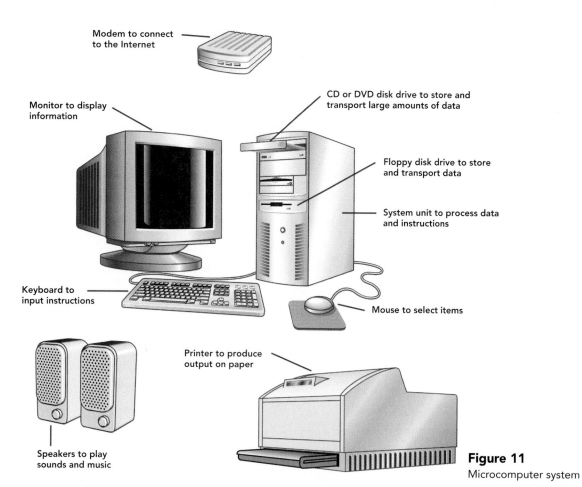

Modem to connect to the Internet

CD or DVD disk drive to store and transport large amounts of data

Monitor to display information

Floppy disk drive to store and transport data

System unit to process data and instructions

Keyboard to input instructions

Mouse to select items

Printer to produce output on paper

Speakers to play sounds and music

Figure 11
Microcomputer system

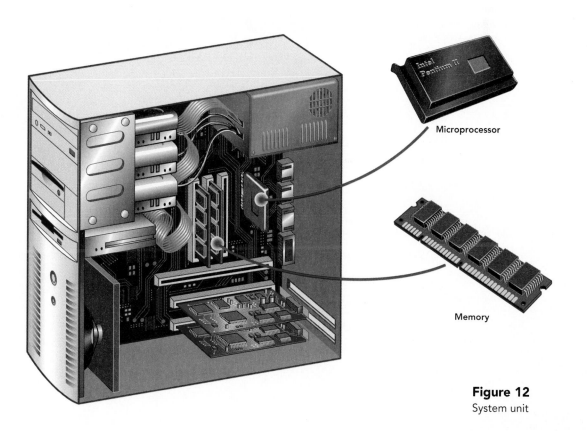

Microprocessor

Memory

Figure 12
System unit

TV Tuner Cards and Video Clips

Want to watch your favorite television program while you work? Perhaps you would like to include a video clip from television and include it in a class presentation. It's easy using a video TV card.

TV Signal

(Analog)

Computer Signal

(Digital)

How It Works

A video capture card converts analog signals from a television or VCR into digital signals that your computer can process. Once the card has been installed, you can view, capture, and use television video clips in a variety of ways.

Viewing

You can be running an application such as PowerPoint and view your favorite TV shows, by taking the steps shown in Figure A.

Figure A

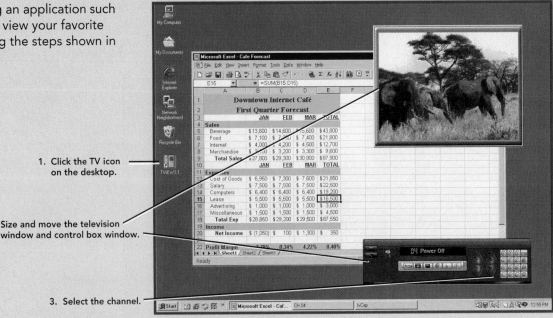

1. Click the TV icon on the desktop.

2. Size and move the television window and control box window.

3. Select the channel.

1. Specify where to save the video clip (e.g., on your internal hard disk).

2. Click the *Record* button to start recording.

Figure B

3. Click the *Stop* button to stop recording.

Capturing

You can capture the video playing in the TV window into a digital file by taking the steps shown in Figure B.

Figure C

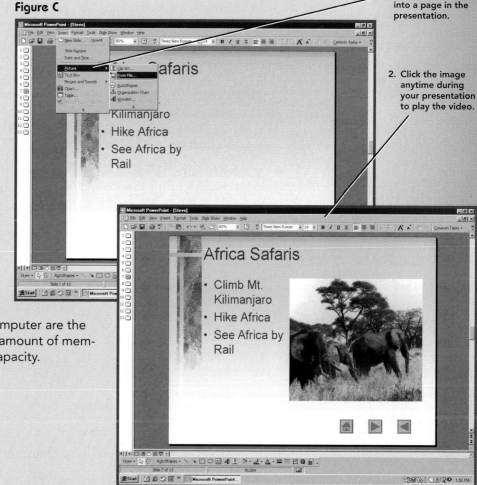

1. Insert the video clip into a page in the presentation.

2. Click the image anytime during your presentation to play the video.

Using

Once captured in a file, a video can be used in any number of ways. It can be added to a Web page, attached to an e-mail, or added to a class presentation.

For example, you could include a video clip into a PowerPoint presentation by taking the steps shown in Figure C.

TV tuner cards are relatively inexpensive and easy to install. Some factors limiting their performance on your computer are the speed of your processor, the amount of memory, and secondary storage capacity.

TV tuner cards are continually changing and some of the specifics presented in this Making IT Work for You may have changed. See our Web site at http://www. mhhe.com/it/oleary/IT.mhtml for possible changes and to learn more about this application of technology.

Figure 14
Monitor

Figure 15
A 3½" floppy disk

Figure 16
An optical disk

Figure 13
Keyboard and mouse

The most common input devices are the **keyboard** and the **mouse**. (See Figure 13.) **Output devices** translate information from the computer into a form that humans can understand. The most common output devices are **monitors** (see Figure 14) and **printers**.

- **Secondary storage devices:** Unlike memory, **secondary storage devices** hold data and programs even after electrical power to the computer system has been turned off. **Floppy disks** are widely used to store and transport data from one computer to another. (See Figure 15.) They are called floppy because data is stored on a very thin flexible, or floppy, plastic disk. **Hard disks** are typically used to store programs and very large data files. Using a rigid metallic platter, hard disks have a much greater capacity and are able to access information much faster than floppy disks. **Optical disks** use laser technology and have the greatest capacity. (See Figure 16.) The two basic types of optical disks are **compact discs (CDs)** and **digital versatile** (or **video**) **discs (DVDs)**. (See Making IT Work for You: CD-R Drives and Music from the Internet on pages 20 and 21.)

- **Communications devices: Communications hardware** sends and receives data and programs from one computer or secondary storage device to another. Many microcomputers use a **modem** to convert electronic signals from the computer into electronic signals that can travel over a telephone line and onto the Internet.

Concept Check

✔ List the four types of computers.
✔ Name the four categories of microcomputer hardware.

Data

Data is stored in document, worksheet, database, and presentation files.

Data is used to describe facts about something. When stored electronically in files, data can be used directly as input for the information system.

Four common types of files (see Figure 17) are:

- **Document files**, created by word processors to save documents such as memos, term papers, and letters.

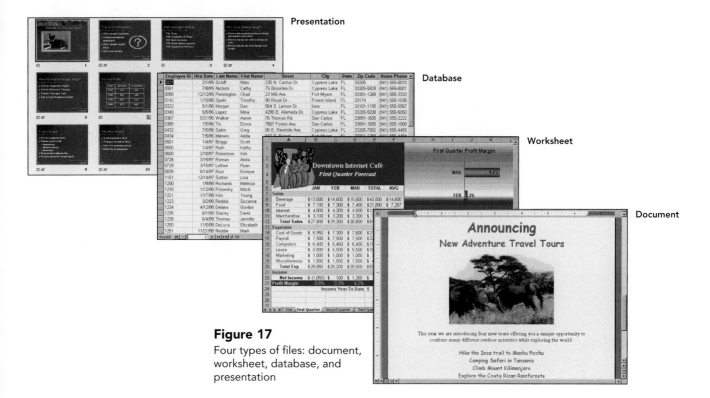

Figure 17

Four types of files: document, worksheet, database, and presentation

- **Worksheet files**, created by electronic spreadsheets to analyze things like budgets and to predict sales.

- **Database files**, typically created by database management programs to contain highly structured and organized data. For example, an employee database file might contain all the workers' names, social security numbers, job titles, and other related pieces of information.

- **Presentation files**, created by presentation graphics programs to save presentation materials. For example, a file might contain audience handouts, speaker notes, and electronic slides.

Concept Check

✔ What is data?

✔ Name four file types in which data can be stored.

Connectivity and the Internet

Connectivity is the microcomputer's ability to communicate with other computers and information sources. The Internet is the largest network in the world.

Connectivity is the capability of your microcomputer to share information with other computers. (See Figure 18.) Data and information can be sent over telephone lines or cable and through the air. Thus, your microcomputer can be *connected* to other computers. It can connect you to the Internet and to many computerized data banks and other sources of information that lie well beyond your desk.

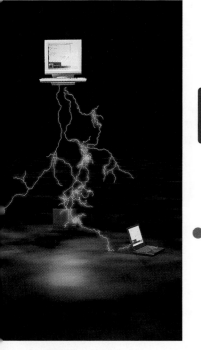

Figure 18

Computers connected together can share information

continued on CE.22

CD-R Drives and Music from the Internet

Did you know that you can use the Internet to locate music, download it to your computer, and create your own compact discs? All it takes is the right software, hardware, and a connection to the Internet.

How It Works

Music is available on the Internet in special compressed music files called MP3s. You can download these music files to your system via your Internet connection. Using your system and some specialized software, you can store and play these files. You can even create a custom CD using a CD-R drive.

Internet   Your System   CD

Downloading Music

There are several sites on the Web that offer free music that you can download to your system. Some Web sites are set up to offer a convenient way to browse and select these files, such as www.mp3.com.

For example, you can download files to your system as shown in Figure A.

Figure A

1. Enter www.mp3.com in the Location box of your browser.

2. Select a featured artist.

3. Select a song to download.

Playing Music

To arrange and play downloaded music files, you need specialized software called a player. WinAmp from Nullsoft (www.winamp.com) is one of the best known.

For example, using WinAmp, you can play music files as shown in Figure B.

Figure B

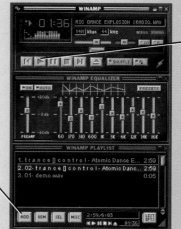

2. Click the *Play* button to play the music.

1. Click the *Add* button to select the music files to play from your hard-disk drive.

Creating a Custom CD

If your computer is equipped with a CD-R or CD-RW drive, you can create your own music CDs. You'll need a blank recordable compact disc and special CD-creation software, such as Easy CD Creator by Adaptec. You use this software to organize and save the music files onto your CD.

For example, using Easy CD Creator, you can create a custom CD as shown in Figure C.

2. Click the *Create CD* button to start the process of recording the CD.

Figure C

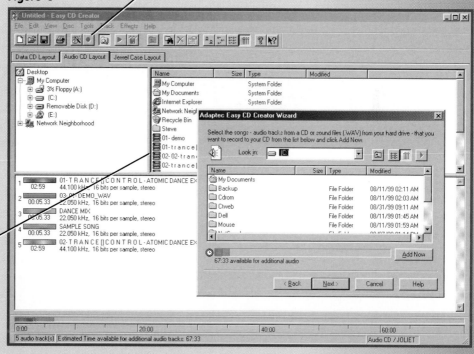

1. Select the music files from your hard drive.

Not all MP3 files can be legally copied. To protect yourself, only download music files from reputable sites.

The Web is continually changing and some of the specifics presented in this Making IT Work for You may have changed. See our Web site at http://www.mhhe.com/ it/oleary/IT.mhtml for possible changes and to learn more about this application of technology.

Connectivity is a very significant development, for it expands the uses of the microcomputer severalfold. Central to the concept of connectivity is the **computer network**. A network is a communications system connecting two or more computers. Networks connect people as close as the next office and as far away as halfway around the world.

The largest network in the world is the **Internet**. It is like a giant highway that connects you to millions of other people and organizations located throughout the world. (See Figure 19.) Unlike typical highways that move people and things from one location to another, the Internet moves your *ideas* and *information*. Rather than moving through geographic space, you move through **cyberspace**—the space of electronic movement of ideas and information. The Web provides an easy-to-use, exciting, multimedia interface to connect to the Internet and to access the resources available in cyberspace.

The Internet was launched in 1969 when the United States funded a project that developed a national computer network called **Advanced Research Project Agency Network (ARPANET)**. The **Web**, also known as **WWW** and the **World Wide Web**, was introduced in 1992 at the **Center for European Nuclear Research (CERN)** in Switzerland. Prior to the Web, the Internet was all text—no graphics, animations, sound, or video. The Web provided a multimedia interface to resources available on the Internet. From these research beginnings, the Internet and the Web have evolved as tools for all of us to use. For example, you can chat with friends and collaborate on group projects using the Internet and instant messaging. (See Making IT Work for You: Instant Messaging on pages 24 and 25.)

Figure 19
The Internet connects millions of people worldwide

Concept Check

✔ Define connectivity.
✔ What is the Internet?

A LOOK TO THE FUTURE

Computer competency is your key to the future.

The purpose of this book is to help you be computer competent not only in the present but also in the future. This will enable you to benefit from three important information technology developments: more powerful software, more powerful hardware, and connectivity to outside information resources. It will also help you remain computer competent and continue to learn in the future.

Powerful Software

The software now available can do an extraordinary number of tasks and help you in an endless number of ways. More and more employers are expecting the people they hire to be able to use it.

Hardware

Microcomputers are now much more powerful than they used to be. Indeed, the newer models have the speed and power of room-size computers of only a few years ago. However, despite the rapid change of specific equipment, their essential features remain unchanged. Thus, the competent end user should focus on these features.

Connectivity, the Internet, and the Web

No longer are microcomputers and competent end users bound by the surface of the desk. Now they can reach past the desk and link with other computers to share data, programs, and information. The Internet and the Web are considered by most to be the two most important technologies for the 21st century.

Security and Privacy

What about people? Is there a downside to all these technological advances? Experts agree that we as a society must be careful about the potential of technology to negatively impact our personal privacy and security. Additionally, we need to be aware of potential physical and mental health risks associated with using technology. Finally, we need to be aware of negative effects on our environment caused by the manufacture of computer-related products.

Changing Times

Are the times changing any faster now than they ever have? Most people think so. Those who were alive when radios, cars, and airplanes were being introduced certainly lived through some dramatic changes. Has technology made our own times even more dynamic? Whatever the answer, it is clear we live in a fast-paced age.

Most businesses have become aware that they must adapt to changing technology or be left behind. Nearly every corporation in the world has a presence on the Internet. Retail stores such as JCPenney and Wal-Mart provide catalog support and sales. Banks such as Wells Fargo and Citibank support home banking and electronic commerce.

Clearly, such changes do away with some jobs—those of many bank tellers and cashiers, for example. However, they create opportunities for other people. New technology requires people who are truly capable of working with it. These are not the people who think every piece of equipment is so simple they can just turn it on and use it. Nor are they those who think each new machine is a potential disaster. In other words, new technology needs people who are not afraid to learn it and are able to manage it. The real issue, then, is not how to make technology better. Rather, it is how to integrate the technology with people.

Instant Messaging

Do you enjoy chatting with your friends? Are you working on a project and need to collaborate with others in your group? Perhaps instant messaging is just what you're looking for. It's easy and free with an Internet connection and the right software.

How It Works

Users register with an instant messaging server and identify friends and colleagues (buddies). Whenever a user is online, the instant messaging server notifies the user of all buddies who are also online and provides support for direct "live" communication.

Getting Started

The first step is to connect to one of the many Web sites that support instant messaging. Once at the site, register, download, and install instant messaging software, and create your buddy list.

For example, you can set up AOL Instant Messenger as shown below.

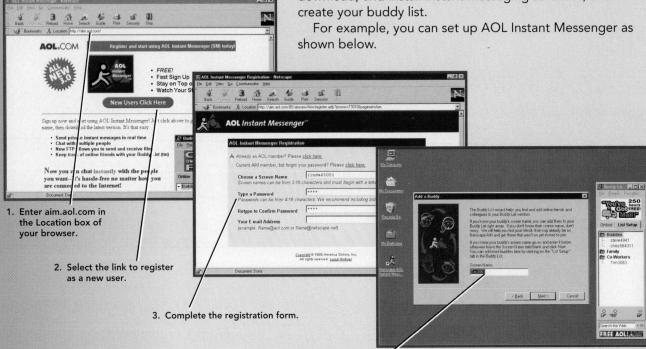

1. Enter aim.aol.com in the Location box of your browser.

2. Select the link to register as a new user.

3. Complete the registration form.

4. After installing the instant messaging software, create your "buddy list."

Communicating with a Friend

Once you have set up your instant messaging software, you can use it to communicate, live, with your online buddies. For example, you could use AOL Instant Messenger as follows:

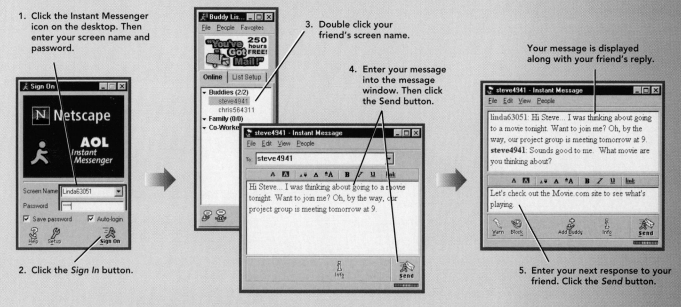

1. Click the Instant Messenger icon on the desktop. Then enter your screen name and password.

2. Click the *Sign In* button.

3. Double click your friend's screen name.

4. Enter your message into the message window. Then click the Send button.

Your message is displayed along with your friend's reply.

5. Enter your next response to your friend. Click the *Send* button.

Collaborating with a Group

You can just as easily communicate or collaborate with a group of people. To conduct a virtual group meeting, all group participants must be signed on and one participant acts as the coordinator.

For example, with AOL Instant Messenger, the coordinator begins as follows:

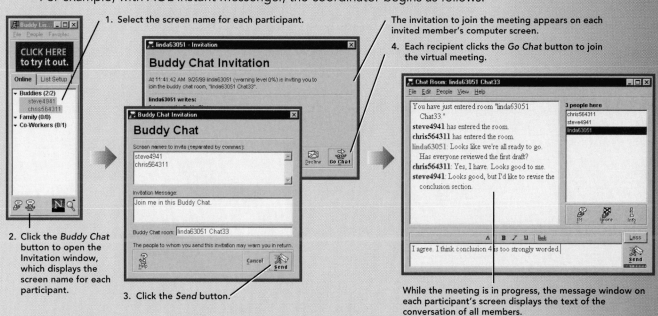

1. Select the screen name for each participant.

2. Click the *Buddy Chat* button to open the Invitation window, which displays the screen name for each participant.

3. Click the *Send* button.

The invitation to join the meeting appears on each invited member's computer screen.

4. Each recipient clicks the *Go Chat* button to join the virtual meeting.

While the meeting is in progress, the message window on each participant's screen displays the text of the conversation of all members.

Most instant messaging servers require that all participants use the same instant messaging software. However, as standards evolve this limitation will likely be overcome.

The Web is continually changing and some of the specifics presented in this Making IT Work for You may have changed. See our Web site at http://www.mhhe.com/it/oleary/IT.mhtml for possible changes and to learn more about this application of technology.

information systems

The way to think about a microcomputer is to realize that it is one part of an **information system**.

Five parts of an information system:

1. **People** are an often-overlooked part. The purpose of information systems is to make people more productive.

2. **Procedures** are rules or guidelines to follow when using software, hardware, and data.

3. **Software (programs)** provides step-by-step instructions to control the computer.

4. **Hardware** consists of the physical equipment.

5. **Data** consists of unprocessed facts including text, numbers, images, and sound. Information is processed data.

people

People are the most important part of an information system. People are touched hundreds of times daily by computers.

Some examples:

Entertainment

Medicine

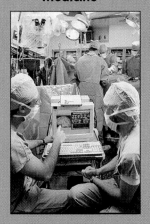

Education

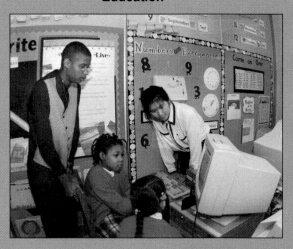

Business

To prepare for your future as a competent end user, you need to understand the basic parts of an information system: people, procedures, software, hardware, and data. Also you need to understand connectivity through the Internet and the Web and to recognize the role of technology in our professional and personal lives.

software

Software or programs consist of system and application software.

System Software

System software—*background* software that manages internal resources. Operating Systems interact with application software and the computer. Utilities are specialized programs that make computing easier.

Application Software

Application software—software that performs useful work on general-purpose problems. Basic applications include:

- Word processors to prepare written documents.
- Spreadsheets to analyze and summarize numerical data.
- Database management systems to organize and manage data.
- Presentation graphics to communicate or persuade.
- Browser to navigate, explore, and find information on the Internet.
- Information managers to maintain electronic calendars, address books, and to-do lists.

Many other more specialized applications are used within certain career paths.

hardware

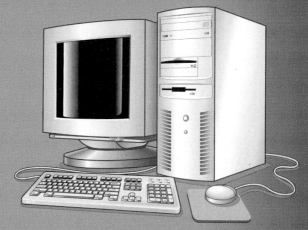

Hardware is the physical equipment in an information system.

Types of Computers

There are four types of computers:

- Supercomputers—the most powerful.
- Mainframe—used by large companies.
- Minicomputers—also known as midrange computers.
- Microcomputers—the fastest growing. Categories include desktop, notebook, and personal digital assistant.

Microcomputer Hardware

The four categories of devices are:

- The system unit contains the electronic circuitry, including the microprocessor and memory.
- Input/output devices are translation units that convert human instruction into machine-readable processes.
- Secondary storage devices store data and programs. Typical media include floppy, hard, and optical disks.
- Communication devices send and receive data and programs from one computer to another. A modem is widely used to connect to the Internet.

Data

Data describes something and is typically stored electronically in a file.

Common types of files are:

Document

Worksheet

Database

Presentation

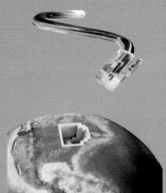

Connectivity

Connectivity is a concept describing the ability of end users to tap into resources well beyond their desktops. Computer **networks** are connected computers that share data and resources.

Internet

The **Internet** is the world's largest computer network. The **Web**, also known as the **World Wide Web** and **WWW**, is an Internet service that provides a multi-media interface to resources available on the Internet.

key terms

Advanced Research Project
  Agency Network (ARPANET)
  CE.22
application software   CE.7
Center for European Nuclear
  Research (CERN)   CE.22
communications hardware   CE.18
compact disc (CD)   CE.18
computer network   CE.22
connectivity   CE.22
cyberspace   CE.19
data   CE.4
database file   CE.19
desktop computer   CE.14
digital versatile (or video) disc
  (DVD)   CE.18
document file   CE.18
floppy disk   CE.18
handheld computer   CE.14
hard disk   CE.18

hardware   CE.4
information   CE.4
information system   CE.4
information technology (IT)   CE.5
input device   CE.14
Internet   CE.22
keyboard   CE.18
mainframe computer   CE.11
memory   CE.14
microcomputer   CE.14
microprocessor   CE.14
midrange computer   CE.14
minicomputer   CE.14
modem   CE.18
monitor   CE.18
mouse   CE.18
notebook computer   CE.14
operating system   CE.7
optical disk   CE.18
output device   CE.18

palmtop computer   CE.14
people   CE.4
personal digital assistant (PDA)
  CE.14
presentation file   CE.19
primary storage   CE.14
printer   CE.18
procedures   CE.4
program   CE.4
random access memory (RAM)
  CE14
secondary storage device   CE.18
software   CE.4
supercomputer   CE.11
system software   CE.7
system unit   CE.14
utilities   CE.7
Web   CE.22
worksheet file   CE.19
World Wide Web (WWW)   CE.22

matching

Match the numbered item with the correct lettered item. Write your answers in the spaces provided.

1. The largest network in the world. ____

2. Storage media that uses very thin, flexible plastic disks. ____

3. Computers small enough to fit on top of or alongside a desk, yet too large to carry around. ____

4. Used to describe facts about something. ____

5. Holds data and program instructions for processing data. ____

6. Most important system software program, interacting between the application software and the computer. ____

7. Midrange, desk-sized computers. ____

8. The capability of your microcomputer to share information with other computers. ____

9. "End-user" software used for general-purpose tasks. ____

10. Translates the processed information from the computer into a form that humans can understand. ____

a. application
   software

b. connectivity

c. data

d. desktop computer

e. floppy disk

f. Internet

g. memory

h. minicomputer

i. operating system

j. output device

true/false

In the spaces provided, write T or F to indicate whether the statement is true or false.

1. Microcomputers are common tools in all areas of life. ____
2. Hardware consists of a monitor, a keyboard, and software. ____
3. Windows 2000 is an application program. ____
4. Memory is also known as primary storage. ____
5. A modem is used to send electronic signals over telephone lines. ____

multiple choice

Circle the letter of the correct answer.

1. Computers are electronic devices that accept instructions, process input, and produce:
   a. information
   b. prewritten programs
   c. data
   d. end users
   e. system software

2. High-capacity computers used primarily by very large organizations or for research purposes:
   a. microcomputers
   b. minicomputers
   c. mainframes
   d. supercomputers
   e. personal computers

3. The microprocessor is located in the:
   a. hard disk
   b. system unit
   c. memory
   d. monitor
   e. keyboard

4. Also called temporary storage, its contents will be lost if electrical power is disrupted or cut off:
   a. secondary storage
   b. basic tools
   c. memory
   d. operating system
   e. hard disk

5. Files containing highly structured and organized data are:
   a. documents
   b. worksheets
   c. databases
   d. graphics
   e. communications

fill-in

Complete each statement in the spaces provided.

1. Microcomputer _____, the physical equipment, falls into four categories: the system unit, input/output, secondary storage, and communication devices.

2. Also known as midrange computers, _____ are frequently used by departments within larger organizations.

3. _____ are guidelines or rules to follow when using software, hardware, and data.

4. _____ storage devices are used to store data and programs even after electrical power has been turned off.

5. _____ are programs used to navigate, explore, and find information on the Internet.

discussion questions

On a separate sheet of paper, respond to each question and statement.

1. Describe the five parts of an information system.

2. How would you distinguish between system software and application software?

3. Compare the four types of computers.

4. What is the difference between memory and secondary storage?

5. What are connectivity, the Internet, and the Web?

critical thinking questions and projects

Read each exercise and answer the related questions on a separate sheet of paper.

1. *Your reasons for learning computing:* How are you already using computer technology? What's happened in the computer-related world in the last six months that you have read about or seen on television? How are companies using computers to stay on the cutting edge? These are some questions you might discuss with classmates to see why computers are an exciting part of life. You might also consider the reasons why you want to gain computer competency. Imagine your dream career. How do you think microcomputers, from what you already know, can help you do the work you want to do? What kind of after-hours interests do you have? Assuming you could afford it, how could a microcomputer bring new skills or value to those interests?

2. *The Internet and the Web:* The Internet and Web are the most exciting connectivity developments today. If you have used the Internet or the Web, discuss your experiences by describing what you used it for, what you liked about it, and what you did not like. If you have not used the Internet or the Web, do you think you will in the near future? What would you use it for?

3. *Privacy and security:* Computer technology offers unlimited opportunities and challenges. We can do so many things faster and better. We can instantly connect to and communicate with people around the world. But have you ever thought about the other side of the coin? Will all of the changes be positive? Will everyone benefit? Discuss these issues and any others that come to mind.

4. *Making IT Work for You:* Review the list of Making IT Work for You topics on page 3. Have you used any of these? If so, identify the topic(s), describe how, when, and whether you found it useful. Assign a rank to each of the five topics based on your interest. (Use 1 to indicate the most interesting.) For each of the first three topics in your ranking, describe why it is interesting to you and how you might use it. Be as specific as possible.

on the web exercises

1. Virtual Libraries

It might surprise you to learn that you can visit libraries on the Web where you can browse through the stacks, research selected topics, and check out books. Several virtual libraries have e-texts, which are entire books on computer, that anyone can download and use. Visit the Web site at http://www.ipl.org. Find a text on a topic that interests you, print out its first page, and write a paragraph on the benefits and shortfalls of using virtual libraries as a resource for your school papers.

2. Ticket Master

Some of the hottest sites on the Web offer the latest music news, present live concerts, and provide updates on your favorite band. Visit the Web site at http://ticketmaster.com. Once connected to that site, check out your favorite band and print out its tour dates or information about its latest album. Write a paragraph describing how you located the information and discuss how the band could better use the Internet to promote its music.

3. Virtual Shopping Malls

Like any community, the Internet community has shopping malls. Visit the Web site at http://shopnow.com. Browse through the mall, find a product that you are familiar with, and print out the information provided on that item. Write a paragraph describing how the prices, services, and selection of the virtual mall compare with those of a traditional mall in your community.

4. Making IT Work for You

Although large organizations have been using information technology for years, individuals like you have only recently begun to use the technology in their everyday lives. The list of Making IT Work for You topics on page 3 presents several everyday uses of technology. Further information about each topic is presented in this chapter and on our Web site. Select one topic that is new to you. Locate and review the Making IT Work for You coverage in this chapter. Visit our Web site at http://www.mhhe.com/it/oleary/IT.mhtml and link to the topic you have selected. Print out the information presented. Write a paragraph or two describing how you might use this technology in your everyday life.

Windows 2000 Basic Skills

L A B 1

Objectives

After completing this lab, you will know how to:

1. Start Windows 2000.
2. Use a mouse.
3. Use menus.
4. Size and move windows.
5. Maximize, minimize, and restore windows.
6. Use Windows Help.
7. Work with multiple open windows.
8. Use My Computer.
9. Print a Help topic.
10. Close all open windows.
11. Shut down Windows 2000.

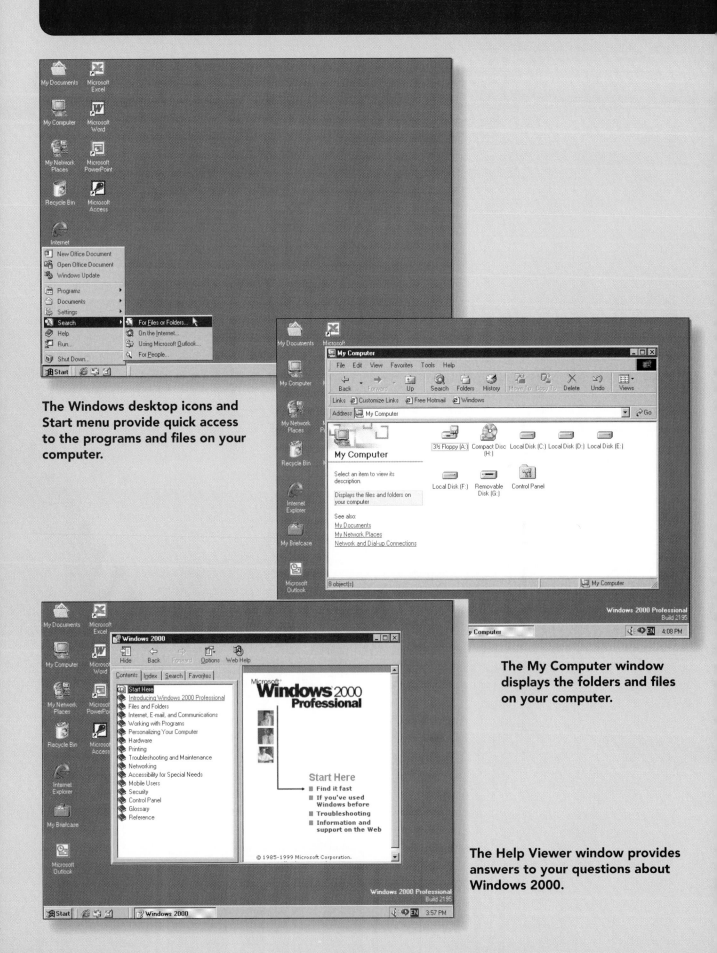

The Windows desktop icons and Start menu provide quick access to the programs and files on your computer.

The My Computer window displays the folders and files on your computer.

The Help Viewer window provides answers to your questions about Windows 2000.

Adventure Travel Tours

As a recent college graduate, you have accepted a job as advertising coordinator for Adventure Travel Tours, a specialty travel company that organizes active adventure vacations. You are responsible for coordinating the advertising program for all locations. Your duties include the creation of brochures, flyers, form letters, news releases, advertisements, and a monthly newsletter, all of which promote Adventure Travel's programs.

The company has recently upgraded to the Windows 2000 operating system, and you have decided that this is a good time to both learn how the new operating system works and to organize the files on your computer. You will begin by using many of the basic Windows fea-

tures that are needed to use a personal computer. This includes learning how to use a mouse, use menus and dialog boxes, start programs, manipulate windows, use the Help system, and explore the contents of your computer.

© Corbis

Starting Windows 2000

The primary purpose of a computer is to run **application software** designed to help you accomplish a task. However, in order to run application software, all computers must first load an operating system that controls the overall activity of the computer.

concept 1

Operating System

1 An **operating system** is a collection of programs that helps the computer manage its resources and that acts as the interface between the user and the computer. The three main functions of an operating system are to manage resources, provide a user interface, and run applications. Managing resources refers to the coordination of all the computer's parts, including keyboard, mouse, printer, monitor storage devices, and memory, so that all parts work together. Users interact with application programs and computer hardware through a **user interface**. Many operating systems use a **graphical user interface (GUI)** in which graphic objects are used to represent features. Running applications refers to the computer running software programs such as a word processor.

The operating system you will learn about in this lab is Microsoft Windows 2000.

Turning on the Computer

When you turn on the computer, the operating system loads automatically and the system and hardware checks are performed.

If your computer is on:

1 ● Press any key on the keyboard to "wake" it up.

Additional Information

Your computer is on if you can hear the fan running and, on most machines, lights are lit on the front.

● If your computer is not on: Flip the power switch located on the back or right side of your computer or push the button on the front of your computer to turn it on.

Additional Information

Do not have any disks in the drives when you start the computer.

HAVING TROUBLE?

The monitor power button and the dials to adjust it are generally located on the front of the monitor.

● If necessary, turn your monitor on and adjust the contrast and brightness.

Your screen should be similar to Figure 1.1.

Additional Information

Use a "strong" password, one that is hard to break. It should be a minimum of seven characters, contain a symbol character in the second through sixth position, and be different from prior passwords. Do not use your name or a common word or name.

Additional Information

Your instructor will provide the necessary user name and password information.

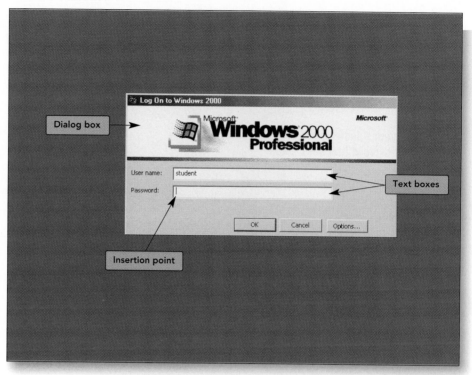

Figure 1.1

The Log On to Windows dialog box is displayed. A **dialog box** appears whenever the program needs to supply additional information to you or needs additional information from you in order to complete a task. In this case, it needs you to enter your personal identification information.

Because multiple users on a single computer are common, as a security measure all users are required to provide the program with a user name and password to access to information stored on the computer. Additionally, because people like to work in different ways, Windows automatically saves changes users have made to suit their personal preferences while they work. These personal settings are then activated when that user logs on again.

Depending on your school's setup, the user name may already be entered and you will only need to enter the password. To enter the requested information, you type it into the appropriate text box. A **text box** is a rectangular area in which you type information. Before typing, the text box must be active and ready to accept information. When active, a blinking vertical bar called an **insertion point** appears in the text box or the content of the text box is highlighted. Pressing the Tab key will move from one feature to another in the dialog box to make it active. If the content of the text box is highlighted, it will be replaced by the new information as you type.

2
- If necessary, press Tab⇥ until the User Name text box is active.

- Type your user name in the User Name text box.

- Press Tab⇥ to move to the Password text box.

- Type your password in the Password text box.

- Press ←Enter.

Additional Information

The password will appear as a series of asterisks as you type it to maintain the privacy of the password.

Another Method

If you know how to use a mouse, you can click in the text boxes to activate them and click [OK] in the dialog box instead of pressing ←Enter.

Your screen may be similar to Figure 1.2

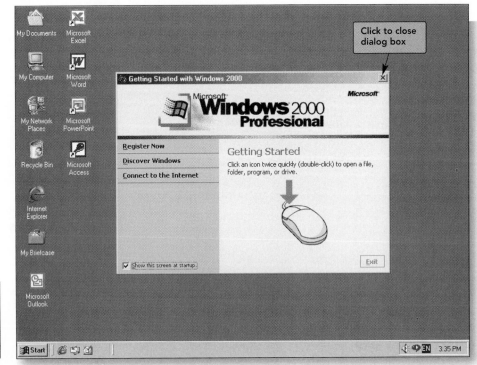

Figure 1.2

Windows 2000 loads your personal settings, and the Getting Started with Windows 2000 box may appear next. Do not be concerned if the Getting Started box is not displayed, as this feature may have been turned off on your computer. You can use this dialog box to register your copy of Windows 2000, to take a tour of the new features of Windows 2000, or to connect to the Internet.

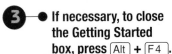

3
- If necessary, to close the Getting Started box, press Alt + F4.

Another Method

If you know how to use a mouse, you can click ⊠ in the upper right corner of the box.

Your screen should be similar to Figure 1.3

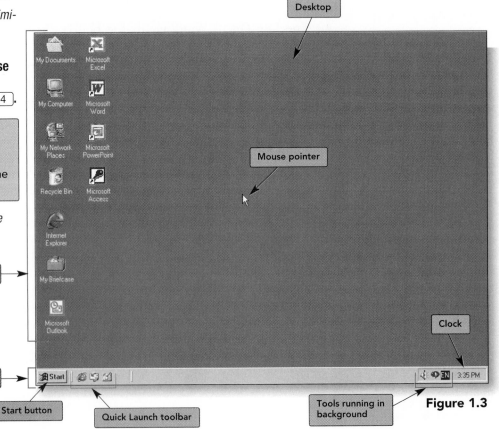

Figure 1.3

Exploring the Desktop

Your screen displays the Windows desktop, from which you access the tools you need to use the computer.

concept 2

Desktop

2 The **desktop** is the opening screen for Windows 2000 and is the place where you begin your work using the computer. It is called a desktop because it provides quick access to the tools you need to complete your work using the computer. The desktop is made up of many items called **objects**. Each object consists of settings and attributes called **properties** that are unique to the object and that affect what the object looks like, what the object can do, or what you can do to the object. Just about all the objects on the desktop have properties associated with them. For example, the small pictures, called **icons**, on the desktop are each made of properties that control what the icon does. The desktop itself is an object that has properties. The properties can be viewed and changed if necessary to suit your needs.

Initially, the Windows 2000 desktop displays six icons that represent functions (described in the table below) needed by most users. Because the desktop can be customized to suit individual needs, your desktop may have been modified from the default Windows 2000 layout. For example, your icons may appear underlined (this indicates how the icon is activated when selected).

Additional Information

You will learn about using a mouse to select items shortly.

Icon		Description
	My Documents	A location where documents you create using an application program are stored.
	My Computer	Used to browse and manage items on a disk.
	My Network Places	Displays the computers on your network.
	Recycle Bin	Stores deleted items that you can later permanently delete or restore.
	Internet Explorer	Starts Internet Explorer or the associated Web browser.
	My Briefcase	Used to transfer information between a desktop and portable computer.

Additional Information

If your taskbar is not visible, it may be set to hide automatically when not in use. To redisplay it, point to the area of the screen (the bottom by default) where the taskbar is located.

At the bottom of the desktop screen is the **taskbar**. The **Start** button on the left end of the bar is used to start a program, open a document, get help, find information, and change system settings. A **button** is a common Windows object that is used to access a feature.

The center of the taskbar is currently blank. It will display **task buttons** representing currently active tasks as you use Windows, making switching between tasks easy. The clock icon on the right end of the taskbar displays the time as maintained by your computer. To the left of the clock are several icons that indicate those tools that are automatically started when you turn on your computer and are running in the background, such as a

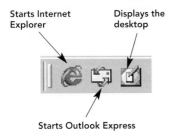

Starts Internet Explorer

Displays the desktop

Starts Outlook Express

speaker if your system includes audio hardware. This area also temporarily displays icons while a tool is in use, such as a printer when printing is in progress.

In addition, the taskbar can display several different **toolbars**. Toolbars contain buttons that provide shortcuts to starting programs or using common features and commands. The default Windows 2000 setup displays the Quick Launch toolbar in the taskbar (shown on the left). This toolbar contains buttons to start different elements of the Microsoft Internet Explorer Web browser program that is included with the Windows 2000 operating system. It also contains a very handy 🔲 Show Desktop button that you will learn about shortly.

Using the Mouse

The ⬚ symbol on your screen is the **mouse pointer**. It is used to interact with objects on the desktop and is controlled by the hardware device called a **mouse** that is attached to your computer.

Most commonly the mouse is a handheld device that you move across the surface of your desk. The most common type is a **mechanical mouse** in which a rubber-coated ball on the bottom of the mouse moves as you move the mouse. The ball's movement is translated into signals that tell the computer how to move the onscreen pointer. The direction the ball moves controls the direction the pointer moves on the screen. Another type of mouse, called an **optical mouse**, emits and senses light to detect mouse movement.

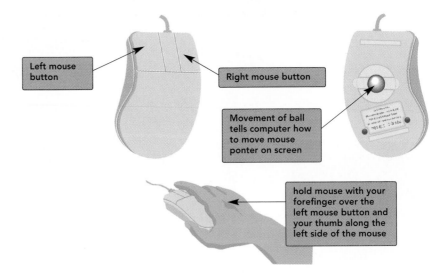

Left mouse button

Right mouse button

Movement of ball tells computer how to move mouse ponter on screen

hold mouse with your forefinger over the left mouse button and your thumb along the left side of the mouse

The mouse pointer changes shape on the screen depending on what it is pointing to. Some of the most common shapes are shown in the table on the next page.

Pointer Shape	Meaning
↖	Normal select
✋	Link select
⧖	Busy
⊘	Area is not available
↖?	Displays Help on selected item
↕	Horizontal/vertical resize
↖	Diagonal resize

On top of the mouse are two or three buttons that are used to choose items on the screen. If your system has a stick, ball, or touch pad, the buttons are located adjacent to the device. Typically, you move the mouse to **point** to items and use the mouse buttons to **click**, **double-click**, and **drag**. These mouse actions are described in the table below.

Action	Description
Point	Move the mouse to position the mouse pointer on the item you want to use.
Click	Press and release the left mouse button.
Right-click	Press and release the right mouse button.
Double-click	Quickly press and release the left mouse button twice.
Drag	Move the mouse while holding down the left or right mouse button.

1 ● Move the mouse in all directions (up, down, left, and right) and note the movement of the mouse pointer.

● Point to  My Computer .

Your screen should be similar to Figure 1.4

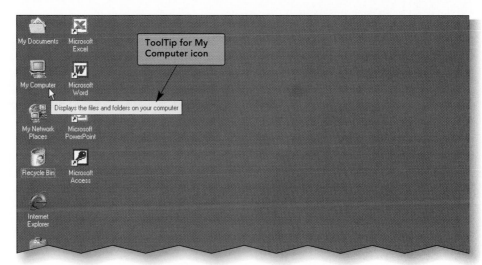

Figure 1.4

The pointer on the screen moves in the direction you moved the mouse. Additionally, many icons and most toolbar buttons will display a **ToolTip** containing a brief description of the item when you rest the mouse pointer on the item for a moment.

2 ● Point to several other icons to view their ToolTips.

● Point to each of the buttons on the taskbar to view their ToolTips.

● If your icons do not display underlines, click on ⬚ , otherwise point to ⬚ to select it.

Additional Information
If your desktop icons display underlines, pointing to the icon both displays the ToolTip and selects (highlights) the icon.

Your screen should be similar to Figure 1.5

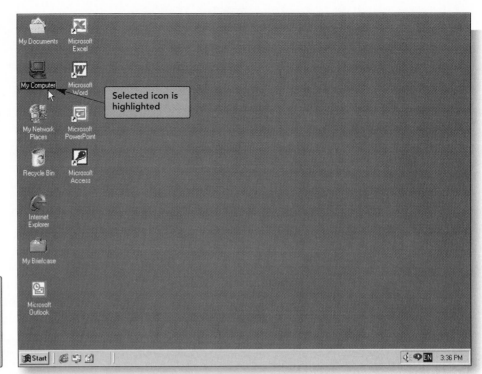

Figure 1.5

The ⬚ icon appears highlighted, indicating it is the selected item and ready to be used.

Note: The procedures in this lab assume that your icons do not display underlines. This means you click on an item to select it and double-click on it to choose and open it. If your icons display underlines, simply point to the item to select it and click on it to choose and open it.

Using Menus

As you learn about Windows 2000, you will find there are many ways to perform the same task. However, using the 🏁Start button is one of the best places to learn how to use Windows 2000. It provides quick and easy access to most features you will use frequently.

Opening the Start Menu

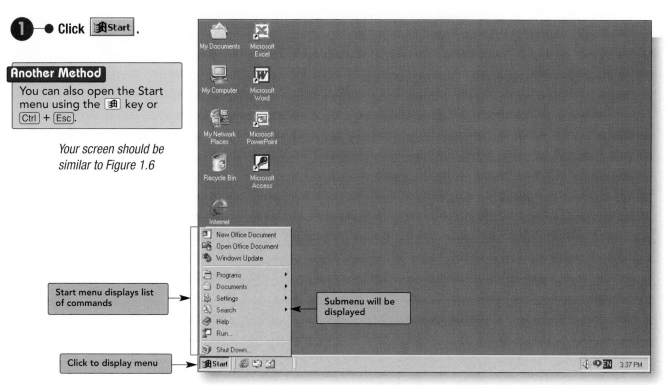

1 ● Click [Start].

Another Method

You can also open the Start menu using the [⊞] key or [Ctrl] + [Esc].

Your screen should be similar to Figure 1.6

Start menu displays list of commands

Submenu will be displayed

Click to display menu

Figure 1.6

The Start menu can be used to access and begin all activities you want to perform on the computer. It is one of many menus you will see in Windows 2000.

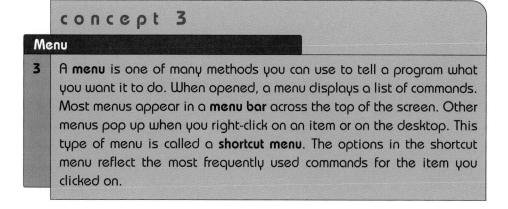

concept 3

Menu

3 A **menu** is one of many methods you can use to tell a program what you want it to do. When opened, a menu displays a list of commands. Most menus appear in a **menu bar** across the top of the screen. Other menus pop up when you right-click on an item or on the desktop. This type of menu is called a **shortcut menu**. The options in the shortcut menu reflect the most frequently used commands for the item you clicked on.

Menus may include the following features (not all menus include all features):

Feature	Meaning
Ellipsis (...)	Indicates a dialog box will be displayed.
▶	Indicates a submenu will be displayed.
ⅴ	Indicates the menu is a short menu. Clicking ⅴ expands the menu to display all options.
Dimmed command	Indicates the command is not available for selection until certain other conditions are met.
Shortcut key	A key or key combination that can be used to execute a command without using the menu.
Checkmark ✔	Indicates a toggle type of command: selecting it turns the feature on or off. A ✔ indicates the feature is on.
Bullet	Indicates that the commands in that group are mutually exclusive: only one can be selected. The bullet indicates the currently selected feature.

The basic Start menu consists of a list of commands that are used to start programs, open documents, customize your system, get Help, search for items on your computer, and more. The icons to the left of each command are graphic representations of the feature. Because the Start menu can be customized, yours may display additional commands.

Selecting Commands

Menus are everywhere in Windows 2000, but they all operate in the same way. Once a menu is open, you can select a command from the menu by pointing to it. A colored highlight bar, called the **selection cursor**, appears over the selected command. If the selected command line displays a ▶, a **submenu** of commands automatically appears when the command is selected. This is commonly called a **cascading menu**.

1 Point to the Shut Down command and slide the mouse pointer up the menu to select the Run, Help, and Search commands.

● Slide the mouse pointer to the right and point to the commands in the Search submenu.

Another Method

You can also move the selection cursor using the four directional arrow keys ⬆, ⬇, ⬅, ➡.

Your screen should be similar to Figure 1.7

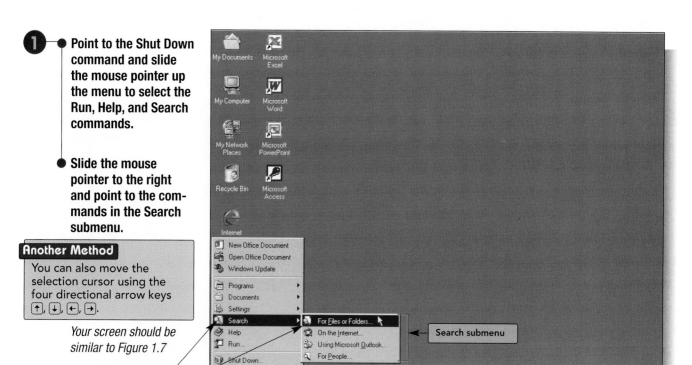

Figure 1.7

Because an arrowhead symbol appears next to the Search command, it displays a submenu of additional commands when selected.

Some menus will display a short version of the available options when the menu is opened. These menus are personalized to the user's needs by displaying only those commands that are frequently used and hiding others.

2 Point to the Settings, Documents, and Programs commands to see the submenus associated with each.

● If necessary, click ⊻ of the Programs submenu to display the expanded menu.

Your screen should be similar to Figure 1.8

Additional Information

The programs appearing on your screen may differ from those in Figure 1.8.

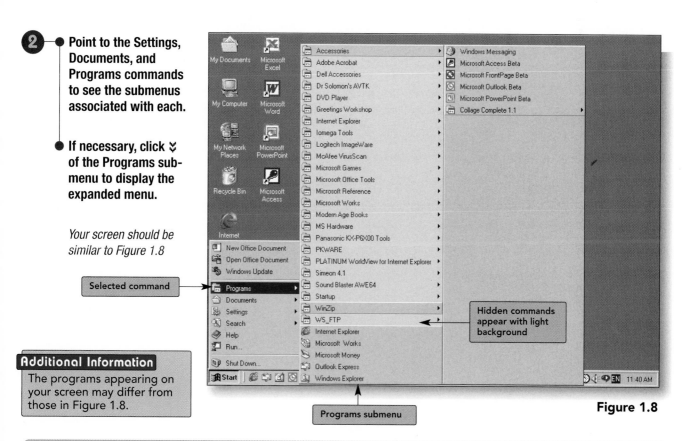

Figure 1.8

The expanded menu displays all the Programs menu options. If your sub-menu was already personalized and displayed ⌄ to expand it, the commands that were hidden appear on a light gray background.

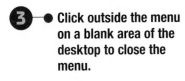 **Click outside the menu on a blank area of the desktop to close the menu.**

Your screen should be similar to Figure 1.9

 Another Method

You can also click ⊞Start again, press the ⊞ key, or Ctrl + Esc to close the Start menu.

Start menu closed again ➔

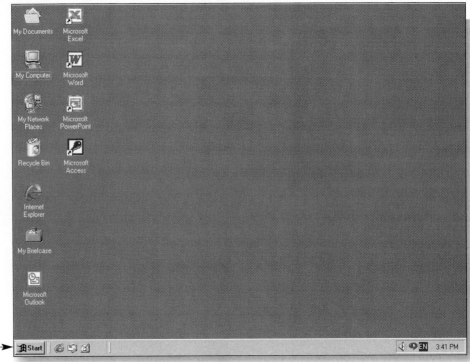

Figure 1.9

Developing the skill for moving the mouse and correctly positioning the pointer takes some time. If you accidentally find yourself in the wrong location or in a command that you did not intend to select, cancel the selected menu as you did above and try again.

Choosing Commands

Next you will use the Start menu to open the Windows 2000 Help program. Once a menu is open and the command selected, you click on the command to choose it. When the command is chosen, the associated action is performed.

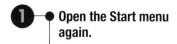
Open the Start menu again.

Click 🎞 Help to choose this command.

Another Method

If your commands display underlined letters, you can type the underlined command letter to choose a command. Also, once a command is selected (highlighted), you can press ⏎Enter to choose it.

Your screen should be similar to Figure 1.10

Additional Information

Some commands have keyboard shortcuts that you can use in place of selecting the command from the menu. The keyboard shortcut to start Windows Help is the 🎞 + F1 .

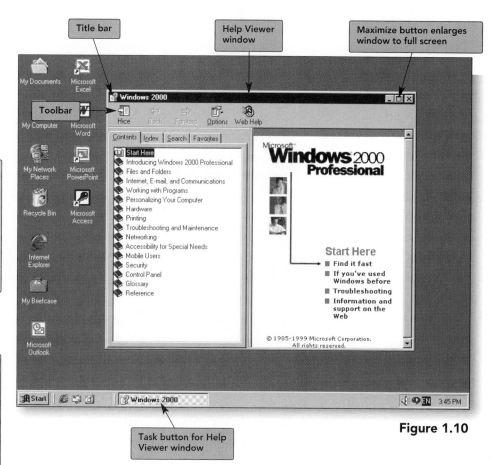

Title bar

Help Viewer window

Maximize button enlarges window to full screen

Toolbar

Task button for Help Viewer window

Figure 1.10

You have executed the Help command, the Start menu is closed, and the Windows 2000 Help program is started.

Working with a Window

HAVING TROUBLE?

Do not be concerned if your window is a different size or displays different information. You will learn to use the Help Viewer window shortly.

The Help program is displayed in a window, called the Help Viewer, on the desktop. The taskbar displays a task button for the open window.

concept 4

Window

4 A **window** is a rectangular section on the screen that is used to display information and other programs. Each program that you open is displayed in its own window. Multiple programs, each in its own window, can be open at the same time. This makes it easy to switch from one project to another as you work.

HAVING TROUBLE?

If your Help window does not display the four tabs as in Figure 1.10, click 🔲 in the toolbar.

All windows have a **title bar** located at the top of the window that displays the program's name, in this case, Windows 2000. It also contains buttons that are used to control the window. Below the title bar is a toolbar containing buttons that are used to navigate within the Help Viewer window. The content of the window is displayed in the large space below the toolbar.

Sizing and Moving a Window

Sometimes the location and size of a window when it opens are not convenient for what you want to do. To make the desktop more workable, you can move and size windows.

concept 5

Sizing and Moving Windows

5 Sizing and moving windows allows you to conveniently view information on your desktop. The size of a window can be adjusted to just about any size you want. You can quickly **minimize** a window to its smallest size, **maximize** a window to its largest size, **restore** a window to its previous size, or close a window entirely. In addition, a window can be custom sized by changing its height and/or width.

A window can be moved anywhere on the desktop. Moving a window simply displays the window at another location on the desktop. It does not change the size of the window.

You will try out these features by sizing and moving the Help Viewer window on your desktop. Your Help Viewer window may be a different size than shown in Figure 1.10. It may even be maximized. This is because Windows remembers and stores in your personal settings the size of a window when you last used it and displays it the same size as it last appeared.

The buttons on the right end of the title bar are used to change a window to several standard sizes, described in the following table.

Button	Description
▬ Minimize	Reduces a window to its smallest size.
❑ Maximize	Enlarges a window to the full screen.
⮽ Restore	Returns a window to its previous size after a window has been maximized or minimized.
☒ Close	Closes the window and exits the application.

First, you will maximize the window.

HAVING TROUBLE?
If your window is already maximized as shown in Figure 1.11, skip step 1.

① ● **Click** ▢ **Maximize in the Help Viewer window title bar.**

Your screen should be similar to Figure 1.11

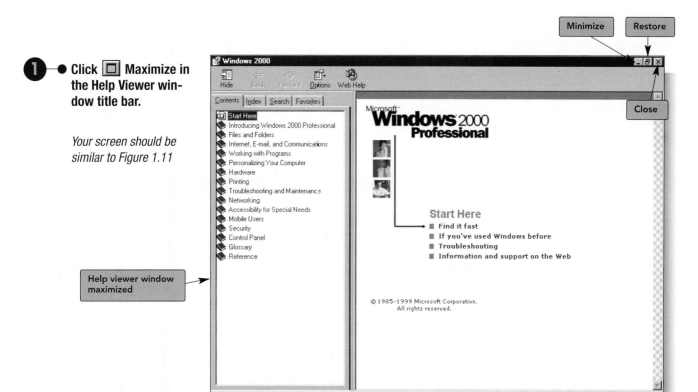

Help viewer window maximized

Figure 1.11

The Help Viewer window now appears the full size of the screen and occupies the entire desktop. Maximizing a window is helpful when you want to be able to view the maximum amount of content possible in the window. When a window is maximized, the Maximize button changes to 🗗 Restore. This button is used to return a window to its previous size.

② ● **Click** 🗗 **Restore.**

Your screen should be similar to Figure 1.12

Additional Information

You can also double-click the window title bar to maximize or restore a window.

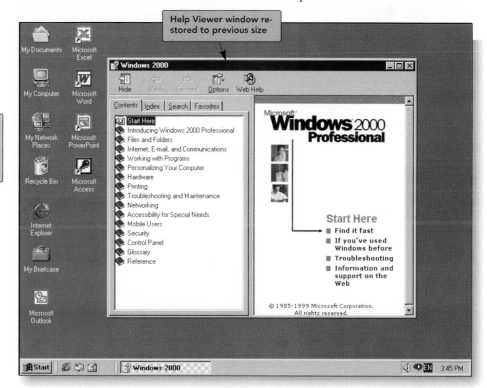

Help Viewer window restored to previous size

Figure 1.12

The Help window is now the same size as it was before it was maximized.

Next you will custom size and shape the window by pointing to the window border and dragging the border in the direction you want to size it. Dragging inward decreases the size, and dragging outward increases the size. To change the height of a window, drag the top or bottom window border. To change the width of a window, drag the side window border. Dragging a corner changes the height and width simultaneously. First you will adjust the height and width of the window.

3 ● Point to a side border of the Help Viewer window and when the pointer changes to ↔, drag the mouse inward and outward to adjust the width of the window.

● Point to a top or bottom window border and when the pointer changes to $\updownarrow$, drag the mouse inward and outward to adjust the height of the window.

● Size the window using the borders until the window size is as in Figure 1.13.

Your screen should be similar to Figure 1.13

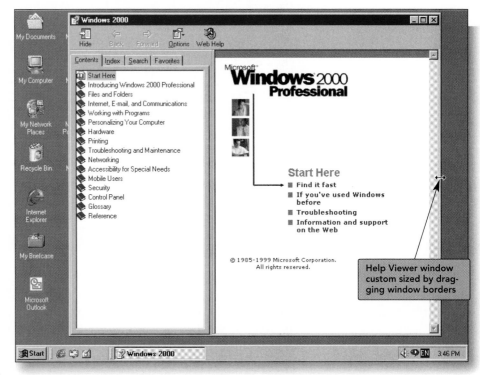

Figure 1.13

Generally, it is faster to size a window by dragging the window corner, because this adjusts both the height and width simultaneously. When you point to a window corner, the pointer changes to $\nwarrow$, indicating the direction in which the window can be sized.

4 ● Point to a corner of the
window and when the
pointer changes to ↖,
drag the mouse in-
ward and outward to
adjust both the height
and width of the win-
dow simultaneously.

● Size the Help Viewer
window until the win-
dow size is as in
Figure 1.14.

*Your screen should be
similar to Figure 1.14*

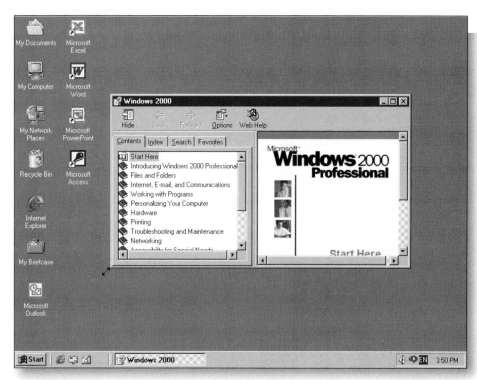

Figure 1.14

Notice as the window is sized that information in the window is reformatted as much as possible to display in the new window space. Once a
window has been custom sized, the only way to return it to the original size
is by resizing the window again.

You can also move a window to another location on the desktop by dragging the window title bar.

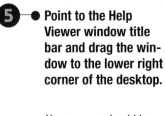

Additional Information
You cannot size a window
that is maximized.

5 ● Point to the Help
Viewer window title
bar and drag the win-
dow to the lower right
corner of the desktop.

*Your screen should be
similar to Figure 1.15*

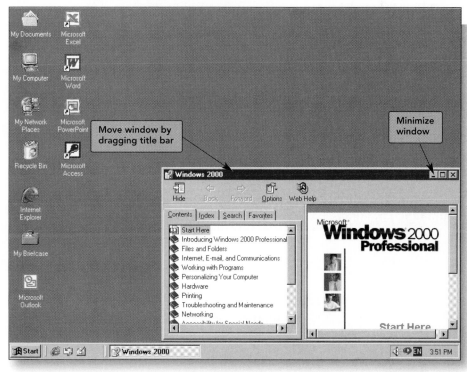

Figure 1.15

Moving a window allows you to see information under it on the desktop or in other open windows while still being able to view the information in the window.

Scrolling a Window

The **scroll bars** on the side and bottom of a space are used with a mouse to bring additional lines of information into view in a space. The vertical scroll bar is used to move up and down, and the horizontal scroll bar is used to move from side to side in the space. The scroll bar consists of **scroll arrows** and a **scroll box**. Clicking the arrows moves the information line by line in the direction of the arrows, allowing new information to be displayed in the space. To move larger distances quickly, you can click above or below the scroll box to move the information up or down in larger increments. Additionally, you can drag the scroll box to move to a general location.

Additional Information

If there is no scroll box in the scroll bar, this indicates that all of the available information is displayed.

1 ● Click ▼ several times in the vertical scroll bar of the left window space to bring more information into view.

● Point to ▼ and hold down the left mouse button for a few seconds to continuously scroll down the information.

● Drag the scroll box to the bottom of the scroll bar.

● Click several times on the scroll bar above the scroll box.

Your screen should be similar to Figure 1.16

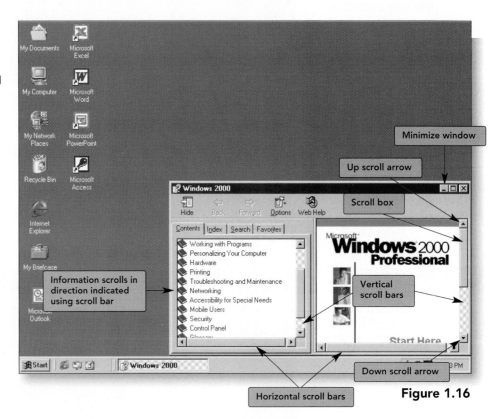

Figure 1.16

Additional Information

In many scroll bars, the size of the scroll box also indicates the relative amount of information available. For example, a small box indicates that only a small amount of the total available information is displayed, whereas a large box indicates that almost all or a large portion of the total amount of available information is displayed.

As you scrolled, the information moved in the direction indicated, allowing new information to be displayed. Did you notice the movement of the scroll box as you scrolled? It moves down along the scroll bar to show your relative position within the area of available information.

Minimizing and Restoring a Window

Often you will want to keep a window open for future use, but you do not want it to occupy space on the desktop. To do this, you can minimize the window.

1 ● **Click**  **Minimize in the Help Viewer window title bar.**

Another Method

You can also click the window's taskbar button to minimize the window.

Your screen should be similar to Figure 1.17

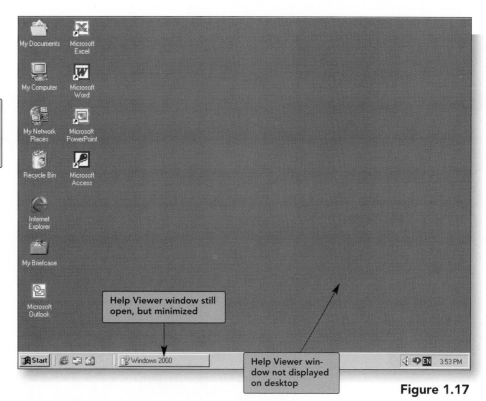

Help Viewer window still open, but minimized

Help Viewer window not displayed on desktop

Figure 1.17

The window is no longer displayed on the desktop. The Help Viewer button in the taskbar, however, is still displayed. This indicates the window is still open, but minimized. To redisplay the window, simply click on its taskbar button.

2 ● **Click**  .

Additional Information

You can click the System menu button in the title bar to display a list of commands that are used to move, size, and otherwise control the window.

Your screen should be similar to Figure 1.18

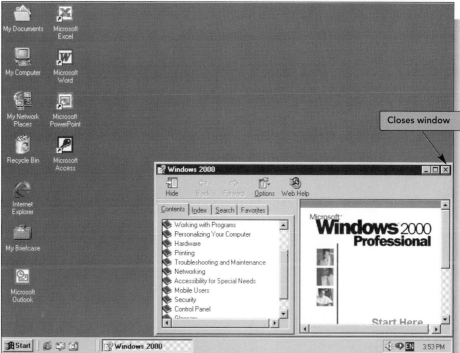

Closes window

Figure 1.18

The Help Viewer window is redisplayed on the desktop in the size and location it last appeared.

Closing a Window

When you are finished using a program, you can close the window and exit the program.

1 ● Click ☒ Close.

Another Method

The keyboard shortcut to close the active window is [Alt] + [F4].

Your screen should be similar to Figure 1.19

Additional Information

If a window is minimized, you can quickly close the program without restoring the window first by choosing Close from the taskbar button's shortcut menu.

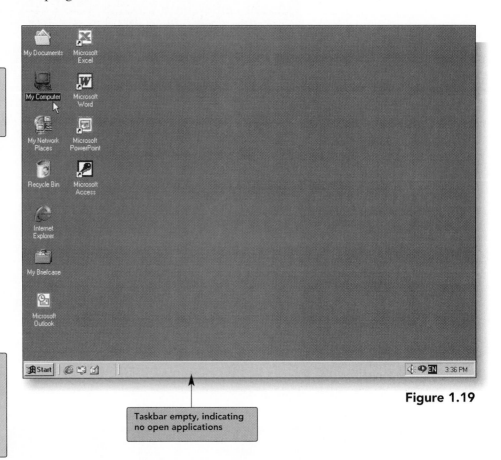

Taskbar empty, indicating no open applications

Figure 1.19

The Help Viewer window is closed and the Help taskbar button is removed, indicating the program is no longer active.

Using Windows 2000 Help

You are now ready to use Help to access information about using Windows 2000. Online help is available in most Windows applications and can be an invaluable resource to learning how to use a program. Because most Help programs operate in a similar manner, learning to use Windows Help will make it easier to use Help in other applications.

1 ● Open the Help Window.

● Size and move the window as in Figure 1.20.

Your screen should be similar to Figure 1.20

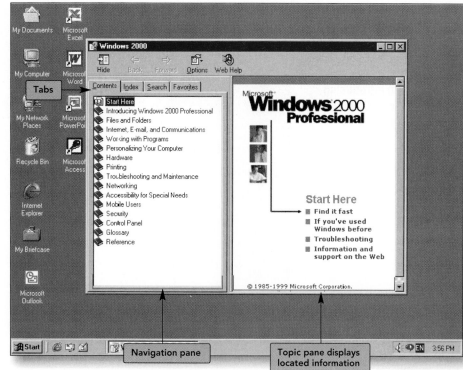

Figure 1.20

Additional Information

Use [Show] to display or [Hide] to hide the navigation pane.

The Help window is divided into two vertical panes. **Panes** divide a window into separate scrollable areas that can display different information. The **navigation pane** on the left displays four folder-like tabs, Contents, Index, Search, and Favorites, which are used to access the four different means of getting Help information as described in the following table. The right pane is the **topic pane** where the located information is displayed.

Tab	Description
Contents	Provides a table of contents listing Help topics that you can browse to locate and select topics of interest.
Index	Provides a scrollable alphabetical list of index entries from which you can select to access topics.
Search	Used to locate every occurrence of a word or phrase that is used in Help.
Favorites	Displays Help topics you have marked as favorites so you can quickly access the topic for viewing.

Using the Contents Tab

First you will use the Contents tab to access Help information by selecting topics from a table of contents listing. To open a tab and make it active, click on it with the mouse. The active tab appears in front of the other tabs and displays the available options for that feature.

1 • **If the Contents tab is not the active tab, click on it.**

• **Point to Introducing Windows 2000 Professional.**

Your screen should be similar to Figure 1.21

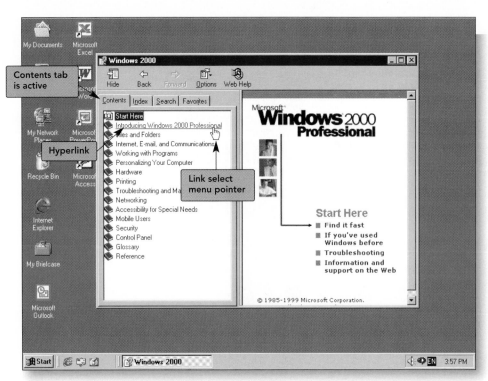

Figure 1.21

Additional Information

The Windows Help system uses Hypertext Markup Language (HTML), a simple programming language that is used to create hyperlinks and format and display information.

The Contents tab displays a table of contents listing of Help topics. Notice that the topic you are pointing to appears in blue text and underlined and that the mouse pointer appears as a 🖑. This indicates the item is a hyperlink. A **hyperlink** typically provides a connection to information at another location. Clicking on a hyperlink jumps to that location and displays the information.

2 • **Click Introducing Windows 2000 Professional.**

• **Click How to Use Help.**

• **Click Find a Help topic.**

Your screen should be similar to Figure 1.22

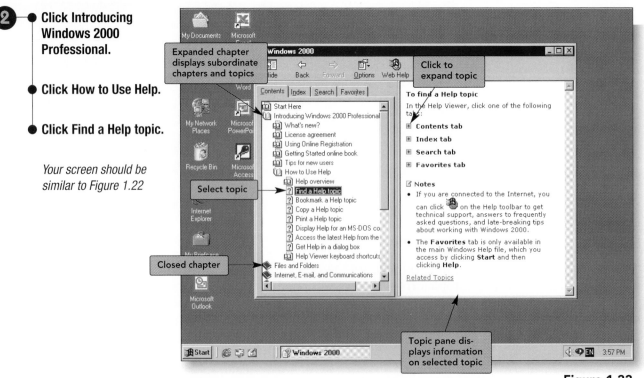

Figure 1.22

Clicking on an item preceded with a ◆ opens a "chapter," which expands to display either additional chapters or specific Help topics. Chapters are preceded with a 🕮 icon, and additional chapters with a 🕮 icon. The topic icon appears as ➕. Subordinate chapters and topics appear indented as in an outline. The topic pane displays information about the selected topic.

3 ● **Read the Help infor-**
mation on how to find
a Help topic.

● **Click ➕ Contents tab**
in the topic pane.

Additional Information
A ToolTip appears when you point to many hyperlinks, providing information about what will happen if you click on the hyperlink.

Your screen should be similar to Figure 1.23

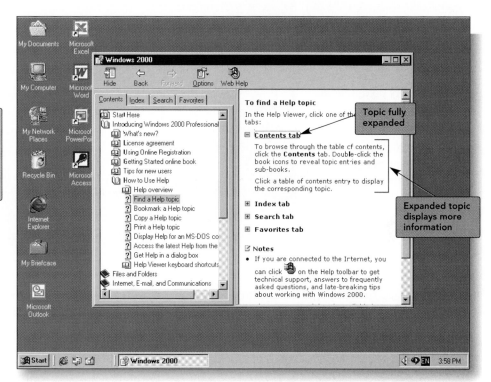

Figure 1.23

More information about the topic is displayed and the ➕ changes to a ➖ indicating the topic content is fully expanded. Now, as more information is displayed in the window, much of the other information is no longer visible. It has moved further down in the window space to allow more information to be displayed.

Using the Index Tab

You will read the Help information about the other tabs, and then use the Index tab to find out what the My Computer icon on the desktop does.

① ● Expand the other three topics and read about how to use each of the tabs.

HAVING TROUBLE?
Scroll the pane to see the additional information.

● Click the Index tab to make it active.

● Type **my computer** in the text box.

● Double-click the "viewing computer contents" topic.

Your screen should be similar to Figure 1.24

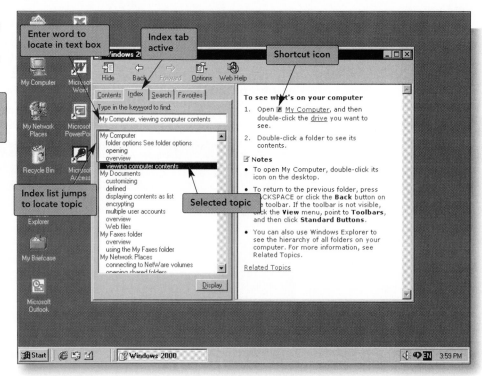

Figure 1.24

Information about how to use My Computer is displayed. Typing a topic in the text box quickly located the information in the index. When you know what topic you want information about, using the Index tab is a lot faster than using the Contents tab.

Next you decide to follow the Help instructions on this topic to see what is on your computer. You will keep the Help window open so you can see the directions while performing the actions. Notice the shortcut icon ⊞ next to the My Computer hyperlink in the topic pane. This indicates that the program will perform the action associated with the link topic, in this case, open the My Computer window.

Additional Information
More typically, the My Computer window is opened by double-clicking the ⊞ icon on the desktop as the directions under the Notes section of the Help window indicate.

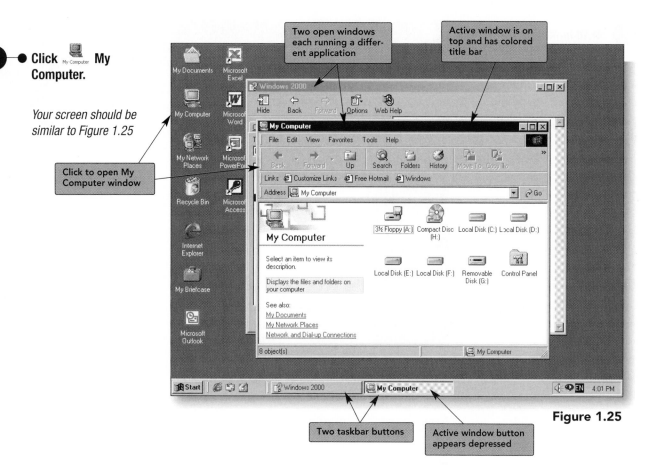

① ● Click [My Computer] **My Computer.**

Your screen should be similar to Figure 1.25

Click to open My Computer window

Two open windows each running a different application

Active window is on top and has colored title bar

Figure 1.25

Two taskbar buttons

Active window button appears depressed

A second window is open on the desktop, and the taskbar displays a button for this open window.

Working with Multiple Open Windows

There are now two programs running at the same time, Windows 2000 Help and Windows Explorer displaying the My Computer window. The capability to run multiple programs at the same time is called **multitasking**. This makes using your computer more like you would actually work, allowing you to switch easily between tasks without having to put one away before beginning the other.

Making a Window Active

The My Computer window is the **active window**, the window that is currently in use. You can tell it is the active window because the taskbar button appears depressed and the window title bar is colored. Multiple windows can be open on the desktop at once, but only one window is active at a time.

When a new window is opened, it appears in the size in which it was last used and in any location on the desktop. The newly opened window is automatically the active window and appears on top of other open windows on the desktop. To see a window that is below another window and make it the active window, you can click on the window's taskbar button or anywhere on the window if it is visible.

1 To make the Help window active, click anywhere in the Help window or click [Windows 2000 Professional].

Another Method

The keyboard shortcut to switch between open items is [Alt] + [Tab↹].

Your screen should be similar to Figure 1.26

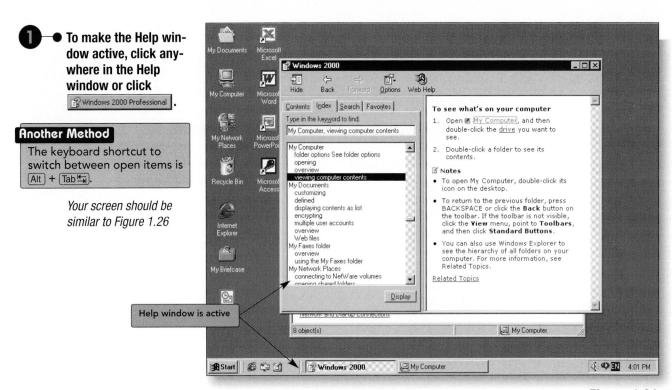

Help window is active

Figure 1.26

Now the active window is on top and the title bar of the Help window is blue. The taskbar button of the active window also appears depressed.

Arranging Windows

It is very common when using your computer that you will have more than one application running at the same time. When working with multiple open windows, it is often convenient to **cascade** or **tile** the windows.

Feature	Description	
Cascade	Layers open windows, displaying the active window fully and only the title bars of all other open windows behind it.	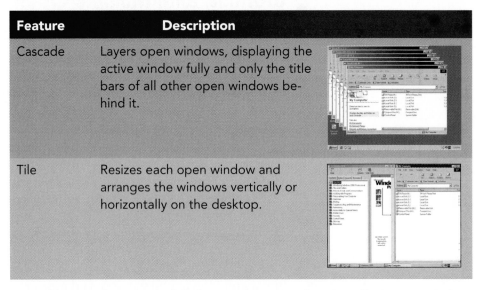
Tile	Resizes each open window and arranges the windows vertically or horizontally on the desktop.	

Cascading windows is useful if you want to work primarily in one window but you want to see the titles of other open windows. Tiling is most useful when you want to work in several applications simultaneously, because it allows you to quickly see the contents of all open windows and move between them. However, the greater the number of open windows, the smaller is the space available to display the tiled window contents.

The taskbar shortcut menu contains commands associated with taskbar settings and arranging open windows. You will cascade the two open windows.

Open windows in cascade arrangement

1 ● **Right-click an empty area on the taskbar to display the shortcut menu.**

● **Choose Cascade Windows.**

Your screen should be similar to Figure 1.27

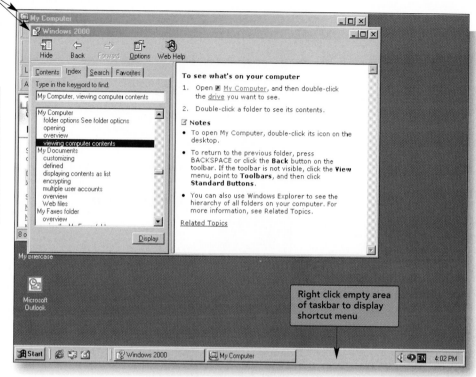

Figure 1.27

Additional Information

Windows that are minimized are not arranged.

The windows are resized and they overlap with the title bars visible. You can click on any visible part of the window to make it active.

2 ● **Make the My Computer window active.**

Your screen should be similar to Figure 1.28

Active window pulled to front of stack

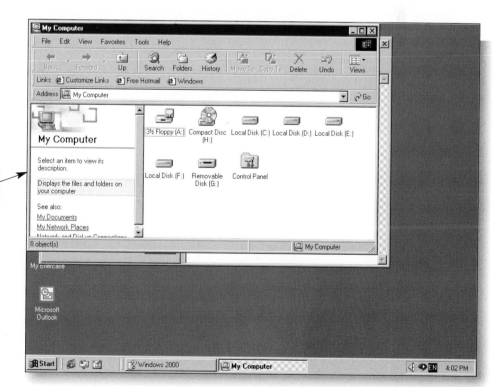

Figure 1.28

The My Computer window is pulled to the front of the stack and covers the other cascaded window. To restore the window size and arrangement as it was prior to cascading the windows, you can use the **Undo** command. Undo allows you to reverse your last action or command.

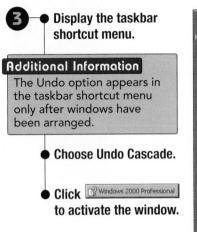

3 ● **Display the taskbar shortcut menu.**

Additional Information
The Undo option appears in the taskbar shortcut menu only after windows have been arranged.

● **Choose Undo Cascade.**

● **Click** [Windows 2000 Professional] **to activate the window.**

Your screen should be similar to Figure 1.29

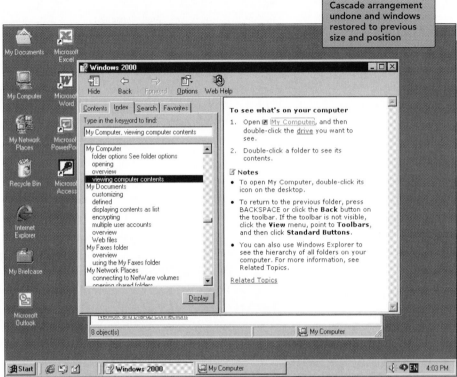

> Cascade arrangement undone and windows restored to previous size and position

Figure 1.29

The windows are arranged and sized again as they were before using the Cascade command. If you do not undo the arrangement before switching to another arrangement, the windows remain in the size and position set by the second arrangement and cannot be returned to their original size without custom sizing and moving the windows. Next you will arrange the windows on the desktop without overlapping.

4 ● **Choose Tile Windows Vertically from the taskbar shortcut menu.**

Your screen should be similar to Figure 1.30

Two open windows tiled vertically

Figure 1.30

Additional Information

Tile Horizontally arranges windows horizontally on the desktop.

The two windows are vertically arranged on the desktop, each taking up one-half of the vertical space.

5 ● **Choose Undo Tile from the taskbar shortcut menu.**

Your screen should be similar to Figure 1.31

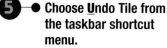

Tile arrangement undone and windows restored to previous size and position

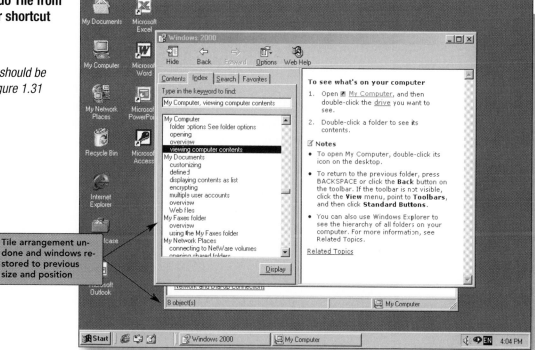

Figure 1.31

Minimizing and Restoring Multiple Windows

Sometimes you may want to minimize all open windows at once so that you can quickly see the entire desktop. You can do this using the Minimize All Windows command on the taskbar shortcut menu. In addition, if the Quick Launch toolbar is displayed in the taskbar, the  Show Desktop button can perform the same action.

1 ● Click  Show Desktop or choose **M**inimize All Windows from the taskbar shortcut menu.

Another Method

The keyboard shortcut is the ⊞ + M.

Your screen should be similar to Figure 1.32

Additional Information

Dialog boxes are minimized only if the  Show Desktop button is used.

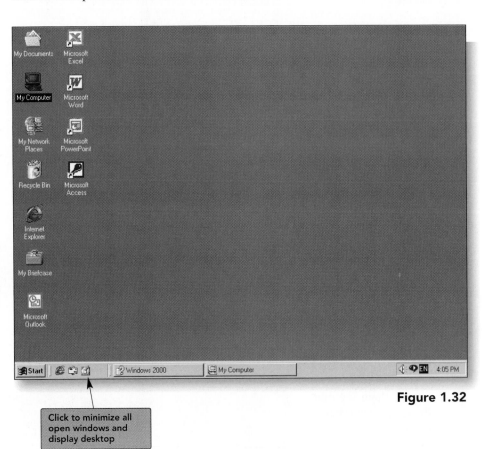

Figure 1.32

Click to minimize all open windows and display desktop

The desktop is cleared of all open windows. This is much quicker than minimizing each window individually. If a dialog box were open, it would be minimized also. It would not, however, appear as a taskbar button. To restore all open windows,

2 ● Click 🖼 **Show Desktop again or choose Undo Minimize All from the taskbar shortcut menu.**

Your screen should be similar to Figure 1.33

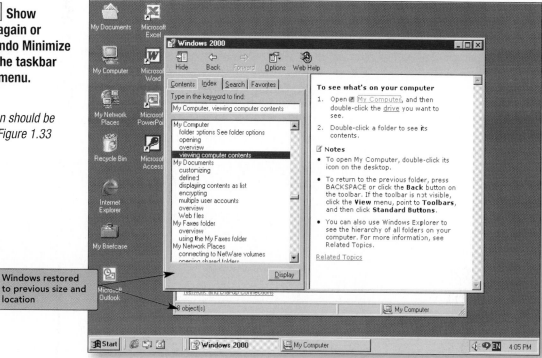

Windows restored to previous size and location

Figure 1.33

Only the windows and dialog boxes that were open on the desktop at the time they were minimized are restored.

Using My Computer

My Computer is used to see the contents of your secondary storage devices such as your hard disk, floppy disk, CD, DVD, and network drives. The contents consist of files and folders.

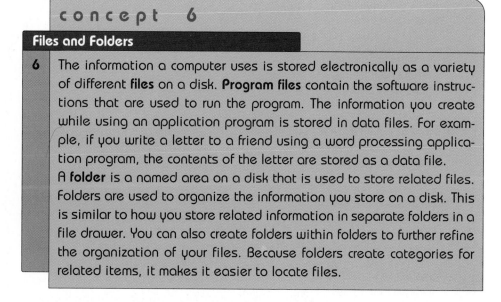

concept 6

Files and Folders

6 The information a computer uses is stored electronically as a variety of different **files** on a disk. **Program files** contain the software instructions that are used to run the program. The information you create while using an application program is stored in data files. For example, if you write a letter to a friend using a word processing application program, the contents of the letter are stored as a data file.

A **folder** is a named area on a disk that is used to store related files. Folders are used to organize the information you store on a disk. This is similar to how you store related information in separate folders in a file drawer. You can also create folders within folders to further refine the organization of your files. Because folders create categories for related items, it makes it easier to locate files.

Windows 2000 includes four default desktop folders, 📁 , 📁 , 📁 , and 📁 .

Exploring the My Computer Window

As with all windows, the title bar displays identifying information about the contents of the window. This information typically consists of the name of the program, the name of the open file, or, as in this case, the name of the folder being viewed. Below the title bar is a menu bar containing six menus that, when selected, display drop-down menus of commands. The menus contain the same features and operate just like the Start menu. The menus are described in the following table.

Menu	Use
File	Used to perform tasks related to files, such as renaming and deleting.
Edit	Used to undo, cut, copy, paste, and select objects within the displayed window.
View	Controls the display of features such as toolbars, icon arrangement, and the status bar.
Favorites	Lists user-defined favorite Web sites and folders.
Tools	Used to connect, synchronize, and disconnect to a network drive, and to change settings associated with folders.
Help	Opens Windows 2000 Help.

1 ● **Size and position the My Computer window as shown in Figure 1.34.**

● **Click on the File menu to display the drop-down menu.**

● **Point to the Edit menu, and then to the View menu.**

● **Point to the three other menus to display their drop-down menus.**

● **Click on a blank area in the window to deactivate the menu bar.**

Your screen should be similar to Figure 1.34

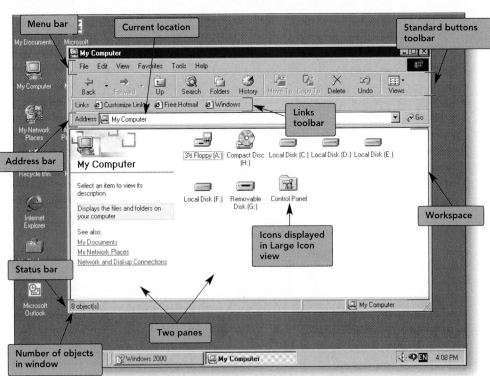

Figure 1.34

By default, the My Computer window displays three toolbars below the menu bar: Standard Buttons, Links, and Address Bar. The buttons on the Standard Buttons toolbar activate the most commonly used menu commands and features in the window. The Links Bar initially contains buttons

HAVING TROUBLE?

If any of these toolbars are not displayed, use View/Toolbars and select the appropriate toolbar from the Submenu.

Additional Information

If the window is not large enough, the left pane is not displayed.

HAVING TROUBLE?

If your left pane displays different information than in Figure 1.34, choose View/Explorer Bar and clear the selection from all options. Then choose Tools/Folder Options and select Enable Web content in folders under Web View.

Additional Information

If the status bar is not displayed choose View/Status Bar to turn it on.

that access various Microsoft Web sites designed to help you locate information. The Address Bar contains a text box that displays the current location you are viewing. You can also use it to enter a location to go to by typing the location address in the text box.

The large area below the toolbars is the **workspace** where the information you are viewing is displayed. In the My Computer folder window, the workspace is divided into two panes. The left pane currently provides directions on how to use the window and links to other folders. The right pane, called the details pane, displays icons representing the drives on your computer and a folder icon. Each icon is identified by a title below the icon. Some or all of the items shown in the table below may be displayed in your My Computer window.

Icon	Representation
	3½ floppy-disk drive
	Hard-disk drive (local disk)
	Network drive
	CD-ROM drive (compact disk)
	Removable disk (zip disk)
Folder Options	Control Panel folder

At the bottom of the window a **status bar** is displayed. The information displayed in the status bar varies with the program you are using and the task being performed. The purpose of the status bar is to advise you of the status of different program conditions and features as you use the program. Currently the status bar tells you the number of objects in the window.

Changing Window Views

Icons in a My Computer can be viewed or displayed in four different ways as described in the following table. These views change the icon size, display order, and the amount of information about the files and folders. Depending upon what you are doing, one view may be more helpful than another.

View	Description
Large Icons	Displays items using large icons.
Small Icons	Displays items using small icons.
List	Displays items in a list.
Details	Displays items in a list with details about each item.

The View menu contains the commands to change the icon display. In addition, the ⊞ button is a drop-down list button, which displays a drop-down list of these menu options when selected. The Large Icon view option (shown in Figure 1.34) is the default setting for My Computer. This view displays large icons arranged alphabetically across rows.

1 ● Click  to open the Views drop-down list.

● Choose Small Icons from the [Views] button drop-down list.

● Large Icons
  Small Icons
  List
  Details

Your screen should be similar to Figure 1.35

Additional Information
A bullet next to an option indicates it is selected.

Another Method
The menu equivalent is View/Small Icons.

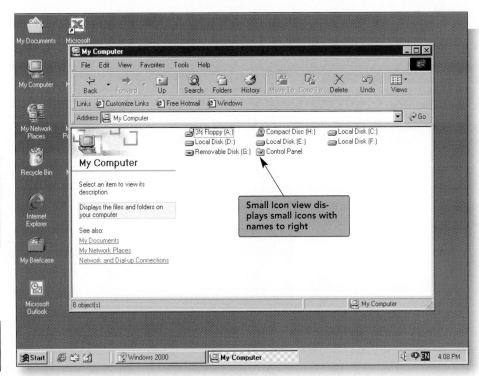

Figure 1.35

Smaller versions of the icons are displayed to the side of each item, allowing more items to be displayed in the window.

2 ● Change the view to List and then Details to see the different arrangements.

● Change the view back to Large Icons.

Your screen should be similar to Figure 1.36

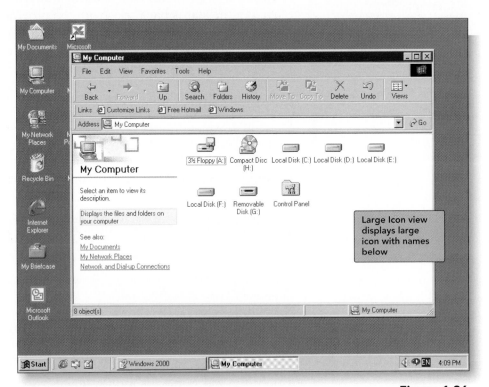

Figure 1.36

In Large Icons view, because the icons are large, fewer folders and files can be displayed in a window at a time. Using this view you may need to scroll the window frequently to locate an object.

Exploring Disk Contents

Initially, My Computer displays an overall view of the organization of the drives on your computer. Next you will view the files and folders on the hard drive of your computer. On most computers the hard drive is the C drive.

1 ● **Maximize the window.**

● **Select the ⬜ icon (or the appropriate hard drive for your system).**

Your screen should be similar to Figure 1.37

Properties of selected object

Status bar

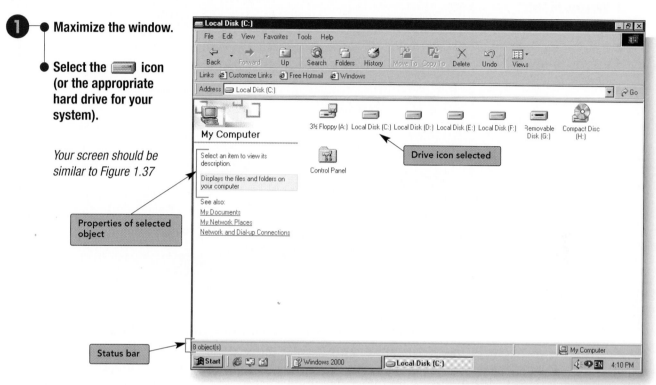

Figure 1.37

Additional Information
Refer to Concept 2: Desktop to review objects and properties.

The hard drive icon is highlighted, indicating it is selected. The left pane displays some basic information about the properties of the selected object. In this case, it displays information about the capacity of the disk, which is visually represented by the pie chart. The status bar also tells you that one object is selected and information about the object's properties.

Choosing a drive icon displays the contents of the disk in that drive. You will look at the contents of your computer's hard drive.

2 ● Double-click [icon] to choose your system's hard disk.

● If necessary, change the view to List.

● If necessary, scroll the window to view the files.

Your screen should be similar to Figure 1.38

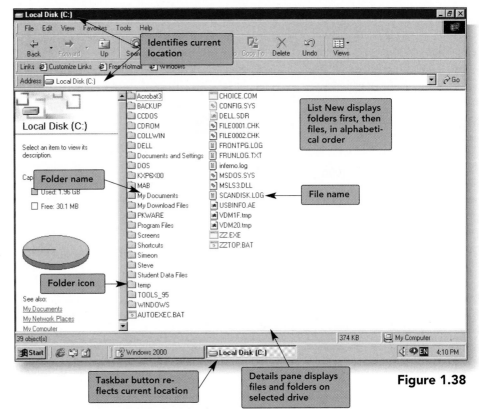

Figure 1.38

The details pane now displays the files and folders on the selected drive. The title bar and Address bar display the name of the location you are currently viewing, and the taskbar button is updated to reflect this change. The files and folders are identified by names that are descriptive of the contents of the file or folder. The folder names are listed first in alphabetical order and are preceded with folder icons [icon]. The individual files are listed following the folders, again in alphabetical order.

You will see many other kinds of icons that represent different types of files on your disk. The various file icons help you distinguish the type of file: a program file, an associated file, or another type of file (generally an unassociated document file). An **associated file** is a file that has a specific application program attached to it that will open when the file is opened. The following table describes several of the file icons.

Icon	Type of File
	Program (executable) file
	System file
	Microsoft Word document file
	Text file
	Movie file
	Sound file
	Graphic file
	Bitmap picture file
	Help file
	Document files that are not associated with an application

● Select several file
  icons and as you do,
  read the brief descrip-
  tion of the selected
  object.

● Restore the window.

*Your screen should be
similar to Figure 1.39*

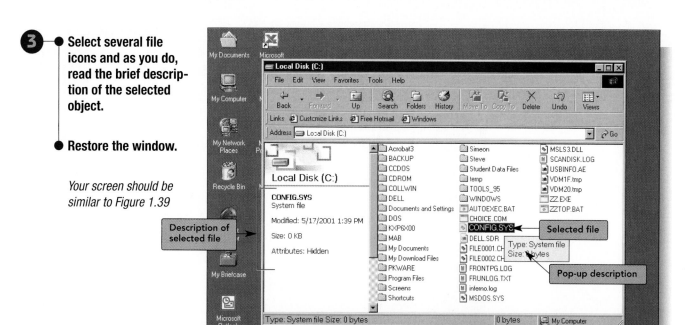

Description of
selected file

Figure 1.39

The left pane displays a brief description of the file and, depending upon
the type of file, it may also display a preview of the contents of the file. The
status bar and a pop-up description also display information about the selected file.

Printing a Help Topic

Now that you have spent some time learning how to use windows, Help,
and My Computer, you decide you want to print a copy of the Help topic
you viewed earlier about how to find a Help topic.

1 ● Click  to make the Help window active.

● If necessary, click [Back].

Your screen should be similar to Figure 1.40

Additional Information

You can also choose Print from the [Options] button drop-down menu to print a selected topic or print all topics within a book on the Contents tab. You can print a pop-up window, such as a definition, by choosing Print Topic from its shortcut menu.

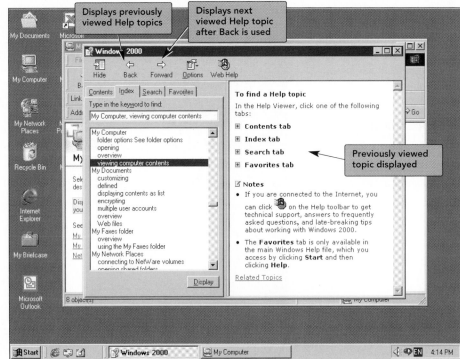

Figure 1.40

Each time you click [Back], the previously viewed Help topic is displayed. The [Forward] button can be used to move forward through Help topics after [Back] has been used. You want to print a copy of this topic with the four topics about the tabs expanded.

2 ● Expand each of the four Help topic tabs.

● Right-click on the topic pane to display the shortcut menu.

● Choose Print.

Your screen should be similar to Figure 1.41

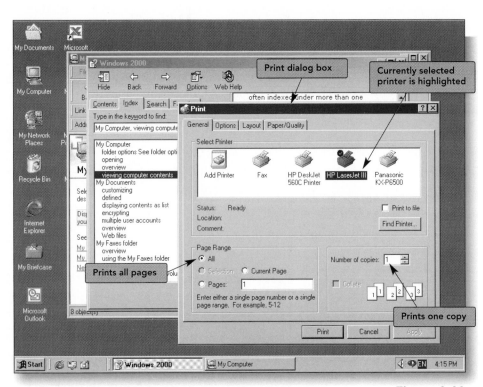

Figure 1.41

From the Print dialog box, you need to specify the printer you will be using and the print settings. The printer that is currently selected is highlighted in the Select Printer section of the dialog box. The Page Range area of the Print dialog box lets you specify how much of the topic you want printed. The range options are described in the following table:

Option	Action
All	Prints the entire document.
Current page	Prints selected page or the page the insertion point is on.
Pages	Prints pages you specify by typing page numbers in the text box.
Selection	Prints selected text only.

The default range setting, All, is the correct setting. In the Copies section, the default setting of one copy of the topic is acceptable.

3 ● **If you need to change the selected printer to another printer, click on the appropriate printer (your instructor will tell you which printer to select) to select it.**

● **Click** `Print` **.**

Your printer should be printing out the Help topic.

Shutting Down Windows 2000

You can shut down Windows 2000 in one of two ways. When you want to stop working and turn off your computer, use the Shut Down command in the Start menu. If, on the other hand, you share a computer and someone else will use it next, use the Log Off command.

1 ● **Close all open windows.**

● **Click** `Start` **.**

● **Choose** 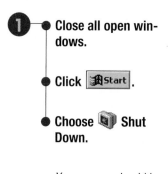 **Shut Down.**

Your screen should be similar to Figure 1.42

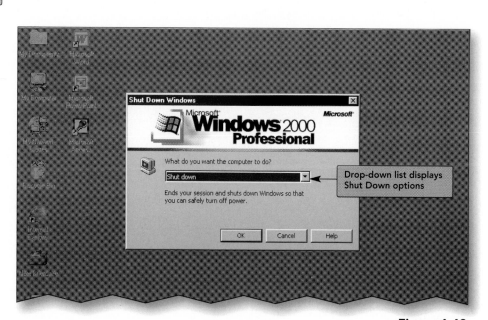

Figure 1.42

From the Shut Down Windows dialog box, you need to specify what you want the computer to do. These options are described in the following table.

Option	Effect
Log Off	Ends your session but leaves the computer running on full power.
Shut Down	Saves any settings you have changed in Windows 2000, writes anything stored in memory to the hard disk, and prepares the computer to be turned off.
Restart	Saves any settings you have changed in Windows 2000, writes anything stored in memory to the hard disk, and restarts the computer. This feature is commonly used when a program stops running and the system freezes up on you. Restarting like this is called a **warm start**. A warm start does not perform a memory check, but it does perform a hardware check.

Another Method

You can also use Ctrl + Alt + Delete to restart the computer.

2 ● Select the Log Off or Shut Down option specified by your instructor.

● Choose [Yes] to confirm your selection.

Warning: If you choose Shut Down the Computer, do not turn off your computer until you see the message indicating it is safe to do so. Otherwise, it is possible that data may be lost.

key terms

active window   WN1.27

application software   WN1.4

associated file   WN1.38

button   WN1.7

cascade   WN1.28

cascading menu   WN1.12

click   WN1.9

desktop   WN1.7

dialog box   WN1.5

double-click   WN1.9

drag   WN1.9

file   WN1.33

folder   WN1.33

graphical user interface (GUI)
    WN1.4

hyperlink   WN1.24

icon   WN1.7

insertion point   WN1.5

maximize   WN1.16

mechanical mouse   WN1.8

menu   WN1.11

menu bar   WN1.11

minimize   WN1.16

mouse   WN1.8

mouse pointer   WN1.8

multitasking   WN1.27

navigation pane   WN1.23

object   WN1.7

operating system   WN1.4

optical mouse   WN1.8

pane   WN1.23

point   WN1.9

program file   WN1.23

property   WN1.7

restore   WN1.16

scroll arrow   WN1.20

scroll bar   WN1.20

scroll box   WN1.20

selection cursor   WN1.12

shortcut menu   WN1.11

status bar   WN1.35

submenu   WN1.12

taskbar   WN1.7

task button   WN1.7

text box   WN1.5

tile   WN1.28

title bar   WN1.15

toolbar   WN1.8

ToolTip   WN1.9

topic pane   WN1.23

Undo   WN1.30

user interface   WN1.4

warm start   WN1.42

window   WN1.15

workspace   WN1.35

command summary

Command	Shortcut	Button	Action
Start Menu		Start	
Help	+ F1		Opens Windows Help program
Log Off			Prepares computer to be used by someone else
Shut Down			Safely shuts down computer before power is turned off
My Computer			
File/Close	Alt + F4		Closes active window
View/Toolbars			Turns on/off display of selected toolbars
View/Status Bar			Turns on/off display of status bar
View/Explorer Bar			Turns on/off display of selected Explorer bars
View/Large Icons			Displays objects with large icons
View/Small Icons			Displays objects with small icons
View/List			Displays objects in a list
View/Details			Displays all folder and file details

screen identification

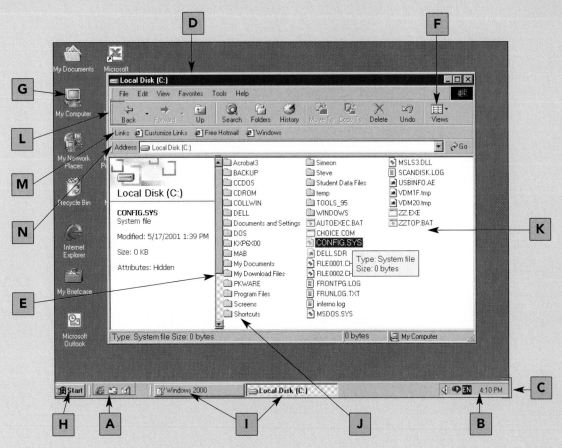

In the following window, several items are identified by letters. Enter the correct term for each item in the space provided.

A. _____   H. _____

B. _____   I. _____

C. _____   J. _____

D. _____   K. _____

E. _____   L. _____

F. _____   M. _____

G. _____   N. _____

discussion questions

1. Different types of computers use different operating systems. Others besides Windows are OS/2, Unix, and the Macintosh operating system. Using the Web as a resource, find information about each of these operating systems. Write a brief report describing the different systems.

2. While using the My Computer window, you looked at the files stored on the hard disk of your computer. Using the library or Web as a resource, describe the construction of the hard disk and explain how a hard disk stores data.

step-by-step

rating system
★ Easy
★ ★ Moderate
★ ★ ★ Difficult

Learning More About Your Computer

★ **1.** Microsoft Help includes the online book, Getting Started, which introduces and explains many of the basic Windows 2000 features. This problem will use the online book to reinforce many of the features presented in this lab.

    a. Start Help. From the Contents tab, open the Introducing Windows 2000 Professional chapter and display the Getting Started online book topic.

    b. Click the Windows 2000 Professional Getting Started shortcut to open the book.

    c. Open Chapter 4—Windows Basics. Read through the Exploring Your Computer book of the chapter and answer the following questions:

      • What is the area that first appears on your screen after you start Windows 2000?

      • What are the small pictures that represent files?

      • How can you get Help information about dialog box options?

      • What do the buttons on the taskbar show you?

      • The right-facing arrow on a menu indicates that a secondary menu called a _____ will be displayed.

      • What is a disk?

      • What is a network?

    d. When you are done, click ✖ to close the Getting Started book.

    e. Close the Help window.

Customizing the Taskbar

★ ★ **2.** The taskbar can be customized in many ways. In this problem, you will learn about other features of the taskbar.

    a. Use Help to find information about sizing the taskbar, setting the date and time, using Auto hide, displaying toolbars in the taskbar, and moving it.

Next, follow the steps below to try out several of these features.

    b. Drag the top border of the taskbar up to increase the size of the taskbar to two rows. What happened to the arrangement of items on the taskbar?

    c. Double-click on the time in the taskbar. What happened?

    d. Use the Help button for information on the Date/Time Properties dialog box. Describe the date and time properties that can be changed. Close the dialog box.

    e. Choose Properties from the taskbar shortcut menu. Describe the five options in this dialog box. Turn on the Auto hide property. Click Apply. What happened to the taskbar?

f. To redisplay the taskbar, move the mouse pointer to the bottom of the window. Turn off the Auto hide taskbar property. Click [OK].

g. Choose Toolbars from the taskbar shortcut menu. Select the Desktop toolbar option. Open the My Computer window using the taskbar button. Close the My Computer window.

h. Remove the Desktop toolbar from the taskbar by clearing the Desktop toolbar option from the taskbar shortcut menu.

i. Resize the taskbar to a single row at the bottom of the screen.

j. Close the Help Viewer window.

k. The taskbar can be moved along any border of the desktop. Move it to each border and describe what happens to the desktop and the taskbar. Return the taskbar to the bottom of the screen.

on your own

Window's Security Features

★★ 1. Windows 2000 has built-in security features. Use what you learned about Help in this lab to locate information on security. Hand-write a paragraph on each of the following: certificates, local security policy, and passwords.

Organizing Your Work

LAB 2

objectives

After completing this lab, you will know how to:

1.	Use Windows Explorer.
2.	Create, name, and delete folders.
3.	Select, move, copy, and delete files.
4.	Run applications.
5.	Open, edit, save and print files.

**Storing related files in separate folders keeps
your computer organized.**

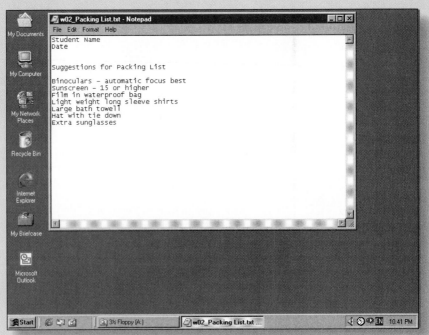

**Notepad can be used to quickly create simple
text documents.**

Adventure Travel Tours

As advertising coordinator, you create many different types of files that are used for different purposes to promote the Adventure Travel Tours company. You often find that it takes you a considerable amount of time to locate a file. Consequently, you decide you need to organize the files on your computer. Organizational skills are very important skills in any profession. When you are disorganized, it takes much longer to complete tasks accurately. In this lab you will learn to use Windows Explorer to organize the folders and files on

your disk. You will learn how to create folders and copy and move files into folders to make it easy to quickly locate files.

Additionally, you will use a simple text editing application, Notepad, to create a packing list for a river rafting adventure. The features you will use to edit and print this document are features that are common to all applications that run under Windows. Learning about many of these features now will make it easier for you to learn to use new applications in the future.

© Corbis

The following concepts will be introduced in this lab:

1	**Hierarchy**	The graphic representation of the organization of folders on a disk is called a hierarchy.
2	**Folder and File Names**	When a file or folder is created, it must be assigned a file name that identifies its contents.
3	**Copy and Move**	All Windows applications include features that allow you to copy and move selected information from one location to another.
4	**Drag and Drop**	Common to all Windows applications is the ability to copy or move selections using the drag and drop feature.
5	**Saving Files**	When you save a document you are working on, a permanent copy of your onscreen document is electronically stored as a file on a disk.

Using Windows Explorer

When looking at the contents of your computer in Lab 1, you used My Computer to display the files and folders on your computer. Another way to view this information is to use Windows Explorer. **Windows Explorer** provides another method of viewing and navigating your computer contents.

Starting Windows Explorer

You will start Windows Explorer and use it to view the contents of your computer.

1
- If necessary turn on the computer and enter your user identification information.
- Right-click 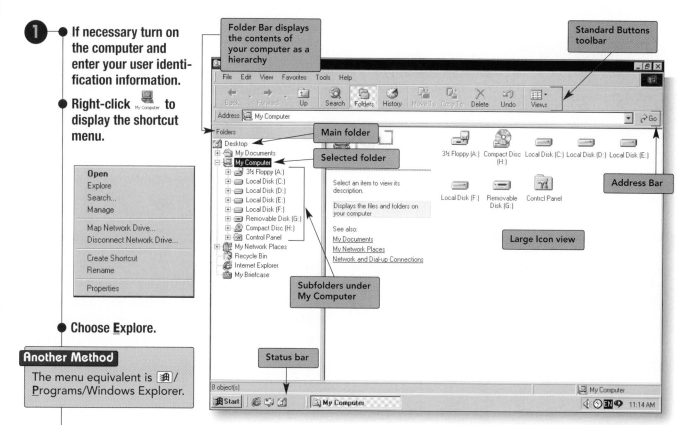 to display the shortcut menu.

Open
Explore
Search...
Manage
Map Network Drive...
Disconnect Network Drive...
Create Shortcut
Rename
Properties

- Choose **E**xplore.

Another Method

The menu equivalent is 🔳/ **P**rograms/**W**indows Explorer.

Figure 2.1

- If necessary, maximize the window.

- If necessary, use the View menu to display the Standard Buttons toolbar with text labels, display the Address bar, display the status bar, and set the icon view to Large Icons.

- If necessary, click 📁 Folders to display the Folders Bar.

Another Method

The menu equivalent is **V**iew/**E**xplorer Bar/Folders.

Additional Information

Because Windows remembers the last-used folder settings, you may need to turn on and off different features to make your Explorer window look like Figure 2.1.

Your screen should be similar to Figure 2.1

Additional Information

Your window will display different folders and icons than those in Figure 2.1.

Exploring the Explorer Window

Additional Information

You can adjust the size of the panes by dragging the bar that separates them.

Because you used the Explorer option in the My Computer Shortcut menu to start the Windows Explorer program, the window displays the contents of the My Computer folder in the details pane. Additionally, the pane on the left displays the Folders Bar.

The primary purpose of the Folders Bar is to help you navigate through and organize the folders and files on a disk. It displays the information about your computer's disk drive as a hierarchy.

concept 1

Hierarchy

1   The graphic representation of the organization of folders on a disk is called a **hierarchy**. The top-level folder of a disk is the **main folder**, also called the **root folder**. On the hard disk, the main folder is represented by the Desktop icon (see Figure 2.1). On a floppy disk, the main folder is generally represented by the drive icon. The main folder always appears at the top of the hierarchy. Folders created in the main folder appear indented below the main folder and are visually connected by the leftmost vertical line. **Subfolders** appear indented below other folders and are connected by another vertical line. Because of the branching nature of the hierarchy, it is sometimes also called a **tree**.

The folders that appear indented and connected by a vertical line under the Desktop icon are the same as the icons that represent these folders on the desktop. The subfolders under My Computer appear indented and are connected vertically by a line.

The contents of the selected folder in the Folders Bar are displayed in the details pane. In this case, because you started Windows Explorer from the My Computer icon, the My Computer folder is selected, indicating it is open. The details pane shows icons for the drives on your computer and the same folders as you saw when you viewed it using My Computer window.

Displaying Folder Contents

Choosing a different item in the Folders Bar opens the item and displays the contents of the item in the details pane. First you will display the contents of the hard drive.

1 ● Click 🖾 Local Disk (C:) (or the appropriate drive for your system) in the Folders Bar.

Your screen should be similar to Figure 2.2

Additional Information
If you start Windows Explorer using the Programs menu, the window opens with the contents of your local disk drive displayed.

Additional Information
The ⊞ appears only if the object contains folders or subfolders.

1 ● Click ⊞ to the left of the Local Disk (C:) icon.

Your screen should be similar to Figure 2.3

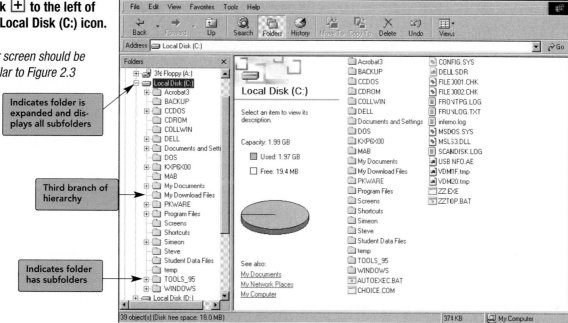

Number of items in folder

Free disk space

Details pane displays contents of selected drive (C:)

Figure 2.2

Now the details pane displays the contents of the selected item. If the selected item contains folders, they are displayed first, in alphabetical order, followed by the files. The status bar displays information about the number of objects and the disk properties of the selected item.

Expanding and Collapsing Folders

You can also display the folders in the Folders Bar. To do this you click the ⊞ to the left of the drive icon to expand the hierarchy.

Indicates folder is expanded and displays all subfolders

Third branch of hierarchy

Indicates folder has subfolders

Figure 2.3

The Folders Bar displays the folders on your hard drive as a third branch on the hierarchy. Notice that the ⊞ changed to a ⊟, which shows that the drive icon is fully open or expanded. You can also expand a folder that contains subfolders.

2 ● **If necessary, scroll the Folders Bar to see the Program Files folder icon.**

● **Expand the Program Files folder.**

Your screen should be similar to Figure 2.4

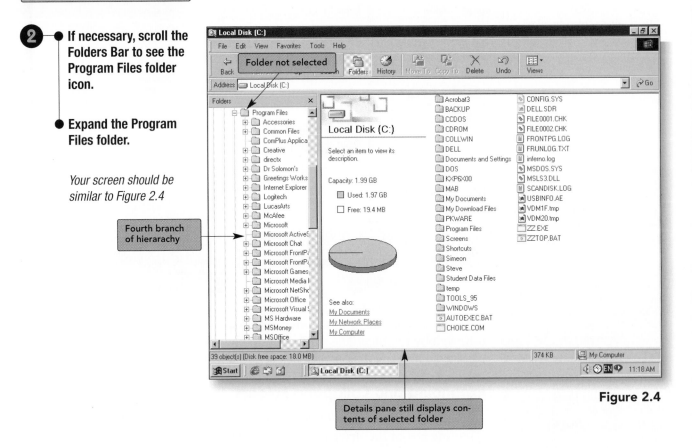

Figure 2.4

Details pane still displays contents of selected folder

The folders in the Program Files folder appear as a fourth branch of the hierarchy. Notice, however, that the details pane still displays the contents of the Local Disk C. This is because the Program Files folder is not yet selected. To see the contents of this folder,

3 Click the Program Files folder name.

Your screen should be similar to Figure 2.5

Selected folder is current folder

HAVING TROUBLE?
If your screen does not contain the advisory message shown in Figure 2.5, double-click on the Accessories folder name in the folders bar and skip to the end of this page.

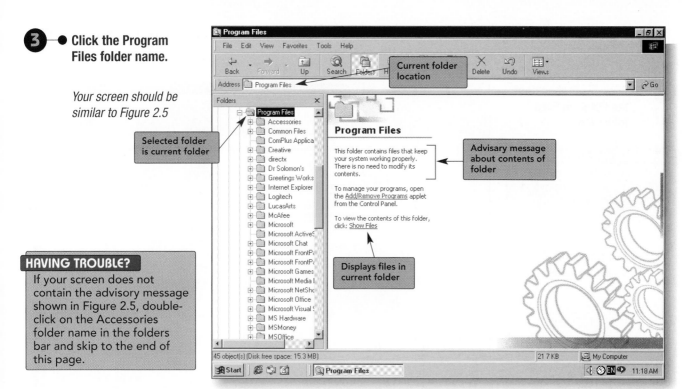

Figure 2.5

Additional Information
The status bar may also indicate the number of hidden files. Hidden files are files that Windows does not display by default to protect them from accidentally being altered.

The folder name is highlighted, and the folder icon appears as 🗀, indicating the folder is open. When a folder is open, it is the **current folder** or the folder that will be affected by your next actions. The name of the current folder appears in the Address bar and in the title bar. Normally, the contents of the current folder are displayed in the details pane. However, on some folders, Microsoft displays an advisory message indicating that you should not need to modify the files in this folder. You will view the contents of the Programs folder and then open the Accessories folder.

4 Click Show Files in the details pane.

● Double-click on the Accessories folder name in the Folders Bar.

Your screen should be similar to Figure 2.6

Current folder

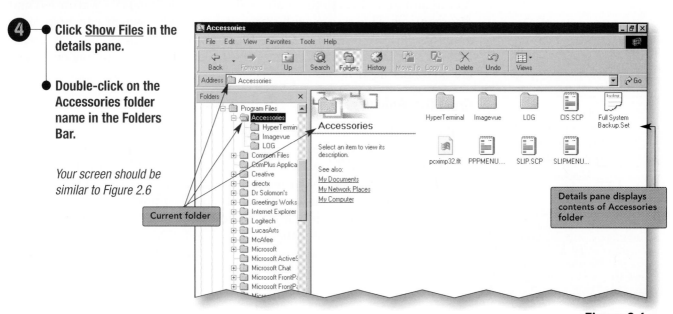

Figure 2.6

Double-clicking on a closed folder both expands it and opens it. Now the Accessories folder is current, and the contents are displayed in the details pane. Finally, you will hide or collapse the display of the Program Files folder again in the Folders Bar.

5 ● Click ⊟ to the left of the Program Files folder icon.

Additional Information

You can also double-click on an open folder to expand or hide the folders in the Folders Bar.

Your screen should be similar to Figure 2.7

HAVING TROUBLE?

Your screen may not display the same text under Program Files as indicated in Figure 2.7.

Figure 2.7

Working with Folders

Now that you understand how Windows is used to organize folders and files, you will learn how to create folders to organize the files on your disk. As you add more files to the main folder of a disk, it gets very crowded and disorganized. This is especially true of hard disks, which can hold large amounts of data. To help organize files into like categories, you can create folders. You can also easily remove folders and all their contents once they are no longer needed.

Creating Folders

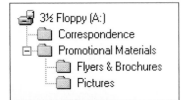

Additional Information

Before a disk can be used, it must be formatted. If your disk is not already formatted, refer to On Your Own Exercise 1 before continuing.

As the advertising coordinator for Adventure Travel Tours, you create many different types of documents to promote the different products offered by the company. You will create folders for the related files to help organize files. The folder and subfolder hierarchy you will create is shown at the left.

The first folder you will create will be used to hold promotional documents such as flyers and brochures you develop for Adventure Travel Tours. To indicate where you want the folder created, the drive or folder must be current first. You will create your new folder directly under the main folder of a blank floppy disk.

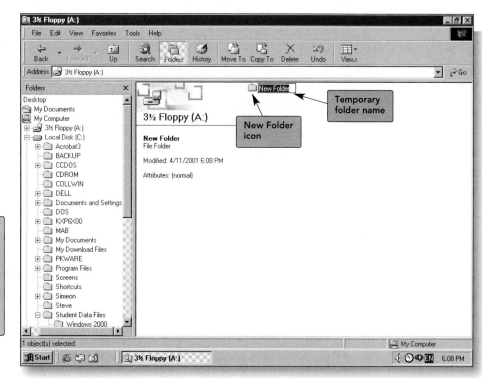

Figure 2.8

① ● Insert a blank disk in drive A (or the appropriate drive for your system).

● Click 3½ Floppy (A:) in the Folders Bar.

● Change the view to List view.

Additional Information

This text assumes drive A is the drive you will use for your data disk. If your system is different, select the appropriate drive for your system in place of A throughout this lab.

● Choose File/New/Folder.

Your screen should be similar to Figure 2.8

A New Folder icon is displayed in the details pane. The temporary folder name, New Folder, is highlighted, and the insertion point is displayed at the end of the folder name. This indicates that Windows 2000 is waiting for you to replace the default name with a descriptive name for the folder you are creating.

concept 2

Folder and File Names

2   When a folder or file is created, it must be assigned a **file name** that identifies its contents. The name you assign a folder or file must be unique for the location it is in. For example, if you give a new file the same name as an existing file in the same folder, the contents of the original file will be replaced by the contents of the new file.

In addition to a name, an extension may be added. A **file name extension** is up to three characters and is separated from the file name by a period. Generally, a file name extension is used to identify the type of file. This information establishes the file association that Windows uses to identify the proper program to use to open the file. Most application programs automatically add the identifying file name extension to any files created using the program. For instance, a file created using Microsoft Word has a file name extension of "doc." A folder extension is not generally used and is never supplied by the operating system.

The parts of a file name are shown below.

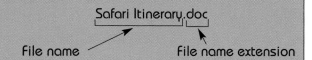

Safari Itinerary.doc

File name   File name extension

You need to replace the default folder name with a name that is descriptive of the folder contents. Windows 2000 and programs that are designed to operate under Windows 2000 allow you to use long folder and file names of up to 215 characters, including spaces. They can contain the letters A to Z, the numbers 0 to 9, and any of the following special characters: underscore (_), caret (^), dollar sign ($), tilde (~), exclamation point (!), number sign (#), percent sign (%), ampersand (&), hyphen (-), braces ({}), parentheses (), "at" sign (@), apostrophe ('), and the grave accent (`). Spaces are allowed in file names, but the following characters are not allowed: \ / : * ? > < |. The same character restrictions apply to file name extensions.

2 ● With the text "New Folder" highlighted, type **Promotional Materials**.

● Press ⏎Enter.

Additional Information
If you make a typing error, use the Backspace key to delete the characters to the left of the insertion point.

Your screen should be similar to Figure 2.9

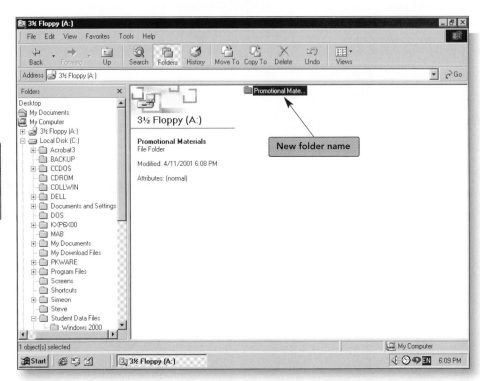

Figure 2.9

The folder name appears exactly as you typed it (including case). The insertion point is no longer displayed, but the folder is still selected.

Next you want to create another folder under the main folder to hold correspondence files, such as letters and memos. Although the Promotional Materials folder is the selected folder, the main folder is still current.

3 Create a new folder named **Correspondence.**

Additional Information
The File menu now includes additional commands that can be used with the selected item.

Your screen should be similar to Figure 2.10

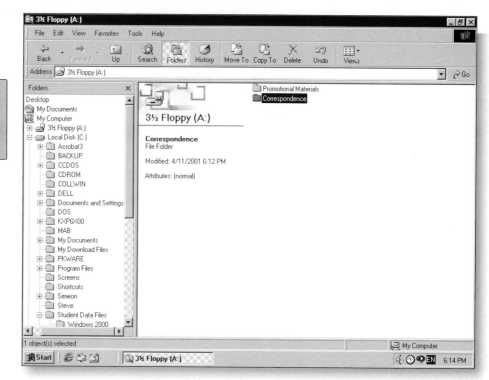

Figure 2.10

The Correspondence folder is displayed in the details pane.

4 Expand the A floppy drive icon to display the folders in the Folders Bar.

Your screen should be similar to Figure 2.11

Folders appear alphabetically in Folder Bar

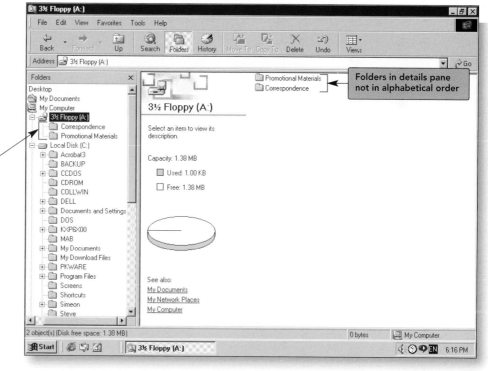

Figure 2.11

The two folders you created appear in alphabetical order in the Folders Bar. However, the two new folders are not yet displayed in alphabetical order in the details pane.

5 ● **Choose View/Arrange Icons/by Name.**

Your screen should be similar to Figure 2.12

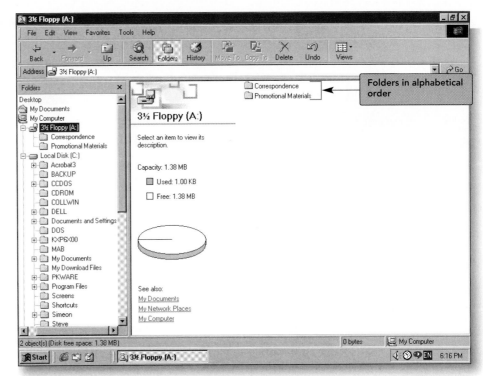

Figure 2.12

The folders now appear in alphabetical order in the details pane.

Because you create many different types of promotional materials, such as flyers, brochures, advertisements, and catalogs, you want to further subdivide your files in the Promotional Materials folder by the type of material. You also use pictures in these materials, which you want to include in a separate subfolder. You will create subfolders under the Promotional Materials folder for flyers, brochures, and pictures. When creating a subfolder, you must first make the folder under which it is to appear the current folder.

6 ● **Open the Promotional Materials folder in the Folders Bar.**

● **Create a subfolder named Flyers.**

● **Create a second subfolder named Brochures in the Promotional Materials folder. (Make sure the Promotional Materials folder is current first.)**

● **Create a third subfolder named Pictures in the Promotional Materials folder.**

● **Arrange the folders alphabetically by name.**

● **Then, to display the folders in the Folders Bar, expand the Promotional Materials folder.**

Your screen should be similar to Figure 2.13

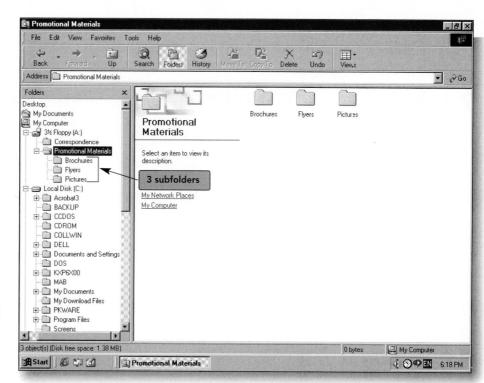

Figure 2.13

The new folders are displayed in the details pane, and ⊞ appears next to the Promotional Materials folder in the Folders Bar to show that the folder is expanded and contains subfolders.

Renaming Folders

As you think about your folder organization, you decide to combine flyers and brochures into one folder. You will rename the folder first to reflect this change so that it is more descriptive of the information it contains.

1 ● **Right-click on the Brochures folder icon to display the shortcut menu.**

● **Choose Rename.**

Your screen should be similar to Figure 2.14

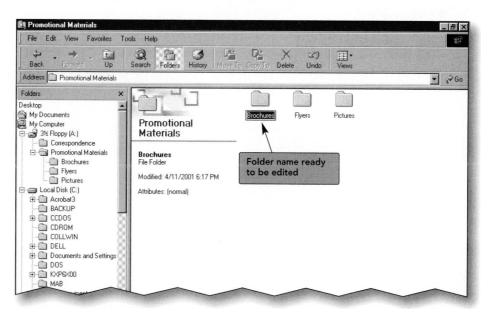

Figure 2.14

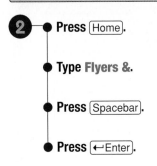

Another Method
You can also use the Rename command on the File menu.

The folder name appears highlighted and with an insertion point, just as a new folder name appears. To move the insertion point to the beginning of the file name and add the text "Flyers &" to the folder name,

2 • Press Home.

• Type **Flyers &**.

• Press Spacebar.

• Press ←Enter.

Your screen should be similar to Figure 2.15

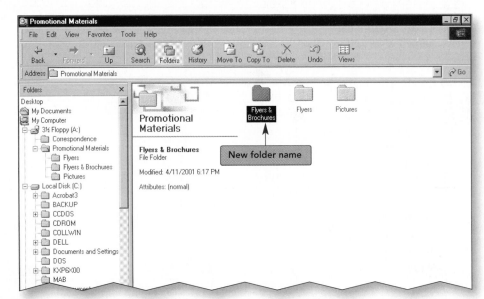

Figure 2.15

The folder name changes to its new name, Flyers & Brochures.

Deleting Folders

Next, since you no longer need the folder you created for flyers, you will delete it. If you delete a folder that contains subfolders and files, all the files and subfolders contained within that folder will be removed.

1 • Select the Flyers folder icon.

• Press Delete.

Another Method
The menu equivalent is File/Delete.

Your screen should be similar to Figure 2.16

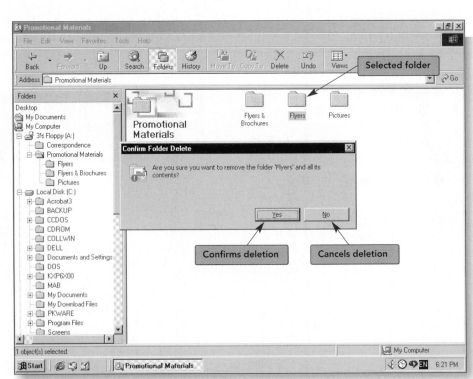

Figure 2.16

The Confirm Folder Delete message box asks you to confirm that you want to delete the folder and its contents. This is especially important when deleting items from a floppy disk, because they are permanently deleted. Files and folders that are deleted from the hard disk are not permanently deleted, but are placed in the Recycle Bin where they are held until they are permanently deleted from that location. If you changed your mind, choosing  would cancel the procedure.

2 ● **Click** Yes .

Your screen should be similar to Figure 2.17

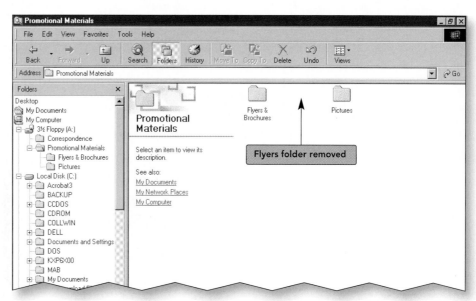

Figure 2.17

The Flyers folder is removed.

Working with Files

Once you have created folders, they can be used to store files. One of the major purposes for using Windows Explorer is to help you manage the files on your computer. This commonly involves copying and moving files to other locations, either on the same disk or to another disk.

concept 3

Copy and Move

3 All Windows applications include features that allow you to copy and move selected items from one location to another. When an item is copied, the item remains in the original location, and a duplicate is created in the new location. When an item is moved, it is deleted from the original location, and a duplicate is created in the new location.

Selecting a File

Now that you have organized your disk into folders, you will copy the files needed to complete this lab (and others your instructor may be using) to the disk. The files you will copy should be in a folder on your hard disk. First you need to open the folder containing the data files.

① ● **Locate and expand the Student Data Files folder.**

● **Open the Windows 2000 folder.**

HAVING TROUBLE?

This text assumes the files are in a folder named Student Data Files on your hard drive. If your school uses a different folder name, or your computer is on a network and the data files are in a folder at another location, your instructor will provide additional instructions.

Your screen should be similar to Figure 2.18

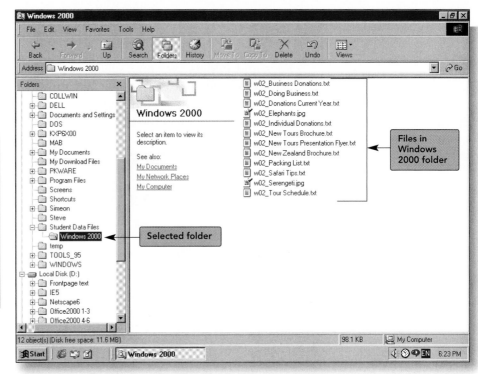

Figure 2.18

HAVING TROUBLE?

If your files do not display file extensions, choose **T**ools/Folder Options/View and clear the Hide file extensions for known file type option.

The Details pane displays the files at the selected location. You will copy the file named Tour Schedule to your disk. To specify which file you want to copy, you must first select it by highlighting it.

② ● **Click on** w02_Tour Schedule.

Your screen should be similar to Figure 2.19

Figure 2.19

The Tour Schedule icon is highlighted, indicating it is selected. The details pane containing the highlight is the **active pane**, or the pane that will be affected by the next action you perform.

Copying and Moving Files Using the Menu

You can move and copy items using several different procedures. The basic procedure uses the Cut, Copy, and Paste commands on the Edit menu. Toolbar shortcuts for these commands are also found on the Standard toolbars of most applications. The location that contains the information you want to cut or copy is called the **source**. The location where you want to copy or move the items to called the **destination**. After using Cut or Copy, a duplicate of the selection is copied to a temporary storage area in memory called the **Clipboard**.

1 ● **Choose Edit/Copy.**

● **Click 3½ Floppy (A:) from the Folders Bar to specify the destination.**

● **Choose Edit/Paste.**

Another Method

The keyboard shortcut to copy is Ctrl + C, and to paste is Ctrl + V.

Your screen should be similar to Figure 2.20

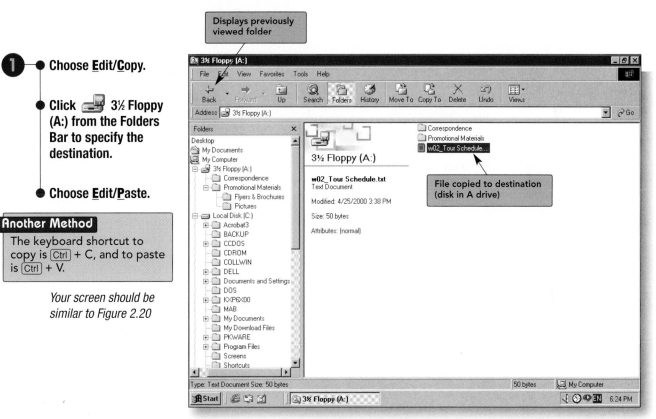

Figure 2.20

A Copying message box is briefly displayed as the file is copied. This box shows the progress of the copy procedure and indicates the amount of time remaining until the procedure is complete.

The file is copied from the Clipboard into the main folder of the floppy disk, and the details pane displays the name of the copied file. You are now ready to copy the rest of the files to your disk.

Another Method

The menu equivalent is View/Go to/Back and the keyboard equivalent is [Alt] + [←].

Your screen should be similar to Figure 2.21

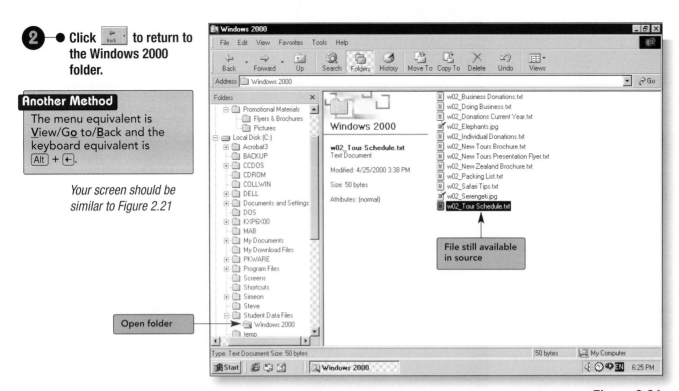

Figure 2.21

Additional Information

The [Back] button redisplays folders that were previously displayed during the current session.

The previous folder is displayed. Notice that the Tour Schedule file is still displayed in the Windows 2000 folder. Because you copied the file, it is now in both the Windows 2000 folder and on your disk.

Next you need to copy the other Windows 2000 data files to the main folder of your disk. Rather than select and copy each file individually, you will select all the files in the folder and copy them at the same time.

3 ● Choose Edit/Select All.

Another Method

The keyboard shortcut for this command is [Ctrl] + A.

Your screen should be similar to Figure 2.22

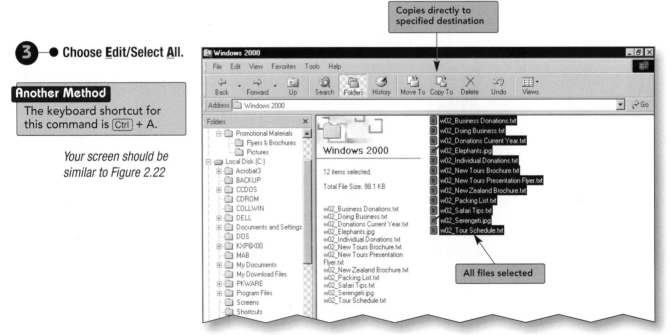

Figure 2.22

All the file icons in the current folder are selected. Instead of using Copy and Paste commands on the menu, you can use the Copy To toolbar button. This button makes the process easier by allowing you to copy files directly to the destination disk without having to select it first.

4 ● Click 🔲.

Your screen should be similar to Figure 2.23

Select location to copy to

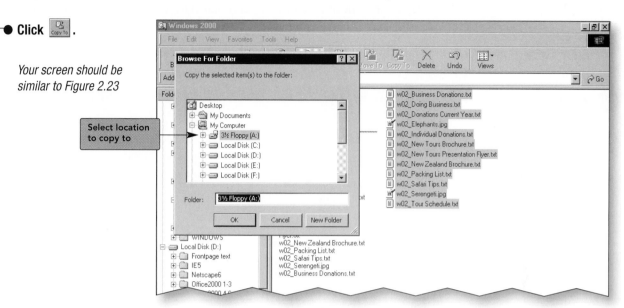

Figure 2.23

In the Browse for Folder dialog box, you need to specify the destination where you want the files copied. Your destination will be the disk in the floppy drive.

5 ● If necessary, expand the My Computer folder.

● Click 🖫 3½ Floppy (A:).

● Click OK.

Your screen should be similar to Figure 2.24

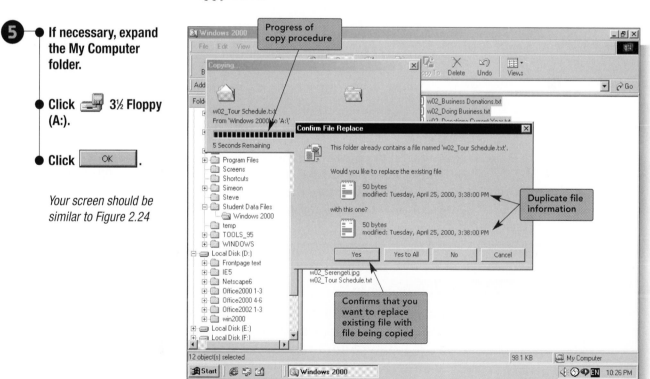

Figure 2.24

The Copying message box is displayed as the files are copied. In addition, because the w02_Tour Schedule file is already on the disk in drive A, a

Confirm File Replace dialog box appears. Windows 2000 displays this message to prevent you from accidentally writing over a file with another that has the same name. The dialog box shows the size of the duplicate files and date and time the files were last modified. Because you just copied the w02_Tour Schedule file, you can overwrite it without changing its contents, or you can choose No to bypass this operation and continue. You will bypass copying this file again and then verify that the files were copied to the A drive.

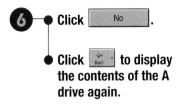

6 ● Click [No] .

● Click [← Back] to display the contents of the A drive again.

Your screen should be similar to Figure 2.25

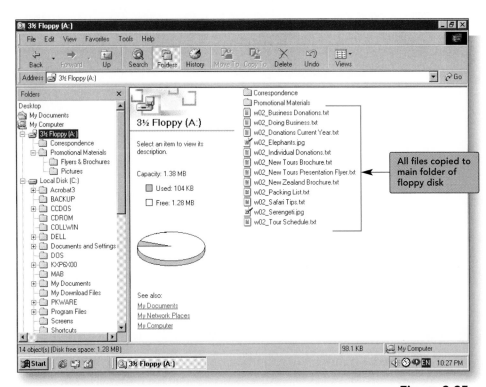

All files copied to main folder of floppy disk

Figure 2.25

Copying and Moving Files by Dragging

Now that all the files are in the root folder, you want to move some of them into the folders you created. First you will move the file w02_Tour Schedule from the main folder into the Promotional Materials folder. Another way to copy or move a file is to drag and drop the selection.

concept 4

Drag and Drop

4 Common to all Windows applications is the ability to copy or move selections using the **drag and drop** feature. Dragging a selection moves or copies it to the destination you are pointing to when you release the mouse button.

 If you drag a file to a destination on the same disk, it will be moved. If you drag a file to a destination on another disk, it will be copied. You can hold down ⇧Shift while dragging to always move a file, or Ctrl to copy a file. If you drag holding down the right mouse button, a shortcut menu appears with options to either copy or move the selection.

You will drag and drop the w02_Tour Schedule file from the root folder to the Promotional Materials folder in the Folders Bar. The destination for the item you want to drag and drop should be visible in the window.

Additional Information

You can also move or copy a file to a folder displayed in the details pane.

1 ● **Select the w02_Tour Schedule file icon.**

● **With the mouse pointer on the selected file icon, drag it to the Promotional Materials folder in the Folders Bar.**

Additional Information

The mouse pointer appears as 🖑 while moving a file using drag and drop.

● **When the pointer is positioned over the Promotional Materials folder and the folder is selected, release the mouse button.**

Additional Information

A circle/slash symbol ⊘ is displayed when the mouse pointer is in an area where the file cannot be copied or moved.

Your screen should be similar to Figure 2.26

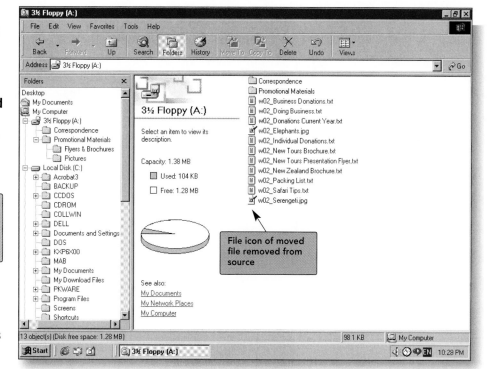

Figure 2.26

A Moving message box appears as the file is moved. When the move is complete, the file icon is removed from the source location. However, now you realize you really wanted to move the file into the Correspondence folder. You will quickly undo the previous action and move the file to the correct folder. The Undo feature is available in most software application programs. In some programs you can undo multiple actions, up to a certain limit. Others, as in Windows 2000, allow you to undo only your last action. You will find that some actions you perform cannot be undone. If the Undo command is unavailable, it appears dimmed and you cannot cancel your last action.

Additional Information

Undo on the taskbar only allows you to undo window arrangements.

Another Method

You can also move a file using the Cut and Paste commands on the Edit or shortcut menu or the toolbar button 🗐.

② ● Click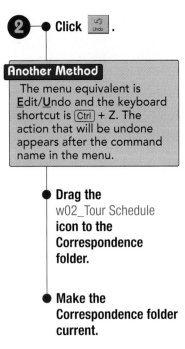

Another Method

The menu equivalent is Edit/Undo and the keyboard shortcut is Ctrl + Z. The action that will be undone appears after the command name in the menu.

● **Drag the** w02_Tour Schedule **icon to the Correspondence folder.**

● **Make the Correspondence folder current.**

Your screen should be similar to Figure 2.27

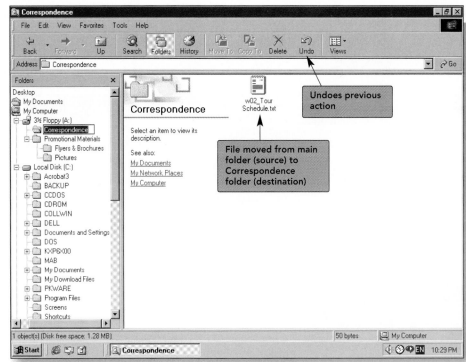

Figure 2.27

The file icon for the file you moved is now displayed in the Correspondence folder.

Selecting Multiple Files

Next you want to move several files into the same folder. Rather than moving the files individually, you can select several files to copy or move at the same time. First you will move three adjacent files, w02_New Tours Brochure, w02_New Tour Presentations Flyer, and w02_New Zealand Brochure, from the main folder to the Brochures & Flyers subfolder.

Additional Information

Another way to select multiple consecutive files is to drag to create a box around the files.

To quickly select adjacent files, click on the first item, then hold down ⇧Shift while clicking on the last item. If a file you do not want selected is included in the group, hold down Ctrl while pointing to the file to deselect it, leaving all others selected. Likewise, you can add other files to the selection by holding down Ctrl while selecting them.

1 ● **Make the main folder of your data disk current.**

● **Select the** w02_New Tours Brochure **icon.**

● **Hold down** ⟨⇧ Shift⟩ **and click on the** w02_New Zealand Brochure **icon.**

Your screen should be similar to Figure 2.28

Number of selected objects

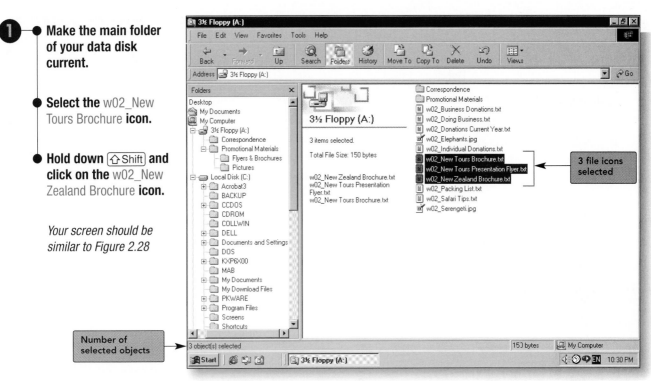

Figure 2.28

The three file icons are selected, and the status bar indicates that three objects are selected.

2 ● **Drag the selected files to the Flyers & Brochures subfolder under the Promotional Materials folder.**

Next you want to move two files that are not next to each other, w02_Serengeti and w02_Elephants, to the Pictures subfolder. To quickly select files that are scattered throughout the file list, hold down ⟨Ctrl⟩ while clicking on the file icons.

3 ● **Select the**
w02_Elephants **file**
icon.

● **Hold down** Ctrl.

● **Select the**
w02_Serengeti **file**
icon.

● **If necessary, deselect**
any other files that
you may have selected
accidentally.

Additional Information
To deselect a file (remove the
highlight), click on it again
while holding down Ctrl.

● **Release** Ctrl.

Your screen should be
similar to Figure 2.29

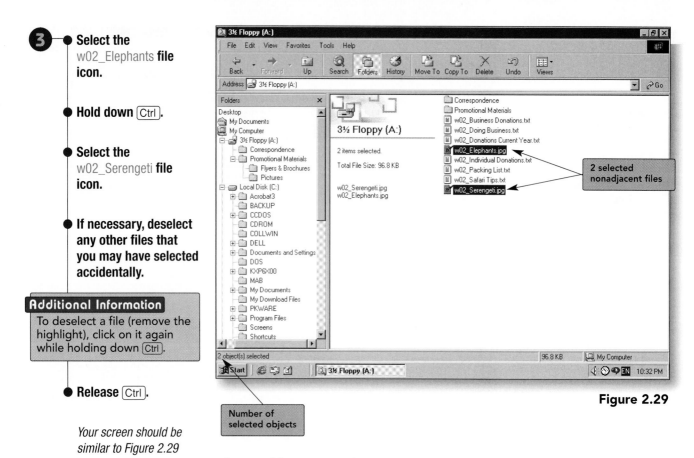

Figure 2.29

The two file icons are highlighted, and the status bar indicates that two objects are selected.

4 ● **Move the files to the Pictures subfolder.**

Renaming and Deleting Files

Like folders, you want the names of files to be descriptive of their contents. The Tour Schedule file actually contains the proposed schedule for the year 2002, so you decide to rename this file 2002 Tour Schedule.

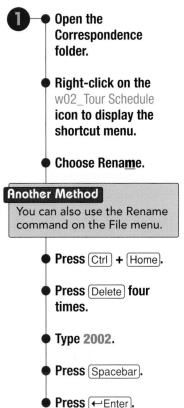

1 ● **Open the Correspondence folder.**

● **Right-click on the** w02_Tour Schedule **icon to display the shortcut menu.**

● **Choose Rename.**

Another Method

You can also use the Rename command on the File menu.

● **Press** [Ctrl] + [Home].

● **Press** [Delete] **four times.**

● **Type** 2002.

● **Press** [Spacebar].

● **Press** [←Enter].

Your screen should be similar to Figure 2.30

Additional Information

When an item is deleted from the hard disk, it is moved to the Recycle Bin, a special folder used to store deleted items until they are permanently removed. This protects you from accidentally deleting files or folders that you might want later. You can then permanently remove the files or restore them to their original location.

Figure 2.30

The file name changes to its new name, 2002 Tour Schedule. Likewise, just like folders, you can easily delete files you no longer need. You will delete the file w02_Safari Tips, since the information it contains has been incorporated into another document.

2 ● Make the main folder of your data disk current.

● Select the w02_Safari Tips **file** icon.

● Click ☒ Delete.

● Click [Yes] to confirm the deletion.

Another Method

You can also press Delete to delete an item.

Additional Information

You cannot use Undo to reverse the action of deleting an item from a floppy disk.

Your screen should be similar to Figure 2.31

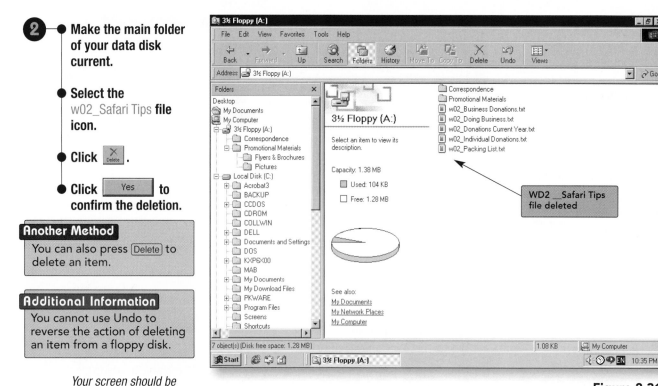

Figure 2.31

The file is removed from the main folder of the disk, and its icon is no longer displayed in the details pane.

3 ● Minimize the Windows Explorer window.

Running Applications

The primary activity a computer is used for is to run application programs to accomplish various tasks, such as creating a letter or a picture. In addition to the programs that run as part of Windows 2000, such as Windows Explorer, Windows 2000 includes several small programs that are designed to help you with your work, or amuse you while passing time. Some, but not all, are installed automatically on the hard disk of the computer when Windows 2000 is installed. Others must be added individually. Among these additional programs is Notepad, a basic text-editing program that is used to create simple text documents that do not require any special formatting.

Starting Notepad

Recently you went on the Adventure Travel Tours Colorado River rafting trip. Upon your return, you used Notepad to jot down several items to include in the suggested packing list for this trip. Since creating this document, you thought of another item to include in the list. You will view, modify, and print this document using Notepad.

1 ● Choose 📖/**P**rograms/
Accessories/Notepad.

● If necessary, size the
Notepad window to
the approximate size
as in Figure 2.32

*Your screen should be
similar to Figure 2.32*

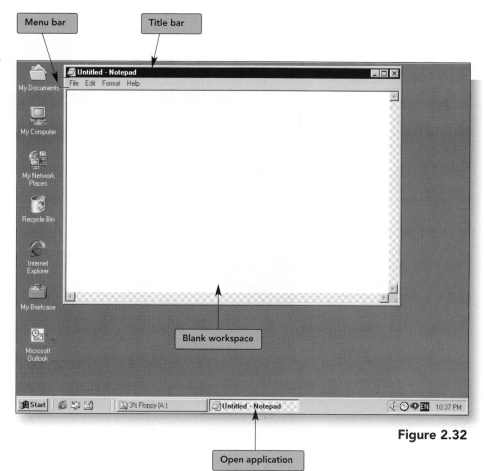

Figure 2.32

The Notepad application program is opened in its own window. As in the
other Windows 2000 programs, the Notepad window includes a title bar
and menu bar. The large blank area below the menu is the workspace where
your work is displayed.

Opening a File

When Notepad first opens, a blank workspace is ready for you to begin typing to create a new document. Alternatively, as you will do in this case, you
can open and then modify an existing document. As in all Windows applications, the Open command on the File menu is used to open files.

① ● Choose **F**ile/**O**pen.

Another Method
The keyboard shortcut is
[Ctrl] + O.

*Your screen should be
similar to Figure 2.33*

Places bar

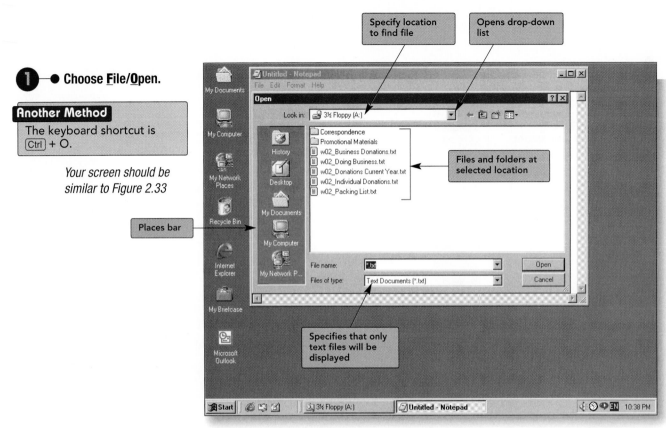

Figure 2.33

The Open dialog box is used to specify the location and name of the file you want to open. This dialog box is common to all applications running under Windows 2000. You can specify the location by selecting from the Look In drop-down list, or from the Places Bar along the left side of the dialog box. The five icons in the Places Bar provide shortcuts to places on your computer from which you can open a file.

Icon	Displays
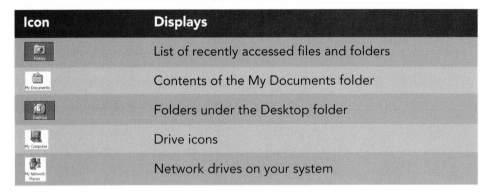 History	List of recently accessed files and folders
My Documents	Contents of the My Documents folder
Desktop	Folders under the Desktop folder
My Computer	Drive icons
My Network Places	Network drives on your system

② ● If necessary, select [icon] 3½ Floppy (or the drive containing your data files) from the Look In drop-down list.

Now the file list box displays the names of all folders and text files in the main folder of your disk. Only text files with a file extension of .txt are displayed, because the Files of Type list box shows that the currently selected type is text documents.

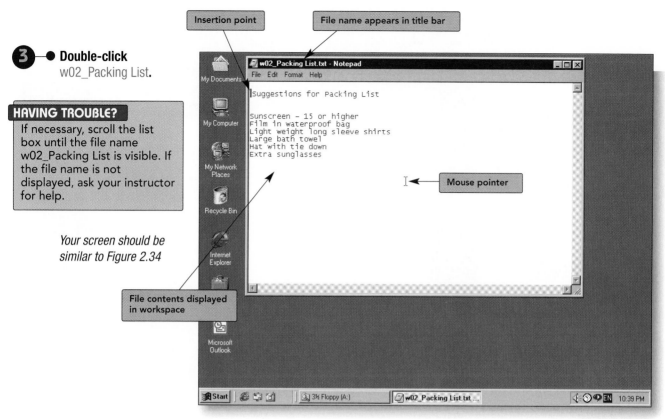

3 ● **Double-click**
w02_Packing List.

HAVING TROUBLE?
If necessary, scroll the list box until the file name w02_Packing List is visible. If the file name is not displayed, ask your instructor for help.

Your screen should be similar to Figure 2.34

Figure 2.34

The file is loaded and displayed in the workspace, and the file name is displayed in the title bar after the program name. The insertion point in the upper left corner of the document shows where the next character will appear when you begin to type. When the mouse pointer is positioned in the workspace, it appears as an I-beam, just as it does in a text box or a dialog box, and is used to position the insertion point in the document.

Editing a Document

While typing you may make typing errors, or you might want to change what you have typed. One of the advantages of using a computer is that you can easily change or **edit** your documents. The changes you make can be as simple as correcting spelling or adding or removing some text, or as complicated as rearranging the content and redesigning the layout of the document.

You want to add an item to the list and include your name and the current date at the top of the document. To add the item to the top of the list, you must first move the insertion point to that location. You can use the directional keys or the mouse to move the insertion point within the text. The directional arrow keys move the insertion point one space in the direction indicated by the arrow. To move the insertion point with the mouse, position the I-beam at the location in the text where you want the insertion point to be and click the left mouse button.

As you are typing, do not be concerned if you make mistakes, as they can be easily removed and corrected. The two most common means to remove text are to use the [Backspace] key to delete unwanted characters to the left of the insertion point, or the [Delete] key to remove the character to the right. Then you can retype the text correctly.

1 ● **Press** ↓ **(three times).**

● **Type Binoculars -**
 automatic focus best.

● **Click on the top line of**
 the document.

● **Type your name.**

● **Press** ←Enter**.**

Your screen should be
similar to Figure 2.35

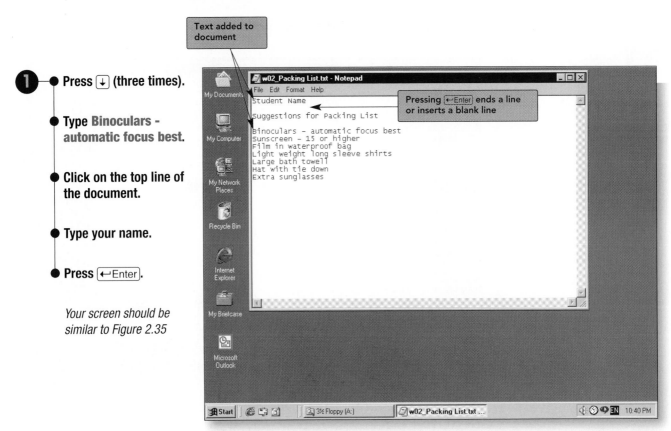

Figure 2.35

Pressing ←Enter ends a line and moves the insertion point to the beginning
of the next line. When the insertion point is at the beginning of a line and
←Enter is pressed, a blank line is created.

2 ● **Type the current date.**

● **Press** ←Enter **twice.**

Your screen should be
similar to Figure 2.36

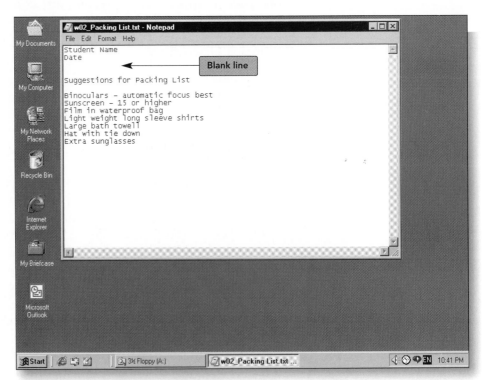

Figure 2.36

Printing a Document

Next you want to print a copy of the document.

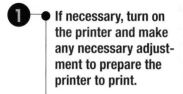 ● **If necessary, turn on the printer and make any necessary adjustment to prepare the printer to print.**

● **Choose File/Print.**

Another Method
The keyboard shortcut for the Print command is
[Ctrl] + P.

Your screen should be similar to Figure 2.37

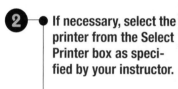 ● **If necessary, select the printer from the Select Printer box as specified by your instructor.**

● **Click**  Print .

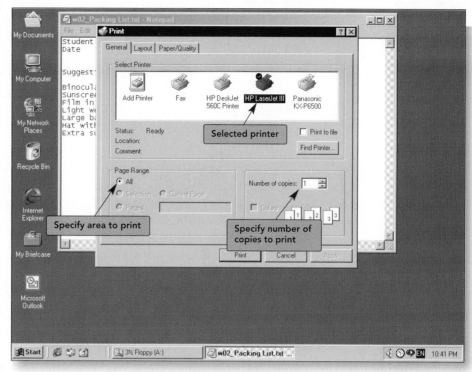

Figure 2.37

The printer indicator icon 🖨 is displayed in the taskbar while printing is in progress. If you double-click on the indicator, the Printer dialog box is displayed so you can see the printer status and settings and cancel a print job if needed.

Saving a File

Now you will save the document with the changes you made to it.

concept 5

Saving Files

5 When you save a document you are working on, a permanent copy of your onscreen document is electronically stored as a file on a disk. While working on a document, the changes you make are stored temporarily in the computer's memory. Not until you save the document as a file on a disk are you safe from losing your work due to a power failure or other mishap. Although many programs create automatic backup files if your work is accidentally interrupted, it is still a good idea to save your work frequently.

Additional Information

When you save a file for the first time, either command can be used.

Another Method

The Save command keyboard shortcut is Ctrl + S.

Two commands found on the File menu of all Windows programs can be used to save a file: Save and Save As. The Save command saves a document using the same location and file name as the existing disk file, by replacing the contents of the file with the changes you made. The Save As command allows you to select a different location and/or provide a different file name. This command lets you save both an original version of a document and a revised document as two separate files. You want to save the document with a more descriptive file name.

1 ● **Choose File/Save As.**

Your screen should be similar to Figure 2.38

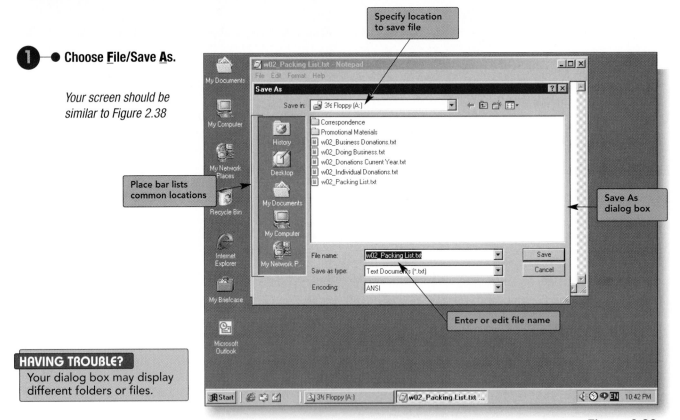

HAVING TROUBLE?

Your dialog box may display different folders or files.

Figure 2.38

Whenever you save a file for the first time or use the Save As command, the Save As dialog box is displayed so you can specify where you want the file saved and the file name. Like the Open dialog box, the Save As dialog box is common to all programs running under Windows 2000. You will save the file to the same location on your data disk with a different file name.

② **Click at the beginning of the file name in the File Name text box.**

● Delete w02_ and type River Rafting before the existing file name.

Your screen should be similar to Figure 2.39

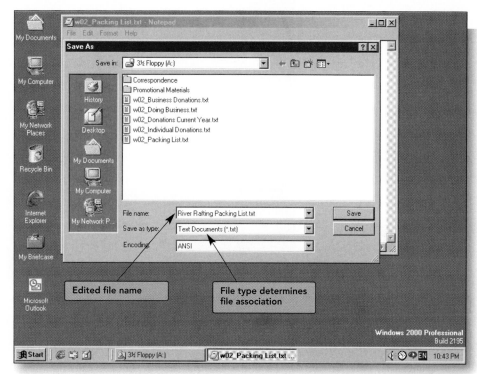

Figure 2.39

Additional Information

Your computer may associate the file with another word processor or with Notepad.

The Save As Type drop-down list box displays the name of the application that will be associated with the saved file. You can change the association by selecting another file type from the drop-down list, or by including a specific file extension when naming the file to override the selection. The file extension is used by Windows to determine the application program to load when a document is opened. In this case, Notepad will automatically add a .txt extension to the file name, establishing the file type as a text file.

3 ● Click [Save].

Your screen should be similar to Figure 2.40

New file name

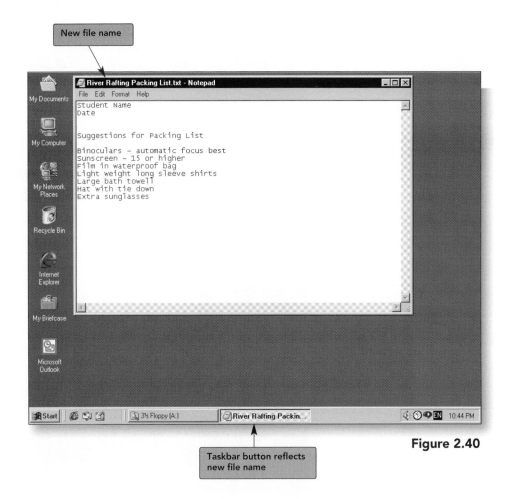

Figure 2.40

Taskbar button reflects new file name

The document is saved to the disk using the specified file name. The new file name now appears in the title bar and in the taskbar button.

4 ● **Close the Notepad window.**

● **Display the Windows Explorer window.**

Your screen should be similar to Figure 2.41

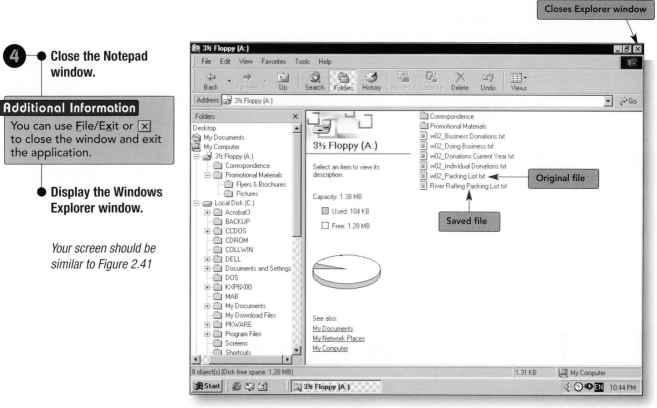

Figure 2.41

The original file you opened and the file you edited and saved are listed in the details pane.

5 ● **Close the Windows Explorer window.**

● **Choose Shut Down or Log Off from the Start menu as appropriate.**

If you are turning the computer off, wait until the screen message is displayed indicating that it is safe to shut off your computer.

lab review

LAB 2
Organizing Your Work

key terms

active pane WN2.19	edit WN2.31	root folder WN2.6
Clipboard WN2.19	file name WN2.11	source WN2.19
current folder WN2.9	file name extension WN2.11	subfolder WN2.6
destination WN2.19	hierarchy WN2.6	tree WN2.6
drag and drop WN2.22	main folder WN2.6	Windows Explorer WN2.4

command summary

Command	Shortcut	Button	Action
Windows Explorer			
/Programs/Windows Explorer			Starts Windows Explorer program
File/New/Folder			Creates a new folder
File/Delete			Sends selected item to Recycle Bin or deletes it from a floppy disk
File/Rename			Changes name of selected item
Edit/Undo	Ctrl + Z	Undo	Undoes last command or action
Edit/Cut	Ctrl + X		Removes selected object and places it in Clipboard
Edit/Copy	Ctrl + C		Copies selected object to Clipboard
Edit/Paste	Ctrl + V		Pastes object from Clipboard to new location
Edit/Select All	Ctrl + A		Selects all items in active window
View/Arrange Icons/by Name			Arranges icons alphabetically by file name
View/Go to/Back	Alt + ←	Back	Displays previous folder location
Notepad			
/Programs/Accessories/Notepad			Starts Notepad application program
File/Open	Ctrl + O		Opens an existing file
File/Save	Ctrl + S		Saves a file with same name
File/Save As			Saves a file with a new name
File/Print	Ctrl + P		Prints document
File/Exit		X	Closes an application

lab exercises

screen identification

Use the figure below to identify each action and match it with its result.
For example, clicking A (Action 1.) expands the folder (Result f.).

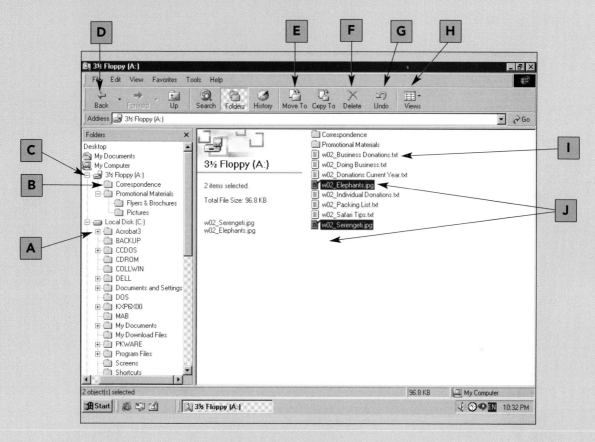

Action	Result	
1. Clicking A	_____ **a.**	moves or copies file
2. Clicking B	_____ **b.**	moves selected item
3. Clicking C	_____ **c.**	collapses the folder
4. Clicking D	_____ **d.**	selects file
5. Clicking E	_____ **e.**	changes display of icons in details pane
6. Clicking F	_____ **f.**	expands the folder
7. Clicking G	_____ **g.**	redisplays previously displayed folders
8. Clicking H	_____ **h.**	makes folder current
9. Clicking I	_____ **i.**	deletes selected item
10. Clicking J	_____ **j.**	undoes the last action

step-by-step

Editing a Document

★ **1.** While doing research for a paper, you created the document wd02_Doing Business. This file should be in your data files.

   a. Start Notepad and open the w02_Doing Business document.

   b. At the top of the document, add the title **Doing Business on the Internet**. Enter two blank lines below the title.

   c. Enter your name and the current date below the last paragraph.

   d. Print the document.

   e. Save the document as E-Business. Close Notepad.

Managing Files and Folders

★★ **2.** You have accepted an internship for a local charity. The charity keeps records on donations, volunteers, and donors. You would like to set up a disk to keep track of the files you create for the charity.

   a. Using Windows Explorer, create two new folders on a floppy disk and name them Donations and People. Under the People folder create two subfolders, Volunteers and Donors.

   b. Make the main folder active. Copy w02_Donations Current Year, w02_Volunteer, w02_Business Donations, and w02_Individual Donations from the Student Data File location to the main folder of your floppy disk.

   c. Move the file w02_Donations Current Year from the main folder to the Donations folder. Rename the file 2002 Donations.

   d. Copy the w02_Volunteer file to the Volunteers subfolder. Rename the file Volunteer.

   e. Delete the w02_Volunteer file from the main folder.

   f. Copy the two files, w02_Business Donations and w02_Individual Donations, from the main folder to the Donors subfolder. Rename the files Business Donations and Individual Donations.

   g. Confirm that all the files have been copied or moved to the folders.

   h. Close Windows Explorer.

on your own

Formatting a Disk

★★ **1.** Before a disk can be used, it must be formatted. This prepares a disk to accept information and files. Most disks are sold preformatted and can be used immediately. Others, however, need to be formatted by the user. Use Help to find out about formatting disks. Follow the instructions in Help to format a floppy disk (make sure the disk does not contain any files you want to keep). Include your name on the volume label.

Things-To-Do

★★ **2.** You are planning a very busy day and need to work up a brief list of the items you need to accomplish. Use Notepad to create a list of at least six items. Include a title for the list and your name and the date below the list. Save and print the list.

Introduction to the Internet and Web

objectives

After completing this lab, you will know how to:

1.	Enter a URL.
2.	Select links.
3.	Use frames.
4.	Use search services to find information.
5.	Search the Web by topic and keyword.
6.	Send and reply to e-mail.
7.	Print and delete e-mail.
8.	Save and print Web pages.

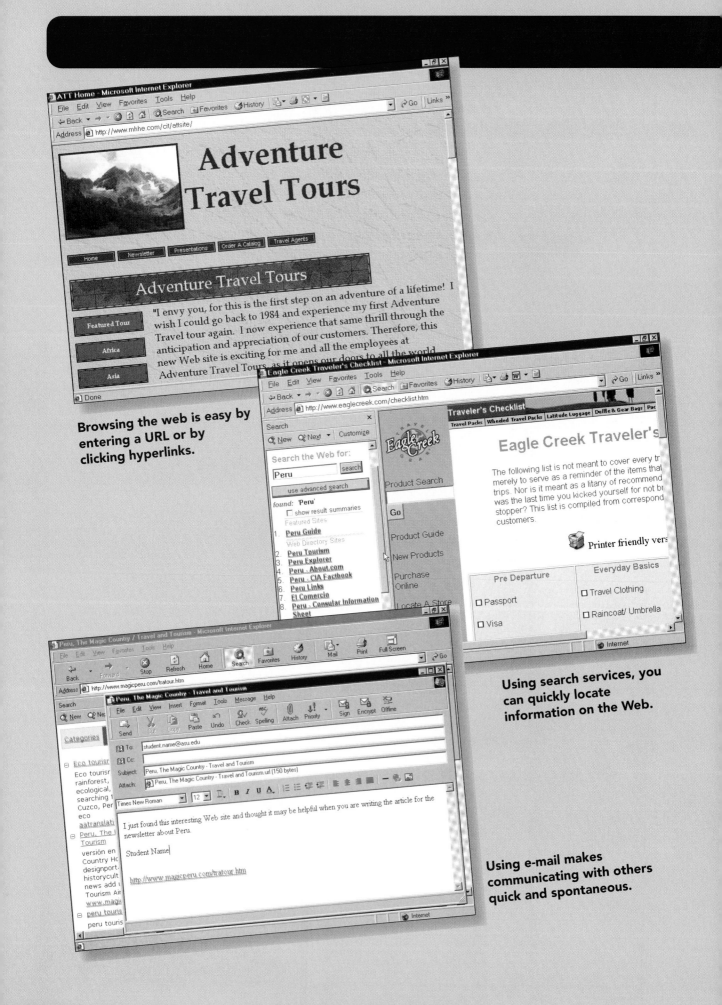

Browsing the web is easy by entering a URL or by clicking hyperlinks.

Using search services, you can quickly locate information on the Web.

Using e-mail makes communicating with others quick and spontaneous.

Adventure Travel

As advertising coordinator for the corporate head-quarters of Adventure Travel Tours, a specialty travel agency that organizes active adventure vacations, you are responsible for all types of promotional materials to be used by the travel agencies located throughout the United States.

One of your responsibilities is the development of materials for the company's

Web site. Your supervisor has asked you to review the current Web site and to make suggestions for improvements. Also, he wants you to search the Web to locate sites for general travel information and information on Peru, the country that will be featured in the next month's newsletter.

The following concepts will be introduced in this lab:

1.	**Web Pages and Web Sites**	A Web page is a text file that has been created using a special programming language called HyperText Markup Language (HTML), and that contains links to other Web pages and graphics. Each Web site consists of interconnected pages that have a common theme and design.
2.	**Web Site Address**	Each Web page has its own address, called the Uniform Resource Locator (URL), which provides location information used to navigate through the Internet to access a page.
3.	**Hypertext Link**	A hypertext link, also called a hyperlink or simply a link, is a connection to another Web page or to another location on the current page.
4.	**Frame**	Frames divide the Web browser's display into separate, scrollable areas. Each frame can display a different Web page.
5.	**Search Service**	Search services are huge databases of Web pages and Internet sites that are used to locate information.
6.	**Topic search**	A topic search is conducted by selecting a category and continuing to select subcategories until your search has been narrowed and a list of relevant documents appears.
7.	**Keyword Search**	If you are looking for a specific concept or a phrase, use the keyword search method by entering a descriptive word or phrase in the search text box.
8.	**E-Mail Address**	On the Internet, each person has a unique e-mail address or means of identification.

What Are the Internet and the Web?

Want to communicate with a friend across town, in another state, or even in another country? Perhaps you would like to send a drawing, a photo, or just a letter. Looking for travel or entertainment information? Perhaps you're researching a term paper or exploring different career paths. Where do you start? For these and other information-related activities, try the Internet and the Web. They are the 21st-century information resources designed for all of us to use.

What is the **Internet**? It is a network of thousands of computer networks that allows computers to communicate with each other. The popular term for the Internet is the "information highway." Like a highway, the Internet connects you to millions of other people and organizations. Unlike typical highways that move people and things from one location to another, the Internet moves your ideas and information. Rather than moving through geographic space, you move through cyberspace—the space of electronic movement of ideas and information.

The uses for the Internet are many and varied. The most popular use is to send e-mail (electronic mail) messages. A second use is to send (upload) or receive (download) files between computers. A third is to participate in discussion groups, such as mailing lists and newsgroups, that allow you to

communicate with large numbers of people about specific topics. Finally, surfing the Web is another very popular use of the Internet.

What is the **Web**? The Web (**World Wide Web** or **WWW**) provides an easy-to-use, exciting, multimedia interface to connect to the Internet and to access the resources available in cyberspace. The Web consists of information organized into Web pages containing text and graphic images. But most importantly, a page contains hypertext links, or highlighted keywords and images that lead to related information. Clicking on the links quickly transports you to the location where that information is located. The links may take you to other pages, text files, graphic images, movies, or audio clips. The Web allows users to view millions of pages of information by jumping from one related source to another by clicking on links.

How Do You Access the Internet?

Many schools and businesses have direct access to the Internet using special high-speed communication lines and equipment. Students and employees are typically provided access through the organization's local area network (LAN) or through their own personal computers.

Another way to access the Internet is through an Internet Service Provider (ISP) such as America Online and Microsoft Network. To access the ISP, you use your personal computer, modem, and telecommunications software to log onto the online service. Your computer connects to a larger computer, which runs special software that provides access to the Internet. You pay a fee for use of their service.

How Do You Access the Web?

Once you have your Internet connection, then you need special software called a **browser** to access the Web. Browsers are used to connect you to remote computers, open and transfer files, display text and images, and provide in one tool an uncomplicated interface to the Internet and the Web. At one time, browsers were considered specialized programs used primarily by computer professionals. Now, browsers are widely used by almost everyone who uses a computer.

The most common activities you use a browser for are to navigate the Web, find information on the Web, and to communicate with others.

Navigating the Web using IE5

Navigating the Web means to move from one Web site to another. Often called surfing or browsing the Web, this activity is like reading a magazine and jumping not only from one article to another within the magazine, but also from one magazine to different magazines, books, movies, and so on.

You will use one of the most widely used browsers, Microsoft's Internet Explorer (IE5), to navigate to the Adventure Travel Tours' Web site and look at the Web pages on the site.

concept 1

Web Pages and Web Sites

1

A **Web page** is a text file that has been created using a special programming language called **HyperText Markup Language (HTML)**, and that contains links to other Web pages and graphics. The Web page is stored on a computer called a **server**, where it can be accessed and displayed using a browser program. A server may contain several Web sites. Each **Web site** consists of interconnected pages that have a common theme and design. Each Web page is designed by the people at the Web site and will contain information unique to that site.

Web pages are interactive. This means the user can send information or commands to the Web site, which control a program running on the Web server, and receive a response from the site. Web pages can also use multimedia. This includes the ability to add animation to a page, display video, and run audio files.

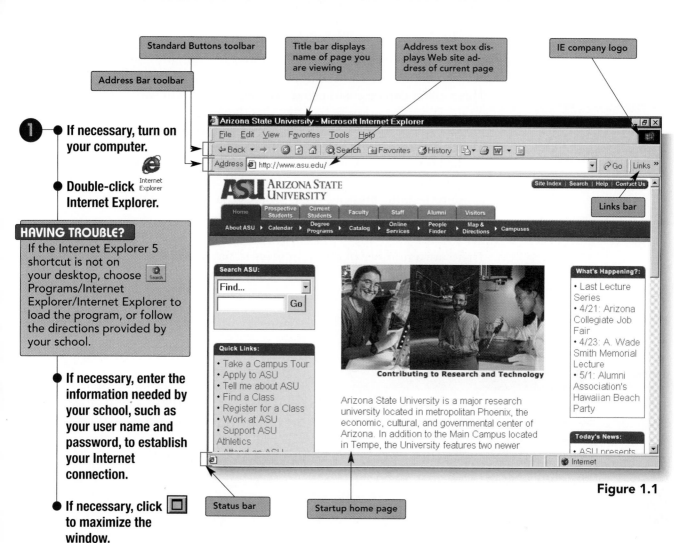

Standard Buttons toolbar

Address Bar toolbar

Title bar displays name of page you are viewing

Address text box displays Web site address of current page

IE company logo

1 • **If necessary, turn on your computer.**

• **Double-click Internet Explorer.**

HAVING TROUBLE?

If the Internet Explorer 5 shortcut is not on your desktop, choose Programs/Internet Explorer/Internet Explorer to load the program, or follow the directions provided by your school.

• **If necessary, enter the information needed by your school, such as your user name and password, to establish your Internet connection.**

• **If necessary, click ▢ to maximize the window.**

Your screen should be similar to Figure 1.1

Links bar

Status bar

Startup home page

Figure 1.1

The Internet Explorer 5 browser window is displayed on your screen. When Internet Explorer first starts, it displays the **startup home page**. This is a page that the Internet Explorer program has been set to load by default. This most likely is your school's home page. A **home page** is the first page of information for a Web site. Generally, home pages include a brief welcome with information about the site and a table of contents that will take you to other pages of information within the Web site. Even though at present your screen displays different information, the components of the browser window are the same.

As in other Windows applications, the window has a title bar, Minimize ▬, ▢, and ⧉ Maximize/Restore buttons, ☒ Close button, menu bar, toolbars, status bar, and scroll bars. The title bar displays the name of the page you are currently viewing. The six pull-down menus below the title bar when selected display Internet Explorer (IE) commands that allow you to control the screen appearance and how IE performs, as well as provide Help information and general file utilities such as saving and printing. On the right edge of the menu bar is the Internet Explorer company logo, which animates whenever a page transfer is in progress.

By default three toolbars, Standard Buttons, Links bar, and Address bar, are displayed when IE is first opened. The Standard Buttons toolbar contains shortcuts for the most widely used commands, including those used to navigate among pages. The Links bar initially contains buttons that access various Microsoft pages designed to help you locate information. This toolbar can be customized to display buttons to your favorite locations on the Web. The Address bar contains the Address text box where you enter the Web address location of a page you want to display in the main window. Currently, the address for your home page is displayed.

Additional Information
You will learn more about Web addresses shortly.

The large center area of the window is the **main window** where the content of a Web page is displayed. The status bar below the main window area contains a status message area, progress bar, and a security level indicator.

Entering a URL

There are a number of different ways to navigate from one site or one Web page to another. One of the most common ways is to directly enter a Web site address.

concept 2

Web Site Address

2   Each Web page has its own address, called the **Uniform Resource Locator (URL)**, which provides location information used to navigate through the Internet to access a page. Although URLs appear complicated, they are actually quite easy to decipher. The URL consists of several parts specifying the protocol, server, and path name of the item. Most begin with http://www or some variation. The URL for the Arizona State University home page is:

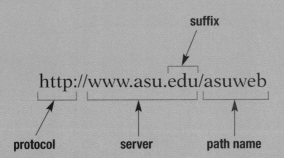

The protocol identifies the type of server where the information is stored. For Web pages, the protocol is HTTP, for HyperText Transfer Protocol. A colon and two forward slashes (//) always follow the protocol. The server, also known as the domain, typically identifies the name of the computer system that stores the information. It typically begins with "www," indicating the site is part of the World Wide Web. The server name also includes a suffix, which identifies the type of server. For example, the suffix .com indicates the server is a commercial server, and .edu indicates it is an educational server. The last part is the path name, which indicates where the information is located on the server. Each part of the path is preceded with a single forward slash (/).

Typing the URL in the Address box will take you instantly to that location. When typing a URL, you must enter it exactly, including uppercase or lowercase. However, like most browsers, Internet Explorer allows you to omit the protocol http://, as this is assumed. If the URL begins with a protocol different than http://, however, you must type it. It is also often unnecessary to type the www part of the URL or the suffix .com.

Additionally, Internet Explorer includes an AutoComplete feature that will attempt to complete the URL for you if there is a URL that was previously entered in the Address box that matches the letters you type. If you enter an incorrect URL, an error message will appear.

To see the Adventure Travel Tours' Web site, you will enter the site's URL in the address box. As the content of the home page for the site is transferred or **downloaded** from the server location to your location, notice that the Internet Explorer company logo animates. The status message area also shows information such as the total and remaining number of items being loaded and the URL. The progress bar appears and visually shows the download percentage completed.

Additional Information
You can find URLs for many Web sites in books, news articles, on TV, and through discussion groups.

Additional Information
The Address box stores the last 14 URLs that were entered.

Another Method
You can also click ▾ in the Address box to display a menu of up to the last 14 URLs that have been entered in the Address box. Choosing a URL from the menu displays the page again.

Additional Information
Clicking, pressing Esc, or choosing <u>V</u>iew/<u>S</u>top will cancel a transfer immediately.

1 ● **Click in the Address box.**

Additional Information
The current URL is highlighted and will be replaced by the new text as you type.

● **Type www.mhhe.com/cit/attsite.**

● **Click** Go.

Another Method
You can also press ←Enter to complete the address.

Another Method
You can also use <u>F</u>ile/<u>O</u>pen or Ctrl + O to display the Open dialog box in which you enter the URL.

Your screen should be similar to Figure 1.2

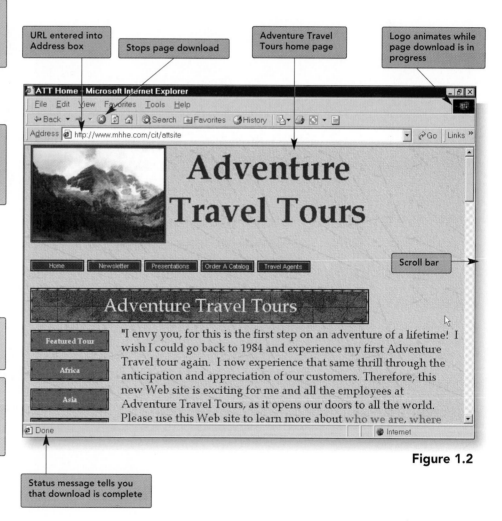

URL entered into Address box

Stops page download

Adventure Travel Tours home page

Logo animates while page download is in progress

Scroll bar

Status message tells you that download is complete

Figure 1.2

The main window displays the Adventure Travel Tours' home page, and the title bar displays the name of the current page. A vertical scroll bar appears whenever the main window is not large enough to fully display the entire page contents. To see more of the page contents, you can scroll the window.

② ● Scroll the window to the bottom of the page.

Your screen should be similar to Figure 1.3

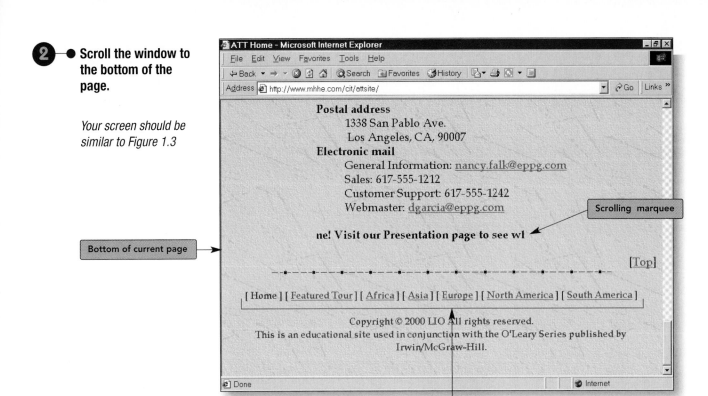

Bottom of current page

Figure 1.3

Selecting Links

The bottom of the page displays a scrolling marquee, a visitor counter, and several hypertext links.

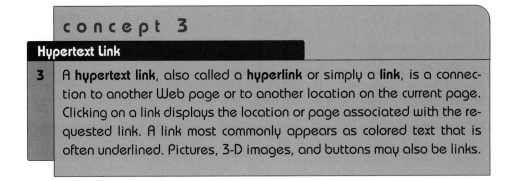

concept 3

Hypertext Link

3 A **hypertext link**, also called a **hyperlink** or simply a **link**, is a connection to another Web page or to another location on the current page. Clicking on a link displays the location or page associated with the requested link. A link most commonly appears as colored text that is often underlined. Pictures, 3-D images, and buttons may also be links.

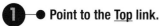

1 ● Point to the <u>Top</u> link.

Your screen should be similar to Figure 1.4

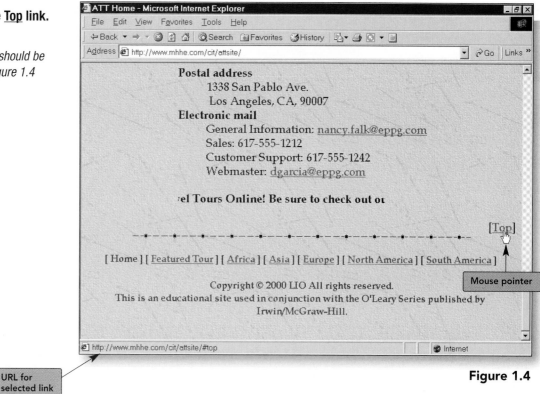

URL for selected link

Figure 1.4

Notice that the mouse pointer shape changed to a hand 🖑, indicating you are pointing to a hypertext link. In addition, the URL for this link appears in the status message area.

2 ● Click <u>Top</u>.

Your screen should be similar to Figure 1.5

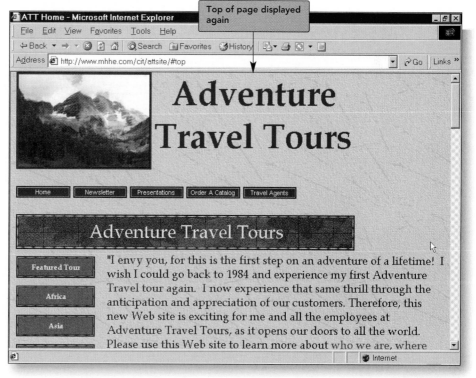

Top of page displayed again

Figure 1.5

HAVING TROUBLE?
Click a link only once and then watch the progress bar. Clicking again cancels the first operation and starts loading the page again. Be patient.

When you click this link, the top of the home page is displayed, saving you the trouble of scrolling back to the top of the page. This type of link is most often used when a Web page is a long document.

3 ● Click <u>where we are</u>.

Your screen should be similar to Figure 1.6

Section of page displayed by checking 'where we are' link

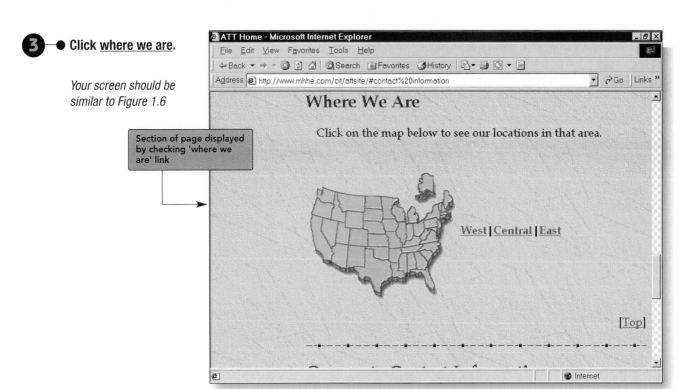

Figure 1.6

The section of the page relating to Where We Are immediately appears at the top of the window. As you can see, this is much faster than scrolling.

Other links display a new page of information in the browser. When you click on a link, the location that the link refers to is transferred from the server location to your location. In addition to text links, buttons and other graphic objects can be links. Watch the information in the status bar while the new page is loaded.

Name of current page

Address of current page

4 ● Click <u>Top</u> to return to the top of the page.

● Click **Featured Tour**.

Your screen should be similar to Figure 1.7

Clicking Featured Tour button displays associated page

Figure 1.7

The title bar displays the name of the current page, and the Address box shows the page's URL.

5 ● **Scroll to bottom of the page.**

● **Click** [Home].

● **Scroll to the bottom of the page.**

Your screen should be similar to Figure 1.8

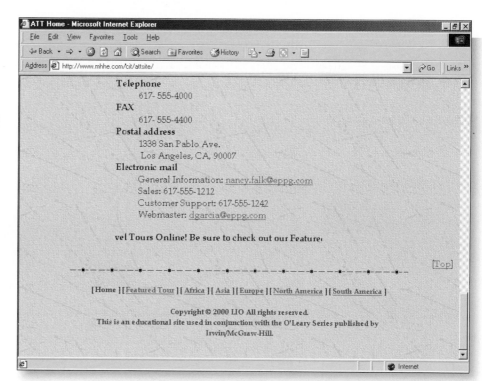

Figure 1.8

Additional Information

Many of the links on the Adventure Travel Web site may appear as followed links if a previous user on your computer recently selected them.

The home page of the Web site is displayed again. You have probably noticed that links are displayed in different colors. The default text colors for links are blue and purple. A link that appears blue indicates it has not been selected recently. This is called an unvisited or **unfollowed link**. A purple link indicates that the link has been recently used, and is thus called a visited or **followed link**. It will remain a followed link for a set period of time, depending upon your program setup (the default is 20 days). Links can also be in different colors, depending upon the colors used in the design of the Web site.

Using Frames

Next you want to check out the newsletter.

1 • Click [Top].

• Click [Newsletter].

Your screen should be similar to Figure 1.9

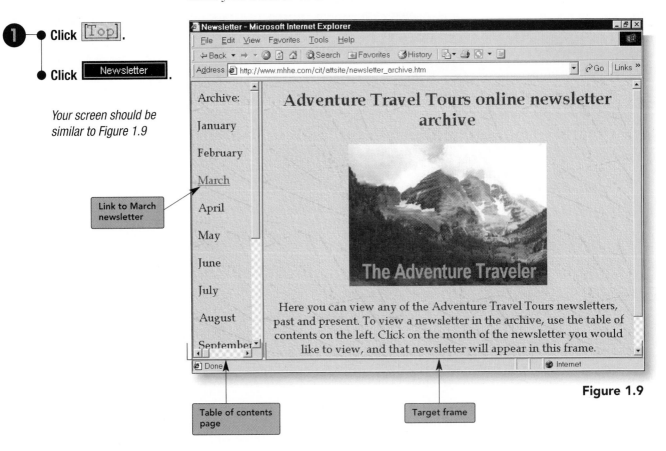

Link to March newsletter

Table of contents page

Target frame

Figure 1.9

The browser's display area is divided into two windows called frames.

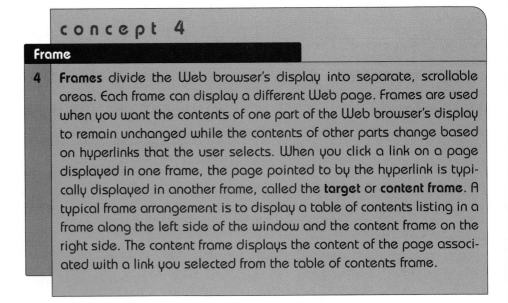

concept 4

Frame

4 **Frames** divide the Web browser's display into separate, scrollable areas. Each frame can display a different Web page. Frames are used when you want the contents of one part of the Web browser's display to remain unchanged while the contents of other parts change based on hyperlinks that the user selects. When you click a link on a page displayed in one frame, the page pointed to by the hyperlink is typically displayed in another frame, called the **target** or **content frame**. A typical frame arrangement is to display a table of contents listing in a frame along the left side of the window and the content frame on the right side. The content frame displays the content of the page associated with a link you selected from the table of contents frame.

2 ● Click March in the table of contents frame.

Your screen should be similar to Figure 1.10

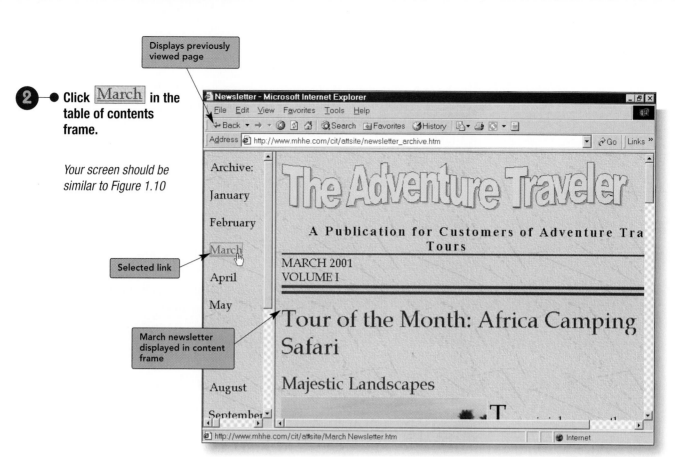

Displays previously viewed page

Selected link

March newsletter displayed in content frame

Figure 1.10

The March newsletter is displayed in the content frame. The frame on the left does not change, allowing you to quickly select a different category. Internet Explorer loads the text of a page first, followed by images. Images first appear as empty boxes containing a small image icon ⊠. As the image is loaded, it replaces the box.

After looking at the newsletter, you want to return to the previous page. However, because the March newsletter page does not include a link back to the Newsletter page, you will use the ⌐Back ▾ button on the browser toolbar.

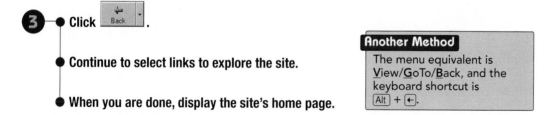

3 ● Click ⌐Back ▾.

● Continue to select links to explore the site.

● When you are done, display the site's home page.

Another Method

The menu equivalent is View/GoTo/Back, and the keyboard shortcut is Alt + ←.

Additional Information

Clicking ⌐→⌐ will display the next page you viewed. ⌐→⌐ is only available after using ⌐←⌐. The menu equivalent is View/GoTo/Forward, and the keyboard shortcut is Alt + →.

After looking over the content of the Web site, you think that the addition of a Travel Resources page containing links to Web sites that provide both general travel information and information directly related to tour locations would be a great addition to the site. You decide you will spend some time browsing the Web to locate appropriate sites to reference.

Finding Information on the Web

The Web is a massive collection of interrelated Web pages. With so much available information, locating the precise information you need can be difficult. Fortunately, a number of search tools have been developed and are available to you on certain Web sites that provide search services to help you find information.

concept 5

Search Service

5 **Search services** also called **search providers**, are huge databases of Web pages and Internet resources that are used to locate information on the Web. Some search services organize the information by categories such as art, computers, entertainment, news, and so on. Each category is further organized into subcategories. Many also offer reviews and ratings of the sites.

Because no one search service has all the Web pages on the Web in its index, and because the search services use different techniques and search different types of Web resources, it is advisable to use more than one engine when conducting a search. It is also helpful to know which tools may be best suited to find the type of information you need. See the following table for a brief description of many of the most popular search services.

Search Service	URL# (all URLs begin with http://)	Description
Yahoo	www.yahoo.com	Easy-to-navigate and comprehensive, subject-based categories. Most useful for browsing and general searching to locate popular sites.
Excite	www.excite.com	Includes over 50 million Web pages, and 65,000 reviewed sites. Fast, big and easy to use, with site reviews and travel guides.
Lycos	www.lycos.com	A large database that includes a site's URL, title, and first 20 lines from which it automatically generates an abstract.
AltaVista	www.alta-vista.com	One of the largest search service databases with over 250 million Web pages. Best place if trying to find obscure piece of information.
MSN WebSearch	www.search.msn.com	Large, easy to use and intuitive search service.
Northern Light	www.nlsearch.com	Maintains a large index of pages. Sorts by relevance and filters duplicate links.

Since the Adventure Travel Web site contains information about trips and tours in many locations, you want to begin by finding several sites that provide general advice on travel, rather than information about a specific topic. You decide to use Yahoo! to locate information on travel.

Type www.yahoo.com in the Address box.

Press ⏎Enter.

Your screen should be similar to Figure 1.11

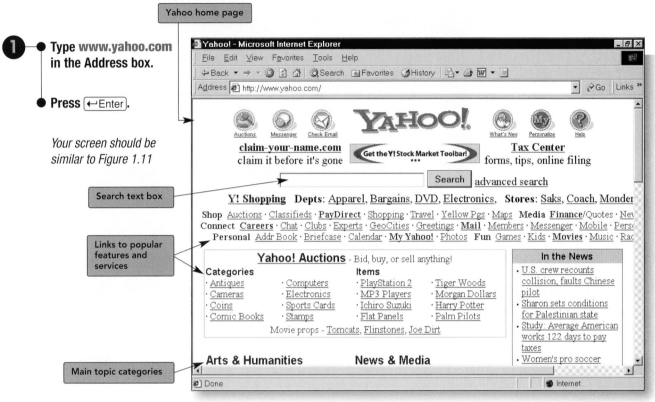

Figure 1.11

Note: If you receive a message indicating you cannot connect to a site, it may be that the maximum number of users is accessing the location. Resubmit your request several times and you will probably get on. If not, skip to the section, "Searching by Keyword," on page IN.21 and return to this section later.

The Yahoo! Web site interface consists of a link at the top of the page that will quickly take you to different locations on the site, a search text box, links to shopping, and the list of main topic area links.

Searching by Topic

The two basic means of searching are by navigating through topic lists or by entering a keyword or phrase into a search text box. Some search services offer both methods, others only one. Yahoo! offers both, but because it categorizes its sites, topic searches are most frequently used.

concept 6

Topic Search

6 A **topic search** is conducted by selecting a category and continuing to select subcategories until your search has been narrowed and a list of relevant documents appears. Using this method, you navigate through a hierarchy of topic listings that group the items in the database into subject categories, such as art, business, and sports. The main subject groupings are further categorized into subtopics; for example, the sports group may have subdivisions of cycling, baseball, and soccer. As you continue to make selections from the topic groups, you narrow the number of listings that will be available to those that more precisely match the information you are seeking. Use a topic search when you are looking for general information.

You want to find general travel information.

1 • Scroll the page to see the entire main topic listing.

• Click Travel under Recreation and Sports.

• Scroll the page to see the Categories list.

Your screen should be similar to Figure 1.12

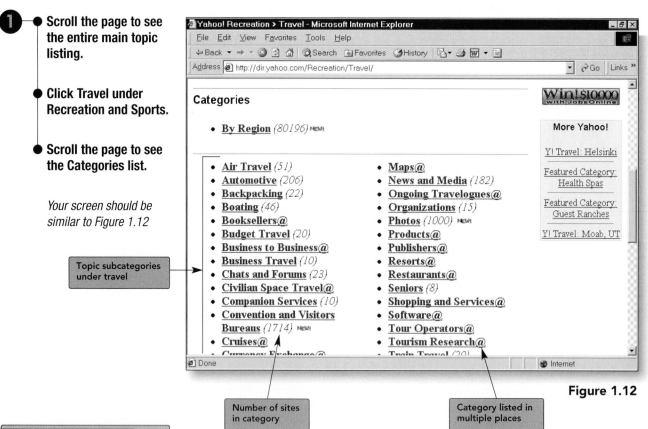

Figure 1.12

Additional Information

The number following a link tells you the number of Web sites that are directly under that topic and the @ symbol means the category is listed in multiple places.

Now a list of travel topics is available, from which you can further narrow your search. You decide to check out the travel tips.

2 ● Click Travel Tips and Tools.

● Scroll the page to see the categories.

Your screen should be similar to Figure 1.13

Additional travel trip categories

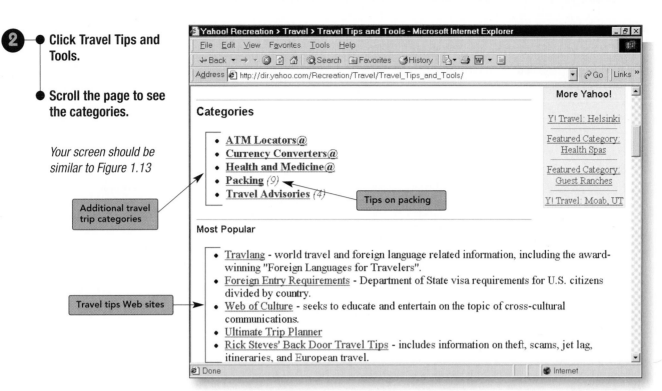

Figure 1.13

This page includes five other category listings as well as a listing of the most popular travel tips and tools Web pages. You decide to narrow your search even more to tips about packing specifically.

3 ● Click Packing.

Your screen should be similar to Figure 1.14

Path of topic selections

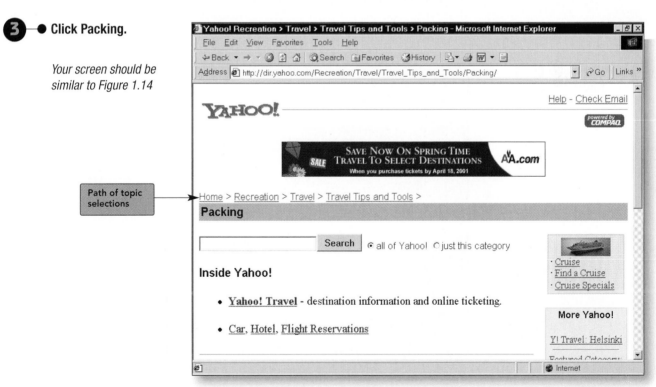

Figure 1.14

The path of selections you have made is displayed above the current category name (Home> Recreation > Travel > Travel Tips and Tools). The previously selected category is now a link back to that page.

4 ● Scroll the page to
see the listing of links
to Web pages on
packing.

*Your screen should be
similar to Figure 1.15*

Page title is hyper-
link to Web site

Description of
contents

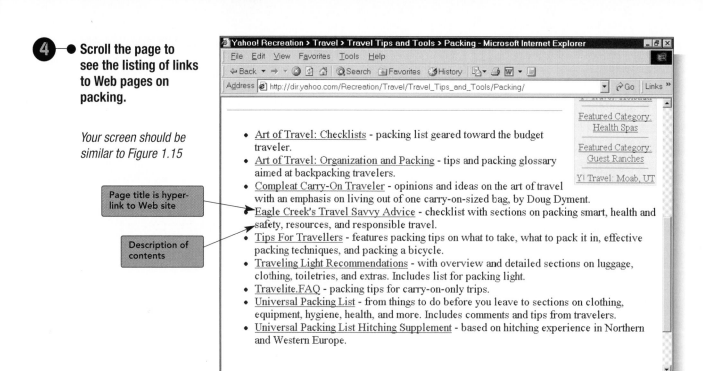

Figure 1.15

This time there are no other categories to select. A list of Web pages specifically about packing is available. Each item in the list consists of the page
title as a hypertext link to the site and a brief description of the site. You
think, from the description, that the Eagle Creek's site may contain content
that would be useful in your Travel Resources Web page, and you want to
check out this site.

5 ● Click Eagle Creek's
Travel Savvy Advice.

*Your screen should be
similar to Figure 1.16*

Page of selected Web
site downloaded and
displayed in browser

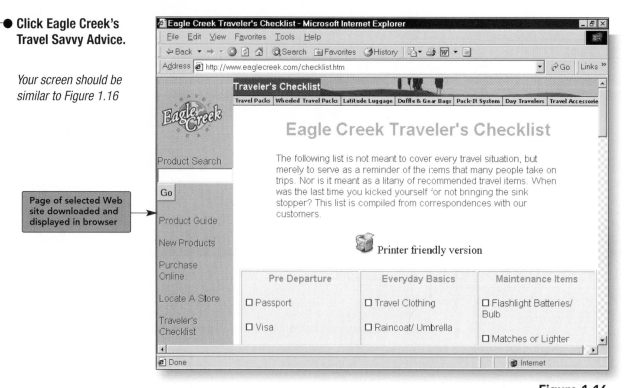

Figure 1.16

The requested page is downloaded. The checklist looks like a good resource for travelers and one that you would like to include on the Travel Resources Web page.

Searching by Keyword

Next you would like to find information about Peru. You will choose a different search service and conduct a search by entering keywords in a search text box. Another way to find a search service is to use Internet Explorer's Search bar.

Search Assistant open in Search bar

1 ● Click [Search].

Another Method

The menu equivalent is View/Explorer Bar/Search and the keyboard shortcut is Ctrl + E.

Your screen should be similar to Figure 1.17

Enter keyword in search text box

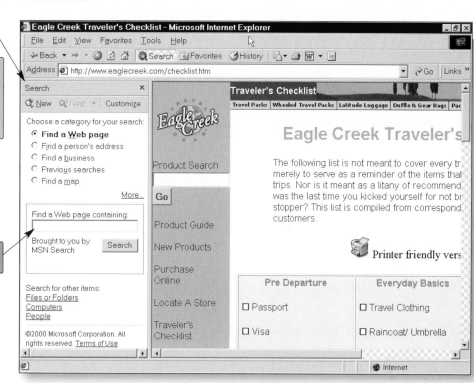

Figure 1.17

The Search bar opens and the Search Assistant feature is activated. To locate information, you enter a keyword in the text box.

concept 7

Keyword Search

7 If you are looking for a specific concept or a phrase, use the **keyword search** method. A **keyword** is a descriptive word or phrase that is entered in the search text box. The search program compares this text with some part of the text it has stored in its database—title, URL, text, a description, abstract, or review—then it displays a list of all pages in its database that contain the text you specified.

If the search yields too few results or "hits," your keyword may be too specific or the incorrect term. Try again using different or less specific or fewer words. Conversely, if you get too many hits, you may want to narrow the field by using more specific words.

2 ● Type **peru**.

● Click [Search].

● Scroll the Search bar to see the results.

Additional Information

In general, use lowercase letters when entering keywords as lowercase words will match any case.

Your screen should be similar to Figure 1.18

Search results for keyword of peru

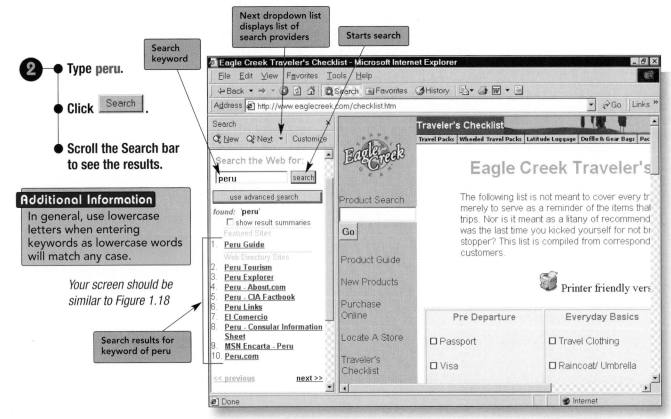

Next dropdown list displays list of search providers

Starts search

Search keyword

Figure 1.18

By default, the MSN Search provider is used and displays the search results related to the search term "peru." After quickly looking at the search result titles, you decide to see what results another search provider will find. You can quickly search using another provider without having to retype the keyword by selecting the provider from the Next drop-down list.

3 ● Click [▼] to open the next drop-down list.

● Choose Alta Vista.

● Scroll the list of results.

Additional Information

All search providers include links to move forward and backwardsthrough the available results.

Your screen should be similar to Figure 1.19

AltaVista Web pages search results

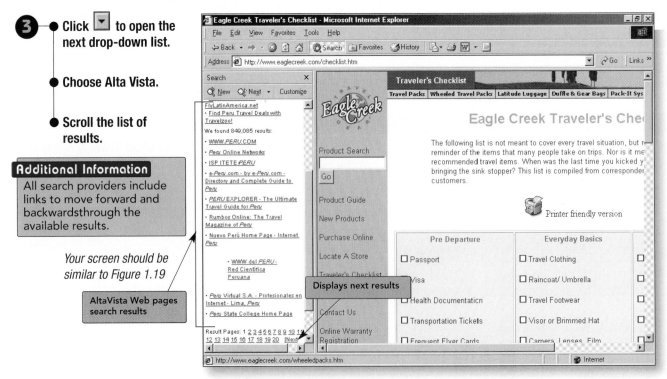

Displays next results

Figure 1.19

AltaVista displays another set of search results. After quickly looking at these, you decide to change the search keyword to locate information on tourism in Peru. You can specify a new search or refine your current search by restricting the new search to the located documents. You will refine the search of the currently displayed results.

4 ● Scroll to the top of the search bar.

● Following the word "Peru" in the Search text box, type **+ tourism**.

● Click show site abstracts.

● Click search.

● Scroll the Search bar to display the results.

Your screen should be similar to Figure 1.20

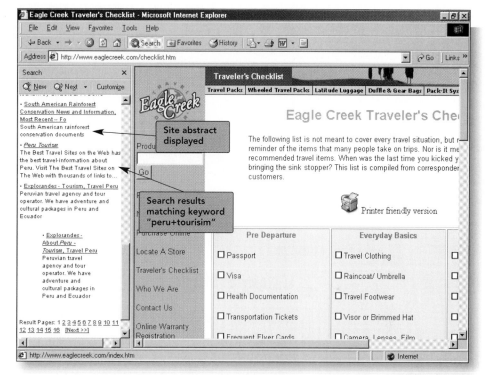

Figure 1.20

When you enter multiple words, Web pages containing all of the keywords are located. However, because you included a "+" between keywords, only sites that contain both words are displayed. Generally, the more specific you can make the keyword query, the better the results. If you know the specific type of information you are looking for, it is faster and more efficient to use a keyword search rather than a topic search.

Additionally, because you selected the option to display site abstracts, a brief description of the site is displayed.

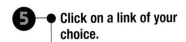

5 ● Click on a link of your choice.

● Click ✕ in the Search bar to close it.

Your selected site should appear full screen similar to the one in Figure 1.21

Figure 1.21

The browser window displays the Web page you selected. To redisplay the Search bar and the abstracted sites, you could use the [🔍 Search] button on the Address toolbar.

Using E-Mail

Note: You need an e-mail address to complete this section, and Outlook Express or another e-mail program must be properly set up on your system. If not, skip to the section, "Saving and Printing Web Pages," on page IN.32.

You think this looks like a good site for information about Peru for the next newsletter. You want to send the address of the site to the person writing this article. To do this, you will send it in an e-mail message. **E-mail**, or electronic mail, one of the original forms of communicating on the Internet, allows individuals to send and receive written messages via computer. The ability to communicate with others over the Internet is one of the prime reasons for its success and popularity.

Composing an E-Mail Message

You can quickly create an e-mail message that includes the Web page as part of the message from within Internet Explorer.

1 • Choose <u>F</u>ile/<u>S</u>end/<u>L</u>ink By E-mail.

• Size the New Message window as in Figure 1.22.

Your screen should be similar to Figure 1.22

New Message window opened

Attachment

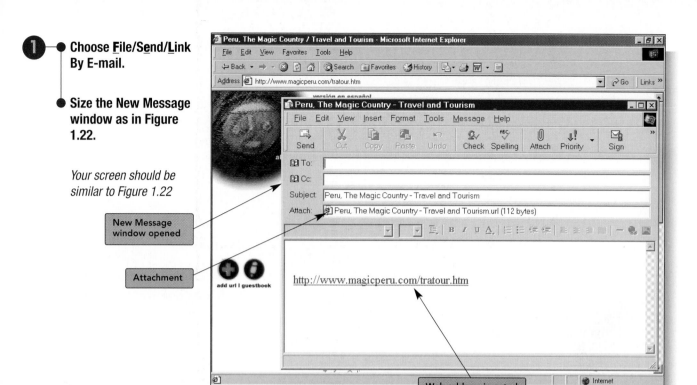

Web address inserted as hyperlink

Figure 1.22

HAVING TROUBLE?
If Outlook Express is not your default e-mail program, your screen will look slightly different.

Additional Information
You can attach a file using the [Attach] button and specifying the location and name of the file to attach.

The Microsoft Outlook Express New Message window is opened, and the Web address of the site you are viewing is automatically entered in the message area as a hyperlink. The page is also an attachment to the e-mail message. An **attachment** is a file that is included with an e-mail message. The ability to send attachments is a very convenient feature. For example, if you are working on a group project, you can attach the file containing your section of the project to another member of your group. This makes it easy to get information to each other without having to meet in person. You can attach files of any type, including text, sound, graphics, and Web pages.

In the To section of the window, you enter the e-mail address of the recipient. In this case, to demonstrate how e-mail works, you will send a message to yourself.

concept 8

E-Mail Address

8   On the Internet, each person has a unique e-mail address or means of identification. The Internet uses an e-mail address system called the **Domain Name System (DNS)**, which consists of three parts: a unique user name, a domain name, and a domain code, as shown below.

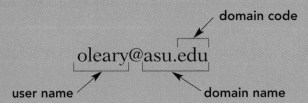

The user name identifies a particular user or group of users at a domain. The user name consists of one word and can contain special characters such as an underscore. It is separated from the domain name with the @ ("at") symbol. The domain name distinguishes a computer from a group of computers. The domain code identifies the type of use. The most common domains are commercial organizations or educational and research institutions. The domain code is generally a three-letter abbreviation; for example, edu stands for education and com for commercial. Periods, called dots, separate the domain code from the rest of the domain name. The number of dots in the domain name varies depending on how the address is structured for a particular computer.

In the Subject section, you can enter a brief description of the contents of the message. In this case, the subject line has also been automatically completed with the name of the attached Web page. The Attach section displays the Web page name and file size of the attachment.

2 • **If necessary, click in the To: field and enter your e-mail address.**

Additional Information
E-mail addresses are not case sensitive.

Your screen should be similar to Figure 1.23

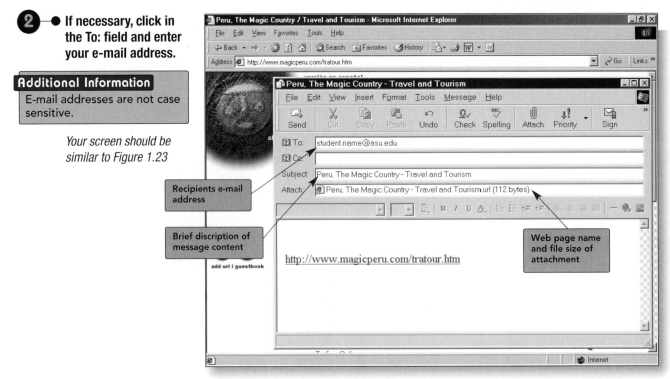

Figure 1.23

Next you will add a short message in the message area. Like a word processor, the text will wrap automatically to the beginning of the next line when it reaches the right edge of the window. Therefore, you do not need to press ⏎Enter at the end of each line. Press ⏎Enter only when you need to end a line or to insert a blank line.

3 ● Click at the top of the message area.

● Press ⏎Enter twice.

● Move to the top of the message and type I just found this interesting Web site and thought it may be helpful when you are writing the article for the newsletter about Peru.

● Press ⏎Enter twice.

● Type your name.

Your screen should be similar to Figure 1.24

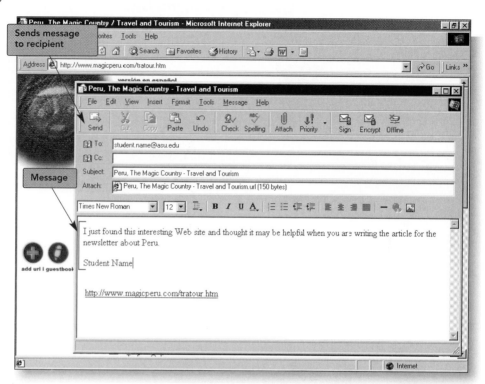

Figure 1.24

Sending a Message

Before sending an e-mail message, you should reread it for accuracy and clarity. Then when the message is complete, you can send it.

1 ● Check the message and correct any errors.

● Click 📤 Send.

Your screen should display your selected site full screen similar to the one in Figure 1.25

Figure 1.25

The New Message window is closed, and the Explorer window is displayed again. How do you know the message was sent? Always assume that it was. If it is not sent, it is bounced back to you with a message from your mail administrator indicating the reason why. The most common reason is an incorrectly entered e-mail address.

Checking Incoming Mail

You will use Outlook Express to look at the message you just sent.

1 ● Open the 📧 drop-down list and choose **Read Mail.**

HAVING TROUBLE?
If Outlook Express is not your default e-mail program, contact your instructor for alternative directions for completing this section.

Your screen should be similar to Figure 1.26

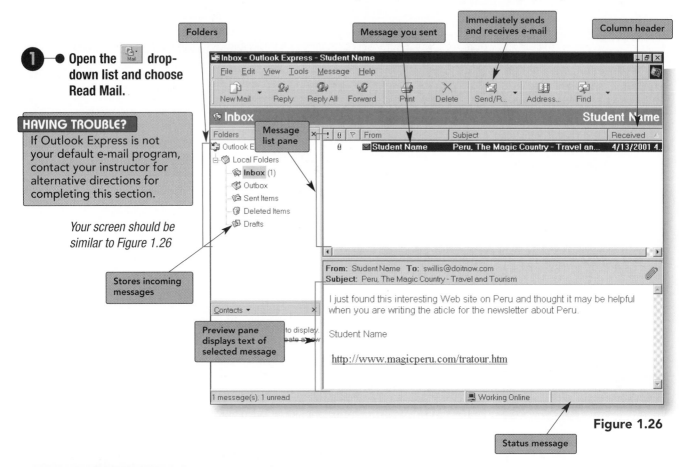

Figure 1.26

Additional Information
By default, Outlook checks for new mail every 30 minutes. You can check for mail manually by clicking 📧 at any time.

When you start Outlook Express, it automatically checks for incoming mail. A message box is briefly displayed that advises you of the number of new messages waiting to be delivered and the progress of the delivery as the messages are downloaded to your computer.

Incoming messages are stored in the Inbox folder. This folder is one of many folders that are used to organize and store your e-mail messages. The following table describes these folders.

Additional Information

Your folder list may include additional or different folders than described here.

Folder	Stores
Inbox	Incoming messages
Outbox	Messages that were not sent
Sent Items	Messages that were sent
Deleted Items	Messages that have been deleted
Drafts	Messages that you are still working on

Additional Information

When you first use Outlook Express to access your mail account, you may receive a welcome e-mail message.

HAVING TROUBLE?

If your new message is not displayed, wait a few minutes, then click [Send/Recv] to try again.

Another Method

Use View/Columns to specify the columns to display and the order. You can also drag to change the column order.

HAVING TROUBLE?

You may need to scroll the message list window horizontally to see the additional columns of information.

The right side of the window is divided into two horizontal panes. The upper right pane displays the message list. The message you sent yourself should be displayed here. The message list contains information about each message. Typically the columns display the message priority, the name and/or e-mail address of the sender, the subject of the message, and the date and time the message was received. Additionally, the message list may display the recipient's name, the size of the message, and the date the message was sent. The columns may also appear in a different order.

The lower right pane is the preview pane where the contents of the selected (highlighted) message are displayed. The status bar shows a count of the total number of messages in the folder and the number that have not been read.

2 ● **If necessary, click the the message you sent.**

Your screen should be similar to Figure 1.27

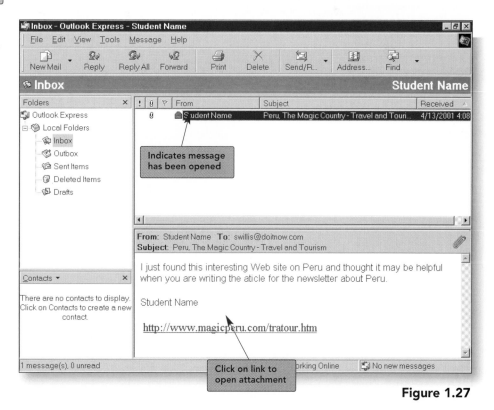

Figure 1.27

When a message header is highlighted, the mail icon automatically changes from a closed letter ✉ to an open letter 📭 after a preset number of seconds (5 is the default). If the message is long, you can use the scroll bar to read it or you can double-click on the message header to display the message in a separate message window.

Now, to read the attachment, you simply click the link. If there is no link, clicking the Attach message header allows you to open or save the attachment. The associated program is automatically opened and the attachment displayed. In this case, IE5 would open and the page would be displayed. For an attachment to be read by recipients, they must have the appropriate software program.

Warning: Open only attachments whose source you trust. Protect your computer by using a virus-checker program to check the attachment before opening it on your computer. Then, if you are unsure of an attachment, save it to your disk rather than open it so that the virus-checker program can check it first.

When you are finished reading a message, you can either reply to it, forward it, file it, delete it, or just leave it. Many times you will want to reply to the message. When the message header is highlighted or you are viewing the message, it is not necessary to type in the recipient's address and subject information. The 📩 Reply command will automatically enter the sender's address as the recipient for you. The original subject text is also automatically entered following Re: in the Subject line. Outlook Express quotes the entire original message by copying it into the body of the reply. The quoted text may be preceded with a line in the left margin or with carets (>). If the original message is long and you are replying to only part of the message, edit the quoted text to include just enough to provide a context for the message and no more. Then add your own new message to the reply, just as you did when composing a new message.

Some messages you receive will contain information that you will want to keep or take with you to another location. You can save these messages in a folder using the File/Save As command, or you can print them out.

Printing a Message

You will find that many times you will want to print a copy of a message. You will print a copy of the message you sent.

1 ● **If necessary, prepare your printer to print.**

● **If necessary, select the message.**

● **Click** 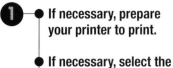.

Another Method

The menu equivalent is File/Print, and the keyboard shortcut is [Ctrl] + P.

● **If necessary, select the appropriate printer for your system.**

● **Click** OK .

Your printed output should be similar to Figure 1.28

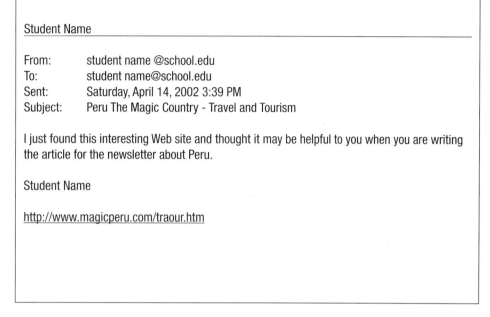

Student Name

From:	student name @school.edu
To:	student name@school.edu
Sent:	Saturday, April 14, 2002 3:39 PM
Subject:	Peru The Magic Country - Travel and Tourism

I just found this interesting Web site and thought it may be helpful to you when you are writing the article for the newsletter about Peru.

Student Name

http://www.magicperu.com/traour.htm

Figure 1.28

Deleting a Message

Often, messages once read are no longer needed. To clear your Inbox of unneeded mail, you can quickly delete messages. You will delete the message you just printed.

1 ● **With the message selected, click** ✕ Delete.

Another Method

The menu equivalent is Edit/Delete, and the keyboard shortcut is [Ctrl] + D.

Additional Information

You can also use drag and drop to move messages to different folders to help organize your messages.

Your screen should be similar to Figure 1.29

HAVING TROUBLE?

If your Inbox does not display the lined-out message marked for deletion, choose View/Current View/Show Deleted Messages.

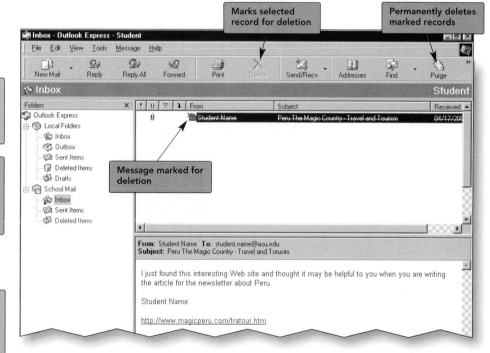

Figure 1.29

The deleted message icon appears as , and the message header is lined out, indicating it is marked for deletion. Next, you will permanently remove the message.

3 — ● Click 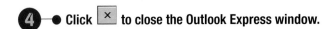 .

Your screen should be similar to Figure 1.30

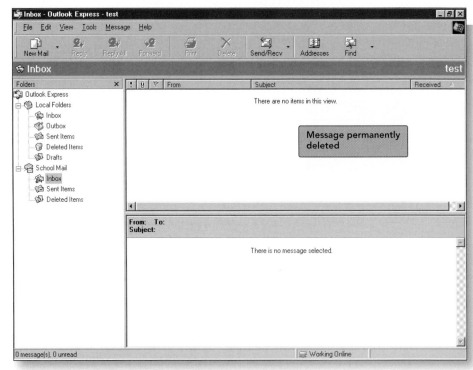

Figure 1.30

When items are deleted, the folder is compacted to a size just large enough to hold the remaining mail.

4 — ● Click ✕ to close the Outlook Express window.

Saving and Printing Web Pages

As you have learned, when you click on a link to a page, sound, or video, the Web page file is downloaded and temporarily stored on your computer system. You can also save a Web page's text, graphics, or links, or the entire page, in permanent files on a disk. Often you may want to save page content to disk rather than read it online. This saves both online time (important when you are paying for time with a service provider) and paper. You can then print the saved files. Alternatively, you can print the page you are currently viewing without saving it first.

Saving Web Pages

You will save the entire Eagle Creek Traveler's Checklist page to a floppy disk. This site provides a specially formatted page designed just to be printed. These pages generally do not include the Web page links and other miscellaneous information that you would not want included on your printout. You will save and print this version.

1 ● **Display the Eagle Creek Traveler's Checklist Web page.**

HAVING TROUBLE?
Click 🔙 repeatedly to return to this page.

● **Close the Search bar.**

● **Click the Printer Friendly Version link.**

Your screen should be similar to Figure 1.31

Printer friendly version of checklist

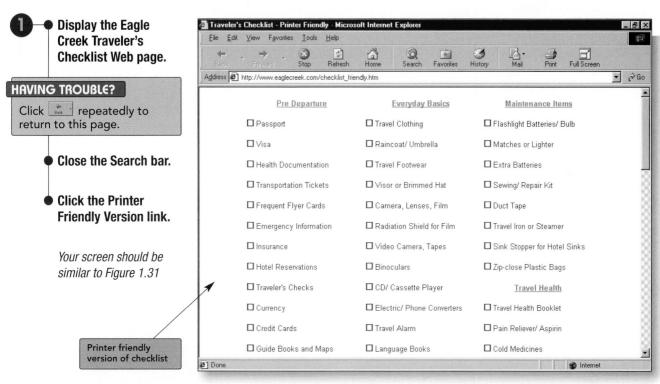

Figure 1.31

The page is opened in a second Internet Explorer window. As you can see, only the checklist is included in this version.

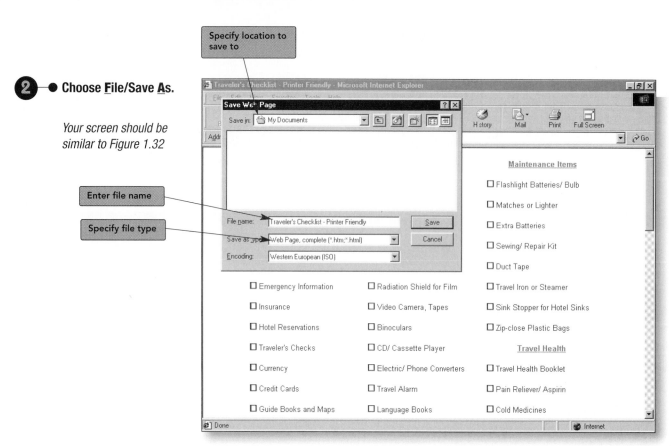

2 ● **Choose File/Save As.**

*Your screen should be
similar to Figure 1.32*

Figure 1.32

In the Save Web Page dialog box, you specify the location to save the file,
the file name, and the file type. The file type options are described in the
following table.

File Type Option	File Type	Description
Web Page, complete	.htm, .html	Saves all the files needed to display the page in its original format, including graphics and frames.
Web Archive	.mht	Saves all files needed to display the page in a single MIME-encoded file for e-mail.
Web Page, HTML only	.htm, .html	Saves the information on the page, maintaining the formatting but without the associated graphics, sounds, or other files.
Text File	.txt	Saves only the text on the page without retaining any of the original page's formatting.

3 ● **Specify the appropriate location for your data files.**

● **Change the file name to** Traveler's Checklist**.**

● **Change the file type to Text File (*.txt).**

● **Click** 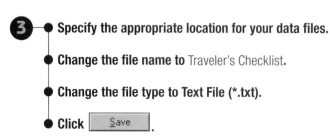**.**

The text from the Web page is saved to your disk.

Viewing Saved Pages

You can view and edit the text of Web pages you saved while you were on-line using a text editor or word processor offline. You will display the checklist in Notepad.

1 • Click ⊞/Start/
Programs/Accessories
/NotePad.

• Click File/Open.

• From the Files of Type
drop-down list, select
Text Documents (*.txt).

• Browse to find the
location where you
saved the Web page.

• Select the file
Traveler's Checklist, and
click ⬛ Open ⬛.

• If necessary, click ⬛
to maximize the
window.

*Your screen should be
similar to Figure 1.33*

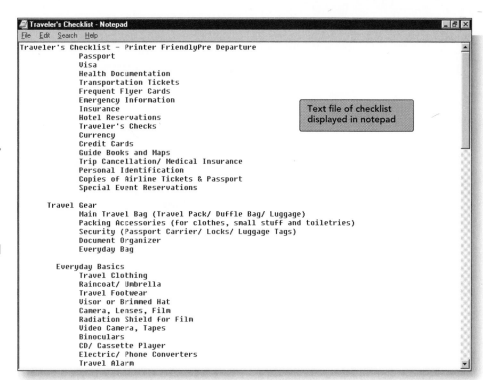

Text file of checklist
displayed in notepad

Figure 1.33

You want to make a few adjustments to the document.

2 • Click at the end of the
word "Checklist" on
the first line and press
Delete until the text
"Printer Friendly" is
removed.

• Press ←Enter 3 times.

• Press Tab ⇄.

• Click on the second
line and type your
name.

*Your screen should be
similar to Figure 1.34*

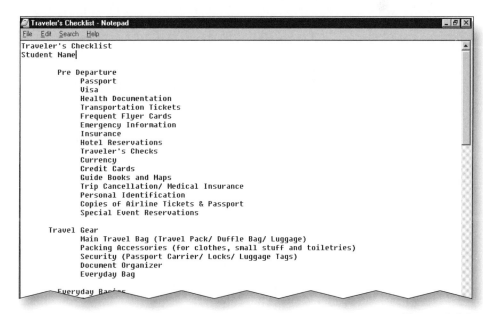

Figure 1.34

3 • Close Notepad, saving the file again.

When copying and saving information from a Web page, be aware of the copyright protection associated with the page. This information is usually displayed at the bottom of the page. You may need the author's permission if you plan to use the information commercially; otherwise, cite appropriately by giving credit as in a footnote of a research paper.

Printing a Web Page

It is also convenient to simply print the contents of the current page. Before printing, you want to modify the information displayed in the header of the printout.

1 ● **Choose File/Page Setup.**

Your screen should be similar to Figure 1.35

> Character combinations specify information to display

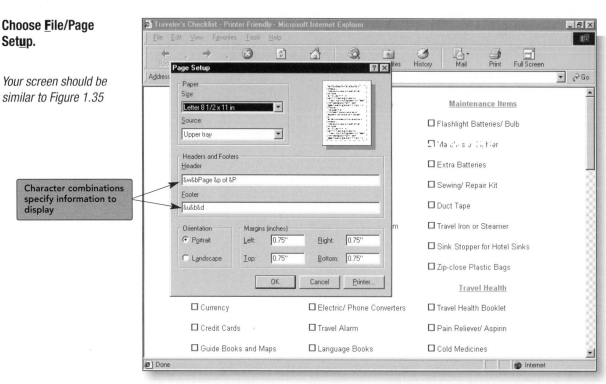

Figure 1.35

The header and footer text boxes display an "&" followed by a character. The different character combinations instruct the program to display certain information when printed. You will display Help for a list of the meaning of these characters and then edit the footer information.

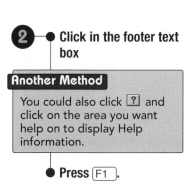

2 ● **Click in the footer text box**

Another Method

You could also click [?] and click on the area you want help on to display Help information.

● **Press** [F1].

Your screen should be similar to Figure 1.36

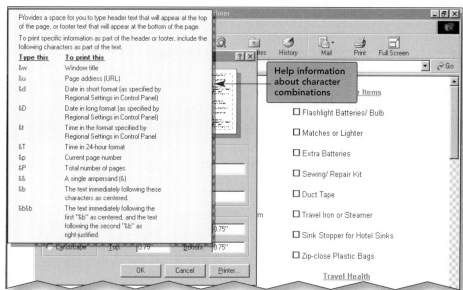

Figure 1.36

The Help box describes the different character combinations and resulting printed output. You want to display your name instead of the Web site address in the footer.

3 ● **Press** [Esc] **to clear the Help information.**

● **Delete the characters "&u" from the footer text box.**

● **Type your name in the footer text box.**

● **Click** OK .

● **Choose File/Print.**

● **Select the appropriate printer for your system from the Printer Name drop-down list box.**

● **Click** OK .

Additional Information

You can print a portion of a Web page by clicking and dragging to select the text and images you want, then clicking the Selection option from the Print dialog box.

Another Method

Clicking [🖨] on the Standard Buttons toolbar immediately prints the page using the default printer settings.

Figure 1.37

Your printout of the first page is shown in Figure 1.37

You are now ready to exit the Internet Explorer program.

4 ● Click **X** in both of the Internet Explorer windows.

Another Method
The menu equivalent is
File/Close.

● If necessary, disconnect from the Internet.

lab review

Introduction to the Internet and Web

key terms

attachment IN.25
browser IN.5
content frame IN.14
download IN.9
Domain Name System (DNS)
 IN.26
e-mail IN.24
followed link IN.13
frame IN.14
home page IN.7
hyperlink IN.10

hypertext link IN.10
HyperText Markup Language
 (HTML) IN.6
Internet IN.4
keyword IN.21
keyword search IN.21
link IN.10
main window IN.8
search service IN.16
search provider IN.16
server IN.6

startup home page IN.7
target frame IN.14
topic search IN.18
unfollowed link IN.13
Uniform Resource Locator
 (URL) IN.8
Web IN.5
Web page IN.6
Web site IN.6
World Wide Web (WWW) IN.5

command summary

Command	Shortcut	Button	Action
Internet Explorer			
File/**O**pen	Ctrl + O		Opens a Web page
File/Save **A**s			Saves current page to disk
File/Page Set**u**p			Specifies page settings for printing
File/**P**rint		Print	Prints current page or frame
File/Se**n**d/**L**ink by E-mail			Opens New Message window with link to current Web site and Web page file attached
File/**C**lose		X	Exits Internet Explorer
View/**E**xplorer Bar/**S**earch		Search	Displays Search bar
View/**G**o to/**B**ack	Alt + ←	Back	Displays last viewed page
View/**G**o to/**F**orward	Alt + →	Forward	Displays next viewed page after using Back
View/Sto**p**	Esc	Stop	Cancels a page transfer
Outlook Express			
File/**S**end Message			Sends new message
Edit/**D**elete	Ctrl + D	Delete	Marks message for deletion
Edit/**U**ndelete			Restores item marked for deletion
Edit/**P**urge Deleted Messages		Edit	Permanently deletes marked messages
Edit/Mark as U**n**read			Marks message as unread
View/**C**urrent **V**iew/Show Deleted Messages			Displays messages marked for deletion
View/**C**olumns			Displays selected column headers

lab exercises

screen identification

In the following Internet Explorer screen, several items are identified by letters. Enter the correct term for each item in the spaces that follow.

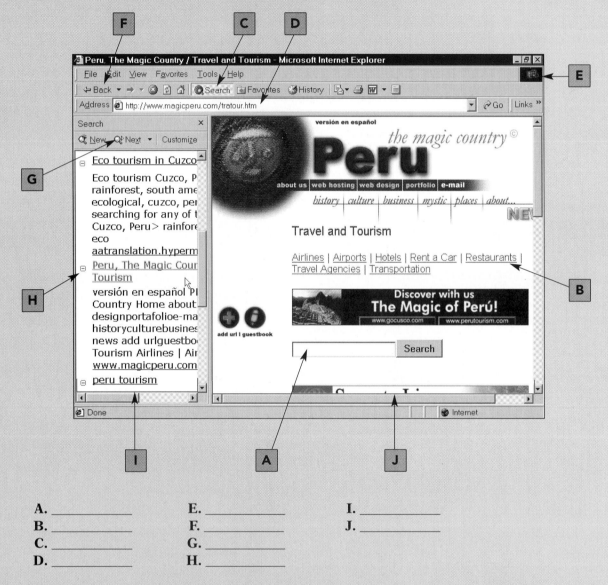

A. _____ E. _____ I. _____
B. _____ F. _____ J. _____
C. _____ G. _____
D. _____ H. _____

Sports Company Web site

★ 1. The Sports Company is a chain of discount sporting goods stores located in large metropolitan areas throughout the United States. The company has recently decided to take advantage of the Internet by creating a site on the Web to market their products and advertise the company. In addition to the traditional commercial aspects of the site, such as a catalog of products, online order forms, and location information, they have included the first issue of "The Sports Company Update," the monthly newsletter, to provide customers with health- and fitness-related information. You will explore the Sports Company Web site, print the home page, and save a page and picture to a file.

   a. Start Internet Explorer and go to The Sports Company Web site at http://www.mhhe.com/sportsco.

   b. Click the Where Are We link and locate the address of the store in Tempe, AZ. Print this page.

   c. Display the newsletter and save the page to your disk in text only file format using the file name Sports Company.

   d. Return to the site's home page. Send yourself an e-mail that includes a link to this page.

   e. Using any word processor program, open the text file Sports Company. Add your name and the current date to the top of the file, resave the file, and print it.

   f. Read the e-mail message you sent yourself. Print the message.

   g. Exit all programs, saving any changes you made to files.

```
Student Name
Current Date

Sports Company Home Page Special of the Month
        Who are we?
        Where are we?
        Newsletter
        Catalogs
        Golf
        Camping
        Fitness

        Feedback
        This site is under
        construction...
        check back often to see our new features. Coming soon...
         Search for a specific
         catalog item using our
         Search feature.
        New Products page The Sports Company


        Welcome to The Sports Company! Thanks for stopping by our home page. We
        are located in major metropolitan areas throughout the U.S. and specialize
        in providing high quality athletic equipment and apparel at reasonable
        prices. So, check out our store nearest you. Or check out our catalogs for
        a quick and convenient online shopping experience.
        Shopping is easy!!!
        Browse our catalogs and choose from over 2,500 items! Click Catalogs to
        see a complete list of catalogs organized by sporting activity. Or select
        from on this page one of our three most popular catalogs. To order:
           Complete an on-line order form or call our toll-free number.
           Our ordering system offers secure on-line ordering.
           We also include free surface shipping to anywhere in the U.S.
        Who are we?
        The Sports Company was founded in August, 1975. The original location in
        Red Bank, New Jersey is still operating. This is a family run business
        that understands the need for personalized attention as well as
        competitive prices.
        Where are we?
        Click the area of the country then select from the list of locations by
        state.
           West|Central|East
        Top | Catalogs | Specials | Feedback | Who are we? | Where are we?
        Golf | Camping | Fitness
        Copyright © 1997 LIO All rights reserved.
        This is an educational site used in conjuction with the O'Leary text
        "Using Netscape Communicator 4" and "Using Internet Explorer 4" from
        Irwin/McGraw-Hill.
```

Exploring a Web site

★ ★ **2.** One of the most popular comic strips is Dilbert. Like many other comic strips, Dilbert has its own Web site. You will explore this site, print a comic strip, and save a page to a file.

   a. Start Internet Explorer and go to the Dilbert site at http://www.unitedmedia.com/comics/dilbert/.

   b. Explore the site and find the answers to the following questions: What are the names of two characters? Who is the creator of Dilbert? What's behind the scenes at DTV?

   c. Locate and read the biography of Scott Adams. Save it in text file format using the file name Adams.

   d. Print the most recent Sunday strip.

   e. Exit Internet Explorer.

   f. Using any word processor program, open the Adams text file you saved. Remove any extra information. Select the undesired text and press the (Delete), leaving only the biography portion of the text. Add your name and the current date to the top of the file, resave the file, and print it.

> Dilbert Books
> I have written four original best selling books: The Dilbert
> Principle, Dogbert's Top Secret Management Handbook, The Dilbert
> Future, and The Joy of Work. The first two were #1 New York Times
> Best Sellers.
>
> Including strip reprint books there are 22 Dilbert books with over
> 10 million copies in print.
>
> Newspapers
> Dilbert appears in 2,000 newspapers in 56 countries, making it one
> of the most successful syndicated comic strips in history.

> Student Name
> Current Date
>
> BIOGRAPHY OF SCOTT ADAMS
>
> Early Years
> I was born 6/8/57 and raised in Windham, New York, in the Catskill
> mountains. I graduated high-school as valedictorian because the
> other 39 people in my class couldn't spell "valedictorian."
>
> I moved to Northern California in 1979 after college and have lived
> in the San Francisco Bay Area since.
>
> Education
>   Hartwick College, Oneonta New York, BA in economics, 1979.
>   University of California at Berkeley, MBA, 1986.
>   Certified Hypnotist, Clement School of Hypnosis, San Francisco,
>   1981.
> Day Jobs
> I worked at Crocker National Bank, San Francisco, 1979 to 1986, in a
> number of humiliating and low paying jobs: teller (robbed twice at
> gunpoint), computer programmer, financial analyst, product manager,
> and commercial lender.
>
> I moved from the bank to Pacific Bell, San Ramon, California, and
> worked there from 1986 through June 1995. I worked in a number of
> jobs that defy description but all involve technology and finances.
> The most recent job was in a laboratory, finding ways to use digital
> phone lines and also running the company's BBS. My business card
> said "engineer" but I'm not an engineer by training.
>
> From 1989 until 1995 I worked my day job while doing the Dilbert
> comic strip mornings, evenings and weekends.
>
> How I Became a Syndicated Cartoonist
> Dilbert is a composite of my co-workers over the years. He emerged
> as the main character of my doodles. I started using him for
> business presentations and got great responses. A co-worker
> suggested I name the character Dilbert. Dogbert was created so
> Dilbert would have someone to talk to.
>
> On the advice of a kind cartoonist I bought a book called "1988
> Artist Markets" and followed the instructions on how to get
> syndicated. I drew fifty sample strips and mailed copies to the
> major cartoon syndicates. United Media called a few weeks later and
> offered a contract. I accepted.
>
> Dilbert was launched in 1989 after several months of further
> developing the strip. That was my first cartooning for profit.

Additional Web Exploration

★ ★ ★ **1.** Everywhere you look you see references to Web pages. Write down several URLs from articles in your local newspaper or that you see on TV. Use Internet Explorer to visit and explore these sites. Save two pages of interest to a floppy disk in plain text format. Open the text file using any word processor and add your name and the current date to the top of the page. Print the text file.

Introduction to Microsoft Office XP

What is Office XP?

Microsoft Office XP is a suite of applications that can be used individually and that are designed to work together seamlessly. The applications include tools used to create, discuss, communicate, and manage projects. If you share a lot of documents with other people, these features facilitate access to common documents. This version has expanded and refined the communication and collaboration features and integration with the World Wide Web. In addition, several new interface features are designed to make it easier to perform tasks and help users take advantage of all the features in the applications.

The Office XP suite is packaged in different combinations of components. The major components and a brief description are provided in the following table.

Component	Description
Word 2002	Word processor
Excel 2002	Spreadsheet
Access 2002	Database manager
PowerPoint 2002	Presentation graphics
Outlook 2002	Desktop information manager
FrontPage 2002	Web page authoring
Publisher	Desktop publishing
SharePoint	Team Web sites

The four main components of Office XP—Word, Excel, Access, and PowerPoint—are described in more detail in the following sections.

Word 2002

Word 2002 is a word processing software application whose purpose is to help you create text-based documents. Word processors are one of the most flexible and widely used application software programs. A word processor can be used to manipulate text data to produce a letter, a report, a memo, an e-mail, message or any other type of correspondence. Two documents you will produce in the first two Word labs, a letter and flyer, are shown here.

February 18, 2001

Dear Adventure Traveler,

Imagine hiking and paddling your way through the rain forests of Costa Rica, under the stars in Africa, or following in the footsteps of the ancient Inca as you backpack the Inca trail to Machu Picchu. Turn these dreams of adventure into memories you will forever by joining Adventure Travel Tours on one of our four new adventure tours.

To tell you more about these exciting new adventures, we are offering presentations in your area. These presentations will focus on the features and cultural region. We will also show you pictures of the places you will visit and activities participate in, as well as a detailed agenda and package costs. Plan on attending of following presentations:

Date	Time	Location	Room
January 5	7:00 PM	Town Center Hotel	Room 284B
February 3	7:30 PM	Airport Manor	Conference Room A
March 8	7:00 PM	Country Inn	Mountainside Room

In appreciation of your past patronage, we are pleased to offer you a 10% discount price of any of the new tour packages. You must book the trip at least 60 days pr departure date. Please turn in this letter to qualify for the discount.

Our vacation tours are professionally developed solely for your enjoyment. W almost everything in the price of your tour while giving you the best possible value dollar. All tours include:

- **Professional tour manager and local guides**
- **All accommodations and meals**
- **All entrance fees, excursions, transfers and tips**

We hope you will join us this year on another special Adventure Travel Tour Your memories of fascinating places and challenging physical adventures should li long, long time. For reservations, please see your travel agent, or contact Adventure Tra at 1-800-777-0004. You can also visit our new Web site at www.AdventureTravelTours

Best regards,

Student Name

A letter containing a tabbed table, indented paragraphs, and text enhancements is quickly created using basic Word features.

Announcing
New Adventure Travel Tours

This year we are introducing four new tours, offering you a unique opportunity to combine many different outdoor activities while exploring the world.

Hike the Inca trail to Machu Picchu
Camp on safari in Tanzania
Climb Mt. Kilimanjaro
Explore the Costa Rican rain forests

Attend an Adventure Travel presentation to learn about some of the earth's greatest unspoiled habitats and find out how you can experience the adventure of a lifetime.

Presentation dates and times are January 5 at 7 PM, February 3 at 7:30 PM, and March 8 at 7 PM. All presentations are held at convenient hotel locations located in downtown Los Angeles, Santa Clara and at the airport.

Call us at 1-800-777-0004 for presentation locations, a full color brochure, and itinerary information, costs, and tour dates.

A flyer incorporating many visual enhancements such as colored text, varied text styles, and graphic elements is both eye-catching and informative.

The beauty of a word processor is that you can make changes or corrections as you are typing. Want to change a report from single spacing to double spacing? Alter the width of the margins? Delete some paragraphs and add others from yet another document? A word processor allows you to do all these things with ease.

Word 2002 includes many group collaboration features to help streamline how documents are developed and changed by group members. You can also create and send e-mail messages directly from within Word using all its features to create and edit the message. You can also send an entire document as your e-mail message, allowing the recipient to edit the document directly without having to open or save an attachment.

Word 2002 is also closely integrated with the World Wide Web, detecting when you type a Web address and automatically converting it to a hyperlink. You can also create your own hyperlinks to locations within documents, or to other documents, including those at external locations such as a Web site or file server. Its many Web-editing features, including a Web Page Wizard that guides you step by step, help you quickly create a Web page. You will see how easy it is when you create the Web page shown below in the Working Together tutorial.

A Web page created in Word and displayed in the Internet Explorer browser.

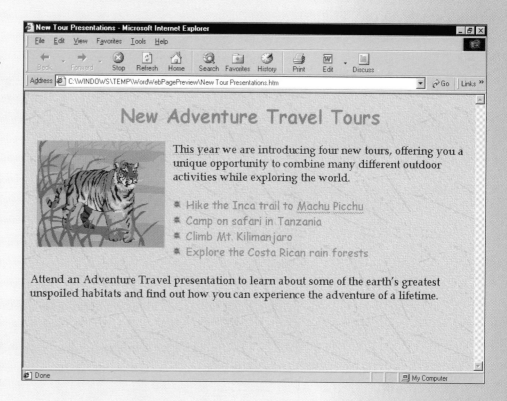

Excel 2002

Excel 2002 is an electronic worksheet that is used to organize, manipulate, and graph numeric data. Once used almost exclusively by accountants, worksheets are now widely used by nearly every profession. Marketing professionals record and evaluate sales trends. Teachers record grades and calculate final grades. Personal trainers record the progress of their clients. Excel includes many features that not only help you create a well-designed worksheet, but one that produces accurate results. Formatting features include visual enhancements such as varied text styles, colors, and graphics. Other features help you enter complex formulas and identify and correct formula errors. You can also produce a visual display of data in the form of graphs or charts. As the values in the worksheet change, charts referencing those values automatically adjust to reflect the changes.

Excel also includes many advanced features and tools that help you perform what-if analysis and create different scenarios. And like all Office XP applications, it is easy to incorporate data created in one application into another. Two worksheets you will produce in Labs 2 and 3 of Excel are shown here.

A worksheet showing the quarterly sales forecast containing a graphic, text enhancements, and a chart of the data is quickly created using basic Excel features.

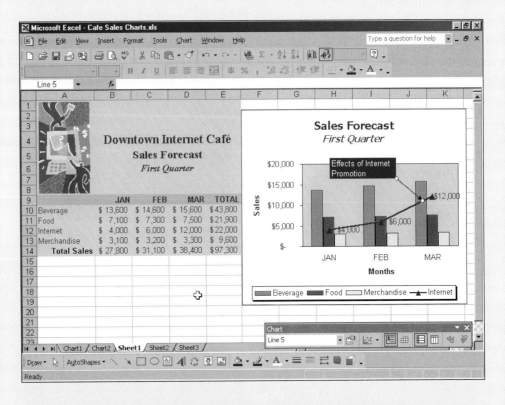

A large worksheet incorporating more complex formulas, visual enhancements such as colored text, varied text styles, and graphic elements is both informative and attractive.

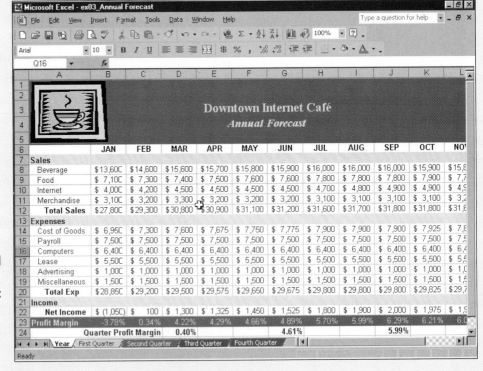

You will see how easy it is to analyze data and make projections using what-if analysis and what-if graphing in Lab 3 and to incorporate Excel data in a Word document as shown in the figures below.

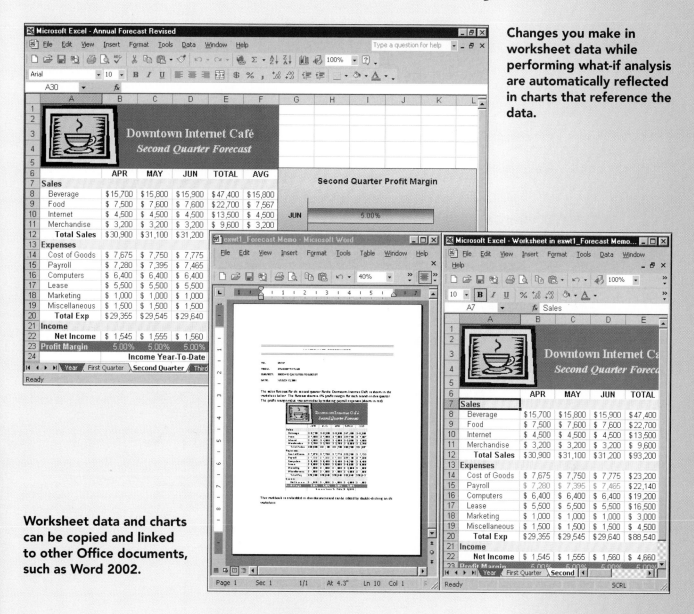

Changes you make in worksheet data while performing what-if analysis are automatically reflected in charts that reference the data.

Worksheet data and charts can be copied and linked to other Office documents, such as Word 2002.

Access 2002

Access 2002 is a relational database management application that is used to create and analyze a database. A database is a collection of related data. In a relational database, the most widely used database structure, data is organized in linked tables. Tables consist of columns (called fields) and rows (called records). The tables are related or linked to one another by a common field. Relational databases allow you to create smaller and more manageable database tables, since you can combine and extract data between tables.

The program provides tools to enter, edit, and retrieve data from the database as well as to analyze the database and produce reports of the output. One of the main advantages of a computerized database is the ability to quickly add, delete, and locate specific records. Records can also be easily rearranged or sorted according to different fields of data, resulting in multiple table arrangements that provide more meaningful information for different purposes. Creation of forms makes it easier to enter and edit data as well. In the Access labs you will create and organize the database table shown below.

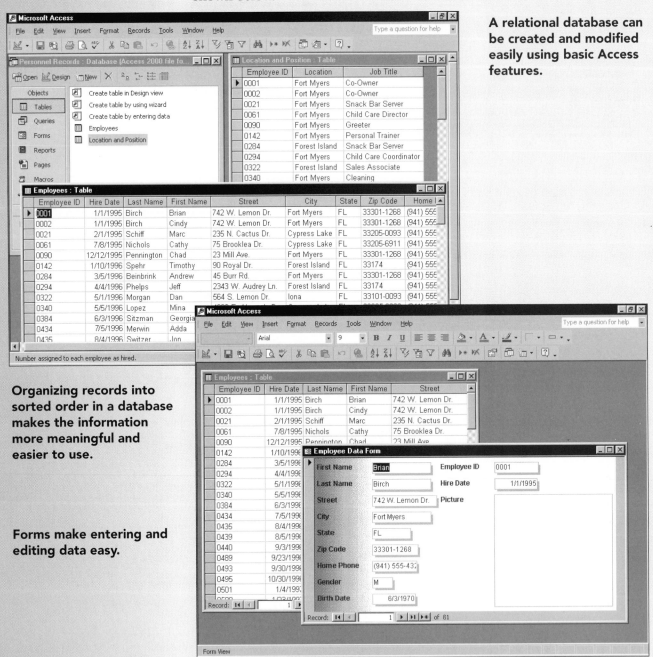

A relational database can be created and modified easily using basic Access features.

Organizing records into sorted order in a database makes the information more meaningful and easier to use.

Forms make entering and editing data easy.

Another feature is the ability to analyze the data in a table and perform calculations on different fields of data. Additionally, you can ask questions or query the table to find only certain records that meet specific conditions to be used in the analysis. Information that was once costly and time-consuming to get is now quickly and readily available. This information can then be quickly printed out in the form of reports ranging from simple listings to complex, professional-looking reports in different layout styles, or with titles, headings, subtotals, or totals.

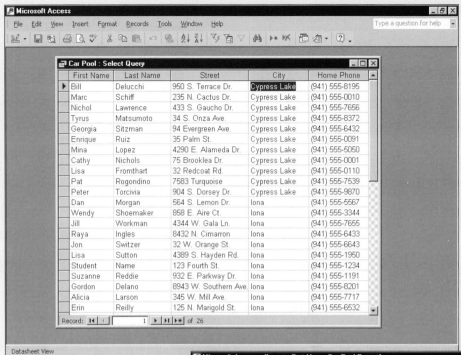

A database can be queried to locate and display only specified information.

A professional-looking report can be quickly generated from information contained in a database.

PowerPoint 2002

PowerPoint 2002 is a graphics presentation program designed to help you produce a high-quality presentation that is both interesting to the audience and effective in its ability to convey your message. A presentation can be as simple as overhead transparencies or as sophisticated as an on-screen electronic display. In the first two PowerPoint labs you will create and organize the presentation shown on the next page.

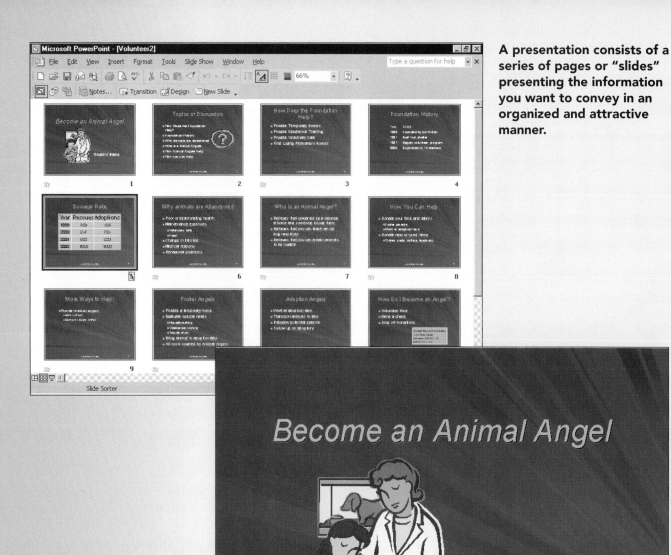

A presentation consists of a series of pages or "slides" presenting the information you want to convey in an organized and attractive manner.

When running an onscreen presentation, each slide of the presentation is displayed full-screen on your computer monitor or projected onto a screen.

Common Office XP Features

Additional Information
Please read the Before You Begin and Instructional Conventions sections in the Overview to Word 2002 (WDO.4) before starting this section.

Now that you know a little about each of the applications in Microsoft Office XP, we will take a look at some of the features that are common to all Office applications. This is a hands-on section that will introduce you to the features and allow you to get a feel for how Office XP works. Although Word 2002 will be used to demonstrate how the features work, only common features will be addressed. These features include using menus, the Office Assistant and Office Help, task panes, toolbars, and starting and exiting an application. The features that are specific to each application will be introduced individually in each lab.

Starting an Office Application

There are several ways to start an Office application. One is to use the New Office Document command on the Start menu and select the type of document you want to create. Another is to use the Documents command on the Start menu and select the document name from the list of recently used documents. This starts the associated application and opens the selected document at the same time. The two most common ways to start an Office XP application are by choosing the application name from the Start menu or by clicking a desktop shortcut for the program if it is available.

1 ● Click **🏁Start** to display the Start menu.

● Select Programs.

● Choose **W Microsoft Word**.

or

1 ● Double-click the **W** shortcut on the desktop. Microsoft Word

2 ● If necessary, click **□** in the title bar to maximize the window.

Your screen should be similar to Figure 1

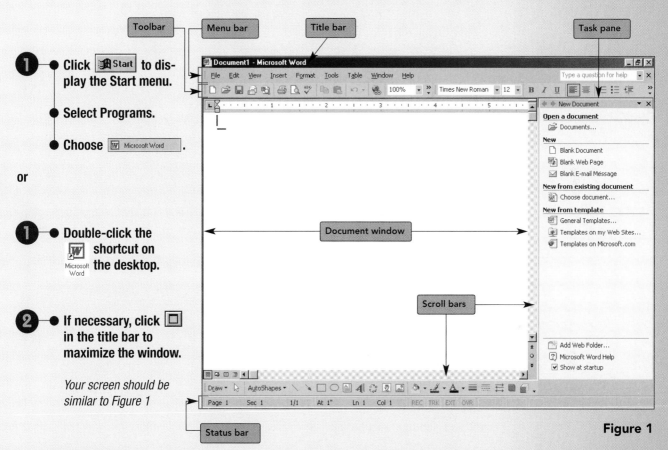

Figure 1

Additional Information
Application windows can be sized, moved, and otherwise manipulated like any other windows on the desktop. Refer to your text or, if available, to the *Introduction to Windows 2000* labs for information about working with windows.

The Word program is started and displayed in a window on the desktop. The left end of the application window title bar displays the file name followed by the program name, Microsoft Word. The right end of the title bar displays the **□** Minimize, **🗗** Restore, and **✕** Close buttons. They perform the same functions and operate in the same way as in Windows 98 and 2000.

The **menu bar** below the title bar displays the application's program menu. The right end displays the document window's **✕** Close button. As you use the Office applications, you will see that the menu bar contains many of the same menus, such as File, Edit, and Help. You will also see several menus that are specific to each application.

The **toolbars** located below the menu bar contain buttons that are mouse shortcuts for many of the menu items. Commonly, the Office applications will display two toolbars when the application is first opened: Standard and Formatting. They may appear together on one row (as in Figure 1), or on separate rows.

The large center area of the program window is the **document window** where open application files are displayed. Currently, there is a blank Word document open. The **task pane** is displayed on the right side of the document window. Task panes provide quick access to features as you are using the application. As you perform certain actions, different task panes automatically open. In this case, since you just started an application, the New Document task pane is automatically displayed, providing different ways to create a new document or open an existing document.

The **status bar** at the bottom of the window displays location information and the status of different settings as they are used. Different information is displayed in the status bar for different applications.

On the right and bottom of the document window, are vertical and horizontal scroll bars. A **scroll bar** is used with a mouse to bring additional lines of information into view in a window. The vertical scroll bar is used to move up or down, and the horizontal scroll bar moves side to side in the window.

As you can see, many of the features in the Word window are the same as in other Windows applications. The common user interface makes learning and using new applications much easier.

Using Menus

A **menu** is one of many methods you can use to accomplish a task in a program. When opened, a menu displays a list of commands.

1 ● **Click File to open the File menu.**

Your screen should be similar to Figure 2

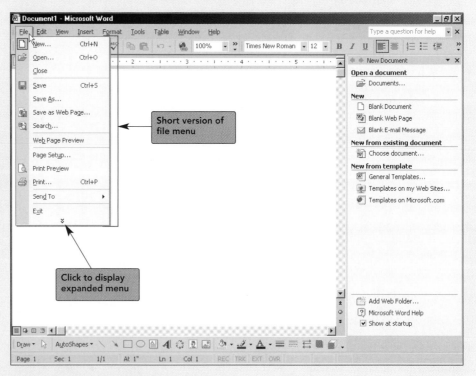

Figure 2

When an Office program menu is first opened, it may display a short version of commands. The short menu is a personalized version of the menu that displays basic and frequently used commands and hides those used less often. An expanded version will display automatically after the menu is open for a few seconds (see Figure 3).

Your screen should be
similar to Figure 3

Expanded File menu

Previously hidden
commands are displayed

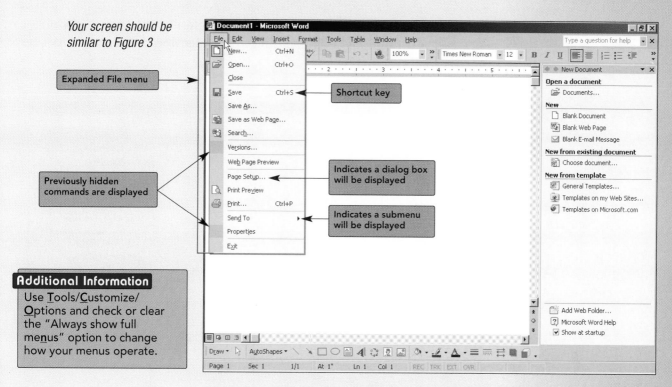

Additional Information
Use **T**ools/**C**ustomize/
Options and check or clear
the "Always show full
me**n**us" option to change
how your menus operate.

Figure 3

When the menu is expanded the hidden commands are displayed. Once
one menu is expanded, others are expanded automatically until you choose
a command or perform another action.

2 ● **Point to each menu in the menu bar to see the full menu for each.**

● **Point to the File menu again.**

Many commands have images next to them so you can quickly associate
the command with the image. The same image appears on the toolbar button for that feature. Menus may include the following features (not all
menus include all features):

Feature	Meaning
Ellipsis (...)	Indicates a dialog box will be displayed
▶	Indicates a submenu will be displayed
Dimmed	Indicates the command is not available for selection until certain other conditions are met
Shortcut key	A key or key combination that can be used to execute a command without using the menu
Checkmark	Indicates a toggle type of command. Selecting it turns the feature on or off. A checkmark indicates the feature is on.

Once a menu is open, you can select a command from the menu by pointing to it. A colored highlight bar, called the **selection cursor**, appears over the selected command.

3 ● **Point to the Send To command to select it and display the submenu.**

Your screen should be similar to Figure 4

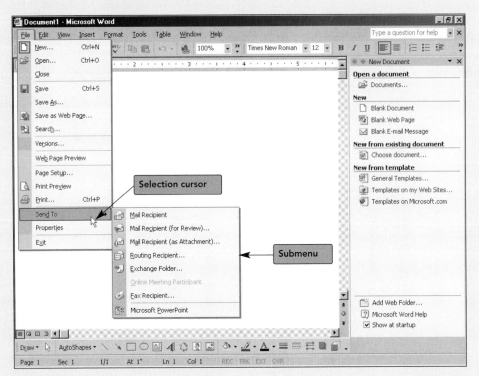

Figure 4

Then to choose a command, you click on it. When the command is chosen, the associated action is performed. You will use a command in the Help menu to access the Microsoft Office Assistant and Help features.

Note: If your screen displays the Office Assistant character as shown in Figure 5, skip step 4.

4 • **Point to Help.**

• **Click Show the Office Assistant to choose the command.**

Your screen should be similar to Figure 5

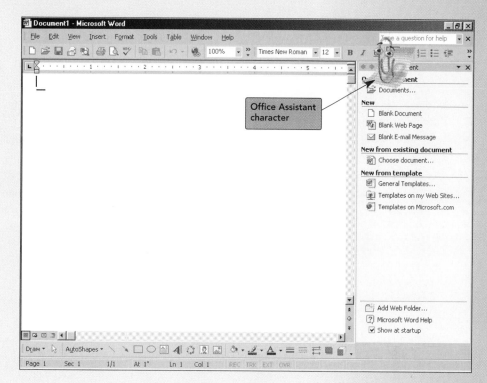

Office Assistant character

Figure 5

HAVING TROUBLE?
If the Assistant does not appear, this feature has been disabled. If this is the case, choose Help/Microsoft Word Help or press F1 and skip to the section "Using Help."

The command to display the Office Assistant has been executed, and the Office Assistant character is displayed. The default Assistant character is Clippit shown in Figure 5. Because there are eight different characters from which you can select, your screen may display a different Assistant character.

Using the Office Assistant

When the Office Assistant is on, it automatically suggests help topics as you work. It anticipates what you are going to do and then makes suggestions on how to perform a task. In addition, you can activate the Assistant at any time to get help on features in the Office application you are using. Clicking on the Assistant character activates it and displays a balloon in which you can type the topic you want help on. You will ask the Office Assistant to provide information on the different ways you can get help while using the program.

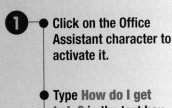

1 ● **Click on the Office Assistant character to activate it.**

● **Type How do I get help? in the text box.**

● **Click** 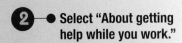 .

Another Method

You could also press ⏎Enter to begin the search.

Your screen should be similar to Figure 6

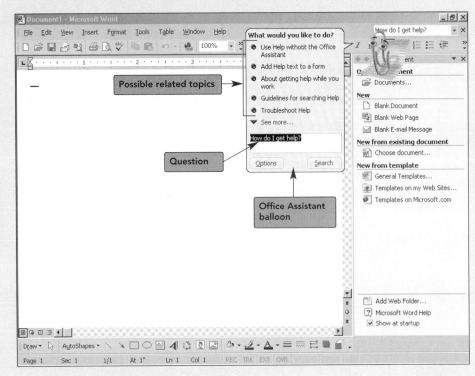

Possible related topics

Question

Office Assistant balloon

Figure 6

The balloon displays a list of related topics from which you can select.

2 ● **Select "About getting help while you work."**

Additional Information

Clicking See more... displays additional topics.

Your screen should be similar to Figure 7

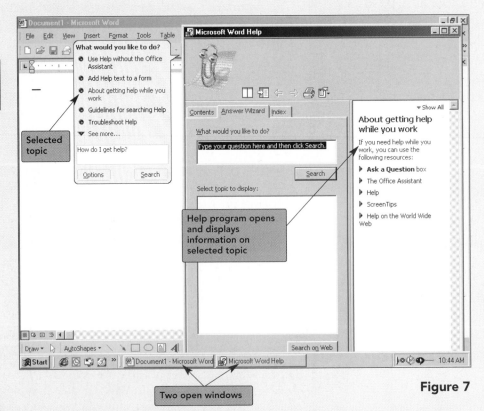

Selected topic

Help program opens and displays information on selected topic

Two open windows

Figure 7

Another Method

You can also choose **H**elp/Microsoft Word **H**elp, or click 🔘 or press F1 to start Help.

The Help program opens and displays the selected topic. Because Word Help is a separate program within Office, it appears in its own window. The Help window overlaps the Word window so that it is easy to read the information in Help while referring to the application office window. The taskbar displays a button for both open windows.

Now that Help is open, you no longer need to see the Assistant. To access commands to control the Office Assistant, you will display the object's shortcut menu by right-clicking on the Assistant character. **Shortcut menus** display the most common menu options related to the selected item only.

3 ● **Right-click the Assistant to display the shortcut menu.**

● **Choose Options.**

● **Click Use the Office Assistant to clear the option.**

● **Click** OK **.**

● **Click** □ **to maximize the Help window.**

● **If necessary, click** ◁▤ **to display the Tabs frame.**

Your screen should be similar to Figure 8

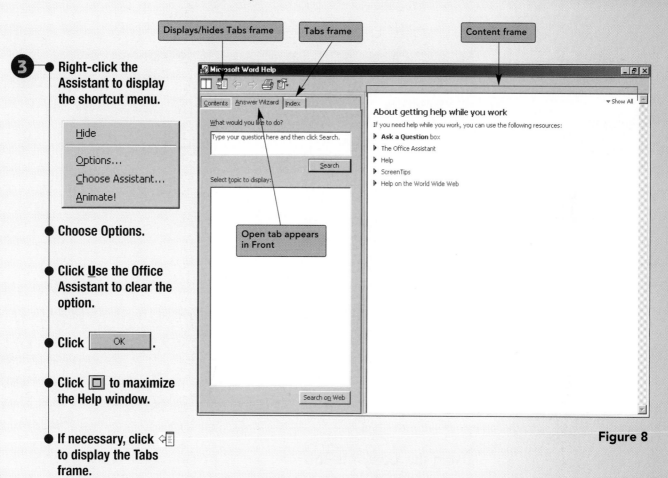

Figure 8

Using Help

In the Help window, the toolbar buttons help you use different Help features and navigate in Help.

The Help window is divided into two vertical frames. **Frames** divide a window into separate, scrollable areas that can display different information. The left frame in the Help window is the Tabs frame. It contains three folder-like tabs, Contents, Answer Wizard, and Search, that provide three different means of getting Help information. The open tab appears in front of the other tabs and displays the available options for the feature. The right frame is the content frame where the content for the selected topic is displayed.

1 ● **Click the Contents tab to open it.**

Your screen should be similar to Figure 9

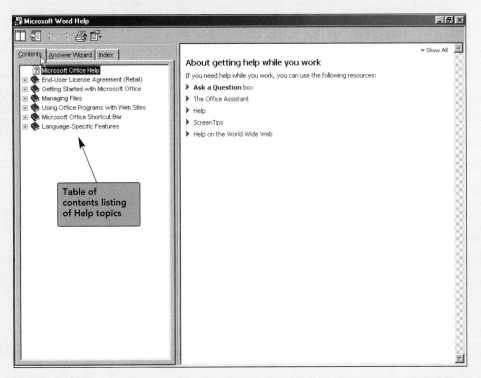

Table of contents listing of Help topics

Figure 9

Using the Contents Tab

The Contents tab displays a table of contents listing of topics in Help. Clicking on an item preceded with a ⊞ opens a "chapter," which expands to display additional chapters or specific Help topics.

1
- Click ⊞ next to **Getting Started with Microsoft Office.**

- Click ⊞ next to **Getting Help.**

- Click **About getting help while you work.**

Your screen should be similar to Figure 10

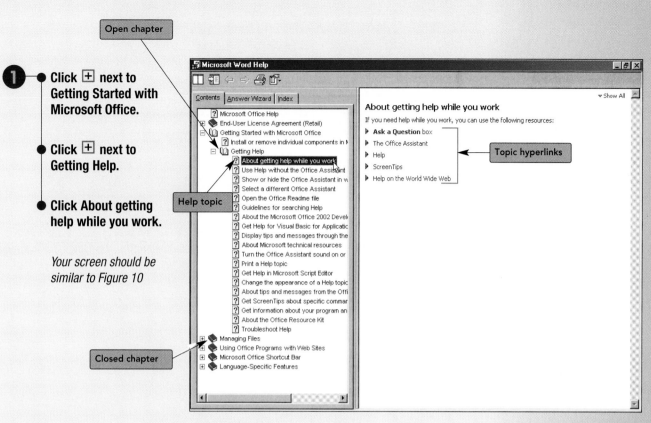

Figure 10

You have opened two chapters and selected a Help topic. Open chapters are preceded with a 📖 icon and topics with a ❓ icon.

Using a Hyperlink

The Help topic tells you about five resources you can use to get help. Each resource is a **hyperlink** or connection to additional information in the current document, in online Help, or on the Microsoft Office Web site. It commonly appears as colored or underlined text. Clicking the hyperlink accesses and displays the information associated with the hyperlink. A hyperlink preceded with a ▶ indicates clicking the link will display additional information about the topic.

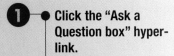

1 ● **Click the "Ask a Question box" hyperlink.**

● **Click the "The Office Assistant" hyperlink.**

Your screen should be similar to Figure 11

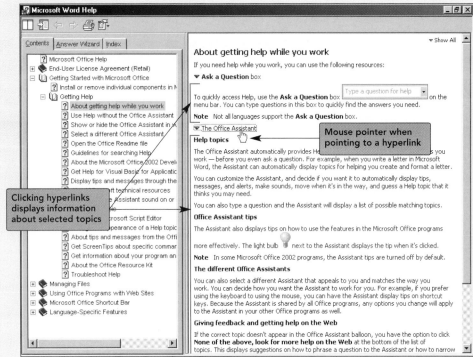

Figure 11

Additional Information

Clicking the scroll arrows scrolls the text in the frame line by line, and dragging the scroll box up or down the scroll bar moves to a general location within the frame area.

The content frame displays additional information about the two selected topics. Now, because there is more information in the content frame than can be displayed at one time, you will need to use the vertical scroll bar to scroll the additional information into the frame as you read the Help information. Also, as you are reading help, you may see text that appears as a hyperlink. Clicking on the text will display a definition of a term.

2 ● **Using the scroll bar, scroll the content frame to read the information on this topic.**

● **Click the "shortcut keys" hyperlink.**

Your screen should be similar to Figure 12

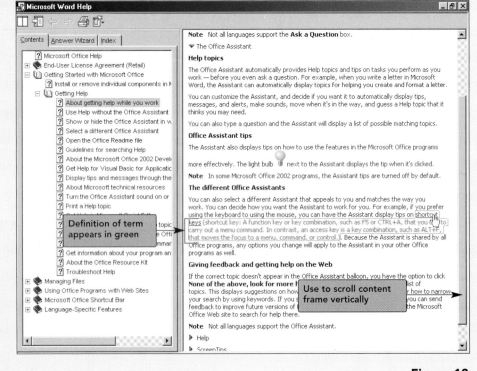

Figure 12

Scrolling the frame displays the information at the bottom of the frame while the information at the top of the frame is no longer visible. The end of the Help information is displayed in the frame. A definition of the term "shortcut keys" is displayed in green text.

3 ● **Click on the definition to clear it.**

● **Click on the Use Help without the Office Assistant topic in the Contents tab.**

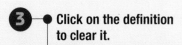

Additional Information
Pointing to a topic in the content frame that is not fully visible displays the full topic in a ScreenTip box.

Your screen should be similar to Figure 13

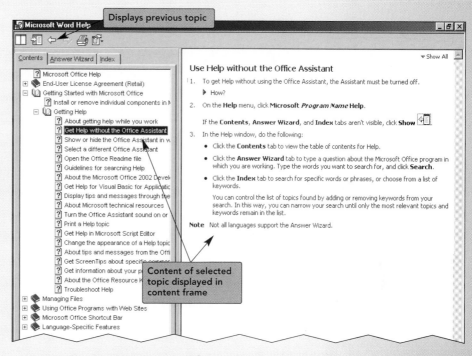

Figure 13

The content frame now displays the Help information about the selected topic. To quickly return to the previous topic,

4 ● **Click** ⬅ **Back.**

Your screen should be similar to Figure 14

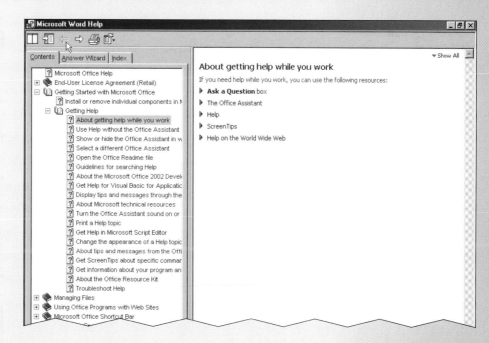

Figure 14

The topic is redisplayed as it originally appeared, without the topic selections expanded.

Using the Index Tab

To search for Help information by entering a word or phrase for a topic, you can use the Index tab.

1 ● **Open the Index tab.**

HAVING TROUBLE?
If the Index tab is not visible in the frame, click the ▶ scroll button to display it.

Your screen should be similar to Figure 15

Enter word or phrase to locate

Alphabetical list of keywords

Open tab

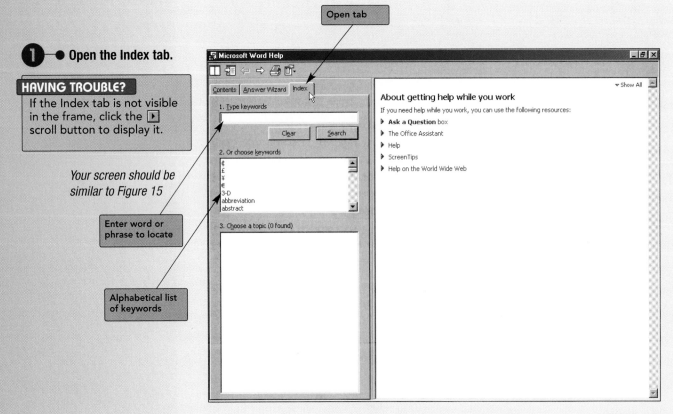

Figure 15

The Index tab consists of a text box where you can type a word or phrase that best describes the topic you want to locate. Below it is a list box displaying a complete list of Help keywords in alphabetical order. You want to find information about using the Index tab.

2 • Type **index** in the text box.

• Click [Search].

Your screen should be similar to Figure 16

19 Help topics containing keyword "index"

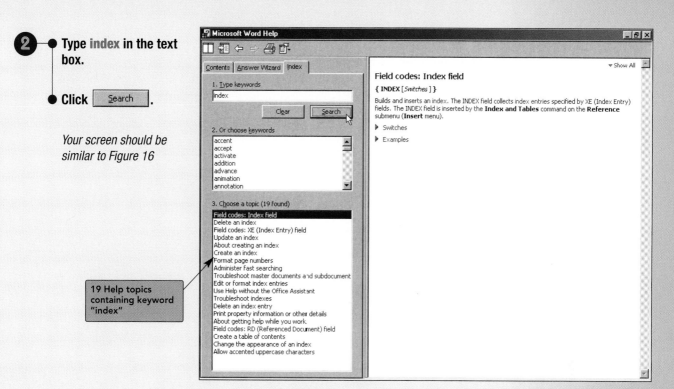

Figure 16

The topic list displays 19 Help topics containing this word, and the content frame, displays the information on the first topic. However, many of the located topics are not about the Help Index feature. To narrow the search more, you can add another word to the keyword text box.

3 • Click in the text box.

• Type **help** following the word "index."

• Click [Search].

Your screen should be similar to Figure 17

Two topics contain both keywords

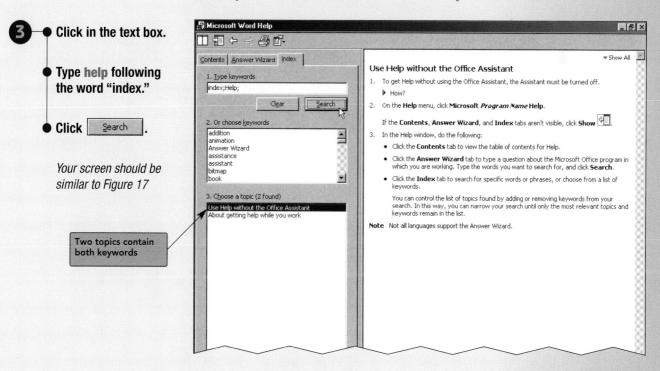

Figure 17

Now only two topics were located that contain both keywords. The first topic in the list is selected and displayed in the content frame.

Using the Answer Wizard

Another way to locate Help topics is to use the Answer Wizard tab. This feature works just like the Office Assistant and the Answer box to locate topics. You will use this method to locate information on toolbars.

1 ● **Open the Answer Wizard tab.**

● **Type How do I use toolbars? in the text box.**

● **Click** Search **.**

Your screen should be similar to Figure 18

Topics related to your search

Additional Information

The search term does not need to be worded as a question. It can also be a word or phrase.

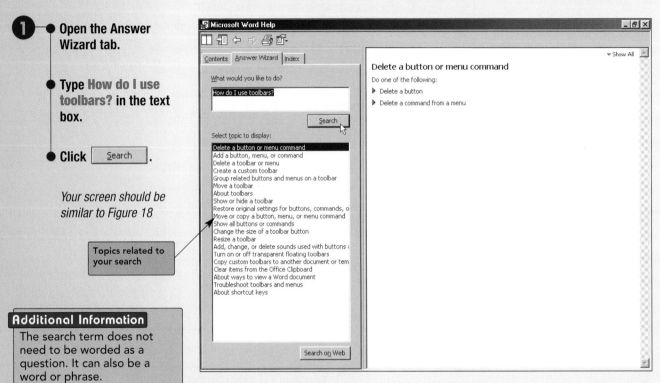

Figure 18

The topic list box displays all topics that the Answer Wizard considers may be related to the question you entered.

2 ● **Select "About toolbars" from the topic list.**

● **Click Show All.**

Your screen should be similar to Figure 19

Selected topic

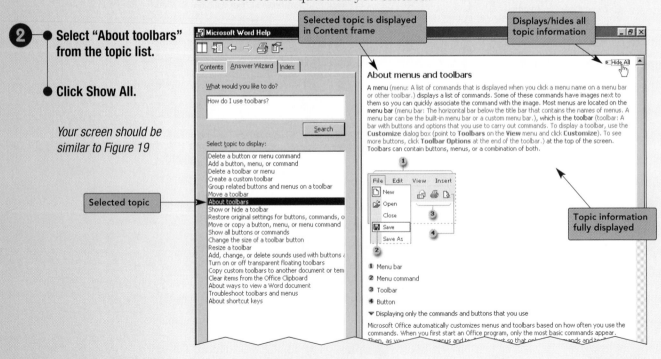

Figure 19

All topics are expanded and definitions displayed.

3 ● Read the information about this topic.

● Click ☒ to close Help.

Your screen should be similar to Figure 20

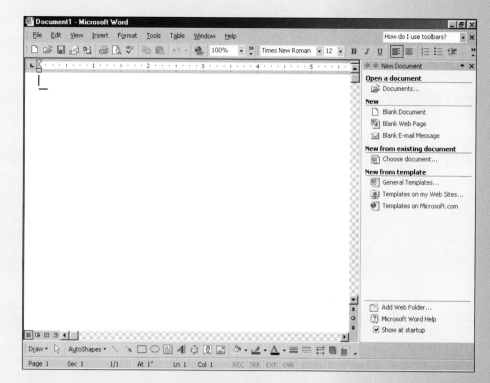

Figure 20

The Help window is closed, and the Word window is displayed again.

HAVING TROUBLE?
Your system must have an Internet connection to access the Microsoft Office Web site. If you do not have that, skip this section.

Getting Help on the Web

A final source of Help information is the Microsoft Office Web site. If a Help topic begins with "Web," clicking it takes you to the Web site and displays the topic in your Help window. You can also connect directly to this site from any Office application using the Help menu.

1 ● **Choose Help/Office on the Web.**

● **If necessary, enter your user information and make the appropriate selections to connect to the Internet.**

● **If necessary, click United States.**

Your screen should be similar to Figure 21

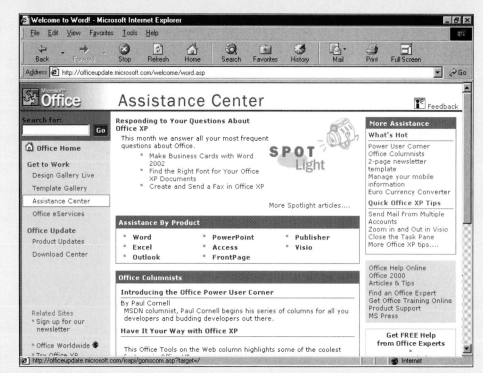

Figure 21

The browser application on your system is started and displays the Microsoft Office Web site. Now you could select any of the hyperlinks to further explore the site.

2 ● **Read the information on this page.**

● **Click ⊠ Close to close the browser.**

● **If necessary, disconnect from the Internet.**

The Word application window is displayed again.

Using Toolbars

While using Office XP, you will see that many toolbars open automatically as different tasks are performed. Toolbars initially display the basic buttons. Like menus, they are personalized automatically, displaying those buttons you use frequently and hiding others. The More Buttons ⟩ button located at the end of a toolbar displays a drop-down button list of those buttons that are not displayed. When you use a button from this list, it then is moved to the toolbar, and a button that has not been used recently is moved to the More Buttons list.

Initially, Word displays two toolbars, Standard and Formatting, on one row below the menu bar (see Figure 22). The Standard toolbar contains buttons that are used to complete the most frequently used menu commands. The Formatting toolbar contains buttons that are used to change the appearance or format of the document.

HAVING TROUBLE?
Your screen may display different toolbars in different locations. This is because the program displays the settings that were in effect when it was last exited.

1 ● **Right-click on any toolbar to display the shortcut menu.**

Your screen should be similar to Figure 22

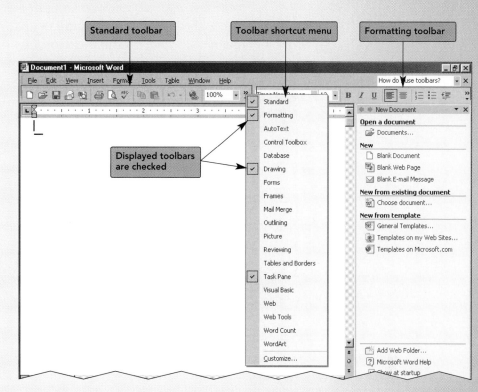

Standard toolbar

Toolbar shortcut menu

Formatting toolbar

Displayed toolbars are checked

Figure 22

Additional Information

The customize option can be used to change features of toolbars and menus.

The toolbar shortcut menu displays a list of toolbar names. The Formatting, Standard, and Task Pane options should be checked, indicating they are displayed. Clicking on a toolbar from the list will display it on-screen. Clicking on a checked toolbar will hide the toolbar.

2 ● **Click Task Pane to clear the checkmark.**

Your screen should be similar to Figure 23

Docked toolbars display move handle

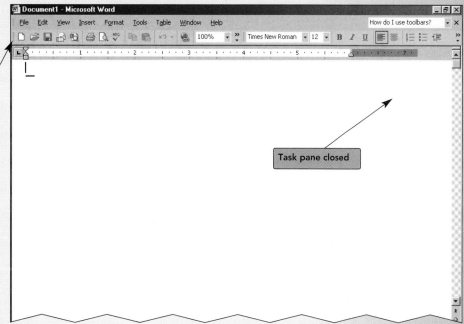

Task pane closed

Figure 23

The task pane is closed. When a toolbar is open, it may appear docked or floating. A docked toolbar is fixed to an edge of the window and displays a vertical bar ‖ called the move handle, on the left edge of the toolbar. Dragging this bar up or down allows you to move the toolbar. If multiple toolbars share the same row, dragging the bar left or right adjusts the size of the toolbar. If docked, a toolbar can occupy a row by itself, or several can be on a row together. A floating toolbar appears in a separate window.

3 ● Drag the move handle of the Standard toolbar into the document window.

Another Method

You can also double-click the top or bottom edge of a docked toolbar to change it to a floating toolbar.

Your screen should be similar to Figure 24

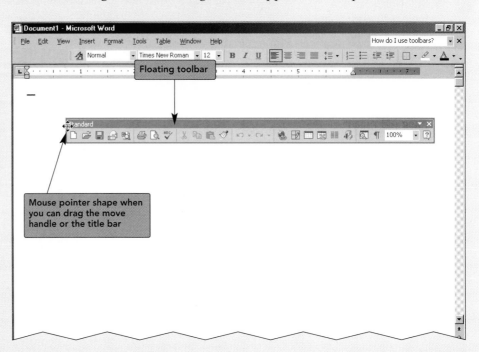

Figure 24

The Standard toolbar is now floating and can be moved to any location in the window by dragging the title bar. If you move it to the edge of the window, it will attach to that location and become a docked toolbar. A floating toolbar can also be sized by dragging the edge of toolbar.

4 ● Drag the title bar of the floating toolbar to move it to the row below the Formatting toolbar.

● Move the Formatting toolbar below the Standard toolbar.

Your screen should be similar to Figure 25

Additional Information

You can permanently display the toolbars on two rows using **T**ools/**C**ustomize/ **O**ptions or by choosing **C**ustomize/**O**ptions from the toolbar shortcut menu and selecting "Show Standard and Formatting toolbars on two rows."

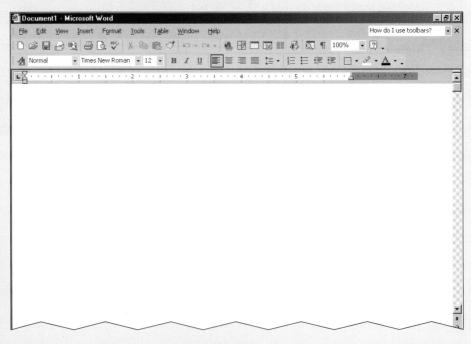

Figure 25

The two toolbars now occupy two rows. To quickly identify the toolbar buttons, you can display the button name by pointing to the button.

5 ● **Point to any button on the Standard toolbar.**

Your screen should be similar to Figure 26

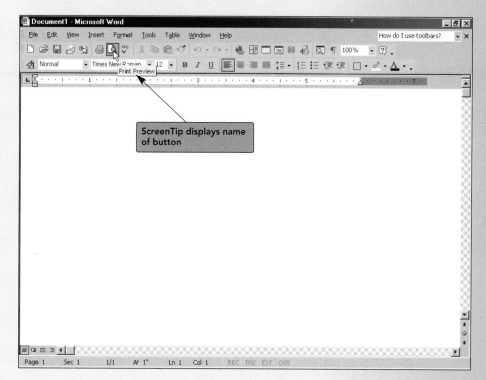

ScreenTip displays name of button

Figure 26

A ScreenTip containing the button name appears next to the mouse pointer.

Exiting an Office Application

The Exit command on the File menu can be used to quit most Windows programs. Alternatively, you can click the ☒ Close button in the program window title bar.

1 ● **Click ☒ Close.**

The program window is closed and the desktop is visible again.

lab review

Starting an Office Application

command summary

Command	Shortcut	Button	Action
Start/Programs			Opens program menu
File/Exit	Alt + F4		Exits Office program
View/Toolbars			Hides or displays toolbars
View/Task Pane			Hides or displays task pane
Tools/Customize/Options			Changes settings associated with toolbars and menus
Help/Microsoft Word Help	F1	?	Opens Help window
Help/Show the Office Assistant			Displays Office Assistant

The O'Leary Series

Microsoft®
Office XP

Overview of Word 2002

What Is Word Processing?

Word 2002 is a word processing software application whose purpose is to help you create any type of written communication. A word processor can be used to manipulate text data to produce a letter, a report, a memo, an e-mail message or any other type of correspondence. Text data is any letter, number, or symbol that you can type on a keyboard. The grouping of the text data to form words, sentences, paragraphs, and pages of text results in the creation of a document. Through a word processor you can create, modify, store, retrieve, and print part or all of a document.

February 18, 2001

Dear Adventure Traveler,

Imagine hiking and paddling your way through the rain forests of Costa Rica, under the stars in Africa, or following in the footsteps of the ancient Inca as you backp the Inca trail to Machu Picchu. Turn these dreams of adventure into memories you w forever by joining Adventure Travel Tours on one of our four new adventure tours.

To tell you more about these exciting new adventures, we are offerin presentations in your area. These presentations will focus on the features and cultu region. We will also show you pictures of the places you will visit and activities participate in, as well as a detailed agenda and package costs. Plan on attending o following presentations:

Date	Time	Location	Room
January 5	7:00 PM	Town Center Hotel	Room 284B
February 3	7:30 PM	Airport Manor	Conference Room
March 8	7:00 PM	Country Inn	Mountainside Room

In appreciation of your past patronage, we are pleased to offer you a 10% disco price of any of the new tour packages. You must book the trip at least 60 days pr departure date. Please turn in this letter to qualify for the discount.

Our vacation tours are professionally developed solely for your enjoyment. W almost everything in the price of your tour while giving you the best possible valu dollar. All tours include:

- Professional tour manager and local guides
- All accommodations and meals
- All entrance fees, excursions, transfers and tips

We hope you will join us this year on another special Adventure Travel Tour Your memories of fascinating places and challenging physical adventures should li long, long time. For reservations, please see your travel agent, or contact Adventure Tra at 1-800-777-0004. You can also visit our new Web site at www.AdventureTravelTour

Best regards,

Student Name

Announcing
New Adventure Travel Tours

This year we are introducing four new tours, offering you a unique opportunity to combine many different outdoor activities while exploring the world.

Hike the Inca trail to Machu Picchu
Camp on safari in Tanzania
Climb Mt. Kilimanjaro
Explore the Costa Rican rain forests

Attend an Adventure Travel presentation to learn about some of the earth's greatest unspoiled habitats and find out how you can experience the adventure of a lifetime.

Presentation dates and times are January 5 at 7 PM, February 3 at 7:30 PM, and March 8 at 7 PM. All presentations are held at convenient hotel locations located in downtown Los Angeles, Santa Clara and at the airport.

Call us at 1-800-777-0004 for presentation locations, a full color brochure, and itinerary information, costs, and tour dates.

Visit Our
Web site at
AdventureTravelTours.com

A letter and flyer created using Word 2002.

Word processors are one of the most widely used applications software programs. Putting your thoughts in writing, from the simplest note to the most complex book, is a time-consuming process. Even more time-consuming is the task of editing and retyping the document to make it better. Word processors make errors nearly nonexistent—not because they are not made, but because they are easy to correct. Word processors let you throw away the correction fluid, scissors, paste, and erasers. Now, with a few keystrokes, you can easily correct errors, move paragraphs, and reprint your document.

Word 2002 Features

Word 2002 excels in its ability to change or edit a document. Editing involves correcting spelling, grammar, and sentence-structure errors. In addition, you can easily revise or update existing text by inserting or deleting text. For example, a document that lists prices can easily be updated to reflect new prices. A document that details procedures can be revised by deleting old procedures and inserting new ones. This is especially helpful when a document is used repeatedly. Rather than recreating the whole document, you change only the parts that need to be revised.

Revision also includes the rearrangement of selected areas of text. For example, while writing a report, you may decide to change the location of a single word or several paragraphs or pages of text. You can do it easily by cutting or removing selected text from one location, then pasting or placing the selected text in another location. The selection can also be copied from one document to another.

Another time saver is word wrap. As you enter text you do not need to decide where to end each line, as you do on a typewriter. When a line is full, the program automatically wraps the text down to the next line.

To help you produce a perfect document, Word 2002 includes many additional support features. The AutoCorrect feature checks the spelling and grammar in a document as text is entered. Many common errors are corrected automatically for you. Others are identified and a correction suggested. While you enter text, the AutoComplete feature may suggest entire phrases that can be quickly inserted based on the first few characters you type. The words and phrases are included in a list of AutoText entries provided with Word 2002, or they may be ones you have included yourself. A thesaurus can be used to display alternative words that have a meaning similar or opposite to a word you entered. A Find and Replace feature can be used to quickly locate specified text and replace it with other text throughout a document.

A variety of Wizards are included in Word 2002 that provide step-by-step assistance while you produce many common types of documents, such as business letters, faxes, resumes, or reports. Templates also can be used to produce many of these documents without the step-by-step guidance provided by the Wizard.

You can also easily control the appearance or format of the document. Formatting includes such operations as changing the line spacing and margin widths, adding page numbers, and displaying page headers and footers. You can also quickly change how your text is aligned with the left or right margin. For example, text can be centered between the margins, or justified—evenly aligned on both the left and right margins. Perhaps the most noticeable formatting feature is the ability to apply different fonts (type styles and sizes) and text appearance changes such as bold, italics, and color to all or selected portions of the document. Additionally, you can add color shading behind individual pieces of text or entire paragraphs and pages to add emphasis. Automatic formatting can be turned on to automatically format text as you type by detecting when to apply selected formats to text as it is entered. In addition, Word 2002 includes a variety of tools that automate the process of many common tasks, such as creating tables, form letters, and columns.

Group collaboration on projects is common in industry today. Word 2002 includes many features to help streamline how documents are developed and changed by group members. A discussion feature allows multiple people to insert remarks in the same document without having to route the document to each person or reconcile multiple reviewers' comments. A feature called versioning allows you to save multiple versions of the same document so that you can see exactly who did what on a document and when. You can easily consolidate all changes and comments from different reviewers in one simple step and accept or reject changes as needed.

To further enhance your documents, you can insert many different types of graphic elements. You can select from over 150 borderline styles that can be applied to areas of text such as headings, or around graphics or entire pages. The drawing tools supplied with Word 2002 can be used to create your own drawings, or you can select from over 100 adjustable AutoShapes and modify them to your needs. All drawings can be further enhanced with 3-D effects, shadows, colors, and textures. Additionally, you can produce fancy text effects using the WordArt tool. More complex pictures can be inserted in documents by scanning your own, using supplied or purchased clip art, or downloading images from World Wide Web.

Word 2002 is closely integrated with the World Wide Web. It detects when you are typing a Web address and converts it to a hyperlink automatically for you. You can also create your own hyperlinks to locations within documents, or to other documents, including those at external locations such as a Web site or file server. Word's many Web-editing features help you quickly create a Web page. Among these is a Web Page Wizard that guides you step by step through the process of creating a Web page. Themes can be used to quickly apply unified design elements and color schemes to your Web pages. Frames can be created to make your Web site easier for users to navigate. Pictures, graphic elements, animated graphics, sound, and movies can all be used to increase the impact of your Web pages.

You can also create and send e-mail messages directly from within Word 2002, using all its features to create and edit the message. You can also send an entire document directly by e-mail. The document becomes the message. This makes collaboration easy because you can edit the document directly without having to open or save an attachment.

Case Study for Word 2002 Labs

As a recent college graduate, you have accepted a job as advertising coordinator for Adventure Travel Tours, a specialty travel company that organizes active adventure vacations. The company is headquartered in Los Angeles and has locations in other major cities throughout the country. Your duties include the creation of brochures, flyers, form letters, news releases, advertisements, and a monthly newsletter, all of which promote Adventure Travel's programs. You are also responsible for working on the company Web site.

Brief Version

Lab 1: Adventure Travel has developed four new tours for the upcoming year and needs to promote them, partly through informative presentations held throughout the country. Your first job as advertising coordinator is to create a flyer advertising the four new tours and the presentations about them.

Lab 2: Your next project is to create a letter to be sent to past clients along with your flyer. The letter briefly describes Adventure Travel's four new tours and invites clients to attend an informational presentation.

Lab 3: Part of your responsibility as advertising coordinator is to gather background information about the various tour locations. You will write a report providing information about Tanzania and Peru for two of the new tours.

Working Together: Adventure Travel has a company Web site. You will convert the flyer you developed to promote the new tours and presentations to be used on the Web site.

Before You Begin

To the Student

The following assumptions have been made:

- Microsoft Word 2002 has been properly installed on your computer system.

- You have the data files needed to complete the series of Word 2002 labs and practice exercises. These are supplied by your instructor.

- You are already familiar with how to use Microsoft Windows and a mouse.

To the Instructor

A complete installation of Office XP is required in which all components are available to students while completing the labs.

Please be aware that the following settings are assumed to be in effect for the Word 2002 program. These assumptions are necessary so that the screens and directions in the labs are accurate.

- The New Document Task Pane is displayed when Word is started. (Use Tools/Options/View/Startup Task Pane.)

- The ScreenTips feature is active. (Use Tools/Customize/Options/Show ScreenTips on Toolbar.)

- The status bar is displayed. (Use Tools/Options/View/Status bar.)

- The horizontal and vertical scroll bars are displayed. (Use Tools/Options/View.)
- The Wrap to Window setting is off. (Use Tools/Options/View.)
- The SmartTags feature is installed and active. (Use Tools/Options/View/SmartTags.)
- The Mark Formatting inconsistencies option is off. (Use Tools/Options/Edit.)
- The Paste Options buttons are displayed. (Use Tools/Options/Edit/Show Paste Options buttons.)
- Background repagination is on. (Use Tools/Options/General.)
- The Standard and Formatting toolbars are displayed on two rows. (Tools/Customize/Options.)
- Full menus are always displayed. (Use Tools/Customize/Options.)
- The Normal view is on. Zoom is 100 percent. (Use View/Normal; View/Zoom/100%.)
- The Drawing toolbar is on and displayed at the bottom of the window. (Use View/Toolbars/Drawing.)
- Language is set to English (US). (Use Tools/Language/Set Language.)
- The Office Assistant feature is off. (Right-click on the Assistant character, choose Options, and clear the Use the Office Assistant option.)
- All default settings for the Normal document template are in effect.

In addition, all figures in the manual reflect the use of a standard VGA display monitor set at 800 by 600. If another monitor setting is used, there may be more or fewer lines of text displayed in the windows than in the figures. This setting can be changed using Windows setup.

Microsoft Office Shortcut Bar

The Microsoft Office Shortcut Bar (shown below) may be displayed automatically on the Windows desktop. Commonly, it appears in the right side of the desktop; however, it may appear in other locations, depending upon your setup. The Shortcut Bar on your screen may also display different buttons. This is because the Shortcut Bar can be customized to display other toolbar buttons.

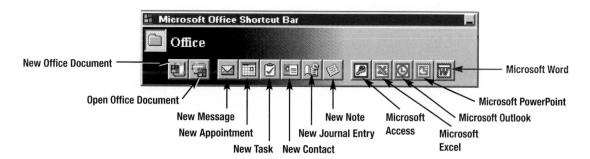

The Office Shortcut Bar makes it easy to open existing documents or to create new documents using one of the Microsoft Office applications. It can also be used to send e-mail, add a task to a to-do list, schedule appointments using Schedule+, or access Office Help.

Instructional Conventions

Hands-on instructions you are to perform appear as a sequence of numbered steps. Within each step, a series of bullets identifies the specific actions that must be performed. Step numbering begins over within each topic heading throughout the lab.

Command sequences you are to issue appear following the word "Choose." Each menu command selection is separated by a /. If the menu command can be selected by typing a letter of the command, the letter will appear underlined and bold. Items that need to be selected will follow the word "Select" and will appear in black text. You can select items with the mouse or directional keys. (See Example A.)

Example A

Choose File/Open.

Select My Documents from the Look In drop-down menu.

Commands that can be initiated using a button and the mouse appear following the word "Click." The icon (and the icon name if the icon does not include text) is displayed following "Click." The menu equivalent and keyboard shortcut appear in an Another Method margin note when the action is first introduced. (See Example B.)

Example B

Click 🖿 Open.

> **Another Method**
> The menu equivalent is File/**O**pen and the keyboard shortcut is [Ctrl]+O.

Plain blue text identifies file names you need to select or enter. Information you are asked to type appears in blue and bold. (See Example C.)

Example C

Open the document wd01_Flyer.

Type Adventure Travel presents four new trips.

The O'Leary Series

Microsoft® Word 2002

Brief Edition

Creating and Editing a Document

LAB 1

objectives

After completing this lab, you will know how to:

1.	Develop a document as well as enter and edit text.
2.	Insert and delete text and blank lines.
3.	Display formatting marks.
4.	Use AutoCorrect, AutoText, and AutoComplete.
5.	Use automatic spelling and grammar checking.
6.	Save, close, and open files.
7.	Select text.
8.	Undo and redo changes.
9.	Change fonts and type sizes.
10.	Bold and color text.
11.	Change alignment.
12.	Insert, size, and move pictures.
13.	Preview and print a document.

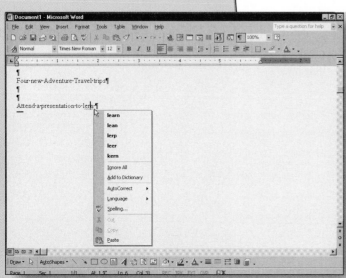

Entering and editing text is simplified with many of Word's AutoCorrect features.

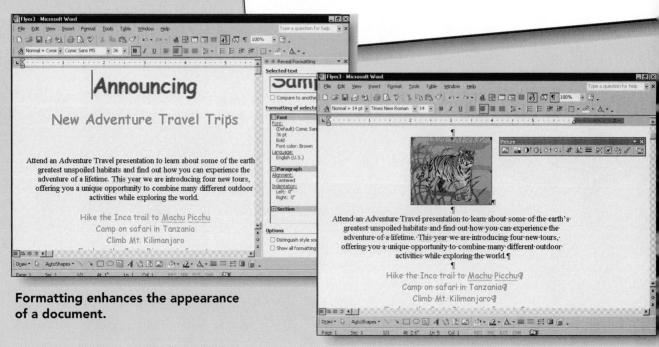

Formatting enhances the appearance of a document.

Pictures add visual interest to a document.

Adventure Travel Tours

As a recent college graduate, you have accepted a job as advertising coordinator for Adventure Travel Tours, a specialty travel company that organizes active adventure vacations. The company is headquartered in Los Angeles and has locations in other major cities throughout the country. You are responsible for coordination of the advertising program for all locations. This includes the creation of many kinds of promotional materials: brochures, flyers, form letters, news releases, advertisements, and a monthly newsletter. You are also responsible for creating Web pages for the company Web site.

Adventure Travel is very excited about four new tours planned for the upcoming year. They want to promote them through informative presentations held throughout the country. Your first job as advertising coordinator will be to create a flyer advertising the four new tours and the presentations about them. The flyer will be modified according to the location of the presentation.

The software tool you will use to create the flyer is the word processing application Microsoft® Word 2002. It helps you create documents such as letters, reports, and research papers. In this lab, you will learn how to enter, edit, and print a document while you create the flyer (shown left) to be distributed in a mailing to Adventure Travel Tours clients.

© Corbis

1	**Template**	A template is a document file that includes predefined settings that are used as a pattern to create many common types of documents.
2	**Grammar Checker**	The grammar checker advises you of incorrect grammar as you create and edit a document, and proposes possible corrections.
3	**AutoText and AutoComplete**	The AutoText feature includes entries, such as commonly used phrases, that can be quickly inserted into a document. As you type the first few characters of an AutoText entry the AutoComplete feature suggests the remainder of the AutoText entry you may want to use.
4	**AutoCorrect**	The AutoCorrect feature makes some basic assumptions about the text you are typing and, based on these assumptions, automatically corrects the entry.
5	**Spelling Checker**	The spelling checker advises you of misspelled words as you create and edit a document, and proposes possible corrections.
6	**Word Wrap**	The word wrap feature automatically decides where to end a line and wrap text to the next line based on the margin settings.
7	**Font and Font Size**	A font, also commonly referred to as a typeface, is a set of characters with a specific design that has one or more font sizes.
8	**Alignment**	Alignment is how text is positioned on a line between the margins or indents. There are four types of paragraph alignment: left, centered, right, and justified.
9	**Graphics**	A graphic is a non-text element or object, such as a drawing or picture, that can be added to a document.

Introducing Word 2002

Adventure Travel Tours has recently upgraded their computer systems at all locations across the country. As part of the upgrade, they have installed the latest version of the Microsoft Office suite of applications, Office XP. You are very excited to see how this new and powerful application can help you create professional letters and reports as well as eye-catching flyers and newsletters.

Starting Word 2002

You will use the word processing application included in the Office suite, Word 2002, to create a flyer promoting the new tours and presentations.

1 ● **Start the Word application.**

HAVING TROUBLE?

See "Common Office XP Features" on page I.9 for information on how to start the application and for a discussion of features common to all Office XP applications.

● **If necessary, maximize the Word application window.**

● **To display the standard window view, choose View/Normal.**

Your screen should be similar to Figure 1.1

Additional Information

You will learn about the different document views shortly.

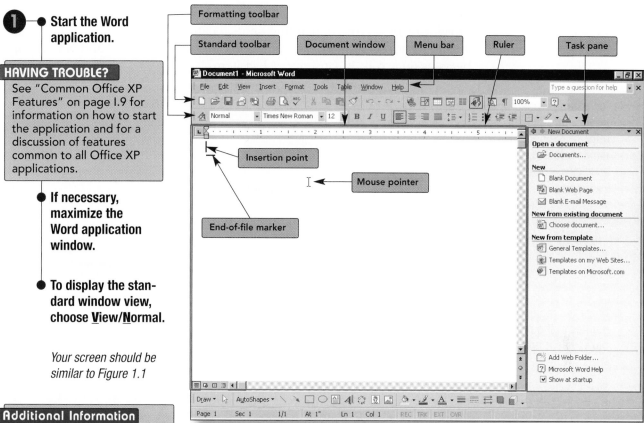

Figure 1.1

Exploring the Word Window

The menu bar below the title bar displays the Word program menu. It consists of nine menus that provide access to the commands and features you will use to create and modify a document.

The toolbars, normally located below the menu bar, contain buttons that are mouse shortcuts for many of the menu items. The **Standard toolbar** contains buttons for the most frequently used menu commands. The **Formatting toolbar** contains buttons that are used to change the appearance or format of the document. Word includes 19 toolbars, many of which appear automatically as you use different features. Your screen may display other toolbars if they were on when the program was last exited.

The task pane is displayed on the right side of the window. Word includes eight task panes, which are displayed depending on the task being performed. Since you just started Word, the New Document task pane is automatically displayed. This task pane provides different ways to create a new document or open an existing document.

The large area to the left of the task pane is the document window. It currently displays a blank Word document. The **ruler**, displayed at the top of the document window, shows the line length in inches and is used to set margins, tab stops, and indents. The **insertion point**, also called the **cursor**, is the blinking vertical bar that marks your location in the document. The solid horizontal line is the **end-of-file marker**. Because there is nothing in this document, the insertion point appears at the first character space on the first line.

HAVING TROUBLE?

If your toolbars are on a single row, choose Tools/Customize/Options/Show Standard and Formatting toolbars on two rows.

HAVING TROUBLE?

If your task pane is not displayed, choose View/Task Pane. If the ruler is not displayed, choose View/Ruler.

The mouse pointer may appear as an I-beam I (see Figure 1.1) or a left- or right-facing arrow, depending on its location in the window. When it appears as an I-beam, it is used to move the insertion point, and when it appears as an arrow, it is used to select items.

1 ● **Move the mouse pointer into the left edge of the document window to see it appear as** ⮡.

● **Move the mouse pointer to the menu bar to see it appear as** ⬉.

Your screen should be similar to Figure 1.2

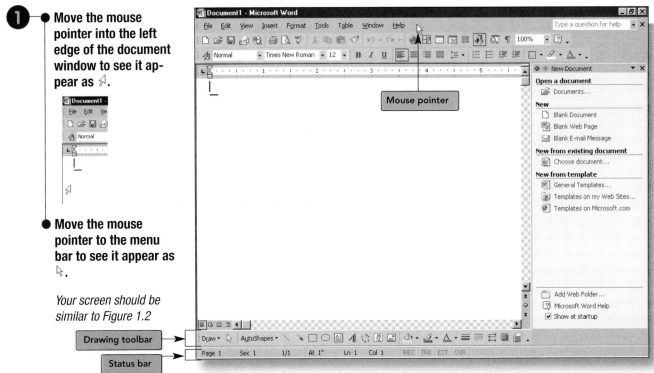

Figure 1.2

HAVING TROUBLE?

If the Drawing toolbar is not displayed, choose View/Toolbars/Drawing.

Below the document window, the **Drawing toolbar** is displayed. It contains buttons that are used to create and enhance drawing objects.

The indicators on the **status bar** show both the location of the text that is displayed in the document window as well as the location of the insertion point in a document. The numbers following the indicators specify the exact location in the document. The indicators are described in the following table.

Indicator	Meaning
Page	Indicates the page of text displayed onscreen.
Sec	Indicates the section of text displayed onscreen. A large document can be broken into sections.
1/1	Indicates the number of the pages displayed on screen, and the total number of pages in the document.
At	Indicates the vertical position in inches of the insertion point from the top of the page.
Ln	Indicates the line of text where the insertion point is located.
Col	Indicates the horizontal position of the insertion point in number of characters from the left margin.

Creating New Documents

When you first start Word 2002, a new blank Word document is opened. It is like a blank piece of paper that already has many predefined settings. These settings, called **default** settings, are generally the most commonly used settings and are stored as a document template.

concept 1

Template

1 A **template** is a document file that includes predefined settings that can be used as a pattern to create many common types of documents. Every Word document is based on a document template (see the examples below).

Default document settings are stored in the **Normal template**. Whenever you create a new document using this template, the same default settings are used. The Normal document template is referred to as a **global template** because it contains settings that are available to all documents.

Many other templates are available within Word and at the Microsoft Office Template Gallery on the Microsoft Web site that are designed to help you create professional-looking documents. They include templates for different styles of memos, letters, reports, faxes, and Web pages. Unlike global templates, the settings included in these specialized templates are available only to documents based on that template. You can also design and save your own document templates.

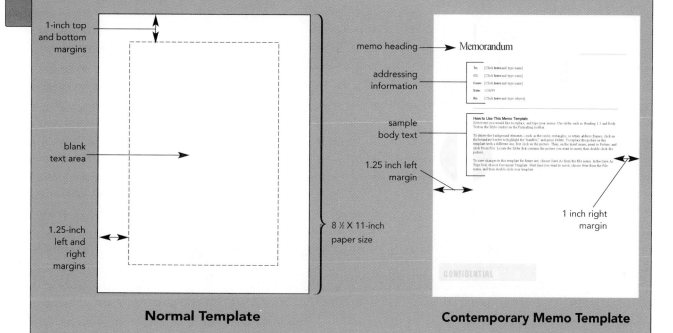

1-inch top and bottom margins

blank text area

1.25-inch left and right margins

8 ½ X 11-inch paper size

Normal Template

memo heading

addressing information

sample body text

1.25 inch left margin

1 inch right margin

Contemporary Memo Template

Using the Normal Template

When you first start Word, it displays a new blank document based on the Normal template. The Normal document template settings include 1-inch top and bottom margins, and 1.25-inch left and right margins. Other default settings include a standard paper-size setting of 8.5 by 11 inches, tab stops at every half inch, and single line spacing.

To verify several of the default settings, you can look at the information displayed in the status bar (see Figure 1.3). As you can see from the first three indicators in the status bar, page 1 of section 1 of a document consisting of only 1 page (1/1) is displayed on your screen. The next three indicators show the position of the insertion point. Currently, the insertion point is positioned at the 1-inch location from the top of the page, on line 1 from the top margin and column 1 from the left margin. The ruler displays dimmed tab marks below each half-inch position, showing the default tab stops of every half inch.

Viewing and Zooming a Document

To more easily verify several of the Normal template settings, you can switch to another document view. Word includes several views that are used for different purposes. You can change views using the View menu commands or the view buttons located to the left of the horizontal scroll bar. The main document views are described in the table below.

Document View	Command	Button	Effect on Text
Normal	View/Normal		Shows text formatting and simple layout of the page. This is the best view to use when typing, editing, and formatting text.
Web Layout	View/Web Layout		Shows the document as it will appear when viewed in a Web browser. Use when creating Web pages or documents that will be displayed on the screen only.
Print Layout	View/Print Layout		Shows how the text and objects will appear on the printed page. This is the view to use when adjusting margins, working in columns, drawing objects, and placing graphics.
Outline	View/Outline		Shows the structure of the document. This is the view to use to move, copy, and reorganize text in a document.

The view you see when first starting Word is the view that was in use when the program was last exited. Currently, your view is normal view, as shown in Figure 1.3. You can tell which view is in use by looking at the view buttons. The button for the view that is in use appears recessed as if it were depressed.

In addition, you can change the amount of information displayed in the document window by "zooming in" to get a close-up view or "zooming out" to see more of the document at a reduced view. The default display, 100 percent, shows the characters the same size they will be when printed. You can increase the onscreen character size up to five times normal display (500 percent) or reduce the character size to 10 percent. You will "zoom out" on the document to see the entire width of the page.

1 ● **Open the** `100%` ▼
Zoom drop-down menu (on the Standard toolbar).

HAVING TROUBLE?

Click the ▼ in the `100%` ▼ button to open the drop-down menu.

● **Choose Page Width.**

Another Method

The menu equivalent is View/Zoom/Page Width.

Your screen should be similar to Figure 1.3

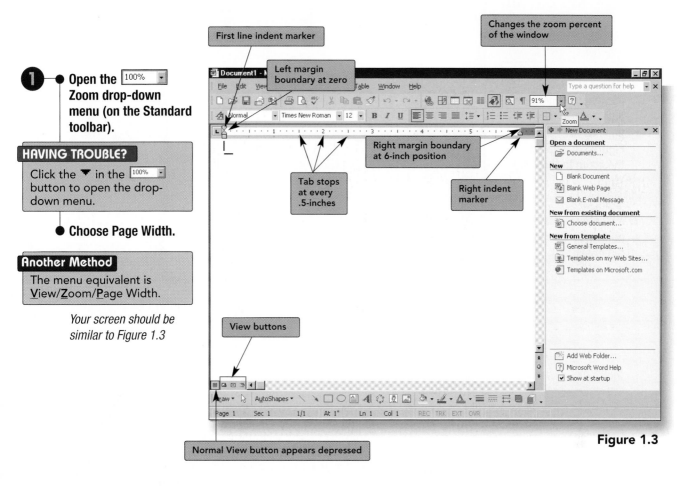

Figure 1.3

HAVING TROUBLE?

If your zoom percentage is different, this is a function of the monitor you are using.

To view the document at page width, the zoom percentage as shown in the Zoom box is 91 percent. You can verify several more Normal template settings by looking at the information displayed in the ruler. The margin boundaries on both ends of the ruler show the location of the left and right margins. The symbol ▽ at the zero position on the ruler is the first line indent marker and marks the location of the left paragraph indent. The symbol △ on the right end of the ruler line at the 6-inch position marks the right paragraph indent. The default paragraph indent locations are the same as the margin settings. The ruler shows that the distance between the left and right margins is 6 inches. Knowing that the default page size is 8.5 inches wide, this leaves 2.5 inches for margins: 1.25 inches for equal-sized left and right margins.

Although in normal view at page width you can see the default document settings, they are even easier to see when you are in print layout view. The zoom for each view is set independently.

2 ● Click 🔲 **Print Layout View** (located to the left of the horizontal scroll bar).

● **If your screen does not display the top and sides of the page as in Figure 1.4, change the zoom to Page Width.**

● **Move the mouse pointer to the center of the document.**

1.25-inch left margin

Three sides of page visible: left, top, and right

1.25-inch right margin

Click and Type pointer

1-inch top margin

Vertical ruler

Print Layout View button

Figure 1.4

Your screen should be similar to Figure 1.4

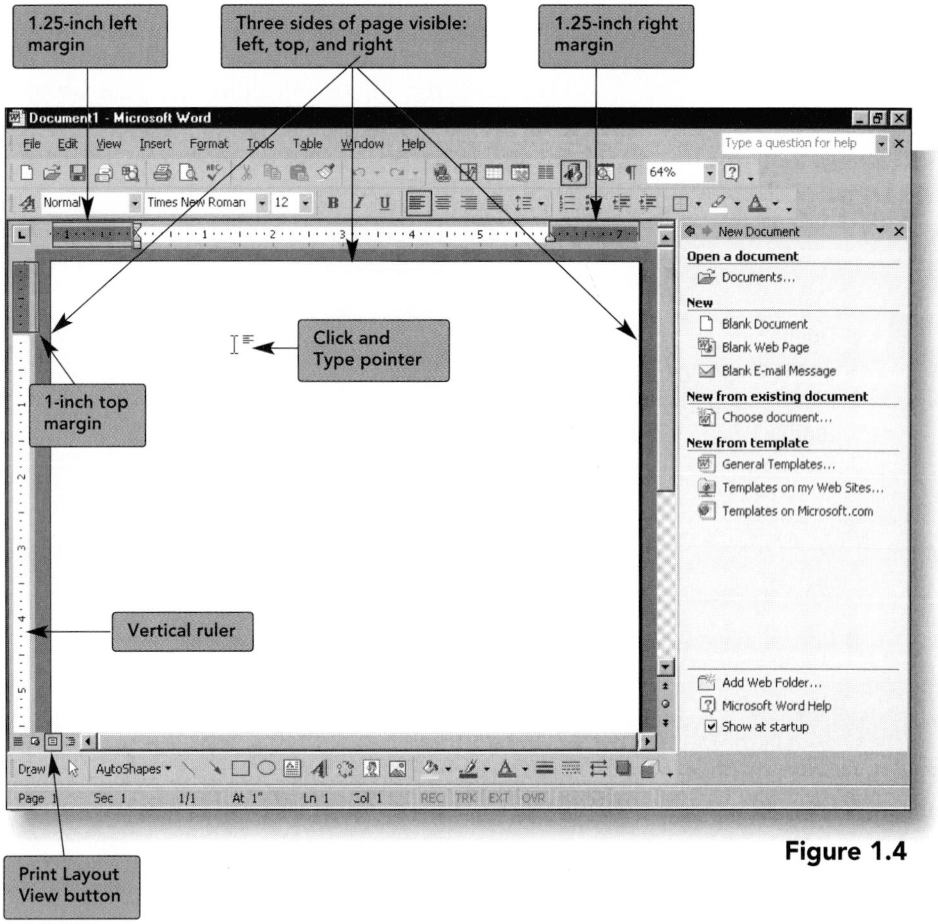

Print layout view displays the current page of your document as it will appear when printed. The top edge of the paper is visible below the horizontal ruler, and the left and right edges are visible along the sides of the window. The top margin is 1 inch from the top of the page, and the left margin setting is 1.25 inches from the left edge of the page.

This view also displays a vertical ruler that shows the vertical position of text. Also notice in this view that the mouse pointer appears as $I^{\equiv}$ when positioned over the document. This is the Click and Type pointer, which indicates the Click and Type feature is on. This feature allows you to quickly insert text into a blank area of a document while applying certain design features automatically. You will learn more about this feature in later labs.

You will use the Normal template in Normal view at the standard zoom percentage of 100 percent to create the flyer about this year's new tours. You will also close the New Document task pane to allow more space in the document window for viewing the document.

● Click 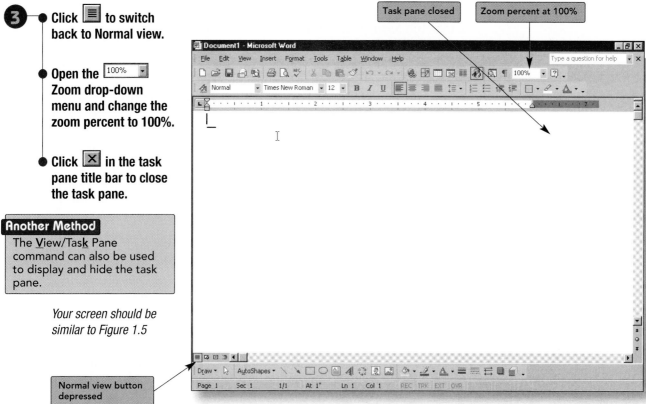 to switch back to Normal view.

● Open the `100%` Zoom drop-down menu and change the zoom percent to 100%.

● Click ☒ in the task pane title bar to close the task pane.

Another Method

The <u>V</u>iew/Tas<u>k</u> Pane command can also be used to display and hide the task pane.

Your screen should be similar to Figure 1.5

Normal view button depressed

Task pane closed | Zoom percent at 100%

Figure 1.5

Developing a Document

Your first project with Adventure Travel Tours is to create a flyer about four new tours. The development of a document follows several steps: plan, enter, edit, format, and preview and print.

Step	Description
Plan	The first step in the development of a document is to understand the purpose of the document and to plan what your document should say.
Enter	After planning the document, you enter the content of the document by typing the text using the keyboard. Text can also be entered using the handwriting and speech recognition features.
Edit	Making changes to your document is called **editing**. While typing, you are bound to make typing and spelling errors that need to be corrected. This is one type of editing. Another is to revise the content of what you have entered to make it clearer, or to add or delete information.
Format	Enhancing the appearance of the document to make it more readable or attractive is called **formatting**. This step is usually performed when the document is near completion. It includes many features such as boldfaced text, italics, and bulleted lists.
Preview and Print	The last step is to preview and print the document. Previewing displays the document onscreen as it will appear when printed, allowing you to check the document's overall appearance and make any final changes before printing.

You will find that you will generally follow these steps in the order listed above for your first draft of a document. However, you will probably retrace steps such as editing and formatting as the final document is developed.

During the planning phase, you spoke with your manager regarding the purpose of the flyer and the content in general. The primary purpose of the flyer is to promote the new tours. A secondary purpose is to advertise the company in general.

You plan to include specific information about the new tours in the flyer as well as general information about Adventure Travel Tours. The content also needs to include information about the upcoming new tour presentations. Finally, you want to include information about the Adventure Travel Web site.

Entering Text

Now that you understand the purpose of the flyer and have a general idea of the content, you are ready to enter the text.

Text is entered using the keyboard. As you type, many of Word's features make entering text much easier. These features include checking for spelling and grammar errors, auto correction, and word wrap. You will see how these features work next.

Typing Text

To enter text in a new document, simply begin typing the text. On the first line of the flyer you will enter "Announcing four new Adventure Travel trips." As you enter the text, do not be concerned if you make errors. You will learn how to correct them shortly.

1 ● **Type Announcing four new Adventure Travel trips.**

Your screen should be similar to Figure 1.6

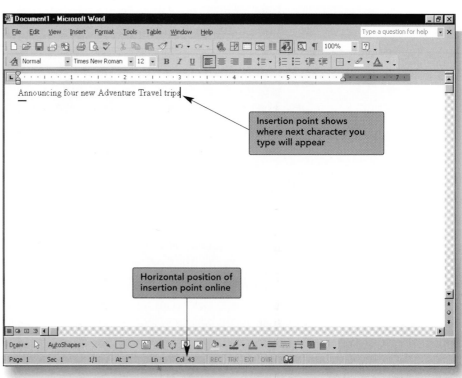

Figure 1.6

Notice that as you type, the insertion point moves to the right and the character appears to the left of the insertion point. The location of the insertion point shows where the next character will appear as you type. Also, the status bar reflects the new horizontal position of the insertion point on the line. It shows the insertion point is currently positioned on column 43 of line 1.

Ending a Line and Inserting Blank Lines

Now you are ready to complete the first line of the announcement. To end a line and begin another line, you simply press ←Enter. The insertion point moves to the beginning of the next line. If you press ←Enter at the beginning of a line, a blank line is inserted into the document. If the insertion point is in the middle of a line of text and you press ←Enter, all the text to the right of the insertion point moves to the beginning of the next line.

1 ● Press ←Enter 3 times.

Your screen should be similar to Figure 1.7

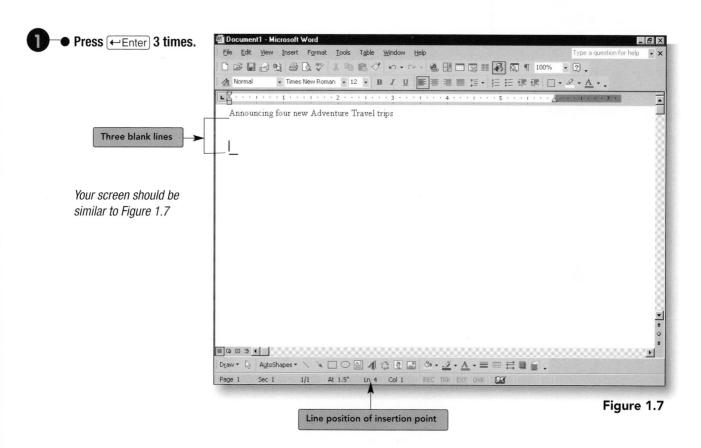

Figure 1.7

Pressing the first ←Enter ended the first line of text and inserted a blank line. The next two inserted blank lines. The status bar now shows that the insertion point is positioned on line 4, column 1 of the page.

Displaying Formatting Marks

While you are creating your document, Word automatically inserts **formatting marks** that control the appearance of your document. Word's default screen display does not show this level of detail. Sometimes, however, it is helpful to view the underlying formatting marks. Displaying these marks makes it easy to see, for example, if you have added an extra space between words or at the end of a sentence.

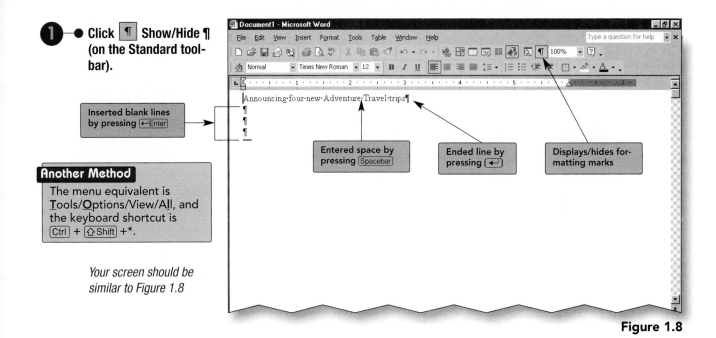

Click ¶ **Show/Hide ¶ (on the Standard toolbar).**

Inserted blank lines by pressing ←Enter

Entered space by pressing Spacebar

Ended line by pressing ←

Displays/hides formatting marks

Another Method

The menu equivalent is Tools/Options/View/All, and the keyboard shortcut is Ctrl + ⇧Shift +*.

Your screen should be similar to Figure 1.8

Figure 1.8

Additional Information

You can display selected formatting marks using Tools/Options/View and selecting the formatting marks you want to see.

The document now displays the formatting marks. The ¶ character on the line above the insertion point represents the pressing of ←Enter that created the blank line. The ¶ character at the end of the text represents the pressing of ←Enter that ended the line and moved the insertion point to the beginning of the next line. Between each word, a dot shows where the Spacebar was pressed. Formatting marks do not appear when the document is printed. You can continue to work on the document while the formatting marks are displayed, just as you did when they were hidden.

Moving through Text

Once text is entered into a document, it is important to know how to move around within the text to correct errors or make changes. Either the mouse or the keyboard can be used to move through the text in the document window. Depending on what you are doing, the mouse is not always the quickest means of moving. For example, if your hands are already on the keyboard as you are entering text, it may be quicker to use the keyboard rather than take your hands off to use the mouse. Therefore, you will learn how to move through the document using both methods.

Moving Using the Keyboard

You use the arrow keys located on the numeric keypad or the directional keypad to move the insertion point in a document. The directional keys and key combinations are described in the table on the next page.

Key	Movement
→	One character to right
←	One character to left
↑	One line up
↓	One line down
Ctrl + →	One word to right
Ctrl + ←	One word to left
Home	Left end of line
End	Right end of line

Additional Information

You can use the directional keys on the numeric keypad or the dedicated directional keypad area. If using the numeric keypad, make sure the Num Lock feature is off, otherwise numbers will be entered in the document. The Num Lock indicator light above the keypad is lit when on. Press Num Lock to turn it off.

Holding down a directional key or key combination moves quickly in the direction indicated, saving multiple presses of the key. Many of the Word insertion point movement keys can be held down to execute multiple moves. You will use many of these keys to quickly move through the text.

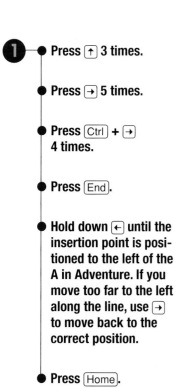

1
- Press ↑ 3 times.
- Press → 5 times.
- Press Ctrl + → 4 times.
- Press End.
- Hold down ← until the insertion point is positioned to the left of the A in Adventure. If you move too far to the left along the line, use → to move back to the correct position.
- Press Home.

Your screen should be similar to Figure 1. 9

Insertion point at top of document

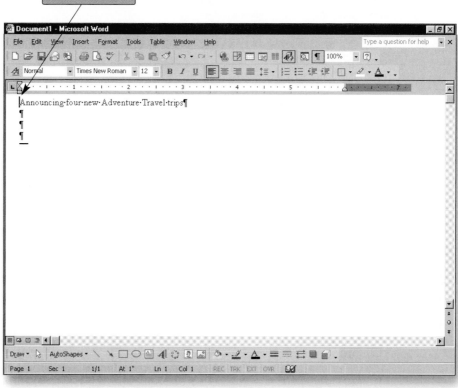

Figure 1.9

Additional Information

The insertion point will attempt to maintain its horizontal position in a line of text as you move up or down through the document.

The insertion point first moved up three lines, then five character spaces to the right, four words to the right, then quickly to the end of the line. You then held down the direction key to quickly move character by character to the left, and finally to the beginning of the line and down two lines to the blank line where you started.

Moving Using the Mouse

You use the mouse to move the insertion point to a specific location in a document. When you can use the mouse to move the insertion point, it is shaped as an I-beam. However, when the mouse pointer is positioned in the unmarked area to the left of a line (the left margin), it changes to an arrow ⇗. When the mouse is in this area, it can be used to highlight (select) text.

You have decided you want the flyer heading to be on two lines, with the word "Announcing" on the first line. To do this, you will insert a blank line after this word. To quickly move the insertion point to the location in the text where you want to insert the blank line,

Additional Information
You will learn about selecting text using this feature shortly.

1 ● **Click on the "f" in "four."**

● **Move the mouse pointer out of the way so you can see the insertion point better.**

Your screen should be similar to Figure 1.10

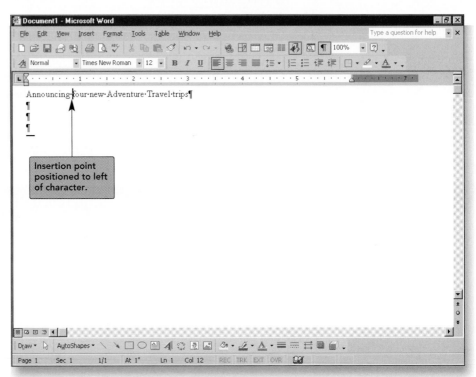

Figure 1.10

The insertion point should now be positioned on one side or the other of the f, with the status bar showing the new location of the insertion point. If it is positioned to the left of the f, this means that the I-beam was positioned more to the left side of the character when you clicked the mouse button. If it is positioned to the right of the f, this means the I-beam was positioned more to the right side of the character when you clicked the mouse button.

Additional Information
Throughout these labs, when instructed to move to a specific letter in the text, this means to move the insertion point to the *left* side of the character.

2

- **If necessary, move to the "f" in "four."**

- **Press ←Enter 2 times.**

- **Press ↓.**

Your screen should be similar to Figure 1.11

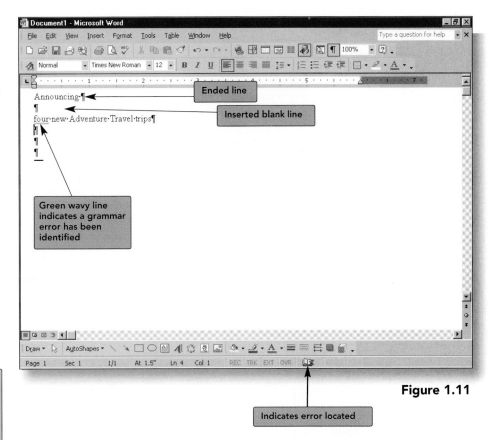

Ended line

Inserted blank line

Green wavy line indicates a grammar error has been identified

Figure 1.11

Indicates error located

The insertion point is positioned at the beginning of the blank line. As you continue to create a document, the formatting marks are automatically inserted and deleted. Notice that a green wavy underline appears under the word "four." This indicates Word has detected an error.

Using Word's Automatic Correcting Features

As you enter text, Word is constantly checking the document for spelling and grammar errors. The Spelling and Grammar Status icon 📖 in the status bar displays an animated pencil icon while you are typing, indicating Word is checking for errors as you type. When you stop typing, it displays either a red checkmark 📖, indicating the program does not detect any errors, or a red X 📖, indicating the document contains an error. In many cases, Word will automatically correct errors for you. In other cases, it identifies the error by underlining it. The different colors and designs of underlines indicate the type of error that has been identified. In addition to identifying the error, Word provides suggestions as to the possible correction needed.

Checking Grammar

In addition to the green wavy line under "four," the Spelling and Grammar Status icon appears as 📖. This indicates a spelling or grammar error has been located. The green wavy underline indicates it is a grammar error.

Grammar Checker

2 The **grammar checker** advises you of incorrect grammar as you create and edit a document, and proposes possible corrections. Grammar checking occurs after you enter punctuation or end a line. If grammatical errors in subject-verb agreements, verb forms, capitalization, or commonly confused words, to name a few, are detected they are identified with a wavy green line. You can correct the grammatical error by editing it or you can display a suggested correction. Because not all identified grammatical errors are actual errors, you need to use discretion when correcting the errors.

---

1 ● **Right-click on the green underline.**

Your screen should be similar to Figure 1.12

Grammar shortcut menu

HAVING TROUBLE?
If the wrong shortcut menu appears, you probably did not have the I-beam exactly positioned on the green wavy line. Press [Esc] or click outside the menu to cancel it and try again.

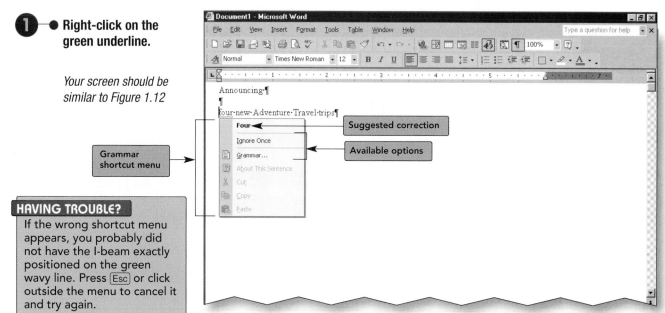

Figure 1.12

The first item on the Grammar shortcut menu is the suggested correction, "Four." It wants you to capitalize the first letter of the word because it is the beginning of a sentence. It also includes three available commands that are relevant to the item, described below.

Command	Effect
Ignore Once	Instructs Word to ignore the grammatical error in this sentence.
Grammar	Opens the grammar checker and displays an explanation of the error.
About This Sentence	Provides help about the grammatical error.

Additional Information
A dimmed menu option means it is currently unavailable.

To make this correction, you could simply choose the correction from the shortcut menu and the correction would be inserted into the document. Although in this case you can readily identify the reason for the error, sometimes the reason is not so obvious. In those cases, you can open the grammar checker to find out more information.

2 ● Choose **Grammar.**

Your screen should be similar to Figure 1.13

Line containing error is selected

Type of error

Location of error

Suggested correction

Click to make suggested correction

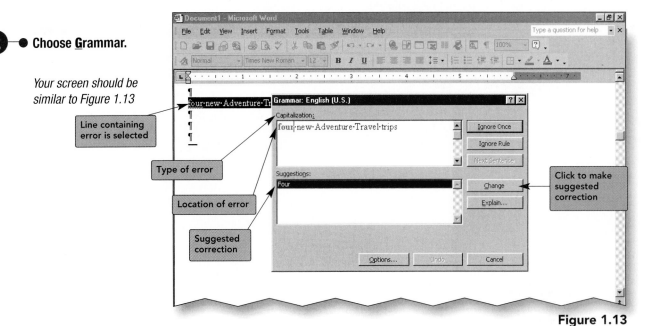

Figure 1.13

The Grammar dialog box identifies the possible grammatical error in the upper text box and the suggested correction in the Suggestions box. The line in the document containing the error is also highlighted (selected) to make it easy for you to see the location of the error. You will make the suggested change.

3 ● Click [Change].

● **Move to the blank line at the end of the document.**

Your screen should be similar to Figure 1.14

Additional Information

Moving the insertion point using the keyboard or mouse deselects or removes the highlight from text that is selected.

Error corrected by capitalizing 'F'

No more errors located

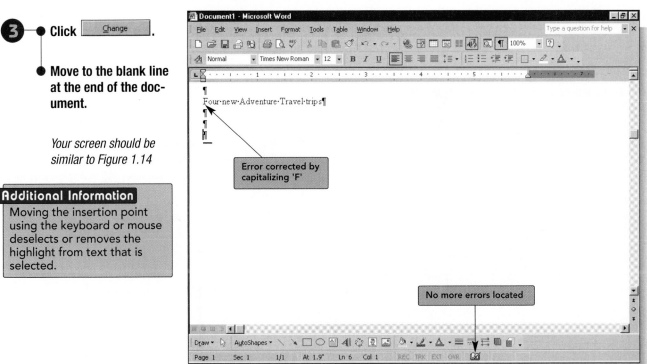

Figure 1.14

The error is corrected, the wavy green line is removed, and the Spelling and Grammar Status icon returns to 📖 .

Using AutoText and AutoComplete

Now you are ready to type the text for the first paragraph of the flyer.

Type atte.

*Your screen should be
similar to Figure 1.15*

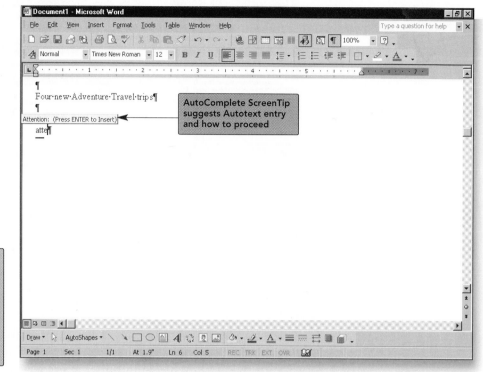

**AutoComplete ScreenTip
suggests Autotext entry
and how to proceed**

HAVING TROUBLE?
If a ScreenTip is not
displayed, choose
Insert/AutoText/AutoText,
select Show AutoComplete
Suggestions, and click
OK to turn on this
feature.

Figure 1.15

A ScreenTip appears displaying "Attention (Press ENTER to Insert):". This
is Word's AutoText and AutoComplete feature.

concept 3

AutoText and AutoComplete

3 The **AutoText** feature includes entries, such as
commonly used phrases, that can be quickly inserted into a document. The AutoText entries can
be selected and inserted into the document
using the Insert/AutoText command. Word's standard AutoText entries include salutations and
closing phrases. You can also add your own entries to the AutoText list, which can consist of
text or graphics you may want to use again.

Common uses are for a company name, mailing
address, and a distribution list for memos.

Additionally, if the **AutoComplete** feature is
on, a ScreenTip appears as you type the first
few characters of an AutoText entry, suggesting
the remainder of the AutoText entry you may
want to use. You can choose to accept the suggestion to insert it into the document, or to ignore it.

The AutoComplete ScreenTip suggests that you may be typing the word
"Attention." In this case, you do not want to enter the suggested word and
will continue typing the word "attend."

2 ● **Type nd.**

Your screen should be similar to Figure 1.16

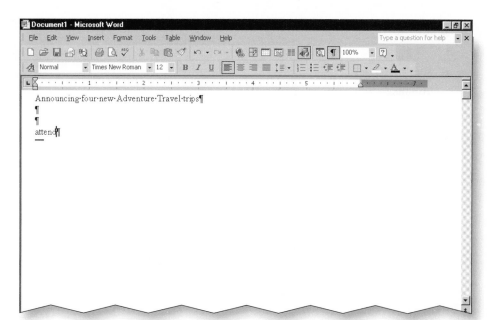

Figure 1.16

The AutoComplete ScreenTip has cleared, and the text as you typed it is displayed.

Using AutoCorrect

To end this word, you need to enter a space. As soon as you complete a word by entering a space or punctuation, the program checks the word for accuracy. This is part of the AutoCorrect feature of Word.

concept 4

AutoCorrect

4 The **AutoCorrect** feature makes some basic assumptions about the text you are typing and, based on these assumptions, automatically corrects the entry. The AutoCorrect feature automatically inserts proper capitalization at the beginning of sentences and in the names of days of the week. It will also change to lowercase letters any words that were incorrectly capitalized due to the accidental use of the Caps Lock key. In addition, it also corrects many common typing and spelling errors automatically.

One way the program automatically makes corrections is by looking for certain types of errors. For example, if two capital letters appear at the beginning of a word, Word changes the second capital letter to a lowercase letter. If a lowercase letter appears at the beginning of a sentence, Word capitalizes the first letter of the first word. If the name of a day begins with a lowercase letter, Word capitalizes the first letter.

Another way the program makes corrections is by checking all entries against a built-in list of AutoCorrect entries. If it finds the entry on the list, the program automatically replaces the error with the correction. For example, the typing error "aboutthe" is automatically changed to "about the" because the error is on the AutoCorrect list. You can also add words to the AutoCorrect list that you want to be automatically corrected.

A third method the program uses to automatically correct errors is to use suggestions from the spelling checker to automatically correct misspelled words. You will learn more about the spelling checker shortly.

1 ● Press Spacebar.

● Point to the word "Attend."

Your screen should be similar to Figure 1.17

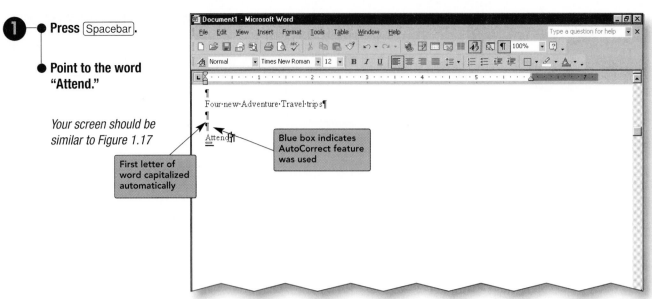

First letter of word capitalized automatically

Blue box indicates AutoCorrect feature was used

Figure 1.17

HAVING TROUBLE?

If your screen does not display the blue box, choose Tools/AutoCorrect Options and select the Show AutoCorrect Options button check box.

Word automatically capitalized the first letter of the word because it determined it is the first word in a sentence. When you rest the mouse pointer near text that has been corrected automatically or move the insertion point onto the word, a small blue box appears under the first character of the word. The blue box changes to the  AutoCorrect Options button when you point directly to it.

2 ● Point to the blue box.

● Click  AutoCorrect Options.

Your screen should be similar to Figure 1.18

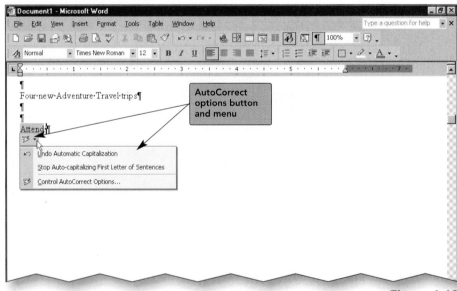

AutoCorrect options button and menu

Additional Information

In some cases, you may want to exclude a word from automatic correction. You can do this by manually adding the word to an exception list using Tools/AutoCorrect Options/Exceptions.

Alternatively, if you use Backspace to delete an automatic correction and then type it again the way you want it to appear, the word will be automatically added to the exceptions list.

Figure 1.18

Each time Word uses the AutoCorrect feature, the AutoCorrect Options button is available. The AutoCorrect Options menu allows you to undo the AutoCorrection or permanently disable the AutoCorrection for the remainder of your document. The Control AutoCorrect Options command can also be used to change the settings for this feature. You want to keep this AutoCorrection.

3 ● Click outside the menu to close it.

Checking Spelling

Next you will continue entering the text for the paragraph. As you enter text, it is also checked for spelling accuracy.

concept 5

Spelling Checker

5 The **spelling checker** advises you of misspelled words as you create and edit a document, and proposes possible corrections. The spelling checker compares each word you type to a **main dictionary** of words supplied with the program. Although this dictionary includes most common words, it may not include proper names, technical terms, and so on. If the word does not appear in the main dictionary, it checks the **custom dictionary**, a dictionary that you can create to hold words you commonly use but that are not included in the main dictionary. If the word does not appear in either dictionary, the program identifies it as misspelled by displaying a red wavy line below the word. You can then correct the misspelled word by editing it. Alternatively, you can display a list of suggested spelling corrections for that word and select the correct spelling from the list to replace the misspelled word in the document.

You will continue to enter the text for the flyer. As you do, it will include several intentional errors. Type the text exactly as it appears.

1 ● If necessary, move to the end of the last line.

● Type a presentaation to lern.

● Press [Spacebar].

Your screen should be similar to Figure 1.19

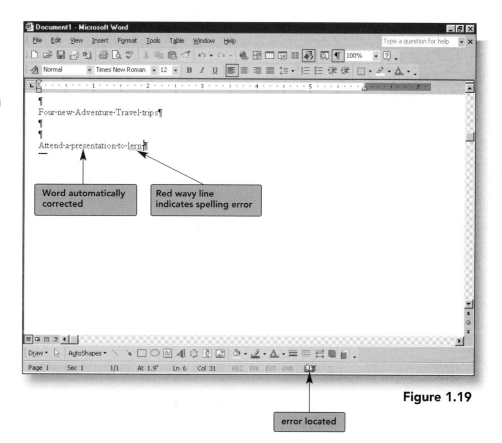

Figure 1.19

This time Word automatically corrected the spelling of "presentation" and identified the word "lern" as misspelled by underlining it with a wavy red line. The AutoCorrect feature corrected the spelling of presentation because it was the only suggested correction for the word supplied by the Spelling Checker. The word "lern" was not corrected because there are several suggested corrections on the Spelling shortcut menu.

The quickest way to correct a misspelled word is to select the correct spelling from a list of suggested spelling corrections displayed on the shortcut menu.

2 ● **Right-click on lern to display the shortcut menu.**

Another Method

You can also position the insertion point on the item you want to display a shortcut menu for and press ⬆Shift + F10 to open the shortcut menu.

Your screen should be similar to Figure 1.20

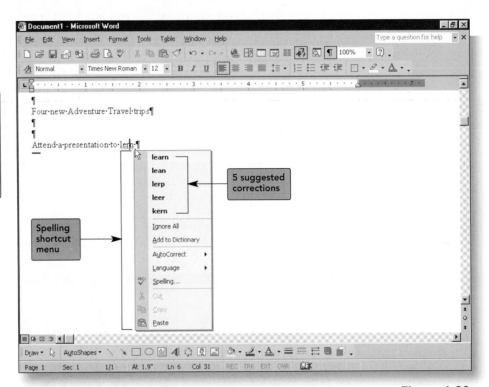

Figure 1.20

A shortcut menu of suggested correct spellings is displayed. In this case, five possible corrections are suggested. If the AutoCorrect feature is on and there is a single suggested spelling correction for a word, the program will automatically replace the incorrect spelling with the suggested replacement, as it did for the word "presentation."

The shortcut menu also includes several related menu options, described in the following table.

Option	Effect
Ignore All	Instructs Word to ignore the misspelling of this word throughout the rest of this session.
Add to Dictionary	Adds the word to the custom dictionary list. When a word is added to the custom dictionary, Word will always accept that spelling as correct.
AutoCorrect	Adds the word to the AutoCorrect list so Word can correct misspellings of it automatically as you type.
Language	Sets the language format, such as French, English or German, to apply to the word.
Spelling	Starts the spell-checking program to check the entire document. You will learn about this feature in Lab 2.

Sometimes there are no suggested replacements, because Word cannot locate any words in its dictionary that are similar in spelling; or the suggestions are not correct. If this happens, you need to edit the word manually. In this case, however the first suggestion is correct.

3 ● **Click learn.**

Your screen should be similar to Figure 1.21

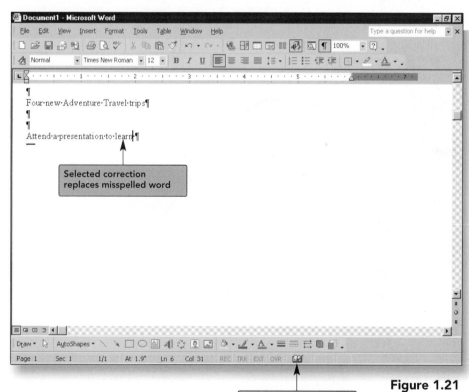

Figure 1.21

no more errors detected

The spelling correction you selected replaces the misspelled word in the document. The Spelling and Grammar status icon returns to , indicating as far as Word is able to detect, the document is free from errors.

Using Word Wrap

Now you will continue entering more of the paragraph. As you type, when the text gets close to the right margin, do not press ⮐Enter to move to the next line. Word will automatically wrap words to the next line as needed.

---

concept 6

Word Wrap

6   The **word wrap** feature automatically decides where to end a line and wrap text to the next line based on the margin settings. This saves time when entering text, as you do not need to press ⮐Enter at the end of a full line to begin a new line. The only time you need to press ⮐Enter is to end a paragraph, to insert blank lines, or to create a short line such as a salutation. In addition, if you change the margins or insert or delete text on a line, the program automatically readjusts the text on the line to fit within the new margin settings. Word wrap is common to all word processors.

---

1  ● Press →.

● Type **about some of the earth's greatest unspoiled habitats and to find out how you can experience the adventure of a lifetime.**

HAVING TROUBLE?
Do not worry about typing errors as you enter this text. You will correct them shortly.

Your screen should be similar to Figure 1.22

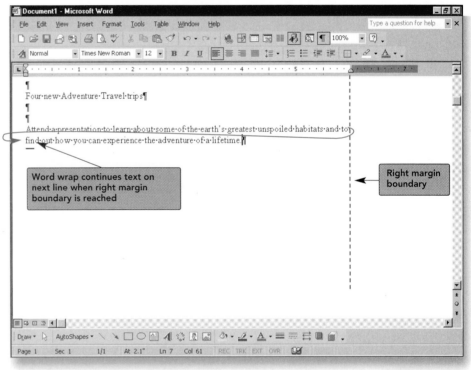

Figure 1.22

The program has wrapped the text that would overlap the right margin to the beginning of the next line. You will continue the paragraph by entering a second sentence.

2 ● Press [Spacebar].

● **Type This year we are introducing four new tours and offering you a unique opportunity to combine many different outdoor activities while exploring the world.**

● Press [←Enter].

● Use the features you learned to correct any identified spelling or grammar errors.

Your screen should be similar to Figure 1.23

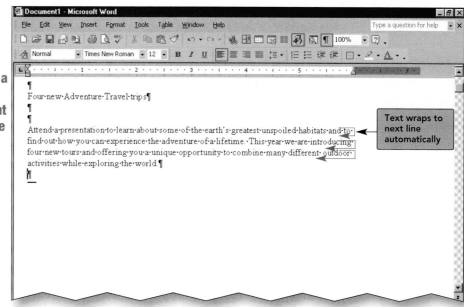

Figure 1.23

Additional Information

Generally, when using a word processor, separate sentences with one space after a period rather than two spaces, which was common when typewriters were used.

Using Smart Tags

You will be attending a meeting in a few minutes, and want to continue working on the document when you get back. You decide to add your name and the current date to the document.

1 ● Move to the end of the document.

● Press [←Enter] to insert another blank line.

● Type your name.

● Press [←Enter].

● Type the month and when the AutoText entry for the complete date appears, press [←Enter] to accept it.

● Press [←Enter] twice.

Your screen should be similar to Figure 1.24

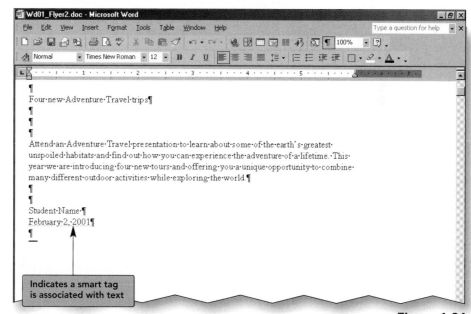

Figure 1.24

HAVING TROUBLE?

If the SmartTag is not identified, choose **T**ools/**A**utoCorrect Options/SmartTags, select "**L**abel text with smart tags" click Recheck Document, and click Yes. If it is still not available, the SmartTag feature has not been installed on your system.

Notice that the date is underlined with a dotted purple line, which indicates a smart tag is attached to the text. The **smart tag** feature recognizes and labels data such as names, addresses, telephone numbers, dates, times, and places as a particular type. The type of data it is recognized as determines what action can be performed with the data. For example, a name and address can be added directly from your document to the Microsoft Outlook Contacts folder. The date is recognized as a date item that can be added to the Outlook Calendar.

Since you do not need to perform any actions with the date, you will remove the Smart Tag. The purple dotted underline is removed indicating a smart tag is no longer associated with the text.

2
- **Point to the date to display the Smart Tag Actions button.**
- **Click [icon] to open the Smart Tag Actions menu.**
- **Choose Remove this Smart Tag.**

You will continue to see Smart Tags as you work through the labs.

Saving, Closing, and Opening Files

Before leaving to attend your meeting you want to save your work to a file and close the file. As you enter and edit text to create a new document, the changes you make are immediately displayed onscreen and are stored in your computer's memory. However, they are not permanently stored until you save your work to a file on a disk. Once a document is saved as a file, it can be closed and opened again at a later time to be further edited.

As a backup against the accidental loss of work due to power failure or other mishap, Word includes an AutoRecover feature. When this feature is on, as you work you may see a pulsing disk icon briefly appear in the status bar. This indicates the program is saving your work to a temporary recovery file. The time interval between automatic saving can be set to any period you specify; the default is every 10 minutes. After a problem has occurred, when you restart the program, the recovery file is automatically opened containing all changes you made up to the last time it was saved by AutoRecover. You then need to save the recovery file. If you do not save it, it is deleted when closed. While AutoRecover is a great feature for recovering lost work, it should not be used in place of regularly saving your work.

Saving a File

You will save the work you have done so far on the flyer. The Save or Save As command on the File menu is used to save files. The Save command or the [icon] Save button will save the active file using the same file name by replacing the contents of the existing file with the document as it appears on your screen. The Save As command allows you to save a file using a new file name or to a new location. This leaves the original file unchanged.

1 ● Choose **File/Save As**.

Your screen should be similar to Figure 1.25

Additional Information

You could also use the Save command to save a new document for the first time, as it will display the Save As dialog box automatically.

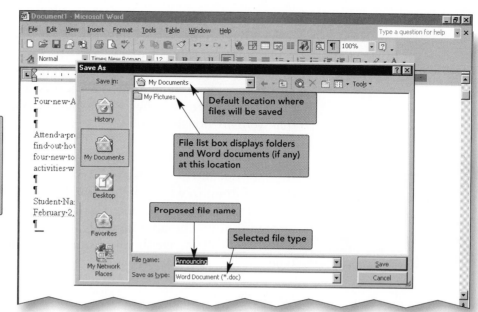

Figure 1.25

The Save As dialog box is used to specify the location to save the file and the file name. The Save In drop-down list box displays the default folder as the location where the file will be saved, and the File Name text box displays the proposed file name. The file list box displays the names of any Word documents in the default location. Only Word-type documents are listed, because Word Document is the specified file type in the Save As Type list box. First you need to change the location where the file will be saved to the drive containing your data disk.

2 ● Open the Save In drop-down list box.

● Select the appropriate location where you want to save your file.

Your screen should be similar to Figure 1.26

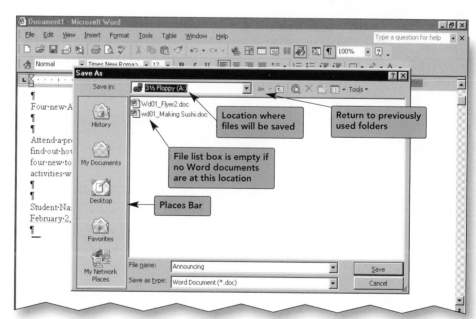

Figure 1.26

Saving, Closing, and Opening Files

Now the large list box displays the names of all Word files, if any, at that location. You can also select the location to save your file from the Places bar along the left side of the dialog box. The icons bring up a list of recently accessed files and folders (History), the contents of the My Documents and Favorites folders, items on the Windows desktop, and the locations on a network. You can also click the ⇦ button in the toolbar to return to folders that were previously opened.

Next you need to enter a file name and specify the file type. The File Name box displays the default file name, consisting of the first few words from the document. The Save as Type box displays "Word Document" as the default format in which the file will be saved. Word documents are identified by the file extension .doc. The file type you select determines the file extension that will be automatically added to the file name when the file is saved. You will change the file name to Flyer and use the default document type.

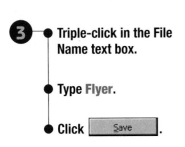

3 ● **Triple-click in the File Name text box.**

● **Type Flyer.**

● **Click** [Save].

Your screen should be similar to Figure 1.27

File name   **Closes document**

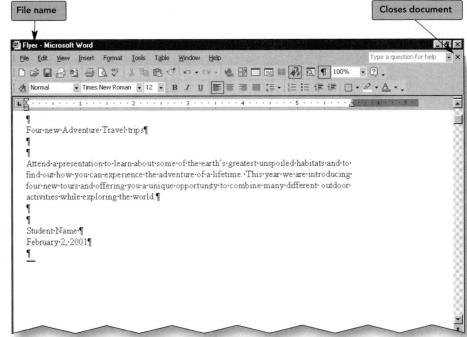

Figure 1.27

The document is saved as Flyer.doc at the location you selected, and the new file name is displayed in the Word title bar.

Closing a File

Finally, you want to close the document while you attend your meeting.

① ● Click ☒ Close
Window in the menu
bar.

Another Method

The menu equivalent is
File/**C**lose and the keyboard
shortcut is Ctrl + F4 .

*Your screen should be
similar to Figure 1.28*

Empty document
window

Status bar
indicators blank

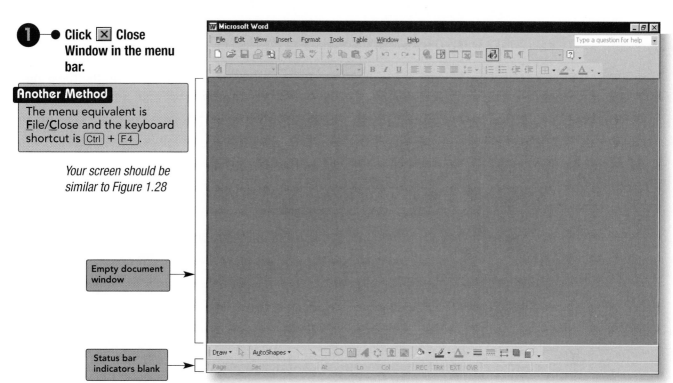

Figure 1.28

Another Method

The menu equivalent is
File/**O**pen and the keyboard
shortcut is Ctrl + O. You can
also click ☞ Open in the
Standard Toolbar.

Because you did not make any changes to the document since saving it, the
document window is closed immediately. If you had made additional
changes, Word would ask if you wanted to save the file before closing it.
This prevents the accidental closing of a file that has not been saved first.
Now the Word window displays an empty document window, and the status bar indicators are blank because there are no open documents.

Opening a File

Additional Information

You can also quickly open a
recently used file by selecting
it from the list of file names
displayed at the bottom of
the File menu and at the top
of the New Document task
pane.

You asked your assistant to enter the remaining information in the flyer for
you while you attended the meeting. Upon your return, you find a note
from your assistant on your desk. The note explains that he had a little trouble entering the information and tells you that he saved the revised file as
Flyer2. You want to open the file and continue working on the flyer.

① ● Choose **V**iew/Tas**k**
Pane.

● Click ☞ More
Documents (in the
Task Pane).

*Your screen should be
similar to Figure 1.29*

Location to open files

Changes dialog box view

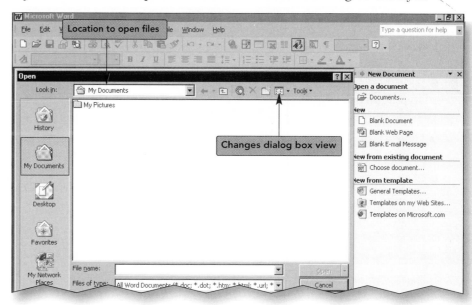

Figure 1.29

In the Open dialog box you specify the location and name of the file you want to open. The Look In drop-down list box displays the last specified location, in the case the location where you saved the Flyer document. The large list box displays the names of all Word documents with the file extensions displayed in the Files of type box. As in the Save As dialog box, the Places bar can be used to quickly access recently used files. When selecting a file to open, it may be helpful to see a preview of the file first. To do this you can change the dialog box view.

2 ● **If the Look In location is not correct, select the location containing your data files from the Look In drop-down list box.**

● **Open the** 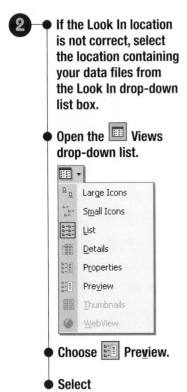 **Views drop-down list.**

● **Choose** **Preview.**

● **Select** wd01_Flyer2.doc.

Your screen should be similar to Figure 1.30

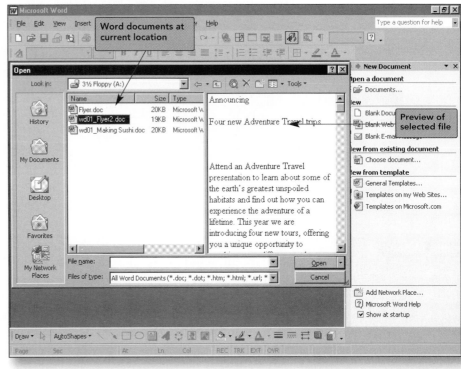

Figure 1.30

A preview of the selected file is displayed in the right pane of the dialog box. You will return the view to the list of file names and open this file.

3 ● **Open the** **Views drop-down list.**

● **Choose List.**

● **Click** Open .

Another Method
You could also double-click the file name to both select and open it.

Your screen should be similar to Figure 1.31

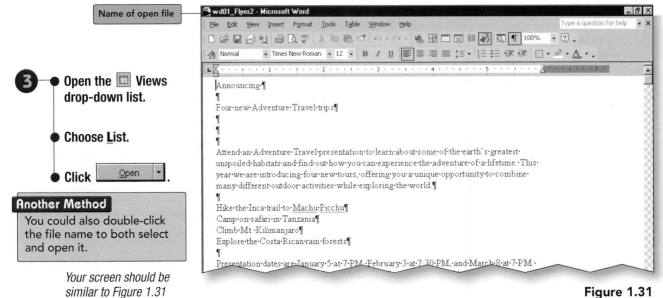

Figure 1.31

The file is opened and displayed in the document window. This file contains the text of the rest of the first draft of the flyer. The formatting marks are displayed because this feature is still on.

Navigating a Document

As documents increase in size, they cannot be easily viewed in their entirety in the document window and much time can be spent moving to different locations in the document. Word includes many features that make it easy to move around in a large document. The most basic is to scroll through a document using the scroll bar or keyboard. Another method is to move directly to a page or other identifiable item in the document, such as a table. You can also quickly return to a previous location, or browse through a document to a previous page or item.

Other features that help move through a large document include searching the document to locate specific items, and using the Document Map or a table of contents. Many of these features you will learn about in later labs.

Scrolling a Document

Additional Information
You can also scroll the document window horizontally using the horizontal scroll bar or the → and ← keys.

Now that more information has been added to the document, the document window is no longer large enough to display the entire document. To bring additional text into view in the window, you can scroll the document using either the scroll bars or the keyboard. Again, both methods are useful, depending on what you are doing. The table below explains the mouse and keyboard techniques that can be used to scroll a document.

Mouse	Action
Click ▼	Moves down line by line.
Click ▲	Moves up line by line.
Click above/below scroll box	Moves up/down window by window.
Drag scroll box	Moves up/down multiple windows.
Click ⬆	Moves to top of previous page.
Click ⬇	Moves to top of next page.
Click ⊙ Select Browse Object	Changes how you want the ⬆ and ⬇ buttons to browse through a document, such as by table or graphic. The default setting is by page.

Key	Action
↓	Down line by line
↑	Up line by line
Page Up	Top of window
Page Down	Bottom of window
Ctrl + Home	Beginning of document
Ctrl + End	End of document

You will use the scroll bar to view the text at the bottom of the flyer.

1 ● Click ▾ in the vertical scroll bar 11 times.

*Your screen should be
similar to Figure 1.32*

Text scrolls up to
allow more text to
appear in window

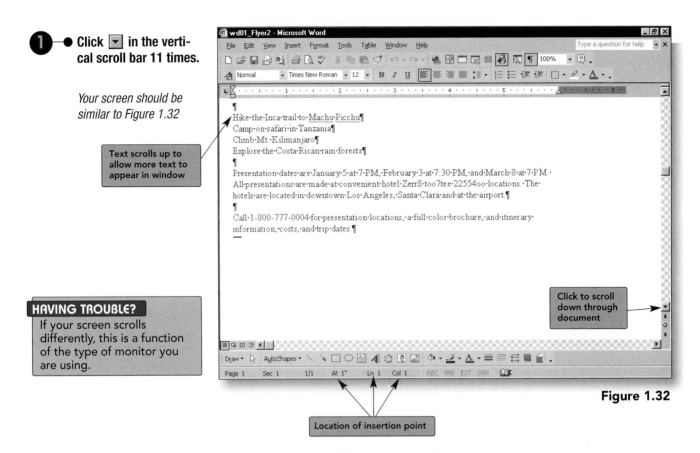

Click to scroll
down through
document

Figure 1.32

HAVING TROUBLE?
If your screen scrolls
differently, this is a function
of the type of monitor you
are using.

Location of insertion point

The text at the beginning of the flyer has scrolled off the top of the document window, and the text at the bottom of the flyer is now displayed. Notice that the insertion point is no longer visible in the document window. The insertion point location information in the status bar shows that the insertion point is still positioned at the top of the document. To actually move the insertion point, you must click in a location in the window.

2 ● Click anywhere in the last line.

You can also scroll the document using the keyboard. While scrolling using the keyboard, the insertion point also moves. The insertion point attempts to maintain its position in a line as you scroll up and down through the document.

3 ● Hold down ↑ for several seconds until the insertion point is on the first line of the flyer.

The document scrolled up in the document window, and the insertion point moved at the same time. In a large document, scrolling line by line can take a while. Observe how the document scrolls as you try out several of the scrolling features that move by larger jumps.

④ ● Click below the scroll box in the scroll bar.

● Drag the scroll box to the top of the scroll bar.

● Press Ctrl + End.

Your screen should be similar to Figure 1.33

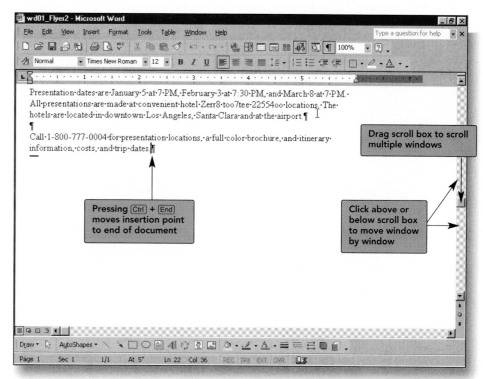

Pressing Ctrl + End moves insertion point to end of document

Drag scroll box to scroll multiple windows

Click above or below scroll box to move window by window

Figure 1.33

The insertion point is now at the end of the document. Using these features makes scrolling a large document much more efficient.

Editing Documents

While entering text and creating a document, you will find that you will want to edit or make changes and corrections to the document. Although many of the corrections are identified and made automatically for you, others must be made manually.

You have decided to make several changes to the text you just entered. The changes you want to make are shown below.

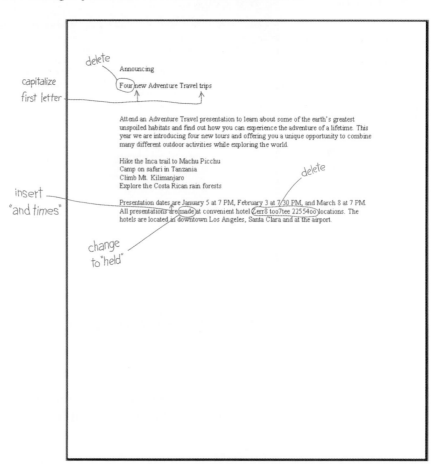

Using Backspace and Delete

Removing typing entries to change or correct them is one of the most basic editing tasks. Like many other features in Word, there are many ways to make corrections. Two of the most important editing keys are the [Backspace] key and the [Delete] key. The [Backspace] key removes a character or space to the left of the insertion point. It is particularly useful when you are moving from right to left (backward) along a line of text. The [Delete] key removes the character or space to the right of the insertion point and is most useful when moving from left to right along a line.

Because the formatting marks are displayed, you noticed there is an extra space after the word "Announcing" that can be deleted.

1

- Press **Ctrl** + **Home** to move to the beginning of the document.

- Press **End**.

- Press **Backspace** once.

Your screen should be similar to Figure 1.34

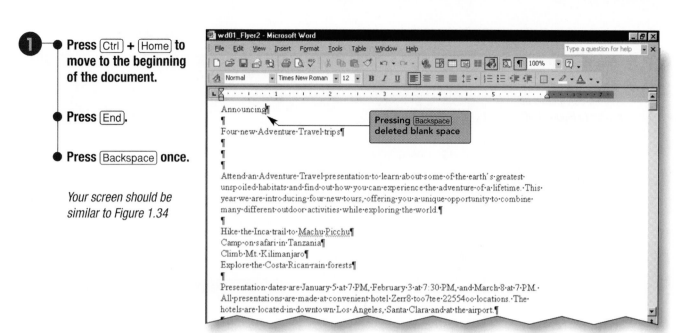

Pressing **Backspace** deleted blank space

Figure 1.34

The blank space and the space formatting mark are deleted.
You also want to capitalize the first letter of each word in the flyer title.

2

- Move to "t" in "trips."

HAVING TROUBLE?
Move to the left of the letter.

- Press **Delete** once.

- Type **T**.

- Move to the "e" in "new."

- Press **Backspace** once.

- Type **N**.

Your screen should be similar to Figure 1.35

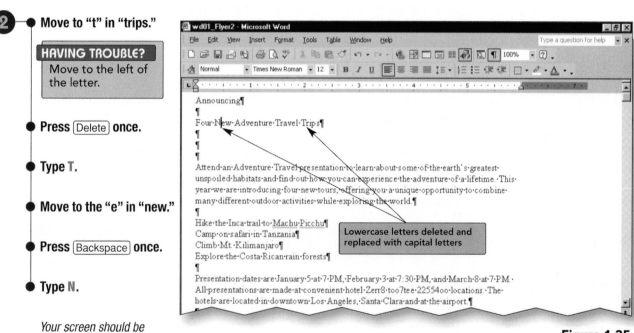

Lowercase letters deleted and replaced with capital letters

Figure 1.35

In many editing situations, it is helpful to display the formatting marks. However, for normal entry of text, you will probably not need the marks displayed.

Formating marks feature off

3 ● **Click ¶ Show/Hide ¶.**

Your screen should be similar to Figure 1.36

Formatting marks hidden

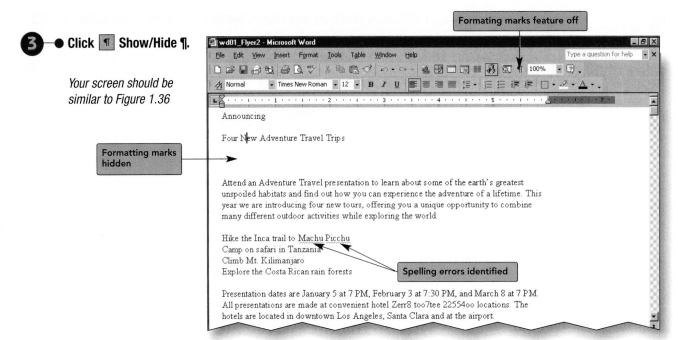

Figure 1.36

The document returns to normal display. Now that you know how to turn this feature on and off, you can use it whenever you want when entering and editing text.

Ignoring Spelling Errors

After entering the text of a document, you should proofread it for accuracy and completeness and modify or edit the document as needed. You first notice that the spelling checker has identified the names of several locations as misspelled, though they are in fact spelled correctly. This is because they are not in the dictionary. You will instruct Word to accept the spelling of these words and all other words it encounters having the same spelling throughout the remainder of the current Word session.

1 ● **Right-click on Machu.**

● **Choose Ignore All.**

● **In the same manner, tell Word to ignore the spelling of Picchu.**

Your screen should be similar to Figure 1.37

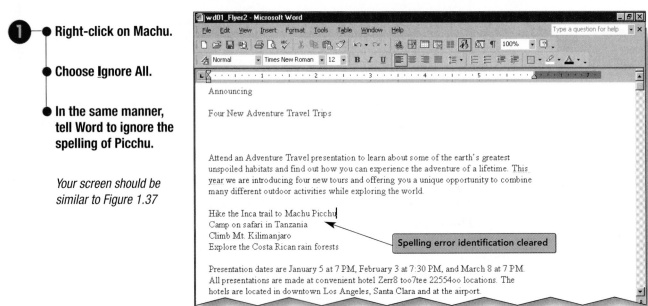

Figure 1.37

The red underlines are removed from each word. If you type any of these words again during this Word session, they will not be identified as misspelled.

Inserting Text

As you continue to check the document, you see that the first sentence of the paragraph below the list of trips is incorrect. It should read: "Presentation dates *and times* are . . ." The sentence is missing the words "and times." In addition, you want to change the word "made" to "held" in the following sentence. These words can easily be entered into the sentence without retyping using either Insert or Overtype mode.

In **Insert mode** new characters are inserted into the existing text by moving the existing text to the right to make space for the new characters. You will insert the words "and times" after the word "dates" in the first sentence.

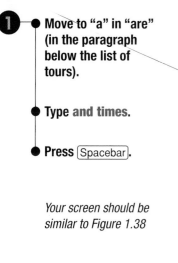

1
- Move to "a" in "are" (in the paragraph below the list of tours).

- Type and times.

- Press Spacebar.

Your screen should be similar to Figure 1.38

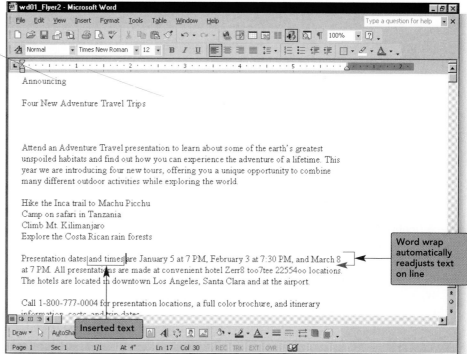

Figure 1.38

The inserted text pushes the existing text on the line to the right, and the word wrap feature automatically readjusts the text on the line to fit within the margin settings.

In the second sentence, you want to change the word "made" to "held." You could delete this word and type in the new word, or you can use the **Overtype mode** to enter text in a document. When you use Overtype mode, new text replaces existing text as you type. You will switch to this mode to change the word.

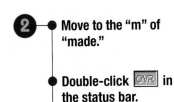

2 ● Move to the "m" of "made."

● Double-click ▭ in the status bar.

● Type **held**.

Your screen should be similar to Figure 1.39

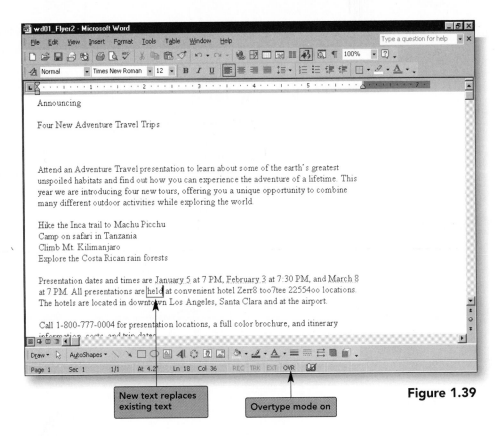

New text replaces existing text

Overtype mode on

Figure 1.39

As each character was typed, the selected character (or space) was replaced with the character being typed. Also notice that the OVR status indicator button letters are now bold, indicating the Overtype mode is on. To turn it off again,

3 ● Double-click ▭.

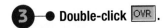

You can also turn Overtype mode on and off by pressing Insert or by choosing Tools/Options/Edit/Overtype mode.

Additional Information

The Ctrl + Backspace key combination deletes text to the left of the insertion point to the beginning of the next group of characters.

Overtype mode is off and Insert mode is restored.

Deleting a Word

Looking back at the title, you decide to delete the word "Four" from the second line. The Ctrl + Delete key combination deletes text to the right of the insertion point to the beginning of the next group of characters. In order to delete an entire word, you must position the insertion point at the beginning of the word.

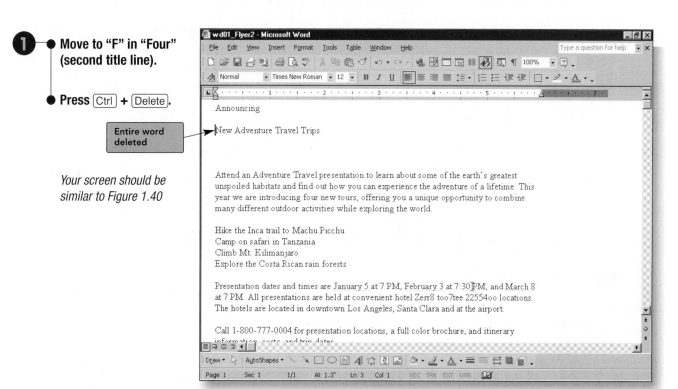

1 ● **Move to "F" in "Four"**
(second title line).

● **Press** Ctrl + Delete.

Entire word deleted

Your screen should be similar to Figure 1.40

Figure 1.40

Selecting and Deleting Text

As you continue proofreading the flyer, you see that the second line of the paragraph below the list of trips contains a section of junk characters. To remove these characters, you could use Delete and Backspace to delete each character individually, or Ctrl + Delete or Ctrl + Backspace to delete each word. This is very slow, however. Several characters, words, or lines of text can be deleted at once by first **selecting** the text and then pressing Delete. Text that is selected is highlighted. To select text, first move the insertion point to the beginning or end of the text to be selected, and then drag the mouse to highlight the text you want selected. You can select as little as a single letter or as much as the entire document.

The section of characters you want to remove follow the word "hotel" in the second line of the paragraph below the list of trips.

1 ● Move to "Z" (second line of paragraph below tour list).

● Drag to the right until all the text including the space before the word "locations" is highlighted.

HAVING TROUBLE?
Hold down the left mouse button while moving the mouse to drag.

Additional Information
When you start dragging over a word, the entire word including the space after it is automatically selected.

Your screen should be similar to Figure 1.41

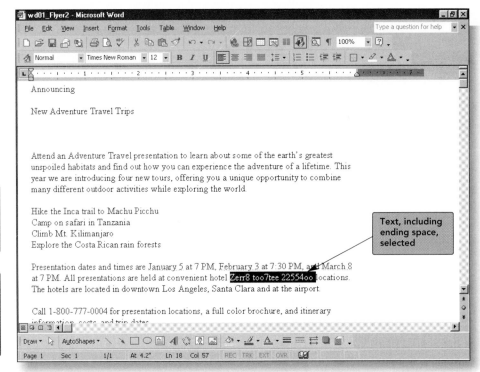

Figure 1.41

The characters you do not want are selected. Text that is selected can then be modified using many different Word features. In this case, you want to remove the selected text.

2 ● Press  Delete .

Another Method
The menu equivalent is Edit/Clear.

You also decide to delete the entire last sentence of the paragraph. You can quickly select a standard block of text. Standard blocks include a sentence, paragraph, page, tabular column, rectangular portion of text, or the entire document. The following table summarizes the techniques used to select standard blocks.

To Select	Procedure
Word	Double-click in the word.
Sentence	Press Ctrl and click within the sentence.
Line	Click to the left of a line when the mouse pointer is ◊.
Multiple lines	Drag up or down to the left of a line when the mouse pointer is ◊.
Paragraph	Triple-click on the paragraph or double-click to the left of the paragraph when the mouse pointer is a ◊.
Multiple paragraphs	Drag to the left of the paragraphs when the mouse pointer is ◊.
Document	Triple-click or press Ctrl and click to the left of the text when the mouse pointer is ◊.
	Use Edit/Select All or the keyboard shortcut Ctrl + A.

You will select and delete the sentence.

3 ● **Hold down** Ctrl **and click anywhere in the third sentence of the paragraph below the list of trips.**

● **Press** Delete.

Your screen should be similar to Figure 1.42

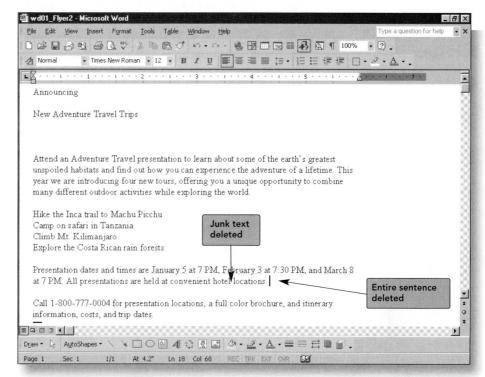

Figure 1.42

Undoing Editing Changes

After removing the sentence, you decide it may be necessary after all. To quickly restore this sentence, you can use ↶ ▾ Undo to reverse your last action or command.

1 ● **Click** ↶ ▾ **Undo.**

Your screen should be similar to Figure 1.43

The menu equivalent is Edit/Undo **(The action to be undone follows the command.) The keyboard shortcut is** Ctrl **+ Z.**

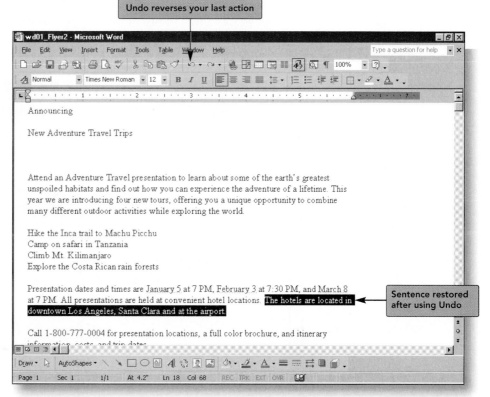

Figure 1.43

Undo returns your last deletion and restores it to its original location in the text, regardless of the current insertion point location. Notice that the Undo button includes a drop-down list button. Clicking this button displays a list of the most recent actions that can be reversed, with the most recent action at the top of the list. When you select an action from the drop-down list, you also undo all actions above it in the list.

2 ● Open the 🔄 ▾ Undo drop-down list.

most recent actions that can be reversed

● Select Delete Word.

Your screen should be similar to Figure 1.44

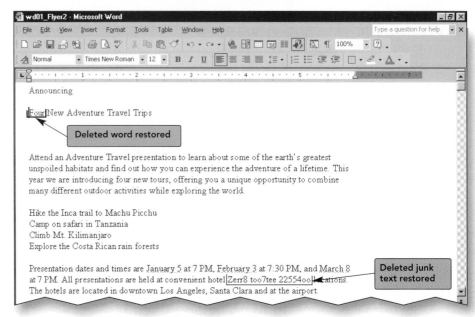

Figure 1.44

The junk characters and the word "Four" are restored. Immediately after you undo an action, the ⟳ ▾ Redo button is available so you can restore the action you just undid. You will restore your corrections and then save the changes you have made to the document to a new file.

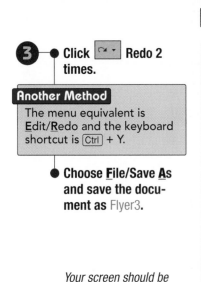

3 ● Click ⟳ ▾ Redo 2 times.

Another Method
The menu equivalent is **E**dit/**R**edo and the keyboard shortcut is Ctrl + Y.

● Choose **F**ile/Save **A**s and save the document as Flyer3.

Your screen should be similar to Figure 1.45

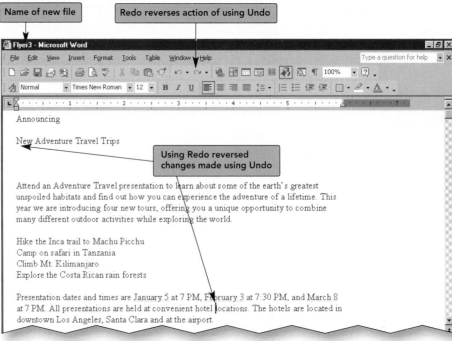

Figure 1.45

forms the actions in the list one by one. The new file name, Flyer3, is displayed in the window title bar. The original document file, wd01_Flyer2 is unchanged.

Formatting a Document

Because this document is a flyer, you want it to be easy to read and interesting to look at. Applying different formatting to characters and paragraphs can greatly enhance the appearance of the document. **Character formatting** consists of formatting features that affect the selected characters only. This includes changing the character style and size, applying effects such as bold and italics to characters, changing the character spacing and adding animated text effects. **Paragraph formatting** features affect an entire paragraph. A paragraph is all text up to and including the paragraph mark. Paragraph formatting features include how the paragraph is positioned or aligned between the margins, paragraph indentation, spacing above and below a paragraph, and line spacing within a paragraph.

Reviewing Document Formatting

Word allows you to quickly review the formatting in a document using the Reveal Formatting task pane.

● Choose Format/Reveal Formatting.

Your screen should be similar to Figure 1.46

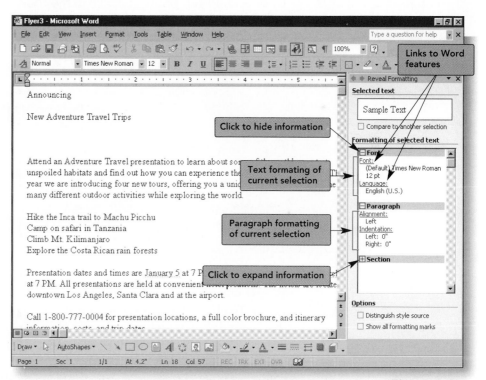

Figure 1.46

The Reveal Formatting task pane displays information about the formatting for the currently selected text and paragraph. It can also be used to modify these settings. The blue underlined text in the task pane indicates items that are direct links to Word features, providing faster access to the feature than using the menu. The mouse pointer appears as a 🖑 when pointing to a link. Clicking the link accesses the feature.

Changing Fonts and Font Sizes

The first formatting change you want to make is to use different fonts and font sizes in the flyer.

concept 7

Font and Font Size

7 A **font**, also commonly referred to as a **typeface**, is a set of characters with a specific design. The designs have names such as Times New Roman and Courier. Using fonts as a design element can add interest to your document and give readers visual cues to help them find information quickly.

There are two basic types of fonts, serif and sans serif. **Serif fonts** have a flair at the base of each letter that visually leads the reader to the next letter. Two common serif fonts are Roman and Times New Roman. Serif fonts generally are used for text in paragraphs. **Sans serif fonts** do not have a flair at the base of each letter. Arial and Helvetica are two common sans serif fonts.

Because sans serif fonts have a clean look, they are often used for headings in documents. It is good practice to use only two types of fonts in a document, one for text and one for headings. Too many styles can make your document look cluttered and unprofessional.

Each font has one or more sizes. **Font size** is the height and width of the character and is commonly measured in **points**, abbreviated "pt." One point equals about 1/72 inch, and text in most documents is 10 pt or 12 pt.

Several common fonts in different sizes are shown in the table below.

Font Name	Font Type	Font Size
Arial	Sans serif	This is 10 pt. This is 16 pt.
Courier New	Serif	This is 10 pt. This is 16 pt.
Times New Roman	Serif	This is 10 pt. This is 16 pt.

To change the font before typing the text, use the command and then type. All text will appear in the specified setting until another font setting is selected. To change a font setting for existing text, select the text you want to change and then use the command. If you want to apply font formatting to a word, simply move the insertion point to the word and the formatting is automatically applied to the entire word.

First you want to increase the font size of all the text in the flyer to make it easier to read.

1 • **Triple-click to the left of the text when the mouse pointer is ⬧ to select the entire document.**

• **Click Font: in the task pane.**

• **If necessary, click the Font tab to open it.**

Your screen should be similar to Figure 1.47

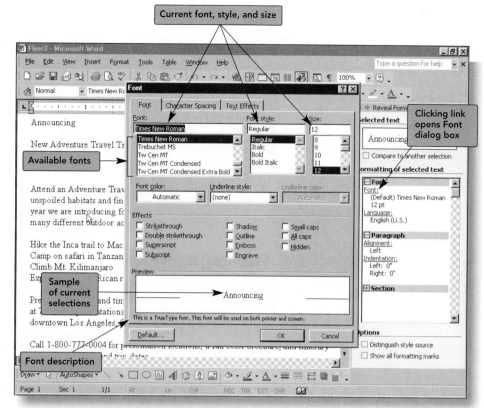

Figure 1.47

The current font settings are displayed, reflecting the Normal template default of Times New Roman with a font size of 12 points. The Preview box displays an example of the currently selected font setting.

Notice the description of the font below the Preview box. It states that the selected font is a TrueType font. **TrueType** fonts are fonts that are automatically installed when you install Windows. They appear onscreen exactly as they will appear when printed. Some fonts are printer fonts, which are available only on your printer and may look different onscreen than when printed. Courier is an example of a printer font.

You will increase the font size to 14 points. As you select the option, the Preview box displays how it will appear.

2 ● Scroll the Size list box and select 14.

● Click [OK].

Another Method
The menu equivalent is Format/Font/Font/Size.

Your screen should be similar to Figure 1.48

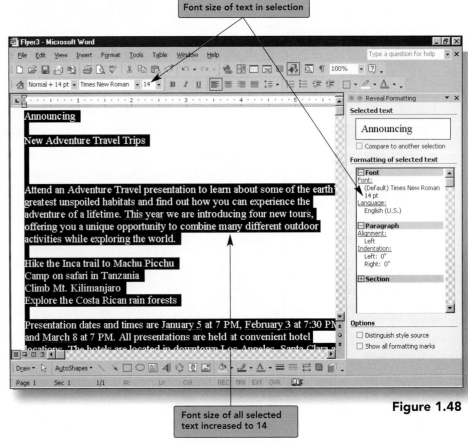

Font size of text in selection

Font size of all selected text increased to 14

Figure 1.48

Additional Information
If a selection includes text of various sizes, the Font Size button will be blank.

The font size of all text in the document has increased to 14 points, making the text much easier to read. The Font Size button in the Formatting tool-bar and in the task pane displays the new point size setting for the text at the location of the insertion point.

Next you will change the font and size of the two title lines. Another way to change the font and size is to use the toolbar buttons.

3

● **Click anywhere on the word "Announcing."**

● **Open the** [Times New Roman ▼] **Font drop-down list.**

● **Scroll the list and choose Comic Sans MS.**

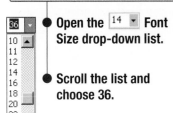

● **Open the** [14 ▼] **Font Size drop-down list.**

● **Scroll the list and choose 36.**

Your screen should be similar to Figure 1.49

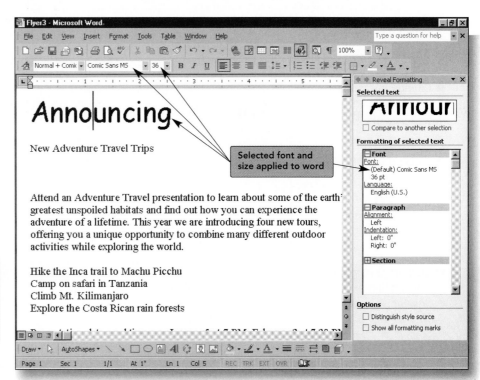

Figure 1.49

The selected font and size have been applied to the word, making the title line much more interesting and eye-catching. The font and font size buttons as well as the task pane reflect the settings in use at the location of the insertion point.

④
- **Select the second title line.**
- **Change the font to Comic Sans MS with a font size of 24.**
- **Select the list of four tours.**
- **Change the font to Comic Sans MS.**
- **Click anywhere on the highlighted text to deselect it.**

Your screen should be similar to Figure 1.50

Figure 1.50

Applying Character Effects

Next you want to liven up the flyer by adding character effects such as color and bold to selected areas. The table below describes some of the effects and their uses.

Format	Example	Use
Bold, italic	**Bold** *Italic*	Adds emphasis
Underline	Underline	Adds emphasis
Strikethrough	Strikethrough	Indicates words to be deleted
Double strikethrough	Double Strikethrough	Indicates words to be deleted
Superscript	"To be or not to be."[1]	Used in footnotes and formulas
Subscript	H_2O	Used in formulas
Shadow	Shadow	Adds distinction to titles and headings
Outline	Outline	Adds distinction to titles and headings
Small caps	SMALL CAPS	Adds emphasis when case is not important
All caps	ALL CAPS	Adds emphasis when case is not important
Hidden		Prevents selected text from displaying or printing
Color	Color Color Color	Adds interest

First you will add color and bold to the top title line.

① ● Click anywhere on the word "Announcing."

● Open the **A ·** Font Color drop-down list.

● Click **■** Brown.

● Click **B** Bold.

Figure 1.51

Another Method

The menu equivalents are Format/<u>F</u>ont/Font/Font Color and /Font Style/Bold. The Bold keyboard shortcut is Ctrl + B.

Your screen should be similar to Figure 1.51

Additional Information

Many of the formatting buttons are toggle buttons. This means that you can click the button to turn on the feature for the selection, and then click it again to remove it from the selection.

The selected color and bold effect have been applied to the entire word. The buttons and task pane information reflect the settings associated with the text at the insertion point. The Font Color button appears in the last selected color. This color can be quickly applied to other selections now simply by clicking the button.

Next you will add color and bold to several other areas of the flyer.

2

- Select the entire second title line.

- Change the color to orange and add bold.

- Select the list of four trips.

- Click 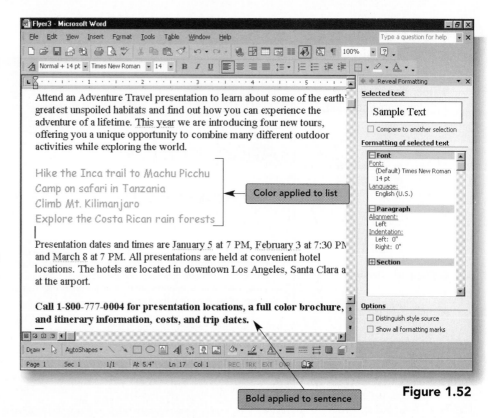 to change the color to orange.

- Bold the last sentence of the flyer.

- Click in the document to deselect the text.

Your screen should be similar to Figure 1.52

Figure 1.52

Setting Paragraph Alignment

The final formatting change you want to make is to change the paragraph alignment.

Alignment

8   **Alignment** is how text is positioned on a line between the margins or indents. There are four types of paragraph alignment: left, center, right, and justified.

Alignment		Effect on Text Alignment
	Left	Aligns text against the left margin of the page, leaving the right margin ragged. This is the most commonly used paragraph alignment type and therefore the default setting in all word processing software packages.
	Center	Centers each line of text between the left and right margins. Center alignment is used mostly for headings or centering graphics on a page.
	Right	Aligns text against the right margin, leaving the left margin ragged. Use right alignment when you want text to line up on the outside of a page, such as a chapter title or a header.
	Justified	Aligns text against the right and left margins and evenly spaces out the words. Newspapers commonly use justified alignment so the columns of text are even.

The alignment settings affect entire paragraphs.

The commands to change paragraph alignment are under the Format/Paragraph menu. However, it is much faster to use the keyboard shortcuts or the buttons on the Formatting toolbar shown below.

Alignment	Command	Keyboard Shortcut	Button
Left	Format/Paragraph/Indents and Spacing/Alignment/Left	Ctrl + L	☰
Center	Format/Paragraph/Indents and Spacing/Alignment/Center	Ctrl + E	☰
Right	Format/Paragraph/Indents and Spacing/Alignment/Right	Ctrl + R	☰
Justified	Format/Paragraph/Indents and Spacing/Alignment/Justified	Ctrl + J	☰

You want to change the alignment of all paragraphs in the flyer from the default of left-aligned to centered.

1

- Press Ctrl + A to select the entire document.

- Click ▤ Center (on the Formatting toolbar).

- Press Ctrl + Home.

Your screen should be similar to Figure 1.53

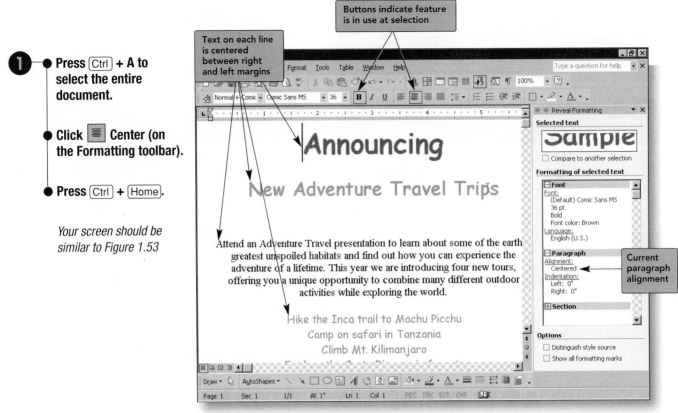

Text on each line is centered between right and left margins

Buttons indicate feature is in use at selection

Current paragraph alignment

Figure 1.53

Each line of text is centered evenly between the left and right page margins. The task pane paragraph alignment setting shows the new alignment is centered. Now that you are finished with formatting the document, you will close the task pane and save the flyer again using the same file name.

2

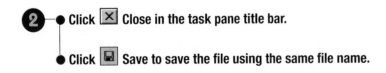

- Click ☒ Close in the task pane title bar.

- Click 🖫 Save to save the file using the same file name.

Additional Information

Saving a file frequently while you are making changes protects you from losing work due to a power outage or other mishap.

Working with Graphics

Finally, you want to add a graphic to the flyer to add interest.

9 A **graphic** is a non-text element or object, such as a drawing or picture, that can be added to a document. An **object** is an item that can be sized, moved, and manipulated.

A graphic can be a simple **drawing object** consisting of shapes such as lines and boxes that can be created using features on the Drawing toolbar. A drawing object is part of your Word document. A **picture** is an illustration such as a graphic illustration or a scanned photograph. Pictures are graphics that were created from another program and are inserted in your Word document as embedded objects. An **embedded object** becomes part of the Word document and can be opened and edited using the **source program**, the program in which it was created. Several examples of drawing objects and pictures are shown below.

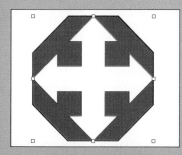
drawing object

graphic illustration

photograph

Add graphics to your documents to help the reader understand concepts, to add interest, and to make your document stand out from others.

Inserting a Picture

You want to add a picture to the flyer below the two title lines. Picture files can be obtained from a variety of sources. Many simple drawings called **clip art** are available in the Clip Organizer that comes with Office XP. You can also create picture files using a scanner to convert any printed document, including photographs, to an electronic format. Most images that are scanned and inserted into documents are stored as Windows bitmap files (.bmp). All types of pictures, including clip art, photographs, and other types of images, can be found on the Internet. These files are commonly stored as .jpg or .pcx files. Keep in mind that any images you locate on the Internet may be copyrighted and should only be used with permission. You can also purchase CDs containing graphics for your use.

You decide to check the Clip Organizer to find a suitable graphic.

> **Additional Information**
> You can also scan a picture and insert it directly into a Word document without saving it as a file first.

1 ● **Click ¶ Show/Hide to display paragraph marks.**

● **Move to the middle blank line below the second title line.**

● **Click 🖼 Insert Clip Art (on the Drawing toolbar).**

Another Method

The menu equivalent is Insert/Picture/Clip Art.

Your screen should be similar to Figure 1.54

Figure 1.54

The Insert Clip Art task pane appears in which you can enter a word or phrase that is representative of the type of picture you want to locate. The media clips are organized by topic and are identified with several keywords that describe the clip. You can also specify the locations to search and the type of media files, such as clip art, movies, photographs, or sound, to display in the results. You want to find clip art and photographs of animals.

2 ● **In the Search text box, type animals.**

● **If All Collections is not displayed in the Search In text box, select Everywhere from the drop-down list.**

HAVING TROUBLE?

Click the box next to an option to select or deselect (clear the checkmark).

● **Open the Results Should Be drop-down list, select Photographs and Clip Art and deselect all other options.**

● **Click Search .**

Your screen should be similar to Figure 1.55

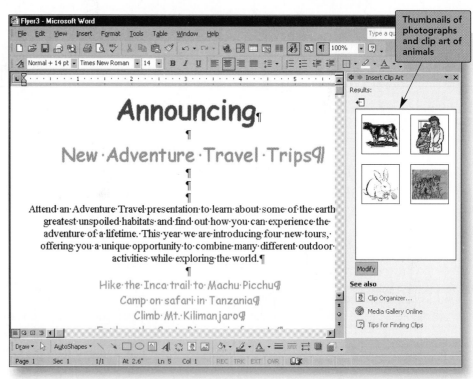

Figure 1.55

The Results area displays thumbnails, miniature representations of pictures, of all located clip art and photographs of animals. You decide to try the picture of the tiger. Pointing to a thumbnail displays the keywords associated with the picture and information about the picture properties. It also displays a drop-down list bar that accesses the item's shortcut menu.

3 ● **Point to the thumbnail of the tiger.**

Keywords → animals, cats, natures, tigers...
Properties → 145 (w) x 117 (h) pixels, 18 KB, WMF

● **Click** ┆ **to open the shortcut menu.**

Additional Information

The shortcut menu commands are used to work with and manage the items in the Clip Organizer.

● **Choose Insert.**

Another Method

You could also simply click on the graphic to insert it in the document.

● **Click** ☒ **in the task pane title bar to close it.**

Your screen should be similar to Figure 1.56

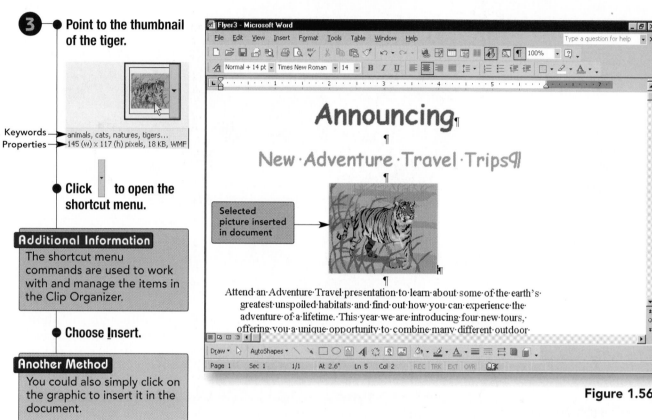

Figure 1.56

The picture is inserted in the document at the insertion point. It is centered because the paragraph formatting in which it was placed is centered. Although you think this graphic looks good, you want to see how a photograph of an elephant you recently received from a client would look instead. The photograph has been saved as a picture image.

● Click 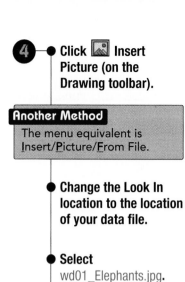 Insert Picture (on the Drawing toolbar).

Another Method
The menu equivalent is Insert/Picture/From File.

● Change the Look In location to the location of your data file.

● Select wd01_Elephants.jpg.

● Click Insert.

Your screen should be similar to Figure 1.57

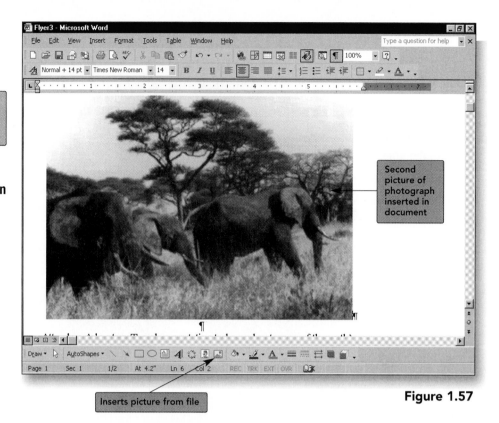

Second picture of photograph inserted in document

Inserts picture from file

Figure 1.57

The elephant picture is inserted below the clip art. Although the photograph looks good, you think the clip art will look better when the flyer is printed.

5 ● Click  Undo.

Your screen should be similar to Figure 1.58

Clicking Undo quickly reverses last action

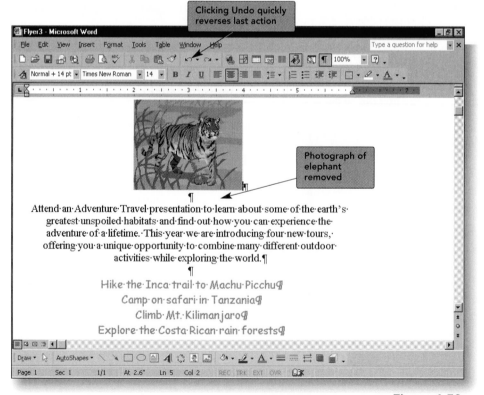

Photograph of elephant removed

Attend·an·Adventure·Travel·presentation·to·learn·about·some·of·the·earth's· greatest·unspoiled·habitats·and·find·out·how·you·can·experience·the· adventure·of·a·lifetime.··This·year·we·are·introducing·four·new·tours,· offering·you·a·unique·opportunity·to·combine·many·different·outdoor· activities·while·exploring·the·world.¶
¶
Hike·the·Inca·trail·to·Machu·Picchu¶
Camp·on·safari·in·Tanzania¶
Climb·Mt.·Kilimanjaro¶
Explore·the·Costa·Rican·rain·forests¶

Figure 1.58

The last action you performed is reversed, and the photograph is removed from the document.

Sizing a Picture

Usually, when a graphic is inserted, its size will need to be adjusted. A graphic object can be manipulated in many ways. You can change its size, add captions, borders, or shading, or move it to another location. A graphic object can be moved anywhere on the page, including in the margins or on top of or below other objects, including text. The only places you cannot place a graphic object are into a footnote, endnote, or caption.

In this case, you want to increase the picture's size. To do this, you must first select the object.

Click on the picture.

Your screen should be similar to Figure 1.59

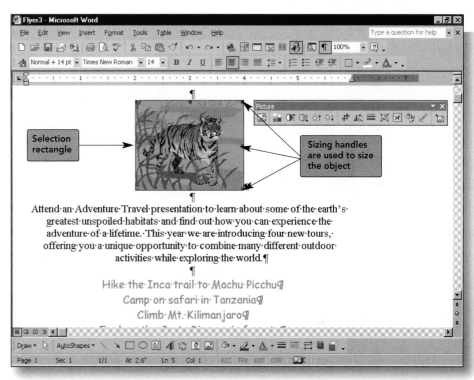

Figure 1.59

The picture is surrounded by a **selection rectangle** and eight boxes, called **sizing handles**, indicating it is a selected object and can now be deleted, sized, moved, or modified. The handles are used to size the object.

The Picture toolbar is also automatically displayed. Its buttons (identified below) are used to modify the selected picture object. Your Picture toolbar may be floating or may be docked along an edge of the window, depending on where it was when last used.

Additional Information

A selected graphic object can be moved by dragging it to the new location and deleted by pressing Delete.

HAVING TROUBLE?

If the Picture toolbar is not displayed, right-click on any toolbar to open the shortcut menu and select Picture, or use View/Toolbars/Picture.

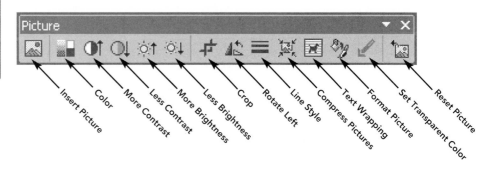

You want to increase the image to approximately 3 inches wide by 3.25 inches high.

2 ● **Point to the lower right corner handle.**

Additional Information

The mouse pointer changes to ↔ when pointing to a handle. The direction of the arrow indicates the direction in which you can drag to size the graphic.

Additional Information

Dragging a corner handle maintains the original proportions of the graphic.

● **With the pointer as a ↖, drag outward from the picture to increase the size to approximately 3 by 3.25 inches (use the ruler as a guide and refer to Figure 1.60).**

Another Method

You can also size a picture to an exact measurement using Format/Picture, and specify a height or width in the Size tab.

● **Click anywhere in the document to deselect the graphic.**

● **Click ¶ Show/Hide.**

● **Click 💾 Save.**

Your screen should be similar to Figure 1.60

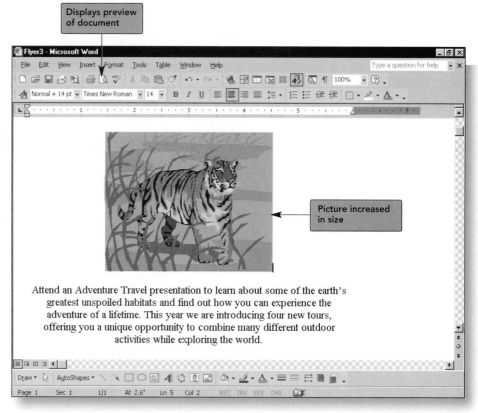

Displays preview of document

Picture increased in size

Attend an Adventure Travel presentation to learn about some of the earth's greatest unspoiled habitats and find out how you can experience the adventure of a lifetime. This year we are introducing four new tours, offering you a unique opportunity to combine many different outdoor activities while exploring the world.

Figure 1.60

Previewing and Printing a Document

Although you still plan to make several formatting changes to the document, you want to give a copy of the flyer to the manager to get feedback regarding the content and layout. To save time and unnecessary printing and paper waste, it is always a good idea to first preview onscreen how your document will appear when printed.

Previewing the Document

Previewing your document before printing it allows you to look over each page and make necessary adjustments before printing it.

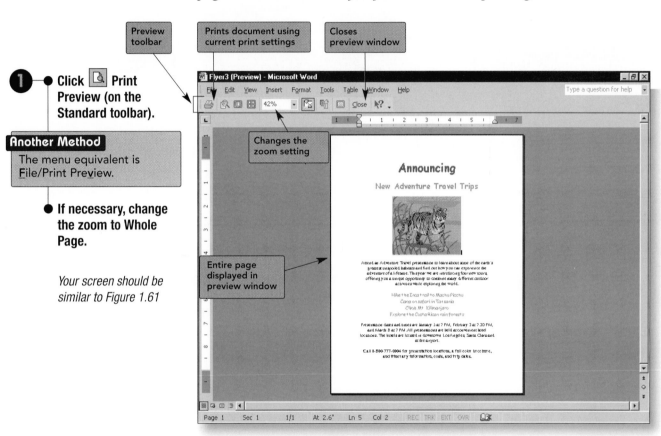

1 ● Click 🔍 **Print Preview (on the Standard toolbar).**

Another Method
The menu equivalent is File/Print Preview.

● **If necessary, change the zoom to Whole Page.**

Your screen should be similar to Figure 1.61

Figure 1.61

The print preview window displays a reduced view of how the current page will appear when printed. This view allows you to check your page layout before printing. The flyer looks good and does not appear to need any further modifications immediately.

The preview window also includes its own toolbar. You can print the letter directly from the preview window using the 🖨 Print button; however, you do not want to send the document directly to the printer just yet. First you need to add your name to the flyer and check the print settings.

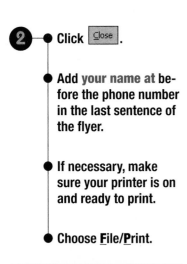

2 ● Click `Close` **.**

● **Add your name at before the phone number in the last sentence of the flyer.**

● **If necessary, make sure your printer is on and ready to print.**

● **Choose File/Print.**

Another Method

The keyboard shortcut for the Print command is `Ctrl` + P. Clicking Print on the Standard toolbar will print the active document immediately using the current print settings.

Your screen should be similar to Figure 1.62

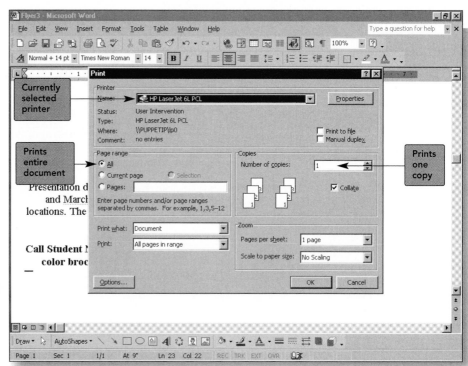

Figure 1.62

Note: Please consult your instructor for printing procedures that may differ from the following directions.

From the Print dialog box, you need to specify the printer you will be using and the document settings. The printer that is currently selected is displayed in the Name drop-down list box in the Printer section of the dialog box.

The Page Range area of the Print dialog box lets you specify how much of the document you want printed. The range options are described in the following table:

Option	Action
All	Prints entire document.
Current page	Prints selected page or page the insertion point is on.
Pages	Prints pages you specify by typing page numbers in the text box.
Selection	Prints selected text only.

The default range setting, All, is the correct setting. In the Copies section, the default setting of one copy of the document is acceptable. You will print using the default print settings.

If you need to change the selected printer to another printer, open the Name drop-down list box and select the appropriate printer (your instructor will tell you which printer to select).

Click **.**

Your printer should be printing out the document. The printed copy of the flyer should be similar to the document shown here.

Announcing

New Adventure Travel Trips

Attend an Adventure Travel presentation to learn about some of the earth's greatest unspoiled habitats and find out how you can experience the adventure of a lifetime. This year we are introducing four new tours, offering you a unique opportunity to combine many different outdoor activities while exploring the world.

Hike the Inca trail to Machu Picchu
Camp on safari in Tanzania
Climb Mt. Kilimanjaro
Explore the Costa Rican rain forests

Presentation dates and times are January 5 at 7 PM, February 3 at 7:30 PM, and March 8 at 7 PM. All presentations are held at convenient hotel locations. The hotels are located in downtown Los Angeles, Santa Clara and at the airport.

Call Student Name at 1-800-777-0004 for presentation locations, a full color brochure, and itinerary information, costs, and trip dates.

Exiting Word

The Exit command in the File menu is used to quit the Word program. Alternatively, you can click the ☒ Close button in the application window title bar. If you attempt to close the application without first saving your document, Word displays a warning asking if you want to save your work. If you do not save your work and you exit the application, all your changes are lost.

Click ☒ Close.

Click  **to save the changes you made to the file.**

The Windows desktop is visible again.

Another Method
The keyboard shortcut for the Exit command is Alt + F4.

concept summary

LAB 1

Creating and Editing a Document

Template (WD1.7)

A template is a document file that includes predefined settings that are used as a pattern to create many common types of documents.

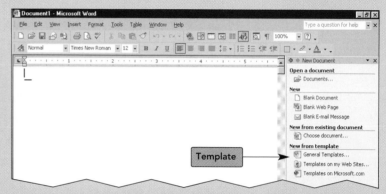

Grammar Checker (WD1.18)

The **grammar checker** advises you of incorrect grammar as you create and edit a document, and proposes possible corrections.

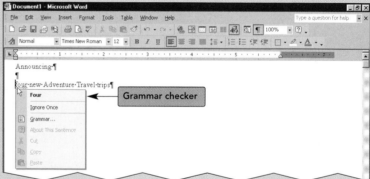

AutoText and AutoComplete (WD1.20)

The **AutoText** feature includes entries, such as commonly used phrases, that can be quickly inserted into a document. As you type the first few characters of an AutoText entry, the **AutoComplete** feature suggests the remainder of the AutoText entry you may want to use.

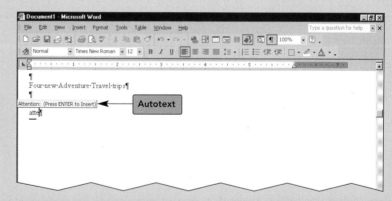

AutoCorrect (WD1.21)

The **AutoCorrect** feature makes some basic assumptions about the text you are typing and, based on these assumptions, automatically corrects the entry.

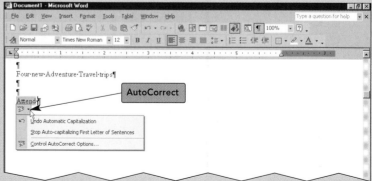

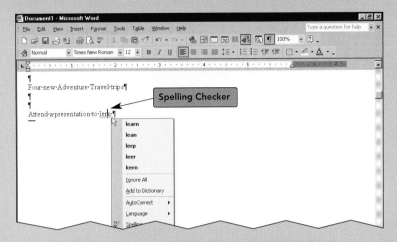

The **spelling checker** advises you of misspelled words as you create and edit a document, and proposes possible corrections.

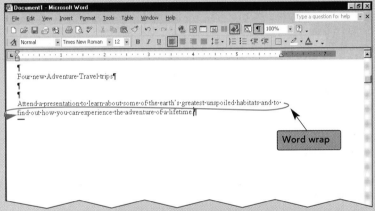

Word Wrap (WD1.26)

The **word wrap** feature automatically decides where to end a line and wrap text to the next line based on the margin settings.

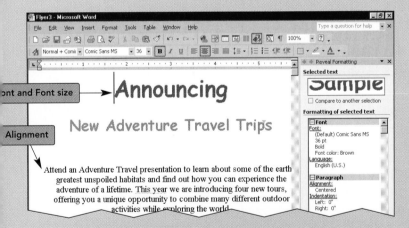

Font and Font Size (WD1.46)

A **font**, also commonly referred to as a typeface, is a set of characters with a specific design that has one or more font sizes.

Alignment (WD1.53)

Alignment is how text is positioned on a line between the margins or indents. There are four types of paragraph alignment: left, centered, right, and justified.

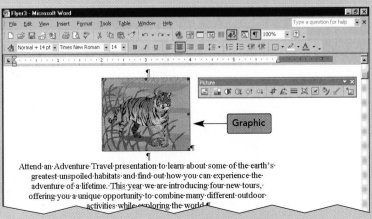

Graphics (WD1.55)

A **graphic** is a non-text element or object, such as a drawing or picture, that can be added to a document.

key terms

alignment WD1.53	format WD1.11	sans serif font WD1.46
AutoComplete WD1.20	formatting mark WD1.13	select WD1.41
AutoCorrect WD1.2	Formatting toolbar WD1.5	selection rectangle WD1.59
AutoText WD1.20	global template WD1.7	serif font WD1.46
character formatting WD1.45	grammar checker WD1.18	sizing handles WD1.59
clip art WD1.55	graphic WD1.55	SmartTag WD1.27
cursor WD1.5	Insert mode WD1.39	source program WD1.55
custom dictionary WD1.23	insertion point WD1.5	spelling checker WD1.23
default WD1.7	main dictionary WD1.23	Standard toolbar WD1.5
drawing object WD1.55	Normal template WD1.7	template WD1.7
Drawing toolbar WD1.6	object WD1.55	thumbnail WD1.57
edit WD1.11	Overtype mode WD1.39	TrueType WD1.47
embedded object WD1.55	paragraph formatting WD1.45	typeface WD1.46
end-of-file marker WD1.5	picture WD1.55	word wrap WD1.26
font WD1.46	points WD1.46	
font size WD1.46	ruler WD1.5	

MOUS skills

The Microsoft Office User Specialist (MOUS) certification program is designed to measure your proficiency in performing basic tasks using the Office 2002 applications. Getting certified demonstrates that you have the skills and provides a valuable industry credential for employment. After completing this lab, you have learned the following Word Microsoft Office User Specialist skills:

Skill	Description	Page
Inserting and	Insert, modify, and move text and symbols	WD1.39
Modifying text	Correct spelling and grammar usage	WD1.23, WD1.18
	Apply and modify text formats	WD1.45
	Apply font and text effects	WD1.45
Creating and Modifying Paragraphs	Modify paragraph formats	WD1.53
Formatting Documents	Preview and print documents	WD1.61
Managing Documents	Save documents using different names and file formats	WD1.28
Working with Graphics	Insert images and graphics	WD1.55

command summary

Command	Shortcut	Key Button	Action
File/New	Ctrl + N	🗋	Opens new document
File/Open	Ctrl + O	📂	Opens existing document file
File/Close	Ctrl + F4	✕	Closes document
File/Save	Ctrl + S	💾	Saves document using same file name
File/Save As			Saves document using a new file name, type, and/or location
File/Print Preview		🔍	Displays document as it will appear when printed
File/Print	Ctrl + P	🖨	Prints document using selected print settings
File/Exit	Alt + F4	✕	Exits Word program
Edit/Undo	Ctrl + Z	↩ ▾	Restores last editing change
Edit/Redo	Ctrl + Y	↪ ▾	Restores last Undo or repeats last command or action
Edit/Select All	Ctrl + A		Selects all text in document
View/Normal		☰	Shows text formatting and simple layout of page
View/Web Layout		▣	Shows document as it will appear when viewed in a Web browser
View/Print Layout		▣	Shows how text and objects will appear on printed page
View/Outline		▤	Shows structure of document
View/Task Pane			Displays or hides task pane
View/Toolbars			Displays or hides selected toolbar
View/Ruler			Displays/hides horizontal ruler bar
View/Zoom/Page width			Fits display of document within right and left margins
Insert/AutoText/AutoText/Show AutoComplete suggestions			Turns on AutoComplete feature
Insert/Picture/Clip Art		🖼	Accesses Clip Organizer and inserts selected clip
Insert/Picture/From File		🖼	Inserts selected picture
Format/Font/Font/Font		Times New Roman ▾	Changes typeface
Format/Font/Font/Font Style/Bold	Ctrl + B	**B**	Makes selected text bold

command summary (continued)

Command	Shortcut	Key Button	Action
Format/Font/Font/Size		`10 ▼`	Changes font size
Format/Font/Font/Color		`A`	Changes text to selected color
Format/Paragraph/Indents and Spacing/Alignment/Center	Ctrl + E	`≡`	Centers text between left and right margins
Format/Paragraph/Indents and Spacing/Alignment/Justified	Ctrl + J	`≣`	Aligns text equally between left and right margins
Format/Paragraph/Indents and Spacing/Alignment/Left	Ctrl + L	`≣`	Aligns text to left margin
Format/Paragraph/Indents and Spacing/Alignment/Right	Ctrl + R	`≣`	Aligns text to right margin
Format/Reveal Formatting			Opens Reveal Formatting task pane
Format/Picture			Change format settings associated with selected picture
Tools/AutoCorrect Options/Show AutoCorrect Options buttons			Displays or hides AutoCorrect option buttons
Tools/Customize/Options/Show Standard and Formatting toolbars			Displays Standard and Formatting toolbars on two rows
Tools/Options/Edit/Overtype Mode	Insert	`OVR`	Switches between Insert and Overtype modes
Tools/Options/View/All	Ctrl + ⇧Shift + *	`¶`	Displays or hides formatting marks

lab exercises

Terminology

screen identification

1. In the following Word screen, letters identify important elements. Enter the correct term for each screen element in the space provided.

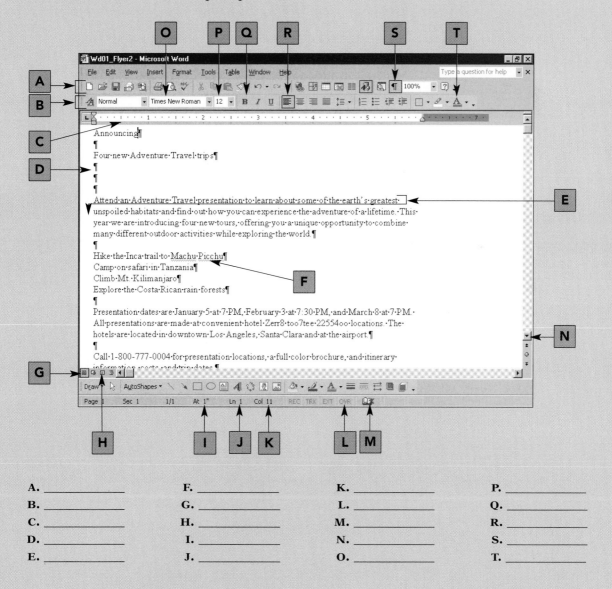

A. _____ F. _____ K. _____ P. _____

B. _____ G. _____ L. _____ Q. _____

C. _____ H. _____ M. _____ R. _____

D. _____ I. _____ N. _____ S. _____

E. _____ J. _____ O. _____ T. _____

lab exercises

matching

Match the item on the left with the correct description on the right.

1. 🔍 _____ **a.** new text writes over existing text

2. template _____ **b.** type style that can be applied to text

3. font _____ **c.** moves to the top of the document

4. OVR _____ **d.** feature that automatically begins a new line when text reaches the right margin

5. alignment _____ **e.** images that enhance a document

6. Ctrl + Home _____ **f.** displays the print preview window

7. graphics _____ **g.** predesigned document that is used as a pattern to create many common types of documents

8. 💾 _____ **h.** font size measurement

9. word wrap _____ **i.** controls paragraph positioning between the margins

10. point _____ **j.** saves a document using the same file name

multiple choice

Circle the correct response to the questions below.

1. Document development follows these steps.
    a. plan, edit, enter, format, preview, and print
    b. enter, edit, format, preview, and print
    c. plan, enter, edit, format, preview, and print
    d. design, enter, edit, format, preview, and print

2. The Word feature that makes some basic assumptions about the text entered and automatically makes changes based on those assumptions is _____.
    a. AutoChange
    b. AutoCorrect
    c. AutoText
    d. AutoFormat

3. Words that are not contained in the main dictionary can be added to the _____ dictionary.
    a. custom
    b. additional
    c. add to
    d. user defined

4. The feature that allows you to preview a document before it is printed is _____.
    a. print review
    b. page review
    c. page preview
    d. print preview

5. When text is evenly aligned on both margins it is _____.
  a. center aligned
  b. justified
  c. left aligned
  d. right aligned

6. Words that may be spelled incorrectly in a document are indicated by a _____.
  a. green wavy line
  b. red wavy line
  c. blue wavy line
  d. purple dotted underline

7. Font sizes are measured in _____.
  a. inches
  b. points
  c. bits
  d. pieces

8. A _____ is a document file that includes predefined settings that can be used as a pattern to create many common types of documents.
  a. template
  b. predesign
  c. design document
  d. format document

9. The _____ feature automatically decides where to end a line and where the next line of text begins based on the margin settings.
  a. line wrap
  b. word wrap
  c. wrap around
  d. end wrap

10. A set of characters with a specific design is called a(n) _____.
  a. style
  b. font
  c. AutoFormat
  d. design

true/false

Check the correct answer to the following questions.

1.	A wavy red line indicates a potential grammar error.	True	False
2.	A template is a predesigned document.	True	False
3.	The first three steps in developing a document are: plan, enter, and edit.	True	False
4.	Text can be entered in a document in either the Insert or Overtype mode.	True	False
5.	The Delete key erases the character to the right of the insertion point.	True	False
6.	The automatic word wrap feature checks for typing errors.	True	False
7.	The Word document file name extension is .wrd.	True	False
8.	Font sizes are measured in inches.	True	False
9.	Word inserts hidden marks into a document to control the display of text.	True	False
10.	The AutoCorrect feature automatically identifies and corrects certain types of errors.	True	False

lab exercises

Concepts

fill-in

1. A small blue box appearing under a word or character indicates that the
   _____ feature was applied.

2. If a word is underlined with purple dots, this indicates a(n) _____.

3. The _____ feature displays each page of your document in a reduced size so you can see the page layout.

4. To size a graphic evenly, click and drag the _____ in one corner of the graphic.

5. It is good practice to use only _____ types of fonts in a document.

6. When you use _____, new text replaces existing text as you type.

7. The _____ sits on the right side of the window and contains buttons and icons to help you perform common tasks, such as opening a blank document.

8. Use _____ when you want to keep your existing document with the original name and make a copy with a new name.

9. The _____ window displays a reduced view of how the current page will appear when printed.

10. The _____ feature includes entries, such as commonly used phrases, that can be quickly inserted into a document.

discussion questions

1. Discuss several uses you may have for a word processor. Then explain the steps you would follow to create a document.

2. Discuss how the AutoCorrect and Spelling and Grammar Checker features help you as you type. What types of corrections does the AutoCorrect feature make?

3. Discuss how word wrap works. What happens when text is added? What happens when text is removed?

4. Discuss three ways you can select text. Discuss when it would be appropriate to use the different methods.

5. Describe how the Undo and Redo features work. What are some advantages of these features?

6. Discuss how graphics can be used in a document. What should you consider when adding graphics to a document? Can the use of a graphic change the reader's response to a document?

Hands-On Exercises

step-by-step

Writing a Memo

★ 1. Universal Industries is starting a casual Friday policy. Ms. Jones, the Vice President of Human Resources, has sent a memo informing employees of this new policy. Your completed memo is shown here.

    a. Open a blank Word document and create the memo with the following text. Press Tab↹ twice after you type colons (:) in the To, From, and Date lines. This will make the information following the colons line up evenly. Enter a blank line between paragraphs.

To: [Your Name]
From: Ms. Jones
Date: [Current date]
RE: Business Casual Dress Code

Effective next Friday, business casual will be allowed in the corporate facility on Fridays and the day before a holiday break. Business casual is sometimes difficult to interpret. For men, it is a collared shirt and tailored trousers. For women, it is a pantsuit or tailored trousers or skirt. Business casual is not jeans, t-shirts, or exercise clothes. A detailed dress code will be available on the company Intranet.

Thank you for your cooperation in this matter.

CSJ/xxx

To: Student Name
From: Ms. Jones
Date: February 17, 2002
RE: Business Casual Dress Code

Effective next Friday, business casual will be allowed in the corporate facility on Fridays and the day before a holiday break. Business casual is sometimes difficult to interpret. For men, it is a collared shirt and tailored trousers. For women, it is a pantsuit or tailored trousers or skirt. Business casual is not jeans, t-shirts, or exercise clothes. A detailed dress code will be available on the company Intranet.

Thank you for your cooperation in this matter.

CSJ/xxx

    b. Correct any spelling and grammar errors that are identified.
    c. Change the font size for the entire memo to 14 pt.
    d. Change the alignment of the memo body to justified.
    e. Insert a blank line under the Date line and insert the AutoText reference line "RE:".
    f. Press Tab↹ twice and type **Business Casual Dress Code**.
    g. Save the document as Dress Code on your data disk.
    h. Preview and print the document.

Writing a Short Article

★ ★ **2.** You work for a health organization that produces a newsletter for patients. The upcoming issue will focus on the effects of stress and how to handle stress. You have located information about the top stresses and want to include this information in a short article. Your completed article is shown here.

a. Enter the following information in a new Word document, pressing ⏎Enter where indicated.

Top Stresses ⏎Enter (3 times)

The National Study of Daily Experiences has found over 50 different types of stress. However, 60 percent of all stresses people experience are from the top stresses listed below. ⏎Enter (2 times)

Arguments or tense moments ⏎Enter

Disagreement on how something gets done at work ⏎Enter

Concern over physical health of others ⏎Enter

Work overload and demands ⏎Enter

Worry about others' problems ⏎Enter

Financial issues ⏎Enter

Disciplining children ⏎Enter

Family disagreements ⏎Enter

Late for or miss an appointment ⏎Enter

Value differences ⏎Enter

Home overload and demands ⏎Enter

Household, car repairs ⏎Enter

Tension over chores ⏎Enter

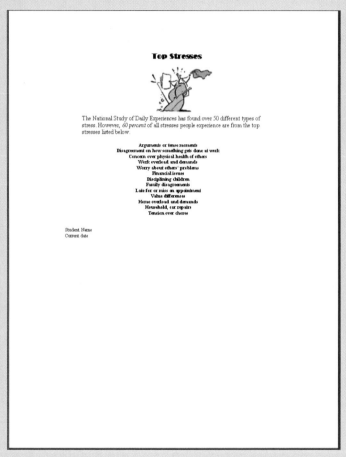

b. Correct any spelling or grammar errors. Save the document as Top Stresses.
c. Turn on the display of formatting marks. Remove any blank spaces at the end of short lines. *Hint:* Use Show/Hide Formatting marks.
d. Change the title font to Broadway (or a font of your choice), 16 pt.
e. Center the title.
f. Center and bold the list of stresses.
g. Add italics and bold to the text "60 percent."
h. Insert the clip art named wd01_Stress from your data file below the title. Size it appropriately and center it below the title.
i. Add your name and the current date on separate lines several lines below the list. Left-align both lines.
j. Preview, then print the document.
k. Save the document again.

Creating a Sales Promotion Flyer

★★ **3.** You are owner of Executive Style, a new clothing boutique that specializes in career wear for men
★ and women. In preparation for an upcoming sale, you want to create a flyer that you can give
customers and also post in the window of other local businesses. Your completed flyer is shown
here.

a. Open a new Word document and enter
the following text, pressing ⎵Enter
where indicated.

Celebrate their birthdays with style ⎵Enter
(2 times)

PRESIDENT'S DAY STOREWIDE SALE ⎵Enter
(4 times)

Starting Wednesday, February 14, we will be
taking an additional 20% off all regularly priced
spring fashion merchandise. Plus take an extra
25% off our entire stock of all fall and winter
clearance fashions for a total savings of 40-60%.
This sale ends Monday, February 19, so hurry in
for the best selection. ⎵Enter (3 times)

Executive Style ⎵Enter (3 times)

2314 Telegraph Avenue ⎵Enter

Store Hours: Monday - Saturday 10 a.m. - 9 p.m.
and Sunday 12 p.m. to 5:30 p.m. ⎵Enter

b. Correct any spelling and grammar errors that are identified.

c. Save the document as Executive Style.

d. Turn on the display of formatting
marks. Center the entire document.

e. Change the first line to a font color of
red, font type of Copperplate Gothic
Light or a font of your choice, and size
of 24 pt.

f. Change the second line to a font color of blue, font type of Copperplate Gothic Bold or a font
of your choice, and size of 36 pt.

g. Increase the font size of the paragraph to 16 points.

h. Bold the store name "Executive Style" and change the font color to red and the font size to 24
points.

i. Insert the pictures named wd01_Executive1 and wd01_Executive2 (from your data files) side by side
on the middle blank line below the second title line.

j. Resize the graphics to be approximately 2 by 3 inches (they should be the same size) using the
ruler as a guide.

k. Add your name and the current date, left-aligned, on separate lines two lines below the last
line. Turn off the display of formatting marks.

l. Preview the document. If necessary, reduce the size of the pictures so the entire flyer fits on
one page. Save and print the flyer.

Creating an Advertisement

★ ★ ★ **4.** You own a bed and breakfast inn in the Pocono Mountains. You are going to advertise the B&B in a local travel guide. Your completed advertisement is shown here.

a. Open a blank Word document and type the following information to create the first draft of the ad.

Pocono Mountain Retreat
124 Mountain Laurel Trail
Pocono Manor, PA 18349

Phone: 1-717-839-5555
Host: [Your Name]

Number of rooms: 4
Number of private baths: 1
Maximum number sharing baths: 4
Double rate for shared bath: $85.00
Double rate for private bath: $95.00
Single rate for shared bath: $65.00
Single rate for private bath: $75.00
Open: All year
Breakfast: Continental
Children: Welcome, over 12

Located in the heart of the Poconos is this rustic country inn where you can choose to indulge yourself in the quiet beauty of the immediate surroundings or take advantage of the numerous activities at nearby resorts, lakes, and parks.

In the winter shuttle buses will transport you to the Jack Frost and Big Boulder ski resorts. We have trails for cross-country skiing right on the property. In the summer you can be whisked away to beautiful Lake Wallenpaupack for swimming and boating. The fall foliage is beyond compare. You can hike our nature trails and take in the breathtaking scenery at any time of year.

In the evenings you can relax in front of a cozy fire or take advantage of the Pocono nightlife. The choice is yours!

Be sure to call well in advance for reservations during the winter and summer months.

Pocono Mountain Retreat
124 Mountain Laurel Trail
Pocono Manor, PA 18349

Phone: 1-717-839-5555
Host: [Your Name]

Number of Rooms: 4
Number of private baths: 1
Maximum number sharing baths: 4
Double rate for shared bath: $85.00
Double rate for private bath: $95.00
Single rate for shared bath: $65.00
Single rate for private bath: $75.00
Open: All year
Breakfast: Continental
Pets: No
Children: Welcome, over 12

Located in the heart of the Poconos is this rustic country inn where you can choose to indulge yourself in the quiet beauty of the immediate surroundings or take advantage of the numerous activities at nearby resorts, lakes, and parks.

In the winter, shuttle buses will transport you to the Jack Frost and Big Boulder ski resorts. We have trails for cross-country skiing right on the property. In the summer you can be whisked away to beautiful Lake Wallenpaupack for swimming and boating. The fall foliage is beyond compare, and you can hike our nature trails and take in the breathtaking scenery at any time of year.

In the evenings, you can relax in front of a cozy fire take advantage of Pocono nightlife. The choice is yours!

Be sure to call well in advance for reservations during the winter and summer months.

b. Correct any spelling and grammar errors that are identified. Ignore the spellings of proper names.

c. Save the document as B&B Ad.

d. Bold and center the first three lines. Change the font to Comic Sans MS (or a font of your choice), 16 pt. Add color of your choice to the three lines.

e. Bold and center the phone number and host lines.

f. Insert the text **Pets: No** above Children: Welcome, over 12.

g. Center the list of features.

h. Change the font size of the four paragraphs to 11 pt and change the alignment to justified.

i. Insert the clip art named wd01_Sunshine (from your data files) above the phone number. Size it appropriately and center it.

j. Save the document again. Preview and print the document.

Writing an Article for the Campus Newspaper

★★ **5.** Each month the campus newspaper runs a column on cooking. This month's article is about
★   making sushi. You started the column a few days ago and just need to continue the article by
adding instructions about making California rolls. Your completed article is shown here.

a. Open the file file named wd01_Making
Sushi and enter the following text at the
end of the document. Include one blank
line above and below the title and above
the Ingredients and Directions headings.

Making California Rolls

California rolls are a great way to introduce
sushi to the novice, as there is no raw fish in
the roll. This recipe calls for imitation crabmeat, but if your budget can handle the cost,
use real crabmeat.

Ingredients:
Nori seaweed
Prepared sushi rice
Avocado, peeled and cut into sixteenths
Imitation crabmeat
Cucumber, peeled, seeded, and julienned

Directions:
Cut one sheet of Nori seaweed in half and
place on a bamboo mat. With a wooden
spoon, spread a thin layer of sushi rice on
the seaweed leaving a strip uncovered at
each end to seal the roll. At one end, add two
strips of cucumber, one slice of avocado, and
one piece of imitation crabmeat. Beginning
at the end with the cucumber, avocado, and crabmeat, roll the seaweed over once. Pull up the bamboo
mat and use it to help you roll the rest of the way until you reach the other end of the seaweed wrap.
Place the roll seam side down and with a sharp knife, cut the roll into 1/4 or 1/2-inch wide slices.

Making Sushi

Your next dinner party can be a big success when you get everyone
involved in making sushi. You need just a few basic items for the
preparation. If you live in a large city, you may find these at your local
grocery store. Your best bet is to find an Asian grocery in your city.

Sushi Basics:
A bamboo-rolling mat (Makisu)
Cutting board
Sharp knife
Wasabi
Pickled ginger
Soy sauce

Making California Rolls

California rolls are a great way to introduce sushi to the novice, as there
is no raw fish in the roll. This recipe calls for imitation crabmeat, but if
your budget can handle the cost, use real crabmeat.

Ingredients:
Nori seaweed
Prepared sushi rice
Avocado, peeled and cut into sixteenths
Imitation crabmeat
Cucumber, peeled, seeded, and julienned

Directions:
Cut one sheet of Nori seaweed in half and place on a bamboo mat. With a wooden spoon,
spread a thin layer of sushi rice on the seaweed leaving a strip uncovered at each end to
seal the roll. At one end, add two strips of cucumber, one slice of avocado, and one piece
of imitation crabmeat. Beginning at the end with the cucumber, avocado, and crabmeat,
roll the seaweed over once. Pull up the bamboo mat and use it to help you roll the rest of
the way until you reach the other end of the seaweed wrap. Place the roll seam side down
and with a sharp knife, cut the roll into ¼ or ½-inch wide rolls.

Student Name - Current Date

b. Correct any spelling and grammar errors. Save the document as Making Sushi2.
c. Center the main title, "Making Sushi." Change the font to Impact with a point size of 24.
d. Center the subtitle "Making California Rolls." Change the font to Impact with a point size of
18.
e. Add a color of your choice to the title and subtitle.
f. Bold and increase to 14 pt the type size of the introductory sentences in each section.
g. Bold the words "Sushi Basics" and the colon that follows them.
h. Bold the word "Ingredients" and the colon that follows it.
i. Bold the word "Directions" and the colon that follows it.
j. Insert the pictue wd01_Sushi (from your data files) below the main title of the article.
k. Size the picture to be 2 inches wide (use the ruler as a guide). Center it below the title.
l. Add your name and the current date two lines below the last line.
m. Save the document again. Preview and print the document.

Writing a Career Report

★ **1.** Locate an article in the newspaper or magazine about careers and/or employment. Summarize the article in a few paragraphs. Add a title to the document and your name and the current date below the title. Center the title lines. Justify the paragraphs. Below the summary, include a reference to the source you used. Save the document as Career Report.

Creating a Family Reunion Invitation

★★ **2.** You are in charge of designing an invitation for an upcoming family reunion. The reunion will be held on July 26, 2002, at the Grand Hotel in Las Vegas. Design an invitation that includes all the information your relatives need to know to attend the event, including location, time, and family contacts. Be sure to use at least two colors of text, two sizes of text, two blank lines, and two kinds of paragraph alignment within your invitation. Include a graphic of your choice from the Clip Organizer. Save the document as Reunion.

Writing a Computer Lab Rules Memo

★★ **3.** Using Hands-On Exercise 1 as a model, create a memo from yourself to the rest of your class that explains the five most important rules to follow while working in the computer lab. Use a piece of clip art to liven up your memo. Format the document in the Arial typeface, 16 pt. Use different font colors for each rule. Save the document as Lab Rules.

Creating a Lost Animal Flyer

★★★ **4.** You agreed to baby-sit your best friend's pet monkey, Pom-Pom. Everything was going well until Pom-Pom ran away. Write and design a poster to place around your neighborhood and attract as much attention as possible. You want to make sure people will contact you with any information they may have about Pom-Pom. Insert a suitable graphic from the Clip Organizer to accent your poster. Size the graphic appropriately. Save the document as Pom-Pom.

Creating a Cruise Flyer

★★★ **5.** Adventure Travel Tours is offering a great deal on a cruise to Spain, Italy, and Greece. Using the features of Word 2002 you have learned so far, create a flyer that will advertise this tour. Search the Web to locate information about places in the tour countries and to obtain graphics you may want to include in the flyer. Right-click on the images you located and use the Save Image As command to download and save them. Insert them into the flyer using the Insert/Picture/From File command. Size and position them appropriately. Save the document as Cruise Flyer.

Improving Your Writing Skills

Word processors, when used skillfully, can help you improve the quality of your writing. Because word processors make it easy to make corrections and change what you type, they allow you to concentrate on expressing your ideas. However, you still need to decide how you want your ideas organized. The Web offers lots of information on how to improve your writing skills. Locate information about this topic, and create a list of ten tips that you think will be helpful when creating and editing documents. Save the document as Writing Tips.

Revising and Refining a Document

LAB **2**

objectives

After completing this lab, you will know how to:

1.	Use the Spelling and Grammar tool and the Thesaurus.
2.	Move, cut, and copy text and formats.
3.	Work with multiple documents.
4.	Control document paging.
5.	Find and replace text.
6.	Insert the current date.
7.	Change margins, line spacing, and indents.
8.	Create a tabbed table and an itemized list.
9.	Add color highlighting and underlines to text.
10.	Create and remove a hyperlink.
11.	Add AutoText and Autoshapes.
12.	Edit in Print Preview.

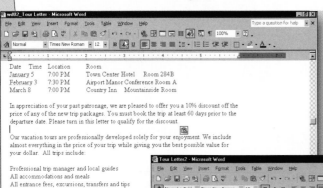

Features such as the Spelling Checker, Thesaurus, Move and Copy, and Find and Replace make it easy to revise and refine your documents.

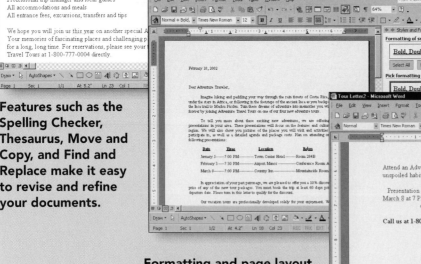

Formatting and page layout changes such as margin adjustments, indented paragraphs, and tabbed tables help improve the readability and style of the document.

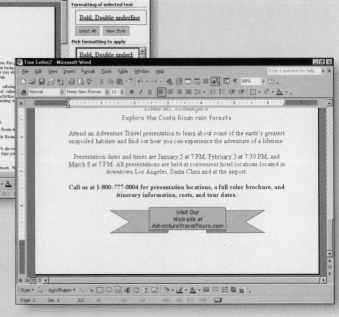

Graphic enhancements such as AutoShapes and additional color add interest to a document.

Adventure Travel Tours

After creating the rough draft of the trip announcement flyer, you showed the printed copy to your manager at Adventure Travel Tours. Your manager then made several suggestions for improving the flyer's style and appearance. In addition, you decided to write a letter to be sent to past clients along with your flyer. The letter briefly describes Adventure Travel's four new tours and invites clients to attend an informational presentation. Your manager likes the idea, but also wants the letter to include information about the new Adventure Travel Web site and a 10 percent discount for early booking.

© Corbis

In this lab, you will learn more about editing documents so you can reorganize and refine both your flyer and a rough draft of the letter to clients. You will also learn to use many more of the formatting features included in Word 2002 so you can add style and interest to your documents.

Formatting features can greatly improve the appearance and design of any document you produce, so that it communicates its message more clearly. The completed letter and revised flyer are shown here.

1

2

3

4

5

6

7

8

The following concepts will be introduced in this lab:

1	**Thesaurus** Word's Thesaurus is a reference tool that provides synonyms, antonyms, and related words for a selected word or phrase.
2	**Move and Copy** Text and graphic selections can be moved or copied to new locations in a document or between documents, saving you time by not having to retype the same information.
3	**Page Break** A page break marks the point at which one page ends and another begins. There are two types of page breaks that can be used in a document: soft page breaks and hard page breaks.
4	**Find and Replace** To make editing easier, you can use the Find and Replace feature to find text in a document and replace it with other text as directed.
5	**Field** A field is a placeholder that instructs Word to insert information into a document.
6	**Page Margin** The page margin is the blank space around the edge of the page. Standard single-sided documents have four margins: top, bottom, left, and right.
7	**Indents** To help your reader find information quickly, you can indent paragraphs from the margins. Indenting paragraphs sets them off from the rest of the document.
8	**Bulleted and Numbered Lists** Whenever possible, use bulleted or numbered lists to organize information and make your writing clear and easy to read.

Revising a Document

After speaking with the manager about the letter's content, you planned the basic topics that need to be included in the letter: to advertise the new tours, invite clients to the presentations, describe the early-booking discount, and promote the new Web site. You quickly entered the text for the letter, saved it as Tour Letter, and printed out a hard copy. As you are reading the document again, you mark up the printout with the changes and corrections you want to make. The marked up copy is shown here.

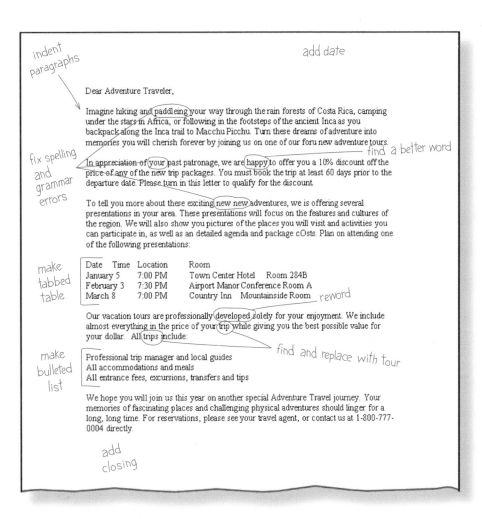

Spell-Checking the Entire Document

The first correction you want to make is to clean up the spelling and grammar errors that Word has identified.

1 ● **Start Word and open the file** wd02_Tour Letter.

● **If necessary, switch to Normal view with a zoom of 100%.**

Your screen should be similar to Figure 2.1

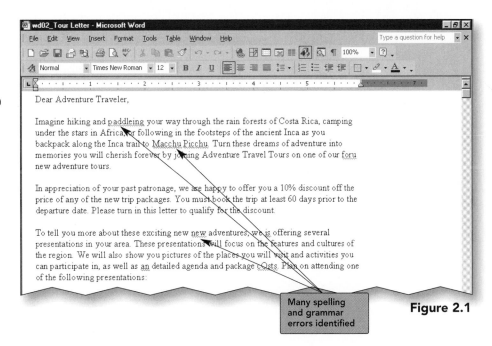

Figure 2.1

To correct the misspelled words and grammatical errors, you can use the shortcut menu to correct each individual word or error, as you learned in Lab 1. However, in many cases you may find it more efficient to wait until you are finished writing before you correct errors. Rather than continually breaking your train of thought to correct errors as you type, you can manually turn on the spelling and grammar checker to locate and correct all the errors in the document at once.

● Click 🧐 Spelling and Grammar.

Another Method

The menu equivalent is Tools/Spelling and Grammar and the keyboard shortcut is F7.

● If necessary, select the Check grammar option to turn on grammar checking.

Your screen should be similar to Figure 2.2

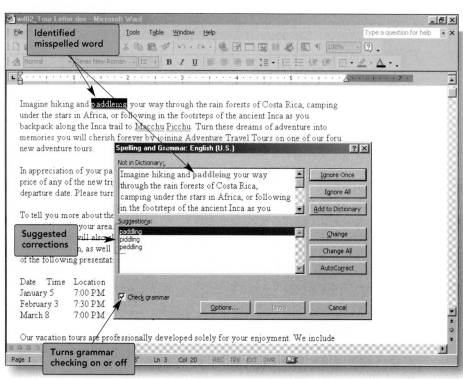

Figure 2.2

Additional Information

You can also double-click the Spelling and Grammar status icon 📖 to move to the next spelling or grammar error and open the spelling shortcut menu.

The Spelling and Grammar dialog box is displayed, and the spelling and grammar checker has immediately located the first word that may be misspelled, "paddleing." The sentence with the misspelled word in red is displayed in the Not in Dictionary text box, and the word is highlighted in the document.

The Suggestions list box displays the words the spelling checker has located in the dictionary that most closely match the misspelled word. The first word is highlighted. Sometimes the spelling checker does not display any suggested replacements. This occurs when it cannot locate any words in the dictionaries that are similar in spelling. If there are no suggestions, the Not in Dictionary text box simply displays the word that is highlighted in the text.

Additional Information

The [Change All] option replaces the same word throughout the document with the word you select in the Suggestions box.

To change the spelling of the word to one of the suggested spellings, highlight the correct word in the list and then choose [Change]. If there were no suggested replacements, and you did not want to use any of the option buttons, you could edit the word yourself by typing the correction in the Not in Dictionary box. In this case, the correct replacement, "paddling" is already highlighted.

Another Method

You can also press [←Enter] or double-click on the correctly spelled word in the Suggestions list to both select and change it.

Your screen should be similar to Figure 2.3

Additional Information

On your own computer system, you would want to add words to the custom dictionary that you use frequently and that are not included in the standard dictionary, so they will be accepted when typed correctly and offered as a suggested replacement when not.

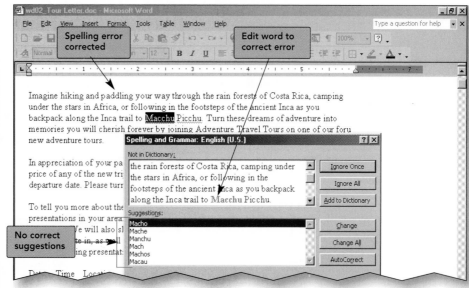

Figure 2.3

The spelling checker replaces the misspelled word with the selected suggested replacement and moves on to locate the next error. This time the error is the name of the Inca ruins at Machu Picchu. The word "Macchu" is spelled incorrectly; there is no correct suggestion, however, because the word is not found in the dictionary. You will correct the spelling of the word by editing it in the Not in Dictionary text box.

4 ● Change the spelling of the word to **Machu** in the Not in Dictionary box.

● Click [Change].

Your screen should be similar to Figure 2.4

Additional Information

You can also edit words directly in the document and then click [Resume] to continue using the spelling and grammar checker.

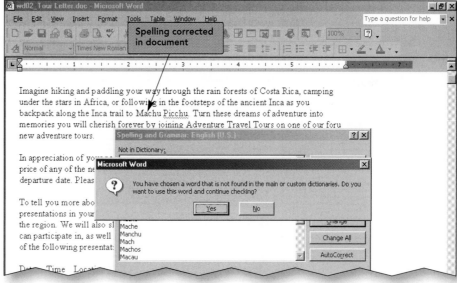

Figure 2.4

Word displays a question dialog box advising you that the correction to the word is not found in its dictionaries, and asking you to confirm that you want to continue.

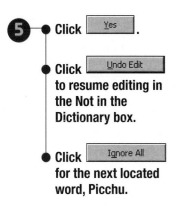

⑤ ● Click [Yes] .

● Click [Undo Edit] to resume editing in the Not in the Dictionary box.

● Click [Ignore All] for the next located word, Picchu.

Your screen should be similar to Figure 2.5

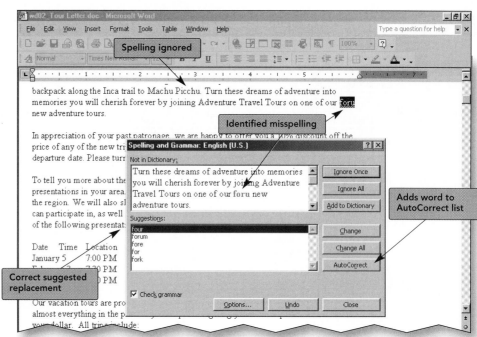

Figure 2.5

Additional Information

The [Ignore Once] option accepts the word as correct for this occurrence only.

The spelling of the word "Picchu" is ignored, and the word is no longer identified as misspelled.

The next located error, "foru," is a typing error that you make frequently when typing the word four. The correct spelling is selected in the Suggestions list box. You want to change it to the suggested word and add it to the list of words that are automatically corrected.

⑥ ● Click [AutoCorrect] .

HAVING TROUBLE?

If a dialog box appears telling you an AutoCorrect entry already exists for this word, simply click [Yes] to continue.

Your screen should be similar to Figure 2.6

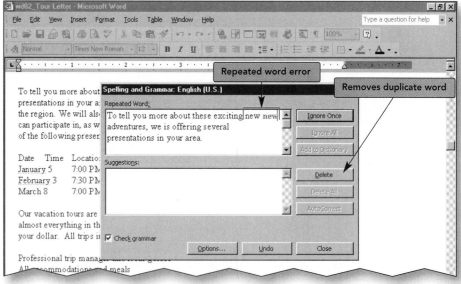

Figure 2.6

The word is corrected in the document. Because you also added it to the AutoCorrect list, in the future whenever you type this word incorrectly as "foru," it will automatically be changed to "four." The next located error identifies the duplicate words "new."

The next four errors that will be identified and their cause are shown in the following table

Identified Error	Cause	Action	Result
new	Repeated word	Delete	Duplicate word "new" is deleted
we is	Subject-verb disagreement	Change	we are
cOsts	Inconsistent capitalization	Change	costs
an detailed	Grammatical error	Change	a

7 ● Click [Delete] to delete the repeated word "new."

● Continue to respond to the Spelling and Grammar checker by clicking [Change] for the next three identified errors.

● Click [OK] in response to the message telling you that the spelling and grammar check is complete.

● Move to the top of the document and save the revised document as Tour Letter2 to the appropriate data file location.

Your screen should be similar to Figure 2.7

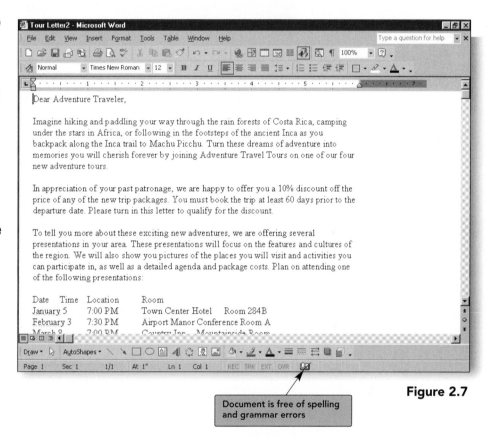

Document is free of spelling and grammar errors

Figure 2.7

Using the Thesaurus

The next text change you want to make is to find a better word for "happy" in the sentence about the 10 percent discount. To help find a similar word, you will use the thesaurus tool.

concept 1

Thesaurus

1 The **thesaurus** is a reference tool that provides synonyms, antonyms, and related words for a selected word or phrase. **Synonyms** are words with a similar meaning, such as "cheerful" and "happy." **Antonyms** are words with an opposite meaning, such as "cheerful" and "sad." Related words are words that are variations of the same word, such as "cheerful" and "cheer." The Thesaurus can help to liven up your documents by adding interest and variety to your text.

To identify the word you want looked up and to use the thesaurus,

1 ● **Move to anywhere in the word "happy" (first sentence, second paragraph).**

● **Choose Tools/Language/Thesaurus.**

Another Method
The keyboard shortcut is ⇧Shift + F7. You can also choose Synonyms from the shortcut menu and select a word from the list.

Your screen should be similar to Figure 2.8

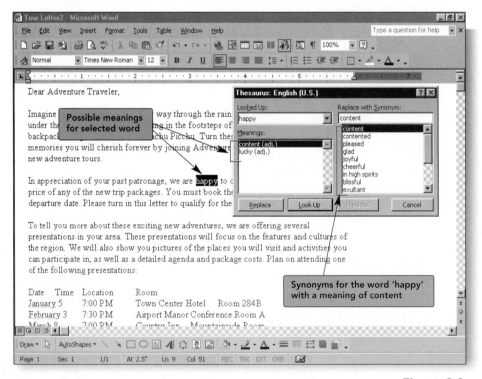

Figure 2.8

The Thesaurus dialog box displays a list of possible meanings for the selected word. From this list you can select the most appropriate meaning for the word. The currently selected meaning, "content," is appropriate for this sentence. The words in the Replace with Synonym box are synonyms for the word "happy" with a meaning of "content." The best choice from this list is "pleased."

Select "pleased."

Click Replace .

Your screen should be similar to Figure 2.9

Additional Information

If a synonym, antonym, or related word is not found, the thesaurus displays an alphabetical list of entries that are similar in spelling to the selected word.

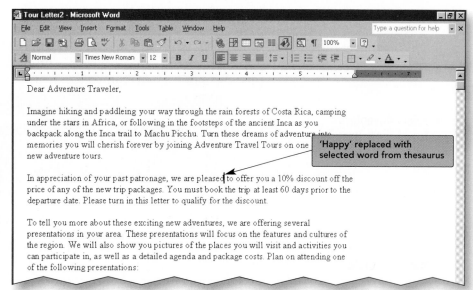

Figure 2.9

Word replaces the word "happy" with the word you selected from the thesaurus.

Moving and Copying Selections

After looking over the letter, you decide to add the company name in several other locations and to change the order of paragraphs. To quickly make these changes, you can move and copy selections.

---

concept 2

Move and Copy

2 Text and graphic selections can be moved or copied to new locations in a document or between documents, saving you time by not having to recreate the same information. A selection that is moved is cut from its original location, called the **source**, and inserted at a new location, called the **destination**. A selection that is copied leaves the original in the source and inserts a duplicate at the destination.

When a selection is cut or copied, the selection is stored in the system Clipboard, a temporary Windows storage area in memory. It is also stored in the Office Clipboard. The system Clipboard holds only the last cut or copied item, whereas the Office Clipboard can store up to 24 items that have been cut or copied. This allows you to insert multiple items from various Office documents and paste all or part of the collection of items into another document.

Using Copy

You want to include the company name in the last paragraph of the letter in two places. Since the name is already entered in the first paragraph, instead of typing the name again, you will copy it.

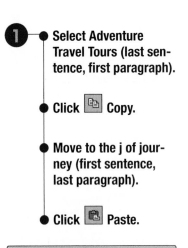

1 ● **Select Adventure Travel Tours (last sentence, first paragraph).**

● **Click** 📋 **Copy.**

● **Move to the j of journey (first sentence, last paragraph).**

● **Click** 📋 **Paste.**

Another Method

The menu equivalent to copy is **E**dit/**C**opy and the keyboard shortcut is Ctrl + C. The menu equivalent to paste is **E**dit/**P**aste and the keyboard shortcut is Ctrl + V.

Your screen should be similar to Figure 2.10

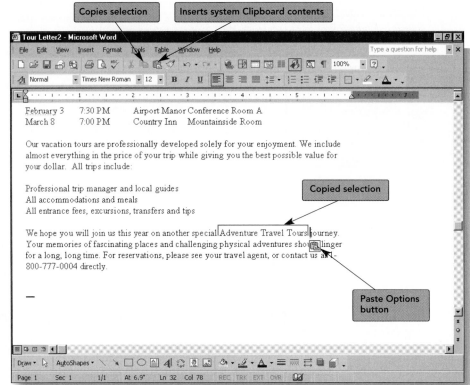

Figure 2.10

The copied selection is inserted at the location you specified. The 📋 Paste Options button appears automatically whenever a selection is pasted. It is used to control the format of the pasted item.

2 ● **Click the** 📋 **Paste Options button.**

Your screen should be similar to Figure 2.11

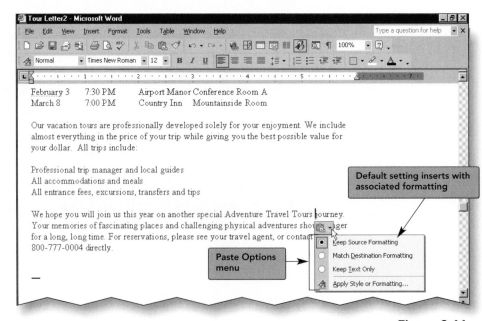

Figure 2.11

The options are used to specify whether to insert the item with the same formatting as it had in the source, to change it to the formatting of the surrounding destination text, or to insert text only (from a selection that is a combination of text and graphics). You can also apply new formatting to the selection. The default, to use the formatting from the source, is appropriate. Next, you want to insert the company name in place of the word "us" in the last sentence of the letter.

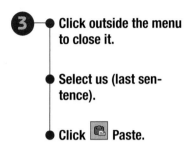

- Click outside the menu to close it.

- Select us (last sentence).

- Click ⬚ Paste.

Your screen should be similar to Figure 2.12

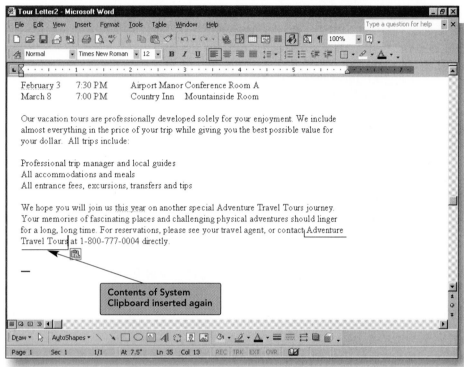

Figure 2.12

The selected text was deleted and replaced with the contents of the system Clipboard. The system Clipboard contents remain in the Clipboard until another item is copied or cut, allowing you to paste the same item multiple times.

Using Cut and Paste

You want the paragraph about the 10 percent discount (second paragraph) to follow the list of presentation dates. To do this, you will move the paragraph from its current location to the new location. The Cut and Paste commands on the Edit menu are used to move selections. You will use the shortcut menu to select the Cut command.

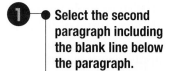

1 ● **Select the second paragraph including the blank line below the paragraph.**

HAVING TROUBLE?
Drag in the space to the left of the paragraph to select it.

● **Right-click on the selection or press ⇧Shift + F10 to display the shortcut menu.**

Another Method
The Cut shortcuts are ✄ or Ctrl + X.

● **Choose Cu*t*.**

Your screen should be similar to Figure 2.13

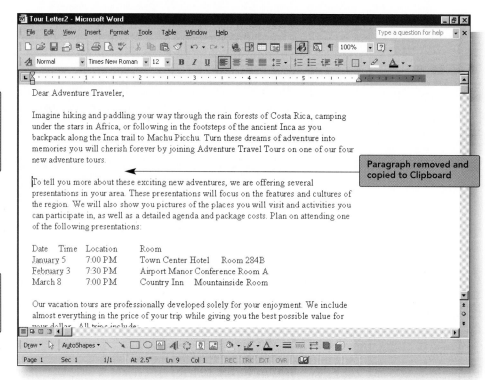

Figure 2.13

The selected paragraph is removed from the source and copied to the Clipboard. Next you need to move the insertion point to the location where the text will be inserted and paste the text into the document from the Clipboard.

2 ● **Move to the "O" in "Our" (at the beginning of the paragraph below list of presentation dates).**

● **Click 📋 Paste.**

Another Method
You can also choose Paste from the shortcut menu.

● **If necessary, scroll down to view the pasted paragraph.**

Your screen should be similar to Figure 2.14

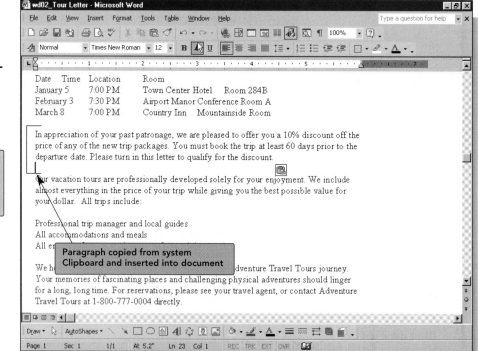

Figure 2.14

The deleted paragraph is reentered into the document at the insertion point location. That was a lot quicker than retyping the whole paragraph!

Using Drag and Drop

Additional Information

You can also use drag and drop to copy a selection by holding down [Ctrl] while dragging. The mouse pointer shape is ⚞.

Finally, you also decide to move the word "directly" in the last paragraph so that the sentence reads ". . . contact Adventure Travel Tours directly at 1-888-777-0004." Rather than use Cut and Paste to move this text, you will use the **drag and drop** editing feature. This feature is most useful for copying or moving short distances in a document. To use drag and drop to move a selection, point to the selection and drag it to the location where you want the selection inserted. The mouse pointer appears as ⚞ as you drag, and a temporary insertion point ⫿ shows you where the text will be placed when you release the mouse button.

1 ● **Select directly (last word in last paragraph).**

● **Drag the selection to before "at" in the same sentence.**

Additional Information

You can also move or copy a selection by holding down the right mouse button while dragging. When you release the mouse button, a shortcut menu appears with the available move and copy options.

Your screen should be similar to Figure 2.15

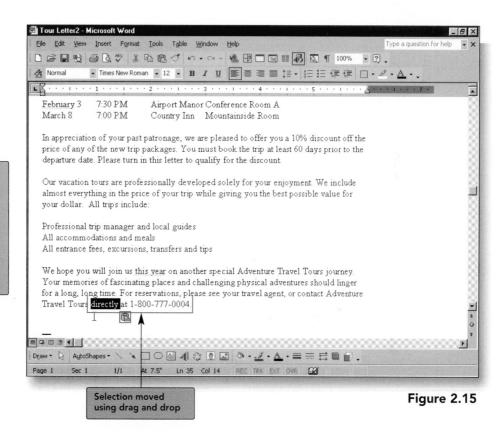

Selection moved using drag and drop

Figure 2.15

The selection is moved to the new location.

Working with Multiple Documents

Next you want to open the flyer document so that you can copy the flyer into the letter document. All Office XP applications allow you to open and use multiple files at the same time. Each file is displayed in a separate application window.

Opening a Second Document

Additional Information

It is always a good idea to save your work before opening another file.

You made several of the changes to the flyer suggested by the manager. You will save the document you are working with then open the revised flyer.

1 Click 💾 Save.

● **Open the** wd02_Flyer4 **document.**

Additional Information

Sometimes you may want to open several files at once. To do this you can select multiple files by holding down Ctrl while clicking on each file name. If the files are adjacent, you can click the first file name, hold down ⇧Shift, and click on the name of the last file.

Your screen should be similar to Figure 2.16

Figure 2.16

The flyer document is opened and displayed in a separate window. It contains the insertion point, which indicates that it is the **active document**, or the document you can work in. The taskbar displays a button for each open document window; it can be used to quickly switch from one window to the other.

Copying between Documents

You plan to include the flyer with the letter to be mailed to clients. You also want to keep the flyer document in a separate file, because it will be printed separately to be given to clients when they come to the office. To include the flyer with the letter document, you will copy the flyer contents into the letter document.

1 ● **Select the entire flyer.**

HAVING TROUBLE?
Triple-click in the left margin to quickly select the entire document.

● **Click** 🖹 **Copy.**

● **Click** 🔲Tour Letter.... **in the taskbar.**

Another Method
You can also use [Alt] + [Tab↹] or the Window menu to switch from one open document window to another.

● **Move to the blank line below the last paragraph of the letter.**

● **Click** 🖺 **Paste.**

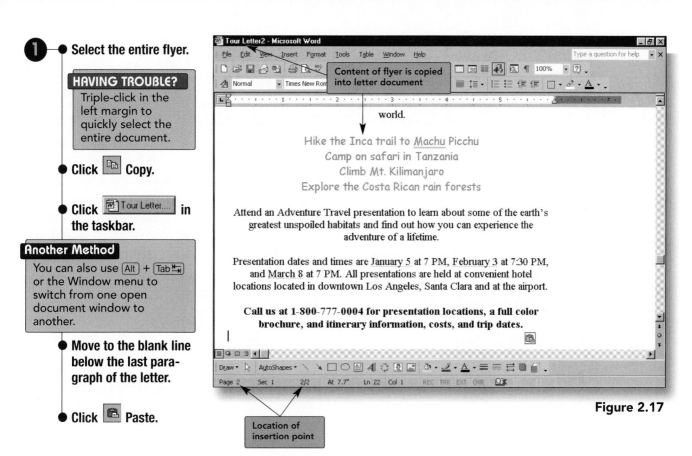

Your screen should be similar to Figure 2.17

Figure 2.17

The letter now consists of two pages. Notice the status bar shows the insertion point location is on page 2/2.

Controlling Document Paging

As text and graphics are added to a document, Word automatically starts a new page when text extends beyond the bottom margin setting. The beginning of a new page is identified by a page break.

Page Break

3 A **page break** marks the point at which one page ends and another begins. There are two types of page breaks that can be used in a document: soft page breaks and hard page breaks. As you fill a page with text or graphics, Word inserts a **soft page break** automatically when the bottom margin is reached and starts a new page. As you add or remove text from a page, Word automatically readjusts the placement of the soft page break.

Many times, however, you may want to force a page break to occur at a specific location. To do this you can manually insert a **hard page break**. This instructs Word to begin a new page regardless of the amount of text on the previous page. When a hard page break is used, its location is never moved regardless of the changes that are made to the amount of text on the preceding page. All soft page breaks that precede or follow a hard page break continue to automatically adjust. Sometimes you may find that you have to remove the hard page break and reenter it at another location as you edit the document.

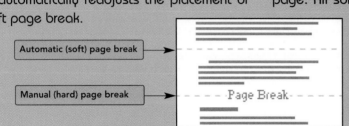

Automatic (soft) page break

Manual (hard) page break — Page Break —

To see where the second page begins,

① ● **Drag the scroll box upward until the flyer title is displayed.**

Additional Information

As you drag the scroll box, a ScreenTip displays the number of the page that is displayed in the window.

Your screen should be similar to Figure 2.18

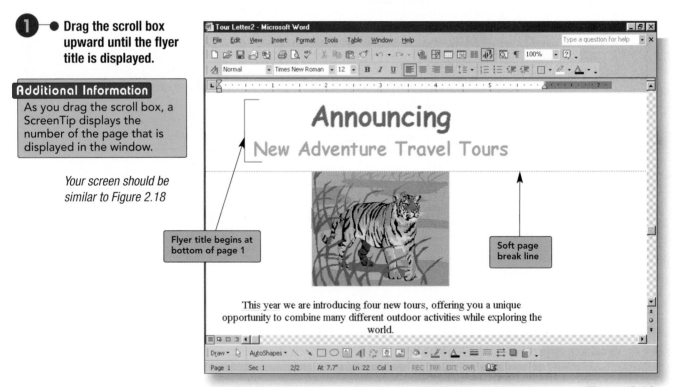

Flyer title begins at bottom of page 1

Soft page break line

Figure 2.18

To show where one page ends and another begins, Word displays a dotted line across the page to mark the soft page break.

Inserting a Hard Page Break

Many times the location of the soft page break is not appropriate. In this case, the location of the soft page break displays the flyer title on the bottom of page 1 and the remaining portion of the flyer on page 2. Because you want the entire flyer to print on a page by itself, you will manually insert a hard page break above the flyer title.

1 ● **Move to the end of the last line of the letter.**

● **Press** [Ctrl] + [←Enter].

Another Method

The menu equivalent is Insert/**B**reak/ **P**age break.

● **Save the document again.**

Your screen should be similar to Figure 2.19

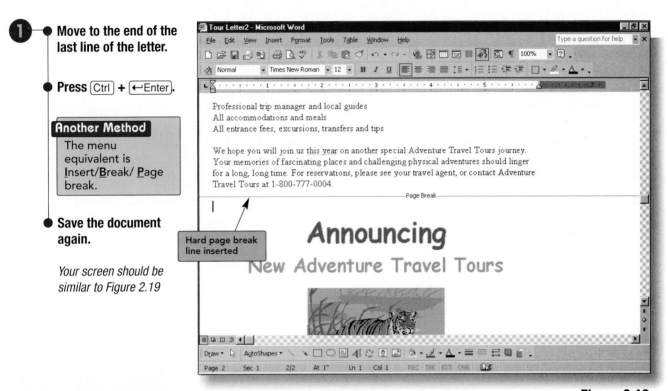

Figure 2.19

Additional Information

To remove a hard page break, simply select the hard page break line and press [Delete].

A dotted line and the words "Page Break" appear across the page above the flyer title, indicating that a hard page break was entered at that position.

Finding and Replacing Text

As you continue proofing the letter, you notice that you frequently used the word "trip." You think that the letter would read better if the word "tour" was used in place of "trip" in some instances.

concept 4

Find and Replace

4 To make editing easier, you can use the Find and Replace feature to find text in a document and replace it with other text as directed. For example, suppose you created a lengthy document describing the type of clothing and equipment needed to set up a world-class home gym, and then you decided to change "sneakers" to "athletic shoes." Instead of deleting every occurrence of "sneakers" and typing "ath-

letic shoes," you can use the Find and Replace feature to perform the task automatically.

You can also find and replace occurrences of special formatting, such as replacing bold text with italicized text, as well as find and replace formatting marks. This feature is fast and accurate; however, use care when replacing so that you do not replace unintended matches.

Finding Text

First you will use the Find command to locate all occurrences of the word "trip" in the document.

1 ● **Move the insertion point to the top of the document.**

> **Another Method**
> Reminder: Use ⌃Ctrl + Home to quickly move to the top of the document.

● **Choose Edit/Find.**

> **Another Method**
> The keyboard shortcut is ⌃Ctrl + F. You can also open the Find and Replace dialog box by clicking the ⊙ Select Browse Object button in the vertical scroll bar and selecting 🔍 Find from the menu.

Your screen should be similar to Figure 2.20

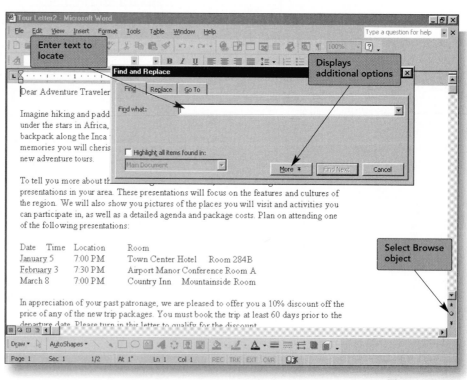

Figure 2.20

The Find and Replace dialog box is used to define the information you want to locate and replace. In the Find What text box, you enter the text you want to locate. In addition, you can use the search options to refine the search. To see these options,

2 ● Click [More ▼].

*Your screen should be
similar to Figure 2.21*

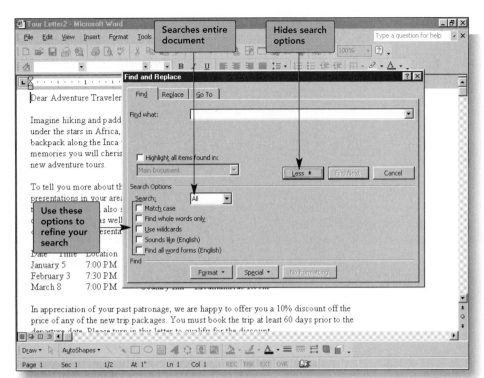

Figure 2.21

The additional options in the Find and Replace dialog box can be combined in many ways to help you find and replace text in documents. They are described in the table below.

Option	Effect on Text
Match case	Finds only those words in which the capitalization matches the text you typed.
Find whole words only	Finds matches that are whole words and not part of a larger word. For example, finds "cat" only and not "catastrophe" too.
Use wildcards	Fine-tunes a search; for example, c?t finds "cat" and "cot" (one-character matches), while c*t finds "cat" and "court" (searches for one or more characters).
Sounds like (English)	Finds words that sound like the word you type; very helpful if you do not know the correct spelling of the word you want to find.
Find all word forms (English)	Finds and replaces all forms of a word; for example, "buy" will replace "purchase," and "bought" will replace "purchased."

When you enter the text to find, you can type everything lowercase, because the Match Case option is not selected. If Match Case is not selected, the search will not be **case sensitive**. This means that lowercase letters will match both upper- and lowercase letters in the text.

Also notice that the Search option default setting is All, which means Word will search the entire document, including headers and footers. You can also choose to search Up or Down the document. These options search in the direction specified but exclude the headers, footers, footnotes, and comments from the area to search. Because you want to search the entire document, All is the appropriate setting. You will hide the search options again and begin the search.

Note: You will learn about headers, footers, footnotes, and comments in later labs.

3 ● Click [Less ‡] to close the advanced search options.

● Type **trip** in the Find What text box.

● Click [Find Next].

Your screen should be similar to Figure 2.22

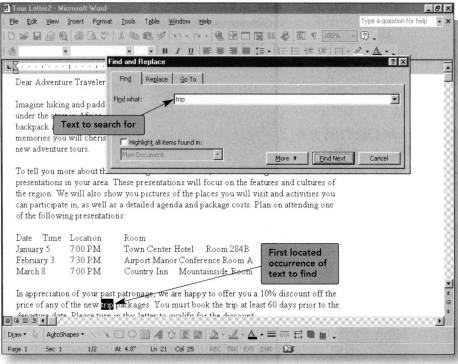

Figure 2.22

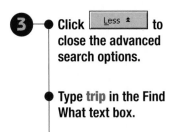

Additional Information

If the search does not begin at the top of the document, when Word reaches the end of the document it asks if you want to continue searching from the beginning of the document. You can also highlight text to restrict the search to a selection.

Word searches for all occurrences of the text to find beginning at the insertion point, locates the first occurrence of the word "trip" and highlights it in the document.

4 ● Continue to click [Find Next] to locate all occurrences of the word.

● Click [OK] when Word indicates the entire document has been searched.

The word "trip" is used six times in the document.

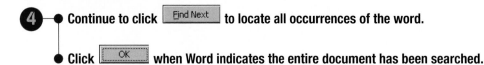

Replacing Text

You decide to replace three occurrences of the word "trip" in the letter with "tour" where appropriate. You will use the Replace function to specify the text to enter as the replacement text.

1 ● **Open the Replace tab.**

Your screen should be similar to Figure 2.23

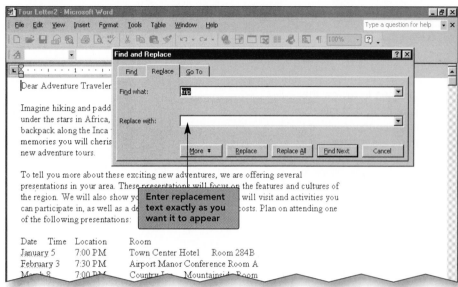

Figure 2.23

The Replace tab includes a Replace With text box in which you enter the replacement text. This text must be entered exactly as you want it to appear in your document. To find and replace the first occurrence of the word "trip" with "tour,"

2 ● **Type tour in the Replace With text box.**

● **Click** 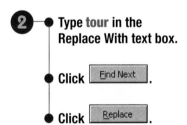 **Find Next** .

● **Click** **Replace** .

Your screen should be similar to Figure 2.24

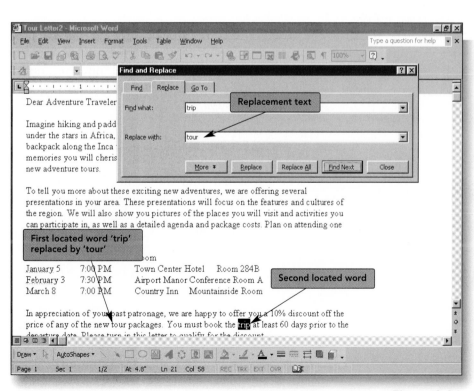

Figure 2.24

Word replaced the first located word with "tour" and has highlighted the second occurrence of the word "trip." You do not want to replace this occurrence of the word. To continue the search without replacing the highlighted text,

3 ● Click [Find Next] .

● **Replace the next located occurrence.**

● **Continue to review the document, replacing all other occurrences of the word "trip" with "tour,"** *except* **on the final line of the flyer.**

● **Click** [Find Next] .

● **Click** [OK] **to close the information dialog box.**

● **Click** [Close] **to close the Find and Replace dialog box.**

Your screen should be similar to Figure 2.25

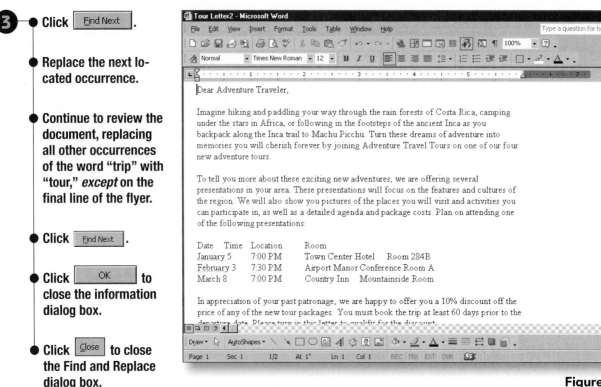

Figure 2.25

When using the Find and Replace feature, if you wanted to change all the occurrences of the located text, it is much faster to use [Replace All] . Exercise care when using Replace All, however, because the search text you specify might be part of another word and you may accidentally replace text you want to keep.

Inserting the Current Date

The last text change you need to make is to add the date to the letter. The Date and Time command on the Insert menu inserts the current date as maintained by your computer system into your document at the location of the insertion point. You want to enter the date on the first line of the letter, four lines above the salutation.

- **Move to the "D" in "Dear" at the top of the letter.**

- **Press** (←Enter) **4 times to insert four blank lines.**

- **Move to the first blank line.**

- **Choose** <u>I</u>**nsert/Date and** <u>T</u>**ime.**

Your screen should be similar to Figure 2.26

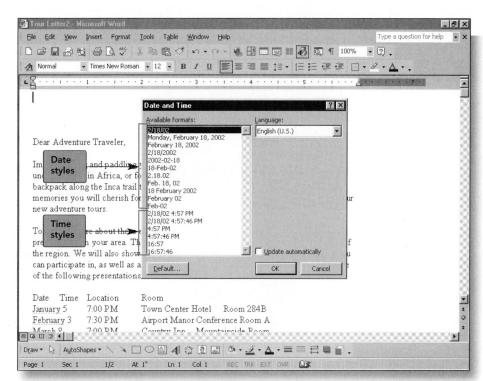

Figure 2.26

From the Date and Time dialog box, you select the style in which you want the date displayed in your document. The Available Formats list box displays the format styles for the current date and time. You want to display the date in the format Month XX, 2XXX, the third format setting in the list.

- **Select the third format setting.**

Your screen should be similar to Figure 2.27

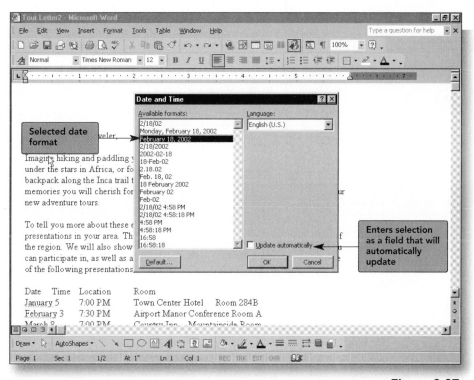

Figure 2.27

Automatically Updating the Date

You also want the date to be updated automatically whenever the letter is sent to new Adventure travelers. You use the Update Automatically option to do this by entering the date as a field.

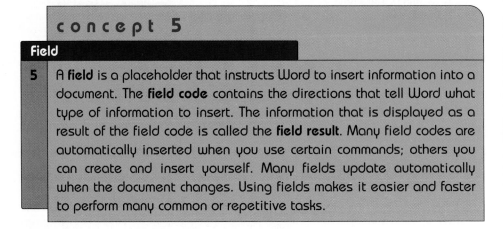

concept 5

Field

5 A **field** is a placeholder that instructs Word to insert information into a document. The **field code** contains the directions that tell Word what type of information to insert. The information that is displayed as a result of the field code is called the **field result**. Many field codes are automatically inserted when you use certain commands; others you can create and insert yourself. Many fields update automatically when the document changes. Using fields makes it easier and faster to perform many common or repetitive tasks.

1 ● If necessary, select **Update Automatically** to display the checkmark.

● Click [OK].

● Press [↵].

Additional Information

You can use [Alt] + [⇧ Shift] + D to insert the current date as a field in the format MM/DD/YY.

Your screen should be similar to Figure 2.28

HAVING TROUBLE?

The date in Figure 2.28 will be different from the date that appears on your screen.

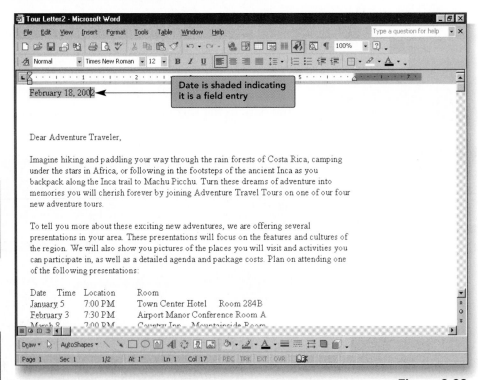

Figure 2.28

The date is entered in the document in the format you selected. When the insertion point is positioned on a field entry, it appears shaded. To see the underlying field code,

2 ● **Right-click on the field.**

● **Choose Toggle Field Codes.**

Your screen should be similar to Figure 2.29

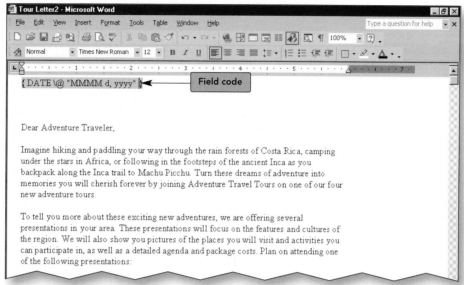

Figure 2.29

The field code includes the field characters, field type, and instructions. Whenever this document is printed, Word will print the current system date using this format.

3 ● **Press** ⇧Shift + F9 .

● **Save the document again.**

Your screen should be similar to Figure 2.30

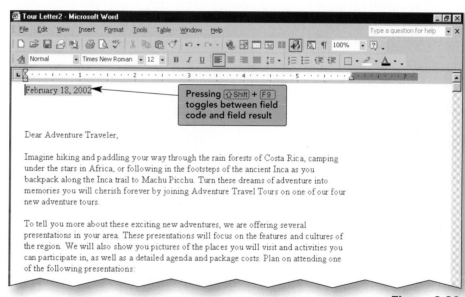

Figure 2.30

The field result is displayed again.

Additional Information

You can press Alt + F9 to show or hide field codes for all fields in a document.

Modifying Page Layout

Next the manager has suggested that you make several formatting changes to improve the appearance of the letter and flyer. Many formatting features that can be used in a document affect the layout of an entire page. These formatting features include page margin settings, vertical alignment of text on a page, headers and footers, and orientation of text on a page.

Changing Margin Settings

One of the first changes you will make is to change the page margin settings.

concept 6

Page Margin

6 The **page margin** is the blank space around the edge of a page. Generally, the text you enter appears in the printable area inside the margins. However, some items can be positioned in the margin space. You can set different page margin widths to alter the appearance of the document.

Standard single-sided documents have four margins: top, bottom, left, and right. Double-sided documents with facing pages, such as books and magazines, also have four margins: top, bottom, inside, and outside. These docu-

ments typically use mirror margins in which the left page is a mirror image of the right page. This means that the inside margins are the same width and the outside margins are the same width. (See the illustrations below.)

You can also set a "gutter" margin that reserves space on the left side of single-sided documents, or on the inside margin of double-sided documents, to accommodate binding. There are also special margin settings for headers and footers. (You will learn about these features in Lab 3.)

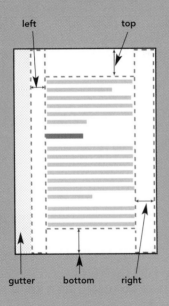

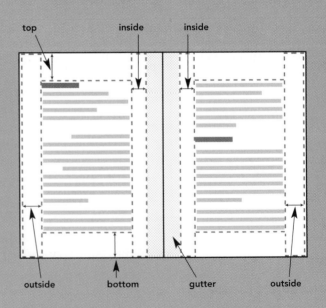

To make it easier to see how your planned margin setting changes will look on the page, you will first change the document view to Print Layout view and Page Width zoom.

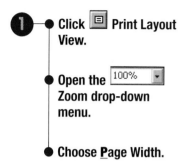

1 ● Click 🖾 **Print Layout View.**

● Open the 100% ▾ **Zoom drop-down menu.**

● Choose **Page Width.**

Your screen should be similar to Figure 2.31

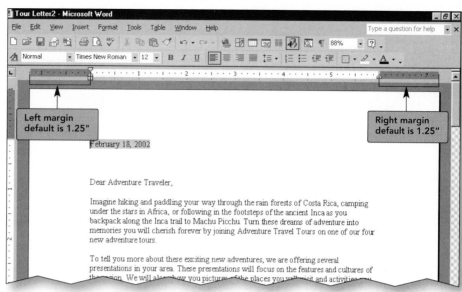

Figure 2.31

The default left and right margin settings of 1.25 inches are now easy to see. As you make changes to the margin settings next, you will be able to easily see the change in the layout of the document on the page.

You would like to see how the letter would look if you changed the right and left margin widths to 1 inch. The Page Setup command on the File menu is used to change settings associated with the layout of the entire document.

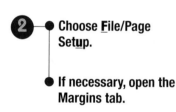

2 ● Choose **File/Page Setup.**

● If necessary, open the **Margins tab.**

Your screen should be similar to Figure 2.32

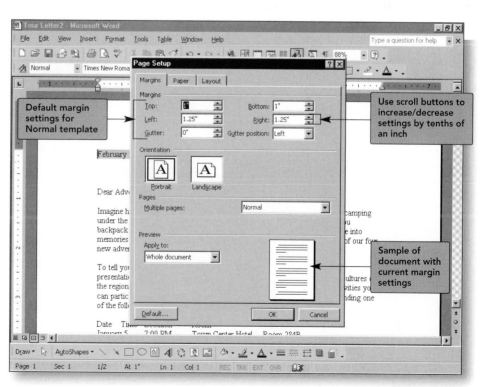

Figure 2.32

The Margins tab of the Page Setup dialog box displays the default margin settings for a single-sided document. The Preview box shows how the current margin settings will appear on a page. New margin settings can be entered by typing the value in the text box, or by clicking the 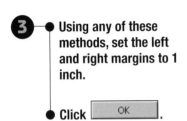 and scroll buttons or pressing the ⬆ or ⬇ keys to increase or decrease the setting by tenths of an inch.

3 ● Using any of these methods, set the left and right margins to 1 inch.

● Click OK.

Your screen should be similar to Figure 2.33

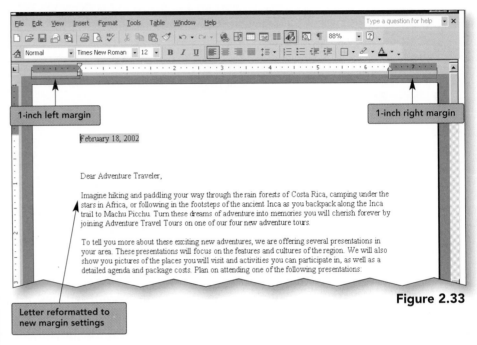

1-inch left margin

1-inch right margin

February 18, 2002

Dear Adventure Traveler,

Imagine hiking and paddling your way through the rain forests of Costa Rica, camping under the stars in Africa, or following in the footsteps of the ancient Inca as you backpack along the Inca trail to Machu Picchu. Turn these dreams of adventure into memories you will cherish forever by joining Adventure Travel Tours on one of our four new adventure tours.

To tell you more about these exciting new adventures, we are offering several presentations in your area. These presentations will focus on the features and cultures of the region. We will also show you pictures of the places you will visit and activities you can participate in, as well as a detailed agenda and package costs. Plan on attending one of the following presentations:

Figure 2.33

Letter reformatted to new margin settings

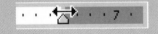
You can see that the letter has been reformatted to fit within the new margin settings. You would like to see what both pages look like at the same time.

4 ● Change the zoom setting to Two Pages.

Your screen should be similar to Figure 2.34

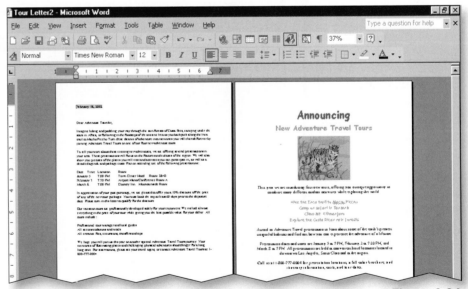

Figure 2.34

Both pages are displayed in the document window. Although the text is difficult to read, you can easily see the layout of the pages and that the margin settings have been changed for both pages.

More Paragraph Formatting

To give the document more interest, you can indent paragraphs, use tabs to create tabular columns of data, and change the line spacing. These formatting features are all paragraph formats that affect the entire selected paragraph.

Indenting Paragraphs

Business letters typically are either created using a block layout style or a modified block style with indented paragraphs. In a block style, all parts of the letter, including the date, inside address, all paragraphs in the body, and closing lines, are evenly aligned with the left margin. The block layout style of your letter has a very formal appearance. The modified block style, on the other hand, has a more casual appearance. In this style, certain elements such as the date, all paragraphs in the body, and the closing lines are indented from the left margin. You want to change the letter style from the block paragraph style to the modified block style.

concept 7

Indents

7 To help your reader find information quickly, you can indent paragraphs from the margins. Indenting paragraphs sets them off from the rest of the document. There are four types of indents you can use to stylize your documents.

Indent	Effect on Text	Indent	Effect on Text
Left	Indents the entire paragraph from the left margin. To outdent or extend the paragraph into the left margin, use a negative value for the left indent.	First Line	Indents the first line of the paragraph. All following lines are aligned with the left margin.
Right	Indents the entire paragraph from the right margin. To outdent or extend the paragraph into the right margin, use a negative value for the right indent.	Hanging	Indents all lines after the first line of the paragraph. The first line is aligned with the left margin. A hanging indent is typically used for bulleted and numbered lists.

You will begin by indenting the first line of the first paragraph.

1
- **Return the zoom to Page Width.**

- **Move to anywhere in the first paragraph.**

- **Choose Format/Paragraph.**

- **If necessary, open the Indents and Spacing tab.**

  Your screen should be similar to Figure 2.35

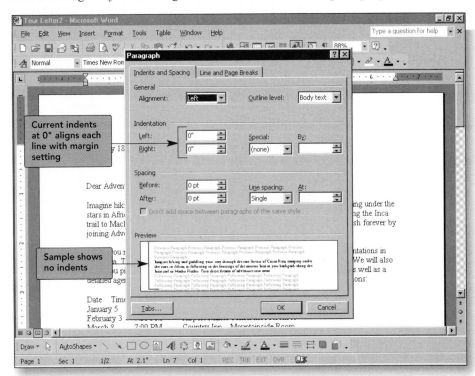

Figure 2.35

The Indents and Spacing tab shows that the left and right indentation settings for the current paragraph are 0. This setting aligns each line of the paragraph with the margin setting. Specifying an indent value would indent each line of the selected paragraph the specified amount from the margin. However, you only want to indent the first line of the paragraph.

2
- **From the Special drop-down list box, select First line.**

  Your screen should be similar to Figure 2.36

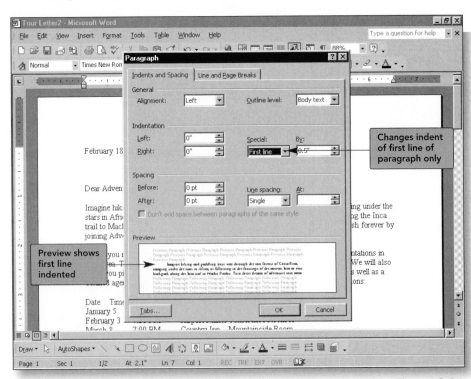

Figure 2.36

The default first line indent setting of 0.5 inch displayed in the By text box is acceptable. The Preview area shows how this setting will affect a paragraph.

Your screen should be similar to Figure 2.37

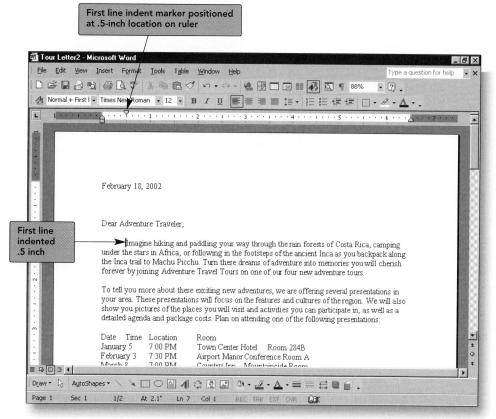

Figure 2.37

The first line of the paragraph indents a half inch from the left margin. The text in the paragraph wraps as needed, and the text on the following line begins at the left margin. Notice that the first line indent marker on the ruler moved to the 0.5-inch position. This marker controls the location of the first line of text in the paragraph.

A much quicker way to indent the first line of a paragraph is to press Tab↹ at the beginning of the paragraph. Pressing Tab↹ indents the first line of the paragraph to the first tab stop from the left margin. A **tab stop** is a marked location on the horizontal ruler that indicates how far to indent text when the Tab key is pressed. The default tab stops are every .5 inch.

4 ● **Move to the beginning of the second paragraph.**

● **Press** `Tab ↹`.

Your screen should be similar to Figure 2.38

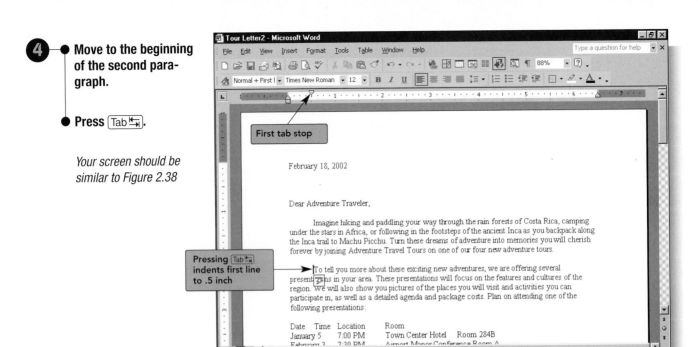

First tab stop

Pressing `Tab ↹` indents first line to .5 inch

Figure 2.38

You can indent the remaining paragraphs individually, or you can select the paragraphs and indent them simultaneously by either using the Format menu or dragging the upper indent marker ▽ on the ruler.

Dragging the first line indent marker indents the first line of each paragraph in a selection

5 ● **Select the remaining text on page 1.**

● **Drag the First Line Indent marker on the ruler to the 0.5-inch position.**

Additional Information
A ScreenTip identifies the First Line Indent marker when you point to it.

● **If necessary, scroll the window to display the entire selection.**

Your screen should be similar to Figure 2.39

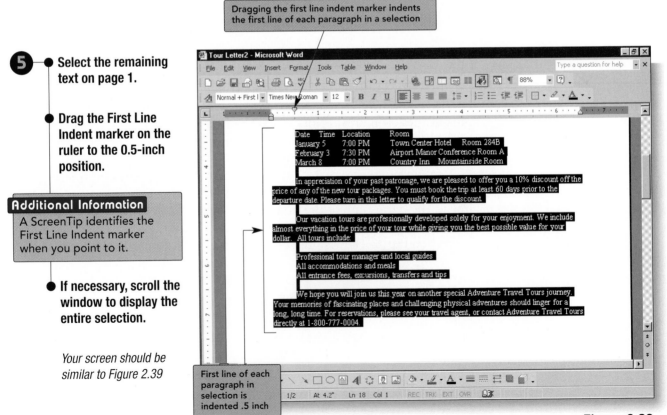

First line of each paragraph in selection is indented .5 inch

Figure 2.39

The first line of each paragraph in the selection is indented. Notice that each line of the date and time information is also indented. This is because each line ends with a paragraph mark. Word considers each line a separate paragraph.

Setting Tab Stops

Next you want to improve the appearance of the list of presentation times and dates. The date and time information was entered using tabs to separate the different columns of information. However, because the default tab stops are set at every 0.5 inch, the columns are not evenly spaced. You want to reformat this information to appear as a tabbed table of information so that it is easier to read as shown in the figure below.

Date	Time	Location	Room
January 5	7:00 PM	Town Center Hotel	Room 284B
February 3	7:30 PM	Airport Manor	Conference Room A
March 8	7:00 PM	Country Inn	Mountainside Room

To improve the appearance of the data, you will create custom tab stops that will align the data in evenly spaced columns. The default tab stops of every 0.5 inch are visible on the ruler as light vertical lines below the numbers. As with other default settings, you can change the location of tab stops in the document.

You can also select from five different types of tab stops that control how characters are positioned or aligned with the tab stop. The following table explains the five tab types, the tab marks that appear in the tab alignment selector box (on the left end of the horizontal ruler) and the effects on the text.

Tab Type	Tab Mark	Effects on Text	Example
Left	⌊	Extends text to right from tab stop	left
Center	⊥	Aligns text centered on tab stop	center
Right	⌟	Extends text to left from tab stop	right
Decimal	⊥	Aligns text with decimal point	35.78
Bar	I	Draws a vertical line through text at tab stop	

To align the data, you will place three left tab stops at the 1.5-inch, 2.75-inch, and 4.5-inch positions. You can quickly specify custom tab stop locations and types using the ruler. To select a type of tab stop, click the tab alignment selector box to cycle through the types. Then, to specify where to place the selected tab stop type, click on the location in the ruler. As you specify the new tab stop settings, the table data will align to the new settings.

1

- Select the line of table headings and the three lines of data.

- If necessary, click the tab alignment selector box until the left tab icon ⬜ appears.

- Click the 1.5-inch position on the ruler.

- Click the 2.75-inch and the 4.5-inch positions on the ruler.

- Click anywhere in the table to deselect it.

Your screen should be similar to Figure 2.40

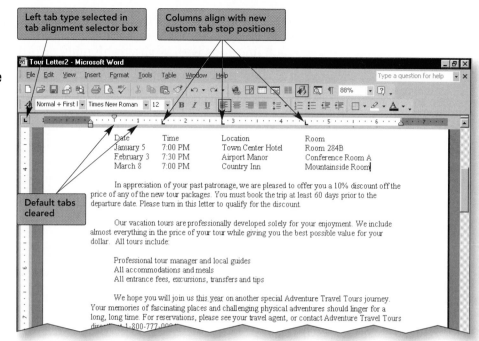

Figure 2.40

The three tabbed columns appropriately align with the new tab stops. All default tabs to the left of the custom tab stops are cleared. After looking at the columns, you decide the column headings would look better centered over the columns of data. To make this change, you will remove the three custom tabs for the heading line by dragging them off the ruler and then add three center tab stops.

2

- Move to anywhere in the heading line.

- Drag the three left tab stop marks off the ruler.

- Click the tab alignment selector box until the center tab icon ⬜ appears.

- Set a center tab stop at the .75-inch, 1.75-inch, 3.25-inch, and 5-inch positions.

Your screen should be similar to Figure 2.41

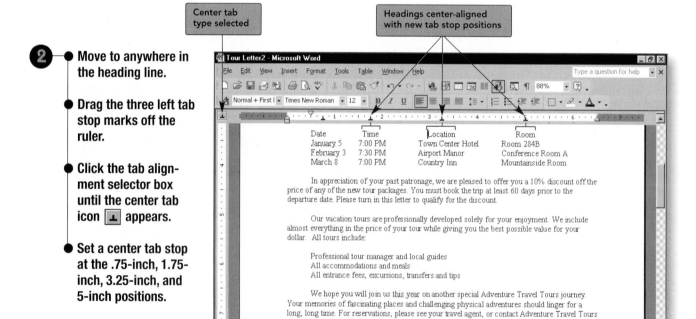

Figure 2.41

The Time, Location, and Room headings are appropriately centered on the tab stops. However, the Date heading still needs to be indented to the .75 tab stop position by pressing [Tab↹].

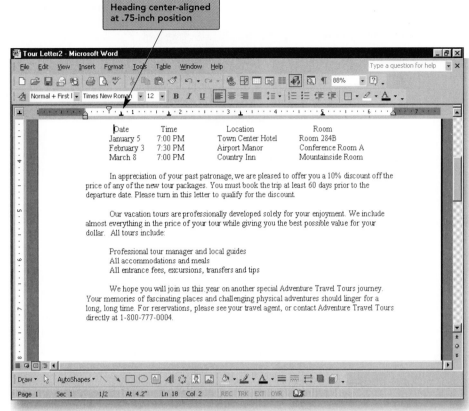

Heading center-aligned at .75-inch position

Date	Time	Location	Room
January 5	7:00 PM	Town Center Hotel	Room 284B
February 3	7:30 PM	Airport Manor	Conference Room A
March 8	7:00 PM	Country Inn	Mountainside Room

In appreciation of your past patronage, we are pleased to offer you a 10% discount off the price of any of the new tour packages. You must book the trip at least 60 days prior to the departure date. Please turn in this letter to qualify for the discount.

Our vacation tours are professionally developed solely for your enjoyment. We include almost everything in the price of your tour while giving you the best possible value for your dollar. All tours include:

Professional tour manager and local guides
All accommodations and meals
All entrance fees, excursions, transfers and tips

We hope you will join us this year on another special Adventure Travel Tours journey. Your memories of fascinating places and challenging physical adventures should linger for a long, long time. For reservations, please see your travel agent, or contact Adventure Travel Tours directly at 1-800-777-0004.

Figure 2.42

The Date heading is now centered at the .75-inch tab stop. As you can see, setting different types of tab stops is helpful for aligning text or numeric data vertically in columns. Using tab stops ensures that the text will indent to the same set location. Setting custom tab stops instead of pressing [Tab] or [Spacebar] repeatedly is a more professional way to format a document, as well as faster and more accurate. It also makes editing easier because you can change the tab stop settings for several paragraphs at once.

Adding Tab Leaders

To make the presentation times and location data even easier to read, you will add tab leaders to the table. **Leader characters** are solid, dotted, or dashed lines that fill the blank space between tab stops. They help the reader's eye move across the blank space between the information aligned at the tab stops.

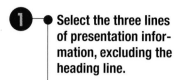

1 ● **Select the three lines of presentation information, excluding the heading line.**

● **Choose F_ormat/T_abs.**

Your screen should be similar to Figure 2.43

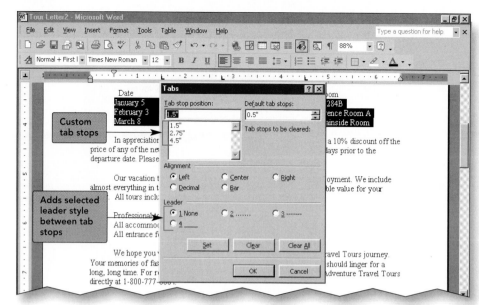

Figure 2.43

Notice that the Tabs dialog box displays the custom tabs you set on the ruler. You can set tab positions in the dialog box by entering the tab positions in the text box. The current tab leader setting is set to None for the 1.5-inch tab stop. You can select from three styles of tab leaders. You will use the third tab leader style, a series of dashed lines. The tab leader fills the empty space to the left of the tab stop. Each tab stop must have the leader individually set.

2 ● **Select 3 -------.**

● **Click** ___Set___ **.**

● **Select the 2.75-inch tab stop setting from the Tab Stop Position list box.**

● **Select 3 -------.**

● **Click** ___Set___ **.**

● **In a similar manner, set the tab leader for the 4.5-inch tab.**

● **Click** ___OK___ **.**

● **Click in the table to deselect the text.**

Your screen should be similar to Figure 2.44

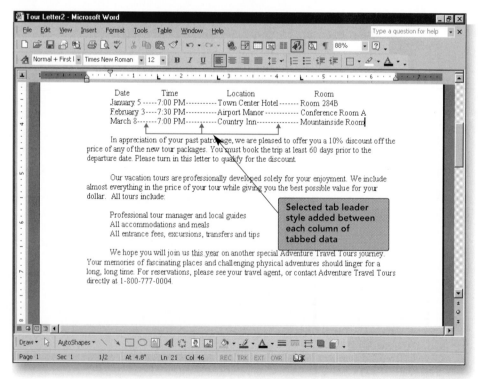

Figure 2.44

The selected leader style has been added to the blank space between each column of tabbed text.

Changing Line Spacing

You also want to increase the line spacing in the table to make the presentation data even easier to read. **Line spacing** is the vertical space between lines of text. The default setting of single line spacing accommodates the largest font in that line, plus a small amount of extra space.

1 ● Select the table including the heading line.

● Choose Format/Paragraph.

● If necessary, open the Indents and Spacing tab.

● Open the Line Spacing drop-down list.

Your screen should be similar to Figure 2.45

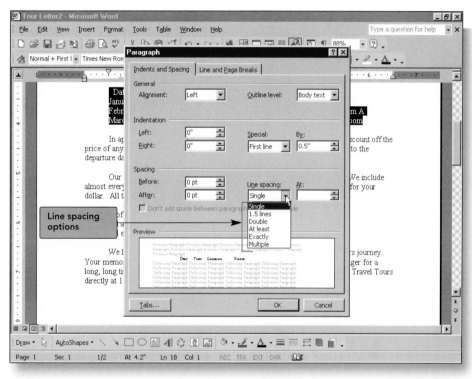

Figure 2.45

The line spacing options are described in the table below.

1.5 lines	Spacing is one and a half times that of single line spacing.
Double	Spacing is twice that of single line spacing.
At least	Uses a value specified in points in the At text box as the minimum line spacing amount that can accommodate larger font sizes or graphics that would not otherwise fit within the specified spacing.
Exactly	Uses a value specified in points in the At text box as a fixed line spacing amount that is not changed, making all lines evenly spaced.
Multiple	Uses a percentage value in the At text box as the amount to increase or decrease line spacing. For example, entering 1.3 will increase the spacing by 33 percent.

2
- Choose 1.5 lines from the Line Spacing drop-down list.
- Click [OK].

Another Method
You can also use Ctrl + # to change the line spacing to the number specified.

- Click in the table to deselect the text.

Your screen should be similar to Figure 2.46

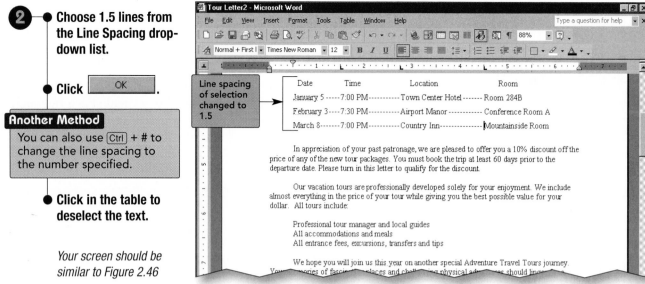

Figure 2.46

The line spacing within the selection has increased to 1.5 spaces.

Justifying Paragraphs

The final paragraph formatting change you want to make to the letter is to change the alignment of all paragraphs in the letter from the default of left-aligned to justified.

1
- Select the text on page 1 only.
- Click [≡] Justify.

Another Method
The menu equivalent is Format/Paragraph/Indents and Spacing/Alignment/Justified.

- Deselect the text and move to the top of the document.

Your screen should be similar to Figure 2.47

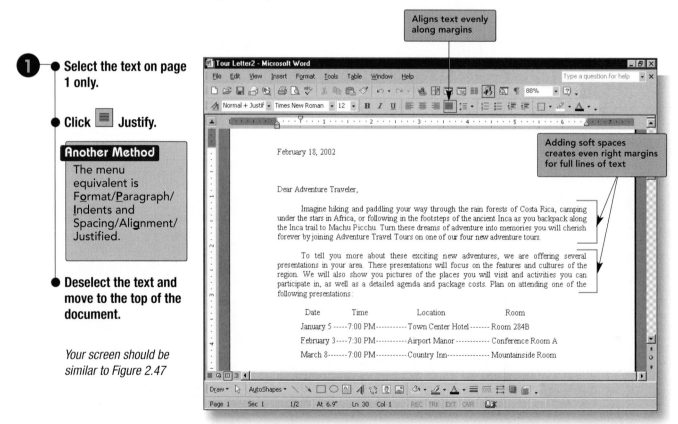

Figure 2.47

All full lines now end even with the right margin. To do this, Word inserts extra spaces, called **soft spaces**, between words to push the text to the right margin. The soft spaces are adjusted automatically whenever additions and deletions are made to the text.

More Character Formatting

As you look at the letter, you still feel that the table of presentation dates and times does not stand out enough. You can add emphasis to information in your documents by formatting specific characters or words. Applying color shading behind text is commonly used to identify areas of text that you want to stand out. It is frequently used to mark text that you want to locate easily as you are revising a document. Italics, underlines, and bold are other character formats that add emphasis and draw the reader's attention to important items. Word applies character formatting to the entire selection or to the entire word at the insertion point. You can apply formatting to a portion of a word by selecting the area to be formatted first.

Adding Color Highlighting

First, you want to see how a color highlight behind the tabbed table of presentation times and locations would look.

1
- Open the [highlight icon] Highlight drop-down list.

- Select the turquoise color from the color palette.

Additional Information

The mouse pointer appears as ✍ when positioned on text, indicating the highlighting feature is on.

- Select the entire table.

Another Method

You can also select the area you want to highlight first and then click [icon] to apply the current color selection.

- Click [icon] to turn off the highlighting feature.

Another Method

You can also press [Esc] to turn off highlighting.

Your screen should be similar to Figure 2.48

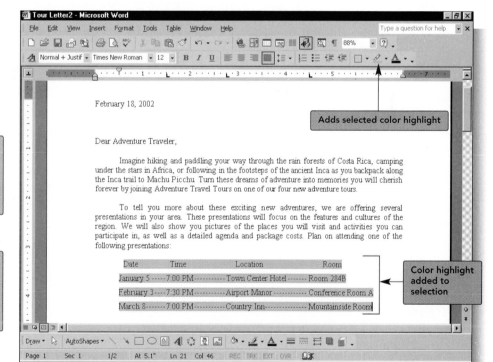

Figure 2.48

Although the highlight makes the table stand out, it does not look good.

Underlining Text

Instead, you decide to bold and underline the headings. In addition to the default single underline style, there are 15 other types of underlines.

1
- Click [↶ ▾] **Undo.**

- Click on the Date heading.

- Click [**B**] **Bold.**

- Choose **Format/Font.**

- If necessary, open the **Font** tab.

- Open the **Underline style drop-down list box.**

Your screen should be similar to Figure 2.49

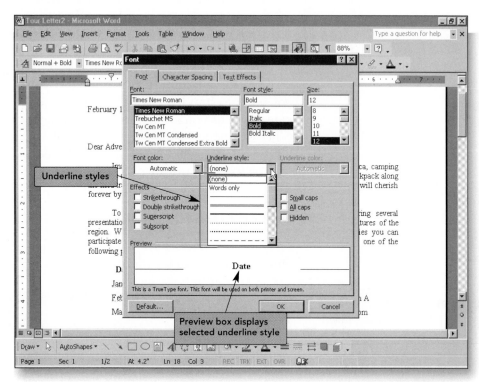

Figure 2.49

The None option removes underlining from a selection, and the Words Only option displays underlines under words in the selection only, not under the spaces between words. The Words Only option uses the default single underline style.

- Select several underline styles and see how they appear in the Preview box.

- Select the double underline style.

 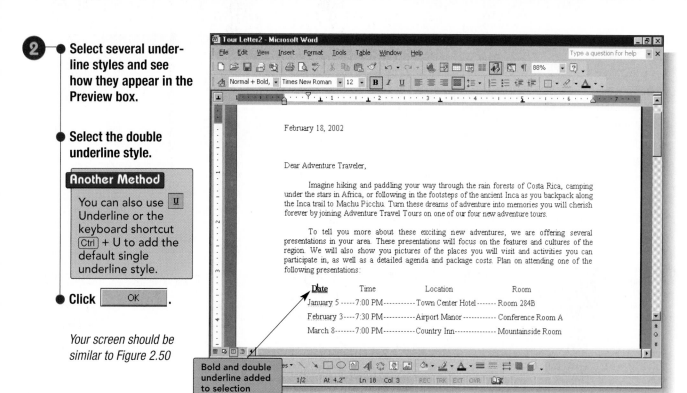
- Click [OK].

Your screen should be similar to Figure 2.50

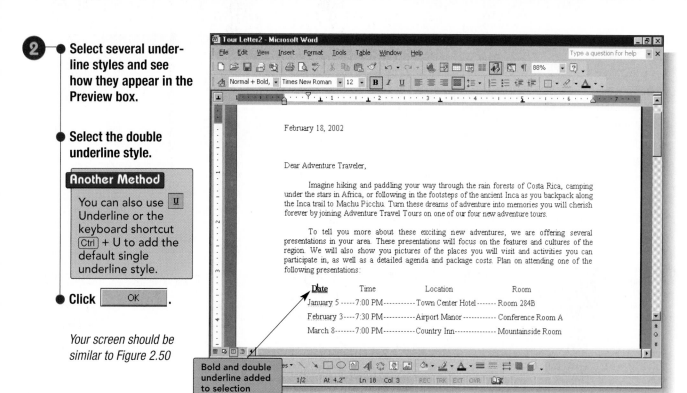

Figure 2.50

Copying Formats with Format Painter

You want to quickly apply the same formats to the other headings. To do this you can use the **Format Painter**. This feature applies the formats associated with the current selection to new selections. If the selection is a paragraph (including the paragraph mark), the formatting is applied to the entire paragraph. If the selection is a character, the format is applied to a character, word, or selection you specify. To turn on the feature, move the insertion point to the text whose formats you want to copy and click the ▨ Format Painter button. Then select the text you want the formats applied to. The format is automatically applied to an entire word simply by clicking on the word. To apply the format to more or less text, you must select the area. If you double-click the ▨ Format Painter button, you can apply the format multiple times.

1 • **If necessary, click on the Date heading.**

• **Double-click 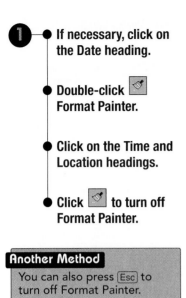 Format Painter.**

• **Click on the Time and Location headings.**

• **Click to turn off Format Painter.**

Another Method
You can also press Esc to turn off Format Painter.

Your screen should be similar to Figure 2.51

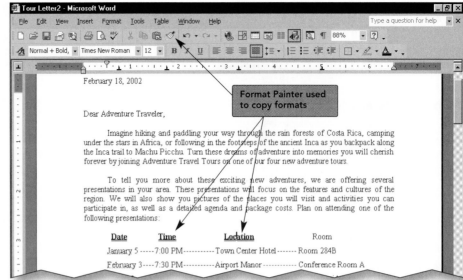

Figure 2.51

Applying Formats Using the Styles and Formatting Task Pane

The last heading to format is Room. Another way to apply existing formatting is to use the Styles and Formatting task pane.

1 • **Click Styles and Formatting on the Formatting toolbar.**

Your screen should be similar to Figure 2.52

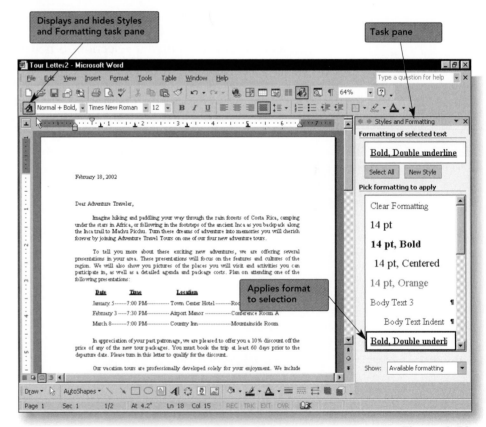

Figure 2.52

This Styles and Formatting task pane displays the formatting associated with the selected text at the top of the pane. All other formatting in use in the document is listed in the scroll box. To apply an existing format to a selection, you can pick the format from this list.

2 ● **Click on the Room table heading.**

● **Click**

Bold, Double underline .

Your screen should be similar to Figure 2.53

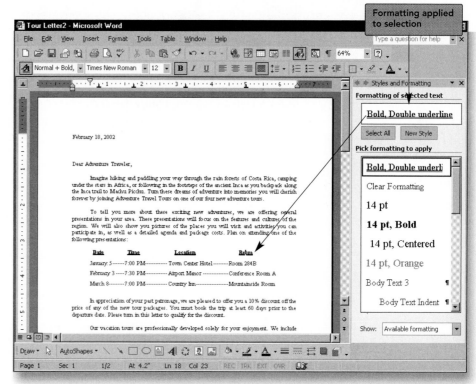

Figure 2.53

The selected formatting is applied to the word. The list box also now displays the last selected formatting at the top of the list to make it easier to select it again.

3 ● **Click** 📇 **Styles and Formatting to turn off the task pane.**

● **Save the document again.**

● Creating Lists

The next change you want to make is to display the three lines of information about tour features as an itemized list so that they stand out better from the surrounding text.

Bulleted and Numbered Lists

8 Whenever possible, use bulleted or numbered lists to organize information and to make your writing clear and easy to read. A list can be used whenever you present three or more related pieces of information.

Use a **bulleted list** when you have several items that logically fall out from a paragraph into a list. A bulleted list displays one of several styles of bullets before each item in the list. You can select from several types of symbols to use as bullets and you can change the color, size, and position of the bullet.

Use a **numbered list** when you want to convey a sequence of events, such as a procedure that has steps to follow in a certain order. A numbered list displays numbers or letters before the text. Word automatically increments the number or letter as you start a new paragraph. You can select from several different numbering schemes to create your numbered lists.

Use an **outline numbered list** style to display multiple outline levels that show a hierarchical structure of the items in the list. There can be up to nine levels.

Numbering a List

Because both bullet and number styles automatically will indent the items when applied, you first need to remove the indent from the three tour features. Then you will try a numbered list style to see how it looks.

1 ● Select the three tour features.

● Drag the First Line Indent marker on the ruler back to the margin boundary.

● Choose **Format/Bullets and Numbering.**

● Open the **Numbered** tab.

Your screen should be similar to Figure 2.54

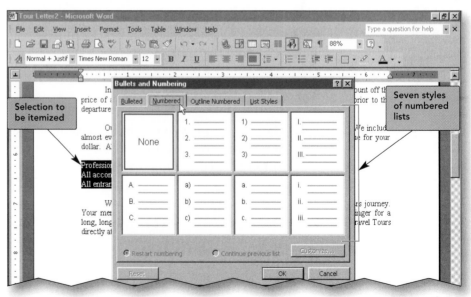

Figure 2.54

The Bullets and Numbering dialog box displays examples of seven numbered list styles. The document default is None. You can also change the appearance of the styles using the Customize option. The first style to the right of None is the style you will use.

2 ● **Select the first numbered list style.**

● Click [OK].

Another Method

You can also click [≡] Numbering to insert the last used numbering style.

Your screen should be similar to Figure 2.55

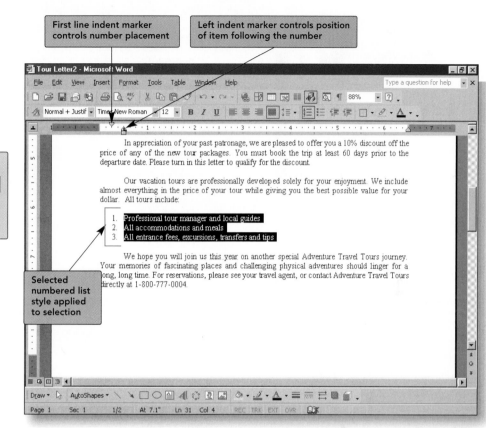

First line indent marker controls number placement

Left indent marker controls position of item following the number

Selected numbered list style applied to selection

In appreciation of your past patronage, we are pleased to offer you a 10% discount off the price of any of the new tour packages. You must book the trip at least 60 days prior to the departure date. Please turn in this letter to qualify for the discount.

Our vacation tours are professionally developed solely for your enjoyment. We include almost everything in the price of your tour while giving you the best possible value for your dollar. All tours include:

1. Professional tour manager and local guides
2. All accommodations and meals
3. All entrance fees, excursions, transfers and tips

We hope you will join us this year on another special Adventure Travel Tours journey. Your memories of fascinating places and challenging physical adventures should linger for a long, long time. For reservations, please see your travel agent, or contact Adventure Travel Tours directly at 1-800-777-0004.

Figure 2.55

Additional Information

You can also create bulleted and numbered lists as you type. To create a bulleted list, type an asterisk (*) followed by a space, and then type the text. To create a numbered list, type a number, type a period followed by a space, and then type the text. When you press [←Enter], Word automatically creates a list and adds numbers or bullets to the next line. To turn off the list, press [←Enter] twice.

A number is inserted at the 0.25-inch position before each line, and the text following the number is indented to the 0.5-inch position. In an itemized list, the first line indent marker on the ruler controls the position of the number or bullet, and the left indent marker controls the position of the item following the number or bullet. The left indent marker creates a hanging indent. If the text following each bullet were longer than a line, the text on the following lines would also be indented to the 0.5-inch position.

Bulleting a List

After looking at the list, you decide it really would be more appropriate if it were a bulleted list instead of a numbered list.

Bullet style replaces numbered list style

Applies last used numbered list style

Applied last used bullet style

① ● Click 📋 Bullets.

Another Method
You can also use Format/Bullets and Numbering/Bulleted.

● Click in the selection to deselect it.

Your screen should be similar to Figure 2.56

Additional Information
To remove bullets or numbers, select the text and choose Format/Bullets and Numbering, and then select the None option, or click 📋 or 📋 again.

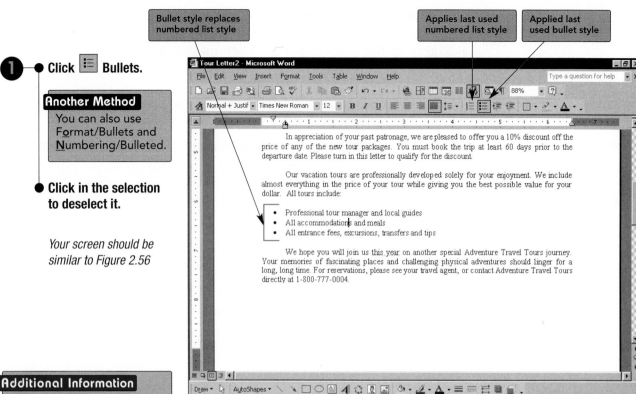

Figure 2.56

The last used bullet style replaces the number.

Using Hyperlinks

The manager has also asked you to add information about the company's Web site to the letter and flyer. You will include the Web site's address, called a **URL** (Uniform Resource Locator), in the document. Word automatically recognizes URLs you enter and creates a hyperlink of the entry. A **hyperlink** is a connection to a location in the current document, another document, or to a Web site. It allows the reader to jump to the referenced location by clicking on the hyperlink text when reading the document on the screen.

Creating a Hyperlink

First you will add the Web site address to the last line of the letter.

1 ● **Add the following sentence after the phone number in the last paragraph:** You can also visit our new Web site at www.AdventureTravelTours.com.

● **Press** (←Enter) **twice.**

Your screen should be similar to Figure 2.57

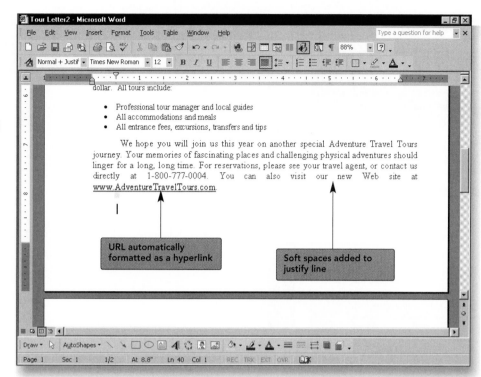

Figure 2.57

The Web address is automatically formatted in blue and underlined, indicating the entry is a hyperlink. The **AutoFormat** feature makes certain formatting changes automatically to your document. These formats include formatting a Web address, replacing ordinals (1st) with superscript (1st), fractions (1/2) with fraction characters (½) and applying a bulleted list format to a list if you type an asterisk (*) followed by a space at the beginning of a paragraph. These AutoFormat features can be turned off if the corrections are not needed in your document.

Removing a Hyperlink

Because this is a document you plan to print, you do not want the text displayed as a link. Since the hyperlink was created using the AutoFormat feature, you can undo the correction or turn it off using the AutoCorrect Options button. You also do not like how the line appears with the addition of soft spaces needed to justify it. To fix this, you decide to remove the word "directly" from the preceding sentence.

1 Point to the hyperlink.

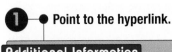

Additional Information

A ScreenTip appears when you point to a hyperlink with instructions on how to follow a link.

special Adventure Travel Tours journey. physical adventures should http://www.adventuretraveltours.com/ agent, or contact Adventure **CTRL + click to follow link** www.AdventureTravelTours.com.

● **Open the AutoCorrect Options menu.**

Additional Information

You can turn off the AutoCorrect feature so the hyperlinks are not created automatically using **Stop Automatically Creating Hyperlinks.**

● **Choose Undo Hyperlink.**

Another Method

You could also click [↰ ▾] Undo to remove the hyperlink autoformatting, or right-click on the hyperlink and select **Remove Hyperlink** from the shortcut menu.

● **Delete the word "directly" from the previous sentence.**

Your screen should be similar to Figure 2.58

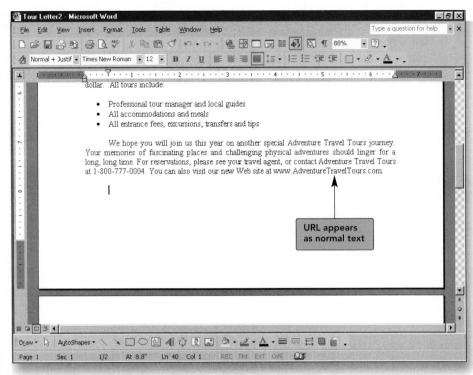

Figure 2.58

The Web address now appears as normal text. The appearance of the paragraph is also greatly improved with the deletion of the word.

Adding an AutoText Entry

While looking at the letter, you realize that the closing lines have not been added to the document. You can quickly insert text and graphics that you use frequently using the AutoText feature. As you learned in Lab 1, Word includes a list of standard AutoText entries that consists of standard phrases such as salutations and closings. You will use the AutoText feature to add a standard closing to the letter.

1 Move to the second blank line at the end of the letter.

● Choose Insert/AutoText/ Closing.

● Choose Best regards.

● Press (←Enter) 3 times.

● Type your name.

● Finally, indent both closing lines to the 3.5-inch position.

● Save the document again.

Your screen should be similar to Figure 2.59

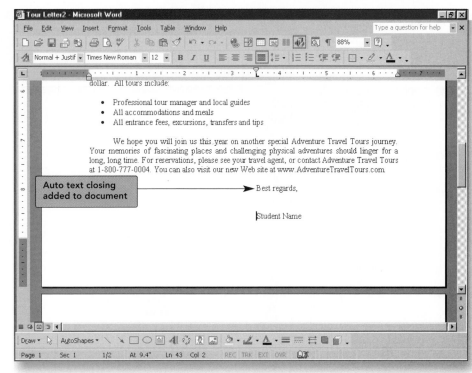

Figure 2.59

Using AutoShapes

You also want to add a special graphic to the flyer containing information about the Web site to catch the reader's attention. To quickly add a shape, you will use one of the ready-made shapes called **AutoShapes** that are supplied with Word. These include such basic shapes as rectangles and circles, a variety of lines, block arrows, flowchart symbols, stars and banners, and callouts. Additional shapes are available in the Clip Organizer. You can also combine AutoShapes to create more complex designs.

Inserting an AutoShape

You want to add a graphic of a banner to the bottom of the flyer.

1
- Press Ctrl + End to move to the bottom of the flyer.

- If necessary, click 📝 Drawing to display the Drawing toolbar.

- Click AutoShapes ▾.

- Select Stars and Banners.

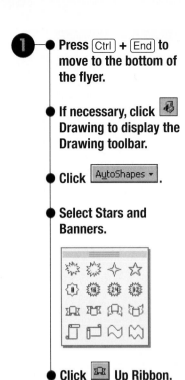

- Click 🎀 Up Ribbon.

Another Method
The menu equivalent is Insert/Picture/AutoShapes.

Your screen should be similar to Figure 2.60

Figure 2.60

A drawing canvas is inserted in the document in which you can draw a picture. All items drawn in the drawing canvas stay as a complete picture within your document and can be moved and resized as a unit. The Drawing Canvas toolbar is used to control features associated with the drawing canvas.

2
- Click in the drawing canvas to insert the autoshape.

- Drag the side middle handles to increase the AutoShape size to that shown in Figure 2.61.

Additional Information
To maintain the height and width proportions of the AutoShape, hold down Shift while you drag.

Your screen should be similar to Figure 2.61

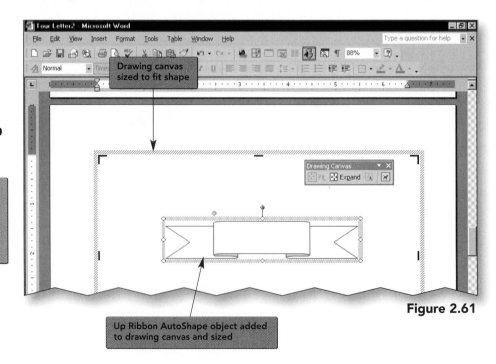

Figure 2.61

Up Ribbon AutoShape object added to drawing canvas and sized

Filling the AutoShape with Color

The AutoShape can also be enhanced using many of the features on the Drawing toolbar, such as adding a fill color and line color.

1 ● Open the  Fill Color drop-down menu in the Drawing toolbar.

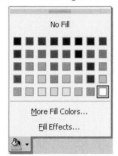

● Select the gold fill color.

● In the same manner, open the Line Color menu in the Drawing toolbar and select a color of your choice.

Your screen should be similar to Figure 2.62

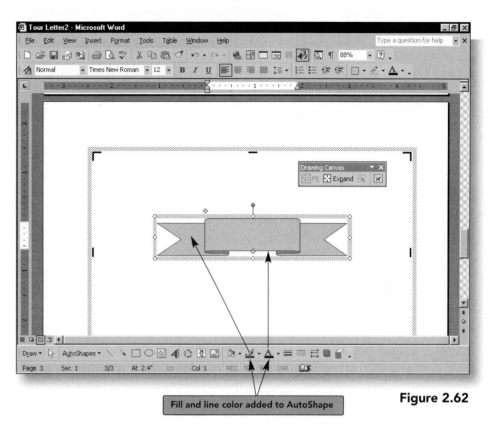

Fill and line color added to AutoShape

Figure 2.62

Adding Text to an AutoShape

Next you will add text to the AutoShape.

1

● **Right-click on the shape to open the shortcut menu.**

● **Choose Add Te_x_t.**

● **Change the font settings to Arial, size 12, bold, italic, centered, and a font color of brown.**

● **Type Visit our.**

● **Press [←Enter].**

● **Type Web site at.**

● **Press [←Enter].**

● **Type AdventureTravel Tours.com.**

● **If necessary, adjust the AutoShape size to fully display the text.**

● **Zoom to Whole Page and scroll the window as in Figure 2.63.**

Your screen should be similar to Figure 2.63

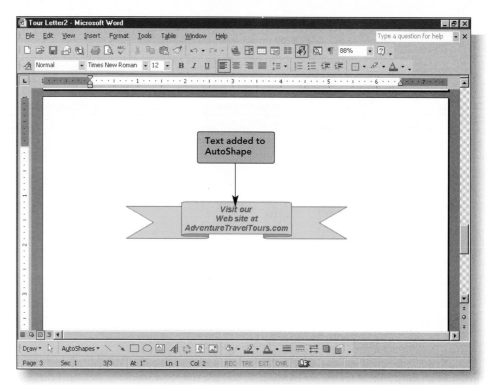

Figure 2.63

Next, you need to move the AutoShape to the bottom of the flyer. In order for the object to fit in this space, you can either make the drawing canvas smaller by sizing it to fit the AutoShape or delete the drawing canvas object. Since the Autoshape is a single object it is not necessary to use the drawing canvas (which is designed to keep multiple objects together). To remove the drawing canvas, you first need to drag the AutoShape off the drawing canvas, then select the drawing canvas and delete it.

2

● **Drag the AutoShape object to move and center it between the margins in the space at the bottom of the flyer.**

● **Click on page 3 to select the drawing canvas and press [Delete].**

● **Return the zoom to Page Width.**

Your screen should be similar to Figure 2.64

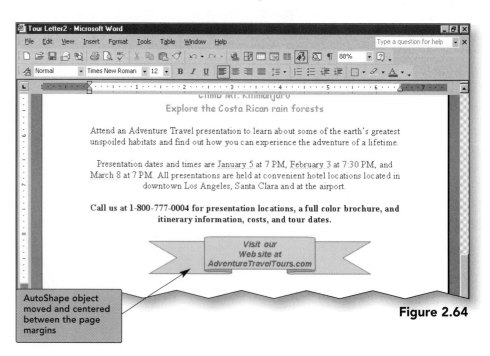

Figure 2.64

Editing While Previewing

Next you will preview and make any final changes to the letter before printing it. When previewing a large document, it is often useful to see multiple pages at the same time to check formatting and other items. Additionally, you can quickly edit while previewing, to make final changes to your document.

Previewing Multiple Pages

First, you want to display both pages of your document in the preview window. You can view up to six pages at the same time in the preview window.

1
- Press Ctrl + Home to move to the top of the document.

- Click 🔲 Print Preview.

- Click 🎛 Multiple pages.

- Click to select 1x2 pages.

HAVING TROUBLE?
Point to the icons on the Multiple Pages drop-down menu to highlight the number of pages and click while selected.

Your screen should be similar to Figure 2.65

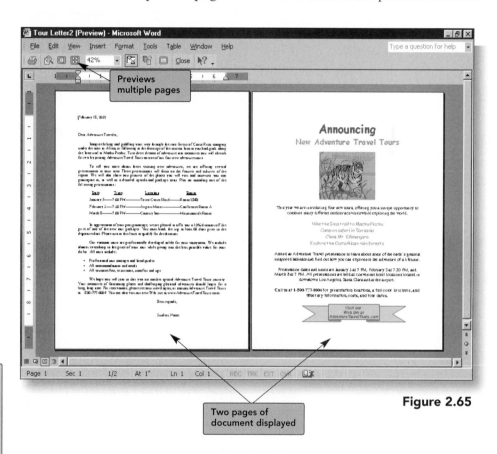

Figure 2.65

Editing in Print Preview

Now that you can see the entire letter, you see that the date needs to be indented to the 3.5-inch tab position. While in Print Preview, you can edit and format text. The mouse pointer can be a magnifying glass 🔍 or an I-beam when it is positioned on text in the document. The 🔍 indicates that when you click on a document, the screen will toggle between the Whole Page view you currently see and 100 percent magnification. The I-beam means you can edit the document.

1 ● If your mouse pointer is not 🔍, click 🔍 to turn on this feature.

● Click near the date in the document.

Your screen should be similar to Figure 2.66

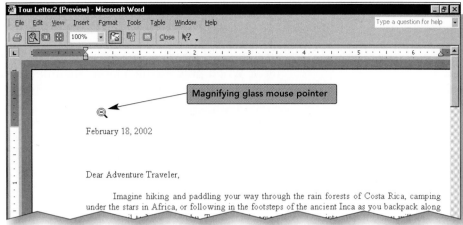

Figure 2.66

The text is displayed in the size it will appear when printed (100 percent zoom). Now that the document is large enough to work in, you will switch from zooming the document to editing it.

2 ● Click 🔍 Magnifier.

● Move the mouse pointer to point to an area containing text.

Your screen should be similar to Figure 2.67

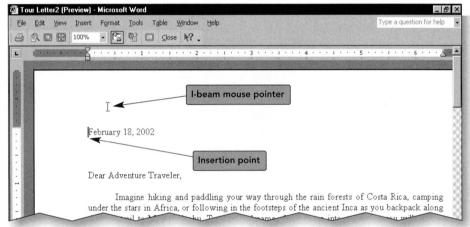

Figure 2.67

When positioned near text, the mouse pointer changes to an I-beam and the insertion point is displayed. Now you can edit the document as in Normal view.

3 ● If necessary, click 🔲 View Ruler to display the ruler.

Additional Information

Pointing to the top or left edge of the window will temporarily display the ruler if the ruler display is off.

● Move to the beginning of the date.

● Indent the date to the 3.5-inch position.

Your screen should be similar to Figure 2.68

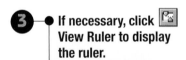

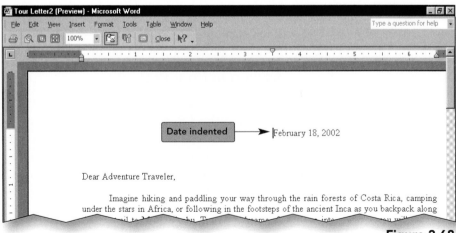

Figure 2.68

While looking at the document, you decide to emphasize some of the text by adding bold. Because you are using Print Preview, the Formatting toolbar buttons are not displayed. You could display the Formatting toolbar or you could use the Format menu to change the text. Another quick way, however, is to use the keyboard shortcut.

4 ● **Select the three bulleted items.**

● **Press** Ctrl **+ B.**

● **Click** 🔍 **Magnifier.**

Another Method

The 100% ▼ Zoom button can also be used to specify the magnification.

● **Click the document.**

Your screen should be similar to Figure 2.69

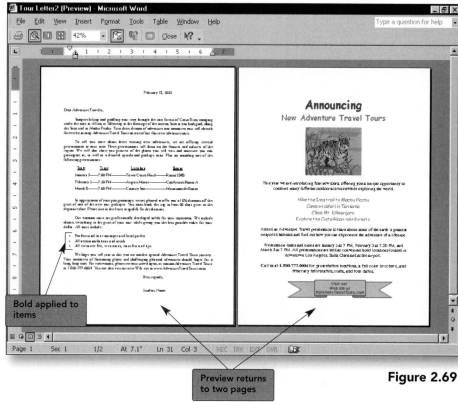

Bold applied to items

Preview returns to two pages

Figure 2.69

Now that the document has been edited and formatted the way you want, you will print a copy of the letter from the Print Preview window using the default print settings.

Note: If you need to specify a different printer, you will need to close the Preview window and use the Print command on the File menu.

5 ● **Click** 🖨 **Print.**

● **Close the Print Preview window.**

● **If necessary, change the view to Normal and the zoom percentage to 100%.**

● **Close and save the** Tour Letter2 **document.**

● **Close the** wd02_Flyer4 **document.**

● **Exit Word.**

The printed output should be similar to the document shown in Figure 2.69.

LAB 2

Revising and Refining a Document

Thesaurus (WD2.10)

Word's **Thesaurus** is a reference tool that provides synonyms, antonyms, and related words for a selected word or phrase.

Move and Copy (WD2.11)

Text and graphic selections can be **moved** or **copied** to new locations in a document or between documents, saving you time by not having to retype the same information.

Page Break (WD2.18)

A **page break** marks the point at which one page ends and another begins. There are two types of page breaks that can be used in a document: soft page breaks and hard page breaks.

Find and Replace (WD2.20)

To make editing easier, you can use the **Find and Replace** feature to find text in a document and replace it with other text as directed.

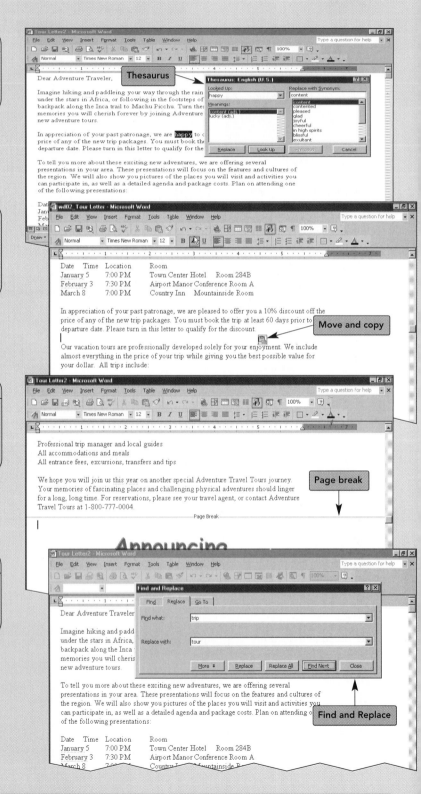

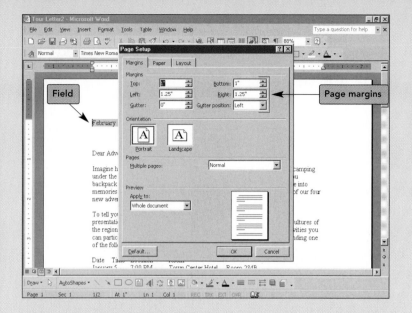

Field (WD2.26)

A **field** is a placeholder that instructs Word to insert information into a document.

Page Margins (WD2.28)

The **page margin** is the blank space around the edge of the page. Standard single-sided documents have four margins: top, bottom, left, and right.

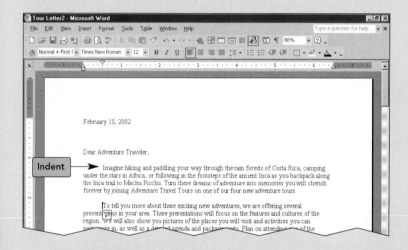

Indents (WD2.31)

To help your reader find information quickly, you can **indent** paragraphs from the margins. Indenting paragraphs sets them off from the rest of the document.

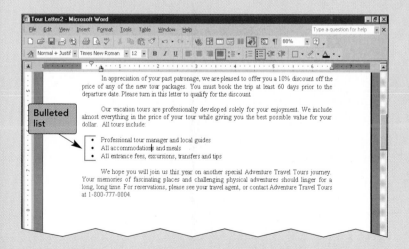

Bulleted and Numbered Lists (WD2.46)

Whenever possible, use **bulleted** or **numbered lists** to organize information and make your writing clear and easy to read.

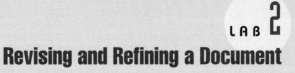

lab review

key terms

active document WD2.16	field code WD2.26	page break WD2.18
antonym WD2.10	field result WD2.26	page margin WD2.28
AutoFormat WD2.49	Format Painter WD2.43	soft page break WD2.18
AutoShape WD2.51	hard page break WD2.18	soft space WD2.41
bulleted list WD2.46	hyperlink WD2.48	source WD2.11
case sensitive WD2.21	leader character WD2.37	synonym WD2.10
destination WD2.11	line spacing WD2.39	tab stop WD2.33
drag and drop WD2.15	numbered list WD2.46	Thesaurus WD2.10
field WD2.26	outline numbered list WD2.46	URL WD2.48

mous skills

The Microsoft Office User Specialist (MOUS) certification program is designed to measure your proficiency in performing basic tasks using the Office XP applications. Getting certified demonstrates that you have the skills and provides a valuable industry credential for employment. After completing this lab, you have learned the following Microsoft Office User Specialist skills:

Skill	Description	Page
Inserting and Modifying text	Apply and modify text formats	WD2.48
	Correct spelling and grammar usage	WD2.5
	Apply font and text effects	WD2.41
	Enter and format Date and Time	WD2.24
Creating and Modifying paragraphs	Modify paragraph formats	WD2.28
	Set and modify tabs	WD2.31
	Apply bullet, outline, and numbering formats to paragraphs	WD2.46
Formatting Documents	Modify document layout and page setup options	WD2.28
	Preview and print documents, envelopes, and labels	

command summary

Command	Shortcut Keys	Button	Action
File/Page Setup			Changes layout of page including margins, paper size, and paper source
Edit/Cut	Ctrl + X	✂	Cuts selection to Clipboard
Edit/Copy	Ctrl + C	📋	Copies selection to Clipboard
Edit/Paste	Ctrl + V	📋	Pastes item from Clipboard
Edit/Find	Ctrl + F		Locates specified text
Edit/Replace	Ctrl + H		Locates and replaces specified text
Insert/Break/Page break	Ctrl + Enter		Inserts hard page break
Insert/Date and Time			Inserts current date or time, maintained by computer system, in selected format
Insert/AutoText			Enters predefined text at insertion point
Insert/Picture/AutoShapes		AutoShapes ▾	Inserts selected AutoShape
Format/Font/Font/Underline style/Single	Ctrl + U	U	Underlines selected text with a single line
Format/Paragraph/Indents and Spacing/Special/First Line			Indents first line of paragraph from left margin
Format/Paragraph/Indents and Spacing/Line Spacing	Ctrl + #		Changes amount of white space between lines
Format/Bullets and Numbering		☰ ☰	Creates a bulleted or numbered list
Format /Tabs			Specifies types and position of tab stops
Tools/Spelling and Grammar	F7	✓	Starts Spelling and Grammar tool
Tools/Language/Thesaurus	Shift + F7		Starts Thesaurus tool

Terminology

screen identification

1. In the following Word screen, letters identify elements. Enter the correct term for each screen element in the space provided.

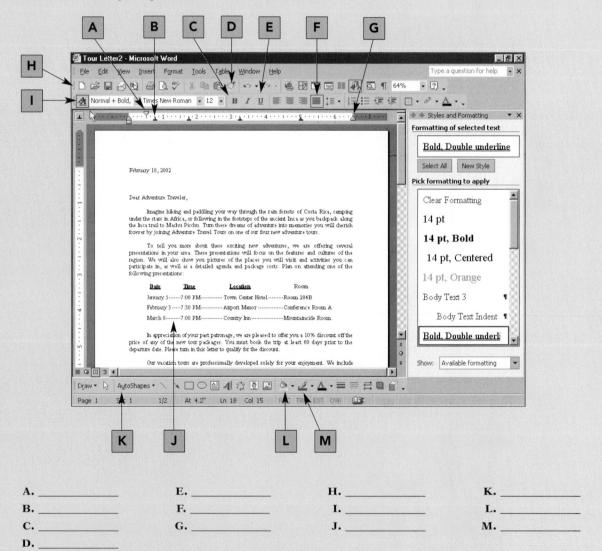

A. _____   E. _____   H. _____   K. _____

B. _____   F. _____   I. _____   L. _____

C. _____   G. _____   J. _____   M. _____

D. _____

matching

Match the item on the left with the correct description on the right.

1. ▤ _____ **a.** toggles between field text and field code

2. ⇧Shift + F9 _____ **b.** used to spell- and grammar-check the document

3. ☷ _____ **c.** adds bold to a selection

4. Ctrl + ↵Enter _____ **d.** indents text to next tab stop

5. Ctrl + B _____ **e.** creates even left and right margins

6. ABC✓ _____ **f.** adds color shading behind selection

7. ✏ ▾ _____ **g.** removes text from the document and stores it in the system Clipboard

8. Tab ↹ _____ **h.** sets a centered tab stop

9. ✂ _____ **i.** creates a bulleted list

10. ⊥ _____ **j.** inserts a hard page break

multiple choice

Circle the correct response to the questions below.

1. A _____ page break is inserted manually by the user.
   a. hard
   b. soft
   c. fixed
   d. floating

2. The _____ feature locates and automatically changes text in a document.
   a. search and replace
   b. find and change
   c. locate and change
   d. find and replace

3. The thesaurus in Word provides _____ .
   a. synonyms
   b. antonyms
   c. related words
   d. all the above

4. The field _____ contains the directions that tell Word what type of information to insert.
   a. results
   b. code
   c. placeholder
   d. format

5. The blank space around the edge of the page is called the _____ .
   a. gutter
   b. indent
   c. margin
   d. white space

6. The _____ indent positions the first line of a paragraph at the left margin with all following lines indented.
   a. left
   b. right
   c. first line
   d. hanging

7. To convey a sequence of events in a document, you should consider using a _____ .
   a. bulleted list
   b. numbered list
   c. organization list
   d. paragraph list

8. A tab stop is the_____ point along a line to which text will indent when you press [Tab].
   a. starting
   b. stopping
   c. beginning
   d. ending

9. The feature most useful for copying or moving short distances in a document is _____ .
   a. drag and drop
   b. drop and drag
   c. move and place
   d. drag and place

10. _____ are solid, dotted, or dashed lines that fill the blank space between tab stops.
   a. tab leaders
   b. leader characters
   c. leader tabs
   d. tab characters

true/false

Circle the correct answer to the following questions.

1. The white space between the text and the edge of the paper is the margin.	True	False
2. A bulleted list conveys a sequence of events.	True	False
3. Indents are used to set paragraphs off from the rest of the text.	True	False
4. Tab leaders are used to separate columns of text.	True	False
5. The spelling checker identifies synonyms for common words.	True	False
6. The Find and Replace feature is used to locate misspelled words in a document.	True	False
7. Soft page breaks are automatically inserted whenever the text reaches the bottom margin.	True	False
8. Field placeholders define the information to be inserted in a document.	True	False
9. Hyperlinks are usually colored and underlined in Word documents.	True	False
10. Formatting and text editing can be done in the print preview window.	True	False

Concepts

fill-in

1. Use a _____ list to convey a sequence of events and a _____ when you have several items that logically fall out from a paragraph into a list.

2. A selection that is moved is cut from its original location, called the _____, and inserted at a new location, called the _____.

3. As you add or remove text from a page, Word automatically _____ the placement of the soft page break.

4. The thesaurus is a reference tool that provides _____, _____ and _____ for a selected word or phrase.

5. The page margin is the _____ space around the edge of a page.

6. A(n)_____ code instructs Word to insert the current date in the document using the selected format whenever the document is printed.

7. Line spacing is the _____ space between lines of text.

8. Use a(n) _____ list style to show a hierarchal structure of the items in the list.

9. Double-sided documents with facing pages typically use _____ margins in which the left page is a mirror image of the right page.

10. When a selection is moved or copied, the selection is stored in the _____ Clipboard, a temporary Windows storage area in memory.

discussion questions

1. Use Help for more information about the AutoFormat feature. Discuss how the AutoFormat feature works and the two ways it can be used.

2. Discuss how the AutoText feature works. When might you want to consider adding words to the AutoText feature? Will added words be recognized in other documents?

3. Discuss the different ways information can be moved within a document. Explain which method is most appropriate in certain circumstances.

4. Discuss how field codes are used in Word documents. What other field codes are available (list several)? Why are field codes important in documents that are reused?

5. Discuss the problems that can be associated with finding and replacing text. What can you do to avoid some of these problems?

Hands-On Exercises

step-by-step

Creating a Checklist

★ 1. You work as a lab assistant in the computer lab. Each week, the lab assistants are responsible for cleaning the computers. You've decided to create a checklist of items that need to be performed to keep the computers clean. Your completed checklist is shown here:

   a. Open the file wd02_Cleaning Checklist.

   b. Use the spelling and grammar checker to correct the identified errors.

   c. Set line spacing for the entire document to 1.5. Set the right and left margins to 1.5 inches.

   d. Bold, color, center, and increase the font size of the main title to 24.

   e. Center the introductory paragraph below the main title.

   f. Move the second sentence in the introductory paragraph below the paragraph. Leave 4 blank lines above and one below the sentence. Highlight the sentence in yellow.

   g. Bold, highlight, and center the subtitles, "Monitor," "Keyboard," and "CPU."

   h. Find and delete each occurrence of "Once a week, " (Hint: leave the Replace With text box empty to delete). Capitalize the first word of the sentence where each deletion occurred.

   i. Select the lines of text below each subtitle and create an itemized list using the solid square bullet style.

Computer Cleaning Checklist

The following items need to be completed on a weekly basis. The cleaning supplies are located in the storeroom on the third shelf.

Drinks in the Lab

Before cleaning, always turn off the computer and unplug the keyboard.

CPU
- Clean the exterior of the box.
- Once a month, vacuum the exterior of the box.

Monitor
- Wipe the screen with a lint-free cloth that is lightly sprayed with an ammonia-free cleaner. Dry the screen thoroughly.
- Wipe the outside of the monitor case, paying special attention to the area around the air vents.

Keyboard
- Turn the keyboard 45 degrees on its edge with the keys facing down and tap the bottom to loosen dust, crumbs, and particles.
- Wipe down the keyboard with a cloth moistened with cleaner. Wrap your finger in the cloth and clean each key individually.

Student Name
Current Date

   j. Use drag and drop to move the "CPU" section above the "Monitor" section.

   k. Add the AutoShape "No" symbol from the Basic Shapes menu to the document.

   l. Add the text **Drinks in the Lab** to the shape. Bold and center the text.

   m. Add a red fill color to the shape. Move the AutoShape to the space below the introductory paragraph. Center the AutoShape between the margins. Delete the Drawing canvas.

   n. Add your name and the current date several lines below the last line on the page.

   o. Save the document as Cleaning Checklist2. Print the document.

Creating a Table

★ **2.** You recently attended a Career Fair and met with many different companies. At the end of the day, you decided to pursue job opportunities with four of the companies. To keep track of the companies, you want to put the key items into a table so you can easily compare them. Your completed document is shown here.

a. Open a new document and set the left and right page margins to 1 inch.

b. Set the line spacing to double.

c. Enter the title **Final 4 Companies** centered on the first line.

d. Apply formats of your choice to the title line.

e. Several lines below the title, place left tab stops at .25, 1.75, and 5.0 inches and a center tab at 4.25 inches on the ruler.

f. Enter the word **Company** at the first tab stop, **Product/Service** at the second tab stop, **Size** at the third tab stop, and **Location** at the fourth tab stop.

g. Enter the rest of the information shown here into the table.

Final 4 Companies

Company	Product/Service	Size	Location
Brown	Telecommunications	12,000	Memphis
GROTAN	Trucking	5,000	Minneapolis
Kriken	Software Development	2,500	San Jose
Matrox	Software Development	3,500	San Diego

Student Name

February 18, 2001

Brown	Telecommunications	12,000	Memphis
GROTAN	Trucking	5,000	Minneapolis
Kriken	Software development	2,500	San Jose
Matrox	Software development	3,500	San Diego

h. Change the font size of the table headings to 18 points and the remainder of the table to 14 points. Add bold, color, and an underline style of your choice to the table headings.

i. Add your name and the current date as a field using the Date and Time command several lines below the table.

j. Save the document as Career Fair and print it.

Preparing an Article

★★ **3.** To complete this exercise, you must have completed Hands-On Exercise 5 in Lab 1. You are still working on the column for the campus newspaper. You need to add information to the article and make several formatting changes to the document. Your completed article is shown here:

a. Open the document Making Sushi2 you created in Practice Exercise 5 in Lab 1.

b. Copy the contents of the file wd02_Rice into the article above the "Making California Rolls" section.

c. Save the document using the file name Making Sushi3.

d. Format the newly inserted section using the same formats as in the "Making California Rolls" section.

e. Change the top margin to 1.5 inches. Change the right and left margins to 1 inch.

f. Indent all the lists to the 1-inch position.

g. Change the directions in both sections to an itemized numbered list.

h. Use the thesaurus to find a better word for "big" in the first sentence.

i. Replace the date in the last line with a date field.

j. Preview, and then print the document.

k. Save the document using the same file name.

Making Sushi

Your next dinner party can be a huge success when you get everyone involved in making sushi. You need just a few basic items for the preparation. If you live in a large city, you may find these at your local grocery store. Your best bet is to find an Asian grocery in your city.

Sushi Basics:
A bamboo-rolling mat (Makisu)
Cutting board
Sharp knife
Wasabi
Pickled ginger
Soy sauce

Making Sushi Rice

Great sushi starts with the rice. If you master this process all you need to add is really good fish. The trick involves fanning the rice as it cools to help evaporate the moisture. The end result should be sticky rice with a glossy texture.

Ingredients:
Medium grain rice
Water
1 tablespoon rice vinegar
1 tablespoon sugar
Dash salt

Directions:
1. Make the rice according to the package directions.
2. After the rice is cooked, put it into the wooden bowl and lightly flatten it.
3. Pour vinegar, sugar, and salt into a small bowl and mix until dissolved.
4. Drizzle the vinegar mixture onto the rice and mix it using the wooden spoon fanning the rice as you mix.
5. When the rice is sticky with a glossy texture, cover the bowl with a damp towel.
6. Let the rice reach room temperature before you use it.

Making California Rolls

California rolls are a great way to introduce sushi to the novice, as there is no raw fish in the roll. This recipe calls for imitation crabmeat but if your budget can handle the cost use real crabmeat.

Ingredients:
Nori seaweed
Prepared sushi rice
Avocado, peeled and cut into sixteenths
Imitation crabmeat
Cucumber, peeled, seeded, and julienned

Directions:
1. Cut one sheet of Nori seaweed in half and place on a bamboo mat.
2. With a wooden spoon, spread a thin layer of sushi rice on the seaweed leaving a strip uncovered at each end to seal the roll.
3. At one end, add two strips of cucumber, one slice of avocado, and one piece of imitation crabmeat.
4. Beginning at the end with the cucumber, avocado, and crabmeat, roll the seaweed over once. Pull up the bamboo mat and use it to help you roll the rest of the way until you reach the other end of the seaweed wrap.
5. Place the roll seam side down and with a sharp knife, cut the roll into ¼ or ½-inch wide rolls.

Student Name - April 18, 2001

Writing a Thank You Letter

★ ★ **4.** Your experience at the career fair was very positive. There is one company that you are very interested in and want to pursue further. You have quickly written a draft of a thank-you letter, but now need to revise it to fix mistakes and add more details of what you would like to discuss with the Human Resources representative. Your completed letter is shown below.

a. Open the file wd02_Thank-You Letter.

b. Replace "[Current Date]" with a date field using the form of the date shown in the final document. Indent the date to the 3-inch position.

c. Bullet the list using a bullet style of your choice.

d. Change the word "focus" in the first bulleted item to a similar word using the thesaurus to find a suitable synonym.

e. Change the left and right and top margins to 1.5 inch.

f. Using the AutoText feature, insert a closing on the second line under the last paragraph.

g. Replace "[Student Name]" with your name in the closing. Indent both closing lines to the 3-inch position.

h. Perform a spelling and grammar check to eliminate errors.

i. Save your letter as Thank-You Letter2 and print it. Sign it just above your name.

April 18, 2001

Brown Telecom
35 Pioneer Avenue
Memphis, TN 47143

Dear Ms. Jones:

Thank you for spending time with me at the West Valley Career Fair last Wednesday. I have attached another copy of my resume and want to point out some highlights that are of particular interest to your company:

- MBA with a concentration on the Global Economy
- Internship for major telecommunications firm in Munich
- Fluent in German and French

I am very interested in the position we discussed and would like to set up a time when we could explore the opportunity further. I will call you later this week to set up a time that is convenient for you.

Sincerely,

Student Name

Creating a Flyer

★ ★ **5.** You work for the Downtown Internet Cafe, which sells fresh roast coffee and coffee beverages.
★   You want to create a document describing the roast coffee varieties and prices. Using tab settings,
       create a table of coffee varieties and prices according to the following specifications. Your
       completed flyer is shown here:

a. Open a new document.

b. Enter the title **DownTown Internet Cafe** on the first line. Add three blank lines.

c. Enter **Roast Coffee** on line 4 followed by two blank lines.

d. Center the first line, make it brown, and change the font size to 48 pt.

e. Center the second line, make it brown, and change the font size to 22 pt.

f. On line seven, place left tab stops at .75 and 2.5 inches and a center tab at 5.25 inches.

g. Enter the word **Coffee** at the first tab stop, **Description** at the second tab stop, and **Cost/Pound** at the third tab stop.

h. Enter the rest of the information for the table shown in the final document.

i. Add tab leaders between the data in the table.

j. Increase the font of the table headings to 14 pt. Add bold, color, and an underline style of your choice to the table headings.

k. Open the file wd02_Coffee Flyer. Copy the first three paragraphs and insert them above "Roast Coffee" in the new document.

DownTown Internet Café

Coffee Sale

Tired of brewing a wimpy cup of coffee that just doesn't have the punch you crave? Then head on over for our huge sale. You'll never buy bland supermarket coffee again.

Through January, take $2 off the regular coffee prices shown below.

Roast Coffee

Coffee	Description	Cost/Pound
Colombian Blend	Classic body and aroma	$11
French Roast	Sophisticated taste	$10
Kenyan	Robust and deep flavor	$12
Arabian Blend	Strong yet subtle	$11

You can also order online at *www.somecoffee.com* today and get coffee delivered right to your door! But hurry, our sale won't last forever.

Student Name - February 19, 2002

l. Center the words "Coffee Sale." Make them bold, font size 24 pt, and a color of your choice.

m. Make the paragraphs bold, centered, and 14 pt, and set their line spacing to double.

n. Increase the font size of the line above "Roast Coffee" to 18 pt. Reset its line spacing to single. Insert a blank line below it.

o. Copy the remaining paragraph from the wd02_Coffee Flyer document, and insert it at the bottom of the new document. Include two blank lines between the table and the paragraph.

p. Bold and center the final paragraph.

q. Increase the top, left and right margins to 1.5 inch.

r. Create the Explosion 1 AutoShape. Enter and center the word **Sale!** in red within it, and choose the gold fill color. Size the shape appropriately. Move the shape above the title line. Delete the drawing canvas.

s. Add your name and a field with the current date several lines below the final paragraph.

t. Save the document as Coffee Flyer2 and print it.

Applying for an Internship

★ 1. Your first year as a law student is going well and you are looking for a summer internship with a local law firm. You just had an interview with Christine Kent of the Kent, Johnson, and Smyth law firm and want to write a follow-up letter thanking her for her time and reiterating how you think you would be best qualified for this position. Write a business letter directed to Ms. Kent. Include your qualifications in the form of a bulleted list. Be sure to also include the date, a salutation, two justified paragraphs, a closing, and your name as a signature. Use the business letter in Hands-On Exercise 4 as a model. Save the document as Internship Letter and print the letter.

Insurance Survey

★ 2. The Arizona Department of Insurance conducted a survey in October, 2000 comparing the cost of a six-month car insurance premium in different areas of the state. The comparison was based on a 48-year-old married couple with a clean driving record. The same criteria for type and year of automobile and miles driven to work were used as well as the amount of insurance coverage.

Create a tabbed table using the information shown below. Bold and underline the column heads. Add style 2 tab leaders to the table entries. Above the table, write a paragraph explaining the table contents.

Insurance Company	Phoenix	Tucson	Flagstaff
AAA Preferred	$1,279	$1,116	$ 775
Farmers	1,461	1,432	1,023
Allstate	1,605	1,617	1,268
American Family	1,341	1,206	817

Include your name and the date below the table. Save the document as Insurance Comparison and print the document.

To-Do List

★★ 3. Many people create lists of things they need to do each day or each week. In this problem, you will create a list of things you need to do for the week. Create a numbered "to do" list of all the things you have to do this week (or all the things you would like to do this week) either in order of importance or in chronological order. Add a title that includes your name and the current date as a field. Use the formatting techniques you have learned to improve the appearance of the list. Create an AutoShape containing the words "To-Do List". Display it above the list. Save the document as To Do List. Print the document.

New Employee Memo

★★ 4. Adventure Travel has recently hired a new sales representative, Amity Zeh. You need to write a memo introducing Amity to the sales staff. Address the memo to the sales staff and add appropriate From, Date, and RE: lines. Using a bulleted list, describe Amity Zeh's past experience as an assistant manager at a movie theater and the skills you think she learned there. Describe as well her new function of selling Adventure Travel tours. Justify your paragraphs and indent the first lines. Add two AutoShapes to accent your memo. Save the document as New Staff Memo and print the memo.

Advertising Flyer

★ ★ 5. Create a flyer to advertise something you have for sale (used car, used stereo, and so on). Integrate
★ the following features into the flyer:

Different fonts in different sizes, colors, and styles
Bulleted or numbered list
Indents
An AutoShape
A graphic
A tabbed table with tab leaders

Include your name as the contact information. Save the document as For Sale Flyer and print the flyer.

on the web

Your political science class is studying the 2000 presidential election. Your instructor has divided the class into three groups and assigned each group a research project. Your group is to find out how Americans voted for the presidential candidates by age and sex. Use the Web to research this topic and write a one-page report on your findings. Include a table of the data you found. Use other features demonstrated in this lab, including AutoShapes, indents, bulleted lists, font colors, and so forth to make your report attractive and easy to read. Be sure to reference your sources on the Web for the data you located. Include your name and the current date below the report. Save the report as Election Results and print your report.

Creating Reports and Tables

objectives

After completing this lab, you will know how to:

1.	Create and modify an outline.
2.	Hide spelling and grammar errors.
3.	Use Click and Type.
4.	Apply styles.
5.	Create and update a table of contents.
6.	Create a section break.
7.	Center a page vertically.
8.	Create footnotes.
9.	Use Document Map.
10.	Wrap text around graphics.
11.	Add captions and cross-references.
12.	Create and format a simple table.
13.	Sort a reference list.
14.	Add headers, footers, and page numbers.
15.	Print selected pages and save to a new folder.

A table of contents listing can be created quickly from heading styles in a document.

Tanzania and Peru
Table of Contents

Student Name

Current Date

Tanzania

Geography and Climate

"In the midst of a great wilderness, full of wild beasts…I fancied I saw a summit…covered with a dazzlingly white cloud (qtd. in Cole 56). This is how Johann Krapf, the first outsider to witness the splendor of Africa's highest mountain, described Kilimanjaro. The peak was real, though the white clouds he "fancied" he saw were the dense layer of snow that coats the mountain.[1]

Tanzania is primarily a plateau that slopes gently downward into the country's five hundred miles of Indian Ocean coastline. Nearly three-quarters of Tanzania is dry savannah, so much so that the Swahili word for the central plateau is *nyika*, meaning "wasteland." Winding through these flatlands is the Great Rift Valley, which forms narrow and shallow lakes in its long path. Several of these great lakes form a belt-like oasis of green vegetation. Contrasting with the severity of the plains are the coastal areas, which are lush with ample rainfall. In the north the plateau slopes dramatically into Mt. Kilimanjaro.

Figure 1- Lions in the Serengeti

Ngorongoro Conservation Area

Some of Tanzania's most distinguishing geographical features are found in the Ngorongoro Conservation Area.[2] The park is composed of many craters and gorges, as well as lakes, forest, and plains. Among these features is the area's namesake, the Ngorongoro Crater. The Crater is a huge expanse, covering more than one hundred square miles. On the Crater's floor, grasslands blend into swamps, lakes, rivers, and woodland. Also within the Conservation Area's perimeter is the Olduvai Gorge, commonly referred to as the "Cradle of Mankind," where in 1931 the stone tools of prehistoric man were found. This find subsequently led to the discovery of the remains of humans who lived 1.75 million years ago.

Serengeti Plain

Adjacent to the western edge of the Ngorongoro Conservation Area is the Serengeti Plain. Its area is approximately 5,700 square miles, and its central savanna supports many grazing animals with plentiful water and lush grasses. Its southern portion is dry, receiving an average of only twenty inches of rainfall annually. The north is wooded grassland with watercourses and tributaries to larger rivers. Only two seasons occur on the Serengeti: dry and wet. The dry season occurs between June and October and the wet season between November to May.

---
[1] Mt. Kilimanjaro is 19,340 feet high, making it the fourth tallest mountain in the world.
[2] The Conservation Area is a national preserve spanning 3,196 square miles.

Wrapping text around graphics, adding figure captions, footnotes, headers, and footers are among many features that can be used to enhance a report.

---

coming from the east. Some areas in the south are considered drier than the Sahara. Conversely, there are a few areas in this region where mountain rivers meet the ocean that are green with life and do not give the impression of being in a desert at all.

La Sierra

Inland and to the east is the mountainous region called La Sierra, encompassing Peru's share of the Andes mountain range. The southern portion of this region is prone to volcanic activity, and some volcanoes are active today. La Sierra is subject to a dry season from May to September, which is winter in that part of the world. La Sierra is moderate by day, and can be freezing in some areas during the night. Temperatures are moderate annual precipitation. The weather is typically sunny, with moderate as well as the Sacred Valley of the Incas. The former Incan capital Cuzco is in this region, as well as the Sacred Valley of the Incas. This region also contains Lake Titicaca, the world's highest navigable lake[3]

La Selva

La Selva, a region of tropical rainforest, is the easternmost region in Peru. This region, with the eastern foot of the Andes Mountains, forms the Amazon Basin, into which numerous rivers flow. The Amazon River begins at the meeting point of the two dominant rivers, the Ucayali and Marañon. La Selva is extremely wet, with some areas exceeding an annual precipitation of 137 inches. Its wettest season occurs from November to April. The weather here is humid and extremely hot.

Region	Annual Rainfall (Inches)	Average Temperature (Fahrenheit)
La Costa	2	68
La Sierra	35	54
La Selva	137	80

Culture

Historical Culture

Peru is where the Incas built their homes and cities. They lived in the southern portion of La Sierra until around 1300 CE[4], when they moved north to the fertile Cuzco Valley. From here they built their empire, overrunning and assimilating neighboring lands and cultures. They organized into a socialist-type theocracy under an emperor – the Inca – whom they worshipped as a deity. The Inca Empire reached its maximum size by the late fifteenth and early sixteenth centuries.

In 1532 the Spanish explorer Francisco Pizarro landed in Peru. He saw great opportunity in seizing the empire because of the rich gold deposits in the Cuzco Valley, and did so with superior armament. This opened the door for masses of gold- and adventure-seeking conquistadors to join in the pursuit, who brought with them both modern weaponry and

---
[3] Lake Titicaca is 12,507 feet above sea level.
[4] Common Era (CE) is the period dating from the birth of Christ.

Including tables and using table formats makes the report attractive and easy to read.

Works Cited

Camerapix Publishers International. *Spectrum Guide to Tanzania*. Edison: Hunter, 1992.

Cole, Tom. *Geographic Expeditions*. San Francisco: Geographic Expeditions, 1999.

Hudson, Rex A., ed. "Peru: A Country Study." *The Library of Congress – Country Studies*. 1992. <http://lcweb2.loc.gov/frd/cs/petoc.html#pe0049> (11 Jan. 2001).

"The Living Edens: Manu – Peru's Hidden Rainforest." *PBS Online*. <http://www.pbs.org/edens/manu> (11 Jan. 2001).

Valdizan, Mónica V. "Virtual Peru." 9 Jan. 1999. http://www.xs4all.nl/~govertme/visitperu/ (11 Jan. 2001).

Lists can be quickly sorted to appear in alphabetical order.

1
2
3
4
5
6
7
8

Adventure Travel Tours

Adventure Travel Tours gives out information on their tours in a variety of forms. Travel brochures, for instance, contain basic tour information in a promotional format and are designed to entice potential clients to sign up for a tour. More detailed regional information packets are given to people who have already signed up for a tour, so they can prepare for their vacation. These packets include facts about each region's climate, geography, and culture. Additional informational formats include pages on Adventure Travel's Web site and scheduled group presentations.

Part of your responsibility as adver-

tising coordinator is to gather the information that Adventure Travel will publicize about each regional tour. Specifically, you have been asked to provide information for two of the new tours: the Tanzania Safari and the Machu Picchu trail. Because this information is used in a variety of formats, your research needs to be easily adapted. You will therefore present your facts in the form of a general report on Tanzania and Peru.

In this lab, you will learn to use many of the features of Word 2002 that make it easy to create an attractive and well-organized report. A portion of the completed report is shown on the left.

© Corbis

The following concepts will be introduced in this lab:

1	**Style**	A style is a set of formats that is assigned a name and can be quickly applied to a selection.
2	**Section**	To format different parts of a document differently, you can divide a document into sections.
3	**Footnote and Endnote**	A footnote is a source reference or text offering additional explanation that is placed at the bottom of a page. An endnote is also a source reference or long comment that typically appears at the end of a document.
4	**Text Wrapping**	You can control how text appears around a graphic object by specifying the text wrapping style.
5	**Captions and Cross References**	A caption is a title or explanation for a table, picture, or graph. A cross-reference is a reference from one part of a document to related information in another part.
6	**Table**	A table is used to organize information into an easy-to-read format of horizontal rows and vertical columns.
7	**Sort**	Word can quickly arrange or sort paragraphs in alphabetical, numeric, or date order based on the first character in each paragraph.
8	**Header and Footer**	A header is a line or several lines of text at the top of each page just above the top margin line. A footer is text at the bottom of every page just below the bottom margin line.

Creating and Modifying an Outline

After several days of research, you have gathered many notes from various sources including books, magazines, and the Web. However, the notes are very disorganized and you are having some difficulty getting started on writing the report. Often the best way to start is by creating an outline of the main topics.

Word makes it easy to create and view document content as an outline using Outline view. Outline view shows the hierarchy of topics in a document by displaying the different heading levels indented to represent their level in the document's structure, as shown in the example at left. The arrangement of headings in a hierarchy of importance quickly shows the relationship between topics. You can use Outline view to help you create a new document or to view and reorganize the topics in an existing document.

- **Tanzania**
  - *Culture*
  - *Geography*
    - Climate
  - *Animal Life*
- **Peru**
  - *Culture*
    - Historical Culture
      - **Machu Picchu**
    - Current Culture
  - *Geography and Climate*
    - La Costa
    - La Sierra
    - La Selva
  - *Animal Life*

Using Outline View

You will use Outline view to help you organize the main topics of the report.

Start Word.

Close the task pane.

Click 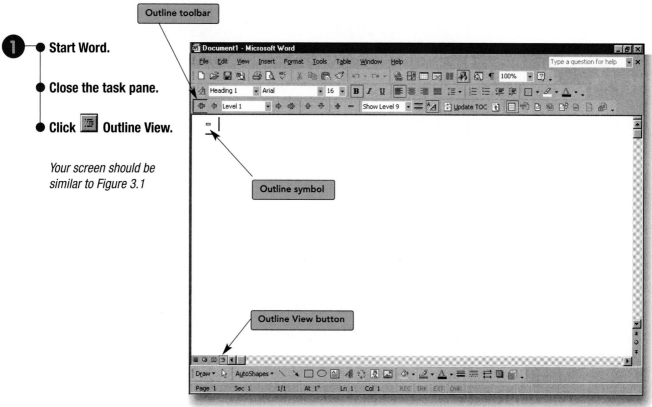 Outline View.

Your screen should be similar to Figure 3.1

Outline toolbar

Outline symbol

Outline View button

Figure 3.1

The Outline toolbar is displayed. It contains buttons that make it easy to modify the outline. The first line of the blank document displays an outline symbol. There are three outline symbols (□, ✚, and ❑) that are used to identify the levels of topics in the outline and to quickly reorganize topics. You will begin by entering the main topic headings for the report.

2 ● **Type the following headings, pressing (←Enter) after each except the last:**

Tanzania

Climate

Geography

Animal Life

Peru

Culture

Historical Culture

Machu Picchu

Current Culture

Geography and Climate

La Costa

La Sierra

La Selva

Animal Life (do not press (←Enter))

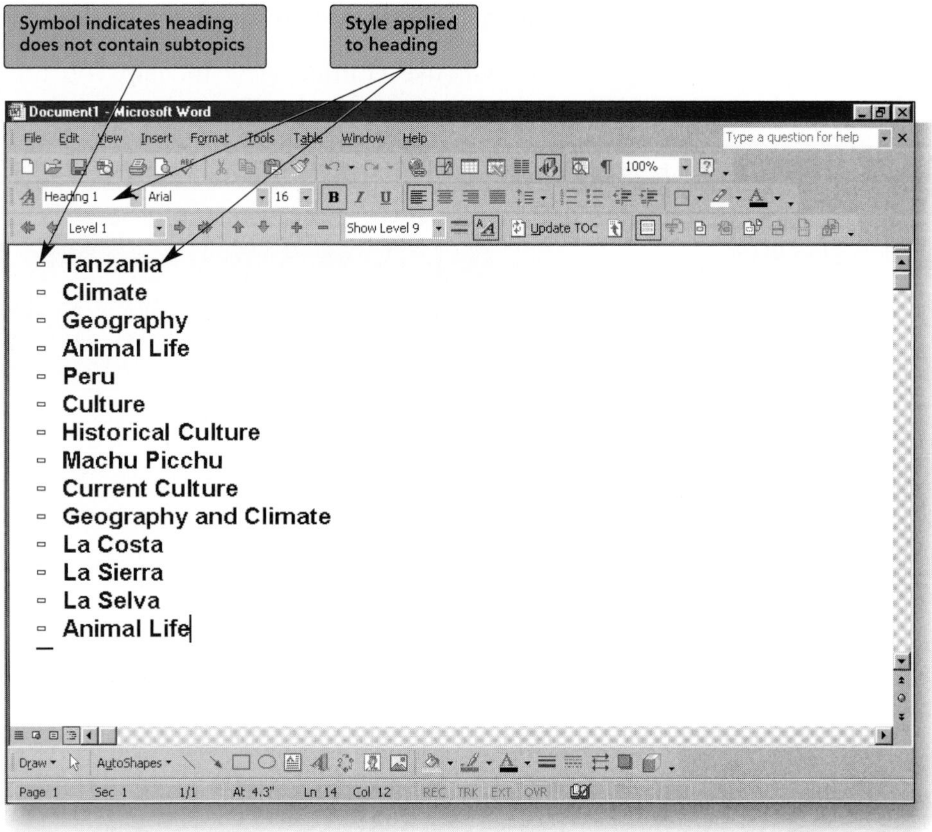

Figure 3.2

● **Correct any misspelled words and use Ignore All for any identified proper names.**

Your screen should be similar to Figure 3.2

Each heading is preceded with the ▭ outline symbol, which indicates the heading does not contain subtopics. As you create a new document in Outline view, Word automatically applies built-in heading styles to the text as it is entered in the outline.

concept 1

Style

1   A **style** is a set of formats that is assigned a name and can be quickly applied to a selection. Word includes 75 predefined styles, and you can create your own custom styles. Many styles are automatically applied when certain features, such as footnotes, are used. Others must be applied manually to selected text.

   Styles can be applied to characters or paragraphs. **Character styles** consist of a combination of any character formats in the Fonts dialog box that affect selected text. **Paragraph styles** are a combination of any character formats and para-

graph formats that affect all text in a paragraph. A paragraph style can include all the font settings that apply to characters, as well as tab settings, indents, and line settings that apply to paragraphs. The default paragraph style is Normal, and it includes character settings of Times New Roman, 12 pt, and paragraph settings of left indent at 0, single line spacing, and left alignment. In addition, many paragraph styles are designed to affect specific text elements such as headings, captions, and footnotes.

Each topic you entered is initially formatted with a Heading 1 style. **Heading styles** are one of the most commonly used styles. They are designed to identify different levels of headings in a document. Heading styles include combinations of fonts, type sizes, bold, and italics. The first four heading styles and the formats associated with each are shown in the table below:

Heading Level	Appearance
Heading 1	Arial 16 pt bold
Heading 2	*Arial 14 pt bold, italic*
Heading 3	Arial 13 pt bold
Heading 4	Times New Roman 14 pt bold

The most important heading in a document should be assigned a Heading 1 style. This style is the largest and most prominent. The next most important heading should be assigned the Heading 2 style, and so on. Headings give the reader another visual cue about how the information is grouped in your document.

Changing Outline Levels

Next you need to arrange the headings by outline levels. As you rearrange the topic headings and subheadings, different heading styles are applied based upon the position or level of the topic within the outline hierarchy. Headings that are level 1 appear as the top level of the outline and appear in a Heading 1 style, level 2 headings appear indented below level 1 headings and appear in a Heading 2 style, and so on.

The outline symbols are used to select and move the heading to a new location or level within the document. Dragging the outline symbol to the right or left changes the level. To demote a heading to a lower level, drag the symbol to the right; to promote a heading to a higher level, drag the symbol to the left. As you drag the symbol, a vertical solid gray line appears at each outline level to show where the heading will be placed.

1 ● Drag the ▢ symbol of the Climate heading to the right one level.

Additional Information

The mouse pointer changes to ✛, indicating dragging it will move the heading.

Your screen should be similar to Figure 3.3

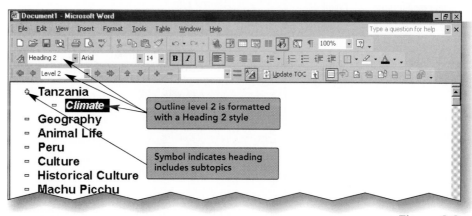

Figure 3.3

First you will make the Climate topic heading a subtopic below the main heading of Tanzania.

The Climate heading has changed to a Heading 2 style, and the heading is indented one level to show it is subordinate to the heading above it. The Tanzania heading now displays a ✛ outline symbol, which indicates the topic heading includes subtopics. You can also click ◄ Promote and ► Demote on the outlining toolabar to change outline levels.

2 ● **Click on the Geography topic.**

● **Click ► Demote 2 times.**

Your screen should be similar to Figure 3.4

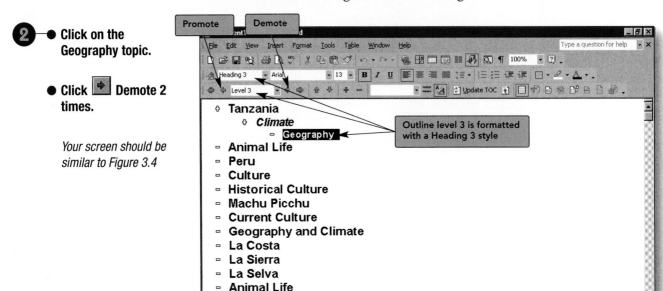

Figure 3.4

The Geography heading is now a Heading 3 style and is indented two levels in the outline.

3 ● **Demote the remaining topics to the heading levels shown below.**

Animal Life	Level 2
Culture	Level 2
Historical Culture	Level 3
Machu Picchu	Level 4
Current Culture	Level 3
Geography and Climate	Level 2
La Costa	Level 3
La Sierra	Level 3
La Selva	Level 3
Animal Life	Level 2

Your screen should be similar to Figure 3.5

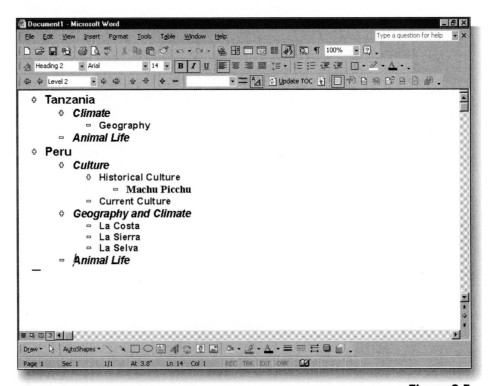

Figure 3.5

Moving and Inserting Outline Topics

Another Method

You can also click ⬆ Move Up and ⬇ Move Down to move a topic.

Next you want to change the order of topics. To move a heading to a different location, drag the outline symbol up or down. As you drag, a horizontal line shows where the heading will be placed when you release the mouse button.

1
- Drag the Geography heading up above the Climate heading.

- Promote the Geography heading to a level 2.

- Demote the Climate heading to a level 3.

  Your screen should be similar to Figure 3.6

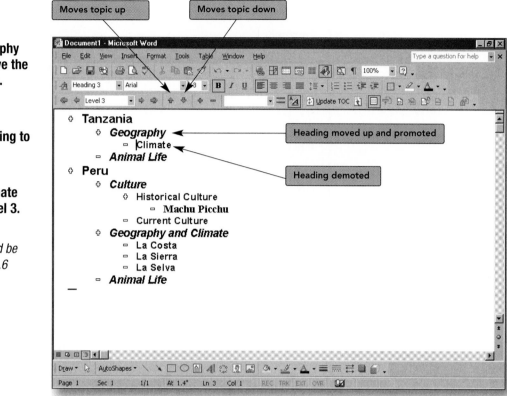

Figure 3.6

As you check the outline, you realize you forgot a heading for Culture under Tanzania.

2
- Move to the beginning of the Geography heading for Tanzania.

- Press ⏎Enter to insert a blank topic heading.

- Type Culture on the blank heading line.

  Your screen should be similar to Figure 3.7

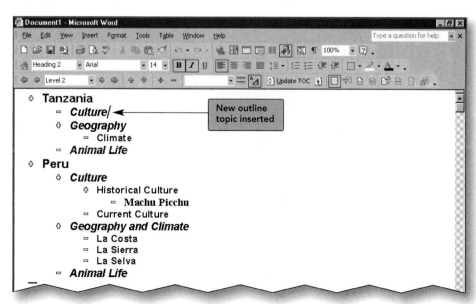

Figure 3.7

When you're satisfied with the organization, you can switch to Normal view or Print Layout view to add detailed body text and graphics.

3 ● **Switch to Normal view.**

Your screen should be similar to Figure 3.8

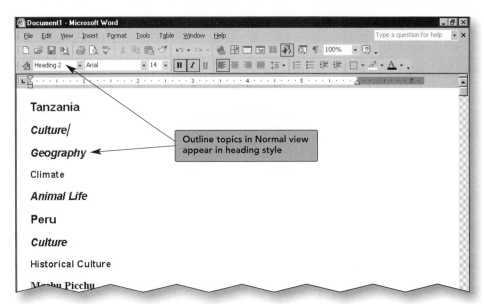

Figure 3.8

The topic headings appear left-aligned on the page in the style that was applied to the text as you created the outline.

Collapsing and Expanding the Outline

You have continued to work on the report during the day and have entered most of the information for the different topics. To see the information that has been added to the report,

1 ● **Open the file**
  wd03_Tour Research.

● **Switch to Outline view.**

● **Scroll the window to view the entire document.**

● **Return to the top of the document.**

Your screen should be similar to Figure 3.9

HAVING TROUBLE?
Your outline may display less text than in Figure 3.9. This is because Outline view reflects the settings that were in effect on your computer when this feature was last used.

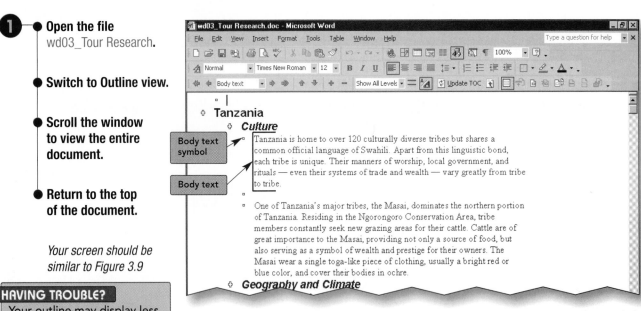

Figure 3.9

The document is displayed as an outline with the topic headings indented appropriately. The body text appears below the appropriate heading. Any text not identified with a heading style is considered body text. The small square to the left of a paragraph identifies it as body text.

In Outline view, you can display as much or as little of the document text as you want. To make it easier to view and reorganize the document's structure, you can "collapse" the document to show just the headings you want. Alternatively, you can display part of the body text below each heading or the entire body text. You can then easily move the headings around until the order is logical, and the body text will follow the heading. The table below shows how you can collapse and expand the amount of text displayed in Outline view.

To Collapse	Do This
Text below a specific heading level	Select the lowest heading you want to display from the [All] Show Level drop-down menu.
All subheadings and body text under a heading	Double-click ✛ next to the heading.
Text under a heading, one level at a time	Click the heading text, and then click [−] Collapse.
All body text	Select Show All Levels from the [Show Level 4 ▾] Show Level drop-down menu.
All body text except first line	Click [≡] Show First Line Only.
To Expand	**Do This**
All headings and body text	Select Show All Levels from the [Show Level 4 ▾] Show Level drop-down menu.
All collapsed subheadings and body text under a heading	Double-click ✛ next to the heading.
Collapsed text under a heading, one level at a time	Click the heading text, then click [+] Expand.

To see more of the outline, you will collapse the display of the text under the Geography and Climate heading.

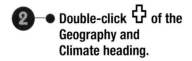

2 ● Double-click ✛ of the Geography and Climate heading.

Your screen should be similar to Figure 3.10

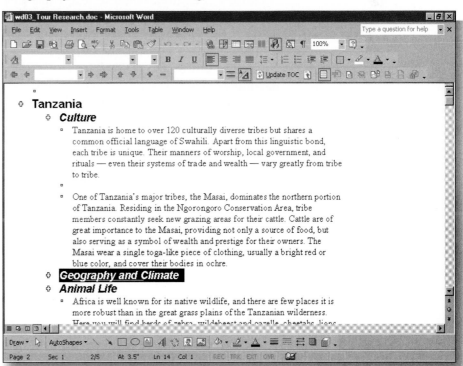

Figure 3.10

All the body text below this heading is hidden. You would like to see only the three heading levels of the document, not the body text, so you can quickly check its organization.

3 ● **Open the** Show Level 4 ▾ **Show Level drop-down list.**

● **Choose Show Level 3.**

Your screen should be similar to Figure 3.11

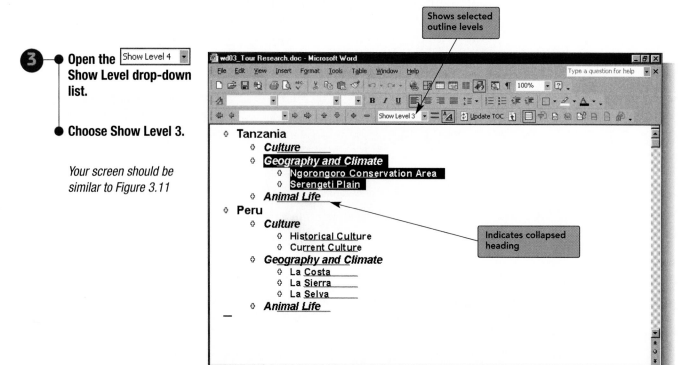

Figure 3.11

Now only the three heading levels are displayed. The gray line below a heading means the heading includes hidden or collapsed headings or body text.

As you look at the organization of the report, you decide to move the discussion of culture to follow the Geography and Climate section. Moving headings in Outline view quickly selects and moves the entire topic, including subtopics and all body text.

● **Drag the Culture heading in the Tanzania
section down to above
the Animal Life head-
ing in the same
section.**

● **Drag the Culture heading in the Peru section
down to above the
Animal Life heading in
the same section.**

*Your screen should be
similar to Figure 3.12*

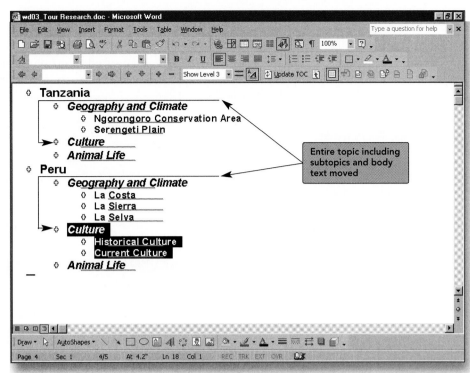

Figure 3.12

When you move or change the level of a heading that includes collapsed
subordinate text, the collapsed text is also selected. Any changes you make
to the heading, such as moving, copying, or deleting it, also affect the collapsed text. To verify this, you will display all body text again.

● **Choose Show All
Levels from the
Show Level 4 ▾ Show
Level drop-down list.**

● **Scroll the report to see
the top of the Peru
Culture section.**

● **Click in the document
to deselect the text.**

*Your screen should be
similar to Figure 3.13*

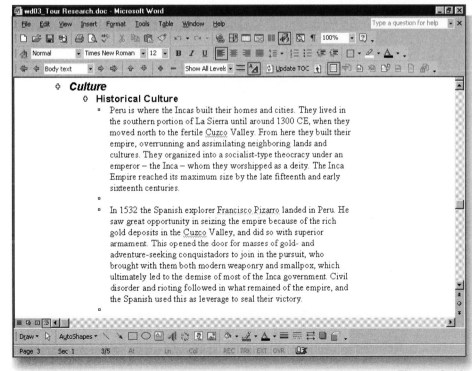

Figure 3.13

The subtopics and body text appear below the heading you moved.

Saving to a New Folder

Next you will save the unnamed document 1 and the changes you made to the research document in a folder that you will use to hold files related to the report. You can create a new folder at the same time you save a file.

1 ● **Choose File/Save As.**

● **Change the Save In location to the appropriate location for your data files.**

● **Click  Create New Folder.**

Your screen should be similar to Figure 3.14

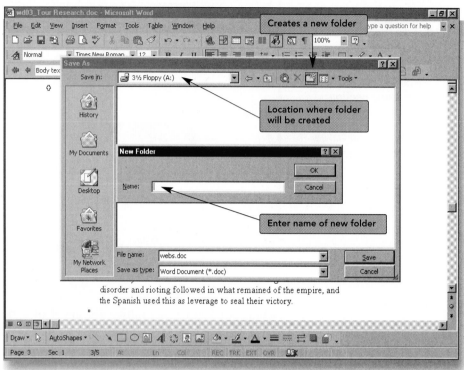

Figure 3.14

Additional Information

See "Saving, Closing, and Opening Files" in Lab 1 for file-naming rules.

In the New Folder dialog box, you enter the folder name. The rules for naming folders are the same as for naming files, except they typically do not include an extension.

2 ● **Type Report in the Name text box.**

● **Click OK.**

● **Enter the file name Tour Research2.**

● **Click Save.**

● **Switch to document 1 containing the outline document.**

● **Save the outline to the Report folder with the file name Research Outline.**

● **Close the Research Outline document.**

The documents are saved in the newly created folder, Report.

Hiding Spelling and Grammar Errors

As you have been working on the report, you have noticed that many spelling and grammar errors are identified. However, they are mostly for proper names and words that are not in the dictionary. While working on a document, you can turn off the display of these errors so that they are not distracting as you work.

1 ● **Choose Tools/Options.**

● **Open the Spelling & Grammar tab.**

Your screen should be similar to Figure 3.15

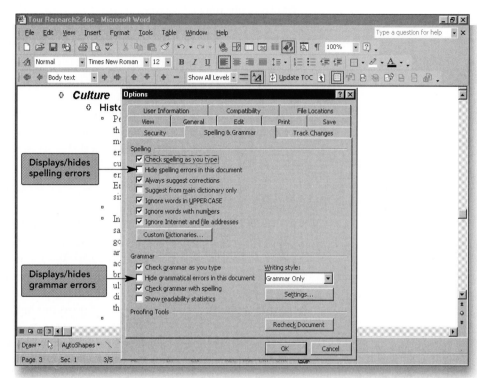

Figure 3.15

The Options dialog box is used to change the way many features in Word operate. The Spelling and Grammar tab displays options that control how these features operate. Checkmarks next to options indicate the setting is on. You want to turn off the display of spelling and grammar errors.

2 ● **Select Hide spelling errors in this document.**

● **Select Hide grammatical errors in this document.**

● **Click** OK **.**

Your screen should be similar to Figure 3.16

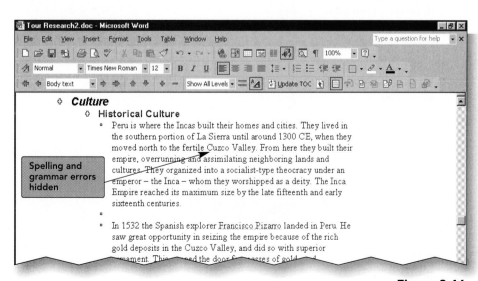

Figure 3.16

The red and green wavy lines are no longer displayed. You can still run spelling and grammar checking manually to check errors at any time.

Formatting Documents Automatically

Now that you are finished reorganizing the report, you want to add a title page. Generally, this page includes information such as the report title, the name of the author, and the date. You also want this page to include a table of contents list.

When preparing research reports, two styles of report formatting are commonly used: MLA (Modern Language Association) and APA (American Psychological Association). Although they require the same basic information, they differ in how this information is presented. For example, MLA style does not include a separate title page, but APA style does. The report you will create in this lab will use many of style requirements of the MLA. However, because this report is not a formal report to be presented at a conference or other academic proceeding, some liberties have been taken with the style to demonstrate features in Word.

Using Click and Type

You will create a new page above the first report topic and enter the title information in Print Layout view using the Click and Type feature. This feature, available in Print Layout and Web Layout views, is used to quickly insert text, graphics, and other items in a blank area of a document, avoiding the need to enter blank lines. This feature also applies the paragraph formatting needed to position an item at the location you clicked.

1 ● **Switch to Print Layout view.**

● **Press** Ctrl + Home **to move to the top of the document.**

● **Press** Ctrl + ←Enter **to insert a hard page break and create a blank page above it.**

● **Move to the top of the blank new page.**

● **Move the mouse pointer from left to right across the page and observe the change in the mouse pointer.**

Your screen should be similar to Figure 3.17

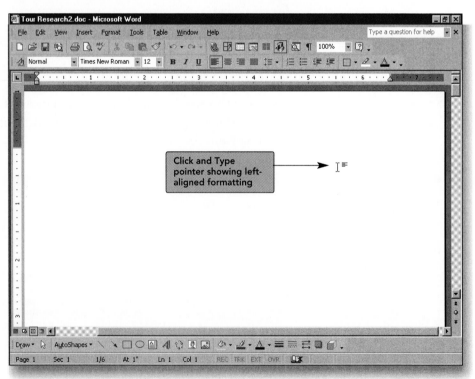

Click and Type pointer showing left-aligned formatting

Figure 3.17

Print Layout view includes formatting "zones" that control the formatting that will be applied. As you move the mouse pointer through the zones, the I-beam pointer displays an icon that indicates which formatting will be applied when you double-click at that location (See the following table). This is the Click and Type pointer.

Pointer shape	Formatting applied
I≡	Align left
I≡	Align center
≡I	Align right
I≡	Left indent
I⊞	Left text wrap
⊞I	Right text wrap

To enable the Click and Type pointer, first click on a blank area, then, as you move the mouse pointer the pointer shape indicates how the item will be formatted. Double-clicking on the location in the page moves the insertion point to that location and applies the formatting to the entry. You will enter the report title centered on the page.

2 ● Click on the center of the page at the .5-inch vertical ruler position.

● Double-click at this location while the mouse pointer is a ≡ .

● Type the report title, **Tanzania and Peru**.

Your screen should be similar to Figure 3.18

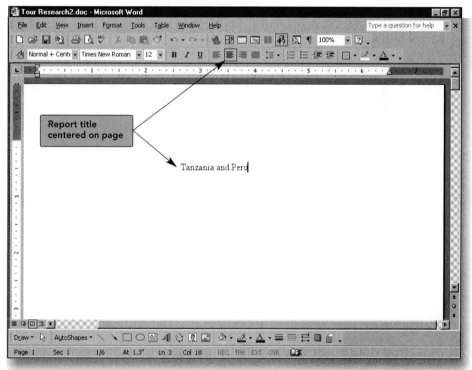

Figure 3.18

Next you will add a heading for the table of contents listing you will create, and you will enter your name and date at the bottom of the title page.

● **Double-click on the center of the page at the 1.5-inch vertical ruler position while the mouse pointer is a** ⊥ .

● **Enter the title** Table of Contents.

● **In the same manner, enter** your name **centered at the 3-inch vertical ruler position.**

● **Press** ⎆Enter.

● **Enter the current date centered below your name.**

Your screen should be similar to Figure 3.19

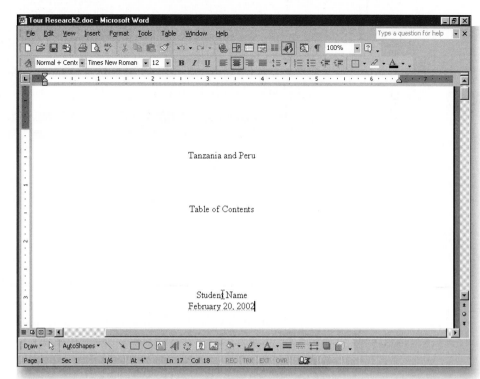

Figure 3.19

Applying Styles

Next you want to improve the appearance of the main title. You can do this quickly by applying a style to the title.

Displays/hides styles and formatting task pane

Task pane

1
● **Move to anywhere in the Tanzania and Peru title.**

● **Click** 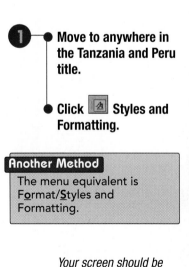 **Styles and Formatting.**

Another Method

The menu equivalent is Format/Styles and Formatting.

Your screen should be similar to Figure 3.20

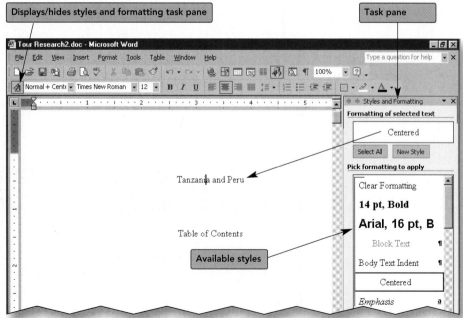

Available styles

Figure 3.20

The Styles and Formatting task pane appears. Within this task pane, you can apply styles, create new styles, and modify existing styles. The "Formatting of selected text" box shows that the text of the current selection is centered. The "Pick formatting to apply" list box displays the names of all available formatting, including those that you have applied directly, in alphabetical order. The names are formatted using the associated formatting. You want to display the complete list of styles and apply the Title style to the text.

<table>
<tr>
<td>

2 ● **Select All styles from the Show drop-down list box.**

● **Scroll the "Pick formatting to apply" list and choose Title.**

Additional Information

Pointing to the style name displays a ScreenTip of information about the format settings used in the style. Click on the style to choose it.

HAVING TROUBLE?

If you accidentally apply the wrong style, reselect the text and select the correct style. To return the style to the default, select Normal.

Your screen should be similar to Figure 3.21

</td>
<td>

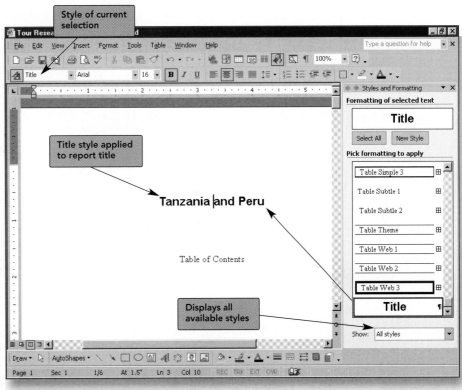

Figure 3.21

</td>
</tr>
</table>

Notice that the entire title appears in the selected style. This is because a Title style is a paragraph style, affecting the entire paragraph at the insertion point. Also notice that the Style drop-down list button in the Formatting toolbar now displays "Title" as the style applied to the selection. This style includes formatting settings of Arial, 16 pt, and bold.

Next you want to apply a Subtitle style to the Table of Contents heading. Another way to select a style is from the [Normal ▼] Style drop-down menu.

3
● **Close the Styles and Formatting task pane.**

● **Move the insertion point to anywhere in the Table of Contents heading.**

● **Open the** Normal + Cent ▾ **Style drop-down menu.**

Your screen should be similar to Figure 3.22

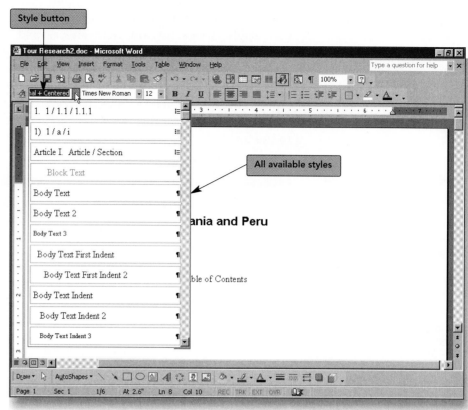

Figure 3.22

The Style drop-down menu displays all available styles. The style names are listed in alphabetical order and appear formatted in that style.

4
● **Scroll the Style drop-down menu and choose Subtitle.**

Your screen should be similar to Figure 3.23

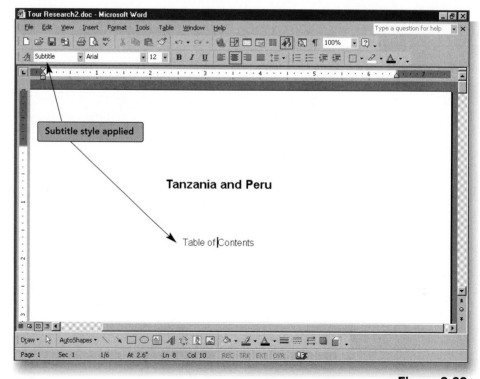

Figure 3.23

Creating a Table of Contents

Now you are ready to create the table of contents. A table of contents is a listing of the topic headings that appear in a document and their associated page references (see the sample below). It shows the reader at a glance what topics are included in the document and makes it easier for the reader to locate information. Word can generate a table of contents automatically once you have applied heading styles to the document headings.

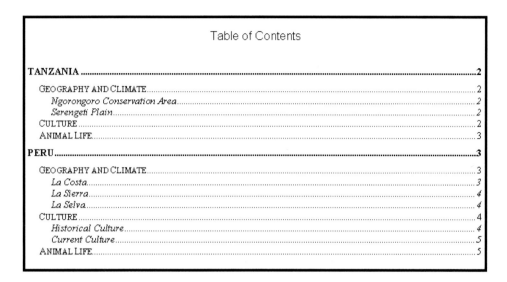

Generating a Table of Contents

You want the table of contents listing to be displayed several lines below the table of contents heading on the title page.

1 ● **Move to the second blank line below the Table of Contents heading.**

> **HAVING TROUBLE?**
>
> If needed, use ¶ Show/Hide to help locate the position in the document.

● **Choose Insert/ Reference/Index and Tables.**

● **Open the Table of Contents tab.**

Your screen should be similar to Figure 3.24

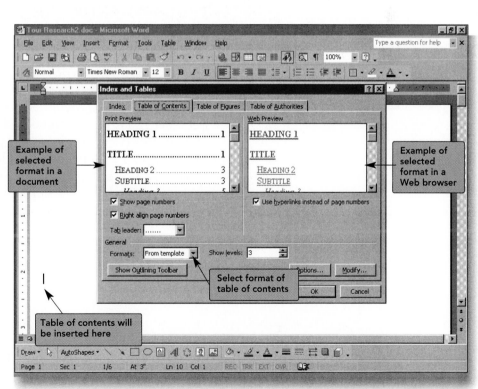

Example of selected format in a document

Example of selected format in a Web browser

Select format of table of contents

Table of contents will be inserted here

Figure 3.24

From the Table of Contents tab, you first need to select the format or design of the table of contents. The Formats drop-down list box displays the name of the default table of contents style, From Template, which is supplied with the Normal template. The Preview boxes display an example of how the selected format will look in a normal printed document or in a document when viewed in a Web browser. The From Template format option is used to design your own table of contents and save it as a template by modifying the existing format. You want to use one of the predesigned formats.

2 ● **Open the Formats drop-down list box.**

● **Choose Formal.**

Your screen should be similar to Figure 3.25

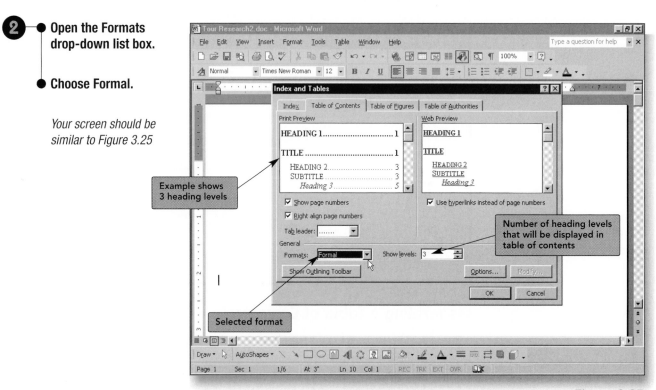

Example shows 3 heading levels

Number of heading levels that will be displayed in table of contents

Selected format

Figure 3.25

The Print Preview area shows this style will display the page numbers flush with the right margin, and with a series of tab leaders between the heading and the page number. This format will display in the table of contents all entries in the document that are formatted with Headings 1, 2, and 3, as well as Title and Subtitle styles. You want the table of contents to also include topics formatted with the Heading 4 style, but to exclude those formatted with the Title and Subtitle styles. You will modify the settings for the Formal format and turn off the use of these styles.

3 ● Change the level number in the Show Levels text box to 4.

● Click Options... .

Your screen should be similar to Figure 3.26

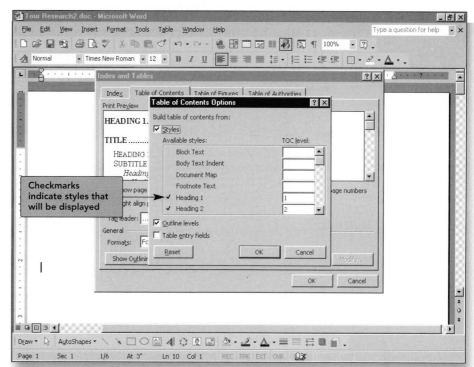

Checkmarks indicate styles that will be displayed

Figure 3.26

The Table of Contents Options dialog box shows the styles that are used to build the table of contents. The checkmark indicates which styles Word will look for in the document to use as items to include in the table of contents, and the number indicates the level at which they will be displayed. To clear a style selection, simply delete the number from the TOC level text box.

4 ● Scroll the Available Styles list to see the Subtitle and Title selections.

● Delete the numbers from the Subtitle and Title text boxes to clear the checkmarks.

● Click OK .

Your screen should be similar to Figure 3.27

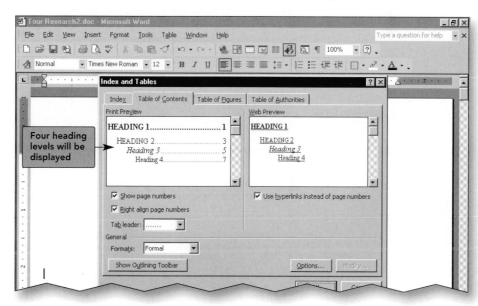

Four heading levels will be displayed

Figure 3.27

The Print Preview area now shows that four levels of headings will be reflected in the table of contents listing, and the title and subtitle will not be included. Now you are ready to generate the listing.

5 ● Click [OK].

Your screen should be similar to Figure 3.28

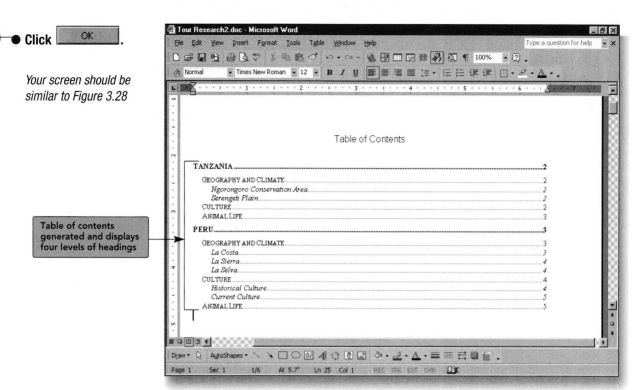

Table of contents generated and displays four levels of headings

Figure 3.28

Word searches for headings with the specified styles, sorts them by heading level, references their page numbers, and displays the table of contents using the Formal style in the document. The headings that were assigned a Heading 1 style are aligned with the left margin, and subordinate heading levels are indented as appropriate.

Using a Table of Contents Hyperlink

When a table of contents is generated, each entry is a field that is a hyperlink to the heading in the document.

1 ● Click anywhere in the table of contents list.

Your screen should be similar to Figure 3.29

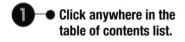
Additional Information

Pointing to an entry in a table of contents displays a ScreenTip with directions on how to follow the hyperlink.

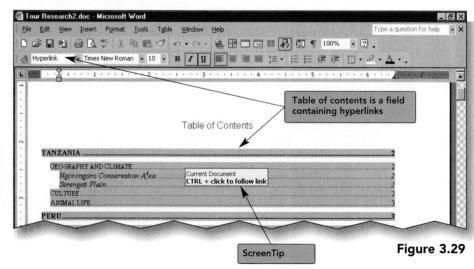

Table of contents is a field containing hyperlinks

ScreenTip

Figure 3.29

Notice that the text in the table of contents is shaded, indicating it is a field. This means it can be updated to reflect changes you may make at a later time in your document. Also notice that the Style list box displays "Hyperlink." Each line in the table of contents has been changed to a hyperlink. Now simply holding down Ctrl while clicking on a link will move you directly to that location in the document.

2 ● **Hold down Ctrl and click the Peru table of contents line.**

Additional Information
The mouse pointer shape changes to a ⏚ when holding down Ctrl and pointing to a hyperlink.

Your screen should be similar to Figure 3.30

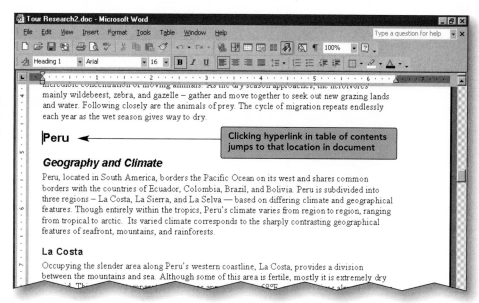

Figure 3.30

The insertion point jumps to that location in the document.

Formatting Document Sections

You want to change the layout of the title page so that the text on the page is centered vertically between the top and bottom page margins. Because page layout settings affect entire documents, to make this change to the title page only you need to divide the document into sections.

concept 2

Section

2 To format different parts of a document differently, you can divide a document into **sections**. Initially a document is one section. To separate it into different parts, you insert section breaks. The **section break** identifies the end of a section and stores the document format settings, such as margins and page layout, associated with that section of the document.

Creating a Section Break

Because the page layout you want to use on the title page is different than the rest of the document, you need to divide the document into two sections. You will delete the hard page break line you inserted and replace it with a section break.

1 ● Switch to Normal view.

● Move to the bottom of page 1.

● Delete the hard page break line.

HAVING TROUBLE?
To remove a hard page break, click on the page break line and press Delete.

● Choose Insert/Break.

Your screen should be similar to Figure 3.31

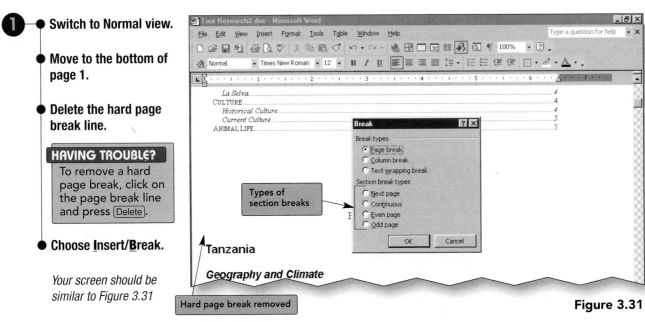

Figure 3.31

In the Break dialog box, you specify the type of section break you want to insert. The three types of section breaks, described in the following table, control the location where the text following a section break begins.

Option	Action
Next Page	Starts the new section on the next page.
Continuous	Starts the new section on the same page.
Odd or Even	Starts new section on the next odd or even numbered page.

You want the new section to start on the next page.

2 ● Select Next page.

● Click OK.

● Delete any blank lines above the Tanzania heading.

Your screen should be similar to Figure 3.32

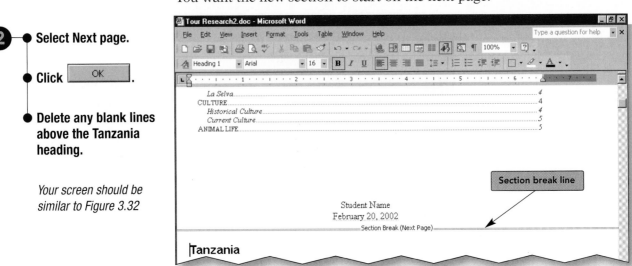

Figure 3.32

A double dotted line and the words "Section Break" identify the type of document break that was inserted.

Centering a Page Vertically

Finally, you are ready to change the layout of the title page to centered vertically.

1 ● **Switch back to Print Layout view.**

● **Move to anywhere in the title page.**

● **Zoom to Whole Page.**

● **Choose File/Page Setup.**

● **If necessary, open the Layout tab.**

Your screen should be similar to Figure 3.33

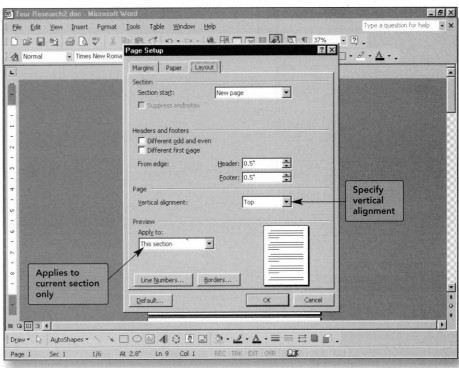

Figure 3.33

Additional Information

If you do not create a section break first, Word will automatically insert a section break for you if you change the formatting of selected text, such as inserting columns or centering selected text vertically on a page.

From the Vertical Alignment drop-down list box, you specify how the text is to be aligned on the page vertically. In addition, from the Apply To drop-down list box you need to specify what part of the document you want to be aligned to the new setting. Because you already divided the document into sections, this setting is already appropriately selected. You only need to specify the vertical alignment.

● From the **V**ertical Alignment drop-down list, select Center.

● Click OK .

● Click 🖫 to save the changes you have made to the document.

Your screen should be similar to Figure 3.34

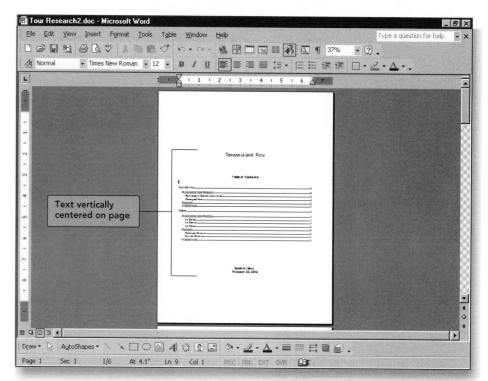

Figure 3.34

Now you can see that the text on the title page is centered vertically between the top and bottom margins. Word required a section break at this location because a different page format, in this case vertical alignment, was used on this page than the rest of the document.

Footnoting a Document

This document already includes parenthetical source references entered according to the MLA style for research papers. However, you still have several reference notes you want to include in the report as footnotes to help clarify some information.

concept 3

Footnote and Endnote

3 A **footnote** is a source reference or text offering additional explanation that is placed at the bottom of a page. An **endnote** is also a source reference or long comment that typically appears at the end of a document. You can have both footnotes and endnotes in the same document. Footnotes and endnotes consist of two parts, the note reference mark and the note text. The **note reference mark** is commonly a superscript number appearing in the document at the end of the material being referenced (for example, text). It can also be a character or combination of characters. The **note text** for a footnote appears at the bottom of the page on which the reference mark appears. The footnote text is separated from the document text by a horizontal line called the **note separator**. Endnote text appears as a listing at the end of the document.

Adding Footnotes

The first footnote reference you want to add is the height of Mt. Kilimanjaro. This note will follow the reference to the mountain at the end of the first paragraph in the Geography and Climate section for Tanzania. To identify where you want the footnote number to appear in the document, you position the insertion point at the document location first.

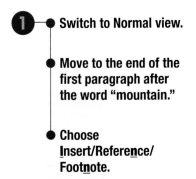

1 ● **Switch to Normal view.**

● **Move to the end of the first paragraph after the word "mountain."**

● **Choose Insert/Reference/ Footnote.**

Another Method

The keyboard shortcut to insert a footnote using the default settings is [Alt] + [Ctrl] + F.

Your screen should be similar to Figure 3.35

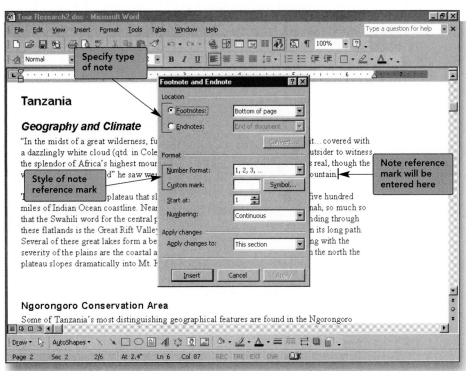

Figure 3.35

In the Footnote and Endnote dialog box, you specify whether you want to create footnotes or endnotes and the type of reference mark you want to appear in the document: a numbered mark or a custom mark. A custom mark can be any nonnumeric character, such as an asterisk, that you enter in the text box. You want to create numbered footnotes, so the default settings of Footnote and AutoNumber are acceptable.

2 Click [Insert].

Your screen should be similar to Figure 3.36

Document pane

Footnote number

Note pane

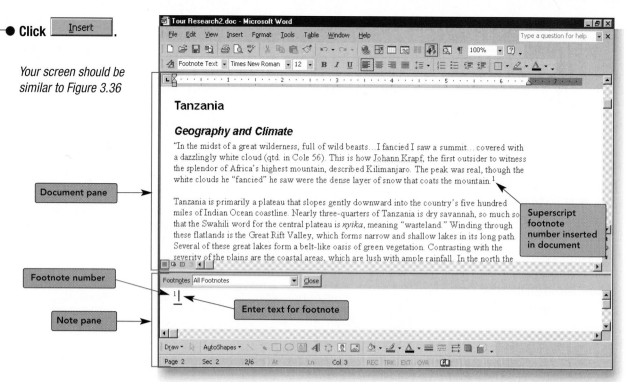

Superscript footnote number inserted in document

Enter text for footnote

Figure 3.36

The document window is now horizontally divided into upper and lower panes. A **pane** is a portion of the document that you can view and scroll independently. The report is displayed in the document pane. The footnote number, 1, appears as a superscript in the document where the insertion point was positioned when the footnote was created. The **note pane** displays the footnote number and the insertion point. This is where you enter the text for the footnote. When you enter a footnote, you can use the same menus, commands, and features as you would in the document window. Any commands that are not available are dimmed.

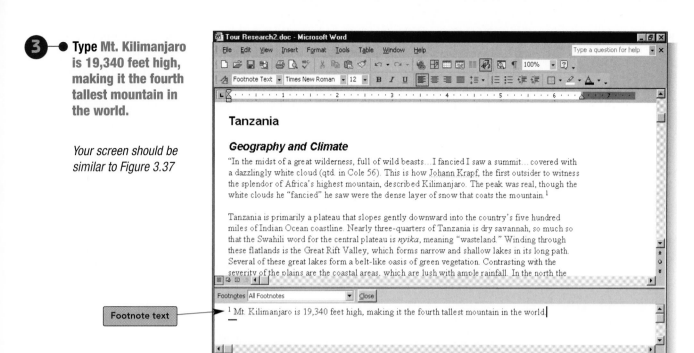

3 • **Type** Mt. Kilimanjaro is 19,340 feet high, making it the fourth tallest mountain in the world.

Your screen should be similar to Figure 3.37

Footnote text →

Figure 3.37

Using the Document Map

The second footnote you want to add is in the Geography and Climate section under Peru. To quickly move to that location in the document, you can use the Document Map feature. **Document Map** displays document headings, and is used to quickly navigate through the document and keep track of your location in it.

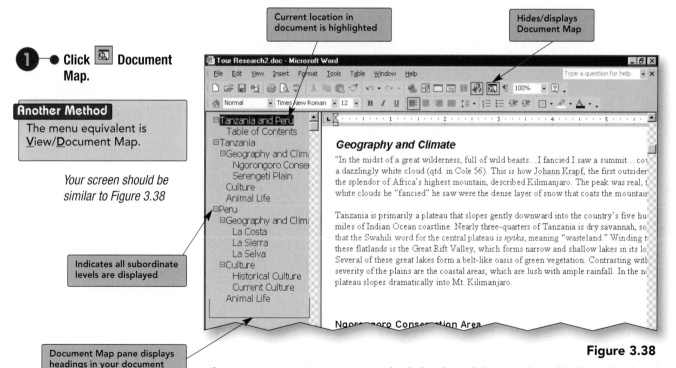

Current location in document is highlighted

Hides/displays Document Map

1 • **Click** [icon] **Document Map.**

Another Method
The menu equivalent is View/Document Map.

Your screen should be similar to Figure 3.38

Indicates all subordinate levels are displayed

Document Map pane displays headings in your document

Figure 3.38

The Document Map pane on the left edge of the window displays the headings in your document. The document pane on the right displays the document in Normal view.

All text that is formatted with a heading style is displayed in the Document Map pane. Notice the ⊟ symbol to the left of many of the headings in the Document Map; this indicates that all subordinate headings are displayed. A ⊞ symbol would indicate that subordinate headings are not displayed. When your document does not contain any headings formatted with heading styles, the program automatically searches the document for paragraphs that look like headings (for example, short lines with a larger font size) and displays them in the Document Map. If it cannot find any such headings, the Document Map is blank. The highlighted heading shows your location in the document. Clicking on a heading in the Document Map quickly jumps to that location in the document.

2 ● **Change the zoom to Page Width.**

● **Click on La Sierra in the Document Map.**

Your screen should be similar to Figure 3.39

Selected heading

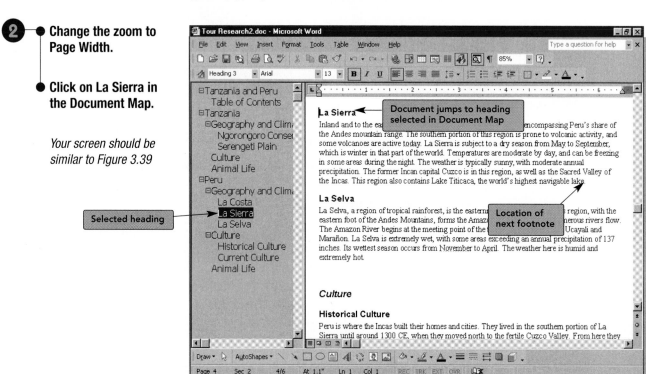

Figure 3.39

The selected heading is displayed at the top of the window and highlighted in the Document Map. You can now quickly locate the text you want to reference. You want to add a note about Lake Titicaca.

3
- **Click at the end of the paragraph following the word "lake."**

- **Choose Insert/Reference/ Footnote/ Insert .**

Your screen should be similar to Figure 3.40

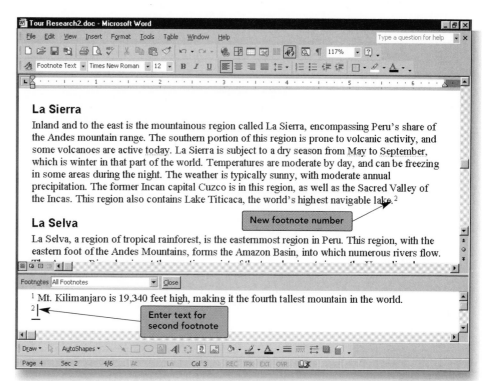

Figure 3.40

The footnote number 2 is automatically entered at the insertion point location. The note pane is active again, so you can enter the text for the second footnote. The Document Map pane is temporarily hidden while the note pane is displayed. When you close the note pane, the Document Map pane will be displayed again.

4
- **In the footnote pane, type Lake Titicaca is 12,507 feet above sea level.**

Your screen should be similar to Figure 3.41

Additional Information

To delete a footnote or endnote, highlight the reference mark and press Delete. The reference mark and associated note text are removed, and the following footnotes are renumbered.

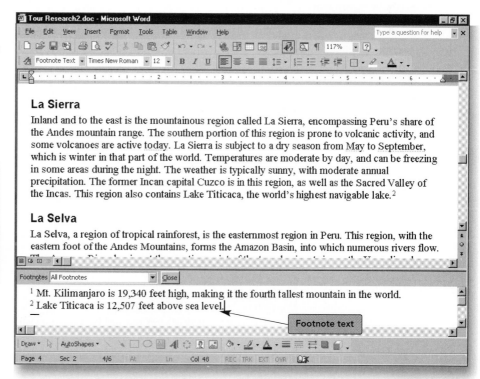

Figure 3.41

Now you realize that you forgot to enter a footnote earlier in the document, on page 2.

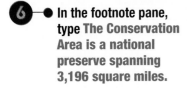

5 ● Click Close on the note pane.

● Click Ngorongoro Conservation Area in the Document Map.

● Move to the end of the first sentence of the first paragraph, following the word "Area."

● Insert a footnote at this location.

Your screen should be similar to Figure 3.42

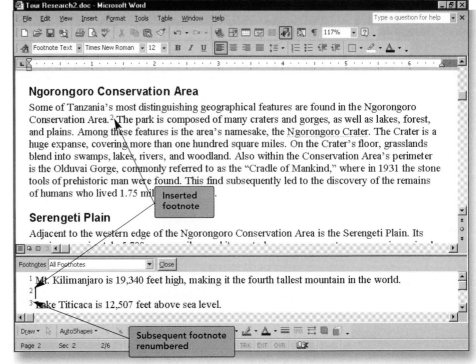

Figure 3.42

Notice that this footnote is now number 2 in the document, and a blank footnote line has been entered in the note pane for the footnote text. Word automatically adjusted the footnote numbers when the new footnote was inserted.

6 ● In the footnote pane, type **The Conservation Area is a national preserve spanning 3,196 square miles.**

Your screen should be similar to Figure 3.43

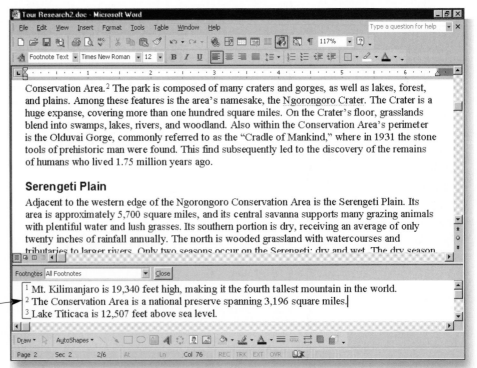

Figure 3.43

You are finished entering footnotes for now.

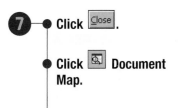

- Click [Close].

- Click 🔲 Document Map.

- If necessary scroll to see the bottom of this page.

Your screen should be similar to Figure 3.44

Additional Information

You can hide and display the note pane any time by using the View/Footnotes command or by double-clicking on a note reference mark.

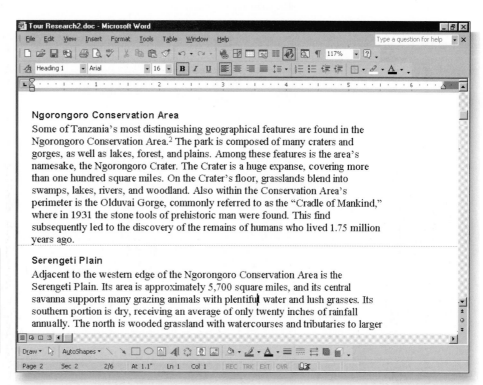

Figure 3.44

Viewing Footnotes

In Normal view, footnotes are not displayed at the bottom of the page. Instead, to see the footnote text, you point to the note reference mark and the footnote is displayed as a ScreenTip.

- Point to note reference mark 2 in the document.

Your screen should be similar to Figure 3.45

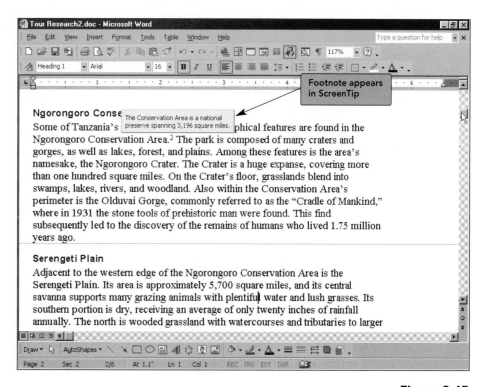

Figure 3.45

In Print Layout view, footnotes are displayed as they will appear when the document is printed.

2 • **Switch to Print Layout view and set the zoom to 75 percent.**

• **Scroll to the bottom of page 2 to see the footnotes.**

Additional Information

If you drag the scroll box, a ScreenTip will identify the page and topic that will be displayed when you stop dragging the scroll box.

Additional Information

If the zoom percentage is too small, the footnote numbers will not display correctly.

Your screen should be similar to Figure 3.46

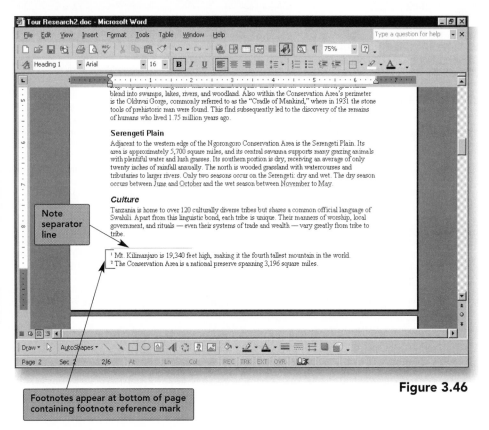

blend into swamps, lakes, rivers, and woodland. Also within the Conservation Area's perimeter is the Olduvai Gorge, commonly referred to as the "Cradle of Mankind," where in 1931 the stone tools of prehistoric man were found. This find subsequently led to the discovery of the remains of humans who lived 1.75 million years ago.

Serengeti Plain

Adjacent to the western edge of the Ngorongoro Conservation Area is the Serengeti Plain. Its area is approximately 5,700 square miles, and its central savanna supports many grazing animals with plentiful water and lush grasses. Its southern portion is dry, receiving an average of only twenty inches of rainfall annually. The north is wooded grassland with watercourses and tributaries to larger rivers. Only two seasons occur on the Serengeti: dry and wet. The dry season occurs between June and October and the wet season between November to May.

Culture

Tanzania is home to over 120 culturally diverse tribes but shares a common official language of Swahili. Apart from this linguistic bond, each tribe is unique. Their manners of worship, local government, and rituals — even their systems of trade and wealth — vary greatly from tribe to tribe.

Note separator line

¹ Mt. Kilimanjaro is 19,340 feet high, making it the fourth tallest mountain in the world.
² The Conservation Area is a national preserve spanning 3,196 square miles.

Figure 3.46

Footnotes appear at bottom of page containing footnote reference mark

The footnotes are displayed immediately above the bottom margin separated from the text by the note separator line. They appear at the bottom of the page containing the footnote reference mark.

Inserting a Footnote in Print Layout View

As you continue to check the document, you decide you want to explain the CE abbreviation following the date 1300 in the Historical Culture section. While in Print Layout view, you can insert, edit, and format footnotes just like any other text. After using the command to insert a footnote, the footnote number appears in the footnote area at the bottom of the page, ready for you to enter the footnote text.

- Move the insertion point after "CE" in the second sentence below Historical Culture on page 4.

- Insert a footnote at this location.

- Type **Common Era (CE) is the period dating from the birth of Christ.**

- Click 🖫 Save to save the changes you have made to the document.

Your screen should be similar to Figure 3.47

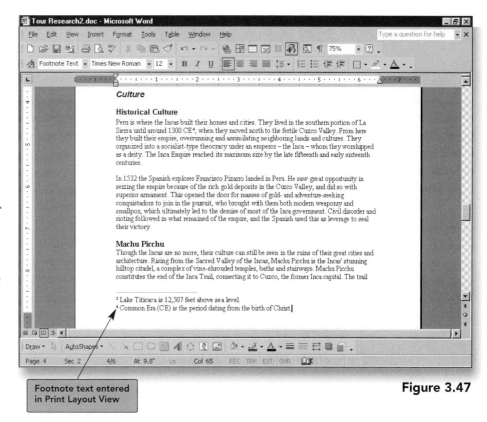

Footnote text entered in Print Layout View

Figure 3.47

Formatting Picture Layout

Next you want to add a picture in the report to complement the subject of the first topic. You want the text in the document where the picture will be inserted to wrap around the picture. To do this, you change the text-wrapping layout for the picture.

concept 4

Text Wrapping

4 You can control how text appears around a graphic object by specifying the text wrapping style. The text in the paragraph may wrap around the object in many different ways as shown below.

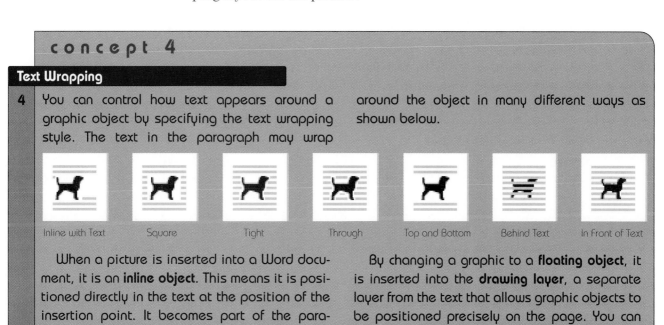

Inline with Text   Square   Tight   Through   Top and Bottom   Behind Text   In Front of Text

When a picture is inserted into a Word document, it is an **inline object**. This means it is positioned directly in the text at the position of the insertion point. It becomes part of the paragraph, and any paragraph alignment settings that apply to the paragraph also apply to the picture.

By changing a graphic to a **floating object**, it is inserted into the **drawing layer**, a separate layer from the text that allows graphic objects to be positioned precisely on the page. You can change an inline object to a floating picture by changing the wrapping style of the object.

You will insert the picture file wd03_Lions.jpg next to the second paragraph on page 2.

1 ● Use the Document Map to move to the Geography and Climate head under Tanzania.

● Move to the beginning of the second paragraph.

● Close the Document Map and change the zoom to Text Width.

● Insert the picture wd03_ Lions **from your data files.**

● Reduce the size of the picture to approximately 2 by 2 inches.

● If necessary, display the Picture toolbar.

Your screen should be similar to Figure 3.48

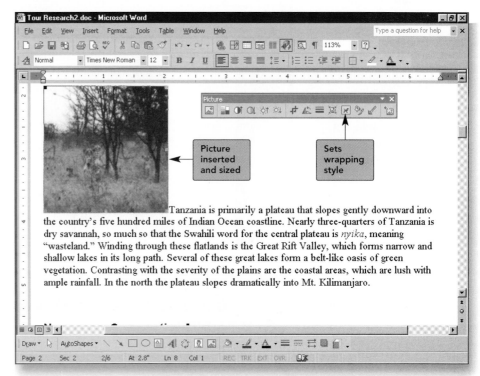

Figure 3.48

The picture has been inserted as an inline object and appears at the beginning of the paragraph like the first text characters of the paragraph. The text continues to the right of the picture.

Wrapping Text around Graphics

You want the text to wrap to the right side of the picture.

1 ● Click 🖼 **Text Wrapping on the Pictures toolbar.**

Your screen should be similar to Figure 3.49

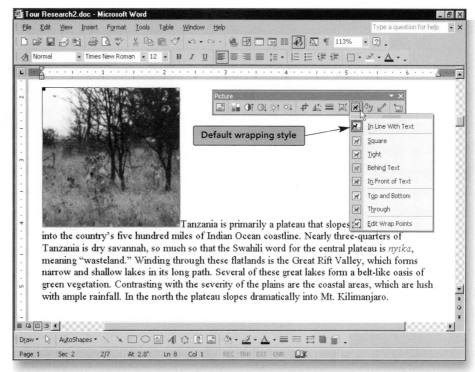

Figure 3.49

The default wrapping style, In Line with Text, is selected. You want to change the style to Square.

2 ● Click 🖼 **Square.**

● **If necessary, resize the picture until the text wraps around it as in Figure 3.50.**

Your screen should be similar to Figure 3.50

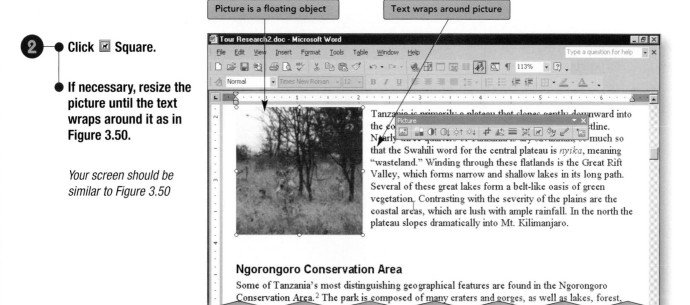

Figure 3.50

The picture is changed to a floating object that can be placed anywhere in the document, including in front of or behind other objects including the text.

Because the picture is aligned with the left margin, the text wraps to the right side of the object. If you moved the picture, because the wrapping style is Square, the text would wrap around the object on all sides.

3 ● Move the picture to the center of the paragraph to see how the text wraps around it.

Your screen should be similar to Figure 3.51

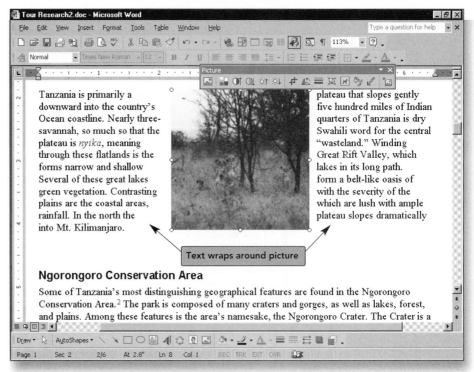

Figure 3.51

The text wraps on all sides of the object, depending on its location in the text.

4 ● Move the picture back to the left margin and aligned with the top of the paragraph. (See Figure 3.50).

● Insert the picture wd03_Parrots to the left of the first paragraph in the Animal Life section under Peru on page 5.

● Change the wrapping style to Square.

● Click 🖫 to save the document.

Your screen should be similar to Figure 3.52

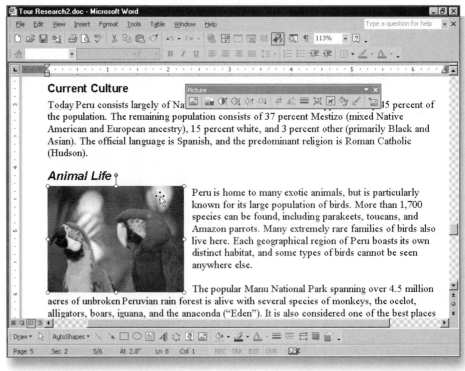

Figure 3.52

Referencing Figures

Referencing figures in a document helps the reader locate information quickly. Using captions and cross-references are two ways that you can link items together in a document. If the reader is viewing the document online, the captions and cross-references become hyperlinks to allow the reader to jump around in the document.

concept 5

Captions and Cross-References

5 A **caption** is a title or explanation for a table, picture, or graph. Word can automatically add captions to graphic objects as they are inserted, or you can add them manually. The caption label can be changed to reflect the type of object to which it refers, such as a table, chart, or figure. In addition, Word automatically numbers graphic objects and adjusts numbering when objects of the same type are added or deleted.

A **cross-reference** is a reference from one part of a document to related information in another part. Once you have captions, you can also include cross-references. For example, if you have a graph in one part of the document that you would like to refer to in another section, you can add a cross-reference that tells the reader what page the graph is on. A cross-reference can also be inserted as a hyperlink, allowing you to jump to another location in the same document or in another document.

Adding a Figure Caption

Next you want to add a caption below the picture of the lions.

1 ● Move to the blank line below the lion picture.

● Choose **Insert/Reference/Caption.**

Your screen should be similar to Figure 3.53

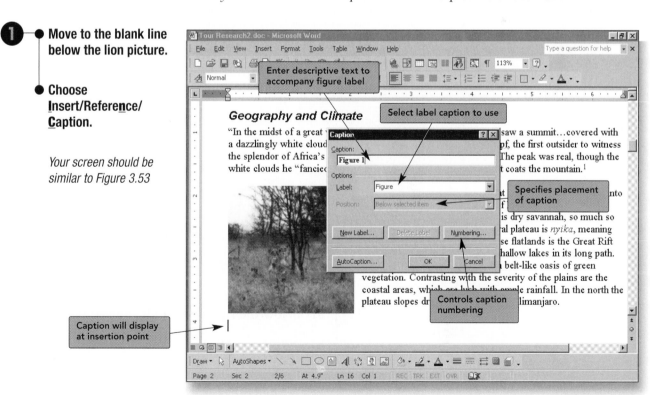

Figure 3.53

The Caption options are described in the table on the next page.

Option	Description
Label	Select from one of three default captions: Table, Figure, or Equation.
Position	Specify the location of the caption, either above or below a selected item. When an item is selected, the Position option is available.
New Label	Create your own captions.
Numbering	Specify the numbering format and starting number for your caption.
AutoCaption	Turns on the automatic insertion of a caption (label and number only) when you insert selected items into your document.

The most recently selected caption label and number appear in the Caption text box. You want the caption to be Figure 1, and you want to add additional descriptive text.

2 ● In the Caption text box, following "Figure 1," type - **Lions in the Serengeti.**

● Click [OK].

Your screen should be similar to Figure 3.54

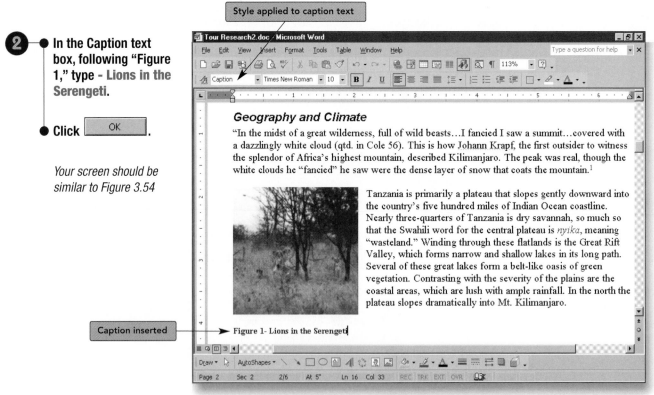

Figure 3.54

The caption label appears below the figure. It can be moved like any other text.

Adding a Cross-Reference

In the Animal section of the report, you discuss the animals found in the Serengeti. You want to include a cross-reference to the picture at this location.

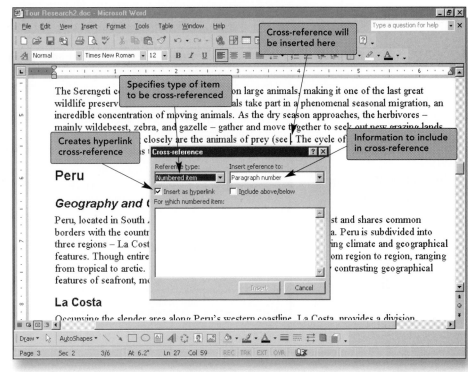

1
- Move to after the word "prey" in the third paragraph in the Animal Life section (page 3).

- Press Spacebar.

- Type (see .

- Press Spacebar.

- Choose Insert/Reference/ Cross-reference.

Your screen should be similar to Figure 3.55

Figure 3.55

In the Cross-reference dialog box, you specify the type of item you are referencing and how you want the reference to appear. You want to reference the lions picture, and you want only the label "Figure 1" entered in the document.

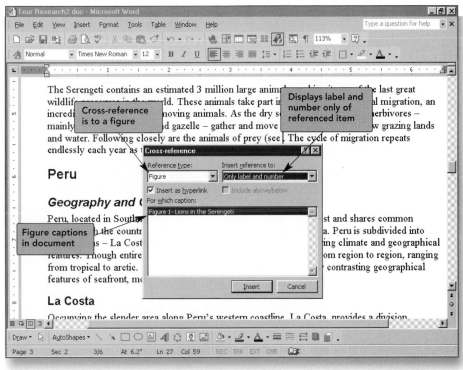

2
- From the Reference Type drop-down list box, select Figure.

- From the Insert Reference To drop-down list box, select Only label and number.

Your screen should be similar to Figure 3.56

Figure 3.56

The For Which Caption list box lists all figure captions in the document. Because there is only one figure in this document, the correct figure caption is already selected. Notice that the Insert as Hyperlink option is selected by default. This option creates a hyperlink between the cross-reference and the caption. The default setting is appropriate.

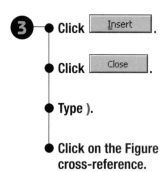

● Click **Insert**.

● Click **Close**.

● Type).

● Click on the Figure cross-reference.

Your screen should be similar to Figure 3.57

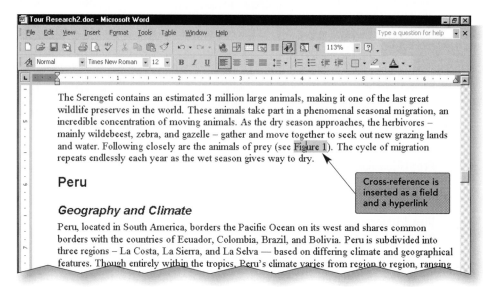

Figure 3.57

A cross-reference is entered into the document as a field. Therefore, if you insert another picture or item that is cross-referenced, the captions and cross-references will renumber automatically. If you edit, delete, or move cross-referenced items, you should manually update the cross-references using Update Field. When you are working on a long document with several figures, tables, and graphs, this feature is very helpful.

Using a Cross-Reference Hyperlink

Next, you want to use the cross-reference hyperlink to jump to the source it references.

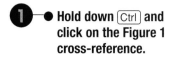

● Hold down Ctrl and click on the Figure 1 cross-reference.

Your screen should be similar to Figure 3.58

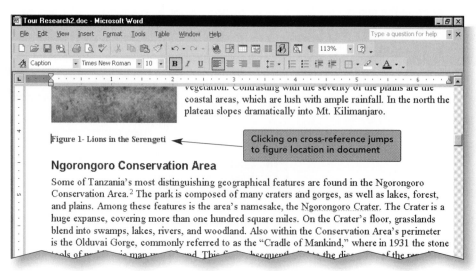

Figure 3.58

The document jumps to the caption beneath the figure.

Creating a Simple Table

Next you want to add a table comparing the rainfall and temperature data for the three regions of Peru.

---

concept 6

Table

6 A **table** is used to organize information into an easy-to-read format of horizontal rows and vertical columns. The insertion of a row and column creates a **cell** in which you can enter data or other information.

Tables are a very effective method for presenting information. The table layout organizes the information for readers and greatly reduces the number of words they have to read to interpret the data. Use tables whenever you can to make your documents easier to read.

The table you want to create will display columns for regions, rainfall, and temperature. The rows will display the data for each region. Your completed table will be similar to the one shown below.

Region	Annual Rainfall (Inches)	Average Temperature (Fahrenheit)
La Costa	2	68
La Sierra	35	54
La Selva	137	80

Inserting a Table

Word includes several different methods you can use to create tables. One method (Table/Convert/Text to Table) will quickly convert text that is arranged in columns into a table. Another uses the Draw Table feature to create any type of table, but is most useful for creating complex tables that contain cells of different heights or a varying number of columns per row. The third method, which you will use, initially creates a simple table consisting of the same number of rows and columns.

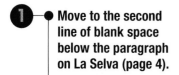

1 ● Move to the second line of blank space below the paragraph on La Selva (page 4).

● Click 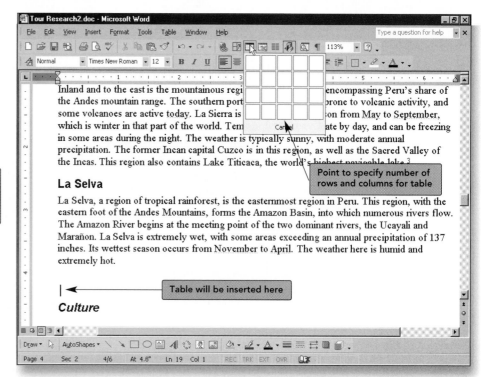 Insert Table (on the Standard toolbar).

Your screen should be similar to Figure 3.59

Figure 3.59

The Insert Table drop-down menu displays a grid in which you specify the number of rows and columns for the table. Moving the mouse pointer over the grid highlights the boxes in the grid and defines the table size. The dimensions are reflected in the bottom of the grid.

2 ● Point to the boxes in Insert Table drop-down grid to highlight a 3-by-3 section.

● Click on the lower right corner of the selection.

Your screen should be similar to Figure 3.60

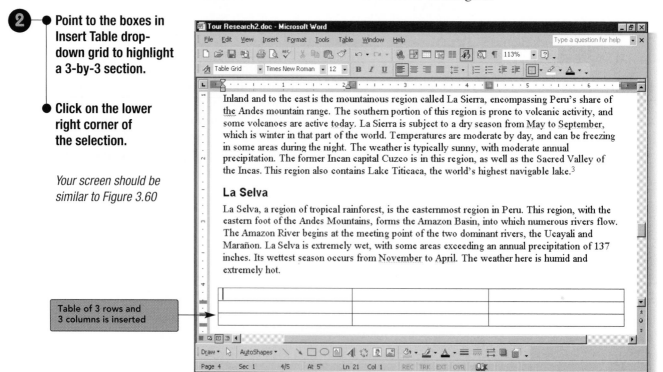

Figure 3.60

A table the full width of the page is drawn. It has equal sized columns and is surrounded by a black borderline.

Entering Data in a Table

Now you are ready to enter information in the table. Each cell contains a single line space where you can enter data. Cells in a table are identified by a letter and number, called a **table reference**. Columns are identified from left to right beginning with the letter A, and rows are numbered from top to bottom beginning with the number 1. The table reference of the top left-most cell is A1 because it is in the first column (A) and first row (1) of the table. The second cell in column 2 cell B2. The fourth cell in column 3 is C4.

	Jan	Feb	Mar	Total
East	7	7	5	19
West	6	4	7	17
South	8	7	9	24
Total	21	18	21	60

You can move from one cell to another by using the arrow keys or by clicking on the cell. In addition, you can use the keys shown in the table below to move around a table.

> **Additional Information**
>
> Pressing [Tab⇥] when in the last cell of a row moves to the first cell of the next row.

To Move To	Press
Next cell in row	[Tab⇥]
Previous cell in row	[⇧ Shift] + [Tab⇥]
First cell in row	[Alt] + [Home]
Last cell in row	[Alt] + [End]
First cell in column	[Alt] + [Page Up]
Last cell in column	[Alt] + [Page Down]
Previous row	[↑]
Next row	[↓]

The mouse pointer may also appear as a solid black arrow when pointing to the table. When it is a ⬇, you can click to select the entire column. When it is ⬀, you can click to select a cell. You will learn more about this feature shortly.

You will begin by entering the information for La Costa in cells A1 through C1. You can type in the cell as you would anywhere in a normal document.

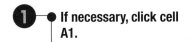

● If necessary, click cell A1.

● Type **La Costa**.

● Press **Tab ⇥**.

● In the same manner, type **2** in cell B1 and **68** in cell C1.

● Continue entering the information shown below, using **Tab ⇥** to move to the next cell.

Cell	Entry
A2	La Sierra
B2	35
C2	54
A3	La Selva
B3	137
C3	80

Your screen should be similar to Figure 3.61

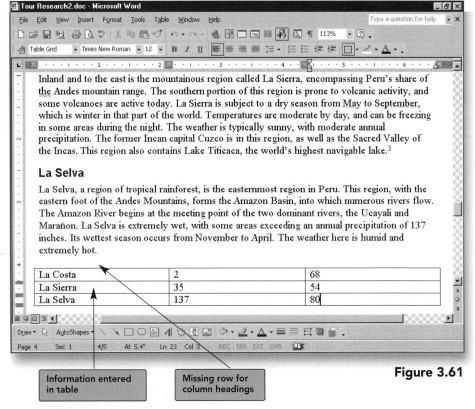

Information entered in table

Missing row for column headings

Figure 3.61

Inserting a Row

After looking at the table, you realize you forgot to include a row above the data to display the column headings.

● Move to any cell in row 1.

● Choose **Table/Insert/Rows Above**.

● Click in the new row to deselect the row.

Your screen should be similar to Figure 3.62

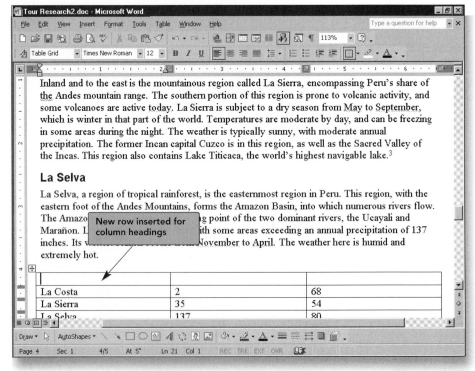

New row inserted for column headings

Figure 3.62

Now you are ready to add the text for the headings.

2 ● In cell A1 type **Region**.

● In cell B1 type **Annual Rainfall**.

● Press ←Enter to insert a second line in the cell.

● Type **(Inches)**.

● In cell C1 type **Average Temperature** on the first line and **(Fahrenheit)** on the second.

Your screen should be similar to Figure 3.63

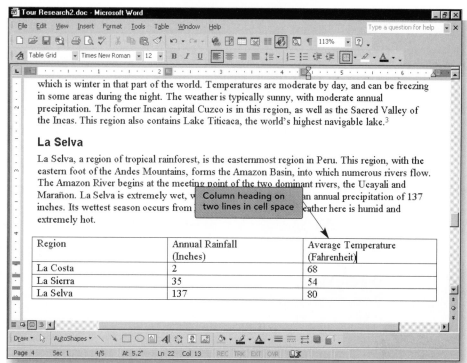

Figure 3.63

Sizing a Table

The table is much larger than it needs to be. To quickly reduce the overall table size, you can drag the resize handle □. This handle appears whenever the mouse pointer rests over the table. Once the table is smaller, you then want to center it between the margins.

1 ● Drag the □ resize handle to decrease the width of the table to 5 inches (see Figure 3.64).

● Click ⊞ to select the entire table.

● Click ≡ Center.

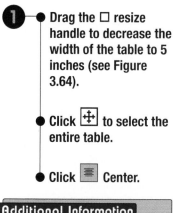

Additional Information

You can also drag the ⊞ move handle to move the table to any location.

Your screen should be similar to Figure 3.64

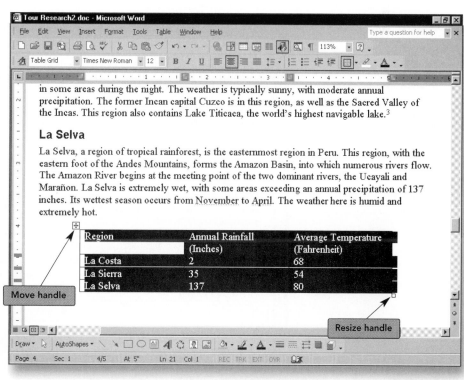

Figure 3.64

Formatting a Table

To enhance the appearance of the table, you can apply many different formats to the cells. This is similar to adding formatting to a document, except the formatting affects the selected cells only.

You want the entries in the cells A1 through C1, and B2 through C4, to be centered in their cell spaces. As you continue to modify the table, many cells can be selected and changed at the same time. You can select areas of a table using the Select command on the Table menu. However, it is often faster to use the procedures described in the table below.

Area to Select	Procedure
Cell	Click the left edge of the cell when the pointer is ⬈.
Row	Click to the left of the row when the pointer is ⬧.
Column	Click the top of the column when the pointer is ⬇.
Multiple cells, rows, or columns	Drag through the cells, rows, or columns when the pointer is ⬇, or select the first cell, row, or column and hold down ⇧Shift while clicking on an other cell, row, or column.
Contents of next cell	Press Tab↹.
Contents of previous cell	Press ⇧Shift + Tab↹.
Entire table	Press Alt + 5 (on the numeric keypad with NumLock off) or click ⊕.

1 ● **Select cells A1 through C1.**

● **Click ▤ Center.**

● **In the same manner, center cells B2 through C4.**

● **Click on any cell of the table.**

Your screen should be similar to Figure 3.65

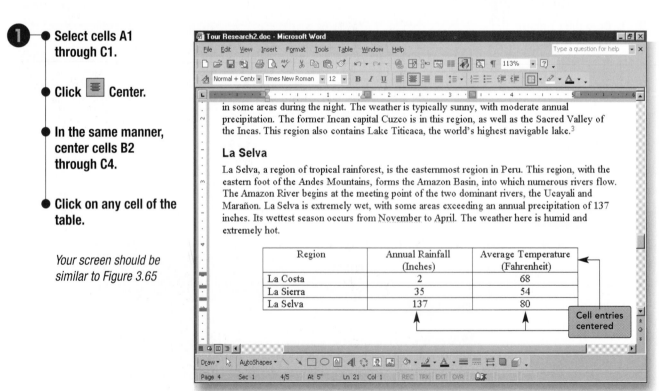

Figure 3.65

A quicker way to apply formats to a table is to use the table AutoFormat feature. This feature includes built-in combinations of formats that can be applied to a table. The AutoFormats consist of a combination of fonts, colors, patterns, borders, and alignment settings.

2 ● **Choose Table/Table AutoFormat.**

Your screen should be similar to Figure 3.66

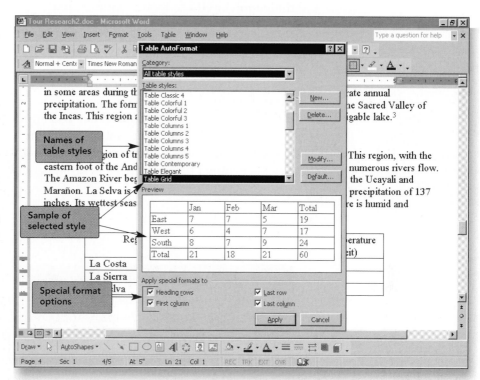

Figure 3.66

From the AutoFormat dialog box, you select the format design you want to apply to the table. The Preview area shows how the selected format will look.

3 ● **Select several names from the Table styles list and look at the samples in the Preview box.**

● **Select Table Colorful 2.**

● **Clear the First Column, Last Row, and Last Column special format options.**

● **Click** Apply.

● **Center the table again.**

● **Click outside the table to deselect it.**

● **Click 🖫 Save.**

Your screen should be similar to Figure 3.67

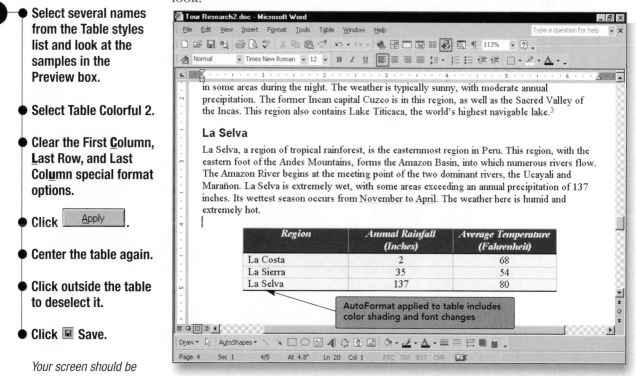

Figure 3.67

Additional Information
Use the Table Normal style to restore the default table style.

The table is reformatted to the new design. The table lines now appear gray, indicating they will not print and are only displayed to help you while entering data on screen. Color shading is applied to the top row along with a change in the text color and italics. Using AutoFormat was much faster than applying these features individually.

Sorting a List

Additional Information
MLA formatting for the Works Cited page also requires that the page is a separate numbered page with the title "Works Cited" centered 1 inch from the top margin. It should also be double-spaced, as is the entire report.

The last page of the report contains the list of works cited in the report. According to the MLA style, each work directly referenced in the paper must appear in alphabetical order by author's last name. The first line is even with the left margin, and subsequent lines of the same work are indented .5 inch. This page needs to be alphabetized and formatted. To quickly arrange the references in alphabetical order, you can sort the list.

concept 7

Sort

7 Word can quickly arrange or **sort** text, numbers or data in lists or tables in alphabetical, numeric, or date order based on the first character in each paragraph. The sort order can be ascending (A to Z, 0 to 9, or earliest to latest date) or descending (Z to A, 9 to 0, or latest to earliest date).

1
- Move to the last page of the document.

- Select the list of references.

- Choose T**a**ble/**S**ort.

Your screen should be similar to Figure 3.68

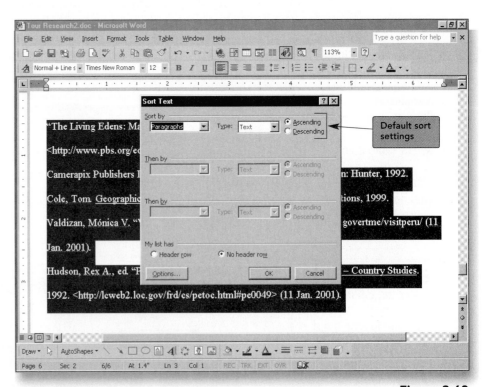

Figure 3.68

The table on the next page describes the rules that are used when sorting.

Sort By	Rules
Text	First, items beginning with punctuation marks or symbols (such as !, #, $, %, or &) are sorted.
	Second, items beginning with numbers are sorted. Dates are treated as three-digit numbers.
	Third, items beginning with letters are sorted.
Numbers	All characters except numbers are ignored. The numbers can be in any location in a paragraph.
Date	Valid date separators include hyphens, forward slashes (/), commas, and periods. Colons (:) are valid time separators. If unable to recognize a date or time, Word places the item at the beginning or end of the list (depending on whether you are sorting in ascending or descending order).
Field results	If an entire field (such as a last name) is the same for two items, Word next evaluates subsequent fields (such as a first name) according to the specified sort options.

When a tie occurs, Word uses the first non-identical character in each item to determine which item should come first.

The default Sort Text settings will sort by text and paragraphs in ascending order.

2 ● Click OK.

● Click ▲ Styles and Formatting.

● Choose the Body Text Indent style.

● Close the task pane.

● Deselect the list of references.

Your screen should be similar to Figure 3.69

Selection is in ascending alphabetical order

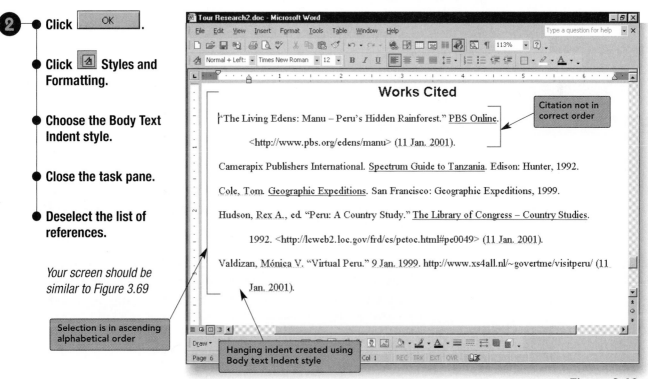

Figure 3.69

The list is in ascending alphabetical order. Entries that are longer than one line appear with a hanging indent. Notice, however, that the citation for "The Living Edens . . ." is still at the top of this list. This is because Word sorts punctuation first. You will need to move this item to below the citation for Hudson.

3 Select the entire "The Living Edens . . ." citation and drag it to below the Hudson citation.

Your screen should be similar to Figure 3.70

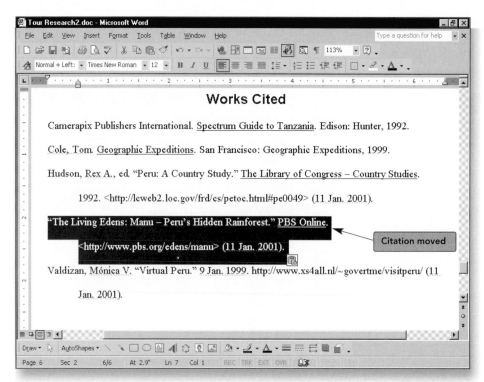

Figure 3.70

Creating Headers and Footers

Next you want to add information in a header and footer to the report.

concept 8

Header and Footer

8 Headers and footers provide information that typically appears at the top and bottom of each page in a document and helps the reader locate information in a document. A **header** is a line or several lines of text at the top of each page just above the top margin line. The header usually contains the title and the section of the document. A **footer** is a line or several lines of text at the bottom of every page just below the bottom margin line. The footer usually contains the page number and perhaps the date. Headers and footers can also contain graphics, such as a company logo.

The same header and footer can be used throughout a document, or a different header and footer can be used in different sections of a document. For example, a unique header or footer can be used in one section and a different one in another section. You can also have a unique header or footer on the first page, or omitted entirely from the first page, or use a different header and footer on odd and even pages.

Adding a Header

You want the report header to display your name and the page number.

- **Move to the Tanzania heading on page 2.**

- **Choose View/Header and Footer.**

Your screen should be similar to Figure 3.71

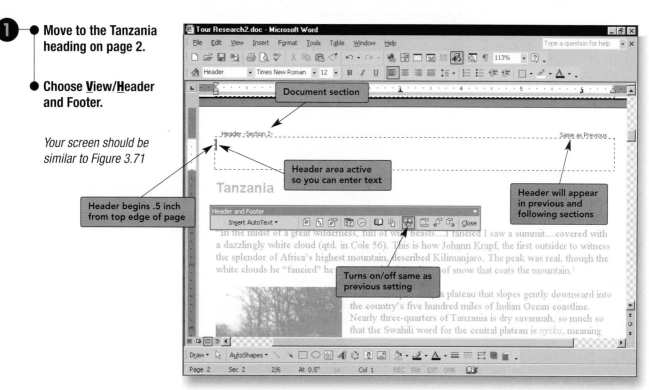

Figure 3.71

The document dims, the header area becomes active, and the Header and Footer toolbar is displayed. Notice that the information above the header area identifies the section location of the document where the insertion point is positioned, in this case, section 2. In addition, in the upper right corner the message "Same as Previous" is displayed. When this setting is on, the header in the sections before and after the section in which you are entering a header will have the same header. Because you do not want the title page in section 1 to have a header, you will turn off the Same as Previous option.

2 ● **Click** 🖳 **Same as Previous.**

Your screen should be similar to Figure 3.72

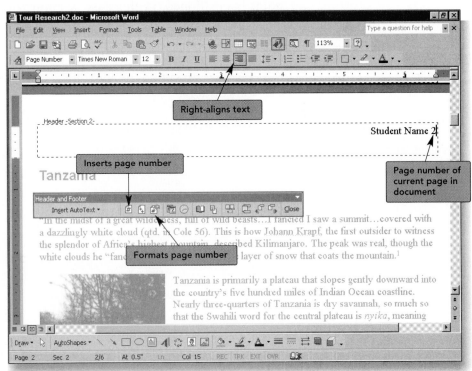

Figure 3.72

Additional Information

MLA style requires that headers and footers be placed .5 inch from the top and bottom of the page. This is the default layout for the Normal template. The header includes the page number preceded by the author's name.

You type in the header as if it were a mini-document. The header and footer text can be formatted just like any other text. In addition, you can control the placement of the header and footer text by specifying where it should appear: left-aligned, centered, or right-aligned in the header or footer space. You will enter your name followed by the page number, right-aligned.

3 ● **Type your name.**

● **Press** Spacebar.

● **Click** 🔢 **Insert Page Number.**

● **Click** ▤ **Align Right.**

Another Method

You can also press Tab⇆ once to center-align and twice to right-align the header text.

Your screen should be similar to Figure 3.73

Figure 3.73

The page number 2 is displayed, because that is the current page in the document. You do not want the title page included in the page numbering, but instead want to begin page numbering with the first page of section 2.

4 ● **Click**  **Format Page Number.**

Another Method
You can also add and format page numbers using Insert/Page Numbers.

Your screen should be similar to Figure 3.74

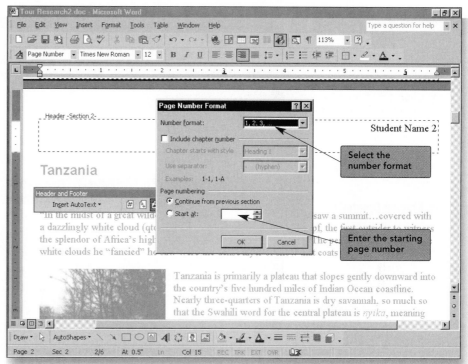

Figure 3.74

The Page Number Format dialog box is used to change the format of page numbers, to include chapter numbers, and to change the page numbering sequence. The default page numbering setting continues the numbering from the first section. To reset the page number sequence to begin section 2 with page 1,

5 ● **Choose Start At.**

Additional Information
The default Start At setting begins numbering with 1.

● **Click** OK .

Your screen should be similar to Figure 3.75

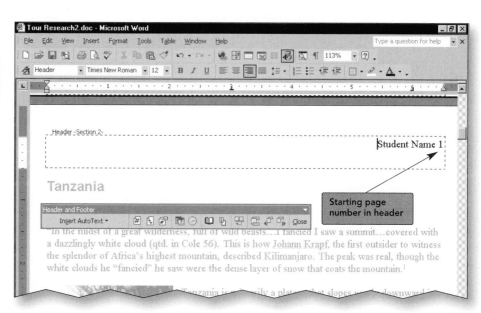

Figure 3.75

The header now displays "1" as the current page number.

Adding a Footer

You want to display the date in the footer. To quickly add this information, you will use an AutoText entry.

1
- Click ⊞ Switch Between Header and Footer.

- Click ⬚ Same as Previous to turn off this option.

- Click [Insert AutoText ▾].

- Choose Created on.

- Right-align the entry.

Your screen should be similar to Figure 3.76

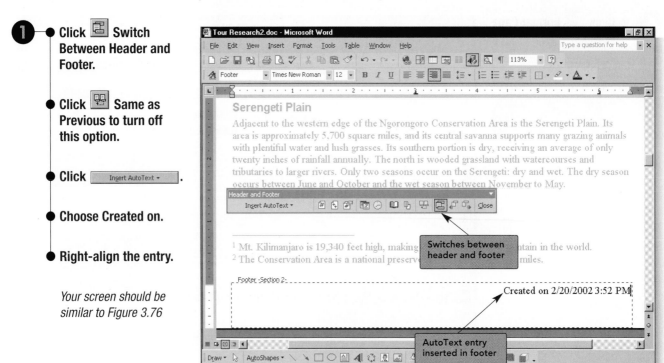

Figure 3.76

The AutoText entry is displayed followed by the date and time.

2 ● Close the Header and Footer toolbar.

● In section 2, scroll down to see the bottom of page 1 and the top of page 2.

Your screen should be similar to Figure 3.77

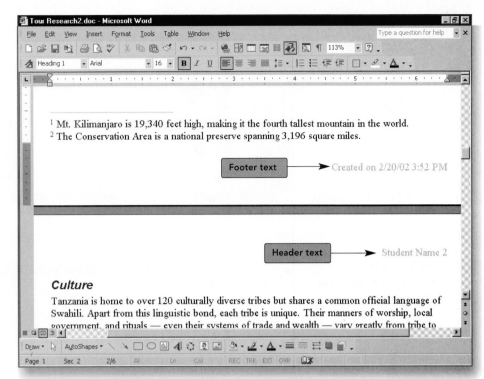

Figure 3.77

The document area is active again, and the header and footer text appears dimmed.

Checking the Document

Before you print the report, you want to check the spelling and grammar of the entire document, including the footnotes, header, and footer. You also want to check the formatting of the document for consistency. Many times when creating a long document, it is easy to format areas differently that should be formatted the same. For example, if your headings are mostly formatted as Heading 2 styles, but you accidentally format a heading with a Heading 3 style, Word can locate the inconsistent formatting and quickly make the appropriate correction for you. Using the formatting consistency checker can give your documents a more professional appearance.

Redisplaying Spelling and Grammar Errors

First you will turn on the display of spelling and grammar errors again and then spell and grammar check the document.

1 ● **Move to the top of page 1 of section 2.**

● **Choose Tools/Options/Spelling and Grammar.**

● **Select Hide spelling errors in this document to clear the checkmark.**

● **Select Hide grammatical errors in this document to clear the checkmark.**

● **Click** `OK` **.**

● **Click** 🔤 **Spelling and Grammar.**

● **Choose Ignore All for all proper names, special terms and abbreviations. Respond appropriately to any other located errors.**

● **Click** `OK` **to end spelling and grammar checking.**

Your screen should be similar to Figure 3.78

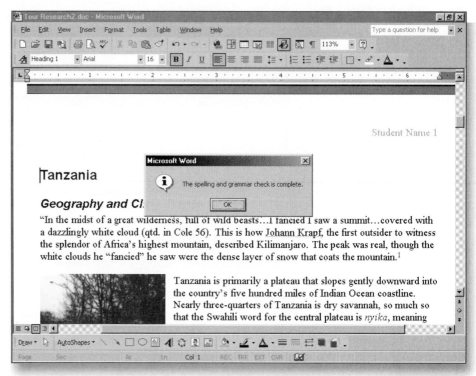

Figure 3.78

The spelling and grammar checker first checked the document text for errors, then footnotes, and finally headers anf footers.

Checking Formatting Inconsistencies

Next, you will turn on the feature to check for formatting inconsistencies. Word identifies inconsistencies with a blue wavy underline.

1 • **Choose Tools/Options.**

• **From the Edit tab, select Mark Formatting Inconsistencies.**

• **Click** [OK] .

• **Right-click on the word Nyika.**

Your screen should be similar to Figure 3.79

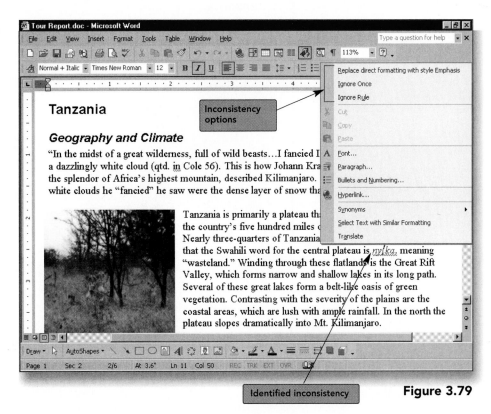

Figure 3.79

The first identified formatting inconsistency is for the italics applied to the word "nyika."

When checking for formatting inconsistencies, Word looks for occurrences of similar formatting that you have applied directly to text, of styles that contain additional direct formatting, and of direct formatting that matches styles that are applied elsewhere in the document. If two occurrences of formatting are markedly different, then they are not identified as inconsistent. However, in cases where the formatting is very similar, they are identified as inconsistent. In this case, the identified inconsistency is because the formatting was applied directly to the word using the italics feature, and the same result could be obtained by using the style Emphasis. Since changing this will not affect how the word looks, you will ignore the suggestion.

2 ● Choose **I**gnore Once.

Your screen should be similar to Figure 3.80

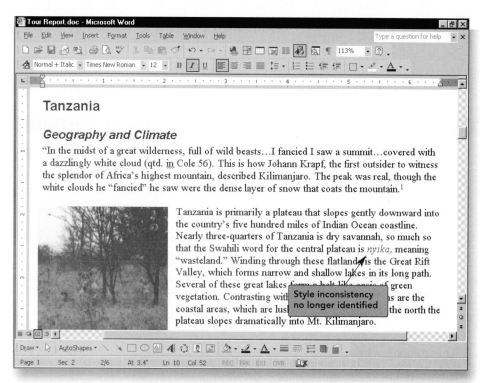

Figure 3.80

The wavy blue underline is cleared from the document.

3 ● Scroll to page 4 to see the next located occurrence in the Machu Picchu heading.

● Right-click on Machu Picchu.

Your screen should be similar to Figure 3.81

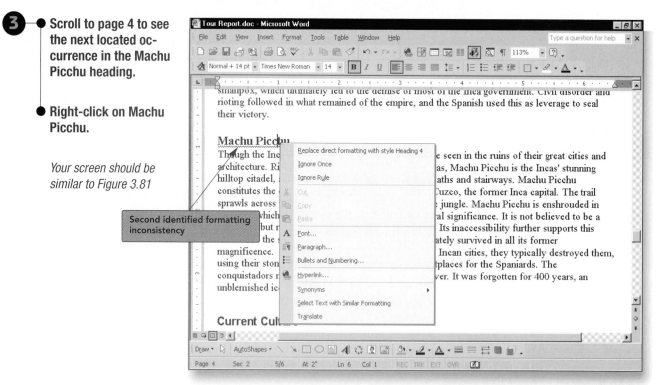

Figure 3.81

The suggested change is to replace the direct formatting of this text (14 points and bold) with the equivalent heading style. Because you want the topic to appear in the table of contents, you will replace the formatting with the Heading 4 style. (The last inconsistency is in the Works Cited heading. You want the heading to appear in the table of contents listing.)

4 ● Choose Replace direct formatting with style Heading 4.

● Move to the Works Cited page.

● Right-click on the Works Cited title.

Your screen should be similar to Figure 3.82

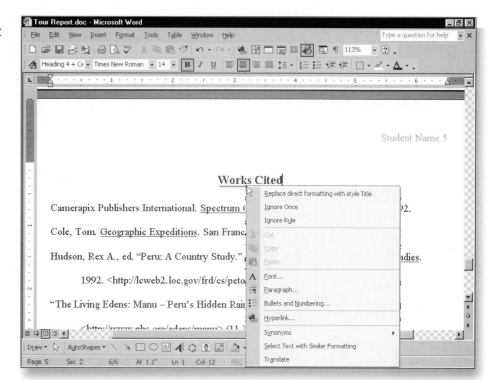

Figure 3.82

The suggested style change is to use the Title style. In this case, you want to change it to a Heading 1 style so it will appear in the table of contents. You will need to make this change directly.

5 ● Choose Heading 1 from the Styles and Formatting task pane list box.

● Click ≡ Center.

● Close the task pane.

● Choose **T**ools/**O**ptions/ Edit/Mark formatting inconsistencies to turn off this feature.

● Click ⌷ OK ⌷.

Your screen should be similar to Figure 3.83

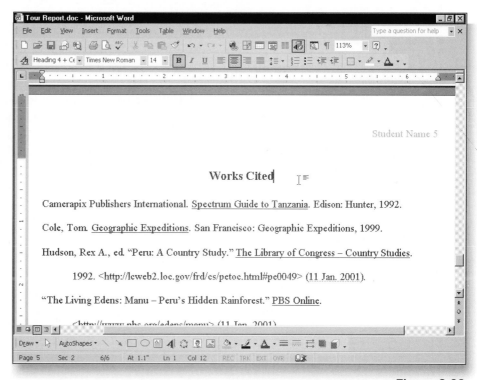

Figure 3.83

1 **Move to the top of the document.**

Right-click on the table of contents to display the shortcut menu.

Choose Update Field.

Another Method
You can also press F9 to quickly update a field.

Choose Update entire table.

Click OK **.**

Scroll the window to see the entire table of contents.

Click outside the table of contents to deselect it.

Your screen should be similar to Figure 3.84

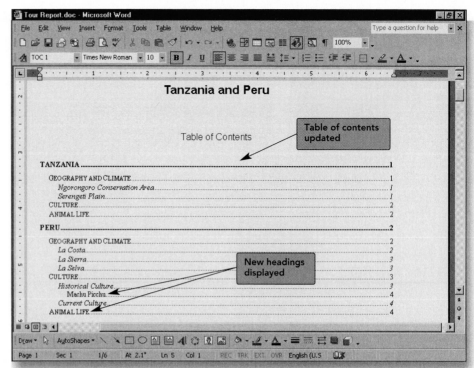

Figure 3.84

Updating a Table of Contents

You have made many modifications to the report since generating the table of contents, so you want to update the listing. Because the table of contents is a field, if you add or remove headings, rearrange topics, or make other changes that affect the table of contents listing, you can quickly update the table of contents. In this case, you have added pictures and a table that may have affected the paging of the document, and you changed two headings to heading styles. You will update the table of contents to ensure that the page references are accurate and that all headings are included.

The page numbers referenced by each table of contents hyperlink have been updated as needed and the two new topics are listed.

Printing Selected Pages

You are now ready to print the report.

- **Click**  **Save.**

- **Preview the report.**

- **Click** 🖽 **Multiple Pages and select 2x3 Pages to display six pages.**

Another Method
The menu equivalent is View/Zoom/Many Pages.

Your screen should be similar to Figure 3.85

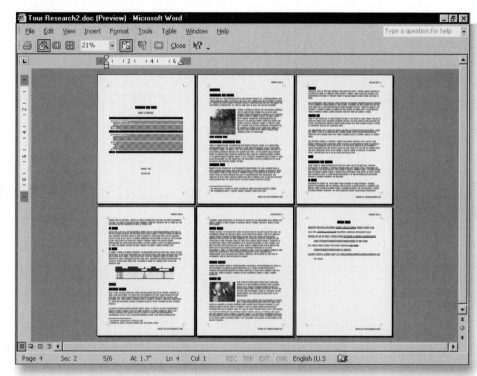

Figure 3.85

You would like to print only the first, second, fourth, and sixth pages of the document. To do this, you use the Print dialog box to select the pages you want to print. When printing pages in different sections, the page number and section number must be identified in the page range.

- **Choose File/Print.**

- **If necessary, select the appropriate printer for your computer system.**

- **Type p1s1, p1s2, p3s2, p5s2 in the Pages text box.**

- **Click** [OK] **.**

- **Click** 🖹 **one page.**

- **Change to Normal view and set the zoom to 100%.**

- **Close the file and exit Word.**

Your printed output should be similar to that shown in the case study at the beginning of the lab.

concept summary

LAB 3
Creating Reports and Tables

Style (WD3.6)

A **style** is a set of formats that is assigned a name.

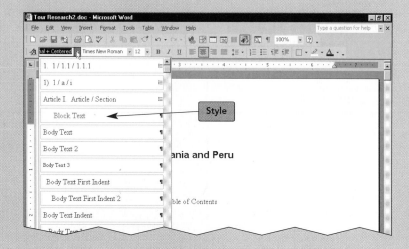

Section (WD3.25)

To format different parts of a document differently, you can divide a document into **sections**.

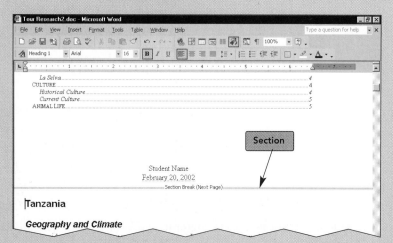

Footnote and Endnote (WD3.28)

A **footnote** is a source reference or text offering additional explanation that is placed at the bottom of a page. An **endnote** is also a source reference or long comment that typically appears at the end of a document.

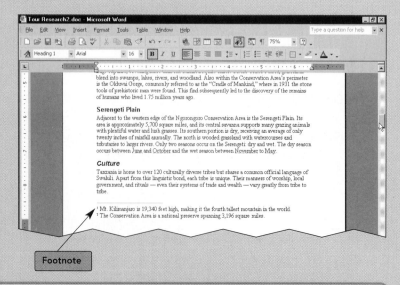

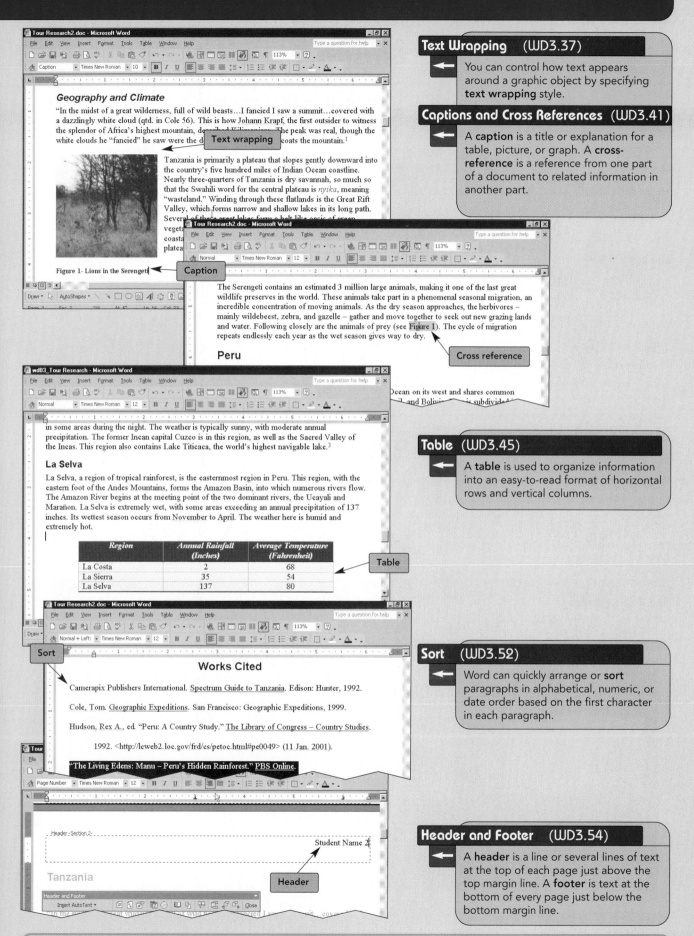

Text Wrapping (WD3.37)

You can control how text appears around a graphic object by specifying **text wrapping** style.

Captions and Cross References (WD3.41)

A **caption** is a title or explanation for a table, picture, or graph. A **cross-reference** is a reference from one part of a document to related information in another part.

Table (WD3.45)

A **table** is used to organize information into an easy-to-read format of horizontal rows and vertical columns.

Sort (WD3.52)

Word can quickly arrange or **sort** paragraphs in alphabetical, numeric, or date order based on the first character in each paragraph.

Header and Footer (WD3.54)

A **header** is a line or several lines of text at the top of each page just above the top margin line. A **footer** is text at the bottom of every page just below the bottom margin line.

LAB **3**

Creating Reports and Tables

key terms

caption WD3.41	footnote WD3.28	pane WD3.30
cell WD3.45	header WD3.54	section WD3.25
character style WD3.6	heading style WD3.6	section break WD3.25
cross-reference WD3.41	inline object WD3.37	sort WD3.52
Document Map WD3.31	note pane WD3.30	style WD3.6
drawing layer WD3.37	note reference mark WD3.28	table WD3.45
endnote WD3.28	note separator WD3.28	table reference WD3.47
floating object WD3.37	note text WD3.28	
footervWD3.54	paragraph style WD3.6	

mous skills

The Microsoft Office User Specialist (MOUS) certification program is designed to measure your proficiency in performing basic tasks using the Office XP applications. Getting certified demonstrates that you have the skills and provides a valuable industry credential for employment. After completing this lab, you have learned the following Microsoft Office User Specialist skills:

Skill	Description	Page
Inserting and Modifying Text	Apply character styles	WD3.6
Creating and Modifying Paragraphs	Apply bullet, outline, and numbering format to paragraphs	WD3.6
	Apply paragraph styles	WD3.6
Formatting Documents	Create and modify a header and footer	WD3.54
	Modify document layout and page setup options	WD3.25
	Create and modify tables	WD3.45
Managing Documents	Manage files and folders for documents	WD3.14

command summary

Command	Shortcut Keys	Button	Action
File/Page Setup/Layout/ Vertical Alignment			Aligns text vertically on a page
View/Document Map		🔲	Displays or hides Document Map pane
View/Header and Footer			Displays header and footer areas
View/Footnotes			Hides or displays note pane
View/Zoom/Many Pages		⊞	Displays two or more pages in document window
Insert/Break/Page/Break	Ctrl + Enter		Inserts a hard page break
Insert/Page Numbers			Specifies page number location
Insert/Reference/Footnote	Alt + Ctrl + F		Inserts footnote reference at insertion point
Insert/Reference/Caption			Inserts caption at insertion point
Insert/Reference/Cross-reference			Inserts cross-reference at insertion point
Insert/Reference/Index and Tables/Table of Contents			Inserts table of contents
Format/Style		Normal ▾	Applies selected style to paragraph or characters
Format/Picture/Layout/ Wrapping Style		🖼	Specifies how text will wrap around picture
Format/Styles and Formatting		🅰	Opens Styles and Formatting task pane
Tools/Options/View/ScreenTips			Turns off and on the display of ScreenTips
Tools/Options/Spelling & Grammar			Changes settings associated with the Spelling and Grammar checking feature
Table/Insert Table		▦	Inserts table at insertion point
Table/Insert/Rows Above			Inserts a new row in table above selected row
Table/Convert/Text to Table			Converts selected text to table format
Table/Table AutoFormat			Applies selected format to table
Table/Sort			Rearranges items in a selection into sorted order

screen identification

1. In the following Word screen, letters identify important elements. Enter the correct screen element in the space provided.

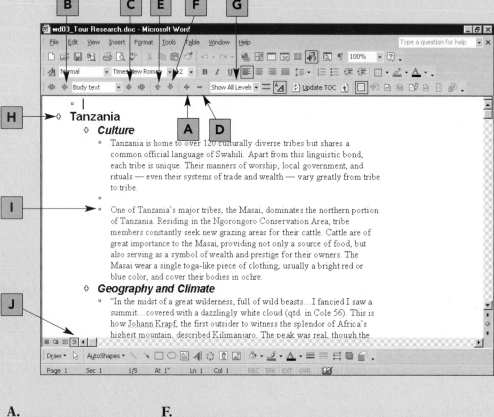

A. _____   F. _____

B. _____   G. _____

C. _____   H. _____

D. _____   I. _____

E. _____   J. _____

matching

Match the item on the left with the correct description on the right.

1. note pane   _____   **a.** text that appears at the bottom of each page below the bottom margin line

2. table of contents   _____   **b.** graphic placed at the insertion point

3. footer   _____   **c.** source reference displayed at the bottom of a page

4. caption   _____   **d.** lower section of workspace that displays footnote text

5. footnote   _____   **e.** instructs Word to end one set of format settings and begin another

6. section break   _____   **f.** a title or explanation for a table, picture, or graph

7. tight wrap   _____   **g.** a listing of the topics that appear in the document

8. Document Map   _____   **h.** text closely follows contours around a graphic

9. inline image   _____   **i.** reference from one part of the document to another part

10. cross-reference   _____   **j.** displays the headings in the document

multiple choice

Circle the correct response to the questions below.

1. Styles can be applied to _____.
   a. characters and paragraphs
   b. documents and paragraphs
   c. words and characters
   d. characters and documents

2. A _____ is inserted automatically when a new page is created in a document.
   a. hard page break
   b. section break
   c. soft page break
   d. page division

3. Source references or text offering additional explanation that are placed at the bottom of a page are _____.
   a. endnotes
   b. footnotes
   c. reference notes
   d. page notes

4. The graphic text-wrapping style(s) that can be used in Word are _____.
   a. inline
   b. square
   c. through
   d. all the above

5. A _____ is a title or explanation for a table, picture, or graph.
   a. statement
   b. cross-reference
   c. caption
   d. footnote

6. A cross-reference is a _____ to another location.
   a. caption
   b. hyperlink
   c. footnote
   d. endnote

7. Text sorted in _____ order appears alphabetically from A to Z.
   a. ordered
   b. descending
   c. ascending
   d. rescending

8. The _____ pane displays the headings in your document.
   a. Document Map
   b. Note
   c. Heading
   d. Outline

9. A _____ object is inserted in the drawing layer and can be positioned precisely on the page.
   a. fixed
   b. floating
   c. layered
   d. pasted

10. A(n)_____displays information in horizontal rows and vertical columns.
    a. Document Map
    b. cell reference
    c. object
    d. table

true/false

Circle the correct answer to the following questions.

1. A style is a named group of formats.	True	False
2. Outline view is the best view to use while entering the body of a document.	True	False
3. The Document Preview pane displays the headings in your document.	True	False
4. A caption can be displayed below a graphic to identify the object.	True	False
5. A cross-reference can be placed within a document to refer back to a figure or other reference in the document.	True	False
6. A hyperlink allows you to jump to another location in a document, another document, or to the Web.	True	False
7. Outline view is used to apply different formats to different parts of a document.	True	False

8. A header is text that prints at the bottom of every page just above the
   bottom margin line.   True   False

9. Footnotes are source references or long comments that typically appear
   at the end of a document.   True   False

10. How text appears surrounding a graphic object depends on the
    text wrapping style.   True   False

Concepts

fill-in

1. A(n)_____ is a named set of formats that affects an entire paragraph.

2. A title or explanation for a table, picture or graph is a(n)_____.

3. Pictures are inserted by default as _____ _____.

4. When you change the wrapping style of a picture, the object changes to a(n)_____
   _____.

5. Use _____ in documents to reference from one part of your document to
   another.

6. The sort order can be either _____ or _____.

7. Headers are displayed _____ the top margin line and footers are displayed _____ the
   bottom margin line.

8. A table consists of horizontal _____, vertical _____, and _____.

9. A cross-reference _____ jumps to the referenced location in the document when clicked.

10. A(n)_____ is typically a source reference that appears at the end of a document.

discussion questions

1. Discuss the differences between footnotes and endnotes. When should notes be added to a
   document?

2. Use Help to learn more about how to position text and graphic objects on a page. Discuss how you
   can move and place graphic objects in a document. Discuss the different wrapping options.

3. Discuss how the Document Map can be used in a document. What must be present for the
   Document Map to display text?

4. Discuss the cross-reference and caption features. When would it be appropriate to use them in a document?

5. Describe the different methods you can use to create a table and explain when they should be used.

6. What is the significance of using a column and row format in tables? How are the rows and columns labeled?

Hands-On Exercises

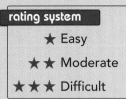

rating system
★ Easy
★★ Moderate
★★★ Difficult

step-by-step

★ Creating an Outline

1. The University Recreation Center provides handouts on different topics related to exercising and health. You are just starting work on a new handout about how to prepare for a workout. To help organize your thoughts, you decide to create an outline of the main topics to be included. Your completed outline is shown here.

   a. Open a new blank document. Switch to Outline view. Turn on formatting marks.

   b. The topics you want to discuss are shown on the next page. Enter these topics at the outline level indicated, pressing [←Enter] at the end of each.

   Student Name   Date

   How to Have an Injury-free Workout

   Warm up Activities

   Low-level aerobics

   5-10 minutes

   Slow stretches

   Benefits

   Increase body temperature

   Warms up muscles

   Increases blood flow

   Stretch

   Stretch all major muscle groups

   Hold 10-20 seconds

   Move slowly and smoothly

   Benefits

   Increase flexibility

   Prevents pulls and strains

   Cool down

   Activities

   Slow stretches

   Low-level aerobics

   5-10 minutes

   Benefits

   Prevents muscle soreness

Stretch (Level 1)
Stretch all major muscle groups (Level 2)
Hold 10–20 seconds (Level 3)
Move slowly and smoothly (Level 3)
Do not bounce (Level 3)
Benefits (Level 2)
Increase flexibility (Level 2)
Prevent pulls and strains (Level 2)
Warm up (Level 1)
Activities (Level 2)
Low-level aerobics (Level 3)
5–10 minutes (Level 4)
Slow stretches (Level 3)
Benefits (Level 2)
Increases body temperature (Level 3)
Warms up muscles (Level 3)
Cool Down (Level 1)
Benefits (Level 2)
Prevents muscle soreness (Level 3)
Activities (Level 2)
Slow stretches (Level 3)
Low-level aerobics (Level 3)
5–10 minutes (Level 4)

c. Move the "Warm up" topic and all subtopics above the "Stretch" topic.
d. In the "Stretch" topic, change the subtopics "Increase flexibility" and "Prevent pulls and strains" to level 3.
e. In the "Cool Down" topic, move "Benefits" below "Activities."
f. Insert a new level 3 line, **Increases blood flow**, as the last subtopic under warm-up benefits. Delete the "Do not bounce" topic under stretch.
g. Turn off formatting marks. Switch to Normal view.
h. Enter your name and the date centered in a header.
i. Print the outline.
j. Save the outline as Workout. Close the file.

★ Modifying an Outline

2. You are preparing a lecture for your class on the Internet and World Wide Web. You have started an outline of topics that you want to discuss, but it still needs some work. Your completed outline is shown here.

a. Open the document wd03_Internet.

b. Enter the title **The Internet and World Wide Web** above the list. Enter a blank line below the title. Apply the Title style to the title.

c. Switch to Outline view.

d. Change the levels of the following topics to the level indicated:
CERN—Level 3
Sends e-mail to and from a list of subscribers—Level 5
Messages sent to your personal inbox—Level 5
E-mail messages are not sent to your personal inbox—Level 5
Messages are posted to news-group sites—Level 5
Research—Level 3

e. Demote the "Use the WWW" topic and all subtopics below it two levels.

f. Delete the topic "E-mail messages are not sent to your personal inbox."

g. Enter the new topic **Public discussions** as the first topic under "Newsgroups" (level 5).

h. Move "Use the WWW" and all subtopics under it to below "Send E-mail."

i. Enter your name and the current date right-aligned in a header.

j. Switch to Print Layout view.

k. Preview and print the outline.

l. Save the outline as Internet2.

Student Name - February 20, 2002

Messages are posted to newsgroup sites

Chat groups

Direct "live" communications

Internet Relay Chat (IRC) is by far the most popular

Student Name - February 20, 2002

The Internet and World Wide Web

The Internet

Definition

History

Advanced Research Project Agency Network (ARPANET)

CERN

Uses

Send E-mail

Use the WWW

Definition

Applications

Communication

Shopping

Web Storefronts

Web Auctions

Research

Entertainment

Participate in Discussion Groups

Mailing Lists

Sends e-mail to and from a list of subscribers

Messages sent to your personal inbox

Newsgroups

Public discussions

★★ Creating a Table

3. You work for the town of Glendale and are putting together a list of the antique shops to give to visitors along with a map showing the location of each shop. You have entered the shop names, specialties, and map locations in a document. You now want to sort the list and display it as a table. Your completed table is shown here.

   a. Open the file wd03_Antique Shops.
   b. Enter the title **Glendale Antique Shops** above the list. Apply the Title style. Include a blank line below the title.
   c. Line up the columns of information by setting left tabs at the 1.5-inch and 3.5-inch positions on the ruler.
   d. Change the order of the list (excluding the heading line) so that it is sorted by the map location number in ascending order.
   e. Select the table text. Choose the Convert Text to Table command on the Table menu to convert the list to a table. Specify 3 columns as the table size, AutoFit to contents and to separate text at tabs.

   f. Apply a table AutoFormat of your choice to the table.
   g. Center the table.
   h. Color the title to match colors used in the table.
   i. Add a header to the document that displays your name left-aligned and the current date, right-aligned.
   j. Print the document.
   k. Save the document as Antique Shops2.

★★ Designing a Flyer

4. The Downtown Internet Cafe is planning a grand opening celebration. You have already started designing a flyer to advertise the event, but it still needs additional work. Your completed flyer is shown on the next page.

   a. Open the file wd03_Cafe Flyer.
   b. Change the left and right margins to 1 inch.
   c. Create the following table of data below the "Users pay . . ." paragraph.

Length of Time	Rate
Hour	$8.00
Half hour	$5.00

   d. Use Table/AutoFit/AutoFit to Contents to size the table to the cell contents.
   e. Apply an AutoFormat of your choice to the table. Center the table.
   f. Add bullets to the four items under "The Downtown Internet Cafe combines." Add a different style bullet before the four items under "What to do at the Cafe."

g. Insert the picture wd03_coffee.wmf to the right of the first four bulleted items.

h. Insert the picture wd03_Computer User.wmf to the left of the second list of bulleted items.

i. Preview the document. Make any editing changes you feel are appropriate.

j. Enter your name and the date centered in the footer.

k. Save the document as Cafe Flyer2.

l. Print the document.

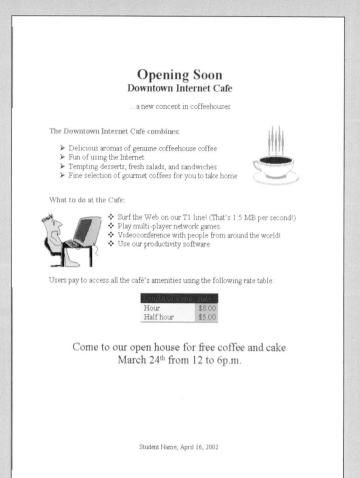

Formatting a Manuscript

★★ 5. You are a freelance writer and have written an article about the top ten scenic drives in the world.
★ You want to enhance the document before submitting it to several travel magazines. Your completed article is shown on the next page.

a. Open the file wd03_Scenic Drives.

b. Create a title page at the top of the document. Include the article title in Title style and your name and the current date centered below the title. Center the title page vertically.

c. Format the names of the top ten drives as Heading 1 styles. (*Hint:* use Format Painter.)

d. On a new page following the title page, add the heading **Table of Contents** formatted as Title style. Create a table of contents listing on this page. Use the Modern style and do not include the Title style headings in the listing.

e. Insert the picture wd03_Mountain to the left of the first paragraph in the Rocky Mountains section. Size the graphic appropriately and wrap the text to the right.

f. Add the following footnote to the end of the first sentence of the third paragraph: **This top 10 list was obtained from the Weissmann Travel Reports in the America Online Traveler's Corner**.

g. Number the pages, excluding the title page.

h. Preview the document and make any adjustments necessary.

i. Save the document as Scenic Drives2. Print the first 3 pages of the document.

Scenic Drives

Student Name
Date

Table of Contents

Top 10 Scenic Drives

The high road, it seems, is the road of choice: Routes through mountainous scenery dominated the nominations you sent in for Top 10 Scenic Drives. As one person wrote about the experience of hitting the top of one Rocky Mountain pass, "you'll think you've reached heaven."

Hyperbole competed with sentiment in many of the nominations we received; multiple exclamation points (AWESOME!!!!!) lined up as thick as billboards along an interstate, and in a few cases, memories of childhood drives revealed just how long it has been since the writer hit the road ("My strongest memories are from looking out the back window of my parents' station wagon").

For those whose memories of beautiful drives needs updating, let the following list of our top 10 picks for Scenic Drives, as nominated by online users and the correspondents and editors of Weissmann Travel Reports, serve as inspiration for your summer travel plans[1]. As usual, this month's ranking is not intended to be a popularity contest; while multiple nominations were taken into consideration when compiling the list, the final results also took into account the writers' ability to convey the beauty they traversed.

1. THE ROCKY MOUNTAINS

Three Rocky roads--Rocky Mountain National Park's Trail Ridge Road, Waterton-Glacier International Peace Park's Going to the Sun Road and the Icefields Parkway, located between Jasper and Banff National Parks in Alberta, Canada, were all nominated as the most scenic drive in the world. Each is lined with spectacular scenery, and for us to try to choose the "best" among them would be like saying that air is more important to human beings than water or food: They all have their strengths, and none could eliminate the others from contention. We're left with a three-way tie. Trail Ridge Road, the highest through-highway in the U.S., begins in Estes Park, Colorado, and winds along a route that takes in terrain ranging from ponderosa pine forests to tundra. Forested canyons, hanging valleys and glacial lakes punctuate the route. Going to the Sun Road, which runs for 50 miles/80 km from Lake McDonald to St. Mary, features stunning and inspiring vistas of alpine scenery (watch for the "Garden Wall," a landmark of the Continental Divide), while the Icefields Parkway is characterized by magnificent lakes, glacial ice fields, waterfalls

---

[1] This top 10 list was obtained from the Weissmann Travel Reports in the America Online Traveler's Corner.

Writing a Report

★ ★
★ **6.** You are a Physical Education major and have written a report on water exercises. The first page of the document is where the table of contents will appear. Pages 2 through 4 contain the body of your report. Several pages of your completed report are shown here. Use the features presented in this lab to add the following to the report:

a. Open the file wd03_Water.

b. Create a new page at the beginning of the document to be used as a title page. Enter the report title, **Acquatic Fitness Routine**, your name, and the date centered on separate lines. Format the report title using the title style.

c. Create a table of contents on the title page below the date.

d. Center the title page vertically.

e. Insert the graphic wd03_Swimmer to the left of the first paragraph of the report. Wrap the text around the graphic. Include a caption below the graphic.

f. Apply additional formats of your choice to the report.

g. Include page numbers right-aligned in a header. Do not number the title page.

h. At the end of the document, create a works cited page following the example in the lab. Enter the following two reference sources:

McEnvoy, Joseph. *Fitness Swimming: Lifetime Programs.* Princeton: Princeton Book Company Publishers, 1995.

President's Council on Physical Fitness and Sports. *AquaDynamics: Physical Conditioning Through Water Exercise.* Washington, DC: Government Printing Office, 1981.

i. Save the document as Water2. Print the report.

Aquatic Fitness Routine
Student Name
February 20, 2002

Table of Contents

1

Figure 1 In-pool Warm-up

In order to achieve and maintain the benefits of exercise, an aquatic exercise program must follow the main principles of a workout. It should begin with warm-up stretches on the pool deck, followed by an in-pool aerobic warm-up session. Then the actual conditioning activity begins, consisting of 20 to 30 minutes of vigorous "aerobic" activity. A cool-down period in the pool can end the session, although a toning period is recommended following the cool-down. The following section discusses the aquatic fitness routine in detail.

Warm-up Stretches

It is very important to include proper warm-up routines before each day's activity. Physiologically, the muscles need to be warmed slowly through increased circulation, and the heart rate needs to be raised gradually. Psychologically, each participant needs to begin to think about the workout and perhaps set some personal goals for the day. Warm-ups are also an important safety precaution. Cold, tight muscles are inefficient for a good workout and may tear with sudden movements.

A general idea to keep in mind while structuring a warm-up routine is to try to simulate the movements of the activity to be performed in the main body of the workout. The warm-up should simulate the workout movement but should be of a much lower intensity. Because of the nature of the exercises, they should be performed before entering the pool.

A good warm-up should move quickly but thoroughly from the top of the body to the bottom of the body. In lap swimming and aerobic workout, special attention should be given to these areas: shoulder complex, obliques, abdominal, groin, hamstrings, quadriceps, gastrocnemius.

Aerobic Warm-up Exercises

Once the participants have entered the pool, they need to slowly raise their heart rates and get their body temperatures acclimated to that of the pool. Some fun activities for a good aerobic warm-up are to walk, jog, skip, or hop back and forth the width of the pool. As further variation, participants can do front kicks or skips and hops across the pool width. Finally, long strides, called skiing, can be used across the pool width. There are several fun games, such as musical kick-board, water basketball, and tug of war, that may be appropriate for your group as an aerobic warm-up. These games should be played for approximately 5 minutes as a warm-up activity.

Conditioning Activities

Circuit Training: Circuit training is a conditioning activity using stations. Different activities are

Creating a FAQ

★ **1.** The city Health Department receives a large number of calls concerning Alzheimer's disease. In response to the need for information on this topic, they are putting together a FAQ (Frequently Asked Questions) sheet with answers to the most frequently asked questions about the disease.

- Open the file wd03_Alzheimer.
- Use the Document Map to locate the headings in the document, and apply appropriate heading levels.
- Number the list of ten warning signs.
- Use the Format Painter to add bold and underlines to the first sentence of each of the ten warning signs.
- Convert the scale for stages of Alzheimer's on the last page to a table (Use Table/Convert text to Table). Apply an AutoFormat of your choice to the table.
- Display a page number at a position of your choice in the footer.
- Include your name and the date in a header.
- Save the document as Alzheimer2 and print the document.

Computers and Children

★ **2.** You are an Elementary Education major and are writing a report about computers and children. You are in the final stages of finishing the report. Use the features presented in this lab to add the following to the report:

- Open the file wd03_Computer.
- Apply appropriate formats to the titles and headings.
- Create a title page above the body of the report. Use appropriate styles, fonts, and sizes.
- Locate and insert an appropriate clip art on the title page.
- Center the title page vertically.
- Add the footnote **Availability of products is limited to stock on hand** after "Look for:" in the section "Software for Kids."
- Add page numbers to the report, excluding the title page.
- Create a bulleted, sorted list of the five software titles at the end of the report.
- Save the document as Computer2.
- Print the document.

Preparing for a Job Search

★ **3.** You are graduating next June and want to begin your job search early. To prepare for how to get a job, locate three sources of information on this topic. Use your school's career services department, the library, newspaper, and magazine articles as sources. Begin by creating an outline of the topics you will include in the report. Using the outline, write a brief report about your findings. Include the following features in your report:

- A title page that displays the report title, your name, the current date, and a table of contents.
- The body of the paper should include at least two levels of headings and a minimum of three footnotes.
- The report layout should include page numbers on the top right corner of every page (excluding the title page). The title page should be vertically aligned.
- Include at least one picture with a caption and cross-reference.
- Include a works cited page with an alphabetical list of your reference sources.
- Save the report as Job Search and print the report.

Writing a Research Paper

★ ★ **4.** Create a brief research report (or use a paper you have written in the past) on a topic of interest to
★   you. The paper must include the following features:
- A title page that displays the report title, your name, the current date, and a table of contents.
- The body of the paper should include at least two levels of headings and a minimum of three footnotes.
- The report layout should include page numbers on the top right corner of every page (excluding the title page). The title page should be vertically aligned.
- Include at least one picture with a caption and cross-reference.
- Include a works cited page with an alphabetical list of your reference sources.
- Save the document as Research and print the report.

on the web

Computer viruses can strike at any time and can cause serious problems. Use the Web as a resource to learn more about them, then write a brief report defining computer viruses. Describe three viruses, what they do, and the effect they could have on a large company. The paper must include the following features:
- A title page that displays the report title, your name, the current date, and a table of contents.
- The body of the paper should include at least two levels of headings and a minimum of three footnotes.
- The report layout should include page numbers on the top right corner of every page (excluding the title page). The title page should be vertically aligned.
- Include at least one picture with a caption and cross-reference.
- Include a works cited page with an alphabetical list of your reference sources.
- Save the document as Computer Viruses and print the report.

Overview to Excel 2002

What Is an Electronic Spreadsheet?

The electronic spreadsheet, or worksheet, is an automated version of the accountant's ledger. Like the accountant's ledger, it consists of rows and columns of numerical data. Unlike the accountant's ledger, which is created on paper using a pencil and a calculator, the electronic spreadsheet is created by a computer system running spreadsheet application software.

In contrast to word processing, which manipulates text, spreadsheet programs manipulate numerical data. The first spreadsheet program, VisiCalc, was introduced in 1979. Since then spreadsheets have evolved into a powerful business tool that has revolutionized the business world.

The electronic spreadsheet eliminates the paper, pencil, and eraser. With a few keystrokes, the user can quickly change, correct, and update the data. Even more impressive is the spreadsheet's ability to perform calculations from very simple sums to the most complex financial and mathematical formulas. The calculator is replaced by the electronic spreadsheet. Analysis

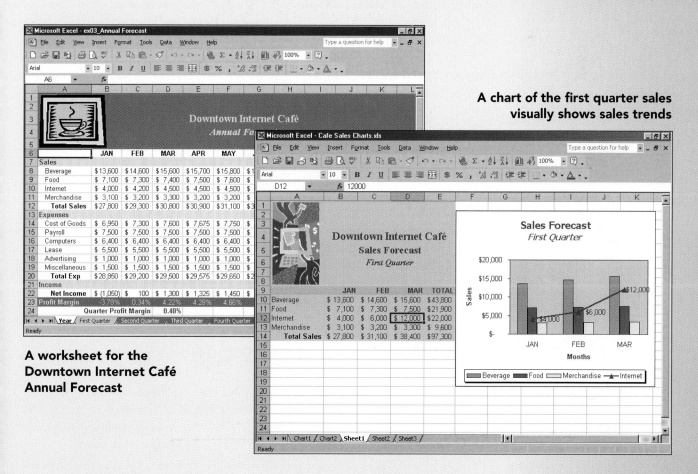

A chart of the first quarter sales visually shows sales trends

A worksheet for the Downtown Internet Café Annual Forecast

of data in the spreadsheet has become a routine business procedure. Once requiring hours of labor and/or costly accountants' fees, data analysis is now available almost instantly using electronic spreadsheets.

Nearly any job that uses rows and columns of numbers can be performed using an electronic spreadsheet. Typical uses include the creation of budgets and financial planning for both business and personal situations.

Excel 2002 Features

Spreadsheet applications help you create well-designed spreadsheets that produce accurate results. These programs not only make it faster to create spreadsheets, they also produce professional-appearing results. Their advantages include the ability to quickly edit and format data, perform calculations, create charts, and print the spreadsheet.

The Microsoft Excel 2002 spreadsheet program uses a workbook file that contains one or more worksheets. Each worksheet can be used to organize different types of related information. Numeric or text data is entered into the worksheet in a location called a cell. These entries can then be erased, moved, copied, or edited. Formulas can be entered that perform calculations using data contained in specified cells. The results of the calculations are displayed in the cell containing the formula.

The design and appearance of the worksheet can be enhanced in many ways. There are several commands that control the format or display of a cell. For instance, numeric entries can be displayed with dollar signs or with a set number of decimal places. Text or label entries can be displayed centered or left- or right-aligned to improve the spreadsheet's appearance. You can further enhance the appearance of the worksheet by changing the type style and size and by adding special effects such as bold, italic, borders, boxes, drop shadows, and shading to selected cells. Columns and rows can be inserted and deleted. The cell width can be changed to accommodate entries of varying lengths.

You can change the values in selected cells and observe their effect on related cells in the worksheet. This is called what-if or sensitivity analysis. Questions that once were too expensive to ask or took too long to answer can now be answered almost instantly and with little cost. Planning that was once partially based on instinct has been replaced to a great extent with facts. However, any financial planning resulting from the data in a worksheet is only as accurate as that data and the logic behind the calculations.

You can also produce a visual display of data in the form of graphs or charts. As the values in the worksheet change, charts referencing those values automatically adjust to reflect the changes. You can also enhance the appearance of a graph by using different type styles and sizes, adding three-dimensional effects, and including text and objects such as lines and arrows.

Case Study for Excel 2002 Labs

The Downtown Internet Café is a new concept in coffeehouses, combining the delicious aromas of a genuine coffeehouse with the fun of using the Internet. You are the new manager for the coffeehouse and are working with the owner, Evan, to develop a financial plan for the next year.

Lab 1: Your first project is to develop a forecast for the Café for the first quarter. You will learn to enter numbers, perform calculations, copy data, label rows and columns, and format entries in a spreadsheet using Excel 2002.

Lab 2: After creating the first quarter forecast for the Downtown Internet Café, you have decided to chart the sales data to make it easier to see the trends and growth patterns. You also want to see what effect a strong advertising promotion of the new Café features will have on the forecasted sales data.

Lab 3: You have been asked to revise the workbook to include forecasts for the second, third, and fourth quarters. Additionally, the owner wants you to create a composite worksheet that shows the entire year's forecast and to change the data to achieve a 5 percent profit margin in the second quarter.

Working Together: Your analysis of sales data for the first quarter has shown a steady increase in total sales. Evan, the Café owner, has asked you for a copy of the forecast that shows the growth in Internet sales if a strong sales promotion is mounted. You will include the worksheet and chart data in a memo to the owner.

Before You Begin

To the Student

The following assumptions have been made:

- Microsoft Excel 2002 has been properly installed on your computer system.

- You have the data files needed to complete the series of Excel 2002 Labs and practice exercises. These files are supplied by your instructor.

- You have completed the McGraw-Hill Windows 98 or 2000 Labs or you are already familiar with how to use Windows and a mouse.

To the Instructor

A complete installation of Office XP is required in which all components are installed and are available to students while completing the labs.

Please be aware that the following settings are assumed to be in effect for the Excel 2002 program. These assumptions are necessary so that the screens and directions in the labs are accurate.

- The New Workbook Task Pane is displayed when Excel is started (Use Tools/Options/View).

- The ScreenTips feature is active (Use Tools/Customize/Options/Show ScreenTips on toolbar).

- The Status bar is displayed (Use Tools/Options/View).

- The horizontal and vertical scroll bars are displayed (Use Tools/Options/View).

- The Paste Options and Show Insert Options buttons are displayed (Use Tools/Options/Edit).

- The Standard and Formatting toolbars are displayed on separate rows (Tools/Customize/Options).

- Full menus are always displayed (Tools/Customize/Options).

- The Normal view is on; Zoom is 100 percent (Use View/Normal; View/Zoom/100%).

- The Office Clipboard is displayed automatically. (Click Options on the Office Clipboard task pane and select Show Office Clipboard Automatically.)

- The Office Assistant feature is not on (Right-click on the Assistant character, choose Options and clear the Use the Office Assistant option.)

- All default settings for a new workbook are in effect.

In addition, all figures in the labs reflect the use of a standard VGA display monitor set at 800 by 600. If another monitor setting is used, there may be more or fewer rows and columns displayed in the window than in the figures. The 800 by 600 setting displays rows 1 through 27 and columns A through L. This setting can be changed using Windows setup.

Microsoft Office XP Shortcut Bar

The Microsoft Office XP Shortcut bar (shown below) may be displayed automatically on the Windows desktop. Commonly, it appears in the right side of the desktop; however, it may appear in other locations, depending upon your setup. The Shortcut bar on your screen may also display different buttons. This is because the Shortcut bar can be customized to display other toolbar buttons.

The Office Shortcut bar makes it easy to open existing documents or to create new documents using one of the Microsoft Office XP applications. It can also be used to send e-mail, add a task to a to-do list, schedule appointments, or access Office Help.

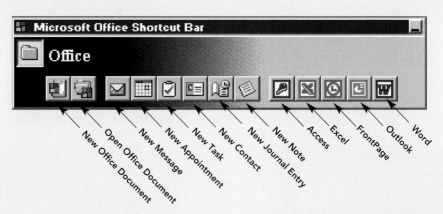

Instructional Conventions

Hands-on instructions you are to perform appear as a sequence of numbered black steps. Within each step, a series of bullets identifies the specific actions that must be performed. Step numbering begins over within each main topic heading throughout the lab.

Command sequences you are to issue appear following the word "Choose." Each menu command selection is separated by a /. If the menu command can be selected by typing a letter of the command, the letter will appear underlined and bold. Items that need to be selected will follow the word "Select" and will appear in black text. You can select items with the mouse or directional keys. (See Example A).

Example A

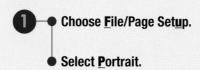

Commands that can be initiated using a button and the mouse appear following the word "Click." The icon (and the icon name if the icon does not include text) is displayed following Click. The menu equivalent and keyboard shortcut appear in a margin note when the action is first introduced. (See Example B).

Example B

Another Method
The menu equivalent is **File/Open** and the keyboard shortcut is Ctrl + O.

Information you are asked to type appears in blue and bold. (See Example C). File names appear in blue.

Example C

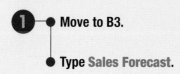

Creating and Editing a Worksheet

objectives

After completing this lab, you will know how to:

1.	Enter, edit, and clear cell entries.
2.	Save, close, and open workbooks.
3.	Specify ranges.
4.	Copy and move cell entries.
5.	Enter formulas and functions.
6.	Adjust column widths.
7.	Change cell alignment.
8.	Format cells.
9.	Insert rows.
10.	Insert and size a ClipArt graphic.
11.	Enter and format a date.
12.	Preview and print a worksheet.

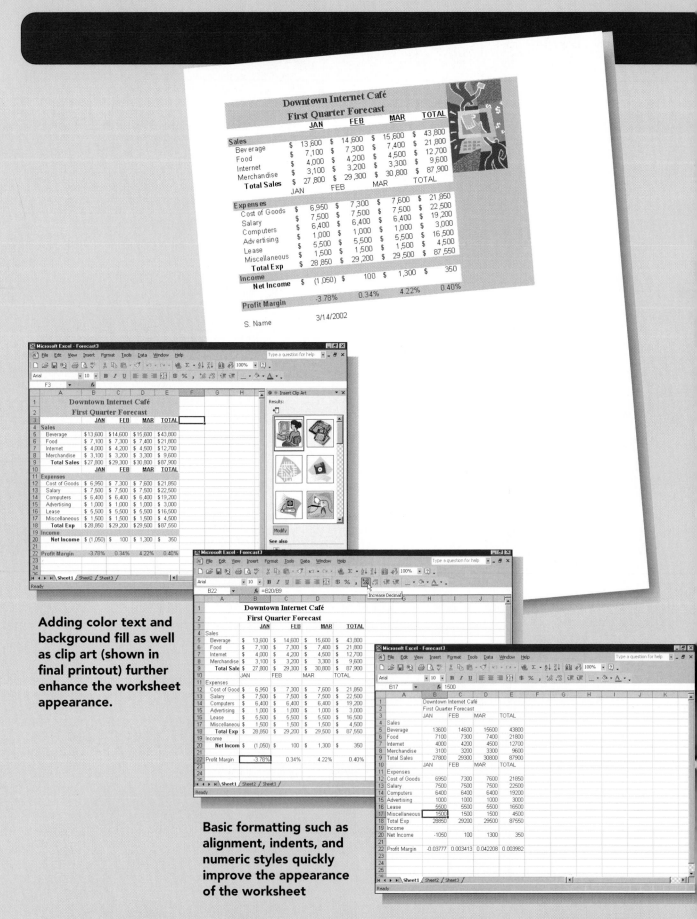

Adding color text and background fill as well as clip art (shown in final printout) further enhance the worksheet appearance.

Basic formatting such as alignment, indents, and numeric styles quickly improve the appearance of the worksheet

Enter labels, numbers, and formulas to create the basic structure of a worksheet.

Downtown Internet Café

You are excited about your new position as manager and financial planner for a local coffeehouse. Evan, the owner, has hired you as part of a larger effort to increase business at the former Downtown Café. Evan began this effort by completely renovating his coffeehouse, installing Internet hookups and outlets for laptops, and changing its name to the Downtown Internet Café. You and Evan expect to increase sales by attracting Internet-savvy café-goers, who, you hope, will use the Downtown Internet Café as a place to meet, study, or just relax.

Evan wants to create a forecast estimating sales and expenses for the first quarter. As part of a good business plan, you and Evan need a realistic set of financial estimates and goals.

In this lab, you will help with the first quarter forecast by using Microsoft Excel 2002, a spreadsheet application that can store, manipulate, and display numeric data. You will learn to enter numbers, perform calculations, copy data, and label rows and columns as you create the basic structure of a worksheet for the Downtown Internet Café. You will then learn how to enhance the worksheet using formatting features and by inserting a ClipArt graphic as shown here.

concept overview

The following concepts will be introduced in this lab:

1	**Template**	A template is a workbook file that includes predefined settings that can be used as a pattern to create many common types of workbooks.
2	**Text and Numeric Entries**	The information or data you enter in a cell can be text, numbers, or formulas.
3	**AutoCorrect**	The AutoCorrect feature makes some basic assumptions about the text you are typing and, based on these assumptions, automatically corrects the entry.
4	**Column Width**	The size or width of a column controls how much information can be displayed in a cell.
5	**Copy and Move**	The contents of worksheet cells can be duplicated (copied) or moved to other locations in the worksheet or between worksheets, saving you time by not having to recreate the same information.
6	**Range**	A selection consisting of two or more cells on a worksheet is a range.
7	**Formulas**	A formula is an equation that performs a calculation on data contained in a worksheet.
8	**Relative Reference**	A relative reference is a cell or range reference in a formula whose location is interpreted in relation to the position of the cell that contains the formula.
9	**Functions**	Functions are prewritten formulas that perform certain types of calculations automatically.
10	**Recalculation**	Whenever a number in a referenced cell in a formula changes, Excel automatically recalculates all formulas that are dependent on the changed value.
11	**Alignment**	Alignment settings allow you to change the horizontal and vertical placement and the orientation of an entry in a cell.
12	**Fonts**	Fonts consist of typefaces, point sizes, and styles that can be applied to characters to improve their appearance.
13	**Number Formats**	Number formats affect how numbers look onscreen and when printed.
14	**Styles**	A style consists of a combination of formats that have been named and that can be quickly applied to a selection.
15	**Graphics**	A graphic is a non-text element or object, such as a drawing or picture that can be added to a document.

Exploring Excel 2002

As part of the renovation of the Downtown Internet Café, new computers and the most current versions of software programs were installed, including the latest version of the Microsoft Office suite of applications, Office XP. You are very excited to see how this new and powerful application can help you create professional budgets and financial forecasts.

Starting Excel 2002

You will use the spreadsheet application Excel 2002 included in the Office suite to create the first quarter forecast for the Café.

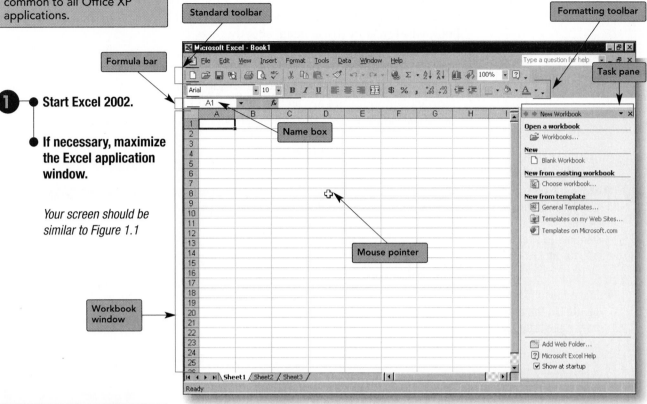

1 ● **Start Excel 2002.**

● **If necessary, maximize the Excel application window.**

Your screen should be similar to Figure 1.1

Figure 1.1

After a few moments, the Excel application window is displayed.

Exploring the Excel Window

The Excel window title bar displays the program name, Microsoft Excel, followed by Book1, the name of the open file. The menu bar below the title bar displays the Excel program menu. It consists of nine menus that provide access to the commands and features you will use to create and modify a worksheet.

The toolbars, normally located below the menu bar, contain buttons that are mouse shortcuts for many of the menu items. The **Standard toolbar** contains buttons that are used to complete the most frequently used menu commands. The **Formatting toolbar** contains buttons that are used to change the appearance or format of the document. Excel includes 23 different toolbars. Many of the toolbars appear automatically as you use different features. Your screen may display other toolbars if they were on when the program was last exited.

Below the toolbars is the formula bar. The **formula bar** displays entries as they are made and edited in the workbook window. The **Name box**, located at the left end of the formula bar, provides information about the selected item. The Edit Formula button is used to create or edit a formula.

The **task pane** is displayed on the right side of the window. There are eight different task panes that display depending on the task being performed. Since you just started Excel, the New Workbook task pane is automatically displayed providing different ways to create a new workbook or open an existing workbook.

The large area to the left of the task pane is the **workbook window**. A **workbook** is an Excel file that stores the information you enter using the program in worksheets. You will learn about the different parts of the workbook window and worksheets shortly.

The mouse pointer can appear as many different shapes. The mouse pointer changes shape depending upon the task you are performing or where the pointer is located on the window. Most commonly it appears as a ⇩ or ⊕. When it appears as a ⊕, it is used to move to different locations in the workbook window and when it appears as a ⇩, it is used to select items.

1 ● **Move the mouse pointer into the center of the workbook window to see it appear as ⊕.**

● **Move the mouse pointer to the menu bar to see it appear as ⇩.**

Workbook window

Your screen should be similar to Figure 1.2

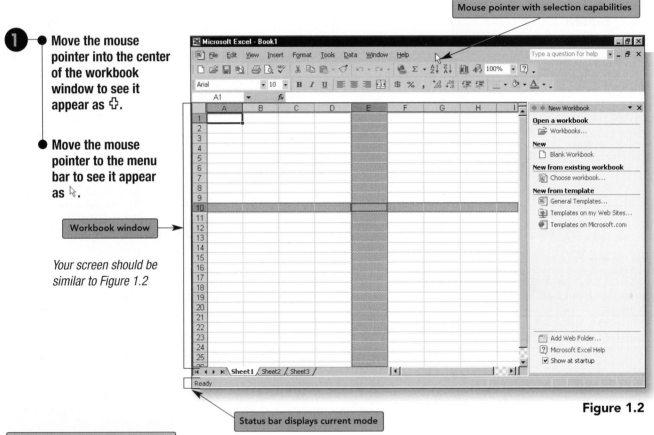

Figure 1.2

The status bar at the bottom of the Excel window displays information about various Excel settings. The left side of the status bar displays the current mode or state of operation of the program, in this case, Ready. When Ready is displayed, you can move around the workbook, enter data, use the function keys, or choose a command. As you use the program, the status bar displays the current mode. The modes will be discussed as they appear throughout the labs.

Finally, your screen may display the Office Assistant. This feature provides quick access to online Help.

Exploring the Workbook Window

The workbook window displays a new blank workbook file containing three blank sheets. A sheet is used to display different types of information, such as financial data or charts. Whenever you open a new workbook, it displays a worksheet.

A **worksheet**, also commonly referred to as a **spreadsheet**, is a rectangular grid of **rows** and **columns** used to enter data. It is always part of a workbook and is the primary type of sheet you will use in Excel. The worksheet is much larger than the part you are viewing in the window. The worksheet actually extends 256 columns to the right and 65,536 rows down.

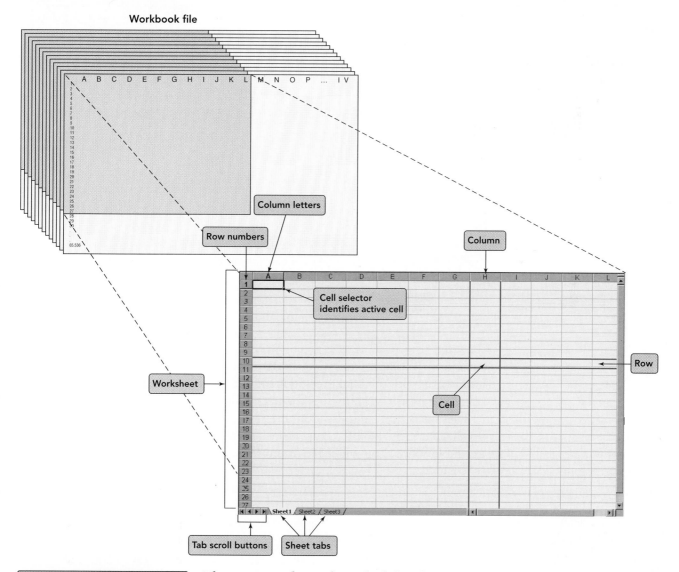

The **row numbers** along the left side and the **column letters** across the top of the workbook window identify each worksheet row and column. The intersection of a row and column creates a **cell**. Notice the heavy border, called the **cell selector**, surrounding the cell located at the intersection of column A and row 1. The cell selector identifies the **active cell**, which is the cell your next entry or procedure affects. Additionally, the Name box in the

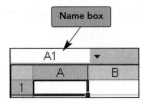

Name box

A1

formula bar displays the **reference**, consisting of the column letter and row number of the active cell. The reference of the active cell is A1.

Each sheet in a workbook is named. The default names are Sheet1, Sheet2, and so on, displayed on **sheet tabs** at the bottom of the workbook window. The name of the **active sheet**, which is the sheet you can work in, appears bold. The currently displayed worksheet in the workbook window, Sheet1, is the active sheet.

1 ● **Click the Sheet2 tab.**

Another Method

You can also press Ctrl + Page Down to move to the next sheet and Ctrl + Page Up to move to the previous sheet.

Your screen should be similar to Figure 1.3

Blank worksheet in Sheet 2

Active sheet

Tab scroll buttons

Sheet tabs

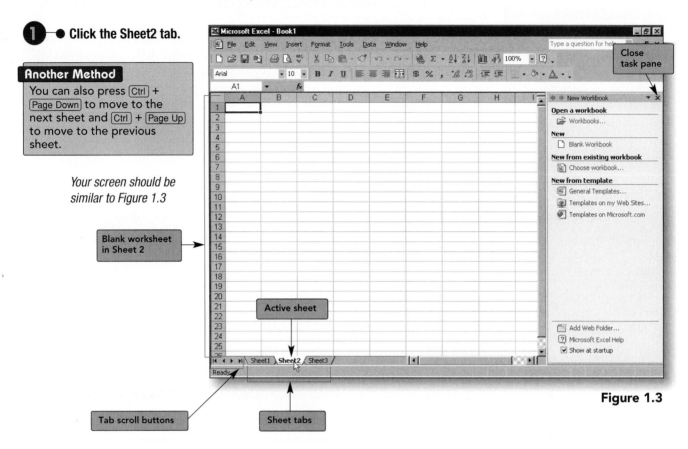

Figure 1.3

An identical blank worksheet is displayed in the window. The Sheet2 tab letters are bold, the background is highlighted, and it appears in front of the other sheet tabs to show it is the active sheet.

The sheet tab area also contains **tab scroll buttons**, which are used to scroll tabs right or left when there are more worksheet tabs than there is available space. You will learn about these features throughout the labs.

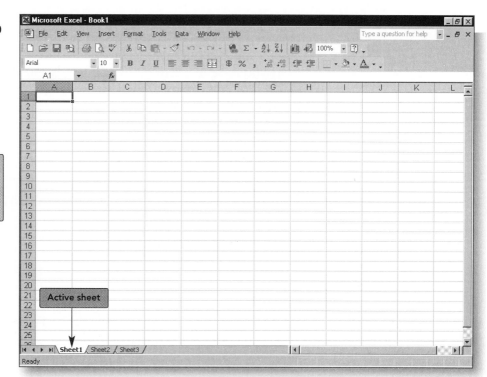

2
- Click the Sheet1 tab to make it the active sheet again.

- Click ⊠ in the task pane title bar to close the task pane.

Another Method
The View/Task Pane command can also be used to hide the task pane.

Your screen should be similar to Figure 1.4

Figure 1.4

With the task pane closed, the workbook window is now the full width of the application window space, allowing much more of the worksheet to be displayed.

Moving around the Worksheet

Either the mouse or the keyboard can be used to move the cell selector from one cell to another in the worksheet. To move using a mouse, simply point to the cell you want to move to and click the mouse button. Depending upon what you are doing, using the mouse to move may not be as convenient as using the keyboard, in which case the directional keys can be used. You will use the mouse, then the keyboard to move the cell selector.

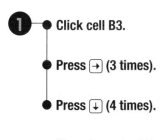
Another Method
You can use the directional keys in the numeric keypad (with NumLock off) or, if you have an extended keyboard, you can use the separate directional keypad area.

1
- Click cell B3.

- Press → (3 times).

- Press ↓ (4 times).

Your screen should be similar to Figure 1.5

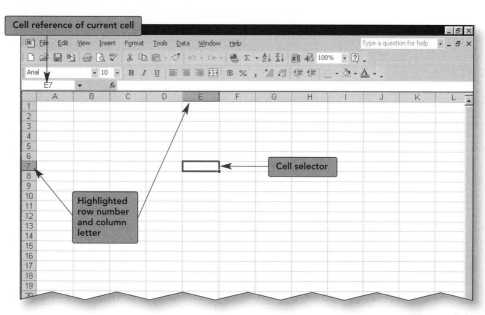

Figure 1.5

The cell selector is now in cell E7, making this cell the active cell. The Name box displays the cell reference. In addition, the row number and column letter appear highlighted to further identify the location of the active cell.

As you have learned, the worksheet is much larger than the part you are viewing in the window. To see an area of the worksheet that is not currently in view, you need to scroll the window. Either the keyboard or the mouse can be used to quickly scroll a worksheet. Again, both methods are useful depending upon what you are doing. The key and mouse procedures shown in the tables that follow can be used to move around the worksheet.

Keys	Action
Page Down	Moves cell selector down one full window
Page Up	Moves cell selector up one full window
Alt + Page Down	Moves cell selector right one full window
Alt + Page Up	Moves cell selector left one full window
Ctrl + Home	Moves cell selector to upper-left corner cell of worksheet
Home	Moves cell selector to beginning of row
End →	Moves cell selector to last-used cell in row
End ↓	Moves cell selector to last-used cell in column

Mouse	Action
Click scroll arrow	Scrolls worksheet one row/column in direction of arrow
Click above/below scroll box	Scrolls worksheet one full window up/down
Click right/left of scroll box	Scrolls worksheet one full window right/left
Drag scroll box	Scrolls worksheet multiple windows up/down or right/left

In addition, if you hold down the arrow keys, the Alt + Page Up or Alt + Page Down keys, or the Page Up or Page Down keys, you can quickly scroll through the worksheet. When you use the scroll bar, however, the cell selector does not move until you click on a cell that is visible in the window.

You will scroll the worksheet to see the rows below row 25 and the columns to the right of column L.

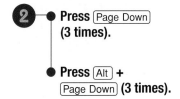

● Press Page Down
   (3 times).

● Press Alt +
   Page Down **(3 times).**

*Your screen should be
similar to Figure 1.6*

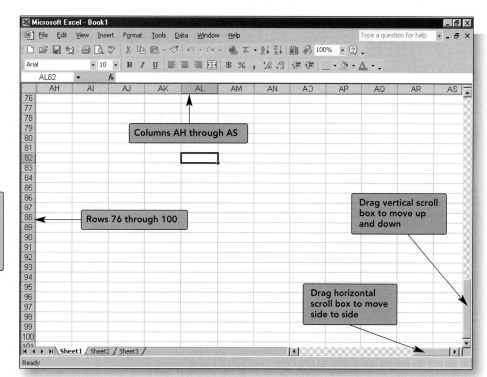

Figure 1.6

The worksheet scrolled downward and left three full windows and the window displays rows 76 through 100 and columns AH through AS of the worksheet. The cell selector is in cell AL82. As you scroll the worksheet using the keyboard, the cell selector also moves.

It is even more efficient to use the scroll bar to move long distances.

3 ● **Slowly drag the vertical scroll box up the scroll bar until row 1 is displayed.**

● **Slowly drag the horizontal scroll box left along the scroll bar until column A is displayed.**

Additional Information
The position of the scroll box
indicates the relative location
of the area you are viewing
within the worksheet and the
size of the scroll box
indicates the proportional
amount of the used area.

*Your screen should be
similar to Figure 1.7*

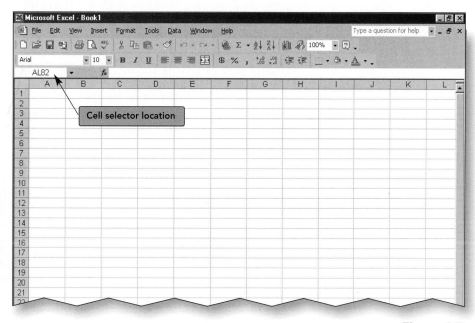

Figure 1.7

Notice that the Name box displays the cell selector location as AL82. When you use the scroll bar to scroll the worksheet, the cell selector does not move.

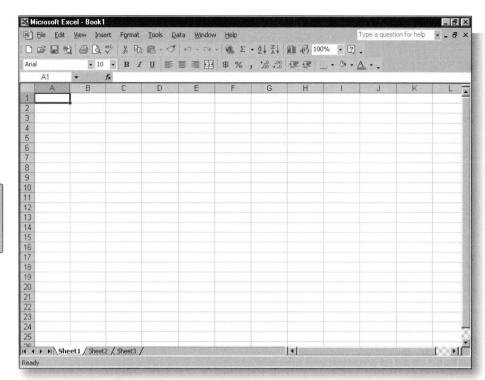

4 ● Practice moving the cell selector around the worksheet using each of the keys presented in the table on page EX1.10.

● Press ⌈Ctrl⌉ + ⌈Home⌉ to move to cell A1.

Another Method

You can also type a cell address in the Name box to move to that location.

Your screen should be similar to Figure 1.8

Figure 1.8

You can use the mouse or the keyboard with most of the exercises in these labs. As you use both the mouse and the keyboard, you will find that it is more efficient to use one or the other in specific situations.

Creating New Workbooks

Now that you are familiar with the parts of the workbook and how to move around, you are ready to create a worksheet showing the forecast for the first three months of operation for the Downtown Internet Café.

Using the Default Workbook Template

When you first start Excel, a new blank Excel workbook is opened. It is like a blank piece of paper that already has many predefined settings. These settings, called **default** settings, are generally the most commonly used settings and are stored as a workbook template.

concept 1

Templates

1 A workbook **template** is a file that includes predefined settings that can be used as a pattern to create many common types of workbooks. Every Excel workbook is based on a template. The default settings for a basic blank workbook are stored in the Book.xlt template file. Whenever you create a new workbook using this template, the same default settings are used.

Many other templates are available within Excel and on the Microsoft Internet site that are designed to help you create professional-looking workbooks. They include templates that create different styles of balance sheets, expense statements, loan amortizations, sales invoices, and timecards. You can also design and save your own workbook templates.

You will use the default workbook template to create the worksheet for the Café. As you create a new workbook, the development progresses through several stages.

Developing a Workbook

Workbook development consists of four steps; planning, entering and editing, testing, and formatting. The objective is to create well-designed worksheets that produce accurate results and are clearly understood, adaptable, and efficient.

Step	Description
1. Plan	Specify the purpose of the workbook and how it should be organized. This means clearly identifying the data that will be input, the calculations that are needed to achieve the results, and the output that is desired. As part of the planning step, it is helpful to sketch out a design of the worksheet to organize the worksheet's structure. The design should include the worksheet title and row and column headings that identify the input and output. Additionally, sample data can be used to help determine the formulas needed to produce the output.
2. Enter and edit	Create the structure of the worksheet using Excel by entering the worksheet labels, data, and formulas. As you enter information, you are bound to make errors that need to be corrected or edited, or you will need to revise the content of what you have entered to make it clearer or to add or delete information.
3. Test	Test the worksheet for errors. Several sets of real or sample data are used as the input, and the resulting output is verified. The input data should include a full range of possible values for each data item to ensure the worksheet can function successfully under all possible conditions.
4. Format	Enhance the appearance of the worksheet to make it more readable or attractive. This step is usually performed when the worksheet is near completion. It includes many features such as boldface text, italic, and color.

As the complexity of the worksheet increases, the importance of following the design process increases. Even for simple worksheets like the one you will create in this lab the design process is important.

During the planning phase, you have spoken with the Café manager regarding the purpose of the workbook and the content in general. The primary purpose is to develop a forecast for sales and expenses for the next year. Evan first wants you to develop a worksheet for the first quarter forecast and then extend it by quarters for the year. After reviewing past budgets and consulting with Evan, you have designed the basic layout for the first quarter forecast for the Café as shown below.

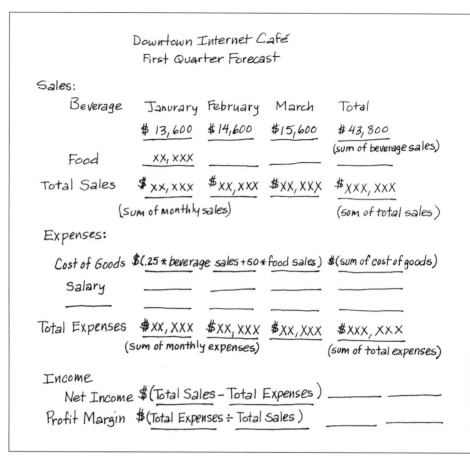

Entering and Editing Data

Now that you understand the purpose of the workbook and have a general idea of the content, you are ready to begin entering the data. You enter data by moving to the cell where you want the data displayed and typing the entry using the keyboard.

As you can see, the budget contains both descriptive text entries and numeric data. These are two types of entries you can make in a worksheet.

concept 2

Text and Numeric Entries

2 The information or data you enter in a cell can be text, numbers, or formulas. **Text** entries can contain any combination of letters, numbers, spaces, and any other special characters. **Number** entries can include only the digits 0 to 9 and any of the special characters, $+ - ( ) , . / \$ \% \Sigma =$. Number entries can be used in calculations. An entry that begins with an equal sign (=) is a **formula**. Formula entries perform calculations using numbers or data contained in other cells. The resulting value from formulas is a **variable** value because it can change if the data it depends on changes. In contrast, a number entry is a **constant** value. It does not begin with an equal sign and does not change unless you change it directly by typing in another entry.

Entering Text

First you will enter the worksheet headings. Row and column **headings** are entries that are used to create the structure of the worksheet and describe other worksheet entries. Generally, headings are text entries. The column headings in this worksheet consist of the three months (January through March) and a total (sum of entries over three months) located in columns B through E. To enter data in a worksheet, you must first select the cell where you want the entry displayed. The column heading for January will be entered in cell B2.

1 ● **Move to B2.**

● **Type J.**

Your screen should be similar to Figure 1.9

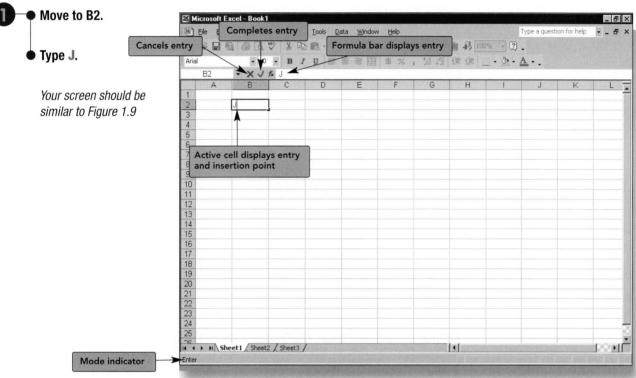

Figure 1.9

Several changes have occurred in the window. As you type, the entry is displayed both in the active cell and in the formula bar. An insertion point appears in the active cell and marks your location in the entry. Two new buttons, ☒ and ☑, appear in the formula bar. They can be used with a mouse to complete your entry or cancel it.

Notice also that the mode displayed in the status bar has changed from Ready to Enter. This notifies you that the current mode of operation in the worksheet is entering data. To continue entering the heading,

2 ● Type **anuary**.

Your screen should be similar to Figure 1.10

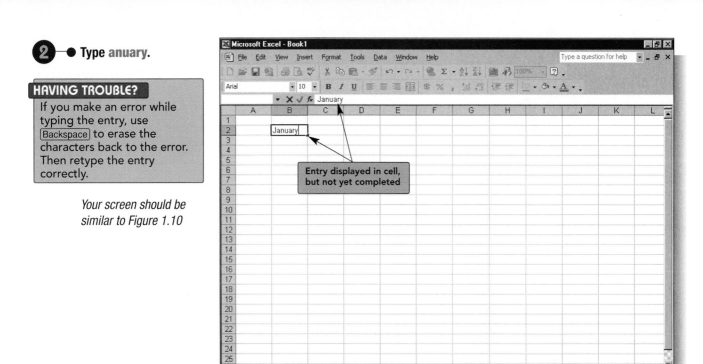

Mode is still Enter

Figure 1.10

Although the entry is displayed in both the active cell and the formula bar, you need to press the [←Enter] key or click ☑ to complete your entry. If you press [Esc] or click ☒, the entry is cleared and nothing appears in the cell. Since your hands are already on the keyboard, it is quicker to press [←Enter] than it is to use the mouse to click ☑.

3 ● Press [←Enter].

Your screen should be similar to Figure 1.11

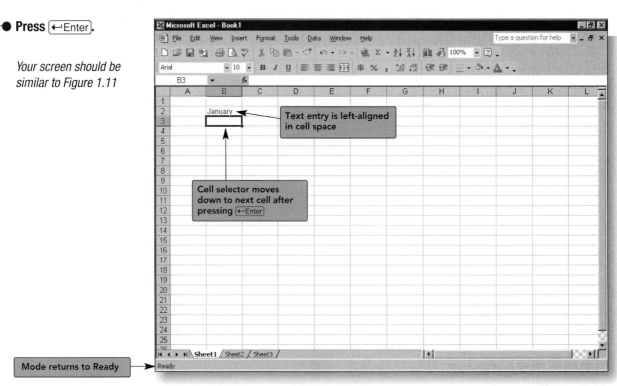

Mode returns to Ready

Figure 1.11

The entry January is displayed in cell B2, and the mode has returned to Ready. In addition, the cell selector has moved to cell B3. Whenever you use the [←Enter] key to complete an entry, the cell selector moves down one cell.

Notice that the entry is positioned to the left side of the cell space. The positioning of cell entries in the cell space is called **alignment**. This is a default setting included in the default workbook template you are using. You will learn more about this feature later in the lab.

Clearing an Entry

After looking at the entry, you decide you want the column headings to be in row 3 rather than in row 2. This will leave more space above the column headings for a worksheet title. The [Delete] key can be used to clear the contents from a cell. To remove the entry from cell B2 and enter it in cell B3,

1 ● Move to B2.

● Press [Delete].

Another Method

The menu equivalent is Edit/Clear/Contents. Clear Contents is also an option on the shortcut menu.

● Move to B3.

● Type January.

● Click ☑.

Your screen should be similar to Figure 1.12

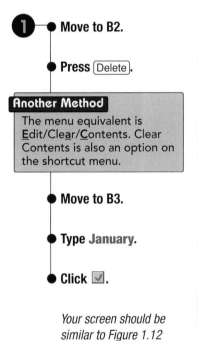

Figure 1.12

The cell selector remains in the active cell when you use ☑ to complete an entry. Because the cell selector is positioned on a cell containing an entry, the contents of the cell are displayed in the formula bar.

Editing an Entry

You would like to change the heading from January to JAN. An entry in a cell can be entirely changed in the Ready mode or partially changed or edited in the Edit mode. To use the Ready mode, you move the cell selector to the cell you want to change and retype the entry the way you want it to appear. As soon as a new character is entered, the existing entry is cleared.

Generally, however, if you need to change only part of an entry, it is quicker to use the Edit mode. To change to Edit mode, double-click on the cell whose contents you want to edit.

Another Method
Pressing the F2 key will also change to Edit mode. The insertion point is positioned at the end of the entry.

Your screen should be similar to Figure 1.13

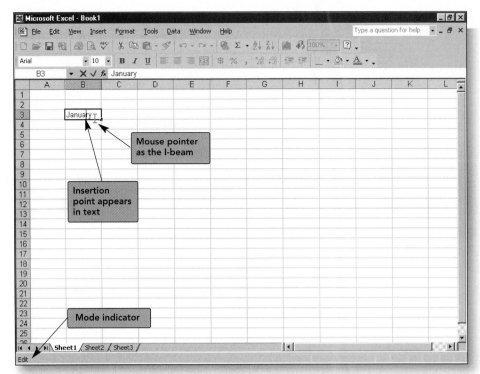

Figure 1.13

The status bar shows that the new mode of operation is Edit. The insertion point appears in the entry, and the mouse pointer changes to an I-beam when positioned on the cell. The mouse pointer can now be used to move the insertion point in the entry by positioning the I-beam and clicking.

In addition, in the Edit mode, the following keys can be used to move the insertion point:

Key	Action
Home	Moves insertion point to beginning of entry
End	Moves insertion point to end of entry
→	Moves insertion point one character right
←	Moves insertion point one character left

Additional Information
You can also use Ctrl + Delete to delete everything to the right of the insertion point.

Once the insertion point is appropriately positioned, you can edit the entry by removing the incorrect characters and typing the correct characters. The Delete key erases characters at the insertion point, and the Backspace key erases characters to the left of the insertion point. You will change this entry to JAN.

2

- If **necessary, move the** insertion point to the end of the entry.

- Press [Backspace] (4 times).

- Press [Home].

- Press [→].

- Press [Caps Lock].

- Press [Insert].

- Type A.

Your screen should be similar to Figure 1.14

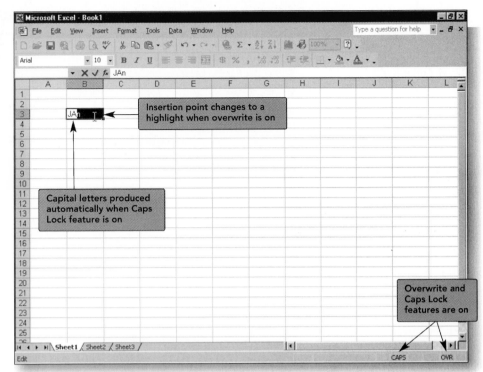

Figure 1.14

The four characters at the end of the entry were deleted using [Backspace]. Turning on the Caps Lock feature produced an uppercase letter A without having to hold down [⇧ Shift]. Finally, by pressing [Insert] the program switched from inserting text to overwriting text as you typed. The insertion point changes to a highlight to show the character will be replaced. The status bar displays CAPS and OVR to let you know these features are on.

Additional Information
The Caps Lock indicator light on your keyboard is lit when this feature is on.

3

- Type N.

- Press [←Enter].

Your screen should be similar to Figure 1.15

Additional Information
Overwrite is automatically turned off when you leave Edit mode or if you press [Insert] again.

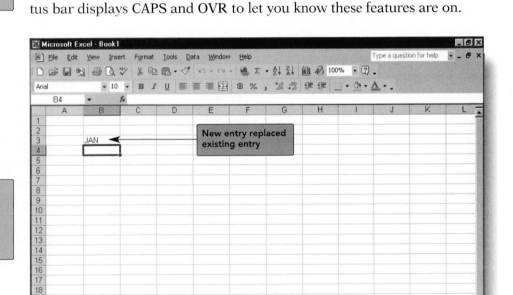

Figure 1.15

The new heading JAN is entered into cell B3, replacing January. As you can see, editing will be particularly useful with long or complicated entries.

Next, you will enter the remaining three headings in row three. You can also complete an entry by moving to any other worksheet cell.

4
● **Move to C3.**

● **Type FEB.**

● **Press → or Tab⇥ or click D3.**

● **Complete the column headings by entering MAR in cell D3 and TOTAL in cell E3.**

● **When you are done, turn off Caps Lock.**

Your screen should be similar to Figure 1.16

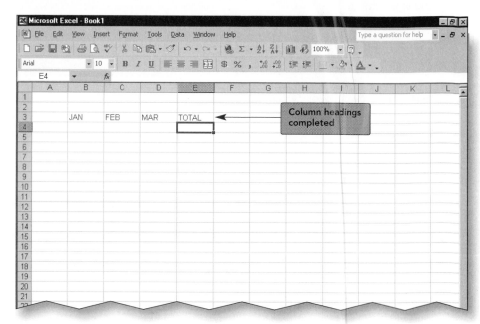

Figure 1.16

The column headings are now complete for the first quarter.

Using AutoCorrect

As soon as you complete an entry in a cell, Excel checks the entry for accuracy. This is part of the automatic correcting feature of Excel.

concept 3

AutoCorrect

3 The **AutoCorrect** feature makes some basic assumptions about the text you are typing and, based on these assumptions, automatically corrects the entry. The AutoCorrect feature automatically inserts proper capitalization at the beginning of sentences and in the names of days of the week. It will also change to lowercase letters any words that were incorrectly capitalized due to the accidental use of the Caps Lock key. In addition, it also corrects many common typing and spelling errors automatically.

One way the program automatically makes corrections is by looking for certain types of errors. For example, if two capital letters appear at the beginning of a word, the second capital letter is changed to a lowercase letter. If a low-ercase letter appears at the beginning of a sentence, the first letter of the first word is capitalized. If the name of a day begins with a lowercase letter, the first letter is capitalized.

Another way the program makes corrections is by checking all entries against a built-in list of words that are commonly spelled incorrectly or typed incorrectly. If it finds the entry on the list, the program automatically replaces the error with the correction. For example, the typing error "aboutthe" is automatically changed to "about the" because the error is on the AutoCorrect list. You can also add words that you want to be automatically corrected to the AutoCorrect list. Words you add are added to the list on the computer you are using and will be available to anyone who uses the machine after you.

Above the column headings, in rows 1 and 2, you want to enter a title for the worksheet. While entering the title, you will intentionally misspell two words to demonstrate how the AutoCorrect feature works.

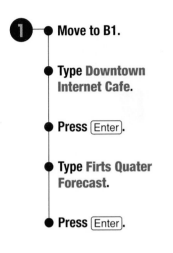

- **Move to B1.**

- **Type Downtown Internet Cafe.**

- **Press** [Enter].

- **Type Firts Quater Forecast.**

- **Press** [Enter].

Your screen should be similar to Figure 1.17

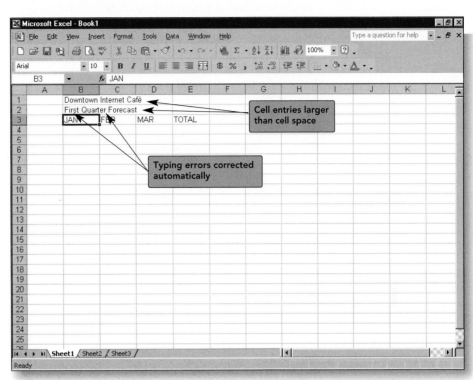

Figure 1.17

The two typing errors were automatically corrected when you completed the entry. When a text entry is longer than the cell's column width, Excel will display as much of the entry as it can. If the cell to the right is empty, the whole entry will be displayed. If the cell to the right contains an entry, the overlapping part of the entry is not displayed.

Next, the row headings need to be entered into column A of the worksheet. The row headings and what they represent are shown on the next page.

Heading	Represents
Sales	
Beverage	Income from sales of drinks (espresso, gourmet coffee, cold drinks)
Food	Income from sales of sandwiches and salads
Internet	Income from Internet connection time charges
Merchandise	Income from sales of Café tee shirts, mugs, and so forth
Total Sales	Sum of all sales
Expenses	
Cost of Goods	Cost of beverage and food items sold
Salary	Personnel expenses
Computers	Monthly payment for computer hardware
Lease	Monthly lease expense
Miscellaneous	Monthly expenses for T1 line, phone, electricity, water, trash removal, etc.
Income	
Net Income	Total sales minus total expenses
Profit Margin	Net income divided by total sales

2 ● Complete the row
headings for the Sales
portion of the work-
sheet by entering the
following headings in
the indicated cells:

Cell	Heading
A4	**Sales**
A5	**Beverage**
A6	**Food**
A7	**Internet**
A8	**Merchandise**
A9	**Total Sales**

HAVING TROUBLE?
Remember to press
Enter or an arrow
key to complete the
last entry.

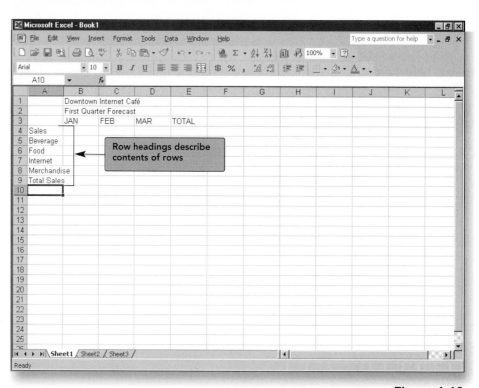

Figure 1.18

*Your screen should be
similar to Figure 1.18*

Entering Numbers

Next, you will enter the expected beverage sales numbers for January through March into cells B5 through D5. As you learned earlier, number entries can include the digits 0 to 9 and any of these special characters: $+ - ( )$, . / \$ % Σ =. When entering numbers, it is not necessary to type the comma to separate thousands or the currency (\$) symbol. You will learn about adding these symbols shortly.

You will enter the expected beverage sales for January first.

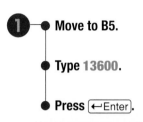

● **Move to B5.**

● **Type** 13600.

● **Press** ⏎Enter.

Your screen should be similar to Figure 1.19

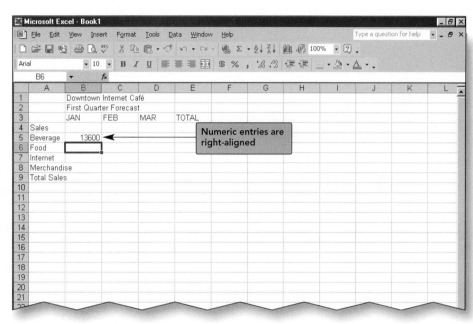

Figure 1.19

Unlike text entries, Excel displays number entries right-aligned in the cell space by default.

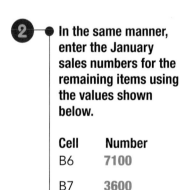

● **In the same manner, enter the January sales numbers for the remaining items using the values shown below.**

Cell	Number
B6	7100
B7	3600
B8	3100

● **Move to A8.**

Your screen should be similar to Figure 1.20

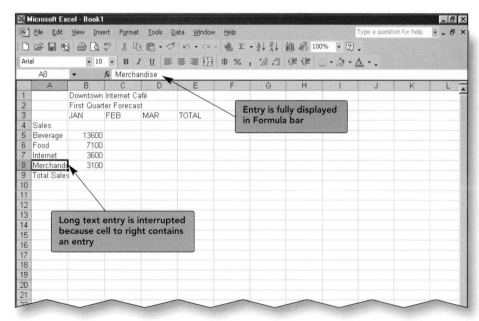

Figure 1.20

After entering the numbers for January in column B, any long headings in column A were cut off or interrupted. Notice that the entry in cell A8 is no longer completely displayed. It is a long text entry and because the cell to the right (B8) now contains an entry, the overlapping part of the entry is shortened. However, the entire entry is fully displayed in the Formula bar. Only the display of the entry in the cell has been shortened.

Changing Column Widths

To allow the long text entries in column A to be fully displayed, you can increase the column's width.

concept 4

Column Width

4   The size or width of a column controls how much information can be displayed in a cell. A text entry that is larger than the column width will be fully displayed only if the cells to the right are blank. If the cells to the right contain data, the text is interrupted. On the other hand, when numbers are entered in a cell, the column width is automatically increased to fully display the entry.

The default column width setting in the default workbook template is 8.43. The number represents the average number of digits that can be displayed in a cell using the standard type style. The column width can be any number from 1 to 255.

When the worksheet is printed, it appears as it does currently on the screen. Therefore, you want to increase the column width to display the largest entry. Likewise, you can decrease the column width when the entries in a column are short.

Dragging the Column Boundary

Additional Information
You can also adjust the size of any row by dragging the row divider line or by using Format/Row/Height.

The column width can be quickly adjusted by dragging the boundary line located to the right of the column letter. Dragging it to the left decreases the column width, while dragging it to the right increases the width. As you drag, a temporary column reference line shows where the new column will appear and a ScreenTip displays the width of the column.

1 ● Point to the boundary line to the right of the column letter A, click and drag the mouse pointer to the right.

● When the ScreenTip displays 15.00, release the mouse button.

Your screen should be similar to Figure 1.21

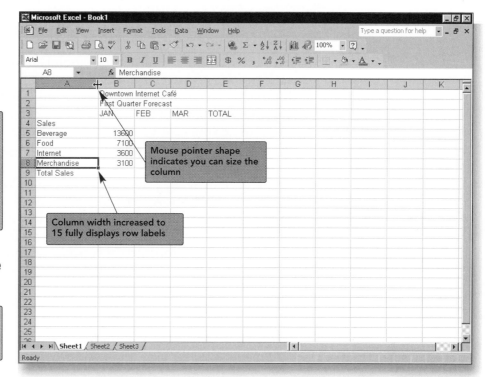

Figure 1.21

Now, however, the column width is wider than needed.

Using AutoFit

Another way to change the column width is to automatically adjust the width to fit the column contents.

1 ● Double-click the A column boundary line.

Your screen should be similar to Figure 1.22

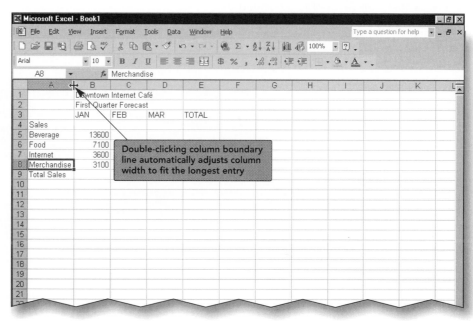

Figure 1.22

The column width is sized to just slightly larger than the longest cell contents.

Saving, Closing, and Opening Workbooks

You have a meeting you need to attend shortly, so you want to save your work to a file and close the file. As you enter and edit data to create a new workbook, the changes you make are immediately displayed onscreen and are stored in your computer's memory. However, they are not permanently stored until you save your work to a file on a disk. Once a workbook is saved as a file, it can be closed and opened again at a later time to be further edited.

As a backup against the accidental loss of work due to power failure or other mishap, Office XP includes an AutoRecover feature. When this feature is on, as you work you may see a pulsing disk icon briefly appear in the status bar. This indicates the program is saving your work to a temporary recovery file. The time interval between automatic saving can be set to any period you specify; the default is every 10 minutes. When you start up again, the recovery file is automatically opened containing all changes you made up to the last time it was saved by AutoRecover. You then need to save the recovery file. If you do not save it, it is deleted when closed. While AutoRecover is a great feature for recovering lost work, it should not be used in place of regularly saving your work.

Saving a New Workbook

You will save the work you have done so far on the workbook. The Save or Save As commands on the File menu are used to save files. The Save command or the 🖫 Save button will save the active file using the same file name by replacing the contents of the existing file with the document as it appears on your screen. The Save As command allows you to save a file with a new file name or to a new location. This leaves the original file unchanged.

Additional Information

When a workbook is saved for the first time, either Save or Save As can be used.

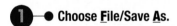

1 ● Choose **F**ile/Save **A**s.

Your screen should be similar to Figure 1.23

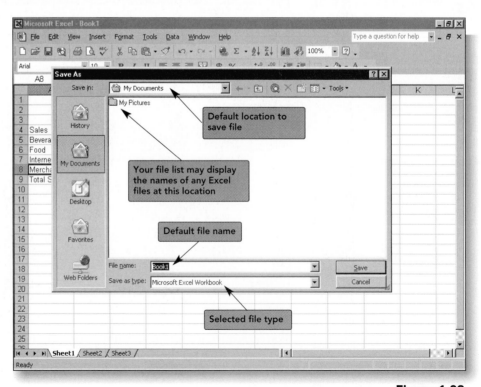

Figure 1.23

This Save As dialog box is used to specify the location to save the file and the file name. The Save In drop-down list box displays the default folder as the location where the file will be saved, and the File Name text box displays the proposed file name. The file list box displays the names of any Excel workbook files in the default location. Only Excel workbook files are listed, because the selected file type in the Save As Type list box is Excel Workbook. First you need to change the location where the file will be saved.

2 ● **Open the Save In drop-down list box.**

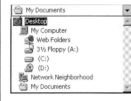

● **Select the appropriate location to save the file.**

HAVING TROUBLE?
If you are saving to a floppy disk and an error message is displayed, check that your disk is properly inserted in the drive and click ___OK___.

Your screen should be similar to Figure 1.24

Additional Information
If your system uses Windows NT, My Network Places is Network Neighborhood; in Windows 98, it is Web Folders.

Additional Information
If your dialog box displays the extension, this is a function of your Windows setup.

Additional Information
In addition to the .xls file type, Excel workbooks can also be saved in several different file formats that have different file extensions depending upon the format.

Additional Information
Windows documents can have up to 215 characters in the file name. Names can contain letters, numbers, and spaces; the symbols \, /, ?, :, *, ", < and > cannot be used.

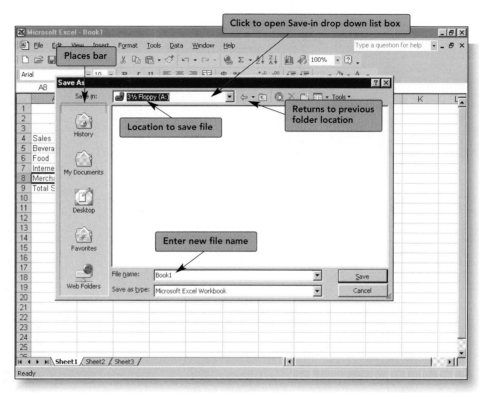

Figure 1.24

If the location you are saving to does not contain other Excel files, your file list will be empty as shown here. Otherwise, your file list may display Excel file names. You can also select the location to save your file from the Places bar along the left side of the dialog box. The icons bring up a list of recently accessed files and folders, the contents of the My Documents and Favorites folder, the Windows desktop, and folders that reside on a network or Web through My Network Places. Selecting a folder from one of these lists changes to that location. You can also click the ⬅ button in the toolbar to return to folders that were previously opened.

Next, you need to enter a file name and specify the file type. The File Name box displays the default file name, Book1. The Save as Type box displays Excel workbook as the default format in which the file will be saved. Workbooks are identified by the file extension .xls. The file type you select determines the file extension that will be automatically added to the file name when the file is saved. You will change the file name to Forecast.

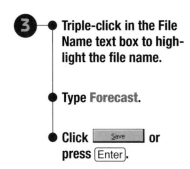

3 ● **Triple-click in the File Name text box to highlight the file name.**

● **Type Forecast.**

● **Click** [Save] **or press** [Enter].

Your screen should be similar to Figure 1.25

Figure 1.25

The new file name is displayed in the application window title bar. The worksheet data that was on your screen and in the computer's memory is now saved at the location you specified in a new file called Forecast.

Closing a Workbook

You are now ready to close the workbook file.

1 ● **Click** ⊠ **Close Window (in the menu bar).**

Because you did not make any changes to the document since saving it, the document window is closed immediately and the Excel window displays an empty workspace. If you had made additional changes, Excel would ask if you wanted to save the file before closing it. This prevents the accidental closing of a file that has not been saved first.

Note: If you are running short on lab time, this is an appropriate place to end your session.

Opening an Existing Workbook

After attending your meeting, you continued working on the Café forecast. To see what has been done so far, you will open the workbook file named ex01_Forecast2.

1 ● Choose **V**iew/Tas**k** Pane.

● Click 📂 **More Workbooks (in the task pane).**

Another Method

The menu equivalent is **F**ile/**O**pen and the keyboard shortcut is Ctrl + O. You can also click 📄 Open in the Standard toolbar.

Additional Information

The **F**ile/**N**ew command or 📄 Blank Workbook on the New Workbook task pane opens a blank new workbook.

Your screen should be similar to Figure 1.26

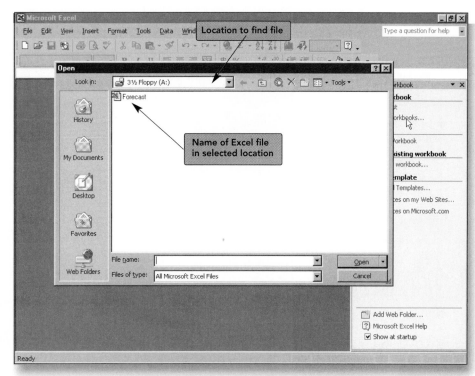

Figure 1.26

In the Open dialog box, you specify the location and name of the file you want to open. The Look In drop-down list box displays the last specified location, in this case the location where you saved the Forecast workbook. The large list box displays the names of all Excel workbooks with the file extensions displayed in the Files of type box. As in the Save As dialog box, the Places bar can be used to quickly access recently used files. When selecting a file to open, it may be helpful to see a preview of the file first. To do this, you can change the dialog box view.

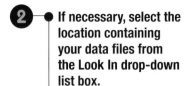

2 If necessary, select the location containing your data files from the Look In drop-down list box.

● Open the 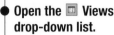 Views drop-down list.

● Choose Pre**v**iew.

● **Select** ex01_Forecast2.

Your screen should be similar to Figure 1.27

Additional Information

To see a preview, the workbook must be saved with the Save preview picture option selected under **F**ile/Proper**t**ies. You will learn about this feature in Lab 2.

3 ● Open the 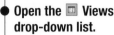 Views drop-down list.

● Choose **L**ist.

● **Select** ex01_Forecast2.

● Click [Open ▾].

Another Method

You could also double-click the file name to both select it and choose [Open ▾].

Your screen should be similar to Figure 1.28

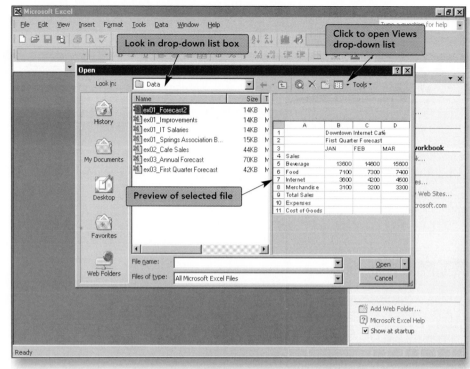

Figure 1.27

A preview of the selected file is displayed in the right pane of the dialog box. To return the view to the list of file names and open this file,

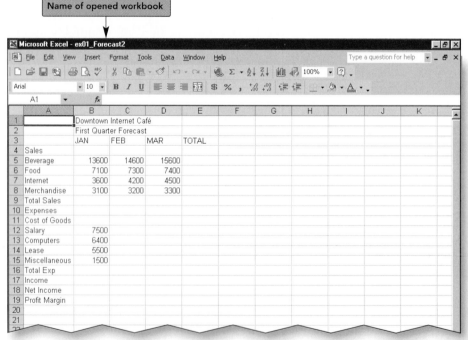

Figure 1.28

The workbook is opened and displayed in the workbook window. The workbook contains the additional sales values for February and March, the expense row headings, and several of the expense values for the month of January.

Duplicating Cell Contents

Next, you want to enter the estimated expenses for salary, computers, lease, and miscellaneous for February and March. They are the same as the January expense numbers. Because these values are the same, instead of entering the same number repeatedly into each cell you can quickly copy the contents of one cell to another. You also want to move information from one location in the worksheet to another.

concept 5

Copy and Move

5 The contents of worksheet cells can be duplicated (copied) or moved to other locations in the worksheet or between worksheets, saving you time by not having to retype the same information. An entry that is copied leaves the original, called the **source** or **copy area**, and inserts a duplicate at a new location, called the **destination** or **paste area**. A selection that is moved is removed or cut from the original location in the source and inserted at the destination.

When a selection is moved or copied, the selection is stored in the system Clipboard, a temporary Windows storage area in memory. The system Clipboard contents are then inserted at the new location specified by the location of the insertion point.

Office XP also includes an Office Clipboard that can store up to 24 items that have been cut or copied. This allows you to insert multiple items from various Office files and paste all or part of the collection of items into another file.

Using Copy and Paste

When using Copy and Paste, you first use the Copy command to copy the cell contents to the system Clipboard. Then you move to the new location where you want the contents copied and use the Paste command to insert the system Clipboard contents into the selected cells. Be careful when pasting to the new location because any existing entries are replaced.

To use the Copy command, you first must select the cell or cells in the source containing the data to be copied. You will copy the value in cell B12 into cells C12 and D12.

1 ● **Move to B12.**

● **Click** 🗐 **Copy.**

Another Method

The menu equivalent is Edit/Copy and the shortcut key is Ctrl + C. Copy is also available on the shortcut menu.

Your screen should be similar to Figure 1.29

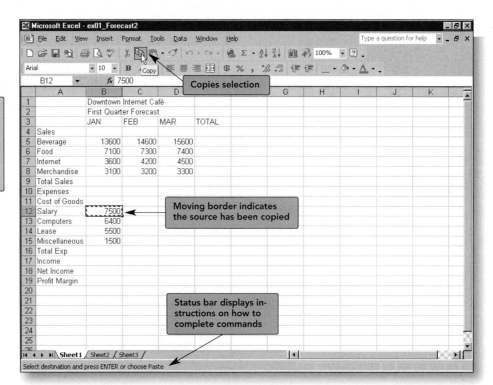

Figure 1.29

A moving border identifies the source and indicates that the contents have been copied to the system Clipboard. The instructions displayed in the status bar tell you to select the destination where you want the contents copied. You will copy it to cell C12.

2 ● **Move to C12.**

● **Click** 🗐 **Paste.**

Another Method

The menu equivalent is Edit/Paste and the shortcut key is Ctrl + V. Paste is also available on the shortcut menu.

Your screen should be similar to Figure 1.30

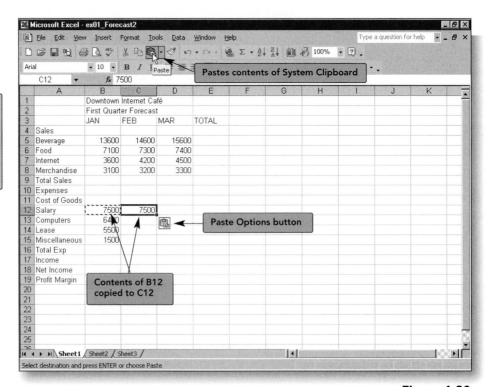

Figure 1.30

The contents of the system Clipboard are inserted at the specified destination location. Each time the paste command is used, the 🗐 Paste Options button is available. Clicking on the button opens the Paste Options menu that allows you to control how the information you are pasting is inserted.

 **Click 🖫 Paste Options.**

Your screen should be similar to Figure 1.31

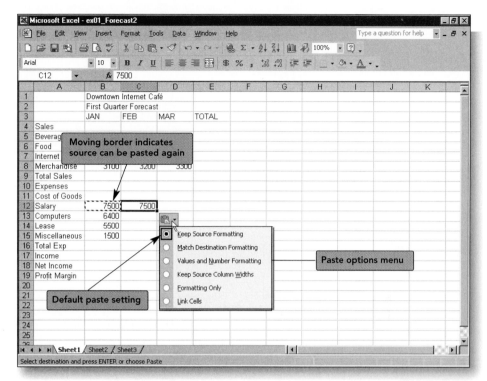

Figure 1.31

The selected option, Keep Source Formatting, will insert the copy exactly as it appears in the source. This is the default paste setting and is appropriate for this and most situations.

4 **Click outside the menu to close it.**

Additional Information
You can cancel a moving border and clear the System Clipboard contents by pressing (Esc).

The moving border is still displayed indicating the system Clipboard still contains the copied entry. Now you can complete the data for the Salary row by pasting the value again from the system Clipboard into cell D12. While the moving border is still displayed, you can also simply press (←Enter) to paste. However, as this method clears the contents of the system Clipboard immediately, it can only be used once.

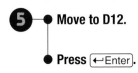

5 Move to D12.

Press ⏎Enter.

Your screen should be similar to Figure 1.32

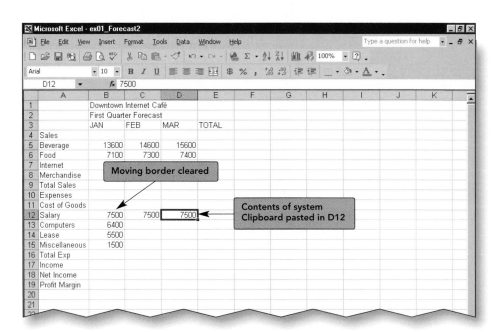

Figure 1.32

The contents of the system Clipboard are inserted at the specified destination location and the moving border is cleared indicating the system Clipboard is empty.

Selecting a Range

Now you need to copy the Computers value in cell B13 to February and March. You could copy and paste the contents individually into each cell. It is much faster, however, to select a paste area that consists of multiple cells, called a range, and paste the contents to all cells in the selection at once.

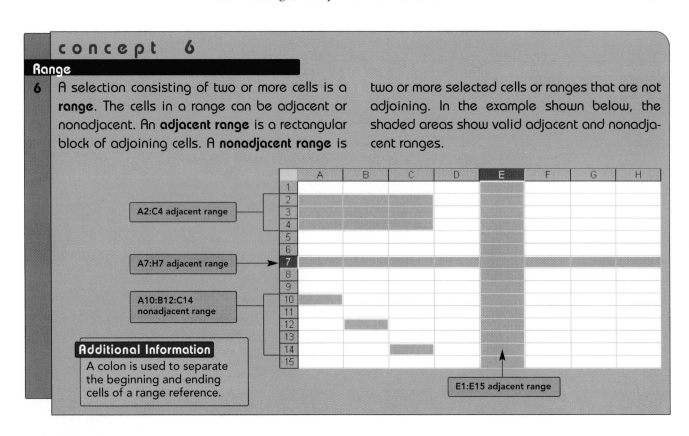

concept 6

Range

6 A selection consisting of two or more cells is a **range**. The cells in a range can be adjacent or nonadjacent. An **adjacent range** is a rectangular block of adjoining cells. A **nonadjacent range** is two or more selected cells or ranges that are not adjoining. In the example shown below, the shaded areas show valid adjacent and nonadjacent ranges.

A2:C4 adjacent range

A7:H7 adjacent range

A10:B12:C14 nonadjacent range

Additional Information

A colon is used to separate the beginning and ending cells of a range reference.

E1:E15 adjacent range

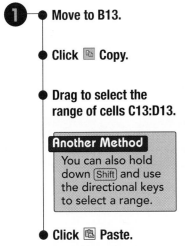

To complete the data for the Computer row, you want to copy the value in cell B13 to the system Clipboard and then copy the system Clipboard contents to the adjacent range of cells C13 through D13. To select an adjacent range, drag the mouse from one corner of the range to the other. If the range is large, it is often easier to select the range by clicking on the first cell of the range, then hold down ⇧Shift while clicking on the last cell of the range.

① ● Move to B13.

● Click ▥ Copy.

● Drag to select the range of cells C13:D13.

Another Method

You can also hold down [Shift] and use the directional keys to select a range.

● Click ▤ Paste.

Additional Information

The paste area does not have to be adjacent to the copy area.

Your screen should be similar to Figure 1.33

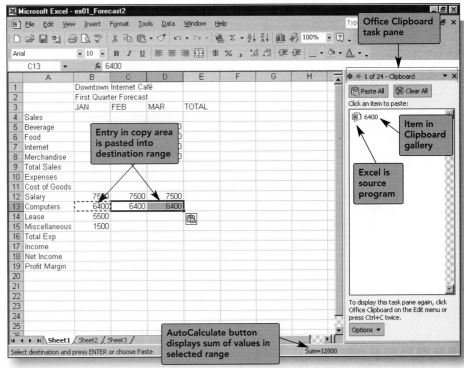

Figure 1.33

The destination range is highlighted and identified by a dark border surrounding the selected cells. The entry copied from cell B13 was pasted into the selected destination range. Also notice the AutoCalculate button in the status bar is now active. This button displays the sum of values in a selected range of cells. It can also display the average, count, minimum, or maximum values in a range by selecting the appropriate option from the button's shortcut menu.

Also, because this is the second consecutive copy you have performed in the workbook, the Office Clipboard task pane automatically opened. As items are copied, an entry representing the copied item is displayed in the

Clipboard gallery. The newest item appears at the top of the gallery. Each entry includes an icon representing the source Office program and a portion of copied text. Because the previous item you copied was cleared from the System Clipboard, only one item is displayed in the gallery. You can click an item in the gallery to paste it or use Paste All to paste all items in the gallery.

Using the Fill Handle

Next you will copy the January Lease expenses to cells C14 through D14 and Miscellaneous expenses to cells C15 through D15. You can copy both values at the same time across the row by first specifying a range as the source. Another way to copy is to drag the **fill handle**, the black box in the lower-right corner of the selection.

HAVING TROUBLE?
If your Office Clipboard task pane is not automatically displayed, choose Edit/Office Clipboard to display it.

1 ● **Drag to select cells B14:B15.**

● **Point to the fill handle and when the mouse pointer is a +, drag the mouse to extend the selection to cells C14:D15.**

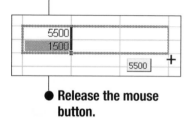

● **Release the mouse button.**

Another Method
The menu equivalent is Edit/Fill/Right or Ctrl + R.

Your screen should be similar to Figure 1.34

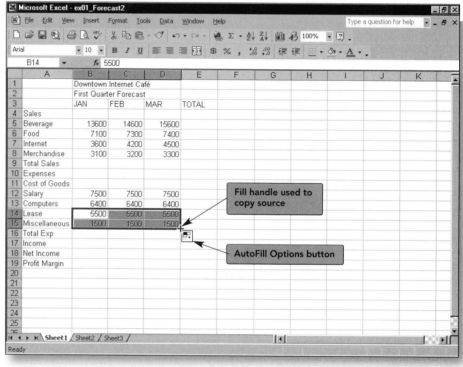

Figure 1.34

The range of cells to the right of the source is filled with the same value as in the source cell. The Fill command does not copy the source to the system Clipboard and therefore an item for the copied selection does not appear in the Office Clipboard task pane gallery. Because the Office Clipboard task pane is no longer needed, it closes automatically. Additionally, you cannot paste the source multiple times. The AutoFill Options button menu commands can be used to modify how the fill operation was performed.

HAVING TROUBLE?
If the Office Clipboard task pane did not close automatically, click ☒ in the task pane to close it.

Inserting Copied Cells

You also decide to include another row of month headings above the expense columns to make the worksheet data easier to read. To do this quickly, you can insert copied data between existing data. To indicate where to place the copied text, you move the cell pointer to the upper-left cell of the area where you want the selection inserted and specify the direction you want to shift the surrounding cells.

1 Copy the contents of cells A3:E3.

● Move to A10.

● Choose Insert/Copied Cells.

● If necessary, select Shift Cells Down from the Insert Paste dialog box.

● Click [OK] on the Task Pane to close it.

● Press [Esc] to clear the moving border.

Your screen should be similar to Figure 1.35

Additional Information

You can insert cut selections between existing cells by choosing Cut **C**ells from the **I**nsert menu.

Additional Information

Holding down [Ctrl] while dragging a selection copies it to the new location.

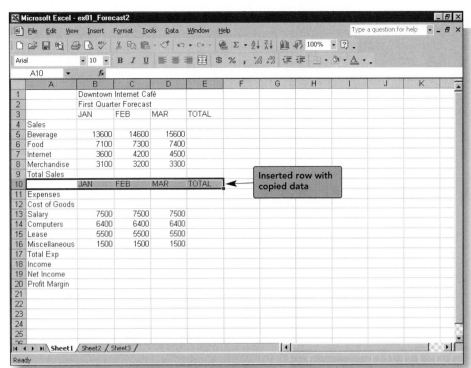

Figure 1.35

The copied data is inserted into the existing row (10) and all entries below are moved down one row.

Moving Entries

You also decide the profit margin row of data would stand out more if a blank row separated it from the net income row. You could remove the cell contents using Edit/Cut and then paste the contents from the system Clipboard into the new location. Alternatively, you can drag the cell border to move the cell contents. Dragging is quickest and most useful when the distance between cells is short and they are visible within the window, whereas Cut and Paste is best for long-distance moves.

1 ● **Move to cell A20.**

● **Point to the border of the selection and when the mouse pointer shape is ⬚, drag the selection down one row to cell A21 and release the mouse button.**

Additional Information

As you drag, an outline of the cell selection appears and the mouse pointer displays the cell reference to show its new location in the worksheet.

● **Choose File/Save As and save the changes you have made to the workbook as Forecast3.**

Your screen should be similar to Figure 1.36

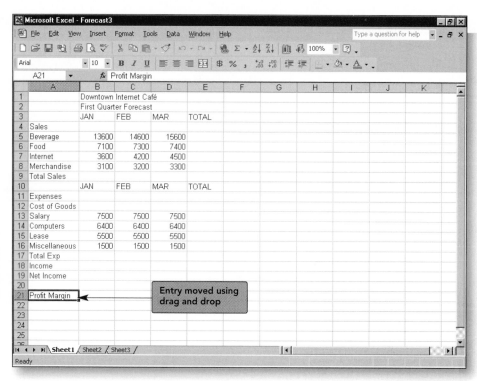

Figure 1.36

The cell contents was moved into cell A21 and cleared from the original cell.

Review of Copying and Moving Methods

To review, you have learned three methods to copy or move an entry:

1. Use the Copy, Cut and Paste commands: Edit/Copy (Ctrl + C) or 🗐, Edit/Cut (Ctrl + X) or ✂, and Edit/Paste (Ctrl + V) or 📋.

2. Use the Edit/Fill command: Right, Left, Up, or Down or drag the fill handle.

3. Drag the cell border of the selection to move. Hold down Ctrl while dragging a selection to copy.

When you use the Copy and Cut commands, the contents are copied to the system Clipboard and can be copied to any location in the worksheet, another workbook, or another application multiple times. When you use Edit/Fill or drag the fill handle, the destination must be in the same row or column as the source, and the source is not copied to the system Clipboard. Dragging the cell border to move or copy also does not copy the source to the system Clipboard.

Working with Formulas

The remaining entries that need to be made in the worksheet are formula entries.

concept 7

Formulas

7 A formula is an equation that performs a calculation on data contained in a worksheet. A formula always begins with an equal sign (=) and uses the following arithmetic **operators** to specify the type of numeric operation to perform: + (addition), − (subtraction), / (division), * (multiplication), % (percent), ^ (exponentiation).

In a formula that contains more than one operator, Excel calculates the formula from left to right and performs the calculation in the following order: percent, exponentiation, multiplication and division, and addition and subtraction (see Example A). If a formula contains operators with the same precedence (for example, addition and subtraction), they are again evaluated from left to right. The order of precedence can be overridden by enclosing the operation you want performed first in parentheses (see Example B). When there are multiple sets of parentheses,

Excel evaluates them working from the innermost set of parentheses out.

Example A: =5*4−3   Result is 17 (5 times 4 to get 20, and then subtract 3 for a total of 17)

Example B: =5*(4−3)   Result is 5 (4 minus 3 to get 1, and then 1 times 5 for a total of 5)

The values on which a numeric formula performs a calculation are called **operands**. Numbers or cell references can be operands in a formula. Usually cell references are used, and when the numeric entries in the referenced cell(s) change, the result of the formula is automatically recalculated.

Entering Formulas

The first formula you will enter will calculate the total Beverage sales for January through March (cell E5) by summing the numbers in cells B5 through D5. You will use cell references in the formula as the operands and the + arithmetic operator to specify addition. A formula is entered in the cell where you want the calculated value to be displayed. As you enter the formula, to help you keep track of the cell references Excel identifies the referenced cell by adding a color to the cell border and using the same color for the cell reference in the formula.

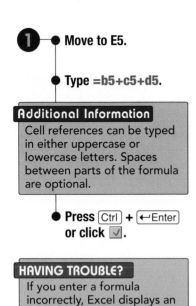

1 • Move to E5.

• Type **=b5+c5+d5.**

Additional Information

Cell references can be typed in either uppercase or lowercase letters. Spaces between parts of the formula are optional.

• Press Ctrl + ←Enter or click ☑ .

HAVING TROUBLE?

If you enter a formula incorrectly, Excel displays an error in the cell or a message box proposing a correction.

Your screen should be similar to Figure 1.37

Figure 1.37

The number 43800 is displayed in cell E5 and the formula that calculates this value is displayed in the formula bar.

Copying Formulas

The formulas to calculate the total sales for rows 5 through 8 can be entered next. Just as you can with text and numeric entries, you can copy formulas from one cell to another.

1 • Copy the formula in cell E5 to cells E6 through E8 using any of the copying methods.

• Move to E6.

Your screen should be similar to Figure 1.38

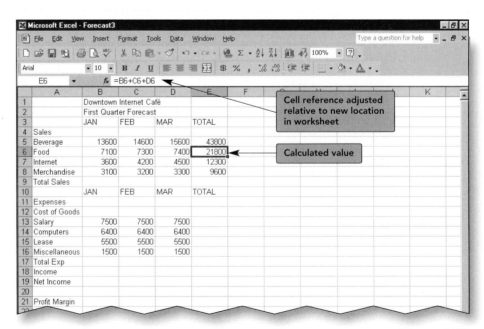

Figure 1.38

The calculated result, 21800 is displayed in the cell. The formula displayed in the formula bar is =B6+C6+D6. The formula to calculate the Food total sales is not an exact duplicate of the formula used to calculate the Beverage total sales (=B5+C5+D5). Instead, the cells referenced in the formula have been changed to reflect the new location of the formula in row 6. This is because the references in the formula are relative references.

concept 8

Relative Reference

8 A **relative reference** is a cell or range reference in a formula whose location is interpreted by Excel in relation to the position of the cell that contains the formula. When a formula is copied, the referenced cells in the formula automatically adjust to reflect the new worksheet location. The relative relationship between the referenced cell and the new location is maintained. Because relative references automatically adjust for the new location, the relative references in a copied formula refer to different cells than the references in the original formula. The relationship between cells in both the copied and pasted formula is the same although the cell references are different.

For example, in the figure here, cell A1 references the value in cell A4 (in this case, 10). If the formula in A1 is copied to B2, the reference for B2 is adjusted to the value in cell B5 (in this case, 20).

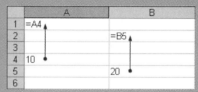

2 ● Move to cell E7 and then to cell E8.

Your screen should be similar to Figure 1.39

Additional Information

If you move cells containing formulas, the formulas are not adjusted relative to their new worksheet location.

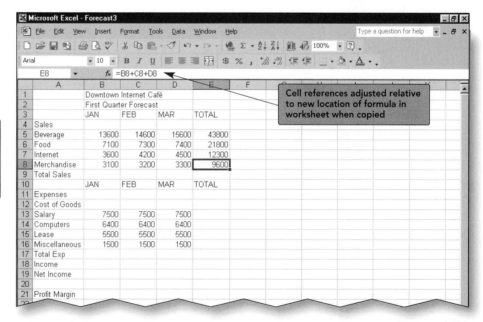

Figure 1.39

The formulas in these cells have also changed to reflect the new row location and to appropriately calculate the total based on the sales.

Entering Functions

Next you will calculate the monthly total sales. The formula to calculate the total sales for January needs to be entered in cell B9 and copied across the row. You could use a formula similar to the formula used to calculate the category sales in column E. The formula would be =B5+B6+B7+B8. However, it is faster and more accurate to use a function.

concept 9

Functions

1 **Functions** are prewritten formulas that perform certain types of calculations automatically. The **syntax** or rules of structure for entering all functions is:

=Function name (argument1, argument2,...)

The function name identifies the type of calculation to be performed. Most functions require that you enter one or more arguments following the function name. An **argument** is the data the function uses to perform the calculation. The type of data the function requires depends upon the type of calculation being performed. Most commonly, the argument consists of numbers or references to cells that contain numbers. The argument is enclosed in parentheses, and commas separate multiple arguments. If a function starts the formula, enter an equal sign before the function name (=SUM(D5:F5)/25).

Additional Information
Use Help for detailed explanations of every function.

Excel includes several hundred functions divided into nine categories. Some common functions and the results they calculate are shown in the following table.

Category	Function	Calculates
Financial	PMT	Calculates the payment for a loan based on constant payments and a constant interest rate
	PV	Returns the present value of an investment; the total amount that a series of future payments is worth now
Time & Date	TODAY	Returns the serial number that represents today's date
	DATE	Returns the serial number of a particular date
	NOW	Returns the serial number of the current date and time
Math & Trig	SUM	Adds all the numbers in a range of cells
	ABS	Returns the absolute value of a number, a number without its sign
Statistical	AVERAGE	Returns the average (arithmetic mean) of its arguments
	MAX	Returns the largest value in a set of values; ignores logical values and text
Lookup & Reference	COLUMNS	Returns the number of columns in an array or reference
	CHOOSE	Chooses a value or action to perform from a list of values, based on an index number

Category	Function	Calculates
Database	DSUM	Adds the numbers in the field (column) or records in the database that match the conditions you specify
	DAVERAGE	Averages the values in a column in a list or database that match conditions you specify
Text	DOLLAR	Converts a number to text, using currency format
	UPPER	Converts text to uppercase
Logical	IF	Returns one value if a condition you specify evaluates to True and another value if it evaluates to False
	AND	Returns True if all its arguments are True; returns False if any arguments are False
Information	ISLOGICAL	Returns True if value is a logical value, either True or False
	ISREF	Returns True if value is a reference

You will use the SUM function to calculate the total sales for January. Because the SUM function is the most commonly used function, it has its own toolbar button.

1 ● **Move to B9.**

● **Click Σ AutoSum.**

Another Method

Pressing [Alt] + = is the keyboard shortcut for AutoSum.

Your screen should be similar to Figure 1.40

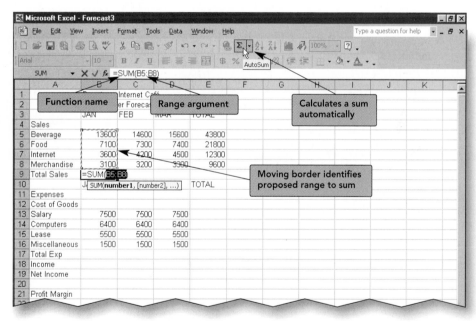

Figure 1.40

Additional Information

The AutoSum button can also calculate a grand total if your worksheet contains subtotals. Select a cell below or to the right of a cell that contains a subtotal and then click Σ AutoSum.

Excel automatically proposes a range based upon the data above or to the left of the active cell. The name of the function followed by the range argument enclosed in parentheses is displayed in the formula bar. To accept the proposed range and enter the function,

2 ● **Click** ☑ **Enter.**

Your screen should be similar to Figure 1.41

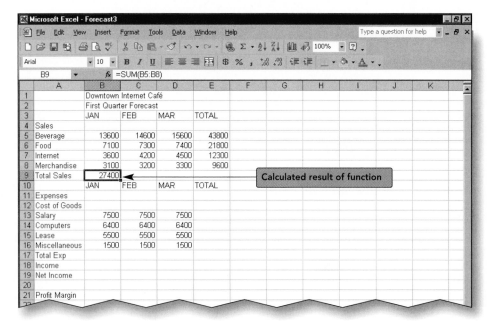

Calculated result of function

Figure 1.41

The result, 27400, calculated by the SUM function is displayed in cell B9. Next you need to calculate the total sales for February and March and the Total column.

3 ● **Copy the function from cell B9 to cells C9 through E9.**

● **Move to C9.**

Your screen should be similar to Figure 1.42

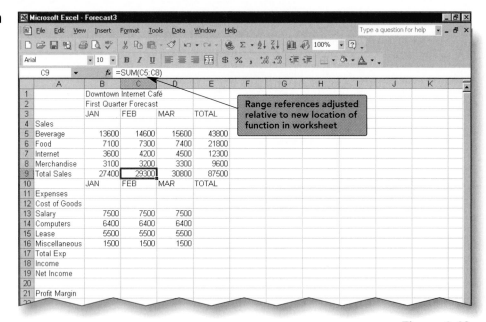

Range references adjusted relative to new location of function in worksheet

Figure 1.42

The result calculated by the function, 29300, is displayed in cell C9 and the copied function is displayed in the formula bar. The range reference in the function adjusted relative to its new cell location because it is a relative reference.

Using Pointing to Enter a Formula

Next you will enter the formula to calculate the cost of goods sold. These numbers are estimated by using a formula to calculate the number as a percent of sales. As a general rule, the Café calculates beverage expenses at 25 percent of beverage sales and food expenses at 50 percent of food sales.

Rather than typing in the cell references for the formula, you will enter them by selecting the worksheet cells. In addition, to make the process of entering and copying entries even easier, you can enter data into the first cell of a range and have it copied to all other cells in the range at the same time by using Ctrl + ←Enter to complete the entry. You will use this feature to enter the formulas to calculate the beverage expenses for January through March. This formula needs to first calculate the beverage cost of goods at 25 percent and add it to the food cost of goods calculated at 50 percent.

1 • Select B12:D12.

• Type =.

• Click cell B5.

Your screen should be similar to Figure 1.43

Mode indicator

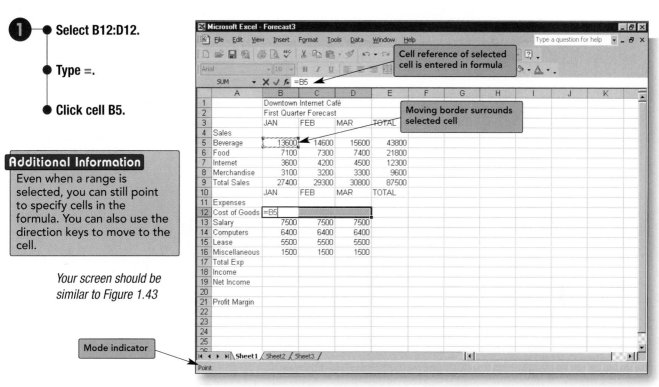

Figure 1.43

Notice that the status bar displays the current mode as Point. This tells you the program is allowing you to select cells by highlighting them. The cell reference, B5, is entered following the = sign. You will complete the formula by entering the percentage value to multiply by and adding the Food percentage to the formula.

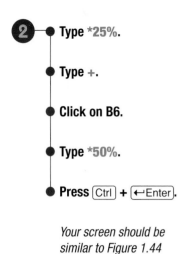

②
● Type ***25%**.

● Type **+**.

● Click on **B6**.

● Type ***50%**.

● Press **Ctrl** + **←Enter**.

Your screen should be similar to Figure 1.44

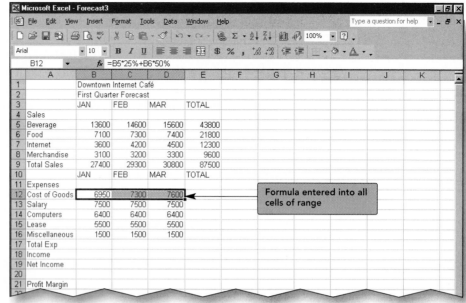

Figure 1.44

The formula to calculate the January cost of goods expense was entered in cell B12 and copied to all cells of the selected range. You can now calculate the total expenses in row 17 and column E. To do this quickly, you will pre-select the range and use the **Σ** AutoSum button. Then you will enter the formula to calculate the net income. Net income is calculated by subtracting total expenses from total sales.

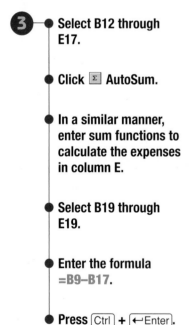

> **Additional Information**
> The cells in the selected range can be adjacent or nonadjacent.

③
● Select **B12** through **E17**.

● Click **Σ** **AutoSum**.

● In a similar manner, enter sum functions to calculate the expenses in column E.

● Select **B19** through **E19**.

● Enter the formula **=B9–B17**.

● Press **Ctrl** + **←Enter**.

Your screen should be similar to Figure 1.45

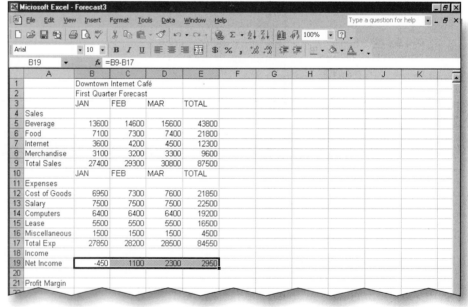

Figure 1.45

The formula is quickly entered into all cells of the range. The final formula you need enter is to calculate the profit margin.

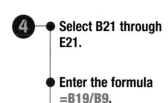

4 ● **Select B21 through E21.**

● **Enter the formula =B19/B9.**

● **Press** Ctrl + ←Enter.

Your screen should be similar to Figure 1.46

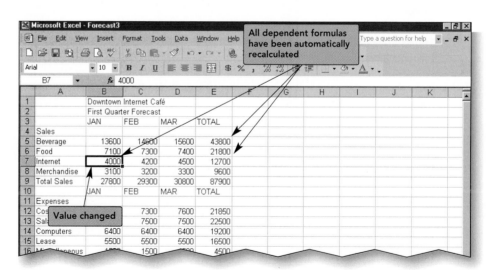

Figure 1.46

The profit margins are calculated and displayed in cells B20 through E20.

Recalculating the Worksheet

Now that you have created the worksheet structure and entered some sample data for the forecasted sales for the first quarter, you want to test the formulas to verify they are operating correctly. A simple way to do this is to use a calculator to verify that the correct result is displayed. You can then further test the worksheet by changing values and verifying that all cells containing formulas that reference the value are appropriately recalculated.

After considering the sales estimates for the three months, you decide that the estimated Internet sales for January are too low and you want to increase this number from 3600 to 4000.

1 ● **Change the entry in cell B7 to 4000.**

Your screen should be similar to Figure 1.47

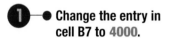

Figure 1.47

The Internet total in cell E7 has been automatically recalculated. The number displayed is now 12700. Likewise, the January total in cell B9 and the grand total in cell E9 have increased by 400 to reflect the change in cell B7.

concept 10

Recalculation

10 Whenever a number in a referenced cell in a formula changes, Excel automatically **recalculates** all formulas that are dependent on the changed value. Because only those formulas directly affected by a change in the data are recalculated, the time it takes to recalculate the workbook is reduced. Without this feature, in large worksheets it could take several minutes to recalculate all formulas each time a number is changed in the worksheet. Recalculation is one of the most powerful features of electronic worksheets.

The formulas in the worksheet are correctly calculating the desired result. The Sales portion of the worksheet is now complete.

Inserting Rows

Finally, you realize you forgot to include a row for the Advertising expenses. To add this data, you will insert a blank row below the Lease row. To indicate where you want to insert a single blank row, move the cell pointer to the row immediately below the row where you want the new row inserted. If you want to insert multiple rows, select a range of rows and Excel inserts the same number of rows you selected in the range.

Additional Information

To delete a row or column, move to it and choose Edit/Delete/Entire Row or Entire Column.

1
- Move to A15.

- Choose Insert/Rows.

- Enter the label **Advertising** in cell A15 and the value **1000** in cells B15 through D15.

- Copy the function from cell E14 to E15 to calculate the Total Advertising expense.

- Move to cell B18.

- Click 🔲 Save to save the worksheet using the same file name.

Your screen should be similar to Figure 1.48

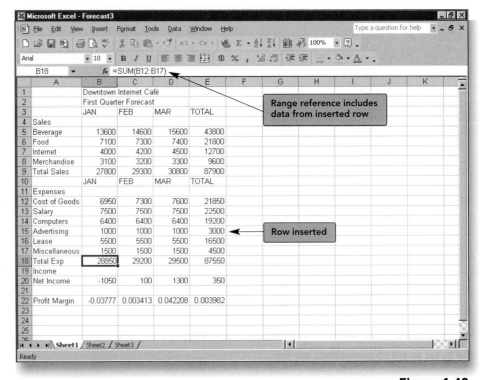

Figure 1.48

The range in the formula to calculate monthly total expenses in row 18 has been revised to include the data in the inserted row. Additionally, the net income in row 20 and profit margin in row 22 have been recalculated to reflect the change in data.

Formatting the Worksheet

Now that many of the worksheet values are entered, you want to improve the appearance of the worksheet by changing the format of the headings. **Format** controls how information is displayed in a cell and includes such features as font (different type styles and sizes), color, patterns, borders, and **number formats** such as commas and dollar signs. Applying different formats greatly improves both the appearance and readability of the data in a worksheet.

Changing Cell Alignment

You decide the column headings would look better if they were right-aligned in their cell spaces. Then they would appear over the numbers in the column. Alignment is a basic format setting that is used in most worksheets.

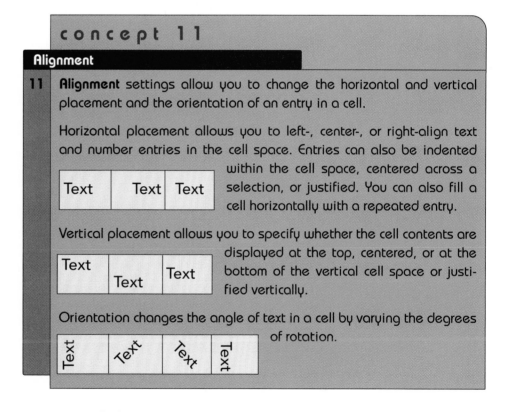

First you will change the column heading in cell B3 to right-aligned.

1 ● **Move to cell B3.**

● **Choose F<u>o</u>rmat/C<u>e</u>lls.**

Another Method
The shortcut key is
Ctrl + 1. Format Cells
is also an option on
the shortcut menu.

● **Open the Alignment
tab.**

*Your screen should be
similar to Figure 1.49*

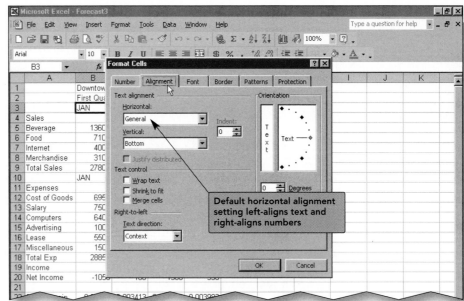

Figure 1.49

The Alignment tab shows the default workbook template alignment settings. The horizontal alignment setting is General. This setting left-aligns text entries and right-aligns number entries. The vertical alignment is set to bottom for both types of entries and the orientation is set to zero degrees rotation from the horizontal position. You want to change the horizontal alignment of the entry to right-aligned.

2 ● **Open the Horizontal
drop-down list box.**

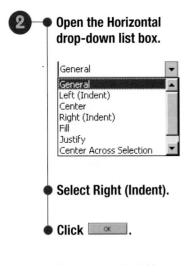

● **Select Right (Indent).**

● **Click** OK **.**

*Your screen should be
similar to Figure 1.50*

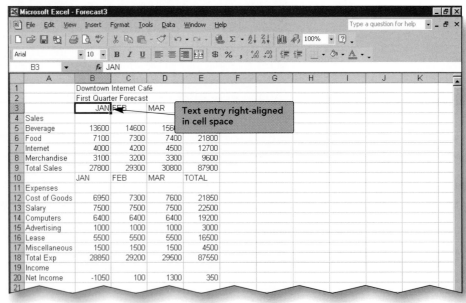

Figure 1.50

A quicker way to change the alignment is to use the Formatting toolbar or keyboard shortcuts shown on the next page.

Formatting toolbar	Keyboard	Action
≣	Ctrl + L	Left align entry
≣	Ctrl + C	Center entry
≣	Ctrl + J	Right align entry

You can quickly align a range of cells by selecting the range and then using the command or button. A quick way to select a range of filled cells is to hold down ⇧Shift and double-click on the edge of the active cell in the direction in which you want the range expanded. For example, to select the range to the right of the active cell, you would double-click the right border. You will use this method to select and right-align the remaining column entries.

Additional Information

If you do not hold down ⇧Shift while double-clicking on a border, the cell selector moves to the last-used cell in the direction indicated.

3 ● **Move to cell C3.**

● **Hold down ⇧Shift and double-click the right cell border of cell C3.**

HAVING TROUBLE?
The mouse pointer must be ⬚ when you click the cell border.

● **Click ≣ Align Right.**

● **In a similar manner, right align the entries in row 10.**

Your screen should be similar to Figure 1.51

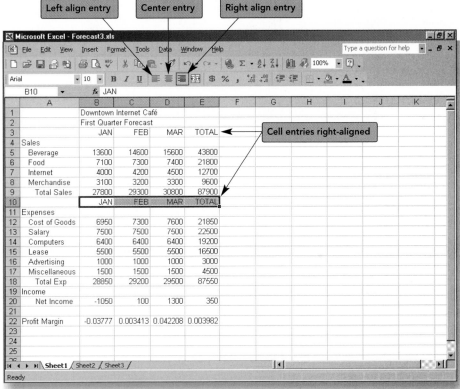

Figure 1.51

The entries in the selected range are right-aligned in their cell spaces.

Indenting Entries

Additional Information

You can also select entire nonadjacent rows or columns by holding down Ctrl while selecting the rows or columns.

Next you would like to indent the row headings in cells A5 through A8 and A12 through A17 from the left edge of the cell. You want to indent the headings in both ranges at the same time. To select nonadjacent cells or cell ranges, after selecting the first cell or range hold down Ctrl while selecting each additional cell or range. You will select the cells and indent their contents.

1 ● Select A5 through A8.

● Hold down Ctrl.

● Select A12 through A17.

● Release Ctrl.

● Click 📊 Increase Indent.

Another Method

The menu equivalent is Format/Cells/Alignment/ Horizontal/Left(Indent)/1.

Your screen should be similar to Figure 1.52

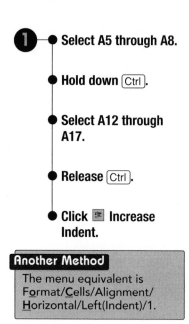

Figure 1.52

Each entry in the selected range is indented two spaces from the left edge of the cell. You would also like to indent the Total Sales, Total Exp, and Net Income headings four spaces.

2 ● Select A9, A18, and A20.

● Click 📊 Increase Indent twice.

Your screen should be similar to Figure 1.53

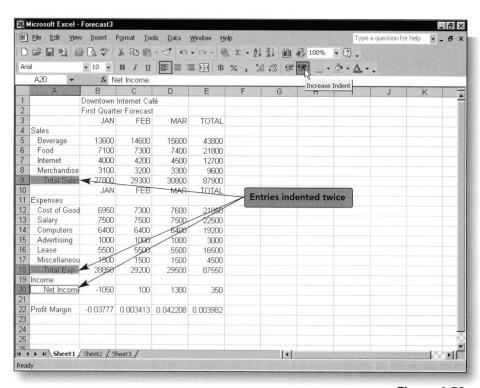

Figure 1.53

Centering across a Selection

Next you want to center the worksheet titles across columns A through E so they are centered over the worksheet data.

● Select A1 through E1.

● Click ▦ Merge and Center.

Your screen should be similar to Figure 1.54

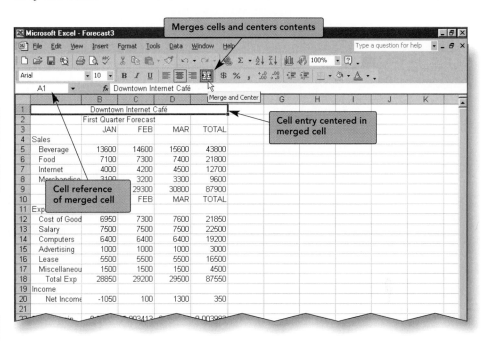

Figure 1.54

The contents of the range are centered in the range. Additionally, the five cells in the selection have been combined into a single large **merged cell**. The cell reference for a merged cell is the upper-left cell in the original selected range, in this case A1. When creating a merged cell and centering the contents, only the contents of the upper-leftmost data in the selected range are centered. If other cells in the range contained data, it would be deleted.

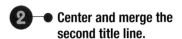

● Center and merge the second title line.

Your screen should be similar to Figure 1.55

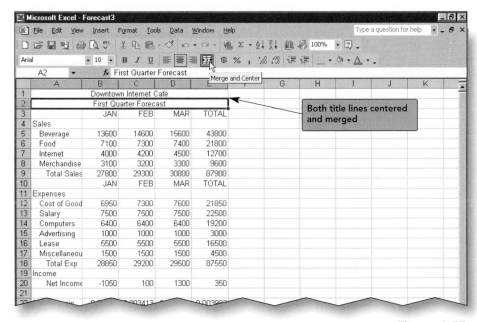

Figure 1.55

Once cells have been merged, you can split them back into their original cells by selecting the merged cell and clicking ▦ to unmerge the cells.

Changing Fonts and Font Styles

Finally, you want to improve the worksheet appearance by enhancing the appearance of the title. One way to do this is to change the font and font size used in the title.

concept 12

Fonts

12 A **font**, also commonly referred to as a **typeface**, is a set of characters with a specific design. The designs have names such as Times New Roman and Courier. Using fonts as a design element can add interest to your document and give readers visual cues to help them find information quickly.

There are two basic types of fonts, serif and sans serif. **Serif** fonts have a flair at the base of each letter that visually leads the reader to the next letter. Two common serif fonts are Roman and Times New Roman. Serif fonts generally are used in paragraphs. **Sans serif** fonts do not have a flair at the base of each letter. Arial and

Helvetica are two common sans serif fonts. Because sans serif fonts have a clean look, they are often used for headings in documents. It is good practice to use only two types of fonts in a document, one for text and one for headings. Too many styles can make your document look cluttered and unprofessional.

Each font has one or more sizes. **Size** is the height and width of the character and is commonly measured in **points**, abbreviated pt. One point equals about 1/72 inch, and text in most documents is 10 pt or 12 pt.

Here are several examples of the same text in various fonts and sizes.

Typeface	Font Size (12 pt/18 pt)
Arial (Sans Serif)	This is 12 pt. This is 18 pt.
Courier New (Serif)	This is 12 pt. This is 18 pt.
Times New Roman (Serif)	This is 12 pt. This is 18 pt.

● **Select A1 and A2.**

● **Open the** `Times New Roman` **Font drop-down list box.**

Another Method

The menu equivalent is Format/Cells/Font/Font.

Your screen should be similar to Figure 1.56

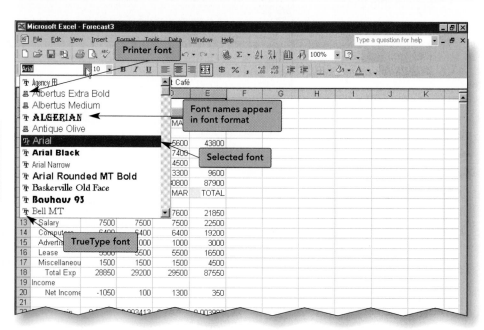

Figure 1.56

The Font drop-down menu displays examples of the available fonts on your system in alphabetical order. The default worksheet font, Arial, is highlighted. Notice the TT preceding the font name. This indicates the font is a TrueType font. TrueType fonts appear onscreen as they will appear when printed. They are installed when Windows is installed. Fonts that are preceded with a blank space or 🖳 are printer fonts. These fonts are supported by your printer and are displayed as closely as possible to how they will appear onscreen, but may not match exactly when printed.

2 ● **Scroll the list and select Times New Roman.**

Your screen should be similar to Figure 1.57

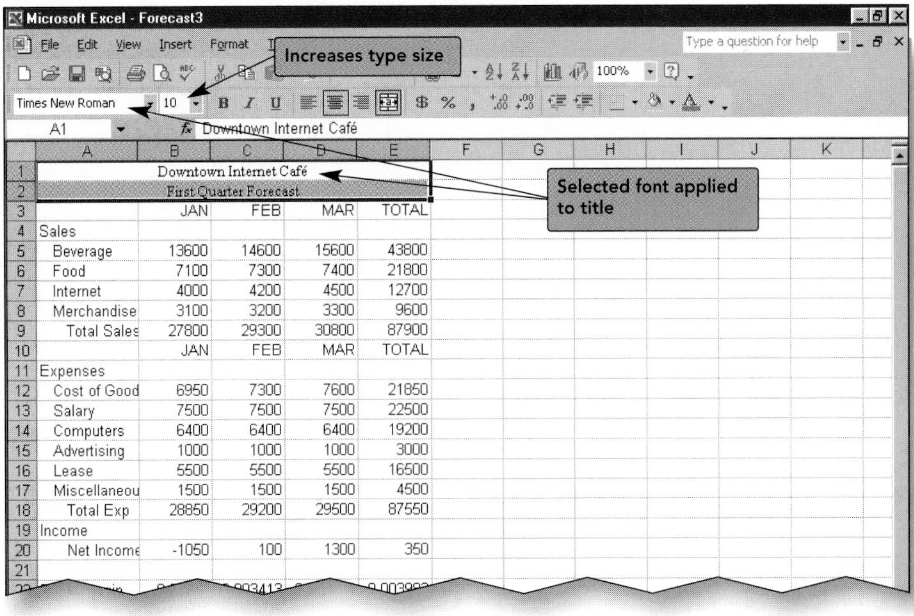

Figure 1.57

The title appears in the selected typeface and the Font button displays the name of the font in the active cell. Next you will increase the font size to 14.

3 ● **Open the ⊡ Font Size drop-down list box.**

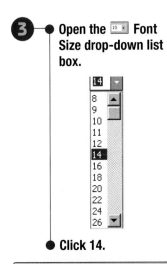

● **Click 14.**

Another Method

The menu equivalent is Format/Cells/Font/Size.

Your screen should be similar to Figure 1.58

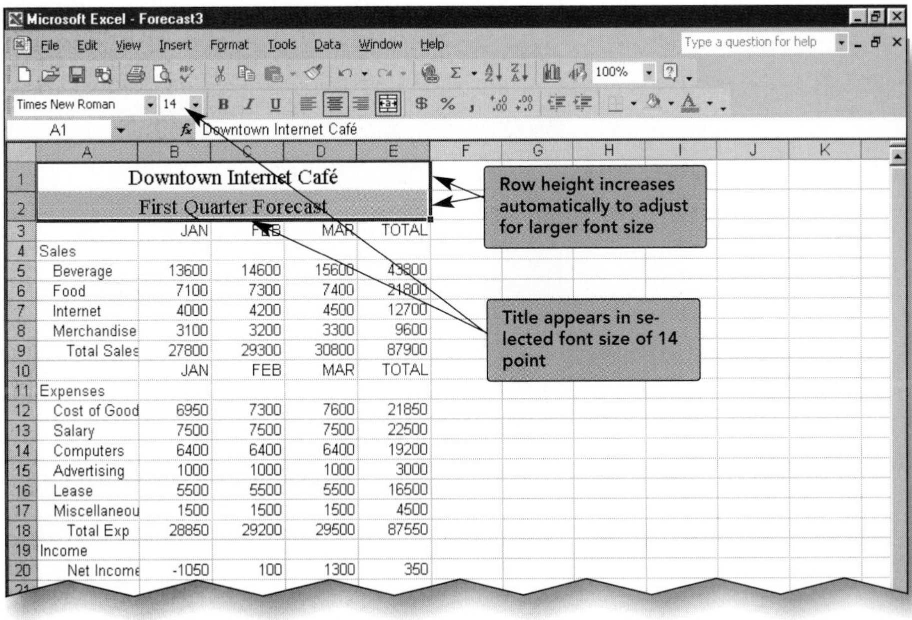

Figure 1.58

Notice that the height of the row has increased to accommodate the larger font size of the heading.

Applying Character Effects

In addition to changing font and font size, you can apply different **character effects** to enhance the appearance of text. The table below describes some of the effects and their uses.

Format	Example	Use
Bold	**Bold**	Adds emphasis
Italic	*Italic*	Adds emphasis
Underline	<u>Underline</u>	Adds emphasis
Strikethrough	~~Strikethrough~~	Indicates words to be deleted
Superscript	"To be or not to be."[1]	Used in footnotes and formulas
Subscript	H_2O	Used in formulas
Color	**Color Color Color**	Adds interest

You want to add bold, italic, and underlines to several worksheet entries. First you will bold the two title lines that are already selected.

Click **B** **Bold.**

> **Another Method**
> The menu equivalent is Format/Cells/Font/Font Style/Bold and the keyboard shortcut is Ctrl + B.

Your screen should be similar to Figure 1.59

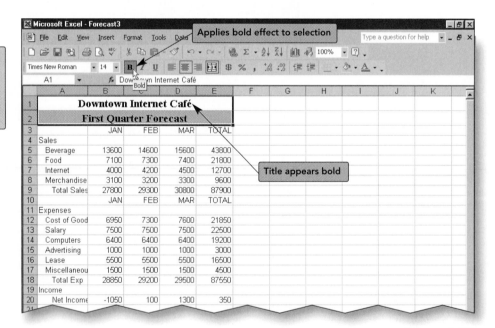

Figure 1.59

Next you would like to bold, underline, and italicize some of the other entries in the worksheet.

2

● Select B3 through E3.

● Click **B** Bold.

● Click **U** Underline.

● Bold and italicize the entries in cells A5 through A8.

Another Method
The menu equivalent for underline is Format/Cells/ Font/Underline/Single or [Ctrl] + U and for italic is Format/Cells/Font/Font Style/Italic or [Ctrl] + I.

Your screen should be similar to Figure 1.60

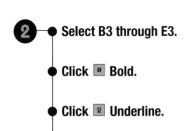

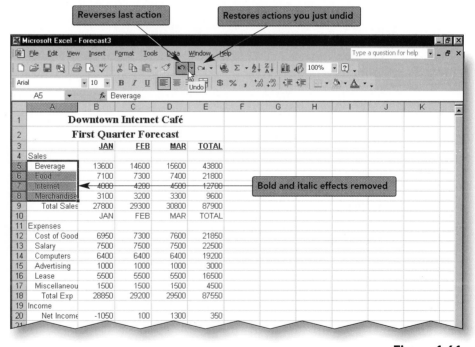

Adds Italic effect   Adds underline effect

Bold and underline applied to labels

Bold and italic applied to labels

Figure 1.60

Using Undo

Sometimes formatting changes you make do not have the expected result. In this case, you feel that the sales category names would look better without the formatting. To quickly undo the last two actions you performed,

1

● Open the Undo drop-down list.

● Move the mouse pointer down the list to highlight the Italic and Bold actions.

Another Method
The menu equivalent is Edit/ Undo or [Ctrl] + Z. You can also click repeatedly to undo the actions in the list one by one.

Your screen should be similar to Figure 1.61

Reverses last action   Restores actions you just undid

Bold and italic effects removed

Figure 1.61

Additional Information
The menu equivalent is Edit/Redo or [Ctrl] + Y.

The two actions you selected are undone. Undo reverses the selected actions regardless of the current cell pointer location. If you change your mind after you Undo an action, the Redo button is available so that you can restore the action you just undid.

Using Format Painter

You do think, however, that the Total Sales, Total Exp, and Net Income labels would look good in bold. You will bold the entry in cell A9 and then copy the format from A9 to the other cells using Format Painter. This feature applies the formats associated with the current selection to new selections. To turn on the feature, move the insertion point to the cell whose formats you want to copy and click the  Format Painter button. Then you select the cell you want the formats applied to. The format is automatically applied to an entire cell contents simply by clicking on the cell. If you double-click the  Format Painter button, you can apply the format multiple times. You will also format the labels in row 10.

1 • **Apply bold to cell A9.**

• **With cell A9 selected, double-click**  **Format Painter.**

When Format Painter is on, the mouse pointer appears as ▲▯.

• **Click A18.**

• **Click A20.**

• **Click**  **Format Painter to turn it off.**

Another Method

You can also press Esc to turn off Format Painter.

• **Use Format Painter to copy the format from cell B3 to cells B10 through E10.**

Your screen should be similar to Figure 1.62

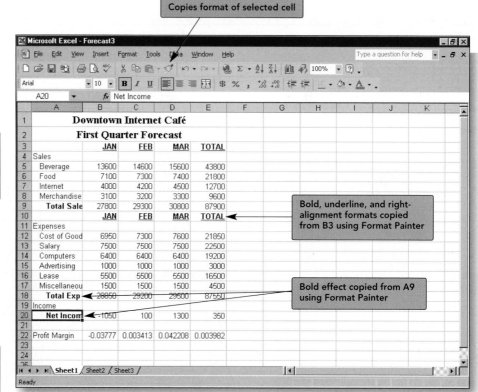

Copies format of selected cell

Bold, underline, and right-alignment formats copied from B3 using Format Painter

Bold effect copied from A9 using Format Painter

Figure 1.62

The formatting was quickly added to each cell as it was selected.

Formatting Numbers

You also want to improve the appearance of the numbers in the worksheet by changing their format.

EX1.58   **Lab 1:** Creating and Editing a Worksheet   www.mhhe.com/oleary

Excel 2002

13 **Number formats** change how numbers look onscreen and when printed, without changing the way the number is stored or used in calculations. When a number is formatted, the formatting appears in the cell and the actual value is displayed in the formula bar.

The default number format setting in a worksheet is General. General format, in most cases, displays numbers just as you enter them, unformatted. Unformatted numbers are displayed without a thousands separator such as a comma, with negative values preceded by a – (minus sign), and with as many decimal place settings as cell space allows. If a number is too long to be fully displayed in the cell, the General format will round numbers with decimals and use scientific notation for large numbers.

First you will change the number format of cells B5 through E8 to display dollar signs, commas, and decimal places.

1 ● Select cells B5 through E9.

● Choose Format/Cells.

Another Method

The keyboard shortcut is Ctrl + 1.

● If necessary, open the Number tab.

● From the Category list box, select Currency.

Your screen should be similar to Figure 1.63

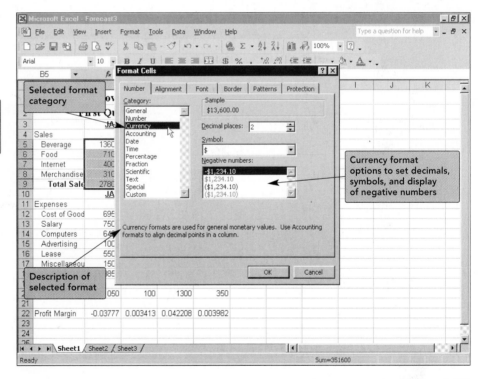

Figure 1.63

The Currency category includes options that allow you to specify the number of decimal places, how negative numbers will appear, and whether a currency symbol such as a dollar sign will be displayed.

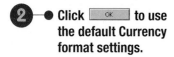

2 ● Click [OK] to use the default Currency format settings.

Your screen should be similar to Figure 1.64

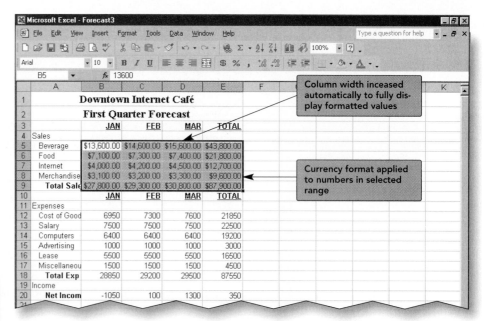

Figure 1.64

The number entries in the selected range appear with a currency symbol, comma, and two decimal places. The column widths increased automatically to fully display the formatted values.

A second format category that displays numbers as currency is Accounting. You will try this format next on the same range. Additionally, you will specify zero as the number of decimal places since all the values are whole values.

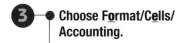

3 ● Choose Format/Cells/Accounting.

● Reduce the decimal places to 0.

● Click [OK].

Your screen should be similar to Figure 1.65

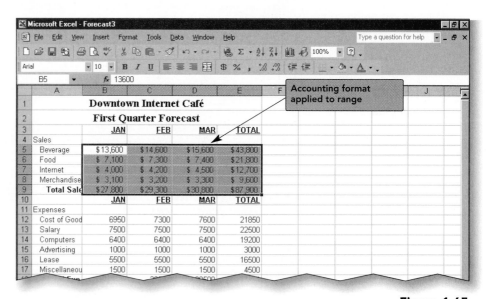

Figure 1.65

The numbers now appear in Accounting format. The primary difference between the Accounting and the Currency formats is that the Accounting format aligns numbers at the decimal place and places the dollar sign in a column at the left edge of the cell space. In addition, it does not allow you to select different ways of displaying negative numbers but displays them in black in parentheses. You decide the Accounting format will make it easier to read the numbers in a column.

Using Styles

You want to apply the same format to the expense range of cells. Another way to apply number formats is to select a predefined format style.

concept 14

Styles

14 A **style** consists of a combination of formats that have been named and that can be quickly applied to a selection. Excel includes six pre-defined styles, or you can create your own custom styles. Normal is the default style used in the Book template. It sets the number format to General and controls other format settings that are applied to all entries, including font type, font size, alignment, and indentation.

Examples of the six predefined styles are shown on the right. Notice the two Currency styles. They will display dollar signs, commas, and two or zero decimal places, just as if you had selected these formats from the Format Cells dialog box.

Style	Example
Normal	89522
Comma	89,522.00
Comma [0]	89,522
Currency	$ 89,522.00
Currency [0]	$ 89,522
Percent	89.52200%

1 ● **Drag to select the range B12 through E20.**

● **Choose Format/Style.**

Your screen should be similar to Figure 1.66

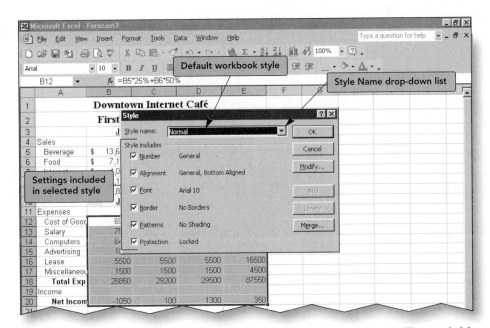

Figure 1.66

The Style dialog box displays the name of the default workbook style, Normal, in the Style Name list box. The check boxes in the Style Includes area of the dialog box show the options that are included in this style and a description or sample. You want to use the Currency $ style.

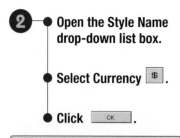

2 ● Open the Style Name drop-down list box.

● Select Currency $.

● Click [OK].

Additional Information

Using $ Currency Style on the Formatting toolbar applies the Accounting number format with two decimal places.

Your screen should be similar to Figure 1.67

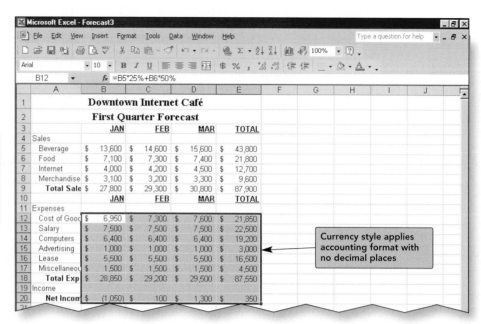

Figure 1.67

The Currency $ style applies the Accounting number format with zero decimal places.

Finally, you want the Profit Margin values to be displayed as percentages with two decimal places.

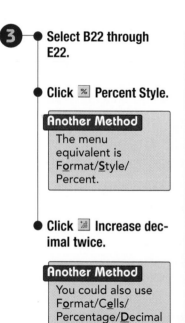

3 ● Select B22 through E22.

● Click % Percent Style.

Another Method

The menu equivalent is Format/Style/Percent.

● Click Increase decimal twice.

Another Method

You could also use Format/Cells/Percentage/Decimal Places/2.

Your screen should be similar to Figure 1.68

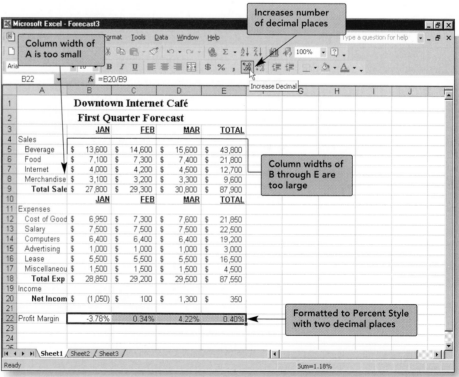

Figure 1.68

Now that the numbers are displayed as a percentage and the number of decimal places has been decreased, the column widths are larger than they need to be. Because Excel does not automatically reduce column widths, you need to make this change yourself. Additionally, you want column A to fully display the row headings. You will use the AutoFit feature to adjust the column widths for all cells in columns A through E.

Column A increased to display longest entry

Columns B through E decreased to the minimum column width needed to display entries

4

● **Click the A column letter and drag to the right to expand the selection to include column E.**

● **Double-click any column border line in the selection to AutoFit the selection.**

Additional Information

You could also press Ctrl + A or click the button at the intersection of the row numbers and column letters to select the entire worksheet and then double-click on any border line to AutoFit the column width of all columns containing entries.

Your screen should be similar to Figure 1.69

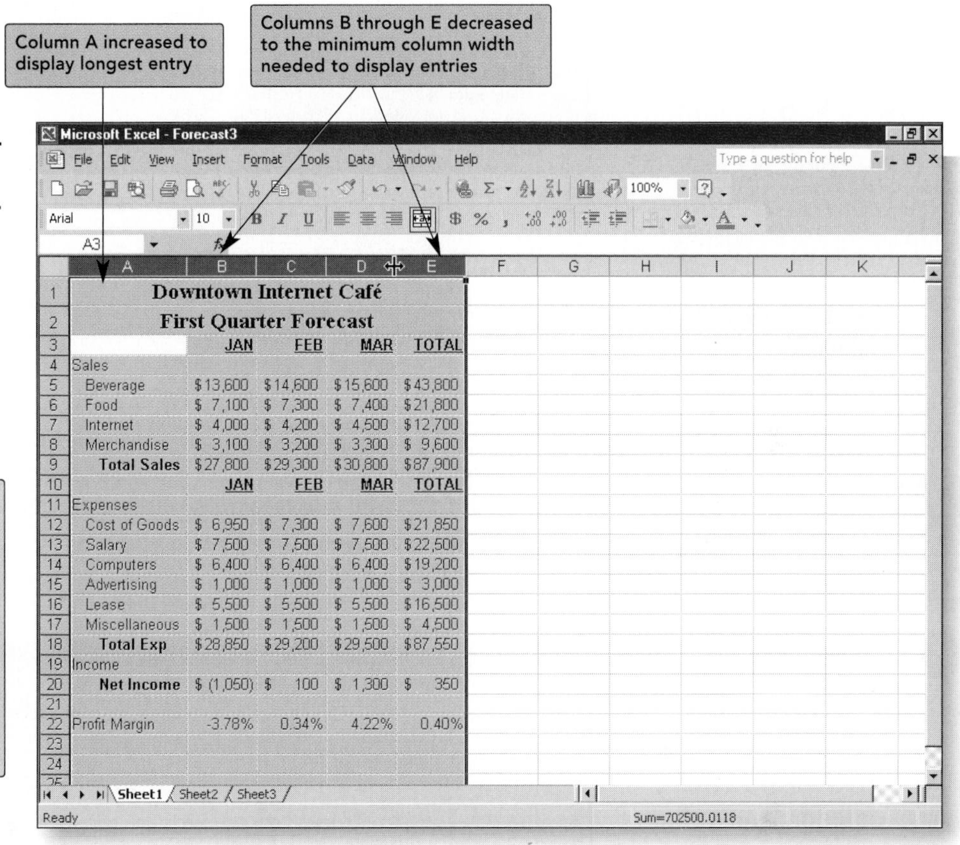

	A	B	C	D	E
1	Downtown Internet Café				
2	First Quarter Forecast				
3		JAN	FEB	MAR	TOTAL
4	Sales				
5	Beverage	$13,600	$14,600	$15,600	$43,800
6	Food	$ 7,100	$ 7,300	$ 7,400	$21,800
7	Internet	$ 4,000	$ 4,200	$ 4,500	$12,700
8	Merchandise	$ 3,100	$ 3,200	$ 3,300	$ 9,600
9	Total Sales	$27,800	$29,300	$30,800	$87,900
10		JAN	FEB	MAR	TOTAL
11	Expenses				
12	Cost of Goods	$ 6,950	$ 7,300	$ 7,600	$21,850
13	Salary	$ 7,500	$ 7,500	$ 7,500	$22,500
14	Computers	$ 6,400	$ 6,400	$ 6,400	$19,200
15	Advertising	$ 1,000	$ 1,000	$ 1,000	$ 3,000
16	Lease	$ 5,500	$ 5,500	$ 5,500	$16,500
17	Miscellaneous	$ 1,500	$ 1,500	$ 1,500	$ 4,500
18	Total Exp	$28,850	$29,200	$29,500	$87,550
19	Income				
20	Net Income	$ (1,050)	$ 100	$ 1,300	$ 350
21					
22	Profit Margin	-3.78%	0.34%	4.22%	0.40%

Figure 1.69

The width of columns B through E automatically decreased to the minimum column width needed to fully display the entries. The width of column A increased to accommodate the longest entry.

Adding Color

The last formatting change you would like to make to the worksheet is to add color to the text and to the background of selected cells. First you will change the color of the text.

①   Select A1 through A2.

   Open the  Font Color palette.

Additional Information
A ScreenTip displays the name of the color as you point to it.

   Select a color of your choice.

Your screen should be similar to Figure 1.70

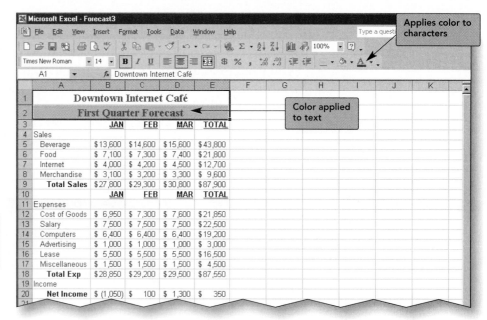

Figure 1.70

The selected color appears in the button and can be applied again simply by clicking the button. Next you will change the cell background color, also called the fill color.

Additional Information
This text uses the cell fill color of tan and the title text color of blue.

②   Open the  Fill Color palette.

   Select a color of your choice.

   Apply the same font color, fill color, and bold to cell A4.

   Use Format Painter to quickly copy the format from cell A4 to cells A11, A19, and A22.

   Apply the same fill color to B4 through E4, B11 through E11, B19 through E19, and B22 through E22.

Your screen should be similar to Figure 1.71

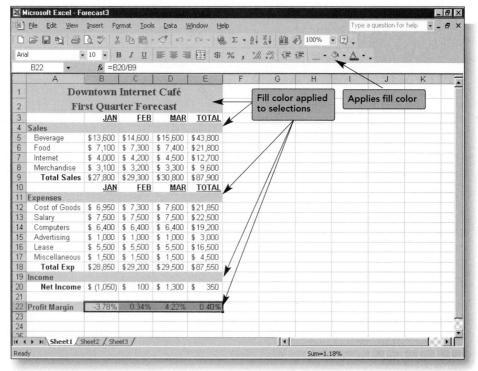

Figure 1.71

EX1.64   **Lab 1:** Creating and Editing a Worksheet

Excel 2002

www.mhhe.com/oleary

● Working with Graphics

Finally you want to add a graphic to add interest. A ClipArt image is one of several different graphic objects that can be added to an Excel document.

Inserting Graphics

You want to insert a graphic to the right of the data in the worksheet. Graphic files can be obtained from a variety of sources. Many simple drawings called **clip art** are available in the Clip Organizer that comes with Office XP. You can also create graphic files using a scanner to convert any printed document, including photographs, to an electronic format. Most images that are scanned are stored as Windows bitmap files (.bmp). All types of graphics, including clip art, photographs, and other types of images, can be found on the Internet. These files are commonly stored as .jpg or .pcx files. Keep in mind that any images you locate on the Internet may be copyrighted and should only be used with permission. You can also purchase CDs containing graphics for your use.

You decide to use the Clip Organizer to find a suitable graphic.

1 ● **Move to F3.**

● **Choose Insert/Picture/Clip Art.**

Your screen should be similar to Figure 1.72

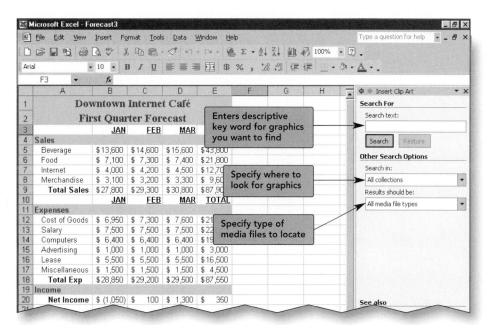

Figure 1.72

The Insert Clip Art task pane appears in which you can enter a key word, a word or phrase that is descriptive of the type of graphic you want to locate. The graphics in the Clip Organizer are organized by topic and are identified with several keywords that describe the graphic. You can also specify the locations to search and the type of media files, such as clip art, movies, photographs or sound, to display in the search results. You want to find clip art and photographs of computers.

2

● In the Search Text box, type computer.

● Open the Results Should Be drop-down list.

● Select Photographs and Clip Art.

● Deselect all other options and click outside the drop-down list to close it.

● Click Search.

Your screen should be similar to Figure 1.73

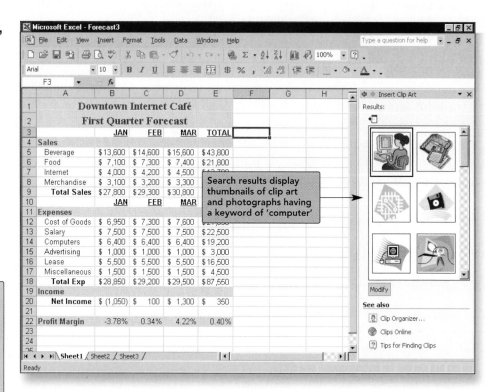

Figure 1.73

The Clip Organizer displays **thumbnails**, miniature images, of all clip art and photographs that are identified with the keyword "computer." You want to use a graphic showing people and a computer.

3 ● Scroll the list and point to the thumbnail of the computer and two people (see Figure 1.74).

● Click on the thumbnail to insert it.

● Click ☒ in the task pane title bar to close it.

HAVING TROUBLE?
If this graphic is not available in the Clip Organizer, choose Insert/Picture/From File and select Internet.wmf from your data file location.

Another Method
You could also choose Insert from the graphics shortcut menu to insert it in the worksheet.

Your screen should be similar to Figure 1.74

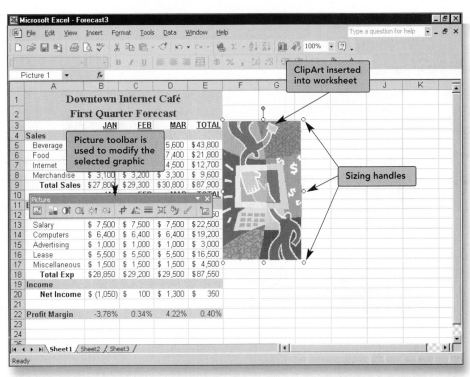

Figure 1.74

Additional Information
A selected graphic object can be deleted by pressing Del.

HAVING TROUBLE?
If the Picture toolbar is not displayed, right-click on any toolbar to open the Shortcut menu and select Picture, or use View/Toolbars/Picture.

Sizing Graphics

The ClipArt image is inserted in the document at the current cell. Once a graphic object is inserted into the workbook, it can be manipulated in many ways. You can change its size, add borders or shading, or move it to another location including in the margin, in headers and footers, or on top of or below other objects. It cannot, however, be placed behind the worksheet data.

You want to reduce the size of the graphic and move it to the top row of the worksheet. The picture is surrounded by eight boxes, called **sizing handles**, indicating it is a selected object and can now be sized and moved anywhere in the document. The handles are used to size the object. A graphic object is moved by dragging it to the new location.

The Picture toolbar is also automatically displayed. Its buttons are used to modify the selected picture object. Your Picture toolbar may be floating or docked along an edge of the window, depending on where it was when last used.

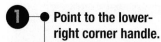

1 ● **Point to the lower-right corner handle.**

Additional Information

The mouse pointer changes to ↘ when you can drag to resize the graphic.

● **Drag the mouse inward to reduce the size of the graphic until the bottom of the graphic is even with row 12.**

Additional Information

Dragging a corner handle maintains the original proportions of the picture.

● **Point to the graphic and drag upward to move the graphic to row 1 of columns F and G.**

● **Click outside the graphic to deselect it.**

● **Add the same background fill color as in the other areas of the worksheet to cells F1:G22.**

Your screen should be similar to Figure 1.75

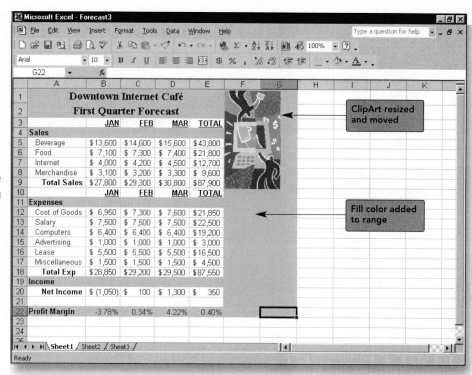

Figure 1.75

The three-month forecast is now complete.

Entering the Date

Now that the worksheet is complete, you want to include your name and the date in the worksheet as documentation.

1
● Enter your first initial and last name in cell A24.

● Enter the current date in cell B24 in the format mm/dd/yy (for example, 10/10/02).

● Move to B24.

● Click 🖫 Save to save the worksheet changes.

Another Method

You can quickly insert the current date using Ctrl + ;.

Your screen should be similar to Figure 1.76

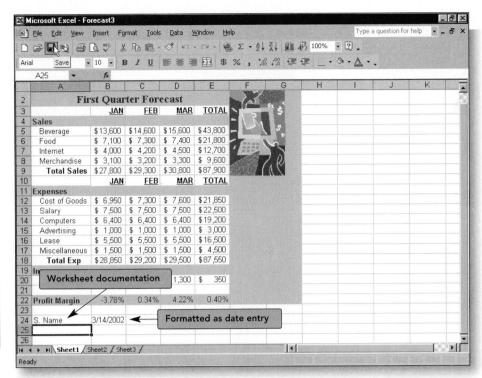

Figure 1.76

Additional Information

Dates, like other numeric entries, can be formatted to display in many different ways. Use Format/Cells/Number/Category/Date to change the date format.

Excel automatically recognized your entry as a date and formatted the entry using the short date format. If you had preceded the date entry with =, Excel would have interpreted it as a formula and a calculation of division would have been performed on the numbers.

Excel stores all dates as serial numbers with each day numbered from the beginning of the century; the date serial number 1 corresponds to the date January 1, 1900, and the integer 65380 is December 31, 2078. The integers are assigned consecutively beginning with 1 and ending with 65,380. They are called **date numbers**. Conversion of the date to a serial number allows dates to be used in calculations.

Previewing and Printing a Workbook

If you have printer capability, you can print a copy of the worksheet. To save time and unnecessary printing and paper waste, it is always a good idea to preview onscreen how the worksheet will appear when printed.

1 Click 🔍 Print Preview.

Another Method

The menu equivalent is File/Print Preview.

Your screen should be similar to Figure 1.77

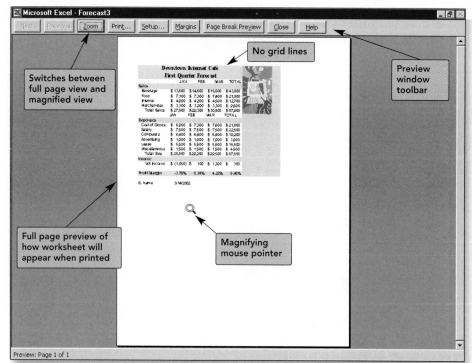

Switches between full page view and magnified view

No grid lines

Preview window toolbar

Full page preview of how worksheet will appear when printed

Magnifying mouse pointer

Preview: Page 1 of 1

Figure 1.77

Additional Information

If you have a monochrome printer, the preview appears in shades of gray as it will appear when printed.

The print preview window displays the worksheet as it will appear on the printed page. Notice that the row and column lines are not displayed and will not print. The worksheet looks good and does not appear to need any further modifications immediately.

The preview window also includes its own toolbar. While previewing, you can change from full-page view to a magnified view using ⎓Zoom⎓ or by clicking on the preview page.

2 Click the worksheet title.

Additional Information

The area you click on is the area that will display in the preview window.

Your screen should be similar to Figure 1.78

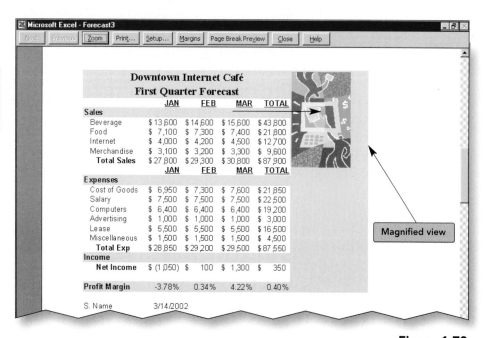

Magnified view

Figure 1.78

The worksheet is displayed in the actual size it will appear when printed. Now you are ready to print the worksheet.

3 ● Click on the worksheet again to return to full-page view.

● Click [Print...].

Your screen should be similar to Figure 1.79

Another Method

You can also use <u>F</u>ile/<u>P</u>rint or the keyboard shortcut [Ctrl] + P from the worksheet window. Clicking 🖨 Print on the Standard toolbar will send the workbook directly to the printer.

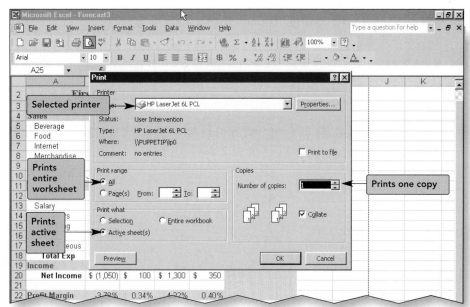

Figure 1.79

Note: Please consult your instructor for printing procedures that may differ from the following directions.

From the Print dialog box, you need to specify the printer you will be using and the document settings. The printer that is currently selected is displayed in the Name drop-down list box in the Printer section of the dialog box.

The Print Range area lets you specify how much of the worksheet you want printed. The range options are described in the following table:

Option	Action
All	Prints the entire worksheet
Pages	Prints pages you specify by typing page numbers in the text box
Selection	Prints selected range only
Active Sheet	Prints the active worksheet
Entire Workbook	Prints all worksheets in the workbook

The default settings of All and Active sheet are correct. In the Copies section, the default setting of one copy of the worksheet is acceptable.

4

- **If necessary, make sure your printer is on and ready to print.**
- **If you need to change the selected printer to another printer, open the Name drop-down list box and select the appropriate printer.**
- **Click OK.**

The printed copy should be similar to the document shown here.

Additional Information

If you do not have a color printer, the colors appear as shades of gray.

Downtown Internet Café
First Quarter Forecast

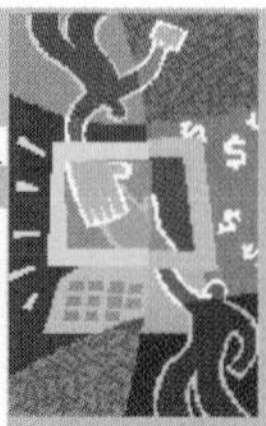

	JAN	FEB	MAR	TOTAL
Sales				
Beverage	$ 13,600	$ 14,600	$ 15,600	$ 43,800
Food	$ 7,100	$ 7,300	$ 7,400	$ 21,800
Internet	$ 4,000	$ 4,200	$ 4,500	$ 12,700
Merchandise	$ 3,100	$ 3,200	$ 3,300	$ 9,600
Total Sales	$ 27,800	$ 29,300	$ 30,800	$ 87,900
	JAN	FEB	MAR	TOTAL
Expenses				
Cost of Goods	$ 6,950	$ 7,300	$ 7,600	$ 21,850
Salary	$ 7,500	$ 7,500	$ 7,500	$ 22,500
Computers	$ 6,400	$ 6,400	$ 6,400	$ 19,200
Advertising	$ 1,000	$ 1,000	$ 1,000	$ 3,000
Lease	$ 5,500	$ 5,500	$ 5,500	$ 16,500
Miscellaneous	$ 1,500	$ 1,500	$ 1,500	$ 4,500
Total Exp	$ 28,850	$ 29,200	$ 29,500	$ 87,550
Income				
Net Income	$ (1,050)	$ 100	$ 1,300	$ 350
Profit Margin	-3.78%	0.34%	4.22%	0.40%

S. Name 3/14/2002

Exiting Excel 2002

The Exit command in the File menu is used to quit the Excel program. Alternatively, you can click the ☒ Close button in the application window title bar. If you attempt to close the application without first saving the workbook, Excel displays a warning asking if you want to save your work. If you do not save your work and you exit the application, all changes you made from the last time you saved are lost.

1 ● **Move to cell A1.**

● **Click** ☒ **(in the application window title bar).**

● **Click** [Yes] **to resave the document.**

> **Additional Information**
> Excel saves the file with the cell selector in the same cell it is in when saved.

Template (EX1.12)

A template is a workbook file that includes predefined settings that can be used as a pattern to create many common types of workbooks.

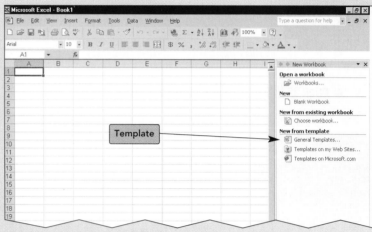

Text and Numeric Entries (EX1.14)

The information or data you enter in a cell can be text, numbers, or formulas.

AutoCorrect (EX1.20)

The AutoCorrect feature makes some basic assumptions about the text you are typing and, based on these assumptions, automatically corrects the entry.

Column Width (EX1.24)

The size or width of a column controls how much information can be displayed in a cell.

Copy and Move (EX1.31)

The contents of worksheet cells can be duplicated (copied) or moved to other locations in the worksheet or between worksheets, saving you time by not having to retype the same information.

Range (EX1.34)

A selection consisting of two or more cells on a worksheet is a range.

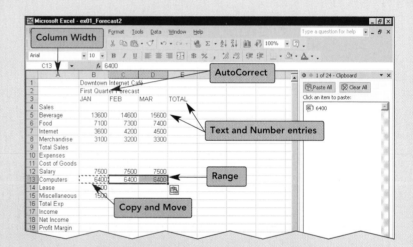

Formulas (EX1.39)

A formula is an equation that performs a calculation on data contained in a worksheet.

Relative Reference (EX1.41)

A relative reference is a cell or range reference in a formula whose location is interpreted by Excel in relation to the position of the cell that contains the formula.

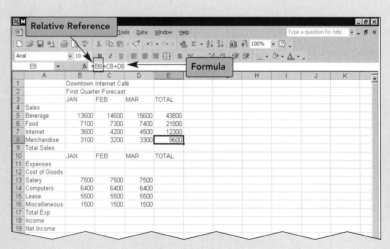

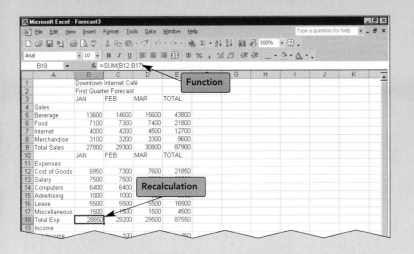

Functions (EX1.42)

← Functions are prewritten formulas that perform certain types of calculations automatically.

Recalculation (EX1.48)

← Excel automatically recalculates formulas whenever a change occurs in a referenced cell.

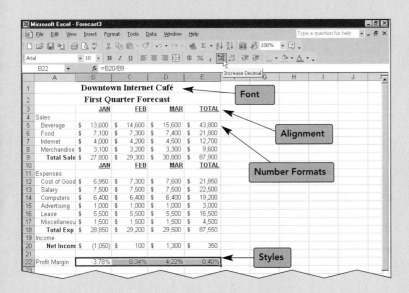

Alignment (EX1.49)

← Alignment settings allow you to change the horizontal and vertical placement and the orientation of an entry in a cell.

Fonts (EX1.54)

← Fonts consist of typefaces, point sizes, and styles that can be applied to characters to improve their appearance.

Number Formats (EX1.59)

← Number formats affect how numbers look onscreen and when printed.

Styles (EX1.61)

← A style consists of a combination of formats that have been named and that can be quickly applied to a selection.

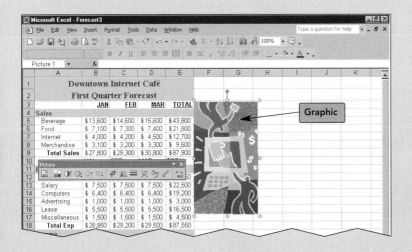

Graphics (EX1.65)

← A graphic is a non-text element or object, such as a drawing or picture, that can be added to a document.

LAB 1

Creating and Editing a Worksheet

key terms

active cell   EX1.7
active sheet   EX1.8
adjacent range   EX1.34
alignment   EX1.17
argument   EX1.42
AutoCorrect   EX1.20
cell   EX1.7
cell selector   EX1.7
character effects   EX1.56
clip art   EX1.65
column   EX1.7
column letter   EX1.7
constant   EX1.14
copy area   EX1.31
date number   EX1.69
defaults   EX1.12
destination   EX1.31
drawing object   EX1.65
embedded object   EX1.65
fill handle   EX1.36
font   EX1.54
format   EX1.49

Formatting toolbar   EX1.5
formula   EX1.14
formula bar   EX1.5
functions   EX1.42
graphic   EX1.65
heading   EX1.15
merged cell   EX1.53
Name box   EX1.5
nonadjacent range   EX1.34
number   EX1.14
number formats   EX1.49
object   EX1.65
operand   EX1.39
operator   EX1.39
paste area   EX1.31
picture   EX1.65
point   EX1.54
range   EX1.34
reference   EX1.8
recalculate   EX1.48
relative reference   EX1.41
row   EX1.7

row number   EX1.7
sans serif   EX1.54
serif   EX1.54
sheet tab   EX1.8
size   EX1.54
sizing handle   EX1.67
source   EX1.31
spreadsheet   EX1.7
Standard toolbar   EX1.5
style   EX1.61
syntax   EX1.42
tab scroll button   EX1.8
task pane   EX1.5
template   EX1.12
text   EX1.14
thumbnail   EX1.66
typeface   EX1.54
variable   EX1.14
workbook   EX1.6
workbook window   EX1.6
worksheet   EX1.7

mous skills

The Microsoft Office User Specialist (MOUS) certification program is designed to measure your proficiency in performing basic tasks using the Office XP applications. Getting certified demonstrates that you have the skills and provides a valuable industry credential for employment. After completing this lab, you have learned the following Microsoft Office User Specialist skills:

Skill	Description	Page
Working with Cells and Cell Data	Insert, delete, and move cells	EX1.36,1.53
	Enter and edit cell data including text, numbers and formulas	EX1.15–1.23,1.39–1.44, 1.54
Managing Workbooks	Manage workbook files and folders	EX1.28
	Save workbooks using different names and file formats	EX1.26
Formatting and Printing Worksheets	Apply and modify cell formats	EX1.54
	Modify row and column formats	EX1.48
	Modify column and row settings	EX1.24
	Apply styles	EX1.61
	Preview and print worksheets and workbooks	EX1.69
Creating and Revising Formulas	Create and revise formulas	EX1.39
	Use statistical, date and time, financial, and logical functions	EX1.42
Creating and Modifying Graphics	Create, modify, and position graphics	EX1.65

command summary

Command	Shortcut Key	Button	Action
File/Open <file name>	Ctrl + O	🖿	Opens an existing workbook file
File/Close		✕	Closes open workbook file
File/Save <file name>	Ctrl + S	🖫	Saves current file on disk using same file name
File/Save As <file name>			Saves current file on disk using a new file name
File/Print Preview		🔍	Displays worksheet as it will appear when printed
File/Print	Ctrl + P	🖶	Prints a worksheet
File/Exit		✕	Exits Excel
Edit/Undo	Ctrl + Z	↶	Undoes last editing or formatting change
Edit/Redo	Ctrl + Y	↷	Restores changes after using Undo
Edit/Copy	Ctrl + C	🗐	Copies selected data to Clipboard
Edit/Office Clipboard			Displays Office Clipboard task pane
Edit/Paste	Ctrl + V	🖆	Pastes selections stored in Clipboard
Edit/Fill			Fills selected cells with contents of source cell
Edit/Clear/Contents	Delete		Clears cell contents
Edit/Delete/Entire Row			Deletes selected rows

command summary (continued)

Command	Shortcut Key	Button	Action
Edit/Delete/Entire column			Deletes selected columns
View/Toolbars			Displays or hides selected toolbar
Insert/Copied Cells			Inserts row and copies text from Clipboard
Insert/Rows			Inserts a blank row
Insert/Columns			Inserts a blank column
Insert/Picture/From File			Inserts picture at insertion point from disk
Format/Cells/Number/Currency			Applies Currency format to selection
Format/Cells/Number/Accounting		$	Applies Accounting format to selection
Format/Cells/Number/Date			Applies Date format to selection
Format/Cells/Number/Percent		%	Applies Percent format to selection
Format/Cells/Number/Decimal places		.00 .00	Increases or decreases the number of decimal places associated with a number value
Format/Cells/Alignment/Horizontal/Left (Indent)		▤	Left-aligns entry in cell space
Format/Cells/Alignment/Horizontal/Center		▤	Center-aligns entry in cell space
Format/Cells/Alignment/Horizontal/Right		▤	Right-aligns entry in cell space
Format/Cells/Alignment/Indent		▤	Indents cell entry
Format/Cells/Alignment/Horizontal/Center Across Selection		▦	Centers cell contents across selected cells
Format/Cells	Ctrl + 1		Changes font and attributes of cells
Format/Cells/Font/Font Style/Bold	Ctrl + B	B	Bolds selected text
Format/Cells/Font/Font Style/Italic	Ctrl + I	I	Italicizes selected text
Format/Cells/Font/Underline/Single	Ctrl + U	U	Underlines selected text
Format/Cells/Font/Color		A ▾	Adds color to text
Format/Cells/Patterns/Color		▨ ▾	Adds color to cell background
Format/Row/Height			Changes height of selected rows
Format/Column/Width			Changes width of columns
Format/Column/Autofit Selection			Changes column width to match widest cell entry
Format/Style			Applies selected style to selection

Terminology

screen identification

In the following worksheet, several items are identified by letters. Enter the correct term for each item in the space provided.

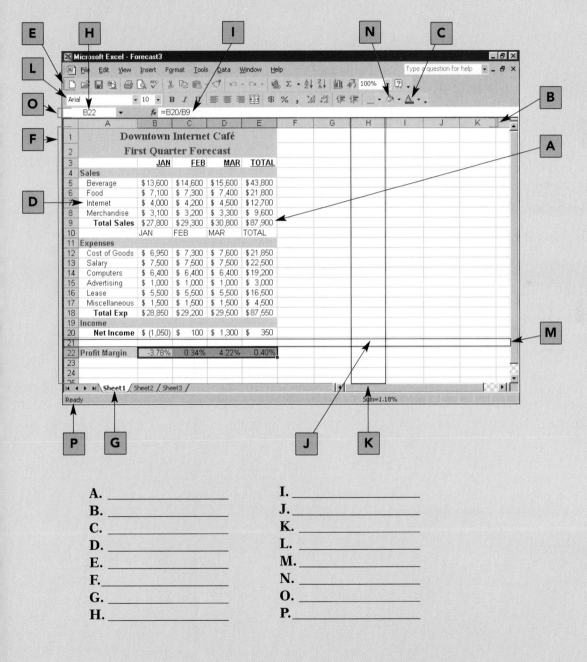

A. _____ I. _____

B. _____ J. _____

C. _____ K. _____

D. _____ L. _____

E. _____ M. _____

F. _____ N. _____

G. _____ O. _____

H. _____ P. _____

matching

Match the lettered item on the right with the numbered item on the left.

1.	source	_____	**a.**	undoes last action
2.	*	_____	**b.**	a set of characters with a specific design
3.	▣	_____	**c.**	the cell you copy from
4.	font	_____	**d.**	two or more worksheet cells
5.	.xls	_____	**e.**	a cell reference
6.	↩▾	_____	**f.**	enters a sum function
7.	=C19+A21	_____	**g.**	an arithmetic operator
8.	range	_____	**h.**	merges cells and centers entry
9.	D11	_____	**i.**	a formula summing two cells
10.	Σ	_____	**j.**	Excel workbook file name extension

multiple choice

Circle the correct response to the questions below.

1. Row and column _____ are entries that are used to create the structure of the worksheet and describe other worksheet entries.
   a. cells
   b. headings
   c. objects
   d. formats

2. _____ entries can contain any combination of letters, numbers, spaces, and any other special characters.
   a. Number
   b. Variable
   c. Constant
   d. Text

3. The _____ feature automatically corrects common typing errors as they are made.
   a. AutoFix
   b. Fixit
   c. AutoComplete
   d. AutoCorrect

4. The _____ is a small black square, located in the lower-right corner of the selection, used to create a series or copy to adjacent cells.
   a. scroll bar
   b. sheet tab
   c. sizing handle
   d. fill handle

5. The values on which a numeric formula performs a calculation are called:
   a. operators
   b. operands
   c. accounts
   d. data

6. Whenever a formula containing _____ references is copied, the referenced cells are automatically adjusted.
   a. relative
   b. automatic
   c. fixed
   d. variable

7. A(n)_____ is a box used to size a selected object.
   a. sizing handle
   b. cell selector
   c. operand
   d. fill handle

8. _____ can be applied to selections to add emphasis or interest to a document.
   a. Alignments
   b. Pictures
   c. Character effects
   d. Text formats

9. The currency number format can display:
   a. dollar signs
   b. commas
   c. decimal places
   d. all the above

10. The integers assigned to the days from January 1, 1900, through December 31, 2099, that allow dates to be used in calculations are called:
    a. date numbers
    b. syntax
    c. number formats
    d. reference

lab exercises

true/false

Circle the correct answer to the following questions.

1. Formulas are used to create, edit, and position graphics.   True   False
2. The default column width setting in Excel is 15.0.   True   False
3. A nonadjacent range is two or more selected cells or ranges that are adjoining.   True   False
4. A formula is an entry that performs a calculation.   True   False
5. When a formula containing relative references is copied, the cell references in the copied formula refer to different cells than the references in the original formula.   True   False
6. Formulas are prewritten statements that perform certain types of calculations automatically.   True   False
7. Recalculation is one of the most powerful features of electronic worksheets.   True   False
8. Font settings allow you to change the horizontal and vertical placement and the orientation of an entry in a cell.   True   False
9. Number formats affect how numbers look onscreen and when printed.   True   False
10. A drawing object is created using a special drawing program that is not included with Excel.   True   False

Concepts

fill-in

Complete the following statements by filling in the blanks with the correct terms.

1. The _____ controls how much information can be displayed in a cell.

2. _____ affect how numbers look onscreen and when printed.

3. _____ placement allows you to specify whether the cell contents are displayed at the top, centered, or at the bottom of the vertical cell space.

4. Pictures are inserted as _____ objects.

5. The _____ feature decreases the recalculation time by only recalculating dependent formulas.

6. By default, text entries are _____ -aligned and number entries are _____ -aligned.

7. A(n) _____ in a formula automatically adjusts for the new location when copied.

8. The values on which a numeric formula performs a calculation are called _____.

9. Without _____ recalculation, large worksheets would take several minutes to recalculate all formulas each time a number was changed.

10. A(n) _____ is the data the function uses to perform the calculation.

discussion questions

1. Discuss four steps in developing a workbook. Why is it important to follow these steps?

2. What types of entries are used in worksheets? Discuss the uses of each type of entry.

3. Discuss how formulas and functions are created. Why are they the power behind workbooks?

4. Discuss the formatting features presented in the lab. Why are they important to the look of the worksheet?

Hands-On Exercises

step-by-step

Park Improvement Bid Analysis

★ 1. Kelly Fitzgerald is an analyst for the city parks and recreation department. One of her responsibilities is to collect and analyze data on future improvements. She has compiled a list of the parks that are scheduled for improvements for the next year and the project bids for each. Follow the directions below to complete the worksheet shown here.

Park Improvement Bids Calendar Year 2005				
Park	Bid 1	Bid 2	Bid 3	Bid 4
West Avenue	$127,000	$154,200	$135,700	$142,800
Amigo	154,500	251,000	202,500	220,300
Canyon Creek	13,600	18,900	15,500	14,700
Mountain View	1,300	2,500	1,800	1,600
East Hill	129,100	154,300	128,500	133,400
Maple Grove	1,200	1,500	1,400	1,600
Thompson-West	10,300	14,200	11,500	10,200
Marshall Way	19,300	19,900	18,900	22,300
Green Mountain	10,200	11,500	12,600	12,500
Blue Bird Pass	29,100	32,500	25,700	28,900
Total	$495,600	$660,500	$554,100	$588,300

Student Name
Date

 a. Open the workbook ex01_Improvements.
 b. Modify the label in cell B2 so that the first letter of each word is capitalized. Increase the font size to 14 point. Center both title lines across columns A through E.
 c. Bold and center the titles in row 5.
 d. Adjust the column widths so that all the data is fully displayed.
 e. In row 16, enter a function to total the Bid 1 and Bid 2 columns.
 f. Format the numbers in rows 6 and 16 using the Currency style with zero decimal places and the numbers in rows 7 through 15 using the Comma style with zero decimal places.
 g. Kelly has just received the last two bids. Enter the following data in the cells indicated.

Row	Col D	Col E
5	Bid 3	Bid 4
6	135700	142800
7	202500	220300
8	15500	14700
9	1800	1600
10	128500	133400
11	1400	1600
12	11500	10200
13	18900	22300
14	12600	12500
15	25700	28900

 h. Format the data to match the style of the corresponding information in columns B and C.

i. Copy the total function to calculate the total for the new bids.

j. Insert a blank row above the Total row.

k. Add font and fill colors to the worksheet, as you like.

l. Insert a Clip Art graphic of your choice from the Clip Organizer. Size and position it appropriately to fit the worksheet.

m. Enter your name and the current date on separate rows just below the worksheet.

n. Move to cell A1. Save the workbook as Park Improvements. Preview and print the worksheet.

Job Trends Analysis Worksheet

★ 2. Lisa Sutton is an employment analyst working for the state of New Jersey. One of her responsibilities is to collect and analyze data on future job opportunities in the state. Lisa has compiled a list of the jobs that are expected to offer the most new positions. Follow the directions below to complete the worksheet shown here.

a. Open the workbook ex01_New Positions.

b. Modify the label in cell B2 so that the first letter of each word is capitalized; move the label in cell B2 to A2; move the label in cell B3 to A3; center the titles across the columns A through D; and finally, increase the font size to 14 point.

Jobs With Most New Positions
1994 - 2005

Title	N.J. Projected New Positions	Avg Pay Per Hour	Percent Above National Average
Systems Analysts/Programmers	27,000	$26.59	14.4%
Nursing Aides and Orderlies	15,400	$9.17	18.3%
Waiters and Waitresses	13,600	$6.09	8.4%
Home Health Aides	13,400	$7.97	1.8%
Marketing and Sales Supv.	12,900	$19.81	25.9%
Janitors and Cleaners	12,500	$8.79	11.3%
Salespersons, retail	11,300	$8.66	4.8%
Cashiers	11,300	$7.44	13.1%
Guards and watch guards	10,200	$8.21	2.8%
Nurse: Registered, Practitioner etc.	9,100	$22.46	15.9%

Student Name
Date

c. Format the numbers in column B as number with a comma to separate thousands and 0 decimal places. Format the numbers in column C as currency with dollar signs and two decimal places. Format the numbers in column D as percent with one decimal place.

d. Insert a new row below row 3 and a new row below row 6.

e. Bold the titles in rows 5 and 6. Underline the titles in row 6. Adjust the column widths so that all the data is fully displayed.

f. Add font and fill colors to the worksheet as you like.

g. Insert a Clip Art graphic of your choice from the Clip Organizer. Size and position it appropriately to fit the page.

h. Enter your name and the current date on separate rows just below the worksheet.

i. Move to cell A1. Save the workbook as Jobs. Preview and print the worksheet.

lab exercises

Comparative U.S. Families at Poverty Level

★ ★ **3.** Mark Ernster works for an agency that provides help to families in poverty. He has been doing some research on the percent of families that fall into this category. He has started a worksheet with data from the years 1990–1999. Follow the directions below to complete the worksheet shown here.

a. Open the workbook ex01_Poverty Level.

b. Edit the title in cell D2 so that the first letter of each word is upper-case except the words 'of' and 'or'. Center the title across columns A through J. Increase the font size to 14 and bold and apply a font color of your choice to the title.

c. Center-align and underline the column headings in row 4. Left-align cells A5 through A14.

d. Calculate the average for the Official percentage in cell B15 using the Average function (=Average(B5:B14)). Format the cell as a percentage with two decimal places. Copy the formula to cells C15 through J15.

e. Next, you would like to calculate the percent of change from 1990 to 1999. Enter the label **Percent Change** in cell A16. Enter the formula **=(B14-B5)/B15** in cell B16. Format the cell as a percentage with two decimal places. Copy the formula to cells C16 through J16.

Percentage of Families At or Below Poverty Level

	Official	NAS	NAS-U	DES	DES-U	NGA	NGA-J	DCM	DCM-U
1990	13.5%	13.7%	16.1%	13.6%	16.7%	13.8%	16.6%	13.6%	16.4%
1991	14.2%	14.5%	16.9%	14.4%	17.6%	14.6%	17.3%	14.3%	17.3%
1992	14.8%	15.1%	17.6%	15.1%	18.3%	15.2%	18.2%	15.0%	18.0%
1993	15.1%	15.8%	18.3%	15.8%	19.0%	15.8%	18.6%	15.7%	18.8%
1994	14.6%	14.6%	17.0%	14.6%	17.5%	14.6%	17.3%	14.5%	17.5%
1995	13.8%	13.8%	16.3%	13.8%	16.9%	13.9%	16.6%	13.8%	16.8%
1996	13.7%	13.6%	16.0%	13.6%	16.7%	13.5%	16.2%	13.7%	16.6%
1997	13.3%	13.3%	15.4%	13.3%	16.0%	13.3%	15.8%	13.3%	15.9%
1998	12.7%	12.5%	14.4%	12.5%	15.1%	12.3%	14.6%	12.5%	15.0%
1999	11.8%	11.7%	13.8%	11.8%	14.3%	11.7%	14.0%	11.9%	14.4%
Average	13.75%	13.86%	16.18%	13.85%	16.81%	13.87%	16.52%	13.83%	16.67%
Percent Change	-12.59%	-14.60%	-14.29%	-13.24%	-14.37%	-15.22%	-15.66%	-12.50%	-12.20%

Legend
Official U.S. government
NAS   National Academy of Sciences methodology - standardized
NAS-U National Academy of Sciences methodology - unstandardized
DES   Different Equivalence Scale: uses three parameters to adjust thresholds by family size, presence of children and family structure (but otherwise similar to NAS) - standardized
DES-U Different Equivalence Scale: uses three parameters to adjust thresholds by family size, presence of children and family structure (but otherwise similar to NAS) - unstandardized
NGA   No Geographic Adjustment (but otherwise similar to NAS) - standardized
NGA-U No Geographic Adjustment (but otherwise similar to NAS) - unstandardized
DCM   Different Child Care Method: assigns fixed amounts of child care expenditures to families based on the number and ages of children present (but otherwise similar to NAS) - standardized
DCM-U Different Child Care Method: assigns fixed amounts of child care expenditures to families based on the number and ages of children present (but otherwise similar to NAS) - unstandardized

Student Name
Date

f. Format the data in cells B5 through J14 as a percentage with one decimal place. Best-fit columns B through J.

g. Adjust the width of column A to fully display the labels.

h. Insert a blank row between rows 14 and 15 and another between rows 16 and 17.

i. Add fill colors to the worksheet as you like.

j. Insert the picture ex01_family. Size and position it to fit on the left side of the title.

k. Enter your name and the current date on separate rows just below the legend.

l. Move to cell A1. Save and replace the workbook as Poverty Level. Preview and print the worksheet.

Information Technology Job and Salary Analysis

★★ **4.** Jake Bell is a writer for a local television station. The station is planning a series about information technology. In his research on this topic, he has found some interesting data on information technology jobs and salaries. He has entered this data into a worksheet but still needs to format the data and perform some analysis of the information. Follow the directions below to complete the worksheet shown here.

a. Open the workbook ex01_IT Salaries.

b. Adjust the width of column A to fully display the row labels.

c. Center the title in row 2 over the worksheet columns A through F. Format the title in row 2 to Tahoma 14 point. Apply a font color and fill color of your choice to row 2.

d. Bold and center the column labels in row 4.

e. Format the data in B6 through D15 using the Comma style and no decimal places.

Information Technology Median Salaries

Management Level	1995	1999	% Change 1995 - 1999	2000	% Change 1999 - 2000
CIO/Vice President	102,500	146,400	42.83%	158,000	7.92%
IS Director	76,650	106,500	38.94%	113,700	6.76%
Manager, Sys. Analysis & Prog.	69,950	91,100	30.24%	97,100	6.59%
Manager, Sys. Prog./Tech. Support	66,200	89,700	35.50%	95,800	6.80%
Network Manager LAN/WAN	56,300	85,200	51.33%	92,100	8.10%
Sys. Analyst/Prog./Proj. Leader	48,250	72,200	49.64%	77,900	7.89%
Database Admin. Manager	64,500	89,000	37.98%	96,500	8.43%
Manager Telecommunications	67,450	79,100	17.27%	84,800	7.21%
Data Center Manager	62,800	73,600	17.20%	77,400	5.16%
PC Work Station Manager	44,650	59,400	33.03%	63,100	6.23%

Student Name
Date

f. Insert a new column between C and D. Calculate the % of change from 1995 to 1999. Format the data as a percentage with two decimal places. (*Hint:* Subtract the 1995 value from the 1999 value and divide the result by the 1995 value.)

g. Calculate the % of change from 1999 to 2000 in column F. Format the data as a percentage with two decimal places.

h. Label the new columns in row 4 **% Change**. Enter **1995–1999** in cell D5 and **1999–2000** in cell F5. Format the headings appropriately. Best-fit the columns to display the labels. Change the widths of columns B, C, and E to the same width as columns D and F.

i. Insert a blank row above row 6.

j. Insert the Disks Clip Art graphic (located in the Computer category of the Clip Organizer or ex01_Disks from your data files) to the right and left of the title on the worksheet. Adjust the size and location of the pictures as necessary.

k. Apply a fill color of your choice behind all rows of the worksheet (except row 2, which already contains a fill color.)

l. Enter your name and the current date on separate rows below the worksheet.

m. Move to cell A1. Save and replace the workbook file as IT Salaries. Preview and print the worksheet.

lab exercises

Homeowners Association Projected Budget

★ ★ ★ **5.** Stuart Philips is president of the Garden Springs Homeowners Association. The Association is planning a large improvement project and wants to project how much there is likely to be in the cash budget after expenses. Using last year's final budget numbers, he wants to create a projected budget for 2004. Follow the directions below to complete the worksheet shown here.

a. Open the workbook file ex01_Springs Budget. Adjust the width of column A to fully display the labels.

b. In column C, calculate a 5 percent increase for all the income numbers for the year 2004. Calculate a 10 percent increase in Administrative and Maintenance expenditures, and a 15 percent increase in Miscellaneous expenditures.

c. Format the data with the Accounting number format.

d. In column D, calculate the totals for Total Income, Total Administrative, Total Maintenance, and Total Expenditures for 2004. In column E, calculate the Total Cash Balance by subtracting the total income from the total expenditures for 2004.

e. Indent the row label subheads and further indent the items under each subhead. Right-align the total labels except for the Total Cash Balance.

f. Delete rows 13 and 14.

g. Change the font type, size, and color of the worksheet title lines to a format of your choice. Center the titles across columns A through E.

h. Apply character effects and color of your choice to the worksheet.

i. Insert a Clip Art image of your choice from the Clip Organizer. Position and size it to fit the worksheet.

j. Enter your name and the current date on separate rows just below the worksheet.

k. Move to cell A1. Save the workbook file as Springs Projected Budget. Preview and print the worksheet.

Garden Springs Homeowners Association		
Projected Budget for 2004		

Income	2003	2004
General Fund:		
Cash on hand	$ 15,907.00	$ 16,702.35
Funds	$ 128,000.00	$ 134,400.00
Receipts		
Member Dues	$ 217,400.00	$ 228,270.00
Transfer Fees	$ 1,500.00	$ 1,575.00
Interest - savings	$ 1,000.00	$ 1,050.00
Total Income	$ 363,807.00	$ 381,997.35
Expenditures		
Administrative		
Administration	$ 7,000.00	$ 7,700.00
Attorney	$ 10,000.00	$ 11,000.00
Audit & Tax Preparation	$ 2,500.00	$ 2,750.00
Insurance	$ 14,000.00	$ 15,400.00
Total Administrative	$ 33,500.00	$ 36,850.00
Maintenance		
Street Repair	$ 90,500.00	$ 99,550.00
Street Cleaning	$ 1,450.00	$ 1,595.00
Snow Removal	$ 14,500.00	$ 15,950.00
Street Signs	$ 5,200.00	$ 5,720.00
Total Maintenance	$ 111,650.00	$ 122,815.00
Miscellaneous		
Miscellaneous	$ 2,800.00	$ 3,220.00
Total Miscellaneous	$ 2,800.00	$ 3,220.00
Total Expenditures	$ 147,950.00	$ 162,885.00
Total Cash Balance	$ 215,857.00	$ 219,112.35

Student Name
Date

Tracking Your Grades

★ ★ **1.** A worksheet can be used to track your grades in a class or for each semester. Design and create a worksheet to record your grades in any class. The worksheet should include grades for at least four test scores showing the number of points you earned on each test and the number of possible points. Include an appropriate title, row and column headings, and formulas to calculate your total points earned and total possible points. Include a formula to calculate your percent. Format the worksheet appropriately using features presented in this lab. Enter real or sample data for the four tests. Include your name and date above the worksheet. Save the workbook as Class Grades and print the worksheet.

Creating a Personal Budget

★ ★ **2.** Create a personal three-month budget using a worksheet. Enter an appropriate title and use descriptive labels for your monthly expenses (food, rent, car payments, insurance, credit card payments, etc.). Enter your monthly expenses (or, if you prefer, any reasonable sample data). Use formulas to calculate total expenses for each month and to calculate the average monthly expenditures for each expense item. Enhance the worksheet using features you learned in this lab. Enter your name and the current date on separate rows just below the worksheet. Save the workbook as Personal Budget. Preview and print the worksheet.

Tracking Sales

★ ★ **3.** Trevor Grey is the new owner and manager of a small custom publishing company. He has four salespeople (Kevin, April, Karen, and Sam) and is planning an intense marketing campaign for the next month. Using the steps in the planning process, plan and create a worksheet for Trevor that can be used to record and analyze sales for that month.

Weekly sales data for each employee will be entered into the worksheet. Using that data, the worksheet will calculate the total monthly sales for each person. Additionally, it will calculate the total weekly sales for the company. Write a short paragraph describing how you used each of the planning steps. Enter sample data in the worksheet. Include your name and the current date on separate rows just below the worksheet. Save the workbook as Weekly Sales. Preview and print the worksheet.

Job Analysis

★ ★ **4.** Use the library and/or the Web to locate information on employment opportunities and salary trends related to your area of study. Create a worksheet to display information relating to job titles, years of experience, and starting and top salaries for positions in your field. Calculate the median salary (the average of the starting and the top salary). Enhance the worksheet using features you learned in this lab. Enter your name and the current date on separate rows just below the worksheet. Save the workbook as Job Analysis. Preview and print the worksheet.

Membership Analysis

★★ 5. LifeStyle Fitness Club wants to analyze their membership growth for the past 3 years. Design and
★ create a worksheet to record the membership enrollment for three years in the three membership
categories: Single, Family, and Senior. Include an appropriate title, row and column headings, and
formulas to calculate total enrollment by category and by year. Include a formula to calculate the
percent growth over the three years. Format the worksheet appropriately using features presented
in this tutorial. Enter sample data for the three years. Include your name and date above the
worksheet. Save the workbook as Membership and print the worksheet.

on the web

Design, planning and testing are very important steps in the development of an accurate
worksheet. A poorly designed worksheet can lead to serious errors in the analysis of data. Use the
Web to find information about spreadsheet errors and spreadsheet design. Write a short paper
summarizing your findings. Include proper citations for your sources. If you are using a word
processor to write the report, save the document as Spreadsheet Design.

Charting Worksheet Data

objectives

After completing this lab, you will know how to:

1.	Select a chart data range.
2.	Change the type of chart.
3.	Move the chart location.
4.	Format chart elements.
5.	Add chart titles and move the legend.
6.	Create a combination chart.
7.	Change worksheet data.
8.	Add data labels, text boxes, and arrows.
9.	Create, explode, and rotate a pie chart.
10.	Apply patterns and color.
11.	Size and align a sheet on a page.
12.	Add predefined headers and footers.
13.	Document, preview, and print a workbook.

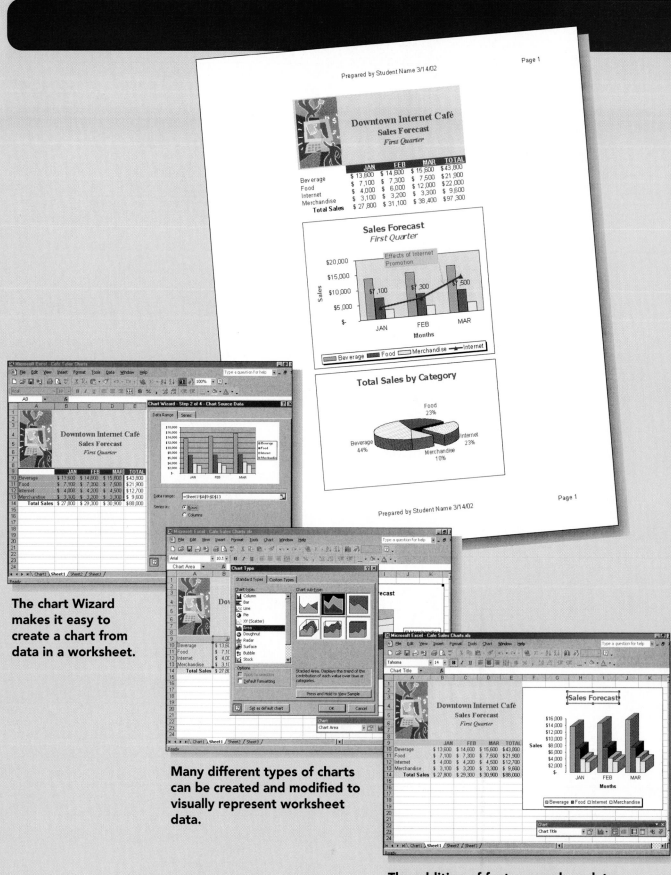

The chart Wizard makes it easy to create a chart from data in a worksheet.

Many different types of charts can be created and modified to visually represent worksheet data.

The addition of features such as data labels, text boxes, arrows, and color add emphasis to the chart.

Downtown Internet Café

After creating the first quarter forecast for the Downtown Internet Café, you contacted several other Internet cafes to inquire about their startup experiences. You heard many exciting success stories! Internet connections attract more customers and the typical customer stays longer at an Internet café than at a regular café. As a result, they end up spending more money.

You now believe that your initial sales estimates are too low. You too should be able to increase sales dramatically. In addition to sales of coffee and food items to customers, the Café also derives sales from charging for Internet connection time. In your discussions with other Internet café managers, you have found that Internet connection sales account for ap-

proximately 25 percent of their total sales. You would like to launch an aggressive advertising campaign to promote the new Internet aspect of the Downtown Internet Café. You believe that the campaign will lead to an increase in sales not only in Internet connection time but also in food and beverage sales.

To convince Evan, you need an effective way to illustrate the sales growth you are forecasting. In this lab, you will learn to use Excel 2002's chart-creating and formatting features to produce several different charts of your sales estimates, as shown on the preceding page.

The following concepts will be introduced in this lab:

1	**Chart**	A chart is visual representation of data that is used to convey information in an easy-to-understand and attractive manner. Different types of charts are used to represent data in different ways.
2	**Chart Elements**	Chart elements consist of a number of parts that are used to graphically display the worksheet data.
3	**Chart Objects**	A chart object is a graphic object that is created using charting features included in Excel. A chart object can be inserted into a worksheet or into a special chart sheet.
4	**Group**	Because it consists of many separate objects, a chart object is a group. A group is two or more objects that behave as a single object when it is moved or sized.
5	**Data Label**	Data labels provide additional information about a data marker.
6	**Text Box**	A text box is a rectangular object in which you type text. Text boxes can be added to a sheet or an embedded chart.
7	**Header and Footer**	Lines of text displayed above the top margin or below the bottom margin of each page are called headers and footers.

Learning About Charts

Creating charts of the sales projections makes it easy to visually understand numeric data. Excel 2002 can create many types of charts from data in a worksheet.

You have decided to chart the sales forecast data for the Downtown Internet Café to better see the sales trends. The sales data is in a separate workbook file.

1  **Open the file**
ex02_Cafe Sales.

Your screen should be similar to Figure 2.1

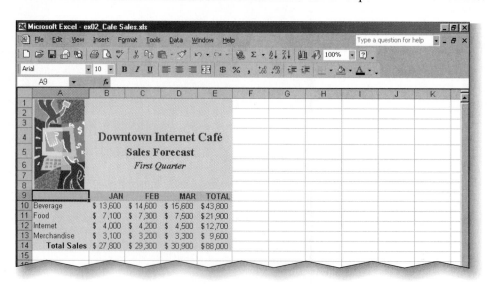

Figure 2.1

Although the worksheet shows the sales data for each category, it is hard to see how the different categories change over time. To make it easier to see the sales trends, you decide to create a chart of this data.

concept 1

Charts

1   A **chart** is visual representation of data that is used to convey information in an easy-to-understand and attractive manner. Different types of charts are used to represent data in different ways. The type of chart you create depends on the type of data you are charting and the emphasis you want the chart to impart.

     Excel 2002 can produce 14 standard types of graphs or charts, with many different sub-types for each standard type. In addition, Excel includes professionally designed built-in custom charts that include additional formatting and chart refinements. The basic chart types and how they represent data are described in the following table.

Type	Description	Type	Description
	Area charts show the magnitude of change over time by emphasizing the area under the curve created by each data series.		Radar charts display a line or area chart wrapped around a central point. Each axis represents a set of data points.
	Bar charts display data as evenly spaced bars. The categories are displayed along the Y axis and the values are displayed horizontally, placing more emphasis on comparisons and less on time.		XY (scatter) charts are used to show the relationship between two ranges of numeric data.
	Column charts display data as evenly spaced bars. They are similar to bar charts, except that categories are organized horizontally and values vertically to emphasize variation over time.		Surface charts display values as what appears to be a rubber sheet stretched over a 3-D column chart. These are useful for finding the best combination between sets of data.
	Line charts display data along a line. They are used to show changes in data over time, emphasizing time and rate of change rather than the amount of change.		Bubble charts compare sets of three values. It is like a scatter chart with the third value displayed as the size of bubble markers.
	Pie charts display data as slices of a circle or pie. They show the relationship of each value in a data series to the series as a whole. Each slice of the pie represents a single value in the series.		A stock chart is a high-low-close chart. It requires three series of values in this order.
			Cylinder charts display values with a cylindrical shape.
	Doughnut charts are similar to pie charts except that they can show more than one data series.		Cone charts display values with a conical shape.
			Pyramid charts display values with a pyramid shape.

Creating a Single Data Series Chart

All charts are drawn from data contained in a worksheet. To create a new chart, you select the worksheet range containing the data you want displayed as a chart plus any row or column headings you want used in the chart. Excel then translates the selected data into a chart based upon the shape and contents of the worksheet selection.

A chart consists of a number of parts that are important to understand so that you can identify the appropriate data to select in the worksheet.

concept 2

Chart Elements

2   A chart consists of a number of parts or elements that are used to graphically display the worksheet data. In a two-dimensional chart, the selected worksheet data is visually displayed within the X- and Y-axis boundaries. The **X axis**, also called the **category axis**, is the bottom boundary line of the chart and is used to label the data being charted, such as a point in time or a category. The left boundary line of the chart is the **Y axis**, also called the **value axis**. This axis is a numbered scale whose numbers are determined by the data used in the chart. Typically the X-axis line is the horizontal line and the Y-axis line is the vertical line. In 3-D charts there can also be an additional axis, called the **Z axis**, which allows you to compare data within a series more easily. This axis is the vertical axis. The X and Y axes delineate the horizontal surface of the chart.

Other basic elements of a 2-dimensional chart are:

Element	Description
category names	Labels that correspond to the headings for the worksheet data that is plotted along the X axis.
plot area	The area within the X- and Y-axis boundaries where the chart appears
data series	Related data points that are distinguished by different colors or patterns
data marker	A bar, dot, or other symbol that represents one number from the worksheet.
chart gridlines	Lines extending from the axis line across the plot area that make it easier to read the chart data.
legend	A box that identifies the chart data series
chart title	A descriptive label displayed above the charted data that explains the contents of the chart.
category-axis title	A descriptive label displayed along the X axis
value-axis title	A descriptive label displayed along the Y axis

The basic parts of a two-dimensional chart are shown in the figure below.

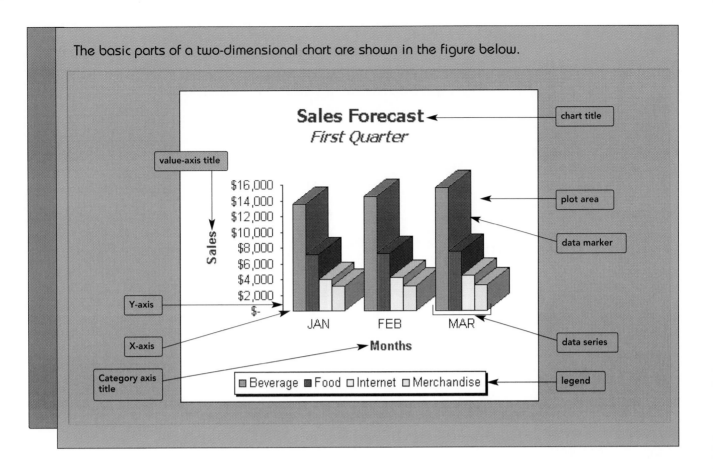

Selecting the Data to Chart

The first chart you want to create will show the total sales pattern over the three months. This chart will use the month labels in cells B9 through D9 to label the X-axis. The numbers to be charted are in cells B14 through D14. In addition, the label Total Sales in cell A14 will be used as the chart legend, making the entire range A14 through D14.

	A	B	C	D
9		JAN	FEB	MAR
10	Beverage	$ 13,600	$ 14,600	$ 15,600
11	Food	$ 7,100	$ 7,300	$ 7,500
12	Internet	$ 4,000	$ 4,200	$ 4,500
13	Merchandise	$ 3,100	$ 3,200	$ 3,300
14	Total Sales	$ 27,800	$ 29,300	$ 30,900

Notice that the two ranges, B9 through D9 and A14 through D14, are not adjacent and are not the same size. When plotting nonadjacent ranges in a chart, the selections must form a rectangular shape. To do this, the blank cell A9 will be included in the selection. You will specify the range and create the chart.

1 ● **Select A9 through D9.**

● **Hold down** Ctrl.

● **Select A14 through D14.**

Your screen should be similar to Figure 2.2

Selected non-adjacent ranges

Starts the Chart Wizard

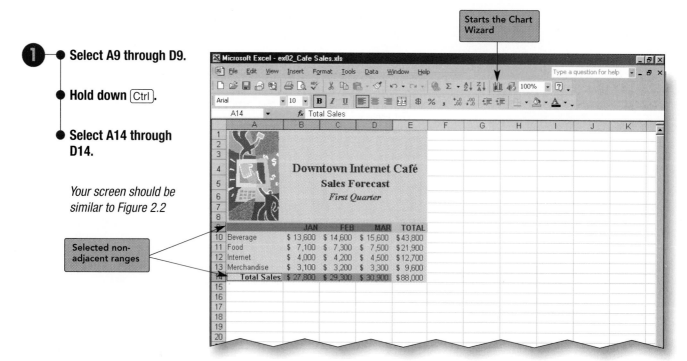

Figure 2.2

Additional Information

Office XP includes many different Wizards that provide step-by-step guidance to help you quickly perform many complicated tasks.

1 ● **Click** 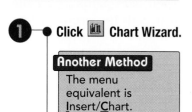 **Chart Wizard.**

Another Method

The menu equivalent is Insert/Chart.

● **Move the Chart Wizard dialog box to the right to see as much of the worksheet as possible.**

HAVING TROUBLE?

Drag the title bar of the dialog box to move it.

Your screen should be similar to Figure 2.3

Using Chart Wizard

Next you will use the Chart Wizard to help you create the chart. Chart Wizard is an interactive program that guides you through the steps to create a chart by asking you questions and creating a chart based on your responses.

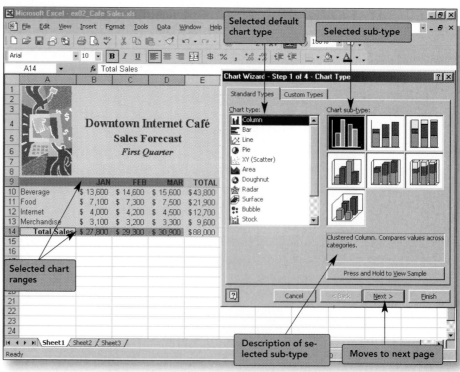

Selected default chart type

Selected sub-type

Selected chart ranges

Description of selected sub-type

Moves to next page

Figure 2.3

The first step is to select the chart type from the Chart Type list box. The default chart type is a column chart. Each type of chart includes many variations. The variations associated with the column chart type are displayed as buttons in the Chart Sub-type section of the dialog box. The default column sub-type is a clustered column. A description of the selected sub-type is displayed in the area below the sub-type buttons. You will use the default column chart type and move to the next step.

2 ● Click `Next >`.

Your screen should be similar to Figure 2.4

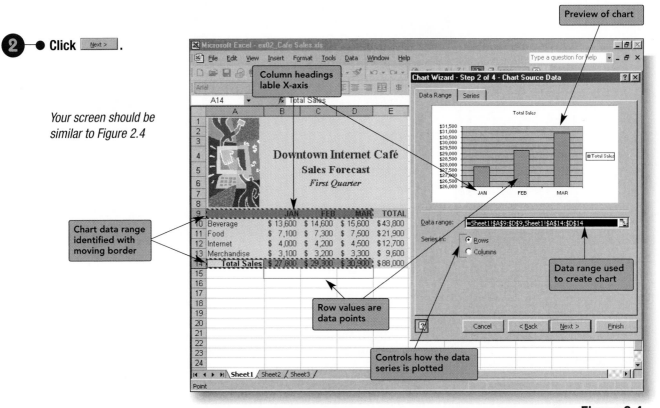

Figure 2.4

In the second Chart Wizard dialog box, you specify the data range on the worksheet you want to plot. Because you selected the data range before starting the Chart Wizard, the range is correctly displayed in the Data range text box. In addition, the data range is identified with a moving border in the worksheet. The dialog box also displays a preview of the chart that will be created using the specified data and selected chart type.

The two Series In options change how Excel plots the data series from the rows or columns in the selected data range. The orientation Excel uses by default varies depending upon the type of chart selected and the number of rows and columns defined in a series. The worksheet data range that has the greater number of rows or columns appears along the X-axis and the smaller number is charted as the data series. When the data series is an equal number of rows and columns, as it is in this case, the default is to plot the rows. The first row defines the X-axis category labels and the second row the plotted data. The content of the first cell in the second row is used as the legend text. To accept the default settings,

3 ● Click  .

● If necessary, open the Titles tab.

Your screen should be similar to Figure 2.5

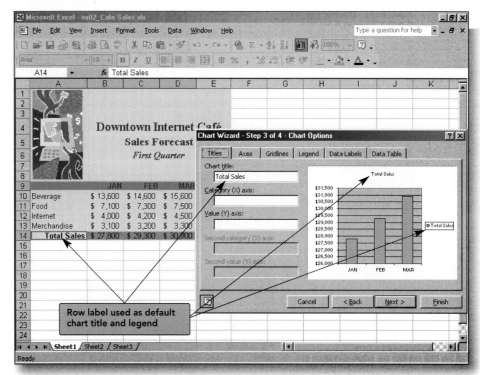

Figure 2.5

In the step 3 dialog box, you can turn some standard options on and off and change the appearance of chart elements such as a legend and titles. To clarify the data in the chart, you will add a more descriptive chart title as well as titles along the X and Y axes. As you add the titles, the preview chart will update to display the new settings.

4 ● In the Chart Title text box, replace the default title with **Downtown Internet Cafe Sales**.

● Press **Tab**.

HAVING TROUBLE?
Do not use **Enter** after typing the title text as this is the same as clicking . Click **< Back** if needed to return to the previous Wizard step.

● In the Category (X) Axis text box, enter **Months**.

● In the Value (Y) Axis text box, enter **Total Sales**.

Your screen should be similar to Figure 2.6

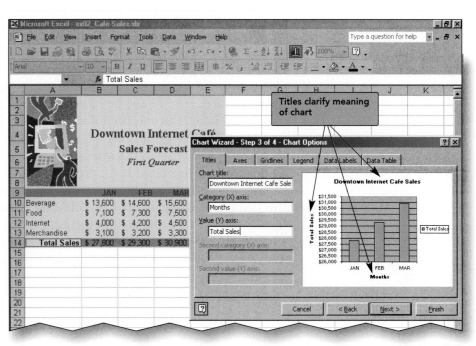

Figure 2.6

The titles clearly describe the information displayed in the chart. Now, because there is only one data range, and the category title fully explains this data, you decide to clear the display of the legend.

5 ● **Open the Legend tab.**

● **Click Show Legend to clear the checkmark.**

Your screen should be similar to Figure 2.7

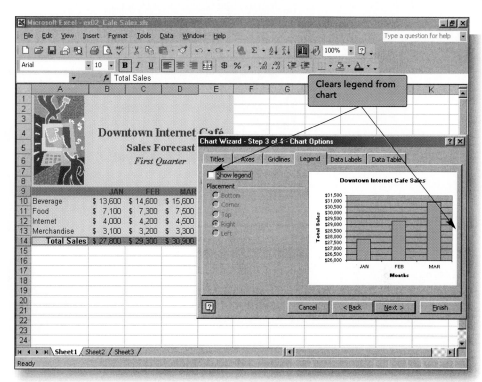

Figure 2.7

The legend is removed and the chart area resized to occupy the extra space.

6 ● **Click** `Next >`.

Your screen should be similar to Figure 2.8

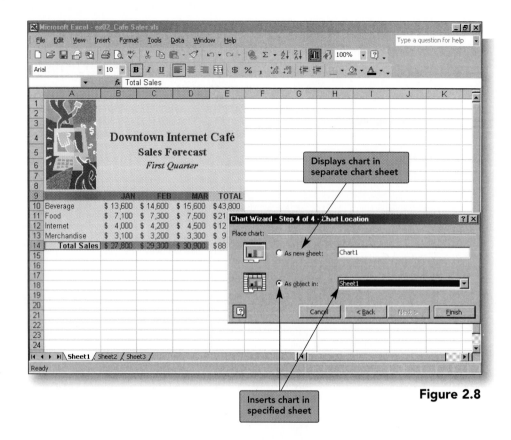

Figure 2.8

In the last step, you specify where you want the chart displayed in the worksheet. A chart can be displayed in a separate chart sheet or as an object in an existing sheet.

concept 3

Chart Objects

3 A **chart object** is a graphic object that is created using charting features included in Excel. A chart object can be inserted into a worksheet or into a special chart sheet.

Charts that are inserted into a worksheet are embedded objects. An **embedded chart** becomes part of the sheet in which it is inserted and is saved as part of the worksheet when you save the workbook file. Like all graphic objects, an embedded chart object can be sized and moved in a worksheet. A worksheet can contain multiple charts.

A chart that is inserted into a separate chart sheet is also saved with the workbook file. Only one chart can be added to a chart sheet and it cannot be sized and moved.

You would like this chart displayed as an object in the Sales worksheet. This is the default selection. You have provided all the information needed by the Wizard to create the chart.

7 ● Click ⎣ Finish ⎦.

● **If necessary, move the Chart toolbar to the bottom right corner of the window.**

HAVING TROUBLE?
If your chart toolbar is not automatically displayed, open it by selecting it from the toolbar shortcut menu. Move toolbars by dragging the title bar of the floating toolbar or the move handle ⫶ of a docked toolbar.

Your screen should be similar to Figure 2.9

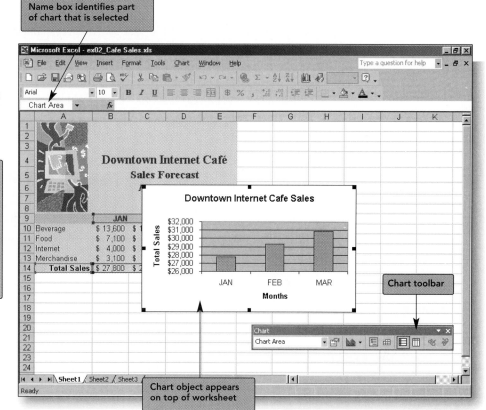

Figure 2.9

The chart with the settings you specified using the Chart Wizard is displayed on the worksheet. It covers some of the worksheet data because it is a separate chart object that can be moved and sized within the worksheet.

Notice that the Name box displays Chart Area. The Name box identifies the part of the chart that is selected, in this case the entire chart and all its contents.

Also notice that the Chart toolbar is automatically displayed whenever a chart is selected. The Chart toolbar contains buttons for the most frequently used chart editing and formatting features. These buttons are identified below.

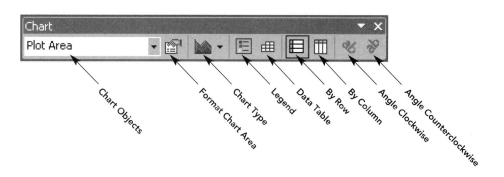

Moving and Sizing a Chart

You want to move the chart so that it is displayed to the right of the worksheet data. In addition, you want to increase the size of the chart. A selected chart object is moved by pointing to it and dragging it to a new location. When you move the mouse pointer into the selected chart object, it will display a chart tip to advise you of the chart element that will be affected by your action. When moving the entire chart, the chart tip must display Chart Area.

- **Move the mouse pointer to different elements within the chart and note the different chart ScreenTips that appear.**

- **With the chart ScreenTip displaying Chart Area, drag the chart object so that the upper-left corner is in cell F4.**

Additional Information

The mouse pointer changes to a ⊕ while dragging to move an object.

Your screen should be similar to Figure 2.10

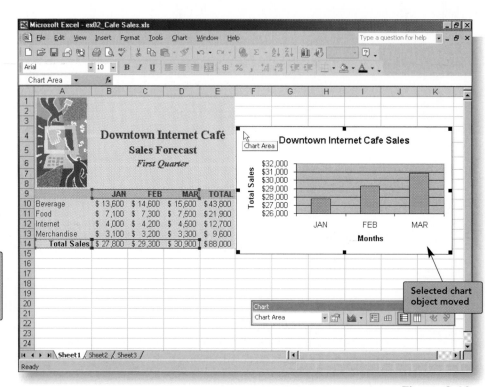

Figure 2.10

Next you will increase the size of the chart by dragging a sizing handle. This is the same as sizing a graphic object.

2 ● Point to the lower-center sizing handle, hold down Alt, and drag the chart box down until it is displayed over cells F4 through K20.

Your screen should be similar to Figure 2.11

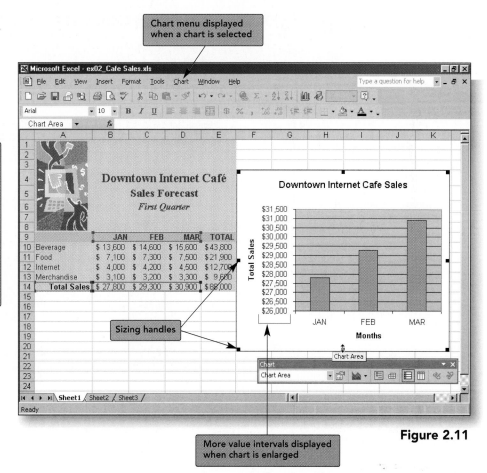

Chart menu displayed when a chart is selected

Sizing handles

More value intervals displayed when chart is enlarged

Figure 2.11

As you enlarge the chart, more value intervals are displayed along the Y axis, making the data in the chart easier to read. Additionally, the fonts in the chart scale proportionally as you resize the chart. The chart includes standard formats that are applied to the selected chart sub-type, such as a shaded background in the plot area and blue columns.

It is now easy to see how the worksheet data you selected is represented in the chart. Each column represents the total sales for that month in row 14. The month labels in row 9 have been used to label the X axis category labels. The range or scale of values along the Y axis is determined from the data in the worksheet. The upper limit is the maximum value in the worksheet rounded upward to the next highest interval.

Changing the Chart Location

Although this chart compares the total sales for the three months, you decide you are more interested in seeing a comparison for the sales categories. You could delete this chart simply by pressing Delete while the chart is selected. Instead, however, you will move it to a separate worksheet in case you want to refer to it again.

When a chart is selected, the Data menu changes to the Chart menu. In addition, many of the commands under the other menus change to commands that apply to charts only. The Chart menu contains commands that can be used to modify the chart.

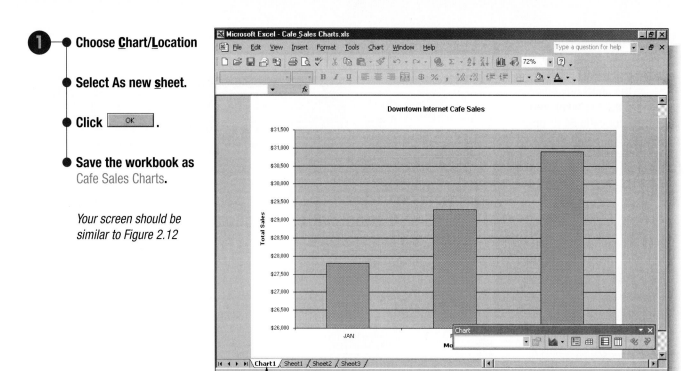

- **1** • Choose **Chart/Location**

  • Select **As new sheet.**

  • Click **OK**.

  • Save the workbook as Cafe Sales Charts.

  Your screen should be similar to Figure 2.12

Figure 2.12

Chart displayed in separate sheet

The column chart is now an object displayed in a separate chart sheet. Generally, you display a chart in a chart sheet when you want the chart displayed separately from the associated worksheet data. The chart is still automatically linked to the worksheet data from which it was created.

The new chart sheet named Chart1 was inserted to the left of the worksheet, Sheet1. The Chart sheet is the active sheet, or the sheet you are currently viewing and working in.

Creating a Multiple Data Series Chart

Now you are ready to continue your analysis of sales trends. You want to create a second chart to display the sales data for each category for the three months. You could create a separate chart for each category and then compare the charts; however, to make the comparisons between the categories easier, you will display all the categories on a single chart.

The data for the three months for the four categories is in cells B10 through D13. The month headings (X-axis data series) are in cells B9 through D9, and the legend text is in the range A10 through A13.

1 ● **Click the Sheet1 tab.**

● **Select A9 through D13.**

● **Click** 📊 **Chart Wizard.**

● **Click** [Next >] .

Your screen should be similar to Figure 2.13

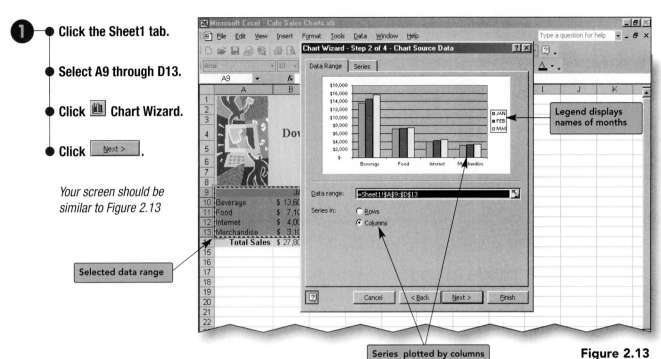

Selected data range

Series plotted by columns

Legend displays names of months

Figure 2.13

When plotting the data for this chart, the Chart Wizard selected Columns as the data series orientation because there are fewer columns than rows in the data range. This time, however, you want to change the data series to Rows so that the months are along the X axis.

2 ● **Select Rows.**

Your screen should be similar to Figure 2.14

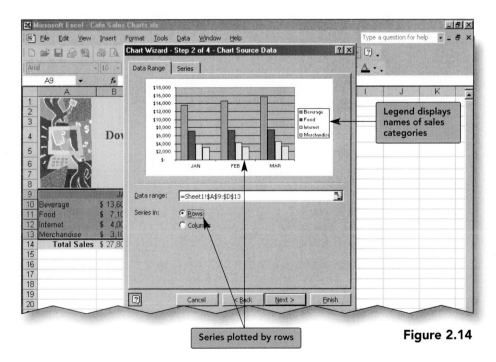

Legend displays names of sales categories

Series plotted by rows

Figure 2.14

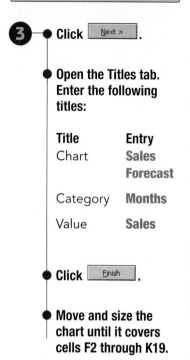
The sample chart is redrawn with the new orientation. The column chart now compares the sales by month rather than by category. The Legend displays the names of the sales categories. Next, you will specify the chart titles and finish the chart.

3 • Click Next >.

• Open the Titles tab. Enter the following titles:

Title	Entry
Chart	**Sales Forecast**
Category	**Months**
Value	**Sales**

• Click Finish.

• Move and size the chart until it covers cells F2 through K19.

Your screen should be similar to Figure 2.15

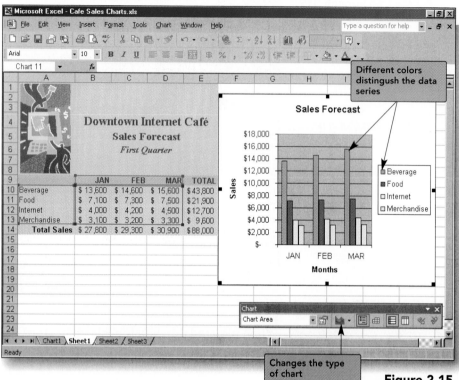

Figure 2.15

A different column color identifies each data series and the legend identifies the categories. The column chart shows that sales in all categories are increasing, with the greatest increase occurring in beverage sales.

Changing the Chart Type

Next you would like to see how the same data displayed in the column chart would look as a line chart. A line chart displays data as a line and is commonly used to show trends over time. This is easily done by changing the chart type using the [image] Chart Type button on the Chart toolbar.

1 ● **Open the** 🖼 **Chart Type drop-down list.**

Another Method

The menu equivalent is Chart/Chart Type.

● **Click** 📈 **Line Chart.**

Your screen should be similar to Figure 2.16

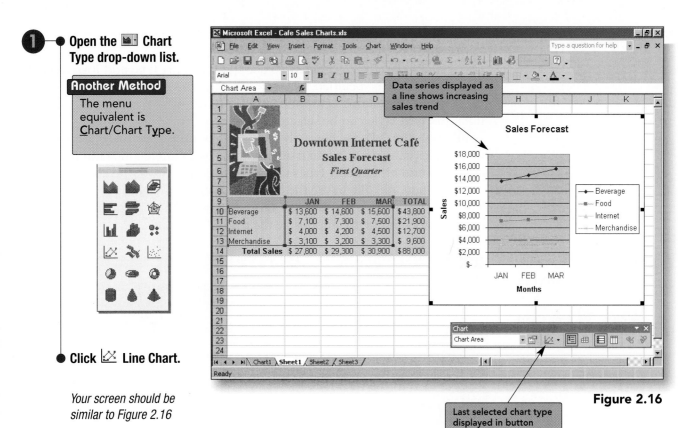

Figure 2.16

The line chart shows the increasing sales trend from month to month. Notice the 🖼 Chart Type button displays a line chart, reflecting the last-selected chart type. You still don't find this chart very interesting so you will change it to a 3-D bar chart next.

2 ● **Open the** 🖼 **Chart Type drop-down list.**

● **Click** 📊 **3-D Bar Chart.**

Your screen should be similar to Figure 2.17

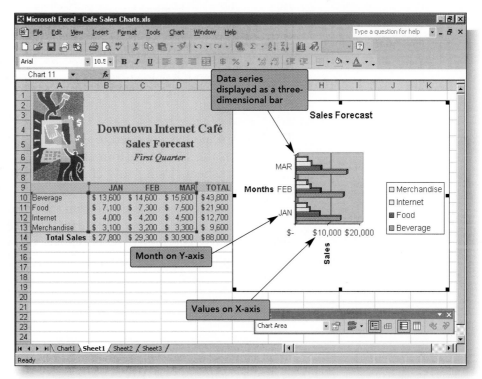

Figure 2.17

The 3-D bar chart reverses the X and Y axes and displays the data series as a three-dimensional bar.

As you can see, it is very easy to change the chart type and format once the data series are specified. The same data can be displayed in many different ways. Depending upon the emphasis you want the chart to make, a different chart style can be selected.

Although the 3-D bar chart shows the sales trends for the three months for the sales categories, again it does not look very interesting. You decide to look at several other chart types to see if you can improve the appearance.

First you would like to see the data represented as an area chart. An area chart represents data the same as a line chart but, in addition, it shades the area below each line to emphasize the degree of change.

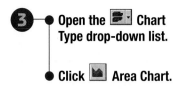

● **Open the [icon] Chart Type drop-down list.**

● **Click [icon] Area Chart.**

Your screen should be similar to Figure 2.18

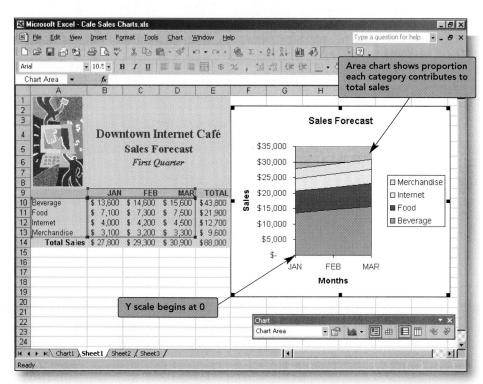

Figure 2.18

The Y-axis scale has changed to reflect the new range of data. The new Y-axis range is the sum of the four categories, or the same as the total number in the worksheet. Using this chart type, you can see the magnitude of change each category contributes to the total sales in each month.

Again you decide this is not the emphasis you want to show and will continue looking at other types of charts. Because not all chart types are available from the Chart Type drop-down list, you will use the Chart Type menu option in the Chart menu instead.

4 ● **Choose Chart/Chart Type.**

Your screen should be similar to Figure 2.19

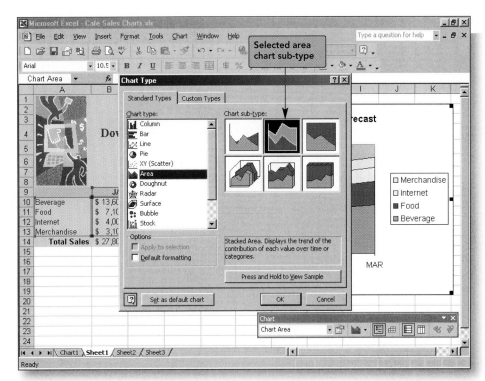

Figure 2.19

The Chart Type dialog box contains the same options as the Chart Wizard— Step 1 dialog box. The current chart type, Area, is the selected option. You want to see how this data will look as a stacked column chart.

5 ● **Select** ▐▌▌ **Column.**

● **Select** ▦ **Stacked column with a 3-D visual effect.**

● **Click and hold**

Press and Hold to View Sample .

Your screen should be similar to Figure 2.20

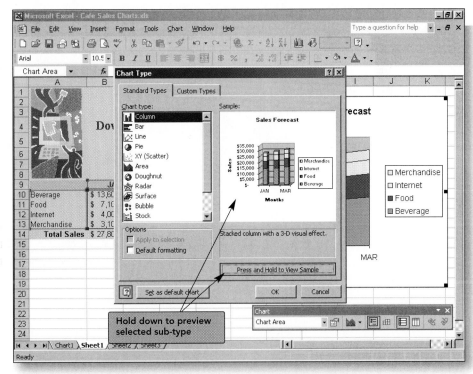

Figure 2.20

The sample chart is redrawn showing the data as a stacked-column chart. This type of chart also shows the proportion of each sales category to the total sales. To see what other types of charts are available,

Creating a Multiple Data Series Chart   **EX2.21**

6 ● **Open the Custom Types tab.**

● **Click 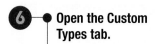 Area Blocks.**

Your screen should be similar to Figure 2.21

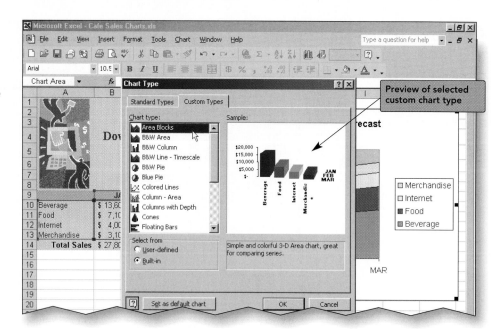

Figure 2.21

The Sample area shows how the data you selected for the chart will appear in this style. Custom charts are based upon standard types that are enhanced with additional display settings and custom formatting. Although this is interesting, you feel the data is difficult to read.

7 ● **Select several other custom chart types to see how the data appears in the Sample area.**

● **Select 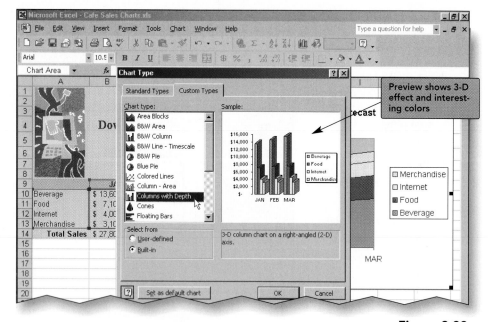 Columns with Depth.**

Your screen should be similar to Figure 2.22

Figure 2.22

This chart shows the sales for each category for each month with more interesting colors and three-dimensional depth.

8 ● Click ▭ OK ▭ .

Your screen should be similar to Figure 2.23

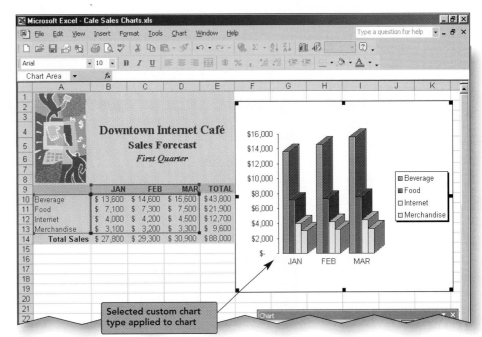

Figure 2.23

Adding Chart Titles

Unfortunately, when applying a custom chart type, the chart titles are deleted and you need to add them again.

1 ● Choose **C**hart/Chart Opt**i**ons.

● In the Titles tab, enter the following titles:

Title	Entry
Chart	**Sales Forecast**
Category	**Months**
Value	**Sales**

Your screen should be similar to Figure 2.24

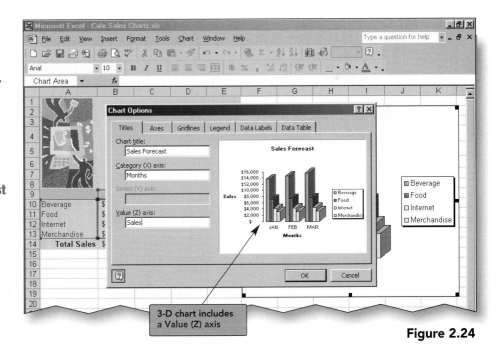

Figure 2.24

Notice that this time instead of entering the Value axis data in the Y axis, you entered it in the Z axis. This is because the Y axis is used as a Series axis on a three-dimensional chart. This three-dimensional chart only has one series of data so the Y axis is not used.

Moving the Legend

While looking at the preview chart, you decide to move the legend below the X axis.

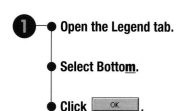

● **Open the Legend tab.**

● **Select Botto<u>m</u>.**

● **Click** OK **.**

Your screen should be similar to Figure 2.25

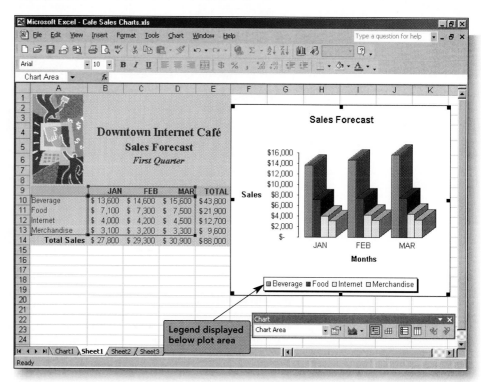

Figure 2.25

The legend is centered below the plot area of the chart and resized to fit the space.

Formatting Chart Elements

Next you want to improve the appearance of the chart by applying formatting to the different chart parts. All the different parts of a chart are separate objects. Because a chart consists of many separate objects, it is a group.

concept 4

Groups

4 A **group** is two or more objects that behave as a single object when moved or sized. A chart consists of many separate objects. For example, the chart title is a single object within the chart object. Some of the objects in a chart are also groups that consist of other objects. For example, the legend is a group object consisting of separate items, each identifying a different data series.

Other objects in a chart are the axis lines, a data series, a data marker, the entire plot area, or the entire chart.

The first formatting change you want to make is to improve the appearance of the chart title. An entire group or each object in a group can be individually selected and then formatted or edited. By selecting the entire group, you can format all objects within the group at once. Alternatively, you can select an object within a group and format it individually.

1 ● **Click on the chart title to select it.**

Your screen should be similar to Figure 2.26

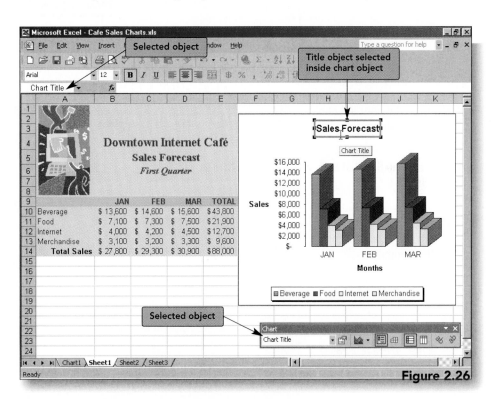

Figure 2.26

The title object is surrounded by a dotted border indicating it is a selected object and that the text inside it can be modified. In addition, the Name box and Chart Objects button display Chart Title as the selected chart object.

As different objects in the chart are selected, the commands on the Format menu change to commands that can be used on the selected object. In addition, the 🔲 Format Object button on the Chart toolbar can be used to format the selected object.

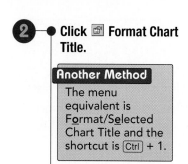

2 ● Click 📰 **Format Chart Title.**

> **Another Method**
>
> The menu equivalent is **F**ormat/**Se**lected Chart Title and the shortcut is Ctrl + 1.

● **Open the Font tab.**

Your screen should be similar to Figure 2.27

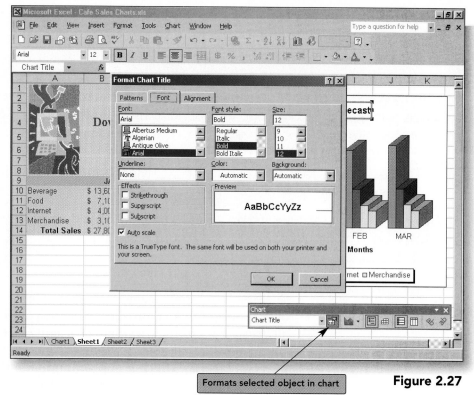

Formats selected object in chart

Figure 2.27

The Format Chart Title dialog box is used to change the patterns, font, and placement of the title.

3 ● Scroll the Font list and select Tahoma.

● Scroll the Size list and select 14.

● Open the Color list and select Indigo (1st row, 7th column).

● Click [OK].

Your screen should be similar to Figure 2.28

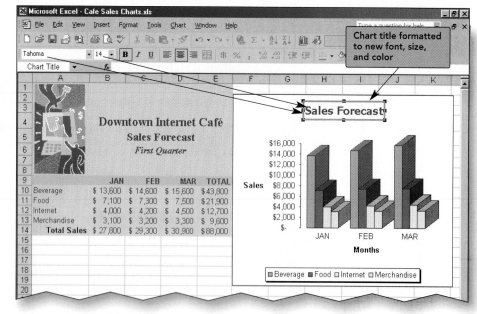

Chart title formatted to new font, size, and color

Figure 2.28

Next you want to change the color of the axis titles. A quicker way to make many formatting changes is to use the Formatting toolbar buttons.

4 • **Click the category-axis title Months.**

• **Open the** 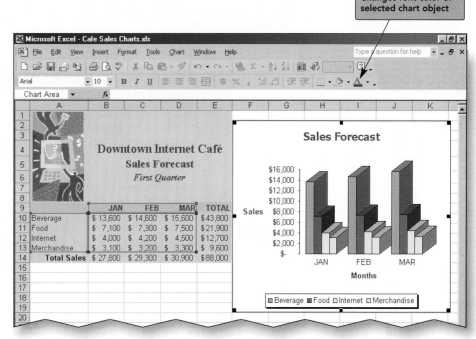 **Font Color palette and change the color to Indigo.**

• **Change the color of the Sales title to Indigo in the same manner.**

• **Click outside the title to deselect it.**

Your screen should be similar to Figure 2.29

Figure 2.29

Changing Orientation

You also want to change the orientation of the Sales title along the axis so that it is parallel with the axis line. To do this, you will rotate the label 90 degrees. You can quickly select a chart object and open the related Format dialog box by double-clicking the object.

1 • **Double-click the Sales title to open the Format Axis Title dialog box.**

• **Open the Alignment tab.**

• **Drag the Orientation indicator line upward to rotate the text 90 degrees.**

Additional Information

You can use ✍ Angle Text Downward or ✍ Angle Text Upward on the Chart toolbar to quickly change the angle of a label to 45 degrees.

Your screen should be similar to Figure 2.30

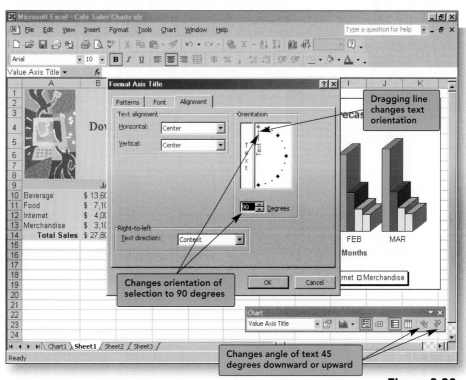

Figure 2.30

You could also enter a positive number in the Degrees box to rotate the selection from lower left to upper right or a negative number to rotate text in the opposite direction. Alternatively, you can use the Degrees scroll buttons to increase and decrease the degrees.

● Click [OK].

Your screen should be similar to Figure 2.31

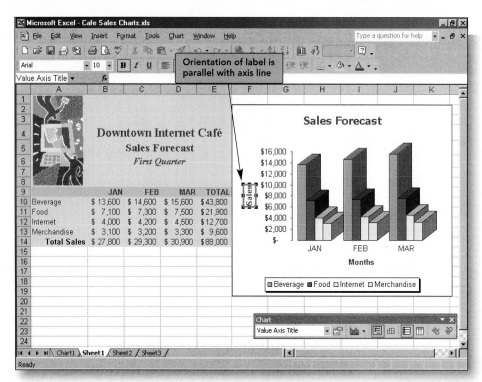

Figure 2.31

The Sales label is now displayed parallel with the Y-axis line.

Finally, you want to add a second line to the chart title. You want the subtitle to be in a smaller font size and italicized. You can select individual sections of text in an object and apply formatting to them just as you would format any other text entry.

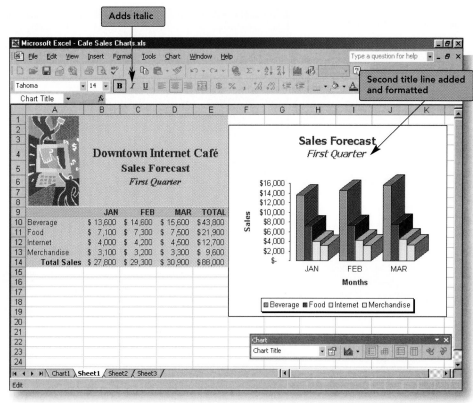

3
- Select the chart title.

- Click at the end of the title to place the insertion point.

- Press ←Enter.

- Type **First Quarter**.

- Drag to select the words First Quarter.

- Click *I* Italic.

- Choose 12 from the 14 ▾ Font Size drop-down list.

- Click in the title to deselect it.

- Save the workbook using the same file name.

Your screen should be similar to Figure 2.32

Figure 2.32

Creating a New Chart from an Existing Chart

Now you want to create another chart that will emphasize the sales trend for the Internet connection data series. This chart will use the same data series and titles as the current chart. Rather than recreate much of the same chart for the new chart, you will create a copy of the column chart and then modify it. The original chart remains in the workbook unchanged.

Copying a Chart

Copying a chart object is the same as copying any other Excel data or objects.

1 ● **Select the entire chart.**

> **HAVING TROUBLE?**
> When the chart ScreenTip displays Chart Area, click on the chart.

● **Click** 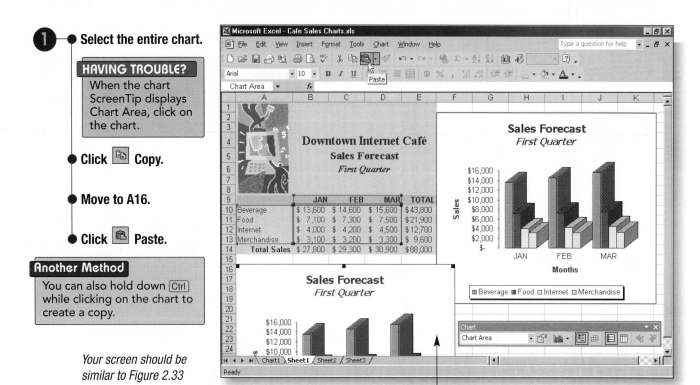 **Copy.**

● **Move to A16.**

● **Click** **Paste.**

> **Another Method**
> You can also hold down Ctrl while clicking on the chart to create a copy.

Your screen should be similar to Figure 2.33

Copy of chart

Figure 2.33

2 ● **Change the location of the new chart to a new chart sheet (Chart2).**

> **HAVING TROUBLE?**
> Select the chart and choose Chart/Location.

● **Move to Sheet1.**

Creating a Combination Chart

To emphasize the Internet data, you want to display the data series as a line and all other data series as columns. This type of chart is called a **combination chart**. It uses two or more chart types to emphasize different information. Because you cannot mix a three-dimensional chart type with a one-dimensional chart type, you first need to change the chart type for the entire chart to a standard one-dimensional column chart. Then you can change the Internet data series to a line.

1 ● Select the chart and change the chart type to Column Chart.

● Click on one of the yellow columns to select the Internet data series.

HAVING TROUBLE?

Sometimes when there are many objects close together, it is easier to select the object from the Chart Objects drop-down list.

● From the 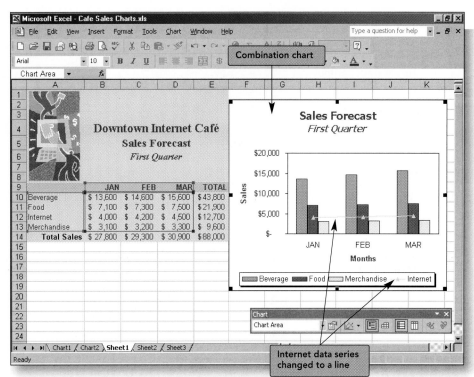 Chart Type drop-down menu, select ⟋ Line.

Your screen should be similar to Figure 2.34

Figure 2.34

A combination chart makes it easy to see comparisons between groups of data or to show different types of data in a single chart. In this case, you can now easily pick out the Internet sales from the other sales categories.

Adding Data Labels

You would like to display data labels containing the actual numbers plotted for the Internet sales on the combination chart.

concept 5

Data Labels

5 **Data labels** provide additional information about a data marker. They can consist of the value of the marker, the name of the data series or category, a percent value, or a bubble size. The different types of data labels that are available depend on the type of chart and the data that is plotted.

Value data labels are helpful when the values are large and you want to know the exact value

for one data series. Data labels that display a name are helpful when the size of the chart is large and it is hard to tell what value the data point is over. The percent data label is used when you want to display the percent of each series on charts that show parts of the whole. Bubble size is used on bubble charts to help the reader quickly see how the different bubbles vary in size.

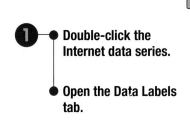

1 ● **Double-click the Internet data series.**

● **Open the Data Labels tab.**

Your screen should be similar to Figure 2.35

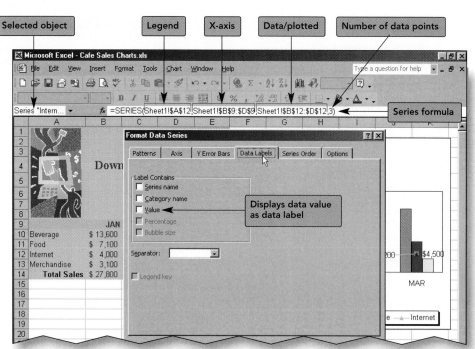

Figure 2.35

Notice that the formula bar displays a **series formula**. This formula links the chart object to the source worksheet, Sheet1. The formula contains four arguments: a reference to the cell that includes the data series name (used in the legend), references to the cells that contain the categories (X-axis numbers), references to the numbers plotted, and an integer that specifies the number of data series plotted.

2 ● **Select Value.**

● **Click** OK .

Your screen should be similar to Figure 2.36

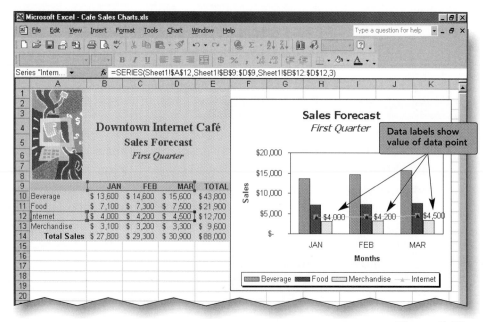

Figure 2.36

Data labels containing the actual values for Internet sales are displayed next to the data points on the line in the chart.

Changing Data Series Fill Colors

To enhance the appearance of a chart, you can change the format of the data series from the default colors to colors of your choice. As the yellow line is difficult to see on a white background, you want to change the color of the line to make it more visible.

1 ● **Double-click the Internet data series line to open the Format Data Series dialog box.**

● **Open the Patterns tab.**

Your screen should be similar to Figure 2.37

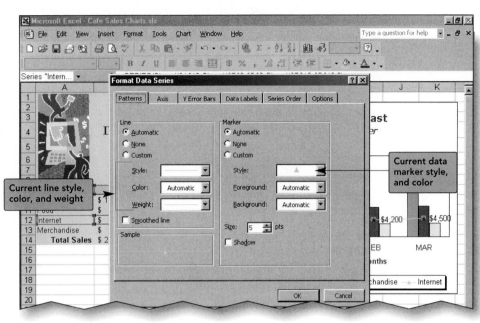

Figure 2.37

The current line and data marker settings are displayed in the Patterns tab. The Sample area shows how your selections will appear.

2 ● **Open the Line Color palette and change the color to blue.**

● **Open the Line Weight drop-down list and increase the line weight setting by one.**

● **Change the Foreground and Background marker color to blue.**

● **Click ▭ OK ▭.**

Your screen should be similar to Figure 2.38

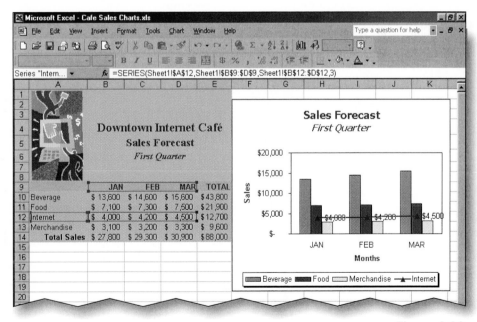

Figure 2.38

Changing Plot Area Colors

Although changing the line color increased its visibility, you think that changing the color of the plot area would also help. You could use the Format Plot Area dialog box to change the color or the ▨ Fill Color button on the Formatting toolbar.

1
- Select the plot area.
- Open the  Fill Color drop-down list.
- Choose tan.

Your screen should be similar to Figure 2.39

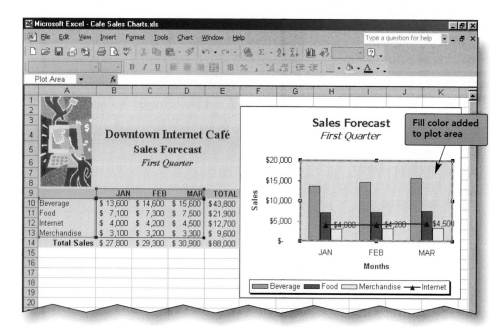

Figure 2.39

Changing Worksheet Data

After checking the worksheet and reconsidering the amounts you have budgeted for the different categories, you now feel that you have underestimated the increase in Internet sales. You are planning to heavily promote the Internet aspect of the Café and anticipate that Internet usage will increase dramatically in February and March and then level off in the following months. You want to change the worksheet to reflect this increase.

1
- Change the February Internet sales value to 6000.
- Change the March Internet sales value to 12000.

Your screen should be similar to Figure 2.40

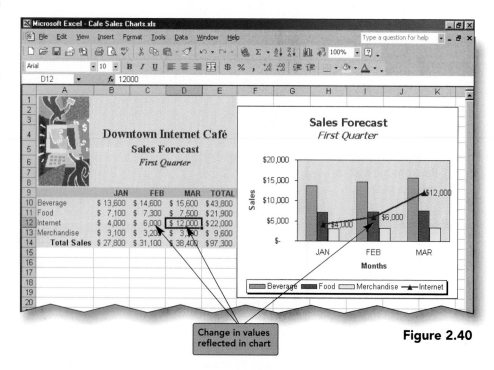

Change in values reflected in chart

Figure 2.40

The worksheet has been recalculated and all charts that reference those worksheet cells have been redrawn to reflect the change in the data for the Internet sales. Since the chart document is linked to the source data, changes to the source data are automatically reflected in the chart.

2 — ● **Look at the charts in the Chart1 and Chart2 sheets to see how they have changed to reflect the change in data.**

Your screen should be similar to Figure 2.41

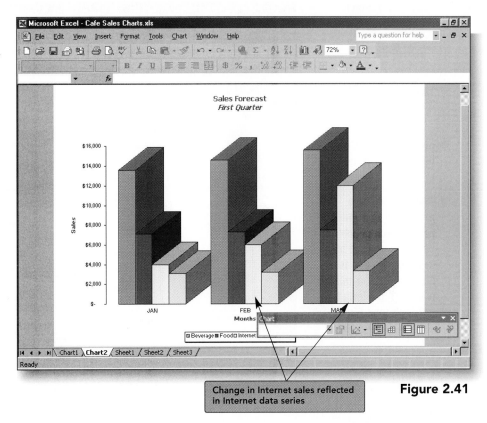

Change in Internet sales reflected in Internet data series

Figure 2.41

The Internet Sales column reflects the change in data in both charts.

Adding a Text Box

Sometimes the information you want to convey in a chart is complicated and may need clarification. In this case, although the chart reflects the Internet sales changes you made in the worksheet, it does not identify the reason for the increase. This information can be entered in a text box.

concept 6

Text Box

6 A **text box** is a rectangular object in which you type text. Text boxes can be added to a sheet or a chart object. To add it to a chart, the chart object must be selected first, otherwise the text box is added to the worksheet. A text box that is part of a chart object can only be sized and moved within the chart object. If you move the chart object, the text box moves with it because it is part of the group. If you do not add it to the chart, it will not move as part of the chart if you move the chart to another location.

Text that is entered in a text box wraps to fit within the boundaries of the text box. This feature is called **word wrap** and eliminates the need to press [Enter] to end a line. If you change the size and shape of the text box, the text automatically rewraps on the line to adjust to the new size.

You will add a text box containing the text Internet Promotion to draw attention to the increase in Internet sales. A text box is created using the  Text Box button on the Drawing toolbar.

1 ● **Switch to Sheet1.**

● **Select the chart.**

● **Click** 🖌 **Drawing (on the Standard toolbar).**

● **Click** 📄 **Text Box (on the Drawing toolbar).**

● **Move the mouse pointer to the space above the February columns of data and drag to create a text box that is approximately 1 1/2 inch by 1/2 inch (see Figure 2.42).**

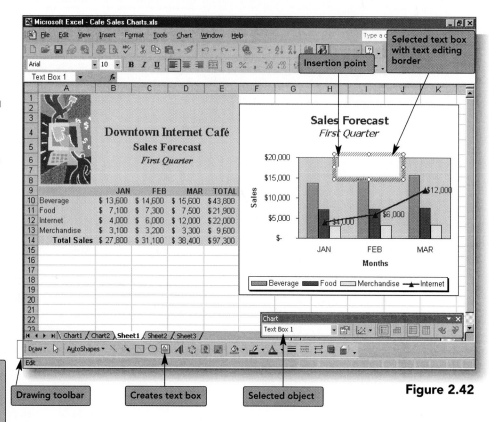

Figure 2.42

Drawing toolbar   Creates text box   Selected object

> **Additional Information**
> The mouse pointer appears as ↓, indicating a text box will be created as you drag the mouse.

Your screen should be similar to Figure 2.42

> **Additional Information**
> A dotted border around a selected object indicates that you can format the box itself. Clicking the hatched border changes it to dotted border.

The text box is a selected object and is surrounded with a hatched border that indicates you can enter, delete, select, and format the text inside the box. It also displays an insertion point indicating that it is waiting for you to enter the text. As you type the text in the text box, do not be concerned if all the text is not visible within the text box. You will resize the box if needed to display the entire entry.

2 ● Type **Effects of Internet Promotion.**

● **If necessary, adjust the size of the text box by dragging the sizing handles until it is just large enough to fully display the text on two lines.**

● **Click outside the text box to deselect it.**

Your screen should be similar to Figure 2.43

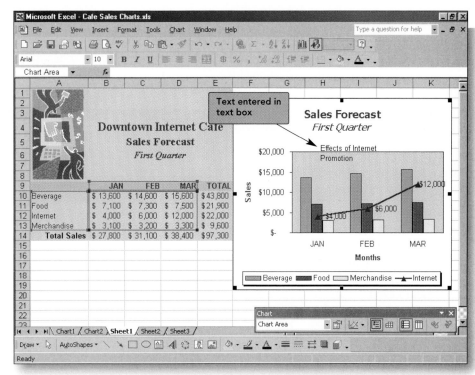

Figure 2.43

The text in the text box is difficult to read because it overlaps the plot area and the box does not include a border line or fill color. To make it stand out better, you will add a fill color to the text box.

3 ● **Select the text box.**

● **Click the hatched text box border to turn off text editing (the insertion point disappears).**

Additional Information

The text box border is dotted and the insertion point is not displayed, indicating you can edit the text box.

● **Open the** 🎨▾ **Fill Color drop-down list and select Indigo.**

Additional Information

You can use the 🎨▾ and 🅰▾ buttons on either the Formatting or Drawing toolbars.

● **From the** 🅰▾ **Font Color list, select White.**

● **Readjust the size of the text box and move it to the position displayed in Figure 2.44.**

Your screen should be similar to Figure 2.44

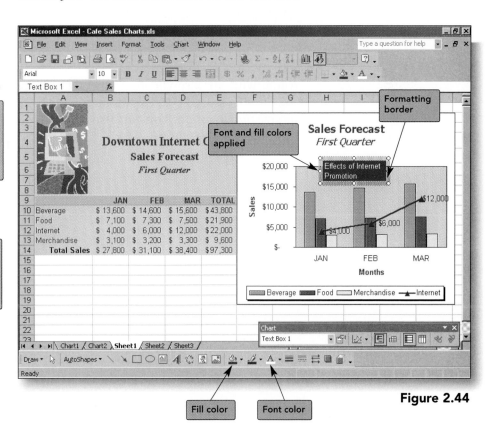

Fill color   Font color

Figure 2.44

Adding Arrows

Next you want to draw an arrow from the text box to the Internet data series line. Like a text box, an arrow is a separate object that can be added to a worksheet or a chart.

1 ● Click  Arrow (on the Drawing toolbar).

Additional Information

The mouse pointer appears as a +.

● To draw the arrow, click on the lower-right corner of the text box and drag to the Internet line. (See Figure 2.45)

Additional Information

If you hold down ⇧Shift while dragging, a straight horizontal line is drawn.

Your screen should be similar to Figure 2.45

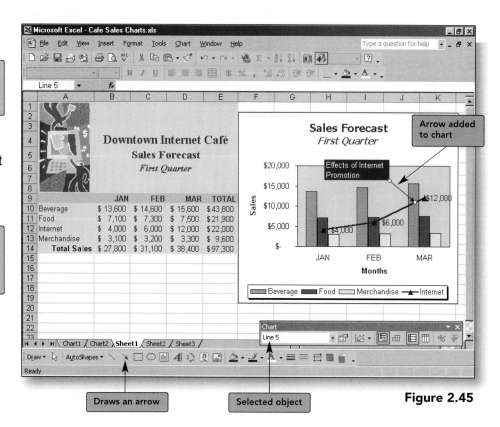

Draws an arrow

Selected object

Figure 2.45

A line with an arrowhead at the end is displayed. The arrow is automatically a selected object. The handles at both ends of the arrow let you adjust its size and location. You can also change the color and weight of the line to make it stand out more.

2 • If necessary, move and size the arrow to adjust its position as in Figure 2.46.

• Click ✎ Line Color and select Indigo.

• Click ▤ Line Style and increase the line weight to 1 1/2 point.

• Deselect the arrow.

• Click 🖫 Save.

Your screen should be similar to Figure 2.46

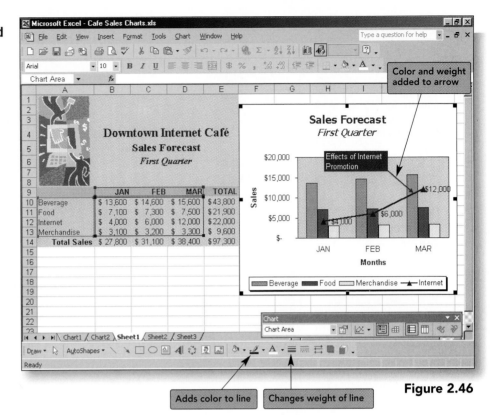

Adds color to line   Changes weight of line

Figure 2.46

Creating and Formatting a Pie Chart

The last chart you will make will use the Total worksheet data in column E. You want to see what proportion each type of sales are of all sales for the quarter. The best chart for this purpose is a pie chart.

A pie chart compares parts to the whole in a similar manner to a stacked-column chart. However, in pie charts, there are no axes. Instead, the worksheet data that is charted is displayed as slices in a circle or pie. Each slice is displayed as a percentage of the total.

Selecting the Pie Chart Data

The use of X (category) and data series settings in a pie chart is different from their use in a column or line chart. The X series labels the slices of the pie rather than the X axis. The data series is used to create the slices in the pie. Only one data series can be specified in a pie chart.

The row labels in column A will label the slices and the total values in column E will be used as the data series.

In addition to creating a chart using the Wizard, you can create a chart by selecting the chart type from the Chart Type toolbar button after the data series has been selected.

Additional Information

You can also create a chart using the default chart type (column) in a new chart sheet by selecting the data range and pressing F11.

1 ● Select A10 through A13 and E10 through E13.

HAVING TROUBLE?
Hold down Ctrl while selecting nonadjacent ranges.

● If necessary, display the Chart toolbar.

● Open the ⊞ Chart Type drop-down menu and choose ◉ 3-D Pie Chart.

Your screen should be similar to Figure 2.47

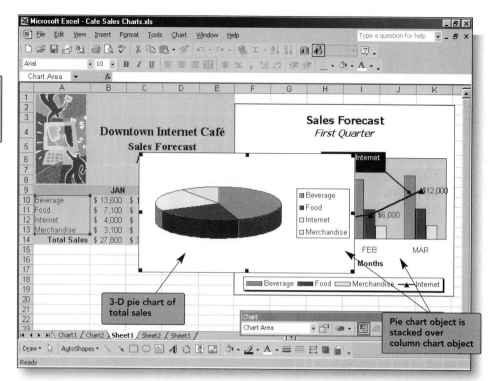

Figure 2.47

A three-dimensional pie chart is drawn in the worksheet. Each value in the data series is displayed as a slice of the pie chart. The size of the slice represents the proportion each sales category is of total sales.

As objects are added to the worksheet, they automatically **stack** in individual layers. The stacking order is apparent when objects overlap. Stacking allows you to create different effects by overlapping objects. Because you can rearrange the stacking order, you do not have to add or create the objects in the order in which you want them to appear.

2 ● Move the combination chart to top-align with cell A16 below the worksheet data.

● Move and size the pie chart to be displayed over cells F1 through K14.

Additional Information
Hold down Alt while moving to snap the chart to the cells.

Your screen should be similar to Figure 2.48

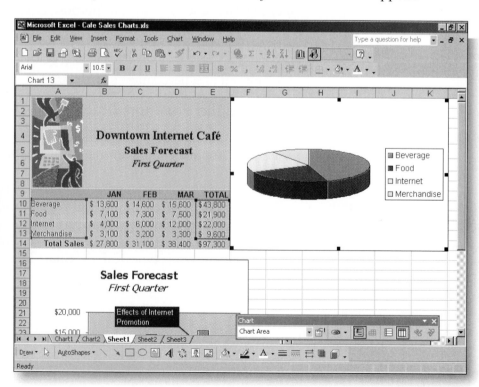

Figure 2.48

Formatting the Pie Chart

To clarify the meaning of the chart, you need to add a chart title. In addition, you want to turn off the legend and display data labels instead to label the slices of the pie.

1 ● **Choose Chart/Chart Options.**

● **Open the Titles tab.**

● **In the Chart Title text box, enter Total Sales by Category.**

● **Open the Legend tab and clear the Show Legend option.**

> **Another Method**
> You can also click
> 🔲 Legend to turn on/off the display of the legend.

● **Open the Data Labels tab and select the Category name and Percentage options.**

● **Click [OK].**

Your screen should be similar to Figure 2.49

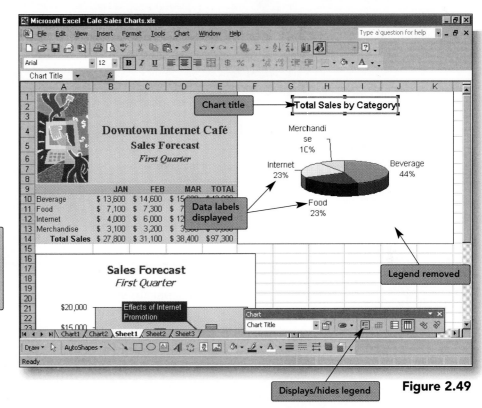

Figure 2.49

The pie chart is redrawn to show the data labels and percents. The data label text box size is based on the size of the chart and the text is appropriately sized to fit in the box. Because the default size of data labels is a little too large, the entire Merchandise label does not appear on one line. To fix this, you will change the font of the data label text. You also want to enhance the appearance of the data labels and title.

Change the title to Tahoma, 14 pt and Indigo.

Select the data labels.

Change the font to Arial Narrow.

Change the font color to Indigo.

Your screen should be similar to Figure 2.50

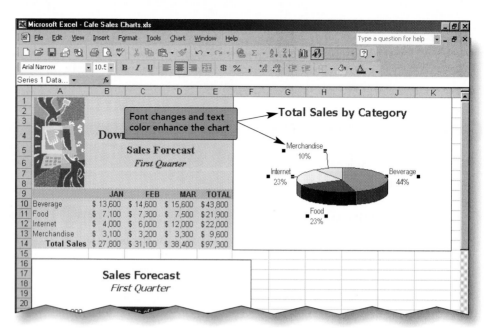

Figure 2.50

Exploding and Rotating the Pie

Next, you want to separate slightly or **explode** the Internet slice of the pie to emphasize the data in that category.

Select the Internet slice.

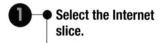

HAVING TROUBLE?

To select an object within a group, select the group first and then select the object within the group. Selection handles surround the selected object.

Drag the selected slice away from the pie.

Additional Information

If all slices on the pie are selected, dragging one slice explodes all slices at the same time.

Your screen should be similar to Figure 2.51

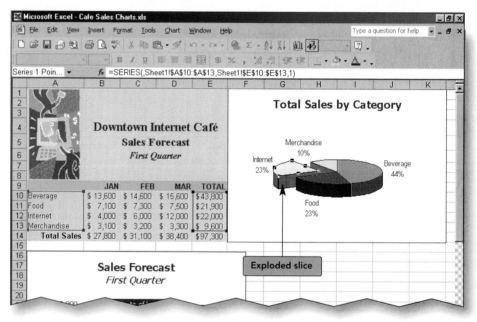

Figure 2.51

The slice is separated from the rest of the pie chart. You also want to change the position of the Internet slice so that it is toward the front of the pie. When a pie chart is created, the first data point is placed to the right of the middle at the top of the chart. The rest of the data points are placed in order to the right until the circle is complete. To change the order in which the slices are displayed, you can rotate the pie chart.

2 ● **Double-click the Internet data series slice.**

● **Open the Options tab.**

● **Change the Angle of first slice setting to 180 degrees.**

● **Click** OK .

Your screen should be similar to Figure 2.52

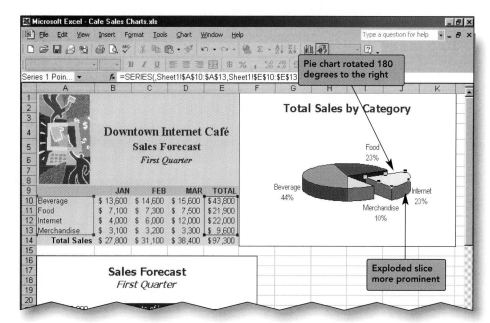

Figure 2.52

The entire pie chart has rotated 180 degrees to the right and now the Internet data slice appears toward the front of the chart.

Applying Patterns and Color

The last change you would like to make is to add patterns to the pie chart data points. As you have seen, when Excel creates a chart each data series (or data point in the case of a pie chart) is automatically displayed in a different color. Although the data series are easy to distinguish from one another onscreen, if you do not have a color printer the colors are printed as shades of gray and may be difficult to distinguish. To make the data series more distinguishable on a black-and-white printer, you can apply a different pattern to each data series object.

1 ● **Double-click the Beverage data series slice.**

● **Open the Patterns tab.**

Your screen should be similar to Figure 2.53

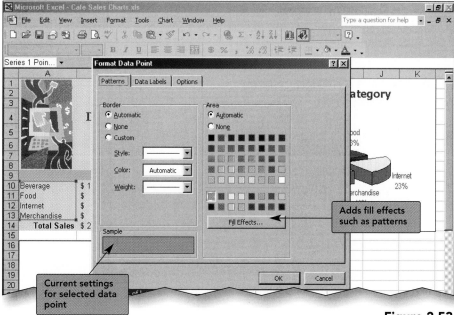

Figure 2.53

The options available in the Pattern tab vary depending upon the type of data point that is selected. In this case, because the selected data point is a pie slice, the options let you change the border and the background area. The current setting for the selected data point is displayed in the sample area. This consists of a black border with a fill color of periwinkle blue. You will add a pattern.

Click Fill Effects... .

Open the Pattern tab.

Your screen should be similar to Figure 2.54

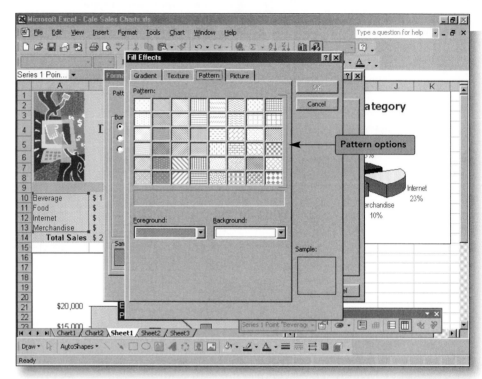

Figure 2.54

From the Fill Effects dialog box, you can change options for gradients, textures, patterns, and pictures used in formatting the selected object. You will add a pattern to the existing fill.

From the Pattern palette, select a pattern of your choice.

Click OK **(twice) to close both dialog boxes.**

Your screen should be similar to Figure 2.55

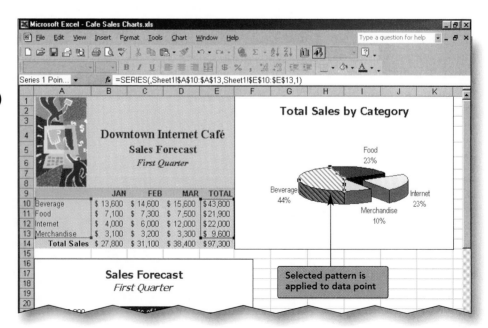

Figure 2.55

The pattern is applied to the selected data point. Next you will add a pattern to the Internet data series slice.

4 ● **Double-click the Internet data series slice.**

● **Click** [Fill Effects...] **.**

● **Open the Pattern tab.**

Your screen should be similar to Figure 2.56

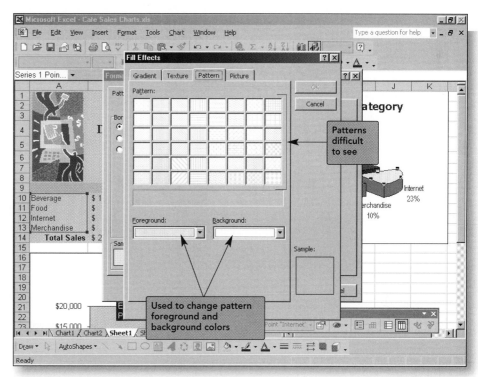

Figure 2.56

Because yellow is a light color, it is difficult to see the patterns in the Fill Effects dialog box. A pattern consists of a foreground color and a background color. The default foreground color is the same as the fill color and the background color is white. To increase the contrast, you can change the color selection of either.

5 ● **From the Foreground color drop-down list, select a darker color of your choice.**

● **Select a different pattern.**

● **Click** [OK] **(twice).**

Your screen should be similar to Figure 2.57

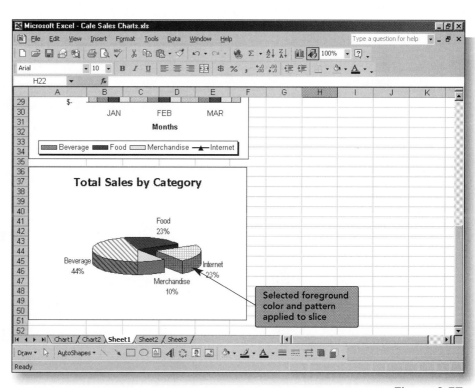

Figure 2.57

You will leave the other two data points without patterns. Finally you want to make the pie chart plot area larger.

6 ● **Select the plot area.**

● **Drag the sizing handle outward to increase the pie chart size slightly as in Figure 2.58.**

● **Select the pie chart and move it below the combination chart to top-align with cell A36.**

● **Deselect the chart.**

● **Close the Chart toolbar.**

● **Save the workbook.**

Your screen should be similar to Figure 2.58

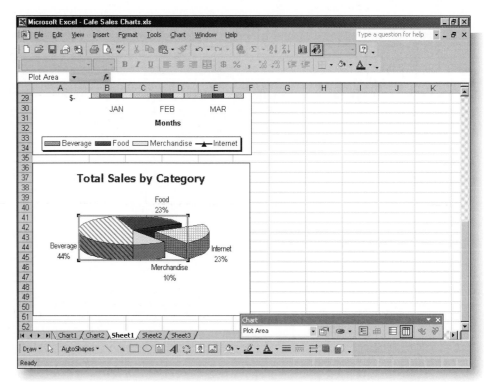

Figure 2.58

Documenting a Workbook

Now you are ready to preview and print the worksheet and charts. Before doing this, however, you will add documentation to the workbook. Each workbook includes summary information that is associated with the file.

1 ● **Choose File/Properties.**

● **Select each tab in the Properties dialog box and look at the recorded information.**

● **Open the Summary tab.**

Your screen should be similar to Figure 2.59

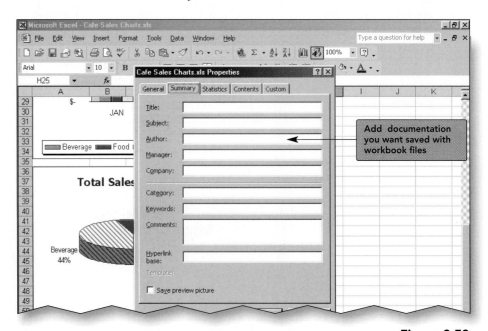

Figure 2.59

The Summary tab is used to specify information you want associated with the file such as a title, subject, author, keywords, and comments about the workbook file. Additionally, you can specify to save a picture of the first page of the file for previewing in the Open dialog box. This information helps you locate the workbook file you want to use as well as indicate the objectives and use of the workbook.

2 ● Enter the following information in the Summary tab.

Title   **Downtown Internet Cafe**

Subject   **Sales Forecast**

Author   **your name**

● Select the Save preview picture option.

● Click [OK].

Your chart should be similar to Figure 2.60

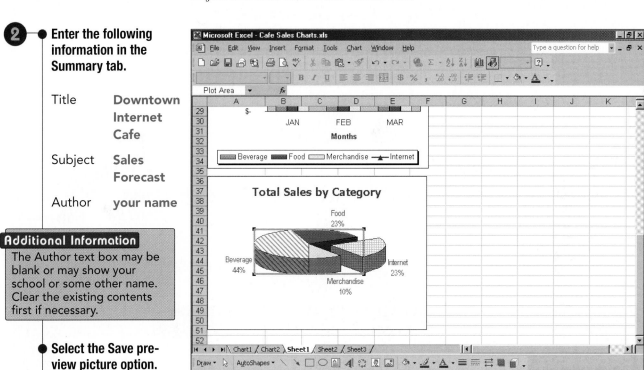

Figure 2.60

Preparing the Workbook for Printing

It is very important before printing charts to preview how they will appear when printed. Formats that look good onscreen may not produce good printed results.

Before printing, you can change the layout of the worksheet and charts to improve the appearance of the printed output. The size and alignment of the worksheet can be changed to make it more attractive on the paper. Additionally, you can include information in a header on each page.

Previewing the Workbook

Your workbook file includes two new chart sheets and a worksheet. You decide the worksheet would look better with more space between the data and charts. You will adjust the placement of the charts and then preview the entire workbook. To preview them all at once, you need to change the print setting to print the entire workbook first.

1 ● **Move the combination chart to top-align with cell A18.**

● **Move the pie chart to top-align with cell A40.**

Your screen should be similar to Figure 2.61

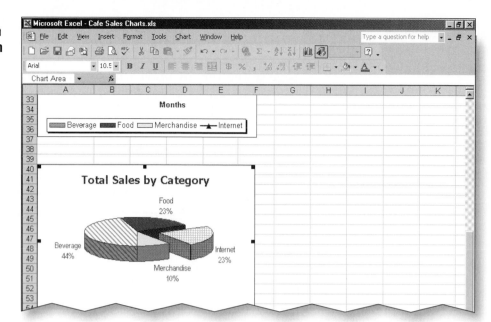

Figure 2.61

2 ● **Deselect the chart object.**

● **Choose File/Print/Entire workbook.**

● **Click** Preview **.**

● **If necessary, reduce the zoom to see the full page.**

Your screen should be similar to Figure 2.62

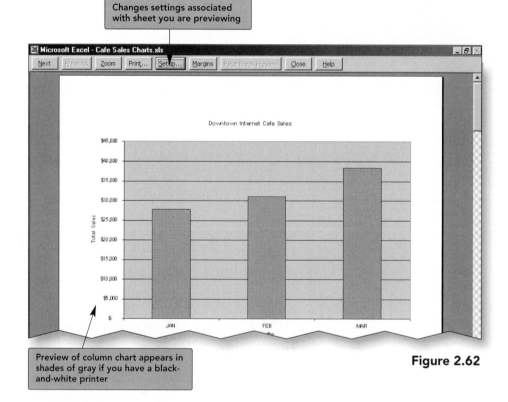

Figure 2.62

Because the column chart is on a separate chart sheet, it is displayed on a page by itself. In addition, if you are not using a color printer, the preview displays the chart colors in shades of gray as it will appear when printed on a black-and-white printer. You will change the print setting associated with this chart sheet to fix this problem. The Print Preview toolbar buttons are used to access many print and page layout changes while you are previewing a document.

3 Click Setup....

• Open the Chart tab.

Your screen should be similar to Figure 2.63

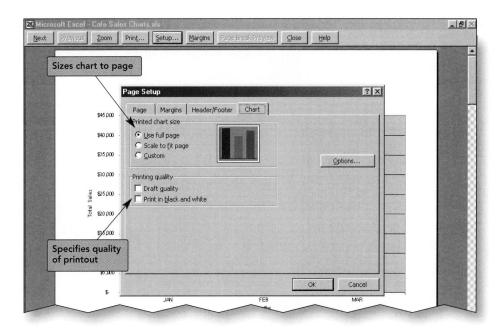

Figure 2.63

Additional Information

You can print an embedded chart without the worksheet by selecting it before using the command to print.

Because chart sheets print only one chart on a page, the default setting is to size the chart to fill the entire page. The Draft Quality setting suppresses the printing of graphics and gridlines, thereby reducing printing time. The black-and-white option applies patterns to data series in place of colors while leaving other areas in shades of gray. If there is a single data series, it is changed to solid black. On a color printer, all other areas are still printed in color when this option is selected.

4 • Select Print in black and white.

• Click OK.

Your screen should be similar to Figure 2.64

Another Method

The menu equivalent is File/Page Setup/Chart/Print in black and white.

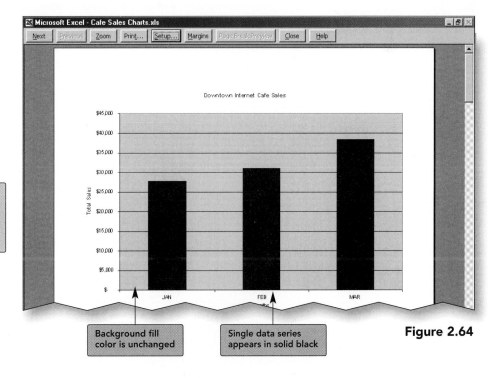

Figure 2.64

The data series changes to black and the background fill has not changed.

5 ● Click Next to see the chart in the next Chart sheet.

Your screen should be similar to Figure 2.65

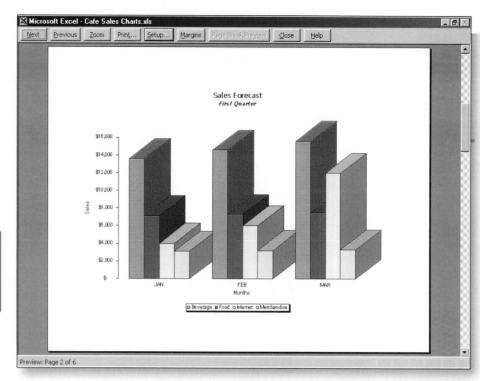

Figure 2.65

Chart 2 looks as if it will print satisfactorily using the default print settings.

6 ● Click Next to see the worksheet and charts in Sheet 1.

Your screen should be similar to Figure 2.66

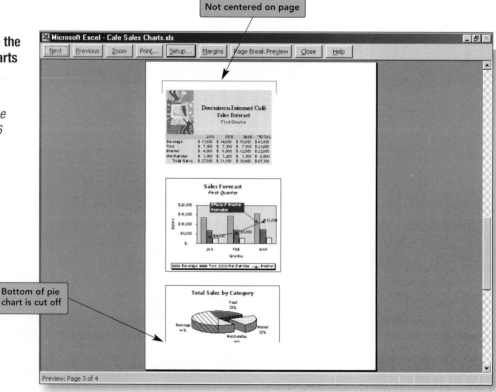

Figure 2.66

You can now see that the bottom of the pie chart exceeds the page margins and will not print on the page. You can also see that the printout will not appear balanced between the page margins. You will make several changes to the layout of the page to correct these problems.

Sizing the Worksheet

First you will reduce the worksheet and chart sizes so that they will fit on one page. Although you could resize the charts in the worksheet, a quicker way is to use the scaling feature to reduce or enlarge the worksheet contents by a percentage or to fit it to a specific number of pages. You want to have the program scale the worksheet to fit on one page.

1 ● Click Setup....

● If necessary, open the Page tab.

● Select **Fit** to.

● Click OK.

Your screen should be similar to Figure 2.67

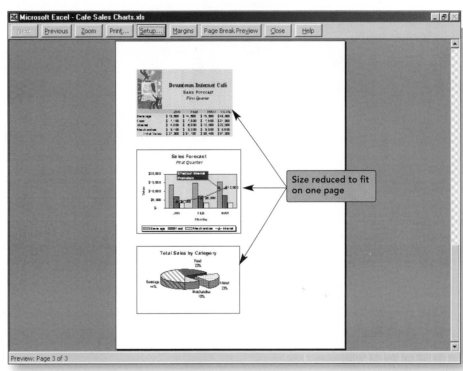

Figure 2.67

The size of the worksheet and charts has been reduced and they now fit on a single page.

Aligning a Sheet on a Page

You would also like to center the worksheet horizontally on the page. The default worksheet margin settings include 1-inch top and bottom margins and .75-inch right and left margins. The **margins** are the blank space outside the printing area around the edges of the paper. The worksheet contents appear in the printable area inside the margins. You want to center the worksheet data horizontally within the existing margins.

1 ● Click Setup....

● **Open the Margins tab.**

● **Select Hori<u>z</u>ontally.**

Your screen should be similar to Figure 2.68

Another Method

The menu equivalent is <u>F</u>ile/Page Set<u>u</u>p/Margins/ Hori<u>z</u>ontally.

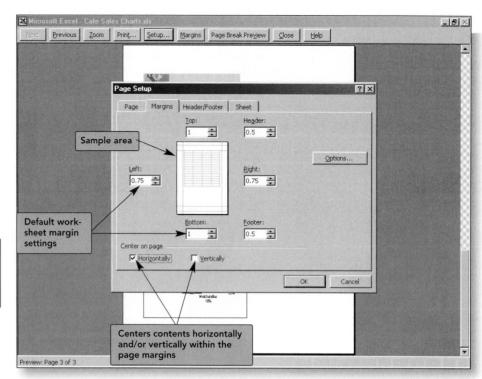

Figure 2.68

The sample area shows the effect of this change on the page layout.

Adding Predefined Headers and Footers

Finally, you want to include your name and the date in a header.

concept 7

Header and Footer

7 A **header** is a line or several lines of text that appears at the top of a page just above the top margin line. A **footer** is a line or several lines of text that appears at the bottom of a page just below the bottom margin line. Information that is commonly placed in a header or footer includes the date and page number.

You can select from predefined header and footer text or enter your own custom text. The information contained in the predefined header

and footer text is obtained from the document properties associated with the workbook and from the program and system settings.

Header and footer text can be formatted like any other text. In addition, you can control the placement of the header and footer text by specifying where it should appear: left-aligned, centered, or right-aligned in the header or footer space.

You will add a predefined header to the worksheet that displays your name, the date and page number.

1
- Open the Header/Footer tab.
- Open the Header drop-down list box and select the Prepared By [your name] [date], Page 3 option.

Another Method
The menu equivalent is File/ Page Setup/Header/Footer.

Your screen should be similar to Figure 2.69

Additional Information
Predefined footers can be added by selecting the footer option from the Footer drop-down list.

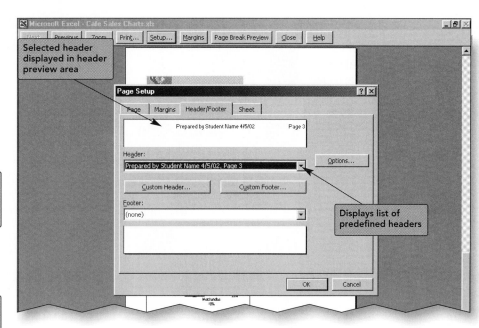

Figure 2.69

The selected header is displayed in the header area of the dialog box. It could then be edited or formatted to meet your needs.

2
- Click  .

Your screen should be similar to Figure 2.70

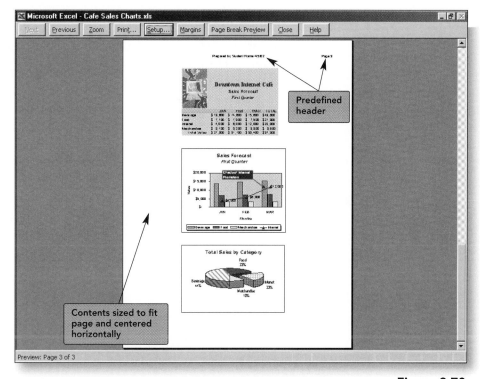

Figure 2.70

The preview window displays the worksheet centered horizontally between the right and left margins. The header you selected is displayed above the top margin line. It now appears the way you want it to look when printed.

3 ● Add a predefined footer to each of the chart sheets that displays your name, page number, and date.

HAVING TROUBLE?

Click Previous to display previous sheets.

Your screen should be similar to Figure 2.71

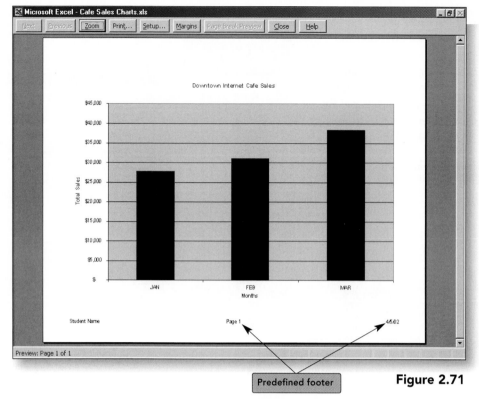

Predefined footer

Figure 2.71

Printing the Workbook

Printing a worksheet that includes charts requires a printer with graphics capability. However, the actual procedure to print is the same as printing a worksheet that does not include charts.

1 ● Click Print... .

● Move to cell A9 of Sheet1.

● If necessary, close the Chart and Drawing toolbars.

● Exit Excel, saving the workbook again.

The workbook documentation and page layout settings you specified have been saved with the workbook file.

Your printed output should be similar to that shown here.

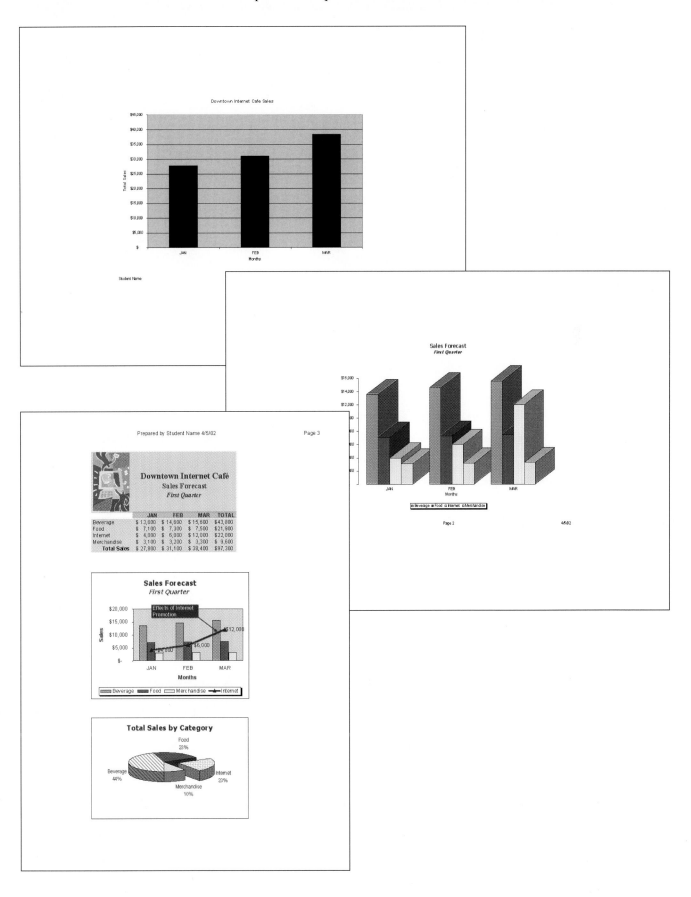

LAB 2
Organizing Your Work

Chart (EX2.5)

A **chart** is visual representation of data that is used to convey information in an easy-to-understand and attractive manner. Different types of charts are used to represent data in different ways.

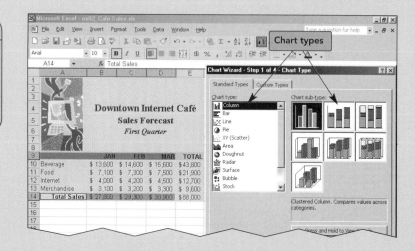

Chart Elements (EX2.6)

Chart elements consist of a number of parts that are used to graphically display the worksheet data.

Chart Objects (EX2.12)

A **chart object** is a graphic object that is created using charting features included in Excel. A chart object can be inserted into a worksheet or into a special chart sheet.

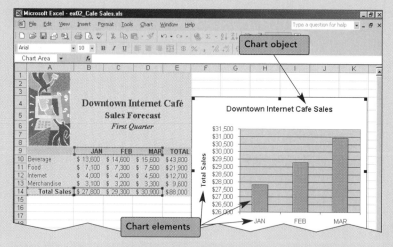

Group (EX2.25)

Because it consists of many separate objects, a chart object is a group. A **group** is two or more objects that behave as a single object when moved or sized.

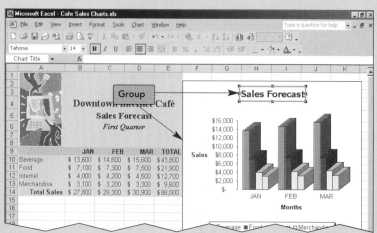

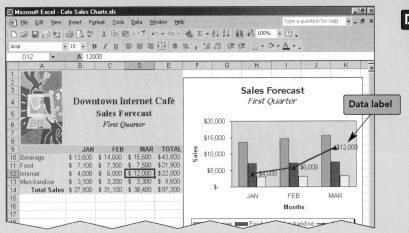

Data Label (EX2.31)

Data labels provide additional information about a data marker.

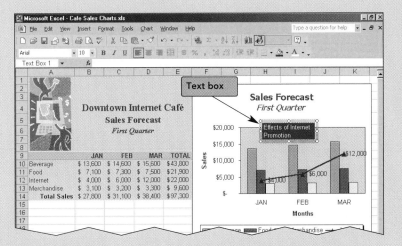

Text Box (EX2.35)

A **text box** is a rectangular object in which you type text. Text boxes can be added to a sheet or to a chart object.

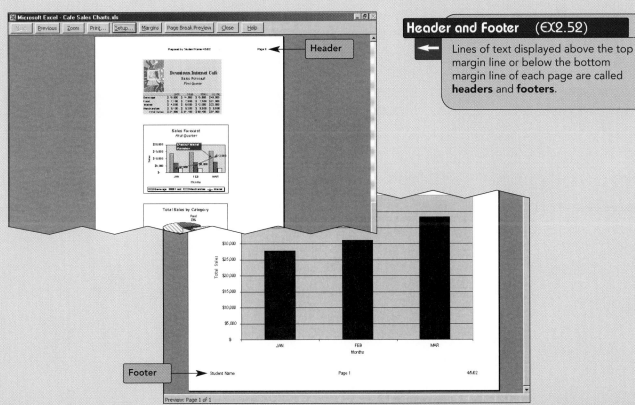

Header and Footer (EX2.52)

Lines of text displayed above the top margin line or below the bottom margin line of each page are called **headers** and **footers**.

lab review

key terms

category-axis EX2.6	data series EX2.6	stack EX2.40
category-axis title EX2.6	embedded chart EX2.12	text box EX2.35
category name EX2.6	explode EX2.42	value axis EX2.6
chart EX2.5	footer EX2.52	value-axis title EX2.6
chart gridlines EX2.6	group EX2.25	word wrap EX2.35
chart object EX2.12	header EX2.52	X axis EX2.6
chart title EX2.6	legend EX2.6	Y axis EX2.6
combination chart EX2.30	margins EX2.51	Z axis EX2.6
data label EX2.31	plot area EX2.6	
data marker EX2.6	series formula EX2.32	

mous skills

The Microsoft Office User Specialist (MOUS) certification program is designed to measure your proficiency in performing basic tasks using the Office XP applications. Getting certified demonstrates that you have the skills and provides a valuable industry credential for employment. After completing this lab, you have learned the following Microsoft Office User Specialist skills:

Skill	Description	Page
Formatting and Printing Worksheets	Modify Page Setup options for worksheets	EX2.51
Creating and Modifying Graphics	Create, modify, and position and print charts	EX2.49

command summary

Command	Shortcut Keys	Button	Action
File/Print/Entire Workbook			Prints all the sheets in a workbook
File/Properties/Summary			Specify information to document file
File/Page Setup/Header/Footer			Adds header and/or footer
File/Page Setup/Chart/ Print in black and white			Prints chart in black and white
File/Page Setup/Margins/ Horizontally			Horizontally centers contents between margins
File/Page Setup/Page/Fit to			Sizes print area to fit on a specified number of pages
Insert/Chart			Starts the Chart Wizard
Format/Selected Data Series/ Data Labels			Adds data labels to data points
Format/Selected Legend	Ctrl + 1		Changes format of legend
Format/Selected Chart Title	Ctrl + 1		Changes format of selected chart title
Format/Selected Data Series	Ctrl + 1		Changes format of selected data series
Chart/Chart Type			Changes type of chart
Chart/Chart Options/Legend/ Show Legend			Displays/Hides legend
Chart/Location			Places chart in selected worksheet or chart sheet

lab exercises

Terminology

In the following worksheet and chart, letters identify important elements. Enter the correct term for each screen element in the space provided.

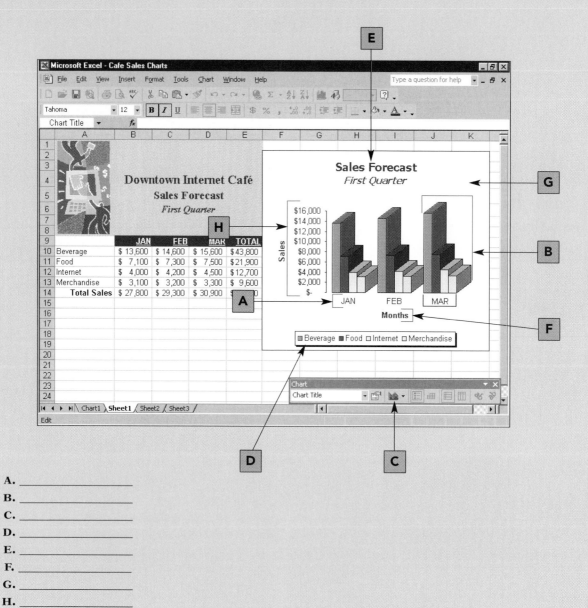

A. _____

B. _____

C. _____

D. _____

E. _____

F. _____

G. _____

H. _____

matching

Match the lettered item on the right with the numbered item on the left.

1. ⬚⬛   _____   **a.** numbered scale along left boundary line of the chart

2. data marker   _____   **b.** bottom boundary line of the chart

3. ⬛   _____   **c.** identifies each number represented in a data series

4. X-axis   _____   **d.** area of chart bounded by X- and Y-axes

5. explode   _____   **e.** changes the type of chart

6. plot area   _____   **f.** identifies the chart data series names and data markers

7. column chart   _____   **g.** a chart that displays data as vertical columns

8. Value axis   _____   **h.** starts the Chart Wizard

9. legend   _____   **i.** to separate wedge slightly from other wedges of pie

10. combination chart _____   **j.** includes mixed data markers

multiple choice

Circle the correct response to the questions below.

1. A(n) _____ links a chart object to the source worksheet.
   a. embedded chart
   b. stack
   c. series formula
   d. data marker

2. The _____ names displayed along the X-axis correspond to the headings for the worksheet data that is plotted along the X-axis.
   a. variable
   b. category
   c. value
   d. option

3. A _____ identifies the chart data series names and data markers that correspond to each data series.
   a. category
   b. value axis
   c. legend
   d. data label

4. Charts that are inserted into a worksheet are called:
   a. embedded objects
   b. attached objects
   c. inserted objects
   d. active objects

5. A(n) _____ represents data like a line chart and shades the area below each line to emphasize the degree of change.
   a. combination chart
   b. area chart
   c. surface chart
   d. doughnut chart

6. _____ can consist of the value of the marker, the name of the data series or category, a percent value, or a bubble size.
   a. legends
   b. X axis
   c. Y axis
   d. data labels

7. A(n) _____ is a rectangular object in which you type text.
   a. text box
   b. label
   c. input box
   d. embedded object

8. A _____ displays the data values as columns stacked upon each other.
   a. line chart
   b. bar chart
   c. stacked-column chart
   d. combination chart

9. Charts that display data as slices of a circle and show the relationship of each value in a data series to the series as a whole are called:
   a. area charts
   b. value charts
   c. pie charts
   d. bar charts

10. A chart that uses two or more chart types to emphasize different information is called a(n):
   a. area chart
   b. pie chart
   c. bar chart
   d. combination chart

true/false

Circle the correct answer to the following questions.

1. The plot area is visually displayed within the X- and Y-axis boundaries.   True   False
2. A bar chart displays data as a line and is commonly used to show trends over time.   True   False
3. The Y-axis title line is called the category-axis title.   True   False
4. An entire group or each object in a group can be individually selected and then formatted or edited.   True   False
5. A series formula links the chart object to the source worksheet.   True   False
6. Value data labels are helpful when the values are large and you want to know the exact value for one data series.   True   False
7. Text that is entered in a text box wraps to fit within the boundaries of the text box.   True   False
8. Separating slightly or exploding a slice of a pie chart emphasizes the data.   True   False
9. Patterns can be added to slices of a pie chart to make it easier to read.   True   False
10. A header is a line or several lines of text that appears at the bottom of each page just below the top margin.   True   False

Concepts

fill-in questions

Complete the following statements by filling in the blanks with the correct terms.

1. A visual representation of data in an easy-to-understand and attractive manner is called a(n) _____.

2. A(n) _____ describes the symbols used within the chart to identify different data series.

3. The bottom boundary of a chart is the _____ and the left boundary is the _____.

4. A chart that is inserted into a worksheet is a(n) _____ object.

5. A(n) _____ is a line or several lines of text that appears at the top of each page just below the top margin.

6. A(n) _____ is two or more objects that behave as a single object.

7. _____ provide additional information about a data marker.

8. A(n) _____ identifies the chart data series names and data markers that correspond to each data series.

9. The _____ is a numbered scale whose numbers are determined by the data used in the chart.

10. A chart that is inserted into a separate chart sheet is also saved with the _____ file.

discussion questions

1. Define each of the following terms and discuss how they are related to one another: chart type, chart element, and chart object.

2. Discuss how column and bar charts represent data. How do they differ from pie charts?

3. What type of information would best be represented by a line chart?

4. Describe how a 3-D column chart differs from a 2-D column chart.

lab exercises

step-by-step

Charting U.S. Home Values

★ 1. Kevin Young works for a real estate company and has been collecting information on sales prices for existing homes across the country. Kevin wants to graph some of the data in the worksheet for his upcoming presentation on home prices in the Midwest. The completed worksheet with charts is shown here.

a. Open the workbook file ex02_Real Estate Prices.

b. Create a line chart on a separate sheet showing the housing prices for the four years for the Midwest only. Title the chart appropriately. Remove the legend.

c. Make the line heavier and change the line and data marker color. Change the fill of the plot area to a gradient effect with two colors of your choice.

d. Add data labels that display the values. Increase the size of the data labels and position them below the line.

e. Increase the size of the chart title and axis labels and add a text color of your choice. Save the workbook as Real Estate Charts.

f. Create a column chart in the worksheet showing housing prices for the four regions for the four years. The X axis will display the years and the regions will be the legend. Title the chart appropriately. Move the legend to the bottom of the chart.

g. Position the chart below the worksheet data and size it appropriately. Increase the size of the chart title and add color. Turn off the plot area fill color.

h. Document the workbook file by adding your name as author and include a preview picture.

i. Preview the workbook. Add a predefined header to the worksheet and chart sheet that displays your name, page number, and date. Center the worksheet horizontally on the page. Print the worksheet. Print the chart sheet

j. Save the workbook again.

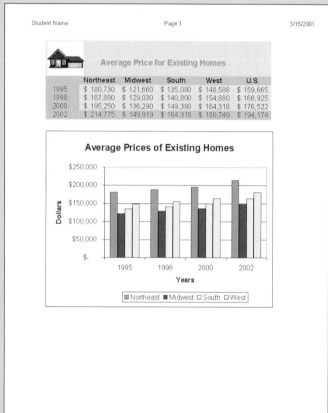

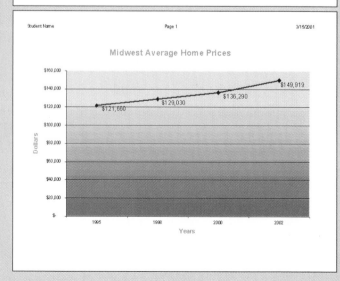

Bengal Tiger Populations

★★ **2.** Jennifer's environmental studies paper is on the endangered Bengal tiger. She has some data saved in a worksheet on the estimated number of tigers in 1997. She has asked you to help her chart the data and make the worksheet look more attractive. The completed worksheet with charts is shown here.

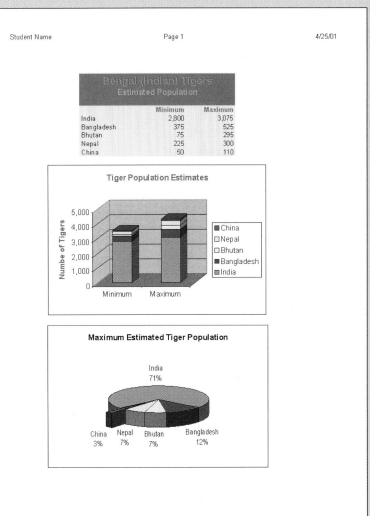

a. Open the workbook ex02_Tiger Data.

b. Use ChartWizard to create a stacked column with 3-D effect chart of the data in cells B6 through D11. Plot the data series from the rows. Enter the chart title **Tiger Population Estimates**. Enter the Value (Z) axis title of **Number of Tigers**. Embed the chart in the worksheet.

c. Size the chart over cells A13 through E30.

d. Rotate the Z-axis title 90 degrees. Change the chart and axis title color to green. Change the color for the China data series to green.

e. Save the workbook as **Tiger Charts**.

f. Create a 3-D pie chart in the worksheet showing the maximum tiger population estimates. Include the title **Maximum Estimated Tiger Population** and display the category name and percents as data labels. Do not include a legend.

g. Move the pie chart below the column chart and size it over cells A32 through E48.

h. Change the data label font to Arial Narrow. Rotate the chart 230 degrees. Explode the China slice. Change the color of the China slice to green.

i. Change the maximum estimated tiger population for China to 110.

j. Document the workbook file by adding your name as author.

k. Preview the worksheet. Add a predefined header to the worksheet that displays your name, page number, and date. Center the worksheet horizontally on the page.

l. Print the worksheet on one page.

m. Save the workbook again.

Tracking Winter Bird Populations

★★ **3.** Richard Johnson volunteers for the Downtown City Park Bird Observation Society. He has compiled a worksheet of the number of bird observations in the park for the last year. He would like a chart that shows the society how the winter bird population differs by month and a chart that shows the total number of bird sightings this year. The completed worksheet with charts is shown here.

a. Open the file ex02_Birds.

b. Chart the monthly data for the 3 types of birds as a line chart. Set the series to be displayed in Rows.

c. Enter the Chart title **Bird Observations by Month**, and the Value (Y) axis as **Number of Birds**. Display the legend below the chart.

d. Position the chart over cells A11 through N27.

e. Add color and font refinements to the chart titles as you like. Change the plot area color to blue. Change the Fox Sparrow data series color to red.

f. Save the workbook as Bird Observations.

g. Create another chart of the data in columns A and N as a 3-D Pie Chart. Title the chart **Total Bird Observations**. Turn off the legend and use the category name and percentage to label the data labels.

h. Position the chart over cells A29 through N45. Add color and font refinements to the chart title as you like. Rotate the chart 120 degrees so the Pied-billed Grebe slice is at the front of the chart. Increase the size of the plot area. Change the data label point size to 12. Explode the Pied-billed Grebe slice.

i. Document the workbook file by adding your name as author. Save the workbook with a picture preview.

j. Preview the worksheet. Add a predefined header to the worksheet that displays your name, page number, and date. Center the worksheet horizontally on the page. Print the worksheet.

k. Save the workbook file again.

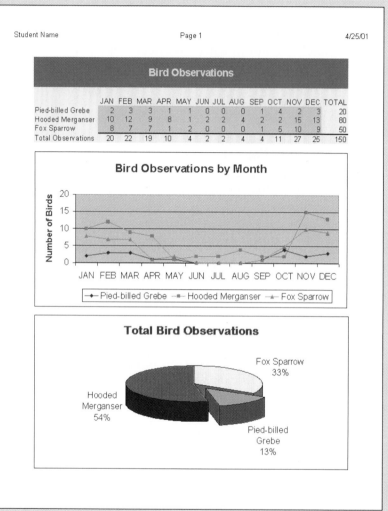

Student Name   Page 1   4/25/01

Bird Observations

	JAN	FEB	MAR	APR	MAY	JUN	JUL	AUG	SEP	OCT	NOV	DEC	TOTAL
Pied-billed Grebe	2	3	3	1	1	0	0	0	1	4	2	3	20
Hooded Merganser	10	12	9	8	1	2	2	4	2	2	15	13	80
Fox Sparrow	8	7	7	1	2	0	0	0	1	5	10	9	50
Total Observations	20	22	19	10	4	2	2	4	4	11	27	25	150

Children's Athletic Programs

★ **4.** Carol Hayes is the program coordinator for Fitness Lifestyles, a physical conditioning and health center. She is proposing to management that they increase their emphasis on child fitness. To reinforce the need for this type of investment, she has found some recent data about growth in the number of children (in millions) participating in sports. She wants to create several charts of this data to emphasize the demand.

a. Create a worksheet of the following data.

	1992	1995	2000
Baseball	3320	3421	3694
Basketball	6125	6200	7420
In-line Skating	1893	7110	8176
Running/Jogging	3510	3429	3257
Slow-pitch Softball	3652	3946	4261
Soccer	2585	2674	3510
Touch Football	4500	4040	4363
Volleyball	3620	3941	4295

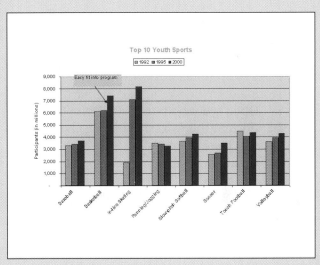

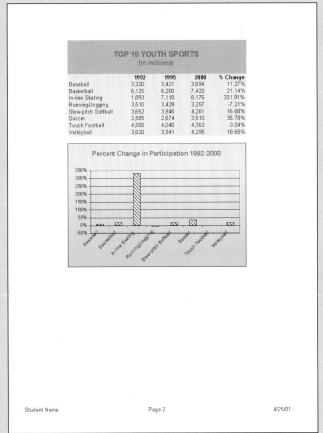

b. Add an appropriate title over the data and format the numbers to show commas with no decimal places. Calculate the percent change from 1992 to 2000 in column E (2000 value − 1992 value)/1992 value). Add a column heading. Enhance the worksheet as you like to improve its appearance. Save the workbook as Youth Sports Charts.

c. Create a clustered column chart of the worksheet data in columns A through D as a new sheet. Enter a chart title and Y axis title. Include a text box and arrow pointing to the increase in basketball and indicate that this would be an easy fit into the existing program. Enhance the chart using features presented in the lab.

d. Create an embedded column chart in the worksheet showing the Gain/Loss data for the sports. Include the title **Percent Change in Participation 1992–2000**. Remove the legend and format the Y-axis to a font size of 12 and no decimal places. Format the X-axis to a font size of 12 and display the labels at a 45-degree angle.

e. Move the chart below the worksheet and re-size.

f. Enhance the chart using features presented in the lab.

g. Document the workbook by adding your name as author. Save the workbook with a picture preview.

h. Preview the worksheet. Add a predefined footer to the worksheet that displays your name, page number, and date to both sheets. Center the worksheet horizontally on the page. Print the worksheet and the area chart.

i. Save the workbook again.

Salaries in Higher Education

★ ★ 5. Wendy Murray's class is studying career opportunities. Part of her class is interested in pursuing
★ careers in higher education. She has done some research and found data that she entered into a worksheet. She would like to chart the data to make an impression on her students.

a. Open the workbook ex02_Higher Education.

b. Format the worksheet using the features you have learned.

c. Create an embedded column chart for the six levels for the four school categories and Average. Move the legend to the bottom of the chart.

d. Display the chart below the worksheet. Change the Average data to a line. Display the average values as data labels. Format the chart to your liking.

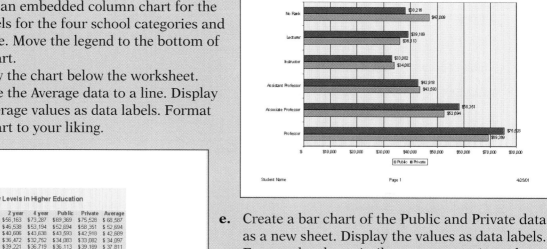
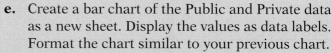

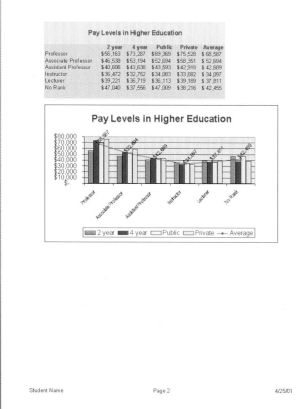

e. Create a bar chart of the Public and Private data as a new sheet. Display the values as data labels. Format the chart similar to your previous chart.

f. Document the workbook file by adding your name as author. Save the workbook with a preview picture.

g. Preview the worksheet. Add a predefined footer to the worksheet and chart sheets that displays your name, page number, and date. Center the worksheet horizontally on the page. Print the worksheet and the charts.

h. Save the workbook file as Higher Education Charts.

Market Seminar

★ **1.** Tom Duggan is preparing for an upcoming job market seminar he is presenting. He has collected data comparing the average hourly pay rate for several professional jobs in the state to the U.S. average rates. He thinks the information would be much more meaningful and have greater impact if it was presented in a chart. Using the data in the workbook ex02_ Job Market, create an appropriate chart of the data for Physicians and Surgeons, Podiatrists, Dentists, and Lawyers on a separate chart sheet. Include appropriate chart titles. Add a pattern to the data series and change the plot area fill color. Enhance the chart in other ways using different font sizes and font colors. Position the legend at the bottom of the chart. Document the workbook by adding your name as author. Add a predefined header to the chart sheet that displays your name, page number, and date. Save the workbook as Seminar and print the chart.

Grade Tracking

★ **2.** Create a worksheet that tracks your grades. It can be a record of the test scores you received this semester, or it can be a record of your GPA each semester. Create an embedded chart that best represents your grade trends. Use the formatting techniques you have learned to change the appearance of the worksheet and the chart. Save the workbook as Grades. Include a header or footer that displays your name and the current date in the worksheet. Print the worksheet with the chart.

Stock Market Workbook

★ ★ **3.** You are interested in the stock market. Use Help to learn more about the Stock chart type. Pick four related stocks and create an embedded stock chart of the data. Save the worksheet with the chart as Stocks. Include a header or footer that displays your name and the current date in the worksheet. Print the worksheet and the chart.

Win/Loss Data

★ ★ **4.** Kevin Tillman has started a new job with Baseball Statistics, Inc. He would like some help creating a worksheet that contains team win/loss records for the last five years. He asks you to search the Web for records. Choose a MLB team of your choice and locate the win/loss record for the last five years. Enter the data into a worksheet. Enhance the worksheet using the features you have learned. Create an embedded chart that displays the information over the five years. Include a header or footer that displays your name and the current date in the worksheet. Save the workbook as Statistics. Print the worksheet with the chart.

Insurance Comparisons

★ ★ **5.** Robert Sanchez is thinking about purchasing a new SUV. However, he is concerned about the insurance rates for the vehicles he is considering. Before purchasing, he wants to find out the insurance rates on the vehicles he is evaluating. Select three different comparable SUVs and use the Web or visit several insurance agents to get the insurance premium cost information for the same amount of coverage from two different insurance companies. Use your own personal information as the basis for the insurance quotes. Create a worksheet that contains the SUV models, purchase price, and insurance premium quotes for each vehicle. Create an embedded chart of the data that shows the models and premiums. Enhance the chart appropriately. Include a header or footer that displays your name and the current date in the worksheet. Save the workbook as Insurance. Print the worksheet and chart.

Managing and Analyzing a Workbook

LAB 3

objectives

After completing this lab, you will know how to:

1.	Spell-check a sheet.
2.	Use Paste Function.
3.	Use absolute references.
4.	Copy, move, and name sheets.
5.	Use Autofill.
6.	Reference multiple sheets.
7.	Zoom the worksheet.
8.	Split windows and freeze panes.
9.	Use What-If analysis and Goal Seek.
10.	Change page orientation.
11.	Add custom headers and footers.
12.	Print selected sheets.

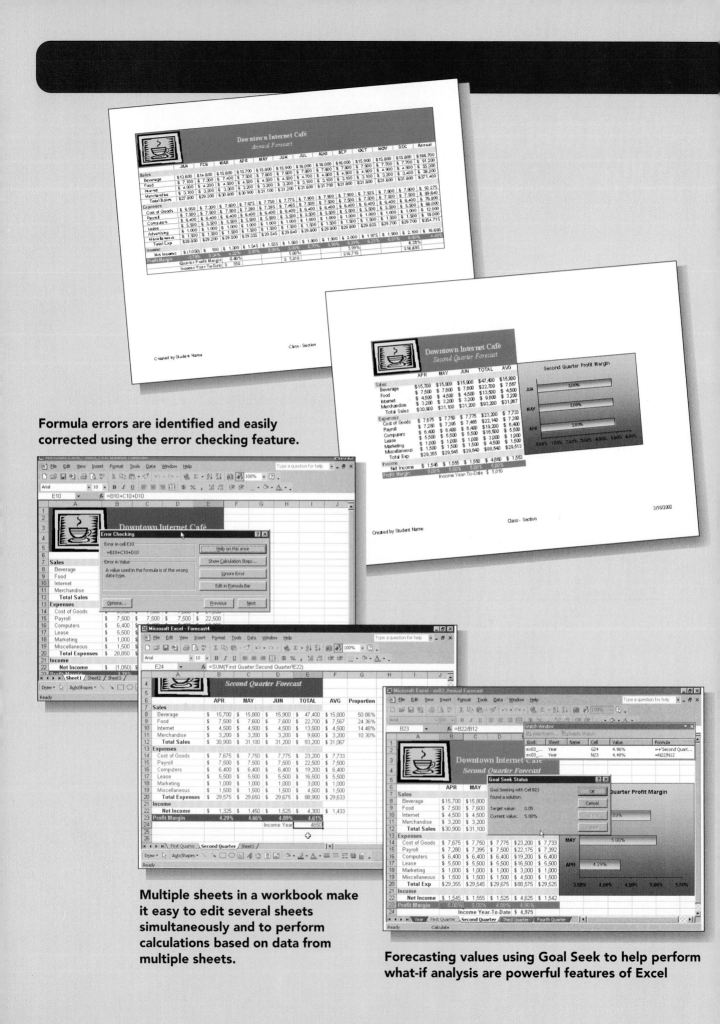

Formula errors are identified and easily corrected using the error checking feature.

Multiple sheets in a workbook make it easy to edit several sheets simultaneously and to perform calculations based on data from multiple sheets.

Forecasting values using Goal Seek to help perform what-if analysis are powerful features of Excel

Downtown Internet Café

You present your new, more optimistic, first quarter forecast for the Downtown Internet Café to Evan, who has made several formatting and design changes. In addition, he asks you to include an Average calculation and to extend the forecast for the next three quarters. Moreover, he wants to hold back on your idea of an aggressive Internet sales promotion. The Café's funds are low due to the cost of the recent renovations. Evan feels, therefore, that you should stick with a more conservative forecast of income derived from Internet sales.

After discussing the situation, you agree that the Café will likely lose money during the

first month of operations. Then the Café should show increasing profitability. Evan stresses that the monthly profit margin should reach 5 per cent in the second quarter.

As you develop the Café's financial forecast, the worksheet grows in size and complexity. You will learn about features of Excel 2002 that help you manage a large workbook efficiently. You will also learn how you can manipulate the data in a worksheet to reach a goal using the what-if analysis capabilities of Excel. The completed annual forecast is shown here.

Correcting Worksheet Errors

Excel 2002 includes several tools to help you find and correct errors in both text and formula entries. Text errors, such as spelling and typing errors, can be located quickly and corrected using the spelling checker. Potential problems in formulas are identified and can be corrected using the formula error checking features.

Checking Spelling

After talking with Evan, the owner of the Café, about the first quarter forecast, you are ready to begin making the changes he suggested. Evan returned the workbook file to you containing the changes he made to the format of the worksheet. To see the workbook file with these changes,

① ● **Start Excel 2002.**

● **Open the workbook**
ex03_First Quarter
Forecast.

*Your screen should be
similar to Figure 3.1*

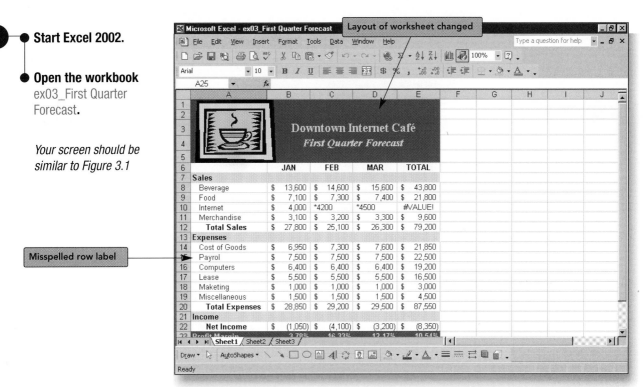

Figure 3.1

As you can see, Evan made several formatting changes to the worksheet. He found a new graphic and changed the fill and text colors to coordinate with the picture. Additionally, he made several changes to the row labels. For example, the Salary label has been replaced with Payroll. However, the new label is misspelled. Just to make sure there are no other spelling errors, you will check the spelling of all text entries in this worksheet.

concept 1

Spell Checking

1 The **spelling checker** locates all misspelled words, duplicate words, and capitalization irregularities in the active worksheet and proposes the correct spelling. This feature works by comparing each word to a dictionary of words. If the word does not appear in the **main dictionary** or in a custom dictionary, it is identified as misspelled. The main dictionary is supplied with the program; a **custom dictionary** is one you can create to hold words you commonly use but that are not included in the main dictionary.

When you check spelling, the entire active worksheet including cell values, text boxes, headers and footers, and text in embedded charts is checked. It does not check spelling in formulas or text that results from formulas. You can also restrict the area to be checked by first selecting a range. If the formula bar is active when you check spelling, only the contents of the formula bar are checked.

Excel begins checking all worksheet entries from the active cell forward. To check the spelling in the worksheet,

② ● Click ☑ **Spelling.**

Another Method

The menu equivalent is **T**ools/**S**pelling and the keyboard shortcut is F7.

Your screen should be similar to Figure 3.2

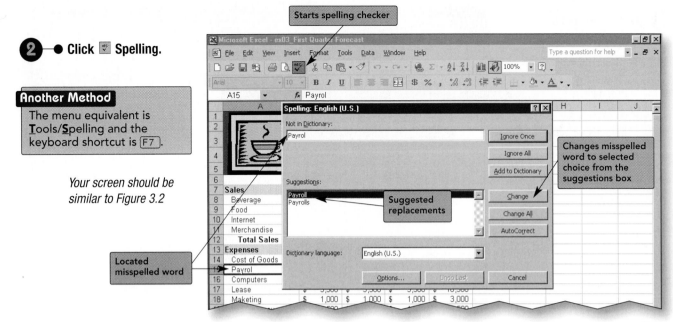

Starts spelling checker

Changes misspelled word to selected choice from the suggestions box

Suggested replacements

Located misspelled word

Figure 3.2

Additional Information

Spell checking operates the same way in all Office XP programs. The dictionaries and AutoCorrect entries are shared between Office applications.

The spelling checker immediately begins checking the worksheet for words that it cannot locate in its main dictionary. The cell selector moves to the first cell containing a misspelled word, in this case Payrol, and the Spelling dialog box is displayed. The word it cannot locate in the dictionary is displayed in the Not in Dictionary text box. The Suggestions text box displays a list of possible replacements. If the selected replacement is not correct, you can select another choice from the suggestions list or type the correct word in the Not in Dictionary text box.

The option buttons shown in the table below have the following effects:

Option	Effect
Ignore Once	Leaves selected word unchanged
Ignore All	Leaves this word and all identical words in worksheet unchanged
Change	Changes selected word to word highlighted in Suggestions text box
Add to Dictionary	Adds selected word to a custom dictionary so Excel will not question this word during subsequent spell checks
Change All	Changes this word and all identical words in worksheet to word highlighted in Suggestions text box
AutoCorrect	Adds a word to the AutoCorrect list so the word will be corrected as you type

You want to accept the suggested replacement, Payroll.

3 ● Click [Change].

*Your screen should be
similar to Figure 3.3*

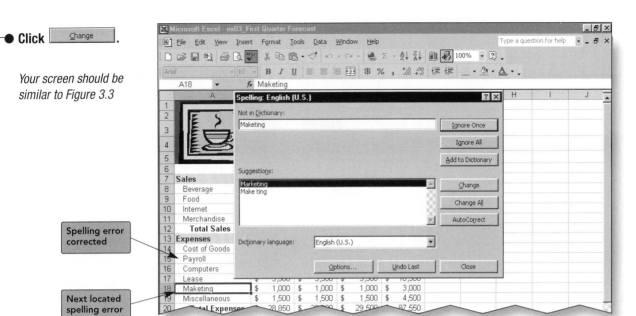

**Spelling error
corrected**

**Next located
spelling error**

Figure 3.3

The correction is made in the worksheet, and the program continues checking the worksheet and locates another error, Maketing.

4 ● **Change this word to
Marketing.**

*Your screen should be
similar to Figure 3.4*

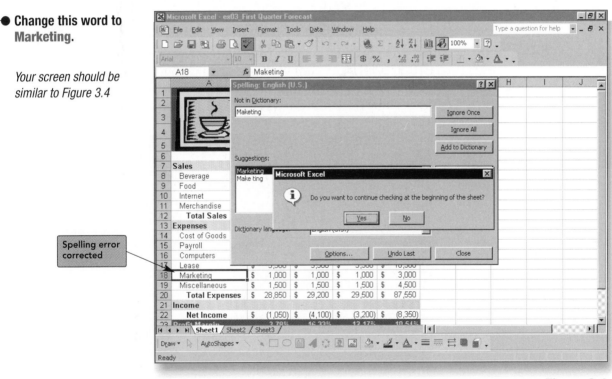

**Spelling error
corrected**

Figure 3.4

The program continues checking the worksheet. When it reaches the end of the sheet, because the cell selector was not at the beginning of the sheet when checking started, the program asks if you want to continue checking at the beginning of the sheet. When no other errors are located, a dialog box is displayed, informing you that the entire worksheet has been checked.

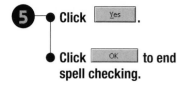

5 ● Click [Yes].

● Click [OK] to end spell checking.

Your screen should be similar to Figure 3.5

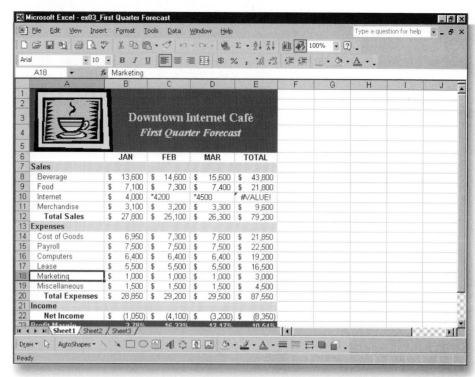

Figure 3.5

Correcting Formula Errors

As you continue to check over the worksheet, you notice a problem in cell E10. If a formula cannot properly calculate a result, an error value is displayed and a triangle appears in the top-left corner of the cell. Each type of error value has a different cause as described in the following table.

Error value	Cause
#####	Column not wide enough to display result or negative date or time is used
#VALUE!	Wrong type of argument or operand is used
#DIV/0!	Number is divided by zero
#NAME?	Text in formula not recognized
#N/A	Value not available
#REF!	Cell reference is not valid
#NUM!	Invalid number values
#NULL!	Intersection operator is not valid

You can correct each identified error individually or use the formula checker to check them all, one at a time. To correct them individually, select the cell and click ⌖ Error Options to display the menu of options that can be used to correct the problem. The formula checker is similar to the spelling checker in that it goes to each location in the worksheet containing a formula error, identifies the problem, and suggests corrections. You will use the formula checker to correct this error and check the entire worksheet for others.

1 ● **Choose Tools/Error Checking.**

● **If necessary, move the dialog box to see the located formula error.**

Your screen should be similar to Figure 3.6

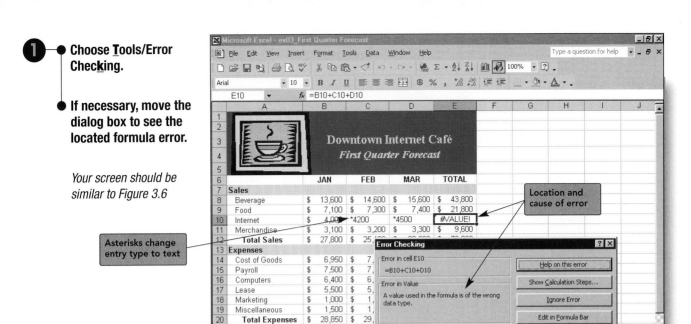

Figure 3.6

The Error Checking dialog box identifies the location and cause of the error. In this case, when Evan changed the Internet sales values back to the original estimates, he included an * in the cell entry to make sure you noticed the change. Because Excel interprets this entry as a text entry, it cannot be used in this formula.. To correct the problem, you need to enter the values correctly.

2 ● **Move to cell C10 and enter 4200.**

● **Enter 4500 in cell D10.**

Your screen should be similar to Figure 3.7

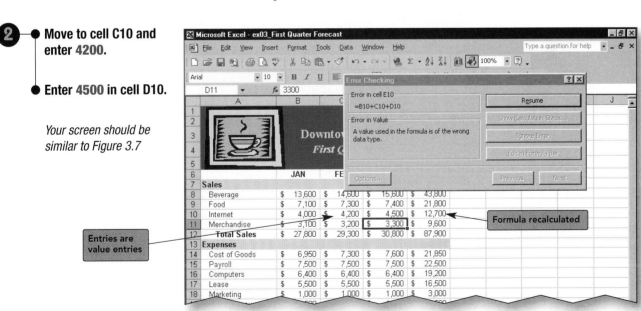

Figure 3.7

Cell E10 now displays the correctly calculated result. The two values you entered will need to be formatted again to Accounting. You will continue checking the worksheet for formula errors and, when error checking is complete, you will reformat the values.

3 • Click 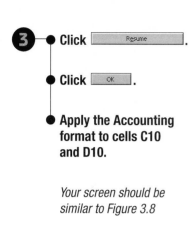 Resume .

• Click OK .

• Apply the Accounting format to cells C10 and D10.

Your screen should be similar to Figure 3.8

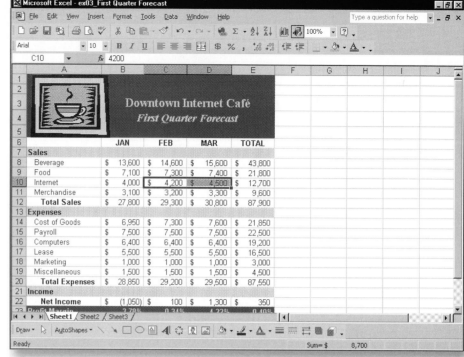

Figure 3.8

Now you are ready to make several of the changes requested by Evan. First you will add a column showing the average values for the first quarter.

4 • Enter the heading **AVG** in cell F6.

• Move to F8.

Your screen should be similar to Figure 3.9

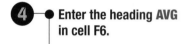 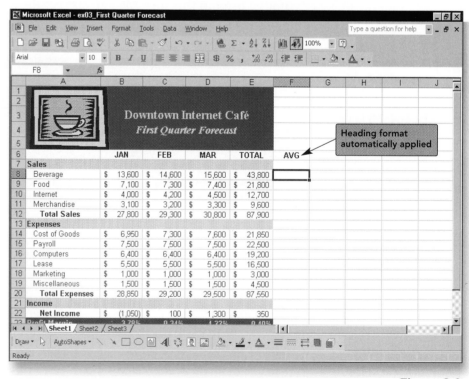

Figure 3.9

Notice the new heading is already appropriately formatted to bold and centered. This is because Excel automatically extends formats to new cells if the format of at least three of the last five preceding columns appears that way.

In addition to the SUM function, you can also use Σ AutoSum to enter several other commonly used functions. This includes functions to calculate an Average, Minimum, Maximum, and Count.

5 ● **Open the Σ AutoSum drop-down menu.**

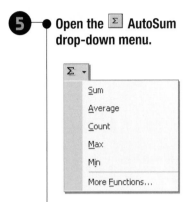

● **Choose Average.**

Your screen should be similar to Figure 3.10

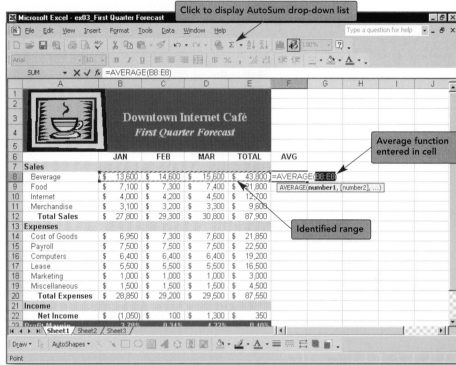

Figure 3.10

Excel identifies the range of cells B8 through E8 for the function argument. Because it incorrectly includes the total value in cell E8, you need to specify the correct range.

6 ● **Drag to select cells B8 through D8.**

● **Press ←Enter.**

Your screen should be similar to Figure 3.11

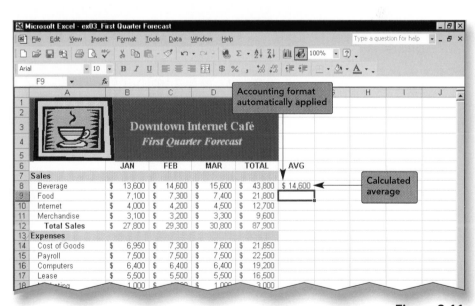

Figure 3.11

The average of the beverage sales for the quarter, 14,600, is calculated and displayed in cell F8. Notice that Excel again extended the format to the new cell, saving you the step of applying the Accounting format.

Next you need to copy the function down column F.

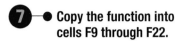

7 ● **Copy the function into cells F9 through F22.**

Your screen should be similar to Figure 3.12

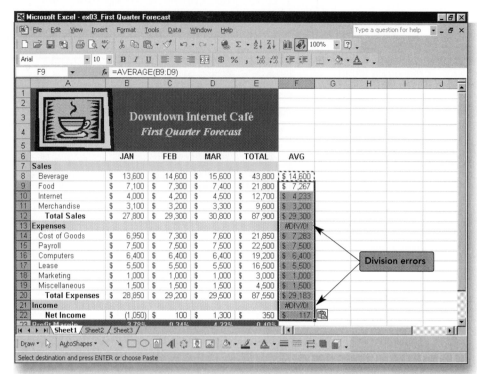

Figure 3.12

The average value has been correctly calculated for each row. Notice, however, that two cells display the error value #DIV/0! indicating the cells contains a formula error.

8 ● **Move to cell F13.**

● **Point to** ◇ **Error Options.**

Your screen should be similar to Figure 3.13

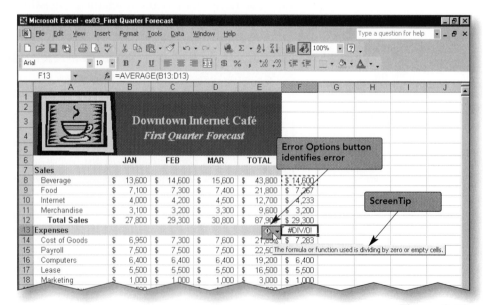

Figure 3.13

The Error Options button displays a ScreenTip identifying the cause of the error; in this case the formula is attempting to divide by zero or empty cells. This time you will individually correct the error.

9 • Click ⊗ **Error Options.**

• **Choose Edit in Formula Bar.**

Your screen should be similar to Figure 3.14

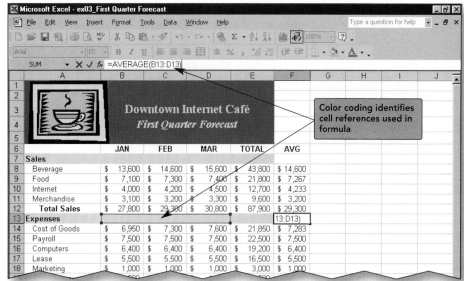

Figure 3.14

Notice that the cell references in the formula are color coded to match the borders Excel displays around the referenced worksheet cells. It is designed to provide visual cues to the relationships between the cells that provide values to the formulas or the cells that depend on the formulas. You can now easily see the error is caused by references to blank cells when the function was copied. Since you do not need this formula, you will delete it.

10 • Press Esc.

• Press Delete.

Your screen should be similar to Figure 3.15

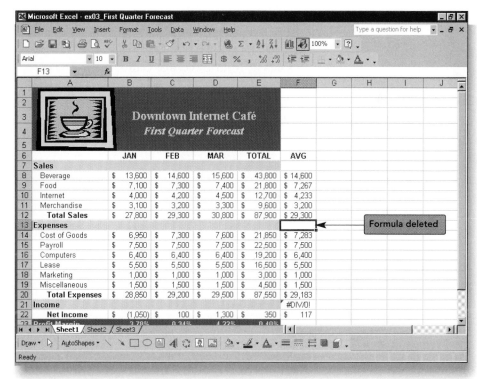

Figure 3.15

Likewise, you need to delete the function that was copied into cell F21. You will clear the entry in this cell using the fill handle.

11 • **Move to cell F21.**

• **Point to the fill handle and when the mouse pointer changes to +, drag upward until the cell is gray.**

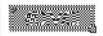

• **Release the mouse button.**

Your screen should be similar to Figure 3.16

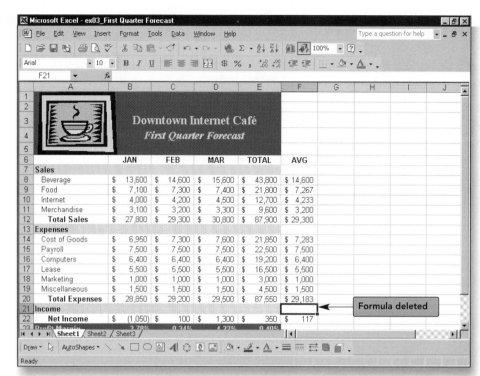

Figure 3.16

Using Absolute References

While looking at the sales data in the worksheet, you decide it may be interesting to find out what contribution each sales item makes to total sales. To find out, you will enter a formula to calculate the proportion of sales by each in column G. The formula to calculate the proportion for beverage sales is Total Beverage Sales/Total Sales.

1 • **Enter the heading Proportion in cell G6.**

• **Enter the formula =E8/E12 in cell G8.**

• **If necessary, move to G8.**

Your screen should be similar to Figure 3.17

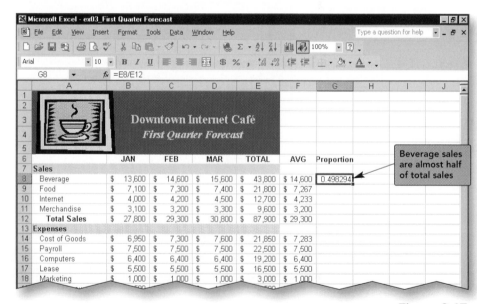

Figure 3.17

The value 0.498294 is displayed in cell G8. This shows that the beverage sales are approximately 50 percent of total sales.

Next, to calculate the proportion for Food Sales, you will copy the formula from G8 to G9. Another quick way to copy cell contents is to drag the cell border while holding down Ctrl. This method is most useful when the distance between cells is short and they are both visible in the window. It cannot be used if you are copying to a larger range than the source range.

2 ● **Point to the border of cell G8 and when the mouse pointer shape is ⬚, hold down Ctrl and drag the mouse pointer to cell G9.**

Your screen should be similar to Figure 3.18

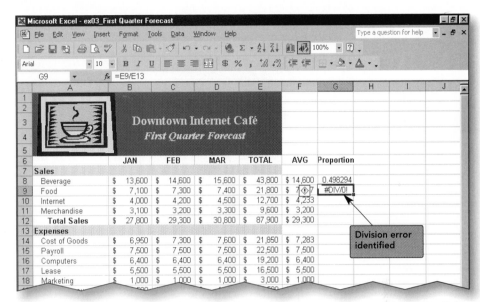

Figure 3.18

You see a #DIV/0! error value is displayed in cell G9 and want to check the formula in that cell.

3 ● **If necessary, move to cell G9.**

● **Choose Edit in Formula Bar from the ⬧ Error Options drop-down menu.**

Your screen should be similar to Figure 3.19

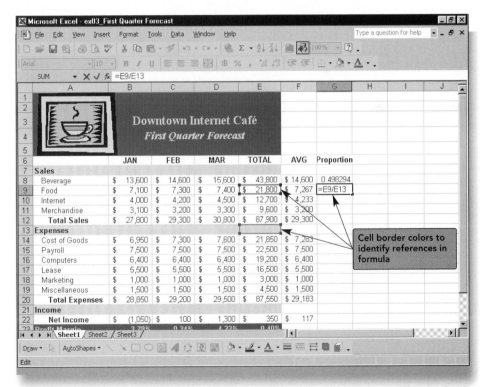

Figure 3.19

You can now see the error occurred because the relative reference to cell E12 adjusted correctly to the new location when the formula was copied and now references cell E13, a blank cell. The formula in G8 needs to be entered so that the reference to the Total Sales value in cell E12 does not change when the formula is copied. To do this, you need to make the cell reference absolute.

concept 2

Absolute References

2   An **absolute reference** is a cell or range reference in a formula whose location does not change when the formula is copied.

To stop the relative adjustment of cell references, enter a $ (dollar sign) character before the column letter and row number. This changes the cell reference to absolute. When a formula containing an absolute cell reference is copied to another row and column location in the worksheet, the cell reference does not change. It is an exact duplicate of the cell reference in the original formula.

A cell reference can also be a **mixed reference**. In this type of reference, either the column letter or the row number is preceded with the $. This makes only the row or column absolute. When a formula containing a mixed cell reference is copied to another location in the worksheet, only the part of the cell reference that is not absolute changes relative to its new location in the worksheet.

The table below shows examples of relative and absolute references and the results when a reference in cell G8 to cell E8 is copied to cell H9.

Cell Contents of G8	Copied to Cell H9	Type of Reference
E8	E8	Absolute reference
E$8	F$8	Mixed reference
$E8	$E9	Mixed reference
E8	F9	Relative reference

You will change the formula in cell G8 to include an absolute reference for cell E12. Then you will copy the formula to cells G9 through G11.

You can change a cell reference to absolute or mixed by typing in the dollar sign directly or by using the ABS (Absolute) key, F4 . To use the ABS key, the program must be in the Edit mode and the cell reference that you want to change must be selected.

4 ● **Move to G8.**

● **Click on the reference to E12 in the formula bar to enter Edit mode and select the reference.**

● **Press** `F4`.

Your screen should be similar to Figure 3.20

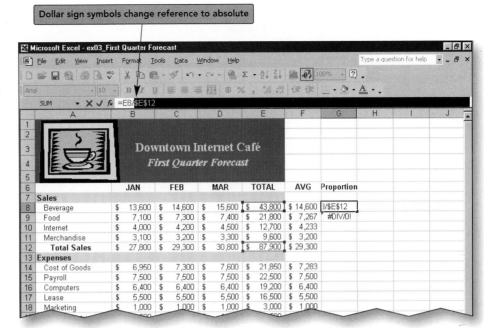

Figure 3.20

The cell reference now displays $ characters before the column letter and row number, making this cell reference absolute. If you continue to press `F4`, the cell reference will cycle through all possible combinations of cell reference types. Leaving the cell reference absolute, as it is now, will stop the relative adjustment of the cell reference when you copy it again.

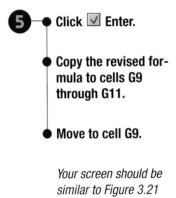

5 ● **Click** ☑ **Enter.**

● **Copy the revised formula to cells G9 through G11.**

● **Move to cell G9.**

Your screen should be similar to Figure 3.21

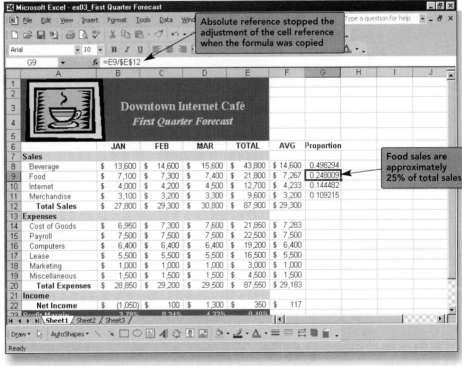

Figure 3.21

The formula when copied correctly adjusted the relative cell reference to Food sales in cell E9 and did not adjust the reference to E12 because it is an absolute reference.

The last change you need to make to the proportion data is to format it to the Percent style.

6

- **Select G8 through G11.**

- **Click ■ Percent Style.**

- **Click ■ Increase Decimal (twice).**

- **Size column G to fit the contents.**

- **Move to cell A6 and save the workbook as** Forecast4.

Your screen should be similar to Figure 3.22

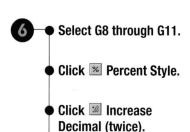

Figure 3.22

The calculated proportion shows the same values that a pie chart of this data would show.

Working with Sheets

Next you want to add the second quarter forecast to the workbook. You want this data in a separate sheet in the same workbook file. To make it easier to enter the forecast for the next quarter, you will copy the contents of the first quarter forecast in Sheet1 into another sheet in the workbook. Then you will change the month headings, the title, and the number data for the second quarter. Finally, you want to include a formula to calculate a year-to-date total for the six months.

Copying Between Sheets

You want to copy the worksheet data from Sheet1 to Sheet2. Copying between sheets is the same as copying within a sheet, except that you switch to the new sheet to specify the destination.

1 • Select the worksheet range A1 through G23.

• Click 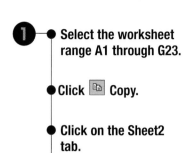 Copy.

• Click on the Sheet2 tab.

• Click 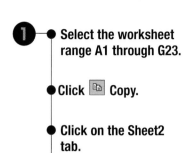 Paste.

Your screen should be similar to Figure 3.23

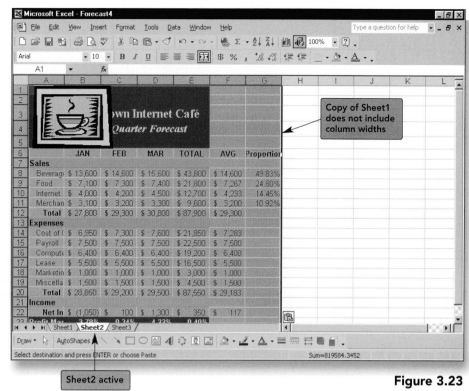

Figure 3.23

All the worksheet data and formatting, except for the column width settings, are copied into the existing Sheet2. You want to include the column width settings from the source.

2 • Click  Paste Options.

• Choose Keep Source Column **W**idths.

Your screen should be similar to Figure 3.24

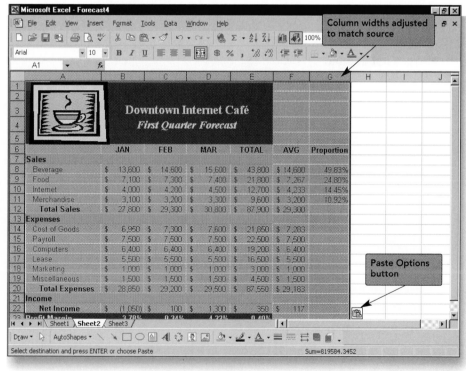

Figure 3.24

Sheet2 now contains a duplicate of the first quarter forecast in Sheet1.

Renaming Sheets and Coloring Sheet Tabs

As more sheets are added to a workbook, remembering what information is in each sheet becomes more difficult. To help clarify the contents of the sheets, you can rename the sheets.

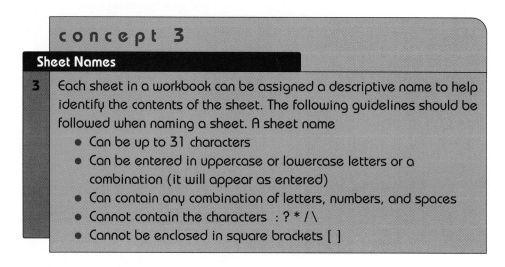

concept 3

Sheet Names

3 Each sheet in a workbook can be assigned a descriptive name to help identify the contents of the sheet. The following guidelines should be followed when naming a sheet. A sheet name

- Can be up to 31 characters
- Can be entered in uppercase or lowercase letters or a combination (it will appear as entered)
- Can contain any combination of letters, numbers, and spaces
- Cannot contain the characters : ? * / \
- Cannot be enclosed in square brackets [ ]

Double-clicking the sheet tab activates the tab and highlights the existing sheet name. The existing name is cleared as soon as you begin to type the new name. You will change the name of Sheet1 to First Quarter and Sheet2 to Second Quarter.

1 ● **Double-click the Sheet1 tab.**

● **Type First Quarter.**

● **Press** ⎆Enter.

● **Change the name of the Sheet2 tab to Second Quarter.**

Another Method

The menu equivalent is Format/Sheet/Rename.

Your screen should be similar to Figure 3.25

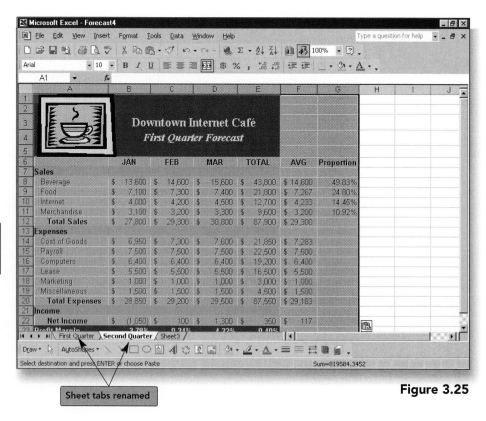

Sheet tabs renamed

Figure 3.25

To further differentiate the sheets, you can add color to the sheet tabs.

2

- **Right-click on the First Quarter tab.**

- **Choose Tab Color from the shortcut menu.**

- **Select yellow from the color pallet.**

- **Click** OK **.**

- **In the same manner, change the color of the Second Quarter sheet tab to green.**

Another Method

The menu equivalent is Format/Sheet/Tab Color.

Your screen should be similar to Figure 3.26

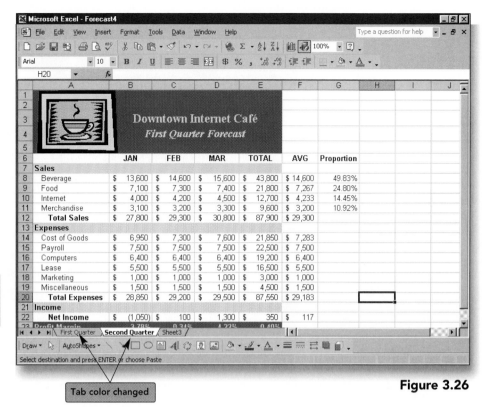

Tab color changed

Figure 3.26

Filling a Series

Now you can change the worksheet title and data in the second quarter sheet.

1

- **Change the title in cell B4 to Second Quarter Forecast.**

- **Change the month heading in cell B6 to APR.**

Your screen should be similar to Figure 3.27

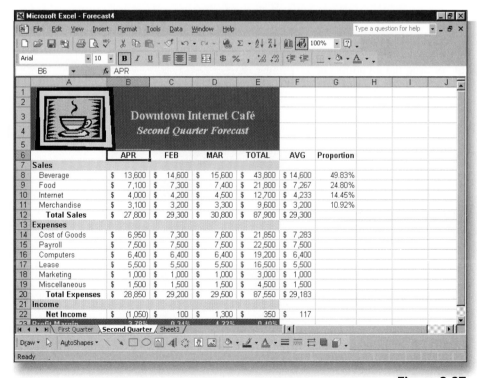

Figure 3.27

Now you need to change the remaining month headings to MAY and JUN. You will use the AutoFill feature to enter the month headings.

concept 4

AutoFill

4 The **AutoFill** feature makes entering a series of headings easier by logically repeating and extending the series. AutoFill recognizes trends and automatically extends data and alphanumeric headings as far as you specify.

Dragging the fill handle activates the AutoFill feature if Excel recognizes the entry in the cell as an entry that can be incremented. When AutoFill extends the entries, it uses the same style as the original entry. For example, if you enter the heading for July as JUL (abbreviated with all letters uppercase), all the extended entries in the series will be abbreviated and uppercase. Dragging down or right increments in increasing order, and up or left increments in decreasing order. A linear series increases or decreases values by a constant value, and a growth series multiplies values by a constant factor.

Initial Selection	Extended series
Qtr1	Qtr2, Qtr3, Qtr4
Mon	Tue Wed Thu
Jan, Apr	Jul, Oct, Jan

Additional Information

A starting value of a series may contain more than one item that can be incremented, such as JAN-02, in which both the month and year can increment. You can specify which value to increment by selecting the appropriate option from the AutoFill Options menu.

The entry in cell B6, APR, is the starting value of a series of months. You will drag the fill handle to the right to increment the months. The mouse pointer displays the entry that will appear in each cell as you drag.

② ● Drag the fill handle of cell B6 to extend the range from cell B6 through cell D6.

Additional Information

If you do not want a series created when you drag the fill handle, hold down Ctrl as you drag and the entries will be copied, not incremented.

Your screen should be similar to Figure 3.28

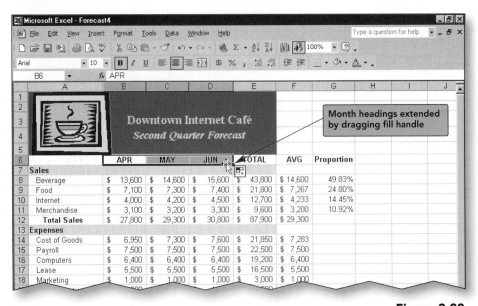

Figure 3.28

Referencing Multiple Sheets

Finally, you need to update the forecast for April through June beverage, food, Internet, and merchandise sales. Then you will enter a formula to calculate the year-to-date income total using data from both sheets.

1 ● **Enter the following values in the specified cells.**

Cell	Number
B8	15700
C8	15800
D8	15900
B9	7500
C9	7600
D9	7600
B10	4500
C10	4500
D10	4500
B11	3200
C11	3200
D11	3200

Your screen should be similar to Figure 3.29

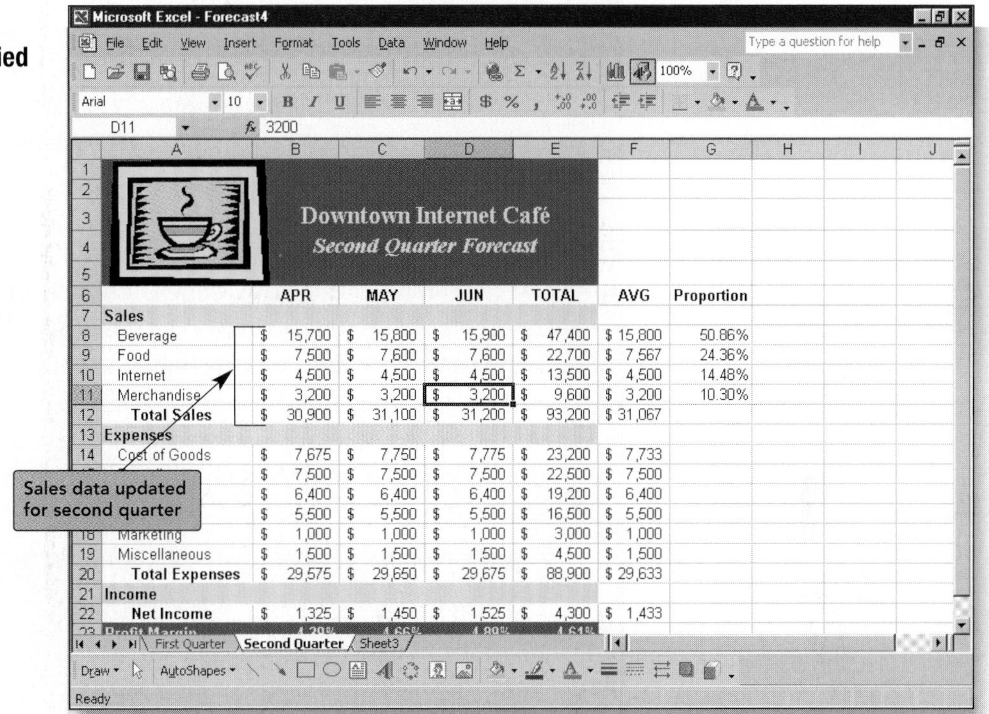

Sales data updated for second quarter

Figure 3.29

The worksheet has been recalculated and now contains the data for the second quarter.

Now you can enter the formula to calculate a year-to-date income total. The formula to make this calculation will sum the total income numbers from the First Quarter sheet in cell E22 and the Second Quarter sheet in cell E22. To reference data in another sheet in the same workbook, you enter a formula that references cells in other worksheets.

concept 5

Sheet and 3-D References

5 A formula that contains references to cells in other sheets of a work-book allows you to use data from multiple sheets and to calculate new values based on this data. The formula contains a **sheet reference** consisting of the name of the sheet, followed by an exclamation point and the cell or range reference. If the sheet name contains non-alphabetic characters, such as a space, the sheet name (or path) must be enclosed in single quotation marks.

If you want to use the same cell or range of cells on multiple sheets, you can use a **3-D reference**. A 3-D reference consists of the names of the beginning and ending sheets enclosed in quotes and separated by a colon. This is followed by an exclamation point and the cell or range reference. The cell or range reference is the same on each sheet in the specified sheet range. If a sheet is inserted or deleted, the range is automatically updated. 3-D references make it easy to analyze data in the same cell or range of cells on multiple worksheets.

Reference	Description
=Sheet2!B17	Displays the entry in cell B17 of Sheet2 in the active cell of the current sheet
=Sheet1!A1+Sheet2!B2.	Sums the values in cell A1 of Sheet1 and B2 of Sheet2
=SUM(Sheet1:Sheet4!H6:K6)	Sums the values in cells H6 through K6 in Sheets 1, 2, 3, and 4
=SUM(Sheet1!H6:K6)	Sums the values in cells H6 through K6 in Sheet1
=SUM(Sheet1:Sheet4!H6)	Sums the values in cell H6 of Sheets 1, 2, 3, and 4

Just like a formula that references cells within a sheet, a formula that references cells in multiple sheets is automatically recalculated when data in a referenced cell changes.

You will enter a descriptive text entry in cell D24 and then use a 3-D reference in a SUM function to calculate the year-to-date total in cell E24.

The SUM function argument will consist of a 3-D reference to cell E22 in the First and Second Quarter sheets. Although a 3-D reference can be entered by typing it using the proper syntax, it is much easier to enter it by pointing to the cells on the sheets. To enter a 3-D reference, select the cell or range in the beginning sheet and then hold down ⇧Shift and click on the sheet tab of the last sheet in the range. This will include the indicated cell range on all sheets between and including the first and last sheet specified.

2 ● **In cell D24 enter and right-align the entry Income Year-To-Date.**

● **Move to E24.**

● **Click Σ AutoSum.**

● **Click cell E22.**

● **Hold down ⇧Shift and click the First Quarter tab.**

● **Release ⇧Shift.**

● **Press ⏎Enter.**

● **Move to E24.**

Your screen should be similar to Figure 3.30

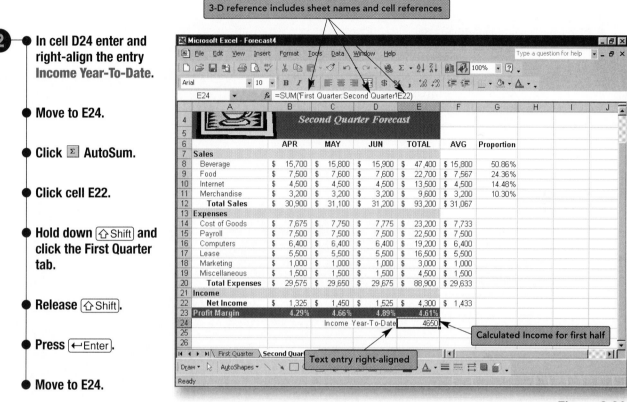

Figure 3.30

The calculated number 4650 appears in cell E24 and the function containing a 3-D reference appears in the formula bar.

You have now completed the forecast for the first half of the year.

● Change the format of cell E24 to Accounting with zero decimal places.

● Enter your name in the workbook file properties as the author.

● Add a predefined header containing your name, page number, and the date to both sheets.

● Preview the entire workbook. Print both worksheets.

● Close and save the workbook file.

Your printed output of the second quarter sheet should be similar to that shown here.

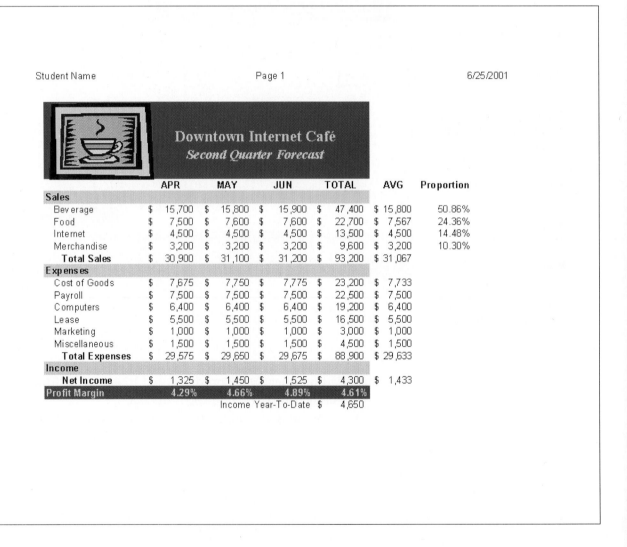

Note: If you are running short on lab time, this is an appropriate place to end this session and begin again at a later time.

Deleting and Moving Sheets

You presented the completed first and second quarterly forecasts to Evan. He is very pleased with the results and now wants you to create worksheets for the third and fourth quarters and a combined annual forecast. Additionally, Evan has asked you to include a column chart of the data for each quarter. Finally, after looking at the forecast, Evan wants the forecast to show a profit margin of 5 percent for each month in the second quarter.

You have already made several of the changes requested and saved them as a workbook file. To see the revised and expanded forecast,

1 ● **Open the workbook file** ex03_Annual Forecast**.**

Your screen should be similar to Figure 3.31

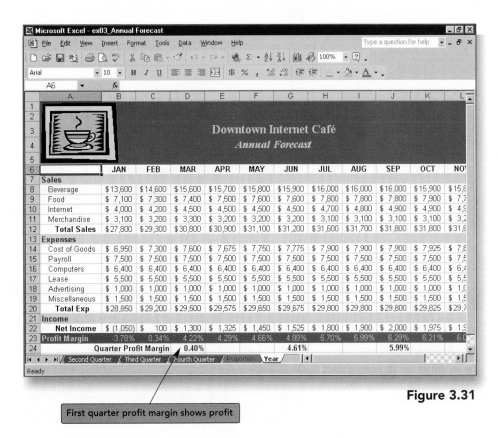

First quarter profit margin shows profit

Figure 3.31

The workbook file now contains six sheets: First Quarter, Second Quarter, Third Quarter, Fourth Quarter, Proportion, and Year. The Proportion sheet contains the proportion of sales values from the first and second quarters. The Year sheet contains the forecast data for the entire 12 months. Each quarter sheet also includes a chart of the profit margin for that quarter. As you can now easily see, the profit margin by the end of the first quarter is showing a profit.

2 ● **Click on each of the Quarter sheet tabs to view the quarterly data and profit margin chart.**

● **Display the Proportion sheet.**

Your screen should be similar to Figure 3.32

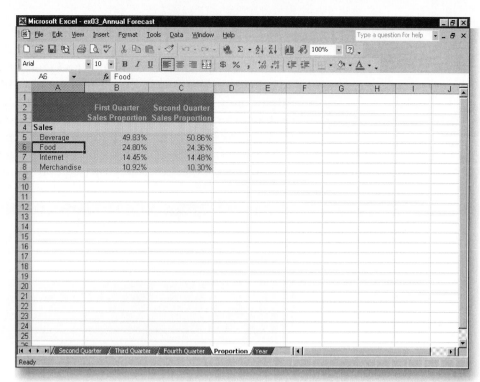

Figure 3.32

You decide this data, although interesting, is not needed in the forecast workbook and want to delete the entire sheet.

3 ● **Choose Edit/Delete Sheet.**

● **Click** [Delete] **to confirm that you want to permanently remove the sheet.**

Your screen should be similar to Figure 3.33

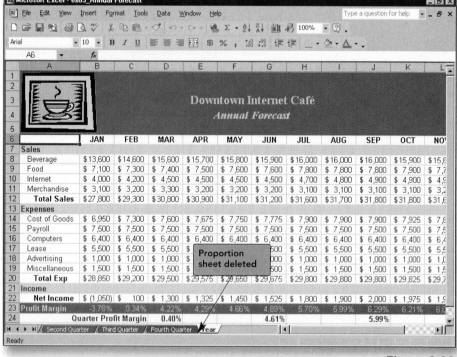

Figure 3.33

The entire sheet is deleted, and the Year sheet is now the active sheet. Next you want to move the Year sheet from the last position in the workbook to the first. You can quickly rearrange sheets in a workbook by dragging the sheet tab to the new location. The symbol ▼ indicates where the sheet will appear.

4 ● Drag the Year tab to the left end of the First Quarter tab.

Another Method

You can also use Edit/Move or Copy Sheet to move a sheet to another location in the workbook.

Your screen should be similar to Figure 3.34

	JAN	**FEB**	**MAR**	**APR**	**MAY**	**JUN**	**JUL**	**AUG**	**SEP**	**OCT**	**NO'**

Microsoft Excel - ex03_Annual Forecast

File Edit View Insert Format Tools Data Window Help

Arial 10 B I U $ % , A6

Downtown Internet Café
Annual Forecast

	A	B	C	D	E	F	G	H	I	J	K	L
7	**Sales**											
8	Beverage	$13,600	$14,600	$15,600	$15,700	$15,800	$15,900	$16,000	$16,000	$16,000	$15,900	$15,8
9	Food	$ 7,100	$ 7,300	$ 7,400	$ 7,500	$ 7,600	$ 7,600	$ 7,800	$ 7,800	$ 7,800	$ 7,900	$ 7,7
10	Internet	$ 4,000	$ 4,200	$ 4,500	$ 4,500	$ 4,500	$ 4,500	$ 4,700	$ 4,800	$ 4,900	$ 4,900	$ 4,9
11	Merchandise	$ 3,100	$ 3,200	$ 3,300	$ 3,200	$ 3,200	$ 3,200	$ 3,100	$ 3,100	$ 3,100	$ 3,100	$ 3,2
12	**Total Sales**	$27,800	$29,300	$30,800	$30,900	$31,100	$31,200	$31,600	$31,700	$31,800	$31,800	$31,8
13	**Expenses**											
14	Cost of Goods	$ 6,950	$ 7,300	$ 7,600	$ 7,675	$ 7,750	$ 7,775	$ 7,900	$ 7,900	$ 7,900	$ 7,925	$ 7,8
15	Payroll	$ 7,500	$ 7,500	$ 7,500	$ 7,500	$ 7,500	$ 7,500	$ 7,500	$ 7,500	$ 7,500	$ 7,500	$ 7,5
16	Comput			00	$ 6,400	$ 6,400	$ 6,400	$ 6,400	$ 6,400	$ 6,400	$ 6,400	$ 6,4
17	Lease		00	$ 5,500	$ 5,500	$ 5,500	$ 5,500	$ 5,500	$ 5,500	$ 5,500	$ 5,500	$ 5,5
18	Advertis		00	$ 1,000	$ 1,000	$ 1,000	$ 1,000	$ 1,000	$ 1,000	$ 1,000	$ 1,000	$ 1,0
19	Miscellaneous	00	$ 1,500	$ 1,500	$ 1,500	$ 1,500	$ 1,500	$ 1,500	$ 1,500	$ 1,500	$ 1,5	
20	**Total Exp**	$28,850	$29,200	$29,500	$29,575	$29,650	$29,675	$29,800	$29,800	$29,800	$29,825	$29,7
21	**Income**											
22	**Net Income**	$ (1,050)	$ 100	$ 1,300	$ 1,325	$ 1,450	$ 1,525	$ 1,800	$ 1,900	$ 2,000	$ 1,975	$ 1,9
23	**Profit Margin**	-3.78%	0.34%	4.22%	4.29%	4.66%	4.89%	5.70%	5.99%	6.29%	6.21%	6.0
24	Quarter Profit Margin		0.40%				4.61%			5.99%		

Sheet moved by dragging tab

Year / First Quarter / Second Quarter / Third Quarter / Fourth Quarter

Ready

Figure 3.34

Managing Large Sheets

Now that the workbook is much larger you are finding that it takes a lot of time to scroll to different areas within and between sheets. To make managing large sheets easier, you can zoom a sheet, split the workbook window, and freeze panes.

Zooming the Worksheet

The Year sheet displays all of the quarterly data. The entire sheet, however, is not visible in the window. You can change how much information is displayed in the window to make it easier to navigate, view, and select worksheet data by adjusting the zoom percentage. The default zoom setting is 100 percent. This setting displays data onscreen the same size that it will appear on the printed page. You can reduce or enlarge the amount of information displayed onscreen by changing the magnification from between 10 to 400 percent. You want to decrease the zoom percent to display more information in the window.

Additional Information

The Zoom feature is common in all Office XP programs.

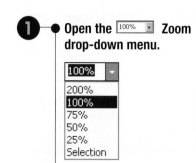

1 **Open the** `100%` **Zoom drop-down menu.**

> 200%
> **100%**
> 75%
> 50%
> 25%
> Selection

Additional Information

The Selection option adjusts the percentage to fit the selected range in the current window size.

● **Choose 75%.**

Another Method

The menu equivalent is View/Zoom.

Your screen should be similar to Figure 3.35

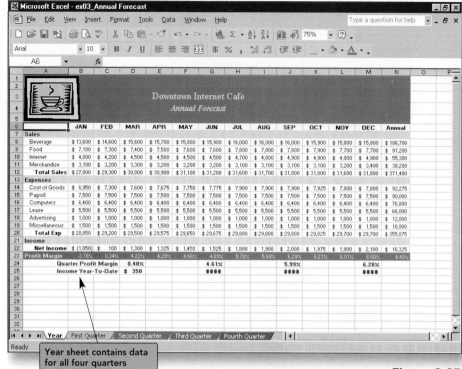

Year sheet contains data for all four quarters

Figure 3.35

You can now see the entire worksheet.

2 **Reduce the zoom percent to 50%.**

Your screen should be similar to Figure 3.36

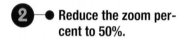

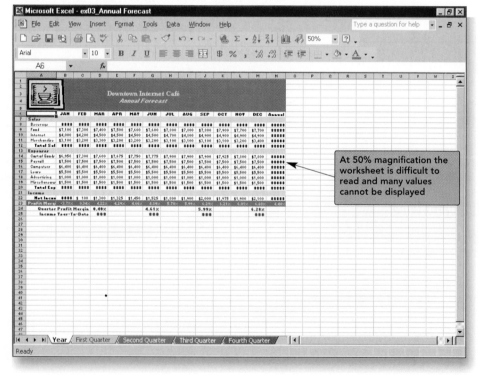

At 50% magnification the worksheet is difficult to read and many values cannot be displayed

Figure 3.36

Additional Information

Pointing to the #### error value will display the cell value in a ScreenTip.

As you reduce the percentage, more worksheet area is visible in the window. However, it gets more difficult to read and many cells display the error value ##### because the column width is not wide enough to fully display the result.

Going to a Specific cell

Most of the monthly values in the Year sheet, such as cell B8, contain linking formulas that reference the appropriate cells in the appropriate quarter sheets. Others, such as the total formulas and the formula to calculate the income, do not reference cells outside the Year worksheet.

To see several of the formulas in cells that reference the quarter sheets,

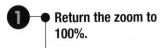

Return the zoom to 100%.

Move to B8.

Move to E12.

Move to H16.

Your screen should be similar to Figure 3.37

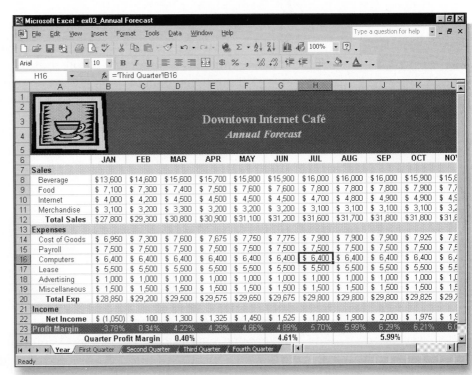

Figure 3.37

Each of these cells contained a formula that referenced a cell in the appropriate quarter sheet. To see the total formulas for the year in column N, you will move to cell N16 using the GoTo feature.

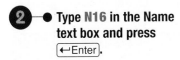

Type N16 in the Name text box and press ⏎Enter.

Another Method

The menu equivalent is Edit/GoTo and the keyboard shortcut is Ctrl + G or F5.

Your screen should be similar to Figure 3.38

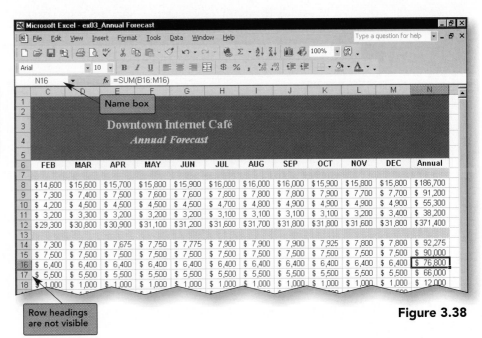

Figure 3.38

The cell selector jumps directly to cell N16 in the total column. The formula in this cell calculates the total of the values in row 16 and does not reference another sheet. However, it is difficult to know what the numbers represent in this row because the row headings are not visible. For example, is this number the total for the lease expenses, advertising expenses, or miscellaneous expenses? Without scrolling back to see the row headings, it is difficult to know.

Splitting Windows

Whenever you scroll a large worksheet, you will find that information you may need to view in one area scrolls out of view as you move to another area. Although you could reduce the zoom percent to view more of a worksheet in the window, you still may not be able to see the entire worksheet if it is very large. And as you saw, continuing to reduce the zoom makes the worksheet difficult to read and prevents some values from fully displaying. To view different areas of the same sheet at the same time, you can split the window.

concept 6

Split Windows

6   A sheet window can be split into sections called **panes** to make it easier to view different parts of the sheet at the same time. The panes can consist of any number of columns or rows along the top or left edge of the window. You can divide the sheet into two panes either horizontally or vertically, or into four panes if you split the window both vertically and horizontally.

Each pane can be scrolled independently to display different areas of the sheet. When split vertically, the panes scroll together when you scroll vertically, but scroll independently when you scroll horizontally. Horizontal panes scroll together when you scroll horizontally, but independently when you scroll vertically.

Panes are most useful for viewing a worksheet that consists of different areas or sections. Creating panes allows you to display the different sections of the worksheet in separate panes and then to quickly switch between panes to access the data in the different sections without having to repeatedly scroll to the areas.

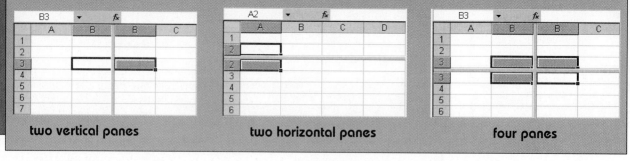

two vertical panes   two horizontal panes   four panes

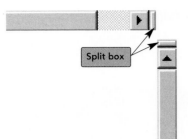

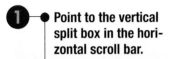

Dragging the split box at the top of the vertical scroll bar downward creates a horizontal split, and dragging the split box at the right end of the horizontal scroll bar leftward creates a vertical split.

You will split the window into two vertical panes. This will allow you to view the titles in column A at the same time as you are viewing data in column N.

1 ● **Point to the vertical split box in the horizontal scroll bar.**

Additional Information

The mouse pointer changes to a ↔ to show you can drag to create a split.

● **Drag to the left and position the bar between columns D and E.**

Your screen should be similar to Figure 3.39

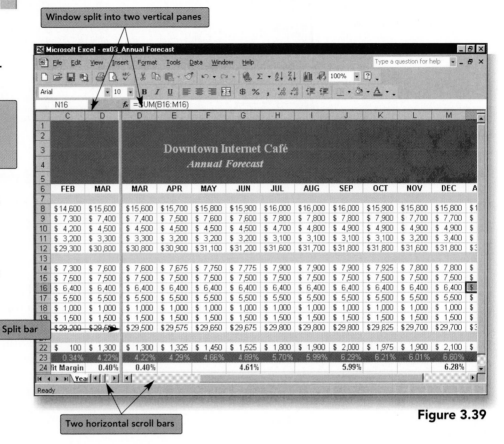

Figure 3.39

Additional Information

The Window/Split command can be used to quickly create a four-way split at the active cell.

There are now two vertical panes with two separate horizontal scroll bars. The highlighted cell selector is visible in the right pane. The left pane also has a cell selector in cell N16, but it is not visible because that area of the worksheet is not displayed in the pane. When the same area of a worksheet is visible in multiple panes, the cell selector in the panes that are not active is highlighted whereas the cell selector in the active pane is clear. The active pane will be affected by your movement horizontally. The cell selector moves in both panes, but only the active pane scrolls.

You will scroll the left pane horizontally to display the month headings in column A.

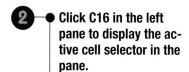

2 ● **Click C16 in the left pane to display the active cell selector in the pane.**

● **Press ← twice.**

Your screen should be similar to Figure 3.40

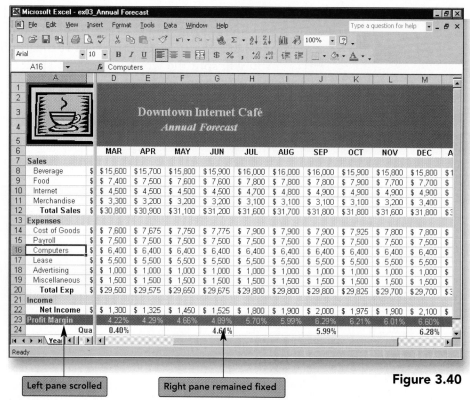

Left pane scrolled

Right pane remained fixed

Figure 3.40

The right pane did not scroll when you moved horizontally through the left pane to display the row headings. The cell selector in the right pane is in the same cell location as in the left pane (A16), although it is not visible. You want to change the location of the split so that you can view an entire quarter in the left pane in order to more easily compare quarters.

3 ● **Drag the split bar to the right three columns.**

● **Click cell E16 in the right pane.**

● **Press End →.**

● **Press → (three times).**

Your screen should be similar to Figure 3.41

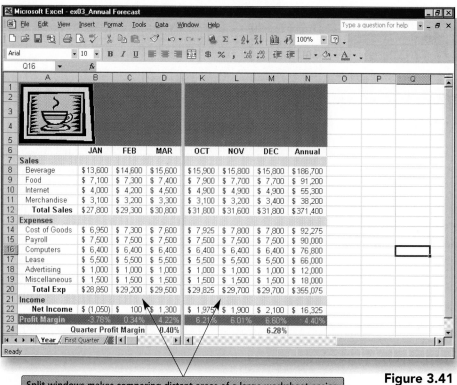

Split windows makes comparing distant areas of a large worksheet easier

Figure 3.41

Now you can easily compare the first quarter data to the last quarter data. As you can see, creating panes is helpful when you want to display and access distant areas of a worksheet quickly. After scrolling the data in the panes to display the appropriate worksheet area, you can then quickly switch between panes to make changes to the data that is visible in the pane. This saves you the time of scrolling to the area each time you want to view it or make changes to it. You will clear the horizontal split from the window.

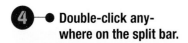

4 ● **Double-click any- where on the split bar.**

Another Method

The menu equivalent is Window/Remove Split.

Your screen should be similar to Figure 3.42

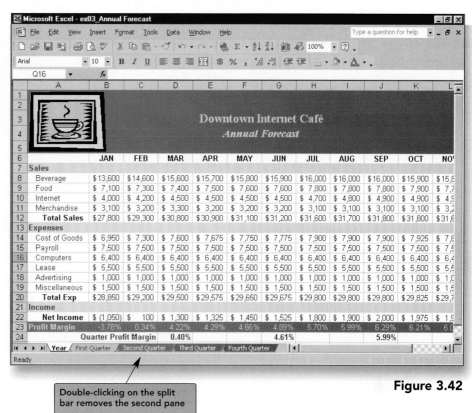

Double-clicking on the split bar removes the second pane

Figure 3.42

Freezing Panes

Another way to manage a large worksheet is to freeze panes.

concept 7

Freeze Panes

7 **Freezing panes** prevents the data in the pane from scrolling as you move to different areas in a worksheet. You can freeze the information in the top and left panes of a window only. This feature is most useful when your worksheet is organized using row and column headings. It allows you to keep the titles on the top and left edge of your worksheet in view as you scroll horizontally and vertically through the worksheet data.

You want to keep the month headings in row 6 and the row headings in column A visible in the window at all times while looking at the Income and Profit Margin data beginning in row 21. To do this, you will create four panes with the upper and left panes frozen.

When creating frozen panes, first position the worksheet in the window to display the information you want to appear in the top and left panes. This is because data in the frozen panes cannot be scrolled like data in regular panes. Then move to the location specified in the following table before using the Windows/Freeze Panes command to create and freeze panes.

To Create	Cell Selector Location	Example
Two horizontal panes with the top pane frozen	Move to the leftmost column in the window and to the row below where you want the split to appear.	**Top Pane Frozen** 9 Food $ 7,100 $ 7,300 10 Internet $ 4,000 $ 4,200 11 Merchandise $ 3,100 $ 3,200 12 Total Sales $ 27,800 $ 29,300 20 Total Exp $ 28,850 $ 29,200 21 Income
Two vertical panes with the left pane frozen	Move to the top row of the window and to the column to the right of where you want the split to appear.	**Left Pane Frozen** 9 Food $ 7,600 $ 7,600 10 Internet $ 4,500 $ 4,500 11 Merchandise $ 3,200 $ 3,200 12 Total Sales $ 31,100 $ 31,200 13 Expenses 14 Cost of Goods $ 7,750 $ 7,775
Four panes with the top and left panes frozen	Move to the cell below and to the right of where you want the split to appear.	**Top and Left Pane Frozen** 6 MAY JUN 7 Sales 8 Beverage $ 15,800 $ 15,900 9 Food $ 7,600 $ 7,600 10 Internet $ 4,500 $ 4,500 11 Merchandise $ 3,200 $ 3,200

You want to split the window into four panes with the month column headings at the top of the window and the row headings in column A at the left side of the window.

1 ● Scroll the window
until row 6 is the top
row in the window.

● Move to B7.

● Choose
Window/Freeze Panes.

*Your screen should be
similar to Figure 3.43*

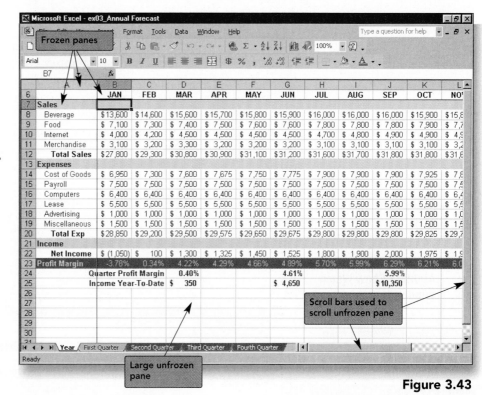

Figure 3.43

The window is divided into four panes at the cell selector location. Only one
set of scroll bars is displayed because the only pane that can be scrolled is
the larger lower-right pane. You can move the cell selector into a frozen
pane, but the data in the frozen panes will not scroll. Also, there is only one
cell selector that moves from one pane to another over the pane divider,
making it unnecessary to click on the pane to make it active before moving
the cell selector in it.

Because Evan has asked you to adjust the profit margin values, you want
to view this area of the worksheet only.

2 ● Use the vertical scroll
bar to scroll the win-
dow until row 21 is
below row 6.

● Move to cell G24.

*Your screen should be
similar to Figure 3.44*

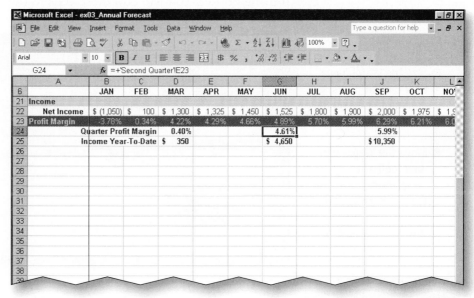

Figure 3.44

Now the Income and profit margin data is displayed immediately below the
month headings in row six. The data in rows 7 through 20 is no longer visible, allowing you to concentrate on this area of the worksheet.

Watching Cells

While using a workbook with large worksheets and/or multiple sheets, you may want to keep an eye on how changes you make to values in one area effect cells in another. For example, if you change a value in one sheet that is referenced in a formula in another, you can view the effect on the calculated value using the Watch Window toolbar.

You will be changing values in the second quarter sheet next and want to be able to see the effect on the linked formulas in the Year sheet at the same time.

1 ● Select cells G24 and N23.

● Choose **T**ools/Formula A**u**diting/Show **W**atch Window.

● Click  from the Watch window toolbar.

Your screen should be similar to Figure 3.45

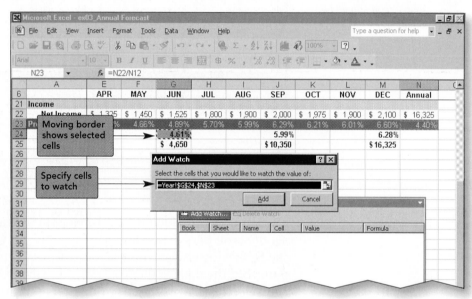

Figure 3.45

The Add Watch dialog box is used to specify the cells you want to see in the Watch Window toolbar. The currently selected cells are identified with a moving border. You will add these cells to the Watch Window.

2 ● Click **Add** .

● Size the Watch window toolbar just large enough to display the two cell values rows.

● Move the Watch window toolbar to the upper-right corner of the workbook window.

Your screen should be similar to Figure 3.46

Figure 3.46

The values in the selected cells as well as the formula and location information are displayed in the Watch Window. The toolbar will remain open on top of the workbook as you move from one sheet to another.

Forecasting Values

Evan has asked you to adjust the forecast for the second quarter to show a profit margin of at least 5 percent for each month. After some consideration, you decide you can most easily reduce monthly payroll expenses by carefully scheduling employee work during these three months. Reducing the monthly expense will increase the profit margin for the quarter. You want to find out what the maximum payroll value you can spend during that period is for each month to accomplish this goal. The process of evaluating what effect changing the payroll expenses will have on the profit margin is called what-if analysis.

concept 8

What-If Analysis

8   **What-if analysis** is a technique used to evaluate the effects of changing selected factors in a worksheet. This technique is a common accounting function that has been made much easier with the introduction of spreadsheet programs. By substituting different values in cells that are referenced by formulas, you can quickly see the effect of the changes when the formulas are recalculated.

You can perform what-if analysis by manually substituting values or by using one of the what-if analysis tools included with Excel.

Performing What-If Analysis Manually

To do this, you will enter different payroll expense values for each month and see what the effect is on that month's profit margin. You will adjust the May payroll value first.

1 ● Make the Second Quarter sheet active.

● Enter **7300** in cell C15.

Your screen should be similar to Figure 3.47

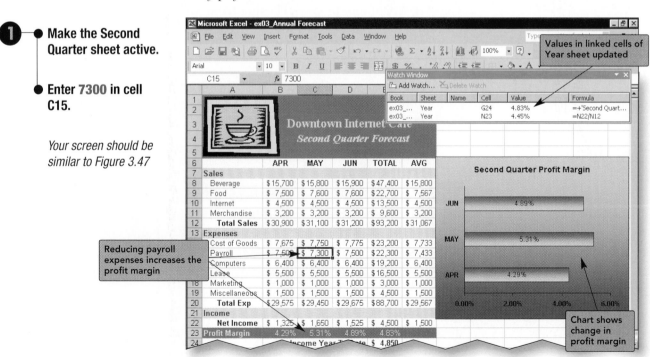

Figure 3.47

Now by looking in cell C23, you can see that decreasing the payroll expenses has increased the profit margin for the month to 5.31 percent. This is more than you need. Also notice the chart has changed to reflect the change in May's profit margin. The Watch Window shows that the values in the two linked cells in the Year sheet were updated accordingly.

You will continue to enter payroll values until the profit margin reaches the goal.

2 ● **Enter 7400 in cell C15.**

● **Enter 7390 in cell C15.**

● **Enter 7395 in cell C15.**

Your screen should be similar to Figure 3.48

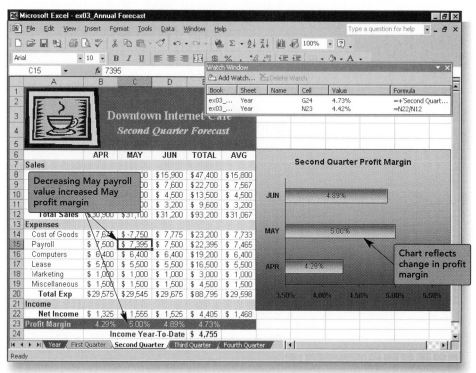

Figure 3.48

That's it! Reducing the payroll value from 7500 to 7395 will achieve the 5% profit margin goal for the month.

Using Goal Seek

It usually takes several tries to find the appropriate value when manually performing what-if analysis. A quicker way is to use the what-if analysis Goal Seek tool provided with Excel.

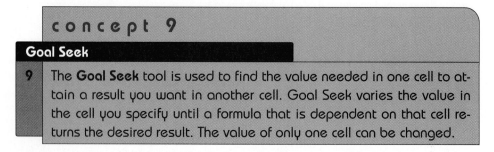

concept 9

Goal Seek

9   The **Goal Seek** tool is used to find the value needed in one cell to attain a result you want in another cell. Goal Seek varies the value in the cell you specify until a formula that is dependent on that cell returns the desired result. The value of only one cell can be changed.

You will use this method to find the payroll value for April that will produce a 5 percent profit margin for that month. The current profit margin value is 4.29 percent in cell B23.

1 ● Move to B23.

● Choose **T**ools/**G**oal
Seek.

*Your screen should be
similar to Figure 3.49*

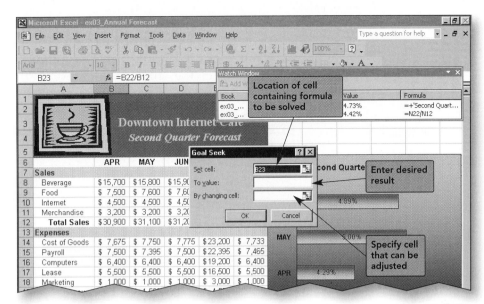

Figure 3.49

In the Goal Seek dialog box, you need to specify the location of the cell containing the formula to be solved, the desired calculated value, and the cell containing the number that can be adjusted to achieve the result. You want the formula in cell B23 to calculate a result of 5 percent by changing the payroll number in cell B15. The Set Cell text box correctly displays the current cell as the location of the formula to be solved. You will enter the information needed in the Goal Seek dialog box.

2 ● Click in the To **V**alue
text box and enter the
value **5.00%**.

● Click in the By
Changing Cell text box
and then click on cell
B15 in the worksheet
to enter the cell
reference.

● Click ● OK .

*Your screen should be
similar to Figure 3.50*

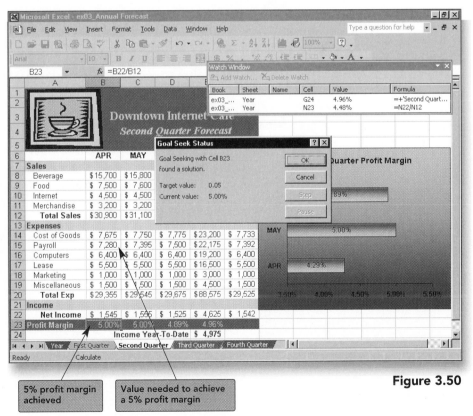

Figure 3.50

The Goal Seek Status dialog box tells you it found a solution that will achieve the 5 percent profit margin. The payroll value of 7280 that will achieve the desired result has been temporarily entered in the worksheet. You can reject the solution and restore the original value by choosing [Cancel]. In this case, however, you want to accept the solution.

Your screen should be
similar to Figure 3.51

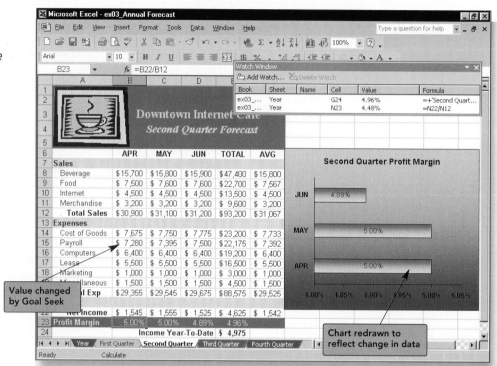

Figure 3.51

The payroll value is permanently updated and the chart redrawn to reflect the change in profit margin for April.

Changing Values Using a Chart

Finally, you need to adjust the June payroll value. This time you will find the value by dragging the June chart data marker to the 5% position on the chart. As you drag the data marker, a dotted bar line will show the new bar length and a ChartTip will display the new profit margin value. An indicator on the X axis also marks your location. Releasing the mouse button with the bar at the new position specifies the new value and opens the Goal Seek dialog box.

1 ● Click on the June data series bar twice (slowly) to select the individual bar.

Additional Information
The bar is surrounded by eight selection handles.

● Drag the middle selection handle on the right end of the bar to increase the length of the bar. When the bar ChartTip value is 0.05 or as close as you can get, release the mouse button.

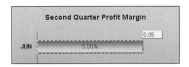

Your screen should be similar to Figure 3.52

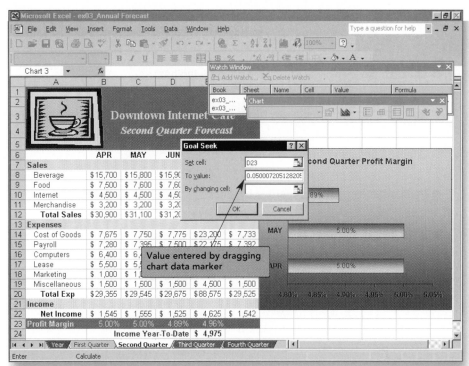

Figure 3.52

Dragging the data marker specifies the value you want to change to and the location of the cell containing the formula. The Goal Seek dialog box is displayed. The Set Cell location and value to attain are entered. Depending on the value you were able to attain by dragging the data marker, you may still need to adjust the value to the exact value of 0.05. You also need to specify the cell location of the value to change.

2 ● If necessary, edit the To **V**alue contents to 0.05.

● Enter cell D15 in the By changing cell text box.

● Click [OK].

● Click [OK] to accept the solution.

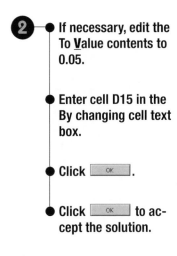

Your screen should be similar to Figure 3.53

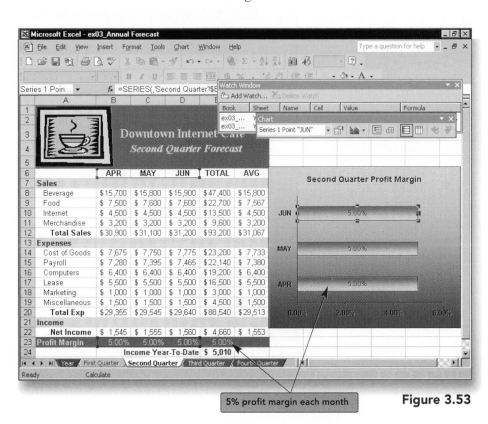

5% profit margin each month

Figure 3.53

The second quarter values are now at the 5 percent profit margin objective. The Watch Window also reflects te change in cell G24.

3 ● Click ⊠ Close to close the Watch Window toolbar.

● Make the Year sheet active to further verify that the profit margin values for the second quarter were updated.

● Choose **W**indow/Un**f**reeze Panes.

● Update the workbook properties by entering your name as author.

● Save the revised forecast as Annual Forecast Revised.

Customizing Print Settings

Now you are ready to print the workbook. Because your worksheet looks great on your screen, this does not mean it will look good when printed. Many times you will want to change the print and layout settings to improve the appearance of the output. Customizing the print settings by changing the orientation of the page, centering the worksheet on the page, hiding gridlines, and adding custom header and footer information are just a few of the ways you can make your printed output look more professional.

Changing Page Orientation

First you want to preview all the sheets in the workbook.

1 ● Right-click a sheet tab and choose Select All Sheets from the shortcut menu.

> **Additional Information**
> The tabs of all sheets appear white indicating they are selected; the active sheet tab name is bold.

● Click 🔍 Print Preview.

Your screen should be similar to Figure 3.54

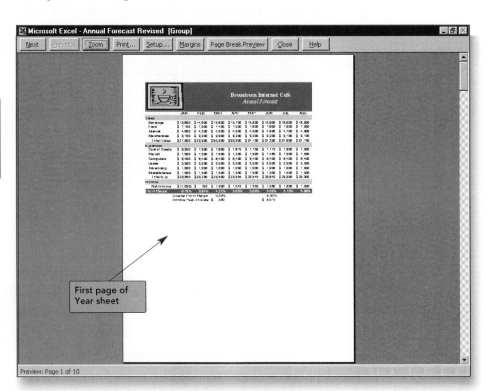

First page of Year sheet

Figure 3.54

The first page of the Year worksheet is displayed in the Preview window. Notice that the entire sheet does not fit across the width of the page. To see the second page,

Click Next.

Your screen should be similar to Figure 3.55

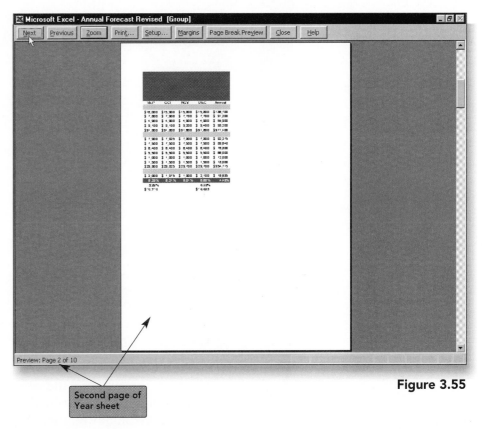

Second page of Year sheet

Figure 3.55

The last five columns of data appear on the second page. Although you could use the Fit To feature to compress the worksheet to a single page, this would make the data small and difficult to read. Instead you can change the orientation or the direction the output is printed on a page. The default orientation is **portrait**. This setting prints across the width of the page. You will change the orientation to **landscape** so that the worksheet prints across the length of the paper. Then you will use the Fit To feature to make sure it fits on one page with the new orientation.

In addition, notice that the total number of pages to be printed is 10. This is because each quarter sheet also requires two pages to print in portrait orientation. You will also change the orientation of these sheets to landscape.

3
- Click Previous .

- Click Setup... .

- If necessary, open the Page tab.

- Select **L**andscape.

- Select **F**it to.

- Click OK .

Your screen should be similar to Figure 3.56

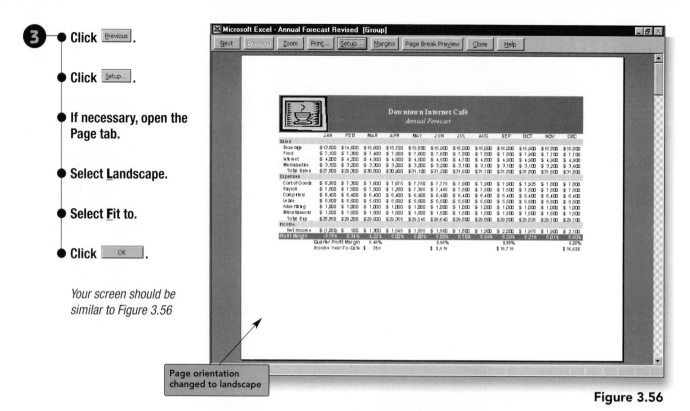

Page orientation changed to landscape

Figure 3.56

Displaying Gridlines and Centering on Page

The entire worksheet now easily fits across the length of the page. Because the worksheet is large, you also feel the worksheet may be easier to read if the row and column gridlines were printed. In addition, you want the worksheet to be centered horizontally on the page.

1
- Click Setup... .

- From the Sheet tab, select **G**ridlines.

- From the Margins tab, select Hori**z**ontally.

- Click OK .

Your screen should be similar to Figure 3.57

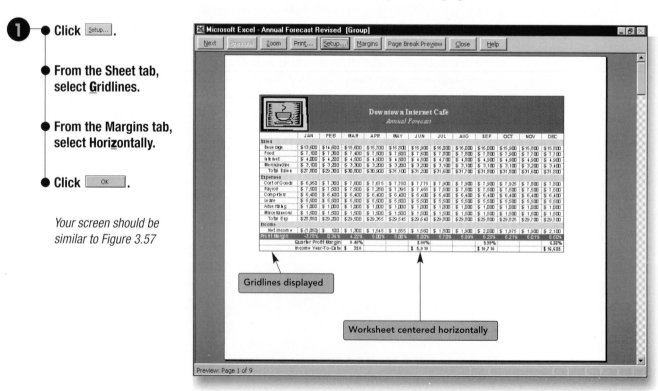

Gridlines displayed

Worksheet centered horizontally

Figure 3.57

The Preview screen is recreated showing how the sheet will appear centered horizontally and with gridlines.

Next, you want to change the orientation to landscape for the four quarterly sheets and to center them both horizontally and vertically on the page. Rather than change each sheet individually in the Preview window, you can make this change to the four sheets at the same time in the worksheet window.

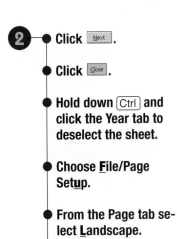

● Click **Next**.

● Click **Close**.

● Hold down Ctrl and click the Year tab to deselect the sheet.

● Choose **File/Page Setup**.

● From the Page tab select **Landscape**.

● From the Margins tab select **Horizontally** and **Vertically**.

● Click **Print Preview**.

Your screen should be similar to Figure 3.58

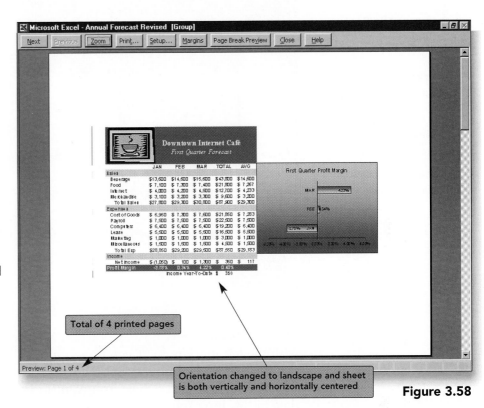

Total of 4 printed pages

Orientation changed to landscape and sheet is both vertically and horizontally centered

Figure 3.58

The worksheet is displayed in landscape orientation and centered both horizontally and vertically on the page. You can also see from the total number of pages to print (four) that the same changes have been made to the four selected sheets.

Adding Custom Headers and Footers

Additional Information

Be careful when making changes to multiple sheets as these changes may replace data on other sheets.

You would also like to add a custom footer to all the sheets. It is faster to add the footer to all sheets at the same time. If you make changes to the active sheet when multiple sheets are selected, the changes are made to all other selected sheets.

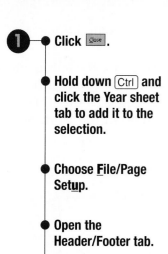

1
● Click [Close].

● Hold down [Ctrl] and
click the Year sheet
tab to add it to the
selection.

● Choose **F**ile/**P**age
Set**u**p.

● Open the
Header/Footer tab.

● Click [Custom Footer...].

*Your screen should be
similar to Figure 3.59*

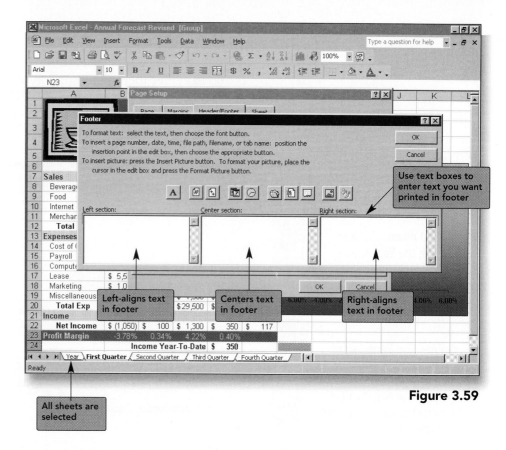

All sheets are
selected

Figure 3.59

The Left Section text box will display the footer text you entered aligned
with the left margin, the Center Section will center the text, and the Right
Section will right-align the text. The insertion point is currently positioned
in the Left Section text box. You want to enter your name, class, and the
date in this box. You will enter your name and class by typing it directly in
the box. Instead of typing the date, however, you will enter a code that will
automatically insert the current date whenever the worksheet is printed.

The buttons above the section boxes (identified below) are used to enter the codes for common header and footer information.

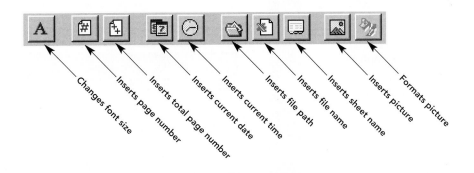

Type Created by [your name].

Press Tab ↹.

Enter the name of your class and the section or time.

Press Tab ↹.

Click ▦ **Date.**

Your screen should be similar to Figure 3.60

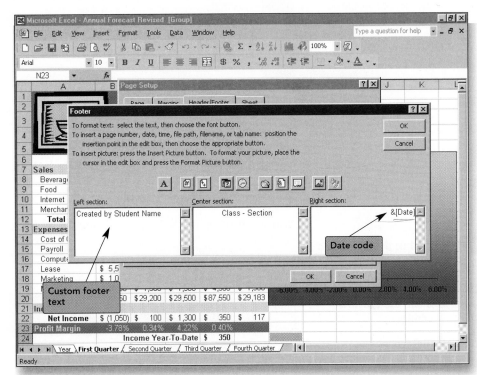

Figure 3.60

You want to make one final check to see how the footer will look before printing the workbook.

● **Click** [OK].

● **Click** [Print Preview].

● **Look at the other sheets to confirm that the footer was added to them as well.**

● **Display the Year sheet again.**

Your screen should be similar to Figure 3.61

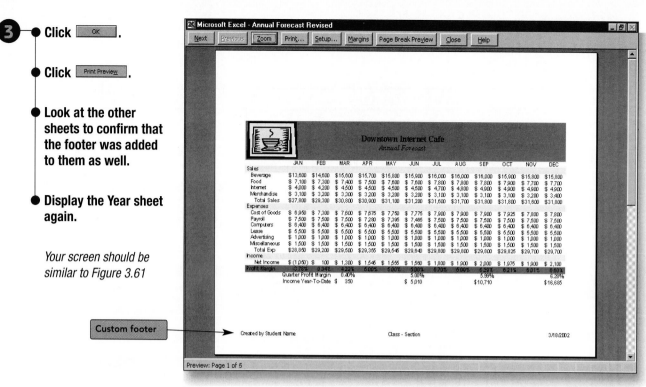

Custom footer

Figure 3.61

The footer as you entered it appears on all selected worksheets.

Printing Selected Sheets

You want to print the Year and Second Quarter worksheets only.

● **Best fit the Year sheet and display grid lines again.**

● **Close the Preview window.**

● **Right-click on a sheet tab and choose Ungroup Sheets.**

● **If necessary, make the Year sheet active.**

● **Save the file again.**

● **Hold down** [Ctrl] **and click the Second Quarter Sheet tab to add it to the selection of sheets to print.**

● **Click** 🖨 **Print.**

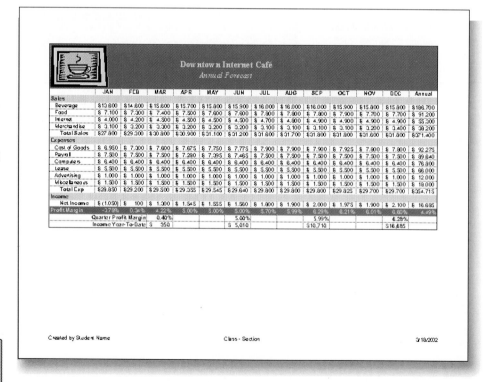

HAVING TROUBLE?

If you need to specify print settings that are different from the default settings on your system, use File/Print to print the worksheet.

Your printed output should look like that shown here and on the next page.

2 **Close the workbook and exit Excel.**

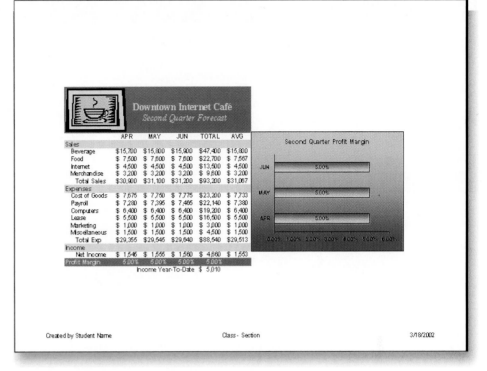

concept summary

Spell Checking (EX3.5)

The spell-checking feature locates all misspelled words, duplicate words, and capitalization irregularities in the active worksheet and proposes the correct spelling.

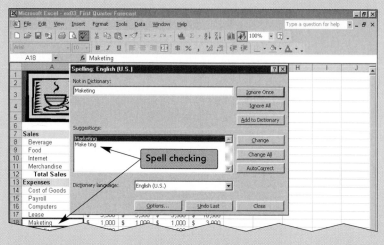

Absolute References (EX3.16)

An absolute reference is a cell or range reference in a formula whose location does not change when the formula is copied.

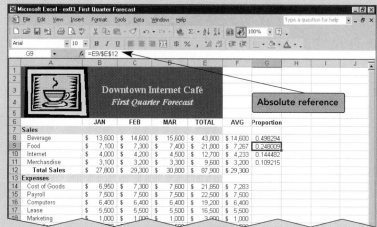

Sheet Names (EX3.20)

Each sheet in a workbook can be assigned a descriptive name to identify the contents of the sheet.

AutoFill (EX3.22)

The AutoFill feature makes entering long or complicated headings easier by logically repeating and extending the series.

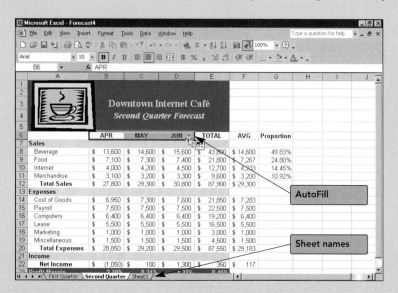

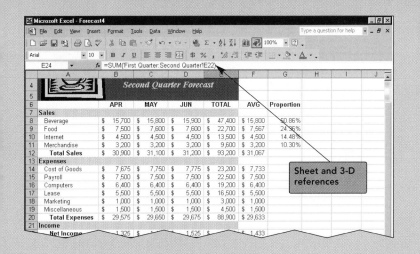

Sheet and 3-D References (EX3.24)

A formula containing sheet and 3-D references to cells in different worksheets in a workbook allows you to use data from other worksheets and to calculate new values based on this data.

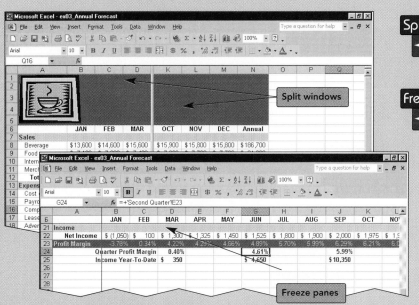

Split Windows (EX3.32)

A sheet window can be split into sections called panes to make it easier to view different parts of the sheet at the same time.

Freeze Panes (EX3.35)

Freezing panes prevents the data in the panes from scrolling as you move to different areas in the worksheet.

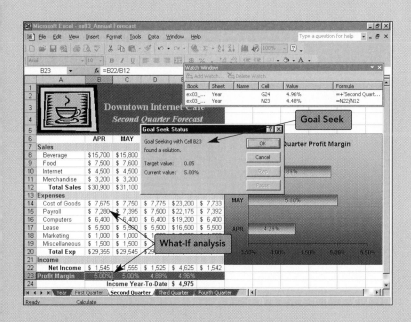

What-If Analysis (EX3.39)

What-if analysis is a technique used to evaluate the effects of changing selected factors in a worksheet.

Goal Seek (EX3.40)

Goal Seek is a tool that is used to find the value needed in one cell to attain a result you want in another cell.

Managing and Analyzing a Workbook

key terms

3-D reference EX3.24	mixed reference EX3.16
absolute reference EX3.16	pane EX3.32
AutoFill EX3.22	portrait EX3.45
custom dictionary EX3.5	Sheet reference EX3.24
freeze panes EX3.35	Spelling Checker EX3.5
Goal Seek EX3.40	what-if analysis EX3.39
landscape EX3.45	
main dictionary EX3.5	

mous skills

After completing this lab, you have learned the following Microsoft Office User Specialist skills:

Skill	Description	Page
Working with Cells and Cell Data	Check spelling	EX3.4
Formatting and Printing Worksheets	Modify row and column settings	EX3.5
	Modify Page Setup options for worksheets	EX3.44
	Preview and print worksheets and workbooks	EX3.44
Modifying Workbooks	Insert and delete worksheets	EX3.27
	Modify worksheet names and positions	EX3.25
	Use 3-D references	EX3.24
Creating and Revising Formulas	Create and revise formulas	EX3.11
	Use statitical, date and time, financial, and logical functions in formulas	EX3.11

command summary

Command	Shortcut Keys	Button	Action
<u>E</u>dit/<u>M</u>ove or Copy Sheet			Moves or copies selected sheet
<u>F</u>ile/Page Set<u>u</u>p/Page/<u>L</u>andscape			Changes orientation to landscape
<u>I</u>nsert/<u>F</u>unction	⇧Shift + F3	f_x	Inserts a function
F<u>o</u>rmat/S<u>h</u>eet/<u>R</u>ename			Renames sheet
F<u>o</u>rmat/<u>S</u>tyle/<u>S</u>tyle name/Currency			Applies currency style to selection
F<u>o</u>rmat/<u>S</u>tyle/<u>S</u>tyle name/Percent		%	Changes cell style to display percentage
<u>T</u>ools/<u>S</u>pelling	F7	ABC✓	Spell-checks worksheet
<u>T</u>ools/<u>G</u>oal Seek			Adjusts value in specified cell until a formula dependent on that cell reaches specified result
<u>T</u>ools/Formula A<u>u</u>diting/Show <u>W</u>atch Window			Opens the Watch Window toolbar
<u>V</u>iew/<u>Z</u>oom		100% ▾	Changes magnification of window
<u>W</u>indow/Un<u>f</u>reeze			Unfreezes window panes
<u>W</u>indow/<u>F</u>reeze Panes			Freezes top and/or leftmost panes
<u>W</u>indow/<u>S</u>plit			Divides window into four panes at active cell
<u>W</u>indow/Remove <u>S</u>plit			Removes split bar from active worksheet

lab exercises

Terminology

screen identification

In the following worksheet and chart, several items are identified by letters. Enter the correct term for each item in the space provided.

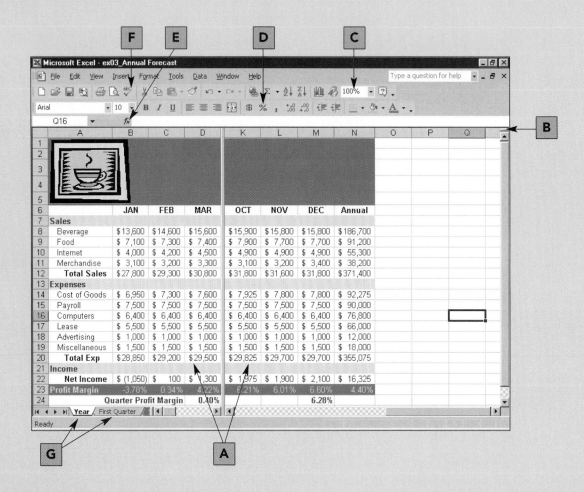

A. _____

B. _____

C. _____

D. _____

E. _____

F. _____

G. _____

matching

Match the lettered item on the right with the numbered item on the left.

1. 'Second Quarter!'A13	_____	a. default page orientation
2. pane	_____	b. spell-checks worksheet
3. portrait	_____	c. pane that contains the cell selector
4. F7	_____	d. the sections of a divided window
5. Sheet1:Sheet3!H3:K5	_____	e. sheet reference
6. #DIV/0!	_____	f. mixed cell reference
7. landscape	_____	g. 3-D reference
8. M34	_____	h. indicates division by zero error
9. active pane	_____	i. prints across the length of the paper
10. $B12	_____	j. absolute cell reference

multiple choice

Circle the correct response to the questions below.

1. _____ styles display dollar signs, commas, and two or zero decimal places.
   a. currency
   b. comma
   c. normal
   d. percent

2. The cell reference to adjust row 4 without adjusting column C is:
   a. C4
   b. C4
   c. $C4
   d. C$4

3. The number 32534 displayed with the Currency[0] style would appear as _____ in a cell.
   a. 32,534
   b. $32534
   c. $32,534
   d. $32,534.00

4. Each sheet in a workbook can be assigned a descriptive name called a:
   a. sheet name
   b. reference name
   c. content name
   d. label name

5. A(n) _____ holds words you commonly use but that are not included in the dictionary supplied with the program.
   a. AutoFill
   b. custom dictionary
   c. spell checker
   d. main dictionary

6. A _____ reference is a reference to the same cell or range on multiple sheets in the same workbook.
   a. copied
   b. 3-D
   c. sheet
   d. workbook

7. A division of the worksheet window that allows different areas of the worksheet to be viewed at the same time is called a:
   a. window
   b. part
   c. pane
   d. section

8. The information in the worksheet can be _____ in the top and left panes of a window only.
   a. frozen
   b. fixed
   c. aligned
   d. adjusted

9. A common accounting function that helps evaluate data by allowing the user to adjust values to see the effect is called:
   a. auto calculate
   b. what-if analysis
   c. AutoFill
   d. value analysis

10. A cell address that is part absolute and part relative is called:
    a. absolute reference
    b. frozen
    c. adjusted
    d. mixed reference

true/false

Circle the correct answer to the following questions.

1.	=SUM(Sheet15:Sheet50!H6) sums the values in cell H6 of sheets 15 and 50.	True	False
2.	An absolute reference is a cell or range reference in a formula whose location does not change when the formula is copied.	True	False
3.	G8 is an absolute reference.	True	False
4.	If you hold down Ctrl while you drag the fill handle the entries will be incremented.	True	False
5.	You can freeze the information in the top and left panes of a window only.	True	False
6.	The sheet reference consists of the name of the sheet separated from the cell reference by an exclamation point.	True	False
7.	The Window/Split command can be used to quickly create a four-way split at the active cell.	True	False

8. To create two horizontal panes with the left pane frozen, move the cell   True   False
selector in the top row of the window and select the column to the left of
where you want the split to appear.

9. Dragging the fill handle activates the AutoFill feature and recognizes the   True   False
cell entry as one that can be incremented.

10. Goal Seek varies the value in the cell you specify until a formula that is   True   False
dependent on that cell returns the desired result.

Concepts

fill-in

Complete the following statements by filling in the blanks with the correct terms.

1. Excel checks spelling by comparing text entries to words in a(n) _____.

2. A(n) _____ is used to identify the contents of a sheet.

3. Changing the page orientation to _____ prints across the length of the page.

4. A(n) _____ reference is a cell or range reference in a formula whose location does not
change when the formula is copied.

5. _____ is used to evaluate the effects of changing selected factors in a worksheet.

6. _____ panes prevents the data in the pane from scrolling as you move to different areas
in a worksheet.

7. A(n) _____ allows you to use data from other worksheets and to calculate values based
on this data.

8. When a window is _____, each pane can be scrolled independently.

9. Use _____ to make entering long or complicated headings easier by logically repeating
and extending the series.

10. Use _____ to find the value in a single cell to achieve the result you want in another cell.

discussion questions

1. Define, compare, and contrast relative references, sheet references, and 3-D references. Provide a
brief example of each.

2. Discuss how absolute and mixed cell references can be used in a worksheet. What is an advantage
of using these types of references over a relative cell reference?

3. Discuss the differences between splitting a window and freezing a window. When would it be
appropriate to split a window? When would it be appropriate to freeze a window?

4. Discuss the differences between what-if analysis and Goal Seek. Under what conditions would it be
more appropriate to use what-if analysis. When would it be more appropriate to use Goal Seek?

Hands-On Exercises

step-by-step

Sandwich Shop Sales Forecast

★ **1.** Nick Walsh owns seven Sandwich Shop franchises. He has created a worksheet to record each store's first quarter sales. Nick would like you to extend this first quarter sales worksheet to another worksheet that provides a sales forecast for the second quarter. The completed worksheets are shown here.

a. Open the workbook ex03_Sandwich Shop. Spell-check the worksheet and correct any misspelled words. Insert a copy of Sheet1 before Sheet2. Rename the Sheet1 tab to **1st Quarter Sales** and then rename Sheet1(2) tab to **2nd Quarter Sales**. Add color to the tabs.

b. In the 2nd Quarter Sales sheet, change the monthly labels to **Apr**, **May**, and **June** using AutoFill.

c. Enter the following projected April sales figures:

Type	Number
8th Avenue	19000
Price-Guadalupe	14250
Mountain Avenue	13000
Sunland Drive	7800
E. Thomas Road	9500
99th Street	3500
W. Monroe Street	5250

d. A new advertising campaign for May and June is expected to increase monthly sales. May sales for each location is expected to be 10 percent more than April sales and June sales are expected to be 15 percent more than May. Enter formulas to calculate May and June sales for the 8th Avenue location and then copy these formulas into the other appropriate cells.

e. Enter and bold the heading **Projected Sales** in cell C2. Center the heading over columns C and D.

f. Enter, bold, italicize, and right-align the heading **Sales Year-To-Date**: in cell D14. In cell E14, enter a formula to calculate the total sales for the first six months by summing cells E11 on both sheets. Format the value to currency with two decimal places.

g. Make the following changes in both sheets:
- Format the numbers to currency with two decimal places.
- Format the column headings to centered, bold, and underlined.
- Format the worksheet title to 14 pt, center it across columns A through E, and add a color and font of your choice.
- Indent, bold, and italicize the Total row heading.
- Bold and italicize the Total row values.
- Add a custom header that contains your name and the date right-aligned to both work sheets.

h. Preview the workbook. Save the workbook as Sandwich Shop2. Print the workbook.

Forecasting Sales

★ **2.** West's Bed and Bath is a small privately owned retail store. Their accountant, Jeremy, has just completed the budgeted income statement for the first quarter. You are going to use this statement to test the sensitivity of Sales to Net Income. The completed worksheet is shown here.

a. Open the workbook ex03_West Income Statement. Examine the contents of the cells under Jan. You will notice that Sales and Fixed Costs are values while the other entries are formulas. This is also the case for the cells for Feb through Jun.

b. Jeremy has been told there may be a rent increase beginning in February that will increase fixed costs to 1755. Update the fixed expense values to see the effect of this increase.

c. Next Jeremy would like to know what level of sales would be necessary to generate a February Net Income of $5000, March of $5100, and $5500 for April through June. Use Goal Seek to answer these questions and update the sales figures.

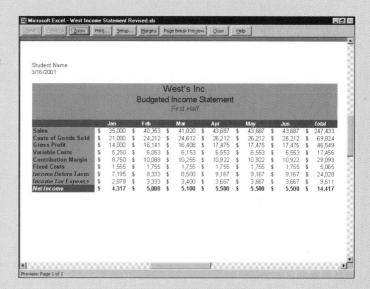

d. Add a custom header that contains your name and the date left-aligned. Change the print orientation to landscape. Save the workbook as West Income Statement2. Print the workbook.

lab exercises

Tracking Hours Worked

★★ **3.** Parker Brent works for United Can Corp. He is paid $8.50 per hour plus time and a half for overtime. For example, this past Monday Parker worked 10 hours. He earned $68 (8 hours times $8.50 per hour) for regular time plus $25.50 (2 hours times $8.50 per hour times 1.5) for overtime for a total of $93.50. He has started to create a worksheet to keep track of weekly hours. You are going to complete this worksheet and create another that Parker will use to schedule next week's hours. The completed worksheets are shown here.

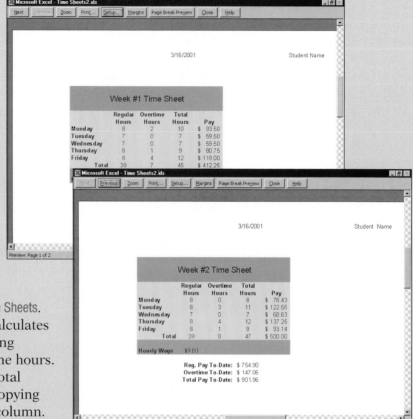

a. Open the workbook ex03_Time Sheets. Enter a formula in E8 that calculates Monday's total hours by adding Monday's regular and overtime hours. Enter formulas to calculate total hours for the other days by copying the formula in E8 down the column. Center the total hours in the cells.

b. Using an absolute reference to the Hourly Wage in cell C15, enter a formula in cell F8 to calculate Monday's pay. Be sure to include regular and overtime pay in the formula. Enter formulas to calculate pay for the other days by copying the formula in cell F8 down the column. Calculate the total Pay. Format the Pay column using the Accounting format with two decimal places.

c. Parker has received his work schedule for next week and would like to record those times by extending the current worksheet to a second week. Insert a copy of Sheet1 before Sheet2. Rename the Sheet1 tab to **First Week** and then rename Sheet1(2) tab to **Second Week**. Add color to the tabs.

d. In the Second Week sheet, change the title in cell B4 to **Week #2 Time Sheet** and enter the following work hours.

	Regular Hours	Overtime Hours
Monday	8	0
Tuesday	8	3
Wednesday	7	0
Thursday	8	4
Friday	8	1

e. Enter, bold, and right-align the following labels:

Reg. Pay To-Date: in cell D17

Overtime To-Date: in cell D18

Total Pay To-Date: in cell D19

f. Enter a formula in cell E17 to calculate the regular pay to date by summing cells C13 on both sheets and multiplying by the hourly wage. Enter a similar formula in cell E18 for overtime pay to date. Calculate the total pay to date in cell E19. Format these values using the Accounting format with two decimal places.

Parker is thinking about asking for a raise from $8.50 to $9.00 to be effective next week. To evaluate the impact of the raise, change the hourly rate in the Week 2 sheet.

g. Use Goal Seek to determine the hourly rate required to achieve a weekly total pay of $500 for Week 2.

h. Add a custom header to both sheets that contains the date centered and your name right-aligned. Preview the workbook. Save the workbook as Time Sheets2. Print the workbook.

Calculating Total Points and GPA

★ 4. Amy Marino is a college student who has just completed the first two years of her undergraduate program as a business major. In this exercise, you will calculate semester and cumulative totals and GPA for each semester. The completed worksheet for Spring 2002 is shown here.

a. Open the workbook ex03_Grade Report. Look at the four sheets. Rename the sheet tabs **Fall 2000**, **Spring 2001**, **Fall 2001**, and **Spring 2002**. Add color to the tabs.

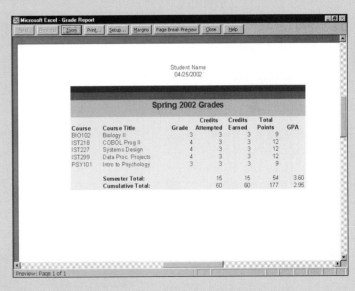

b. You need to enter the formulas to calculate the Total Points and GPA for the four semesters. You will do this for all four sheets at the same time. Select the four sheets. In the Fall 2000 sheet, multiply the Grade by the Credits Earned to calculate Total Points for Intro to Business. Copy that formula down the column. Sum the Credits Attempted, Credits Earned, and Total Points columns and display the results in the Semester Total row.

c. In cell G13, divide the Semester Total's Total Points by the Semester Total's Credits Earned to calculate the GPA for the semester. Use what-if analysis to see what Amy's GPA would be if she had earned a 3 instead of a 2 in Western Civ. Change the grade back to a 2.

d. Look at each sheet to see that the formulas were entered and the calculations performed.

e. Go to cell D14 in the Fall 2000 sheet. Enter the reference formula **=D13** to copy the Semester Total Credits Attempted number to the Cumulative Total row. Copy the formula to cells E14 and F14 to calculate Credits Earned and Total Points.

f. Go to the Spring 2001 sheet and calculate a Cumulative Total for Credits Attempted by summing the Spring 2001 Semester Total and the Fall 2000 Cumulative Total. (*Hint:* You can use pointing to enter the Cumulative Totals formula.)

g. Copy that formula to the adjacent cells to calculate Cumulative Totals for Credits Earned and Total Points. Repeat this procedure on the Fall 2001 and Spring 2002 sheets.

h. Go to the Fall 2000 sheet. Select all four sheets. In cell G14, calculate the GPA for the Cumulative Total. Format the Semester Total GPA and the Cumulative Total GPA to display two decimals. Look at each sheet to see the cumulative GPA for each semester. (*Hint:* Amy's cumulative GPA at the end of the Spring 2002 semester is 2.95.) Display the Sheet tab shortcut menu and ungroup the sheets.

i. Go to the Fall 2000 sheet and preview the workbook. Add a custom header that contains your name and the date center-aligned to the sheets. Save the workbook file as Grade Report2. Print the Spring 2002 sheet centered horizontally on the page.

Preparing the Homeowners Association Budget

★★ **5.** Stuart Philips is president of the Garden Springs Homeowners Association. He has nearly
★ completed a six-month budget for the association. Stuart wants to complete the six-month budget, and extend it for the next six months; The completed second half budget is shown here.

a. Open the workbook ex03_Springs Forecast. Spell-check and correct any errors in the workbook.

b. Enter the function to calculate the Average in cell I6. Copy the function down the column. Clear any cells that contain division by zero errors.

c. Insert a copy of Sheet1 before Sheet2. Rename the Sheet1 tab to **First Half** and rename Sheet2 to **Second Half**. Add color to the tabs.

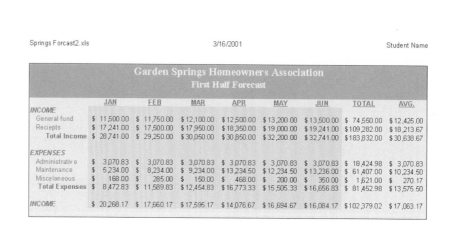

d. Use the AutoFill feature to replace the months JAN through JUN with JUL through DEC on the Second Half sheet. Update the title of the Second Half sheet to **Second Half Forecast.**

e. Stuart expects Receipts for July to increase by 2 percent over June and then to increase 1 percent per month beginning August until the end of the year. Create a formula to calculate the receipts for July by taking the receipts figure from June in the First Half sheet and multiplying it by 1.02. Create a formula to calculate August's receipts by taking the receipts in July and multiplying it by 1.01. Copy this formula down and across to calculate the remaining receipts.

f. The maintenance and miscellaneous expenses for July through December are difficult to determine. At this point Stuart would like to plug in values that average the expenses for the first half of the year. Enter **10200** for Maintenance expense and **270** for Miscellaneous expense for July. Copy the values to August through December.

g. Add a custom header that contains the file name left-aligned, the date centered, and your name right-aligned. Preview the workbook. Save the workbook as Springs Forecast2. Print the Second Half worksheet using landscape orientation.

African Safari Cost Analysis

★★ **6.** Alice, a travel analyst for Adventure Travel Tours, is evaluating the profitability of a planned African Safari package. She has researched competing tours and has determined that a price of $4,900 is appropriate. Alice has determined the following costs for the package.

Item	Cost
Air transport	$1,800 per person
Ground transportation	$360 per person
Lodging	$775 per person
Food	$750 per person
Tour Guides	$3,000
Administrative	$1,200
Miscellaneous	$4,000

Alice has started a worksheet to evaluate the revenues and costs for the African Safari. She wants to know how many travelers are needed to break even (revenues equal costs), how many are needed to make $5,000, and how many are needed to make $10,000. The three worksheets of the completed analysis are shown here and on the next page.

a. Open the workbook ex03_African Safari. Notice that Alice has already entered the tour price and an estimated number of travelers.

b. Spell-check and correct any errors in the workbook.

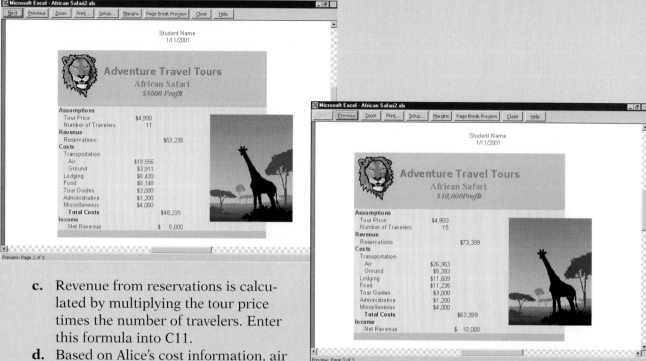

c. Revenue from reservations is calculated by multiplying the tour price times the number of travelers. Enter this formula into C11.

d. Based on Alice's cost information, air transportation is $1800 times the number of travelers. Enter this formula into B14. Enter formulas into B15, B16, and B17 for the other expenses (see table above) related to the number of travelers.

e. Enter the remaining expenses into cells B18, B19, and B20.

f. Calculate total costs in cell C21. Net revenue is the difference between revenue from reservations and total costs. Enter this formula into cell C23.

g. Format the currency values in the worksheet to Currency with no decimal places.

h. Use Goal Seek to determine the number of travelers required to just break even (net revenue equals zero).

i. Rename the sheet tab to **Break Even**. Insert a copy of the Break Even sheet before Sheet2 and rename the tab of the copy **$5000**. Add color to the tabs.

j. In the $5000 sheet, change the title in B5 to **$5,000 Profit**. Use Goal Seek to determine the number of travelers needed to produce a net revenue of $5,000.

k. Insert a copy of the $5000 sheet before Sheet2 and rename the tab of the copy to $10,000. Change the title in B5 to **$10,000 Profit**. Use Goal Seek to determine the number of travelers needed to produce a net revenue of $10,000.

l. Preview the workbook. Add a custom header that contains your name and the date center-aligned to the three sheets. Center the worksheet horizontally. Save the workbook file as African Safari2. Print the workbook.

lab exercises

on your own

Expanding Budget Projections

★ 1. In On Your Own exercise 2 of Lab 1, Personal Budget, you created a workbook for a three-month budget. Extend this workbook by adding two additional sheets. One sheet is to contain a budget for the next six months. The final sheet is to present a full year's summary using 3-D references to the values in the appropriate sheets.

Consider making a special purchase, such as a car, a new computer, or perhaps taking a trip. On a separate line below the total balance in the summary sheet, enter the amount you would need. Subtract this value from the total balance. If this value is negative, reevaluate your expenses and adjust them appropriately. Format the sheets using the features you have learned in the first three labs. Add a custom header on all sheets that includes your name. Preview, print, and save the workbook as Personal Budget2.

Program Expense Comparisons

★★ 2. Obtain yearly income and expense data for three major art programs at your college or university. In a workbook, record each program's data in a separate sheet. In a fourth sheet, calculate the total income, total expenses, and net income for each program. Also in this sheet, calculate the overall totals for income, expense, and net income. Format the sheets using the features you have learned in the first three labs. Add a custom header on all sheets that includes your name. Preview, print, and save the workbook as Art Expenses.

Stock Data Analysis

★★ 3. Select three stocks listed on the New York Stock Exchange. Using the Internet or the library, determine each stock's month-ending price for the past year. In a workbook containing four sheets, record each stock's prices in separate worksheets. In a fourth sheet, calculate the average, standard deviation, and maximum and minimum for each of the three stocks. Also, in the final sheet, chart the average data for the three stocks. Format the sheets using the features you have learned in the first three labs. Add a custom header on all sheets that includes your name. Preview, print, and save the workbook as Stock Analysis.

on the web

★★ Owning and managing a small business is a dream of many college students. Do some research on the Web and choose a business that interests you. Create a projected worksheet for four quarters in separate worksheets. In a fifth sheet, show the total for the year. Include a year-to-date value in each quarterly sheet. In the last quarter sheet, select one expense and determine what value the expense would have to have been so that the net income for that quarter would have been 10 percent higher than the current level. Format the sheets using the features you have learned in the first three labs. Add a custom header on all sheets that includes your name. Preview, print, and save the workbook as My Business.

Overview to Microsoft Access 2002

What Is a Database?

Somewhere at home, or maybe in your office, you probably have a file cabinet or desk drawer filled with information. Perhaps you have organized the information into drawers of related information, and further categorized that information into file folders. This is a database.

As organized as you might be, it takes time to locate a specific piece of information by manually opening drawers and searching through the folders. You can just imagine how much time would be required for a large company to manually search through its massive amounts of data. These companies use electronic database management systems. Now you too can use electronic database management systems to store, organize, access, manipulate, and present information in a variety of ways.

In this series of labs you will learn how to design and create a computerized database using Access 2002 and you will quickly appreciate the many advantages of a computerized database.

Access 2002 Features

Access 2002 is a relational database management system. In relational database systems, data is organized in tables that are related or linked to one another. Each table consists of rows, called records, and columns, called fields.

For example, a state's motor vehicle department database might have an address table. Each row (record) in the table would contain address information about one individual. Each column (field) would contain just one piece of information, for example, zip codes. The address table would be linked to other tables in the database by common fields. For example, the address table might be linked to a vehicle owner's table by name and linked to an outstanding citation table by license number (see example below).

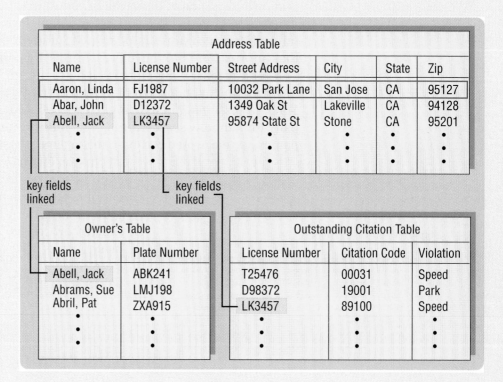

Access 2002 is a powerful program with numerous easy-to-use features including the ability to quickly locate information, add, delete, modify and sort records, analyze data, and produce professional-looking reports. Some of the basic Access 2002 features are described next.

Find Information

Once you enter data into the database table, you can quickly search the table to locate a specific record based on the data in a field. In a manual system, you can usually locate a record by knowing one key piece of information. For example, if the records are stored in a file cabinet alphabetically by last name, to quickly find a record you must know the last name. In a computerized database, even if the records are sorted or organized by last name, you can still quickly locate a record using information in another field.

Add, Delete, and Modify Records

Using Access, it is also easy to add and delete records from the table. Once you locate a record, you can edit the contents of the fields to update the record or delete the record entirely from the table. You can also add new records to a table. When you enter a new record, it is automatically placed in the correct organizational location within the table.

Sort Records

The capability to arrange or sort records in the table according to different field can provide more meaningful information. You can organize records by name, department, pay, class, or any other category you need at a particular time. Sorting the records in different ways can provide information to different departments for different purposes.

Analyze Data

Using Access, you can analyze the data in a table and perform calculations on different fields of data. Instead of pulling each record from a filing cabinet, recording the piece of data you want to use, and then performing the calculation on the recorded data, you can simply have the database program perform the calculation on all the values in the specified field. Additionally, you can ask questions or query the table to find only certain records that meet specific conditions to be used in the analysis. Information that was once costly and time-consuming to get is now quickly and readily available.

Generate Reports

Access includes many features that help you quickly produce reports ranging from simple listings to complex, professional-looking reports. You can create a simple report by asking for a listing of specified fields of data and restricting the listing to records meeting designated conditions. You can create a more complex professional report using the same restrictions or conditions as the simple report, but you can display the data in different layout styles, or with titles, headings, subtotals, or totals.

Case Study for Labs 1–3

You have recently accepted a job as employment administrator for Lifestyle Fitness Club. The club has recently purchased Microsoft Access 2002, and you are using it to update their manual system for recording employee information.

Lab 1: You will learn how to design and create the structure for a computerized database and how to enter and edit records in the database. You will also print a simple report of the records you enter in the database file.

Lab 2: You will continue to build, modify, and use the employee database of records. You will learn how to sort the records in a database file to make it easier to locate records. Additionally, you will create a form to make it easier to enter and edit data in the database file.

Lab 3: You will learn how to query the database to locate specific information. You will also learn how to create a report and link multiple tables.

Working Together: You will learn how to share information between applications by incorporating database information from Access into a Word memo.

Before You Begin

To the Student

The following assumptions have been made:

- Microsoft Access 2002 has been properly installed on the hard disk of your computer system.
- The data files needed to complete the series of labs and practice exercises are supplied by your instructor.
- You have completed the O'Leary Series Windows 98 or 2000 modules or you are already familiar with how to use Windows and a mouse.

To the Instructor

It is assumed that the complete version of the program has been installed prior to students using the labs. In addition, please be aware that the following settings are assumed to be in effect for the Access 2002 program. These assumptions are necessary so that the screens and directions in the manual are accurate.

- The New File Task Pane is displayed on startup (use Tools/Options/View).
- The status bar is displayed (use Tools/Options/View).
- The New Object shortcuts are displayed in the Object list (use Tools/Options/View).
- The Database toolbar is displayed (use Tools/Customize/Options).
- Full menus are always displayed (use Tools/Customize/Options).
- The ScreenTips feature is active (use Tools/Customize/Options).
- The Office Assistant feature is not on (click on the Assistant, click Options, and clear the Use the Office Assistant option).
- All default datasheet settings are in effect, including font settings of Arial 10 pt.

In addition, all figures in the manual reflect the use of a standard VGA display monitor set at 800 by 600. If another monitor setting is used, there may be more or fewer lines displayed in the windows than in the figures. This setting can be changed using Windows setup.

Microsoft Office Shortcut Bar

The Microsoft Office Shortcut Bar (shown below) may be displayed automatically on the Windows desktop. Commonly, it appears in the right side of the desktop; however, it may appear in other locations, depending upon your setup. The Shortcut Bar on your screen may display different buttons. This is because the Shortcut Bar can be customized to display other toolbar buttons.

The Office Shortcut Bar makes it easy to open existing documents or to create new documents using one of the Microsoft Office applications. It can also be used to send e-mail, add a task to a to-do list, schedule appointments using Schedule[+], or access Office Help.

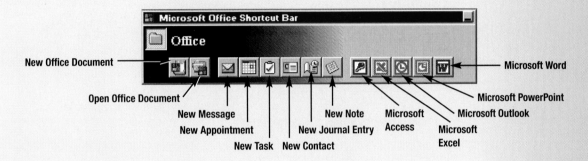

Instructional Conventions

Hands-on instructions you are to perform appear as a sequence of numbered steps. Within each step, a series of bullets identifies the specific actions that must be performed. Step numbering begins over within each topic heading throughout the lab.

Command sequences you are to issue appear following the word "Choose." Each menu command selection is separated by a /. If the menu command can be selected by typing a letter of the command, the letter will appear underlined and bold. Items that need to be highlighted will follow the word "Select." You can select items with the mouse or directional keys. (See Example A.)

Example A

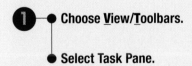

1 • Choose **V**iew/**T**oolbars.

   • Select Task Pane.

Commands that can be initiated using a button and the mouse appear following the word "Click." The icon (and the icon name if the icon does not include text) is displayed following "Click." The menu equivalent and keyboard shortcut appear in a margin note when the action is first introduced. (See Example B.)

Example B

1 — ● Click  Open.

Another Method

The menu equivalent is **F**ile/**O**pen and the keyboard shortcut is Ctrl + O.

Plain blue text identifies file names you need to open. Information you are asked to type appears in blue and bold. (See Example C.)

Example C

1 ● Click Open.

● **Select** Employee Records.

● **Move to a new blank record.**

● **Type** Smith.

The O'Leary Series

Microsoft® Access 2002

Brief Edition

Creating a Database

objectives

After completing this lab, you will know how to:

1.	Plan and create a database.
2.	Create a table.
3.	Define field names, data types, field properties, and primary key fields.
4.	Save the table structure.
5.	Change views.
6.	Enter and edit data in Datasheet view and Data Entry.
7.	Insert a picture.
8.	Adjust column widths.
9.	Use the Best Fit feature.
10.	Delete records.
11.	Preview and print a table.
12.	Change page orientation.
13.	Close and open a table and database.

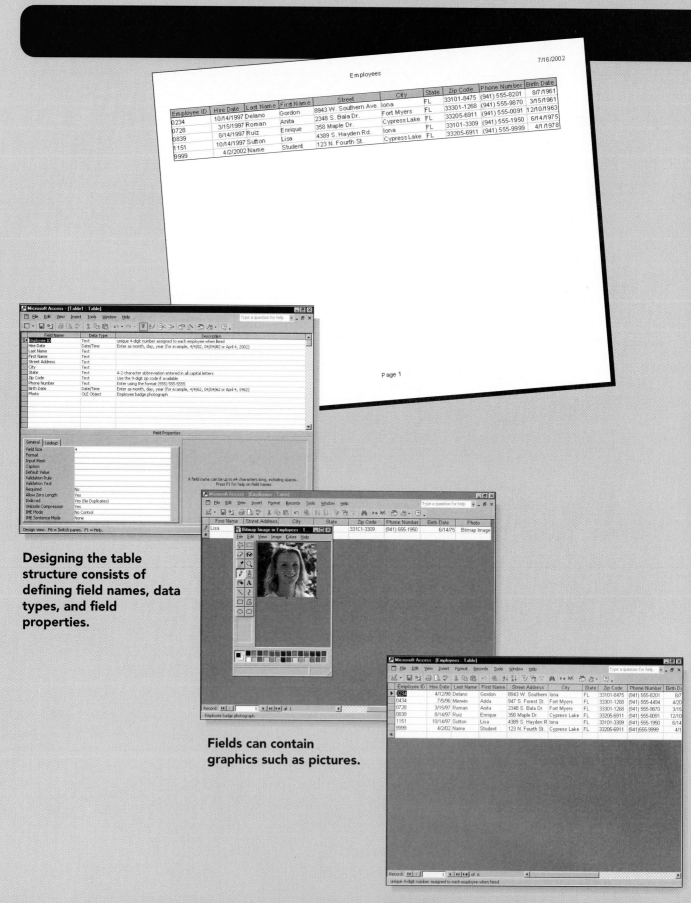

Designing the table structure consists of defining field names, data types, and field properties.

Fields can contain graphics such as pictures.

Entering data in a table creates records of information.

Lifestyle Fitness Club

You have recently accepted a new job as employment administrator with Lifestyle Fitness Club. Like many fitness centers, Lifestyle Fitness Club includes exercise equipment, free weights, aerobic classes, tanning and massage facilities, swimming pool, steam room and sauna, and child care facilities. In addition, they promote a healthy lifestyle by including educational seminars on good nutrition and proper exercise. They also have a small snack bar that serves healthy drinks, sandwiches, and snacks.

The Lifestyle Fitness Clubs are a franchised chain of clubs that are individually owned. You work at a club owned by Brian and Tami Birch, who also own two others in Florida. Accounting and employment functions for all three clubs are handled centrally at the Fort Myers location.

You are responsible for maintaining the employment records for

all employees, as well as records for traditional employment activities such as hiring and benefits. Currently the Club employment records are maintained on paper forms and stored in file cabinets organized alphabetically by last name. Although the information is well organized, it still takes time to manually leaf through the folders to locate the information you need and to compile reports from this data.

The Club has recently purchased new computers, and the owners want to update the employee record-keeping system to an electronic database management system. The software tool you will use to create the database is the database application Microsoft Access 2002. In this lab, you will learn about entering, editing, previewing, and printing a database while you create it and a table of basic employee information.

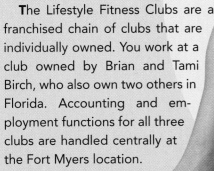

© Corbis

The following concepts will be introduced in this lab:

1	**Database**	A database is an organized collection of related information. Typically, the information in a database is stored in a table consisting of vertical columns and horizontal rows.
2	**Object**	An object is an item, such as a table or report, that can be created, selected, and manipulated as a unit.
3	**Field Name**	A field name is used to identify the data stored in the field.
4	**Data Type**	The data type defines the type of data the field will contain.
5	**Field Property**	A field property is a characteristic that helps define a field. A set of field properties is associated with each field.
6	**Primary Key**	A primary key is a field that uniquely identifies each record.
7	**Graphic**	A graphic is a non-text element or object, such as a drawing or picture, which can be added to a table.
8	**Column Width**	Column width refers to the size of a field column in a datasheet. It controls the amount of data you can see on the screen.

Introducing Access 2002

The Lifestyle Fitness Club recently purchased the Microsoft Office XP application software suite. You are very excited to learn how to use this new and powerful application to store and maintain the club's records.

Starting Access

You will use the Access database management program to create several different databases of information.

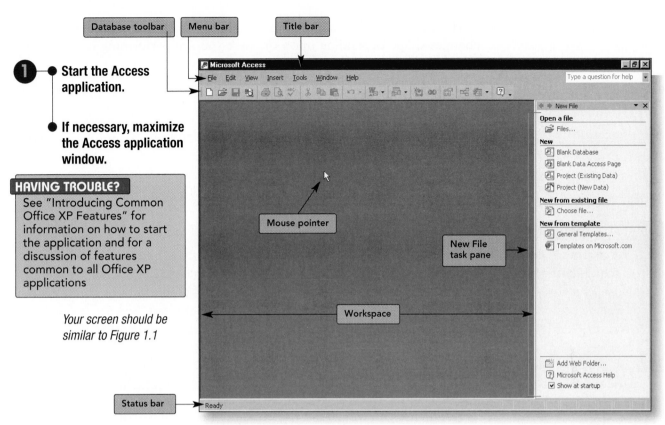

Start the Access application.

If necessary, maximize the Access application window.

HAVING TROUBLE?
See "Introducing Common Office XP Features" for information on how to start the application and for a discussion of features common to all Office XP applications

Your screen should be similar to Figure 1.1

Figure 1.1

HAVING TROUBLE?
If your screen looks slightly different, this is because Access remembers settings that were on when the program was last used.

The Access application window, with the New File task pane open in it, is displayed.

Exploring the Access Window

The menu bar below the title bar displays the Access program menu. It consists of seven menus that provide access to the commands and features you will use to create and modify a database. The menus and commands that are available at any time vary with the task you are performing.

Toolbars, normally located below the menu bar, contain buttons that are mouse shortcuts for many of the menu items. Access uses many different toolbars. Most toolbars appear automatically as you perform different tasks and open different windows. The **Database toolbar** is initially displayed and contains buttons that are used to access basic database features. Your screen may display other toolbars if they were on when the program was last exited.

HAVING TROUBLE?
If the New File task pane is not displayed, choose View/Toolbars/Task Pane.

The task pane is displayed on the right side of the window. Different task panes are displayed depending on the task being performed. Because you just started Access, the New File task pane is automatically displayed, providing different ways to create a new database file or open an existing file.

Another Method
The File/New command or the keyboard shortcut Ctrl + N also opens the New File task pane.

The large area to the left of the task pane is the **workspace**, where different Access windows are displayed as you are using the program. Just below the workspace, the status bar provides information about the task you are working on and the current Access operation. In addition, the status bar displays messages such as instructions to help you use the program more efficiently.

The mouse pointer appears as ⌖ on your screen. The mouse pointer changes shape depending upon the task you are performing or where the pointer is located on the window.

● Creating a New Database

The Lifestyle Fitness Club plans to use Access 2002 to maintain several different types of databases.

concept 1

Databasse

1   A **database** is an organized collection of related information. Typically, the information in a database is stored in a **table** consisting of vertical columns and horizontal rows. Each row contains a **record**, which is all the information about one person, thing, or place. Each column is a **field**, which is the smallest unit of information about a record. Access databases can contain multiple tables that can be linked to produce combined output form all tables. This type of database is called a **relational database**. See the "Overview to Access 2002" for more information about relational databases.

The database you will create will contain information about each Club employee. Other plans for using Access include keeping track of members and inventory. To keep the different types of information separate, the club plans to create a database for each group.

Creating a new database follows several basic steps: plan, create, enter and edit, and preview and print.

Step	Description
Plan	The first step in the development of a database is to understand the purpose of the database.
Create	After planning the database, you create tables to hold data by defining the table structure.
Enter and Edit	After setting up the table, you enter the data to complete each record. While entering data, you may make typing and entry errors that need to be corrected. This is one type of editing. Another is to revise the structure of the tables by adding, deleting, or redefining information in the table.
Preview and Print	The last step is to print a hard copy of the database or report. This step includes previewing the document onscreen as it will appear when printed. Previewing enables you to check the document's overall appearance and to make any final changes needed before printing.

You will find that you will generally follow these steps in order as you create your database. However, you will probably retrace steps as the final database is developed.

Planning a Database

Your first step is to plan the design of your database tables: how many tables, what data they will contain, and how they will be related. You need to decide what information each table in the employee database should contain and how it should be structured or laid out.

You can obtain this information by analyzing the current record-keeping procedures used throughout the company. You need to understand the existing procedures so your database tables will reflect the information that is maintained by different departments. You should be aware of the forms that are the basis for the data entered into the department records, and of the information that is taken from the records to produce periodic reports. You also need to find out what information the department heads would like to be able to obtain from the database that may be too difficult to generate using their current procedures.

After looking over the existing record-keeping procedures and the reports that are created from the information, you decide to create several separate tables of data in the database file. Creating several smaller tables of related data rather than one large table makes it easier to use the tables and faster to process data. This is because you can join several tables together as needed.

The main table will include the employee's basic information, such as employee number, name, birth date, and address. Another will contain work location information only. A third will contain data on pay rate and hours worked each week. To clarify the organization of the database, you sketched out the structure for the employee database as shown below.

Employee Database

Employee Table

Emp #	Last Name	First Name	Street	City	State	Zipcode	Phone	Birth Date
7721	Brown	Linda	——	——	——	——	——	——
7823	Duggan	Michael	——	——	——	——	——	——
:	:	:	:	:	:	:	:	:

link on common field

link on common field

Location

Emp #	Location
7721	Iona
7823	Fort Myers
:	:

Pay Rate

Emp #	Pay	Hours
7721	8.25	30
7823	7.50	20
:	:	:

Creating and Naming the Database File

Now that you have decided on the information you want to include in the tables, you are ready to create a new database to hold the table information.

1 ● **Click**  **in the New File task pane.**

Your screen should be similar to Figure 1.2

HAVING TROUBLE?
The default location, folders, and files displayed on your screen may be different from what is shown here.

Additionally, your screen may not display the file extensions, if the setting has been turned off in Windows on your system.

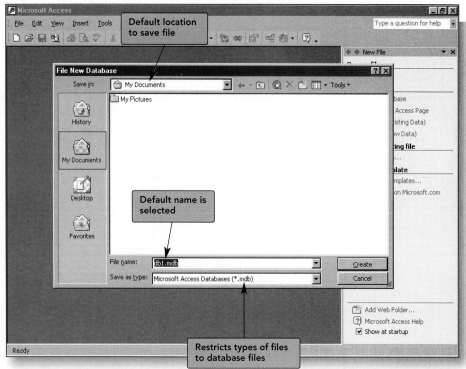

Figure 1.2

The File New Database dialog box is displayed. The first step is to specify a name for the database file and the location where you want the file saved. By default, Access opens the My Documents folder as the location to save the file. The file list section of the dialog box displays the names of folders and database files in the default location. Only database file names are displayed because the file type is restricted to Access Databases in the Save As Type text box. The default file name db1 appears in the File Name text box. You want the program to store the database on your data disk using the name Lifestyle Fitness Employees. Notice that the default name is highlighted, indicating it is selected and will be replaced as you type the new name.

2 **Type** Lifestyle Fitness
Employees.

*Your screen should be
similar to Figure 1.3*

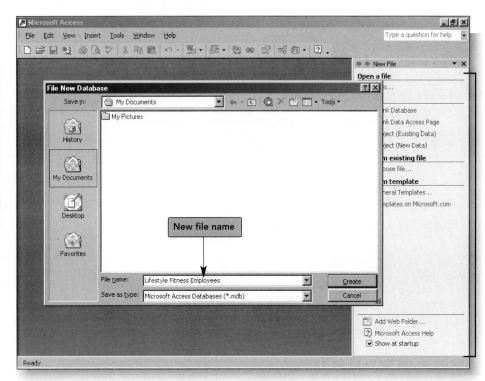

Figure 1.3

The default file name is replaced with the new file name. Next you need to
change the location to the appropriate location for your data files. You can
do this by selecting the location from the Save In drop-down list or from the
icons in the Places bar along the left side of the dialog box. The icons bring
up a list of recently accessed files and folders (History), the contents of the
My Documents and Favorites folders, and the Windows Desktop. When you
select a folder from one of these lists, the display changes to that location.

3 **Open the Save In list
box and change the
Save In location to the
appropriate drive for
your system.**

*Your screen should be
similar to Figure 1.4*

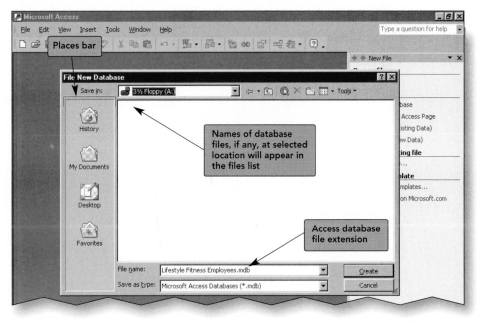

Figure 1.4

Now the file list section displays the names of all Access files on your data
disk. Notice that the program added the .mdb file extension to the file
name. This is the default extension for Access database files.

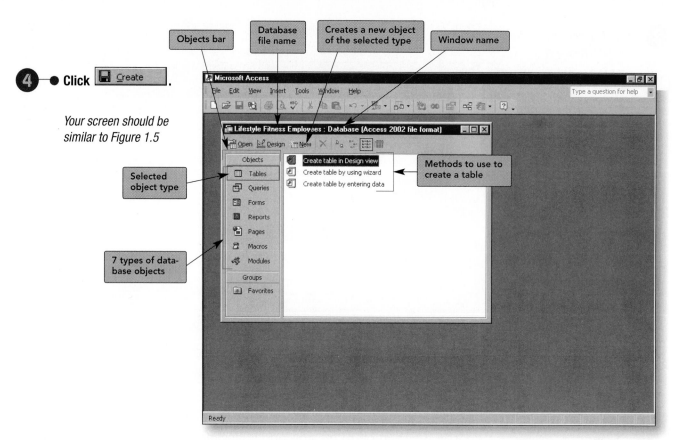

4 ● Click 🖫 **Create** .

Your screen should be similar to Figure 1.5

Objects bar

Database file name

Creates a new object of the selected type

Window name

Selected object type

Methods to use to create a table

7 types of database objects

Figure 1.5

The Database window opens in the workspace and displays the name of the database, Lifestyle Fitness Employees, followed by the name of the window in the window title bar.

Creating a Table

The Database window is used to help you quickly create, open, or manage database objects.

concept 2

Object

2 An Access database is made up of several types of **objects**, such as a table or report, consisting of many elements. An object can be created, selected, and manipulated as a unit. The database objects are described below.

Object	Use
Table	Stores data
Query	Finds and displays selected data
Form	View, add, and update data in tables
Report	Analyze and print data in a specific layout

The table object is the basic unit of a database and must be created first, before any other types of objects are created. Access displays each different type of object in its own window. You can display multiple object windows in the workspace; however, you cannot open more than one database file at a time.

The Objects bar along the left edge of the Database window organizes the database objects into object types and groups, and is used to quickly access the different database objects. The currently selected object is Tables. The object list box to the right of the object bar displays three ways you can create a table. It will also display the names of objects of the selected object type once they are created.

After naming the database, your next step is to create the new table to hold the employee information by defining the structure of the table.

● Click **New**.

Your screen should be similar to Figure 1.6

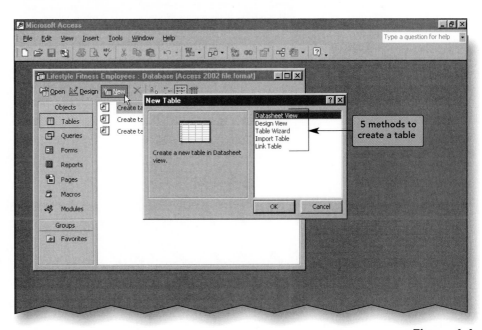

Figure 1.6

Additional Information

Access includes many different Wizards that can be used to create different Access objects.

Additional Information

You will learn about other views later in this lab.

The New Table dialog box provides five different ways to create a table. The first three, Datasheet View, Design View, and Table Wizard, are the most commonly used. They are the same three methods that are listed in the object list box. The Datasheet and Design View options open different windows in which you can create a new custom table from scratch. The Table Wizard option starts the Table Wizard feature, which lets you select from predesigned database tables. The Wizard then guides you through the steps to create a table for you based upon your selections.

You will use the Design View option to create the table.

2 ● Select Design View.

● Click [OK].

● If necessary, click □ in the Table window title box to maximize the window.

Your screen should be similar to Figure 1.7

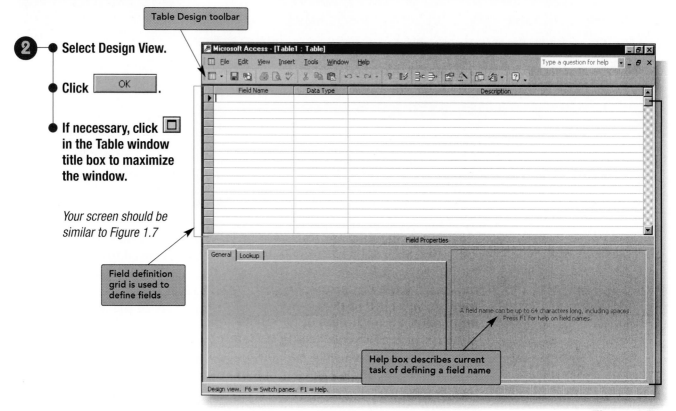

Figure 1.7

The Table Design window is opened and displayed over the Database window in the workspace. This window also has its own toolbar, the Table Design toolbar, which contains the standard buttons as well as buttons that are specific to this window.

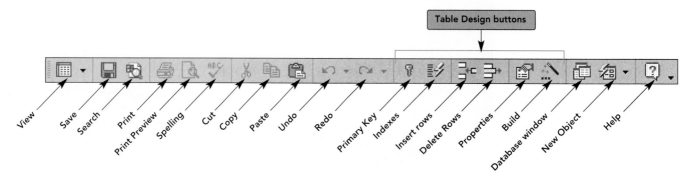

The upper section of the table Design window consists of a field definition grid where you define each field to include in the table. Each row in the grid is where a field is defined by entering the required information in each of the columns.

Defining Field Names

You decide to include the data currently maintained in the personnel folder on each employee in one table using the following 11 fields: Employee Number, Date Hired, Last Name, First Name, Street, City, State, Zip Code, Phone Number, Birth Date, and Picture. The first step is to give each field a field name.

concept 3

Field Name

3 A **field name** is used to identify the data stored in the field. A field name should be descriptive of the contents of the data to be entered in the field. It can be up to 64 characters long and can consist of letters, numbers, spaces, and special characters, except a period, an exclamation point, an accent grave (`), and brackets ([]). You also cannot start a field name with a space. Examples of field names are: Last Name, First Name, Address, Phone Number, Department, Hire Date, or other words that describe the data. It is best to use short field names to make the tables easier to manage.

In the lower right section of the table Design window, a Help box provides information on the task you are performing in the window. Because the insertion point is positioned in the Field Name text box, the Help box displays a brief description of the rules for entering a valid field name.

The first field of data you will enter in the table is the employee number, which is assigned to each employee when hired. Each new employee is given the next consecutive number, so no two employees can have the same number. It is a maximum of four digits. The ▶ to the left of the first row indicates the current field.

1 ● Type **Employee Number.**

Additional Information

The field name can be typed in uppercase or lowercase letters. It will be displayed in your database table exactly as you enter it.

Your screen should be similar to Figure 1.8

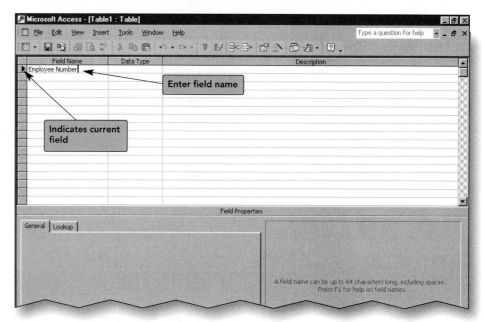

Figure 1.8

You realize that "Employee ID" is the more common term used on company forms, so you decide to use this as the field name instead. To change the field name, you will edit the entry.

2 ● Press Backspace 6 times to delete the word "Number" (until only "Employee" and a space following it remain).

Another Method

You can also select (highlight by dragging or double-clicking on a word) the word "Number" and press the Delete key to erase it.

● Type **ID**.

● Press ↵Enter.

Another Method

Using the Tab↹ or → key has the same effect as pressing ↵Enter. It stores any entered data and moves the insertion point to the next column to the right. Pressing ⇧Shift + Tab↹ or ← moves the insertion point to the left one column.

Your screen should be similar to Figure 1.9

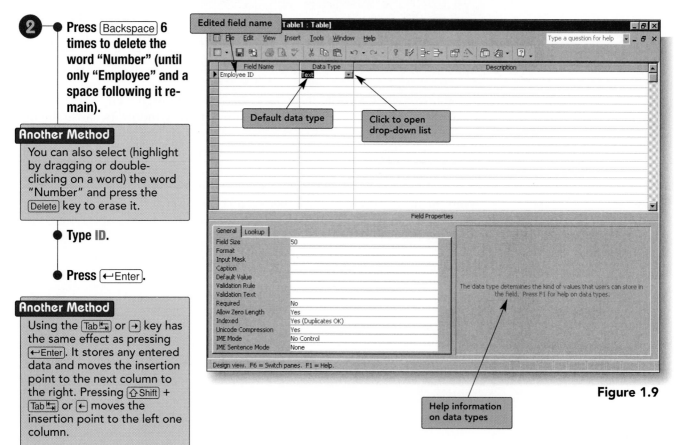

Figure 1.9

The insertion point has moved to the Data Type column, where the default data type of Text is automatically entered.

Defining Data Types

You know that the Employee ID will always be a number, so you decide to check out what other options there are for the Data Type field.

1 • Click ▼ to open the Data Type drop-down menu.

Your screen should be similar to Figure 1.10

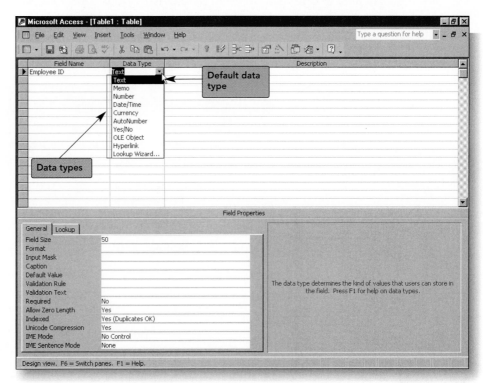

Figure 1.10

concept 4

4 The **data type** defines the type of data the field will contain. Access uses the data type to ensure that the right kind of data is entered in a field. It is important to choose the right data type for a field before you start entering data in the table. You can change a data type after the field con- tains data, but if the data types are not com- patible, such as a text entry in a field whose data type accepts numbers only, you may lose data. The data types are described in the fol- lowing table.

Data Type	Description
Text	Text entries (words, combinations of words and numbers, numbers that are not used in calculations) up to 255 characters in length. Names and phone numbers are examples of Text field entries. Text is the default data type.
Memo	Text that is variable in length and usually too long to be stored in a Text field. A maximum of 65,535 characters can be entered in a Memo field.
Number	Digits only. Number fields are used when you want to perform calculations on the values in the field. Number of Units Ordered is an example of a Number field entry.
Date/Time	Any valid date. Access allows dates from January 1, 100 to December 31, 9999. Access correctly handles leap years and checks all dates for validity.
Currency	Same as the Number field, but formatted to display decimal places and a currency symbol.
AutoNumber	A unique, sequential number that is automatically incremented by one when- ever a new record is added to a table. Once a number is assigned to a record, it can never be used again, even if the record is deleted.
Yes/No	Accepts only Yes or No, True or False, and On or Off entries.
OLE Object	An object, such as a graphic (picture), sound, document, or spreadsheet, that is linked to or embedded in a table.
Hyperlink	Accepts hyperlink entries that are paths to an object, document, Web page, or other destinations.
Lookup Wizard	Creates a Lookup field where you can enter a value or choose from a list of values from another table or query.

Even though a field such as the Employee ID field may contain numeric entries, unless the numbers are used in calculations, the field should be assigned the Text data type. This allows other characters, such as the parentheses or hyphens in a telephone number, to be included in the entry. Also, by specifying the type as Text, any leading zeros (for example, in the zip code 07739) will be preserved, whereas leading zeros in a Number type field are dropped (which would make this zip code incorrectly 7739).

2 ● Click ▼ to close the Data Type drop-down menu without changing the selection.

Another Method

You can also press [Esc] to close the menu.

Your screen should be similar to Figure 1.11

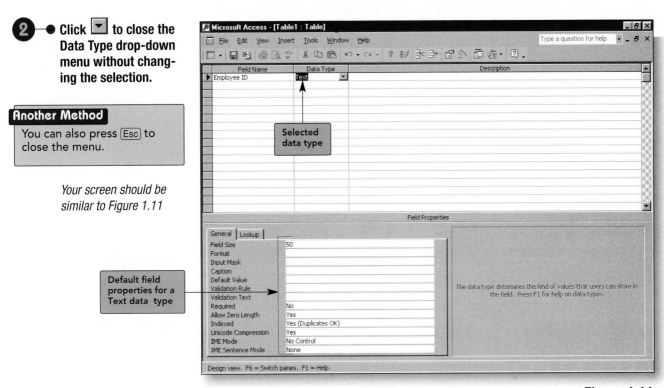

Figure 1.11

Defining Field Properties

In the Field Properties area of the dialog box, the General tab displays the default field property settings associated with the current data type (which in this case is Text).

concept 4

4 A **field property** is a characteristic that helps define a field. A set of field properties is associated with each field. Each data type has a different set of field properties. Setting field properties enhances the way your table works. Some of the more commonly used properties and their functions are described in the following table.

Field Property	Description
Field Size	Sets the maximum number of characters that can be entered in the field.
Format	Specifies how data displays in a table and prints.
Input Mask	Simplifies data entry by controlling what data is required in a field and how the data is to be displayed.
Caption	Specifies a field label other than the field name.
Default Value	Automatically fills in a certain value for this field in new records as you add to the table. You can override a default value by typing a new value into the field.
Validation Rule	Limits data entered in a field to values that meet certain requirements.
Validation Text	Specifies the message to be displayed when the associated Validation Rule is not satisfied.
Required	Specifies whether or not a value must be entered in a field.
Allow Zero Length	Specifies whether or not an entry containing no characters is valid.
Indexed	Sets a field as an index field (a field that controls the order of records). This speeds up searches on fields that are searched frequently.

First, you need to set the **field size** for the Employee ID field. By default, Access sets a Text field size to 50. Although Access uses only the amount of storage space necessary for the text you actually store in a Text field, setting the field size to the smallest possible size can decrease the processing time required by the program. Additionally, if the field data to be entered is a specific size, setting the field size to that number restricts the entry to the maximum number.

Since the employee ID will never be more than four digits long, you want to change the field size from the default of 50 to 4.

1 • **Click the Field Size property text box.**

Another Method

You can also press the F6 key to switch between the upper and lower areas of the Table Design window.

• **Double-click on 50 to select it.**

• **Type 4 to replace the default entry.**

Your screen should be similar to Figure 1.12

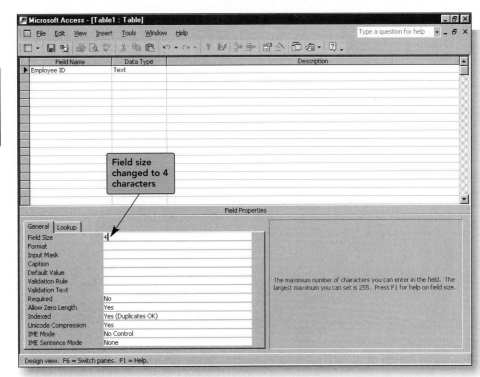

Figure 1.12

Entering a Field Description

To continue defining the Employee ID field, you will enter a description of the field in the Description text box. Although it is optional, a field description makes the table easier to understand and update because the description is displayed in the status bar when you enter data into the table.

1 • **Click the Description text box for the Employee ID field.**

• **Type A unique 4-digit number assigned to each employee when hired.**

Additional Information

The Description box scrolls horizontally as necessary to accommodate the length of the text entry.

Your screen should be similar to Figure 1.13

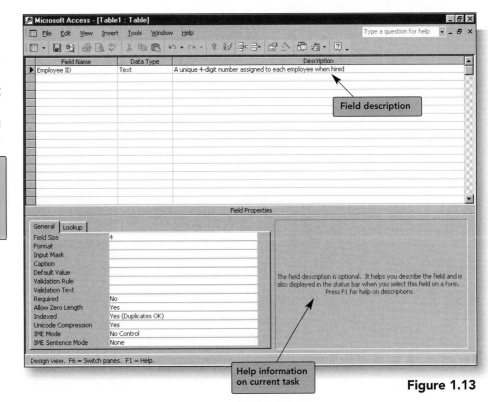

Figure 1.13

Defining a Primary Key Field

Next you want to make the Employee ID field a primary key field.

1 ● Click  Primary Key.

Another Method

The menu equivalent is Edit/Primary Key.

Your screen should be similar to Figure 1.14

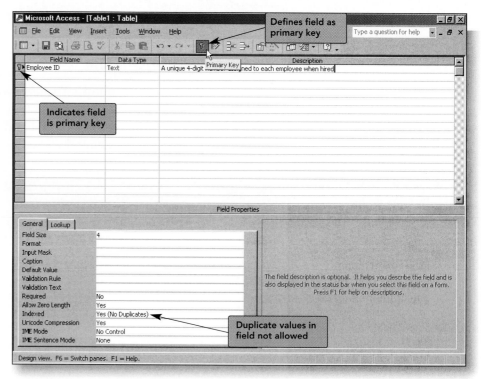

Figure 1.14

The icon appears in the column to the left of the field name, showing that this field is a primary key field. Now that this is the primary key field, the Indexed property setting has changed to Yes (No Duplicates). This setting prohibits duplicate values in a field.

Defining Additional Fields

The second field will display the date the employee started working at Lifestyle Fitness Club in the form of month/day/year.

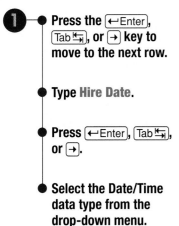

1
- Press the ⏎Enter, Tab⇆, or → key to move to the next row.

- Type **Hire Date**.

- Press ⏎Enter, Tab⇆, or →.

- Select the Date/Time data type from the drop-down menu.

Another Method
You can also enter the data type by typing the first character of the type you want to use. For example, if you type D, the Date/Time data type will be automatically selected and displayed in the field.

Your screen should be similar to Figure 1.15

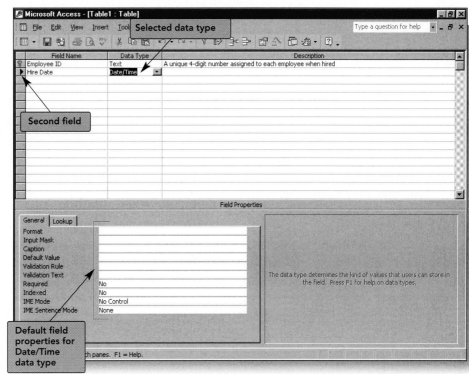

Figure 1.15

The default field properties for the selected data type are displayed. This time you want to change the format of the field so that the date will display as mm/dd/yyyy, regardless of how it is entered.

2
- Click in the Format property box.

- Click ▼ to open the drop-down list of Format options.

Your screen should be similar to Figure 1.16

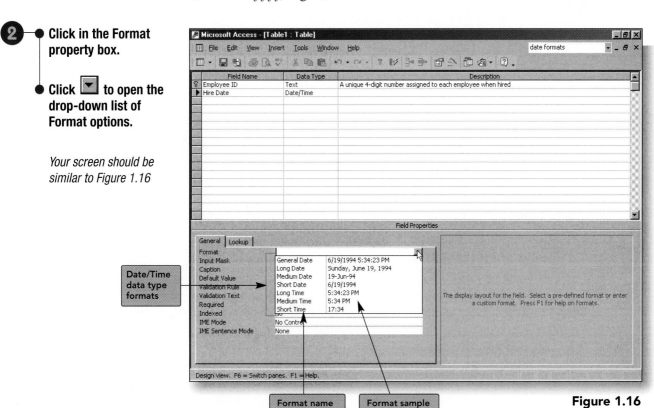

Figure 1.16

The names of the seven predefined layouts for the Date/Time field type are displayed in the list. An example of each layout appears to the right of the name. The General Date format is the default format. It displays dates using the Short Date format. If a time value is entered it will also display the time in the Long Time format.

3 ● **Choose General Date.**

● **In the Description text box of the Date Hired field, enter the following description: Enter as month, day, year (for example, 4/4/02, 04/04/02 or April 4, 2002).**

Additional Information

Access automatically assumes the first two digits of a year entry. If you enter a year that is between /30 and /99, Access reads this as a twentieth-century date (1930 to 1999). A year entry between /00 and /29 is assumed to be a twenty-first century date (2000 to 2029).

Your screen should be similar to Figure 1.17

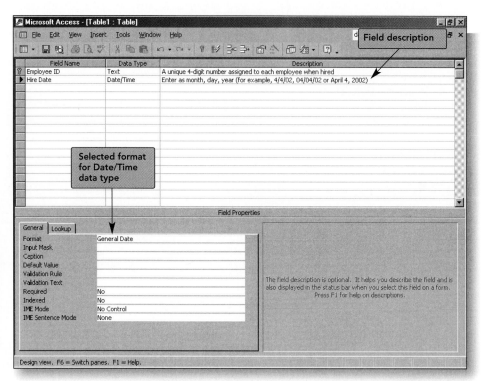

Figure 1.17

The third field is a Text field type that will contain the employee's last name. Because the field name is descriptive of the field contents, a description is not needed.

4 ● **Move to the third row.**

● **Type Last Name.**

● **Press ⏎Enter, Tab⇥, or → three times.**

Your screen should be similar to Figure 1.18

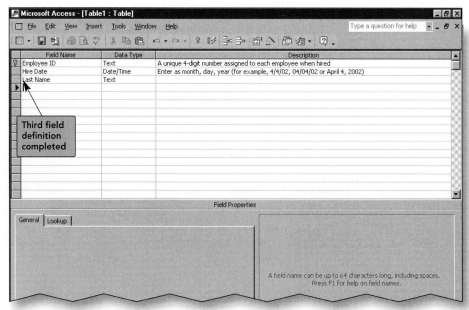

Figure 1.18

In the same manner, enter the information shown in the table on the right for the next eight fields.

When you have completed the eight additional fields, your field definition grid should be similar to Figure 1.19

Field Name	Data Type	Description	Field Size/ Format
First Name	Text		50
Street Address	Text		50
City	Text		50
State	Text	A 2-character abbreviation entered in all capital letters	2
Zip Code	Text	Use the 9-digit zip code if available	10
Phone Number	Text	Enter using the format (555) 555-5555	15
Birth Date	Date/Time	Enter as month, day, year (for example, 4/4/62, 04/04/62 or April 4, 1962)	General Date
Photo	OLE object	Employee badge photograph	

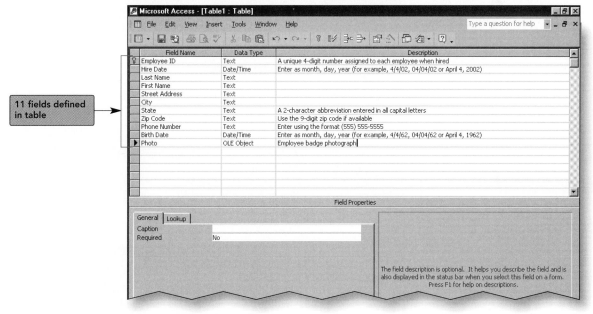

11 fields defined in table

Figure 1.19

Editing Field Definitions

After looking over the fields, you decide to change the field sizes of the Last Name, First Name, and City fields to 20-character entries. Positioning the insertion point in any column of a field will display the properties for that field.

1 ● **Move to any column in the Last Name field.**

● **Change the field size to 20.**

● **In a similar manner, change the field size for the First Name and City fields to 20.**

● **Carefully check your field definition grid to ensure that each field name and field type was entered accurately and make any necessary corrections.**

Your screen should be similar to Figure 1.20

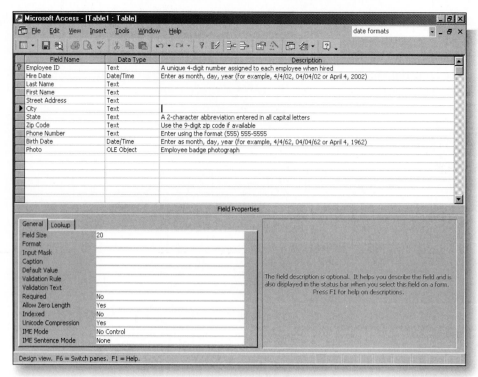

Figure 1.20

Saving the Table Structure

Once you are satisfied that your field definitions are correct, you save the table design by naming it.

1 ● Click  Save.

Another Method

The menu equivalent is File/Save and the keyboard shortcut is Ctrl + S.

Your screen should be similar to Figure 1.21

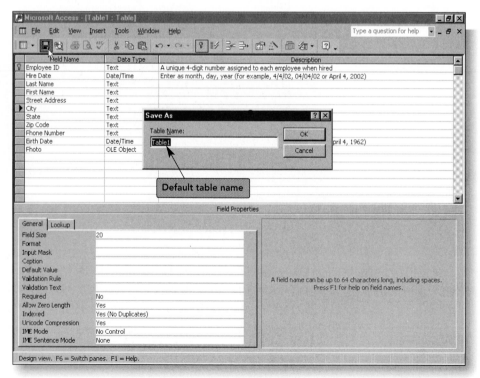

Figure 1.21

In the Save As dialog box, you want to replace the default name, Table1, with a more descriptive name. A table name follows the same set of standard naming conventions or rules that you use when naming fields. It is acceptable to use the same name for both a table and the database, although each table in a database must have a unique name. You will save the table using the table name "Employees."

Type Employees.

Click OK.

The table structure is saved with the database file. You have created a table named "Employees" in the Lifestyle Fitness Employees database file.

Entering and Editing Table Data

Now that the table structure is defined and saved, you can enter the employee data into the new table, and change that data as necessary. In order to do this, you need to switch views.

Switching Views

Access uses several different window formats, called **views** to display and work with the objects in a database. Each view includes its own menu and toolbar designed to work with the object in the window. The views that are available change according to the type of object you are working with. The basic views are described in the following table.

View	Purpose
Design view	Used to create a table, form, query, or report.
Datasheet view	Provides a row-and-column view of the data in tables, forms, and queries.
Form view	Displays the records in a form.
Preview	Displays a form, report, table, or query as it will appear when printed.

The ▦▾ View button is a toggle button that switches between the different available views. The graphic in the button changes to indicate the view that will be displayed when selected. The View button appears as ▨▾ for Design view and ▦▾ for Datasheet view. Clicking the ▾ in the View button displays a drop-down list of the available views from which you can choose.

You enter and display table data in Datasheet view, which is the view you will switch to right now.

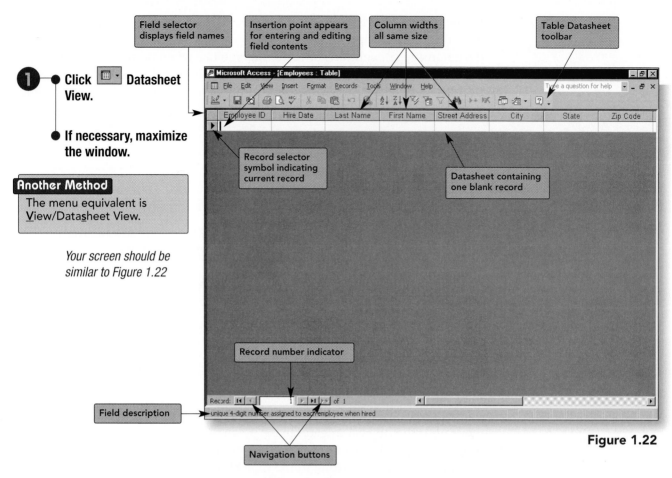

1 ● Click 🔲 ▾ **Datasheet View.**

● If necessary, maximize the window.

Another Method

The menu equivalent is View/Datasheet View.

Your screen should be similar to Figure 1.22

Field selector displays field names

Insertion point appears for entering and editing field contents

Column widths all same size

Table Datasheet toolbar

Record selector symbol indicating current record

Datasheet containing one blank record

Record number indicator

Field description

Navigation buttons

Figure 1.22

The Datasheet view window displays the table in a row-and-column format called a **datasheet**. Each field is a column of the table, and the field names you entered in Design view are displayed as column headings. The column heading area is called the **field selector** for each column. Below the field selector is a blank row where you will enter the data for a record. To the left of the row is the **record selector** symbol ▶, which indicates which record is the **current record**, or the record containing the insertion point.

The bottom of the window displays a horizontal scroll bar, navigation buttons, and a record number indicator. The **record number indicator** shows the number of the current record as well as the total number of records in the table. Because the table does not yet contain records, the indicator displays "Record: 1 of 1" in anticipation of your first entry. On both sides of the record number are the **navigation buttons**, which are used to move through records with a mouse.

In addition, this view displays a Table Datasheet toolbar containing the standard buttons as well as buttons (identified in the following illustration) that are specific to the Table Datasheet view window.

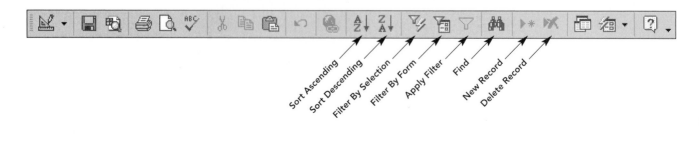

Sort Ascending Sort Descending Filter By Selection Filter By Form Apply Filter Find New Record Delete Record

Notice also in this view that the column widths are all the same, even though you set different field sizes in the Table Design window. This is because the Table Datasheet view window has its own default column width setting.

Entering Data in Datasheet View

You can enter and delete records and edit field data in existing records using this view. The insertion point is positioned in the Employee ID field, indicating the program is ready to accept data in this field. The status bar displays the description you entered for the field. The data you will enter for the first record is shown in the following table. (Do not enter any of this data until you are instructed to do so in the following steps.)

Field Name	Data
Employee ID	1151
Hire Date	October 14,1997
Last Name	Sutton
First Name	Lisa
Street Address	4389 S. Hayden Rd.
City	Iona
State	FL
Zip Code	33101-3309
Phone Number	(941) 555-1950
Birth Date	June 14, 1975
Photo	Friend1.bmp

When you enter data in a record, it should be entered accurately and consistently. The data you enter in a field should be typed exactly as you want it to appear. This is important because any printouts of the data will display the information exactly as entered. It is also important to enter data in a consistent form. For example, if you decide to abbreviate the word "Street" as "St." in the Street field, then it should be abbreviated the same way in every record where it appears. Also be careful not to enter a blank space before or after a field entry. This can cause problems when using the table to locate information.

To see how field properties can help ensure data accuracy, you will first try to enter an Employee ID number that is larger than the field size of 4 that you defined in Table Design view.

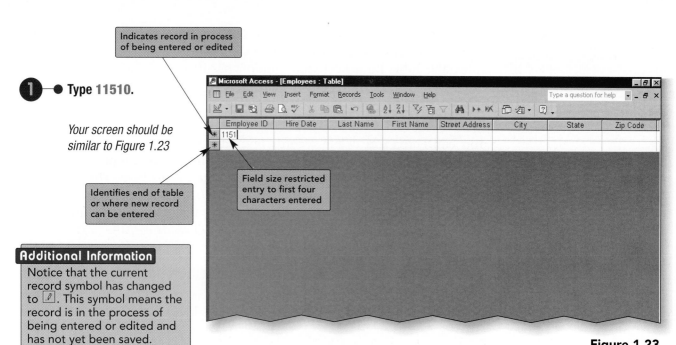

1 ● Type **11510.**

Your screen should be similar to Figure 1.23

Indicates record in process of being entered or edited

Identifies end of table or where new record can be entered

Field size restricted entry to first four characters entered

Additional Information

Notice that the current record symbol has changed to ✏. This symbol means the record is in the process of being entered or edited and has not yet been saved.

Figure 1.23

The program accepted only the first four digits, and would not let you type a fifth. The field size restriction helps control the accuracy of data by not allowing an entry larger than specified.

Next, you will intentionally enter an invalid hire date to see what happens.

2 ● Press ←Enter, Tab⇆, or → to move to the Hire Date field.

● Type **10/41/1997.**

● Press ←Enter, Tab⇆, or →.

Your screen should be similar to Figure 1.24

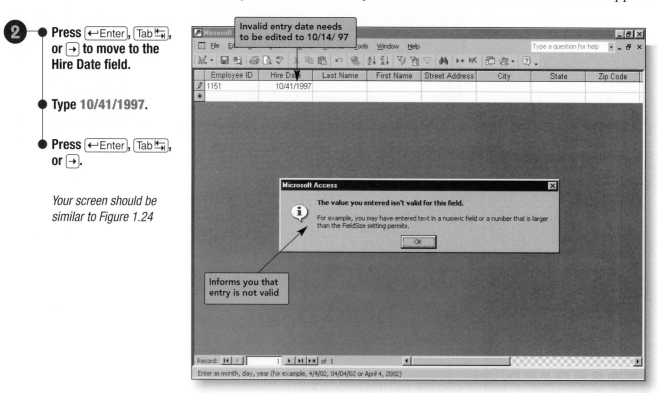

Invalid entry date needs to be edited to 10/14/97

Informs you that entry is not valid

Figure 1.24

An informational message box is displayed advising you that the entry is not valid. In this case, the date entered (10/41/1997) could not be correct because there cannot be 41 days in a month. Access automatically performs some basic validity checks on the data as it is entered based upon the field type specified in the table design. This is another way Access helps you control data entry to ensure the accuracy of the data.

Editing Data

You will need to edit the date entry to correct it. To position the insertion point in the field entry, click at the location where you want it to appear. The keyboard keys shown in the table below can also be used to move the insertion point in an entry and to make changes to individual characters in the entry.

Key	Effect
← or →	Moves insertion point left or right one character.
Ctrl + ← or Ctrl + →	Moves insertion point left or right one word.
↓	Moves insertion point to current field in next record.
Home or End	Moves insertion point to beginning or end of field in single-line field.
Ctrl + Home or Ctrl + End	Moves insertion point to beginning or end of field in multiple-line field.
Delete	Deletes character to right of insertion point.
Backspace	Deletes character to left of insertion point.

1 ● Click [OK] to close the message box.

● Press ← (5 times).

● Press [Delete] (2 times).

● Type **14**.

Additional Information
You can cancel changes you are making in the current field at any time before you move on to the next field. Just press [Esc] and the original entry is restored.

● Press [Tab ⇥].

Your screen should be similar to Figure 1.25

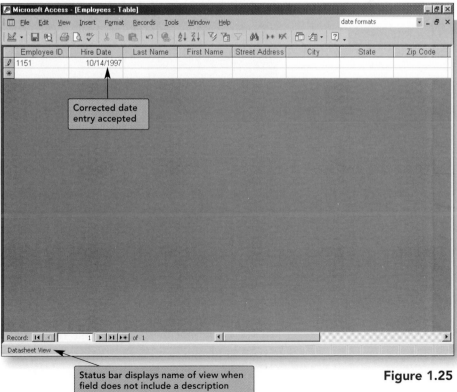

Corrected date entry accepted

Status bar displays name of view when field does not include a description

Figure 1.25

The corrected date is accepted, and the insertion point moves to the Last Name field. The year in the date changed to four digits, which reflects the date format you specified in the field's property.

Because no description was entered for this field, the status bar displays "Datasheet View," the name of the current view, instead of a field description.

2 ● **Enter the data shown in the table on the right for the remaining fields, typing the information exactly as it appears.**

Your screen should be similar to Figure 1.26

Field Name	Data
Last Name	Sutton
First Name	Lisa
Street Address	4389 S. Hayden Rd.
City	Iona
State	FL
Zip Code	33101-3309
Phone Number	(941) 555-1950
Birth Date	6/14/75

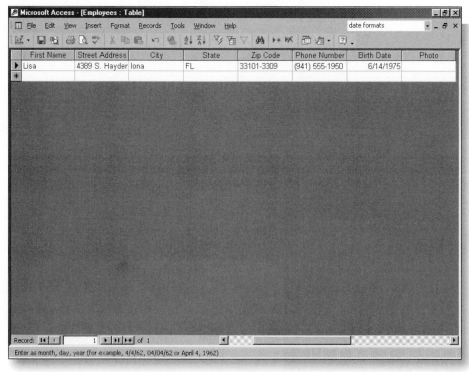

Figure 1.26

All the information for the first record is now complete, except for the Photo field.

Inserting a Picture

To complete the information for this record, you need to insert a picture of Lisa in the Photo field. A picture is one of several different types of graphic objects that can be added to a database table.

concept 8

Graphic

8 A **graphic** is a non-text element or object, such as a drawing or picture, which can be added to a table. A graphic can be a simple **drawing object** consisting of shapes such as lines and boxes that can be created using a drawing program such as Paint. A **picture** is an illustration such as a scanned photograph. Other types of graphic objects that can be added are a worksheet created in Excel or a Word document. Examples of several graphic objects are shown below.

Graphic objects can be inserted in a table as bound or unbound objects. A **bound object** is stored in a table and connected to a specific record and field. Each record can have its own graphic object. An **unbound object** is associated with the table as a whole, not with a specific record, and does not change when you move from record to record. An unbound object is often used to display decorative pictures, a background picture, or an informational text item, such as a company logo.

Photograph

Clip Art

Drawing Object

Picture files can be obtained from a variety of sources. Many simple drawings, called **clip art**, are available in the Clip Organizer that comes with Office XP. You can also create graphic files using a scanner to convert any printed document, including photographs, to an electronic format. Most images that are scanned and inserted into documents are stored as Windows bitmap files (.bmp). All types of graphics, including clip art, photographs, and other types of images, can be found on the Internet. These files are commonly stored as .jpg or .pcx files. Keep in mind that any images you locate on the Internet may be protected by copyright and should be used only with permission. You can also purchase CDs containing graphics for your use.

You have not organized the employees' badge photographs yet, but you want to demonstrate to the Club owners how this feature works, so you decide to insert a picture of a friend. Then, after the database design is completed, you will insert all the employees' photographs into the appropriate field. You have a recent picture of your friend that you scanned and saved in a file, which you will insert in the Photo field for Lisa Sutton.

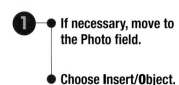

1 ● If necessary, move to the Photo field.

● Choose **I**nsert/**O**bject.

Your screen should be similar to Figure 1.27

HAVING TROUBLE?
The items in the Object Type list will reflect programs on your system.

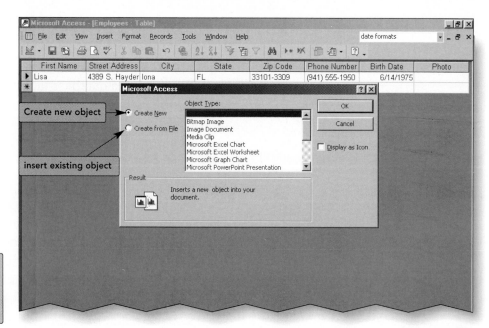

Figure 1.27

This dialog box asks you to specify whether you want to create a new object or insert an existing object. Because your friend's picture is already created and stored as a file, you will use the Create from File option and specify the location of the file.

2 ● Select **Create from File.**

● Click **Browse...**.

Your screen should be similar to Figure 1.28

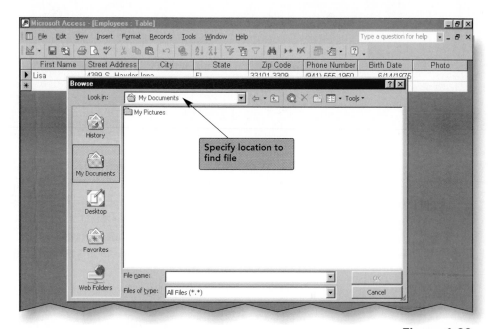

Figure 1.28

This Browse dialog box is used to locate and select the name of the file you want to insert. The Look In drop-down list box displays the location where the program will look for files, and the file list box displays the names of all files (if any) at that location. First you may need to change the location to the location containing your data files.

3 ● If necessary, open the
Look In drop-down list
box and specify the lo-
cation of your data
files.

*Your screen should be
similar to Figure 1.29*

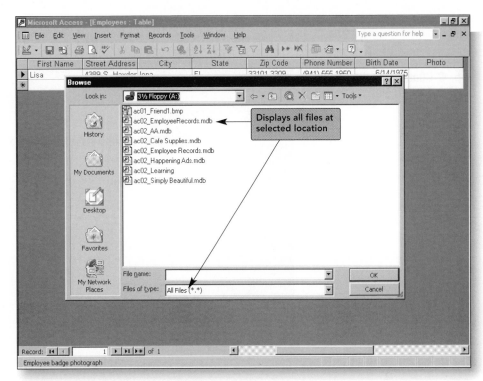

Figure 1.29

The Browse dialog box displays the names of all files on your data disk.
When selecting a file to insert, it may be helpful to see a preview of the file
first. To do this, you can change the dialog box view.

4 ● Open the 🞇 Views
drop-down list.

● Choose Pre**v**iew.

● Click the file name
ac01_Friend1 **in the file
list box.**

HAVING TROUBLE?
If necessary, scroll the file list
box to locate the file. If
ac01_Friend1 is not displayed
in the file list, ask your
instructor for help.

*Your screen should be
similar to Figure 1.30*

Figure 1.30

A preview of the file is displayed in the right side of the Browse dialog box.

You see that it is the picture you want, so you can select it as the object file to be inserted.

5 • **Change the dialog box view to List.**

• **Double-click the** ac01_Friend1 **file name.**

Your screen should be similar to Figure 1.31

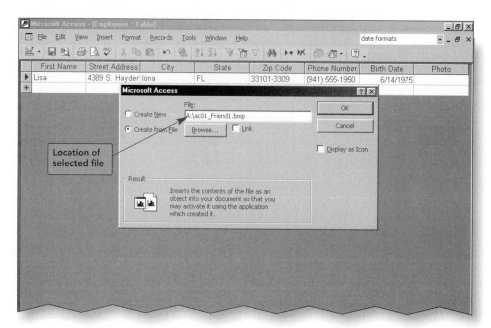

Figure 1.31

The object dialog box is displayed again with the path to the selected object displayed in the File text box. When inserting an object, you can specify if you want to display the object as an icon instead of the picture. Using this setting saves a lot of disk space, because only an icon appears for the object rather than the complete object. Although the future plan is to include a photograph for each employee and display it as an icon, for the test picture you want to display the photo itself.

6 • **Click**  **.**

Your screen should be similar to Figure 1.32

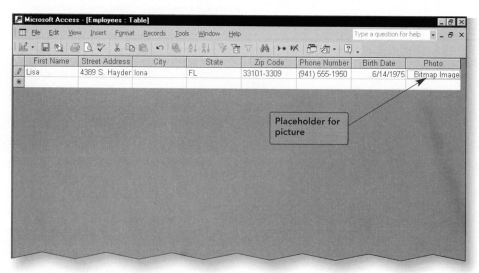

Figure 1.32

The picture object was inserted as a bound object, because it is associated with the Photo field. In Datasheet view, the field displays a text placeholder such as "Package" or "Bitmap Image" instead of the picture. The actual placeholder you will see will depend upon the software your computer used to import the image into Access.

You can now display the photograph from the Photo field to check that it has in fact been inserted there.

Double-click on the Photo field entry.

Your screen should be similar to Figure 1.33

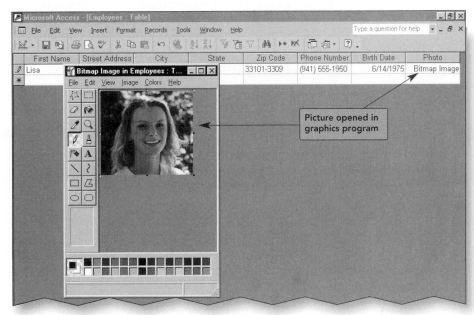

Additional Information

The graphic can be further manipulated using the graphics program features.

The picture object is opened and displayed in the associated graphics program, in this case, Paint. Yours may open and display in a different graphics program.

● **Click** **X** **Close in the Paint window title bar to close the application.**

● **Press** **←Enter**.

Your screen should be similar to Figure 1.34

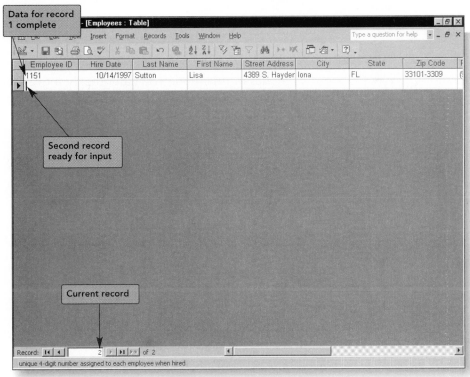

Figure 1.34

The data for the first record is now complete.

The insertion point moves to the first field on the next row and waits for input of the employee number for the next record. As soon as the insertion point moves to another record, the data is saved to the table file and the number of the new record appears in the status bar. The second record was automatically assigned the record number 2.

Navigating a Datasheet

Next you will check the first record for accuracy.

1 ● Point to the left end of the Employee ID field for the first record. When the mouse pointer appears as ⇧, click the mouse button.

Your screen should be similar to Figure 1.35

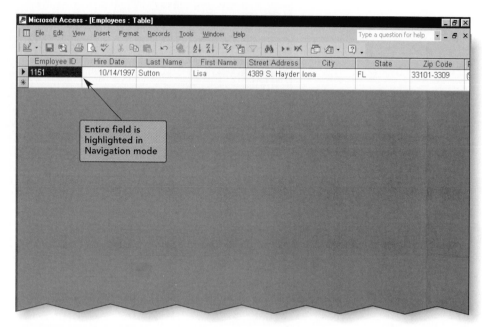

Figure 1.35

The entire field is selected (highlighted), and you have activated Navigation mode. In this mode you can quickly move from field to field in a datasheet using the keyboard keys shown in the following table.

Key	Moves highlight to
→ or Tab ⇥	Next field
← or ⇧ Shift + Tab ⇥	Previous field
Home or End	First or last field in current record
↓	Current field in next record
↑	Current field in previous record
Home	First field in record
End	Last field in record

Because the entire field contents is selected, if you type, the selection will be replaced with the new text. If you use Delete or Backspace, the entire highlighted field contents are deleted. Next, you will select the Street Address field in order to check its contents.

2 ● **Press** → **4 times.**

● **Click the Street Address field with the mouse pointer shape as an I-beam** I.

Your screen should be similar to Figure 1.36

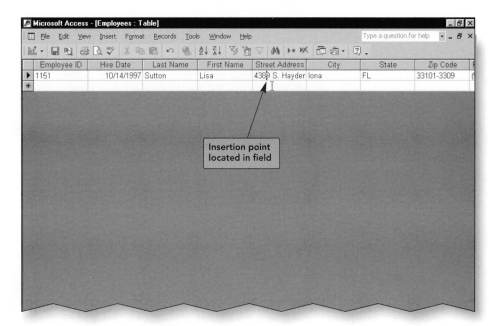

Figure 1.36

The insertion point is positioned in the field, and you could now edit the field contents if necessary. The beginning of the field looks fine, but because the column width is too narrow, you cannot see the entire entry. You will move the insertion point to the end of the address so you can check the rest of the entry.

3 ● **Press** End.

Your screen should be similar to Figure 1.37

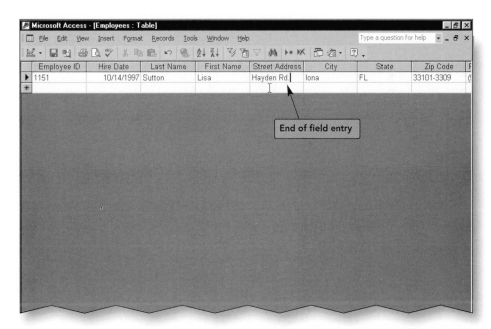

Figure 1.37

The text scrolled in the field, and the insertion point is positioned at the end of the entry. However, now you cannot see the beginning of the entry, which makes it difficult to edit.

Another way to view the field's contents is to expand the field.

4 ● **Press** ⟨⇧ Shift⟩ + ⟨F2⟩.

*Your screen should be
similar to Figure 1.38*

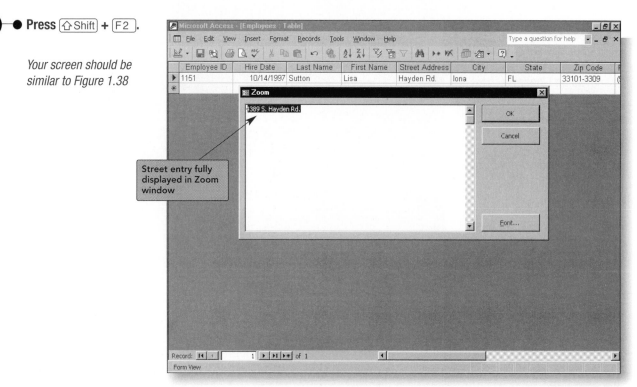

Street entry fully
displayed in Zoom
window

Figure 1.38

The entry is fully displayed in a separate Zoom window. You can edit in the
window just as you would in the field.

5 ● **If the entry contains an error, correct it.**

● **Click** ⟨ OK ⟩.

● **Press** ⟨Tab ⇥⟩.

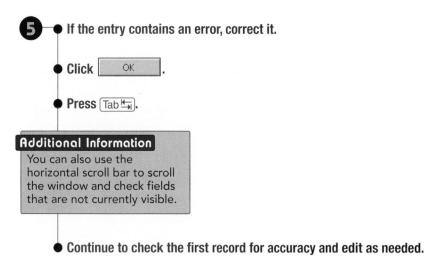

Additional Information
You can also use the
horizontal scroll bar to scroll
the window and check fields
that are not currently visible.

● **Continue to check the first record for accuracy and edit as needed.**

6 **Enter the data shown in the table on the right for the second record.**

● **Press [←Enter] twice to skip the Photo field and complete the record.**

● **Check the second record for accuracy and edit it if necessary.**

Your screen should be similar to Figure 1.39

Field Name	Data
Employee ID	0434
Hire Date	July 5, 1996
Last Name	Merwin
First Name	Adda
Street Address	947 S. Forest St.
City	Fort Myers
State	FL
Zip Code	33301-1268
Phone Number	(941) 555-4494
Birth Date	April 20, 1970

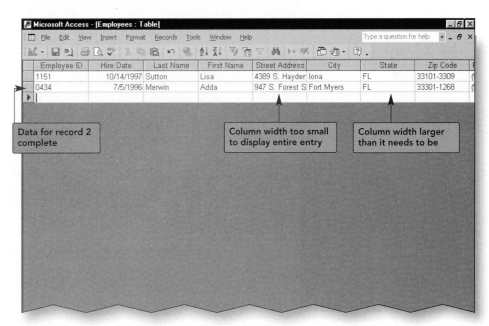

Figure 1.39

Notice that the dates changed automatically to the format set in the date property field.

Changing Column Width

Additional Information
You will learn how to do more table formatting in future labs.

The first thing you want to do is make the columns wider so you can see each complete field entry without having to move to the field and scroll or expand the field box. There are several ways that you can manipulate the rows and columns of a datasheet so that it is easier to view and work with the table data.

Resizing a Column

As you have noticed, some of the fields (such as the Street field) do not display the entire entry, while other fields (such as the State field) are much larger than the field's column heading or contents. This is because the default width of a column in the datasheet is not the same size as the field sizes you specified in Design view.

To quickly resize a column, simply drag the right column border line in the field selector in either direction to increase or decrease the column width. The mouse pointer shape is ✛ when you can drag to size the column. As you drag, a column line appears to show you the new column border. When you release the mouse button, the column width will be set. First you will increase the width of the Street field so the entire address will be visible.

1 ● Point to the right column border line in the field selector for the Street Address field name.

● When the mouse pointer is ✛, drag the border to the right until you think the column width will be long enough to display the field contents.

● Adjust the column width again if it is too wide or not wide enough.

Another Method
You can also adjust the column width to a specific number of characters using Format/Column Width.

Your screen should be similar to Figure 1.40

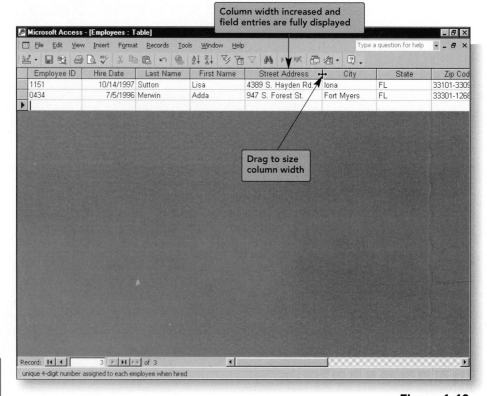

Figure 1.40

Using Best Fit

Rather than change the widths of all the other columns individually, you can select all columns and change their widths at the same time. To select multiple columns, point to the column heading in the field selector area of the first or last column you want to select. Then, when the mouse pointer changes to ↓, click, and without releasing the mouse button, drag in either direction across the column headings.

1 ● **Point to the Employee ID field name.**

● **When the mouse pointer is ↓, drag to the right across all column headings.**

● **Use the horizontal scroll bar to bring the first field column back into view in the window.**

Your screen should be similar to Figure 1.41

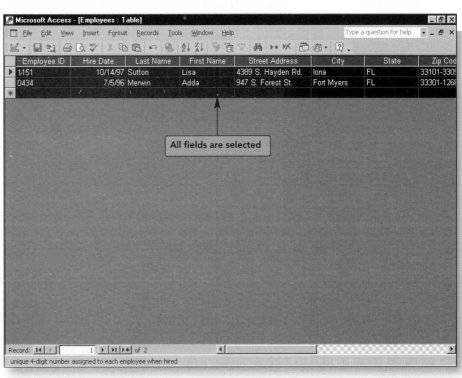

Figure 1.41

Multiple columns are highlighted. Now, if you were to drag the column border of any selected column, all the selected columns would change to the same size. However, you want the column widths to be adjusted appropriately to fit the data in each column. To do this, you can double-click the column border to activate the Best Fit feature. The **Best Fit** feature automatically adjusts the column widths of all selected columns to accommodate the longest entry or column heading in each of the selected columns.

2 ● Double-click any column border line (in the field selector) within the selection when the mouse pointer is ↔.

● Click anywhere on the table to deselect the datasheet.

Another Method

You can also use the Format/Column Width menu equivalent and click ⬚Best Fit in the Column Width dialog box. The Column Width command is also on the shortcut menu when an entire column is selected.

Your screen should be similar to Figure 1.42

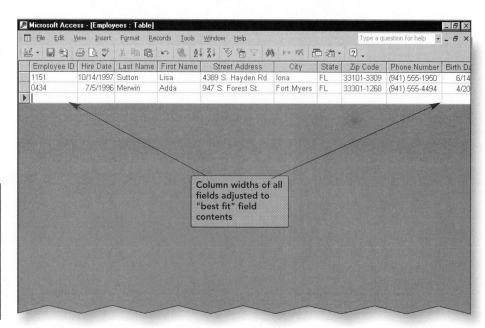

Figure 1.42

Now you can see the complete contents of each field. You are also no longer in Navigation mode, because the insertion point is visible in the field.

3 ● Check each of the records again and edit any entries that are incorrect.

● Add the record in the table on the right as record 3.

● Press ⏎Enter twice to skip the Photo field and complete the record.

Your screen should be similar to Figure 1.43

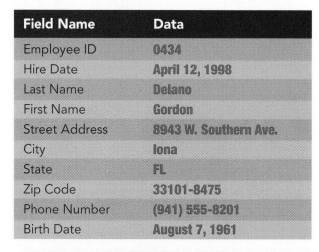

Field Name	Data
Employee ID	0434
Hire Date	April 12, 1998
Last Name	Delano
First Name	Gordon
Street Address	8943 W. Southern Ave.
City	Iona
State	FL
Zip Code	33101-8475
Phone Number	(941) 555-8201
Birth Date	August 7, 1961

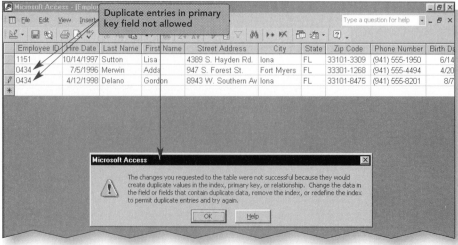

Figure 1.43

As soon as you complete the record, an error message dialog box appears indicating that Access has located a duplicate value in a key field. The key field is Employee ID. You realize you were looking at the employee number from the previous record when you entered the employee number for this record. You need to clear the message and enter the correct number.

4 ● Click ⬚ OK ⬚.

● Press Home.

● Change the Employee ID for record 3 to **0234**.

● Press ↓.

Your screen should be similar to Figure 1.44

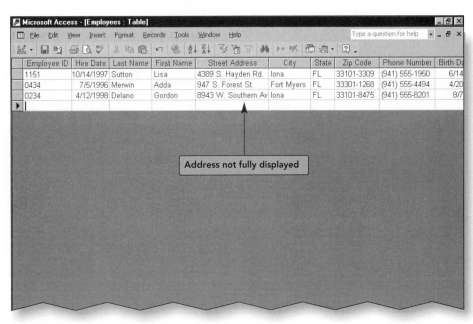

Address not fully displayed

Figure 1.44

The record is accepted with the new employee number. However, you notice that the address for this record does not fully display in the Street Address field. It has a longer address than either of the other two records.

5 ● Double-click the right border of the Street Address field to best fit the field column.

Your screen should be similar to Figure 1.45

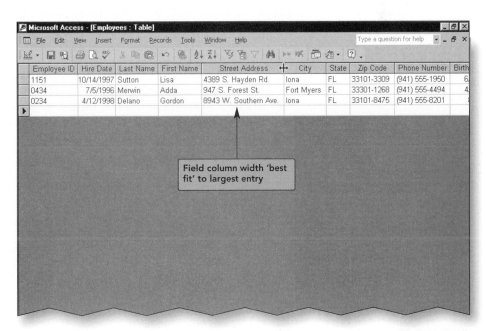

Field column width 'best fit' to largest entry

Figure 1.45

Displaying Records in Primary Key Order

When you add new records in a datasheet, the records are displayed in the order you enter them. However, they are stored on disk in order by the primary key field. You can change the display on the screen to reflect the correct order by using the ⇧Shift + F9 key combination.

6 ● Press ⇧Shift + F9 .

Your screen should be similar to Figure 1.46

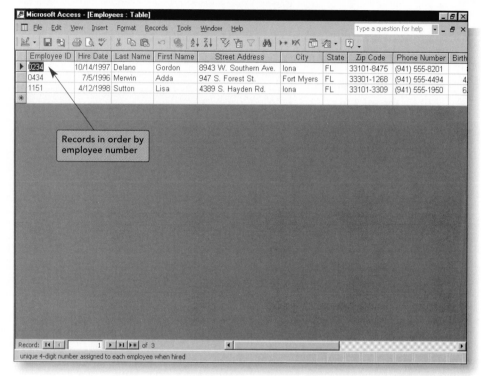

Records in order by employee number

Figure 1.46

The records are now in order by employee number. This is the order determined by the primary key field.

Adding Records in Data Entry

Next you want to add several more employee records to the table. Another way to add records is to use the Data Entry command. Using this command hides all existing records in the datasheet and displays a blank datasheet area in which you can enter data. The advantage to using this command is that it prevents accidental changes to existing table data.

Your screen should be similar to Figure 1.47

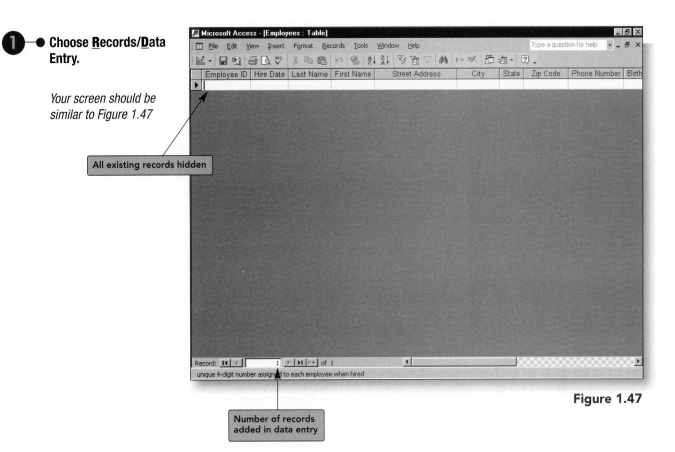

All existing records hidden

Number of records added in data entry

Figure 1.47

The existing records are hidden, and the only row displayed is a blank row where you can enter a new record. The status bar displays "1 of 1." This number reflects the number of new records as they are added in Data Entry rather than all records in the table.

You will add three more records to the table. If data for some fields, such as the City, State, or Zip Code, is the same from record to record, you can save yourself some typing by copying the data from one of the other records. Just select the field contents and click 🔃 Copy. Then move to the field where you want the copy to appear and click 📋 Paste.

Another Method

The menu equivalents are **E**dit/**C**opy or Ctrl + C and **E**dit/**P**aste or Ctrl + V. You can also press Ctrl + ' to duplicate an entry in the same field of the previous record.

1 ● Enter the data for the two records shown in the table on the right.

● Enter a final record using your first and last names. Enter **9999** as your employee number and the current date as your date hired. The information you enter in all other fields can be fictitious.

● Best fit any columns that do not fully display the field contents.

● Check each of the records and correct any entry errors.

Your screen should be similar to Figure 1.48

Field	Record 1	Record 2
Employee ID	0839	0728
Hire Date	August 14, 1997	March 15, 1997
Last Name	Ruiz	Roman
First Name	Enrique	Anita
Street	358 Maple Dr.	2348 S. Bala Dr.
City	Cypress Lake	Fort Myers
State	FL	FL
Zip Code	33205-6911	33301-1268
Phone Number	(941) 555-0091	(941) 555-9870
Birth Date	December 10, 1963	March 15, 1961

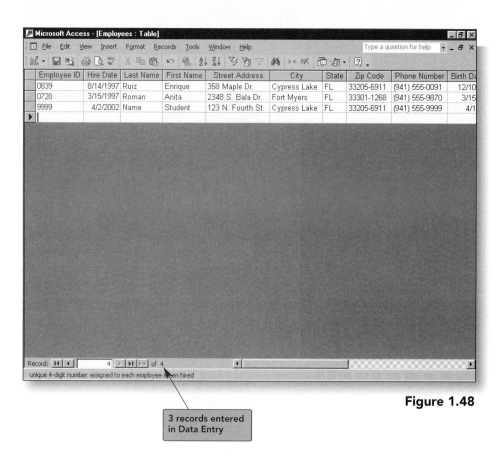

3 records entered in Data Entry

Figure 1.48

Now that you have entered the new records, you can redisplay all the records in the table.

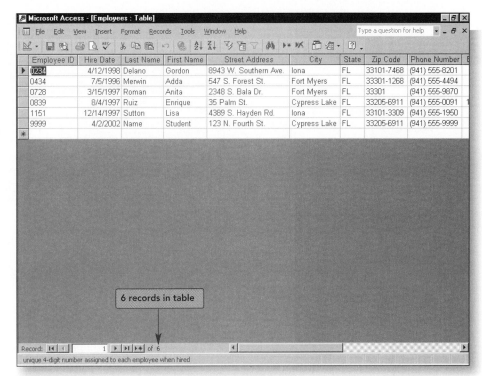

Figure 1.49

There is now a total of 6 records in the table. The records are displayed in
the datasheet in sorted order by employee number. If you had added the
new records in Datasheet view, they would not appear in primary key field
order until you updated the table display. This is another advantage of
using Data Entry.

Deleting Records

While you are entering the employee records, you find a memo from one of
your managers stating that Adda Merwin is no longer working at the club
and asking you to remove her record from the employee files.

You can remove records from a table by selecting the entire record and
pressing the Delete key. This method is useful when you have multiple
records to be deleted that you can select and delete as a group. It is quicker,
however, to use the 🔲 Delete Record button when you want to remove individual records. This is because the entire record is both selected and
deleted at the same time.

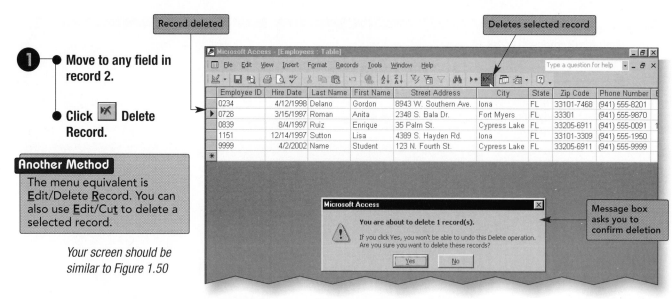

1 • Move to any field in record 2.

   • Click 🗙 Delete Record.

Another Method

The menu equivalent is Edit/Delete Record. You can also use Edit/Cut to delete a selected record.

Your screen should be similar to Figure 1.50

Figure 1.50

This message box asks you to confirm that you really want to delete the selected record. This is because this action cannot be reversed.

2 • Click Yes to confirm that you want to delete the record.

Your screen should be similar to Figure 1.51

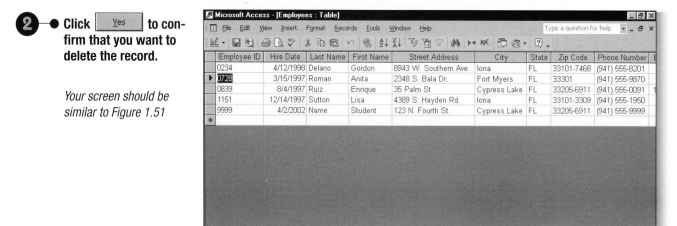

Figure 1.51

The table now consists of five employee records. You decide to print out the table as it stands now and get your managers' approval before you begin entering the rest of the employee records.

Previewing and Printing a Table

Now, you want to print a copy of the records in this table. Before printing the table, you will preview on screen how it will look when printed.

Previewing the Table

Previewing a table displays each page in a reduced size so you can see the layout. Then, if necessary, you can make changes to the layout before printing, to both save time and avoid wasting paper.

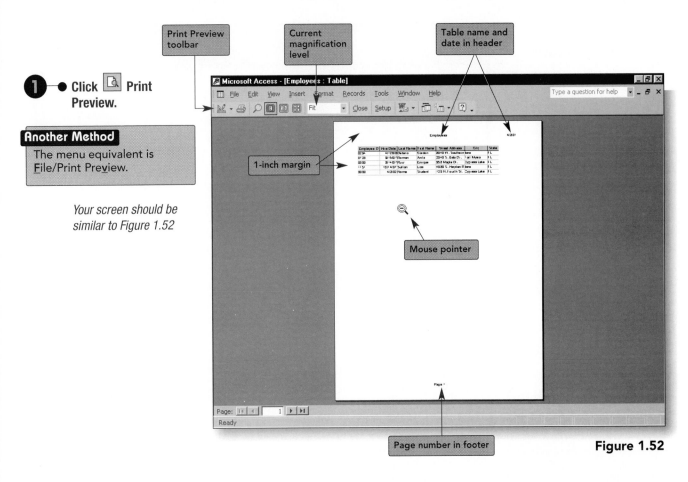

1 ● Click 📷 Print Preview.

Another Method

The menu equivalent is File/Print Preview.

Your screen should be similar to Figure 1.52

Figure 1.52

Labels in figure:
- Print Preview toolbar
- Current magnification level
- Table name and date in header
- 1-inch margin
- Mouse pointer
- Page number in footer

The Print Preview window displays a reduced view of how the table will appear when printed. The document will be printed using the default report and page layout settings, which include such items as 1-inch margins, the table name and date displayed in a header, and the page number in a footer.

To better see the information in the table, you can change the magnification level of the Preview window. The current magnification level, Fit, is displayed in the [Fit ▼] button in the Print Preview toolbar. This setting adjusts the magnification of the page to best fit in the size of the window. Notice that the mouse pointer is a 🔍 Magnifying glass when it is positioned on the page. This indicates that you can click on the page to switch between the Fit magnification level and the last used level.

2 ● Click on the table name in the header.

Additional Information

The location where you click will determine the area that is displayed initially.

Your screen should be similar to Figure 1.53

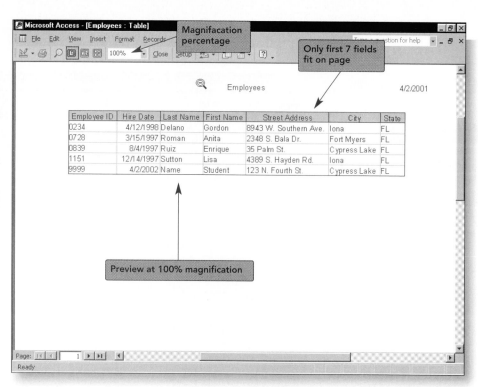

Additional Information

You can also use <u>V</u>iew/<u>Z</u>oom or the Fit Zoom button on the Print Preview toolbar to increase the character size up to ten times the normal display (1000 percent) or reduce it to 10 percent.

Figure 1.53

The table appears in 100 percent magnification. This is the size it will appear when printed. Notice, however, that because the table is too wide to fit across the width of a page, only the first seven fields are displayed on the page. Tables with multiple columns are typically wider than what can fit on an 8½ by 11 piece of paper. You would like to see both pages displayed onscreen.

3 ● Click ▣ Two pages.

Your screen should be similar to Figure 1.54

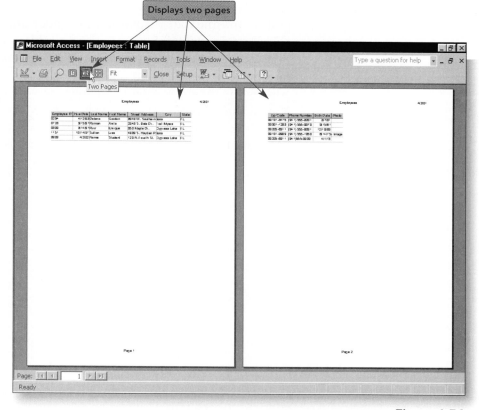

Figure 1.54

Changing the Page Orientation

Rather than print the table on two pages, you decide to see if changing the orientation of the table will allow you to print it on one page. **Orientation** refers to the direction that text prints on a page. Normal orientation is to print across the width of an 8½-inch page. This is called **portrait** orientation. You can change the orientation to print across the length of the paper. This is called **landscape** orientation.

You already know from seeing the table in Print Preview that it will not fit on one page in the default portrait orientation, so you need to change it to landscape.

● Click Setup.

Another Method
The menu equivalent is File/Page Setup.

Your screen should be similar to Figure 1.55

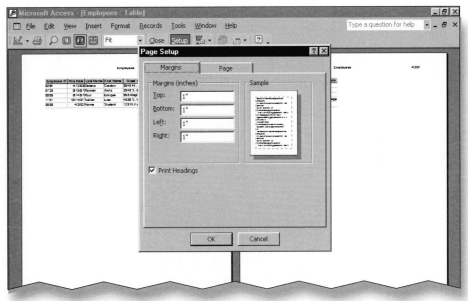

Figure 1.55

The Page Setup dialog box lets you specify the basic layout for your table. There are two types of layout changes that you can make, Margins and Page. The orientation setting is on the Page tab.

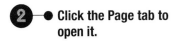
● **Click the Page tab to open it.**

Your screen should be similar to Figure 1.56

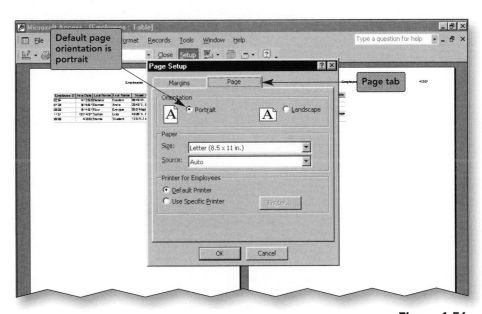

Figure 1.56

The Orientation panel shows how text will print in each orientation. You select the desired orientation by clicking on its radio button.

3 ● **Select Landscape.**

● **Click** OK .

Your screen should be similar to Figure 1.57

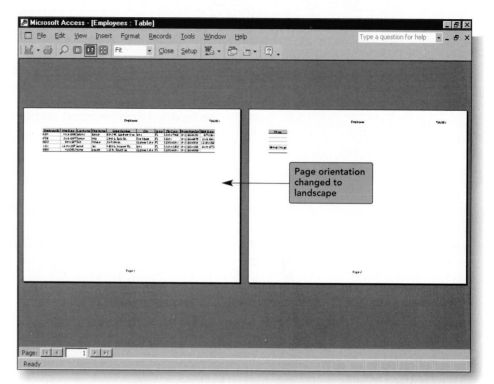

Page orientation changed to landscape

Figure 1.57

The Print Preview view now shows all but the Photo field of the table will print on one page. Because none of the employee photos have actually been inserted yet (and the photos would not actually print as part of the table — only the placeholders would), you decide that this is acceptable for now and will go ahead and print the table.

Printing a Table

The 🖨 Print button on the toolbar will immediately start printing the report using the default print settings. However, if you want to check the print settings first, you need to use the Print command.

1 • If necessary, make sure your printer is on and ready to print.

• Choose **File/Print**.

Another Method

The keyboard shortcut is Ctrl + P.

Your screen should be similar to Figure 1.58

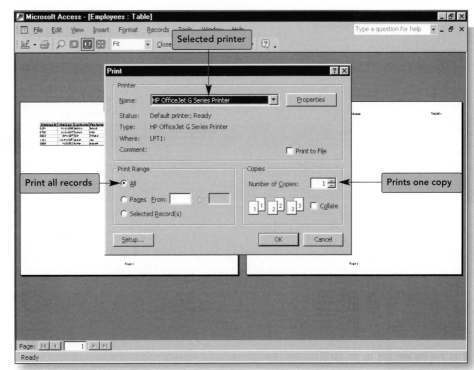

Figure 1.58

HAVING TROUBLE?

Please consult your instructor for printing procedures that may differ from the directions given here.

From the Print dialog box, you specify the printer you will be using and the document settings. The printer that is currently selected is displayed in the Name drop-down list box in the Printer section of the dialog box.

The Page Range area of the Print dialog box lets you specify how much of the document you want printed. The range options are described in the following table.

Option	Action
All	Prints the entire document.
Pages	Prints pages you specify by typing page numbers in the text box.
Selected Records	Prints selected records only.

Because the second page contains the Photo field, you decide to print only the first page of the table.

2 • If you need to change the selected printer to another printer, open the Name drop-down list box and select the appropriate printer (your instructor will tell you which printer to select).

• Select **Pages**.

• Type **1** in both the **From** and **To** text boxes.

• Click ⬛ OK ⬛.

Previewing and Printing a Table **AC1.53**

A status message box is displayed briefly, informing you that the table is being printed. Your printed copy should be similar to the printout shown here.

				Employees					7/16/2002

Employee ID	Hire Date	Last Name	First Name	Street	City	State	Zip Code	Phone Number	Birth Date
0234	10/14/1997	Delano	Gordon	8943 W. Southern Ave.	Iona	FL	33101-8475	(941) 555-8201	8/7/1961
0728	3/15/1997	Roman	Anita	2348 S. Bala Dr.	Fort Myers	FL	33301-1268	(941) 555-9870	3/15/1961
0839	8/14/1997	Ruiz	Enrique	358 Maple Dr.	Cypress Lake	FL	33205-6911	(941) 555-0091	12/10/1963
1151	10/14/1997	Sutton	Lisa	4389 S. Hayden Rd.	Iona	FL	33101-3309	(941) 555-1950	6/14/1975
9999	4/2/2002	Name	Student	123 N. Fourth St.	Cypress Lake	FL	33205-6911	(941) 555-9999	4/1/1978

You can now close the Print Preview window and return to Datasheet view.

3 ● Click 🔲 One page.

● Click Close .

Your screen should look similar to Figure 1.59

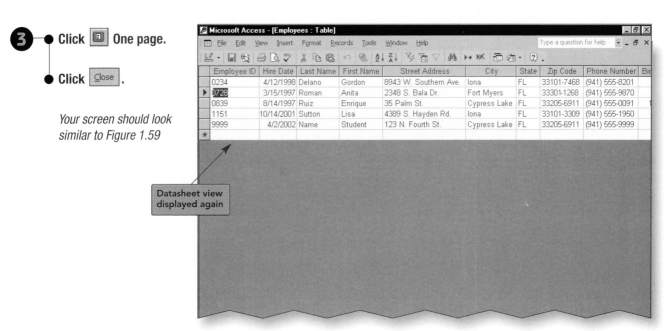

Datasheet view displayed again

Figure 1.59

Closing and Opening a Table and Database

You are ready to show your managers your printed table and get approval on how you set up the data. But first you need to close the table and database that you created.

Closing a Table and Database

You close a table by closing its window and saving any layout changes you have made since your last Access session.

1 ● Click ✕ Close Window in the menu bar.

Another Method

The menu equivalent is File/Close.

Your screen should look similar to Figure 1.60

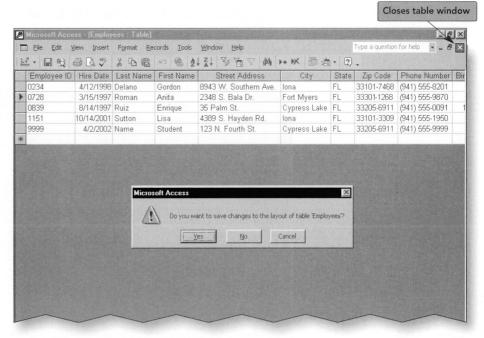

Closes table window

Figure 1.60

Because you changed the column widths of the table in Datasheet view, you are prompted to save the layout changes before the table is closed. If you do not save the table, your column width settings will be lost.

2 ● Click [Yes].

Your screen should be similar to Figure 1.61

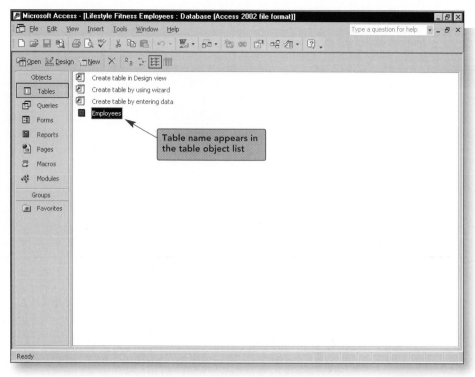

Figure 1.61

The Database window is displayed again. The name of the table you created appears in the Table object list. Next, you will close the database.

3 ● Click ☒ **Close Window in the menu bar.**

Your screen should be similar to Figure 1.62

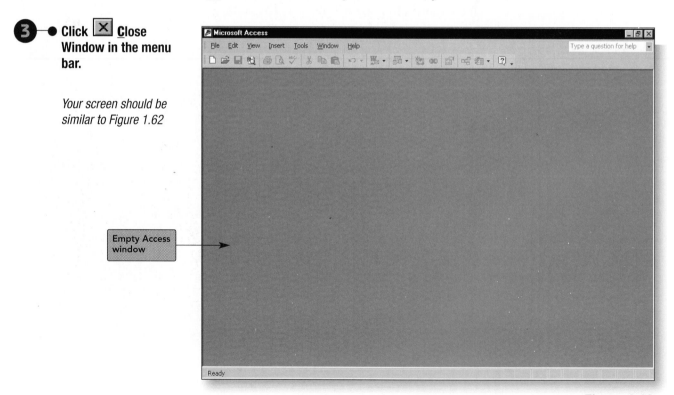

Figure 1.62

You are left with an empty Access application window. The main Access menu commands and buttons are still available, however, for you to create new and access existing database files.

Opening a Table and Database

You want to make sure you know how to access your table of employee records, so you will reopen it and then close it again.

1 ● Click  Open.

Another Method

The menu equivalent is File/Open and the keyboard shortcut is Ctrl + O. You can also display the New File task pane and select the file name from the Open a File list or select More Files if the file you want to open is not listed.

● If necessary, open the Look In drop-down list and select the location of your data files.

Your screen should be similar to Figure 1.63

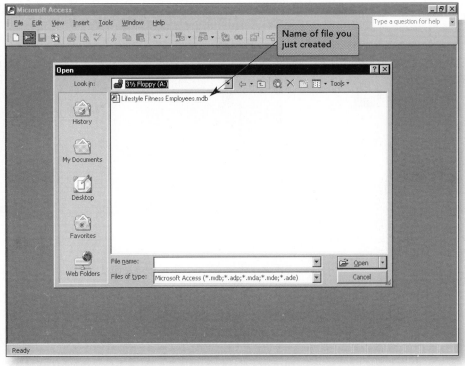

Name of file you just created

Figure 1.63

HAVING TROUBLE?

If the file extension is not displayed, this is because the setting to display extensions in Windows has been turned off on your system.

Now the name of the database file you just created is displayed in the list box. Your list box may display additional database file names.

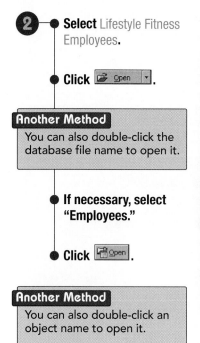

Select Lifestyle Fitness Employees.

Click 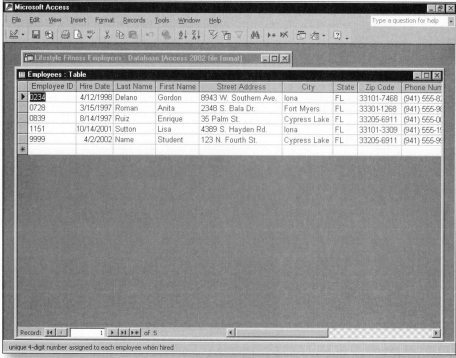 Open.

Another Method
You can also double-click the database file name to open it.

If necessary, select "Employees."

Click 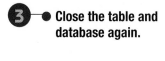 Open.

Another Method
You can also double-click an object name to open it.

Your screen should be similar to Figure 1.64

Employee ID	Hire Date	Last Name	First Name	Street Address	City	State	Zip Code	Phone Num
0234	4/12/1998	Delano	Gordon	8943 W. Southern Ave.	Iona	FL	33101-7468	(941) 555-8:
0728	3/15/1997	Roman	Anita	2348 S. Bala Dr.	Fort Myers	FL	33301-1268	(941) 555-9(
0839	8/14/1997	Ruiz	Enrique	35 Palm St.	Cypress Lake	FL	33205-6911	(941) 555-0(
1151	10/14/2001	Sutton	Lisa	4389 S. Hayden Rd.	Iona	FL	33101-3309	(941) 555-1!
9999	4/2/2002	Name	Student	123 N. Fourth St.	Cypress Lake	FL	33205-6911	(941) 555-9!

unique 4-digit number assigned to each employee when hired

Figure 1.64

The table of employee records is displayed in Datasheet view again, just as it was before you saved and closed the table.

Close the table and database again.

Your screen should be similar to Figure 1.65

Closes Access

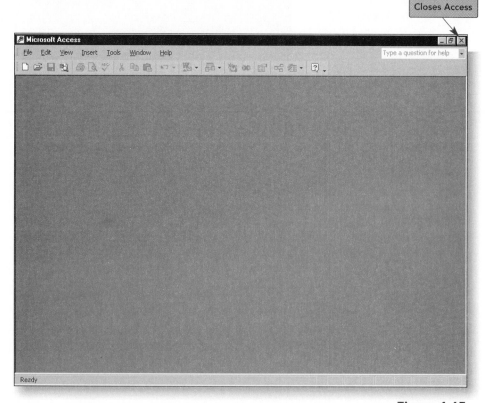

Figure 1.65

Notice that this time you were not prompted to save the table because you did not make any layout changes.

www.mhhe.com/oleary

Access 2002

Exiting Access

You will continue to build and use the table of employee records in the next lab. Until then, you can exit Access and return to the Windows desktop.

1 ● Click  Close in the Access window title bar.

Another Method

The menu equivalent is File/Exit.

Warning: If you are using a floppy disk, do not remove it from the drive until you exit Access.

concept summary

LAB 1

Creating a Database

Database (AC1.6)

A **database** is an organized collection of related information. Typically, the information in a database is stored in a table consisting of vertical columns and horizontal rows.

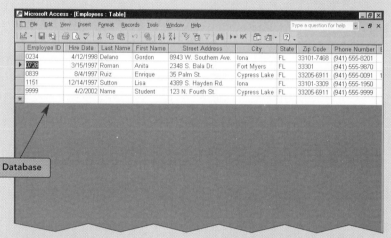

Database

Object (AC1.11)

An **object** is an item, such as a table or report, that can be created, selected, and manipulated as a unit.

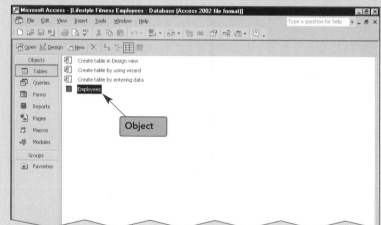

Object

Field Name (AC1.13)

A **field name** is used to identify the data stored in the field.

Data Type (AC1.16)

The **data type** defines the type of data the field will contain.

Field Property (AC1.18)

A **field property** is a characteristic that helps define a field. A set of field properties is associated with each field.

Field Property

Field name

Data type

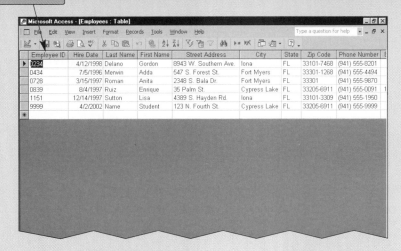

Primary Key (AC1.20)

A **primary key** is a field that uniquely identifies each record.

Graphics

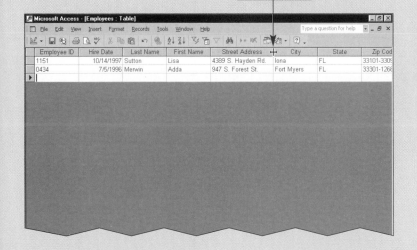

Graphics (AC1.31)

A **graphic** is a non-text element or object, such as a drawing or picture, which can be added to a table.

Column width

Column Width (AC1.40)

Column width refers to the size of a field column in Datasheet view. It controls the amount of data you can see on the screen.

key terms

Best Fit   AC1.41

bound object   AC1.31

clip art   AC1.31

column width   AC1.40

current record   AC1.26

database   AC1.6

Database toolbar   AC1.5

datasheet   AC1.26

data type   AC1.16

drawing object   AC1.31

field   AC1.6

field name   AC1.13

field property   AC1.18

field selector   AC1.26

field size   AC1.18

graphic   AC1.31

landscape   AC1.51

navigation buttons   AC1.26

Navigation mode   AC1.36

object   AC1.11

orientation   AC1.51

picture   AC1.31

portrait   AC1.51

primary key   AC1.20

record   AC1.6

record number indicator   AC1.26

record selector   AC1.26

relational database   AC1.6

table   AC1.6

unbound object   AC1.31

view   AC1.25

workspace   AC1.5

mous skills

The Microsoft Office User Specialist (MOUS) certification program is designed to measure your proficiency in performing basic tasks using the Office XP applications. Getting certified demonstrates that you have the skills and provides a valuable industry credential for employment. After completing this lab, you have learned the following Access 2002 Microsoft Office User Specialist skills:

Skill	Description	Page
Creating and Using Databases	Create Access databases	AC1.8
	Open database objects in different views	AC1.25
	Move among records	AC1.36
Creating and Modifying Tables	Create and modify tables	AC1.10, AC1.23
	Modify field properties	AC1.18
Viewing and Organizing Information	Enter, edit, and delete records	AC1.27, AC1.47

command summary

Command	Shortcut Keys	Button	Action
File/New	Ctrl + N		Opens New File task pane
File/Open	Ctrl + O		Opens an existing database
File/Close		X	Closes open window
File/Save	Ctrl + S		Saves database object
File/Page Setup		Setup	Setting page margins and page layout for printed output
File/Print Preview			Displays file as it will appear when printed
File/Print	Ctrl + P		Specifies print settings and prints current database object
File/Exit		X	Closes Access
Edit/Cut	Ctrl + X		Removes selected item and copies to the Clipboard
Edit/Copy	Ctrl + C		Duplictes selected item and copies to the Clipboard
Edit/Paste	Ctrl + V		Inserts copy of item in clipboard
Edit/Select Record			Selects current record
Edit/Delete Record			Deletes selected record
Edit/Delete Rows			Deletes selected field in Design view
Edit/Primary Key			Defines a field as a primary key field
View/Toolbars/Task Pane			Displays task pane
View/Datasheet View			Displays table in Datasheet view
View/Zoom/%		Fit	Displays previewed database object at specified percentage
Insert/Rows			Inserts new field in table in Design view
Insert/Object			Inserts an object into current field
Format/Column Width			Changes width of table columns in Datasheet view
Records/Remove Filter/Sort			Displays all records in table
Records/Data Entry			Hides existing records and displays Data Entry window

Terminology

screen identification

In the following Access screen, several items are identified by letters. Enter the correct term for each item in the spaces provided.

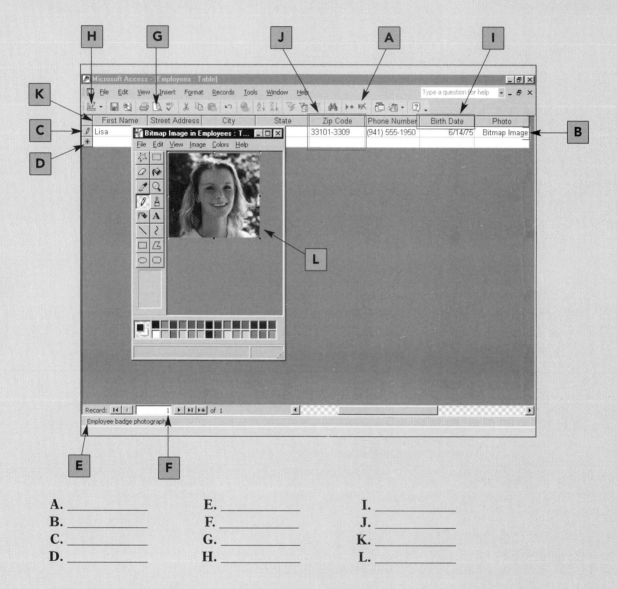

A. _____   E. _____   I. _____
B. _____   F. _____   J. _____
C. _____   G. _____   K. _____
D. _____   H. _____   L. _____

matching

Match the numbered item with the correct lettered description.

1. record _____
2. view
3. relational database _____
4. primary key _____
5. Best Fit _____
6. field size _____
7. data type _____
8. Design view _____
9. Datasheet view _____
10. unbound object _____
_____

a. an object associated with the table as a whole and not connected to a specific field

b. collection of related fields

c. a way of looking at table data

d. used to define the table structure

e. feature used to adjust column width to field contents

f. controls the type of data a field can contain

g. field used to order records

h. displays table in row and column format

i. contains multiple tables linked by a common field

j. controls the maximum number of characters that can be entered in a field

multiple choice

Circle the letter of the correct response.

1. The field property that limits a text data type to a certain size is called _____.
   a. label control
   b. operator
   c. field size
   d. field property

2. The steps of database development include planning, creating, and _____ data.
   a. entering
   b. graphing
   c. developing
   d. organizing

3. You can use the Objects _____ located at the left of the Database window to select the type of object you want to work with.
   a. bar
   b. buttons
   c. properties
   d. tabs

4. A field name is used to identify the _____ stored in a field.
   a. characters
   b. keys
   c. data
   d. graphics

5. The _____ type defines the type of data the field contains.
   a. property
   b. entry
   c. data
   d. specification

6. Field size, format, input mask, caption, and default value are _____.
   a. key elements
   b. field properties
   c. navigating modes
   d. data types

7. The record selector symbol indicates which record is the _____.
   a. bound control
   b. primary key
   c. destination file
   d. current record

8. The _____ mode is used to move from field to field and to delete an entire field entry.
   a. Edit
   b. Browser
   c. Entry
   d. Navigation

9. The _____ is a field that uniquely identifies each record.
   a. format
   b. table
   c. table definition
   d. primary key
   e. text property

10. You can examine the objects in your database using different window formats called _____.
   a. views
   b. masks
   c. tables
   d. dialog objects
   e. perspectives

true/false

Circle the correct answer to the following statements.

1. There is one specific view that is used to edit table data.	True	False
2. The first step in database development is planning.	True	False
3. Tables, forms, and reports are objects.	True	False
4. Field names are used to define properties for a database.	True	False
5. Text, memo, number, and date/time are data types.	True	False
6. Data properties are a set of characteristics that are associated with each field.	True	False
7. A person's first name is often used as the primary key.	True	False
8. You may lose data if your data and data type are incompatible.	True	False
9. Drawings and pictures can be added to a database.	True	False
10. While column width does not affect the amount of data that you can see on the screen, it does affect the amount of data that you can enter into a field.	True	False

Concepts

fill-in

Complete the following statements by filling in the blanks with the correct terms.

1. Database information is stored in _____.

2. Relational databases define _____ between tables by having common data in the tables.

3. The first step in developing a database is _____.

4. The _____ defines the type of data that can be entered in a field.

5. A(n) _____ is an item made up of different elements.

6. The set of characteristics associated with a field are the _____.

7. A descriptive label called a(n) _____ is used to identify the data stored in a field.

8. The _____ data type is used to format numbers with dollar signs and decimal places.

9. A(n) _____ is a field that uniquely identifies each record in a table.

10. _____ view allows the user to enter, edit, and delete records in a table.

discussion questions

Answer the following questions by preparing written responses.

1. Discuss several uses you may have for a relational database. Then explain the steps you would follow to create the first table.

2. Discuss why it is important to plan a database before creating it. How can proper planning save you time later?

3. Discuss the difference between a bound and an unbound object.

4. Design view and Datasheet view are two of the Access views. Discuss when it would be appropriate to use each of these views.

5. Discuss why it is important to choose the correct data type for a field. What may happen to the data if you change the data type?

Hands-On Exercises

step-by-step

Creating a Client Database

★ **1.** Simply Beautiful is a day spa with several Tri-County locations. Up until now the spa's owner, Maria Dell, has kept separate records at each location. She is finding, however, that several of the spa's clients frequent more than one location. Therefore, Ms. Dell has asked you to build a database that will enable her to keep information about the spa's clients in one central location. When you are finished, a printout of your completed database table should look like that shown here.

Clients   5/9/2001

Client #	Last Name	First Name	Home Phone	Work Phone	Cell Phone	Street Address	City	State
100-01	Marchand	Ellen	(803) 555-4515	(803) 555-6226	(803) 555-2112	818 Southern Ave.	Columbia	SC
100-02	Finch	Terrence	(803) 555-0091	(803) 555-2831	(803) 555-3087	919 Port Ct.	Orangeburg	SC
100-03	Lawry	Rachel	(803) 555-1748	(803) 555-4279	(803) 555-8301	248 S. Tram Rd.	Lexington	SC
100-04	[Your last name]	[Your first name]	(803) 555-1212	(803) 555-9335	(803) 555-5555	387 Main Street	Wateree	SC

Clients   5/9/2001

Zip Code	E-mail
29201	ellen@mail.com
29115	terr@set.net
29071	law@mail.com
29044	student@ed.net

Page 2

To create the client database, follow these steps:

a. Create a database named Beautiful. Design a table using the following field information:

Field Data	Type	Description	Field Size
Client #	Text	A unique 5-digit number	6
Last Name	Text		25
First Name	Text		25
Home Phone	Text		15
Work Phone	Text		15
Cell Phone	Text		15
Street Address	Text		30
City	Text		25
State	Text	2-letter abbreviation	2
Zip Code	Text		10
E-mail	Text		30

b. Make the Client No. field the primary key field.
c. Save the table as Clients.
d. Switch to Datasheet view and enter the following records into the table:

Record 1	Record 2	Record 3	Record 4
100-01	100-02	100-03	100-04
Marchand	Finch	Lawry	[Your last name]
Ellen	Terrence	Rachel	[Your first name]
(803) 555-4515	(803) 555-0091	(803) 555-1748	(803) 555-1212
(803) 555-6226	(803) 555-2831	(803) 555-4279	(803) 555-9335
(803) 555-2112	(803) 555-3087	(803) 555-8301	(803) 555-5555
818 Southern Ave.	919 Port Ct.	248 S. Tram Rd.	387 Main Street
Columbia	Orangeburg	Lexington	Wateree
SC	SC	SC	SC
29201	29115	29071	29044
Ellen@mail.com	Terr@set.net	Law@mail.com	Student@ed.net

e. Adjust the column widths appropriately.
f. Change the page orientation to landscape.
g. Preview, print, save, and close the table.

Creating an Advertiser Database

★★ 2. You are a member of the homeowner's association for your community. To keep the residents informed about issues and events, the association distributes a monthly newsletter, Happenings. In the past year, there has been a rapid growth in building, including more houses and small office complexes. There are also plans to bring a school, fire station, and shopping center to your community. Consequently, the newsletter is now the size of a small magazine, and the homeowners' dues are not covering the expense of publishing it. The editorial staff has already begun selling ad space in the newsletter to local businesses, and based on your background in database management, they have asked you to set up a database to keep track of the advertiser contact information. You agree to design such a database and tell them you will have something to show them at the next meeting. Your printed database table should look like that shown here.

Advertisers   5/9/2001

Billing #	Business Name	Business Type	Contact Name	Contact Phone	Billing Street	Billing City	Billing State	Billing Zip
01D01	Discount Drugs	Pharmacy	Linda Donaldson	(520) 555-2233	124 Desert Way	Benson	AZ	85602
02A01	Ace Auto	Auto Repair	Frank Mason	(520) 555-3903	595 Main St.	Benson	AZ	85602
03P01	Pen and Ink	Office Supplies	Lu Yung	(520) 555-5050	201 Main St.	Benson	AZ	85602
04W01	Walkwells	Shoe Store	Student Name	(520) 555-3589	101 A Street	Benson	AZ	85602

Page 1

To create the advertiser database, follow these steps:

a. Create a database named Happenings. Design a table using the following field information:

Field Data	Type	Description	Field Size
Billing #	Text	Unique 5-digit billing code and business ID	5
Business Name	Text		25
Business Type	Text		15
Contact Name	Text		30
Contact Phone	Text		15
Billing Street	Text		30
Billing City	Text		25
Billing State	Text		2
Billing Zip	Text		10

b. Make the Billing # field the primary key field.
c. Save the table as **Advertisers**.
d. Switch to Datasheet view and enter the following records into the table, using Copy and Paste for fields that have the same data (such as the city):

Record 1	Record 2	Record 3	Record 4
01D01	02A01	03P01	04W01
Discount Drugs	Ace Auto	Pen and Ink	Walkwells
Pharmacy	Auto Repair	Office Supplies	Shoe Store
Linda Donaldson	Frank Mason	Lu Yung	[Your Name]
(520) 555-2233	(520) 555-3903	(520) 555-5050	(520) 555-3589
124 Desert Way	595 Main St.	201 Main St.	101 A Street
Benson	Benson	Benson	Benson
AZ	AZ	AZ	AZ
85602	85602	85602	85602

e. Switch back to Design view and change the field sizes for Business Name and Business Type to **30** and **20**, respectively. Save the changes.
f. Switch back to Datasheet view and best fit the column widths.
g. Display the records in primary key order.
h. Change the page orientation to landscape.
i. Print, save, and close the table.

Creating a Product Vendor Database

★★ **3.** The Downtown Internet Cafe, which you helped the owner, Evan, get off the ground, is an
★ overwhelming success. The clientele is growing every day, as is the demand for the beverages you
serve. Up until now, the information about the vendors has been kept in an alphabetical card file.
This has become quite unwieldy, however, and Evan would like a more sophisticated tracking
system. For starters, he would like you to create a database containing each supply item and the
contact information for the vendor that sells that item. When you are finished, your printed
database table should look like that shown here.

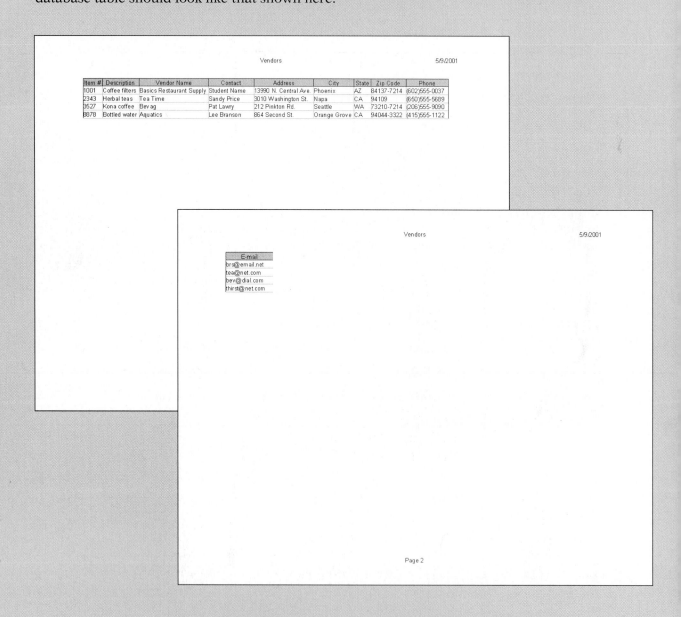

To create the database, follow these steps:

a. Create a database named Supplies. Design a table using the following field information:

Field Data	Type	Description	Field Size
Item #	Text	Unique 4-digit product number	4
Description	Text	Name of product	50
Vendor Name	Text	Name of supplier	50
Contact	Text	First & last name of contact person	50
Address	Text		50
City	Text		50
State	Text	2-letter abbreviation	2
Zip Code	Text	Include the 4-digit extension number if possible	10
Phone	Text	Include the area code in parentheses: (999) 123-4567	15
E-mail	Text	E-mail address of contact person	30

b. Make the Item # field the primary key field.
c. Save the table as Vendors.
d. Enter the following records into the table in Datasheet view:

Record 1	Record 2	Record 3
3527	2343	5721
Kona coffee	Herbal teas	Juice
Bevag	Tea Time	Natural Nectors
Pat Lawry	Sandy Price	Roberta White
212 Pinkton Rd.	3010 Washington St.	747 Manson Ave.
Seattle	Napa	Seattle
WA	CA	WA
73210-7214	94019	73210
(206) 555-9090	(650) 555-5689	(206) 555-0616
bev@dial.com	tea@net.com	nector@dial.com

e. Add the following records into the table in Data Entry:

Record 1	Record 2
8878	1001
Bottled water	Coffee filters
Aquatics	Basics Restaurant Supply
Lee Branson	Mandy Swanson
864 Second St.	13990 N. Central Ave.
Orange Grove	Phoenix
CA	AZ
94044-3213	84137-7214
(415) 555-1122	(602) 555-0037
thirst@net.com	brs@email.net

f. Return to Datasheet view and display the records in primary key order.

g. Adjust the column widths appropriately.

h. Edit the record for Item # 8878 to change the four-digit zip code extension from 3213 to 3322.

i. Delete the record for Natural Nectors.

j. Edit the record for Item # 1001 to replace the current Contact name with your name.

k. Change to landscape orientation.

l. Preview the table.

m. Print, save, and close the table.

Creating an Informational Database

★★ **4.** You have just been hired by Adventure Travel to create and maintain a database containing
★★   information about the tours they offer and the accommodations that are part of each tour
★   package. When you are finished, your printed database table should look like that shown here.

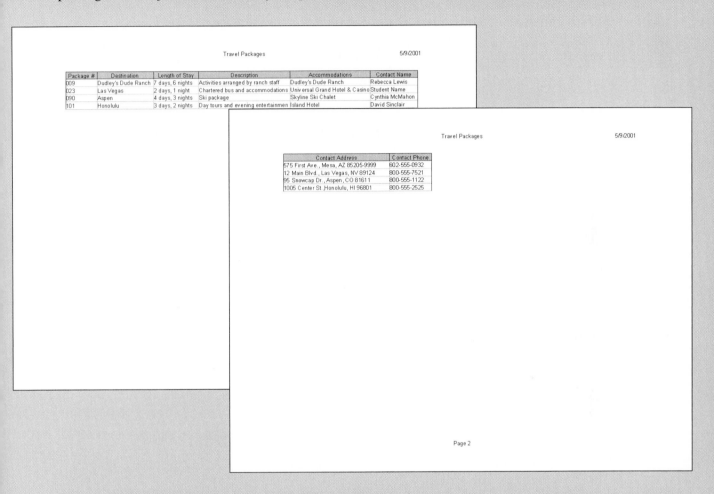

To create the database, follow these steps:

a. Create a database named Adventure Travel. Design a table using the following field information
    and copy repetitive text where possible:

Field Data	Type	Description	Field Size
Package #	Text	Unique 3-digit number	3
Destination	Text		20
Length of Stay	Text	Enter as # days, # nights	20
Description	Text	Package details (20 words or less)	20
Accommodations	Text	Name of hotel, motel, or other lodging	20
Contact Name	Text		20
Contact Address	Text	Street address, city, state, and zip code	20
Contact Phone	Text	Enter as ###-###-#### (e.g., 800-555-5555)	15

b. Make the Package # field the primary key field.

c. Change the Contact Name and Accomodations field sizes to **30** and the Contact Address field size to **50**.

d. Change the size of the Description field to **50** and its description to **10 words or less**.

e. Save the table as **Travel Packages**.

f. Enter the following records into the table in Table Datasheet view:

Record 1	Record 2	Record 3
101	009	212
Honolulu	Dudley's Dude Ranch	Washington, DC
3 days, 2 nights	7 days, 6 nights	7 days, 6 nights
Day tours and evening entertainment	Activities arranged by ranch staff	Tour of capital sites
Island Hotel	Dudley's Dude Ranch	Capitol Motel
David Sinclair	Rebecca Lewis	Lawrence Hallins
1005 Center St., Honolulu, HI 96801	575 First Ave., Mesa, AZ 85205	1000 Capitol Way, Washington, DC 20235
800-555-2525	602-555-0932	202-555-0048

g. Add the following records into the table in Data Entry:

Record 1	Record 2
023	090
Las Vegas	Aspen
2 days, 1 night	4 days, 3 nights
Chartered bus and accommodations	Ski package
Universal Grand Hotel & Casino	Skyline Ski Chalet
Barry Frazier	Cynthia McMahon
12 Main Blvd., Las Vegas, NV 89124	95 Snowcap Dr., Aspen, CO 81611
800-555-7521	800-555-1122

h. Return to Datasheet view and display the records in primary key order.

i. Adjust the column widths appropriately.

j. Edit the record for Package # 023 to replace Barry Frazier's name with your name.

k. Add a four-digit zip code extension of **9999** to the dude ranch address.

l. Delete record 212.

m. Change the orientation to landscape.

n. Preview and print the table, then save and close it.

Creating a Tracking Database

★★★ 5. As a volunteer at the Animal Rescue Foundation, you offer to create an Access database for them, to help them keep track of the animals that are picked up from local shelters. It needs to show when and which animals were boarded at the foundation, placed in foster homes, and placed in adoptive homes. When you are finished, your printed database table should look like that shown here. To create the database, follow these steps:

Tracking 5/9/2001

ID #	Type	Gender	Name	Boarded Date	Foster Date	Adoption Date	Photo
012	Dog	F	Erin	3/2/1998	4/1/1998		Bitmap Image
062	Cat	M	Max	12/9/1998			
123	Cat	M	Puddy	3/23/1998	4/15/1998		
199	Cat	F		1/15/1999		2/1/1999	
752	Horse	F	Student pet	2/7/1999			

Page 1

a. Create a database named Animal Rescue. Design a table using the following field information:

Field Data	Type	Description	Field Size/Format
ID #	Text	Unique 3-digit number given to animal when picked up from shelter	3
Type	Text	Type of animal (cat, dog, horse, etc.)	50
Gender	Text	Enter M (male) or F (female)	1
Name	Text	Name of animal, if any	50
Boarded Date	Date/Time	Date animal was boarded	Short Date
Foster Date	Date/Time	Date animal was placed in foster home	Short Date
Adoption Date	Date/Time	Date animal was adopted	Short Date
Photo	OLE object		

b. Change the field size of Type to 10 and Name to 30.

c. Make the ID # field the primary key field, and save the table as Tracking.

d. Enter six records: two for animals that are still being boarded (make one of these a dog), another two for animals in foster homes, and another two for animals that have been adopted. Enter **[your name]'s Pet** in the Name field of the last new record you add.

e. In Datasheet view, select the Photo field in a record you entered for a dog that is still being boarded. Insert the Whitedog.bmp picture file as an object in the selected field. View the inserted picture.

f. Display the records in primary key order. Adjust the column widths appropriately and change to landscape orientation.

g. Preview and print the table, then save and close the table.

on your own

Music Collection Database

★ **1.** You have just purchased a 200-disk CD carousel and now you would like to organize and catalogue your CDs. You realize that without an updateable list, it will be difficult to maintain an accurate list of what is in the changer. To get the most out of your new purchase you decide a database is in order. Create a new database called Music Collection, and a table called **CD Catalogue.** The table you create should include the Artist's Name, Album title, Genre, and Position Number. Make the Position field the primary key (because you may have multiple CDs by a given artist). Add an entry that includes your name as the artist. Enter at least 15 records. Preview and print the table when you are finished.

Employee Phone List

★★ **2.** When you first started working at Lewis & Lewis, Inc., as an administrative assistant, you knew everyone by name and had no problems taking and transferring calls. However, the company has grown quite a bit and you no longer have everyone's phone extension memorized. Since you are on the computer most of the day, you decide that having this information online would be quite helpful, not only when you receive calls, but also to print out and distribute phone lists within the office. Create a database called Lewis Personnel and a table named **Phone List** that contains the employees' last and first names, position, and extension number, with the extension field as the primary key (because each employee should have a unique phone extension). Enter at least ten records, including one with your name as the employee and a phone extension of **0.** Preview and print the table when you are finished.

Patient Database

★★ **3.** You have been hired to create a patient database by a dentist who just opened his own office. Create a database called Patient Information and a table named **Patient Data.** The database table you set up should contain patient identification numbers, last and first names, addresses, phone numbers, "referred by" information, "patient since" dates, and insurance company information. Use appropriate field sizes and make the ID number field the primary key. Enter at least ten records, using both Data Entry and Datasheet view, adjusting the column widths as necessary. Display the table in primary key order. To practice editing data, change two of the records. Add a record that contains your name as the patient. Preview and print the table.

Expenses Database

★★ **4.** You work in the accounting department at a start-up company called JK Enterprises. One of your
★ duties is to process expense reports, which up until now was a simple task of having the employees fill out a form and submit it to you for payment. You would then cut a check for them

and charge it to the general expense fund of the company. However, the company has grown tremendously in the last year, adding employees and departments at a rapid rate, and the executive team has decided that it is time to start managing the income and expenses on a much more detailed level. To this end, you need to create a database that includes the employee ID, submission date, expense type, and expense amount for each expense report that is turned in. Name the database JK Enterprises and the table **Expenses**. Use the Currency data type for the amount field, and appropriate data types for the remaining fields. Make the employee ID the primary key. Use both Data Entry and Datasheet views to enter at least 15 records, copying and pasting some of the data to minimize your data entry efforts. Adjust the column widths as necessary. Delete one of the records you just entered, and then edit one of the remaining records so it contains your name as the employee. Set the orientation to landscape, and then preview and print the table. You work for Golden Oldies, a small company that locates and sells record albums.

on the web

The current method used to keep track of on-hand inventory is a notebook taped to the storeroom wall with a typewritten list where employees check records in and out. The business and inventory has grown large enough now to warrant an online database. Create a database named Golden Oldies with a table named **Inventory** that contains stock identification numbers, record titles, artist, category (such as jazz, blues, classical, and rock) cost, and inventory on hand. Size the fields as appropriate and assign a primary key to one of them. To obtain title, category, and artist information for records you might sell in this type of company, search for "collectable record albums" on the Web and select an appropriate site. Use this information to enter records into your table, adjusting column widths as necessary. Display the table in primary key order, edit one of the records, delete one of the records, and change the artist's name in one of the records to your name. Set landscape orientation, and then preview and print the table.

Modifying a Table and Creating a Form

LAB 2

objectives

After completing this lab, you will know how to:

1.	Navigate a large table.
2.	Change field format properties.
3.	Set default field values.
4.	Insert a field.
5.	Add validity checks
6.	Hide and redisplay fields.
7.	Find and replace data.
8.	Use Undo.
9.	Sort records.
10.	Create and enter records into a form.
11.	Preview, print, close, and save a form.

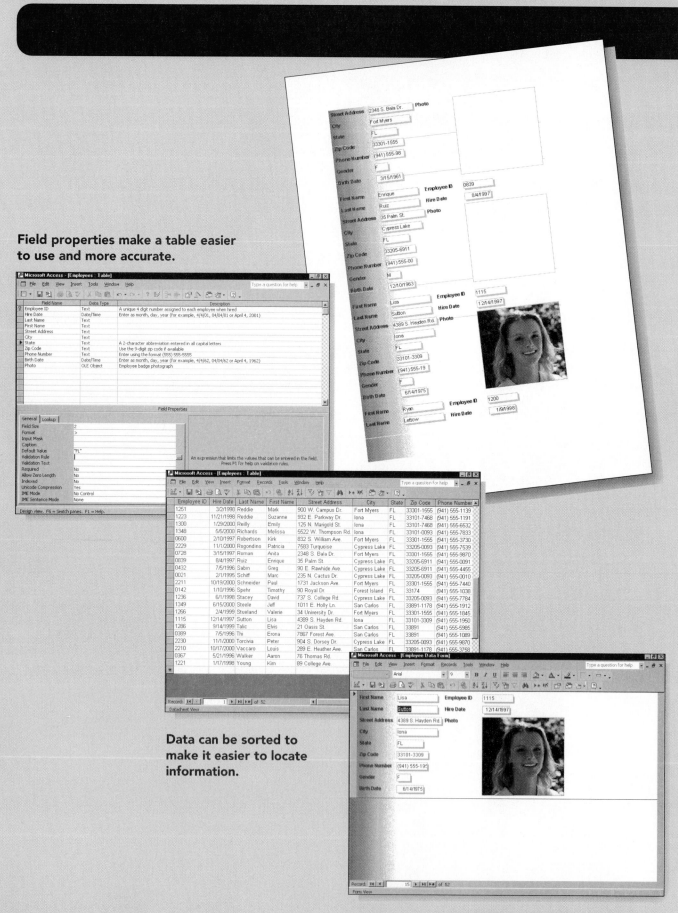

Field properties make a table easier to use and more accurate.

Data can be sorted to make it easier to locate information.

Forms display information in an easy-to-read manner and make data entry easier.

Lifestyle Fitness Club

The Lifestyle Fitness Club owners, Brian and Tami, are very pleased with your plans for the organization of the database and with your progress in creating the first table of basic employee data. As you have seen, creating a database takes planning and a lot of time to set up the structure and enter the data. As you have continued to add more employee records to the table, you have noticed several errors. You also realize that you forgot to include a field for the employee's sex. Even with the best of planning and care, errors occur and the information may change. You will see

how easy it is to modify the database structure and to customize field properties to provide more control over how and what data is entered in a field.

Even more impressive, as you will see in this lab, is the program's ability to locate information in the database. This is where all the hard work of entering data pays off. With a click of a button you can find data that might otherwise take hours to locate. The end result saves time and improves the accuracy of the output.

You will also see how you can make the data you are looking at onscreen more pleasing and easier to read by creating and using a form.

© Corbis

1	**Format Property** You can use the Format property to create custom formats that change the way numbers, dates, times, and text display and print.
2	**Default Value Property** The Default Value property is used to specify a value to be automatically entered in a field when a new record is created.
3	**Validity Check** Access automatically performs certain checks, called validity checks, on values entered in a field to make sure that the values are valid for the field type.
4	**Find and Replace** The Find and Replace feature helps you quickly find specific information and automatically replace it with new information.
5	**Sort** You can quickly rearrange a table's records by sorting the table data in a different order.
6	**Form** A form is a database object used primarily to display records onscreen to make it easier to enter new records and to make changes to existing records.

Navigating a Large Table

You have continued to add more records to the Lifestyle Fitness Employees database. As you entered the data, you know you made data entry errors that still need to be corrected. Additionally, you have found that with the addition of records, it is taking much longer to move around in the datasheet. Typical database tables are very large and consequently can be very inefficient to navigate. Learning how to move around in a large table will save time and help you get the job done faster. You want to open the expanded database which you saved using a new file name, and continue working on and refining the Employees table.

1 ● **Start Access.**

● **In the New File task pane, under Open a File, click**  More files... .

HAVING TROUBLE?
If your task pane is not displayed, choose View/Toolbars/Task Pane.

Another Method
You can also use the File/Open menu equivalent, or the Ctrl + O keyboard shortcut.

● **From the Look In drop-down list box, change the location to the drive containing your data files.**

● **Double-click** ac02_EmployeeRecords.

Your screen should be similar to Figure 2.1

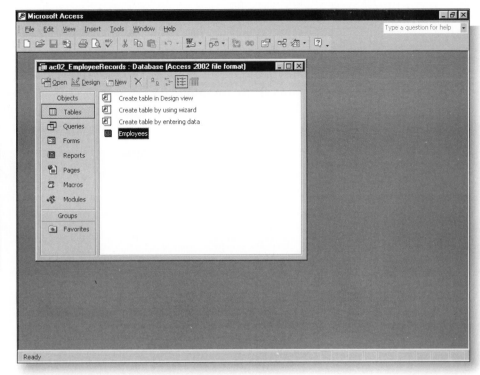

Figure 2.1

The Database window for the Employee Records file is displayed. You will open the "Employees" table containing the additional employee records.

2 ● **Double-click the "Employees" table.**

● **Maximize the Datasheet window.**

Your screen should be similar to Figure 2.2

HAVING TROUBLE?
Your screen may display a different number of records depending on your monitor settings.

Records 1-26 displayed

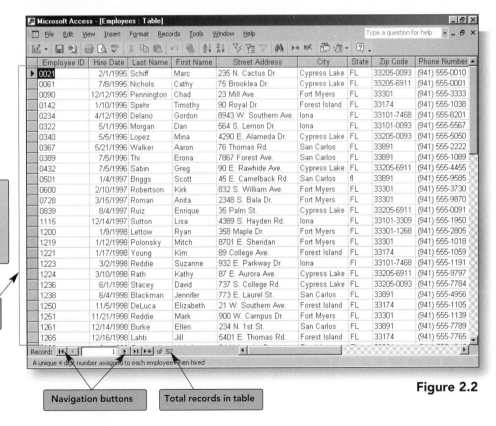

Navigation buttons   Total records in table

Figure 2.2

By default, the Datasheet view of the Table window is displayed. As you can see from the record number indicator, there are now 52 records in the table.

Navigating Using the Keyboard

In a large table, there are many methods you can use to quickly navigate through records in Datasheet view. You can always use the mouse to move from one field or record to another. However, if the information is not visible in the window, you must scroll the window first. The following table presents several keyboard methods that will help you move around in Navigation mode.

Keys	Effect
Page Down	Down one window
Page Up	Up one window
Ctrl + Page Up	Left one window
Ctrl + Page Down	Right one window
Ctrl + End	Last field of last record
Ctrl + Home	First field of first record
Ctrl + ↑	Current field of first record
Ctrl + ↓	Current field of last record

Another Method

You can also move to a specific record by typing its record number in the status bar's record indicator box.

Currently, records 1 through 26 are displayed in the window. You can easily move from one window of records to the next.

3 • Press Page Down.

HAVING TROUBLE?

If your screen displays a different number of records, this is because your monitor size and system setup may be different than those used to create the figures in the text.

Your screen should be similar to Figure 2.3

Records 27-52 displayed

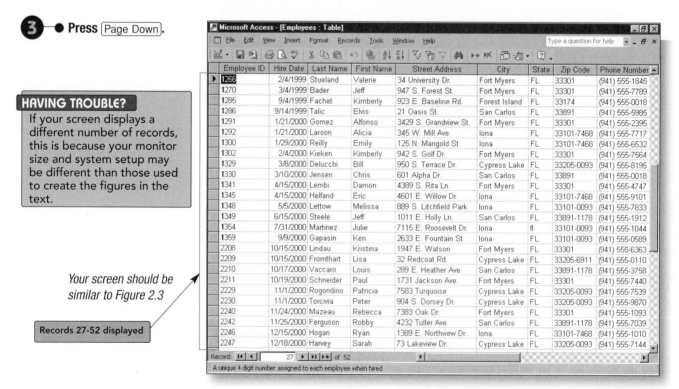

Figure 2.3

Now records 27 through 52 are displayed in the window. The first record in the window is now the current record.

Due to the number and width of the fields, not all fields can be displayed in the window at the same time. Rather than scrolling the window horizontally to see the additional fields, you can quickly move to the right a window at a time.

4 ● **Press** Ctrl + Page Down.

Your screen should be similar to Figure 2.4

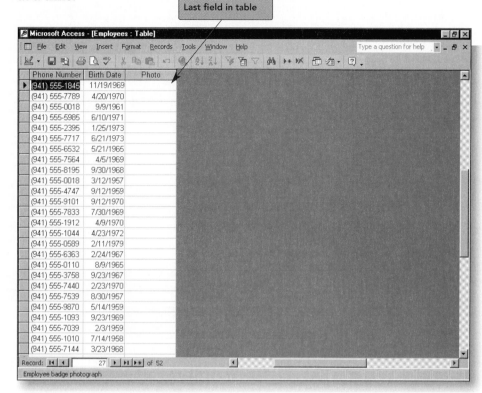

Figure 2.4

The last field in the table is now visible in the window.

Moving Using the Navigation Buttons

The navigation buttons in the status bar also provide navigation shortcuts. These buttons are described in the following table.

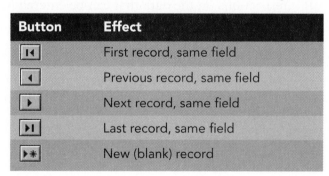

Button	Effect
⏮	First record, same field
◀	Previous record, same field
▶	Next record, same field
⏭	Last record, same field
▶*	New (blank) record

You will use the navigation buttons to move to the same field that is currently selected of the last record and then back to the same field of the first record then you will move to the first field of the first record.

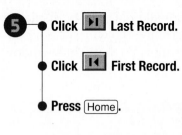

5 ● Click ▶❙ **Last Record.**

● Click ❙◀ **First Record.**

● Press [Home].

Your screen should be similar to Figure 2.5

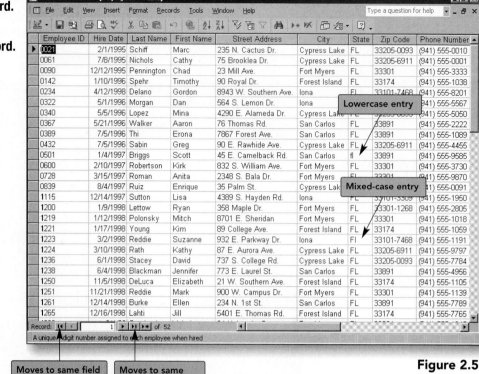

Moves to same field of first record

Moves to same field of last record

Figure 2.5

Customizing and Inserting Fields

As you looked through the records, you noticed that records 11 and 41 have lowercase entries in the State field, and record 19 has a mixed-case entry. You would like all the State field entries to be consistently entered in all uppercase letters. Additionally, you realize that you forgot to include a field for each employee's gender. While developing a table, you can modify and refine how the table operates. You can easily add and delete fields and add restrictions on the data that can be entered in a field as well as define how the data entered in a field will be displayed.

Setting Display Formats

You will begin by fixing the display of the entries in the State field. You do this by setting a display format for the field in Design view.

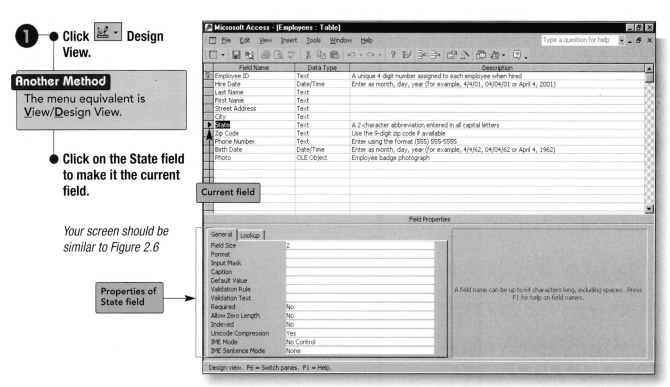

Figure 2.6

The properties associated with the State field are displayed in the General tab. The Format property is used to customize the way an entry is displayed.

concept 1

Format Property

1 You can change the way numbers, dates, times, and text display and print by defining the fields' **Format property**. Format properties do not change the way Access stores data, only how the data is displayed. To change the format of a field, you can select from predefined formats or create a custom format by entering different symbols in the Format text box. Text and Memo Data Types can use any of the four symbols shown in the following table.

Symbol	Meaning	Example
@	A required text character or space	@@@-@@-@@@@ would display 123456789 as 123–45–6789. Nine characters or spaces are required.
>	Forces all characters to uppercase	> would display SMITH whether you entered SMITH, smith, or Smith.
<	Forces all characters to lowercase	< would display smith whether you entered SMITH, smith, or Smith.
&	An optional text character	@@-@@& would display 12345 as 12–345 and 12.34 as 12–34. Four out of five characters are required, and a fifth is optional.

So, to change the State field's display format to all uppercase, you just have to enter the appropriate symbol.

2 ● **Move to the Format field property text box.**

● **Type >.**

Your screen should be similar to Figure 2.7

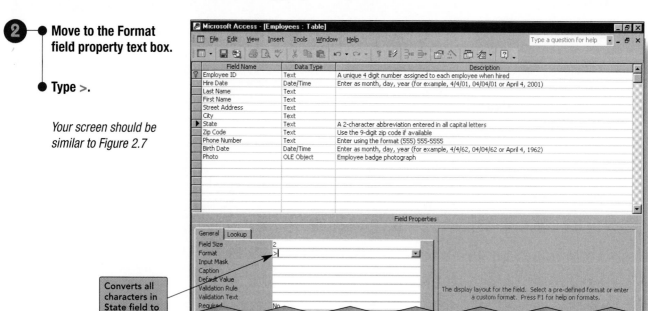

Converts all characters in State field to uppercase

Figure 2.7

Next, you'll see what effect your display format change has made on the existing records.

3 ● **Click 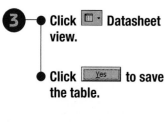 Datasheet view.**

● **Click Yes to save the table.**

Your screen should be similar to Figure 2.8

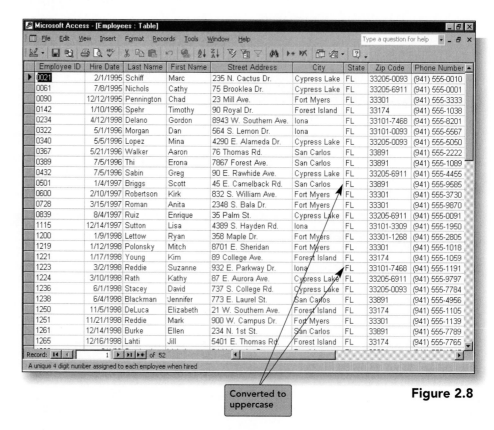

Converted to uppercase

Figure 2.8

In this window, you can see that records 11 (Scott Briggs) and 19 (Suzanne Reddie) now correctly display the state in capital letters.

Setting Default Values

Because all the club locations are in Florida, it is unlikely that any club employees will live in another state. So, rather than having to enter the same state for each record, you can have the State field automatically display FL. This is done by setting the field's Default Value property.

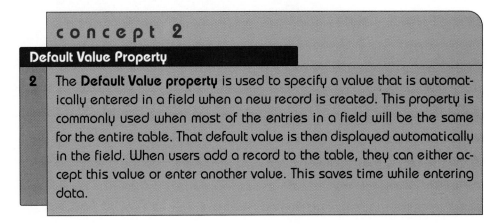

concept 2

Default Value Property

2   The **Default Value property** is used to specify a value that is automatically entered in a field when a new record is created. This property is commonly used when most of the entries in a field will be the same for the entire table. That default value is then displayed automatically in the field. When users add a record to the table, they can either accept this value or enter another value. This saves time while entering data.

You will set the State field's default value to display FL.

● Click ⬚ ▾ Design View.

● Make the State field the current field.

● Click in the Default Value property text box.

● Type **FL**.

● Press (←Enter).

Your screen should be similar to Figure 2.9

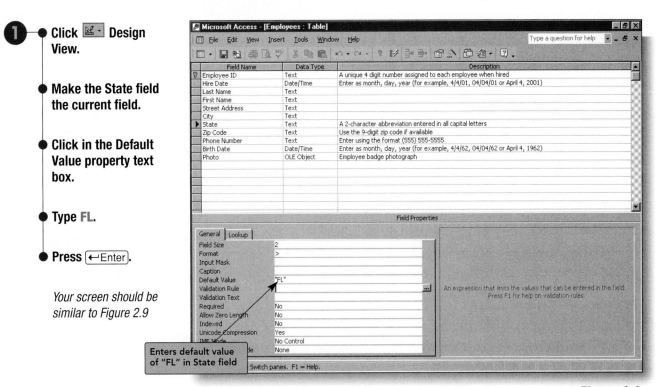

Enters default value of "FL" in State field

Figure 2.9

The default value is automatically enclosed in quotes to identify the entry as a group of characters called a **character string**. To see how setting a default value affects your table, you will return to Datasheet view and look at a new blank record.

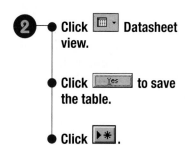

② ● Click ▦▾ **Datasheet view.**

● Click ⬛ Yes ⬛ **to save the table.**

● Click ▸✱.

Your screen should be similar to Figure 2.10

Employee ID	Hire Date	Last Name	First Name	Street Address	City	State	Zip Code	Phone Number
1270	3/4/1999	Bader	Jeff	947 S. Forest St.	Fort Myers	FL	33301	(941) 555-7789
1285	9/4/1999	Fachet	Kimberly	923 E. Baseline Rd.	Forest Island	FL	33174	(941) 555-0018
1286	9/14/1999	Talic	Elvis	21 Oasis St.	San Carlos	FL	33891	(941) 555-5985
1291	1/21/2000	Gomez	Alfonso	3429 S. Grandview St.	Fort Myers	FL	33301	(941) 555-2395
1292	1/21/2000	Larson	Alicia	345 W. Mill Ave.	Iona	FL	33101-7468	(941) 555-7717
1300	1/29/2000	Reilly	Emily	125 N. Marigold St.	Iona	FL	33101-7468	(941) 555-6532
1302	2/4/2000	Kieken	Kimberly	942 S. Golf Dr.	Fort Myers	FL	33301	(941) 555-7564
1329	3/8/2000	Delucchi	Bill	950 S. Terrace Dr.	Cypress Lake	FL	33205-0093	(941) 555-8195
1330	3/10/2000	Jensen	Chris	601 Alpha Dr.	San Carlos	FL	33891	(941) 555-0018
1341	4/15/2000	Lembi	Damon	4389 S. Rita Ln.	Fort Myers	FL	33301	(941) 555-4747
1345	4/15/2000	Helfand	Eric	4601 E. Willow Dr.	Iona	FL	33101-7468	(941) 555-9101
1348	5/5/2000	Lettow	Melissa	889 S. Litchfield Park	Iona	FL	33101-0093	(941) 555-7833
1349	6/15/2000	Steele	Jeff	1011 E. Holly Ln.	San Carlos	FL	33891-1178	(941) 555-1912
1354	7/31/2000	Martinez	Julie	7115 E. Roosevelt Dr.	Iona	FL	33101-0093	(941) 555-1044
1359	9/9/2000	Gapasin	Ken	2633 E. Fountain St.	Iona	FL	33101-0093	(941) 555-0589
2208	10/15/2000	Lindau	Kristina	1947 E. Watson	Fort Myers	FL	33301	(941) 555-6363
2209	10/15/2000	Fromthart	Lisa	32 Redcoat Rd.	Cypress Lake	FL	33205-6911	(941) 555-0110
2210	10/17/2000	Vaccaro	Louis	289 E. Heather Ave.	San Carlos	FL	33891-1178	(941) 555-3758
2211	10/19/2000	Schneider	Paul	1731 Jackson Ave.	Fort Myers	FL	33301	(941) 555-7440
2229	11/1/2000	Rogondino	Patricia	7583 Turquoise	Cypress Lake	FL	33205-0093	(941) 555-7539
2230	11/1/2000	Torcivia	Peter	904 S. Dorsey Dr.	Cypress Lake	FL	33205-0093	(941) 555-9870
2240	11/24/2000	Mazeau	Rebecca	7383 Oak Dr.	Fort Myers	FL	33301	(941) 555-1093
2242	11/25/2000	Ferguson	Robby	4232 Tuller Ave.	San Carlos	FL	33891-1178	(941) 555-7039
2246	12/15/2000	Hogan	Ryan	1389 E. Northview Dr.	Iona	FL	33101-7468	(941) 555-1010
2247	12/18/2000	Harvey	Sarah	73 Lakeview Dr.	Cypress Lake	FL	33205-0093	(941) 555-7144
						FL		

Record: ⏮ ◀ 53 ▶ ⏭ ▶✱ of 53

A unique 4 digit number assigned to each employee whe...

Default value displayed in State field of new record

Figure 2.10

The new blank record at the end of the table displays FL as the default value for the State field.

Inserting a Field

Now you want to add the new field to hold each employee's gender. Although it is better to include all the necessary fields when creating the table structure, it is possible to add or remove fields from a table at a later time. After looking at the order of the fields, you decide to add the Gender field between the Phone Number and Birth Date fields. To do so, you will switch to Design view to insert the new field in the table.

Another Method

You can also add a field in Datasheet view by using Insert/**C**olumn to insert a column where you want the new field to be located, and giving the new column the desired field name. However, you still need to switch to Design view to set the new field's properties.

① ● Click ▨▾ **Design view.**

● **Make the Birth Date field current.**

● Click ▤ᶜ **Insert Rows.**

Another Method

The menu equivalent is Insert/**R**ows. You can also use the Insert Row command on the shortcut menu.

Your screen should be similar to Figure 2.11

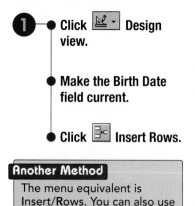
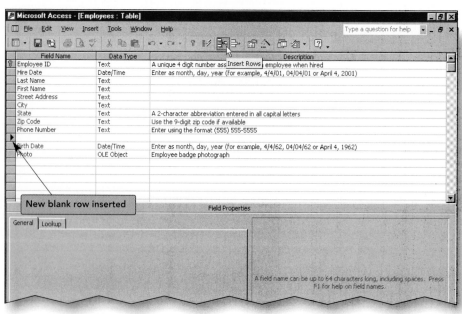

Field Name	Data Type	Description
Employee ID	Text	A unique 4 digit number ass Insert Rows employee when hired
Hire Date	Date/Time	Enter as month, day, year (for example, 4/4/01, 04/04/01 or April 4, 2001)
Last Name	Text	
First Name	Text	
Street Address	Text	
City	Text	
State	Text	A 2-character abbreviation entered in all capital letters
Zip Code	Text	Use the 9-digit zip code if available
Phone Number	Text	Enter using the format (555) 555-5555
Birth Date	Date/Time	Enter as month, day, year (for example, 4/4/62, 04/04/62 or April 4, 1962)
Photo	OLE Object	Employee badge photograph

New blank row inserted

Field Properties

General | Lookup

A field name can be up to 64 characters long, including spaces. Press F1 for help on field names.

Figure 2.11

A new blank row is inserted into the table. Next, you'll name the field and set its properties.

2 Enter the new field definitions from the table on the right.

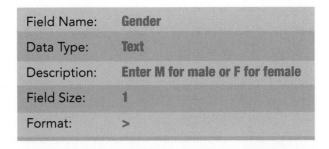

Field Name:	Gender
Data Type:	Text
Description:	Enter M for male or F for female
Field Size:	1
Format:	>

Your screen should be similar to Figure 2.12

New field inserted and defined

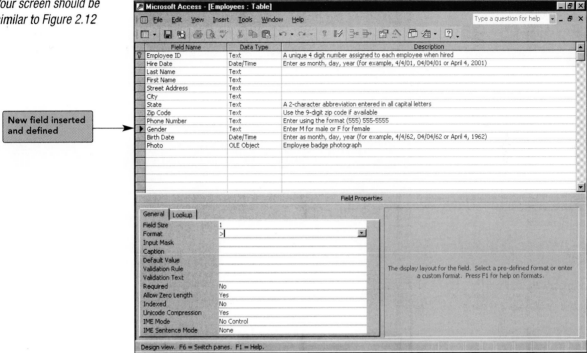

Figure 2.12

Adding Validity Checks

The only two characters you want the Gender field to accept are M for male and F for female. To specify that these two characters are the only entries acceptable in the Gender field, you will add a validity check to it.

Validity Check

3 Access automatically performs certain checks, called **validity checks**, on values entered in a field to make sure that the values are valid for the field type. A Text field type has few restrictions, whereas a Number field type accepts only numeric entries. You can also create your own validity checks for a field, which Access will apply during data entry. A validity check is defined by entering a validation rule for the field's property. A **validation rule** consists of an expression that defines the acceptable values. An **ex-**

pression is a formula consisting of a combination of symbols that evaluates to a single value. Expressions are used throughout Access to create validity checks, queries, forms, and reports.

You can also include a validation text message. **Validation text** is an explanatory message that appears if a user attempts to enter invalid information in a text field for which there is a validity check. If you do not specify a message, Access will display a default error message, which will not clearly describe the reason for the error.

For some examples of possible expressions, see the table below.

Expression	Result
=[Sales Amount] + [Sales Tax]	Sums values in two fields.
="M" OR "F"	Includes M or F entries only.
>=#1/1/95# AND <=#12/31/95#	Includes entries greater than or equal to 1/1/95, and less than or equal to 12/31/95.
="Tennis Rackets"	Includes the entry Tennis Rackets only.

You create an expression by combining identifiers, operators, and values to produce the desired result. An **identifier** is an element that refers to the value of a field, a graphical object, or property. In the expression =[Sales Amount] + [Sales Tax], [Sales Amount] and [Sales Tax] are identifiers that refer to the values in the Sales Amount and Sales Tax fields.

An **operator** is a symbol or word that indicates that an operation is to be performed. A **comparison operator** is a symbol that allows you to make comparisons between two items. The table below describes the comparison operators.

Operator	Meaning
=	Equal to
<>	Not equal to
<	Less than
>	Greater than
<=	Less than or equal to
>=	Greater than or equal to

In addition, the OR and AND operators allow you to enter additional criteria in the same field or different fields.

Values are numbers, dates, or character strings. Character strings such as "M", "F", or "Tennis Rackets" are enclosed in quotation marks. Dates are enclosed in pound signs (#), as in #1/1/95#.

You want to enter a validation check for the Gender field that will only accept M for male and F for female.

The expression is entered in the Validation Rule field of the field's property.

1 ● Move to the Validation Rule field property text box.

● Type **M or F**.

● Press ⏎Enter.

● For the validation text, type **The only valid entry is M or F.**

Your screen should be similar to Figure 2.13

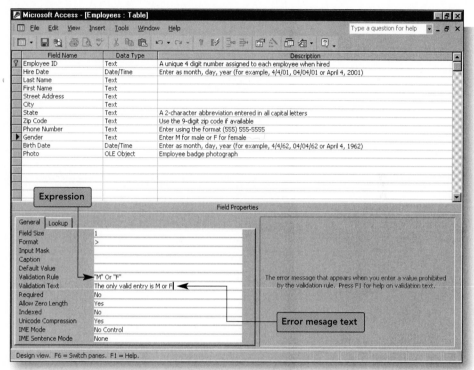

Figure 2.13

The expression states that the acceptable values can only be equal to an M or an F. Notice that Access automatically added quotation marks around the two character strings and changed the "o" in "or" to uppercase. Because the Format property has been set to convert all entries to uppercase, this means that an entry of m or f is as acceptable as M or F.

Next you want to add the data for the Gender field to the table, so you will switch back to Datasheet view.

2 ● Click **Datasheet view.**

● Click **Yes** to save the table.

Your screen should be similar to Figure 2.14

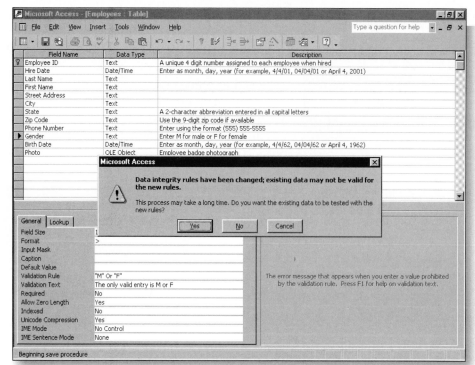

Figure 2.14

A message box advises you that data integrity rules have been changed. When you restructure a table, you often make changes that could result in a loss of data. Changes such as shortening field sizes, creating validity checks, or changing field types can cause existing data to become invalid. Because the field is new, there are no data values to verify, and a validation check is unnecessary at this time.

3 ● Click **No** .

● **Move to the Gender field for record 1.**

Your screen should be similar to Figure 2.15

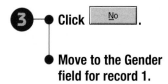

New field inserted

Last Name	First Name	Street Address	City	State	Zip Code	Phone Number	Gender	Birth Dat ▲
Schiff	Marc	235 N. Cactus Dr.	Cypress Lake	FL	33205-0093	(941) 555-0010		3/9/197
Nichols	Cathy	75 Brooklea Dr.	Cypress Lake	FL	33205-6911	(941) 555-0001		5/19/197
Pennington	Chad	23 Mill Ave.	Fort Myers	FL	33301	(941) 555-3333		7/7/196
Spehr	Timothy	90 Royal Dr.	Forest Island	FL	33174	(941) 555-1038		9/9/196
Delano	Gordon	8943 W. Southern Ave.	Iona	FL	33101-7468	(941) 555-8201		8/7/196
Morgan	Dan	564 S. Lemon Dr.	Iona	FL	33101-0093	(941) 555-5567		3/5/196
Lopez	Mina	4290 E. Alameda Dr.	Cypress Lake	FL	33205-0093	(941) 555-5050		2/25/196
Walker	Aaron	76 Thomas Rd.	San Carlos	FL	33891	(941) 555-2222		8/1/196
Thi	Erona	7867 Forest Ave.	San Carlos	FL	33891	(941) 555-1089		5/10/197
Sabin	Greg	90 E. Rawhide Ave.	Cypress Lake	FL	33205-6911	(941) 555-4455		9/30/197
Briggs	Scott	45 E. Camelback Rd.	San Carlos	FL	33891	(941) 555-9585		9/15/197
Robertson	Kirk	832 S. William Ave.	Fort Myers	FL	33301	(941) 555-3730		4/5/196
Roman	Anita	2348 S. Bala Dr.	Fort Myers	FL	33301	(941) 555-9870		3/15/196
Ruiz	Enrique	35 Palm St.	Cypress Lake	FL	33205-6911	(941) 555-0091		12/10/196
Sutton	Lisa	4389 S. Hayden Rd.	Iona	FL	33101-3309	(941) 555-1950		6/14/197
Lettow	Ryan	358 Maple Dr.	Fort Myers	FL	33301-1268	(941) 555-2805		11/15/197
Polonsky	Mitch	8701 E. Sheridan	Fort Myers	FL	33301	(941) 555-1018		3/13/197
Young	Kim	89 College Ave.	Forest Island	FL	33174	(941) 555-1059		4/12/197
Reddie	Suzanne	932 E. Parkway Dr.	Iona	FL	33101-7468	(941) 555-1191		7/14/195
Rath	Kathy	87 E. Aurora Ave.	Cypress Lake	FL	33205-6911	(941) 555-9797		5/30/196
Stacey	David	737 S. College Rd.	Cypress Lake	FL	33205-0093	(941) 555-7784		9/30/195
Blackman	Jennifer	773 E. Laurel St.	San Carlos	FL	33891	(941) 555-4956		1/22/197
DeLuca	Elizabeth	21 W. Southern Ave.	Forest Island	FL	33174	(941) 555-1105		8/21/196
Reddie	Mark	900 W. Campus Dr.	Fort Myers	FL	33301	(941) 555-1139		11/5/197
Burke	Ellen	234 N. 1st St.	San Carlos	FL	33891	(941) 555-7789		9/30/196
Lahti	Jill	5401 E. Thomas Rd.	Forest Island	FL	33174	(941) 555-7765		6/14/196

Record: 14 ◀ [1] ▶ ▶I ▶* of 52

Enter M for male or F for female

Figure 2.15

The new field was added to the table between the Phone Number and Birth Date fields. To verify that the validity check works, you will enter an invalid field value in the Gender field for the first record.

● Type **g**.

● Press ⏎Enter.

Your screen should be similar to Figure 2.16

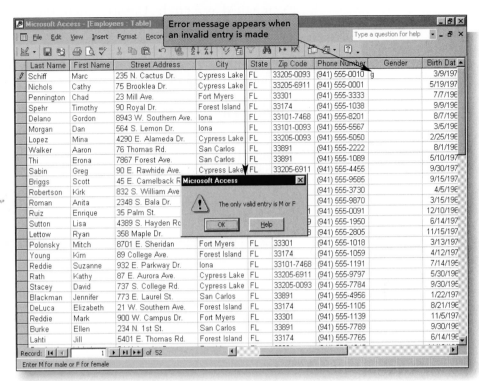

Figure 2.16

Access displays the error message you entered in the Validation Text box of Design view. To clear the error message and correct the entry,

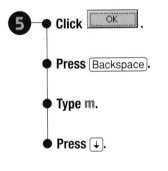

● Click ▭ OK ▭.

● Press Backspace.

● Type **m**.

● Press ↓.

Your screen should be similar to Figure 2.17

Figure 2.17

The entry for the first record is accepted and displayed as an uppercase M.

Hiding and Redisplaying Fields

To enter the gender data for the rest of the fields, you want to use the First Name field as a guide. Unfortunately, the First Name and Gender fields are currently on opposite sides of the screen and will require you to scan your eyes back and forth across each record. You can avoid this by hiding the fields you do not need to see, and then redisplaying them when you are through entering the gender data.

Hiding Fields

A quick way to view two fields side by side (in this case, the First Name and Gender fields) is to hide the fields that are in between (the Street Address through Phone Number fields).

1 ● **Select the Street Address field through the Phone Number field.**

> **Additional Information**
> Drag along the column heads when the mouse pointer is ↓ to select the fields.

● **Choose Format/Hide Columns.**

Your screen should be similar to Figure 2.18

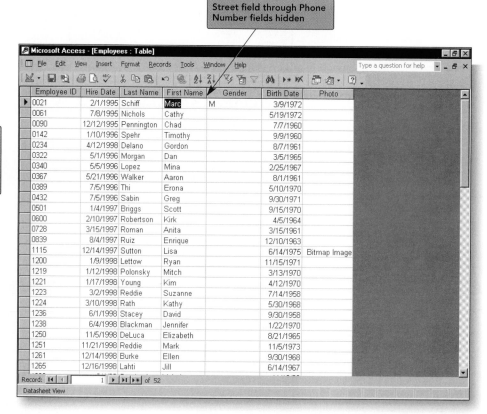

Street field through Phone Number fields hidden

Figure 2.18

Now the First Name and Gender columns are next to each other. You can now refer to the first name in each record to enter the correct gender data.

2 ● Enter the Gender field values for the remaining records by looking at the First Name field to determine whether the employee is male or female.

● Reduce the size of the Gender column using the Best Fit command.

HAVING TROUBLE?
Remember, to best fit data in a column, you double-click on its right border.

Your screen should be similar to Figure 2.19

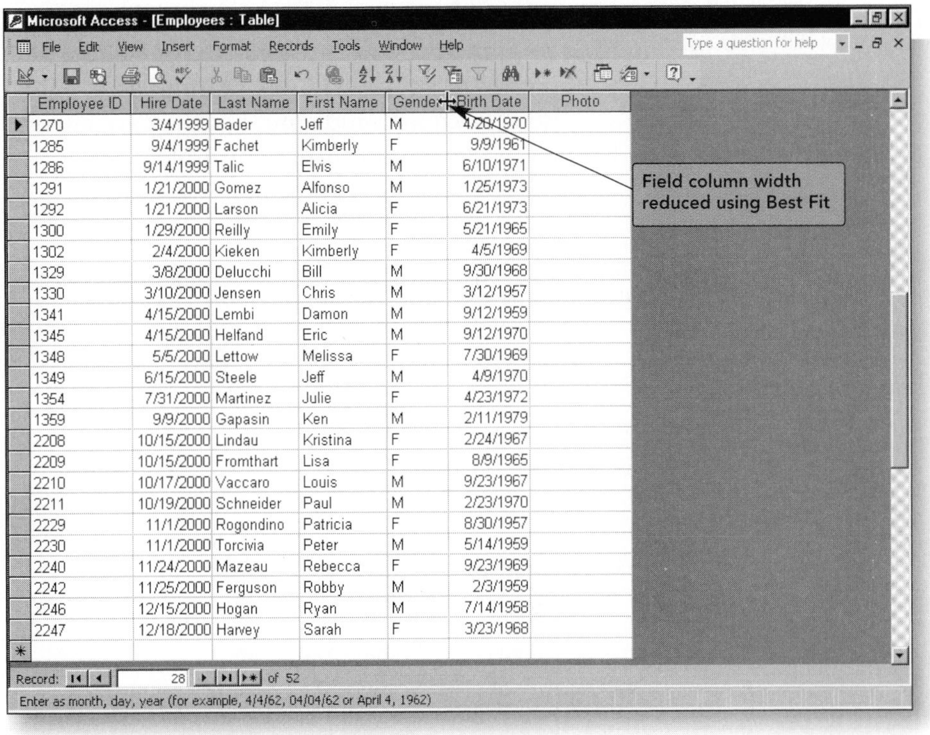

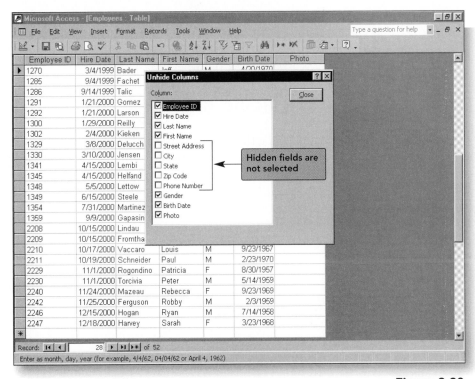

Figure 2.19

Redisplaying Hidden Fields

After you have entered the gender data for all of the records, you can redisplay the hidden fields.

1 ● Choose Format/Unhide Columns.

Your screen should be similar to Figure 2.20

Figure 2.20

You use the Unhide Columns dialog box to select which currently hidden columns you want to redisplay. A checkmark in the box next to a column name indicates that the column is currently displayed; column names with no checkmarks indicate that they are currently hidden. You want to unhide all hidden columns in your table.

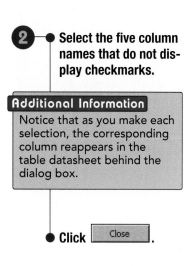

2 ● **Select the five column names that do not display checkmarks.**

Additional Information

Notice that as you make each selection, the corresponding column reappears in the table datasheet behind the dialog box.

● **Click** [Close].

Your screen should be similar to Figure 2.21

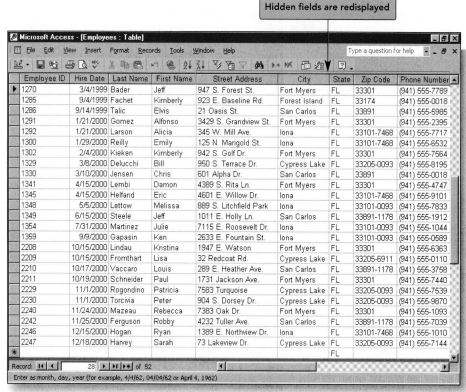

Hidden fields are redisplayed

Figure 2.21

All of the fields are now displayed again, and you can continue to refine your table data.

Finding and Replacing Data

Over the past few days you have received several change request forms to update the employee records. Rather than have to scroll through all the records to locate the ones that need to be modified, you can use the Find and Replace feature.

Find and Replace

4 The **Find and Replace** feature helps you quickly find specific information and automatically replace it with new information. The Find command will locate all specified values in a field, and the Replace command will both find a value and automatically replace it with another. For example, in a table containing supplier and item prices, you may need to increase the price of all items supplied by one manufacturer. To quickly locate these items, you would use the Find command to locate all records with the name of the manufacturer and then update the price appropriately. Alternatively, you could use the Replace command if you knew that all items priced at $9.95 were increasing to $11.89. This command would locate all values matching the original price and replace them with the new price. Finding and replacing data is fast and accurate, but you need to be careful when replacing not to replace unintended matches.

Finding Data

The first change request is for Melissa Lettow, who recently married and has both a name and address change. To quickly locate this record, you will use the Find command.

Move to the Last Name field of record 1.

Click  **Find.**

Another Method

The menu equivalent is **Edit/Find**.

Your screen should be similar to Figure 2.22

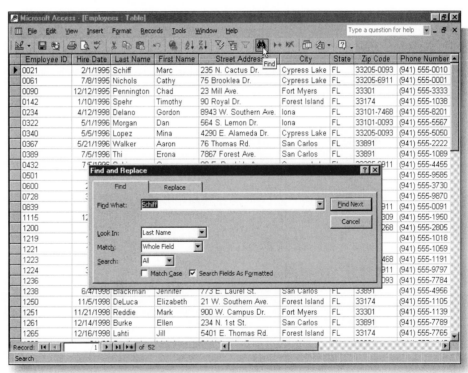

Figure 2.22

You use the Find and Replace dialog box to specify what you are looking for and how you want Access to search the table for it. In the Find What text box, you enter the text you want to locate. You can further refine your search by using the options described in the table on the next page.

Option	Effect
Look In	Searches the current field or the entire table for the specified text.
Match	Locates matches to the whole field, any part of the field, or the start of the field.
Search	Specifies the direction in which the table will be searched: All (search all records), Down (search down or up from the current insertion point location in the field), or Up (search up from the current insertion point location in the field).
Match Case	Finds words that have the same pattern of uppercase letters as entered in the Find What text box. Using this option makes the search case sensitive.
Search Fields as Formatted	Finds data based on its display format.

You are already in the field you want to search, and you want to find a specific last name, so you just need to enter the name in the Find What text box.

2 ● Type **lettow** in the Find What text box.

Additional Information

Because the Match Case option is not selected in the Find and Replace dialog box, it doesn't matter whether you enter the text to be located in uppercase, lowercase, or mixed case letters — Access will ignore the case and look for the specified text.

● Click  .

Your screen should be similar to Figure 2.23

HAVING TROUBLE?

If the Find command did not locate this record, try it again. Make sure that you enter the name "lettow" (upper- or lowercase) correctly and that Last Name is the selected field in the Look In box.

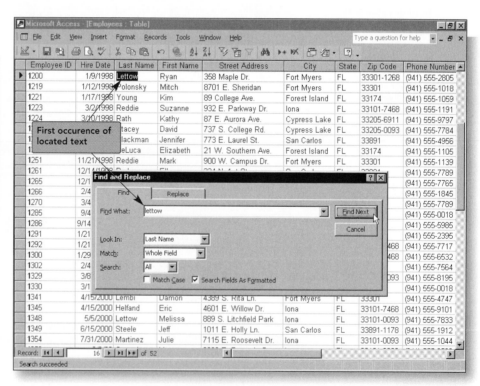

Figure 2.23

Access searches the table and moves to the first located occurrence of the entry you specified. The Last Name field is highlighted in record 16. You need to change the last name from Lettow to Richards.

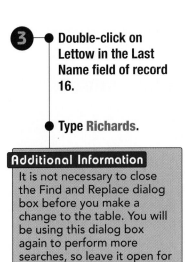

3 ● **Double-click on Lettow in the Last Name field of record 16.**

● **Type Richards.**

Additional Information

It is not necessary to close the Find and Replace dialog box before you make a change to the table. You will be using this dialog box again to perform more searches, so leave it open for now.

● **Press ←Enter.**

Your screen should be similar to Figure 2.24

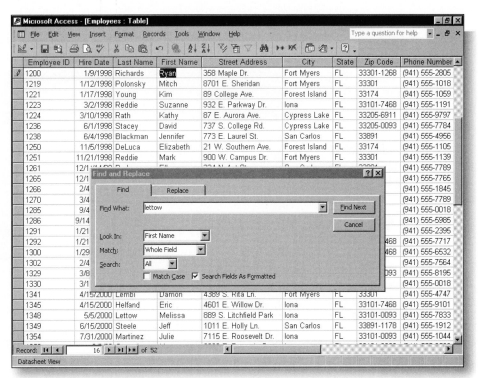

Figure 2.24

Now that the highlight is on the First Name field, you notice this is the record for Ryan Lettow, not Melissa. You changed the wrong record. You will use the Undo command next to quickly fix this error.

Using Undo

Undo will cancel your last action as long as you have not made any further changes to the table. Even if you save the record or the table, you can undo changes to the last edited record by using the Undo Saved Record command on the Edit menu or by clicking  Undo. Once you have changed another record or moved to another window, however, the earlier change cannot be undone. You will use Undo to revert Ryan's record to how it was before you made the change.

1 ● **Click**  **Undo.**

Another Method

The menu equivalent is Edit/Undo Current Field/Record and the keyboard shortcut is Ctrl + Z.

Your screen should be similar to Figure 2.25

Figure 2.25

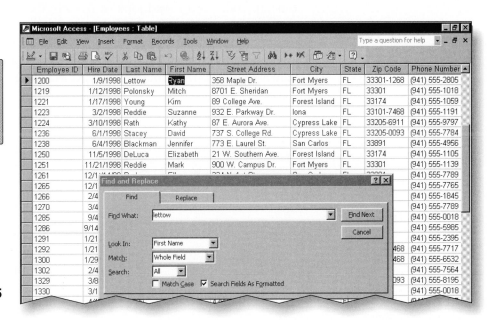

The original field value of Lettow is restored. Now you want to continue the search to locate the next record with the last name of Lettow.

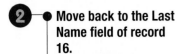

2 ● **Move back to the Last Name field of record 16.**

● **Click** Find Next **in the Find and Replace dialog box.**

● **When Access locates the record for Melissa Lettow (record 39), change her last name to Richards and the street to 5522 W. Thompson Rd.**

Your screen should be similar to Figure 2.26

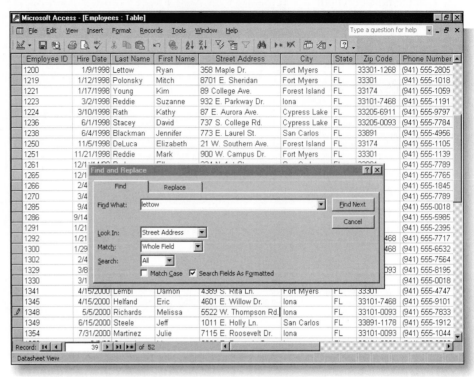

Figure 2.26

The Find method works well when you need to locate an individual field in order to view the data and/or modify it. However, when you need to make the same change to more than one record, the Replace command is the quicker method because it both finds and replaces the data.

Replacing Data

You have checked with the U.S. Postal Service and learned that all zip codes of 33301 have a four-digit extension of 1555. To locate all the records with this zip code, you could look at the Zip Code field for each record to find the match and then edit the field to add the extension. If the table is small, this method would be acceptable. For large tables, however, this method could be quite time consuming and more prone to errors. A more efficient way is to search the table to find specific values in records and then replace the entry with another.

1 Move to the Zip Code field of record 1.

Open the Replace tab.

Another Method

The keyboard shortcut for the Replace command is Ctrl + H.

Your screen should be similar to Figure 2.27

Enter replacement text

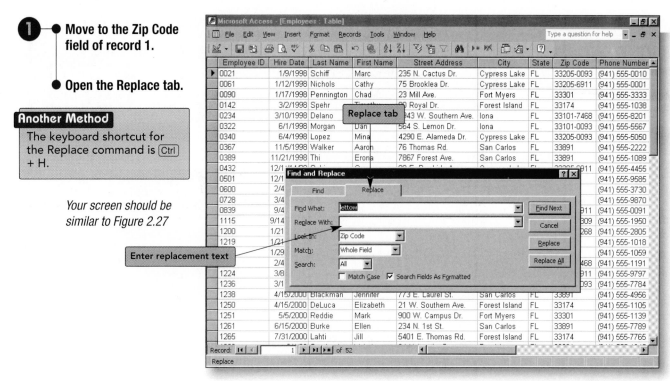

Figure 2.27

The options in the Replace tab are the same, with the addition of a Replace With text box, where you enter the replacement text exactly as you want it to appear in your table.

2 In the Find What text box, type **33301**.

Press Tab⇆ to move to the Replace With text box.

Type **33301-1555**.

Click Find Next.

Your screen should be similar to Figure 2.28

Located entry

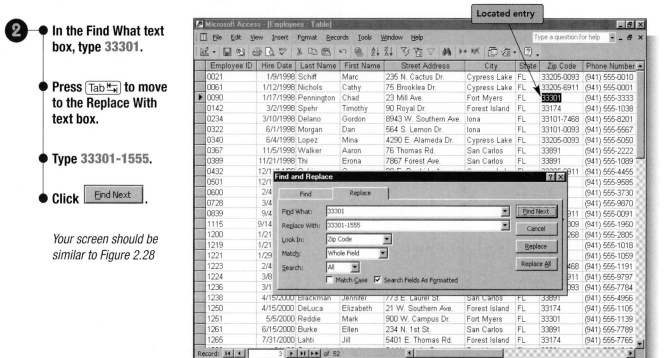

Figure 2.28

HAVING TROUBLE?

If necessary, move the dialog box so you can see the highlighted entry.

Immediately the highlight moves to the first occurrence of text in the document that matches the Find What text and highlights it. You can now replace this text with the click of a button.

3 ● Click [Replace].

Your screen should be similar to Figure 2.29

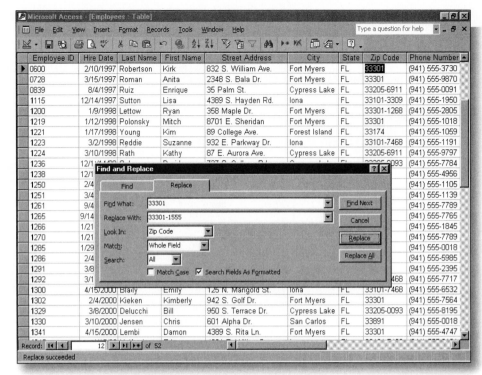

Figure 2.29

The original zip code entry is replaced with the new zip code. The program immediately continues searching and locates a second occurrence of the entry. You decide the program is locating the values accurately, and it will be safe to replace all finds with the replacement value.

Original zip code
replaced with correction

4 ● Click [Replace All].

● Click [Yes] in response to the advisory message.

● Close the Find and Replace dialog box.

Your screen should be similar to Figure 2.30

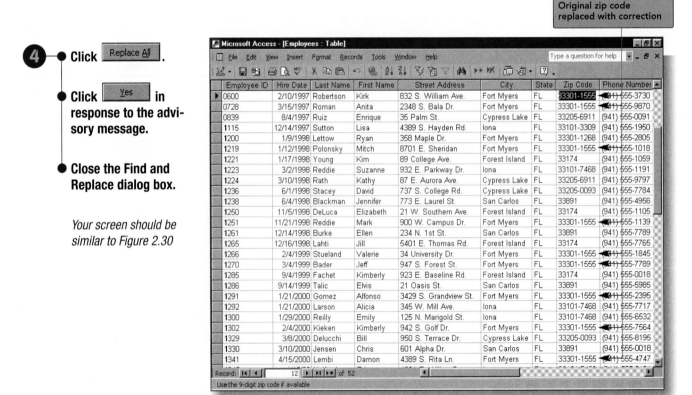

Figure 2.30

All matches are replaced with the replacement text. It is much faster to use Replace All than to confirm each match separately. However, exercise care when using Replace All, because the search text you specify might be part of another field and you may accidentally replace text you want to keep.

Sorting Records

As you may recall from Lab 1, the records are ordered by the primary key field, Employee ID. The Accounting department manager, however, has asked you for an alphabetical list of all employees. To do this, you can sort the records in the table.

concept 5

Sort

5 You can quickly rearrange a table's records by **sorting** the table data in a different order. Sorting data often helps you find specific information quickly. In Access you can sort data in ascending order (A to Z or 0 to 9) or descending order (Z to A or 9 to 0). You can sort all records in a table by a single field, such as State, or you can select adjacent columns and sort by more than one field, such as State and then City. When you select multiple columns to sort, Access sorts records starting with the column farthest left, then moves to the right across the columns. For example, if you want to quickly sort by State, then by City, the State field must be to the left of the City field. Access saves the new sort order with your table data and reapplies it automatically each time you open the table. To return to the primary key sort order, you must remove the temporary sort.

Sorting on a Single Field

You will sort the records on a single field, Last Name. To perform a sort on a single field, you move to the field you want to base the sort on and click the button that corresponds to the type of sort you want to do. In this case, you will sort the Last Name field in ascending alphabetical order.

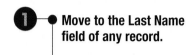

1 • Move to the Last Name field of any record.

• Click ▲↓ Sort Ascending.

Another Method

The menu equivalent is Records/Sort/Sort Ascending.

Your screen should be similar to Figure 2.31

Records are in ascending alphabetical order | Ascending sort | Descending sort

Employee ID	Hire Date	Last Name	First Name	Street Address	City	State	Zip Code	Phone Number
1270	3/4/1999	Bader	Jeff	947 S. Forest St.	Fort Myers	FL	33301	(941) 555-7789
1238	6/4/1998	Blackman	Jennifer	773 E. Laurel St.	San Carlos	FL	33891	(941) 555-4956
0501	1/4/1997	Briggs	Scott	45 E. Camelback Rd.	San Carlos	fl	33891	(941) 555-9585
1261	12/14/1998	Burke	Ellen	234 N. 1st St.	San Carlos	FL	33891	(941) 555-7789
0234	4/12/1998	Delano	Gordon	8943 W. Southern Ave.	Iona	FL	33101-7468	(941) 555-8201
1250	11/5/1998	DeLuca	Elizabeth	21 W. Southern Ave.	Forest Island	FL	33174	(941) 555-1105
1329	3/8/2000	Delucchi	Bill	950 S. Terrace Dr.	Cypress Lake	FL	33205-0093	(941) 555-8195
1285	9/4/1999	Fachet	Kimberly	923 E. Baseline Rd.	Forest Island	FL	33174	(941) 555-0018
2242	11/25/2000	Ferguson	Robby	4232 Tuller Ave.	San Carlos	FL	33891-1178	(941) 555-7039
2209	10/15/2000	Fromthart	Lisa	32 Redcoat Rd.	Cypress Lake	FL	33205-6911	(941) 555-0110
1359	9/9/2000	Gapasin	Ken	2633 E. Fountain St.	Iona	FL	33101-0093	(941) 555-0589
1291	1/21/2000	Gomez	Alfonso	3429 S. Grandview St.	Fort Myers	FL	33301	(941) 555-2395
2247	12/18/2000	Harvey	Sarah	73 Lakeview Dr.	Cypress Lake	FL	33205-0093	(941) 555-7144
1345	4/15/2000	Helfand	Eric	4601 E. Willow Dr.	Iona	FL	33101-7468	(941) 555-9101
2246	12/15/2000	Hogan	Ryan	1389 E. Northview Dr.	Iona	FL	33101-7468	(941) 555-1010
1330	3/10/2000	Jensen	Chris	601 Alpha Dr.	San Carlos	FL	33891	(941) 555-0018
1302	2/4/2000	Kieken	Kimberly	942 S. Golf Dr.	Fort Myers	FL	33301	(941) 555-7564
1265	12/16/1998	Lahti	Jill	5401 E. Thomas Rd.	Forest Island	FL	33174	(941) 555-7765
1292	1/21/2000	Larson	Alicia	345 W. Mill Ave.	Iona	FL	33101-7468	(941) 555-7717
▶ 1341	4/15/2000	Lembi	Damon	4389 S. Rita Ln.	Fort Myers	FL	33301	(941) 555-4747
1200	1/9/1998	Lettow	Ryan	358 Maple Dr.	Fort Myers	FL	33301-1268	(941) 555-2805
2208	10/15/2000	Lindau	Kristina	1947 E. Watson	Fort Myers	FL	33301	(941) 555-6363
0340	5/5/1996	Lopez	Mina	4290 E. Alameda Dr.	Cypress Lake	FL	33205-0093	(941) 555-5050
1354	7/31/2000	Martinez	Julie	7115 E. Roosevelt Dr.	Iona	fl	33101-0093	(941) 555-1044
2240	11/24/2000	Mazeau	Rebecca	7383 Oak Dr.	Fort Myers	FL	33301	(941) 555-1093
0322	5/1/1996	Morgan	Dan	564 S. Lemon Dr.	Iona	FL	33205-0093	(941) 555-5567

Record: 20 ▶ ▶| ▶* of 51

Datasheet View

Figure 2.31

The employee records are displayed in alphabetical order by last name.

Next you want to check the rest of the table to see if there is anything else you need to do.

2 • Use the scroll box to scroll down to record 31.

Additional Information

As you drag the scroll box, the record location is displayed on top of it (for example, "Record 31 of 52").

Your screen should be similar to Figure 2.32

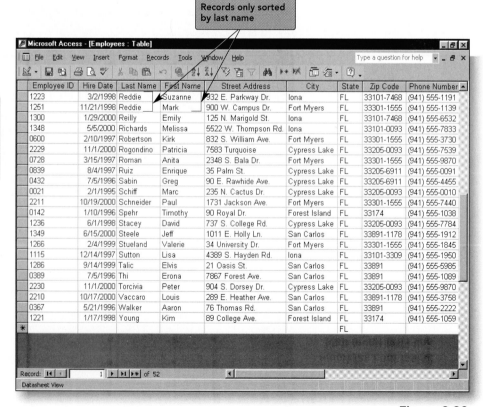

Records only sorted by last name

Employee ID	Hire Date	Last Name	First Name	Street Address	City	State	Zip Code	Phone Number
1223	3/2/1998	Reddie	Suzanne	932 E. Parkway Dr.	Iona	FL	33101-7468	(941) 555-1191
1251	11/21/1998	Reddie	Mark	900 W. Campus Dr.	Fort Myers	FL	33301-1555	(941) 555-1139
1300	1/29/2000	Reilly	Emily	125 N. Marigold St.	Iona	FL	33101-7468	(941) 555-6532
1348	5/5/2000	Richards	Melissa	5522 W. Thompson Rd.	Iona	FL	33101-0093	(941) 555-7833
0600	2/10/1997	Robertson	Kirk	832 S. William Ave.	Fort Myers	FL	33301-1555	(941) 555-3730
2229	11/1/2000	Rogondino	Patricia	7583 Turquoise	Cypress Lake	FL	33205-0093	(941) 555-7539
0728	3/15/1997	Roman	Anita	2348 S. Bala Dr.	Fort Myers	FL	33301-1555	(941) 555-9870
0839	8/4/1997	Ruiz	Enrique	35 Palm St.	Cypress Lake	FL	33205-6911	(941) 555-0091
0432	7/5/1996	Sabin	Greg	90 E. Rawhide Ave.	Cypress Lake	FL	33205-6911	(941) 555-4455
0021	2/1/1995	Schiff	Marc	235 N. Cactus Dr.	Cypress Lake	FL	33205-0093	(941) 555-0010
2211	10/19/2000	Schneider	Paul	1731 Jackson Ave.	Fort Myers	FL	33301-1555	(941) 555-7440
0142	1/10/1996	Spehr	Timothy	90 Royal Dr.	Forest Island	FL	33174	(941) 555-1038
1236	6/1/1998	Stacey	David	737 S. College Rd.	Cypress Lake	FL	33205-0093	(941) 555-7784
1349	6/15/2000	Steele	Jeff	1011 E. Holly Ln.	San Carlos	FL	33891-1178	(941) 555-1912
1266	2/4/1999	Stueland	Valerie	34 University Dr.	Fort Myers	FL	33301-1555	(941) 555-1845
1115	12/14/1997	Sutton	Lisa	4389 S. Hayden Rd.	Iona	FL	33101-3309	(941) 555-1950
1286	9/14/1999	Talic	Elvis	21 Oasis St.	San Carlos	FL	33891	(941) 555-5985
0389	7/5/1996	Thi	Erona	7867 Forest Ave.	San Carlos	FL	33891	(941) 555-1089
2230	11/1/2000	Torcivia	Peter	904 S. Dorsey Dr.	Cypress Lake	FL	33205-0093	(941) 555-9870
2210	10/17/2000	Vaccaro	Louis	289 E. Heather Ave.	San Carlos	FL	33891-1178	(941) 555-3758
0367	5/21/1996	Walker	Aaron	76 Thomas Rd.	San Carlos	FL	33891	(941) 555-2222
1221	1/17/1998	Young	Kim	89 College Ave.	Forest Island	FL	33174	(941) 555-1059
*						FL		

Record: 1 ▶ ▶| ▶* of 52

Datasheet View

Figure 2.32

Now you can see that the records for Suzanne and Mark Reddie are sorted by last name but not by first name. You want all records that have the same last name to be further sorted by first name. To do this, you need to sort using multiple sort fields.

Sorting on Multiple Fields

When sorting on multiple fields, the fields must be adjacent to each other, and the most important field in the sort must be to the left of the secondary field. The Last Name and First Name fields are already in the correct locations for the sort you want to perform. To specify the fields to sort on, both columns must be selected.

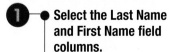

Additional Information
If the columns to sort were not already adjacent, you would hide the columns that are in between. If the columns were not in the correct order, you would move the columns. You will learn how to do this in Lab 3.

1 ● **Select the Last Name and First Name field columns.**

● **Click** 🔼 **Sort Ascending.**

● **Scroll down to record 31 again.**

Your screen should be similar to Figure 2.33

Records sorted by last name and by first name within same last names

Employee ID	Hire Date	Last Name	First Name	Street Address	City	State	Zip Code	Phone Number
1251	3/2/1998	Reddie	Mark	900 W. Campus Dr.	Fort Myers	FL	33301-1555	(941) 555-1139
1223	11/21/1998	Reddie	Suzanne	932 E. Parkway Dr.	Iona	FL	33101-7468	(941) 555-1191
1300	1/29/2000	Reilly	Emily	125 N. Marigold St.	Iona	FL	33101-7468	(941) 555-6532
1348	5/5/2000	Richards	Melissa	5522 W. Thompson Rd.	Iona	FL	33101-0093	(941) 555-7833
0600	2/10/1997	Robertson	Kirk	832 S. William Ave.	Fort Myers	FL	33301-1555	(941) 555-3730
2229	11/1/2000	Rogondino	Patricia	7583 Turquoise	Cypress Lake	FL	33205-0093	(941) 555-7539
0728	3/15/1997	Roman	Anita	2348 S. Bala Dr.	Fort Myers	FL	33301-1555	(941) 555-9870
0839	8/4/1997	Ruiz	Enrique	35 Palm St.	Cypress Lake	FL	33205-6911	(941) 555-0091
0432	7/5/1996	Sabin	Greg	90 E. Rawhide Ave.	Cypress Lake	FL	33205-6911	(941) 555-4455
0021	2/1/1995	Schiff	Marc	235 N. Cactus Dr.	Cypress Lake	FL	33205-0093	(941) 555-0010
2211	10/19/2000	Schneider	Paul	1731 Jackson Ave.	Fort Myers	FL	33301-1555	(941) 555-7440
0142	1/10/1996	Spehr	Timothy	90 Royal Dr.	Forest Island	FL	33174	(941) 555-1038
1236	6/1/1998	Stacey	David	737 S. College Rd.	Cypress Lake	FL	33205-0093	(941) 555-7784
1349	6/15/2000	Steele	Jeff	1011 E. Holly Ln.	San Carlos	FL	33891-1178	(941) 555-1912
1266	2/4/1999	Stueland	Valerie	34 University Dr.	Fort Myers	FL	33301-1555	(941) 555-1845
1115	12/14/1997	Sutton	Lisa	4389 S. Hayden Rd.	Iona	FL	33101-3309	(941) 555-1950
1286	9/14/1999	Talic	Elvis	21 Oasis St.	San Carlos	FL	33891	(941) 555-5985
0389	7/5/1996	Thi	Erona	7867 Forest Ave.	San Carlos	FL	33891	(941) 555-1089
2230	11/1/2000	Torcivia	Peter	904 S. Dorsey Dr.	Cypress Lake	FL	33205-0093	(941) 555-9870
2210	10/17/2000	Vaccaro	Louis	289 E. Heather Ave.	San Carlos	FL	33891-1178	(941) 555-3758
0367	5/21/1996	Walker	Aaron	76 Thomas Rd.	San Carlos	FL	33891	(941) 555-2222
1221	1/17/1998	Young	Kim	89 College Ave.	Forest Island	FL	33174	(941) 555-1059
*						FL		

Record: 1 of 52

Datasheet View

Figure 2.33

The record for Mark Reddie is now before the record for Suzanne. As you can see, sorting is a fast, useful tool. The sort order remains in effect until you remove the sort or replace it with a new sort order. Although Access remembers your sort order even when you exit the program, it does not actually change the table records. You can remove the sort at any time to restore the records to the primary key sort order. You decide to do this now and re-sort the table alphabetically for the Accounting department later, after you have finished making changes to it.

2 ● Choose
Records/Remove
Filter/Sort.

*Your screen should be
similar to Figure 2.34*

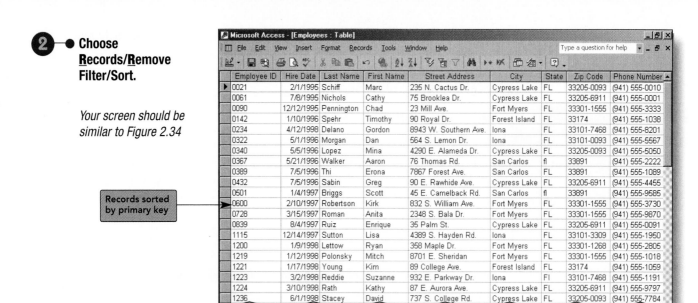

Records sorted
by primary key

Figure 2.34

The table is back to primary key order.

Formatting the Datasheet

Finally, you want to **format** or enhance the appearance of the datasheet on the screen to make it more readable or attractive by applying different effects. Datasheet formats include settings that change the appearance of the cell, gridlines, background and gridline colors, and border and line styles. In addition, you can change the text color and add text effects, such as bold and italics to the datasheet. Datasheet formats affect the entire datasheet appearance and cannot be applied to separate areas of the datasheet.

Changing Background and Gridline Color

You first want to see how changing the color of the datasheet background will look.

1 ● Choose
Format/Datasheet.

*Your screen should be
similar to Figure 2.35*

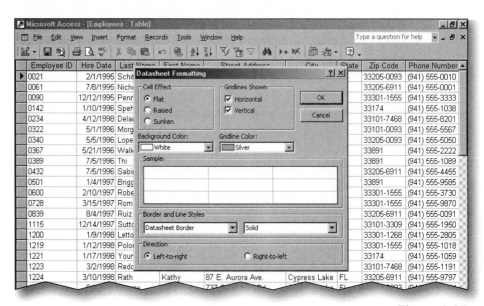

Figure 2.35

The Datasheet Formatting dialog box allows you to make changes to the format and preview how the changes will appear in the sample area. The default datasheet settings are selected. You want to change the background color from the default of white and the gridline color from the default of silver to different colors.

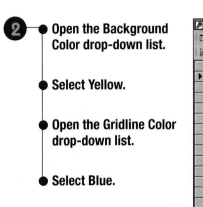

2
- **Open the Background Color drop-down list.**

- **Select Yellow.**

- **Open the Gridline Color drop-down list.**

- **Select Blue.**

Your screen should be similar to Figure 2.36

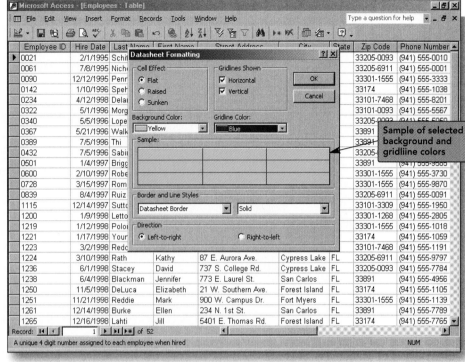

Figure 2.36

The sample area shows how your selections will appear. You will see how the datasheet looks with these new settings next.

3
- **Click [OK].**

Your screen should be similar to Figure 2.37

Datasheet displays in selected background and gridline colors

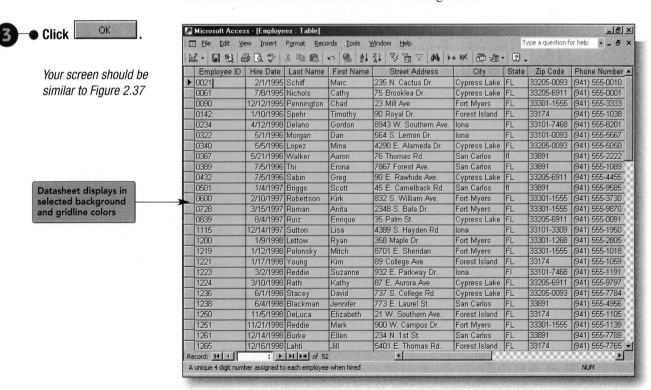

Figure 2.37

Changing the Font Color

The datasheet background and gridline colors brighten the screen appearance, but you think the text is a little difficult to read. You will change the text color to blue and bold. Many of the formatting features can also be applied using the Formatting toolbar. Using the Formatting toolbar to make changes to the datasheet, applies changes instantly.

① ● Display the Formatting toolbar.

● Open the [A ▾] Font/Fore Color drop-down menu.

● Select Blue from the color palette.

● Click [B] Bold.

Your screen should be similar to Figure 2.38

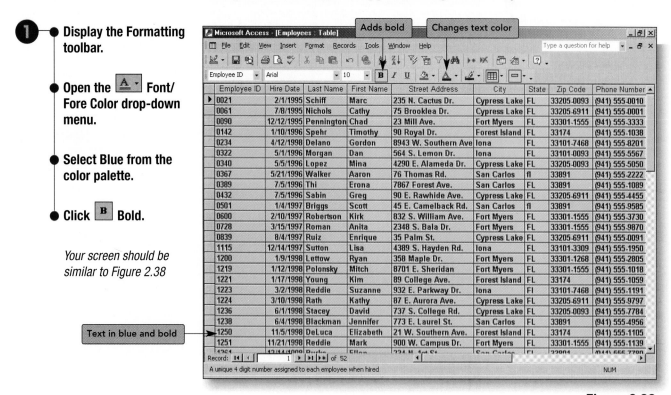

Figure 2.38

The text is now easier to read.

② ● Close the Formatting toolbar.

● Close the table saving your design changes.

You're now back at the Database window for the Employee Records file. Next you will learn how to create and use a form in Access.

NOTE: If you are ending your session now, close the database file and exit Access. When you begin again, load Access and open the Database window for the Employees Records.

Creating and Using Forms

One of your objectives is to make the database easy to use. You know from experience that long hours of viewing large tables can be tiring. Therefore, you want to create an onscreen form to make this table easier to view and use.

concept 6

Forms

6   A **form** is a database object used primarily to display records on-screen to make it easier to enter new records and to make changes to existing records. Forms are based on an underlying table, and include design control elements such as descriptive text, titles, labels, lines, boxes, and pictures. Forms often use calculations as well, to summarize data that is not listed on the actual table, such as a sales total. Forms make working with long lists of data easier. They enable people to use the data in the tables without having to sift through many lines of data to find the exact record.

You want the onscreen form to be similar to the paper form that is completed by each new employee when hired (shown below). The information from that form is used as the source of input for the new record that will be added to the table for the new employee.

EMPLOYEE DATA

First Name _____   Last Name _____
Street   _____
City   _____   State _____ Zip Code _____
Phone Number _____
Gender   _____   Birth Date _____
For Personnel Use Only:
Employee ID _____
Hire Date   _____

Using the Form Wizard

The Form Wizard guides you through the steps required to create a form. This is only one of the methods available for form creation — as with tables, you can create a form in Design view instead. In order to become familiar with all the parts of a form, you will use the Form Wizard to create a form for the "Employees" table.

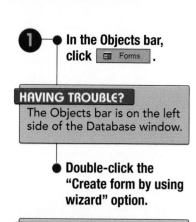

1 ● In the Objects bar, click ⊞ Forms .

HAVING TROUBLE?
The Objects bar is on the left side of the Database window.

● Double-click the "Create form by using wizard" option.

Another Method
You can also click the 🖅New button and select the Form Wizard in the New Form dialog box.

Your screen should be similar to Figure 2.39

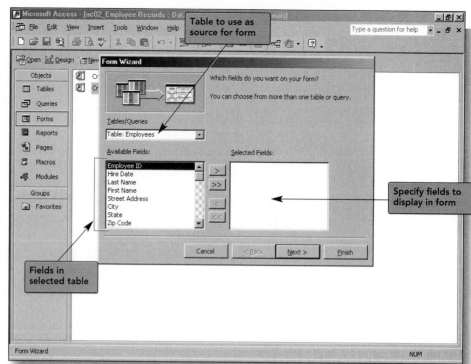

Figure 2.39

Additional Information
If your database contained multiple tables, you could open the Tables/Queries drop-down list to select the appropriate underlying table to use for the form.

The Form Wizard dialog box displays the name of the current table, Employees, in the Tables/Queries list box. This is the underlying table that Access will be use to create the form. The fields from the selected table are displayed in the Available Fields list box. You use this box to select the fields you want included on the form, in the order that you want them to appear. This is called the **tab order** because it is the order that the highlight will move through the fields on the form when you press the [Tab⇆] key during data entry. You decide that you want the fields to be in the same order as they are on the paper form shown in the illustration above.

2 ● Select First Name.

● Click >.

Another Method
You can also double-click on each field name in the Available Fields list box to move the field name to the Selected Fields list box.

Additional Information
The >> button adds all available fields to the Selected Fields list, in the same order that they appear in the Available Fields list.

Your screen should be similar to Figure 2.40

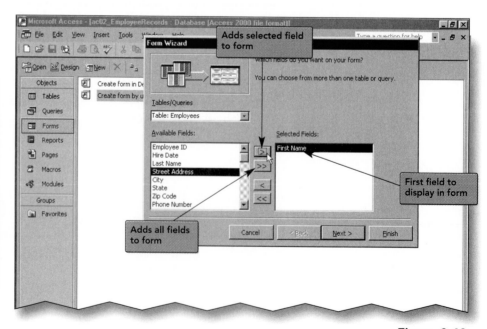

Figure 2.40

The First Name field is removed from the Available Fields list and added to the top of the Selected Fields list box.

3 ● In the same manner, add the following fields to the Selected Fields list in the order shown here:

Last Name

Street Address

City

State

Zip Code

Phone Number

Gender

Birth Date

Employee ID

Hire Date

Photo

Your screen should be similar to Figure 2.41

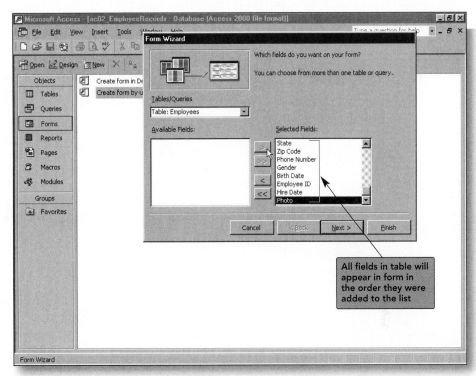

Figure 2.41

When you are done, the Available Fields list box is empty, and the Selected Fields list box lists the fields in the selected order. You are now ready to move on to the next Form Wizard screen.

4 ● Click .

Your screen should be similar to Figure 2.42

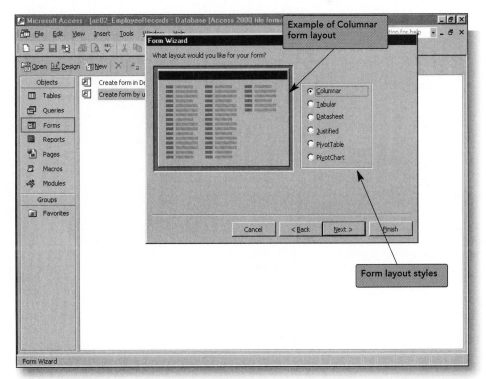

Figure 2.42

In this Form Wizard screen, you are asked to select the layout for the form. Six form layouts are available: The four basic form layouts are described in the following table.

Form	Layout Style	Description
Columnar	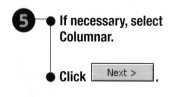	Presents data for the selected fields in columns. The field name labels display down the left side of the column, with the data for each field just to the right of its corresponding label. A single record is displayed in each Form window.
Tabular		Presents data in a table layout with field name labels across the top of the page and the corresponding data in rows and columns under each heading. Multiple records are displayed in the Form Window, each on a single row.
Datasheet		Displays data in rows and columns similar to the Table Datasheet view, but only selected fields display in the order chosen during form design. Displays multiple records, one per row, in the Form window.
Justified		Displays data in rows, with field name labels across the top of the row and the corresponding field data below it. A single record may appear in multiple rows in the Form window in order to fully display the field name label and data.

The columnar layout appears most similar to the paper form currently in use by the Club, so you decide to select that layout for your form.

5 ● **If necessary, select Columnar.**

● **Click** Next > .

Your screen should be similar to Figure 2.43

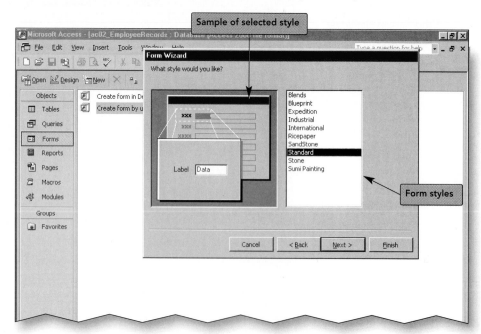

Figure 2.43

In this Form Wizard dialog box, you select from ten different styles for your form. A sample of each style as it is selected is displayed on the left side of the dialog box. Standard is the default selection. You will create the form using the Blends style.

6 ● **Select Blends.**

Additional Information

The last selected form style is the currently selected style.

● **Click** Next > .

Your screen should be similar to Figure 2.44

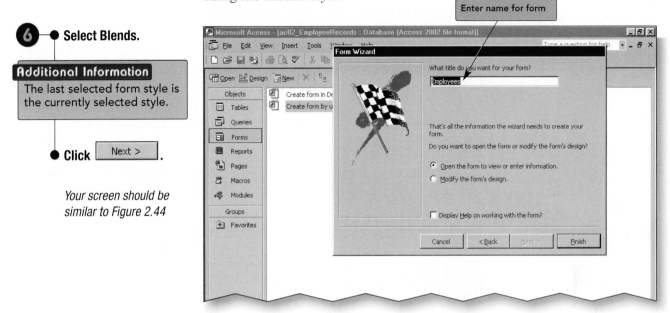

Figure 2.44

In this final Form Wizard dialog box, you need to enter a form title to be used as the name of the form, and you need to specify whether the form should open with data displayed in it. The Form Wizard uses the name of the table as the default form title. You want to change the form's title, and you want to keep the default of displaying the form when you are through creating it.

7 ● **Type Employee Data Form.**

● **Click** Finish .

● **If necessary, maximize the Form window.**

Your screen should be similar to Figure 2.45

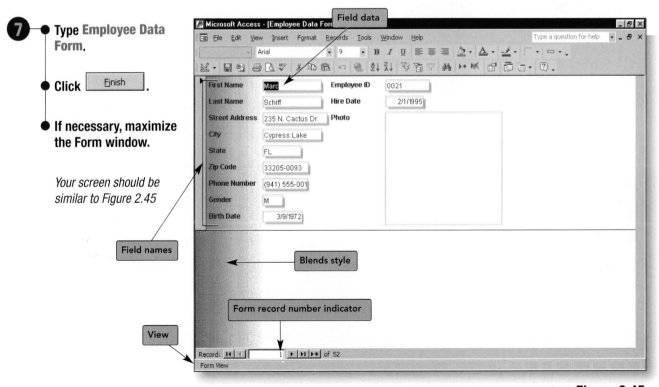

Figure 2.45

The completed form is displayed in the Form view window. The form displays the selected fields in columnar layout using the Blends style. The field name labels are in two columns with the field data text boxes in adjacent columns to the right. The employee information for Marc Schiff, the current record in the table, is displayed in the text boxes.

Navigating in Form View

You use the same navigation keys in Form view that you used in Datasheet view. You can move between fields in the form by using the Tab↹, ←Enter, ⇧Shift + Tab↹, and the directional arrow keys on the keyboard. You can use Page Up and Page Down, as well as the navigation buttons at the bottom of the form, to move between records.

You can also use the Find command to locate and display specific records. The Find command works the same way in a form as in a table. To try this out, you will find and display the record for Lisa Sutton.

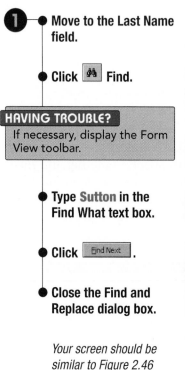

1 ● **Move to the Last Name field.**

● **Click** 🔍 **Find.**

HAVING TROUBLE?
If necessary, display the Form View toolbar.

● **Type Sutton in the Find What text box.**

● **Click** Find Next .

● **Close the Find and Replace dialog box.**

Your screen should be similar to Figure 2.46

Additional Information
You can adjust the size of the panes by dragging the bar that separates them.

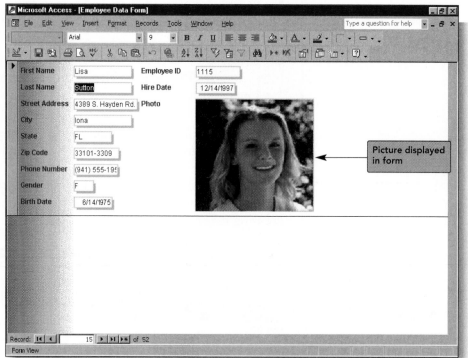

Figure 2.46

Lisa Sutton's record is displayed in the form. Because this record contains the inserted picture in the Photo field, the photo is displayed.

Adding Records in a Form

You need to add a new employee record to the database, whose paper employee record form is shown below. You will add the record in Form view using the information on the paper form for the field entry data.

EMPLOYEE DATA

First Name	Kevin	Last Name	Tillman
Street	89 E. Southern Dr.		
City	Fort Myers	State FL	Zip Code 33301-2316
Phone Number	(941) 555-3434		
Gender	M	Birth Date	April 13, 1971

For Personnel Use Only:

Employee ID   2248

Hire Date   Jan. 12, 2002

1 ● Click 	New Record to display a new blank entry form.

● Enter the data shown in the employee's paper form for the new record.

Additional Information

Press Tab↹ to move from field to field.

Your screen should be similar to Figure 2.47

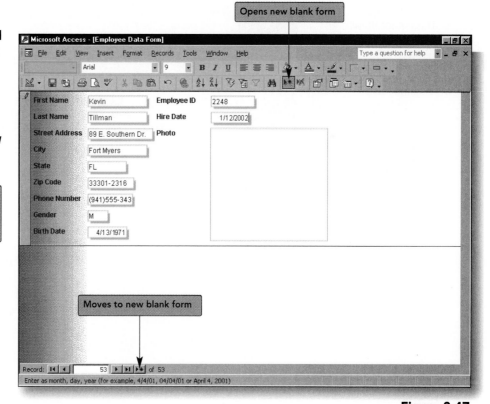

Opens new blank form

Moves to new blank form

Figure 2.47

Using the form makes entering the new employee data much faster because the fields are in the same order as the information in the paper Employee Data form used by the personnel department. When you use the Form Wizard to create a form, most of the field text boxes are appropriately sized to display the data in the field. You probably noticed, however, that the Phone Number field is not quite large enough to display all the numbers. You will learn how to fix this problem in the next lab.

Before you end this lab, you will add a record for yourself.

2 ● **Enter another record using your special Employee ID 9999 and your first and last name. Enter the current date as your Hire Date. The data in all other fields can be fictitious.**

● **Open the [icon] View button drop-down list and click [icon] Datasheet View.**

Another Method

The menu equivalent is View/Datasheet View.

● **Scroll up a few rows to display both new records.**

Your screen should be similar to Figure 2.48

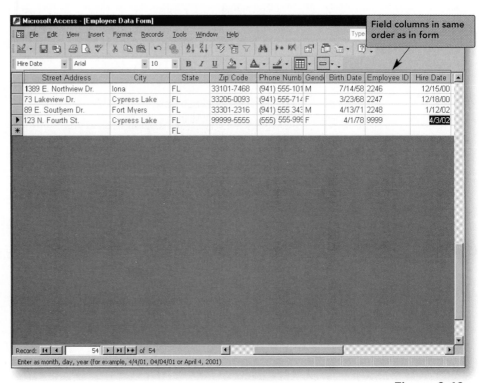

Field columns in same order as in form

Figure 2.48

The Datasheet View of the form data is displayed. Notice that the field columns are now in the same order as in the form.

You will learn how to further manipulate and enhance forms in the next lab, but for now, you want to see how the form you designed looks printed out.

Previewing and Printing a Form

You want to preview and print only the form that displays your record.

● **Switch back to Form view.**

● **Click Print Preview.**

● **Zoom to 100% to see the page better.**

Your screen should be similar to Figure 2.49

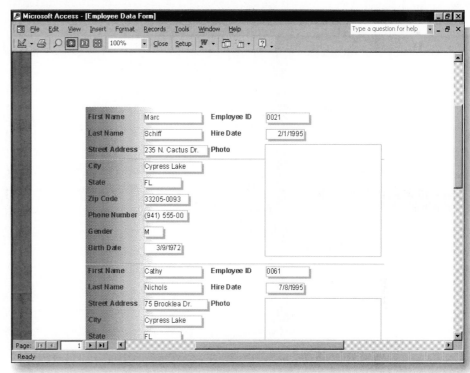

Figure 2.49

Print Preview displays whatever view you were last using. In this case, because you were last in Form view, the form is displayed in the Preview window. Access prints as many records as can be printed on a page in the Form layout. You want to print only the form displaying your record.

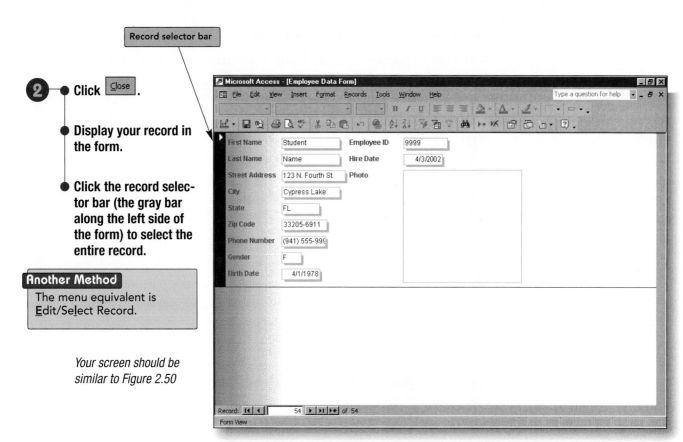

Record selector bar

2 • Click [Close].

• Display your record in the form.

• Click the record selector bar (the gray bar along the left side of the form) to select the entire record.

The menu equivalent is Edit/Select Record.

Your screen should be similar to Figure 2.50

Figure 2.50

Now that the record is selected, you can print the record. The record will print using the current view, in this case Form View.

3 • Choose File/Print.

• Select Selected Records.

• Click [OK].

Closing and Saving a Form

Next you will close the form.

1 Close the Form window.

Your screen should be similar to Figure 2.51

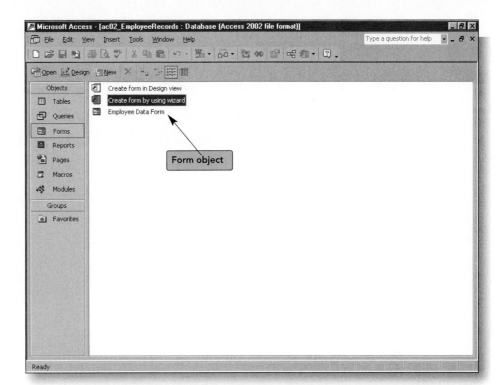

Figure 2.51

The Database window is displayed, showing the new form object name in the forms list box.

2 Exit Access.

Modifying a Table and Creating a Form

Format Property (AC2.9)

You can use the Format property to create custom formats that change the way numbers, dates, times, and text display and print.

Format property

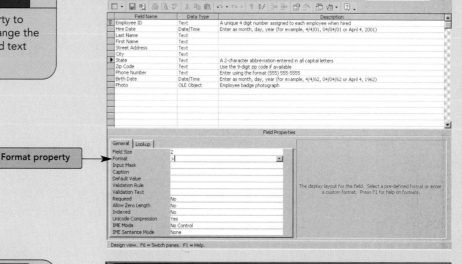

Default Value Property (AC2.11)

The Default Value property is used to specify a value to be automatically entered in a field when a new record is created.

Default value property

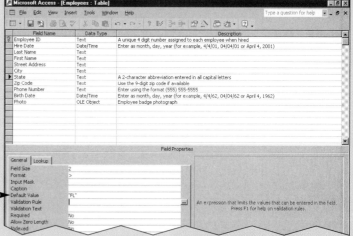

Validity Check (AC2.14)

Access automatically performs certain checks, called **validity checks**, on values entered in a field to make sure that the values are valid for the field type.

Validity check

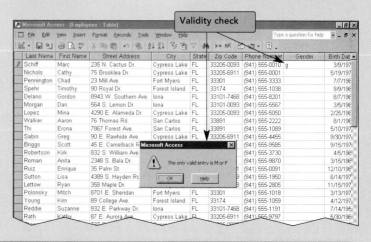

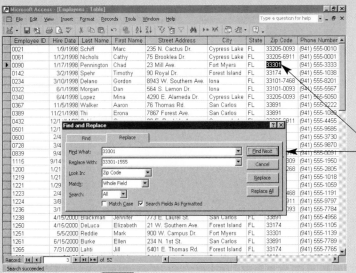

Find and Replace (AC2.21)

The Find and Replace feature helps you quickly find specific information and automatically replace it with new information.

Find and Replace

Sort

Sort (AC2.27)

You can quickly rearrange a table's records by **sorting** the table data in a different order.

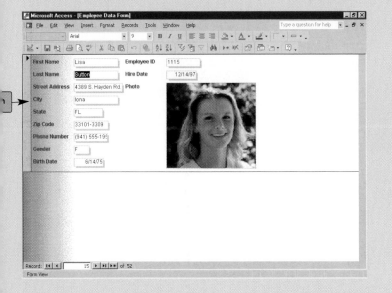

Form (AC2.33)

A **form** is a database object used primarily to display records onscreen to make it easier to enter new records and to make changes to existing records.

key terms

character string AC2.11	identifier AC2.14
comparison operator AC2.14	operator AC2.14
Default Value property AC2.11	sorting AC2.27
expression AC2.14	tab order AC2.34
Find and Replace AC2.21	validation rule AC2.14
form AC2.33	validation text AC2.14
format AC2.30	validity check AC2.14
Format property AC2.9	value AC2.15

mous skills

The Microsoft Office User Specialist (MOUS) certification program is designed to measure your proficiency in performing basic tasks using the Office XP applications. Getting certified demonstrates that you have the skills and provides a valuable industry credential for employment. After completing this lab, you have learned the following Access 2002 Microsoft Office User Specialist skills:

Skill	Description	Page
Creating and Using Databases	Open database objects in multiple views	AC2.40
	Move among records	AC2.6
	Format datasheets	AC2.30
Creating and Modifying Tables	Create and modify tables	AC2.8
	Modify field properties	AC2.8
Creating and Modifying Forms	Create and display forms	AC2.32
Viewing and Organizing Information	Enter and edit records	AC2.39
	Sort records	AC2.27

command summary

Command	Shortcut	Button	Action
Edit/Undo	Ctrl + Z	↶	Cancels last action
Edit/Find	Ctrl + F	🔍	Locates specified data
Edit/Replace	Ctrl + H		Locates and replaces specified data
View/Design View		📐 ▾	Displays Design view
View/Form View			Displays a form in Form view
Insert/Column			Inserts a new field in a table in Datasheet view
Format/Hide Columns			Hides columns in Datasheet view
Format/Unhide Columns			Redisplays hidden columns
Records/Sort/Sort Ascending		⬇	Reorders records in ascending alphabetical order

Terminology

screen identification

In the following Access screen, several items are identified by letters. Enter the correct term for each item in the spaces provided.

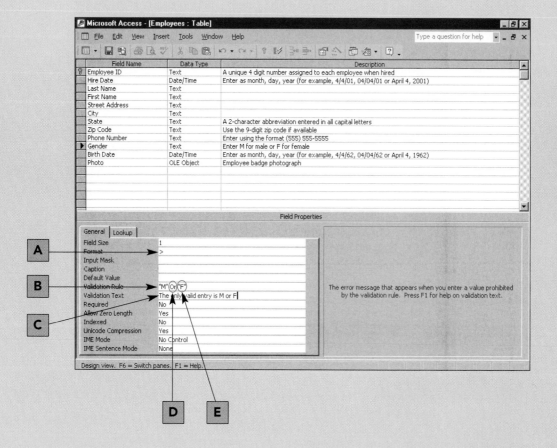

A. _____

B. _____

C. _____

D. _____

E. _____

matching

Match the numbered item with the correct lettered description.

1. match case   _____ **a.** cancels your last action

2. Ctrl + Home   _____ **b.** an expression

3. ⟲   _____ **c.** database object used primarily for onscreen display

4. character string   _____ **d.** moves to the first field of the first record

5. tab order   _____ **e.** makes the search for specified data case sensitive

6. >   _____ **f.** displays Design view

7. sort   _____ **g.** order in which pressing Tab moves through fields in a form

8. ="Y" Or "N"   _____ **h.** a group of characters

9. ◪ ▾   _____ **i.** changes the display order of a table

10. form   _____ **j.** format character that forces all data in a field to uppercase

multiple choice

Circle the letter of the correct response.

1. Format _____ is used to create custom formats that change the way numbers, dates, times, and text display and print.
   a. specification
   b. alignment
   c. range
   d. property

2. Values to be automatically entered into a field are specified in the _____ Value property.
   a. Auto
   b. Initial
   c. Default
   d. Assumed

3. _____ are automatically performed on values entered in a field to make sure that the values are valid for the field type.
   a. Object validations
   b. Security specifications
   c. Form searches
   d. Validity checks

4. You can quickly reorder _____ in a table by sorting the table.
   a. records
   b. columns
   c. fields
   d. objects

5. Forms are based on the underlying table by using design _____ elements.
   a. control
   b. default
   c. property
   d. object

6. To change the format of a field, different _____ are entered in the Format text box.
   a. symbols
   b. buttons
   c. objects
   d. graphics

7. When users add a record to a table, they can either accept the _____ value or enter another value.
   a. default
   b. initial
   c. last
   d. null

8. A(n) _____ is a sequence of characters (letters, numbers, or symbols) that must be handled as text, not as numeric data.
   a. identifier
   b. character string
   c. expression
   d. operator

9. Data sorted in _____ order is arranged alphabetically A to Z or numerically 0 to 9.
   a. increasing
   b. descending
   c. ascending
   d. decreasing

10. _____ are items made up of many elements that can be created, selected, and manipulated as a unit.
   a. Records
   b. Objects
   c. Tables
   d. Forms

true/false

Circle the correct answer to the following statements.

1.	Format properties do not change the way Access stores data.	True	False
2.	The Format property determines the value automatically entered into a field of a new record.	True	False
3.	An identifier is a symbol or word that indicates that an operation is to be performed.	True	False
4.	The Find command will locate specific values in a field and automatically replace them.	True	False

5.	Format properties change the way data is displayed.	True	False
6.	The Default Value property is commonly used when most of the entries in a field will be the same for the entire table.	True	False
7.	Values are numbers, dates, or pictures.	True	False
8.	The Replace command will automatically restore properties to an object.	True	False
9.	Sorting reorders records in a table.	True	False
10.	Forms are database objects used primarily for report generation.	True	False

Concepts

fill-in

Complete the following statements by filling in the blanks with the correct terms.

1. A(n) _____ is a combination of symbols that produces specific results.

2. The _____ property is used to specify a value that is automatically entered in a field when a new record is created.

3. When _____ are performed, Access makes sure that the entry is acceptable in the field.

4. Records can be temporarily displayed in a different order by using the _____ feature.

5. Forms are primarily used for _____ and making changes to existing records.

6. The _____ property changes the way data appears in a field.

7. The four form layouts are _____, _____, _____, and _____.

8. Use _____ to cancel your last action.

9. A(n) _____ is a symbol or word that indicates that an operation is to be performed.

10. To return to _____ order, you must remove the temporary sort.

discussion questions

Answer the following questions by preparing written responses.

1. Discuss several different Format properties and how they are used in a database.

2. Discuss the different types of form layouts and why you would use one layout type over another.

3. Discuss how validity checks work. What are some advantages of adding validity checks to a field? Include several examples.

4. Discuss the different ways records can be sorted. What are some advantages of sorting records?

Hands-On Exercises

step-by-step

Modifying the Client Database and Creating a Client Form

★ 1. Maria Dell is very impressed with the work you have done on the database for the Simply Beautiful Spa (Step-by-Step Exercise 1 of Lab 1). After an initial review of the database, Ms. Dell realizes that the inclusion of additional data in the database can help her with other administrative functions. For example, as part of her future advertising campaigns, she would like to send birthday cards to each of her clients and wonders if it is possible to include birth date information in the database. Also, she would like you to modify some client records, create a form to ease data entry, and print a copy of the form. You have continued to add records to the database and have saved the expanded database file as Simply Beautiful. You are now ready to make the modifications to the Client table and to create a form. Your completed form is shown here.

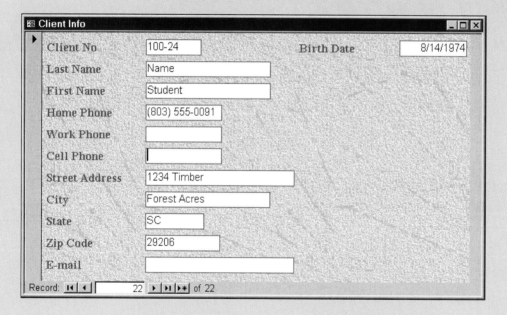

To make the requested changes to the database and create the form, follow these steps:

a. Open the expanded database named ac02_Simply Beautiful and the table named "Clients."

b. In Design view, add the following field to the end of the table:

Field name: **Birth Date**

Data type: **Date/Time**

Description: **Identifies client's birthday**

Field format: **Short date**

c. Make the First Name and Last Name required fields. (Hint: Set the Required property to Yes.)

d. Save the table design changes and return to Datasheet view. Update the table by filling in the new field for each record with appropriate data. Include several birth dates before 01/01/64.

e. Edit the appropriate records to reflect the client changes that Ms. Dell gave you:

- Sally Grimes has moved to **202 S. Jefferson**. The city, state, and zip code will remain the same.

- Mr. Fen Woo has a cell phone number. It is **(301) 555-9076**.

- Barbara Williams wrote down her e-mail address when she was last in. It is **Barbara@smart.com**.

f. Close the table.

g. Use the Form Wizard to create a form for the "Clients" table. Include all fields as listed. Use the columnar layout and Expedition style. Name it **Client Info**.

h. Use the new form to enter the following records:

Record 1	**Record 2**
100-23	100-24
Price	[Your last name]
Georgia	[Your first name]
(301) 555-5522	(301) 555-0091
(301) 555-6321	[no work phone]
(301) 555-3434	[no cell phone]
243 May Avenue	1234 Timber
Lexington	Forest Acres
SC	SC
29071	29206
gprice@mail.com	[no e-mail]
3/21/73	8/14/74

i. Preview and print the form for the second new record you added.

j. Exit Access, saving your changes as needed.

Modifying the Advertiser Database and Creating an Ad Rate Form

★★ **2.** You have completed the advertiser contact portion of your homeowners' Happenings database (Step-by-Step Exercise 2 of Lab 1), and you are ready to expand it to include the ad size, rate, and frequency that the local merchants have contracted for. The ad rate is $50 for a 1/4-page ad, $100 for a 1/2-page ad, and $175 for a full-page ad. You also want to create a data-entry form when you're finished with the basic design. Your completed form is shown here.

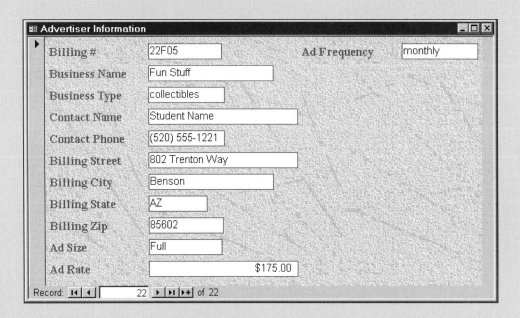

To add the new fields to the database and create the form, follow these steps:

a. Open the expanded database named ac02_Happening Ads and the table named "Advertisers."

b. In Design view, add the following three fields to the end of the table:

Field name: Ad Size

Data type: Text

Description: Enter one of the following: ¼, ½, or Full

Field size: 5

Field name: Ad Rate

Data type: Currency

Description: Contracted rate per ad

Field name: Ad Frequency

Data type: Text

Description: Enter one of the following: Single, Monthly, Bimonthly

Field size: 10

c. Save the table design changes and return to Datasheet view. Update the table by filling in the new fields for each record. Readjust the column widths as necessary.

d. Close and save the table.

e. Use the Form Wizard to create a form for the "Advertisers" table. Include all the table fields in their current order. Use the Columnar layout and Expedition style. Title the form Advertiser Information.

f. Use the new form to enter the following records:

Record 1	Record 2
21H03	22F05
Hearth & Home	Fun Stuff
Furniture Store	Collectibles
Doris Francis	[Your Name]
(912) 555-0022	(912) 555-1221
124 Desert Way	802 Trenton Way
Willcox	Benson
AZ	AZ
85643	85602
1/2	Full
100	175
Bimonthly	Monthly

g. Preview and print the form for the second new record you added.

h. Exit Access, saving your changes as needed.

Modifying the Product Vendor Database and Creating a Vendor Information Form

★★ 3. You and other employees of the Downtown Internet Cafe have been sharing the task of entering
★ product and vendor information into the purchase items Supplies database (Step-by-Step Exercise
3 of Lab 1). You are now ready to add fields that show the inventory on hand and to indicate
special orders so Evan, the cafe owner, knows when to place an order. However, when you open
the database, you noticed that some of the information for the existing fields is missing, incorrect,
or inconsistent. You realize that besides adding the new fields, you need to change some of the
field properties, specify required fields, correct some errors, and create a form to make data entry
easier. When you are finished, you will end up with an easy-to-use data entry form shown here.

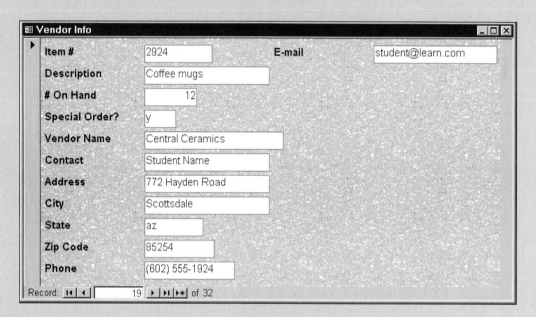

To make the changes and create the form, follow these steps:
a. Open the expanded database named ac02_Cafe Supplies and the table named "Vendors."
b. Use the Replace command to replace item #2579 with the correct item number, 2575. Use the
same command to replace Beverage with their new name, Better Beverages, Inc. Adjust the
Vendor Name column to fit the new name.
c. In Design view, make the Item #, Description, and Vendor Name required fields. Add a Format
property to the State field to force the data in that field to display in all capital letters.

d. Add a field before the Vendor Name to specify the inventory on hand for each item:

Field name: **# On Hand**

Data type: Number

Description: **Number of individual units (bags, boxes, etc.) in stock**

Field size: Integer

e. Add another field before the Vendor Name to specify whether the item is a special order (not regularly stocked):

Field name: **Special Order?**

Data type: Text

Description: **Is this a special order item?**

Field size: **1**

Default value: **N**

Validation rule: **Y or N**

Validation text: **The only valid entry is Y (yes) or N (no)**

f. Return to Datasheet view and update the table by filling in the new fields for each record.

g. Use the Form Wizard to create a columnar form with the SandStone style and include all the table fields in their current order. Use the title **Vendor Info** for the table.

h. Use the new form to add the following purchase items to the table:

Record 1	Record 2
1102	2924
Napkins	Coffee mugs
50	12
N	Y
Basics Restaurant Supply	Central Ceramics
Mandy Swanson	[Your Name]
13990 N. Central Ave.	772 Hayden Road
Phoenix	Scottsdale
AZ	AZ
84137-7214	85254
(602) 555-0037	(602) 555-1924
brs@email.net	student@learn.com

i. Preview and print the form for the second new record you added.

Maintaining a Product Development Database

★ ★ **4.** The EduSoft Company, which develops computer curriculums for grades K–8, has just hired you
★ to update and maintain their software database. Some of the tasks your manager asks you to
accomplish involve correcting some known errors and applying some validation rules. She would
also like you to create a form, shown here, which will make it easier to enter new software titles.

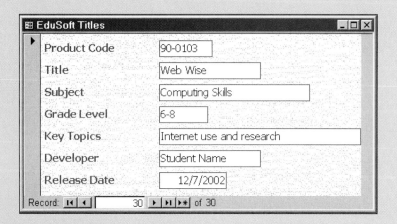

To update the database and create the form, follow these steps:

a. Open the database file named ac02_Learning and the table named "Software."

b. The corrections you need to make to the table are related to the software titles. Sort the table
in ascending order by Title so it will be easier to see the names you need to correct.

c. You have a note that the name of the Figure It series has been changed to Solve It. Use the
Replace command (match the Start of Field to retain the numbers) or navigate through the
table to find the three records with this title and change them.

d. The program called Reading & Writing was never released and has been replaced by separate
reading and writing programs. Find and delete this record.

e. Switch to Design view and add a validity rule and text to the Grade Level field so that it only
allows an entry of K–2, 3–5, or 6–8 (all three valid entries must be in quotes).

f. Add a field above Release Date to specify the name of the lead program developer for each title.

Field name: **Developer**

Data type: Text

Description: **Name of lead program developer**

Field size: **20**

g. Return to Datasheet view and hide the Title through Key Topic columns. Next you need to update the table by filling in the new field for each record. Each lead programmer has a unique
two-digit prefix on their product numbers. Using Teri O'Neill and other names of your choice,
complete the Developer field for each record. For example, Teri O'Neill worked on products
with the 36 prefix. Unhide the columns when you are done.

h. Create a columnar form using the Form Wizard. Use the Sumi Painting style and include all
the fields in their current order. Use the name **EduSoft Titles** for the form.

i. Use the form to enter a new record for a software program called Web Wise, Product Code
90–0103, which is currently in development for grades 6–8 to help them learn to use the
Internet and do research. Enter your name as the developer. Preview and print the form for
this new record. Exit Access, saving changes as needed.

Maintaining a Tracking Database

5. You have continued to add records to the database for tracking the animals that come into and go out of the Animal Rescue Foundation (Step-by-Step Exercise 5 of Lab 1). Now you need to modify the database structure and customize field properties to control the data entered by the Animal Angels volunteers who are assigned this task. You also want to create a form to make it easier for the volunteers to enter the necessary information, as shown here.

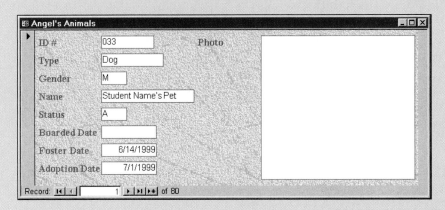

To enhance the Animal Rescue database and create the form, follow these steps:

a. Open the expanded database named ac02_AA and the table named "Animals."

b. In Design view, insert the following field above the Boarded Date field:

Field name: **Status**

Data type: Text

Description: **Enter B (boarded), F (in foster home), or A (adopted)**

Field size: **1**

Format: **>**

c. Make the following additional changes to the database structure:

- Add a validation rule and appropriate validation text to the Gender field to accept only M or F (male or female). Also format the field to display the information uppercase.

- Add a validation rule and appropriate validation text to the Status field to accept only B, F, or A (boarded, foster home, or adopted).

d. Return to Datasheet view and update the table by filling in the new Status field for each record with data of your choice.

e. So you can easily see the current status of the animals to ascertain which still need homes, sort the table in descending order by the Status, Boarded Date, Foster Date, and Adoption Date fields (hold down the [Shift] key and click the Status column and then the Adoption Date column). Change the status of Lemon to **A** and enter today's date as the Adoption Date. Remove the sort filter.

f. Use the Form Wizard to create a columnar form. Use the Expedition style and include all the fields in their current order. Title the form **Angel's Animals**.

g. Add two records using the new form. Enter **[your name]'s Pet** in the Name field of the second record you add, and then select, preview, and print it.

h. Exit Access, saving changes as needed.

lab exercises

Adventure Travel Form

★ 1. You have heard from the employees of Adventure Travel that the database table you created (Step-by-Step Exercise 4 of Lab 1) is a bit unwieldy for them to enter the necessary data, because it now contains so many fields that it requires scrolling across the screen to locate them. You decide to create a form that will make entering data not only easier, but more attractive as well. Open the Adventure Travel database and use the Form Wizard to create a form called **Packages** for the "Travel Packages" table. Use the form to enter one new record with a fictitious client name and another with your name as the client. Select and print the second new record.

Expense Account Tracking

★★ 2. While creating the database table for JK Enterprises (On Your Own Exercise 4 of Lab 1), you learned that some employees have been receiving advances for anticipated expenses (such as for travel). You have also been informed that the executives want to start tracking the expenses by department. You need to add a currency field for the advance amount data and a field to enter the department name (or number, if you prefer). You also need to add a Yes/No field to record whether or not the expense has been paid, with a corresponding validation rule and message. Update the Expenses table to include appropriate values in the new fields in the existing records. Close the table, saving the changes. Then use the Form Wizard to create a data entry form called **JK Expenses** for this table. To test the form, enter a new record with your name as the contact and then select and print the record.

Dental Database Update

★★ 3. The single-dentist office for which you created a patient database (On Your Own Exercise 3 of Lab 1) has now expanded to include a second dentist and receptionist, requiring you to identify required fields and to add more fields that identify which patient is assigned to which dentist. You also decide that creating a form for the database would make it easier for both you and the other receptionist to enter and locate patient information. Open the Patient Information database and "Patient Data" table and make the patient identification number, name, and phone number required fields. Add a Dentist Name field, with the two dentist's names in the field description and an appropriate validation rule and message. Update the table to "assign" some of the patients to one of the dentists and some patients to the other dentist. Sort the table by dentist name to see the results of your new assignments. "Reassign" one of the displayed patients and then remove the sort filter. Close the table, saving the changes. Create a form called **Administration** for the table using the Form Wizard. Enter two new records, one for each of the dentists. Use the Find command to locate the record form that has your name as the patient, and then select and print the displayed record.

Employee Database Update

★★ 4. The management at Lewis & Lewis, Inc. is quite impressed with the employee database you
★   created (On Your Own Exercise 2 of Lab 1). However, they would like you to include home phone numbers and addresses so the database can be used to send mail (such as Christmas cards, 401k information, and tax forms) to employees. Also, you have been asked to create a form that will make it easier for other administrative assistants to enter employee data into the database as well. Open the Lewis Personnel database and "Phone List" table and add home address and phone number fields to it. Update the table to include information in the new fields for the existing records. Sort

the table by employee last name and use the Replace command or table navigation to locate and change the last name of a female employee who has gotten married since you first created the database. Use the same technique to locate and delete a record for an employee who has left the company. Remove the sort filter and close the table, saving the changes. Create a form called **Human Resources** for the table using the Form Wizard. Enter two new records. Use the Find command to locate the record form that has your name as the employee, and then select and print the displayed record.

on the web

You realize that you have left out some very important fields in the "Inventory" table you created in the Golden Oldies database (On the Web Exercise 1 of Lab 1)—fields that identify the sources where you can obtain the vintage records your customers are looking for. Repeat your Web search for collectible record albums and note the resources (for example, online shopping services, specialty stores, or individual collectors who are offering these items at online auctions) for the titles you have included in your table. Add source name and address fields to the table and update it to include this information in the existing records. Sort the records according to the source name field and adjust the column widths to accommodate the new information. Remove the sort filter and close the table, saving the changes. Now, to make data entry easier for the company's employees, create a data entry form called **Collectibles** using the Form Wizard. Use the form to enter a new record with your name as the source, and then print it.

Analyzing Data and Creating Reports

LAB 3

objectives

After completing this lab, you will know how to:

1.	Filter table records.
2.	Create and modify a query.
3.	Move columns.
4.	Query two tables.
5.	Create reports from tables and queries.
6.	Modify a report design.
7.	Change page margins.
8.	Print a selected page.
9.	Compact a database.

Iona to Fort Myers Car Pool Report

First Name	Last Name	Street Address	City	Phone Number
Bill	Delucchi	950 S. Terrace Dr.	Cypress Lake	(941) 555-8195
Lisa	Fromthart	32 Redcoat Rd.	Cypress Lake	(941) 555-0110
Nichol	Lawrence	433 S. Gaucho Dr.	Cypress Lake	(941) 555-7656
Mina	Lopez	4290 E. Alameda Dr.	Cypress Lake	(941) 555-5050
Cathy	Nichols	75 Brooklea Dr.	Cypress Lake	(941) 555-0001
Marc	Schiff	235 N. Cactus Dr.	Cypress Lake	(941) 555-0010
Eric	Helfand	4601 E. Willow Dr.	Iona	(941) 555-9101
Suzanne	Reddie	932 E. Parkway Dr.	Iona	(941) 555-1191
Name	Student	89 Any St.	Iona	(941) 555-3333
Lisa	Sutton	4389 S. Hayden Rd.	Iona	(941) 555-1950

Employee Address Report

First Name	Last Name	Street Address	City	State	Zip Code	Phone Number
Jeff	Bader	947 S. Forest St.	Fort Myers	FL	33301-1555	(941) 555-7789
Andrew	Beinbrink	45 Burr Rd.	Fort Myers	FL	33301-1555	(941) 555-5322
Brian	Birch	742 W. Lemon Dr.	Fort Myers	FL	33301-1555	(941) 555-4321
Tamara	Birch	742 W. Lemon Dr.	Forest Island	FL	33301-1555	(941) 555-4321
William	Bloomquist	43 Kings Rd.	Fort Myers	FL	33174	(941) 555-6432
Anna	Brett	23 Suffolk Ln.	San Carlos	FL	33301-1555	(941) 555-4543
Scott	Briggs	45 E. Camelback Rd.	San Carlos	FL	33891-1605	(941) 555-9385
Ellen	Burke	234 N. 1st St.	Iona	FL	33891-1605	(941) 555-7789
Gordon	Delano	8943 W. Southern Ave.	Forest Island	FL	33101-7468	(941) 555-8201
Elizabeth	DeLuca	21 W. Southern Ave.	Cypress Lake	FL	33174	(941) 555-1105
Bill	Delucchi	950 S. Terrace Dr.	San Carlos	FL	33205-0093	(941) 555-8195
Barbara	Euster	1153 S. Wilson	Forest Island	FL	33891-1605	(941) 555-3211
Kimberly	Fachet	923 E. Baseline Rd.	Forest Island	FL	33174	(941) 555-0018
Daniel	Facqur	5832 Fremont St.	San Carlos	FL	33174	(941) 555-4563
Nancy	Falk	9483 W. Island Dr.	San Carlos	FL	33891-1605	(941) 555-8665
Robby	Ferguson	4232 Tuller Ave.	Cypress Lake	FL	33891-1178	(941) 555-7039
Lisa	Fromthart	32 Redcoat Rd.	Iona	FL	33205-6911	(941) 555-0110
Ken	Gapasin	2633 E. Fountain St.	Fort Myers	FL	33101-0093	(941) 555-0589
Alfonso	Gomez	3429 S. Grandview St.	Cypress Lake	FL	33301-1555	(941) 555-2395
Sarah	Harvey	73 Lakeview St.	Iona	FL	33205-6911	(941) 555-7144
Eric	Helfand	4601 E. Willow Dr.	San Carlos	FL	33101-7468	(941) 555-9101
Karen	Henstreet	999 Solano Dr.	Iona	FL	33891-1605	(941) 555-6325
Ryan	Hogan	1389 E. Northview Dr.	Fort Myers	FL	33101-7468	(941) 555-1010
Karen	Howard	9423 S. Forest Ave.	Iona	FL	33301-1555	(941) 555-5326
Raya	Ingles	8432 N. Cimarron	San Carlos	FL	33101-7468	(941) 555-6433
Chris	Jensen	601 Alpha Dr.		FL	33891-1605	(941) 555-0018

Page 1 of 3

Thursday, April 05, 2001

Custom reports can be generated to display database information in an attractive and meaningful manner.

Microsoft Access - [Employees : Table]

Employee ID	Hire Date	Last Name	First Name	Street Address	City	State	Zip Code	Phone Number	
0322	5/1/1996	Morgan	Dan	564 S. Lemon Dr.	Iona	FL	33101-0093	(941) 555-5567	M
0435	8/4/1996	Switzer	Jon	32 W. Orange St.	Iona	FL	33101-0093	(941) 555-6643	M
0489	9/23/1996	Shoemaker	Wendy	858 E. Aire Ct.	Iona	FL	33101-0093	(941) 555-3344	F
0683	2/23/1997	Workman	Jill	4344 W. Gala Ln.	Iona	FL	33101-7468	(941) 555-7655	F
0692	3/10/1997	Ingles	Raya	8432 N. Cimarron	Iona	FL	33101-7468	(941) 555-6433	F
0765	5/5/1997	Lamm	Chris	382 E. Ladonna Dr.	Iona	FL	33101-7468	(941) 555-8332	M
9999	2/25/1997	Name	Student	89 Any St.	Iona	FL	33101-0093	(941) 555-9999	F
1151	12/14/1997	Sutton	Lisa	4389 S. Hayden Rd.	Iona	FL	33101-0093	(941) 555-1950	F
1223	3/2/1998	Reddie	Suzanne	932 E. Parkway Dr.	Iona	FL	33101-7468	(941) 555-1191	F
1234	4/12/1998	Delano	Gordon	8943 W. Southern Ave	Iona	FL	33101-7468	(941) 555-8201	M
1242	7/24/1998	Player	Allison	234 S. Sycamore	Iona	FL	33101-0093	(941) 555-5532	F
1292	1/21/2000	Larson	Alicia	345 W. Mill Ave.	Iona	FL	33101-7468	(941) 555-7717	F
1300	1/29/2000	Reilly	Emily	125 N. Marigold St.	Iona	FL	33101-7468	(941) 555-6532	F
1345	4/15/2000	Helfand	Eric	4601 E. Willow Dr.	Iona	FL	33101-7468	(941) 555-9101	M
1348	5/5/2000	Richards	Melissa	5401 E. Thomas Rd.	Iona	FL	33101-0093	(941) 555-7833	F
1354	7/31/2000	Martinez	Julie	7115 E. Roosevelt Dr.	Iona	FL	33101-0093	(941) 555-1044	F
1359	9/9/2000	Gapasin	Ken	2633 E. Fountain St.	Iona	FL	33101-0093	(941) 555-0589	M
2246	12/15/2000	Hogan	Ryan	1389 E. Northview Dr.	Iona	FL	33101-7468	(941) 555-1010	M

Filtering a datasheet displays only those records meeting the specified conditions.

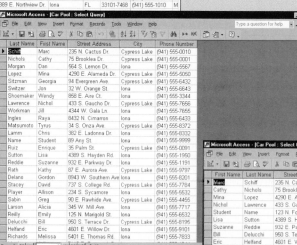

Microsoft Access - [Car Pool : Select Query]

Last Name	First Name	Street Address	City	Phone Number
Schiff	Marc	235 N. Cactus Dr.	Cypress Lake	(941) 555-0010
Nichols	Cathy	75 Brooklea Dr.	Cypress Lake	(941) 555-0001
Morgan	Dan	564 S. Lemon Dr.	Iona	(941) 555-5567
Lopez	Mina	4290 E. Alameda Dr.	Cypress Lake	(941) 555-5050
Sitzman	Georgia	94 Evergreen Ave.	Cypress Lake	(941) 555-6432
Switzer	Jon	32 W. Orange St.	Iona	(941) 555-6643
Shoemaker	Wendy	858 E. Aire Ct.	Iona	(941) 555-3344
Lawrence	Nichol	433 S. Gaucho Dr.	Iona	(941) 555-7656
Workman	Jill	4344 W. Gala Ln.	Iona	(941) 555-7655
Ingles	Raya	8432 N. Cimarron	Iona	(941) 555-6433
Matsumoto	Tyrus	34 S. Onza Ave.	Cypress Lake	(941) 555-8372
Lamm	Chris	382 E. Ladonna Dr.	Iona	(941) 555-8332
Name	Student	89 Any St.	Iona	(941) 555-9999
Ruiz	Enrique	35 Palm St.	Cypress Lake	(941) 555-0091
Sutton	Lisa	4389 S. Hayden Rd.	Iona	(941) 555-1950
Reddie	Suzanne	932 E. Parkway Dr.	Iona	(941) 555-1191
Rath	Kathy	87 E. Aurora Ave.	Cypress Lake	(941) 555-9797
Delano	Gordon	8943 W. Southern Ave	Iona	(941) 555-8201
Stacey	David	737 S. College Rd.	Cypress Lake	(941) 555-7784
Player	Allison	234 S. Sycamore	Iona	(941) 555-5532
Sabin	Greg	90 E. Rawhide Ave.	Cypress Lake	(941) 555-4455
Larson	Alicia	345 W. Mill Ave.	Iona	(941) 555-7717
Reilly	Emily	125 N. Marigold St.	Iona	(941) 555-6532
Delucchi	Bill	950 S. Terrace Dr.	Cypress Lake	(941) 555-8195
Helfand	Eric	4601 E. Willow Dr.	Iona	(941) 555-9101
Richards	Melissa	5401 E. Thomas Rd.	Iona	(941) 555-7833

Record: 1 of 33
Datasheet View

Using a query helps you analyze the information in your database.

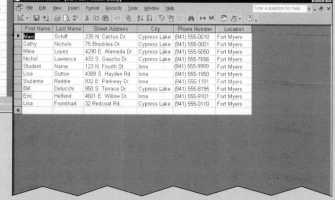

Microsoft Access - [Car Pool : Select Query]

First Name	Last Name	Street Address	City	Phone Number	Location
Marc	Schiff	235 N. Cactus Dr.	Cypress Lake	(941) 555-0010	Fort Myers
Cathy	Nichols	75 Brooklea Dr.	Cypress Lake	(941) 555-0001	Fort Myers
Mina	Lopez	4290 E. Alameda Dr.	Cypress Lake	(941) 555-5050	Fort Myers
Nichol	Lawrence	433 S. Gaucho Dr.	Iona	(941) 555-7656	Fort Myers
Student	Name	123 N. Fourth St.	Iona	(941) 555-9999	Fort Myers
Lisa	Sutton	4389 S. Hayden Rd.	Iona	(941) 555-1950	Fort Myers
Suzanne	Reddie	932 E. Parkway Dr.	Iona	(941) 555-1191	Fort Myers
Bill	Delucchi	950 S. Terrace Dr.	Cypress Lake	(941) 555-8195	Fort Myers
Eric	Helfand	4601 E. Willow Dr.	Iona	(941) 555-9101	Fort Myers
Lisa	Fromthart	32 Redcoat Rd.	Cypress Lake	(941) 555-0110	Fort Myers

A multitable query is the power behind relational databases.

Lifestyle Fitness Club

After modifying the structure of the table of employee records, you have continued to enter many more records. You have also created a second table in the database that contains employee information about location and job titles. Again, the owners are very impressed with the database. They are anxious to see next how the information in the database can be used.

As you have seen, compiling, storing, and updating information in your database is very useful. The real strength of a database program, however, is how it can be used to find the information you need quickly, and manipulate and analyze it to answer specific questions. You will use the information in the tables to provide the answers to several inquiries about the Club employees. As you learn about the analytical features, think what it would be like to do the same task by hand. How long would it take? Would it be as accurate or as well presented? In addition, you will create several reports that present the information from the database attractively.

© Corbis

Filtering Records

Julie Martinez, an employee at the Fort Myers location, is interested in forming a car pool. She recently approached you about finding others who may also be interested. You decide this would be a great opportunity to see how you can use the employee table to find this information. To find the employees, you could sort the table and then write down the needed information. This could be time consuming, however, if you had hundreds of employees in the table. A faster way is to apply a filter to the table records to locate this information.

concept 1

Filter

1 A **filter** is a restriction placed on records in the open datasheet or form to quickly isolate and display a subset of records. A filter is created by specifying a set of limiting conditions, or **criteria**, which you want records to meet in order to be displayed. A filter is ideal when you want to display the subset for only a brief time and then return immediately to the full set of records. You can print the filtered records as you would any form or table. A filter is only temporary, and all records are redisplayed when you remove the filter or close and reopen the table or form. The filter results cannot be saved. However, the last filter criteria you specify are saved with the table, and the results can be quickly redisplayed.

You have continued to enter employee records into the "Employees" table. The updated table has been saved for you as Employees in the Personnel Records database. Before you begin filtering records, you need to open the current database.

1 ● **Start Access.**

● **Open the**
ac03_Personnel Records
database file.

*Your screen should be
similar to Figure 3.1*

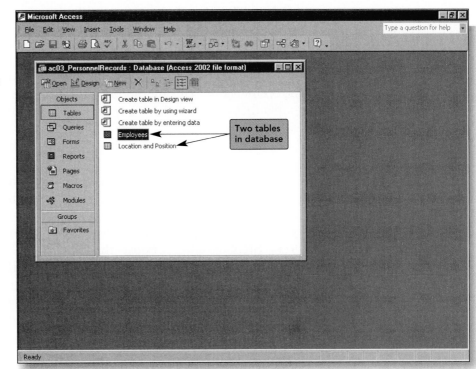

Figure 3.1

The tables list box of the Database window displays the names of two tables
in this database: Employees, and Location and Position. These tables will
be used throughout the lab.

2 ● **Open the "Employees"
table.**

● **Maximize the
datasheet window.**

● **Add your information
as record number 80
using your special ID
number 9999 and your
name. Enter 2/25/97
as your hire date, city
as Iona, and zip code
as 33101-7468. Fill in
the remaining fields as
desired.**

Additional Information

You can copy the zip code
from another record that has
Iona as the city.

● **Return to the first field
of the first record.**

*Your screen should be
similar to Figure 3.2*

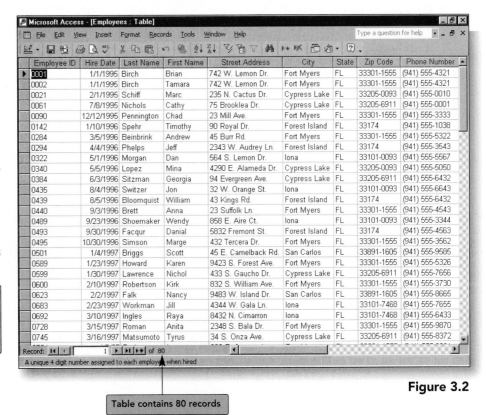

Table contains 80 records

Figure 3.2

Using Filter by Selection

Julie lives in Iona, and wants to find others who work at the same location and live in Iona. You can do this for her quite easily by using the Filter by Selection method. **Filter by Selection** displays only records containing a speccific value. This method is effective when there is only one value in the table that you want Access to use as the criterion for selecting and displaying records.

How the value is selected determines what results will be displayed. Placing the insertion point in a field selects the entire field contents. The filtered subset will include all records containing an exact match. Selecting part of a value in a field (by highlighting it) displays all records containing the selection. For example, in a table for a book collection, you could position the mouse pointer anywhere in a field containing the name of the author Stephen King, choose the Filter by Selection command, and only records for books whose author matches the selected name, "Stephen King," would be displayed. Selecting just "King" would include all records for authors Stephen King, Martin Luther King, and Barbara Kingsolver.

You want to filter the table to display only those records with a City field entry of Iona. To specify the city to locate, you need to select an example of the data in the table.

> **Additional Information**
>
> If the selected part of a value starts with the first character in the field, the subset displays all records with values that begin with the same selected characters.

- ① ● **Move to the City field of record 9.**

  ● **Click** ▼ **Filter by Selection.**

> **Another Method**
>
> The menu equivalent is Records/Filter/Filter by Selection.

Your screen should be similar to Figure 3.3

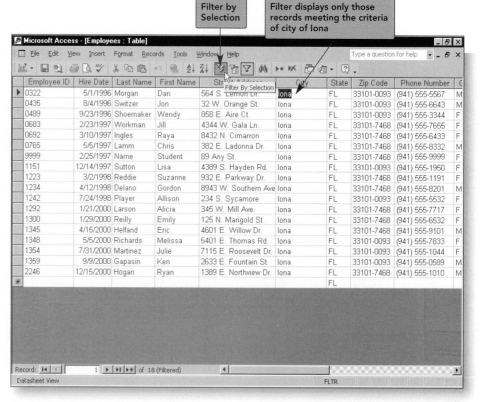

Figure 3.3

The datasheet displays only those records that contain the selected city. All other records are temporarily hidden. The status bar indicates the total number of filtered records (18) and shows that the datasheet is filtered.

After seeing how easy it was to locate this information, you want to locate employees who live in Cypress Lake. This information may help in setting up the car pool, because the people traveling from the city of Iona pass through Cypress Lake on the way to the Fort Myers location. Before creating the new filter, you will remove the current filter and return the table to its full display.

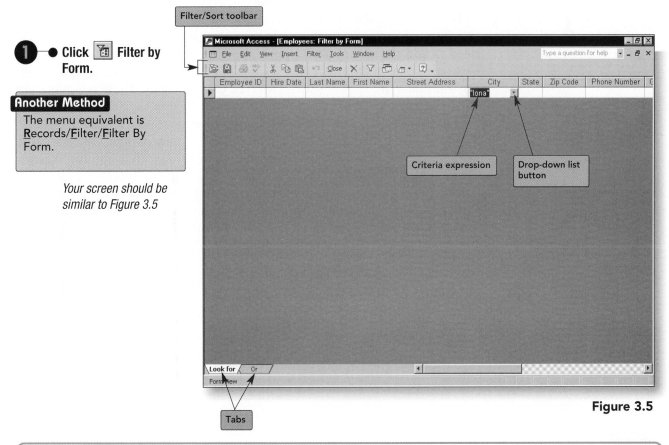

2 ● Click ▽ **Remove Filter.**

Your screen should be similar to Figure 3.4

Figure 3.4

Using Filter by Form

The **Filter by Form** method allows you to perform filters on multiple criteria. In this case, you want to filter the employee data by two cities, Iona and Cypress Lake.

1 ● Click 🖼 **Filter by Form.**

Your screen should be similar to Figure 3.5

Figure 3.5

The Filter by Form window displays a blank version of the current datasheet with empty fields in which you specify the criteria. Notice that at the bottom of the Filter by Form window there are two tabs, Look For and Or. In the Look For tab, you enter the first filter criterion you want to use, and in the Or tab, you enter additional filter criteria. You want to filter the records on one field, City, with an initial criterion of Iona and a second criterion of Cypress Lake.

Also notice that the Filter/Sort toolbar displays several standard buttons as well as buttons specific to filtering records (identified in the following illustration).

To tell Access what specific data you want it to use for the filter criteria, you enter values in the blank field spaces of the record row as criteria expressions. A **criteria expression** is an expression that will select only the records that meet certain limiting criteria. You can create the criteria expression by either typing a value directly in its corresponding field or selecting a value from a drop-down list.

Currently the Look For tab is active and the City field displays "Iona," which is the criterion you specified when you did the Filter by Selection. Notice that the field displays a drop-down list button. Each field has a drop-down button when the field is selected. Clicking this button displays a list of values that are available in that field. You can use this list to select values and build a criteria expression, if necessary.

You do not need to select a different value for the initial criterion because the City field already contains the correct value (Iona). However, you do need to add the second criterion to the filter to include all records with a City field value of Cypress Lake. To instruct the filter to locate records meeting multiple criteria, you use the AND or OR operators. These operators are used to specify multiple conditions that must be met for the records to display in the filter datasheet. The **AND operator** narrows the search, because a record must meet both conditions to be included. The **OR operator** broadens the search, because any record meeting either condition is included in the output.

The AND operator is assumed when you enter criteria in multiple fields. Within a field, typing the word "and" between criteria in the same field establishes the AND condition. The OR operator is established by entering the criterion in the Or tab, or by typing "or" between criteria in the same field.

In this filter, you will use an OR operator so that records meeting either city criterion will be included in the output. To include the city as an OR criterion, you enter the criterion in the Or tab.

2 ● Click the Or tab.

A value must be entered in the Look For tab before the Or tab is available (active). Then, each time you click the Or tab, another Or tab is added to the window to enable you to enter more filter criteria. Again, a value must be entered in each Or tab before the next Or tab is actually available for use (active).

Your screen should be similar to Figure 3.6

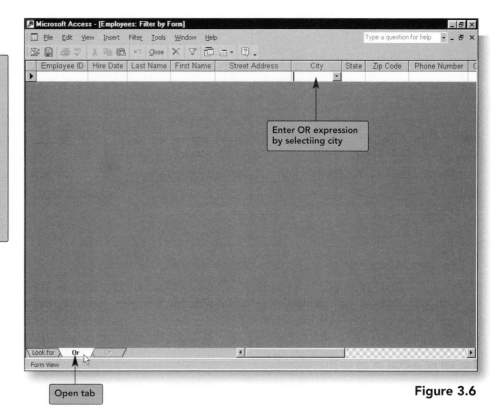

Figure 3.6

The Or tab is opened, and a new blank row is displayed. You will enter this criteria expression by selecting the criterion from the City drop-down list.

3 ● From the City field drop-down list, select Cypress Lake.

You could have typed "Cypress Lake" directly in the City field instead of selecting it from the drop-down list.

Your screen should be similar to Figure 3.7

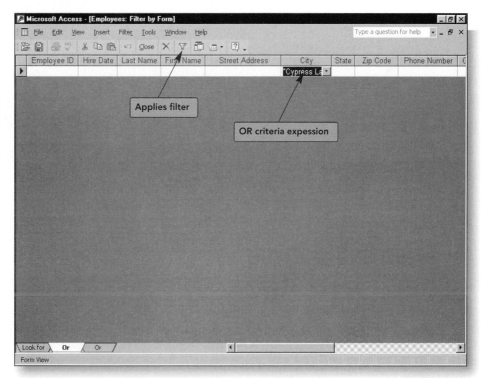

Figure 3.7

The selected criterion is displayed in the City field surrounded by quotes, as required of all text entries used in an expression, and the Look For tab still contains the criterion for the city of Iona. You can now apply the filter.

Click ▽ **Apply Filter.**

Another Method

The menu equivalent is Filter/Apply Filter/Sort.

Your screen should be similar to Figure 3.8

> Filtered database displays only records with a city of Iona or Cypress Lake

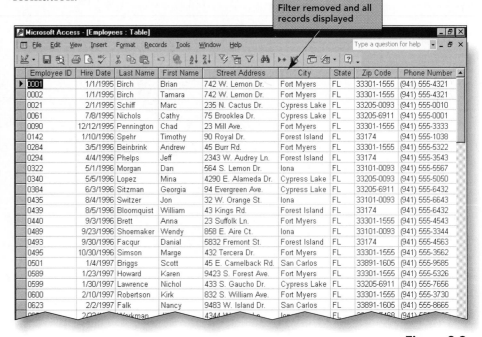

> Number of records meeting filter criteria

Figure 3.8

The filtered datasheet displays the records for all 33 employees who live in the city of Iona or Cypress Lake. After seeing this, you realize that it contains more information about each employee than someone would need (or should even have access to) in order to form a car pool. You decide to remove the filter and try a different method to gather only the necessary information.

Click ▽ **Remove Filter.**

Additional Information

▽ is a toggle button that applies and removes a filter. The filter criteria you last specified are stored with the table, and the results can be redisplayed simply by applying the filter with ▽ again.

Click 🖫 **Save to save the changes you've made to the "Employees" table.**

Your screen should be similar to Figure 3.9

> Filter removed and all records displayed

Figure 3.9

Querying a Database

To obtain exactly the information you need to give Julie for her car pool, you will use a query.

concept 2

Query

2 A **query** is a request for specific data contained in a database. Queries are used to view data in different ways, to analyze data, and even to change existing data. Because queries are based on tables, you can also use a query as the source for forms and reports. The five types of queries are described in the following table.

Query Type	Description
Select query	Retrieves the specific data you request from one or more tables, then displays the data in a query datasheet in the order you specify. This is the most common type of query.
Crosstab query	Summarizes large amounts of data in an easy-to-read, row-and-column format.
Parameter query	Displays a dialog box prompting you for information, such as criteria for locating data. For example, a parameter query might request the beginning and ending dates, then display all records matching dates between the two specified values.
Action query	Makes changes to many records in one operation. There are four types of action queries: a make-table query creates a new table from selected data in one or more tables; an update query makes update changes to records, such as when you need to raise salaries of all sales staff by 7 percent; an append query adds records from one or more tables to the end of other tables; and a delete query deletes records from a table or tables.
SQL query	Created using SQL (Structured Query Language), an advanced programming language used in Access.

Creating a query in Access is much the same as creating a table or a form. You can either create a new query from the Database window by selecting the Queries object and the creation method you want to use, or you can create a new query from within an open table. Because you already have the "Employees" table open, you will use the second method this time.

1 From the [icon] New Object drop-down list, choose **Q**uery.

Your screen should be similar to Figure 3.10

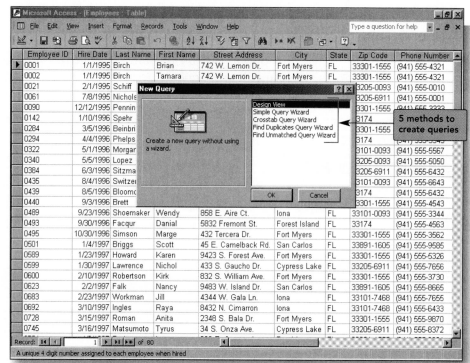

5 methods to create queries

Figure 3.10

The New Query dialog box contains five options for creating queries. You can create a query from scratch in Query Design view or by using one of the four query Wizards. The following table explains the type of query that each of the Wizards creates.

Query Wizard	Type of Query Created
Simple	Select query
Crosstab	Crosstab query
Find Duplicates	Locates all records that contain duplicate values in one or more fields in the specified tables.
Find Unmatched	Locates records in one table that do not have records in another. For example, you could locate all employees in one table who have no hours worked in another table.

Using a Query Wizard

You decide that you want to try the Simple Query Wizard and create a select query to see if it gives you the results you want.

1 Select Simple Query Wizard.

● Click [OK].

Your screen should be similar to Figure 3.11

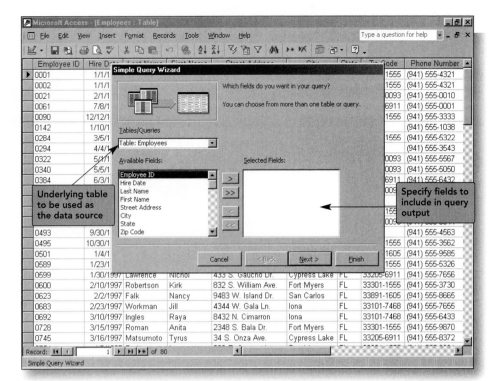

Figure 3.11

In the first Simple Query Wizard dialog box, you specify the underlying table and the fields from the table that will give you the desired query result, just as you did when creating a form. You will use data from the "Employees" table, which is already selected. You need to select the fields you want displayed in the query output.

2 ● Add the Last Name, First Name, Street Address, City, and Phone Number fields to the Selected Fields list.

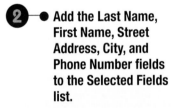

Additional Information

The quickest way to add a field to the Selected Fields list is to double-click its field name in the Available Fields list.

Your screen should be similar to Figure 3.12

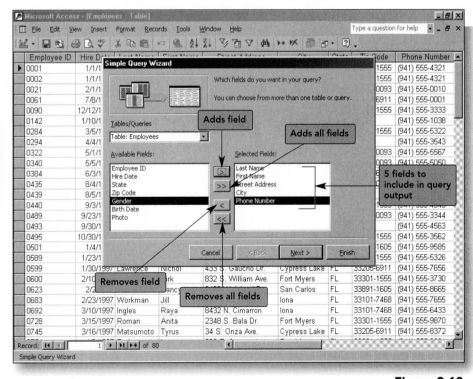

Figure 3.12

After you have selected all the fields that you want to include in your query, you can move on to the next step in the simple query creation.

 **Click** Next > .

Your screen should be similar to Figure 3.13

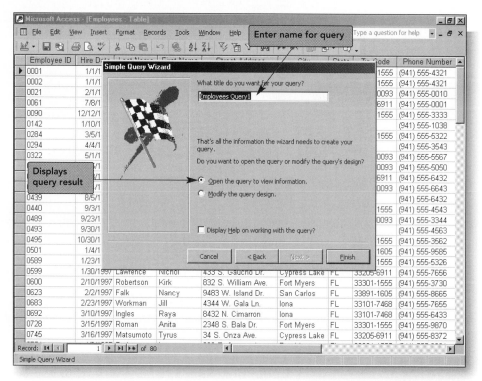

Figure 3.13

In the second Simple Query Wizard dialog box, you specify a name for your query, and whether you want to open it as is or in Design view so you can modify it. You can also have Access display Help messages while you are working on your query by clicking the corresponding box at the bottom of this Wizard screen. You decide that you just want to display the query results, and you want to give the query a name that will identify its purpose.

 **Replace the suggested title in the text box with Car Pool.**

Click Finish .

Your screen should be similar to Figure 3.14

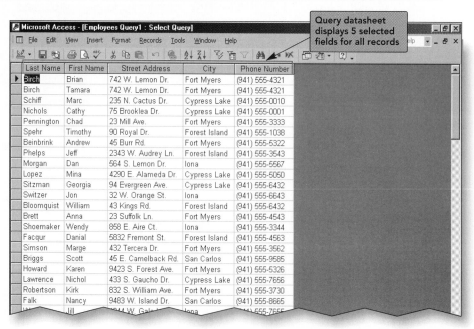

Figure 3.14

The result of the query is displayed in a **query datasheet**. In this case, the query datasheet displays only the five specified fields for all records in the table. Query Datasheet view includes the same menus and toolbar buttons as in Table Datasheet view.

Moving Columns

The order of the fields in the query datasheet reflects the order they were placed in the Selected Fields list. You can still change the display order of the fields by moving the columns to where you want them. To move a column, you first select it and then drag it to its new location.

For the car pool list, there is no reason for the last name to be listed first, so you decide to move the Last Name column to follow the First Name column.

Additional Information
Changing the column order in the query datasheet does not affect the field order in the table, which is controlled by the table design.

1 ● **Select the Last Name column.**

HAVING TROUBLE?
Remember, to select an entire column, you click on its column heading (which in this case, is Last Name) when the mouse pointer is a ↓.

● **Click and hold the mouse button on the Last Name column heading.**

Additional Information
When the mouse pointer is a ▨, it indicates you can drag to move the selection.

● **Drag the Last Name column to the right until a thick black line is displayed between the First Name and Street columns.**

● **Release the mouse button.**

● **Click anywhere in the table to clear the selection.**

Additional Information
You can move fields in Table Datasheet view in the same way.

Your screen should be similar to Figure 3.15

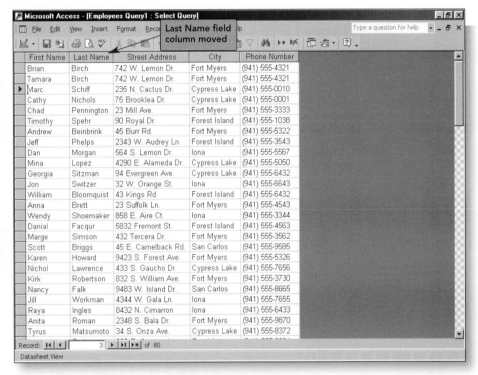

Figure 3.15

Although the query result displays only the fields you want to see, it displays all the employee records in the database. You need to modify the query to include only the records for employees who live in Iona or Cypress Lake.

Modifying a Query

To modify a query to display only selected records, you specify the criteria in the Query Design view window.

① ● **Click** [icon] ▾ **View to switch to the Query Design view.**

Another Method

The menu equivalent is View/Design View.

Your screen should be similar to Figure 3.16

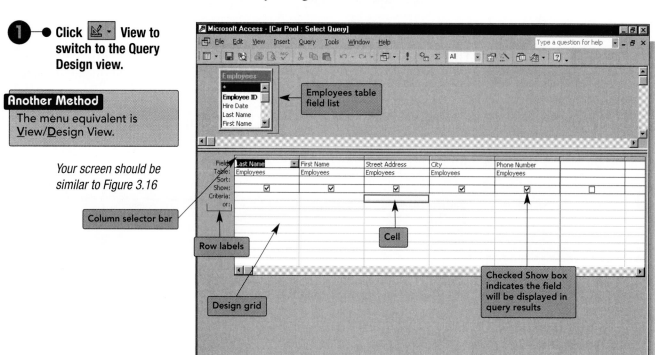

Figure 3.16

Query Design view is used to create and modify the structure of the query. This view automatically displays the Query Design toolbar, which contains the standard buttons as well as buttons (identified below) that are specific to the Query Design view window.

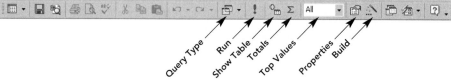

The Query Design window is divided into two areas. The upper area displays a list box of all the fields in the selected table. This is called the **field list**. The lower portion of the window displays the **design grid**. This is where you enter the settings that define the query. Each column in the grid holds the information about each field to be included in the query datasheet. The design grid automatically displays the fields that are specified when a query is created using a Query Wizard.

Above the field names is a narrow bar called the **column selector bar**. It is used to select an entire column. Each **row label** identifies the type of information that can be entered. The intersection of a column and row creates a **cell**. This is where you enter expressions to obtain the query results you need.

The boxes in the Show row are called **Show boxes**. The Show box for a field lets you specify whether you want that field displayed in the query result. A checked box indicates that the field will be displayed; no check means that it will not.

The Criteria row contains the criteria expression (field value or values) and a comparison operator.

The first thing you want to do in this query is locate and display only those records where the city is Iona. In the Criteria row of the City column, you first need to enter a criteria expression to select only those records.

Additional Information

Refer to Lab 2 for a review of expressions and operators.

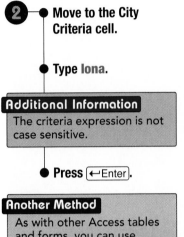

2 ● **Move to the City Criteria cell.**

● **Type Iona.**

Additional Information

The criteria expression is not case sensitive.

● **Press** ←Enter.

Another Method

As with other Access tables and forms, you can use ←Enter, Tab↹, and the arrow keys to move from cell to cell in the Query design grid.

Additional Information

Because you want Access to include all records with a city of Iona, you don't need to enter = (equal to), as it is the assumed comparison operator.

Your screen should be similar to Figure 3.17

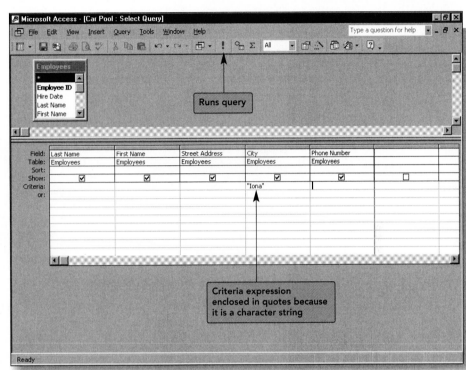

Figure 3.17

The expression is enclosed in quotes because it is a character string. To display the query results, you run the query.

3 ● Click ▣ **Run.**

The menu equivalent is
Query/Run. You can also click
▣▾ Datasheet View to run
the query and display the
query datasheet.

*Your screen should be
similar to Figure 3.18*

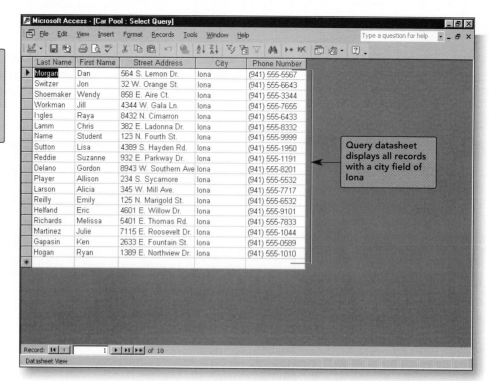

Query datasheet
displays all records
with a city field of
Iona

Figure 3.18

The query datasheet displays only those records meeting the city criterion.
This is the same result as the first simple-query filter you used, except that
it displays only the specified fields.

Next, you will add a second criterion to include Cypress Lake in the result. As with filters, the AND and OR operators are used to combine criteria. If the results must meet both of the specified criteria for a field, this
condition is established by typing the word "and" in a field's Criteria cell as
part of its criteria expression. If the results can meet either of the specified
criteria, this is established by entering the first criteria expression in the
first Criteria cell for the field, and the second expression in the Or cell for
the same field.

Because you want to display the records for employees who live in either
city, you will enter this as an Or condition.

4 ● **Switch to Query
Design view.**

● **In the Or cell of the
City column, type
Cypress Lake.**

● **Press ⏎Enter.**

*Your screen should be
similar to Figure 3.19*

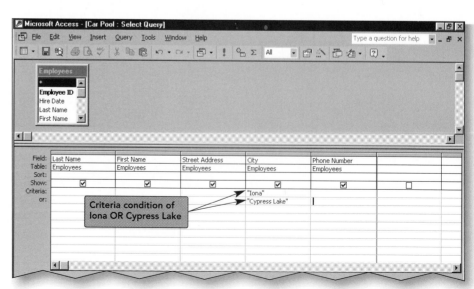

Criteria condition of
Iona OR Cypress Lake

Figure 3.19

"Cypress Lake" is now set as the Or condition, and you are ready to run the query.

5 — Click ! Run.

Additional Information
If an expression is entered incorrectly, an informational box that indicates the source of the error will be displayed when the query is run.

Your screen should be similar to Figure 3.20

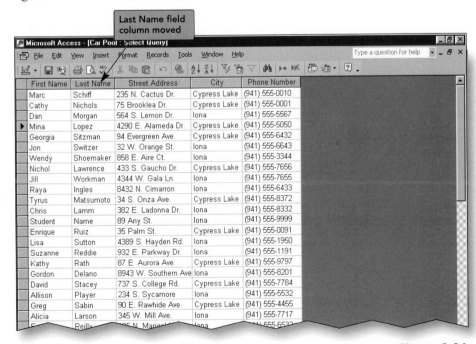

Query datasheet displays all records with a City field of Iona or Cypress Lake

Figure 3.20

The query located 33 records in which the employee met the specified criteria. Notice that the fields are again in the order in which they appear in the design grid, which is not the most convenient way to look at them for your purposes. You will switch the Last Name and First Name columns again.

Last Name field column moved

6 — Move the Last Name column after the First Name column.

— Deselect the column.

Your screen should be similar to Figure 3.21

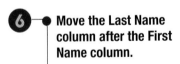

Figure 3.21

While you are working on the car pool query, Brian, the Club owner, stops in and asks if you can find some information quickly for him. Because you plan to continue working on the car pool query later, you will save the query so you do not have to recreate it. This is another advantage of queries over filters. Filters are temporary, whereas queries can be permanently saved with the database.

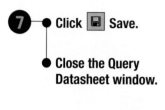

7 ● Click 🖫 Save.

● **Close the Query Datasheet window.**

Your screen should be similar to Figure 3.22

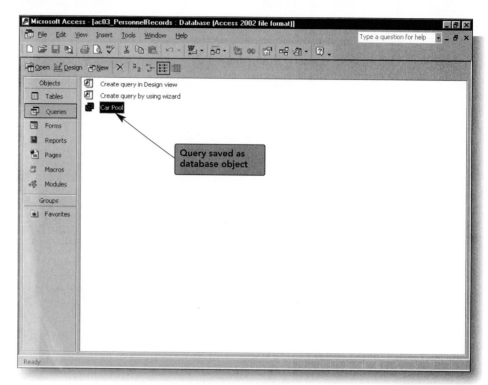

Query saved as database object

Figure 3.22

The query name, "Car Pool," is displayed in the queries list.

Creating a Query in Design View

In January, 2002, the Club celebrates its 10-year anniversary. Brian is planning an anniversary celebration party that month and wants to use the occasion to presnt 3-year and 5-year service awards. He needs to know how many employees are in each category so that he can order the correct number of awards. To help Brian locate these employees, you will create a new query. You decide to create the query directly in Query Design view this time, rather than using a Query Wizard.

1 ● **Double-click Create query in Design view.**

● **If necessary, open the tables tab.**

Your screen should be similar to Figure 3.23

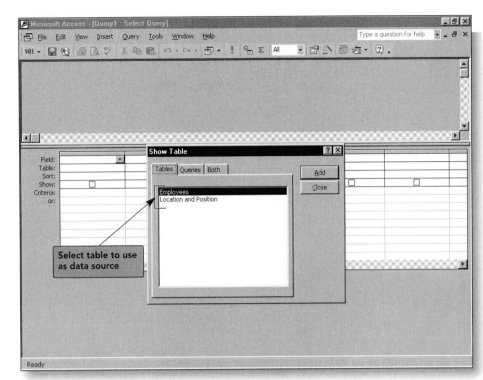

Figure 3.23

The Query Design window is open with the Show Table dialog box open on top of it. The dialog box is used to specify the underlying table or query to use to create the new query. The three tabs—Tables, Queries, and Both—contain the names of the existing tables and queries that can be used as the information source for the query. You need to add the "Employees" table to the query design.

2 ● **In the Tables tab, select the "Employees" table (if it is not already selected).**

● **Click** [Add].

Another Method

You can also double-click the table name to add it to the query design.

● **Click** [Close].

● **If necessary, maximize the Query Design window.**

Your screen should be similar to Figure 3.24

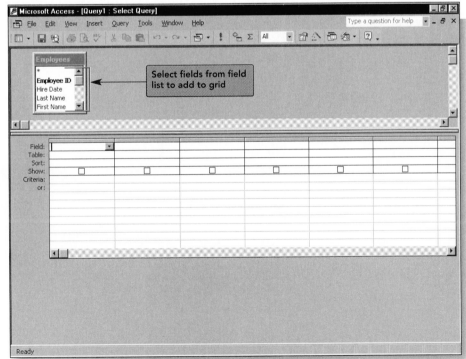

Figure 3.24

A field list for the selected table appears above the design grid. From the field list, you need to add the fields to the grid that you want to use in the query. You can use the following methods to add fields to the design grid:

- Select the field name and drag it from the field list to the grid. To select several adjacent fields, press ⬆Shift while you click the field names. To select nonadjacent fields, pressing Ctrl while clicking the field names. To select all fields, double-click the field list title bar. You can then drag all the selected fields into the grid, and Access will place each field in a separate column.

- Double-click on the field name. The field is added to the next available column in the grid.

- Select the Field cell drop-down arrow in the grid, then choose the field name.

In addition, if you select the asterisk in the field list and add it to the grid, Access displays the table or query name in the field row followed by a period and asterisk. This indicates that all fields in the table will be included in the query results. Using this feature also will automatically include any new fields that may later be added to the table, and will exclude deleted fields. You cannot sort records or specify criteria for fields, however, unless you also add those fields individually to the design grid.

The fields you want to add to the grid for this query are Hire Date, First Name, and Last Name.

3 ● **Double-click Hire Date in the field list to add it to the grid.**

● **Add the First Name field and the Last Name field to the grid, in that order.**

Your screen should be similar to Figure 3.25

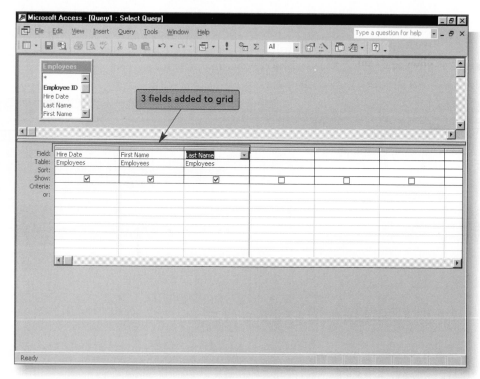

Figure 3.25

Now that you have set up the fields you want to include in this query, you can start entering the criteria that each field must meet to be included in the query results. First, you want to locate all employees who have at least 3 years with the Club. To do this you will use the < and = operators to include all records with a hire of 1/1/99 or earlier.

4 • **In the Hire Date Criteria cell, type <=1/1/99.**

• **Press ←Enter.**

Your screen should be similar to Figure 3.26

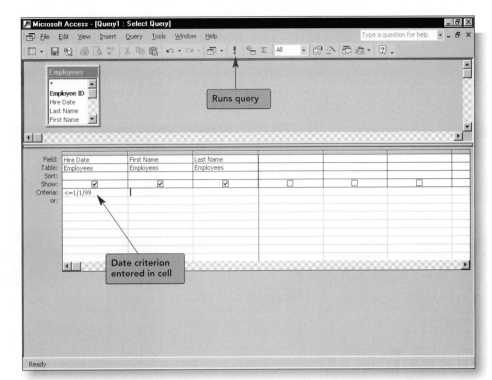

Figure 3.26

The expression appears in the cell as <=#1/1/1999#. Access adds # signs around the date to identify the values in the expression as a date. You decide to run the query to see the results.

5 • **Click ! Run.**

Your screen should be similar to Figure 3.27

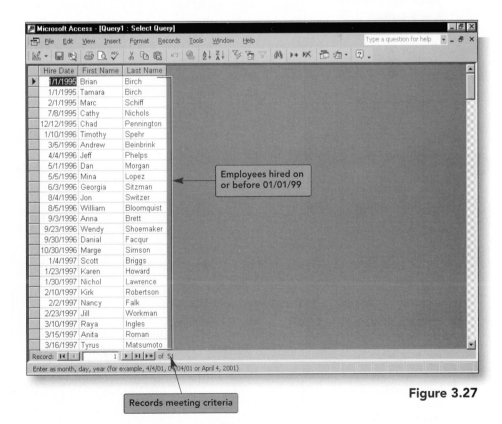

Figure 3.27

The query datasheet displays only those records meeting the date criterion. The record number indicator of the query datasheet shows that 50 employees were hired by January 1999. However, what you really want to find out are those employees who have 3 or more years of service, but less than 5 years. You will refine the search to locate just these employees.

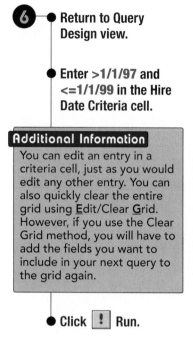

6 ● **Return to Query Design view.**

● **Enter >1/1/97 and <=1/1/99 in the Hire Date Criteria cell.**

Additional Information

You can edit an entry in a criteria cell, just as you would edit any other entry. You can also quickly clear the entire grid using Edit/Clear Grid. However, if you use the Clear Grid method, you will have to add the fields you want to include in your next query to the grid again.

● **Click** ! **Run.**

Your screen should be similar to Figure 3.28

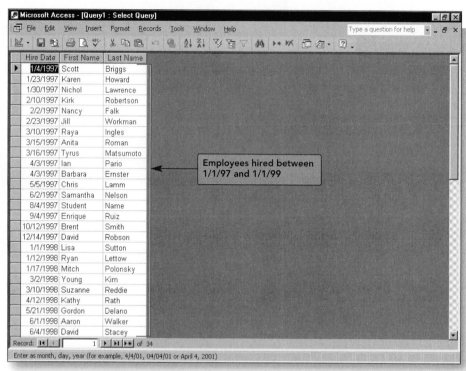

Figure 3.28

The number of employees with at least 3 but less than 5 years with the club is 33. These are the employees who are eligible for the 3-year service awards. You will print out this datasheet for Brian and save the query in case you need it again.

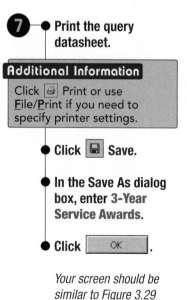

7 ● **Print the query datasheet.**

Additional Information

Click 🖨 Print or use File/Print if you need to specify printer settings.

● **Click** 🖫 **Save.**

● **In the Save As dialog box, enter 3-Year Service Awards.**

● **Click** OK .

Your screen should be similar to Figure 3.29

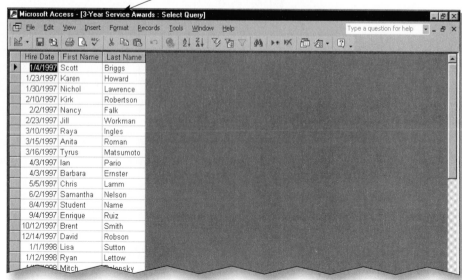

Figure 3.29

For the next level of awards that Brian wants to give out, you need to find the employees with more than 5 years of service.

8 ● **Return to Query Design view and enter <=1/1/97 in the Hire Date Criteria cell.**

● **Run the query.**

Your screen should be similar to Figure 3.30

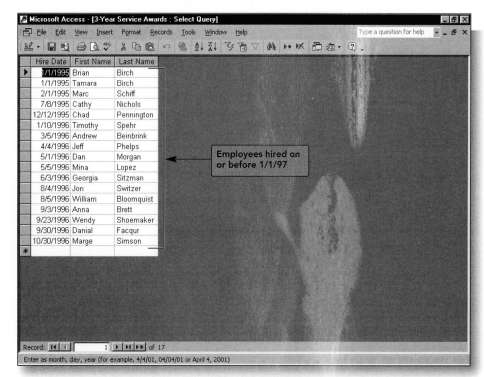

Figure 3.30

The query results show that there are 17 employees who have been with the club for at least 5 years and are eligible for the 5-year service award. You can now print and save this query.

9 ● **Print the query datasheet.**

● **Choose File/Save As and save the query as 5-Year Service Awards.**

● **Close the Query Datasheet.**

Your screen should be similar to Figure 3.31

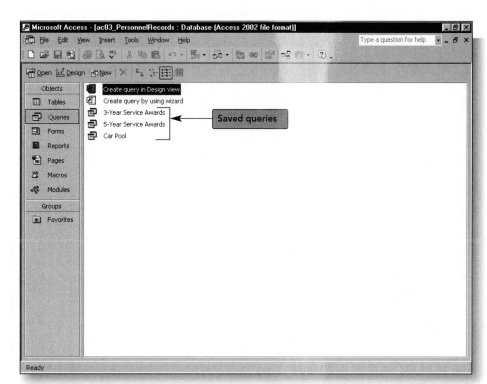

Figure 3.31

The two new queries you saved are listed in the queries object list box. Having provided Brian with the answers he needed, you are ready to get back to work on the car pool query.

Querying Two Tables

The car pool list would be more helpful if it had only the people that work at the Fort Myers location. Because the "Employees" table does not contain this information, you will need to create a query using the information from two tables to get these results. A query that uses more than one table is called a **multitable query**. To bring together two tables in a query, you create a join between the tables.

concept 3

Join

3   A **join** is an association between a field in one table or query and a field of the same data type in another table or query. Joining tables enables you to bring information from different tables in your database together or to perform the same action on data from more than one table. The capability to join tables is what makes relational databases so powerful.

   In order to be joined, the tables must have at least one common field. **Common fields** are of the same data type and contain the same kind of information, but they can have different field names.

   The following diagram shows an example of how, when the Employee ID fields of two tables are joined, a query can be created using data from both tables to provide the requested information.

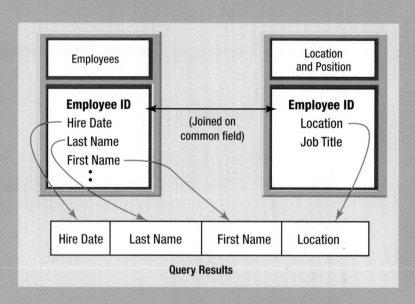

The location information for each employee is in a table named "Location and Position."

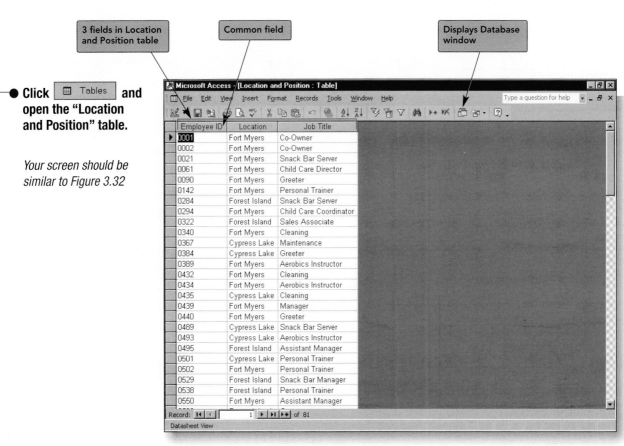

Figure 3.32

The "Location and Position" table contains three fields of data for each employee: Employee ID, Club Location, and Job Title. The Employee ID field is the primary key field and is the common field between the two tables. To display the information on the Fort Myers employees, you need to create a query using information from this table and from the Employees table.

As a starting point, you will open the "Car Pool" query you already created and saved.

2 ● Click  Database Window.

● From the queries object list, open the "Car Pool" query.

● Switch to Query Design view and maximize the window.

● Click  Show Table.

Your screen should be similar to Figure 3.33

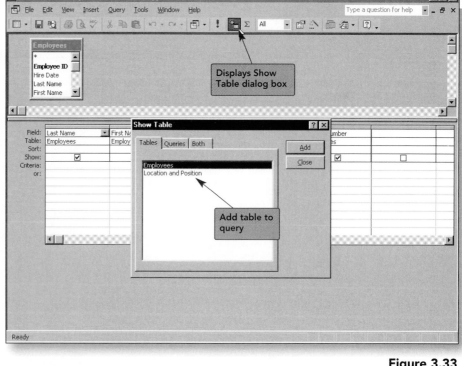

Figure 3.33

From the Query Design window, you need to select the name of the table you want to add to the query.

3 ● On the Tables tab, select "Location and Position."

● Click  Add .

● Close the Show Table dialog box.

Your screen should be similar to Figure 3.34

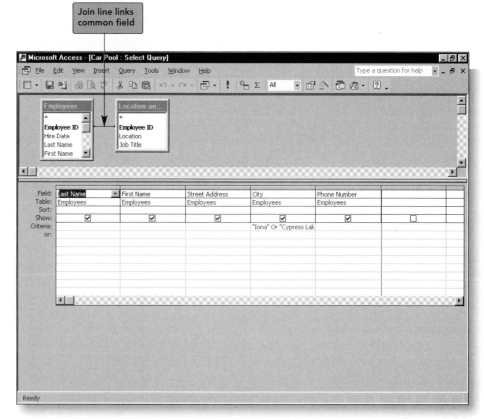

Figure 3.34

The field list for the second table is added to the Query Design window. The **join line** between the two field lists tells Access how the data in those tables are related. When you add multiple tables to a query, Access automatically joins the tables based on the common fields if one of the common fields is a primary key. This is the default join. If the common fields have different names, however, Access does not automatically create the join. Instead, you can create the join manually by dragging from one common field to the other. In this case, the join line indicates that the two tables have been temporarily joined with Employee ID as the common field.

Next you need to add the fields to the grid that you want to use in the query.

4 • **Add the Location field to the design grid.**

• **To specify the location criterion, type the expression Fort Myers in the Location Criteria cell.**

• **Press ⏎Enter.**

Your screen should be similar to Figure 3.35

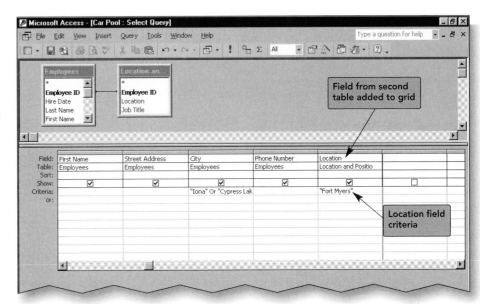

Figure 3.35

This is the only criterion that you need to add to your car pool query, so you can go ahead and display the results.

5 • **Run the query.**

Your screen should be similar to Figure 3.36

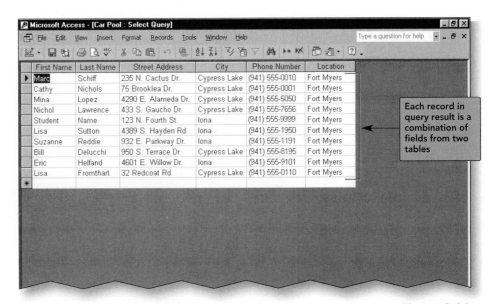

Figure 3.36

The query result shows there are 14 employees who live in either Iona or Cypress Lake and work at the Fort Myers location. Each record in the query result datasheet includes information from both tables. This is because of the type of join used in the query. There are three types of joins:

Join Type	Description
Inner join	Checks records for matching values and when it finds matches, combines the records and displays them as one record in the query results.
Outer join	Each matching record from two tables is combined into one record in the query results. One table contributes all of its records even if the values in its joined field do not match the field values in the other table.
SQL join	Records to be included in the query results are based on the value in one join field being greater than, less than, not equal to, greater than or equal to, or less than or equal to the value in the other join field.

In a query, the default join type is an inner join. In this case, it checked for matching values in the Employee ID fields, combined matching records, and displayed them as one record in the query result.

Next you want to sort the query datasheet by City and Last Name.

6 ● **Move the City column to the left of the Last Name column.**

● **Select the City and Last Name columns.**

● **Click** 🔼 **Sort Ascending.**

● **Move the City column back to its original location, after the Street Address column.**

● **Deselect the City column.**

Your screen should be similar to Figure 3.37

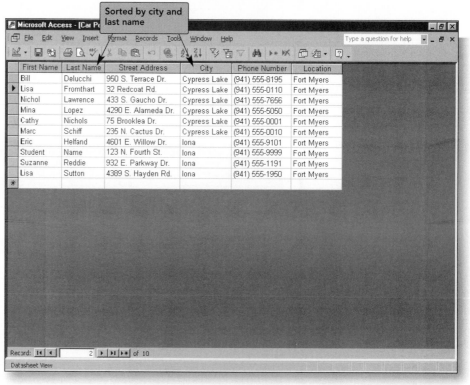

Figure 3.37

This is exactly what you need to give Julie for her car pool, so you decide to print and save the data.

7 ● Print the table.

● Close the query, saving your changes.

● Close the "Location and Position" table.

Your screen should be similar to Figure 3.38

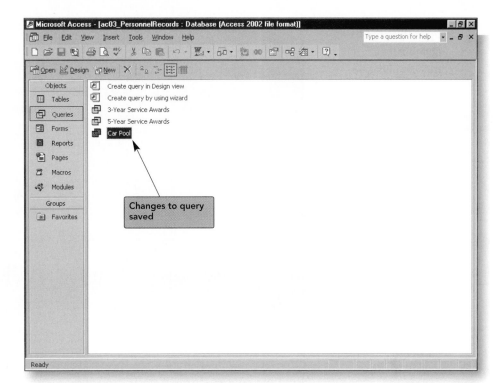

Figure 3.38

Note: If you are running short on time, this is an appropriate point to end your Access session. When you begin again, open the ac03_Personnel Records database.

Creating Reports

Brian showed Tami the printout you gave him of the employees who will get service awards. She sees many uses for the information generated by Access, including the ability to quickly analyze information in the database. As a start, she has asked you to create an address report for all employees sorted by name. You have already created and printed several simple reports using the Print command on the File menu. This time, however, you want to create a custom report of this information.

concept 4

Report

4 A **report** is printed output generated from tables or queries. It might be a simple listing of all the fields in a table, or it might be a list of selected fields based on a query. Access also includes a custom report feature that enables you to create professional-appearing reports. The custom report is a document that includes text formats, styles, and layouts that enhance the display of information. In addition, you can group data in reports to achieve specific results. You can then display summary information, such as totals, by group to allow the reader to further analyze the data. Creating a custom report displays the information from your database in a more attractive and meaningful format.

You will create the address list report using the data in the "Employees" table.

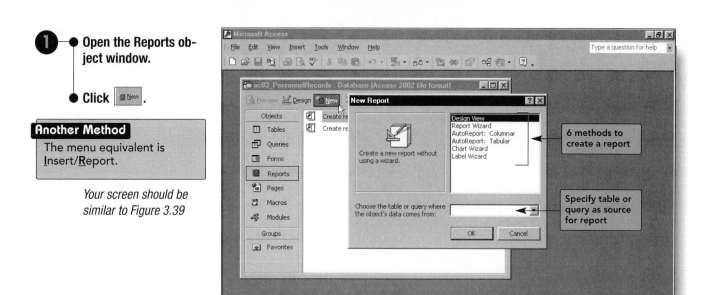

1 ● Open the Reports object window.

● Click [New].

Another Method

The menu equivalent is Insert/Report.

Your screen should be similar to Figure 3.39

Figure 3.39

The New Report dialog box presents six ways to create a report. You can create a report from scratch in Design view, or by using the Report Wizard or one of the AutoReport Wizards. The Report Wizard lets you choose the fields to include in the report and helps you quickly format and lay out the new report. The AutoReport Wizard creates a report that displays all fields and records from the underlying table or query in a predesigned report layout and style.

Using the AutoReport Wizard

You decide to use the AutoReport Wizard to create a columnar report using data in the "Employees" table.

1 ● Select AutoReport: Columnar.

● Select "Employees" from the table selection drop-down list.

● Click [OK].

Your screen should be similar to Figure 3.40

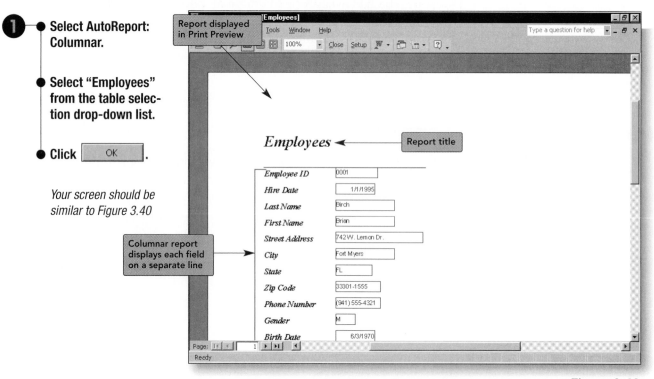

Figure 3.40

HAVING TROUBLE?

Your report may be displayed
with a different style. This is
because when creating an
AutoReport, Access
remembers the last
AutoReport style used on
your machine, then applies
that same style to the new
report. If the AutoReport
command has not been used,
the report will use the basic
style. You will learn how to
change styles later in this lab.

After a few moments, the report is created and displayed in the Print
Preview window. The AutoReport Wizard creates a columnar report that
displays each field on a separate line in a single column for each record.
The fields are in the order they appear in the table. The report appears in a
predefined report style and layout. The report style shown in Figure 3.40
uses the table name as the report title and includes the use of text colors,
various typefaces and sizes, and horizontal lines and boxes.

Just as you can in Table, Form, and Datasheet views, you can use the navigation tools and navigation buttons to move through the pages of a report.

2 ● Click on the page to
change the magnifica-
tion to Fit.

Another Method

The menu equivalent is
View/Zoom/Fit to Window.

*Your screen should be
similar to Figure 3.41*

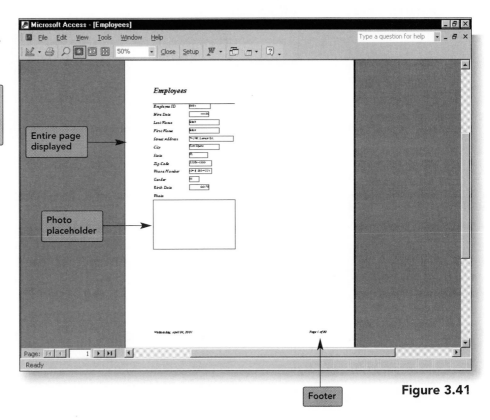

Figure 3.41

Now the entire page is visible, and although most of the text is too small to
read, you can see the entire page layout. The box is a placeholder for the
employee photo. The current date and page number appear at the bottom
of the page in the footer.

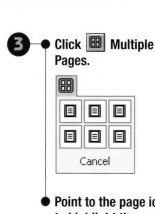

3 ● **Click** **Multiple Pages.**

● **Point to the page icons to highlight the number of pages to display and click when the menu indicates 2×3 pages are selected.**

Your screen should be similar to Figure 3.42

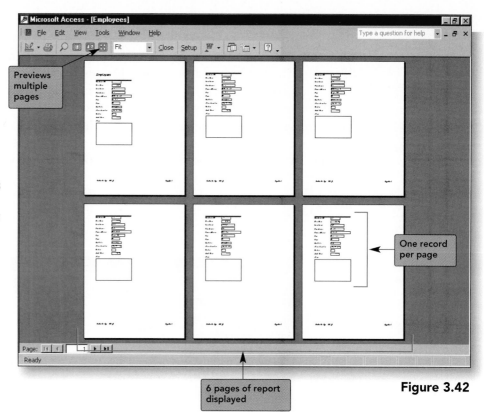

Figure 3.42

The window now displays six pages of your report (two rows of three pages each, or 2×3).

After looking over the columnar report, you decide the layout is inappropriate for your report, because only one record is printed per page. In addition, you do not want the report to include all the fields from the table. So you will close this report file without saving it, and then create a different type of report that better suits your needs.

Additional Information

The View/Pages command can be used to display up to 12 pages, and the button can be used to display up to 20 pages of a report in the window.

4 ● **Click** ☒ **Close.**

HAVING TROUBLE?

Do not click Close on the toolbar. This closes the Print Preview window, but does not close the report window.

● **Click** No .

Your screen should be similar to Figure 3.43

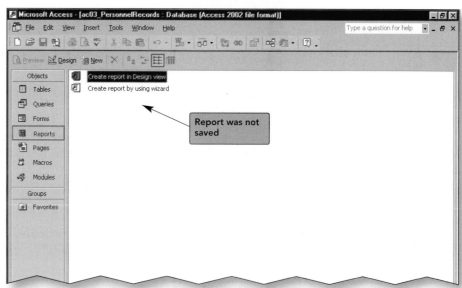

Figure 3.43

Using the Report Wizard

You want the report to display the field contents for each record on a line rather than in a column. You will use the Report Wizard to create this type of report.

1 • In the Reports object window, select Create report by using wizard.

Your screen should be similar to Figure 3.44

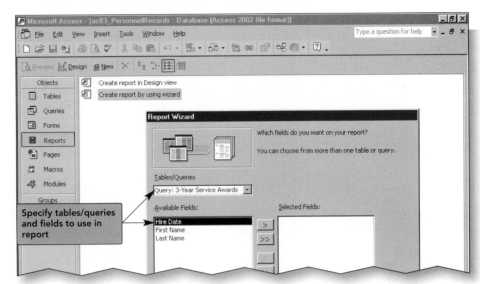

Figure 3.44

The Report Wizard consists of a series of dialog boxes, much like the Form and Query Wizards. As with those Wizards, in the first dialog box you specify the table or query to be used in the report and add the fields you want included.

2 • Select Table: "Employees" from the Tables/Queries drop-down list.

• Add the First Name field to the Selected Fields list.

• Then add the Last Name, Street Address, City, State, Zip Code, and Phone Number fields in that order.

Additional Information

A report does not have to include all the fields from the table or query that is used to create it.

Your screen should be similar to Figure 3.45

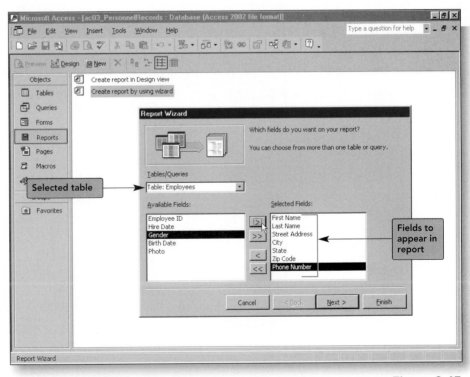

Figure 3.45

All the fields that you want included on the report are now displayed in the Selected Fields list, and you can go on to the next Wizard step.

3 ● Click [Next >].

*Your screen should be
similar to Figure 3.46*

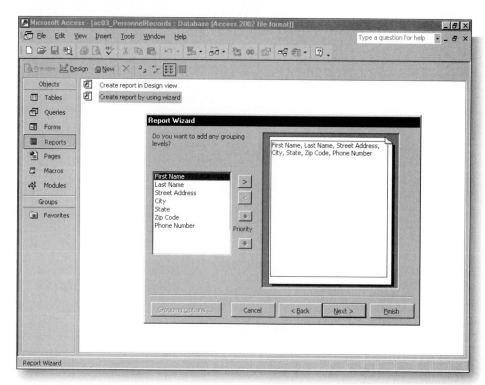

Figure 3.46

In the second Report Wizard dialog box, you specify how to group the data
in the report. Tami does not want the report grouped by any category, so
you do not need to do anything in this dialog box.

4 ● Click [Next >].

*Your screen should be
similar to Figure 3.47*

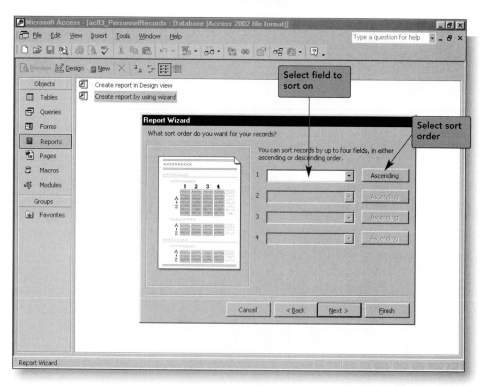

Figure 3.47

This dialog box is used to specify a sort order for the records. A report can
be sorted on up to four fields. You want the report sorted in ascending
order by last name and first name within same last names.

- **Select the Last Name field from the number 1 drop-down list**

- **Select the First Name field from the number 2 drop-down list.**

Additional Information

You can click [Ascending] to change the sort order to descending. Alternately, when the current sort order is descending, the button displays [Descending], and you can click it to change to ascending sort order.

Your screen should be similar to Figure 3.48

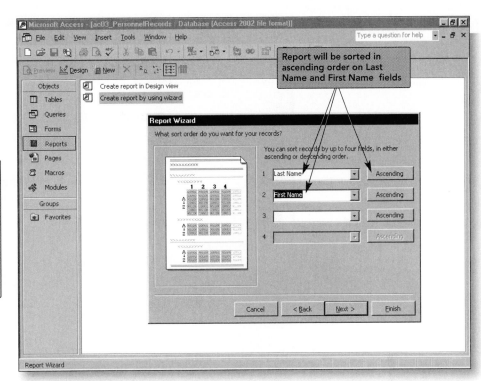

Figure 3.48

The sort fields and order are set and you can go on to the next Wizard step.

- **Click** [Next >].

Your screen should be similar to Figure 3.49

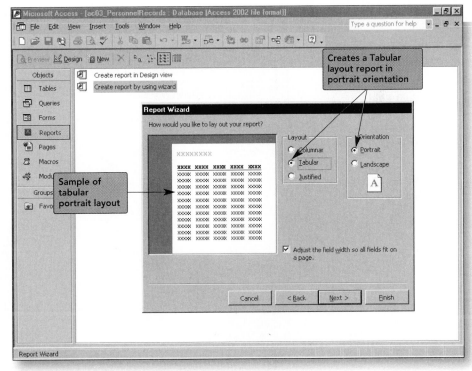

Figure 3.49

This dialog box is used to change the report layout and orientation. The default report settings create a tabular layout using portrait orientation. In addition, the option to adjust the field width so all fields fit on one page is selected. Because this report is only five columns, the default settings are acceptable.

7 ● Click [Next >] .

Your screen should be similar to Figure 3.50

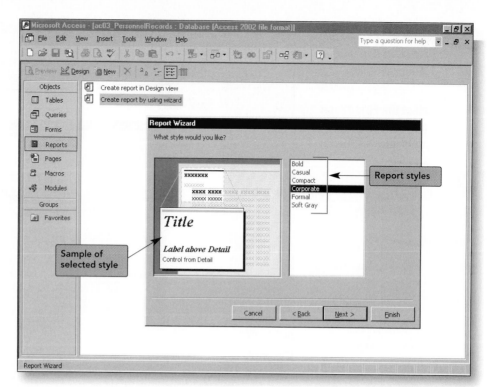

Figure 3.50

From this dialog box you select a style for the report. The preview area displays a sample of each style as it is selected.

8 ● Select each style to preview the style options.

● Select Bold.

● Click [Next >] .

Your screen should be similar to Figure 3.51

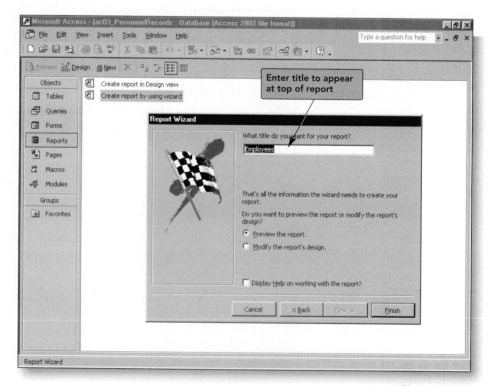

Figure 3.51

The last Report Wizard dialog box is used to add a title to the report and to specify how the report should be displayed after it is created. The only change you want to make is to replace the table name with a more descriptive report title.

9 ● **Type Employee Address Report.**

● **Click** [Finish].

Your screen should be similar to Figure 3.52

Field names

Tabular report in Bold style

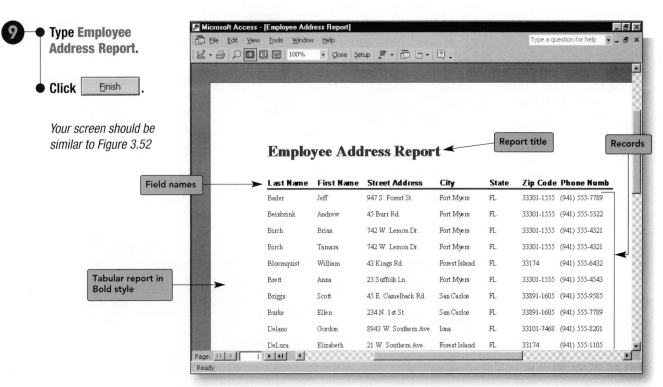

Report title

Records

Employee Address Report

Last Name	First Name	Street Address	City	State	Zip Code	Phone Numb
Bader	Jeff	947 S. Forest St.	Fort Myers	FL	33301-1555	(941) 555-7789
Beinbrink	Andrew	45 Burr Rd.	Fort Myers	FL	33301-1555	(941) 555-5322
Birch	Brian	742 W. Lemon Dr.	Fort Myers	FL	33301-1555	(941) 555-4321
Birch	Tamara	742 W. Lemon Dr.	Fort Myers	FL	33301-1555	(941) 555-4321
Bloomquist	William	43 Kings Rd.	Forest Island	FL	33174	(941) 555-6432
Brett	Anna	23 Suffolk Ln.	Fort Myers	FL	33301-1555	(941) 555-4543
Briggs	Scott	45 E. Camelback Rd.	San Carlos	FL	33891-1605	(941) 555-9585
Burke	Ellen	234 N. 1st St.	San Carlos	FL	33891-1605	(941) 555-7789
Delano	Gordon	8943 W. Southern Ave.	Iona	FL	33101-7468	(941) 555-8201
DeLuca	Elizabeth	21 W. Southern Ave.	Forest Island	FL	33174	(941) 555-1105

Figure 3.52

The program takes a minute to generate the report, during which time Report Design view is briefly displayed. In a few moments, the completed report with the data from the underlying table is displayed in the Print Preview window in the selected Bold report style. The report title reflects the title you specified using the Wizard. The names of the selected fields are displayed on the first line of the report, and each record appears on a separate row below the field names. Notice that the Last Name field is the first field, even though you selected it as the second field. This is because the sort order overrides the selected field order.

Modifying the Report Design

You like the layout of this report, but you still want the Last Name field to follow the First Name field. You also notice that the Phone Number field name is cut off, so you need to change it so it displays correctly. To make these changes, you need to modify the report design.

1 ● Click [icon] ▾ View to switch to Report Design view.

Your screen should be similar to Figure 3.53

Toolbox toolbar

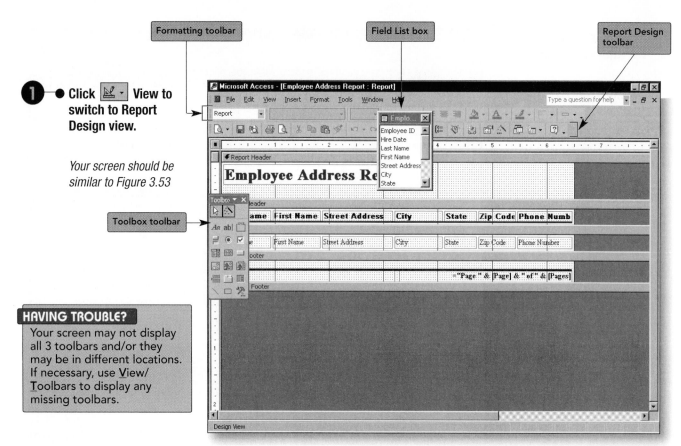

Figure 3.53

The Report Design view is used to create and modify the structure of a report. This view displays three toolbars: Report Design, Formatting, and Toolbox. The Report Design toolbar contains the standard buttons as well as buttons that are specific to the Report Design view window. The Formatting toolbar contains buttons that allow you to make text enhancements. The Toolbox toolbar buttons are used to add and modify report design objects.

In order to have an unobstructed view of and work with the report design, you will move the Toolbox toolbar and close the Employees Field List.

Additionally, the Field List box containing the field names from the "Employees" table may be displayed. The Field List can be used to quickly add additional fields to the report.

Additional Information

Use View/Field List or [icon] to hide and display the Field List.

Additional Information

You can also use View/Toolbox or click [icon] to hide and display.

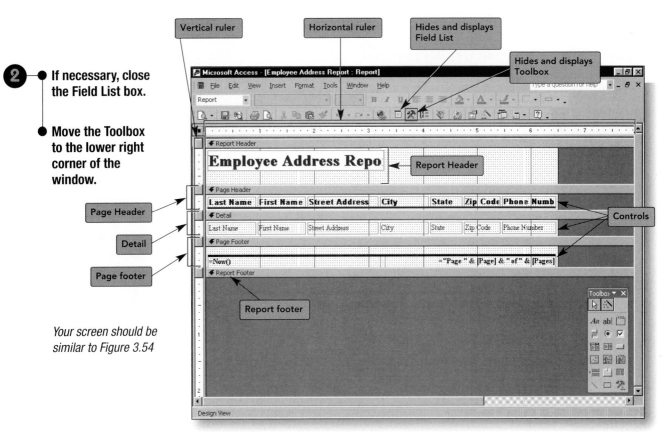

2 • If necessary, close the Field List box.

• Move the Toolbox to the lower right corner of the window.

Your screen should be similar to Figure 3.54

Figure 3.54

The report's contents are displayed in a window that is bordered along the top by a horizontal ruler and along the left by a vertical ruler. These rulers help you correctly place items within the window.

The Report Design window is divided into five sections: Report Header, Page Header, Detail, Page Footer, and Report Footer. The contents of each section appear below the horizontal bar that contains the name of that section. The sections are described in the following table.

Section	Description
Report Header	Contains information to be printed once at the beginning of the report. The report title is displayed in this area.
Page Header	Contains information to be printed at the top of each page. The column headings are displayed in this section.
Detail	Contains the records of the table. The field column widths are the same as the column widths set in the table design.
Page Footer	Contains information to be printed at the bottom of each page, such as the date and page number.
Report Footer	Contains information to be printed at the end of the report. The Report Footer section currently contains no data.

All of the information in a report is contained in boxes, called controls. You make changes to your report design by working with these controls.

concept 5

Controls

5   **Controls** are objects on a form or report that display information, perform actions, or enhance the design. Access provides controls for many types of objects, including labels, text boxes, check boxes, list boxes, command buttons, lines, rectangles, option buttons, and more.

There are two basic types of controls: bound and unbound. A **bound control** is linked to a field in an underlying table. An example of a bound control is a text box that creates a link to the underlying source (usually a field from a table) and displays the field entry in the report or form. An **unbound control** is not connected to a field. Examples of unbound controls are labels, which can be taken from the underlying table associated with a text box or customized with descriptive titles or user instructions. Other unbound controls contain elements that enhance the appearance of the form, such as lines, boxes, and pictures. A text box can also be an unbound control if it is used for user input or to display calculation results.

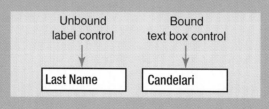

Selecting Controls

Additional Information

You select controls in Form Design view using the same methods you will be learning here.

In this report design, the label controls are displayed in the Page Header section, and the text box controls are in the Detail section. You need to select the Last Name and First Name controls in order to modify their order.

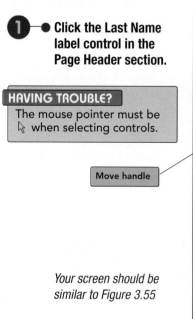

1 ● Click the Last Name label control in the Page Header section.

HAVING TROUBLE?
The mouse pointer must be ⌖ when selecting controls.

Your screen should be similar to Figure 3.55

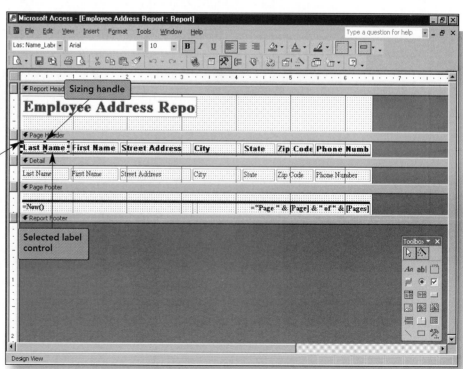

Figure 3.55

The Last Name label control is surrounded by eight small boxes called **sizing handles** that indicate the label control is selected. The sizing handles are used to size the control. In addition, a large box in the upper left corner is displayed. This is a **move handle** that is used to move the selected control.

You also want to select the Last Name text box control.

● Hold down ⇧ Shift and click the **Last Name** text box control in the Detail section.

Your screen should be similar to Figure 3.56

Label and text box controls selected

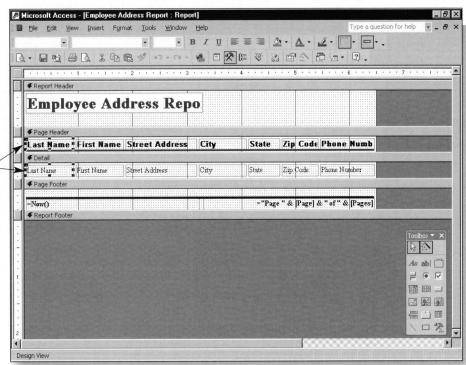

Figure 3.56

Now both controls are selected. Once controls are selected, they can be moved and sized.

Moving Controls

You want to move the Last Name controls to the right of the First Name controls. Controls can be moved to any location in the Report design by dragging them to the new location. The mouse pointer changes to a ✋ shape to indicate that a selected control can be moved. The grid of dots helps you position the controls on the form. It not only provides a visual guide to positioning and sizing controls, but controls are "snapped" to the grid, or automatically positioned on the nearest grid line.

Because you need to swap positions of the two fields, you will first move the Last Name controls to the right, and then you will move the First Name controls to the left.

1 • **Drag the Last Name controls to the right so the right edge of the control is at the 2½" ruler position. (They should not completely obscure the First Name controls, which you will need to select and move next.)**

HAVING TROUBLE?
Do not point to a sizing handle when dragging the control to move it, as this will size the controls.

• **Select both First Name controls and drag them to the left edge of the grid.**

• **Select the Last Name controls again and drag them to between the First Name and Street Address controls.**

Your screen should be similar to Figure 3.57

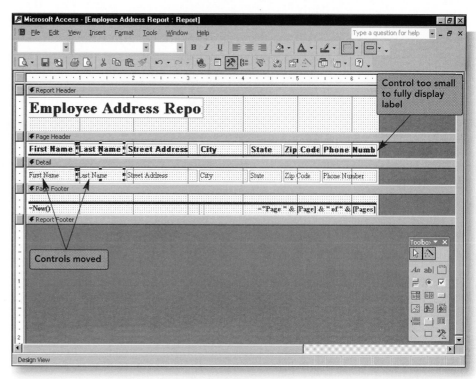

Figure 3.57

Sizing Controls

Next you will increase the size of the Phone Number label control. When you position the mouse pointer on a sizing handle, it changes to a ↔. The direction of the arrow indicates in which direction dragging the mouse will alter the shape of the object. This is similar to sizing a window.

1 • **Select the Phone Number label control in the Page Header section.**

• **Point to the middle handle on the right end of the selected control.**

• **When the mouse pointer appears as ↔, drag the control to the right just until the entire field label is displayed.**

Additional Information
The right edge of the form will automatically increase as you increase the size of the control.

Your screen should be similar to Figure 3.58

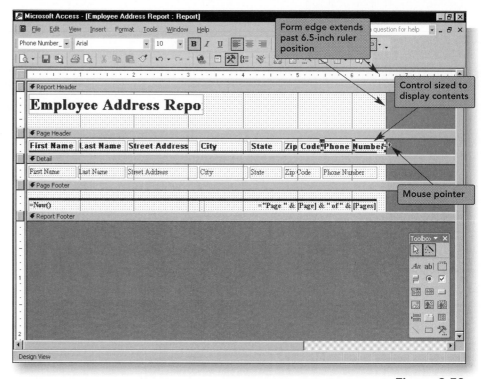

Figure 3.58

Printing a Report

When you are making a lot of design changes to a report, it is a good idea to periodically check how the printed output will look. If you need to make further adjustments, you can return to Design view. Other adjustments can be made using the print page setup options.

Changing Page Margins

You want to preview how the first few pages of the report will appear when printed.

1 ● Click  Print Preview.

● Display three pages of the report.

Your screen should be similar to Figure 3.59

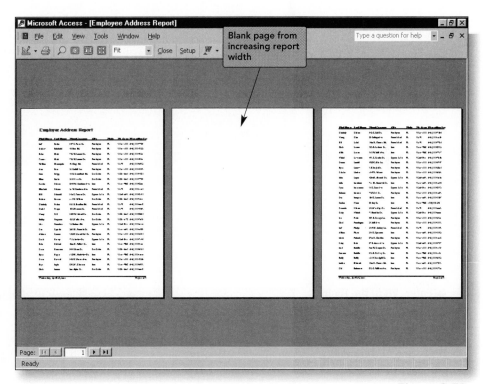

Figure 3.59

A blank page is displayed between the first and third page. This is because as you increased the size of the Phone Number label, the overall report width increased, making it too large to fully display across the width of the page using the default margin settings. The **margin** is the blank space around the edge of a page. You will decrease the right margin to allow the extra space needed to print the width of the report across the page.

2 ● Click Setup .

● **If necessary, open the Margins tab.**

Your screen should be similar to Figure 3.60

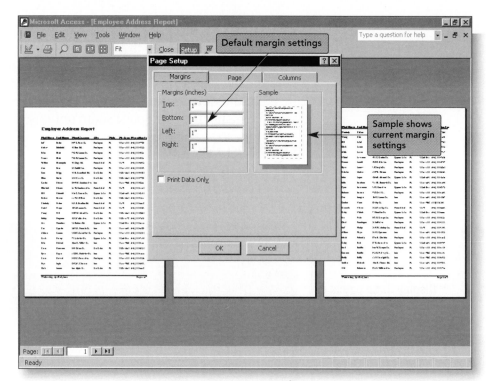

Figure 3.60

The default margin settings are 1 inch on all sides of the page. You will decrease the right margin to .75 inch. The sample will adjust to reflect the change as you enter it.

3 ● **Enter .75 in the Right text box.**

● Click OK .

Your screen should be similar to Figure 3.61

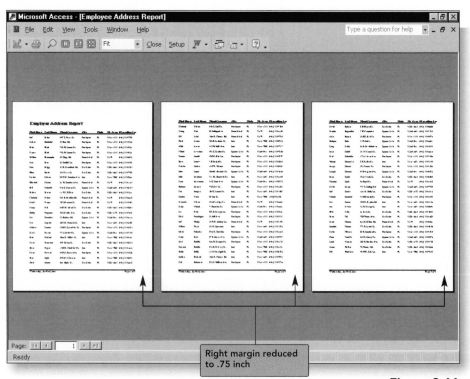

Figure 3.61

Now, everything looks good to you.

Printing a Selected Page

You decide to print out only one page and get Tami's approval before printing the entire report. Just like you can with a table or form, you can print all of the report or only specified pages. You are going to print the page containing your record.

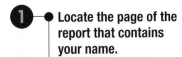

● **Locate the page of the report that contains your name.**

Additional Information

The page number is displayed in the page indicator box. You can use the navigational keys on either side of this box to move from page to page.

● **Choose File/Print.**

Additional Information

The 🖨 Print button prints the entire report.

● **If necessary, select the appropriate printer for your system.**

● **Select Pages.**

Additional Information

The page number is displayed in the page indicator box.

● **Type the page number containing your record in the From and To text boxes.**

Your screen should be similar to Figure 3.62

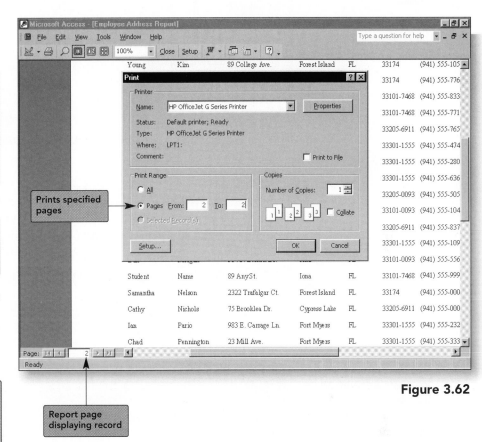

Figure 3.62

Prints specified pages

Report page displaying record

The page you want to print is now specified, and you are ready to send it to the printer.

2 ● Click OK .

● Close the Report window, saving the changes you have made.

Your screen should be similar to Figure 3.63

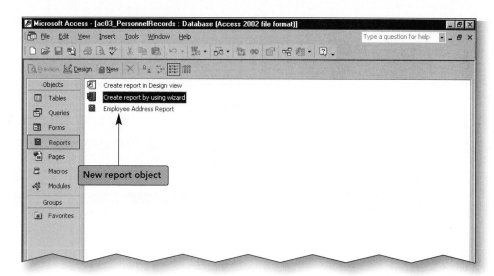

Figure 3.63

The Database window is displayed again, and the report object name is listed in the reports object list. The Report Wizard automatically saves the report using the report title as the object name.

Creating a Report from a Query

You have seen how easy it is to create a report from a table, so you would like to create a report from the "Car Pool" query.

1 ● Use the Report Wizard to create a report based on the "Car Pool" query using the following specifications:

● Include all fields except Location.

● Sort on City first, then Last Name and First Name.

● Select a Tabular layout.

● Use the Casual style.

● Title the report **Iona to Fort Myers Car Pool Report.**

When the Wizard finishes creating the report, your screen should be similar to Figure 3.64

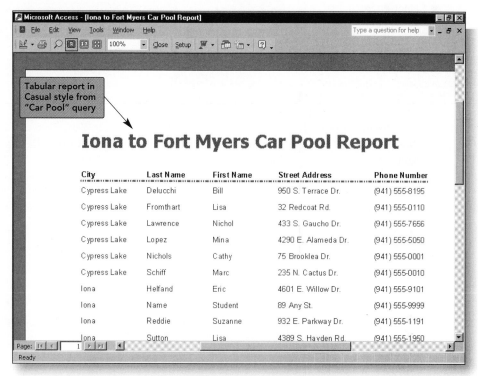

Figure 3.64

You will now do a little quick design work on this report and print it out.

2
- Use Report Design view to change the field order to First Name, Last Name, Street Address, City, and Phone Number order.

- Save the report.

- Preview, and then print the report.

Your completed Car Pool report should look like that shown here.

Iona to Fort Myers Car Pool Report

First Name	Last Name	Street Address	City	Phone Number
Bill	Delucchi	950 S. Terrace Dr.	Cypress Lake	(941) 555-8195
Lisa	Fromthart	32 Redcoat Rd.	Cypress Lake	(941) 555-0110
Nichol	Lawrence	433 S. Gaucho Dr.	Cypress Lake	(941) 555-7656
Mina	Lopez	4290 E. Alameda Dr.	Cypress Lake	(941) 555-5050
Cathy	Nichols	75 Brooklea Dr.	Cypress Lake	(941) 555-0001
Marc	Schiff	235 N. Cactus Dr.	Cypress Lake	(941) 555-0010
Eric	Helfand	4601 E. Willow Dr.	Iona	(941) 555-9101
Suzanne	Reddie	932 E. Parkway Dr.	Iona	(941) 555-1191
Name	Student	89 Any St.	Iona	(941) 555-3333
Lisa	Sutton	4389 S. Hayden Rd.	Iona	(941) 555-1950

Thursday, April 05, 2001   Page 1 of 1

Compacting the Database

As you modify a database, the changes are saved to your disk. When you delete data or objects, the database file can become fragmented and use disk space inefficiently. To make the database perform optimally, you should **compact** the database on a regular basis. Compacting makes a copy of the file and rearranges how the file is stored on your disk.

1
- Choose **T**ools/**D**atabase Utilities/**C**ompact and Repair Database.

- Close the database and exit Access.

LAB 3

Analyzing Data and Creating Reports

Filter (AC3.4)

A filter is a restriction placed on records in the open datasheet or form to temporarily isolate and display a subset of records.

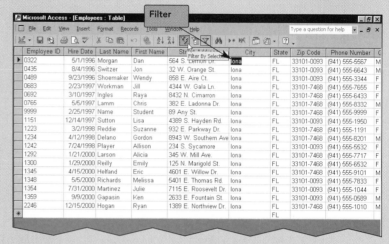

Query (AC3.11)

A query is a request for specific data contained in a database. Queries are used to view data in different ways, to analyze data, and even to change existing data.

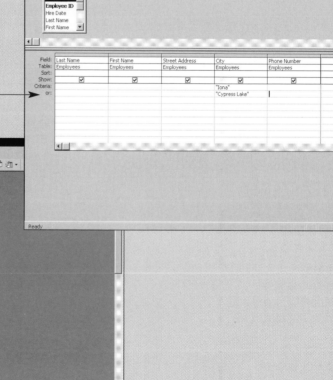

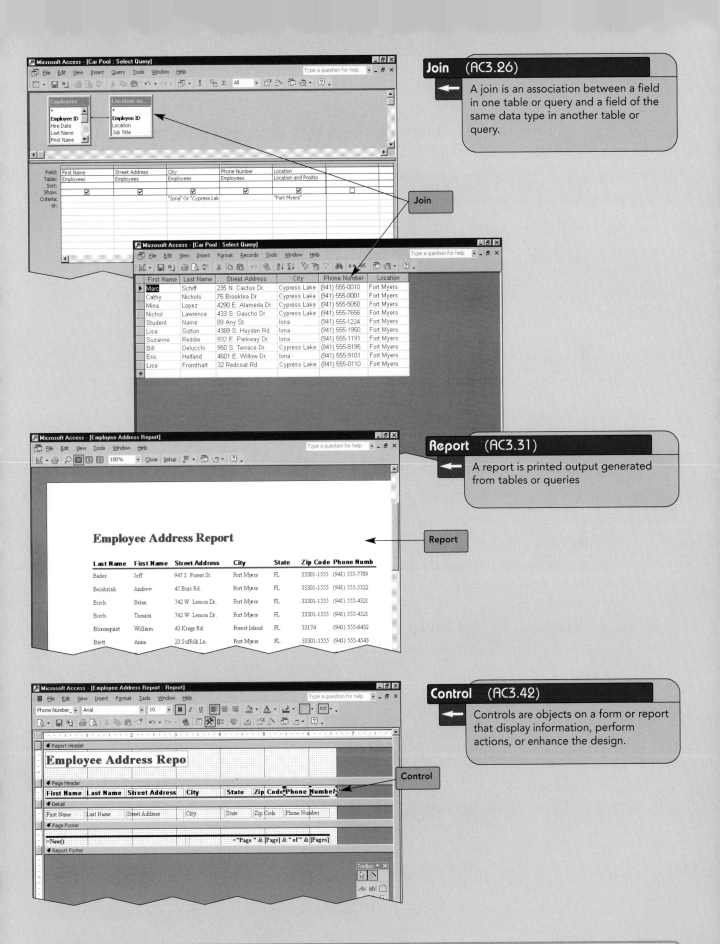

Join (AC3.26)

A join is an association between a field in one table or query and a field of the same data type in another table or query.

Join

Report (AC3.31)

A report is printed output generated from tables or queries

Report

Control (AC3.42)

Controls are objects on a form or report that display information, perform actions, or enhance the design.

Control

key terms

mous skills

The Microsoft Office User Specialist (MOUS) certification program is designed to measure your proficiency in performing basic tasks using the Office XP applications. Getting certified demonstrates that you have the skills and provides a valuable industry credential for employment. After completing this lab, you have learned the following Access 2002 Microsoft Office User Specialist skills:

Skill	Description	Page
Creating and Using Databases	Open datase objects in multiple views	AC3.16, AC3.39
Creating and Modifying Queries	Create and modify Select queries	AC3.12
Viewing and Organizing Information	Create queries	AC3.11
	Sort records	AC3.30, AC3.36
	Filter records	AC3.4
Producing Reports	Create and format reports	AC3.31
	Preview and print reports	AC3.45

Command	Button	Action
Edit/Clear Grid		Clears query grid
Insert/Report	New	Creates a new report object
View/Design View		Displays Design View window
View/Zoom/Fit to Window		Displays entire previewed page
View/Pages		Displays specified number of pages of previewed report
View/Toolbox		Displays/hides Toolbox
Records/Filter/Filter by Form		Displays blank datasheet for entering criteria to filter database to display specific information
Records/Filter/Filter by Selection		Displays only records that contain the same value as in the selected field
Tools/Database Utilities/Compact and Repair Database		Compacts and repairs database file
Filter/Apply Filter/Sort		Applies filter to table
Query/Run		Displays query results in Query Datasheet view
Query/Show Table		Displays Show Table dialog box
Window/Database		Displays Database window

screen identification

In the following Access screen, several items are identified by letters. Enter the correct term for each item in the spaces provided.

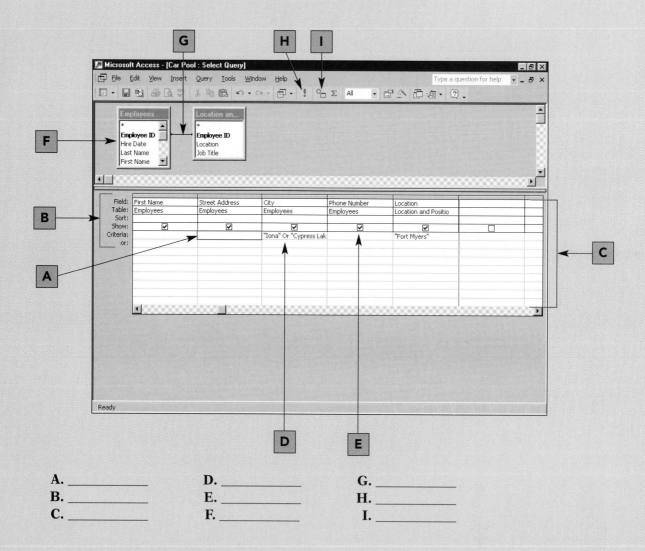

A. _____   D. _____   G. _____
B. _____   E. _____   H. _____
C. _____   F. _____   I. _____

matching

Match the numbered item with the correct lettered description.

1. ⚠ _____ **a.** intersection of a column and row

2. query _____ **b.** a control that is tied to a field in an underlying table

3. multitable query _____ **c.** temporary restriction placed on displayed data to isolate specific records

4. criteria _____ **d.** includes any records containing either condition

5. 🖻 _____ **e.** object that links a form or report to the underlying table

6. filter _____ **f.** runs a query and displays query datasheet

7. OR _____ **g.** used to ask questions about database tables

8. bound _____ **h.** query that uses data from more than one table

9. control _____ **i.** set of limiting conditions

10. cell _____ **j.** accesses Filter By Form feature

multiple choice

Circle the letter of the correct response.

1. A(n) _____ is a restriction placed on records in the open datasheet or form to quickly isolate and display a subset of records.
   a. filter
   b. query
   c. join
   d. property

2. AND and OR are _____.
   a. criteria
   b. operators
   c. elements
   d. properties

3. Select, crosstab, parameter, action, and SQL are different types of _____.
   a. action elements
   b. formats
   c. queries
   d. property elements

4. Inner, outer, and SQL are different types of _____.
   a. joins
   b. queries
   c. filters
   d. reports

5. All information in a report or form is contained in boxes called _____.
   a. filters
   b. criteria
   c. controls
   d. keys

6. A filter is created by specifying a set of limiting conditions or _____.
   a. forms
   b. controls
   c. criteria
   d. objects

7. The operator that broadens a search, because any record meeting either condition is included in the output, is _____.
   a. AND
   b. OR
   c. MOST
   d. ALL

8. A(n) _____ is a question asked of the data contained in a database.
   a. form
   b. inquiry
   c. request
   d. query

9. A(n) _____ is an association that tells Access how data between tables is related.
   a. join
   b. criteria expression
   c. query
   d. object

10. Bound and unbound are types of _____.
    a. buttons
    b. forms
    c. properties
    d. controls

Circle the correct answer to the following statements.

1.	Multiple filter results can be saved.	True	False
2.	The OR operator narrows a search.	True	False
3.	Queries are used to view data in different ways, to analyze data, and to change existing data.	True	False
4.	Values that tell Access how to filter the criteria in a query are called filter expressions.	True	False
5.	Access includes a custom report feature to assist in creating professional-appearing reports.	True	False
6.	Filters use reports to set limiting conditions.	True	False
7.	The AND operator is assumed when you enter criteria in multiple fields.	True	False
8.	A join line shows how different tables are related.	True	False
9.	Reports are printed output generated from tables and queries.	True	False
10.	Controls are text objects.	True	False

Concepts

fill-in

Complete the following statements by filling in the blanks with the correct terms.

1. A(n) _____ is used to isolate and display a specific group of records.

2. The _____ operator narrows the search for records that meet both conditions.

3. The _____ operator narrows the search for records that meet either condition.

4. A(n) _____ is an association that shows how data between tables is related.

5. A(n) _____ retrieves specific data from one or more tables and displays the results in a query datasheet.

6. The _____ of the Query window is where the fields to be displayed in the query datasheet are placed.

7. Tables are joined by relating the _____ between the tables.

8. _____ are used to hold the report data.

9. Custom names in a report are _____ because they are not connected to a field.

10. The _____ comparison operator is used to find values that are less than or equal to another value.

discussion questions

Answer the following questions by preparing written responses.

1. Discuss what filters are and how they can be used in a database. When would it be appropriate to use a filter?

2. Discuss the differences between the AND and OR filter conditions.

3. Discuss what a query can do and some advantages of using queries.

4. Discuss the different types of controls. Give an example of how they can be used to create different report designs.

Hands-On Exercises

step-by-step

Filtering a Database

★ 1. Maria Dell, the owner of the Simply Beautiful Spa, continues to be impressed with your work on the company's database (Step-by-Step Exercise 1 of Lab 2). She is thinking of offering a spa package that would include various anti-aging skin treatments and massages. To get an idea of how much interest there would be in this package among those who currently frequent the spa, Ms. Dell has asked you for a list of clients who are over the age of 35. She doesn't need a formal report right now, so you decide to just filter the existing table and print the filtered datasheet. The printed datasheet is shown here.

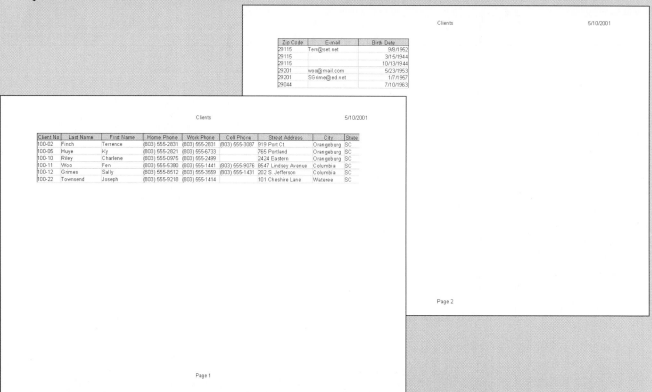

To filter the table, follow these steps:

a. Open the database file named ac02_Simply Beautiful that you modified in Step-by-step Exercise 1 of Lab 2. Open the table named "Clients."

b. Select Filter by Form and enter **<1/1/65** in the Birth Date field. Apply the filter.

c. Enter your name in the last of the displayed fields and print the filtered datasheet in landscape orientation.

d. Remove the filter.

e. Close the table, saving the changes.

f. Compact and repair the database.

Locating Bimonthly Advertisers

★★ 2. The data entry form for the Happenings database is is working well (Step-by-Step Exercise 2 of Lab 2). The printer you use for the Happenings newsletter, however, is raising his prices. You have been quite pleased with the quality of his work and would prefer not to have to go to someone else. Instead, you decide to contact the local merchants who are currently advertising in the newsletter bimonthly to see if they would be willing to increase the frequency of their ads. To do this, you want to create a datasheet that contains the contact information for these merchants, as shown below.

To produce this datasheet, you will perform a query on the "Advertisers" table.

a. Open the database file named ac02_Happening Ads that you modified in Step-by-Step Exercise 2 of Lab 2. Select the Queries object.

b. Use the Query Wizard to run a select query on the "Advertisers" table. Include all the fields in the order listed. Title the query **Bimonthly Advertisers**.

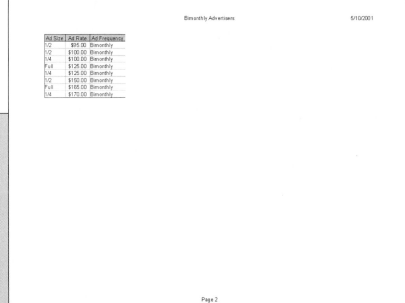

c. In Query Design view, enter **Bimonthly** in the Ad Frequency criteria field. Run the query. Sort the Ad Rate field in ascending sort order. Print the query using landscape orientation.

d. Close the query, saving the changes.

e. Compact and repair the database.

Creating a Stock Report

★★ **3.** Evan, the owner of the Downtown Internet Cafe, has asked you to submit a daily report on all
★ low-quantity items so he can place the necessary orders. With the database you created in Step-
by-Step Exercise 3 of Lab 2, you can use it to mointor inventory levels and respond to Evan's
request. First you decide to run a query to find the low-stock items, and then you can generate the
requested report from the query. Your completed report should look similar to the report below.

To generate the query and
report, follow these steps:

a. Open the database file
named ac02_Cafe Supplies
that you modified in Step-
by-Step Exercise 3 of Lab
2.

b. Use the Query Wizard to
create a query based on
the "Inventory" table.
Include all fields except
Item # in their current
order. Name the query
Low Stock. In Design view,
enter the criteria to display only those records
with an On-Hand # that is
less than 25, and run the
query. Review the result-
ing datasheet.

Vendor Name	Better Beverages, Inc.
Contact	Pat Lawry
Phone	(206) 555-909
E-mail	bev@dial.com
Description	Sumatra coffee
# On Hand	11
Special Order?	N
Vendor Name	Better Beverages, Inc.
Contact	Pat Lawry
Phone	(206) 555-909
E-mail	bev@dial.com
Description	Guatamala coffee
# On Hand	0
Special Order?	N
Vendor Name	Central Ceramics
Contact	[Your Name]
Phone	(602) 555-192
E-mail	student@learn.com
Description	Coffee mugs
# On Hand	12
Special Order?	Y

Thursday, May 10, 2001   Page 3 of 5

c. Upon reviewing the
datasheet, you realize that
it is not in a very useful order. Also, since Evan typically places orders by phone, the address
information is not really necessary. Return to Design view and do the following:

- Apply an ascending sort to the Vendor Name column.
- Delete the four mailing address columns.
- Move the Vendor Name, Contact, Phone, and E-mail columns to the left of the Description
  column.

d. Run the query and review the resulting datasheet. Since the query now looks satisfactory
enough to create a report from it, close the Query window, saving the changes.

e. Use the Report Wizard to create a report based on the "Low Stock" query you just saved.
Include all the listed fields in the following order:

- Vendor Name
- Contact
- Phone
- E-mail
- Description
- # On Hand
- Special Order?

f. Select Vendor Name as the only sort field. Select the Columnar layout and Bold style. Name the report **Order Items**.

g. Preview and print the page of the report that contains your name in the Contact field, and then close the Report window, saving the changes.

h. Compact and repair the database.

Creating a Product Development Report

★ **4.** You are responsible for updating, maintaining, and using EduSoft's database (Step-by-Step Exercise 4 of Lab 2). You are frequently asked to provide reports that show the company's curriculum software products from different vantage points and for different purposes. The most recent request was from product development, asking for a report that shows the math and science titles released over 3 years ago. They plan on using this report to gauge how many titles on those topics will need to be updated in the near future. The report you create for them will look similar to the report shown here.

To create the requested report, follow these steps:

a. Open the database named ac02_Learning that you modified in Step-by-Step Exercise 4 of Lab 2.

b. Use the Query Wizard to create a query based on the "Software" table. Include the following fields in this order: Title, Subject, Grade Level, Release Date. Name the query **Old Math and Science**.

c. In Query Design view, enter **Math** in the first Subject criteria cell and **Science** in the second (or) criteria cell. Enter **<1/1/98** in the Release Date criteria cell. Run the query and review the resulting datasheet. Close the Query window, saving the changes.

96-97 Math and Science Titles

Release Date	Subject	Title	Grade Level
1/20/1996	Science	Try It I	K-2
6/4/1996	Science	Try It II	3-5
9/20/1996	Science	Try It III	6-8
6/14/1997	Math	Solve It I	K-2
9/3/1997	Math	Solve It II	3-5
12/15/1997	Math	Solve It III	6-8

Thursday, May 10, 2001   Page 1 of 1

d. Use the Report Wizard to create a report based on the "Old Math and Science" query you just saved. Include all the fields in the order listed. Select Release Date as the first sort field and Subject as the second sort field. Select the Tabular layout, landscape orientation, and Formal style. Name the report **96-97 Math and Science Titles**.

e. Center the Report Header control at the top of the page.

f. Preview and then print the report. Close the Report window, saving the changes you made.

g. Compact and repair the database.

Creating an Animal Adoption Report

★★ ★ **5.** The Animal Angels volunteers are successfully using the database you created to enter information for all the animals picked up by the organization and boarded, placed in foster care, and/or adopted (Step-by-Step Exercise 5 of Lab 2). Meanwhile, you created another table containing information about the adoptive homes (including names, addresses, and phone numbers). The Animal Rescue Foundation management have now asked you for a report, shown below, of all animals adopted in the past six months and by whom, so the appropriate thank you notes can be sent. Your completed report will be similar to the report shown here.

To create the requested report, follow these steps:

a. Open the database file named ac03_Angels.

b. Open the Queries tab and create a query in Design view. Join the "Animals" and "Adopters" tables, and add the following fields to the design grid in the order listed below:

- Type
- Status
- Adoption Date
- Adopter First Name
- Adopter Last Name
- Adopter Street
- Adopter City
- Adopter State
- Adopter Zip

c. Specify **A** as the Status criteria and **>9/1/98** as the Adoption Date criteria. Run the query and review the resulting datasheet. Select an ascending sort in the Adopter Last Name column. Save the query as **Adoptees** and close the Query window.

d. Use the Report Wizard to create a report based on the "Adoptees" query you just saved. Include the following fields in the order listed below:

- Adopter First Name
- Adopter Last Name
- Adopter Street
- Adopter City
- Adopter State
- Adopter Zip
- Type

e. Select Adopter Last Name as the first sort field and Adopter First Name as the second sort field. Select the Justified layout, landscape orientation, and the Casual style. Name the report **Animal Adoption Report**.

f. Center the Report Header control at the top of the page. Move the Adopter Last Name field before the Adopter First Name field.

g. Preview and then print the report. Close the report window, saving the changes you made.

h. Compact and repair the database.

on your own

Identifying a Product Developer

★ 1. The program manager for the EduSoft Company is requesting a list of software titles that were worked on by Teri O'Neill so he can use it for Teri's review. Open the database named ac02_Learning and the "Software" table you updated in Step-by-Step Exercise 4 of Lab 2. Filter the table to include only those records that have Teri O'Neill in the Developer field. Add your name to one of the software titles (e.g., [Your Name]'s Seeing Stars) and print the filtered datasheet.

Issuing W-2 Forms

★★ 2. As an administrative assistant at Lewis & Lewis, Inc., you are responsible for sending out W2 forms to all of the employees. Use the Lewis Personnel database that you updated in On Your Own Exercise 4 of Lab 2 and create a query that includes only the employee name and home address fields. Save the query as **Home Address**. Run and print the resulting query datasheet.

Expense Account Report

★★ 3. One of the department managers at JK Enterprises has requested a report showing who in her group has submitted an expense report but not yet been paid. In the JK Enterprise database, open the "Expenses" table you updated in On Your Own Exercise 2 of Lab 2. Locate a department that has at least two expense reports that have not been paid. (If there are none, change some of one department's paid fields from Yes to No.) Then run a query that includes all fields except the employee ID. Enter query sort criteria to find only records for employees who have not been paid, and for the department you chose earlier. Apply an ascending sort to the field containing the date the expense report was submitted. Save the query as **Pending** and then use the Report Wizard to create a report named **Pending Expenses** based on the query. Sort the report by the date submitted and then the name fields. Preview and print the report.

Thank You Card Report

★★ 4. The Animal Angels owners have finished sending thank you cards to those who adopted animals
★ in the last six months, and would now like to send cards to those who have provided foster care in the same time period. Using the same techniques you used in Step-by-Step Exercise 5 of this lab, create a query in the ac03_Angels database that joins the "Animals" and "Fosters" tables; includes the animal type, status, and foster home information; and specifies **F** and **>9/1/98** as the Status and Foster Date criteria. Save the query as **Foster** and close the query. Then use the Report Wizard to create a report called **Foster Angels** based on this query. Include all fields except the Status field, with the foster home name and address information fields first and the Type field last. Preview and print the report. Compact and repair the database after closing it.

on the web

The owners of Golden Oldies have decided to expand their offerings to include out-of-print books as well as collectable record albums. Revisit the Web to obtain some book titles and resources and add the appropriate fields to the "Inventory" table of the Golden Oldies database you updated in On the Web Exercise of Lab 2. To create a list of only the new products, filter the table to include the client and book fields (not the record album fields), and print the filtered datasheet. Then create a query called **Complete Products** that includes the records for both product types (record and book), sorted by category. Use the Report Wizard to create a report that is based on the query; include the customer name, product type, category, and source fields; and sort it by customer last name. Preview and print the report.

Overview to PowerPoint 2002

What is a Presentation Program?

You are in a panic! Tomorrow you are to make a presentation to an audience and you want it to be good. To the rescue comes a powerful tool: graphics presentation programs. These programs are designed to help you create an effective presentation, whether to the board of directors of your company or to your fellow classmates. An effective presentation gets your point across clearly and in an interesting manner.

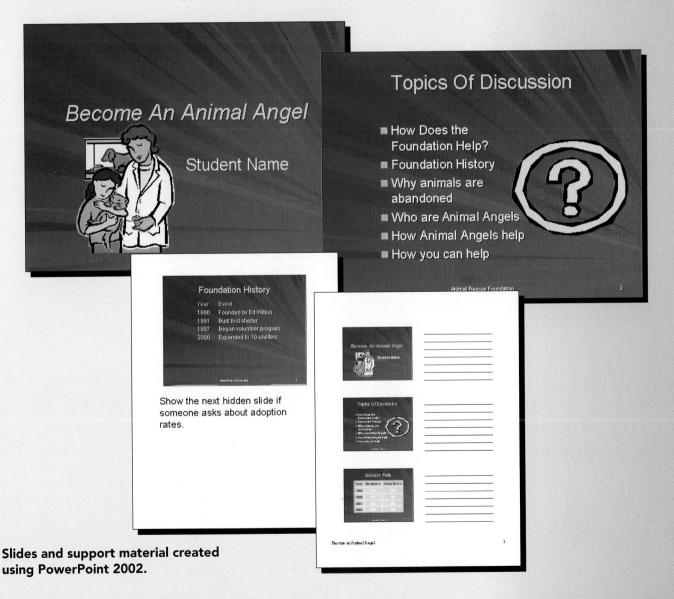

Slides and support material created using PowerPoint 2002.

Graphics presentation programs are designed to help you produce a high-quality presentation that is both interesting to the audience and effective in its ability to convey your message. A presentation can be as simple as overhead transparencies or as sophisticated as an onscreen electronic display. Graphics presentation programs can produce black-and-white or color overhead transparencies, 35mm slides, onscreen electronic presentations called screen shows, Web pages for Web use, and support materials for both the speaker and the audience.

The graphics presentation program includes features such as text handling, outlining, graphing, drawing, animations, clip art, and multimedia support. With a few keystrokes the user can quickly change, correct, and update the presentation. In addition, graphics presentation programs suggest layouts for different types of presentations and offer professionally designed templates to help you produce a presentation that is sure to keep your audience's attention.

• PowerPoint 2002 Features

Creating an effective presentation is a complicated process. Graphics presentation programs help simplify this process by providing assistance in the content development phase, as well as the layout and design phase. In addition, these programs produce the support materials you can use when making a presentation to an audience.

The content development phase includes deciding on the topic of your presentation, the organization of the content, and the ultimate message you want to convey to the audience. As an aid in this phase, PowerPoint 2002 helps you organize your thoughts based on the type of presentation you are making. Several common types of presentations sell a product or idea, suggest a strategy, or report on the progress of a program. Based on the type of presentation, the program suggests ideas and organization tips. For example, if you are making a presentation on the progress of a sales campaign, the program would suggest that you enter text on the background of the sales campaign as the first page, called a slide; the current status of the campaign as the next slide; and accomplishments, schedule, issues and problems, and where you are heading on subsequent slides.

The layout for each slide is the next important decision. Again, PowerPoint 2002 helps you by suggesting text layout features such as title placement, bullets, and columns. You can also incorporate graphs of data, tables, organizational charts, clip art, and other special text effects in the slides.

PowerPoint 2002 also includes professionally designed templates to further enhance the appearance of your slides. These templates include features that standardize the appearance of all the slides in your presentation. Professionally selected combinations of text and background colors, common typefaces and sizes, borders, and other art designs take the worry out of much of the design layout.

Once you have written and designed the slides, you can then have the slides made into black-and-white or color overhead transparencies or 35mm slides. Alternatively, you can use the slides in an onscreen electronic presentation or a Web page for use on the Web. An electronic presentation uses the computer to display the slides on an overhead projection screen. When using this type of presentation, many programs also include a rehearsal feature, allowing you to practice and time your presentation. The length of time to display each slide can be set and your entire presentation can be completed within the allotted time. A presentation can be modified to display on a Web site and run using a Web browser.

Finally, with PowerPoint 2002 you can also print out the materials you have created. You can print an outline of the text showing the titles of the slides and main text but not the art. The outline allows you to check the organizational logic of your presentation. You can also print speaker notes that you can refer to while making your presentation. These notes generally consist of a small printout of each slide with any notes on topics you want to discuss while the slides are displayed. Finally, you can create printed handouts of the slides for the audience. The audience can refer to the slide and make notes on the handout page as you speak.

Case Study for PowerPoint 2002 Labs

You have volunteered at the Animal Rescue Foundation, a nonprofit organization that rescues unwanted animals from local animal shelters and finds foster homes for them until a suitable adoptive family can be found. With your computer skills, you have been asked to create a powerful and persuasive presentation to entice the community to volunteer.

The organization has recently purchased the graphics presentation program Microsoft PowerPoint 2002. You will use this application to create the presentation.

Lab 1: You use PowerPoint to enter and edit the text for your presentation. You also learn how to reorganize the presentation and enhance it with different text attributes and by adding a picture. Finally, you learn how to run a slide show and print handouts.

Lab 2: You learn about many more features to enhance the appearance of your slides. This includes changing the slide design and color scheme and adding clip art, animation, and sound. You also learn how to add transitional effects to make the presentation more interesting. Finally, you create speaker notes to help you keep your cool during the presentation.

Working Together: Demonstrates the sharing of information between applications. First you learn how to copy and embed a table created in Word into a slide. Then you learn how to link a chart created in Excel to another slide.

Before You Begin

To the Student

The following assumptions have been made:

- The Microsoft PowerPoint 2002 program has been properly installed on the hard disk of your computer system. A mouse is also installed.

- The student data files are needed to complete the series of labs. These files are supplied by your instructor.

- You have completed the O'Leary Series Windows 98 or 2000 modules or you are already familiar with how to use Windows 98 or 2000 and a mouse.

To the Instructor

It is assumed that the complete version of the program has been installed prior to students using the labs. In addition, please be aware that the following settings are assumed to be in effect for the PowerPoint 2002 program. These assumptions are necessary so that the screens and directions in the manual are accurate.

- The New Presentation Task Pane is displayed on startup (use Tools/Options/View).

- The status bar is displayed (use Tools/Options/View).

- The Paste Options buttons are displayed (use Tools/Options/Edit).

- The Standard, Formatting, and Drawing toolbars are on (use View/Customize/Toolbars).

- The Standard and Formatting toolbars are displayed on separate rows (use Tools/Customize/Options).

- Full menus are always displayed (use Tools/Customize/Options).

- The Office Assistant feature is enabled but not on (click on the Assistant, click [Options...], and clear the Use the Office Assistant option).

- The Normal view is on (use View/Normal).

- The Clip Organizer is fully installed.

- The automatic spelling check feature is on (use Tools/Options/Spelling and Style/Check spelling as you type).

- The Style check feature is off (use Tools/Options/Spelling and Style and clear the Check Style option).

- All the options in the View tab are selected (use Tools/Options/View).

In addition, all figures in the manual reflect the use of a standard VGA display monitor set at 800 by 600. If another monitor setting is used, there may be more or fewer lines of text displayed in the windows than in the figures. This setting can be changed using Windows setup.

Microsoft Office XP Shortcut Bar

The Microsoft Office XP Shortcut Bar (shown on the next page) may be displayed automatically on the Windows desktop. Commonly, it appears in the right side of the desktop; however, it may appear in other locations depending upon your setup. The Shortcut Bar on your screen may display different buttons. This is because the Shortcut Bar can be customized to display other toolbar buttons.

The Office Shortcut Bar makes it easy to open existing documents or to create new documents using one of the Microsoft Office applications. It can also be used to send e-mail, add a task to a to-do list, schedule appointments using Schedule+, or access Office Help.

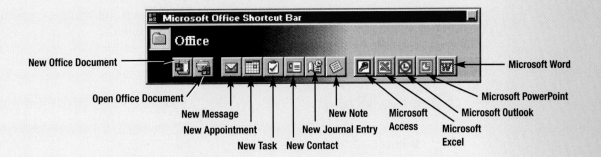

New Office Document

Open Office Document

New Message

New Appointment

New Task   New Contact

New Journal Entry

New Note

Microsoft Access

Microsoft Excel

Microsoft Outlook

Microsoft PowerPoint

Microsoft Word

Instructional Conventions

Hands-on instructions you are to perform appear as a sequence of numbered steps. Within each step, a series of bullets identifies the specific actions that must be performed. Step numbering begins over within each topic heading throughout the lab.

Command sequences you are to issue appear following the word "Choose." Each menu command selection is separated by a /. If the menu command can be selected by typing a letter of the command, the letter will appear underlined and bold. Items that need to be selected will follow the word "Select." You can select items with the mouse or directional keys. (See Example A.)

Example A

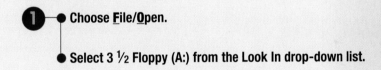

1 ● Choose **File/Open**.

● Select 3 ½ Floppy (A:) from the Look In drop-down list.

Commands that can be initiated using a button and the mouse appear following the word "Click." The icon (and the icon name if the icon does not include text) is displayed following "Click." The menu equivalent and keyboard shortcut appear in a margin note when the action is first introduced. (See Example B.)

Example B

1 ● Click  Open.

Another Method

The menu equivalent is **File/Open** and the keyboard shortcut is Ctrl + O.

Plain blue text identifies file names you need to open. Information you are asked to type appears in blue and bold. (See Example C.)

Example C

1 ● **Click** 🖙 **Open.**

● **Select** Volunteer.

2 ● **Move to slide 1.**

● **Type** How Do I Become an Animal Angel?

Creating a Presentation

LAB 1

Objectives

After completing this lab, you will know how to:

1.	Use the AutoContent Wizard to create a presentation.
2.	View and edit a presentation.
3.	Save and open a presentation.
4.	Check spelling.
5.	Delete, move, and insert slides.
6.	Size and move placeholders.
7.	Run a slide show.
8.	Change fonts and formatting.
9.	Insert pictures and clip art.
10.	Preview and print a presentation.

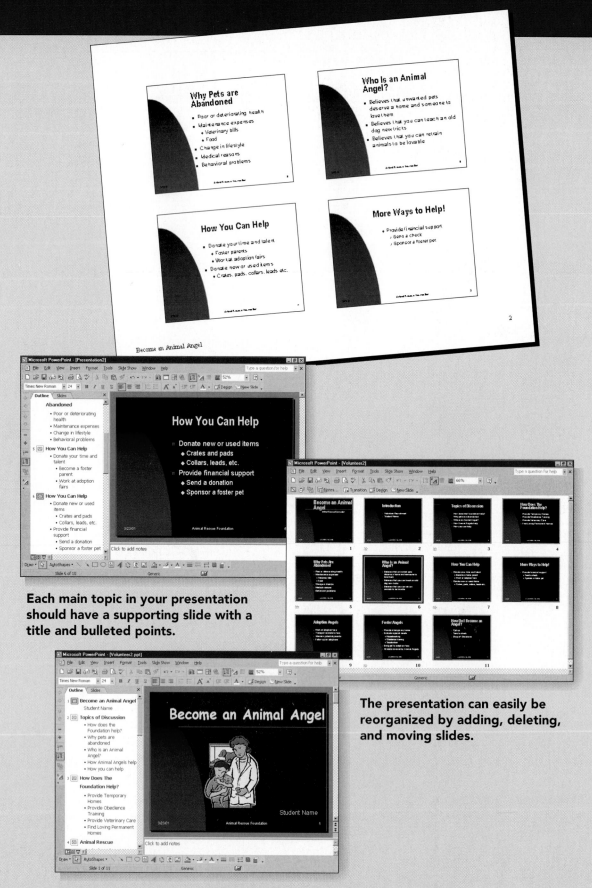

Each main topic in your presentation should have a supporting slide with a title and bulleted points.

The presentation can easily be reorganized by adding, deleting, and moving slides.

Enhance the presentation with the addition of graphics and text colors.

Animal Angels

You have volunteered to help out at the local Animal Rescue Foundation, a nonprofit organization that rescues unwanted pets from local animal shelters and finds foster homes for them until a suitable adoptive family can be found. The agency has a large volunteer group called the Animal Angels that provides much-needed support for the foundation. Because of your computer skills, you have been asked to create a powerful and persuasive presentation to entice more members of the community to join the Animal Angels.

The agency director has just informed you that you need to preview the presentation at the weekly staff meeting tomorrow, and has asked you to present a draft of the presentation by noon today.

Although we would all like to think that our message is the core of the presentation, the presentation materials we use can determine whether or not the message reaches the audience. To help you create the presentation, you will use PowerPoint 2002, a graphics presentation application that is designed to create presentation materials such as slides, overheads, and handouts. Using PowerPoint you can create a high-quality and interesting onscreen presentation with pizzazz that will dazzle your audience.

© Corbis

The following concepts will be introduced in this lab:

1 **Template**   A template is a file that includes predefined settings that can be used as a pattern to create many common types of presentations.

2 **Presentation Styles**   A PowerPoint presentation can be made using five different styles: onscreen presentations, Web presentations, black-and-white or color overheads, and 35mm slides.

3 **Slide**   A slide is an individual "page" of your presentation. The first slide of a presentation is the title slide. Additional slides are used to support each main point in your presentation.

4 **AutoCorrect**   The AutoCorrect feature makes some basic assumptions about the text you are typing and, based on these assumptions, automatically corrects the entry.

5 **Spelling Check**   The spelling checker feature advises you of misspelled words as you create and edit a presentation, and proposes possible corrections.

6 **Layout**   PowerPoint includes 27 predefined slide layouts that can be selected and applied to slides.

7 **Font and Font Size**   A font is a set of characters with a specific design. Each font has one or more sizes. Using fonts as a design element can add interest to your presentation and give your audience visual cues to help them find information quickly.

8 **Graphics**   A graphic is a non-text element or object, such as a drawing or picture, that can be added to a slide.

9 **Stacking Order**   Stacking order is the order objects are inserted in the different layers of the slide. As each object is added to the slide, it is added to the top layer.

Introducing PowerPoint 2002

The Animal Rescue Foundation has just installed the latest version of the Microsoft Office Suite of applications, Office XP, on their computers. You will use the graphics presentation program, Microsoft PowerPoint 2002, included in the office suite to create your presentation. Using this program, you should have no problem creating the presentation in time for tomorrow's staff meeting.

Exploring the PowerPoint 2002 Window

1 ● **Start the Microsoft PowerPoint 2002 application.**

Having Trouble?
See "Introduction to Office XP" on page I.9 for information on how to start the application and for a discussion of features that are common to all Office XP applications.

Your screen should be similar to Figure 1.1

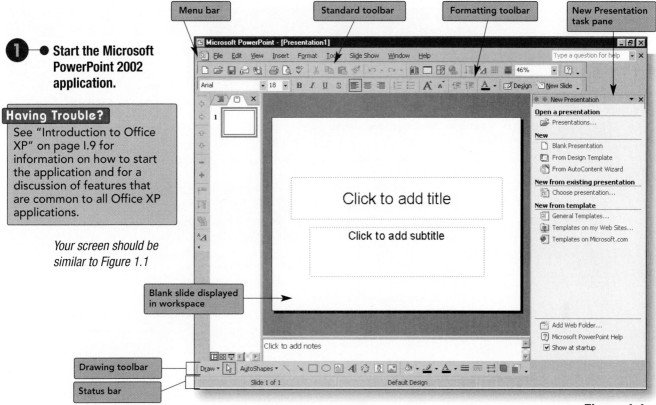

Figure 1.1

The PowerPoint application window is displayed. The menu bar below the title bar displays the PowerPoint program menu. It consists of nine menus that provide access to the commands and features you will use to create and modify a presentation.

Additional Information
Because the Office XP applications remember settings that were on when the program was last exited, your screen may look slightly different.

Normally located below the menu bar are the Standard and Formatting toolbars. The **Standard toolbar** contains buttons that are used to complete the most frequently used menu commands. The **Formatting toolbar** contains buttons that are used to change the appearance or format of the document. In addition, the **Drawing toolbar** is displayed along the bottom edge of the window. It contains buttons that are used to enhance text and create shapes. Other toolbars may be displayed if they were on when the program was last exited.

Additional Information
There are 13 different PowerPoint toolbars.

The large area containing the blank slide is the **workspace** where your presentations are displayed as you create and edit them. Because you just started the program, the New Presentation task pane is automatically displayed. It is used to open an existing presentation or create new presentations. The status bar at the bottom of the PowerPoint window displays messages and information about various PowerPoint settings.

Developing New Presentations

During your presentation you will present information about the Animal Rescue Foundation and why someone should want to join the Animal

Angels volunteer group. As you prepare to create a new presentation, you should follow several basic steps: plan, create, edit, enhance, and rehearse.

Step	Description
Plan	The first step in planning a presentation is to understand its purpose. You also need to find out the length of time you have to speak, who the audience is, what type of room you will be in, and what kind of audiovisual equipment is available. These factors have an impact on the type of presentation you will create.
Create	To begin creating your presentation, develop the content by typing your thoughts or notes into an outline. Each main idea in your presentation should have a supporting slide with a title and bulleted points.
Edit	While typing, you are bound to make typing and spelling errors that need to be corrected. This is one type of editing. Another is to revise the content of what you have entered to make it clearer, or to add or delete information. To do this, you might insert a slide, add or delete bulleted items, or move text to another location.
Enhance	You want to develop a presentation that grabs and holds the audience's attention. Choose a design that gives your presentation some dazzle. Wherever possible add graphics to replace or enhance text. Add effects that control how a slide appears and disappears, and that reveal text in a bulleted list one bullet at a time.
Rehearse	Finally, you should rehearse the delivery of your presentation. For a professional presentation, your delivery should be as polished as your materials. Use the same equipment that you will use when you give the presentation. Practice advancing from slide to slide and then back in case someone asks a question. If you have a mouse available, practice pointing or drawing on the slide to call attention to key points.

After rehearsing your presentation, you may find that you want to go back to the editing phase. You may change text, move bullets, or insert a new slide. Periodically, as you make changes, rehearse the presentation again to see how the changes affect your presentation. By the day of the presentation, you will be confident about your message and at ease with the materials.

During the planning phase, you have spoken with the foundation director regarding the purpose of the presentation and the content in general. The purpose of your presentation is to educate members of the community about the organization and to persuade many to volunteer. In addition, you want to impress the director by creating a professional presentation.

Creating a Presentation

When you first start PowerPoint, a new blank presentation is opened. It is like a blank piece of paper that already has many predefined settings. These settings, called **default** settings, are generally the most commonly used settings and are stored as a presentation template.

Template

1 A **template** is a file that includes predefined settings that can be used as a pattern to create many common types of presentations. Every PowerPoint presentation is based on a template. The default settings for a basic blank presentation are stored in the default design template file. Whenever you create a new presentation using this template, the same default settings are used.

Many other templates are also available within PowerPoint and on the Microsoft Office Template Gallery on the Microsoft Office Web site that are designed to help you create professional-looking presentations. They include design templates, which provied a design concept, fonts, and color scheme; and content templates, which suggest content for your presentation based on the type of presentation you are making. You can also design and save your own presentation templates.

The New Presentation task pane is used to specify how you want to start using the PowerPoint program. It includes three options that provide access to different methods for creating a new presentation. The **AutoContent Wizard** is a guided approach that helps you determine the content and organization of your presentation through a series of questions. Then it creates a presentation that contains suggested content and design based on the answers you provide. You can also create a new presentation beginning with a design template. Finally, you can create a new presentation from scratch using the Blank Presentation option, which uses the default template.

Additional Information

If the Microsoft Office suite is on your system and the Office Shortcut Bar is displayed, you can click 🔲 New Office Document and select the method you want to use to create a new presentation while starting the PowerPoint program.

Using the AutoContent Wizard

Since this is your first presentation created using PowerPoint, you decide to use the AutoContent Wizard.

---

1 ● **From the Presentation task pane, select New From AutoContent Wizard.**

HAVING TROUBLE?
If your Office Assistant appears, choose "No, don't provide help now."

Your screen should be similar to Figure 1.2

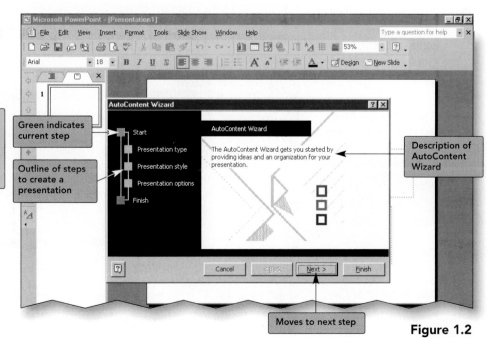

Figure 1.2

The opening dialog box of the AutoContent Wizard briefly describes how the feature works. As the AutoContent Wizard guides you through creating the presentation, it shows you which step you are on in the outline on the left side of the window. The green box identifies the current step.

Click `Next >` .

Additional Information
You can also click the outline box on the left side to move directly to any step.

Your screen should be similar to Figure 1.3

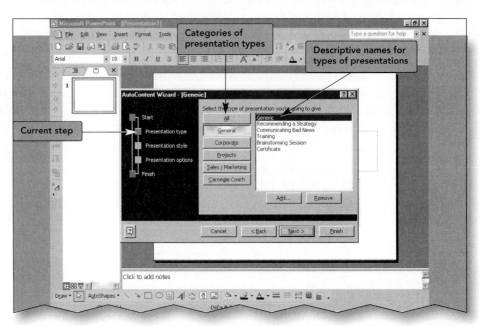

Figure 1.3

In the Presentation Type step, you are asked to select the type of presentation you are creating. PowerPoint includes 24 different types of presentations, each with a different recommended content and design. Each type is indexed under a category. Currently, only the presentation types in the General category are listed, and a descriptive name for each presentation type in this category appears in the list box. You will use the Generic presentation option.

Click on each category button to see the different presentation types in each category.

Select Generic from the General category.

Additional Information
The Generic option is also available under the All category.

Click `Next >` .

Your screen should be similar to Figure 1.4

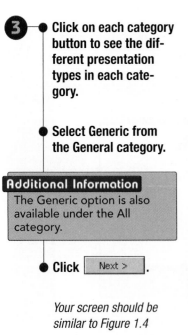

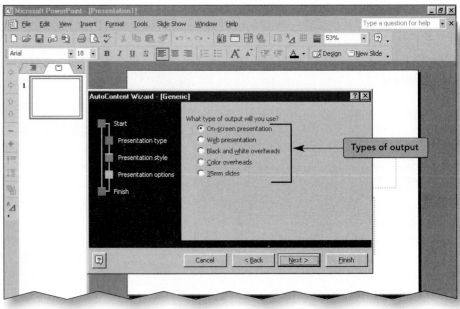

Figure 1.4

In the Presentation Style step, you select the type of output your presentation will use.

The room you will be using to make your presentation is equipped with computer projection equipment, so you will create an on-screen presentation. The Wizard selects the color scheme best suited to the type of output you select. Since On-screen Presentation is the default selection, accept it and move to the next step,

4 ● **Click**  .

Your screen should be similar to Figure 1.5

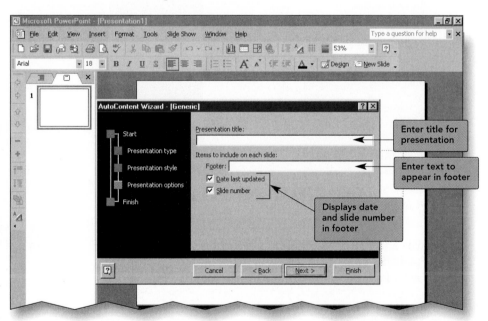

Figure 1.5

In the Presentation Options step, you are asked to enter some basic information that will appear on the title slide and in the footer of each slide in the presentation.

You would like the name of the presentation to appear as the title on the first slide, and the name of the organization, date of the presentation, and the slide number to appear on the footer of each slide. A **footer** is text or graphics that appear at the bottom of each slide. Because the options to display the date that the presentation was last updated and slide number are already selected, you only need to enter the title text and footer text.

5 ● Click in the Presentation title text box to display the insertation point.

● Type **Become an Animal Angel**.

HAVING TROUBLE?

If you make a typing error, use the [Backspace] key to delete the characters to the left of the insertion point and then retype the correct text.

● Press [Tab ⇥].

● Type **Animal Rescue Foundation** in the Footer text box.

Your screen should be similar to Figure 1.6

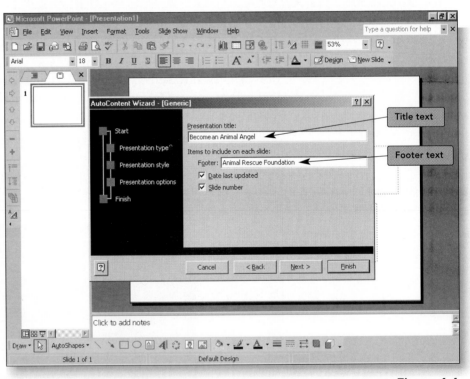

Figure 1.6

You have entered all the information PowerPoint needs to create your presentation.

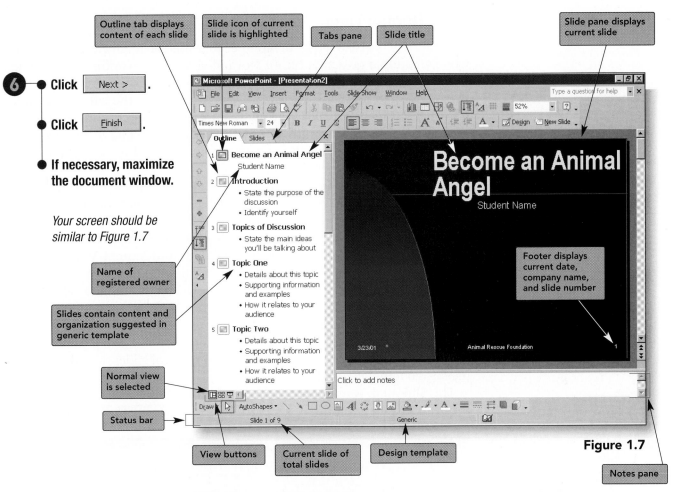

6
● Click [Next >].

● Click [Finish].

● If necessary, maximize the document window.

Your screen should be similar to Figure 1.7

Name of registered owner

Slides contain content and organization suggested in generic template

Normal view is selected

Status bar

Outline tab displays content of each slide

Slide icon of current slide is highlighted

Tabs pane

Slide title

Slide pane displays current slide

Footer displays current date, company name, and slide number

Figure 1.7

View buttons

Current slide of total slides

Design template

Notes pane

Viewing the Presentation

Based on your selections and entries, the AutoContent Wizard creates a presentation and displays it in the workspace. The presentation is initially displayed in Normal view showing the Outline tab. A **view** is a way of looking at a presentation. PowerPoint provides several views you can use to look at and modify your presentation. Depending on what you are doing, one view may be preferable to another. The commands to change views are located on the View menu. In addition, the three view buttons to the left of the horizontal scroll bar can be used to quickly switch from one view to another. The menu commands, buttons, and the three main views are described in the table below.

View	Command	Button	Description
Normal	**V**iew/**N**ormal		Provides three working areas of the window that allow you to work on all aspects of your presentation in one place.
Slide Sorter	**V**iew/Sli**d**e Sorter		Displays a miniature of each slide to make it easy to reorder slides, add special effects such as transitions, and set timing between slides.
Slide Show	**V**iew/Slide Sho**w**		Displays each slide in final form using the full screen space so you can practice or present the presentation.

Using Normal View

Normal view is displayed by default because it is the main view you will use while creating a presentation. In Normal view, three working areas, called **panes**, are displayed. This allows you to work on all components of your presentation in one convenient location. The pane on the left side includes tabs that alternate between viewing the presentation in outline format and as slide miniatures. Currently, the Outline tab is open and displays the title and text for each slide in the presentation. It is used to organize and develop the content of your presentation.

To the left of each slide title in the Outline tab is a slide icon 🖵 and a number that identifies each slide. (See Figure 1.7.) The icon of the current slide is highlighted, and the current slide is displayed in the main working area, called the slide pane. The text for the first slide consists of the title and the footer text you specified when using the AutoContent Wizard. Below the title, the name of the registered owner of the application program is displayed automatically. The other slides shown in the outline tab contain sample text that is included by the Wizard based upon the type of presentation you selected. The sample text suggests the content for each slide to help you organize your presentation's content. The status bar now displays the number of the current slide and total number of slides, and the name of the design template used.

The Slides tab is used to display thumbnails of the entire presentation. A **thumbnail** is a miniature of a slide.

Additional Information

Normal view is often referred to as a tri-pane view because it displays three panes simultaneously.

Additional Information

You can adjust the size of each pane by dragging the splitter bars that border each pane.

1 ● Click on the Slides tab to open it.

Another Method

You can also press Ctrl + ⇧ Shift + Tab ⇆ to switch between the Slide and Outline tabs.

● Scroll the tabs pane to view the rest of the slides.

● Click on the last slide in the Slides tab.

Your screen should be similar to Figure 1.8

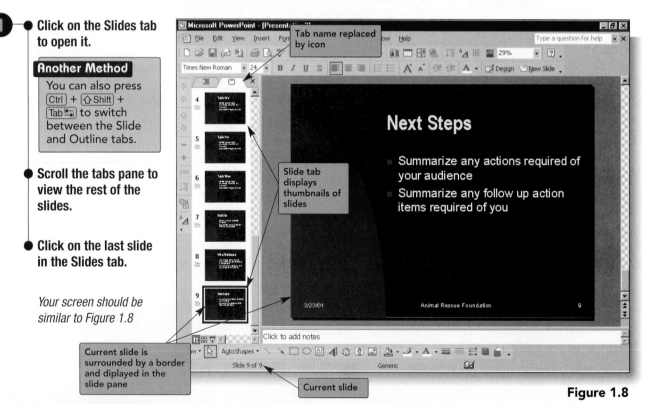

Figure 1.8

Additional Information

You can make the thumbnails larger by increasing the width of the tabs pane.

The tabs pane size is adjusted to just large enough to display the thumbnails. In addition, because the pane is more narrow, the tab names are replaced by icons. You can now see that there are a total of nine slides in the presentation. Clicking on the thumbnail selects the slide, making it the current slide, and displays it in the slide pane. The status bar displays the number of the current slide.

Using Slide Sorter View

The second main view that is used while creating a presentation is Slide Sorter view. This view also displays thumbnails of the slides.

1 ● Click ⊞ **Slide Sorter View.**

HAVING TROUBLE?
The view buttons are located to the left of the horizontal scroll bar. Pointing to a view button displays its name in a ScreenTip.

Your screen should be similar to Figure 1.9

Border surrounds current slide

Slide Sorter view is selected

All slides have the same design style

Slide Sorter view displays miniatures of all slides in presentation

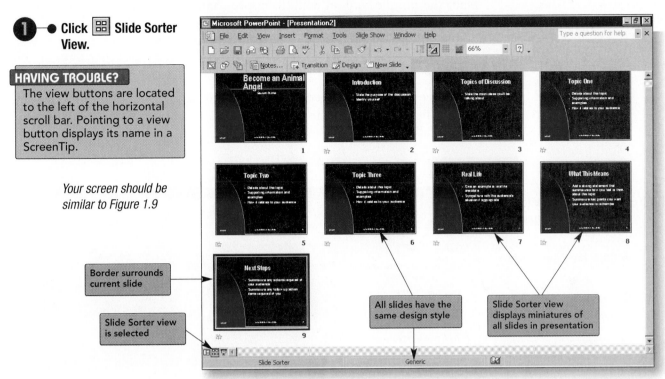

Figure 1.9

This view displays a miniature of each slide in the window. All the slides use the same design style, associated with a generic presentation. The design style sets the background design and color, as well as the text style, color, and layout. The currently selected slide, slide 9, appears with a dark border around it. Clicking on a thumbnail selects the slide and makes it the current slide, or the slide that will be affected by any changes you make.

2 ● **Click on slide 1.**

Your screen should be similar to Figure 1.10

Current slide is affected by any changes you make

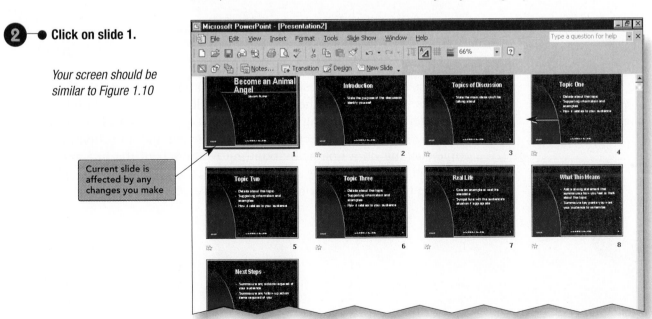

Figure 1.10

Editing a Presentation

After creating a presentation using the AutoContent Wizard, you need to replace the sample content with the appropriate information for your presentation. Editing not only involves text replacements, but rearrangement of bulleted items on slides as well as the order of slides.

Using the Outline Tab

It is easiest to make text-editing changes using the Outline tab in Normal view. When working in the outline tab, it is helpful to have the **Outlining toolbar** displayed. It is used to modify the presentation outline.

1 ● Click ⊞ to switch to Normal view again.

● Click the Outline tab.

● If necessary, display the Outlining toolbar.

HAVING TROUBLE?
Use <u>V</u>iew/<u>T</u>oolbars/Outlining or select Outlining from the toolbar shortcut menu.

Your screen should be similar to Figure 1.11

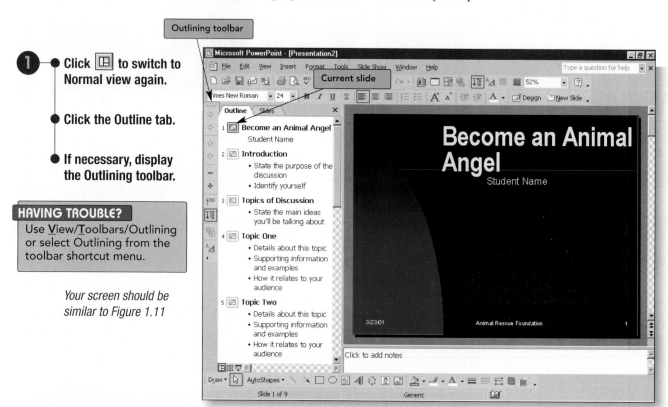

Figure 1.11

Slide 1 is still the current slide. The first change you want to make is to select the owner name on the first slide and delete it. In the Outline tab, you can select text by dragging when the mouse pointer is an I-beam. In addition, you can quickly select an entire paragraph and all subparagraphs by triple-clicking on a line or by pointing to the left of the line and clicking when the mouse pointer is a ✛. If you click the slide icon ▭ to the right of the slide number, all text on the slide is selected.

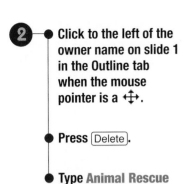

2 ● Click to the left of the owner name on slide 1 in the Outline tab when the mouse pointer is a ✥.

● Press Delete.

● Type **Animal Rescue Foundation.**

HAVING TROUBLE?
If you accidentally drag selected text, it will move. To return it to its original location, use Edit/Undo or click ⟲ ▾ Undo immediately.

Your screen should be similar to Figure 1.12

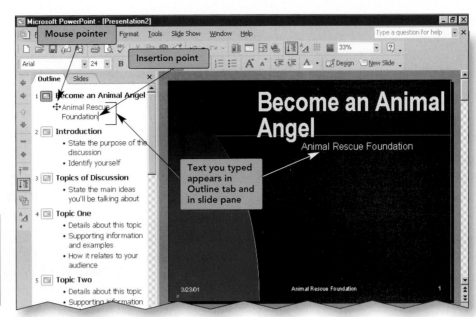

Figure 1.12

The selected text is removed and the new text is entered in the Outline tab as well as in the slide displayed in the slide pane. As you make changes in the Outline tab, the slide pane updates immediately. The next change you want to make is in the Introduction slide. The sample text in this slide recommends that you enter an opening statement to explain the purpose of the discussion and to introduce yourself. You need to replace the sample text next to the first bullet with the text for your slide.

3 ● Click on the slide 2 icon.

● Select the sample text "State the purpose of the discussion."

● Type **volunter** (this word is intentionally misspelled).

● Press Spacebar.

Your screen should be similar to Figure 1.13

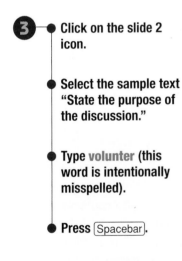

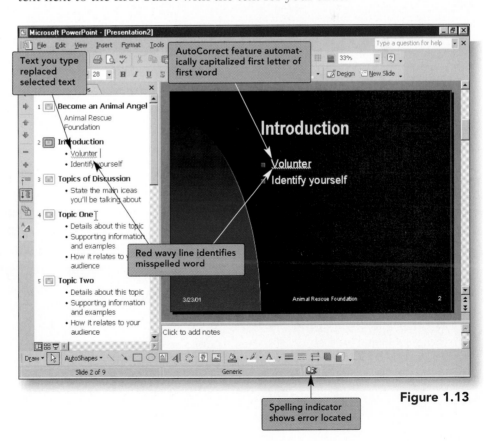

Figure 1.13

Additional Information

Bulleted items in a presentation are capitalized in sentence case format. Ending periods, however, are not included.

As soon as you pressed a key, the selected text was deleted and replaced by the new text you typed. Also, as you enter text, the program checks words for accuracy. First PowerPoint capitalized the first letter of the word. This is part of the AutoCorrect feature of PowerPoint.

concept 4

AutoCorrect

4 The **AutoCorrect** feature makes some basic assumptions about the text you are typing and, based on these assumptions, automatically corrects the entry. The AutoCorrect feature automatically inserts proper capitalization at the beginning of sentences and in the names of days of the week. It will also change to lowercase letters any words that were incorrectly capitalized due to the accidental use of the Caps Lock key. In addition, it also corrects many common typing and spelling errors automatically.

One way the program automatically makes corrections is by looking for certain types of errors. For example, if two capital letters appear at the beginning of a word, the second capital letter is changed to a lowercase letter. If a lowercase letter appears at the beginning of a sentence, the first letter of the first word is capitalized. If the name of a day begins with a lowercase letter, the first letter is capitalized.

Another way the program makes corrections is by checking all entries against a built-in list of words that are commonly spelled incorrectly or typed incorrectly. If it finds the entry on the list, the program automatically replaces the error with the correction. For example, the typing error "aboutthe" is automatically changed to "about the" because the error is on the AutoCorrect list. You can also add words to the AutoCorrect list that you want to be automatically corrected. Any such words are added to the list on the computer you are using and will be available to anyone who uses the machine after you.

Next PowerPoint identified the word as misspelled by underlining it with a wavy red line. In addition, the spelling indicator in the status bar appears as ⊞, indicating the automatic spelling check feature has found a spelling error.

concept 5

Spelling Check

5 The spelling check feature advises you of misspelled words as you create and edit a presentation, and proposes possible corrections. The spelling check compares the word you type to a **main dictionary** of words supplied with the program. Although this dictionary includes most common words, it may not include proper names, technical terms, and so on. If the word does not appear in the main dictionary, the spelling check checks the **custom dictionary**, a dictionary that you can create to hold words you commonly use but that are not included in the main dictionary. If the word does not appear in either dictionary, the program identifies it as misspelled by displaying a red wavy line below the word. You can then correct the misspelled word by editing it. Alternatively, you can display a list of suggested spelling corrections for that word and select the correct spelling from the list to replace the misspelled word in the presentation.

Because you have discovered this error very soon after typing it, and you know that the correct spelling of this word is "volunteer," you can quickly correct it using Backspace. The Backspace key removes the character or space to the left of the insertion point; therefore, it is particularly useful when you are moving from right to left (backward) along a line of text. You will correct this word and continue entering the text for this slide.

Additional Information
The spelling check works just as in the other Microsoft Office XP applications.

4
● **Press** Backspace **twice.**

● **Type er.**

● **Press** Spacebar.

● **Type recruitment.**

Additional Information
As you type, an animated pen appears over the spelling indicator while the spelling check is in the process of checking for errors. When no spelling errors are located, the indicator appears as 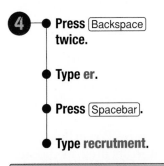.

Your screen should be similar to Figure 1.14

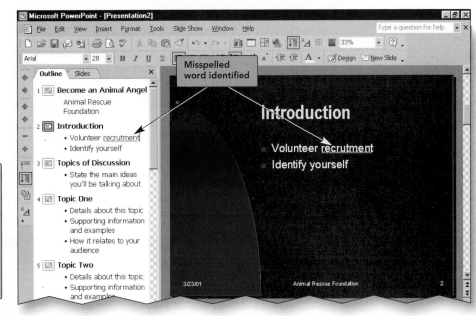

Figure 1.14

Again, the program has identified a word as misspelled. Another way to quickly correct a misspelled word is to select the correct spelling from a list of suggested spelling corrections displayed on the shortcut menu.

5
● **Right-click on the misspelled word in the Outline tab to display the shortcut menu.**

Your screen should be similar to Figure 1.15

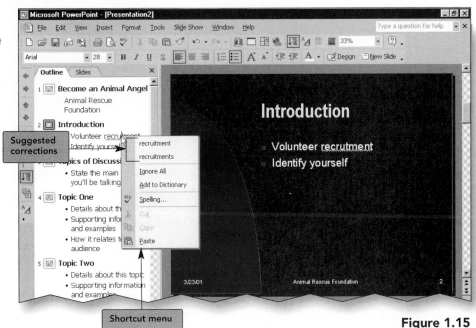

Figure 1.15

This menu displays two suggested correct spellings. The menu also includes several related menu options described below.

Option	Effect
Ignore All	Instructs PowerPoint to ignore the misspelling of this word throughout the rest of this session.
Add to Dictionary	Adds the word to the custom dictionary list. When a word is added to the custom dictionary, PowerPoint will always accept that spelling as correct.
Spelling	Starts the spelling checker to check the entire presentation.

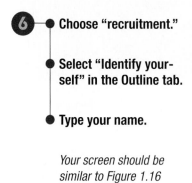

Additional Information

If there is only one suggested spelling correction, the correction is automatically inserted.

Sometimes there are no suggested replacements because PowerPoint cannot locate any words in its dictionary that are similar in spelling, or the suggestions are not correct. If this happens, you need to edit the word manually. You will replace the word with the correct spelling and enter your name on this slide.

6 ● **Choose "recruitment."**

● **Select "Identify yourself" in the Outline tab.**

● **Type your name.**

Your screen should be similar to Figure 1.16

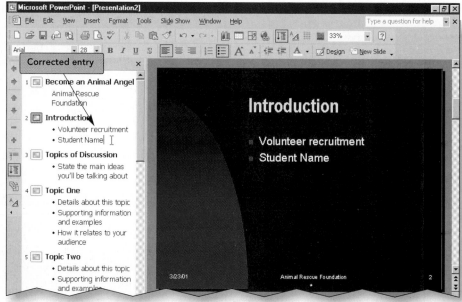

Figure 1.16

You are now ready to update the third slide in your presentation by entering the three main topics you will be discussing. You want to enter each topic on a separate bulleted line. The first bullet is already displayed and contains sample text that you will replace. To add additional lines and bullets, you simply press ←Enter.

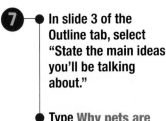

7
- In slide 3 of the Outline tab, select "State the main ideas you'll be talking about."

- Type **Why pets are abandoned**.

- Press ←Enter.

- Type **How you can help**.

- Press ←Enter.

- Type **How does the Foundation help?** (do not press ←Enter).

HAVING TROUBLE?
If you accidentally insert an extra bullet and blank line, press Backspace twice to remove them.

Your screen should be similar to Figure 1.17

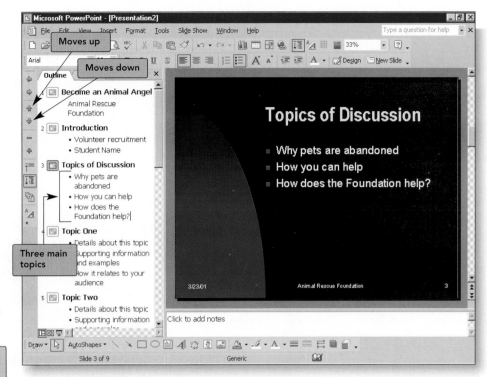

Figure 1.17

You realize that you entered the topics in the wrong order. You want the last item to be the first item in the list. A bulleted point can be moved easily by selecting it and dragging it to a new location, or by using the Move Up or Move Down buttons in the Outlining toolbar. When using the buttons, the insertion point must be on the bulleted item you want to move. You will move the bulleted item on the current line up two lines.

8
- Click Move Up (2 times).

Your screen should be similar to Figure 1.18

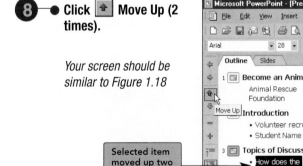

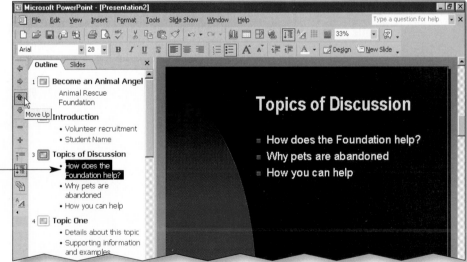

Figure 1.18

Editing in the Slide Pane

Next you want to update the content of the fourth slide. The fourth slide contains the title "Topic One" and a list of three bulleted items. The title and the bulleted list are two separate elements or placeholders on the slide. **Placeholders** are boxes that are designed to contain specific types of items or **objects** such as the slide title text, bulleted item text, charts, tables, and pictures. Each slide can have several different types of placeholders. To indicate which placeholder to work with, you must first select it. You will change the sample text in the title placeholder first in the slide pane.

1 ● **Click on slide 4 in the Outline tab to display it in the slide pane.**

● **Click anywhere on the slide title text in the slide pane.**

Your screen should be similar to Figure 1.19

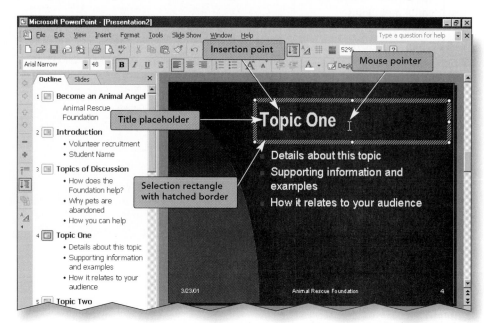

Figure 1.19

Additional Information

A dotted border around a selected object indicates you can format the box itself. Clicking the hatch-marked border changes it to a dotted border.

The title placeholder is now a selected object and is surrounded by a **selection rectangle**. The hatch-marked border of the selection rectangle indicates you can enter, delete, select, and format the text inside the placeholder. An insertion point is displayed to show your location in the text and to allow you to select and edit the text. The mouse pointer appears as an I-beam to be used to position the insertion point. You will enter the new title for this slide.

2 ● **Select the title text.**

HAVING TROUBLE?

Drag to select a portion of the text, double-click to select a word, or triple-click to select a line.

● **Type Why Pets Are Abandoned.**

Your screen should be similar to Figure 1.20

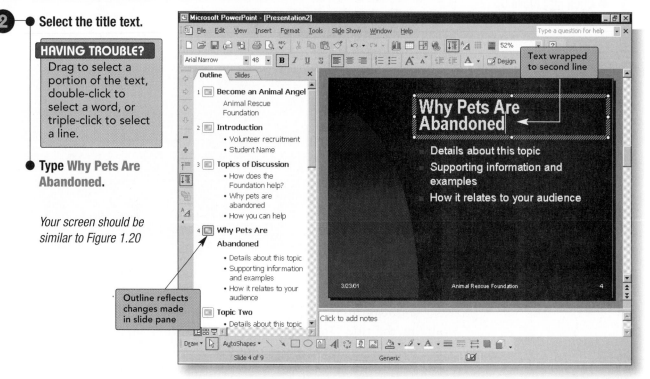

Figure 1.20

Notice that the text automatically wrapped to a second line when the length exceeded the width of the box. The Outline tab reflects the changes as they are made in the slide pane. Next you need to replace the sample text in the bulleted list.

3

- **Click on any of the bulleted items to select the placeholder.**

- **Select all three items in the placeholder box.**

- **Type Poor or deteriorating health.**

- **Press ↵Enter.**

- **Enter the following text for the next three bullets:**

Maintenance expenses

Change in lifestyle

Behavioral problems

Your screen should be similar to Figure 1.21

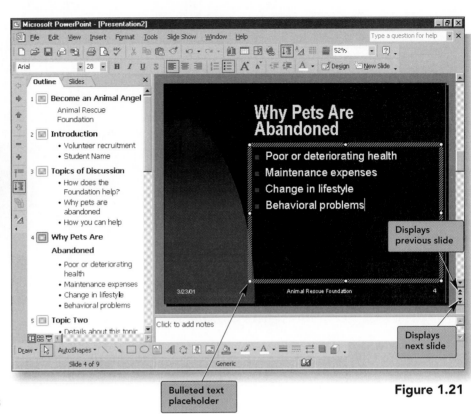

Figure 1.21

Now you are ready to change the text in the next slide. You want this slide to display how the Animal Rescue Foundation helps abandoned pets. In addition to clicking on the slide in the Outline tab, the following features can be used to move to other slides in Normal view.

To Display	Action
Previous slide	Click ⬆
	Click above scroll box
	Press Page Up
Next slide	Click ⬇
	Click below scroll box
	Press Page Down
Any slide	Drag scroll box until the ScreenTip displays the slide you want to view

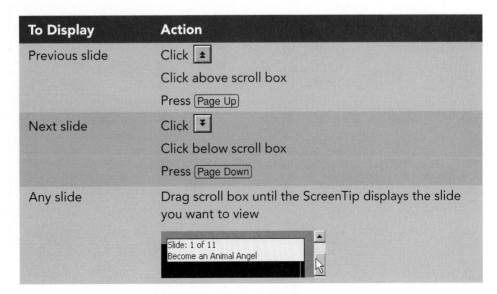

You will enter a new slide title and text for the bulleted items.

4 ● Click ⬛ Next Slide to display slide 5.

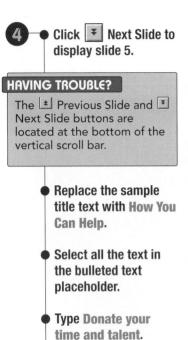

HAVING TROUBLE?
The ⬛ Previous Slide and ⬛ Next Slide buttons are located at the bottom of the vertical scroll bar.

● Replace the sample title text with How You Can Help.

● Select all the text in the bulleted text placeholder.

● Type Donate your time and talent.

● Press ⏎Enter.

Your screen should be similar to Figure 1.22

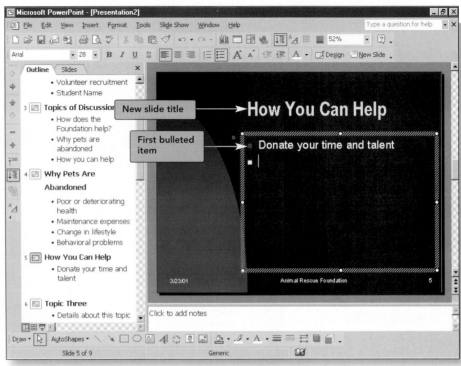

Figure 1.22

Demoting and Promoting Bulleted Items

You want the next bulleted item to be indented below the first bulleted item. Indenting a bulleted point to the right **demotes** it, or makes it a lower or subordinate topic in the outline hierarchy.

1 ● Click ➡ Demote on the Outlining toolbar.

● Type Become a foster parent.

● Press ⏎Enter.

● Type Work at adoption fairs.

● Press ⏎Enter.

Your screen should be similar to Figure 1.23

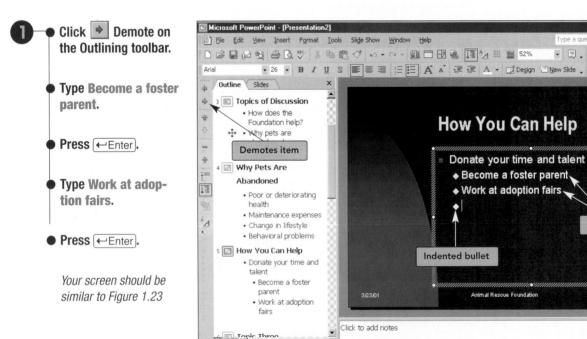

Figure 1.23

Additional Information

You can also demote and promote bulleted items in the Outline tab using the same procedure.

The bullet style of the demoted lines is ◆. When you demote a bulleted point, PowerPoint continues to indent to the same level until you cancel the indent. Before entering the next item, you want to remove the indentation, or **promote** the line. Promoting a line moves it to the left, or up a level in the outline hierarchy.

2 ● Click 🔄 Promote.

● Type Donate new or used items.

● Press ←Enter.

● Enter the following two bulleted items:

Crates and pads

Collars, leads, etc.

Your screen should be similar to Figure 1.24

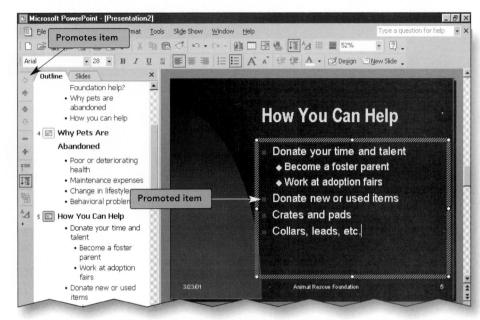

Figure 1.24

You can also promote or demote bulleted items after the text has been entered. The insertion point can be anywhere on the line to be promoted or demoted.

3 ● Demote the items "Crates and pads" and "Collars, leads, etc."

Another Method

You can also press Tab⇄ or ⇧Shift + Tab⇄ to demote or promote an item. However, the insertion point must be at the beginning of the line. The 🔼 Increase Indent and 🔽 Decrease Indent buttons on the Formatting toolbar can also promote and demote outline levels.

Your screen should be similar to Figure 1.25

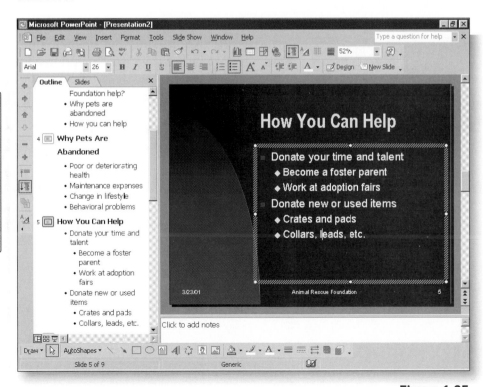

Figure 1.25

You still have three more bulleted items to add to this text placeholder. Notice, however, that the last item is near the bottom of the box. As you type, the text AutoFit feature will automatically reduce the size of the text and line spacing so it fits inside the placeholder.

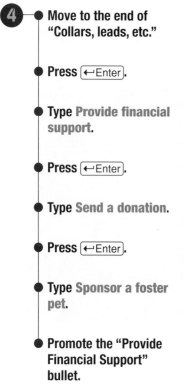

4 ● Move to the end of "Collars, leads, etc."

● Press ⏎Enter.

● Type **Provide financial support**.

● Press ⏎Enter.

● Type **Send a donation**.

● Press ⏎Enter.

● Type **Sponsor a foster pet**.

● Promote the "Provide Financial Support" bullet.

Your screen should be similar to Figure 1.26

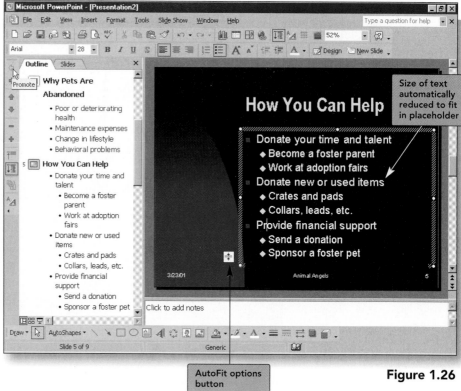

Figure 1.26

As you continued entering more bulleted items, the text size reduced even more. Also notice the ⬍ AutoFit Options button appears next to the placeholder. It contains options that allow you to control the AutoFit feature and to handle the over-spilling text.

Splitting Text Between Slides

Generally when creating slides, it is a good idea to limit the number of bulleted items on a slide to five. It is also recommended that the number of words per bulleted item not exceed five words. This is often called the "5 by 5 rule." In this case, because there are ten bulleted items on this slide, you want to split the slide content between two slides.

1 ● Click the ⊞ AutoFit Options button.

● Choose Split Text Between Two Slides.

Your screen should be similar to Figure 1.27

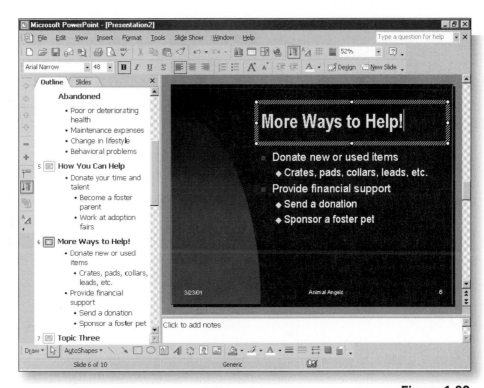

Figure 1.27

A new slide is inserted into the presentation containing the same title as the previous slide and the last two bulleted topic groups. Because the split occurs at a main topic, there are still six bulleted items on the new slide. You will combine two items into one to reduce the number to five and change the title of the slide.

2 ● Click the title placeholder.

● Replace the title text with More Ways to Help!

● Move to the end of the second bulleted item and press [Del].

● Edit the item to be Crates, pads, collars, leads, etc.

Your screen should be similar to Figure 1.28

Figure 1.28

Saving, Closing, and Opening a Presentation

You have just been notified of an important meeting that is to begin in a few minutes. Before leaving for the meeting, you want to save the presentation. As you enter and edit text to create a new presentation, the changes you make are immediately displayed onscreen and are stored in your computer's memory. However, they are not permanently stored until you save your work to a file on a disk. Once a presentation is saved as a file, it can be closed and opened again at a later time to be further edited.

As a backup against the accidental loss of work due to power failure or other mishap, Office XP includes an AutoRecover feature. When this feature is on, as you work you may see a pulsing disk icon briefly appear in the status bar. This indicates the program is saving your work to a temporary recovery file. The time interval between automatic saving can be set to any period you specify; the default is every 10 minutes. When you start up again, the recovery file is automatically opened containing all changes you made up to the last time it was saved by AutoRecover. You then need to save the recovery file. If you do not save it, it is deleted when closed. While AutoRecover is a great feature for recovering lost work, it should not be used in place of regularly saving your work.

Saving the Presentation

Additional Information

When a presentation is saved for the first time, either command can be used.

You will save the work you have done so far on the presentation. The Save or Save As commands on the File menu are used to save files. The Save command or the 🖫 Save button will save the active file using the same file name by replacing the contents of the existing file with the document as it appears on your screen. The Save As command allows you to save a file with a new file name and/or to a new location. This leaves the original file unchanged.

1 ● Choose **F**ile/Save **A**s.

Your screen should be similar to Figure 1.29

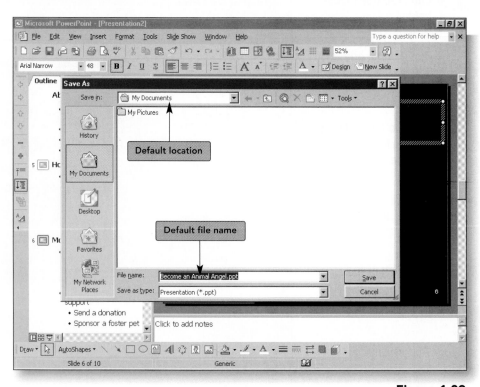

Figure 1.29

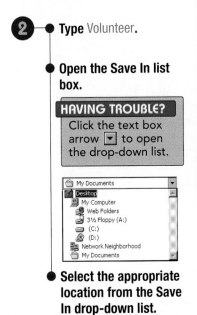
The Save As dialog box is displayed in which you specify the location to save the file and the file name. The Save In list box displays the default location where files are stored. The File Name text box displays the title from the first slide as the default file name. You will change the location to the location where you save your files and the file name. Notice that the default name is highlighted, indicating it is selected and will be replaced as you type the new name.

2 ● **Type** Volunteer.

● **Open the Save In list box.**

HAVING TROUBLE?
Click the text box arrow ▼ to open the drop-down list.

● **Select the appropriate location from the Save In drop-down list.**

HAVING TROUBLE?
If you are saving to a floppy disk and an error message is displayed, check that your disk is properly inserted in the drive and click ⬚ OK ⬚.

Your screen should be similar to Figure 1.30

HAVING TROUBLE?
If your dialog box does not display file extensions, your Windows program has this option deactivated.

Additional Information
If your system uses Windows NT, My Network Places is Network Neighborhood.

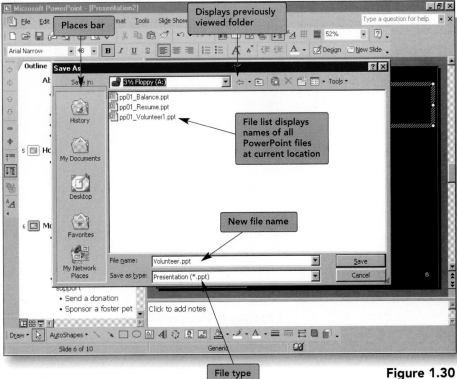

Figure 1.30

The large list box displays the names of any PowerPoint files (if any) stored in that location. Only PowerPoint presentation files are listed, because the selected file type in the Save As Type list box is Presentation. Presentation files have a default file extension of .ppt.

You can also select the save location from the Places bar along the left side of the dialog box. The icons bring up a list of recently accessed files and folders, the contents of the My Documents and Favorites folders, the Windows desktop, and folders that reside on a network or Web through the My Network Places. Selecting a folder from one of these lists changes to that location. You can also click the ⬅ button in the toolbar to return to folders that were previously opened during the current session.

3 ● Click [Save].

Your screen should be similar to Figure 1.31

New file name

Closes document window

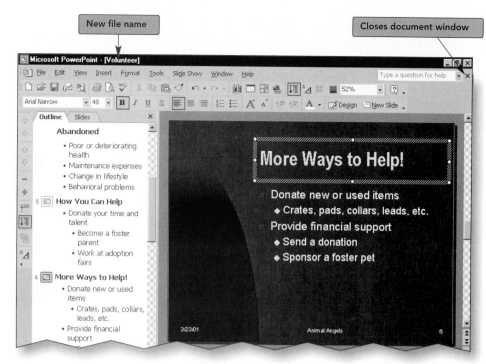

Figure 1.31

The new file name is displayed in the window title bar. The presentation is now saved in a new file named Volunteer. The view in use at the time the file is saved is also saved with the file.

Closing a Presentation

You are now ready to close the file.

1 ● Click ☒ Close Window (in the menu bar).

Another Method
The menu equivalent is File/Close.

Your screen should be similar to Figure 1.32

Blank PowerPoint window

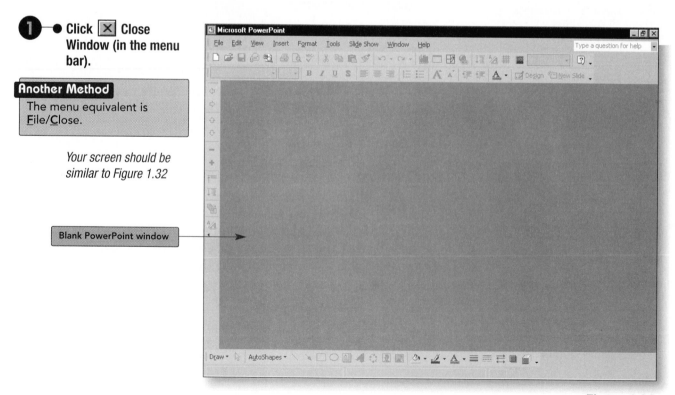

Figure 1.32

The presentation is closed, and a blank PowerPoint window is displayed. Always save your slide presentation before closing a file or leaving the PowerPoint program. As a safeguard against losing your work if you forget to save the presentation, PowerPoint will remind you to save any unsaved presentation before closing the file or exiting the program.

Note: If you are ending your lab session now, choose File/Exit to exit the program.

Opening an Existing Presentation

After returning from your meeting, you hastily continued to enter the information for several more slide and saved the presentation using a new file name. You will open this file to see the information in the new slides and continue working on the presentation.

① • **Choose View/Task Pane.**

• **Click** 🖼 More presentations... **(in the task pane).**

• **If necessary, select the location containing your data files from the Look In drop-down list box.**

Your screen should be similar to Figure 1.33

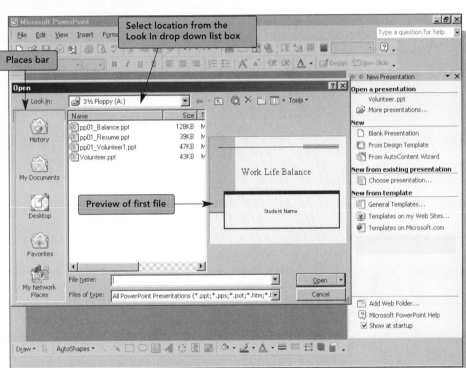

Figure 1.33

In the Open dialog box you specify the location and name of the file you want to open. The Look In drop-down list box displays the last specified location, in this case the location where you saved the Volunteer presentation. The large list box displays the names of all presentations, with the file extensions displayed in the Files of Type box. As in the Save As dialog box, the Places bar can be used to quickly access recently used files. A preview of the first file in the file list is displayed in the right side of the dialog box.

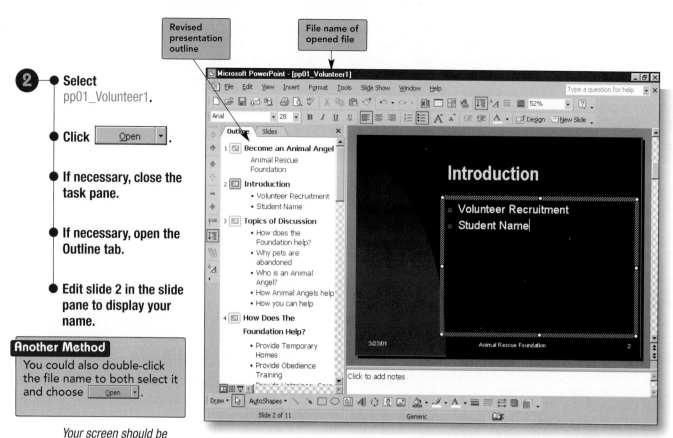

Revised presentation outline

File name of opened file

2 ● **Select** pp01_Volunteer1.

● **Click** [Open ▾].

● **If necessary, close the task pane.**

● **If necessary, open the Outline tab.**

● **Edit slide 2 in the slide pane to display your name.**

Another Method

You could also double-click the file name to both select it and choose [Open ▾].

Your screen should be similar to Figure 1.34

Figure 1.34

Checking Spelling

As you entered the information on the additional slides, you left several typing errors uncorrected. To correct the misspelled words and grammatical errors, you can use the shortcut menu to correct each individual word or error, as you learned earlier. However, in many cases you may find it more efficient to wait until you are finished writing before you correct any spelling or grammatical errors. Rather than continually breaking your train of thought to correct errors as you type, you can check the spelling on all slides of the presentation at once.

1 ● Click ⌨ Spell Check.

Another Method

The menu equivalent is
Tools/Spelling and Grammar
and the keyboard shortcut is
F7 . You can also double-
click the spelling indicator
in the status bar to start
the spelling checker. Using
this method moves to the
first potential spelling error
and displays the shortcut
menu.

*Your screen should be
similar to Figure 1.35*

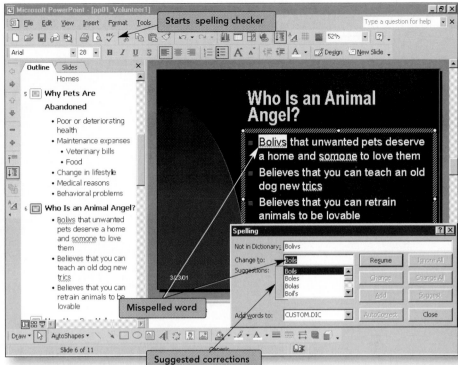

Figure 1.35

Additional Information

The spelling checker
identifies many proper names
and technical terms as
misspelled. To stop this from
occurring, use the **Add**
Words to option to add
those names to the custom
dictionary.

The program jumps to slide 6, highlights the first located misspelled word,
"Bolivs," in the Outline pane, and opens the Spelling dialog box. The
Spelling dialog box displays the misspelled word in the Not in Dictionary
text box. The Suggestions list box displays the words the spelling checker
has located in the dictionary that most closely match the misspelled word.
The first word is highlighted.

Although the list displays several additional suggestions, none of them is
correct. Sometimes the spelling checker does not display any suggested replacements because it cannot locate any words in the dictionaries that are
similar in spelling. If there are no suggestions, the Not in Dictionary text
box simply displays the word that is highlighted in the text. When none of
the suggestions is correct, you need to edit the word yourself by typing the
correction in the Change To text box.

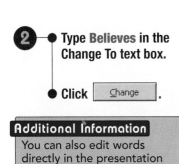

2 ● Type **Believes** in the Change To text box.

● Click [Change].

You can also edit words directly in the presentation and then click [Resume] to continue checking spelling.

Your screen should be similar to Figure 1.36

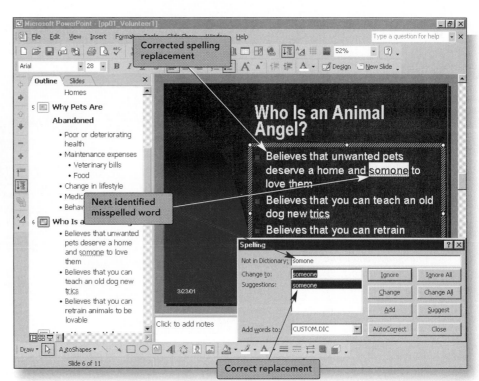

Figure 1.36

The corrected replacement is made in the slide. Once the Spelling dialog box is open, the spelling checker continues to check the entire presentation for spelling errors. The next misspelled word, "somone," is identified. In this case, the suggested replacement is correct.

3 ● Click [Change].

If necessary, move the dialog box to see the located misspelled word.

● Click [Change] to accept the next correction, "tricks."

● Correct any other located spelling errors as needed.

● Click [OK] in response to the message telling you that the spelling check is complete.

● Save the revised presentation as Volunteer2 to the appropriate data file location.

Your screen should be similar to Figure 1.37

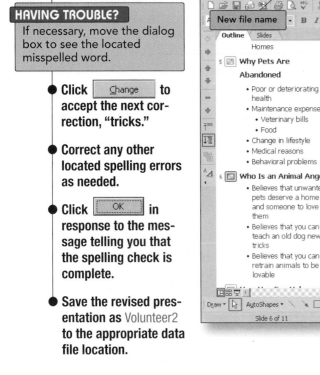
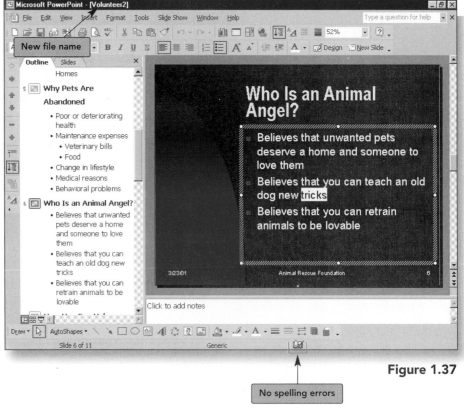

Figure 1.37

Working with Slides

To get a better overall picture of all slides in the presentation, you will switch to Slide Sorter view.

1 ● Click 🔡 **Slide Sorter view.**

Another Method

The menu equivalent is View/Slide Sorter.

Your screen should be similar to Figure 1.38

HAVING TROUBLE?

Do not be concerned if your screen displays a different number of slides per row. This is a function of your monitor settings.

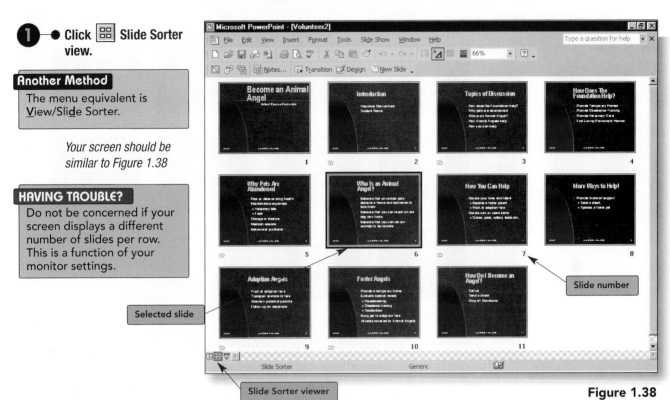

Figure 1.38

Additional Information

This view also has its toolbar that is used to add enhancements to your presentation. You will learn about these features in Lab 2.

Viewing the slides side by side helps you see how your presentation flows. There are still eleven slides in the presentation, but all the sample text that was provided by the AutoContent Wizard has been replaced by the text for the presentation. The slide number appears below each slide. Notice that slide 6, the slide you were last viewing in Normal view, is displayed with a dark border around it. This indicates that the slide is selected.

Deleting Slides

As you look at the slides, you decide the second slide does not really add much to the presentation and you want to delete it.

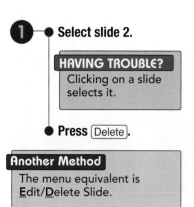

1 • **Select slide 2.**

HAVING TROUBLE?
Clicking on a slide selects it.

• **Press** Delete.

Another Method
The menu equivalent is Edit/Delete Slide.

Your screen should be similar to Figure 1.39

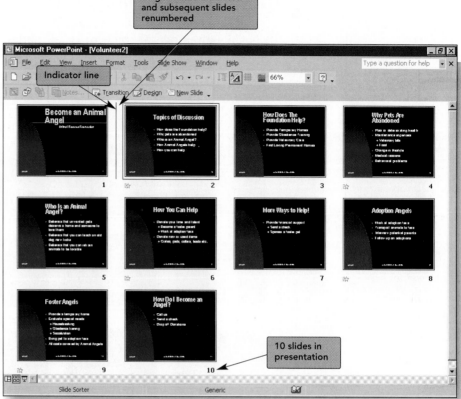

Figure 1.39

The Introduction slide has been deleted, and slides 3 through 11 have been appropriately renumbered 2 through 10. An indicator line appears between slides 1 and 2 where the deleted slide once existed.

Moving Slides

Next you decide to switch the order of slide 8, Adoption Angels, with slide 9, Foster Angels. To reorder a slide in Slide Sorter view, you drag it to its new location using drag and drop. As you drag the mouse pointer, the indicator line appears to show you where the slide will appear in the presentation. When the indicator line is located where you want the slide to be placed, release the mouse button.

1 • Select slide 9.

• Drag the mouse pointer until the indicator line is displayed before slide 8.

• Release the mouse button.

Another Method
You can also use the Edit/Cut and Edit/Paste commands to move slides in Slide Sorter view.

Your screen should be similar to Figure 1.40

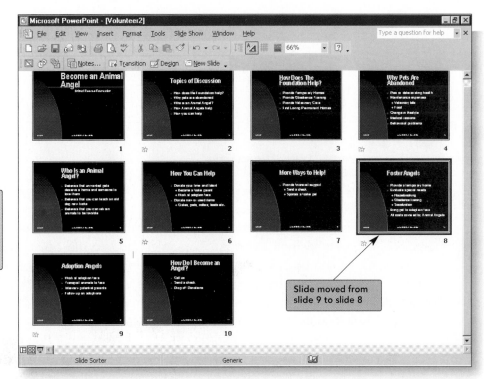

Figure 1.40

The Foster Angels slide is now before the Adoption Angels slide.

Inserting Slides

During your discussion with the foundation director, it was suggested that you add a slide showing the history of the organization. To include this information in the presentation, you will insert a new slide after slide 3.

1 • Click in the space between slide 3 and slide 4.

Additional Information
The indicator line shows you where the new slide will be added.

• Click ⬚ New Slide .

Another Method
The menu equivalent is Insert/New Slide and the keyboard shortcut is Ctrl + M.

Your screen should be similar to Figure 1.41

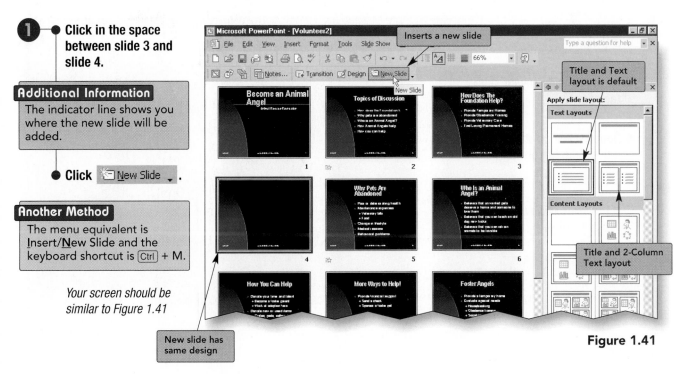

Figure 1.41

A blank new slide is inserted. It has the same design elements as the other slides in the presentation.

Selecting the Slide Layout

The Slide Layout task pane is automatically displayed so that you can select a slide layout for the new slide. The default layout, Title and Text, is selected.

---

concept 6

Layout

6   The **layout** controls the way items are arranged on a slide. A layout contains placeholders for the different items such as bulleted text, titles, charts, and so on. PowerPoint includes 27 predefined layouts that can be selected and applied to slides. For example, there are text layouts that include placeholders for a title and bulleted text, and content layouts that include placeholders for a table, diagram, chart, or clip art.

You can change the layout of an existing slide by selecting a new layout. If the new layout does not include placeholders for objects that are already on your slide (for example, if you created a chart and the new layout does not in-

clude a chart placeholder), you do not lose the information. All objects remain on the slide and the selected layout is automatically adjusted by adding the appropriate type of placeholder for the object. Alternatively, as you add new objects to a slide, the layout automatically adjusts by adding the appropriate type of placeholder. You can also rearrange, size, and format placeholders on a slide any way you like to customize the slide's appearance.

To make creating slides easy, use the predefined layouts. The layouts help you keep your presentation format consistent and, therefore, more professional.

Because this slide will contain two columns of text about the history of the organization, you want to use the two-column text layout.

1 ● **Click** ⊞⊞ **Title and 2-Column Text.**

● **Close the Slide Layout task pane.**

● **Double-click on slide 4 to switch to Normal view.**

Your screen should be similar to Figure 1.42

Additional Information

The layout of an existing slide can be changed using Format/Slide Layout.

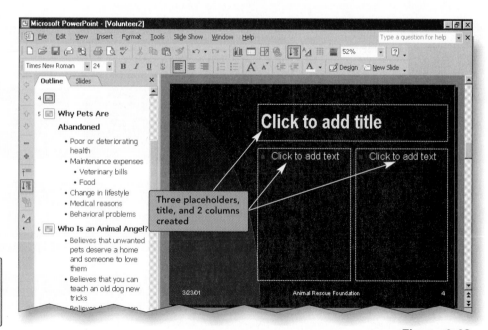

Figure 1.42

The slide displays the three placeholders created by the two-column text layout. Next you will add text to the slide presenting a brief history of the Animal Rescue Foundation. First you will enter the slide title and then the list of dates and events.

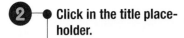

- Click in the title placeholder.

- Type **Animal Rescue Foundation History.**

- Click in the left text placeholder.

- Type **Year.**

- Press **←Enter**.

- Continue entering the information shown below. Remember to press **←Enter** to create a new line.

  1990

  1991

  1997

  2000

- In the same manner, enter the following text in the right text placeholder:

  Event

  Founded by Ed Wilton

  Built first shelter

  Began volunteer program

  Expanded to 10 shelters

  Your screen should be similar to Figure 1.43

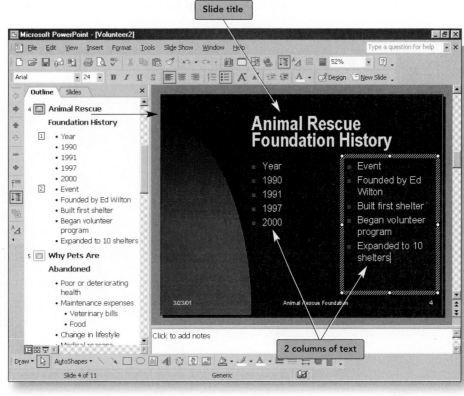

Figure 1.43

The left placeholder is too big for its contents, and the right placeholder is too small. To fix this, you can adjust the size of the placeholders.

Sizing a Placeholder

The eight boxes in the selection rectangle are **sizing handles** that can be used to adjust the size of the placeholder. Dragging the corner sizing handles will adjust both the height and width at the same time, whereas the center handles adjust the side borders to which they are associated. When you point to the sizing handle, the mouse pointer appears as ⟷ indicating the direction you can drag to adjust the size.

1

- **On the right placeholder, drag the left-center sizing handle to the left until each item is on a single line (see Figure 1.44).**
- **Select the left placeholder and drag the right-center sizing handle to the left (see Figure 1.44).**

Your screen should be similar to Figure 1.44

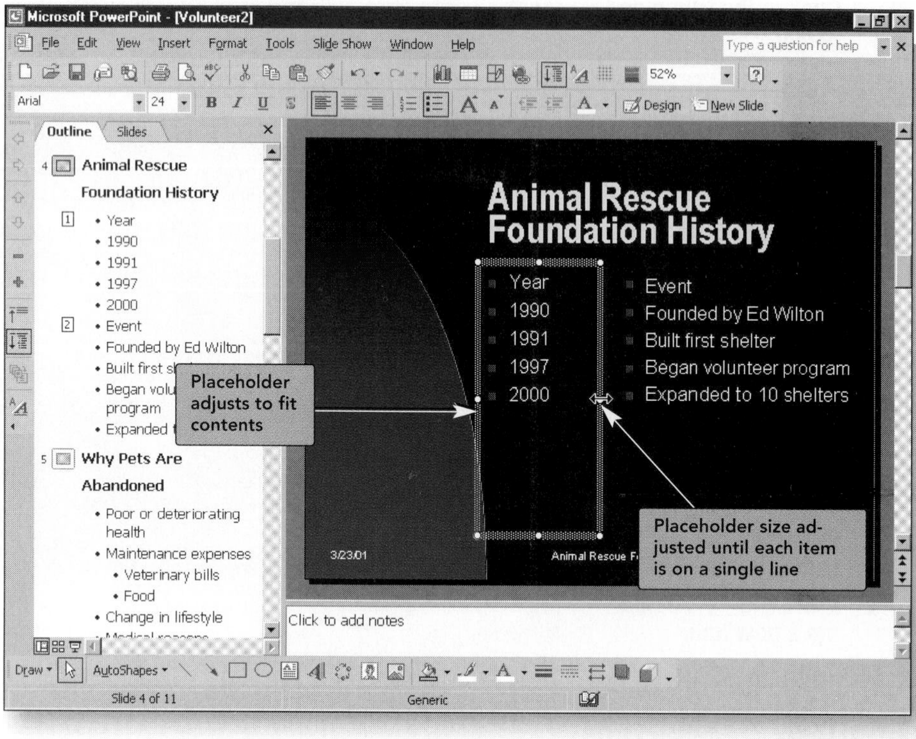

Figure 1.44

Moving a Placeholder

Next you want to move both placeholders so they appear more centered in the space. An object can be moved anywhere on a slide by dragging the selection rectangle. The mouse pointer appears as ✥ when you can move a placeholder. You will select both placeholders and move them at the same time. A dotted outline is displayed as you drag the placeholder to show your new location.

1 ● **With the left place-holder still selected hold down** Ctrl **while clicking on the right placeholder to select both.**

● **Point to the selection rectangle (not a handle) and drag the selected placeholders to their new location (see Figure 1.45).**

● **Click anywhere outside the selected object to deselect it.**

● **Save your changes to the presentation using the same file name.**

HAVING TROUBLE?

Click 🖫 Save to quickly save the presentation.

Your screen should be similar to Figure 1.45

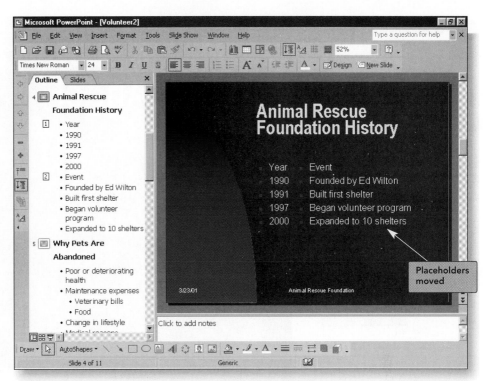

Figure 1.45

Rehearsing a Presentation

Now that the slides are in the order you want, you would like to see how the presentation would look when viewed by an audience. Rather than set up the presentation as you would to present it for an audience, a simple way to rehearse a presentation is to view it electronically on your screen as a slide show. A **slide show** displays each slide full screen and in order. While the slide show is running, you can plan what you want to say to supplement the information provided on the slides.

Using Slide Show View

Additional Information

The slide show will begin with the currently selected slide.

When viewing a slide show, each slide fills the screen, hiding the PowerPoint application window, so you can view the slides as your audience would. You will begin the slide show starting with the first slide.

1 ● Select slide 1 in the Outline tab.

● Click ⬚ Slide Show.

Another Method

The menu equivalent is View/Slide Show and the keyboard shortcut is F5.

Your screen should be similar to Figure 1.46

Slide displayed full screen in Slide Show view →

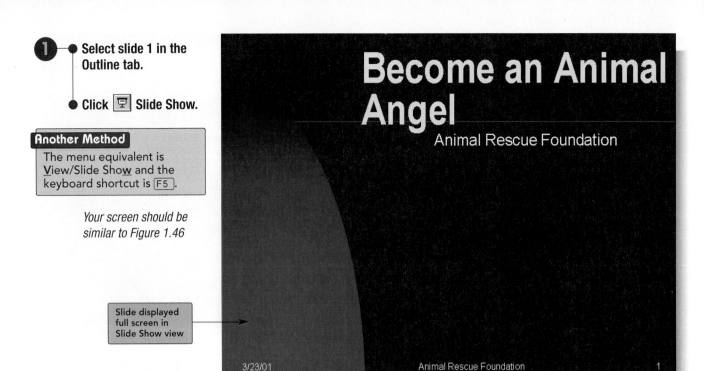

Figure 1.46

Additional Information

Pressing F1 while in Slide Show opens a Help window describing the actions you can use during the slide show.

The presentation title slide is displayed full screen, as it will appear when projected on a screen using computer projection equipment. The easiest way to see the next slide is to click the mouse button. You can also use the keys shown below to move to the next or previous slide.

Another Method

You can also select Next or Previous from the shortcut menu. Moving the mouse pointer in Slide Show displays 🖉△ in the lower left corner of the window. Clicking 🖉△ also opens the shortcut menu.

Next Slide	Previous Slide
Spacebar	Backspace
↵Enter	
→	←
↓	↑
Page Down	Page Up
N (for next)	P (for previous)

2 ● Click to display the next slide.

● Using each of the methods described, slowly display the entire presentation.

● When the last slide displays a black window click again to end the slide show.

Additional Information

You can press [Esc] at any time to end the slide show.

Your screen should be similar to Figure 1.47

Program returns to normal view

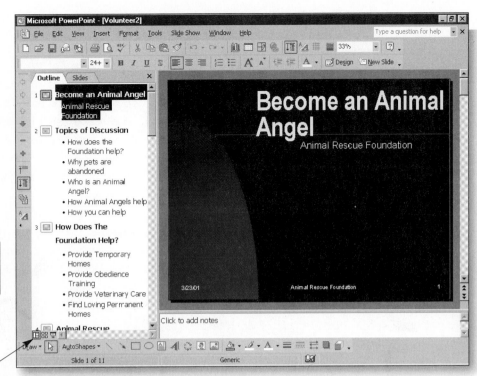

Figure 1.47

After the last slide is displayed, the program returns to the view you were last using, in this case Normal view.

Formatting Slide Text

While looking at the slide show, you decide that the title slide needs to have more impact. You also want to remove the bullets from the items on the history slide. Enhancing the appearance of the slide to make it more readable or attractive is called **formatting**. The default design template includes many basic formatting features already.

Applying different formatting to characters and paragraphs can greatly enhance the appearance of the slide. **Character formatting** features affect the selected characters only. They include changing the character style and size, applying effects such as bold and italics, changing the character spacing, and adding animated text effects. **Paragraph formatting** features affect an entire paragraph. A paragraph is text that has a carriage return from pressing [←Enter] at the end of it. Each item in a bulleted list, title, and subtitle are each paragraphs. Paragraph formatting features include how the paragraph is positioned or aligned between the margins, paragraph indentation, spacing above and below a paragraph, and line spacing within a paragraph.

Changing Fonts

First you will improve the appearance of the presentation title by changing the font of the title text.

Font and Font Size

7 A **font**, also commonly referred to as a **typeface**, is a set of characters with a specific design. The designs have names such as Times New Roman and Courier. Using fonts as a design element can add interest to your presentation and give your audience visual cues to help them find information quickly.

There are two basic types of fonts, serif and sans serif. **Serif** fonts have a flair at the base of each letter that visually leads the reader to the next letter. Two common serif fonts are Roman and Times New Roman. Serif fonts generally are used for text in paragraphs. **Sans serif** fonts do not have a flair at the base of each letter. Arial and Helvetica are two common sans serif fonts. Because sans serif fonts have a clean look, they are often used for headings in documents. It is good practice to use only two or three different fonts in a presentation as too many can distract from your presentation content and look unprofessional.

Each font has one or more sizes. **Font size** is the height and width of the character and is commonly measured in **points**, abbreviated pt. One point equals about 1/72 inch, and text in most documents is 10 pt or 12 pt.

Several common fonts in different sizes are shown in the following table.

Font Name	Font Type	Font Size
Arial	Sans serif	This is 10 pt. This is 16 pt.
Courier New	Serif	This is 10 pt. This is 16 pt.
Times New Roman	Serif	This is 10 pt. This is 16 pt.

To change the font before typing the text, use the command and then type. All text will appear in the specified setting until another font setting is selected. To change a font setting for existing text, select the text you want to change and then use the command. If you want to apply font formatting to a word, simply move the insertion point to the word and the formatting is automatically applied to the entire word.

① ● Select the text "Become an Animal Angel" in the slide pane.

Additional Information
The font used in the title is Arial Narrow, as displayed in the [Arial Narrow ▾] button.

● Open the [Arial Narrow ▾] Font drop-down list.

● Scroll the list and choose Comic Sans MS.

Another Method
The menu equivalent is Format/Font/Font.

Your screen should be similar to Figure 1.48

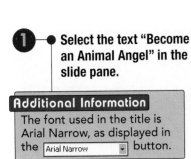

Font of current selection displayed in Font button

Figure 1.48

The text has changed to the new font style, and the Font button displays the font name used in the current selection.

Changing Font Size

The title text is also a little larger than you want it to be.

① ● Click [A̅] Decrease Font Size 2 times.

Additional Information
Use [A̅] Increase Font Size to incrementally increase the point size of selected text.

Another Method
You could also specify the point size from the [24 ▾] Font Size drop-down list or use Format/Font/Size.

Your screen should be similar to Figure 1.49

Additional Information
If a selection includes text in several different sizes, the smallest size appears in the Font Size button followed by a + sign.

Font size of current selection is displayed in Font Size button

Increases font size by increments

Decreases font size by increments

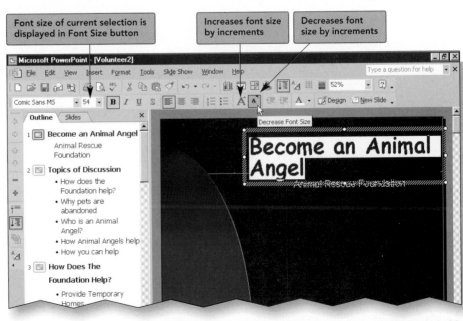

Figure 1.49

The Font Size button displays the point size of the current selection.

2 ● Replace the subtitle text with your name.

● Reduce the size of the subtitle placeholder to fit the contents.

HAVING TROUBLE?
Drag the sizing handles to size the placeholder.

● Size and move the placeholders as shown in Figure 1.50.

Your screen should be similar to Figure 1.50

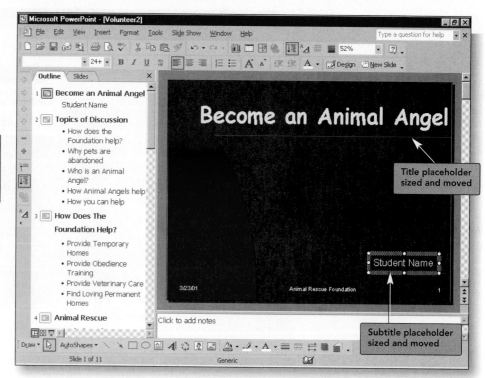

Figure 1.50

Removing Bullets

Next, you want to remove the bullets from the items on the history slide. You can quickly apply and remove bullets using ☰ Bullets on the Formatting toolbar. This button applies the bullet style associated with the design template you are using. Since the placeholder items already include bullets, using this button will remove them.

1

● **Select slide 4.**

● **Select both text place-holders.**

HAVING TROUBLE?

Hold down [Ctrl] while clicking on the placeholders to select both.

● **Click** [≣] **Bullets.**

Another Method

The menu equivalent is Format/**B**ullets and Numbering/Bulleted/None.

● **Save the presentation again.**

Your screen should be similar to Figure 1.51

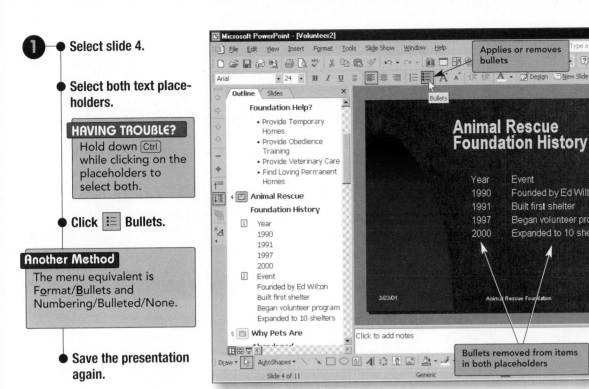

Figure 1.51

The bullets are removed from the items in both placeholders.

Working with Graphics

Next, you want to add a picture to the title slide. A picture is one of several different graphic objects that can be added to a slide.

concept 8

Graphics

1 A **graphic** is a non-text element or object, such as a drawing or picture, that can be added to a slide. A graphic can be a simple **drawing object** consisting of shapes such as lines and boxes that can be created using features on the Drawing toolbar. A drawing object is part of your presentation document. A **picture** is an image such as a graphic illustration or a scanned photograph. Pictures are graphics that were created from another program and are inserted in a slide as embedded objects. An **embedded object** becomes part of the presentation file and can be opened and edited using the **source program**, the program in which it was created. Several examples of drawing objects and pictures are shown below.

Add graphics to your presentation to help the audience understand concepts, to add interest, and to make your presentation stand out from others.

Photograph

Clip Art

We are pleased to announce the grand opening of Tom's Deli

Drawing Object

Inserting a Graphic from the Clip Organizer

You want to add a graphic to the slide below the title line. Graphic files can be obtained from a variety of sources. Many simple drawings called **clip art** are available in the Clip Organizer that comes with Office XP. The Clip Organizer's files, or clips, include art, sound, animation, and movies you can add to a presentation.

You can also create graphic files using a scanner to convert any printed document, including photographs, to an electronic format. Most images that are scanned and inserted into documents are stored as Windows bitmap files (.bmp). All types of graphics, including clip art, photographs, and other types of images, can be found on the Internet. These files are commonly stored as .jpg or .pcx files. Keep in mind that any images you locate on the Internet may be copyrighted and should only be used with permission. You can also purchase CDs containing graphics for your use.

You decide to check the Clip Organizer to find a suitable graphic.

1 ● Make slide 1.

● Click 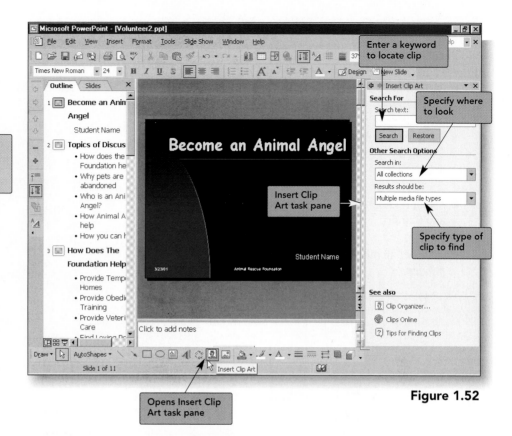 **Insert Clip Art (in the Drawing toolbar).**

Another Method

The menu equivalent is Insert/Picture/Clip Art.

Your screen should be similar to Figure 1.52

Figure 1.52

The Insert Clip Art task pane appears. Every item in the Clip Organizer has been named and assigned several keywords that describe the content of the clip. You can quickly locate clip art by entering a keyword in the Search Text text box. You will search using a keyword. You can also specify the locations to search and the type of media files, such as clip art, movies, photographs, or sound, to display in the results. You want to find clip art and photographs of animals.

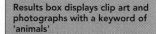
Results box displays clip art and photographs with a keyword of 'animals'

2 In the Search text box, type **animal**.

● Open the Results Should Be drop-down list.

● Select Photographs and Clip Art.

● Deselect all other options.

HAVING TROUBLE?

Make sure all other options are deselected. If there is a checkmark next to an item, click the checkmark to deselect that item.

● Click outside the drop-down list to close it.

● Click Search .

● Point to the 🖼 graphic.

Your screen should be similar to Figure 1.53

Opens short-cut menu

Keywords and graphic size

Figure 1.53

Additional Information

If you do not find a suitable clip in the Clip Organizer, clicking Clips Online in the task pane will take you to the Microsoft Clip Gallery Web site containing thousands of clips that are updated monthly.

The Results box displays thumbnails of all clip art and photographs with a keyword of "animals." You decide to try the graphic of the people and animals. Pointing to a graphic displays its associated keywords and information about its size in a ScreenTip. It also displays a · along the right edge of the graphic that is used to open the graphic shortcut menu. The graphic shortcut menu commands are used to work with and manage the items in the Clip Organizer. You can insert the clip, preview the clip in a larger size, add the clip to your list of Favorites, or find other clips that are similar.

3 ● Click ▎ to open the shortcut menu.

● **Choose** [Insert].

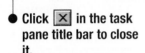

Another Method

You could also simply click on the graphic to insert it in the slide.

● Click ☒ in the task pane title bar to close it.

Your screen should be similar to Figure 1.54

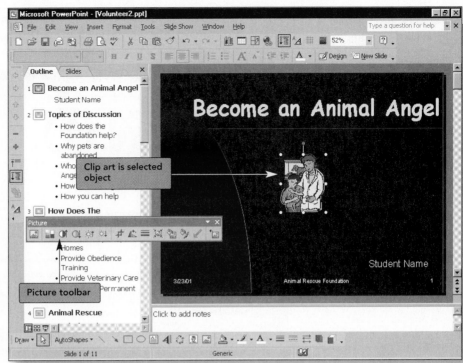

Figure 1.54

The clip art graphic is inserted in the center of the slide. It is a selected object and can be sized and moved like any other selected object. The picture toolbar is also automatically displayed and is used to modify the graphic.

Inserting a Graphic from a File

Although you think this graphic looks good, you want to see how a photograph you recently scanned of a puppy would look instead. The photograph has been saved as pp01_Puppy.jpg.

1 ● Click ▨ Insert
Picture (on the
Drawing toolbar).

Another Method

The menu
equivalent is
Insert/Picture/From
File.

● **Change the location to
your data file location.**

*Your screen should be
similar to Figure 1.55*

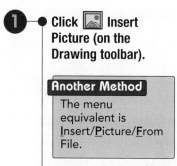

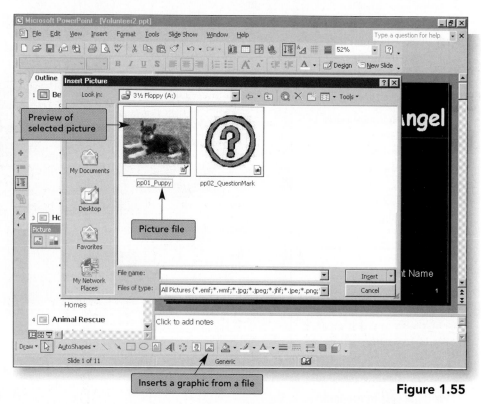

Inserts a graphic from a file

Figure 1.55

HAVING TROUBLE?

If the thumbnail preview is
not displayed, click ▦ Views
and choose Thumbnails.

The Insert Picture dialog box is similar to the Open and Save dialog boxes,
except the only types of files listed are files with picture file extensions. A
thumbnail preview of each picture is displayed above the file name.

2 ● **Select** pp01_Puppy.jpg.

● **Click** ▭ Insert ▾ .

● **Move the picture to
the right to see the
underlying clip art.**

*Your screen should be
similar to Figure 1.56*

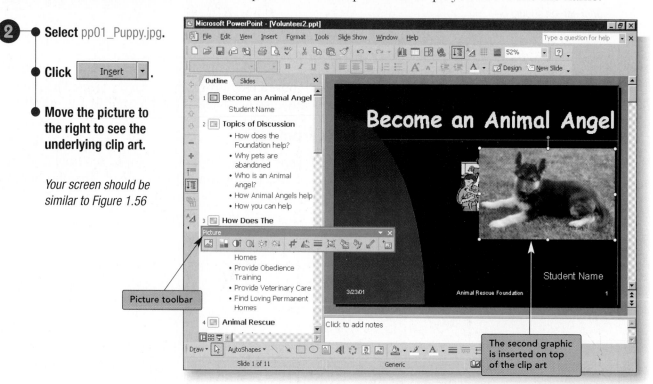

Figure 1.56

The second graphic is inserted on the slide on top of the clip art object. As
objects are added to a slide, they automatically stack in individual layers.

concept 9

Stacking Order

9 **Stacking order** is the order objects are inserted in the different layers of the slide. As each object is added to the slide, it is added to the top layer. Adding objects to separate layers allows each object to be positioned precisely on the page, including in front of and behind other objects. As objects are stacked in layers, they may overlap. To change the stacking order, open the Dr**aw** menu on the Drawing toolbar and select O**r**der.

Additional Information

Sometimes it is easy to lose an object behind another. If this happens, you can press [Tab⇆] to cycle forward or [⇧Shift] + [Tab⇆] to cycle backward through the stacked objects until the one you want is selected.

Since the photograph was the last object added to the slide, it is on the top layer of the stack. Although the photograph looks good, you think the clip art introduces the topic of volunteering better.

3 ● Click  Undo (2 times).

Another Method

The menu equivalent is **E**dit/**U**ndo or [Ctrl] + Z. You could also have simply pressed [Delete] to remove the selected object.

Your screen should be similar to Figure 1.57

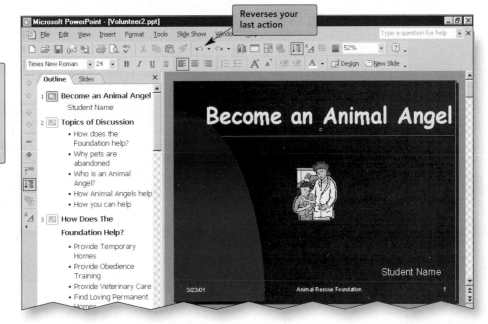

Figure 1.57

Using Undo reverses your last action. Notice that the Undo button includes a drop-down list button. Clicking this button displays a list of the most recent actions that can be reversed, with the most recent action at the top of the list. When you select an action from the drop-down list, you also undo all actions above it in the list.

Sizing and Moving a Graphic

Frequently, when a graphic is inserted, its size or placement will need to be adjusted. A graphic object is sized and moved just like a placeholder. You want to increase the graphic size slightly and position it in the space below the title.

1
- Click on the graphic to select it.

- Drag a corner sizing handle to increase its size to that shown in Figure 1.58.

- Drag the graphic to position it as shown in Figure 1.58.

- Click outside the graphic to deselect it.

Your screen should be similar to Figure 1.58

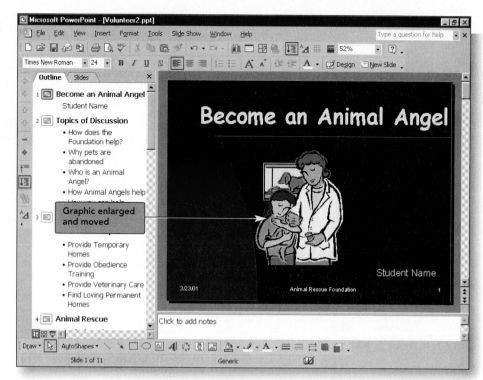

Figure 1.58

Now you think the title slide will make a much better impression. To see how the changes and enhancements you have made to the presentation will look full screen, you will run the slide show again.

2
- Save the presentation again.

- Run the slide show from the first slide.

Printing the Presentation

Although you still plan to make many changes to the presentation, you want to give a copy of the slides to the foundation director to get feedback regarding the content and layout. To save time and unnecessary printing and paper waste, it is always a good idea to preview onscreen how your slides will appear when printed.

Previewing the Presentation

Shading, patterns, and backgrounds that look good on the screen can make printed handouts unreadable, so you want to preview how the printout will look before making a copy for the director.

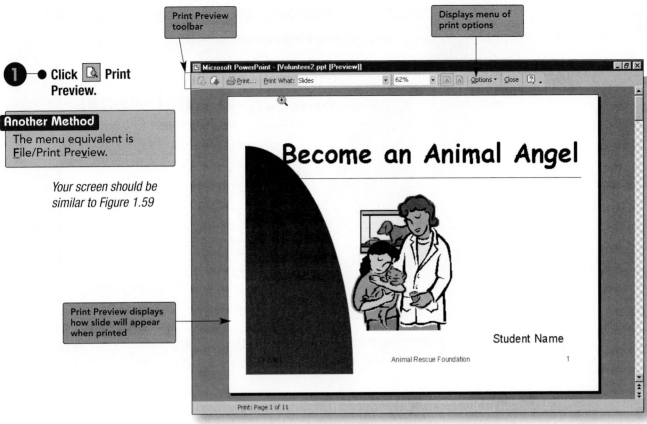

Figure 1.59

The Print Preview window shows how the first slide in the presentation will appear when printed using the selected printer. It is displayed in color if your selected printer is a color printer; otherwise, it appears in black and white or grayscale (shades of gray) as shown in Figure 1.59. Even if you have a color printer, you want to print the slides in grayscale. The Print Preview window also includes its own toolbar that lets you modify the default print settings.

2 ● **If you need to change to grayscale, click** Options ▾ **.**

● **Choose Color/Grayscale/Grayscale.**

The default grayscale setting (shown in Figure 1.59) shows you how the slide would look with some of the background in white, with black text, and with patterns in grayscale.

Printing Handouts

The Preview window displays a single slide on the page as it will appear when printed. You want to print several slides on a page.

Callouts and side notes from the figure:

- Print Preview toolbar
- Displays menu of print options
- **①** ● Click ☐ Print Preview.
- **Another Method** The menu equivalent is File/Print Preview.
- *Your screen should be similar to Figure 1.59*
- Print Preview displays how slide will appear when printed

1 ● **Open the Print What drop-down menu.**

Your screen should be similar to Figure 1.60

Figure 1.60

The Print What option is used to specify the type of presentation document you want to print: slides, handouts, outlines, or note pages. PowerPoint can print only one type of output at a time. The default is slides. The output types are described in the table below.

Output Type	Description
Slides	Prints one slide per page
Handouts	Prints multiple slides per page
Outline View	Prints the slide content as it appears in Outline view
Notes Pages	Prints the slide and the associated notes on a page

Additional Information
You will learn about notes in Lab 2.

You want to print handouts with 4 slides on a page.

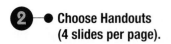

2 ● **Choose Handouts (4 slides per page).**

Your screen should be similar to Figure 1.61

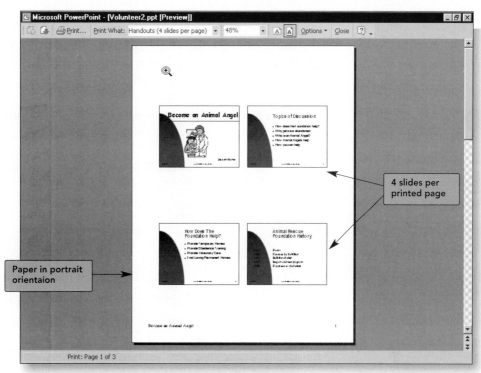

Figure 1.61

Changing Page Orientation

You also want to change the orientation or the direction the output is printed on a page. The default orientation for handouts is **portrait**. This setting prints across the width of the page. You will change the orientation to **landscape** so that the slides print across the length of the paper. Then you will preview the other pages.

1 ● **Click** 🅰 **Landscape.**

● **Use the Preview window scroll bar to view pages 2 and 3 of the handout.**

Your screen should be similar to Figure 1.62

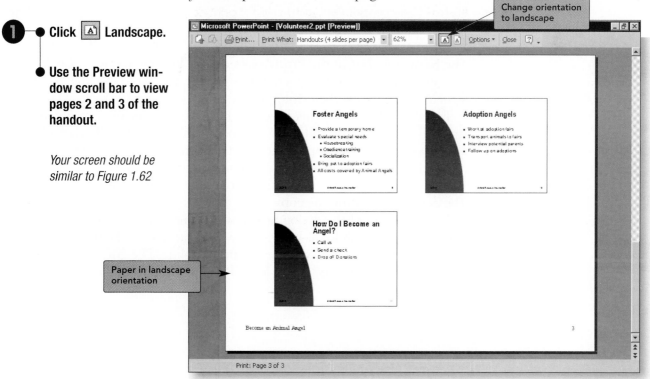

Figure 1.62

The slides are resized to the new page orientation and are slightly larger.

Checking Print Settings

You can print the slides directly from the Preview window using the  Print button; however, you do not want to send it directly to the printer just yet. First you need to check the print settings.

1 ● **Click** `Close` .

● **Choose File/Print.**

Another Method

The keyboard shortcut is `Ctrl` + P. You can use Print on the Standard toolbar if you do not need to make any changes to the default print settings.

Your screen should be similar to Figure 1.63

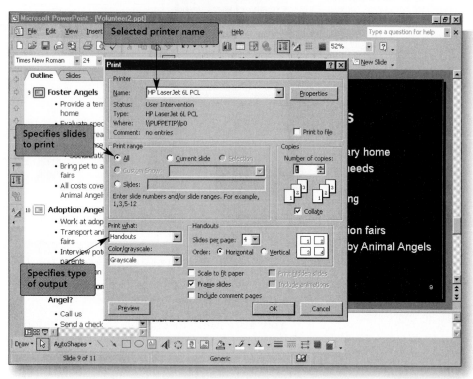

Figure 1.63

Note: Please consult your instructor for printing procedures that may differ from the following directions.

The Name text box in the Printer section displays the name of the selected printer. You may need to specify the printer you will be using. (Your instructor will provide the printer to select).

The Print Range settings specify which slides to print. The default setting, All, prints all the slides, while Current Slide prints only the slide you are viewing. The Slides option is used to specify individual slides or a range of slides to print by entering the slide numbers in the text box. The Copies section is used to specify the number of copies of the specified print range. The default is to print one copy.

At the bottom of the dialog box, PowerPoint displays options that allow you to print color slides as black-and-white slides, to make the slide images fill the paper, and to add a frame around the slide. The grayscale and handout options you specified in the Print Preview window are already selected.

2 ● If you need to select a different printer, open the Name drop-down list and select the appropriate printer.

● If necessary, make sure your printer is on and ready to print.

● Click   OK   .

> The 🖶 Printer icon appears in the status bar, indicating that the program is sending data to the Print Manager. Your handouts should be printing. The first page should be similar to the output shown here.

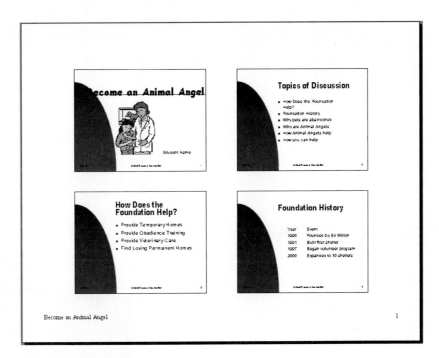

Exiting PowerPoint

> You will continue to work on the presentation in the next tutorial. Now you will exit the PowerPoint program.

1 ● Choose File/Exit.

● If asked to save the file again, choose   Yes   .

LAB 1

Creating a Presentation

Template (PP1.7)

A **template** is a file that includes predefined settings that can be used as a pattern to create many common types of presentations.

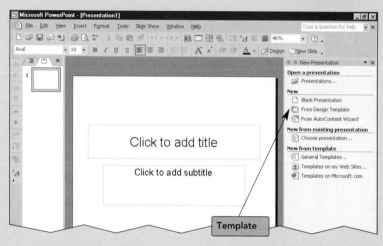

Template

Presentation Style (PP1.9)

A PowerPoint presentation can be made using five different **styles**: onscreen presentations, Web presentations, black-and-white or color overheads, and 35mm slides.

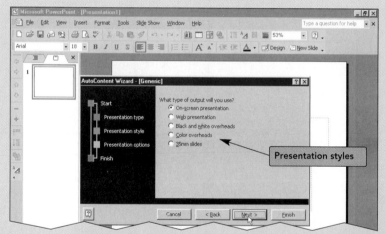

Presentation styles

Slide (PP1.10)

A **slide** is an individual "page" of your presentation. The first slide of a presentation is the title slide. Additional slides are used to support each main point in your presentation.

AutoCorrect (PP1.16)

The **AutoCorrect** feature makes some basic assumptions about the text you are typing and, based on these assumptions, automatically identifies and/or corrects the entry.

Spelling Check (PP1.16)

The **spelling check** feature advises you of misspelled words as you create and edit a presentation, and proposes possible corrections.

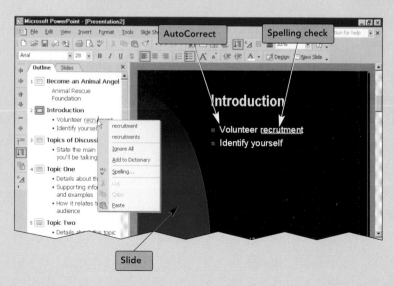

Slide

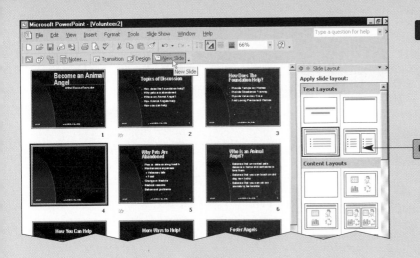

Layout (PP1.36)

PowerPoint includes 27 predefined **slide layouts** that can be selected and applied to slides.

Layout

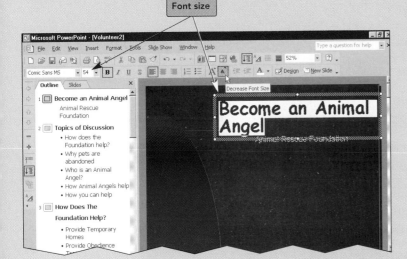

Font size

Font and Font Size (PP1.42)

A **font** is a set of characters with a specific design. Each font has one or more sizes. Using fonts as a design element can add interest to your presentation and give your audience visual cues to help them find information

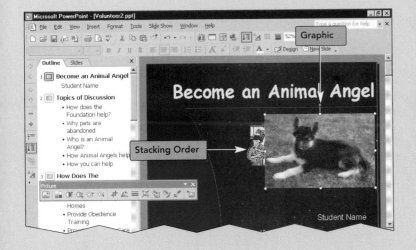

Graphic (PP1.46)

A **graphic** is a non-text element or object, such as a drawing or picture, that can be added to a slide.

Stacking Order (PP1.51)

Stacking order is the order objects are inserted in the different layers of the slide. As each object is added to the slide, it is added to the top layer.

key terms

AutoContent Wizard   PP1.7

AutoCorrect   PP1.16

character formatting   PP1.41

clip art   PP1.46

custom dictionary   PP1.16

default   PP1.6

demote   PP1.22

drawing object   PP1.46

Drawing toolbar   PP1.5

embedded object   PP1.46

font   PP1.42

font size   PP1.42

footer   PP1.10

format   PP1.41

Formatting toolbar   PP1.5

graphic   PP1.46

landscape layout   PP1.55

layout   PP1.36

main dictionary   PP1.16

object   PP1.36

Outlining toolbar   PP1.14

pane   PP1.12

paragraph formatting   PP1.41

picture   PP1.46

placeholder   PP1.20

point   PP1.42

portrait   PP1.55

promote   PP1.23

sans serif   PP1.42

selection rectangle   PP1.20

serif   PP1.42

sizing handles   PP1.20

slide   PP1.10

slide show   PP1.39

source program   PP1.46

stacking order   PP1.51

Standard toolbar   PP1.5

template   PP1.7

thumbnail   PP1.12

typeface   PP1.42

view   PP1.11

workspace   PP1.5

mous skills

The Microsoft Office User Specialist (MOUS) certification program is designed to measure your proficiency in performing basic tasks using the Office XP applications. Getting certified demonstrates that you have the skills and provides a valuable industry credential for employment. After completing this lab, you have learned the following Microsoft Office User Specialist skills:

Skill	Description	Page
Creating Presentations	Create presentations (manually and using automated tools)	PP1.7
	Add slides to and delete slides from presentations	PP1.33, PP1.35
Inserting and Modifying Text	Insert, format, and modify text	PP1.41
Inserting and Modifying Visual Elements	Add tables, charts, clip art, and bitmap images to slides	PP1.46
Modifying Presentation Formats	Rearrange slides	PP1.34
Printing Presentations	Preview and print slides, outlines, handouts, and speaker notes	PP1.52
Managing and Delivering Presentations	Deliver presentations	PP1.39

command summary

Command	Shortcut	Button	Action
File/New	Ctrl + N		Creates new presentation
File/Open	Ctrl + O		Opens existing presentation
File/Close			Closes presentation
File/Save	Ctrl + S		Saves presentation
File/Save As			Saves presentation using new file name and/or location
File/Print Preview			Displays preview of slide
File/Print	Ctrl + P		Prints presentation
File/Exit			Exits PowerPoint program
Edit/Undo	Ctrl + Z		Reverses last action
Edit/Select All	Ctrl + A		Selects all objects on a slide or all text in an object, or (in Outline pane) an entire outline
Edit/Delete Slide	Delete		Deletes selected slide
View/Normal			Switches to Normal view
View/Slide Sorter			Switches to Slide Sorter view
View/Slide Show	F5		Runs slide show
View/Task pane			Displays task pane
View/Toolbars			Displays or hides selected toolbars
Insert/New Slide	Ctrl + M		Inserts new slide
Insert/Picture/Clip Art			Opens Clip Organizer and inserts selected clip art
Insert/Picture/From File			Inserts a picture from file on disk
Format/Font/Font		Arial Narrow	Changes font type
Format/Font/Size		24	Changes font size
Format/Slide Layout			Changes the layout of an existing or new slide
Tools/Spelling	F7		Spell-checks presentation

Terminology

screen identification

In the following PowerPoint screen, several items are identified by letters. Enter the correct term for each item in the spaces that follow.

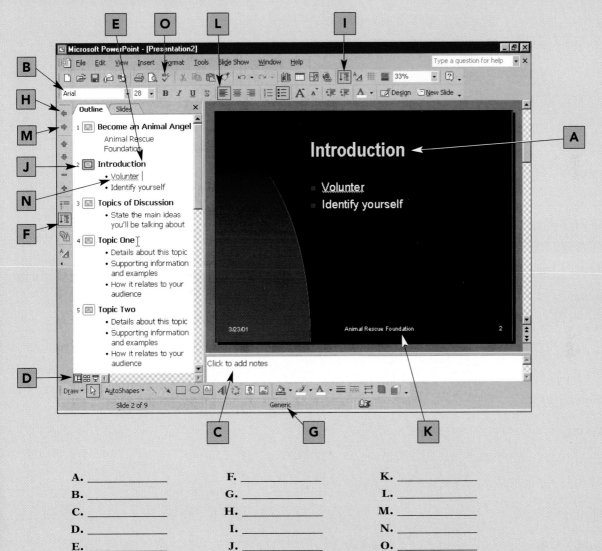

A. _____	F. _____	K. _____
B. _____	G. _____	L. _____
C. _____	H. _____	M. _____
D. _____	I. _____	N. _____
E. _____	J. _____	O. _____

matching

Match the numbered item with the correct lettered description.

1. AutoContent Wizard _____   a. displays slide pane, outline pane, and note pane

2. Normal view _____   b. displays miniatures of each slide

3. placeholder _____   c. guides you through steps to create a presentation

4. selection rectangle _____   d. prints multiple slides per page

5. [⬅] _____   e. indents items in outline

6. .ppt _____   f. displays each slide using the full screen space

7. Slide Sorter view _____   g. used to change the size of an object

8. slide show _____   h. boxes that contain specific types of items or objects

9. sizing handle _____   i. default extension for PowerPoint documents

10. handouts _____   j. allows text entry, deletion, selection, and formatting of an object when border appears hatched

multiple choice

Circle the letter of the correct response.

1. The large area of the screen where presentations are displayed is called the _____ .
   a. work area
   b. workspace
   c. window pane
   d. document area

2. The step in the development of a presentation that focuses on grabbing and holding the audience's attention is _____ .
   a. planning
   b. creating
   c. editing
   d. enhancing

3. PowerPoint can be used to create _____ .
   a. onscreen presentations
   b. Web presentations
   c. black-and-white or color overheads
   d. all the above

4. The first slide of a presentation is the _____ slide.
   a. summary
   b. title
   c. support
   d. introduction

5. _____ view contains three separate panes so that you can work on all aspects of your presentation.
   a. Slide Sorter
   b. Normal
   c. Slide
   d. Outline

6. When the Spelling Checker is used, words are checked against the _____ dictionary first.
   a. custom
   b. official
   c. main
   d. common

7. Boxes containing objects such as the slide title, bulleted text, charts, tables, and pictures are called _____.
   a. placeholders
   b. dialogs
   c. forms
   d. slides

8. A(n)_____is an onscreen display of your presentation.
   a. outline
   b. handout
   c. slide show
   d. slide

9. _____ fonts have a flair at the base of each letter that visually leads the reader to the next letter.
   a. sans serif
   b. serif
   c. printer
   d. display

10. Objects such as charts, drawings, pictures, and scanned photographs that provide visual interest or clarify data are _____.
    a. drawing objects
    b. clip art
    c. graphics
    d. none of the above

true/false

Circle the correct answer to the following questions.

1.	The AutoContent Wizard is a guided approach that helps you determine the content and organization of your presentation through a series of questions.	True	False
2.	The 5 by 5 rule refers to the number of bullets on a slide and the number of words per bullet.	True	False
3.	The Drawing toolbar contains buttons that are used to change the appearance or format of the presentation.	True	False
4.	Onscreen presentations can be designed specifically for the World Wide Web, where a browser serves as the presentation tool.	True	False
5.	A selected placeholder is surrounded with four sizing handles that can be used to move and size the placeholder.	True	False
6.	An object that is embedded is edited using the source program.	True	False
7.	Running a slide show makes the slide fill the screen, hiding the PowerPoint application window, so you can view the slides as your audience would.	True	False
8.	The size of a placeholder can be changed by dragging its sizing handles.	True	False
9.	The font is the height of the character and is commonly measured in points.	True	False
10.	All drawing objects are inserted into the same layer of the presentation.	True	False

lab exercises

Concepts

fill-in

Complete the following statements by filling in the blanks with the correct terms.

1. The first step in creating a presentation is to understand its _____.

2. Practicing or_____ the delivery of your presentation is the final step in presentation development.

3. When selected, a placeholder is surrounded with eight _____.

4. A _____ is an individual "page" of your presentation.

5. In _____ view, the slide pane is enlarged so you can work on enhancing the slides.

6. _____ is a PowerPoint feature that advises you of misspelled words as you create and edit a document and proposes possible corrections.

7. _____ is a set of characters with a specific design.

8. _____ is a set of picture files or simple drawings that comes with Office XP.

9. Boxes that are designed to contain specific types of objects such as the slide title, bulleted text, charts, tables, and pictures are called _____.

10. A _____ is text or graphics that appears at the bottom of each slide.

discussion questions

1. Suppose that you were required to present a report in your economics class and that you have decided to do an electronic presentation. Discuss each of the presentation development steps you would follow. Be as specific as possible.

2. List the different PowerPoint views. Define each and describe how they are typically used.

3. How can fonts and graphics be used to enhance a presentation?

Hands-On Exercises

step-by-step

Balancing Work/Life

★ **1.** Sheila Bowen works in the Human Resources department in your company. She is working on a presentation about maintaining a balance between work and life that she will give to a new group of college interns. She has found some new information to add to the presentation. She also wants to rearrange several slides and make a few other changes to improve the appearance of the presentation. Several slides of the completed presentation are shown here.

a. Open the file pp01_Balance. Enter your name as the subtitle on slide 1.

b. Run the slide show to see what Sheila has done so far.

c. Spell-check the presentation, making the appropriate corrections.

d. Reduce the font size on slide 2 from 28 to 24 points. Size and position the placeholder appropriately. Delete the bullets.

e. Appropriately size and position the graphics on slide 3.

f. Insert the picture pp01_Time on slide 4. Size and position it appropriately. Remove the bullets.

g. Insert the picture pp01_Traffic on slide 5 and size and position it appropriately.

h. Change the layout of slide 7 to Title, Content, and Text. (Hint: Use Format/Slide Layout.) Add three items that are ways you waste time. Insert the pp01_QuestionMark clip art. Size and position it appropriately.

i. Move slide 7 before slide 6.

j. Split the text on slide 7 into 2 slides with 5 bullets each. (Hint: Read the Another Method note in Splitting Text Between Slides.) Enter the title **More Things You Can Do**. Delete the right placeholder on slide 7. Resize the remaining placeholder appropriately.

k. Insert a new slide after slide 5 using the Title and 2-Column Text layout. Add the title **TV Viewing** and the following text in the column placeholders:

Left Column	Right Column
	Hours/Week
Adult men	21.9
Adult women	26.5

Remove the bullets, increase the point size to 32, and size the placeholders appropriately.

l. Run the slide show.

j. Save the presentation as Balance1. Print the slides as handouts (four per page).

You will complete this presentation in Step by Step Exercise 1 of Lab 2.

Writing Effective Resumes

★★ **2.** You work for the career services center of a university and you are planning a presentation on how to write effective resumes and cover letters. A previous employee had started to create such a presentation, but never got around to editing or finalizing it. You need to clean it up and enhance it a bit before presenting it. Several slides of the completed presentation are shown here.

a. Open the PowerPoint presentation pp01_Resume.

b. Run the Spelling Checker and correct any spelling errors.

c. In Normal view, change the font size of the title in the title slide to 40 pt. Resize and move the title placeholder so the title is centered above the red line. Increase the subtitle to 32 pt and size the placeholder to display it on a single line. Move it to the lower right corner of the slide above the slide number.

d. Replace "Student Name" in slide 2 with your name.

e. On slide 5, break each bulleted item into two bullets and split the slide content into 2 slides. Capitalize the first word of each bulleted item and remove unecessary commas.

f. Since there is too much text on slide 7, split the slide content into two slides. Move the Education bullet from slide 8 to slide 7. Add an appropriate title to slide 8.

g. Reorganize the bulleted items on slide 11 so that "Types of cover letters" is the first item. To match the slide order with the way the topics are now introduced, move slide 14 before slide 12.

h. In Normal view, remove the bullet format from the three demoted bulleted paragraphs on slide 12. Press [Tab ⇥] at the beginning of each of these paragraphs so they are indented correctly. Remove the periods at the end of the paragraphs (because they are not complete sentences).

i. Split slide 13 into 2 slides.

j. On slide 15, change the font size of the title "Anatomy of a Good Cover Letter" to 36 pt so it all fits on one line.

k. Break each bulleted item on slide 15 into two or three bullets each as appropriate. Capatalize the first word of each bulleted item. Remove commas and periods at the end of the items. Split the slide content into three slides. Add an appropriate slide title.

l. On the title slide, insert the pp01_Goals clip art. Resize and position it above the subtitle.

m. On slide 3, insert the pp01_Correspondence clip art in the Communications category below the bulleted list. Size and position it appropriately.

n. Save the presentation as Resume1.

o. Run the slide show.

p. Print the slides as handouts (six per page) and close the presentation.

Emergency Driving Techniques

★★ **3.** The department of public safety holds monthly community outreach programs. Next month's topic is about how to handle special driving circumstances, such as driving in rain or snow. You are responsible for presenting the section on how to handle tire blowouts. You have organized the topics to be presented and located several clip art graphics that will complement the talk. Now you are ready to begin creating the presentation. Several slides of the completed presentation are shown here.

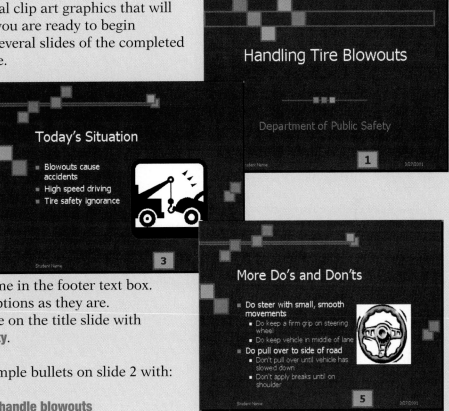

a. Using the AutoContent Wizard, select Recommending a Strategy as the type of presentation, and select On-screen as the style of output for the presentation. Enter **Handling Tire Blowouts** in the Presentation Title text box. Enter your name in the footer text box. Keep the other footer options as they are.

b. Replace the owner name on the title slide with **Department of Public Safety**.

c. Delete slide 2.

d. Replace the title and sample bullets on slide 2 with:
  Title: **Objectives**
  Bullet 1: **Learn how to handle blowouts**
  Bullet 2: **Learn how to prevent blowouts**

e. Replace sample bulleted text in slide 3 with:
  Bullet 1: **Blowouts cause accidents**
  Bullet 2: **High speed driving**
  Bullet 3: **Tire safety ignorance**

f. Change the title of slide 4 to **Tire Safety = Prevention**. Replace the sample bullet text with the following four bulleted items: **Pressure**, **Alignment**, **Rotation**, **Tread**.

g. Change the title of slide 5 to **Pressure** and replace the sample bullet text the following bulleted items:
  Bullet 1: **Under inflation**
  Bullet 2: **Fill to manufacturer's recommendation**
  Bullet 3: **Fill when cool**
  Bullet 4: **Check monthly**

h. Change bullet 1 on slide 5 to **Check monthly for under-inflation**. Delete bullet 4.

i. Change the title of slide 6 to **Rotation** and include the following bulleted items:
  Bullet 1: **Pattern**
    Demoted Bullet 2: **Follow manufacturer's guidelines**
  Bullet 3: **Fix alignment and balance problems first**
  Bullet 4: **Approximately every 6000 miles**

j. Insert a new slide after slide 6 using the Title and Text layout. Add the title **Tread** and the following bulleted items:

> Bullet 1: **Minimum tread 1/16 inch**
> Bullet 2: **Worn treads cause skidding and hydroplaning**
> Bullet 3: **Wear bars visible**
> Bullet 4: **Penny test**

k. Change the order of the bullets 1 and 2 on slide 7.

l. Insert a new slide after slide 7 using the Title and Text layout. Add the title **Alignment** and the following bulleted items:

> Bullet 1: **Misalignment causes uneven and rapid tread wear**
> Bullet 2: **Pulling or vibration**
> Bullet 3: **Correct by tire dealer**

m. Change the order of the slides to Pressure, Alignment, Rotation, and Tread.

n. Insert a new slide after slide 3 using the Title and Text layout. Add the title **Do's and Don'ts of Blowouts** and the following bulleted items:

> Bullet 1: **Don't over react**
> Bullet 2: **Do slow down gradually**
> Demoted Bullet 3: **Don't slam on brakes**
> Demoted Bullet 4: **Don't rapidly take foot off accelerator**
>   Twice demoted bullet 5: **Do ease off gas gradually**
> Bullet 6: **Do steer with small, smooth movements**
>   Demoted Bullet 7: **Do keep a firm grip on wheel**
>   Demoted Bullet 8: **Do keep vehicle in middle of lane**
> Bullet 9: **Do pull over to shoulder of road**
>   Demoted Bullet 10: **Don't pull over until vehicle has slowed down**
>   Demoted Bullet 11: **Don't apply brakes until on shoulder**

o. Split the text on slide 4 between two slides. Title the second slide **More Do's and Don'ts**. Change the font of the title on the title slide to 48 pt and the subtitle to 32 pt.

p. Locate and insert the graphic of a car and tow truck from the Clip Organizer on slide3. Size and position it appropriately.

q. Go online and visit the Microsoft Clip Gallery to locate several other graphics to complement the slides. Size and position them appropriately. (If you cannot go online, use some of the graphics supplied with your data files: Wheel, Tire, Unprepared, Repair.)

r. Run the slide show.

s. Save the presentation as Blowouts.

t. Print the slides as handouts (four per page).

You will complete this presentation in Step by Step Exercise 2 of Lab 2.

Coffee Product Knowledge

★ 4. As the manager of the Downtown Internet Cafe, you want to make a presentation to the other employees about the various blends of coffee that the cafe offers. The purpose of this presentation is to enable employees to answer the many questions that are asked by customers when looking at the Blend of the Day board or choosing the type of coffee beans they want to purchase. Several slides of the completed presentation are shown here.

a. Using the AutoContent Wizard, select Generic as the type of presentation and select Color Overheads as the presentation style. Enter **Coffee Talk** in the Presentation Title text box. Enter your name in the footer text box and keep the other footer settings as they are.

b. Replace the owner name in the title slide with **Downtown Internet Cafe**.

c. Replace the sample bulleted text on slide 2 with the following:
   Bullet 1: **What's in a name?**

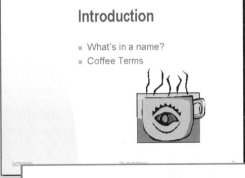

d. Replace the sample bulleted text on slide 3 with the following:
   Bullet 1: **Regular Roasts**
   Bullet 2: **Other Offerings**

e. In Normal view, change the title of slide 4 to **Regular Roasts** and replace the sample bulleted text with the following:
   Bullet 1: **Central and South American**
   Bullet 2: **East African**
   Bullet 3: **Indonesian**

f. Change the title of slide 5 to **Central and South American Coffees** and replace the sample bulleted text with the following:
   Bullet 1: **Colombian**
     Demoted Bullet 2: **Distinctive, heady aroma**
     Demoted Bullet 3: **Clean, mellow, balanced flavor**
   Bullet 4: **Guatemala Antigua**
     Demoted Bullet 5: **Rich and satisfying**
     Demoted Bullet 6: **Lively flavor**
   Bullet 7: **Kona**
     Demoted Bullet 8: **Delicately aromatic**
     Demoted Bullet 9: **Smooth, mild flavor**

g. Change the title of slide 6 to **East African Coffees** and replace the sample bulleted text with the following:
   Bullet 1: **Arabian**
     Demoted Bullet 2: **Strong and sparkling**
     Demoted Bullet 3: **Pungent, winy flavor**
   Bullet 4: **Ethiopian**
     Demoted Bullet 5: **Floral aroma and flavor**
     Demoted Bullet 6: **Moderate body and acidity**
   Bullet 7: **Kenyan**
     Demoted Bullet 8: **Intense flavor and acidity**
     Demoted Bullet 9: **Rich and hearty**

h. Change the title of slide 7 to Indonesian Coffees and replace the sample bulleted text with the following:

Bullet 1: Java
  Demoted Bullet 2: Deep, fragrant aroma
  Demoted Bullet 3: Rich-bodied
Bullet 4: Sumatra
  Demoted Bullet 5: Herbal aroma
  Demoted Bullet 6: Spicy, vibrant flavor

i. Change the title of slide 8 to Other Offerings and replace the sample bulleted text with the following:

Bullet 1: Blends
Bullet 2: Dark Roasts
  Demoted Bullet 3: Espresso (dark)
  Demoted Bullet 4: Italian (darker)
  Demoted Bullet 5: French (darkest)
Bullet 6: Decaffeinated
  Demoted Bullet 7: Traditionally (solvent) processed
  Demoted Bullet 8: Water processed
  Demoted Bullet 9: Regular and dark roasts

j. Change the order of the last two demoted bulleted items in slide 6.

k. Add a second bullet to slide 2 with the text Coffee Terms.

l. Change the title of slide 9 to Coffee Terms. Change the layout to Title and 2-Column Text. (Hint: Use Format/Slide Layout.) Replace the sample bulleted text with the following in the columns indicated:

Left Column	Right Column
Bullet 1: Flavor	Aroma, acidity, and body
Bullet 2: Aroma	Fragrance of brewed coffee
Bullet 3: Acidity	Sharp, lively characteristic of coffee
Bullet 4: Body	Impression of a coffee's weight in the mouth

m. Change the font size of the bulleted items in slide 9 to 24 pt. Remove the bullets from the right column. Size and position the column placeholders to align the information in both columns.

n. Change the font and size of the title and subtitle on the title slide to improve its appearance.

o. On the title slide, insert the clip art pp01_CoffeeShop. Resize and position it below the subtitle.

p. Insert the clip art pp01_CoffeeMug on slide 2. Appropriately size and position the bulleted items and clip art on the slide.

q. Insert the clip art pp01_Cup on slide 3. Appropriately size and position the clip art on the slide.

r. Run the Spelling Checker and correct any spelling errors.

s. Save the presentation as Coffee.

t. Run the slide show.

u. Print the slides as handouts (six per page).

You will complete this presentation in Step by Step Exercise 3 of Lab 2.

Workplace Issues

★ ★ **5.** Tim is preparing for his lecture on "Workplace Issues" for his Introduction to Computers class. He uses PowerPoint to create presentations for each of his lectures. He has organized the topics to be presented and located several clip art graphics that will complement the lecture. He is now ready to begin creating the presentation. Several slides of the completed presentation are shown here.

a. Using the AutoContent Wizard, select Generic as the type of presentation, and select Color Overheads as the style of output for the presentation. Enter **Workplace Issues** in the Presentation Title text box. Enter your name in the footer text box. Keep the other footer options as they are.

b. Replace the owner name on the title slide with **Lecture 4**.

c. Delete slide 2.

d. Replace the sample bulleted text on the new slide 2 with:
> Bullet 1: **Ergonomics**
> Bullet 2: **Ethics**
> Bullet 3: **Environment**

e. Replace the title and sample bulleted text in slide 3 with:
> Title: **Ergonomics**
> Bullet 1: **Definition**
> Bullet 2: **Fit the job to the worker rather than forcing the worker to contort to fit the job**
> Bullet 3: **The study of human factors related to computers**

f. Change the order of bullets 2 and 3 on slide 3. Demote bullets 2 and 3.

g. Change the title of slide 4 to **Mental Health**. Include two bulleted items: **Noise** and **Monitoring**.

h. Change the title of slide 5 to **Physical Health** and include the following bulleted items:
> Bullet 1: **Eyestrain and headache**
> Bullet 2: **Back and neck pain**
> Bullet 3: **Electromagnetic fields**
> Bullet 4: **Repetitive strain injury**

i. Change the title of slide 6 to **Ethics** and include the following bulleted items:
> Bullet 1: **Definition**
> Demoted Bullet 2: **Guidelines for the morally acceptable use of computers in our society**

j. Change the title of slide 7 to **Primary Ethical Issues** and include the following bulleted items:
> Bullet 1: **Privacy**
> Bullet 2: **Accuracy**
> Bullet 3: **Property**
> Bullet 4: **Access**

k. Change the title of slide 8 to **The Environment** and include the following bulleted items:
> Bullet 1: **The Energy Star program**
> Bullet 2: **The Green PC**

l. Insert a new slide after slide 8 using the Title and Text layout. Change the title to **The Green PC** and include the following bulleted items:
    Bullet 1: **System unit**
    Bullet 2: **Display**
    Bullet 3: **Manufacturing**

m. Insert a new slide after slide 9 using the Title and Text layout. Add the title **Personal Responsibility** and the following bulleted items:
    Bullet 1: **Conserving**
    Bullet 2: **Recycling**
    Bullet 3: **Educating**

n. In Slide Sorter view, move slide 5 before slide 4.

o. Change the font of the subtitle on the title slide to Times New Roman and the size to 44 pt.

p. Insert the following graphics in the slides indicated. Size and position them appropriately.
    Slide 1: Board Meeting (from the Clip Organizer)
    Slide 3: pp01_Ergonomics
    Slide 4: pp01_PhysicalHealth
    Slide 5: pp01_MentalHealth
    Slide 6: pp01_Handshake
    Slide 8: Recycling (from Clip Organizer)
    Slide 9: Manufacturing (from Clip Organizer)

q. Run the slide show.

r. Save the presentation as Workplace Issues.

s. Print the slides as handouts (four per page).

You will complete this presentation in Step by Step Exercise 5 of Lab 2.

on your own

Bicycle Safety Presentation

★ 1. As owner of the Better Bikes Company, you have written several articles for your local newspaper on bicycle safety. Based on one of your articles, an elementary school in your town has asked you to do a presentation for their PTA meeting on children's cycling tips. Create your presentation in PowerPoint, using the information in the file pp01_BikeSafety as a resource. Use the AutoContent Wizard and the Generic template. Include your name in the footer. When you are done, run the Spelling Checker, then save your presentation as Better Bike Safety and print it.

You will complete this presentation in On Your Own Exercise 2 of Lab 2.

Telephone Training Course

★★ 2. You are a trainer with Super Software, Inc. You received a memo from your manager alerting you that many of the support personnel are not using proper telephone protocol or obtaining the proper information from the customers who call in. Your manager has asked you to conduct a training class that covers these topics. Using the pp01_Memo data file as a resource, prepare the slides for your class. Use the AutoContent Wizard and select an appropriate presentation type. Include your name in the footer. When you are done, save the presentation as Phone Etiquette and print the handouts.

Visual Aids Training Presentation

★ ★ 3.   You are a trainer with Super Software, Inc. Your manager has asked you to prepare a presentation on various visual aids that one may use in presentation. Using the pp01_VisualAids data file as a resource, create an onsreen presentation using the AutoContent Wizard. Select an appropriate presentation type. Add clip art that illustrates the type of visual aid. Include your name in the footer. When you are done, save the presentation as Presentation Aids and print the handouts.

Job Placement Services

★ ★ 4.   You work at a job placement agency, and you have been asked to do a presentation for new clients that describes the services your company offers and the categories used to list available jobs. Visit a local placement agency or search the Web to gather information about job placement agency services and job listings. Using the AutoContent Wizard, select an appropriate presentation type to create a short presentation. Include your name in the footer. When you are done, save the presentation as Placement Services and print the handouts.

Web Design Proposal

★ ★ 5.   Your company wants to create a Web site, but it is not sure whether to design its own or hire a Web design firm to do it. You have been asked to create a presentation to management relaying the pros and cons of each approach. To gather information, search the Web for the topic "Web design" and select some key points about designing a Web page from one of the "how-to" or "tips" categories. Use these points to create the first part of your presentation and call it something like "Creating Our Own Web Page." Then search the Web for the topic "Web designers" and select two Web design firms. Pick some key points about each firm (for example, Web sites they have designed, design elements they typically use, and/or their design philosophy). Finally, include at least one slide that lists the pros and cons of each approach. Include your name on the title slide. When your presentation is complete, save it as Web Design and print the slide as handouts.

You will expand on this presentation in On Your Own Exercise 4 of Lab 2.

Modifying and Refining a Presentation

L A B 2

objectives

After completing this lab, you will know how to:

1.	Find and replace text.
2.	Create and enhance a table.
3.	Modify graphic objects and create a text box.
4.	Change the presentation's design and color scheme.
5.	Change slide and title masters.
6.	Hide the title slide footer.
7.	Duplicate and hide slides.
8.	Create and enhance AutoShapes.
9.	Add animation, sound, transition, and build effects.
10.	Control and annotate a slide show.
11.	Create speaker notes.
12.	Check style consistency.
13.	Document a file.
14.	Print scaled and framed handouts.

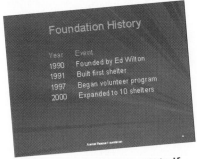

Show the next hidden slide if someone asks about adoption rates.

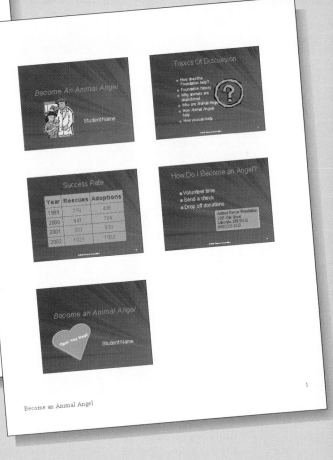

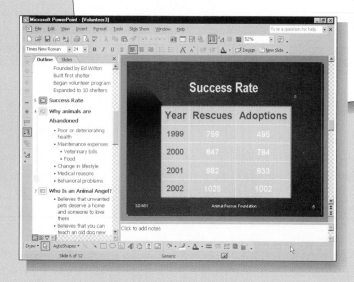

Using tables make data easy to understand.

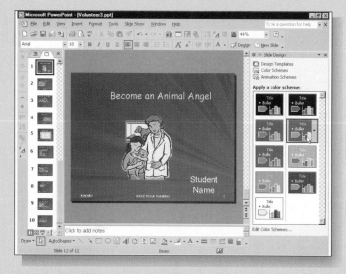

Slide designs and color schemes quickly enhance the look of a presentation.

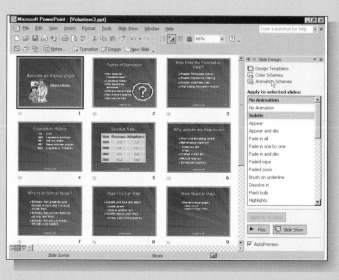

Slide transitions, builds, and special effects add action to a slide show.

Animal Angels

The foundation director was very impressed with your first draft of the presentation to recruit volunteers, and asked to see the presentation onscreen. While viewing it the director made several suggestions to improve both content and design. First, the director wants you to include more information on ways that volunteers can help. Additionally, because the organization has such an excellent adoption rate, the director suggests that you include a table to illustrate the success of the adoption program. It was also suggested that you consider using a different design background and that you include more art and other graphic features to enhance the appearance of the slides. Finally, to keep the audience's attention, the director suggests that you consider adding more action to the slides using the special effects included with PowerPoint.

PowerPoint 2002 gives you the design and production capabilities to create a first-class onscreen presentation. These features include artist-designed layouts and color schemes that give your presentation a professional appearance. In addition, you can add your own personal touches by modifying text attributes, incorporating art or graphics, and including animation to add impact, interest, and excitement to your presentation.

© Corbis

Replacing Text

You have updated the content to include the additional information on ways that volunteers can help Animal Angels. You want to see the revised presentation.

1
- **Start PowerPoint 2002.**

- **Open the file** pp02_Volunteer2.

- **If necessary, switch to Normal view.**

- **Replace Student Name in slide 1 with your name.**

- **Scroll the Outline tab to view the content of the revised presentation.**

Your screen should be similar to Figure 2.1

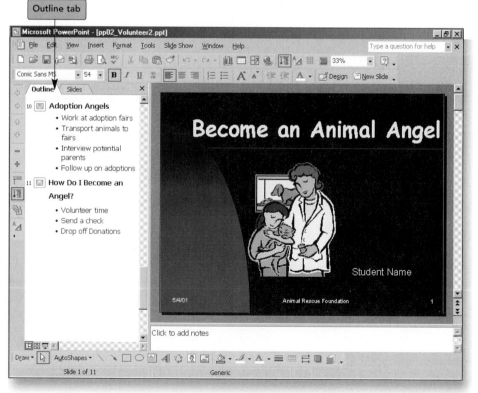

Figure 2.1

As you look at the text in the slides, you decide to edit the presentation by replacing the word "pet" in many locations with the word "animal."

Find and Replace

1 To make editing easier, you can use the Find and Replace feature to both find text in a presentation and replace it with other text as directed. For example, suppose you created a lengthy presentation describing the type of clothing and equipment needed to set up a world-class home gym, and then you decided to change "sneakers" to "athletic shoes." Instead of deleting every occurrence of "sneakers" and typing "athletic shoes," you can use the Find and Replace feature to perform the task automatically. This feature is fast and accurate; however, use care when replacing so that you do not replace unintended matches.

Using Find and Replace

You want to replace selected occurrences of the word "pet" with "animal."

 **Choose Edit/Replace.**

Additional Information
The keyboard shortcut is Control + H. The Edit/Find command locates specified text only.

Your screen should be similar to Figure 2.2

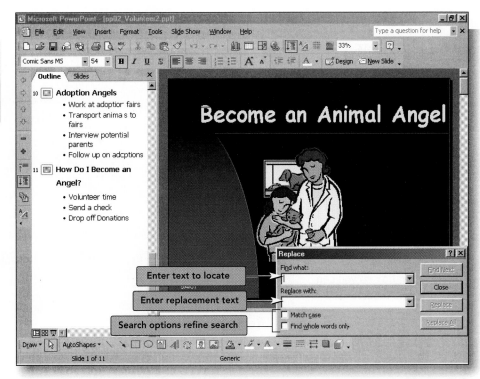

Figure 2.2

In the Find What text box, you enter the text you want to locate. The two options described in the following table allow you to refine how the search for the text you want to locate is conducted.

Option	Effect on Text
Match Case	Distinguishes between uppercase and lower-case characters. When selected, finds only those instances in which the capitalization matches the text you typed in the Find What box.
Find Whole Words Only	Distinguishes between whole and partial words. When selected, locates matches that are whole words and not part of a larger word. For example, finds "cat" only and not "catastrophe" too.

The text you want to replace is entered in the Replace With text box. The replacement text must be entered exactly as you want it to appear in your document. You want to find all occurrences of the complete word "pet" and replace them with the word "animal." You will enter the text to find and replace and begin the search.

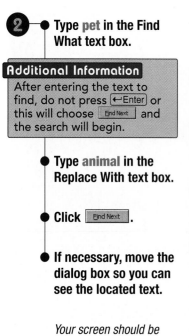

2 ● **Type pet in the Find What text box.**

Additional Information
After entering the text to find, do not press ←Enter or this will choose Find Next and the search will begin.

● **Type animal in the Replace With text box.**

● **Click Find Next.**

● **If neccessary, move the dialog box so you can see the located text.**

Your screen should be similar to Figure 2.3

Additional Information
Find and Replace will highlight located text in whichever pane is current when the procedure started.

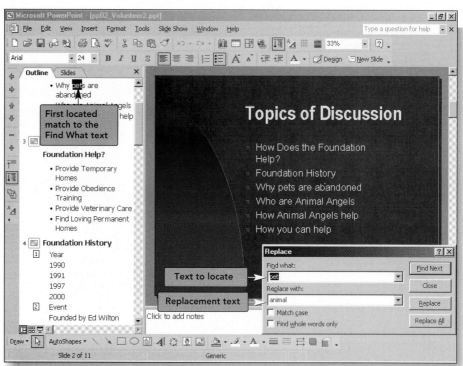

Figure 2.3

Immediately, the first occurrence of text in the presentation that matches the entry in the Find What text box is located and highlighted in the Outline tab. You will replace the located word with the replacement text.

3 ● Click  .

Your screen should be similar to Figure 2.4

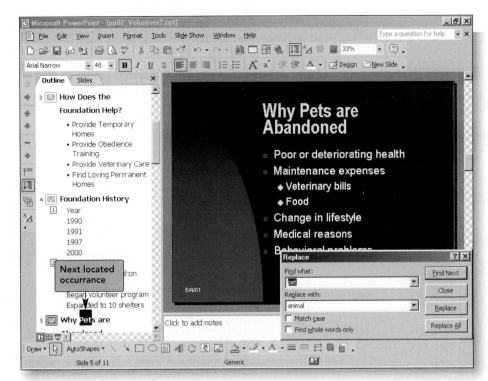

Figure 2.4

The highlighted text is replaced, and the next occurrence of the Find text is located in slide 5. Again, you want to replace this occurrence. If you do not want to replace a word, you can use Find Next to skip to the next occurrence without replacing it. You will continue to respond to the located occurrences.

4 ● Click Replace .

● Click Find Next to skip the third located text in slide 6.

● Replace the fourth located text in slide 8.

● Replace the last located text in slide 9.

● Click OK to end searching.

● Click Close to close the dialog box.

● Save the presentation as Volunteer3.

Your screen should be similar to Figure 2.5

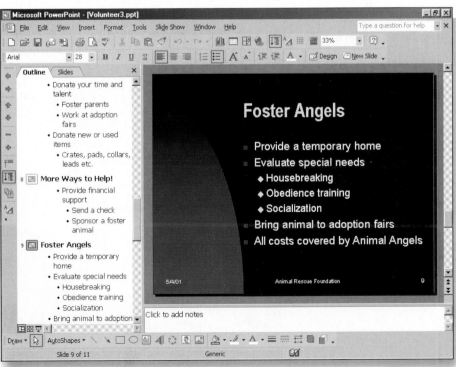

Figure 2.5

If you are changing all the occurrences, it is much faster to use the Replace All command button. Exercise care when using Replace All, however, because the search text you specify might be part of another word and you may accidentally replace text you want to keep.

Creating a Simple Table

During your discussion with the director, it was suggested that you add a slide containing data on the number of adoptions versus rescues. The information in this slide will be presented using a table layout.

concept 2

Table

2 A **table** is made up of rows and columns of **cells** that you can fill with text and graphics. Traditionally, columns are identified from left to right beginning with the letter A, and rows are numbered from top to bottom beginning with the number 1. Tables are commonly used to align numbers in columns and then sort and perform calculations on them. They make it easier to read and understand numbers.

Year	Rescues	Adoptions
1999	759	495
2000	847	784
2001	982	833
2002	1025	1002

Using the Table Layout

To include this information in the presentation, you will insert a new slide after slide 4. Because this slide will contain a table showing the adoption figures, you want to use the table slide layout.

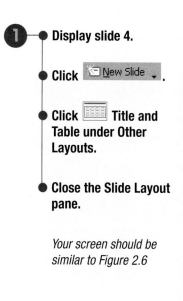

1 ● Display slide 4.

● Click ⬚ New Slide ⬚ .

● Click ⬚ Title and Table under Other Layouts.

● Close the Slide Layout pane.

Your screen should be similar to Figure 2.6

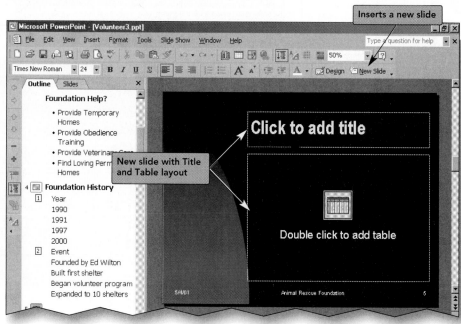

Figure 2.6

A new slide 5 with title and table placeholders is inserted.

Inserting the Table

Next you want to add a slide title and then create the table to display the number of adoptions and rescues.

1 ● **Enter the title Success Rate in the title placeholder.**

● **Double-click the table placeholder.**

Your screen should be similar to Figure 2.7

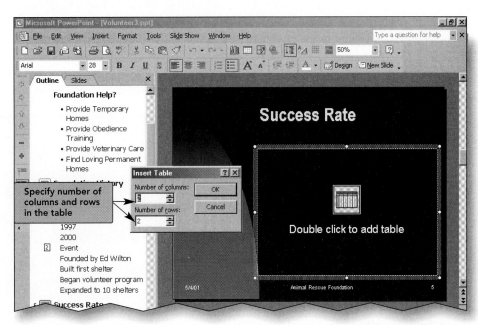

Figure 2.7

In the Insert Table dialog box, you specify the number of rows and columns for the table.

2 ● **Specify 3 columns and 5 rows.**

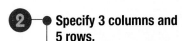

HAVING TROUBLE?
You can type in the number or use the scroll buttons to increase or decrease the number.

● **Click OK.**

● **If necessary, move the Tables and Borders toolbar out of the way or dock it.**

Your screen should be similar to Figure 2.8

HAVING TROUBLE?
If the Tables and Borders toolbar is not displayed automatically, you will need to open it from the Toolbar shortcut menu.

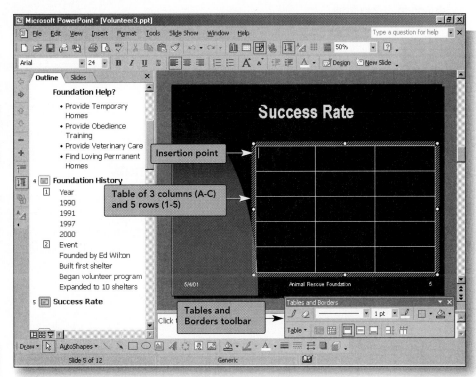

Figure 2.8

A basic table consisting of three columns and five rows is displayed as a selected object. The Tables and Borders toolbar is displayed.

Entering Data in a Table

Now you can now enter the information into the table. The insertion point appears in the top left corner cell ready for you to enter text. To move in a table, click on the cell or use [Tab⇆] to move to the next cell to the right and [⇧Shift] + [Tab⇆] to move to the preceding cell. If you are in the last cell of a row, pressing [Tab⇆] takes you to the first cell of the next row. You can also use the [↑] and [↓] directional keys to move up or down a row. While entering a lot of text in a table, it is easier to use [Tab⇆] to move rather than using the mouse because your hands are already on the keyboard.

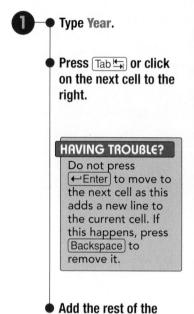

Type Year.

Press [Tab⇆] **or click on the next cell to the right.**

HAVING TROUBLE?
Do not press [←Enter] to move to the next cell as this adds a new line to the current cell. If this happens, press [Backspace] to remove it.

Add the rest of the information shown below to the table.

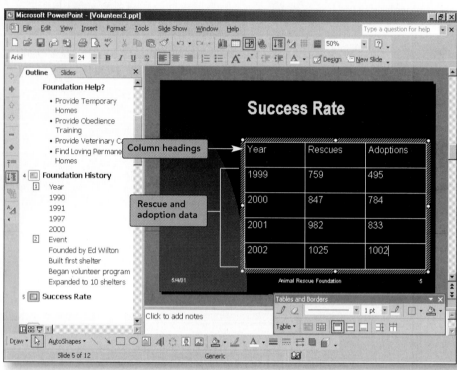

Figure 2.9

	Col. A	Col. B	Col. C
Row 1		**Rescues**	**Adoptions**
Row 2	**1999**	**759**	**495**
Row 3	**2000**	**847**	**784**
Row 4	**2001**	**982**	**833**
Row 5	**2002**	**1025**	**1002**

Your screen should be similar to Figure 2.9

Applying Text Formats

Next you want to improve the table's appearance by formatting the table text. Fonts and font size are two basic text attributes that you have used already. Other text formats are text color, bold, and italics. You can also apply special effects to text such as shadows and embossed text effects.

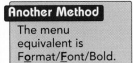

1 Drag to select row 1 containing the column headings and increase the font size to 36 pt.

● Click **B** Bold to bold the selection.

Another Method
The menu equivalent is Format/Font/Bold.

● Click ▲ Font Color (in the Drawing toolbar).

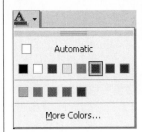

● Click on a dark blue.

Another Method
The menu equivalent is Format/Font/Color.

● Select rows 2 through 5 and increase the font size to 28.

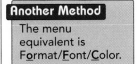

Your screen should be similar to Figure 2.10

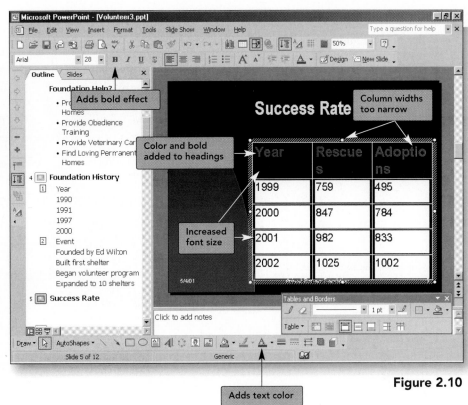

Figure 2.10

Sizing the Table Columns

Because you increased the font size of the headings, two of the headings are too large to display on a single line in the cell space. To fix this, you will adjust the size of the columns to fit their contents. To adjust the column width or row height, drag the row and column boundaries. The mouse pointer appears as a ◂|▸ when you can size the column and ▲▼ when you can size the row.

① Decrease the width of the Year column and then adjust the width of the other two columns as in Figure 2.11.

Your screen should be similar to Figure 2.11

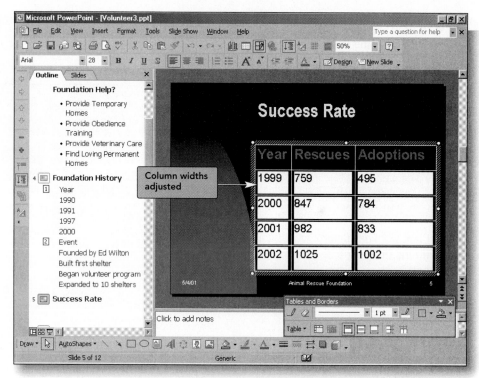

Figure 2.11

Aligning Text in Cells

Now that the columns are more appropriately sized, you want to center the text and data in the cells. To do this, you can change the alignment of the text entries.

concept 3

Alignment

3 **Alignment** controls how text entries are positioned within a space. You can change the horizontal placement of an entry in a placeholder or a table cell. There are four horizontal alignment settings: left, center, right, and justified. You can also vertically align text in a table cell with the top, middle, or bottom of the cell space.

Horizontal Alignment	Effect on Text	Vertical Alignment	Effect on Text
Left	Aligns text against the left edge of the placeholder or cell, leaving the right edge of text, which wraps to another line, ragged.	Top	Aligns text at the top of the cell space.
Center	Centers each line of text between the left and right edges of the placeholder or cell.	Middle	Aligns text in the middle of the cell space.
Right	Aligns text against the right edge of the placeholder or cell, leaving the left edge of multiple lines ragged.	Bottom	Aligns text at the bottom of the cell space.
Justified	Aligns text evenly with both the right and left edges of the placeholder or cell.		

The commands to change horizontal alignment are options under the Format/Alignment menu. However, it is much faster to use the shortcuts shown below.

Alignment	Keyboard Shortcut	Button
Left	Ctrl + L	
Center	Ctrl + E	
Right	Ctrl + R	
Justified	Ctrl + J	

You will center the cell entries both horizontally and vertically in their cell spaces.

① Select the entire table contents.

● Click 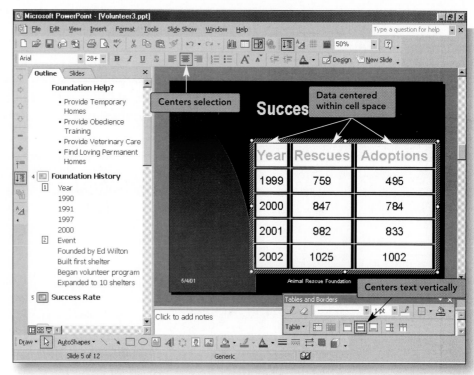 Center (on the Formatting toolbar).

● Click ▤ Center Vertically (on the Tables and Borders toolbar).

Your screen should be similar to Figure 2.12

Figure 2.12

Changing the Border Size and Color

Next, you will add a color to the outside border and increase the thickness or weight of the borderline. The Tables and Borders toolbar is used to make these enhancements.

① Open the `1 pt ▾` Border Width drop-down menu.

● Click `3 pt ──`.

● Click 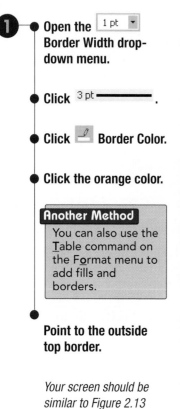 Border Color.

● Click the orange color.

> **Another Method**
> You can also use the Table command on the Format menu to add fills and borders.

● Point to the outside top border.

Your screen should be similar to Figure 2.13

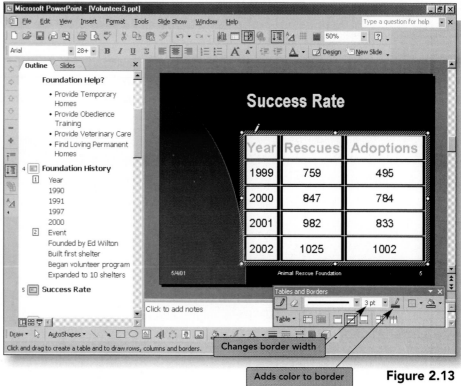

Changes border width

Adds color to border

Figure 2.13

The mouse pointer is a ✐ indicating that the Draw Table feature has been turned on. When on, this feature allows you to add row and column lines to an existing table. It is also used to modify the settings associated with the existing lines. You will drag the mouse pointer over the existing outside border to modify it to the new settings you have selected. As you drag, a dotted line identifies the section of the border that will be modified.

2 ● Drag along the top border to apply the new settings.

> **HAVING TROUBLE?**
> You will need to look carefully to see the dotted line as you drag, as it is difficult to see in the cross-hatch border.

● In the same manner, apply the new border formats to the remaining three sides of the table.

● Click ✐ Draw Table to turn off the Draw Table feature.

Your screen should be similar to Figure 2.14

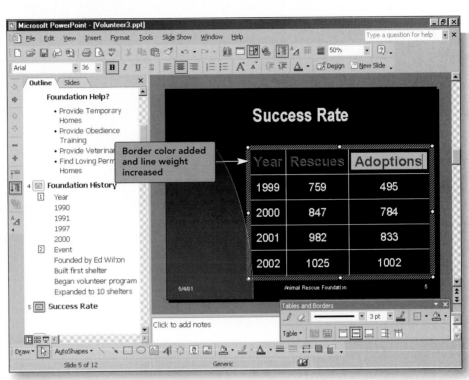

Figure 2.14

Adding Background Fill Color

Finally, you will add a background fill color to the table.

1 ● Select the entire table.

● Click ■ Fill Color.

● Choose More Fill Colors.

● If necessary, open the Standard tab.

Your screen should be similar to Figure 2.15

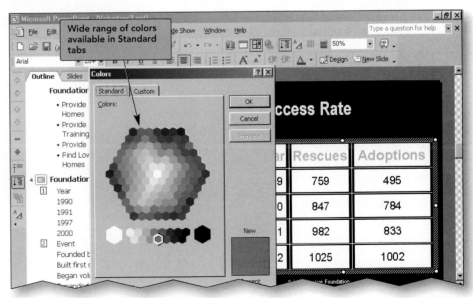

Figure 2.15

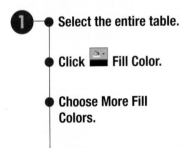

From the Standard tab of the colors dialog box, you can select from a wider range of colors. You want to use a gold color for the table background.

2
- Click on a gold color.
- Click **OK**.
- Click in the table to deselect the table.

Your screen should be similar to Figure 2.16

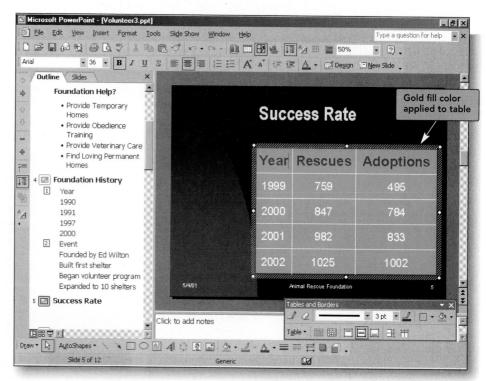

Figure 2.16

The new background table has made it difficult to see the data and row and column lines. To fix this, you will change the color of the lines and data.

3
- Change the font color of the years to the same blue as the column headings.
- Change the font color of the numeric data to a dark color of your choice.
- Change the color of the interior lines to the same orange as the outside border (keep the weight at 1 pt).
- Adjust the position of the table on the slide as in Figure 2-17.
- Click outside the table to deselect it.
- Save the presentation.

Your screen should be similar to Figure 2.17

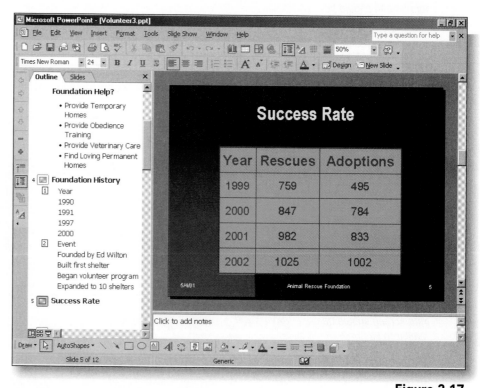

Figure 2.17

The enhancements you added to the table greatly improve its appearance.

Modifying Graphic Objects

Using the Text and Content Layout

You would also like to add a graphic to slide 2. Before doing this you will change the slide layout from the bulleted list style to a style that is designed to accommodate text as well as other types of content such as graphics.

1

● **Display slide 2.**

● **Choose F̲ormat/Slide Lay̲out.**

● **Click ▥ Title, Text, and Content (from the Text and Content Layouts category).**

● **Close the Slide Layout pane.**

Your screen should be similar to Figure 2.18

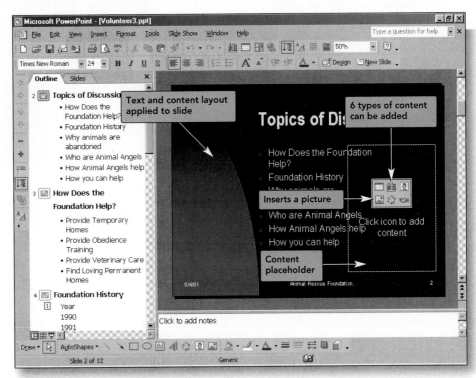

Figure 2.18

Because the slide already contained title and bulleted text placeholders, a content placeholder was added on the right side of the slide, overlapping the bulleted text placeholder. You will add a clip art graphic of a question mark and then size the placeholder. Inside the content placeholder are six icons representing the different types of content that can be inserted. Clicking an icon opens the appropriate feature to add the specified type of content.

● Click  in the content placeholder.

Additional Information

A ScreenTip identifies the item as you point to it.

● If necessary, change the Look In location to the location containing your data files.

● Locate and select the pp02_QuestionMark clip art.

● Click [Insert ▾].

● Size the graphic as in Figure 2.19.

Your screen should be similar to Figure 2.19

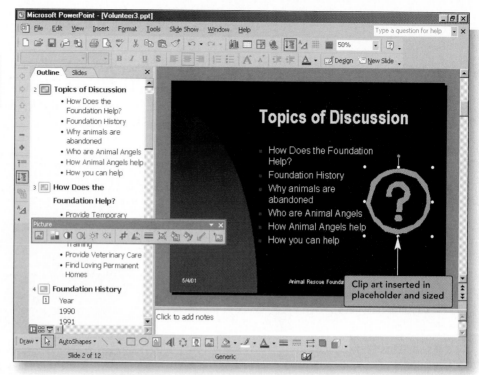

Figure 2.19

Recolor a Picture

Now you want to change the color of the graphic to a bright gold color.

● If necessary, display the Picture toolbar.

● Click 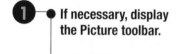 Recolor Picture.

Another Method

The menu equivalent is Format/Picture/Recolor.

Your screen should be similar to Figure 2.20

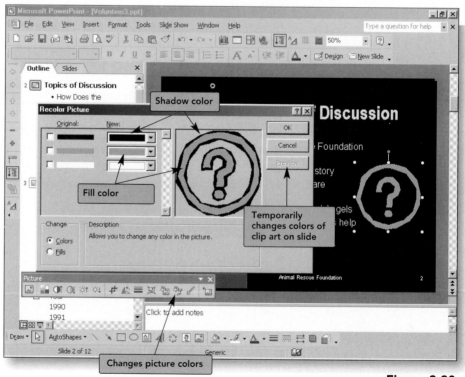

Figure 2.20

The original color of each component of the picture is listed. Selecting the check box for a component allows you to change the color to a new color. You want to change the blue color to gold.

2 ● Select the Original blue color check box.

● Open the New color drop-down menu for the selected component and select gold.

● Click 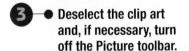 OK .

Additional Information
To restore the original color, clear its check box.

Your screen should be similar to Figure 2.21

3 ● Deselect the clip art and, if necessary, turn off the Picture toolbar.

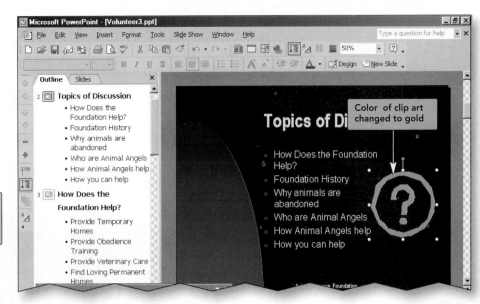

Figure 2.21

Working with Text Boxes

On slide 11, you want to add the organization's name and address. To make it stand out on the slide, you will put it into a text box. A **text box** is a container for text or graphics. The text box can be moved, resized, and enhanced in other ways to make it stand out from the other text on the slide.

Creating a Text Box

First, you create the text box, then you add the content.

1 ● Display slide 12.

● Click in the slide pane.

● Click ▦ Text Box (on the Drawing toolbar).

Another Method
The menu equivalent is Insert/Text Box.

● Point to a blank area below the bullets and click to create a box.

Your screen should be similar to Figure 2.22

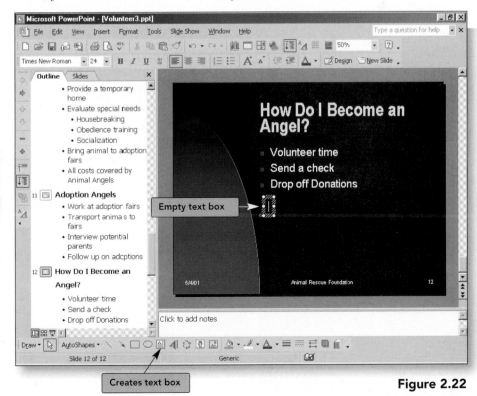

Figure 2.22

The text box is a selected object and is surrounded with a hatched border, indicating you can enter, delete, select, and format the text inside the box.

Adding Text to a Text Box

The text box displays an insertion point, indicating it is waiting for you to enter the text. As you type the text in the text box, it will automatically resize as needed to display the entire entry.

1 • **Type the organization's name and address shown below in the text box. (Press ⏎Enter at the end of a line.)**

**Animal Rescue Foundation
1166 Oak Street
Lakeside, NH 03112
(603) 555-1313**

Your screen should be similar to Figure 2.23

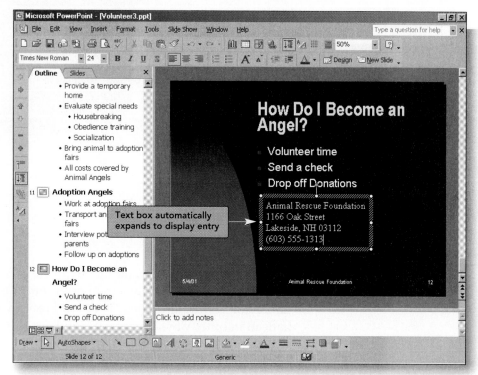

Figure 2.23

Notice that text that is attached to an object, such as a text box, is not displayed in the outline pane.

Enhancing the Text Box

Like any other object, the text box can be sized and moved anywhere on the slide. It can also be enhanced by adding a border, fill color, shadow effect, or a three-dimensional effect to the box. You want to add a border around the box to define the space and add a fill color behind the text.

1 ● Click ▤ Line Style and select a style of your choice from the menu.

● Click 🎨▾ Fill Color and select a color of your choice from the color palette.

● If the text does not look good with the fill color you selected, change the text color to a color of your choice.

● Position the text box as in Figure 2.24.

● Deselect the text box.

● Save the presentation.

Your screen should be similar to Figure 2.24

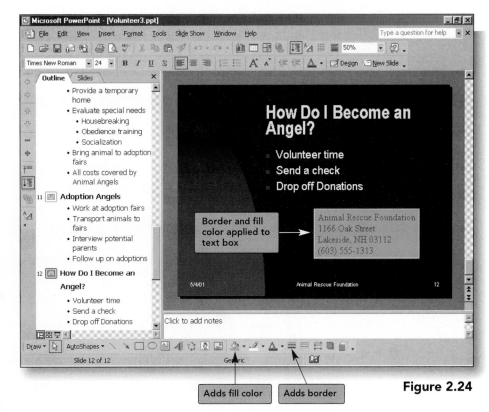

Border and fill color applied to text box

Adds fill color   Adds border

Figure 2.24

The information in the text box now stands out from the other information on the slide.

Changing the Presentation Design

Now you are satisfied with the presentation's basic content and organization. Next you want to change its style and appearance by applying a different design template.

concept 4

Design Template

4   A **design template** is a professionally created slide design that can be applied to your presentation. Design templates contain color schemes, custom formatting, background designs, styled fonts, and other layout and design elements that have been created by artists. PowerPoint has more than 100 design templates from which you can select to quickly give your presentations a professional appearance. Additional design templates are available at the Microsoft Office Template Gallery Web site, or you can create your own custom design templates. Use a design template to ensure that your presentation has a professional, consistent look throughout.

Applying a Design

A design template can be applied to the entire presentation or to selected slides. You want to change the design template for the entire presentation.

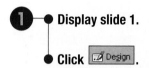

● Display slide 1.

● Click [Design].

Another Method

The menu equivalent is Format/Slide Design.

Your screen should be similar to Figure 2.25

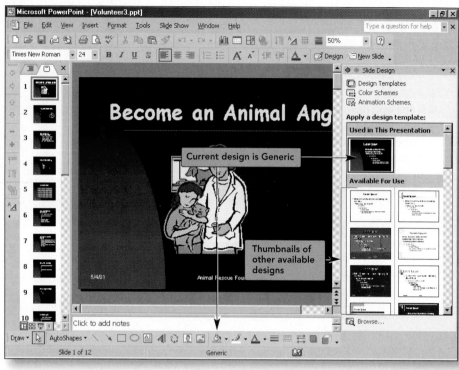

Figure 2.25

Additional Information

Design templates are stored in a file with a .pot file extension.

The Slide Design task pane shows the design that is currently used in the presentation—Generic. Thumbnails of the available design templates are displayed in the Available for Use section of the pane.

2 ● Click ▦ Balance to see how this design would look.

Additional Information

Pointing to the design template thumbnail displays the template name in a ScreenTip. The design templates are in alphabetical order by name.

Your screen should be similar to Figure 2.26

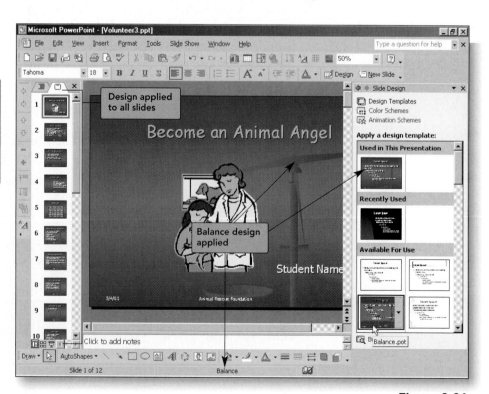

Figure 2.26

The Balance design template is applied to all slides in the presentation. The status bar displays the name of the current design.

You will preview several other design templates, and then use the Beam template for the presentation.

3 ● **Preview several other design templates.**

● **Choose the Beam template design.**

Your screen should be similar to Figure 2.27

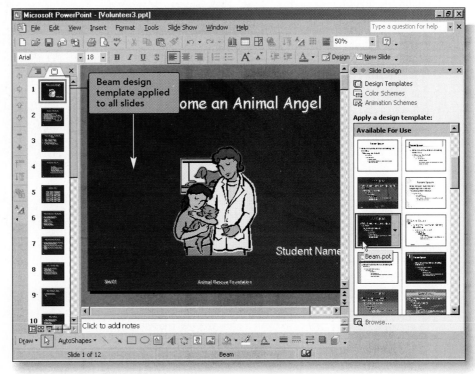

Figure 2.27

The Beam design template has been applied to all slides in the presentation. When a new template design is applied, the text styles, graphics, and colors that are included in the template replace the previous template settings. Consequently, the layout may need to be adjusted. For example, your name may appear on two lines and may cover part of the footer. In addition, although the title is still the font you selected, its font size has been reduced and it is now too small. You will fix that shortly.

4 • If necessary, move your name up slightly so it no longer covers the footer.

• Use the Slide tab to select each slide and check the layout.

• Make the adjustments shown in table below Figure 2.28.

Your screen should be similar to Figure 2.28

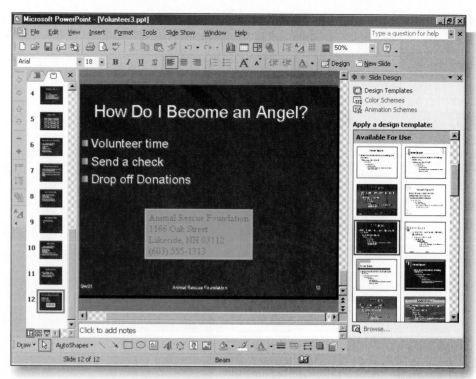

Figure 2.28

Slide	Adjustment
2	Adjust the size and placement of the graphic.
4	Move the two placeholders to display the text centered below the title and change the Year and Event headings to gold.
5	Adjust the size of the table columns and center the table below the title. If necessary, change the table text colors to coordinate with the new design.
12	Move the text box toward the center of the slide as in Figure 2.28.

Changing the Color Scheme

As you review the slides and look at the new design style, you feel the color is too dark. To make the presentation livelier, you decide to try a different color scheme. Each design template has several alternative color schemes from which you can choose.

Display slide 1.

Click  **.**

Your screen should be similar to Figure 2.29

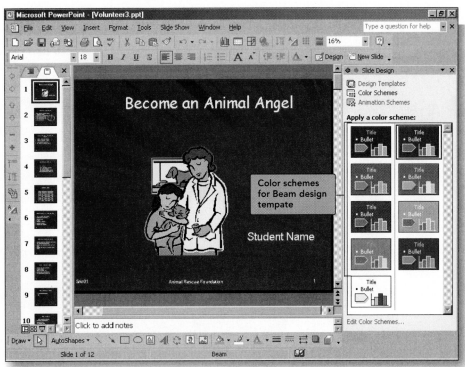

Figure 2.29

The nine color schemes for the Beam design template are displayed in the Slide Design pane. The color scheme with the dark blue background is selected. Each color scheme consists of eight coordinated colors that are applied to different slide elements. Using predefined color schemes gives your presentation a professional and consistent look. You want to see how the teal color scheme would look.

2

Select the teal color scheme (second column, second row).

Your screen should be similar to Figure 2.30

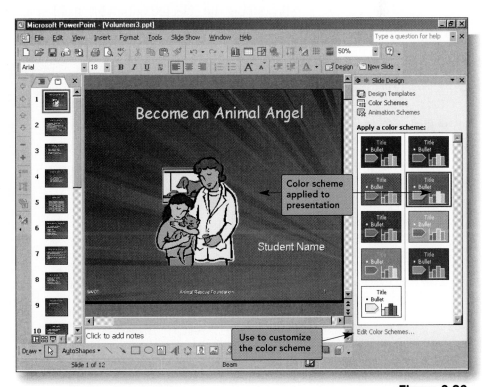

Figure 2.30

The slides display in the selected color scheme. Although you like this color scheme, you think the title would look better in gold to pick up the accent color you have used in the slides. You can customize this scheme by changing the title color.

3 ● **Click** Edit Color Schemes... .

● **Open the Custom tab, if necessary.**

Your screen should be similar to Figure 2.31

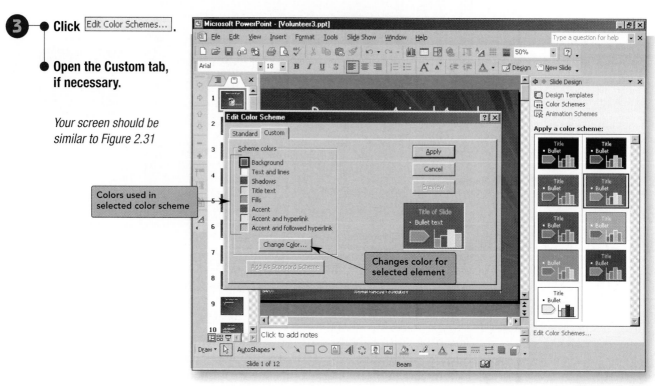

Colors used in selected color scheme

Changes color for selected element

Figure 2.31

The Scheme Colors area of the dialog box shows you the eight colors that are applied to different elements of the template design. The sample box shows how the selected colors are used in a slide. The option to change the background color is selected by default. You want to change the color of the title text.

4 ● **Select Title Text.**

● **Click** Change Color... .

● **If necessary, open the Standard tab.**

Your screen should be similar to Figure 2.32

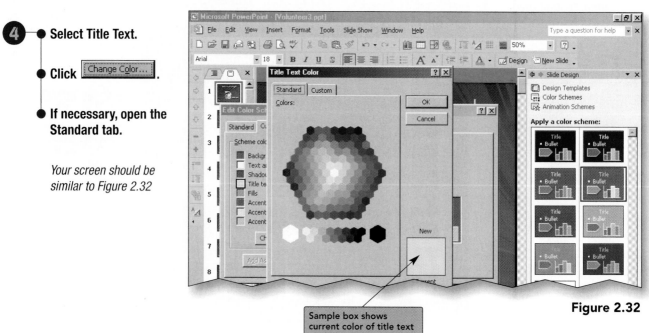

Sample box shows current color of title text

Figure 2.32

The dialog box displays a palette of standard colors. The current color of the title text is selected. The sample box will show the new color you select in the upper half, and the current color in the lower half. Because you have not yet selected a new color, only one color is displayed.

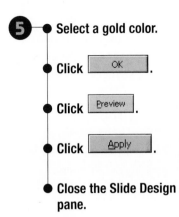

5 ● **Select a gold color.**

● **Click** OK .

● **Click** Preview .

● **Click** Apply .

● **Close the Slide Design pane.**

Your screen should be similar to Figure 2.33

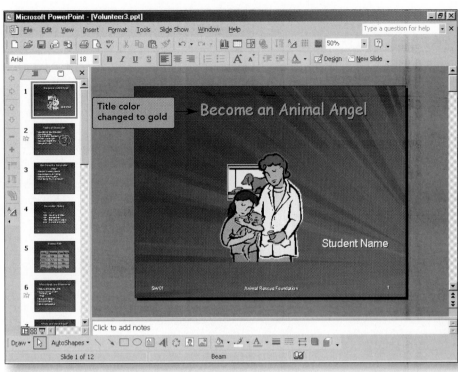

Figure 2.33

The title color has changed on all slides in the presentation. This color gives the presentation much more impact.

Working with Master Slides

While viewing the slides, you think the slide appearance could be further improved by changing the bullet design on all slides. Although you can change each slide individually as you did in Lab 1, you can make the change much faster to all the slides by changing the slide master.

Master

5 A **master** is a special slide that controls the format and placement of titles and text for all slides in your presentation. Each component of a presentation — title slide, slides, notes pages, and handout pages — has a corresponding master. The master contains formatted placeholders for the titles, main text, footnotes, background elements, and so on that appear on each associated slide or page. Any changes you make to a master affect all slides or pages associated with that master. The four masters are described below.

Master	Function
Slide Master	Defines the format and placement of title, body, and footer text, bullet styles, background design, and color scheme of each slide in the presentation.
Title Master	Defines the format and placement of titles and text for slides that use the Title Slide layout.
Handout Master	Defines the format and placement of the slide image, text, headers, footers, and other elements that are to appear on every handout.
Notes Master	Defines the format and placement of the slide image, note text, headers, footers, and other elements that are to appear on all speaker notes.

Each design template comes with its own slide master. When you apply a new design template to a presentation, all slides and masters are updated to those of the new design template.

Using the master to modify or add elements to a presentation ensures consistency and saves time.

You can create slides that differ from the master by changing the format and placement of elements in the individual slide rather than on the master. For example, when you changed the font settings of the title on the title slide, the slide master was not affected. Only the individual slide changed, making it unique. If you have created a unique slide, the elements you changed on that slide retain their uniqueness even if you later make changes to the slide master. That is why the title font did not change when you changed the design template.

Modifying the Slide Master

You will change the bullet style in the slide master so that all slides in the presentation will be changed.

1 ● Choose
View/**M**aster/**S**lide
Master.

Another Method

You also can hold
down ⬆Shift and
click ▣ Normal
View to display the
slide master.

*Your screen should be
similar to Figure 2.34*

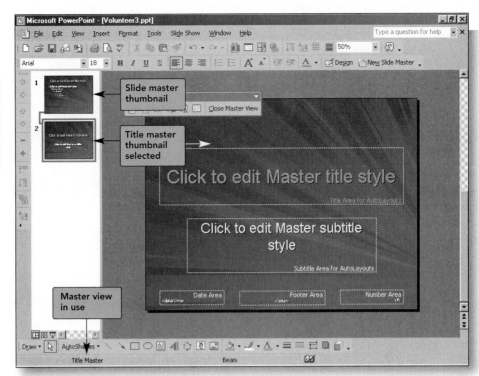

Figure 2.34

Additional Information

Pointing to the master
thumbnail displays a
ScreenTip that identifies the
selected master and the
slides where it is used in the
presentation.

The view has changed to Master view, and the Slide Master View toolbar
may also be displayed. Thumbnails for both the title master and slide master
for the Beam design template appear in the left pane of this view. The
second thumbnail for the title master is selected and the slide pane displays
the master for it. The status bar identifies the master you are viewing. You
want to make changes to the slide master first.

2 ● Point to the first master thumbnail to see
the ScreenTip.

● Click on the first
master thumbnail to
select it.

*Your screen should be
similar to Figure 2.35*

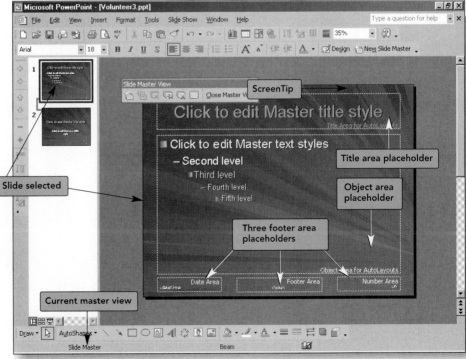

Figure 2.35

The slide master consists of five area placeholders that control the appearance of all slides except a title slide. Each placeholder displays sample text to show you how changes you make in these areas will appear. You make changes to the master slide just like you change any other slide. You will change the graphic that is used for the bullet style in the object area to one that is gold colored.

3 ● **Click the object area to select it.**

● **Choose Format/Bullets and Numbering.**

● **Click** Picture... .

Your screen should be similar to Figure 2.36

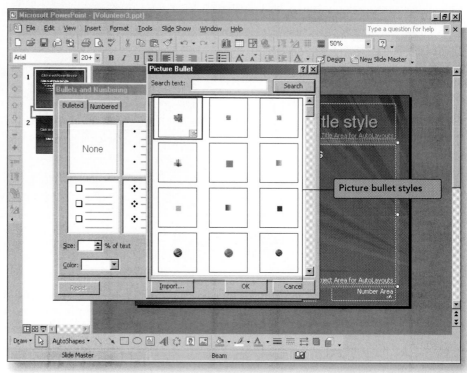

Figure 2.36

From the Picture Bullet dialog box, you can select from any of the bullet styles listed.

4 ● **Double-click** □ **(first bullet, sixth row).**

Your screen should be similar to Figure 2.37

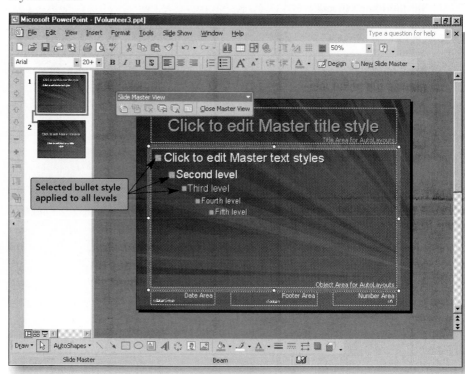

Figure 2.37

The selected bullet style has been applied to all levels of items in the object area.

While looking at the slide master, you decide the object area would look better if it was smaller to allow more blank space on the left and right edge of the slide. Additionally, you decide to delete the date from the footer.

5 ● **Drag the corner of the object area place-holder to decrease the placeholder size and center it below the title placeholder as in Figure 2.38.**

● **Select the Date Area placeholder.**

● **Press** Delete.

Your screen should be similar to Figure 2.38

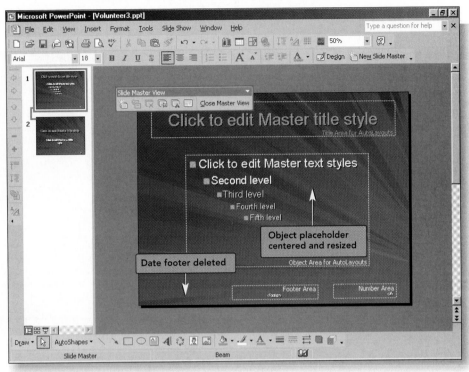

Figure 2.38

You want to see how the changes you have made to the slide master affected the slides.

6 ● **Click** 🔲 **Slide Sorter view.**

Your screen should be similar to Figure 2.39

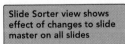

Slide Sorter view shows effect of changes to slide master on all slides

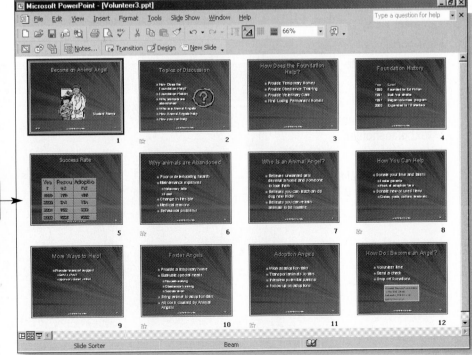

Figure 2.39

You can now see that all slides in the presentation have been modified. The changes to the bullet style, and size and placement of the object text are reflected in all slides. None of the slides, except the title slide, displays the date in the footer.

Modifying the Title Master

Next you want to enhance the appearance of the title slide.

1 ● Display slide 1 in Normal view.

Your screen should be similar to Figure 2.40

Figure 2.40

Earlier, you changed the font, size, and placement of the title and the placement of the subtitle. Although you still like these changes, you want the title to be larger and italicized and the subtitle text smaller. You also want to remove the shadow from the subtitle.

2 ● Display the Slide Master view.

● Display the Title Master.

● Click the master title text placeholder.

Your screen should be similar to Figure 2.41

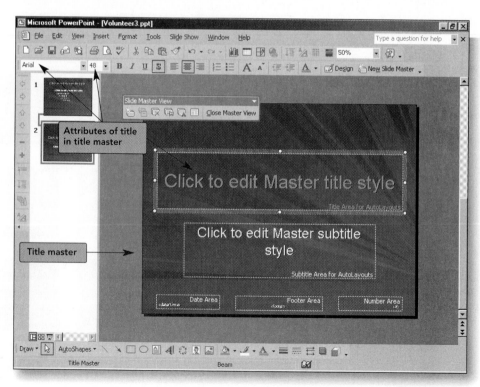

Figure 2.41

Notice that the title master has a slightly different appearance from the title slide in your presentation. This is because you modified the title slide by moving placeholders and changing the font, size, and color, making it a unique slide. The unique changes you made to that slide were not changed when the title master of the Beam design template was applied. The title master attributes reflect the attributes associated with the Beam template, such as the title font of Arial, 48 pt as shown in the toolbar buttons.

3

- Increase the font size to 54.

- Click _I_ Italic.

Another Method

The menu equivalent is Format/Font/Font Style/Italic.

- Choose View/Ruler to display the ruler.

- Decrease the size of the placeholder and center it on the slide as in Figure 2.42.

Additional Information

Use the ruler as a guide for placement of objects on the slide.

- Select the subtitle area placeholder.

- Click Shadow to remove the shadow.

- Decrease the size of the placeholder and move it to the location shown in Figure 2.42.

Your screen should be similar to Figure 2.42

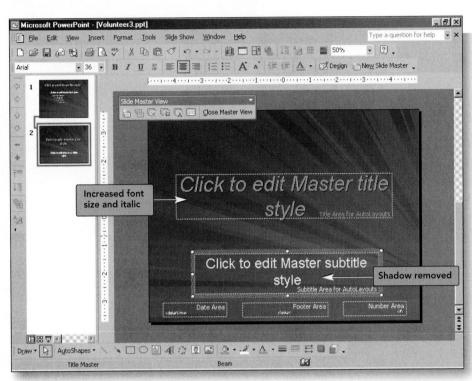

Figure 2.42

You want to see how the title slide looks with the changes you have made.

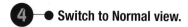

4 ● **Switch to Normal view.**

Your screen should be similar to Figure 2.43

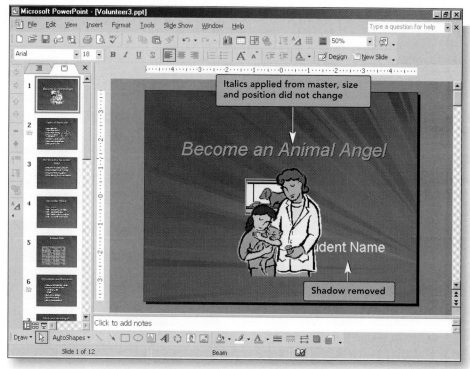

Figure 2.43

Some of the changes you made to the title master were automatically applied to the title slide. However, others were not. This is because the earlier changes made the slide unique, and changes made to an individual slide override the master slide.

Reapplying a Slide Layout

To apply all the settings on the master title slide to the title slide in the presentation, you need to reapply the slide layout.

1 ● **Choose Format/Slide Layout.**

● **Click** ▮ **to open the drop-down menu for the selected layout.**

> Apply to Selected Slides
> Reapply Layout
> Insert New Slide

● **Choose Reapply Layout.**

● **Close the Slide Layout pane.**

Your screen should be similar to Figure 2.44

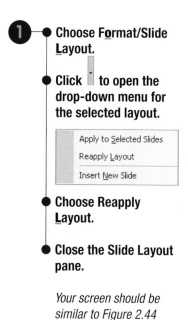

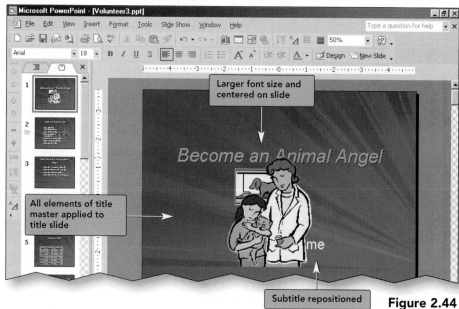

Subtitle repositioned   **Figure 2.44**

All elements of the title master slide have been applied to the title slide. The only adjustment you want to make to the slide is to reposition the graphic.

- Select the graphic and move it to the location shown in Figure 2.45.

- Move the subtitle to the location shown in Figure 2.45.

- Choose **View/Ruler** to hide the ruler again.

- Deselect the placeholder.

Your screen should be similar to Figure 2.45

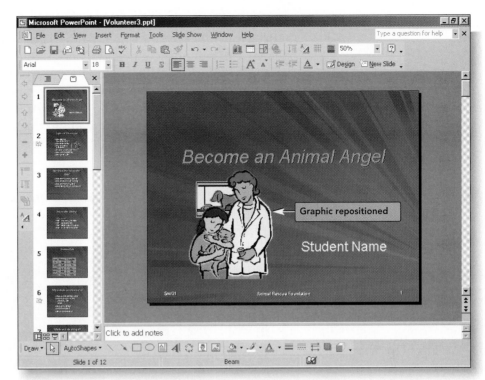

Figure 2.45

Hiding the Title Slide Footer

You would also like to hide the display of the footer information on the title slide. When you created the presentation using the AutoContent Wizard, you specified the information to appear in the center footer area. The title master determines the information displayed in the left and right footer areas. The left footer displays the current date and the right the slide number. The information in the footer can be changed or hidden completely.

- Choose **View/Header** and Footer.

- Open the Slide tab, if necessary.

Your screen should be similar to Figure 2.46

Additional Information

The date on your screen may be displayed different than in Figure 2.46 depending on your Windows settings.

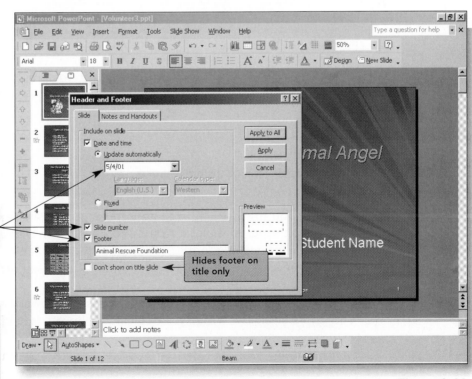

Figure 2.46

The Date and Time option is selected, and the date is set to update automatically using the current system date whenever the presentation is opened. You can also change this option to enter a fixed date that will not change. Additionally, the slide number was preselected, and the text you entered, "Animal Rescue Foundation," appears in the footer text box. You could turn off these options and delete the footer text in order to remove this information from the current slide. Because it is very common to not display this information on a title slide, there is an option to hide it for that type of slide.

2 ● Select Don't show on title slide.

● Click [Apply].

Additional Information

The [Apply] command button applies the current settings to the selected slides only. Using [Apply to All] applies the current setting to the entire presentation, including the corresponding master.

Your screen should be similar to Figure 2.47

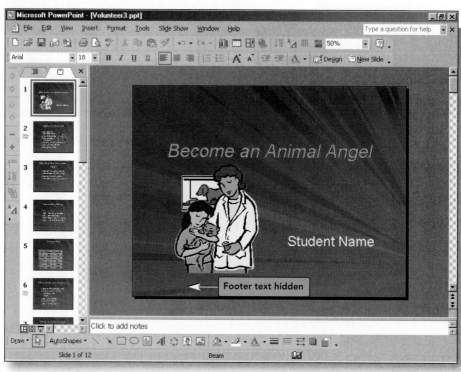

Figure 2.47

Additional Information

You could also delete the three footer areas from the title master to remove them from all title slides.

The entire footer is no longer displayed on the title slide.

You have made many changes to the presentation. You will run the slide show to see how they will look when the presentation is run.

3 ● Click [ ] Slide Show.

● Click on each slide to advance through the presentation.

You think the presentation looks quite good, but you have several changes in mind to make it more interesting. For example, you want to add a concluding slide to mark the end of the presentation, and you want to include several features that will animate the presentation.

Note: If you are ending your session now, save the presentation and exit PowerPoint. When you begin again, open this file.

Duplicating a Slide

Every presentation should have a concluding slide. To create the concluding slide, you will duplicate slide 1. Duplicating a slide creates a copy of the selected slide and places it directly after the selected slide. You can duplicate a slide in any view, but in this case you will use the Outline tab in Slide view to duplicate slide 1 and move it to the end of the presentation.

1

- Click slide 1 in the Outline tab.

- Choose **I**nsert/**D**uplicate Slide.

- Drag slide 2 in the Outline tab to the end of the list of slides.

Your screen should be similar to Figure 2.48

Another Method

You can also duplicate a slide using the Copy and Paste commands on the Edit menu.

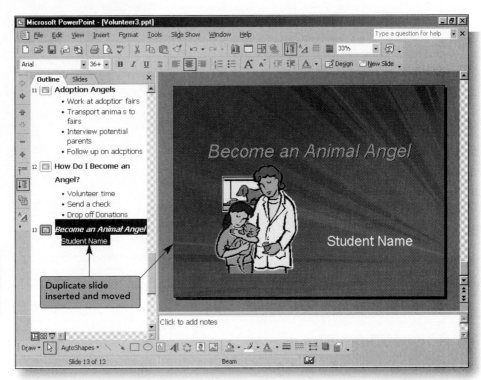

Figure 2.48

Working with AutoShapes

The concluding slide in the presentation needs to be more powerful, as it is your last chance to convince your audience to help the Animal Angels organization. You decide to replace the graphic with another of a heart. To quickly add a shape, you will use one of the ready-made shapes supplied with PowerPoint called **AutoShapes**. These include such basic shapes as rectangles and circles, a variety of lines, block arrows, flowchart symbols, stars and banners, and callouts.

Inserting an AutoShape

1 ● Select the graphic and press (Delete).

● Click AutoShapes ▾ (in the Drawing toolbar).

● Select **B**asic Shapes.

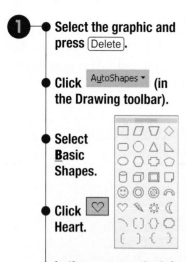

● Click ♡ Heart.

● In the space on the left side of the slide, click and drag downward and to the right to create the heart.

> **Another Method**
> The menu equivalent is Insert/Picture/AutoShapes.

● If necessary, size and position the heart as in Figure 2.49.

> **Additional Information**
> An AutoShape can be sized and moved just like any other object.

> **Another Method**
> To maintain the height and width proportions of the AutoShape, hold down (⇧ Shift) while you drag.

Your screen should be similar to Figure 2.49

> **Additional Information**
> Most shapes can also be inserted from the Clip Organizer as well.

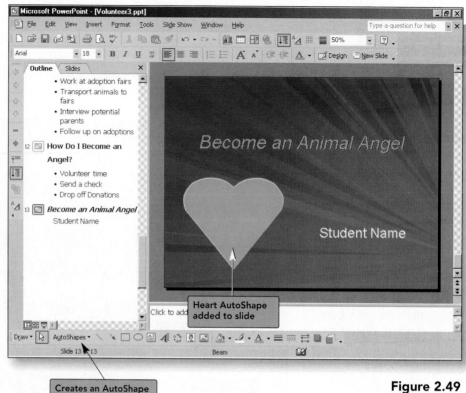

Heart AutoShape added to slide

Creates an AutoShape

Figure 2.49

Adding Text to an AutoShape

Next you will add text to the heart object. Text can be added to all shapes and becomes part of the shape—when the shape is moved, the text moves with it.

1

- Right-click on the AutoShape object to open the shortcut menu, and select Add Text.

- Click **B** Bold.

- Increase the font size to 24 points.

- Change the font color to gold.

- Type Open Your Heart.

- If necessary, adjust the size of the heart.

Your screen should be similar to Figure 2.50

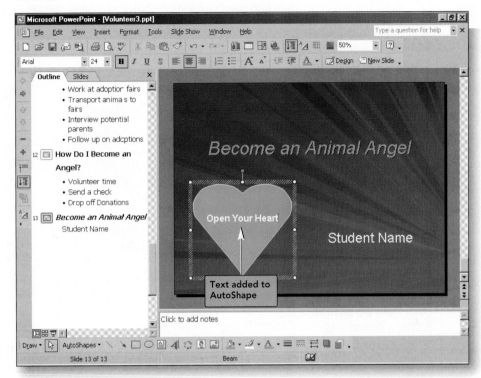

Figure 2.50

Enhancing the AutoShape

Next you will enhance its appearance by adding a shadow behind the heart. Then you will change the color of the shadow so it is easier to see.

● Click ▣ **Shadow Style (on the Drawing toolbar).**

● **Select any shadow style from the pop-up menu.**

● Click ▣ **Shadow/Style and choose Shadow Settings.**

● Click ▣▾ **Shadow Color from the Shadow Settings toolbar and select a color of your choice.**

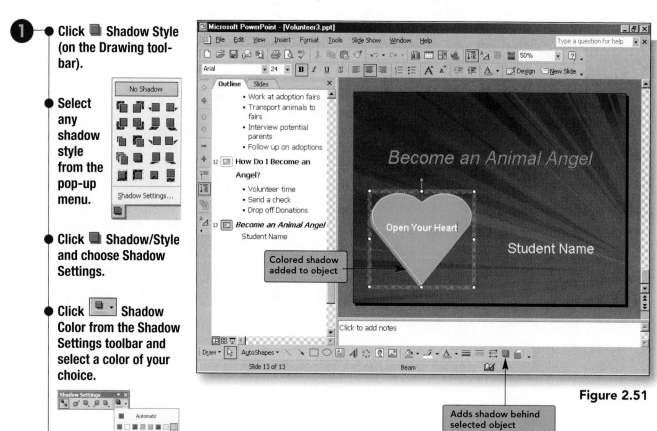

Figure 2.51

Colored shadow added to object

Adds shadow behind selected object

Additional Information

A darker shade of the object's color for a shadow is very effective.

● **Close the Shadow Settings toolbar.**

Your screen should be similar to Figure 2.51

Additional Information

Holding down ⟨⇧Shift⟩ while using the rotate handle rotates the object in 15-degree increments.

Rotating the Object

Finally, you want to change the angle of the object. You can rotate an object 90 degrees left or right, or to any other angle. You will change the angle of the heart to the right using the ● **rotate handle** for the selected object, which allows you to rotate the object to any degree in any direction.

1 Hold down ⇧Shift while you drag the rotate handle to the left one increment.

Additional Information

The mouse pointer appears as 🔄 when positioned on the rotate handle.

Your screen should be similar to Figure 2.52

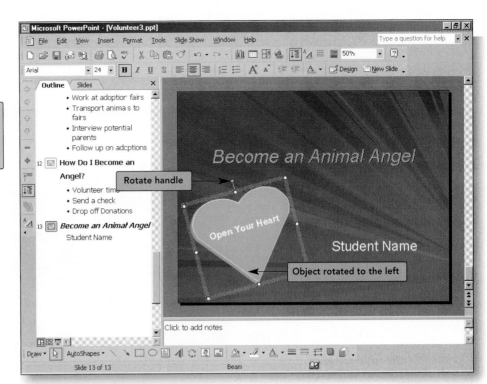

Figure 2.52

Using Special Effects

Next you would like to use some of PowerPoint's special effects to enhance the onscreen presentation.

concept 6

Special Effects

6 Special effects such as animation, sound, slide transitions, and build slides are used to enhance an onscreen presentation.

Animation adds action to text and graphics so they move around on the screen. You can assign sounds to further enhance the effect.

Transitions control how one slide moves off the screen and the next one appears. You can select from many different transition choices. You may choose Dissolve for your title slide to give it an added flair. After that you could use Wipe Right for all the slides until the next to the last, and then use Dissolve again to end the show. As with any special effect, use slide transitions carefully.

Builds are used to display each bullet point, text, paragraph, or graphic independently of the other text or objects on the slide. You set up the

way you want each element to appear (to fly in from the left, for instance) and whether you want the other elements already on the slide to dim or shimmer when a new element is added. For example, since your audience is used to reading from left to right, you could design your build slides so the bullet points fly in from the left. Then, when you want to emphasize a point, bring a bullet point in from the right. That change grabs the audience's attention.

When you present a slide show, the content of your presentation should take center stage. You want the special effects you use, such as animation, builds, and transitions, to help emphasize the main points in your presentation—not draw the audience's attention to the special effects.

Animating an Object and Adding Sound Effects

To further enhance the AutoShape object on the final slide, you will add two special effects, custom animation and sound, to this object.

1 ● **Right-click on the AutoShape object to open the shortcut menu, and select Custom Animation.**

Your screen should be similar to Figure 2.53

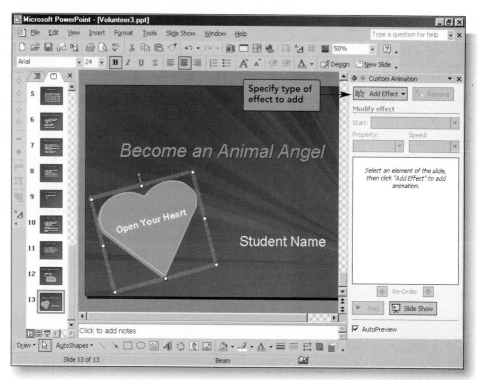

Figure 2.53

The Custom Animation task pane is used to assign animations and sound to all objects on the slide and to determine the order in which they display. You will animate the AutoShape object only. As you make selections, the screen will display the selected animation effect and the list box will display the selected settings for the object.

2 ● **Click** 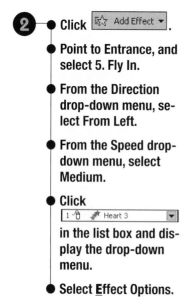 **.**

● **Point to Entrance, and select 5. Fly In.**

● **From the Direction drop-down menu, select From Left.**

● **From the Speed drop-down menu, select Medium.**

● **Click**

● **in the list box and display the drop-down menu.**

● **Select Effect Options.**

Your screen should be similar to Figure 2.54

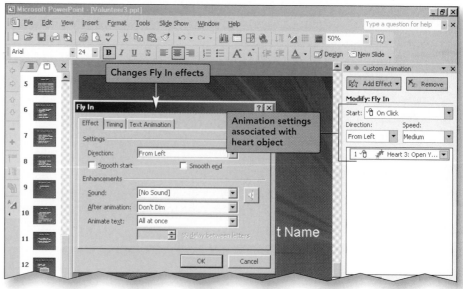

Figure 2.54

The Fly In dialog box includes the setting you already specified for the direction of the effect. You want to include a sound with the fly-in effect. Then you want to see how the animation will work while the presentation is running. When you run a slide show, it will begin at the current slide location. Also, you need to click on the slide to activate the animation and sound effect.

3 ● **From the Sound drop-down menu, choose Chime.**

● **Click** OK .

● **Click** 🖳 Slide Show **in the task pane.**

Additional Information
You must have a speaker and a sound card to hear the sound.

● **Click the slide.**

Your screen should be similar to Figure 2.55

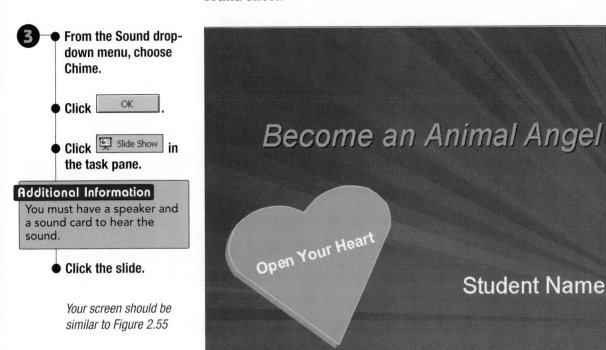

Become an Animal Angel

Open Your Heart

Student Name

Figure 2.55

Slide 13 is displayed in Slide Show view and, after you clicked on the slide, the heart appeared using the fly-in effect and the chime sound played. You can end a slide show at any point by pressing (Esc), and the slide you are viewing becomes the current slide.

4 ● **Press** (Esc) **to end the slide show.**

● **Close the task pane.**

Adding Transition Effects

You would also like to add a transition effect to all the slides.

● Switch to Slide Sorter view and select slide 1.

● Click 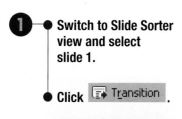 Transition .

Another Method

The menu equivalent is **S**lide Show/Slide **T**ransition.

Your screen should be similar to Figure 2.56

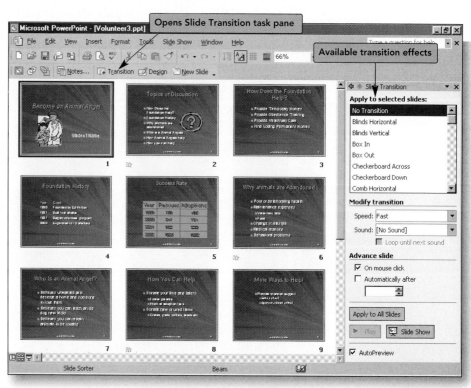

Figure 2.56

In the Slide Transition task pane, the list box displays the names of the transition effects that can be used on the slides. Currently, No Transition is selected. The selected transition effects will be displayed in the slide as they are selected from the list.

● Select a few transition effects to see how they work.

● Scroll the list box and select Shape Diamond.

Your screen should be similar to Figure 2.57

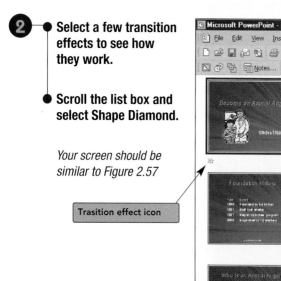

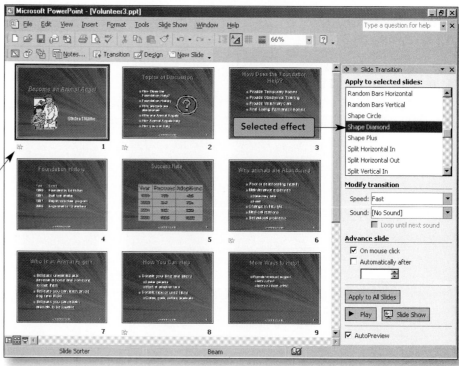

Figure 2.57

A preview of the selected transition effect is displayed on the slide in Slide Sorter view, and a ⚝ transition icon is displayed below slide 1. This indicates that a transition effect has been applied to the slide. Several other slides in the presentation also display a transition effect icon. This is because the AutoContent Wizard automatically used the Cut transition effect on all slides, except the title slide, that were added when the presentation was created originally.

You like how transition effects work and decide to use the Random Transition effect, which will randomly select different transition effects, on all the slides. You will select and change all the slides at once.

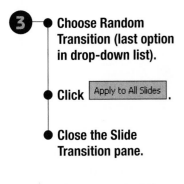

3
- **Choose Random Transition (last option in drop-down list).**

- **Click** `Apply to All Slides`.

- **Close the Slide Transition pane.**

Your screen should be similar to Figure 2.58

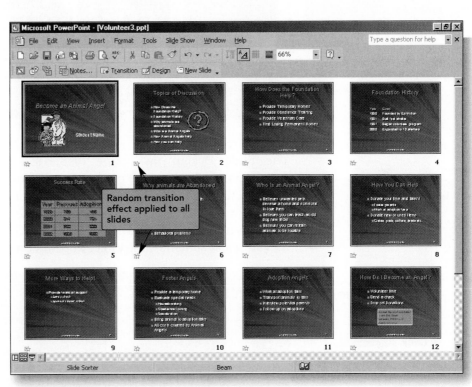

Figure 2.58

The transition icon appears below each slide, indicating that a transition effect has been applied to all slides.

4 Run the slide show from the beginning to see the different effects.

Adding Build Effects

The next effect you want to add to the slides is a build to progressively display each bullet on a slide. When a build is applied to a slide, the slide initially shows only the title. The bulleted text appears as the presentation proceeds. A build slide can also include different build transition effects, which are similar to slide transition effects. The effect is applied to the bulleted text as it is displayed on the slide. You would like to add a build to all slides in the presentation except slides 1, 2, 4, 5, and 13.

1 ● Click  Design .

● Click 🖼 Animation Schemes .

Additional Information

You can also use the Animation Schemes and Custom Animation commands on the Slide Show menu to add sound build effects. To use this option, you must be in Slide view.

Your screen should be similar to Figure 2.59

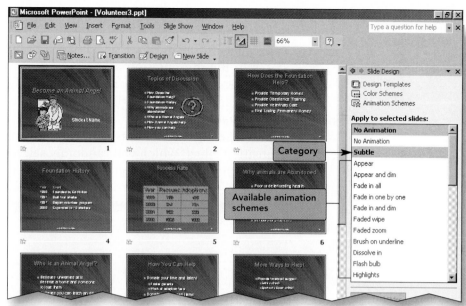

Figure 2.59

Additional Information

Pointing to a scheme name displays a description of the effects in a ScreenTip.

The Slide Design task pane displays a list of animation schemes. **Animation schemes** are preset visual effects that can be added to slide text. Each scheme usually includes an effect for the title as well as the bulleted items. Some schemes include a slide transition effect as well. The schemes are divided into three categories: Subtle, Moderate, and Exciting. As you select schemes, the effect appears on each selected slide.

2 ● Select a few animation schemes.

● Select Wipe.

● Click Apply to All Slides .

● Select slides 1, 2, 4, 5, and 13.

HAVING TROUBLE?

You can select and deselect multiple slides by holding down (Control) while making your selection.

● Click No Animation .

● Select slides 1 and 13.

● Select the Big title effect from the Exciting category.

● Select slide 1 and run the slide show.

● Click to display the subtitle.

Your screen should be similar to Figure 2.60

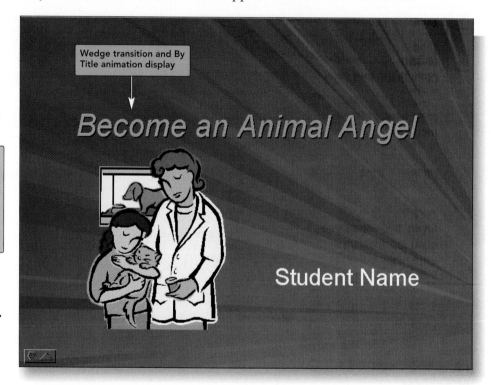

Figure 2.60

The first slide is displayed using the Wedge transition effect and Big Title animation, but did not display the subtitle until you clicked on the slide. When a build is applied to a slide, the body items are displayed only when you click or use any of the procedures to advance to the next slide. This allows the presenter to focus the audience's attention and to control the pace of the presentation.

Controlling the Slide Show

As much as you would like to control a presentation, the presence of an audience usually causes the presentation to change course. PowerPoint has several ways you can control a slide show during the presentation. Before presenting a slide show, you should rehearse the presentation. To help with this aspect of the presentation, PowerPoint includes a Rehearse Timings option on the Slide Show menu that records the time you spend on each slide as you practice your narration. If your computer is set up with a microphone, you could even record your narration with the Record Narration option.

Navigating in a Slide Show

Running the slide show and practicing how to control the slide show help you have a smooth presentation. For example, if someone has a question about a previous slide, you can go backward and redisplay it. You will try out some of the features you can use while running the slide show.

 **Continue to click or press** [Spacebar] **until the title of slide 6 appears.**

Press [Backspace] **(4 times).**

You returned the onscreen presentation to slide 3. But now, because the audience already viewed slide 4, you want to advance to slide 5. To go to a specific slide number, you type the slide number and press [←Enter].

 **Press 5.**

Press [←Enter]**.**

> **Another Method**
> You also can choose **G**o/Slide **N**avigator from the shortcut menu to select a slide to move to.

Sometimes a question from an audience member can interrupt the flow of the presentation. If this happens to you, you can black out the screen to focus attention onto your response.

 **Press B.**

> **Another Method**
> The menu equivalent is S**c**reen/**B**lack Screen on the shortcut menu.

The screen goes to black while you address the topic. When you are ready to resume the presentation, you can bring the slide back.

Click, or press B.

Adding Freehand Annotations

During your presentation, you may want to point to an important word, underline an important point, or draw checkmarks next to items that you have covered. To do this, you can use the mouse pointer during the presentation.

Display slide 6.

Press Spacebar **(5 times) to display the bulleted items.**

To display the mouse pointer, move the mouse on your desktop.

Your screen should be similar to Figure 2.61

Figure 2.61

In its current shape ⬆, you can use the mouse pointer to point to items on the slide. You can also use it to draw on the screen by changing the pointer to a pen, which activates the freehand annotation feature.

Click ⬛ **to display the shortcut menu.**

Select Po**inter Options.**

Another Method
You can also right-click on the screen to display the shortcut menu.

Your screen should be similar to Figure 2.62

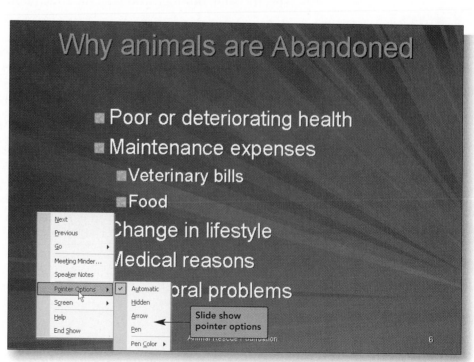

Figure 2.62

The pointer options are described in the following table.

Option	Effect
Automatic	The default option. Hides the pointer if it is not moved for 15 seconds. It reappears when you move the mouse.
Hidden	Hides the pointer until another pointer option is selected.
Arrow	Displays the pointer as an arrow and does not hide it.
Pen	Changes the pointer to a pen and turns on freehand annotation. You can also use Pen Color to turn on the annotation and specify the color of line to draw.

3 ● **Choose Pen.**

Additional Information
The keyboard shortcut is [Control] + P.

4 ● **Move the mouse pointer under "Medical reasons."**

● **Drag the pen pointer until the underline is drawn.**

HAVING TROUBLE?
To draw a straight line, hold down [⇧Shift] while dragging.

Your screen should be similar to Figure 2.63

Additional Information
You can also erase annotations by selecting Screen/Erase Pen from the shortcut menu. The keyboard shortcut is E.

The mouse pointer changes to a ✎. To see how the freehand annotation feature works, you will underline the last bullet. To draw, you drag the pen pointer in the direction you want to draw.

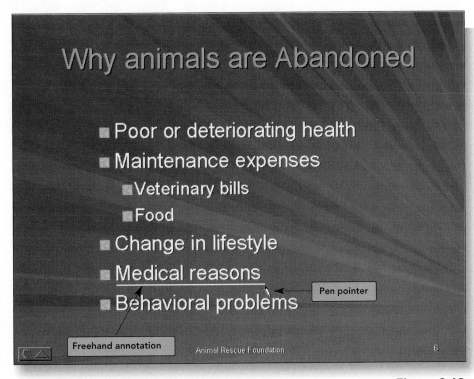

Figure 2.63

5 ● **Practice using the freehand annotator to draw any shapes you want on the slide.**

● **To turn off freehand annotation, select Pointer Options/Automatic from the shortcut menu.**

● **Press [Esc] to end the slide show.**

● **Close the task pane.**

You do not have to be concerned about cluttering your slides with freehand drawings because they are erased when you continue the presentation.

Hiding Slides

As you reconsider the presentation, you decide to show the Success Rate slide only if someone asks about this information. To do this, you will hide the slide. You can hide slides in several views, but the procedure is easiest in Slide Sorter view. Slide Sorter view also has its own toolbar that makes it easy to perform many different tasks in this view. The Formatting toolbar is not displayed because you cannot format slides in this view.

- Select slide 5.

- Click 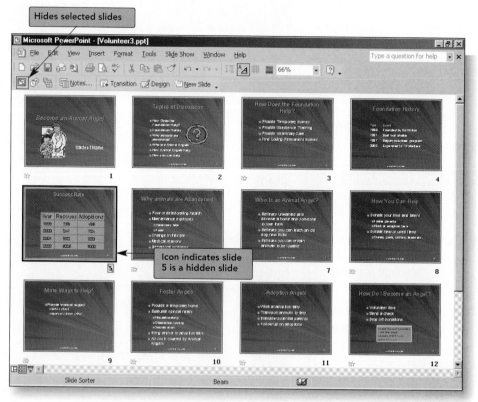 Hide Slide.

Additional Information

The menu equivalent is Slide Show/Hide Slide.

HAVING TROUBLE?

If the Slide Sorter toolbar is not displayed, select it from the Toolbar shortcut menu.

Your screen should be similar to Figure 2.64

Figure 2.64

Notice that the slide number for slide 5 is surrounded by a box with a slash drawn through it. This indicates that the slide is hidden. Next you will run the slide show to see how hidden slides work. You will begin the show at the slide before the hidden slide.

② ● **Select slide 4.**

● **Run the slide show.**

● **Display the next slide, which should be Why Animals are Abandoned.**

Your screen should be similar to Figure 2.65

Figure 2.65

Slide 5 was not displayed because it is hidden. To show how to display a hidden slide, you will run the slide show beginning with slide 4 and then display slide 6.

③ ● **Press** Page Up **twice.**

● **Press H to see slide 5.**

Your screen should be similar to Figure 2.66

Another Method

You can also use **G**o/By **T**itle on the shortcut menu to display a hidden slide.

Hidden slide is displayed

Year	Rescues	Adoptions
1999	759	495
2000	847	784
2001	982	833
2002	1025	1002

Animal Rescue Foundation   5

Figure 2.66

Creating Speaker Notes

When making your presentation, there are some critical points you want to be sure to discuss. To help you remember the important points, you can use **notes pages**. These pages show a miniature of the slide and provide an area to enter speaker notes. You can create notes pages for some or all of the slides in a presentation. Notes pages can also be used to remind you of hidden slides. You decide to create speaker notes on slide 4 to remind you about the hidden slide.

1
- Press Esc to end the slide show.
- Switch to Normal view.
- Display slide 4.
- Click in the Notes pane.
- Type **Show the next hidden slide if someone asks about adoption rates.**

Additional Information
You can enlarge the notes area by dragging the pane divider line.

Your screen should be similar to Figure 2.67

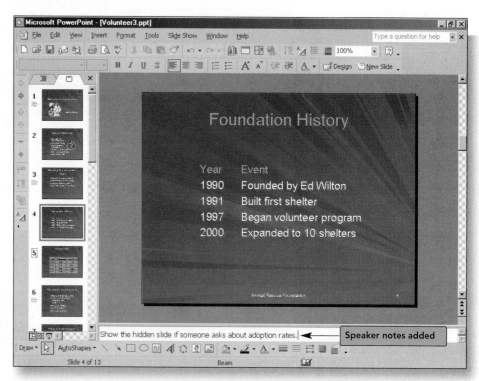

Figure 2.67

You want to see how the notes page will look when printed.

2
- Choose **V**iew/Notes **P**age.

Your screen should be similar to Figure 2.68

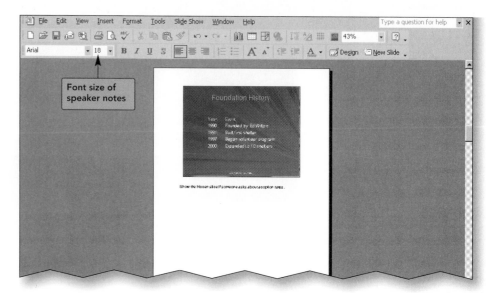

Figure 2.68

The notes pages display the notes you added below the slide that the note accompanies. To make the speaker notes easy to read in a dimly lit room while you are making the presentation, you would like to use a larger type size.

3 ● Click on the note text to select the placeholder.

● Select the note text.

● Increase the font size to 24.

Your screen should be similar to Figure 2.69

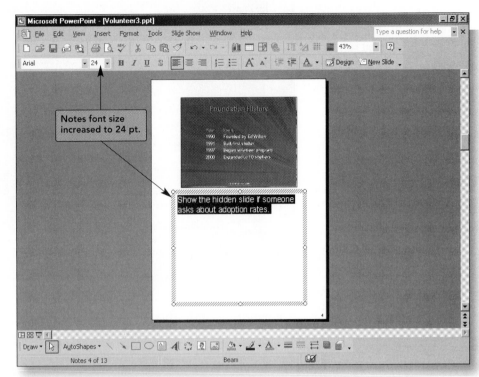

Notes font size increased to 24 pt.

Figure 2.69

Checking the Style

You want to make a final check of the presentation for consistency and style. To do this, you may need to turn on the style checking feature and set the options to check.

1
- Display slide 1 in Normal view.

- Choose Tools/Options.

- Open the Spelling and Style tab and select Check Style.

- If prompted, click [Enable Assistant] to enable the Office Assistant.

- Click [Style Options...].

Your screen should be similar to Figure 2.70

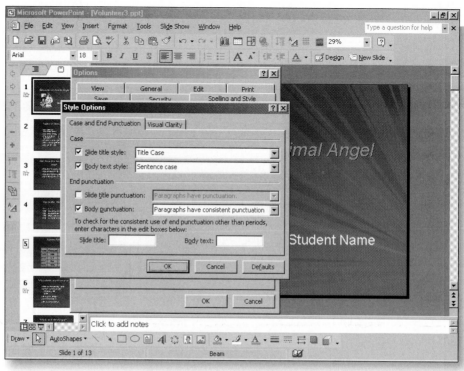

Figure 2.70

You want the style check to check the case of the title and body text, and the end punctuation of the body text.

2
- If necessary, make the appropriate selections from the Case and End Punctuation tab as shown in Figure 2.70.

- Open the Visual Clarity tab.

- Select the same options shown in Figure 2.71.

Your screen should be similar to Figure 2.71

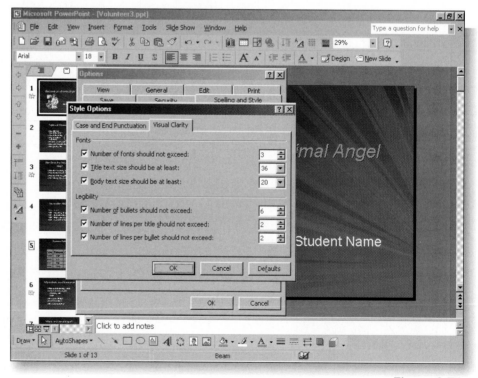

Figure 2.71

When a style check is made, each slide is examined for visual clarity. The default settings use guidelines for proper slide design: the font size is large, the number of fonts used is small, and the amount of text on a slide is limited. For example, the maximum number of bullets per slide is six and number of lines per bullet is two. All these settings help you adhere to good slide design.

The style check feature is only active when the Office Assistant is displayed. It displays a light bulb next to the area in any slides in which it detects a potential problem.

3 ● Click [OK] two times.

● If necessary, click on the slide to display the light bulb.

● Click on the light bulb.

● Move the Assistant character to the upper right corner of the screen.

Your screen should be similar to Figure 2.72

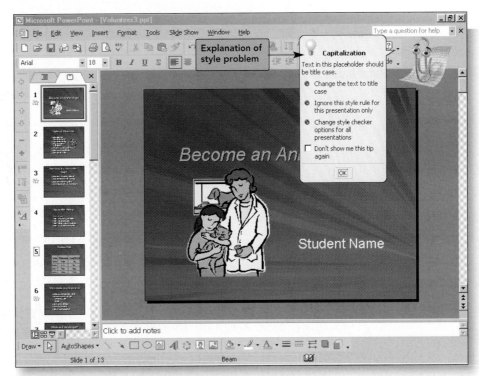

Figure 2.72

The Assistant displays an explanation of the problem it has located, in this case, a capitalization error. The default slide design uses title case (first letter of each word is capitalized) for slide titles.

4 ● Choose Change the text to title case.

Your screen should be similar to Figure 2.73

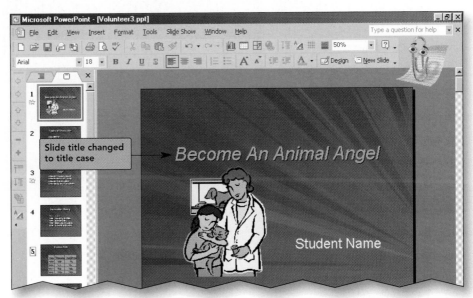

Figure 2.73

To continue checking the style, you need to move to the next slide.

● Click in the scroll bar to display slide 2.

● Click the light bulb.

● Choose Change the text to title case.

● Click the light bulb.

Your screen should be similar to Figure 2.74

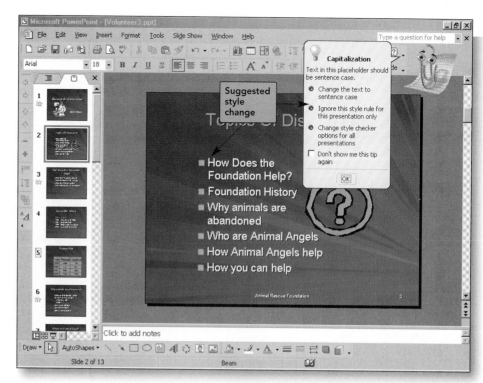

Figure 2.74

The suggested style change is to change the bulleted items to sentence case (first letter of the sentence is capitalized) for body text. No end punctuation is used.

● Choose Change the text to sentence case.

Your screen should be similar to Figure 2.75

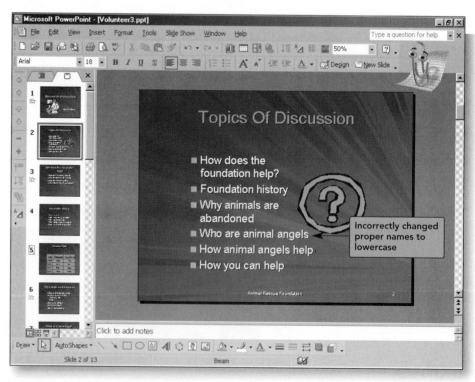

Figure 2.75

Making this change also changed proper names, such as the name of the volunteer group, to lowercase. In this case, you do not want to keep this change. You will undo the change and skip the style check suggestion to clear it.

7 ● Click 🔄 Undo.

● Click the light bulb.

● Click OK to ignore the suggestion for this slide.

● Display slide 3.

● Click the light bulb.

● Choose Change the text to title case.

● Click the light bulb.

● Choose Change the text to sentence case.

Your screen should be similar to Figure 2.76

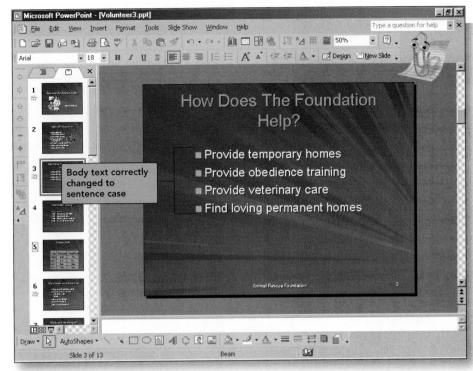

Figure 2.76

The style of the bulleted items is correctly updated.

8 • Continue checking the style on the remaining slides in the presentation, making the changes shown in the table below Figure 2.77.

Your screen should be similar to Figure 2.77

9 • Choose **T**ools/**O**ptions/ Spelling and Style and select **C**heck Style to clear it.

• If necessary, hide the Office Assistant.

HAVING TROUBLE?
Open the Assistant shortcut menu and choose **H**ide.

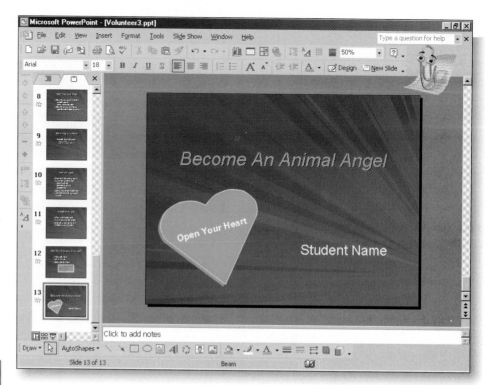

Figure 2.77

Slide	Adjustment
4	Ignore change for this slide.
6	Change the text to title case.
7	Change the text to title case.
7	Click OK to ignore change for this slide.
8	Click OK to ignore change for this slide.
9	Change the text to title case.
10	Click OK to ignore change for this slide.
12	Change the text to sentence case.
13	Change the text to title case.

Documenting a File

Before saving the completed presentation, you want to include file documentation with the file when it is saved.

1 ● **Choose File/Properties.**

● **Open the Summary tab if necessary.**

Your screen should be similar to Figure 2.78

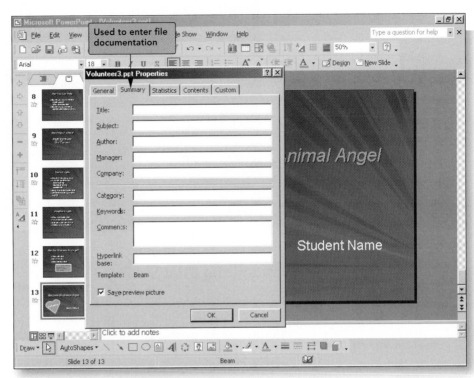

Figure 2.78

The Summary tab text boxes are used for the following:

Option	Action
Title	Enter the presentation title. This title can be longer and more descriptive than the presentation file name.
Subject	Enter a description of the presentation's content.
Author	Enter the name of the presentation's author. By default this is the name entered when PowerPoint was installed.
Manager	Enter the name of your manager.
Company	Enter the name of your company.
Category	Enter the name of a higher-level category under which you can group similar types of presentations.
Keywords	Enter words that you associate with the presentation so the Find File command can be used.
Comments	Enter any comments you feel are appropriate for the presentation.
Hyperlink base	Enter the path or URL that you want to use for all hyperlinks in the document.
Template	Identifies the template that is attached to the file.
Save Preview Picture	Saves a picture of the first slide with the file to display in the Open dialog box.

2

● In the title text box, enter **Animal Angels**.

● In the subject text box, enter **Volunteer recruitment**.

● In the Author text box, enter your name.

● If necessary, select Sa**v**e preview picture.

Your screen should be similar to Figure 2.79

3

● Click .

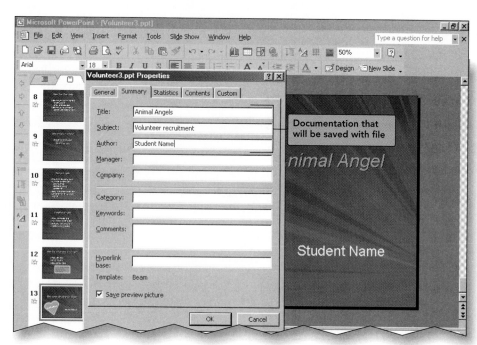

Figure 2.79

Customizing Print Settings

You have created both slides and notes pages for the presentation. Now you want to print the notes page and some of the slides. Just because your presentation looks great on your screen does not mean it will look good when printed. Previewing the presentation allows you to see how it will look before you waste time and paper printing it out. Many times you will want to change the print and layout settings to improve the appearance of the output. Customizing the print settings by changing the orientation of the page, scaling the size of the slides to fill the page, and adding a borderline around each slide are a few of the ways you can make your printed output look more professional.

First you will print the notes page for the slide on which you entered text.

1

● Choose **F**ile/**P**rint.

● From the Print Range area, select **S**lides.

● Type **4**.

● From the Print **W**hat drop-down list box, select Notes Pages.

● Click Preview.

Your screen should be similar to Figure 2.80

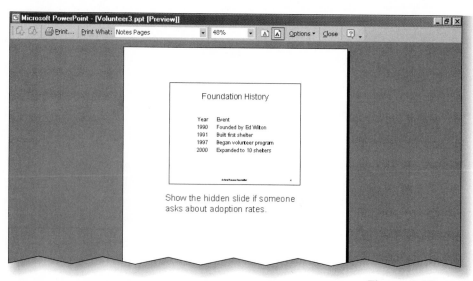

Figure 2.80

The notes page is displayed in portrait orientation as it will appear when printed.

2 ● Click 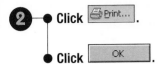 **Print...**

● Click [OK] .

Scaling and Framing

Next you will print a few selected slides to be used as handouts. You will scale the slides to fit the paper in your printer and will add a thin border around the slides as a frame.

1 ● Choose **File/Print**.

● Specify Handouts as the component to print and 6 slides per page.

● Select S**l**ides from the Print Range section.

● In the Slides text box, type **1, 2, 5, 12, 13**.

● Select Scale to **F**it Paper.

● If necessary, select Fra**m**e Slides.

● Click [Preview] .

Your screen should be similar to Figure 2.81

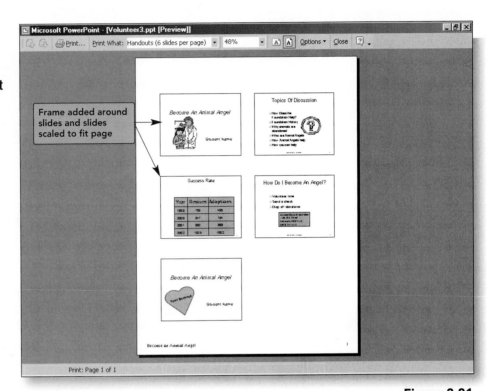

Figure 2.81

The slide images were made as large as possible to fill the printed page, and a thin border was added around each slide.

2 ● If necessary, change the print setting to grayscale.

● Click 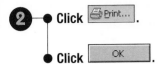 **Print...**

● Click [OK] .

● Save the completed presentation file.

● Exit PowerPoint.

The view you are in when saving the file is the view that will be displayed when the file is opened. The print settings are also saved with the file.

LAB 2

Modifying and Refining a Presentation

Find and Replace (PP2.5)

To make editing easier, you can use the Find and Replace feature to both find text in a presentation and replace it with other text as directed.

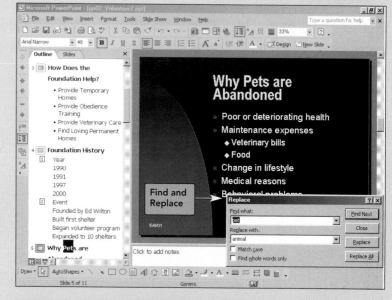

Table (PP2.8)

A table is made up of rows and columns of cells that you can fill with text and graphics.

Alignment (PP2.13)

Alignment settings allow you to change the horizontal placement of an entry in a placeholder or a table cell.

Design Template (PP2.21)

Design templates are professionally created slide designs that can be applied to a presentation.

Master (PP2.28)

A master is a special slide that controls the format and placement of titles and text for all slides in your presentation.

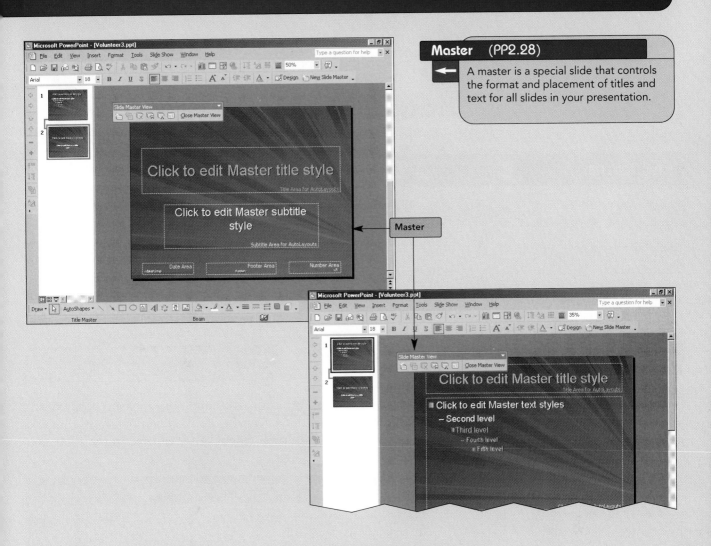

Master

Special Effects (PP2.41)

Special effects such as animation, sound, slide transitions, and build slides are used to enhance the onscreen presentation.

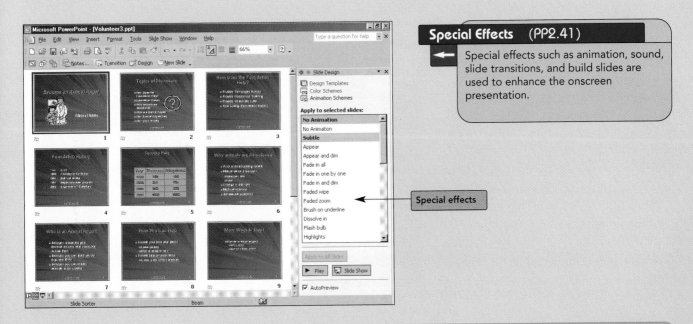

Special effects

lab review

LAB **2**

Modifying and Refining a Presentation

mous skills

The Microsoft Office User Specialist (MOUS) certification program is designed to measure your proficiency in performing basic tasks using the Office XP applications. Getting certified demonstrates that you have the skills and provides a valuable industry credential for employment. After completing this lab, you have learned the following Microsoft Office User Specialist skills:

Skill	Description	Page
Creating Presentations	Add slides to and delete slides from presentations	PP2.8, PP2.37
	Modify headers and footers in the slide master	PP2.31
Inserting and Modifying Text	Insert, format, and modify text	PP2.5, PP2.9
Inserting and Modifying Visual Elements	Add tables, charts, clip art, and bitmap images to slides	PP2.8
	Add OfficeArt elements to slides	PP2.19, PP2.38
	Apply custom formats to tables	PP2.10, PP2.16
Modifying Presentation Formats	Apply formats to presentations	PP2.25, PP2.30, PP2.33
	Apply animation schemes	PP2.42, PP2.46
	Apply slide transitions	PP2.44
	Customize slide formats	PP2.26
	Customize slide templates	PP2.24
	Rearrange slides	PP2.37
	Modify slide layout	PP2.17
Printing Presentations	Preview and print slides, outlines, handouts, and speaker notes	PP2.60
Working with Data from Other Sources	Add sound and video to slides	PP2.43
Managing and Delivering Presentations	Deliver presentations	PP2.47

command summary

Command	Shortcut	Button	Action
File/Properties			Displays statistics and stores information about presentation
Edit/Find	Ctrl + F		Finds selected text
Edit/Replace	Ctrl + H		Replaces selected text
View/Notes Page			Displays notes pages
View/Master/Slide Master			Displays slide master for current presentation
View/Master/Title Master			Displays title master for current presentation
View/Ruler			Displays or hides ruler
View/Header and Footer			Specifies information that appears as headers and footers on slides, notes, outlines, and handout pages
Insert/Duplicate Slide			Inserts duplicate of selected slide
Insert/Picture/AutoShapes			Inserts selected AutoShape object
Insert/Text Box		[⊞]	Adds a text box
Format/Font/Font Style/Bold		[B]	Adds bold effect to selection
Format/Font/Font Style/Italic		[I]	Adds italic effect to selection
Format/Font/Color		[A ▾]	Adds color to selection
Format/Alignment		[≣] [≣] [≣] [≣]	Aligns text in a cell or placeholder to the left, center, right, or justified
Format/Slide Design		[⟀ Design]	Changes appearance of slide by applying a different design template
Format/Slide Layout			Changes or creates a slide layout
Tools/Options/Spelling and Style			Sets spelling and style options
Slide Show/Animation Schemes			Applies selected animation schemes
Slide Show/Slide Transition		[⟀ Transition]	Adds transition effects
Slide Show/Hide Slide		[⟀]	Hides selected slide

Slide Show Shortcut Menu

Command	Shortcut	Button	Action
Go/By Title	H		Displays hidden slide
Go/Slide Navigator			Moves to selected slide
Screen/Black Screen	B		Blacks out screen
Screen/Erase Pen	E		Erases freehand annotations
Pointer Options/Automatic			Hides slide show pointer after 15 seconds of inactivity
Pointer Options/Pen	Ctrl + P		Turns on/off freehand annotation

Terminology

screen identification

In the following PowerPoint screen, several items are identified by letters. Enter the correct term for each item in the spaces that follow.

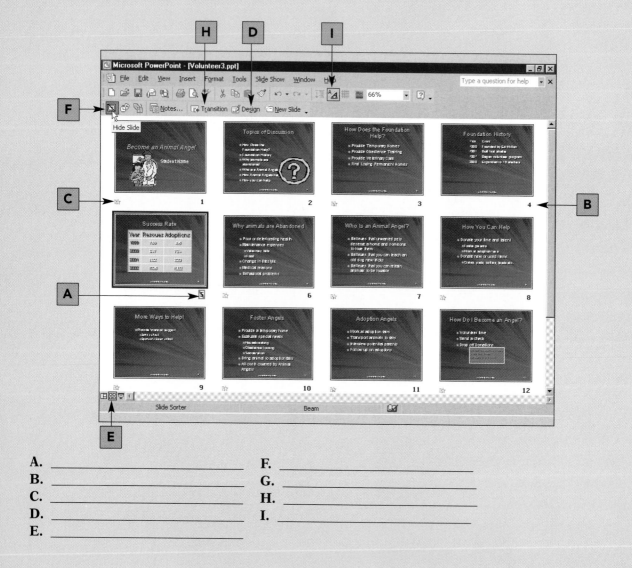

A. _____   F. _____

B. _____   G. _____

C. _____   H. _____

D. _____   I. _____

E. _____

matching

Match the numbered item with the correct lettered description.

1. transitions _____ **a.** shortcut to select all slides

2. ▣ _____ **b.** used to display each bullet point, text, paragraph, or graphic independently on the slide

3. design template _____ **c.** special slide that controls format for the title slide only

4. slide master _____ **d.** hides selected slide

5. builds _____ **e.** shortcut to insert a new slide

6. Ctrl + A _____ **f.** controls how one slide moves off the screen and the next one appears

7. table _____ **g.** defines the background, text format, and placement for each slide

8. Ctrl + M _____ **h.** professionally created slide design that can be applied to a presentation

9. title master _____ **i.** organizes information in rows and columns of cells

10. notes pages _____ **j.** shows a miniature of the slide and provides an area to enter speaker notes

multiple choice

Circle the letter of the correct response.

1. To substitute one word for another in a presentation, you would use the _____ command on the Edit menu.
   a. Find
   b. Locate
   c. Replace
   d. Duplicate

2. A hidden slide can be displayed while running a presentation by pressing the letter _____ .
   a. H
   b. U
   c. B
   d. E

3. A(n) _____ is a special slide that controls the format and placement of titles and text for all slides in a presentation.
   a. handout
   b. notes page
   c. outline slide
   d. master

4. The intersection of a row and column in a table creates a _____ .
   a. block
   b. cell
   c. space
   d. square

5. Slide transitions and build slides are _____ that are used to enhance the onscreen presentation.
   a. animations
   b. slide masters
   c. graphics
   d. special effects

6. Dissolve and Wipe Right are _____.
   a. builds
   b. transitions
   c. animations
   d. all of the above

7. _____ are special effects that control how a bulleted point appears to fly onto the screen.
   a. builds
   b. transitions
   c. graphics
   d. animations

8. _____ adds action to text and graphics so they move around on the screen.
   a. build
   b. transition
   c. graphic
   d. animation

9. _____ are used to define where text and graphics appear on a slide.
   a. effects
   b. placeholders
   c. slide views
   d. animations

10. To help you remember the important points, you can use speaker _____.
   a. notes pages
   b. slide handouts
   c. preview handouts
   d. handouts

true/false

Circle the correct answer to the following questions.

1. Masters are professionally created slide designs that can be applied to your presentation.   True   False

2. AutoShape is an object that can be enhanced using drawing tools and menu commands.   True   False

3. Style checking looks for consistency in punctuation and capitalization.   True   False

4. A master is a special slide on which the formatting for all slides in your presentation is defined.   True   False

5. Alignment controls how text entries are positioned in a placeholder.   True   False

6. A title master defines the format and placement of titles and text for slides that use the title layout.   True   False

7. A handout master defines the format and placement of the slide image, text, headers, footers, and other elements that are to appear on every slide in the presentation.　　True　　False

8. Builds control how one slide moves off the screen and the next one appears.　　True　　False

9. Transitions are used to display each bullet point, text, paragraph, or graphic independently of the other text or objects on the slide.　　True　　False

10. To help you remember the important points, you can use speaker notes pages.　　True　　False

Concepts

fill-in

Complete the following statements by filling in the blanks with the correct terms.

1. _____ are professionally created slide designs that can be applied to your presentation.

2. The _____ master controls format, placement, and all elements that are to appear on every audience handout.

3. _____ refers to attributes such as bold and italics.

4. The _____ slide is a special slide on which the formatting for all slides in your presentation is defined.

5. Pressing the letter H during a presentation displays a _____ slide.

6. PowerPoint includes predefined slide layouts called _____ that are used to control the placement of objects on a slide.

7. _____ adds action to text and graphics so they move around on the screen.

8. A table is made up of _____ and _____ of cells that you can fill with text and graphics.

9. To control how one slide moves off the screen and the next one appears, you can apply _____ effects.

10. _____ are used to display each bullet point, text, paragraph, or graphic independently of the other text or objects on the slide.

discussion questions

1. Discuss how slide masters and design templates can be used to format a presentation.

2. Discuss how slide builds and transitions can be used to enhance a presentation. What should you consider before applying them to a presentation?

3. Discuss how the style checking feature works. Point out the advantages and disadvantages to using this feature.

Hands-On Exercises

step-by-step

Enhancing the Work/Life Presentation

★ 1. To complete this problem, you must have completed Step by Step Exercise 1 in Lab 1. Now Sheila is much more comfortable using PowerPoint and she decides to use her newfound confidence to further enhance the Work/Life Balance presentation. Several slides of the modified presentation are shown here.

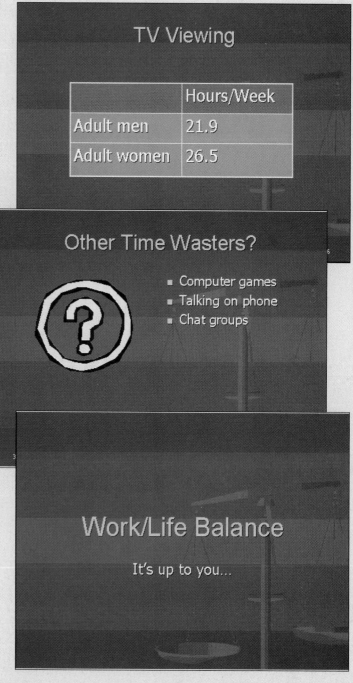

a. Open the file Balance1.

b. Use the Find and Replace command to replace all occurrences of "Work Life" with "Work/Life."

c. Apply a new presentation design and color scheme of your choice to the presentation. Check the presentation to see how the new design has affected all slides, and move and size clip art and bulleted lists as needed.

d. Modify the text color of the titles using the title and slide masters.

e. Change the information in slide 6 to a table. Enhance the table appropriately. Hide the slide. Add a note to the slide citing the source of this data: **Source: Canada General Survey, 1996**.

f. Add a note to slide 5 to remind you to display the hidden slide.

g. Modify the color of the clip art on slide 7 to coordinate with the slide colors.

h. Add the following note to slide 10: **Source: 1999 Ceridian Employer Serivces Work Perk poll**.

i. Duplicate slide 1 and place the duplicate slide at the end of the presentation. Change the subtitle text to **It's up to you...**

j. Add a footer to all slides in the presentation, except the title slides, that displays the slide number, your name, and the date that will update automatically.

k. Add the Dissolve In custom animation and chime sound effect to the clip art on slide 7.

l. Apply transition and animation effects of your choice to the presentation.

m. Check the presentation style and make changes you think are appropriate. Turn the style check feature off when you are done.

n. Run the slide show.

o. Add file documentation and save the presentation as Balance2. Print the slides as handouts (four per page).

Enhancing the ASU Presentation

★ **2.** Bonnie is the Assistant Director of New Admissions at Arizona State University. Part of her job is to make presentations at community colleges and local high schools about the University. She has already created the introductory portion of the presentation and needs to reorganize the topics and make the presentation more visually appealing. Several slides of the modified presentation are shown here.

a. Open the file pp02_ASU Presentation.

b. Run the slide show to see what Bonnie has done so far.

c. Spell-check the presentation, making the appropriate corrections.

d. Move slide 5 before slide 4.

e. Use the Find and Replace command to locate all the occurrences of "Arizona State University" and replace them with "ASU" on all slides except the first and second slides.

f. Enter your name as the subtitle in slide 1. Insert the picture pp02_PalmWalk on the title slide. Size the picture and position the placeholders on the slide appropriately.

g. Demote all the bulleted items on slides 8 and 9 except the first item.

h. Apply a new presentation design of your choice to the presentation. Apply a new slide color scheme. Modify the text color of the titles using the title and slide masters.

i. Duplicate slide 1 and move the duplicate to the end of the presentation. Replace your name with **Apply Now!**

j. Bonnie would like to add some pictures of the buildings at the end of the presentation. Switch to Slide Sorter view and select slides 12, 13, and 14. Apply the Text and Clip Art layout. Insert the picture pp02_Student Services in slide 12, the picture pp02_Library in slide 13, and the picture pp02_Fine Arts in slide 14. (Hint: Use the Insert/Picture command to insert the picture and then drag the inserted picture into the clip art placeholder.)

k. Check the style of the presentation and make any changes you feel are appropriate. Turn the style check feature off when you are done.

l. Add a custom animation and sound to the picture on the title slide.

m. Apply random transitions to all slides in the presentation.

n. Apply the Fly From Right build effect to all the slides with bullet items.

o. Run the slide show.

p. Add file documentation and save the presentation as ASU Presentation1. Print slides 1, 2, and 12–15 as handouts (six per page).

Completing the Emergency Driving Presentation

★★ **3.** To complete this problem, you must have completed Step by Step Exercise 3 in Lab 1. You have completed the first draft of the presentation on tire blowouts, but still have some information to add. Additionally, you want to make the presentation look better using many of the PowerPoint design and slide show presentation features. Several slides of the modified presentation are shown here.

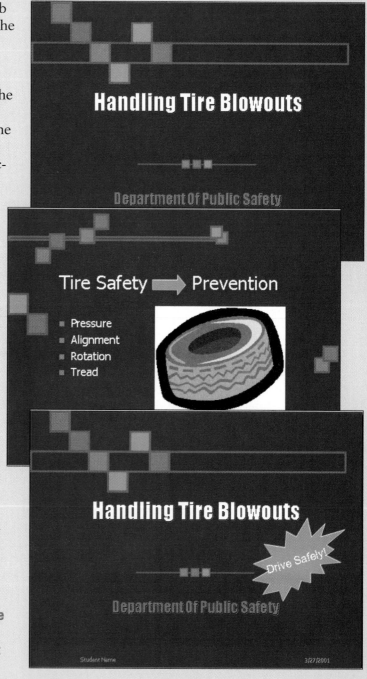

a. Open the presentation Blowouts. If necessary, switch to Normal view.

b. Make the following adjustments to the title master:
- Delete the page number placeholders.
- Change the font of the title and subtitle to Impact or similar font. Add a shadow.

c. On slide 6, replace the = in the title with a right-facing block arrow AutoShape. Add a Fly In from Left custom animation to the AutoShape.

d. Duplicate the title slide and move it to the end of the presentation. Add a drawing object to this slide that includes the text **Drive Safely!**. Format the object and text appropriately.

e. Select an animation scheme of your choice to add transition and build effects to all the slides. Run the slide show.

f. Add the following note to slide 7 in a point size of 18:
Under inflation is the leading cause of tire failure.
Maximum inflation pressure on tire is not recommended pressure.

g. Add the following note to slide 10 in a point size of 18:
Penny test—tread should come to the top of the head of Lincoln.

h. Style-check the presentation and make any necessary changes. Turn off the style-check option when you are done.

i. Add file documentation and save the completed presentation as Blowouts2.

j. Print the notes page for slide 7. Print slides 1, 6, and 11 as handouts with three slides per page.

Enhancing the Coffee Presentation

★ **4.** To complete this problem, you must have completed Step by Step Exercise 4 in Lab 1. Evan, the owner of the Downtown Internet Cafe, was so impressed with your presentation on coffee that he has decided to run it periodically throughout the day on a large screen in the cafe so customers can see it as well. To "spiff it up," he wants you to convert it to an onscreen presentation with more graphics as well as other design and animation effects. Several slides of the modified presentation are shown here.

a. Open the file Coffee.

b. Use the Replace feature to replace both instances of the term "Regular Roasts" with "Coffee Categories." Do the same to replace both instances of the term "Other Offerings" with "Coffee Types."

c. Change the design template to Sumi Painting or a design of your choice. Select a color scheme of your choice. Check the presentation to see how the new design has affected all slides, and move and size clip art and bulleted lists as needed.

d. Change the font of the main title on the title slide to Calisto MT. Use the slide master to change the font color of all first-level bullets to a stronger color.

e. Apply a custom animation and sound of your choice to the coffee cup clip art on slide 2.

f. Change the title of slide 3 to **What's Brewing?**. Delete the clip art.

g. Copy the clip art from slide 2 to slide 3. Add a third bullet to slide 3 with the text: **Coffee Terms**. Delete slide 2.

h. Change the title "Central and South American Coffee" on slide 4 to **Coffees from the Americas**.

i. Insert a new slide with a table format after slide 7. Enter the title, **Coffee Terms**. Create the table with two columns and five rows. Enter **What You Say** as the first column heading and **What It Means** as the second column heading. Copy the terms and definitions from slide 9 into the table. Change the font size of the text as needed. Bold the column headings and put quotation marks around the terms. Center-align the What You Say column. Size the columns and table appropriately. Add a fill color to the table.

j. Delete slide 9.

k. Duplicate the title slide and move the duplicate to the end of the presentation. Delete the clip art. Change the title to **Come have coffee with us . . .** and delete the subtitle text. Change the font size of the subtitle to 32 pt. Move the subtitle to the lower right corner of the slide.

l. Add the following information in a text box on slide 9:

> **Downtown Internet Cafe**
> **122 Main Street * Red Bank**

Add a fill color and border to the text box.

m. Include your name in a footer on all slides. Hide the footer on the title slides.

n. Check the presentation style and make any necessary changes. Turn off the style-check feature when you are done.

o. Set the slide transition to automatically advance after ten seconds. Run the slide show.

p. Add file documentation information and save the completed presentation as Coffee Show.

q. Print slides 1, 2, 8, and 9 as handouts, four per page.

Completing the Workplace Issues Presentation

★★ **5.** To complete this problem, you must have completed Step by Step Exercise 5 in Lab 1. Tim has
★ completed the first draft of the presentation for his class lecture on Workplace Issues, but he still has some information he wants to add to the presentation. Additionally, he wants to make the presentation look better using many of the PowerPoint design and slide show presentation features. Several slides of the modified presentation are shown here.

a. Open the presentation Workplace Issues. If necessary, switch to Normal view.

b. Change the design template to Digital Dots. Change the color scheme to a color of your choice.

c. Change to Slide Sorter view and check the slide layouts. Make the following adjustments:
- Title master:
  - Delete the Date area and Number area placeholders.
  - Change the font of the title to Impact or similar font. Change the font size to 60 pt.
  - Remove the shadow.
  - Change the text color of the sub-title to a color of your choice, bold it, and change it to the same font as the title.
  - Move the title and subtitle placeholders closer to the top of the slide.
- Slide master:
  - Change the bullet style to a picture style of your choice.
  - Reduce the size of the object area placeholder and center it on the slide.

d. Check the slide layouts again in Slide Sorter view and fix the placement and size of the place-holders as needed.

e. Apply the Title, Text, and Content layout to slide 2. Insert the clip art pp02_Arrows into the slide. Modify the AutoShape color to coordinate with the colors in your color scheme. Add a custom animation and sound to the clip art.

f. Change the angle of the clipart in slide 6.

g. Duplicate the title slide and move it to the end of the presentation. Delete the graphic and add a drawing object to this slide that includes the text **End of Class**. Format the object and text ap-propriately.

h. Select an animation scheme of your choice to add transition and build effects to all the slides. Run the slide show.

i. Add the following note to slide 3 in a point size of 18:

Computers used to be the more expensive - focus was to make people adjust to fit computers

Now, people are more expensive - focus is on ergonomics

Objective - design computers and use them to increase productivity and avoid health risks

Physical as well as mental risks

j. Style-check the presentation and make any necessary changes. Turn off the style-check feature when you are done.

k. Add file documentation and save the completed presentation as Workplace Issues2.

l. Print the notes page for slide 3. Print slides 1, 2, 6, and 11 as handouts with four slides per page.

on your own

Successful Interview Techniques

★ **1.** You work at an employment agency and your manager has asked you to create an onscreen presentation about interview techniques. This presentation will be loaded on all the computers that your company makes available to clients for online job searches, and instructions on how to run the presentation will be posted at each workstation. Select a presentation design that you like and create the presentation using the following notes for reference. Add clip art and build effects where applicable. Add your name to a footer on each slide except the title slide. Set the slide transition so that it automatically advances after an appropriate length of time (long enough for the person viewing the presentation to read each slide's contents). Save the presentation as Interview Techcniques. Print all slides of your presentation, 6 per page.

- Before a job interview, you should thoroughly research the company (use the library or the Web). For example, what is one event that occurred in the company within the last five years?
- During the interview, demonstrate your expertise, using a consultant's style of communicating. Create open and clear communication, and effectively respond to open-ended questions. Examples of open-ended questions are: "Tell me about yourself." "What makes you stand out?" "What are your greatest weaknesses?" You should also be ready to answer questions about why you are interviewing with the company and how and where you fit within their organization. You must be prepared to handle both spoken and unspoken objections. And finally, you must justify your salary requirements; don't just negotiate them.

Expanding Bicycle Safety Presentation

★★ **2.** To finish creating the basic Better Bikes Company presentation on cycling tips that you began in Lab 1, On Your Own Exercise 1, turn it into an onscreen presentation with a custom design, clip art, sound, transitions, and builds so it will hold your audience's interest. Add speaker notes and rehearse the presentation before giving it to the school PTA. When you are done, save the presentation as Better Bike Safety2 and print the presentation as handouts and print the notes pages for slides containing notes only.

Promoting a Trip

★★ **3.** Your travel club is planning a trip next summer. You want to visit Rome and Venice and want to prepare a presentation on cost and key tourist attractions to help convince your club to add those cities to the itinerary. Research these two cities on the Web to determine flight costs, train costs between cities, hotel costs, and key tourist attractions. Select an appropriate slide design. Include your name in the footer. When you are done, save the presentation as Travel Italy and print the handouts.

Enhancing the Web Design Presentation

★★ **4.** After completing the Web Design presentation in Lab 1, On Your Own Exercise 5, you decide it
★ needs a bit more sprucing up. First of all, it would be more impressive as an onscreen presentation with a custom design. Also, the pros and cons information would look better as a table, and a few animated clip art pictures, non-standard bullets, builds, and transitions wouldn't hurt. Make these and any other changes that you think would enhance the presentation. When you are done, save as Web Design2 and print the presentation as handouts and print the notes pages for slides containing notes only.

Sharing Favorite Vacation Spots

★ **5.** You and your fellow Getaway Travel Club members have decided that each of you should do a
★ presentation on your favorite vacation spot (one you have already been to or one you would like to
go to). Pick a location and do some research on the Web and/or visit a local travel agency to get
information about your chosen destination. Create a presentation using a custom design and
include clip art, animation, sounds, transitions, and build effects to make the presentation more
interesting. Include your name as a footer or subtitle on at least one slide. Use speaker notes if
necessary to remind yourself of additional information you want to relay that is not included in
the slides. Run the slide show and practice your presentation, then save as Travel Favorites and print
your presentation and notes pages.

Working Together: Word and Your Web Browser

Adventure Travel Tours

Adventure Travel Tours has a World Wide Web (WWW) site. Through it they hope to be able to promote their products and broaden their audience of customers. In addition to the obvious marketing and sales potential, they want to provide an avenue for interaction between themselves and the customer to improve their customer service. They also want the Web site to provide articles of interest to customers. The articles, with topics such as travel background information and descriptions, would change on a monthly basis as an added incentive for readers to return to the site.

You think the flyer you developed to promote the new tours and presentations could be used on the Web site. Word 2002 includes Web-editing features that help you create a Web page quickly and easily. While using the Web-editing features, you will be working with Word and with a Web browser application. This capability of all Office XP applications to work together and with other applications makes it easy to share and exchange information between applications. Your completed Web pages are shown here.

Note: The intent of the Working Together tutorial is to show how two applications work together and to present a basic introduction to creating Web pages. More information about Web page creation is available in Lab 6 of the Introductory text.

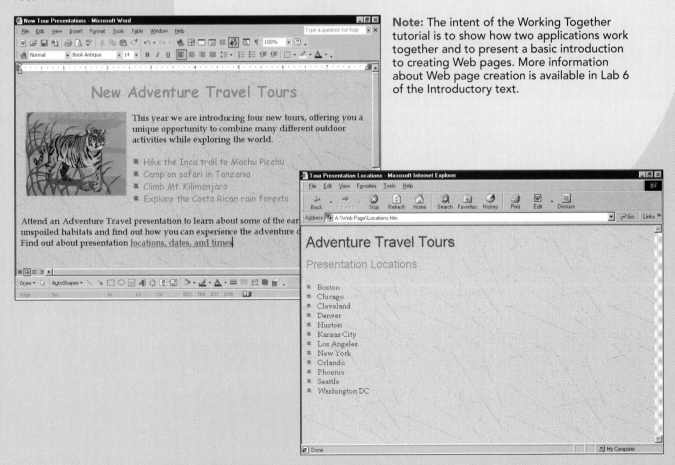

Saving a Word Document as a Web Page

You want to create a Web page on the company's Web site. A **Web page** is a document that can be used on the WWW. The Web page you create will provide information about the tour presentations. Word offers three ways to create or **author** Web pages. One way is to start with a blank Web page and enter text and graphics much as you would a normal document. Another is to use the Web Page Wizard, which provides step-by-step instructions to help you quickly create a Web page. Finally, you can quickly convert an existing Word document to a Web page.

Because the tour flyer has already been created as a Word document and contains much of the information you want to use on the Web page, you will convert it to a Web page document.

1 ● **Start Word.**

● **Open the file** wdwt_Tour Flyer **from the appropriate location.**

● **If necessary, close the New Document task pane.**

Your screen should be similar to Figure 1

Figure 1

Word converts a document to a Web page by adding HTML coding to the document. HTML **(HyperText Markup Language)** is a programming language used to create Web pages. HTML commands control the display of information on a page, such as font colors and size, and how an item will be processed. HTML also allows users to click on hyperlinks and jump to other locations on the same page, other pages in the same site, or other sites and locations on the WWW. HTML commands are interpreted by the browser software you are using. A **browser** is a program that connects you to remote computers and displays the Web pages you request.

When a file is converted to a Web page, the HTML coding is added and it is saved to a new file with an .html file extension.

● **Choose File/Save as Web Page.**

Your screen should be similar to Figure 2

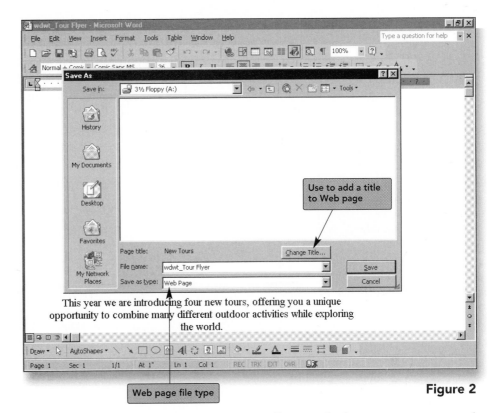

Figure 2

Web page file type

The file type of Web Page is automatically specified. You want to save the Web page using the file name New Tour Presentations in a new folder. You also need to provide a title for the page. This is the text that will appear in the title bar of the Web browser when the page is displayed. You want the title to be the same as the file name.

● **If necessary, change the location to save to the appropriate save location.**

● **Create a new folder named Web Page.**

● **Change the file name to New Tour Presentations.**

● **Click** Change Title... .

● **Change the title to New Tour Presentations.**

● **Click** OK .

● **Click** Save .

Your screen should be similar to Figure 3.

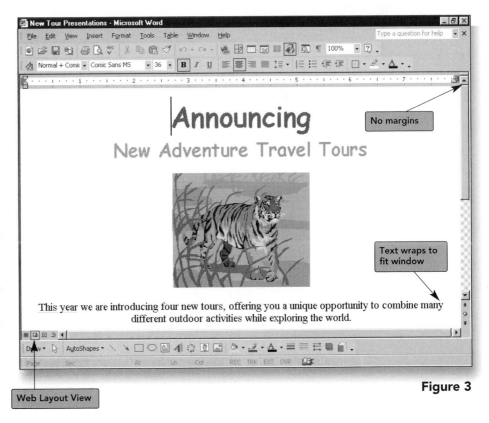

Figure 3

Web Layout View

The flyer has been converted to an HTML document and is displayed in Web Layout view. Although the menu bar contains the same menus, Word customizes some menus, commands, and options to provide the Web page authoring features. This view displays the document as it will appear if viewed using a Web browser. This document looks very much like a normal Word document. In fact, the only visible difference is the margin settings. A Web page does not include margins. Instead, the text wraps to fit into the window space. However, the formatting and features that are supported by HTML, in this case the paragraph and character formatting such as the font style, type size, and color attributes, have been converted to HTML format.

Web Layout view does not display the HTML codes that control the formatting of the Web page. To view these codes, you will switch to HTML Source view.

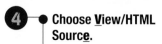

Some formatting features, such as emboss and shadow effects, are not supported by HTML or other Web browsers and are not available when authoring Web pages.

4 ● Choose **View/HTML Source.**

● **If necessary, maximize the window.**

Your screen should be similar to Figure 4

HAVING TROUBLE?
If the HTML Script Editor is not installed on your system, you will not be able to use this feature.

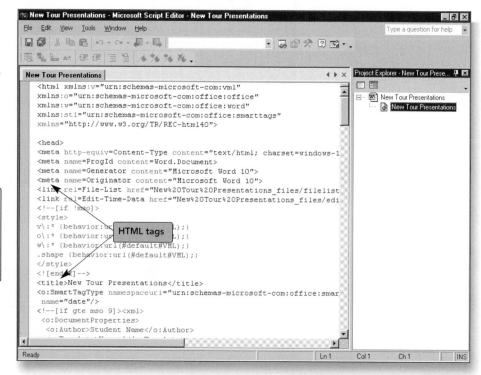

Figure 4

Every item on a Web page has properties associated with it that are encoded in HTML tags. **Tags** are embedded codes that supply information about the page's structure, appearance, and contents. They tell your browser where the title, headings, paragraphs, images, and other information are to appear on the page. Converting this document to HTML format using Word was a lot easier than learning to enter the codes yourself.

5 ● Click ☒ in the title bar to close the Microsoft Script Editor window.

The Web page is displayed in Web Layout view again.

Making Text Changes

Next you want to change the layout of the Web page so that more information is displayed in the window when the page is viewed in the browser. You will delete any unnecessary text first and change the paragraph alignment to left-aligned.

1 ● Select the entire "Announcing" heading line.

● Press ⎣Delete⎦.

● Delete the last two paragraphs in the flyer and the AutoShape.

● Select all the text below the picture.

● Click ▤ Left.

● Add bullets preceding the list of four tours.

● Scroll to the top of the document.

Your screen should be similar to Figure 5

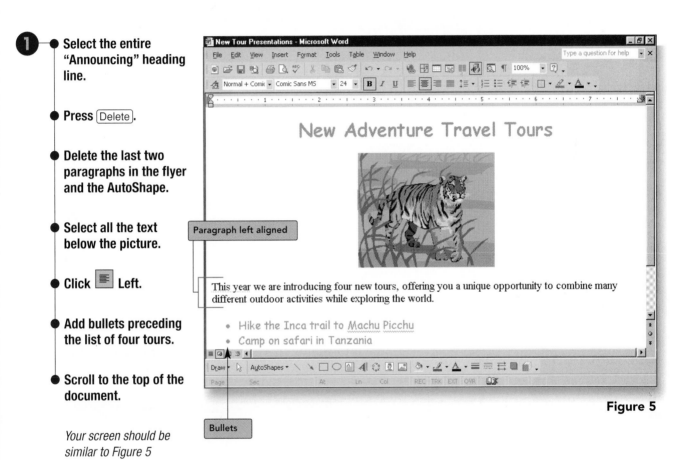

Paragraph left aligned

Bullets

Figure 5

Changing the Picture Layout

You still cannot view all the information in a single window. To make more space, you will move the picture to the left edge of the window and wrap the text to the right around it. Unlike a normal Word document, pictures and other graphic elements are not embedded into the Web page document. Instead they are inserted as inline objects. In an HTML file, an inline image is stored as a separate file that is accessed and loaded by the browser when the page is loaded. However, it can still be moved, sized, and formatted just like embedded picture objects.

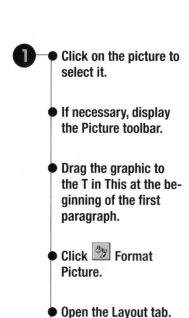

1 ● Click on the picture to select it.

● If necessary, display the Picture toolbar.

● Drag the graphic to the T in This at the beginning of the first paragraph.

● Click 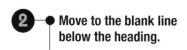 Format Picture.

● Open the Layout tab.

● Select ⊞ Square.

● Change the horizontal alignment to Left.

● Click OK.

Your screen should be similar to Figure 6

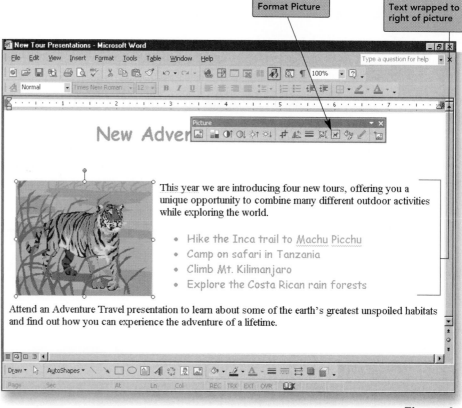

Figure 6

Now almost all the information is visible. You will remove two of the blank lines from below the heading and reduce the size of the picture slightly.

2 ● Move to the blank line below the heading.

● Press Delete twice.

● Reduce the picture size slightly as in Figure 7.

Your screen should be similar to Figure 7

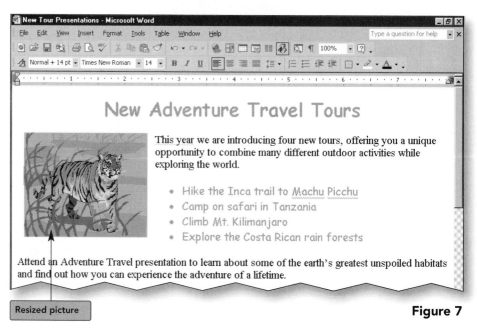

Figure 7

Applying a Theme

Because color and design are important elements of Web pages, you can add a background color and other special effects to a Web page. Many of these special effects are designed specifically for Web pages and cannot be used in printed pages. Like styles, Word includes many predesigned Web page effects, called **themes**, which you can quickly apply to a Web page.

Choose Format/Theme.

Your screen should be similar to Figure 8

Figure 8

The Choose a Theme list displays the names of all the themes that are provided with Word. The preview area displays a sample of the selected theme showing the background design, bullet and horizontal line style, and character formats that will be applied to headings, normal text, and hyperlinks.

- **Select several themes to preview them.**

- **Select the Expedition theme.**

- **Click** OK .

- **Click** 🖫 **to save the changes you have made to the Web page.**

Your screen should be similar to Figure 9

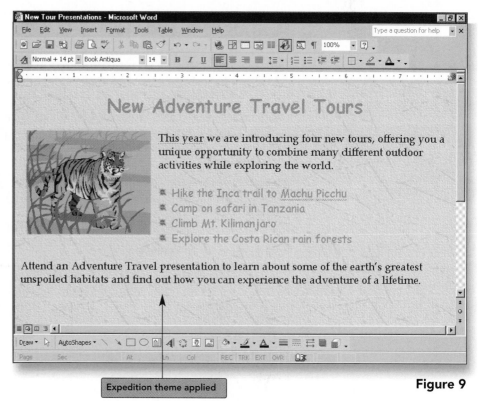

Expedition theme applied

Figure 9

The formatting settings associated with the selected theme are applied to the Web page.

Creating a Hyperlink

Next you want to create another Web page that will contain a list of presentation locations. You will then add a hyperlink to this information from the New Tour Presentations page. As you have learned, a hyperlink provides a quick way to jump to other documents, objects, or Web pages. Hyperlinks are the real power of the WWW. You can jump to sites on your own system and network as well as to sites on the Internet and WWW.

The list of tour locations has already been entered as a Word document and saved as a file named Locations.

1 ● **Open the file**
wdwt_Locations.

● **Save the document as a Web page to your Web Page folder with the file name** Locations **and a page title of Tour Presentation Locations.**

● **Apply the Expedition theme to this page.**

● **Save the page again.**

Your screen should be similar to Figure 10

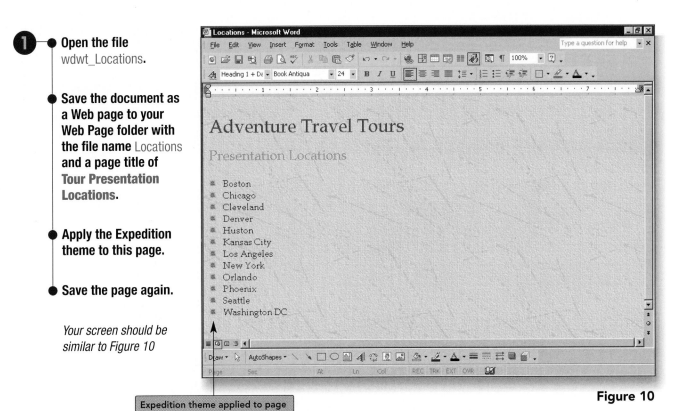

Expedition theme applied to page

Figure 10

Now you are ready to create the hyperlink from the New Tour Presentations page to the Locations page.

2 ● **Switch to the New Tour Presentations window.**

● **Add the following text, left aligned one line below the last paragraph: Find out about presentation locations, dates, and times.**

● **Select the text "locations, dates, and times."**

● **Click** 🔗 **Insert Hyperlink (on the Standard toolbar).**

Another Method
The menu equivalent is Insert/Hyperlink and the keyboard shortcut is Ctrl + K.

Your screen should be similar to Figure 11

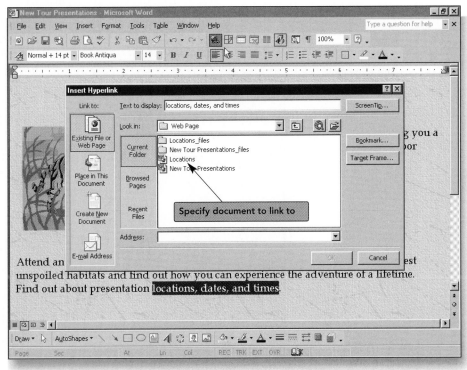

Specify document to link to

Figure 3.11

From the Insert Hyperlink dialog box, you need to specify the name of the document you want to the link connect to.

3

- If necessary, click .

- Click [Current Folder].

- Select Locations.htm from the file list.

- Click [OK].

Your screen should be similar to Figure 12

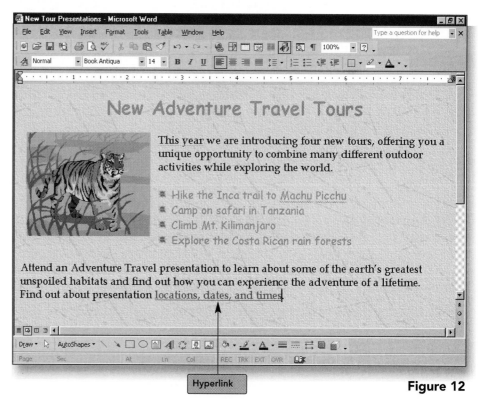

Hyperlink

Figure 12

The selected text appears as a hyperlink in the design colors specified by the theme.

4

- Hold down Ctrl and click the hyperlink.

Your screen should be similar to Figure 13

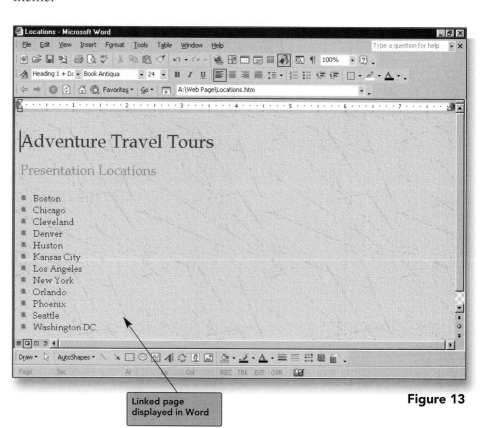

Linked page displayed in Word

Figure 13

Because the Locations document is already open in a window, clicking the hyperlink simply switches to the open window and displays the page. You plan to add hyperlinks from each location to information about dates and times for each location.

Previewing the Page

To see how your Web page will actually look when displayed by our browser, you can preview it in your default browser.

1 ● Click ⇐ **Back to view the previous page.**

● Choose **File/Web Page Preview.**

● If necessary, maximize the browser window.

● If Internet Explorer is your default browser and the Favorites bar is open, click ✕ in the Favorites bar to close it.

Your screen should be similar to Figure 14

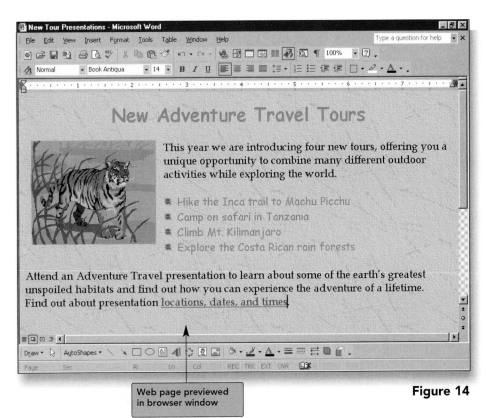

Web page previewed in browser window

Figure 14

The browser on your system is loaded offline, and the Web page you are working on is displayed in the browser window. Sometimes the browser may display a page slightly differently than it appears in Web Page view. In this case, the bullets overlap the edge of the picture. If you do not like the change, you can return to Word and adjust the layout until it displays appropriately in the browser. In this case, however, you will leave it as it is.

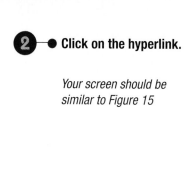

Click on the hyperlink.

*Your screen should be
similar to Figure 15*

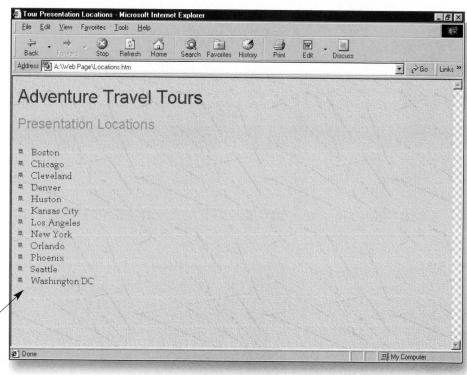

Figure 15

The associated page is displayed in the browser. This page also looks fine
and does not need any additional formatting.

Click ⊠ **in the title bar to exit the browser program.**

Exit Word, saving the changes you made to both documents.

Making a Web Page Public

Now that you have created Web pages, in order for others to see them you
need to make them available on the Internet. The steps that you take to
make your pages public depend on how you want to share them. There are
two main avenues: on your local network or intranet for limited access by
people within an organization, or on the Internet for access by anyone
using the WWW. To make pages available to other people on your network,
save your Web pages and related files, such as pictures, to a network location. To make your Web pages available on the WWW, you need to either install Web server software on your computer or locate an Internet service
provider that allocates space for Web pages.

lab review

Working Together: Word and Your Web Browser

key terms

author   WDWT1.2
browser   WDWT1.2

HTML (Hypertext Markup Language)   WDWT1.2
tag   WDWT1.4

theme   WDWT1.7
Web page   WDWT1.2

mous skills

The Microsoft Office User Specialist (MOUS) certification program is designed to measure your proficiency in performing basic tasks using the Office XP applications. Getting certified demonstrates that you have the skills and provides a valuable industry credential for employment. After completing this lab, you have learned the following Microsoft Office User Specialist skills:

Skill	Description	Page
Workgroup	Preview documents as Web pages	WDWT1.11
Collaboration	Save documents as Web pages	WDWT1.2

command summary

Command	Shortcut Keys	Button	Action
File/Save as Web Page			Saves file as a Web page document
File/Web Page Preview			Previews Web page in browser window
View/HTML Source			Displays HTML source code
Insert/Hyperlink	Ctrl + K	🔗	Inserts hyperlink
Format/Theme			Applies a predesigned theme to Web page

Hands-On Exercises

step-by-step

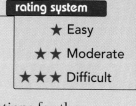
Adding a New Web Page

★ **1.** You want to continue working on the Web pages about the new tour presentations for the Adventure Travel Web site. Your next step is to create links from each location to information about each location's presentation date and times. Your completed Web page for the Los Angeles area is shown here.

   a. In Word, open the Web page file Locations you created in this lab.

   b. Open the document wdwt_LosAngeles. Save the document as a Web page to your Web Page folder with the file name LosAngeles and a page title of **Los Angeles Presentation Information**.

   c. Apply the same design theme to the new page. Change the title to a Heading 1 style. Add color to the table headings. Enhance the Web page with any features you feel are appropriate.

   d. Two lines below the table add the text **Contact [your name] at (909) 555-1212 for more information**.

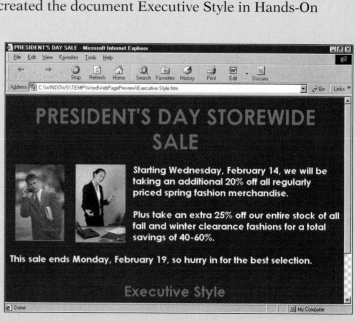

   e. On the Locations page, create a link from the Los Angeles location to the Los Angeles page. Test the link.

   f. Resave both Web pages and preview them in your browser. Print the Los Angeles Web page.

   g. Exit the browser and Word.

Converting a Flyer to a Web Page

★★ **2.** To complete this problem, you must have created the document Executive Style in Hands-On Exercise 3 of Lab 1.

You have decided to modify the Executive Style flyer you created and convert the flyer into a Web page to add to your store's Web site. Your completed Web page is shown here.

   a. Open the file Executive Style you created in Hands-On Exercise 3 in Lab 1.

   b. Convert the flyer to a Web page and save it using the same file name in a new folder. Include an appropriate page title.

   c. Delete the first title line and blank line below it.

   d. Apply the Cascade theme to the page. (If this theme is not available, select another theme of your choice.)

e. Break the paragraph into three paragraphs at each sentence, leaving a blank line between each. Change the three paragraphs to left-aligned.

f. Reduce the size of the pictures. Change the picture text wrapping style to square. Move the pictures to the left of the first two paragraphs. Size the pictures to fit next to the first two paragraphs.

g. Change the color of the title line to red.

h. Preview the page in your browser. Close your browser. Resave the Web page.

i. Use Print Preview to see how the page will appear when printed. The background and white text does not display. Change the text color to lime green and preview the page again. Print the Web page.

j. Exit Word without saving your changes to the page.

Advertising on the Web

★ 3. To complete this problem, you must have completed Hands-On Exercise 4 in Lab 1. You would like to advertise your bed and breakfast inn on the Web. You plan to use the information in the advertisement flyer you created as the basis for the Web pages. Your completed Web pages are shown here.

a. Open the file B&B Ad. Convert the document to a Web page and save it as B&B in a new folder. Include an appropriate page title.

b. Cut the information from "Number of Rooms" to "Children" and paste it to a new Web page. Add the text **Information and Rates** above the list on the new page. Format it with a Heading 1 style. Center it above the list.

c. Save the new page to the folder with the file name Information. Title the page **Information and Rates**.

d. Apply the design theme Waves or a theme of your choice to both pages. Change the B&B name on the first page to a Heading 1 style. Add the text **Information and Rates** below the Host name to the first page and create a link from this text to the Information page. Test the link.

e. Change the layout of the first page to that shown here. Copy the graphic from the first page to the second and change the layout to that shown here.

f. Resave the Web pages and preview them in your browser.

g. Print the pages.

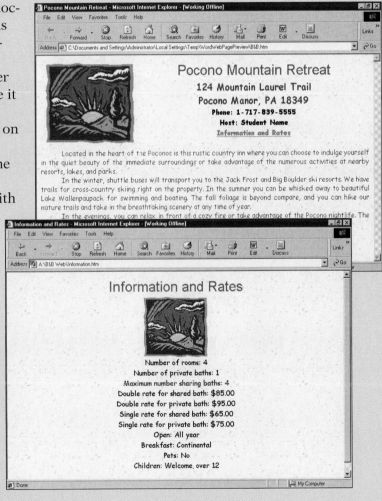

lab exercises

on your own

★ **1.** **Learning about Web Design**

Use Word Help to learn more about Web pages and making Web pages public.

   a. Search in Help for information on Web page design, Web layout, Web sites, and publishing Web pages.

   b. Print the Help pages that might be appropriate for writing a report on using Word to create a Web site.

   c. Write a one-page report in Word summarizing the information you found.

   d. Include your name and the date in a header.

   e. Save the report as Web Design. Print the report.

Working Together: Linking, Embedding, and E-mailing

Evan, the Café owner, is particularly concerned about the first quarter forecast. Your analysis of the sales data for the first quarter shows a steady increase in total sales. However, as you suggested, if a strong sales promotion is mounted, Internet sales will increase sharply. Evan has asked you to send him a memo containing the worksheet data showing the expected sales without a strong sales promotion and the chart showing the projected Internet sales with a sales promotion.

Additionally, Evan wants a copy of the second quarter forecast showing the 5 percent profit margins for each month. He also wants a copy of the workbook file so that he can play with the sales values to see how they would affect the profit margin.

You will learn how to share information between applications while you create these memos. Additionally, you will learn how to send the workbook via e-mail. Your completed document will look like that shown below.

Note: This lab assumes that you already know how to use Word and that you have completed Labs 2 and 3 of Excel. You will need the file Café Sales Charts you created in Lab 2 and Annual Forecast Revised from Lab 3.

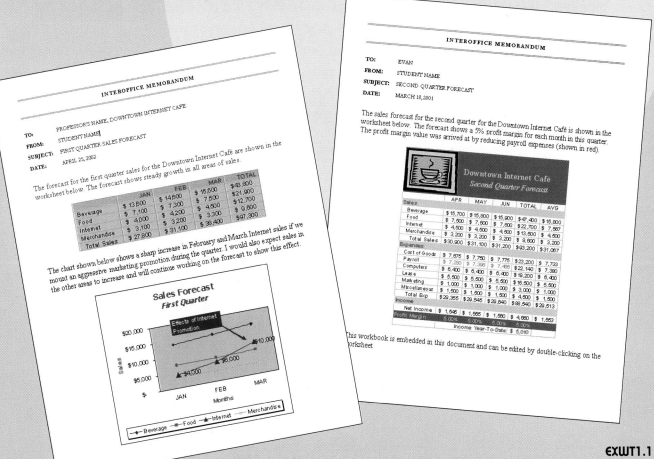

Copying between Applications

The memo to the manager about the analysis of the sales data has already been created using Word. However, you still need to add the Excel worksheet data and charts to the memo. All Microsoft Office applications have a common user interface such as similar commands and menu structures. In addition to these obvious features, they have been designed to work together, making it easy to share and exchange information between applications.

You will begin by copying the worksheet from Excel into a Word document. You can also use the same commands and procedure to copy information from Word or other Office XP applications into Excel.

Copying a Worksheet to a Word Document

1 • **Start Word and open the document** exwt1_Sales Forecast Memo.

• **In the memo header, replace Professor's Name with your instructor's name and Student Name with your name.**

Your screen should be similar to Figure 1

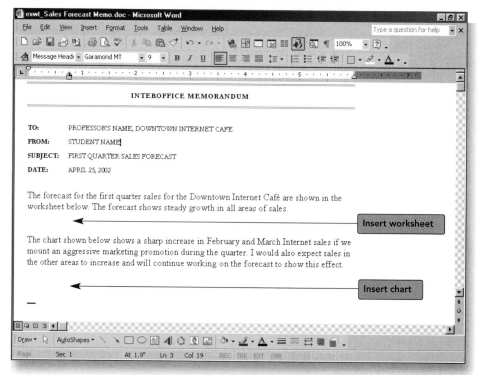

Figure 1

You will insert the worksheet data of the first quarter sales forecast below the first paragraph. Below the second paragraph, you will display the combination chart of sales by category. To insert the information from the Excel workbook file into the Word memo, you need to open the workbook.

2

Start Excel and open the workbook Cafe Sales Charts.

If necessary, move to cell A9 of Sheet1.

Your screen should be similar to Figure 2

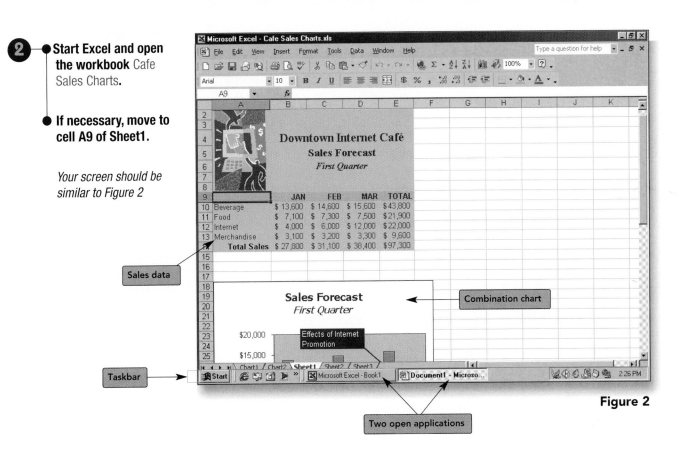

Sales data

Combination chart

Taskbar

Two open applications

Figure 2

There are now two open applications, Word and Excel. Word is open in a window behind the Excel application window. Both application buttons are displayed in the taskbar. There are also two open files, Cafe Sales Charts in Excel and exwt1_Sales Forecast Memo in Word. Excel is the active application and Cafe Sales Charts is the active file.

First you will copy the worksheet data into the Word memo. While using the Excel application, you have learned how to use cut, copy, and paste to move or copy information within the same document. You can also perform these operations between documents in the same application and between documents in different applications. For example, you can copy information from a Word document and paste it into an Excel worksheet. The information is pasted in a format that the application can edit, if possible.

You want to copy the worksheet data in cells A9 through E14 into the memo.

3 ● Select cells A9 through E14.

● Click 🖿 Copy.

● Click [exwt1_Sales Forecast Me...] in the taskbar.

● Move to the second blank line below the first paragraph of the memo.

● Click 🖿 Paste to copy the contents of the Clipboard into the memo.

Your screen should be similar to Figure 3

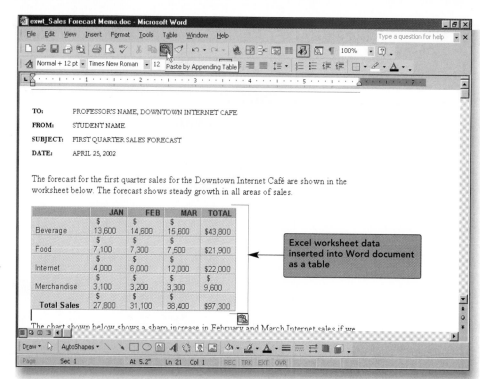

TO: PROFESSOR'S NAME, DOWNTOWN INTERNET CAFE
FROM: STUDENT NAME
SUBJECT: FIRST QUARTER SALES FORECAST
DATE: APRIL 25, 2002

The forecast for the first quarter sales for the Downtown Internet Café are shown in the worksheet below. The forecast shows steady growth in all areas of sales.

	JAN	FEB	MAR	TOTAL
Beverage	$ 13,600	$ 14,600	$ 15,600	$43,800
Food	$ 7,100	$ 7,300	$ 7,500	$21,900
Internet	$ 4,000	$ 6,000	$ 12,000	$22,000
Merchandise	$ 3,100	$ 3,200	$ 3,300	$ 9,600
Total Sales	27,800	31,100	38,400	$97,300

← Excel worksheet data inserted into Word document as a table

The chart shown below shows a sharp increase in February and March Internet sales if we

Figure 3

The worksheet data has been copied into the Word document as a table that can be edited and manipulated within Word. Much of the formatting associated with the copied information is also pasted into the document. You need to adjust the column widths of the table to display the data correctly. Then you will center the table between the margins.

4 ● Choose **Table/Select/Table**.

● **Double-click on the column border of any column to fit the columns to the size of the data.**

● Click 🖿 **Center.**

● **Deselect the table.**

Your screen should be similar to Figure 4

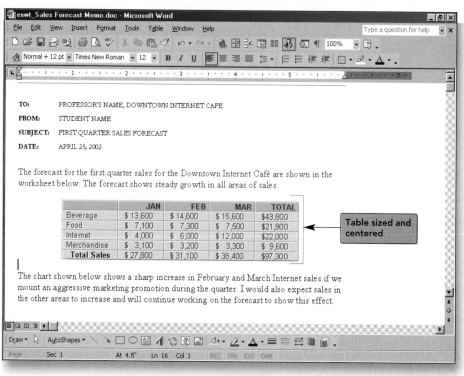

TO: PROFESSOR'S NAME, DOWNTOWN INTERNET CAFE
FROM: STUDENT NAME
SUBJECT: FIRST QUARTER SALES FORECAST
DATE: APRIL 25, 2002

The forecast for the first quarter sales for the Downtown Internet Café are shown in the worksheet below. The forecast shows steady growth in all areas of sales.

	JAN	FEB	MAR	TOTAL
Beverage	$ 13,600	$ 14,600	$ 15,600	$43,800
Food	$ 7,100	$ 7,300	$ 7,500	$21,900
Internet	$ 4,000	$ 6,000	$ 12,000	$22,000
Merchandise	$ 3,100	$ 3,200	$ 3,300	$ 9,600
Total Sales	$ 27,800	$ 31,100	$ 38,400	$97,300

← Table sized and centered

The chart shown below shows a sharp increase in February and March Internet sales if we mount an aggressive marketing promotion during the quarter. I would also expect sales in the other areas to increase and will continue working on the forecast to show this effect.

Figure 4

Next you want to return the Internet sales data in the table to the original forecasted values assuming an aggressive marketing campaign is not mounted.

5 ● **Change the value in C4 to 4,200, in D4 to 4,500 and E4 to 12,700.**

Your screen should be similar to Figure 5

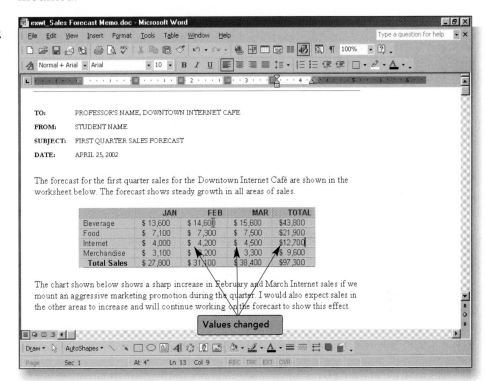

Figure 5

6 ● **Switch to Excel.**

Your screen should be similar to Figure 6

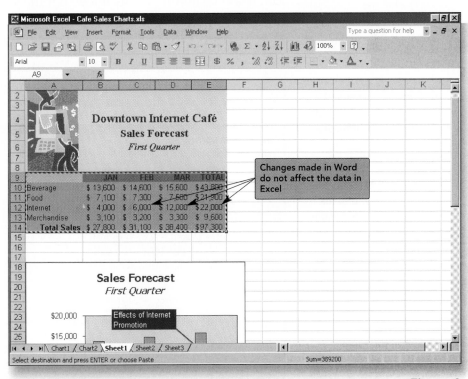

Figure 6

The change in data made in the Word table does not affect the data in the worksheet. This is because the Word table is simply a copy of the Excel worksheet.

Linking between Applications

Next you want to display the combination chart showing the sales trends for Internet sales if an aggressive marketing campaign is mounted below the second paragraph in the memo. You will insert the chart object into the memo as a **linked object**. Information created in one application can also be inserted as a linked object into a document created by another application. When an object is linked, the data is stored in the **source file** (the document it was created in). A graphic representation or picture of the data is displayed in the **destination file** (the document in which the object is inserted). A connection between the information in the destination file to the source file is established by the creation of a link. The link contains references to the location of the source file and the selection within the document that is linked to the destination file.

When changes are made in the source file that affect the linked object, the changes are automatically reflected in the destination file when it is opened. This is called a **live link**. When you create linked objects, the date and time on your machine should be accurate. This is because the program refers to the date of the source file to determine whether updates are needed when you open the destination file.

Linking a Chart Object to a Word Document

You will insert the chart as a linked object. By making the chart a linked object, it will be automatically updated if the source file is edited.

1

- Select the combination chart.

- Click 🖹 Copy to copy the selected chart object to the Clipboard.

- Switch to the Word application and move to the second blank line below the second paragraph of the memo.

- Choose <u>E</u>dit/Paste <u>S</u>pecial.

- Select Paste <u>l</u>ink.

Your screen should be similar to Figure 7

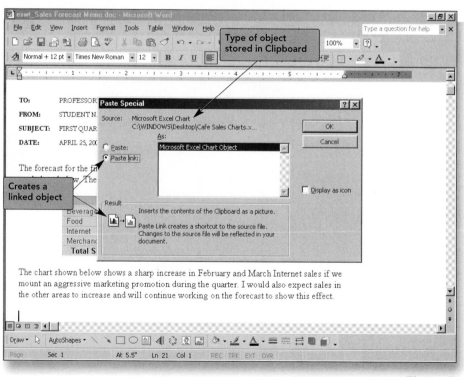

Figure 7

The Paste Special dialog box displays the type of object contained in the Clipboard and its location in the Source area. From the As list box you select the type of format in which you want the object inserted into the destination file. The only available option for this object is as a Microsoft Excel Chart Object. The Result area describes the effect of your selections. In this case, the object will be inserted as a picture and a link will be created to the chart in the source file. Selecting the Display as Icon option changes the display of the object from a picture to an icon. Double-clicking the icon displays the object picture. The default selections are appropriate.

2 ● **Click** [OK].

● **Set the Zoom to 75%.**

● **Position the window so you can see both the worksheet and the chart on the page.**

● **Center the chart object on the page.**

Your screen should be similar to Figure 8

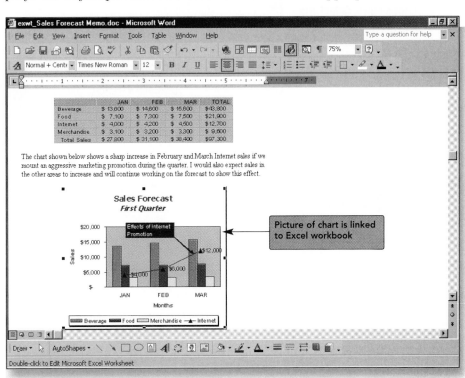

Figure 8

Updating a Linked Object

While reading the memo and looking at the chart, you decide to change the chart type from a combination chart to a line chart. You feel a line chart will show the sales trends for all sales items more clearly. You also decide to lower your sales expectation for Internet sales from 12,000 to 10,000 for March.

To make these changes, you need to switch back to Excel.

1 • **Double-click the chart object.**

Another Method
The menu equivalent is Edit/Linked Worksheet Object/Edit Link.

• **If necessary, select the chart.**

• **Click** 📊 **Chart Type.**

• **Click** 📈 **Line chart.**

• **Change the value in cell D12 to 10000.**

• **Scroll the window to see both the chart and worksheet data.**

Your screen should be similar to Figure 9

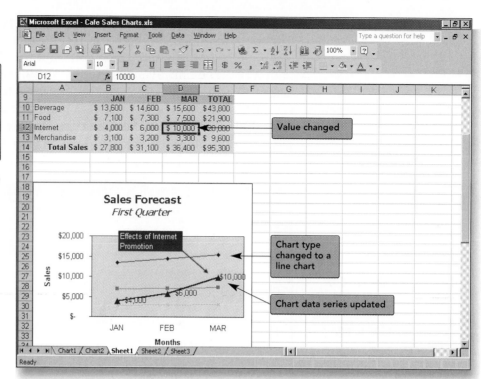

Figure 9

The chart type has changed to a line chart and the chart data series has been updated to reflect the change in data. Now you will look at the memo to see what changes were made to the worksheet and chart.

2 • **Switch to the Word document.**

Your screen should be similar to Figure 10

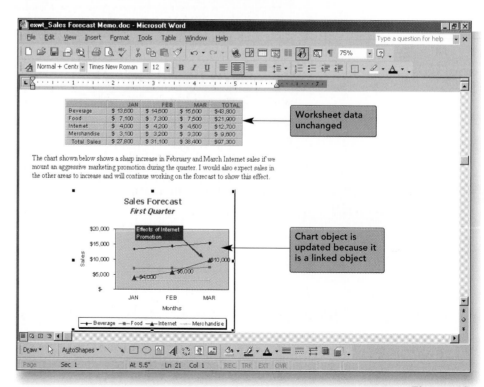

Figure 10

The chart in the memo reflects the change in both chart type and the change in data for the Internet sales. This is because any changes you make in the chart in Excel will be automatically reflected in the linked chart in the Word document. However, because the worksheet data is a word table and not a linked object, it does not reflect the change in data made in Excel.

Editing Links

Whenever a document is opened that contains links, the application looks for the source file and automatically updates the linked objects. If there are many links, updating can take a lot of time. Additionally, if you move the source file to another location or perform other operations that may interfere with the link, your link will not work. To help with situations like these, you can edit the settings associated with links. To see how you do this,

1 ● If necessary, select the chart object.

● Choose **E**dit/Lin**k**s.

Your screen should be similar to Figure 11

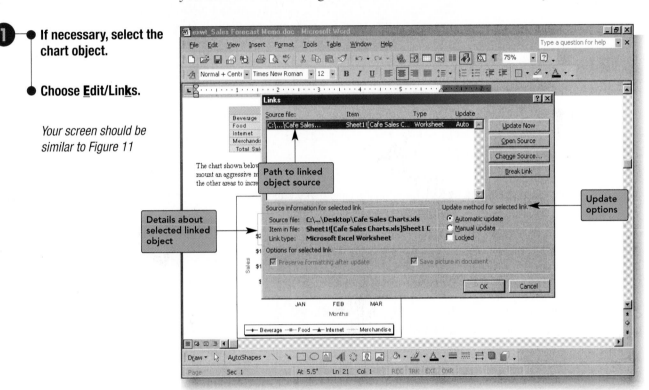

Figure 11

The Links dialog box displays the object path for all links in the document in the list box. The field code specifies the path and name of the source file, the range of linked cells or object name, the type of file, and the update status. Below the list box, the details for the selected link are displayed. The other options in this dialog box are described in the table below.

Option	Effect
Automatic	Updates the linked object whenever the destination document is opened or the source file changes. This is the default.
Manual	The destination document is not automatically updated and you must use the Update Now command button to update the link.
Locked	Prevents a linked object from being updated.
Open Source	Opens the source document for the selected link.
Change Source	Used to modify the path to the source document.
Break Link	Breaks the connection between the source document and the active document.

2 ● Click  .

● **Deselect the chart and save the Word document as** Sales Forecast Memo Linked.

● **Preview, print, then close the document.**

● **Save the Excel workbook as** Cafe Sales Charts Linked **and close the file.**

Embedding an Object in Another Application

The last thing you need to send Evan is a memo that describes and shows the second quarter forecast. To do this, you'll open the memo already created for you in Word and **embed** the sections from the Annual Forecast Revised workbook that Evan wants in the appropriate locations. An object that is embedded is stored in the destination file and becomes part of that document. The entire file, not just the selection that is displayed in the destination file, becomes part of the document. This means that you can modify it without affecting the source document where the original object resides.

Embedding a Worksheet in a Word Document

1 ● **Open the Word document** exwt1_Forecast Memo.

● **In the memo header, replace the Student Name with your name.**

● **Move to the second blank line below the first paragraph of the memo.**

Your screen should be similar to Figure 12

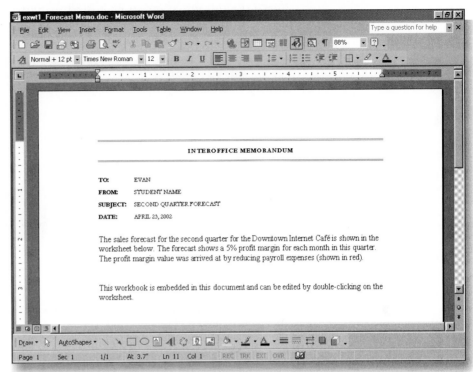

Figure 12

You will embed the first quarter 2002 forecast worksheet in the Word document.

2 ● **Switch to Excel and open the workbook file** Annual Forecast Revised.

● **Make the Second Quarter sheet active.**

● **Copy the range A1 through F24.**

● **Switch to Word.**

● **Choose Edit/Paste Special.**

Additional Information
To embed an entire file, use Insert/Object.

The dialog box on your screen should be similar to Figure 13

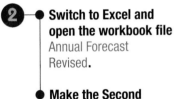

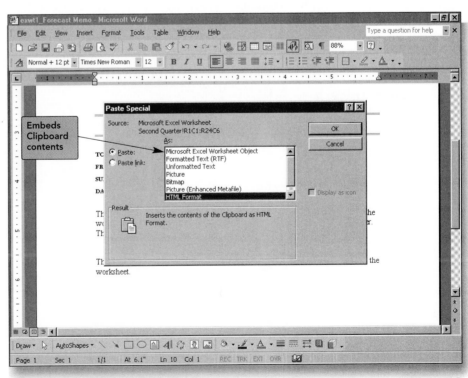

Figure 13

The Paste option inserts or embeds the Clipboard contents in the format you specify from the As list box. To embed the contents of the Clipboard into a document so it can be edited using the server application, select the option that displays the server name, in this case Excel.

3 ● **Select Microsoft Excel Worksheet Object.**

● **Click** OK .

Your screen should be similar to Figure 14

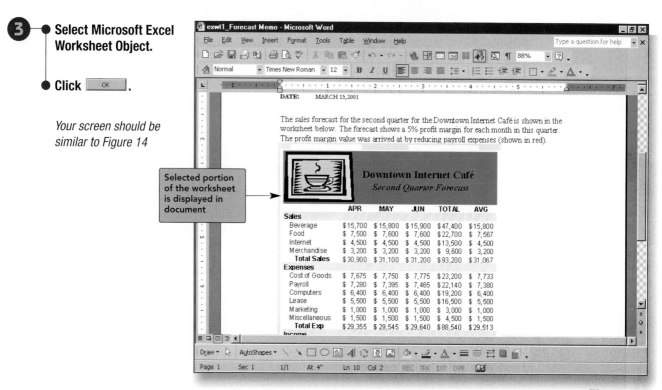

Selected portion of the worksheet is displayed in document

Figure 14

The selected portion of the worksheet is displayed in the memo at the location of the insertion point. As you can see, the object is a bit large.

4 ● **Decrease the size of the worksheet object slightly and center it between the margins.**

Your screen should be similar to Figure 15

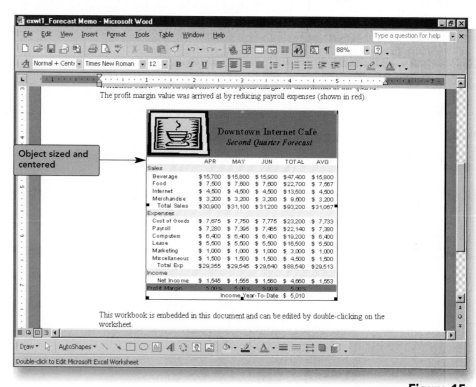

Object sized and centered

Figure 15

Updating an Embedded Object

You want to add color to the payroll range of cells you adjusted to arrive at the 5% profit margin. Because the worksheet is embedded, you can do this from within the Word document. To demonstrate how an embedded object works, you will close the Excel source file and application and edit the worksheet from within the Word document.

1 ● **Switch to Excel.**

   ● **Close the workbook without saving changes and exit Excel.**

The server application is used to edit data in an embedded object. To open the server application and edit the worksheet, you double-click the embedded object.

2 ● **Double-click the worksheet object.**

Your screen should be similar to Figure 16

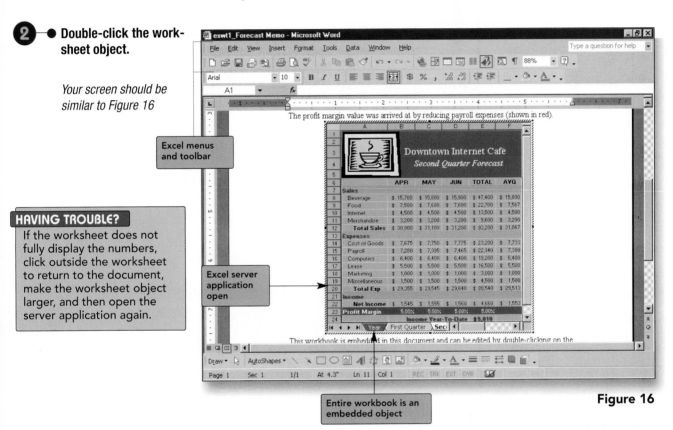

HAVING TROUBLE?
If the worksheet does not fully display the numbers, click outside the worksheet to return to the document, make the worksheet object larger, and then open the server application again.

Excel menus and toolbar

Excel server application open

Entire workbook is an embedded object

Figure 16

Additional Information
The user must have the server application on his or her system to be able to open and edit the embedded object.

The server application, in this case Excel, is opened. The Excel menus and toolbars replace the menus and toolbars in the Word application window. The selected portion of the embedded object is displayed in an editing worksheet window. Now you can use the server commands to edit the object.

3 ● Change the font color of cells B15 through D15 to red.

● Close the server application by clicking anywhere outside the object.

Your screen should be similar to Figure 17

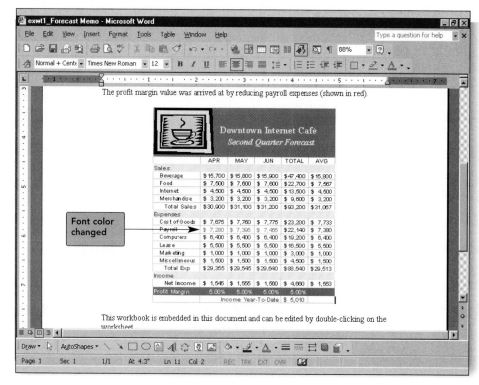

Figure 17

The embedded object in the memo is updated to reflect the changes you made.

E-Mailing the Memo

Finally, you want to e-mail the memo to Evan.

1 ● Click 🖾 **E-mail.**

HAVING TROUBLE?
If you do not have an e-mail program installed, the 🖾 button is not displayed and you will need to skip this section.

Another Method
The menu equivalent is File/Send to/Mail Recipient.

Additional Information
The process to e-mail is the same in Excel.

Your screen should look similar to Figure 18

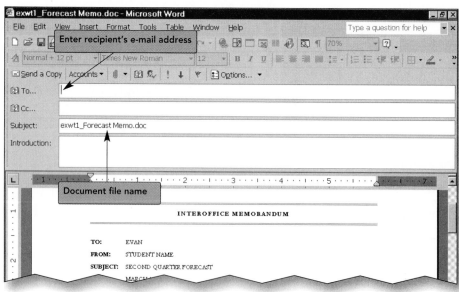

Figure 18

An e-mail message box is displayed at the top of the document. You use the message box to specify the recipient's e-mail address, the e-mail address of anyone you want to send a copy of this message to (cc:), and the subject of the message. You can also use the toolbar buttons to select recipient names from your e-mail address book, attach a file to the message, set the message priority (high, normal, or low priority), include a follow-up message flag, and set other e-mail options. The name of the document appears in the Subject box by default. And finally, you can use the Introduction box to include a brief note along with the copy of the memo.

2 ● Enter the e-mail address of the person you want to send the message to in the To: box.

● In place of the information displayed in the Subject box, enter **Second Quarter Forecast**.

Your screen should look similar to Figure 19

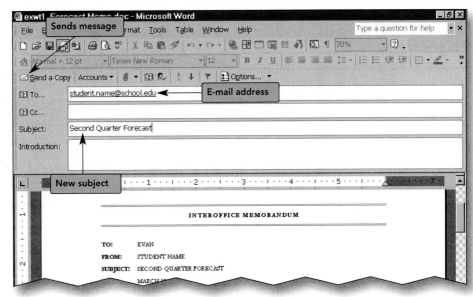

Figure 19

That is all the information that is required to send the e-mail message. You are now ready to send your e-mail message.

3 ● Click .

Your message is sent and the e-mail message box is removed from the screen.

4 ● Save the memo as Second Quarter Forecast.

● Preview and print the memo.

● Exit Word.

Deciding When to Link or Embed Objects

Linking documents is a very handy feature, particularly in documents whose information is updated frequently. If you include a linked object in a document that you are giving to another person, make sure the user has access to the source file and application. Otherwise the links will not operate correctly.

Keep the following in mind when deciding whether to link or embed objects.

Use linking when:	Use embedding when:
File size is important	File size is not important
Users have access to the source file and application	Users have access to the application but not to the source file
The information is updated frequently	The data changes infrequently

Working Together: Linking, Embedding, and E-Mailing

key terms

destination file   EXWT1.6
embed   EXWT1.10
linked object   EXWT1.6
live link   EXWT1.6
source file   EXWT1.6

command summary

Command	Button	Action
File/Send to/Mail Recipient		Sends the active document to the e-mail recipient
Edit/Paste Special		Inserts the object as an embedded object
Edit/Paste Special/Paste Link		Creates a link to the source document
Edit/Links		Modifies selected link
Edit/Linked Object/Edit Link		Modifies selected linked object

Hands-On Exercises

step- by-step

Rescue Foundation Income Memo

★★ **1.** The Animal Rescue Foundation's agency director has asked you to provide her with information about income for 2002. You want to create a memo to her and include a copy of the worksheet analysis of this data in the memo. The completed memo is shown below.

    a. Start Word and open the document exwt1_Rescue Memo.

    b. In the header, replace the From placeholder with your name.

    c. Start Excel and open the workbook exwt1_Contributions.

    d. Insert both worksheets as links below the first paragraph in the Word memo. Size and center the worksheets below the paragraph.

    e. Enter the income of **$2,650** for May raffle ticket sales.

    f. Save the Excel workbook as Contributions2. Exit Excel.

    g. If necessary, adjust the size and placement of the worksheets in the memo. Save the Word document as Rescue Memo Linked. Preview and print the document.

    h. E-mail the memo to your instructor and carbon copy yourself. Include appropriate information in the subject.

Memo

To: Barbara Wood

From: Student Name

CC: Mark Wilson

Date: 04/25/2001

Re: Income

Below is the completed analysis of income for 2002. As you can see, the income for both periods is very close, with Fall/Winter slightly higher.

Animal Rescue Foundation

	March	April	May	June	July	August	Total
Annual Memberships	$4,000	$4,583	$8,395	$2,834	$6,394	$5,481	$30,677
Phone Solicitation	1,200			2,000			3,200
Corporate Donations			12,000			8,000	20,000
Raffle Tickets			2,650				2,650
Pet Shows		7,000					7,000
Other	2,000	2,000	2,000	2,000	2,000	2,000	12,000
Total	$7,200	$13,583	$25,045	$6,834	$7,394	$15,481	$75,527

Animal Rescue Foundation

	September	October	November	December	January	February	Total
Annual Memberships	$6,540	$4,523	$4,395	$1,834	$1,384	$5,481	$24,157
Phone Solicitation	1,200					2,000	3,200
Corporate Donations		15,000				10,000	25,000
Raffle Tickets			2,894				2,894
Pet Shows		9,000					9,000
Other	2,000	2,000	2,000	2,000	2,000	2,000	12,000
Total	$9,740	$30,523	$9,289	$3,834	$3,384	$19,481	$76,251

I would like to set up a meeting for next week to brainstorm about ways we can increase income for next year. Please let me know what your schedules are like so I can set a date and time.

1

Tour Status Memo

★★ **2.** Adventure Travel Tours travel agency sends a monthly status report to all subsidiary offices showing the bookings for the specialty tours offered by the company. Previously the worksheet data was printed separately from the memo. Now you want to include the worksheet in the same document as the memo.

a. Start Word and open the exwt1_Tour Status Report document. Replace Student Name with your name on the From line in the heading.

b. Start Excel and open the exwt1_Adventure Travel Monthly workbook.

c. Copy the worksheet as a linked object into the memo below the paragraph.

d. Enter the following data for the March bookings in the worksheet.

Tour	March Data
Tuolumne Clavey Falls	20
Costa Rica Rainforest	4
Kilimanjaro	4
Machu Picchu	3
Himalayas	6
Tanzania Safari	6

e. Save the workbook as Adventure Travel Monthly2. Exit Excel.

f. Center the worksheet object in the word document.

g. Save the Word document as March Status Report. Print the memo.

h. E-mail the memo to your instructor and carbon copy yourself. Include appropriate information in the subject.

INTEROFFICE MEMORANDUM

TO: ADVENTURE TRAVEL EMPLOYEES
FROM: STUDENT NAME
SUBJECT: TOUR STATUS REPORT
DATE: 3/20/01

The bookings to date for our upcoming specialty tours are displayed in the following table. As you can see the new white water rafting tour to below the Tuolumne Clavey Falls in California is almost full to capacity and we are considering offering a second week. Because several others are also close to capacity you may want to advise any clients who are considering one of these tours to make reservations as soon as possible.

Adventure Travel Tours
Speciality Tours Status Report

Tour	Jan	Feb	Mar	Total	Tour Capacity
Tuolumne Clavey Falls	8	14	20	42	46
Costa Rica Rainforests	5	9	4	18	36
Kilimanjaro	2	2	4	8	15
Machu Picchu	4	8	3	15	30
Himalayas	0	0	6	6	18
Tanzania Safari	4	3	6	13	21

Hotel Occupancy Memo

★★ **3.** Karen works for a large hotel chain in the marketing department. She has recently researched hotel occupancy rates for the Phoenix area and has created a worksheet and stacked-column chart of the data. Now Karen wants to send a memo containing the chart to her supervisor.

a. Start Word and open the document exwt1_Hotel Memo.

b. In the header, replace the placeholder information in brackets with the following:

TO:	**Brad Wise**
FROM:	**Karen Howard**
CC:	**[your name]**
RE:	**Hotel Occupancy**

c. Start Excel and open the workbook exwt1_Hotel Data. Embed the column chart below the paragraph in the Word memo. Center the chart in the memo. Exit Excel.

d. You decide you need to clarify that the data for 2003 and 2004 is projected. Add a second title line **(2003 - 2004 projected)** to the embedded chart in 12 point, italic, no bold.

e. Save the Word document as Hotel Memo2. Preview and print the document.

f. E-mail the memo to your instructor and carbon copy yourself. Include appropriate information in the subject.

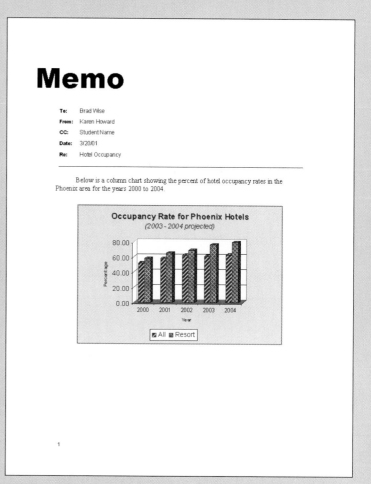

Case Study

Brian, the co-owner of Lifestyle Fitness Club, recently asked you to provide him with a list of all employees who have at least 3 and 5 years of service with the Club. You queried the Employees table in the Personnel Records database and were quickly able to obtain this information. Now you want to include the query results with a brief memo to Brian.

You will learn how to share information between applications while you create the memo. Your memo containing the query results generated by Access will look like the one shown here.

Note: This tutorial assumes that you already know how to use Word and that you have completed Lab 3 of Access. You will need the database file Personnel Records you saved at the end of Lab 3.

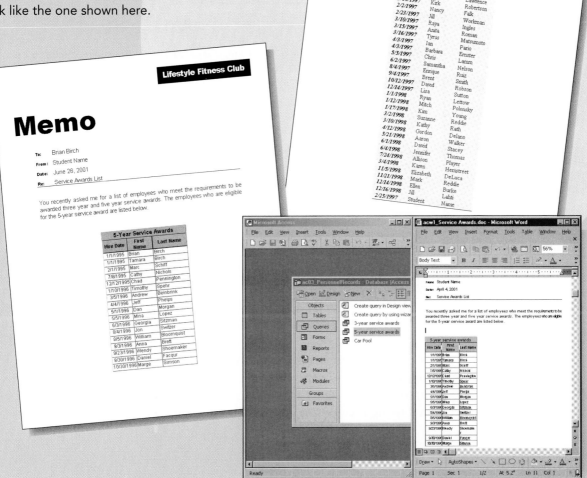

Copying Between Applications

You have already created the memo to Brian and just need to add the information from Access to the memo. All Microsoft Office applications have a common user interface such as similar commands and menu structures. In addition to these obvious features, they have been designed to work together, making it easy to share and exchange information between applications.

As with all Office applications, you can cut, copy, and paste selections within and between tables and objects in an Access database. You can also perform these operations between Access databases and other applications. For example, you can copy a database object or selection into a Word document. The information is inserted in a format the application can recognize.

Copying a Query to a Word Document

You will begin by copying the 5-year query results from Access into a Word memo. You can also use the same commands and procedures to copy information from Word or other Office applications into Access.

First, you need to open the memo document in Word.

1 ● **Start Word and open the document** acw1_Service Awards.

● **Maximize the application and document windows.**

● **If necessary, change to Normal view at Page Width zoom.**

● **In the memo header, replace Student Name with your name.**

● **Scroll the memo so you can see the body of the memo.**

Your screen should be similar to Figure 1

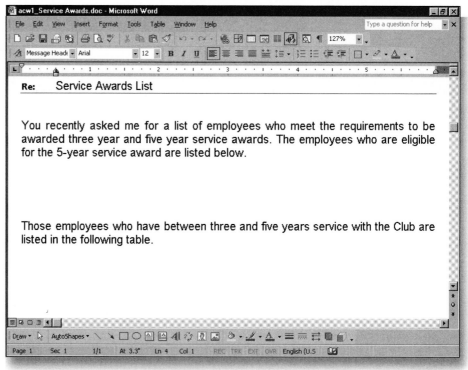

Figure 1

This document contains the text of the memo to Brian. Below each of the paragraphs, you want to display the appropriate list of employees. This information is available in the Personnel Records database file and can be obtained using the Service Awards queries you created and saved.

2 ● **Start Access.**

● **If necessary, maximize the window.**

● **Open the** ac03_Personnel Records **database file.**

● **Open the Queries object list.**

Your screen should be similar to Figure 2

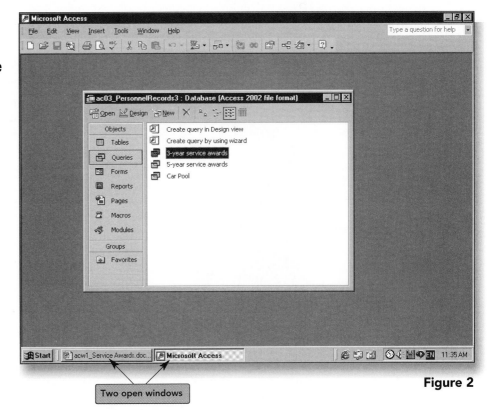

Two open windows

Figure 2

There are now two open applications, Word and Access. Word is open in a window behind the Access application window. Application buttons for all open windows are displayed in the taskbar.

You want to copy the output from the 5-Year Service Awards query below the first paragraph of the memo. You can use Copy and Paste or drag and drop between the Access and Word applications to copy a database object. To use drag and drop, both applications must be open and visible in the window. You can do this by tiling the application windows.

3
Right-click on a blank area of the taskbar to open the shortcut menu.

HAVING TROUBLE?
If your taskbar is hidden, point to the thin line at the bottom of the screen to redisplay it.

Choose Tile Windows Vertically.

Click in the Access window to make it active.

Your screen should be similar to Figure 3

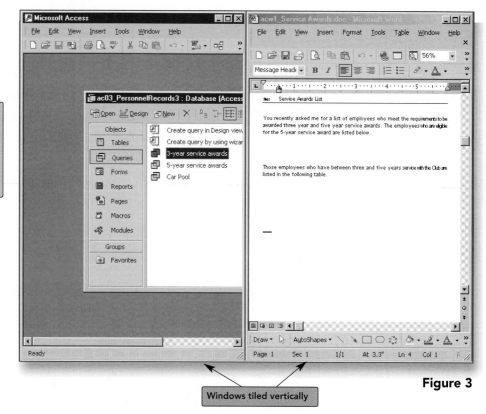

Windows tiled vertically

Figure 3

You can now see the contents of both the Access and Word applications and are ready to copy the query results to below the first paragraph of the memo.

4
Select the 5-year Service Awards object in the Access Database window.

Drag the selected object to the second blank line below the first paragraph of the memo.

Click in the Word document to deselect the table.

Your screen should be similar to Figure 4

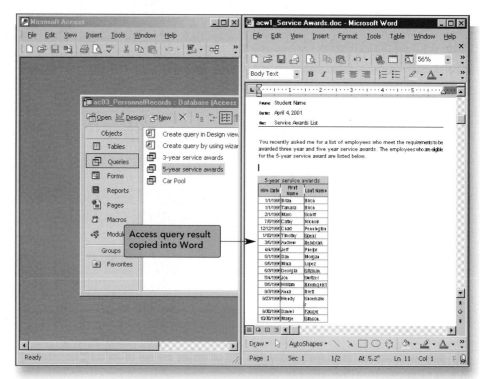

Access query result copied into Word

Figure 4

The query results have been copied into the Word document as a table that can be edited and manipulated within Word. Much of the formatting associated with the copied information is also pasted into the document.

Formatting Copied Data

You think the memo would look better if the Hire Date column of information in the table was centered. You also want to make the table wider so the entire contents of the last name are displayed on a single line, and you want to center it between the margins of the memo.

1
- Click ☐ to maximize the Word window.

- Scroll the table to see Wendy Shoemaker's record.

- Increase the width of the table by dragging the right table border line to the 2.5 inch position on the ruler.

- Move to any row in the Hire Date column and choose Table/Select/Column.

- Click ☰ to center the Hire Date column contents.

- Choose Table/Select/Table to select the entire table.

- Click ☰ to center the table between the margins.

- Deselect the table.

Your screen should be similar to Figure 5

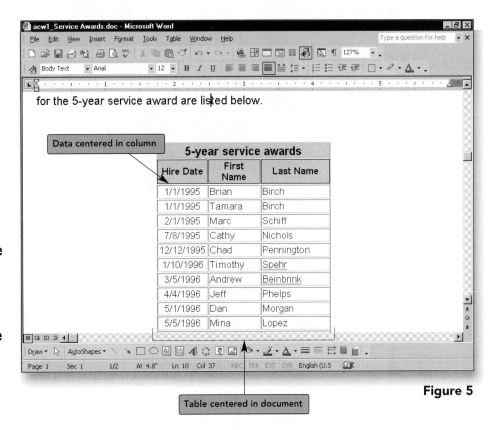

Figure 5

Editing a Copied Object

As you check the information in the table, you notice that Daniel Facqur's first name is misspelled. You want to correct this in both the memo and in the database table.

1 ● Edit the spelling of "Danial" to "**Daniel**" in the Word table.

● Click 🗗 to restore the Word window to tiled vertically.

● Switch to Access and open the "5-year Service Awards query."

● Correct the spelling of Daniel's name in the query results.

Your screen should be similar to Figure 6

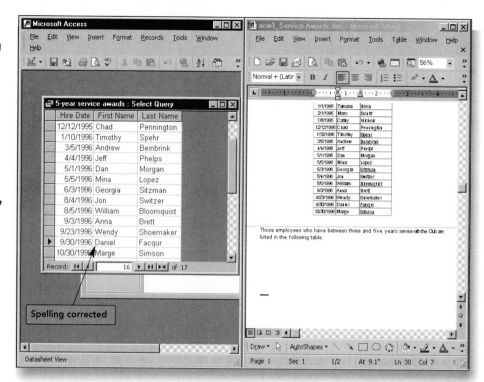

Figure 6

Now the information is correct in both applications.

Your first query table has been copied into the memo and formatted to fit the memo's layout. Next you need to insert the query results showing all employees who have more than 3 years and less than 5 years with the club. As you consider the memo, you are concerned that you may need to make corrections to the database again. If you need to, you want the memo to be automatically updated when you modify the query. To do this you will link the query object to the memo.

Linking between Applications

You will insert the query result into the memo as a **linked object**. Information created in one application can be inserted as a linked object into a document created by another application. When an object is linked, the data is stored in the **source file** (the document it was created in). A graphic representation or picture of the data is displayed in the **destination file** (the document in which the object is inserted). A connection between the information in the destination file to the source file is established by the creation of a link. The link contains references to the location of the source file and the selection within the document that is linked to the destination file.

When changes that affect the linked object are made in the source file, the changes are automatically reflected in the destination file when it is opened. This is called a **live link**. When you create linked objects, the date and time on your machine should be accurate, because the program refers to the date of the source file to determine whether updates are needed when you open the destination file.

Linking a Query to a Word Document

Additional Information
You can also use Word's Insert/Object command to insert an Access file as a linked object.

One way to create a link to the query is with the 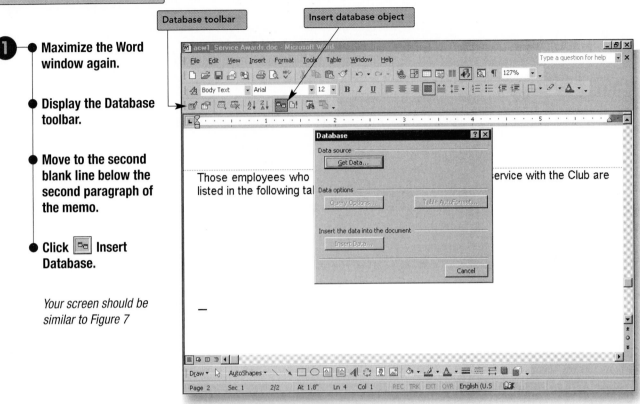 Insert Database button on the Database toolbar of Word. This is the method you will use to link the 3-Year Service Awards query table to the memo.

1
- **Maximize the Word window again.**
- **Display the Database toolbar.**
- **Move to the second blank line below the second paragraph of the memo.**
- **Click** Insert Database.

Your screen should be similar to Figure 7

Figure 7

From the Database dialog box, you need to first select the database file to be inserted into the memo.

2
- **Click** Get Data...
- **Select the location containing your data files from the Look In drop-down list.**
- **Double-click the** ac03_Personnel Records **database file.**

HAVING TROUBLE?
If the database file name is not displayed, change the file type option to All Data Sources.

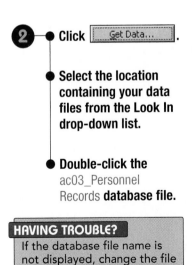 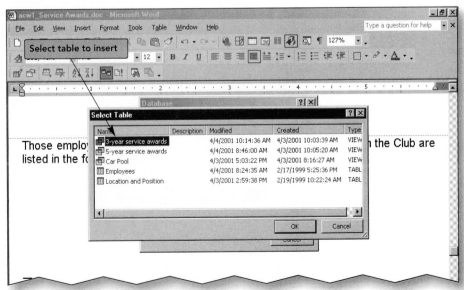

Your screen should be similar to Figure 8

Figure 8

The Select Table dialog box automatically opens to the queries list for Personnel Records. This is because the last object you worked with in this database was a query (the 5-year Service Awards query table, which you just copied into the memo). From this list, you will select the 3-Year Service Awards query to be inserted in the Word document.

3

● **If necessary, select "3-Year Service Awards."**

● **Click** OK **.**

Your screen should be similar to Figure 9

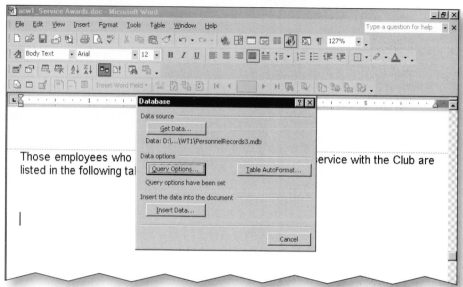

Figure 9

The Database dialog box is displayed again. The Query Options button enables you to modify the query settings. Since you want it to appear as it is, you do not need to use this option. The AutoFormat button lets you select a format to apply to the table. If you do not select a format style, the datasheet is copied into the document as an unformatted table.

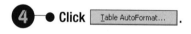

4

● **Click** Table AutoFormat... **.**

Your screen should be similar to Figure 10

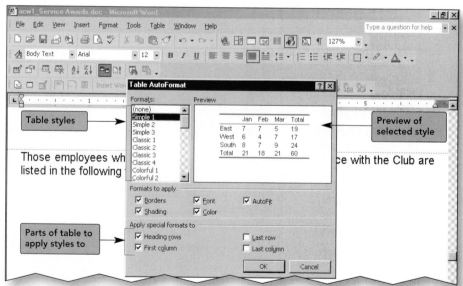

Figure 10

From the Table AutoFormat dialog box, you select the style you want to use and the parts of the table you want to apply it to. You want the formats applied to the heading rows and first column.

5 If necessary, select the Heading rows and First column options as the only two areas to apply special formats.

● Select the Colorful 2 style.

● Click **OK**.

● Click **Insert Data...** from the Database dialog box.

Your screen should be similar to Figure 11

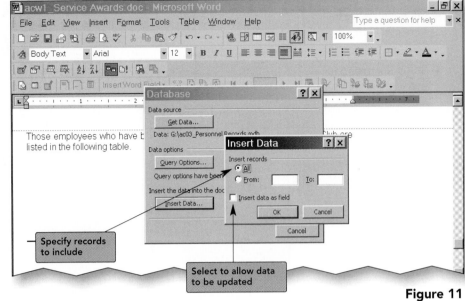

Specify records to include

Select to allow data to be updated

Figure 11

From the Insert Data dialog box, you specify what records to include in the inserted table and whether to insert the data as a field. Inserting it as a field allows the data to be updated whenever the source changes.

6 If necessary, select **All**.

● Select **Insert data as field**.

● Click **OK**.

Your screen should be similar to Figure 12

Query object inserted into Word document using selected AutoFormat style

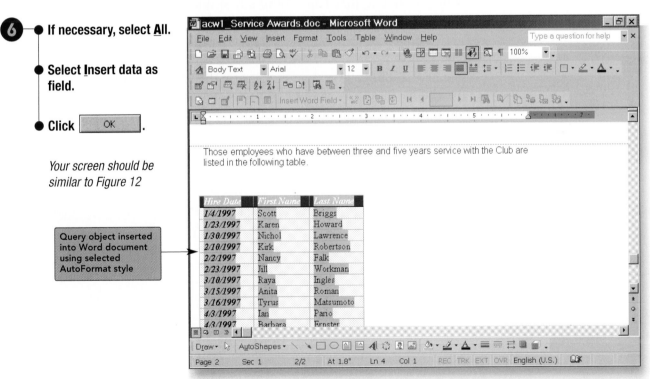

Figure 12

The link to the database file and to the query object is established, and the database table is inserted into the document in the selected format style. The table lists the 33 employees who have between 3 and 5 years with the club.

7 ● Click above the table to deselect it.

● Scroll the memo to see the bottom of the inserted table.

Your screen should be similar to Figure 13

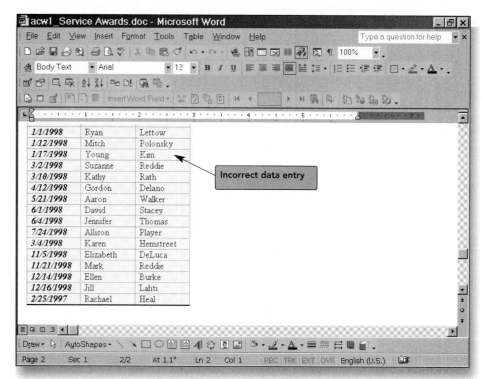

Figure 13

Now you notice that Kim Young's first and last names are reversed. You want to correct this in both the table in Access and in the memo.

Updating a Linked Object

Because you linked the Access object to the Word document, you can make the change in Access, and it will be automatically updated in the memo.

1 ● **Restore the Word window to tiled vertically.**

● **Close the "5-year Service Awards" query.**

● **Open the "3-Year Service Awards" query in Access.**

● **Correct the Last Name and First Name fields in Kim Young's record.**

● **Move to any other record to complete the edit.**

● **Click 🖫 Save.**

● **Switch to the Word memo and click on the table to select it.**

● **Click 🗈! Update Field to update the table contents.**

● **Scroll the memo to confirm that Kim Young's name is now corrected in the table.**

Your screen should be similar to Figure 14

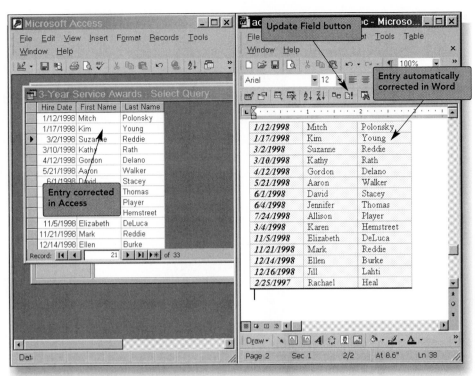

Figure 14

The query results were regenerated and inserted into the document again. The last change you want to make is to center the table. Then you will save and print the memo.

Additional Information

Edits made to a linked object in the destination file do not affect the source file.

2 ● **From the taskbar shortcut menu, choose Undo Tile.**

● **Close the Database and Mail Merge toolbars.**

● **Center the table on the page.**

● **Deselect the table.**

● **Preview both pages of the memo.**

Your screen should be similar to Figure 15

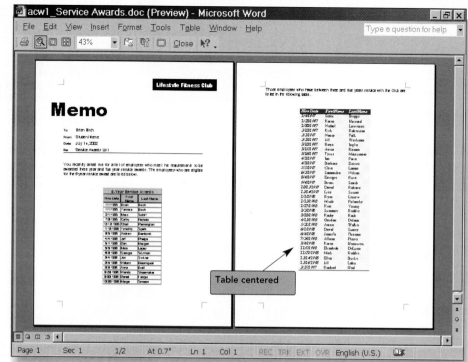

Figure 15

3 ● **Save the memo as** Service Awards Linked.

● **Print the memo and exit Word.**

● **Maximize the Access window.**

● **Close the query and exit Access.**

Your printed memo should look similar to the one shown in the Case Study at the beginning of this lab.

Working Together: Linking Access and Word

key terms

Destination file   ACWT1.6
Linked object   ACWT1.6
Live link   ACWT1.6
Source file   ACWT1.6

lab exercises

Hands-On Exercises

rating system

★ Easy

★★ Moderate

★★★ Difficult

step by step

Spa Marketing Memo

★ **1.** The Simply Beautiful Spa database has been used extensively (Step-by-Step Exercise 1 of Lab 3). Maria Dell, the owner, has asked you for a printed list of clients who are over the age of 35 to get an idea of how much interest there would be in an anti-aging spa package she is considering offering. You already filtered the Clients table to locate this information and now want to include the results in a memo to Maria (shown here).

   a. Open the ac02_Simply Beautiful database and the "Clients" table that you modified in Step-by-Step Exercise 1 of Lab 3. Apply the filter. (If you did not save the table with the filter, create the filter again by entering **<1/1/65** in the Birth date field of the Filter by Form window).

To: Maria Dell
From: Student Name
Date: [Current Date]
Here is the information you requested on the spa clients who are over the age of 35.

Last Name	First Name	Street Address	City	State	Zip Code	E-mail	Birth Date
Finch	Terrence	919 Port Ct.	Orangeburg	SC	29115	Terr@set.net	09/08/1952
Huye	Ky	765 Portland	Orangeburg	SC	29115		03/15/1944
Riley	Charlene	2424 Eastern	Orangeburg	SC	29115		10/13/1944
Woo	Fen	8547 Lindsey Avenue	Columbia	SC	29201	woo@mail.com	05/23/1953
Grimes	Sally	202 S. Jefferson	Columbia	SC	29201	SGrime@ed.net	01/07/1957
Townsend	Joseph	101 Cheshire Lane	Wateree	SC	29044		07/10/1963

b. Hide the Client No., Home Phone, Work Phone, and Cell Phone fields.

c. Open Word and enter the following text in a new document.
TO: Maria Dell
FROM: [Your Name]
DATE: [current date]
Here is the information you requested on the spa clients who are over the age of 35.

d. Select the filter results and use Copy and Paste to copy them into the Word document.

e. Save the memo as Beautiful 35+ Clients. Close the document and exit Word.

f. Unhide the four fields. Remove the filter. Close the table and database.

Low Stock Memo

★★ **2.** Evan, the owner of the Dwontown Internet Cafe, continues to beimpressed with the Cafe's database (Step-by-Step Exercise 3 of Lab 3). Evan has asked you to send him a memo listing of all special-order items and how many of these items are currently in-stock right away. You are not sure how much detail he needs (he didn't say anything about placing any orders), and he is not available for you to ask him right now. You decide to go ahead and create the memo and link the query result to it. This way, you can easily revise the query and update the memo should it be necessary. The completed memo is shown here.

a. Open the ac02_Cafe Supplies database that you modified in Step-by-Step Exercise 3 of Lab 3.

b. Create a new query named "Special Orders" that will display items with Y in the Special Order? field, and include the On Hand, Description, and Vendor Name fields (in that order). Run the query. Save the query.

c. Open Word, and enter the following text in a new document.
TO: Evan
FROM: [your first name]
DATE: [current date]
The following table lists our current special-order inventory. Please let me know if you need additional information.

TO: Evan
FROM: Student Name
DATE: Current Date

The following table lists our current special-order inventory. Please let me know if you need additional information.

Special Order?	# On Hand	Description	Vendor Name
Y	30	Decaf Viennese	Pure Processing
Y	6	Business cards	Pro Printing
Y	1	Coffee mints	Tasty Delights
Y	45	Kenya coffee	Better Beverages, Inc.
Y	2	Ethiopian coffee	Better Beverages, Inc.
Y	0	Kona coffee	Better Beverages, Inc.
Y	12	Coffee mugs	Central Ceramics

d. Insert the query results into the Word document as a linked object and a field. Use an Auto-Format of your choice.

e. Size and center the table appropriately.

f. Change the # on Hand in the query for Decaf Viennese to **30** and for Kenya coffee to **45**. Update the table in the memo.

g. Save the memo as Special Orders. Print the document. Exit Word.

h. Save the query. Close the table and database.

Software Memo

★ **3.** The report you created for EduSoft listing the math and science titles released over 3 years ago has been well received (Step-by-Step Exercise 4 of Lab 3). EduSoft's production development manager has asked you to locate the same information for all titles. You will quickly modify the query to get this information and include it in a memo to the manager (shown here).

    a. Open the ac02_Learning database and the "Old Math and Science" query that you modified in Step-by-Step Exercise 4 of Lab 3.

    b. Modify the query to display all titles that are over 3 years old. Best fit the fields. Save the modified query as "3+ Products."

    c. Open Word and enter the following text in a new document.

    TO: Kaitlin Mann, Product Dev. Mgr.
    FROM: [Your Name]
    DATE: [current date]
    Here is the information you requested on the products EduSoft released over 3 years ago.

TO: Kaitlin Mann, Product Dev.Mgr.
FROM: Student Name
DATE: Current date

Here is the information you requested on the products EduSoft released over 3 years ago.

Title	Subject	Grade Level	Release Date
Say It	Speech	K-2	01/20/1995
Spell It	Spelling	K-2	04/20/1995
Spell It II	Spelling	3-5	07/20/1995
Type It	Typing	K-2	01/15/1996
Read It III	Reading	6-8	03/20/1996
Try It I	Science	K-2	01/20/1996
Try It II	Science	3-5	06/04/1996
Try It III	Science	6-8	09/20/1996
Seeing Stars	Astronomy	3-5	11/07/1996
Rain or Shine	Meteorology	3-5	01/23/1997
Any Body	Anatomy and Biology	6-8	03/15/1997
Solve It I	Math	K-2	06/14/1997
Solve It II	Math	3-5	09/03/1997
Solve It III	Math	6-8	12/15/1997
Tell It	Speech	K-2	01/20/1995

    d. Insert the query results into the Word document as a linked object and a field. Use an AutoFormat of your choice.

    e. Open the "Software" table and add a new record to the table using the following information: **90-0102; Tell It; Speech; K–2; Story Telling; your name; 1/20/1995**.

    f. Run the query again.

    g. Update the memo.

    h. Size and center the table appropriately.

    i. Save the memo as EduSoft 3+. Print the document.

    j. Save the query changes. Close the table and database.

Working Together: Copying, Embedding, and Linking Between Applications

The director of the Animal Rescue Foundation has reviewed the PowerPoint presentation you created and has asked you to include a chart created in Excel showing the adoption success rate. Additionally, the director has provided a list of dates for the upcoming volunteer orientation meetings that she feels would be good content for another slide.

Frequently you will find that you will want to include information that was created using a word processor, spreadsheet, or database application in your slide show. As you will see, it is easy to share information between applications, saving you both time and effort by eliminating the need to recreate information that is available in another application. You will learn how to share information between applications while you create the new slides. The new slides containing information from Word and Excel are shown here.

Note: The Working Together section assumes that you already know how to use Word and Excel 2002 and that you have completed Lab 2 of PowerPoint. You will need the file Volunteer3 you saved at the end of Lab 2 of PowerPoint.

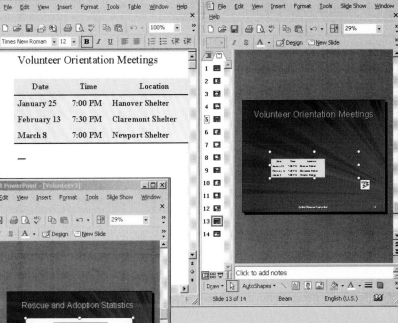

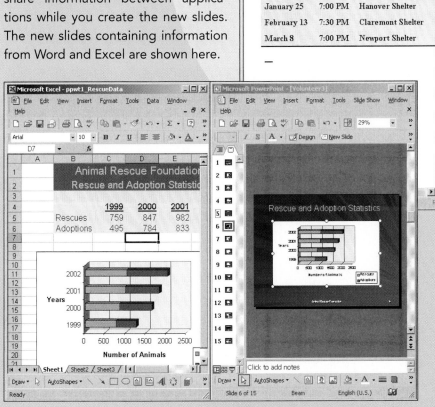

Copying Between Applications

The orientation meeting information has already been entered in a document using Word. All Microsoft Office applications have a common user interface, such as similar commands and menu structures. In addition to these obvious features, they have been designed to work together, making it easy to share and exchange information between applications.

Rather than retype the list of orientation meeting dates provided by the director, you will copy it from the Word document into the presentation. You can also use the same commands and procedures to copy information from PowerPoint or other Office applications into Word.

Copying from Word to a PowerPoint Slide

First you need to modify the PowerPoint presentation to include a new slide for the orientation meeting dates.

1 ● **Start PowerPoint and open the presentation** Volunteer3.

● **Insert a new slide in the Title Only layout after slide 12.**

● **Close the Slide Layout pane.**

Your screen should be similar to Figure 1

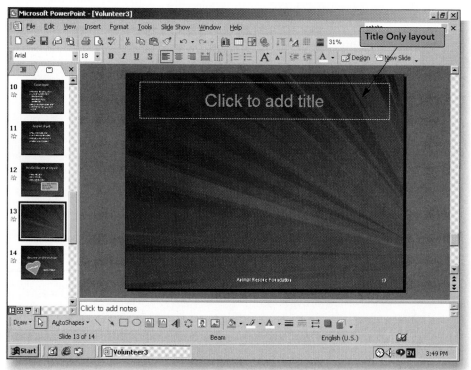

Figure 1

To copy the information from the Word document file into the PowerPoint presentation, you need to open the Word document.

2 ● **Start Word 2002.**

● **Open the document**
ppwt1_Orientation
Meetings.

HAVING TROUBLE?
Use the Start button or
display the desktop and
click  .

*Your screen should be
similar to Figure 2*

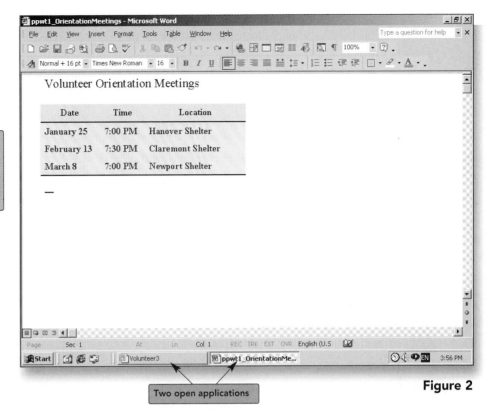

Two open applications

Figure 2

There are now two open applications, Word and PowerPoint. PowerPoint is
open in a window behind the Word application window. Both application
buttons are displayed in the taskbar. There are also two open files,
Orientation Meetings in Word and Volunteer3 in PowerPoint. Word is the
active application, and Orientation Meetings is the active file. To make it
easier to work with two applications, you will tile the windows to view both
on the screen at the same time.

3 ● **Right-click on a blank
area of the taskbar to
open the shortcut
menu.**

● **Select Tile Windows
Vertically.**

● **Click on the Word document window to
make it active.**

*Your screen should be
similar to Figure 3*

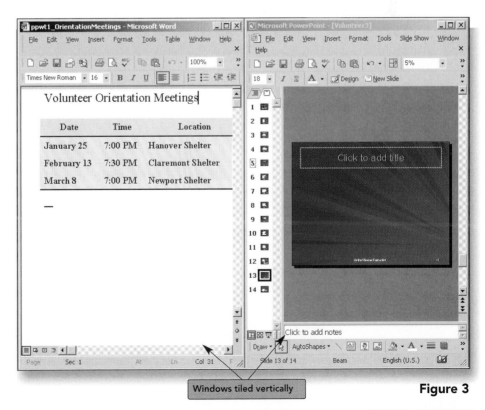

Windows tiled vertically

Figure 3

First you will copy the title from the Word document into the title place-holder of the slide. While using the Word and PowerPoint applications, you have learned how to use cut, copy, and paste to move or copy information within the same document. You can also perform these same operations between documents in the same application and between documents in different applications. The information is pasted in a format that the application can edit, if possible.

4

● Select the title "Volunteer Orientation Meetings."

● Drag the selection using the right mouse button to the title placeholder in the slide.

HAVING TROUBLE?
If you drag using the left mouse button, the selection is moved.

● From the shortcut menu, select Copy.

Another Method
You could also use Copy and Paste to copy the title to the slide.

● Click on the slide to deselect the place-holder.

Your screen should be similar to Figure 4

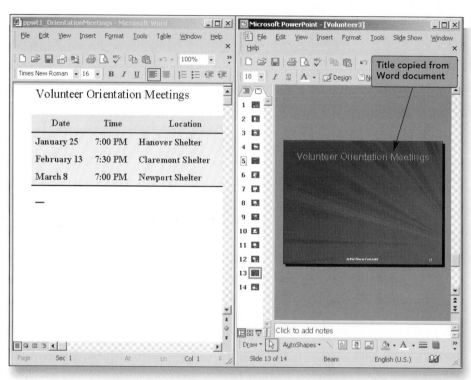

Figure 4

The title has been copied into the slide and can be edited and manipulated within PowerPoint. The formats associated with the slide master are applied to the copied text. If the copied text included formatting, such as color, it would override the slide master settings, just as if you individually formatted a slide to make it unique.

Embedding a Word Table in a PowerPoint Slide

Next you want to display the table of orientation dates below the title in the slide. You will copy and embed the table in the slide. An object that is embedded is stored in the **destination file**, the file that the object is inserted into, and becomes part of that document. The embedded object can be edited using features from the source program, the application in which it was created. This means that you can modify it without affecting the **source file**, the file containing the original object.

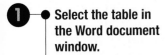

1 ● Select the table in the Word document window.

> **HAVING TROUBLE?**
> Drag to select the entire table or use Table/Select/Table.

● Click 📋 Copy.

● Click on the PowerPoint window.

● Choose Edit/Paste Special.

Your screen should be similar to Figure 5

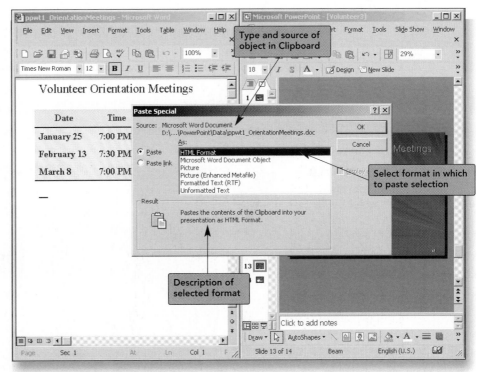

Figure 5

The Paste Special dialog box displays the type of object contained in the Clipboard and its location in the Source area. From the As list box, you select the type of format in which you want the object inserted into the destination file. The default option inserts the copy in HTML (HyperText Markup Language) format. The Result area describes the effect of your selections. In this case, you want the object inserted as a Word Document Object.

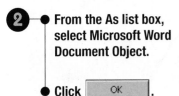

2 ● From the As list box, select Microsoft Word Document Object.

● Click ▢ OK ▢.

Your screen should be similar to Figure 6

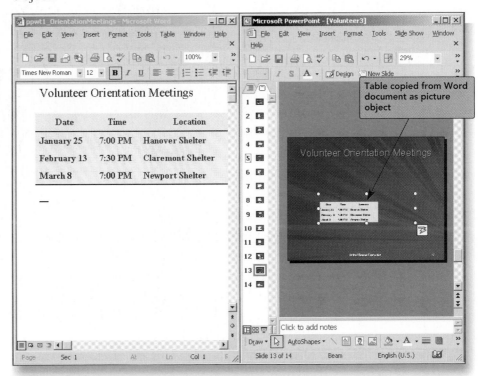

Figure 6

The table, including the table formatting, is copied into the slide. The embedded object can be manipulated using the Picture toolbar. You will trim or crop the object so that the object size is the same size as the table. Then you will increase the size of the object and position it in the slide.

3
- Choose **U**ndo Tile from the Taskbar shortcut menu.

- If necessary, maximize the PowerPoint window and select the table.

- Display the Picture toolbar.

- Click ✂ Crop.

- Position the cropping tool ✂ over a corner crop mark and drag inward to reduce the size of the object to the same size as the table.

Your screen should be similar to Figure 7

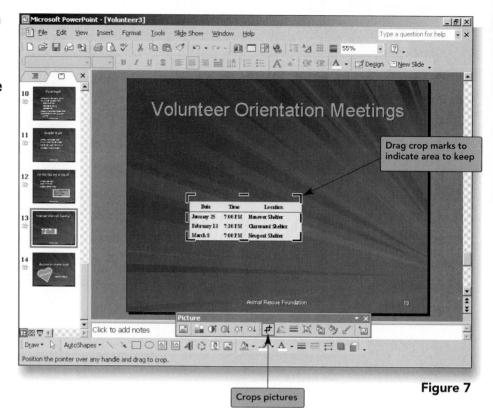

Figure 7

4
- Continue reducing the object size as needed to fit the table.

- Click ✂ Crop to turn off the cropping tool.

- Size and move the table object as in Figure 8.

- Deselect the object.

Your screen should be similar to Figure 8

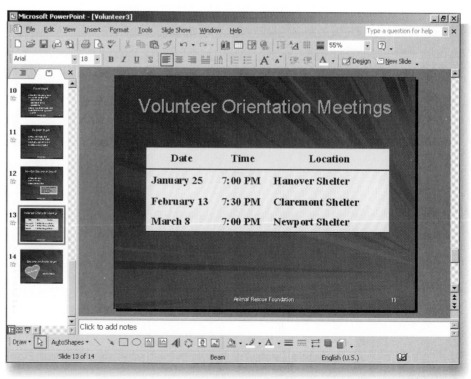

Figure 8

Editing an Embedded Object

As you look at the table, you decide you want to change the appearance of the text in the headings. To do this, you will edit the embedded object using the source program.

1 ● Double-click the table.

Your screen should be similar to Figure 9

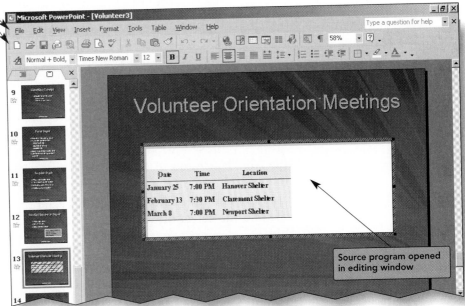

Source program opened in editing window

Figure 9

The source program, in this case Word, is opened. The Word menus and toolbars replace some of the menus and toolbars in the PowerPoint application window. The embedded object is displayed in an editing window. Now you can use the Word commands to edit the object.

2 ● Change the font color of the three headings to blue.

● Left-align the three headings.

● Close the source program by clicking anywhere outside the object.

Your screen should be similar to Figure 10

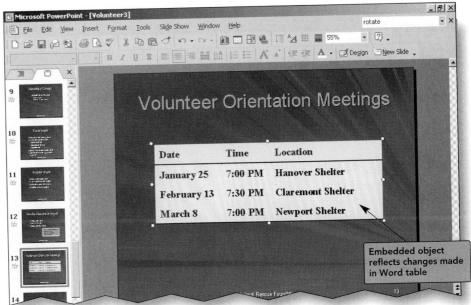

Embedded object reflects changes made in Word table

Figure 10

The embedded object in the PowerPoint slide is updated to reflect the changes you made in the Word table.

3 ● Click ⊞ Orientation Meetings.doc - ... in the taskbar to switch to the Word application.

● Exit Word.

Linking Between Applications

Next you want to copy the chart of the rescue and adoption data into the presentation. You will insert the chart object into the slide as a **linked object**, which is another way to insert information created in one application into a document created by another application. When an object is linked, the data is stored in the source file (the document it was created in). A graphic representation or picture of the data is displayed in the destination file (the document in which the object is inserted). A connection between the information in the destination file to the source file is established by the creation of a link. The link contains references to the location of the source file and the selection within the document that is linked to the destination file.

When changes are made in the source file that affect the linked object, the changes are automatically reflected in the destination file when it is opened. This is called a **live link**. When you create linked objects, the date and time on your machine should be accurate. This is because the program refers to the date of the source file to determine whether updates are needed when you open the destination file.

Linking an Excel Chart to a PowerPoint Presentation

The chart of the rescue and adoption data will be inserted into another new slide following slide 5.

1 ● Insert a new slide following slide 5, using the Title Only layout.

● Close the Slide Layout pane.

● Start Excel 2002 and open the workbook ppwt1_RescueData from your data files.

● Tile the application windows vertically.

Your screen should be similar to Figure 11

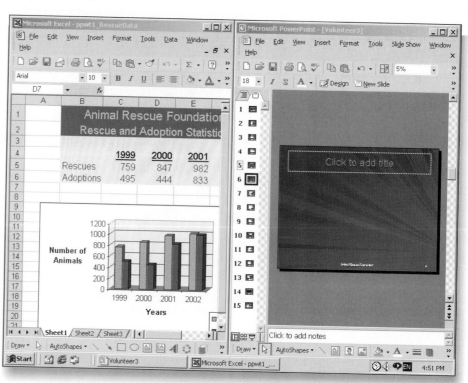

Figure 11

Working Together: Copying, Embedding, and Linking Between Applications

www.mhhe.com/oleary

The worksheet contains the rescue and adoption data for the past four years as well as a column chart of the data. Again, you have two open applications, PowerPoint and Excel. Next you will copy the second title line from the worksheet into the slide title placeholder.

2 ● Select cell B2.

● Click 📋 Copy.

● Switch to the PowerPoint window.

● Select the Title placeholder.

● Choose **Edit/Paste Special** and select Formatted text (RTF).

● Click ⬚ OK ⬚.

● Remove the extra blank lines below the title.

● If necessary, size the placeholder and position the title appropriately on the slide.

● Click on the slide to deselect the placeholder.

Your screen should be similar to Figure 12

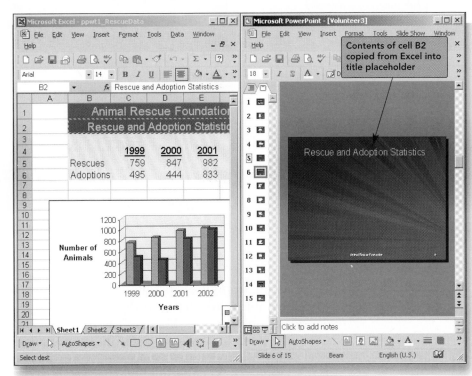

Figure 12

Now you are ready to copy the chart. By making the chart a linked object, it will be automatically updated if the source file is edited.

3 • **Select the entire chart.**

> **HAVING TROUBLE?**
> Click on the chart to select it when the ScreenTip displays Chart Area.

• **Click 🖳 Copy.**

• **Click on the slide.**

• **Choose Edit/Paste Special.**

• **Select Paste Link.**

Your screen should be similar to Figure 13

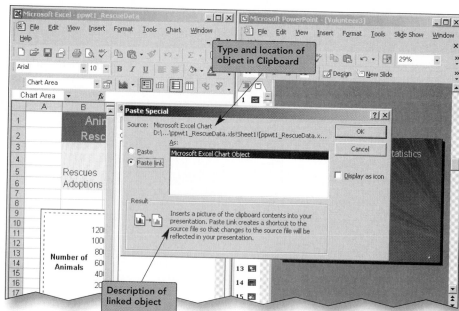

Figure 13

Again, from the As list box, you select the type of format in which you want the object inserted into the destination file. The only available option for this object is as a Microsoft Excel Chart Object. The Result area describes the effect of your selections. In this case, the object will be inserted as a picture, and a link will be created to the chart in the source file. Selecting the Display as Icon option changes the display of the object from a picture to an icon. Double-clicking the icon displays the object picture. The default selections are appropriate.

4 • **Click [OK].**

• **Appropriately size and center the linked object on the slide.**

• **Deselect the object.**

Your screen should be similar to Figure 14

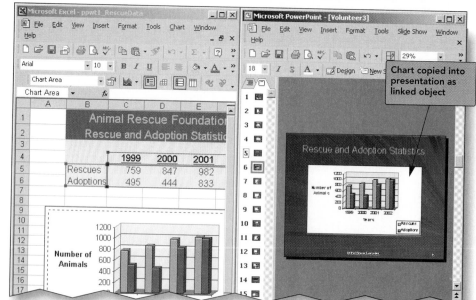

Figure 14

Updating a Linked Object

While looking at the chart in the slide, you decide to change the chart type from a column chart to a bar chart. You feel a bar chart will show the trends more clearly. You also notice the adoption data for 2000 looks very

Working Together: Copying, Embedding, and Linking Between Applications

www.mhhe.com/oleary

low. After checking the original information, you see you entered the wrong value in the worksheet and need to correct the value to 784.

To make these changes, you need to switch back to Excel. Double-clicking on a linked object quickly switches to the open source file. If the source file is not open, it opens the file for you. If the application is not started, it both starts the application and opens the source file.

1 ● **Double-click the chart object in the slide.**

> **Another Method**
> The menu equivalent is Edit/Linked Worksheet Object/Open.

● **In Excel, right-click on one of the columns in the chart and select Chart Type.**

> **Another Method**
> The menu equivalent is Chart/Chart Type.

● **Select Stacked Bar with a 3-D visual effect.**

● **Click** [OK].

● **Edit the value in cell D6 to 784.**

Your screen should be similar to Figure 15

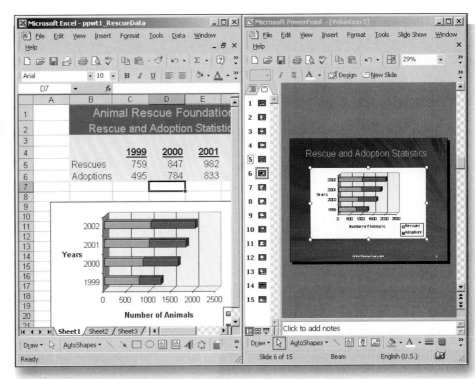

Figure 15

The chart type in both applications has changed to a bar chart, and the chart data series has been updated to reflect the change in data. This is because any changes you make in the chart in Excel will be automatically reflected in the linked chart in the slide.

2 ● **Untile the application windows.**

● **Save the revised workbook as** Rescue Data Linked**.**

● **Exit Excel.**

● **If necessary, maximize the PowerPoint window.**

● **Close the Picture toolbar.**

Editing Links

Whenever a document is opened that contains links, the application looks for the source file and automatically updates the linked objects. If there are many links, updating can take a lot of time. Additionally, if you move the source file to another location, or perform other operations that may interfere with the link, your link will not work. To help with situations like these, you can edit the settings associated with links. You will see how to do this, though you will not actually edit the settings.

1 ● **If necessary, select the chart object.**

● **Choose Edit/Links.**

Your screen should be similar to Figure 16

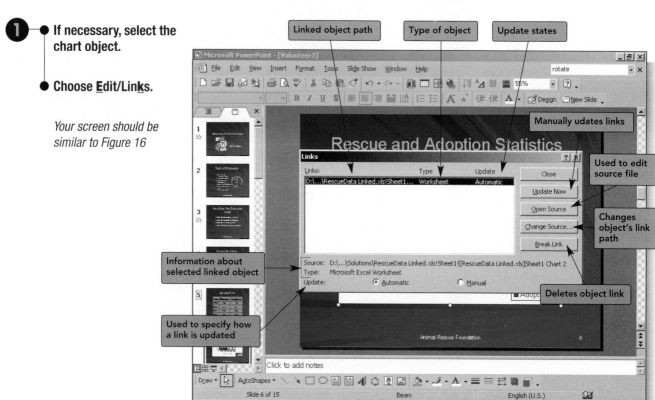

Figure 16

The Links dialog box list box displays information about all links in the document. This includes the path and name of the source file, the range of linked cells or object name, the type of file, and the update status. Below the list box the details for the selected link are displayed. The other options in this dialog box are described in the table on the next page.

Working Together: Copying, Embedding, and Linking Between Applications

Option	Effect
Automatic	Updates the linked object whenever the destination document is opened or the source file changes. This is the default.
Manual	The destination document is not automatically updated and you must use the Update Now command button to update the link.
Locked	Prevents a linked object from being updated.
Open Source	Opens the source document for the selected link
Change Source	Used to modify the path to the source document.
Break Link	Breaks the connection between the source document and the active document

You do not want to make any changes to the link.

2 — • **Click**  .

Linking documents is a very handy feature, particularly in documents whose information is updated frequently. If you include a linked object in a document that you are giving to another person, make sure the user has access to the source file and application. Otherwise the links will not operate correctly.

Printing Slides

Next you will print the two new slides.

1 ● **Use <u>V</u>iew/<u>H</u>eader and Footer to modify the slide footer to display your name on slides 6 and 14 only.**

> **HAVING TROUBLE?**
> Display the slide you want to modify, use the command, and click [<u>Apply</u>] to apply the new footer to the selected slide only.

● **Choose <u>F</u>ile/<u>P</u>rint.**

● **Specify slides 6 and 14 as the slides to print in the Slides text box.**

● **Specify Slides as the type of output.**

● **Preview the output and change the print to grayscale if necessary.**

● **Print the slides.**

● **Save the PowerPoint presentation as** Volunteer3 Linked **and exit PowerPoint.**

Your printed output should be similar to that shown here.

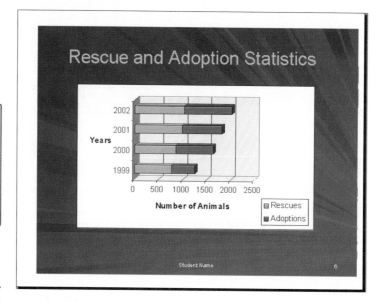

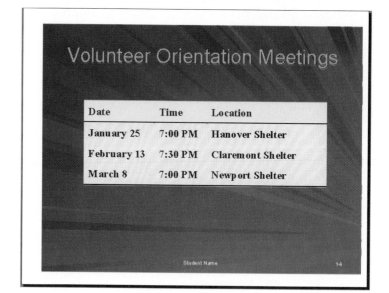

lab review

Working Together: Copying, Embedding, and Linking Between Applications

key terms

destination file   PPWT.4
linked object   PPWT.8
live link   PPWT.8
source file   PPWT.4

mous skills

The Microsoft Office User Specialist (MOUS) certification program is designed to measure your proficiency in performing basic tasks using the Office XP applications. Getting certified demonstrates that you have the skills and provides a valuable industry credential for employment. After completing this lab, you have learned the following Microsoft Office User Specialist skills:

Skill	Description	Page
Working with Data from Other Sources	Import Excel charts to slides	PPWT.8
	Insert Word tables on slides	PPWT.4
Printing Presentations	Preview and print slides	PPWT.14

command summary

Command	Action
Edit/Paste Special/ <Object>	Inserts a selection as an embedded object
Edit/Paste Special/Paste Link	Inserts a selection as an linked object
Edit/Links	Changes settings associated with linked objects
Edit/Linked Object/Open	Opens source application of linked object

Hands-On Exercises

step-by-step

rating system

★ Easy

★★ Moderate

★★★ Difficult

Embedding a Table of Blowout Indicators

★★ **1.** To complete this problem, you must have completed Step-by-Step Exercise 3 in Lab 2. The Blowouts section for the Department of Safety presentation is almost complete. You just need to add some information to the presentation about the indicators of a flat tire. This information is already in a Word document as a table. You will copy and embed it into a new slide. The completed slide is shown here.

a. Start Word and open the ppwt1_BlowoutSigns.

b. Start PowerPoint and open the Blowouts2 presentation.

c. Add a new slide after slide 3 using the Title Only layout.

d. Copy the title from the Word document into the slide title placeholder.

e. Copy the table into the slide as an embedded object. Exit Word.

f. Size and position the object on the slide appropriately.

g. Edit the table to change the table headings to left-aligned and bold.

h. Save the presentation as Blowouts3.

i. Print the new slide.

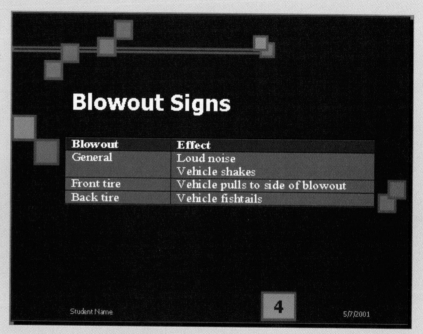

Linking a Table of Coffee Prices

2. To complete this problem, you must have completed Step-by-Step Exercise 4 in Lab 2. Evan, owner of the Downtown Internet Cafe, wants you to include information about special prices on coffee beans in the coffee slide show you created. You will link the coffee price information to the presentation, because the prices change frequently with market conditions and good buys. The completed slide is shown here.

a. Start Word and open the document ppwt1_CoffeePrices.

b. Start PowerPoint and open the presentation Coffee.

c. Add a new slide at the end of the presentation using the Title Only layout.

d. Enter the slide title **. . . Or Take Some Home**.

e. Copy the table of prices into the slide as a linked object.

f. Size and position the object appropriately.

g. In the Word document, change the price of the Kenyan blend to **$9.95**.

h. Save the Word document as Coffee Prices Linked. Exit Word.

i. Save the PowerPoint presentation as Coffee Show Linked.

j. Print the new slide.

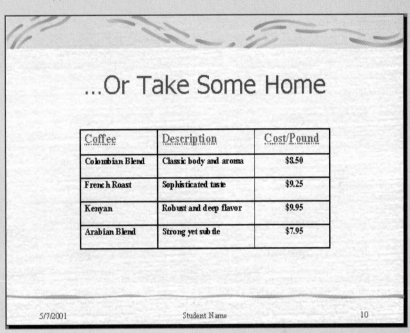

...Or Take Some Home

Coffee	Description	Cost/Pound
Colombian Blend	Classic body and aroma	$8.50
French Roast	Sophisticated taste	$9.25
Kenyan	Robust and deep flavor	$9.95
Arabian Blend	Strong yet subtle	$7.95

5/7/2001   Student Name   10

Lab Exercises   **PPWT.17**

PowerPoint 2002

Linking a Worksheet on Energy Use

★★ **3.** To complete this problem, you must have completed Step-by-Step Exercise 5 of Lab 2. Tim has found some interesting data and wants to include this information in his lecture presentation. The completed slide is shown here.

    a. Start PowerPoint and open the Workplace Issues2 presentation.

    b. Start Excel and open the ppwt1_EnergyUse worksheet.

    c. Add a new slide after slide 10 using the Title Only layout.

    d. Copy the title from cell A3 and A4 into the title placeholder for slide 11. Remove blank lines and spaces. Reapply the slide layout.

    e. Copy the worksheet range A5 through D8 as a linked object into slide 11. Size and position it appropriately.

    f. You notice that the percentage for use of a monitor in the year 2000 seems low. After checking the original source, you see you entered the value incorrectly. In Excel, change the value in cell C7 to **11%**.

    g. Save the worksheet as EnergyUse Linked. Exit Excel.

    h. Save the presentation as Workplace Issues2 Linked.

    i. Print the new slide.

Word Command Summary

Command	Shortcut	Button	Action
File/New	Ctrl + N	◻	Opens new document
File/Open	Ctrl + O	📂	Opens existing document file
File/Close	Ctrl + F4	✕	Closes document file
File/Save	Ctrl + S	💾	Saves document using same file name
File/Save As			Saves document using a new file name, type and/or location
File/Save as Web Page			Saves file as a Web page document
File/Web Page Preview			Previews Web page in browser window
File/Page Setup			Changes layout of page including margins, paper size, and paper source
File/Page Setup/Layout/Vertical Alignment			Aligns text vertically on a page
File/Print Preview		🔍	Displays document as it will appear when printed
File/Print	Ctrl + P	🖨	Prints document using selected print settings
File/Exit	Alt + F4	✕	Exits Word program
Edit/Undo	Ctrl + Z	↺ ▾	Restores last editing change
Edit/Redo	Ctrl + Y	↻ ▾	Restores last Undo or repeats last command or action
Edit/Cut	Ctrl + X	✂	Cuts selected text and copies it to Clipboard
Edit/Copy	Ctrl + C	📋	Copies selected text to Clipboard
Edit/Paste	Ctrl + V	📋	Pastes text from Clipboard
Edit/Select All	Ctrl + A		Selects all text in document
Edit/Find	Ctrl + F		Locates specified text
Edit/Replace	Ctrl + H		Locates and replaces specified text
View/Normal		▤	Displays document in Normal view
View/Web Layout		▣	Shows document as it will appear when viewed in a Web browser
View/Print Layout		▣	Shows how text and objects will appear on the printed page
View/Outline		▤	Shows structure of document
View/Task Pane			Displays or hides task pane
View/Toolbars			Displays or hides selected toolbar
View/Ruler			Displays or hides horizontal ruler

Command	Shortcut	Button	Action
View/Show Paragraph Marks			Displays or hides paragraph marks
View/Document Map		🔍	Displays or hides Document Map pane.
View/Header and Footer			Displays header and footer areas
View/Footnotes			Hides or displays note pane
View/Zoom		100% ▾	Changes onscreen character size
View/Zoom/Page width			Fits display of document within right and left margins
View/Zoom/Whole Page			Displays entire page onscreen
View/Zoom/Many Pages			Displays two or more pages in document window
View/HTML Source			Displays HTML source code
Insert/Break/Page break	Ctrl + ←Enter		Inserts hard page break
Insert/Page Numbers			Specifies page number location
Insert/Date and Time			Inserts current date or time, maintained by computer system, in selected format
Insert/AutoText			Enters predefined text
Insert/AutoText/AutoText/ Show			Turns on AutoText feature
AutoComplete suggestions Insert/Reference/Footnote	Alt + Ctrl + F		Inserts footnote reference at insertion point
Insert/Reference/Caption			Inserts caption at insertion point
Insert/Reference/Cross-reference			Inserts cross-reference at insertion point
Insert/Reference/Index and Tables/ Table of Contents			Inserts table of contents
Insert/Picture/Clip Art			Inserts selected clip art at insertion point
Insert/Picture/From File			Inserts selected picture into document
Insert/Picture/AutoShapes		AutoShapes ▾	Inserts selected AutoShape
Insert/Hyperlink	Ctrl + K	🌐	Inserts hyperlink in Web page
Format/Font/Font/Font		Times New Roman ▾	Changes typeface
Format/Font/Font/Size		12 ▾	Changes type size
Format/Font/Font/Color		A	Changes type color
Format/Font/Font/Font Style/Italic	Ctrl + I	I	Makes selected text italic
Format/Font/Font/Font Style/Bold	Ctrl + B	B	Makes selected text bold
Format/Font/Font/ Underline style/Single	Ctrl + U	U	Underlines selected text
Format/Paragraph/Indents and Spacing/Special/First Line			Indents first line of paragraph from right margin
Format/Paragraph/Indents and Spacing/Alignment/Left	Ctrl + L	▤	Aligns text to left margin
Format/Paragraph/Indents and Spacing/Alignment/Centered	Ctrl + E	▤	Centers text between left and right margins
Format/Paragraph/Indents and Spacing/Alignment/Right	Ctrl + R	▤	Aligns text to right margin

Command	Shortcut	Button	Action
Format/Paragraph/Indents and Spacing/Alignment/Justified	Ctrl + J	⬛	Aligns text equally between left and right margins
Format/Paragraph/Indents and Spacing/Alignment/Line Spacing			Changes amount of space between lines
Format/Theme			Applies a predesigned theme to Web page
Format/Style		Normal ▾	Applies selected style to paragraph or characters
Format/Picture/Layout/Wrapping style			Specifies how text will wrap around picture
Format/Bullets and Numbering		≣ ≣	Creates a bulleted or numbered list
Format/Tabs			Specifies types and position of tab stops
Format/Styles and Formatting			Opens Styles and Formatting task pane
Format/Reveal Formatting			Opens Reveal Formatting task pane
Tools/Spelling and Grammar	F7	✓	Starts Spelling and Grammar tool
Tools/Language/Thesaurus	Shift + F7		Starts Thesaurus tool
Tools/AutoCorrect Options/ Show AutoCorrect Options			Displays or hides AutoCorrect options
Tools/Customize/Options/Show Standard and Formatting toolbars on two rows			Displays Standard and Formatting toolbars on two rows
Tools/Options/Edit/Overtype mode	Ins	OVR	Switches between Insert and Overtype modes
Tools/Options/View/All		¶	Displays or hides formatting marks
Tools/Options/View/ScreenTips			Turns off and on the display of screen tips
Tools/Options/View/All	Ctrl + Shift	¶	Displays or hides special characters
Tools/Options/Edit/Overtype mode		OVR	Switches between insert and overtype modes
Tools/Options/Spelling & Grammar			Changes settings associated with the Spelling and Grammar checking feature
Table/Insert Table		▦	Inserts table at insertion point
Table/Insert/Row Above			Inserts a new row in table above the selected row
Table/Table AutoFormat			Applies selected format to table
Table/Convert/Text to Table			Converts selected text to table format
Table/Sort			Rearranges items in a selection into sorted order
Help/Microsoft Word Help		?	Opens Help window

Excel Command Summary

Command	Shortcut	Button	Action
File/Open <file name>	Ctrl + O		Opens an existing workbook file
File/Close		X	Closes open workbook file
File/Save <file name>	Ctrl + S		Saves current file on disk using same file name
File/Save As <file name>			Saves current file on disk using a new file name
File/Send to/Mail Recipient			Sends the active document to the e-mail recipient.
File/Page Setup/Page/Landscape			Changes orientation to landscape
File/Page Setup/Header/Footer			Adds header and/or footer
File/Print Preview			Displays worksheet as it will appear when printed
File/Print	Ctrl + P		Prints a worksheet
File/Print/Entire Workbook			Prints all the sheets in a workbook
File/Properties			Displays information about a file
File/Exit		X	Exits Excel 2000
Edit/Undo	Ctrl + Z		Undoes last editing or formatting change
Edit/Redo	Ctrl + Y		Restores changes after using Undo
Edit/Copy	Ctrl + C		Copies selected data to Clipboard
Edit/Paste	Ctrl + V		Pastes selections stored in Clipboard
Edit/Paste Special			Inserts the object as an embedded object
Edit/Paste Special/Paste Link			Creates a link to the source document
Edit/Links			Modifies selected link
Edit/Linked Object/Edit Link			Modifies selected linked object
Edit/Fill			Fills selected cells with contents of source cell
Edit/Clear/Contents	Delete		Clears cell contents
Edit/Delete/Entire row			Deletes selected rows
Edit/Delete/Entire column			Deletes selected columns
Edit/Move or Copy Sheet			Moves or copies selected sheet
View/Toolbars			Displays or hides selected toolbar
View/Zoom		100%	Changes magnification of window
Insert/Copied Cells			Inserts row and copies text from Clipboard

Command	Shortcut	Button	Action
Insert/Rows			Inserts a blank row
Insert/Columns			Inserts a blank column
Insert/Chart		🔲	Inserts chart into worksheet
Insert/Function	⇧Shift + F3	ƒ×	Inserts a function
Insert/Picture/From File			Inserts picture at insertion point from disk
Format/Cells/Number/Currency			Applies Currency format to selection
Format/Cells/Number/Accounting		$	Applies Accounting format to selection
Format/Cells/Number/Date			Applies Date format to selection
Format/Cells/Number/Percent		%	Applies Percent format to selection
Format/Cells/Number/Decimal places		.00 / .00	Increases or decreases the number of decimal places associated with a number value
Format/Cells/Alignment/ Horizontal/ Left (Indent)		▤	Left-aligns entry in cell space
Format/Cells/Alignment/ Horizontal/Center		▤	Center-aligns entry in cell space
Format/Cells/Alignment/ Horizontal/Right		▤	Right-aligns entry in cell space
Format/Cells/Alignment/Indent/1		▤	Indents cell entry one space
Format/Cells/Alignment/ Horizontal/Center Across Selection		▦	Centers cell contents across selected cells
Format/Cells/Font			Changes font and attributes of cell contents
Format/Cells/Font/Font Style/Bold	Ctrl + B	B	Bolds selected text
Format/Cells/Font/Font Style/Italic	Ctrl + I	I	Italicizes selected text
Format/Cells/Font/Underline/Single	Ctrl + U	U	Underlines selected text
Format/Cells/Font/Color		A ▾	Adds color to text
Format/Cells/Patterns/Color		♦ ▾	Adds color to cell background
Format/Row/Height			Changes height of selected row
Format/Column/Width			Changes width of columns
Format/Column/AutoFit Selection			Changes column width to match widest cell entry
Format/Sheet/Rename			Renames sheet
Format/Style			Applies selected style to selection
Format/Style/Style name/Currency			Applies currency style to selection
Format/Style/Style name/Percent		%	Changes cell style to display percentage
Format/Selected Data Series/ Data Labels	Ctrl + 1		Inserts data labels into chart
Format/Selected Legend	Ctrl + 1	▤	Changes legend
Format/Selected Chart Title	Ctrl + 1	▤	Changes format of selected chart title

Command	Shortcut	Button	Action
Format/Selected Data Series	Ctrl + 1	▣	Changes format of selected data series
Format/Selected Object		▣	Changes format of embedded objects
Chart/Chart Type		▣ ▾	Changes type of chart
Chart/Chart Options			Adds options to chart
Chart/Location			Moves chart from worksheet to chart sheet
Tools/Spelling	F7	▣	Spell-checks worksheet
Tools/Goal Seek			Adjusts value in specified cell until a formula dependent on that cell reaches specified result
Tools/Formula Auditing/ Show Watch Window			Opens the Watch Window toolbar
Window/Unfreeze Panes			Unfreezes window panes
Window/Freeze Panes			Freezes top and/or leftmost panes
Window/Split			Divides window into four panes at active cell
Window/Remove Split			Removes split bar from active worksheet

Access Command Summary

Command	Shortcut	Button	Action
File/New	Ctrl + N	▯	Opens New File task pane
File/Open	Ctrl + O	▱	Opens an existing database
File/Close		✕	Closes open window
File/Save	Ctrl + S	▤	Saves database object
File/Page Setup/		Setup	Sets page margins and page layout for printed output
File/Print/Pages/From			Prints selected pages
File/Print Preview		▣	Displays file as it will appear when printed
File/Print	Ctrl + P	▤	Specifies print settings and prints current database object
File/Exit		✕	Closes Access
Edit/Undo	Ctrl + Z	↰	Cancels last action
Edit/Cut	Ctrl + X	✂ or ✄	Removes selected item and copies it to the Clipboard
Edit/Copy	Ctrl + C	▤	Duplicates selected item and copies to the Clipboard
Edit/Paste	Ctrl + V	▤	Inserts copy of item in Clipboard
Edit/Select Record			Selects current record
Edit/Select All Records	Ctrl + A		Selects all controls on a form
Edit/Find	Ctrl + F	▨	Locates specified data
Edit/Replace	Ctrl + H		Locates and replaces specified data
Edit/Delete Rows		⮕	Deletes selected field in Design view
Edit/Primary Key		▦	Defines a field as a primary key field
Edit/Clear Grid			Clears query grid
View/Design View		▨ ▾	Displays Design view
View/Datasheet View		▦ ▾	Displays table in Datasheet view
View/Form View			Displays a form in Form view
View/Toolbars/Task Pane			Displays task pane
View/Zoom/%		Fit ▾	Displays previewed database object at specified percentage
Insert/Rows		⮨	Inserts a new field in table in Design view

Command	Shortcut	Button	Action
Insert/Column			Inserts a new field in a table in Datasheet view
Insert/Object			Inserts an object into current field
Insert/Report			Creates a new report object
Filter/Apply Filter/Sort	▽		Applies filter to table
Query/Run	!		Displays query results in Query Datasheet view
Query/Show Table			Displays Show Table dialog box
Format/Column Width			Changes width of table columns in Datasheet view
Format/Column Width/Best Fit			Sizes selected columns to accommodate longest entry or column header
Format/Hide Columns			Hides columns
Format/Unhide Columns			Redisplays hidden columns
Records/Remove Filter/Sort			Displays all records in table
Records/Data Entry			Hides existing records and displays Data Entry window
Records/Sort/Sort Ascending	↓		Reorders records in ascending alphabetical order
View/Toolbox	⚒		Displays/Hides Toolbox
View/Zoom/%			Displays previewed document at specified percentage
View/Zoom/Fit to Window			Displays entire previewed document page
View/Pages			Displays specified number of pages of previewed document
Records/Filter/Filter by Form			Displays blank datasheet for entering criteria to display specific information
Records/Filter/Filter by Selection			Displays only records that contain a specific value
Records/Apply Filter/Sort	▽		Applies filter to table
Tools/Relationships			Defines permanent relationship between tables
Tools/Database Utilities/ Compact and Repair Database			Displays blank datasheet for entering criteria to display specific information
Window/Database			Displays selected window
			Displays Database window

PowerPoint Command Summary

Command	Shortcut	Button	Action
File/New	Ctrl + N	▯	Creates new presentation
File/Open	Ctrl + O	▣	Opens selected presentation
File/Close		▣	Closes presentation
File/Save	Ctrl + S	▣	Saves presentation
File/Save As			Saves presentation using new file name
File/Print Preview		▣	Displays a preview of selected output
File/Print	Ctrl + P	▣	Prints presentation using default print settings
File/Properties			Displays statistics and stores documentation about file
File/Exit		▣	Exits PowerPoint program
Edit/Undo	Ctrl + Z	↺▾	Undoes the last action
Edit/Paste Special			Inserts a selection as an embedded object
Edit/Paste Special/Paste Link			Inserts a selection as a linked object
Edit/Select All	Ctrl + A		Selects all slides in presentation, all text and graphics in active window, or all text in selected object
Edit/Delete Slide	Delete		Deletes selected slide
Edit/Find	Ctrl + F		Finds selected text
Edit/Replace	Ctrl + H		Replaces selected text
Edit/Links			Changes settings associated with linked objects
Edit/Linked Object/Open			Opens the source application of the linked object
View/Normal		▣	Displays current slide in Normal view
View/Slide Sorter		▣	Switches to Slide Sorter view
View/Slide Show	F5	▣	Runs slide show
View/Notes Page			Displays notes pages
View/Master/Slide Master	⇧ Shift + ▣		Displays the slide and title masters for the current presentation
View/Task Pane			Displays or hides task pane
View/Toolbars			Displays or hides toolbars
View/Ruler			Turns on/off display of the ruler

Command	Shortcut	Button	Action
View/**H**eader and Footer			Specifies information that appears as headers and footers on slides, notes, outlines, and handout pages
Insert/**N**ew Slide	Ctrl + M	📧	Inserts new slide
Insert/**D**uplicate Slide			Inserts duplicate of selected slide
Insert/**P**icture/**C**lip Art		🖼	Inserts selected clip art
Insert/**P**icture/**F**rom File			Inserts picture from file on disk
Insert/**P**icture/**A**utoShapes			Inserts an AutoShape object
Insert/Te**x**t box		🔳	Adds a text box object
F**o**rmat/**F**ont/**F**ont		Times New Roman ▾	Changes font typeface
F**o**rmat/**F**ont/F**o**nt Style/Bold	Alt + B	**B**	Adds bold effect to selection
F**o**rmat/**F**ont/F**o**nt Style/Italic	Alt + I	*I*	Adds italic effect to selection
F**o**rmat/**F**ont/**S**ize		24 ▾	Changes font size
F**o**rmat/**F**ont/**C**olor		**A** ▾	Adds color to selected text
Format/Bullets and Numbering		☰ ☰	Applies/removes selected bullet or numbering style
F**o**rmat/**A**lignment/Align **L**eft	Ctrl + L	☰	Left-aligns selection
F**o**rmat/**A**lignment/**C**enter	Ctrl + E	☰	Center-aligns selection
F**o**rmat/**A**lignment/Align **R**ight	Ctrl+R	☰	Right-aligns selection
F**o**rmat/**A**lignment/**J**ustify	Ctrl + J	☰	Justifies selection
F**o**rmat/Slide **L**ayout			Changes or creates a slide layout
F**o**rmat/Slide **D**esign			Applies selected design template to one or all slides in a presentation
Tools/**S**pelling and Grammar	F7	✓	Spell and grammar checks presentation
Tools/**O**ptions/Spelling and Style/Check Style			Checks presentation style
Slide Show/Animation S**c**hemes		No Effect ▾	Adds predesigned builds to selected slides
Slide Show/Slide **T**ransition		📧	Adds transition effects
Slide Show /**H**ide Slide		🔲	Hides selected slide
Slide Show Shortcut Menu			
Go/By **T**itle	H		Displays hidden slide
Go/Slide **N**avigator			Move to specified slide
S**c**reen/**B**lack	B		Blacks out/redisplays screen
S**c**reen/**E**rase	E		Erases freehand annotations
P**o**inter Options/**A**utomatic			Sets pointer to an arrow and hides after 15 seconds of non-use
P**o**inter Options/**P**en	Ctrl + P		Turns on freehand annotation

Word Glossary of Key Terms

active document   The document containing the insertion point and that will be affected by any changes you make.

alignment   The positioning of paragraphs between the margins: left, right, centered, or justified.

antonym   A word with the opposite meaning.

author   The process of designing and creating a Web page.

AutoComplete   A feature that recognizes commonly used words or phrases and can automatically complete them for you if chosen.

AutoCorrect   A feature that makes basic assumptions about the text you are typing and automatically corrects the entry.

AutoFormat   The feature that makes certain formatting changes automatically to your document.

automatic grammar check   The feature that advises you of incorrect grammar as you create and edit a document, and proposes possible corrections.

automatic spelling check   The feature that advises you of misspelled words as you create and edit a document, and proposes possible corrections.

AutoShape   A ready-made shape that is supplied with Word.

AutoText   A feature that provides commonly used words or phrases that you can select and quickly insert into a document.

browser   A program that connects to remote computers and displays Web pages.

bulleted list   Displays items that logically fall out from a paragraph into a list, with items preceded by bullets.

caption   A title or explanation for a table, picture, or graph.

case sensitive   The capability to distinguish between uppercase and lowercase characters.

cell   The intersection of a column and row where data is entered in a table.

character formatting   Formatting features, such as bold and color, that affect the selected characters only.

Character style   A combination of any character formats that affect selected text.

clip art   A collection of graphics that is usually bundled with a software application.

cross-reference   A reference in one part of a document to related information in another part.

cursor   The blinking vertical bar that shows you where the next character you type will appear. Also called the insertion point.

custom dictionary   A dictionary of terms you have entered that are not in the main dictionary of the Spelling Checker.

default   The initial Word document settings that can be changed to customize documents.

destination   The location to which text is moved or copied.

Document Map   Displays the headings in the document.

document window   The area of the application window that displays the contents of the open document.

drag and drop   A mouse procedure that moves or copies a selection to a new location.

drawing layer   The layer above or below the text layer where floating objects are inserted.

drawing object   A simple object consisting of shapes such as lines and boxes.

edit   The process of changing and correcting existing text in a document.

embedded object   An object, such as a picture graphic, that becomes part of the Word document and that can be opened and edited using the program in which it was created.

endnote   A reference note displayed at the end of the document.

end-of-file marker   The horizontal line that marks the end of a file.

field   A placeholder code that instructs Word to insert information in a document.

field code The code containing the instructions about the type of information to insert in a field.

field results The results displayed in a field according to the instructions in the field code.

floating object A graphic object that is inserted into the drawing layer and which can be positioned anywhere on the page.

font A set of characters with a specific design. Also called a typeface.

font size The height and width of a character, commonly measured in points.

footer The line or several lines of text at the bottom of every page just below the bottom margin line.

footnote A reference note displayed at the bottom of the page on which the reference occurs.

format To enhance the appearance of the document to make it more readable or attractive.

Format Painter The feature that applies formats associated with the current selection to new selections.

formatting marks Symbols that are automatically inserted into a document as you enter and edit text and that control the appearance of the document.

Formatting toolbar The toolbar that contains buttons representing the most frequently used text-editing and text-layout features.

frame A division of a window that can be scrolled separately.

global template The normal document template whose settings are available to all documents.

graphic A non-text element in a document.

hard page break A manually inserted page break that instructs Word to begin a new page regardless of the amount of text on the previous page.

header The line or several lines of text at the top of each page just above the top margin line.

heading style A style that is designed to identify different levels of headings in a document.

HTML (Hypertext Markup Language) A programming language used to create Web pages.

hyperlink A connection to locations in the current document, other documents, or Web pages. Clicking a hyperlink jumps to the specified location.

inline object An object that is inserted directly in the text at the position of the insertion point, becoming part of the paragraph.

Insert mode Method of text entry in which new characters are inserted into existing text, which moves to the right to make space for the new characters; the text on the line is reformatted as necessary.

insertion point The blinking vertical bar that shows you where the next character you type will appear on the line. Also called the cursor.

leader characters Solid, dotted, or dashed lines that fill the blank space between tab stops.

line spacing The vertical space between lines of text.

main dictionary The dictionary of terms that comes with Word 2002.

menu Method used to tell a program what you want it to do.

menu bar A bar that displays the menu names that can be selected.

Normal template The document template that is opened when you start Word.

note pane Lower portion of the window that displays footnotes.

note reference mark A superscript number or character appearing in the document at the end of the material being referenced.

note separator The horizontal line separating footnote text from main document text.

note text The text in a footnote.

numbered list Displays items that convey a sequence of events in a particular order, with items preceded by numbers or letters.

object An item that can be sized, moved, and manipulated.

outlined numbered list Displays items in multiple outline levels that show a hierarchical structure of the items in the list.

Overtype mode Method of text entry in which new text types over the existing characters.

page break Marks the point at which one page ends and another begins.

page margin The blank space around the edge of the page.

pane A split portion of the document window that can be scrolled independently.

paragraph formatting Formatting features, such as alignment, indentation, and line spacing, that affect an entire paragraph.

paragraph style A combination of any character formats and paragraph formats that affect all text in a paragraph.

picture An illustration such as a scanned photograph.

point Measure used for height of type; one point equals 1/72 inch.

ruler The ruler located below the Formatting toolbar that shows the line length in inches.

sans serif font A font, such as Arial or Helvetica, that does not have a flair at the base of each letter.

scroll bar A window element located on the right or bottom window border that lets you display text that is not currently visible in the window. It contains scroll arrows and a scroll box.

section A division into which a document can be divided that can be formatted separately from the rest of the document.

section break Marks the point at which one section ends and another begins.

section cursor A colored highlight bar that appears over the selected command in a menu.

select To highlight text.

selection rectangle The rectangular outline around an object that indicates it is selected.

serif font A font, such as Times New Roman, that has a flair at the base of each letter.

shortcut menu A menu of the most common menu options that is displayed by right-clicking on the selected item.

sizing handles Black squares around a selected object that can be used to size the object.

SmartTag A feature that recognizes data such as names, addresses, telephone numbers, dates, times, and places as a particular type. The recognized item can then be quickly added to a Microsoft Outlook feature.

soft page break A page break automatically inserted by Word to start a new page when the previous page has been filled with text or graphics.

soft space A space automatically entered by Word to align the text properly on a single line.

sort To arrange alphabetically or numerically in ascending or descending order.

source The location from which text is moved or copied.

source program The program in which an object was created.

Standard toolbar The toolbar that contains buttons for the most frequently used commands.

status bar A bar displayed at the bottom of the document window that advises you of the status of different program conditions and features as you use the program.

style A set of formats that is assigned a name.

synonym A word with a similar meaning.

tab stop A marked location on the horizontal ruler that indicates how far to indent text when the [Tab] key is pressed.

table Displays information in horizontal rows and vertical columns.

table reference The letter and number (for example, A1) that identify a cell in a table.

tag An HTML code embedded in a Web page document that supplies information about the page's structure.

task pane A pane that provides quick access to features as you are using them.

template A document file that includes predefined settings that can be used as a pattern to create many common types of documents.

theme Predesigned Web page effects that can be applied to a Web page to enhance its appearance.

Thesaurus Word feature that provides synonyms and antonyms for words.

thumbnail A miniture representation of a picture.

toolbar A bar of buttons commonly displayed below the menu bar. The buttons are shortcuts for many of the most common menu commands.

TrueType A font that is automatically installed when you install Windows.

typeface A set of characters with a specific design. Also called a font.

URL The address that indicates the location of a document on the World Wide Web. URL stands for Uniform Resource Locator.

Web page A document that uses HTML to display in a browser.

word wrap A feature that automatically determines where to end a line and wrap text to the next line based on the margin settings.

Excel Glossary of Key Terms

3-D reference: A reference to the same cell or range on multiple sheets in the same workbook.

absolute reference: A cell or range reference in a formula whose location remains the same (absolute) when copied. Indicated by a $ character entered before the column letter or row number or both.

active cell: The cell displaying the cell selector that will be affected by the next entry or procedure.

active pane: The pane that contains the cell selector.

active sheet: A sheet that contains the cell selector and that will be affected by the next action.

adjacent range: A rectangular block of adjoining cells.

alignment: The vertical or horizontal placement and orientation of an entry in a cell.

area chart: A chart that shows trends by emphasizing the area under the curve.

argument: The data used in a function on which the calculation is performed.

AutoFill: Feature that logically repeats and extends a series.

AutoFormat: A built-in combination of formats that can be applied to a range.

automatic recalculation: The recalculation of a formula within the worksheet whenever a value in a referenced cell in the formula changes.

category-axis: Another name for the X-axis of a chart.

category-axis title: A label that describes the X-axis.

category name: Labels displayed along the X-axis in a chart to identify the data being plotted.

cell: The space created by the intersection of a vertical column and a horizontal row.

cell selector: The heavy border surrounding a cell in the worksheet that identifies the active cell.

chart: A visual representation of data in a worksheet.

chart gridlines: Lines extending from the axis lines across the plot area that make it easier to read and evaluate the chart data.

chart object: One type of graphic object that is created using charting features included in Excel 2002. A chart object can be inserted into a worksheet or into a special chart sheet.

chart title: Appears at the top of a chart and is used to describe the contents of the chart.

ClipArt: A collection of graphics that is usually bundled with a software application.

column: A vertical block of cells one cell wide in the worksheet.

column letters: The border of letters across the top of the worksheet that identifies the columns in the worksheet.

combination chart: A chart type that includes mixed data markers, such as both columns and lines.

constant: A value that does not change unless you change it directly by typing in another entry.

copy area: The cell or cells containing the data to be copied.

custom dictionary: An additional dictionary you create to supplement the main dictionary.

data labels: Labels for data points or bars that show the values being plotted on a chart.

data marker: Represents a data series on a chart. It can be a symbol, color, or pattern, depending upon the type of chart.

data series: The numbers to be charted.

date numbers: The integers assigned to the days from January 1, 1900, through December 31, 2099, that allow dates to be used in calculations.

destination: The cell or range of cells that receives the data from the copy area or source.

destination file: A document in which a linked object is inserted.

drawing object: Object consisting of shapes such as lines and boxes that can be created using features on the Drawing toolbar.

embedded chart: A chart that is inserted into another file.

embedded object: Information inserted into a destination file of another application that becomes part of this file but can be edited within the destination file using the server application.

explode: To separate a wedge of a pie chart slightly from the other wedges in the pie.

fill handle: A small black square located in the lower-right corner of the selection that is used to create a series or copy to adjacent cells with a mouse.

font: The typeface, type size, and style associated with a worksheet entry that can be selected to improve the appearance of the worksheet.

footer: A line (or several lines) of text that appears at the bottom of each page just above the bottom margin.

format: Formats are settings that affect the display of entries in a worksheet.

Formatting toolbar: A toolbar that contains buttons used to change the format of a worksheet.

formula: An entry that performs a calculation.

Formula bar: The bar near the top of the Excel window that displays the cell contents.

freeze: To fix in place on the screen specified rows or columns or both when scrolling.

function: A prewritten formula that performs certain types of calculations automatically.

Goal Seek: Tool used to find the value needed in one cell to attain a result you want in another cell.

graphic: A non-text element or object, such as a drawing or picture that can be added to a document.

group: An object that contains other objects.

header: A line (or several lines) of text that appears at the top of each page just below the top margin.

heading: Row and column entries that are used to create the structure of the worksheet and describe other worksheet entries.

landscape: The orientation of the printed document so that it prints sideways across the length of the page.

legend: A brief description of the symbols used in a chart that represent the data ranges.

line chart: A chart that represents data as a set of points along a line.

linked object: Information created in a source file from one application and inserted into a destination file of another application while maintaining a link between files.

live link: A linked object that automatically reflects in the destination document any changes made in the source document when the destination document is opened.

main dictionary: The dictionary included with Office XP.

margins: The blank space around the edge of the paper.

merged cell: A cell made up of several selected cells combined into one.

minimal recalculation: The recalculation of only the formulas in a worksheet that are affected by a change of data.

mixed reference: A cell address that is part absolute and part relative.

name box: The area located on the left side of the formula bar that provides information about the selected item such as the reference of the active cell.

nonadjacent range: Cells or ranges that are not adjacent but are included in the same selection.

number: A cell entry that contains any of the digits 0 to 9 and any of the special characters + = ( ) , . / $ % Σ =.

number formats: Affect how numbers look onscreen and when printed.

object: An element such as a text box that can be added to a workbook and that can be selected, sized, and moved.

operand: A value on which a numeric formula performs a calculation.

operator: Specify the type of calculation to be performed.

order of precedence: Order in which calculations are performed and can be overridden by the use of parentheses.

pane: A division of the worksheet window, either horizontal or vertical, through which different areas of the worksheet can be viewed at the same time.

paste area: The cells or range of cells that receive the data from the copy area or source.

picture: An illustration such as a scanned photograph.

pie chart: A chart that compares parts to the whole. Each value in the data range is a wedge of the pie (circle).

plot area: The area of the chart bounded by the axes.

portrait: The orientation of the printed document so that it prints across the width of the page.

range: A selection consisting of two or more cells in a worksheet.

reference: The column letter and row number of a cell.

relative reference: A cell or range reference that automatically adjusts to the new location in the worksheet when the formula is copied.

row: A horizontal block of cells one cell high in the worksheet.

row numbers: The border of numbers along the left side of the worksheet that identifies the rows in the worksheet.

sans serif font: A font, such as Arial or Helvetica, that does not have a flair at the base of each letter.

selection handles: Small boxes surrounding a selected object that are used to size the object.

selection rectangle: Border around selected object indicating it can be sized or moved.

series formula: A formula that links a chart object to the source worksheet.

serif font: A font, such as Times New Roman, that has a flair at the base of each letter.

sheet reference: Used in references to other worksheets and consists of the name of the sheet enclosed in quotes and is separated from the cell reference by an exclamation point.

sheet tab: On the bottom of the workbook window, the tabs where the sheet names appear.

sizing handle: Box used to size a selected object.

source: The cell or range of cells containing the data you want to copy.

source file: The document that stores the data for the linked object.

spell-checking: Feature that locates misspelled words and proposes corrections.

spreadsheet: A rectangular grid of rows and columns used to enter data.

stack: The order in which objects are added in layers to the worksheet.

stacked-column chart: A chart that displays the data values as columns stacked upon each other.

standard toolbar: A toolbar that contains buttons used to complete the most frequently used menu commands.

style: A named combination of formats that can be applied to a selection.

syntax: Rules of structure for entering all functions.

Tab scroll buttons: Located to the left of the sheet tabs, they are used to scroll sheet tabs right or left.

text: A cell entry that contains text, numbers, or any other special characters.

text box: A rectangular object in which you type text.

thumbnail: Miniature images displayed in the Clip Organizer.

title: In a chart, descriptive text that explains the contents of the chart.

typeface: The appearance and shape of characters. Some common typefaces are Roman and Courier.

value axis: Y axis of a chart that usually contains numerical values.

value axis title: A label that describes the values on the Y axis.

variable: The resulting value of a formula that changes if the data it depends on changes.

what-if analysis: A technique used to evaluate what effect changing one or more values in formulas has on other values in the worksheet.

word wrap: Feature that automatically determines when to begin the next line of text.

workbook: The file in which you work and store sheets created in Excel 2002.

workbook window: A window that displays an open workbook file.

worksheet: Similar to a financial spreadsheet in that it is a rectangular grid of rows and columns used to enter data.

X-axis: The bottom boundary line of a chart.

Y-axis: The left boundary line of a chart.

Z axis: The left boundary line of a 3-D chart.

Access Glossary of Key Terms

action query   Query used to make changes to multiple records in one operation.

AutoReport Wizard   Creates a report, either tabular or columnar, based on a table or query, and adds all fields to the report.

Best Fit   A feature that automatically adjusts column width to fit the longest entry.

bound control   A control that is linked to a field in an underlying table.

bound object   A graphic object that is stored in a table and connected to a specific record and field.

cell   The space created by the intersection of a vertical column and a horizontal row.

character string   A group of characters. [Au: Expand definition? See p. 2-11]

clip art   A collection of simple drawings that is usually included with a software program. [Au: Definition from PP 2000. Pick up from Word or PP 2002 if necessary.]

column selector bar   In Query Design view, the thin gray bar just above the field name in the grid.

column width   The size of a field column in Datasheet view. It controls the amount of data you can see on the screen.

common field   A field that is found in two or more tables. It must have the same data type and the same kind of information in each table, but may have different field names.

compact   The database makes a copy of the file and rearranges how the file is stored on disk foroptimal performance.

comparison operator   A symbol used in expressions that allows you to make comparisons. The > (greater than) and < (less than) symbols are examples of comparison operators.

control   An object in a form or report that displays, information, performs actions, or enhances the design.

criteria   A set of limiting conditions.

criteria expression   An expression that will select only the records that meet certain limiting criteria.

crosstab query   Summarizes large amounts of data in an easy-to-read, row-and-column format.

current record   The record, containing the insertion point, that will be affected by the next action.

database   An organized collection of related information.

Database toolbar   Toolbar that contains buttons that are used to enter and edit data.

datasheet   Data from a table that is displayed in row and column format.

Datasheet form   A form layout that is similar to a table datasheet, in that information is displayed in rows and columns.

data type   Attribute for a field that determines what type of data it can contain.

design grid   The lower part of the Query Design window, which displays settings that are used to define the query.

destination file   The document in which a linked object is inserted.

drawing object   A simple graphic consisting of shapes such as lines and boxes that can be created using a drawing program such as Paint.

expression   Description of acceptable values in a validity check, which can contain any combination of the following elements operators, identifiers, and values.

field A single category of data in a table, the values of which appear in a column of a datasheet.

field list A small window that lists all fields in an underlying table.

field name Label used to identify the data stored in a field.

field property An attribute of a field that affects its appearance or behavior.

field selector A small gray box or bar in datasheets and queries that can be clicked to select the entire column. The field selector usually contains the field names.

field size Field property that limits a text data type to a certain size or limits numeric data to values within a specific range.

filter A restriction placed on records in an open form or datasheet to temporarily isolate a subset of records.

Filter by Form A method that filters records based on multiple criteria that are entered into a blank datasheet.

Filter by Selection A type of filter that displays only records containing a specific value.

form A database object used primarily to display records onscreen to make it easier to enter and make changes to records.

graphic A non-text element or object, such as a drawing or picture, which can be added to a table.

identifier A part of an expression that refers to the value of a field, a graphic object, or property.

join Creates a relationship between tables by linking common fields in multiple tables.

join line In the Query Design window, the line that joins the common fields between one or more table field lists.

landscape Printing orientation that prints a report across the length of the page.

linked object An object that is pasted into another application. The data is stored in the source document, and a graphic representation of the data is displayed in the destination document.

live link A link in which, when the source document is edited, the changes are automatically reflected in the destination document.

margin The blank space around the edge of a page.

move handle The large box in the upper left corner of a selected control that is used to move the control.picture An illustration such as a scanned photograph.

multitable query A query that uses more than one table.

navigation buttons Used to move through records in Datasheet and Form views. Also available in the Print Preview window.

Navigation mode In Datasheet view, when the entire field is highlighted.

object A table, form, or report that can be selected and manipulated as a unit.

operator A symbol or word used to perform an operation.

orientation The direction the paper prints, either landscape or portrait.

portrait Printing orientation that prints the report across the width of a page.

primary key One or more fields in a table that uniquely identify a record.

query Used to view data in different ways, to analyze data, and to change data.

query datasheet Where the result or answer to a query is displayed.

record A row of a table, consisting of a group of related fields.

record number indicator A small box that displays the current record number in the lower left corner of most views. The record number indicator is surrounded by the navigation buttons.

record selector Displayed to the left of the first column; it can be used to select an entire record in Datasheet view.

relational database Database in which a relationship is created by having a common field in the tables. The common field lets you extract and combine data from multiple tables.

report Printed output generated from queries or tables.

row label In the design grid of Query Design view, identifies the type of information that can be entered in the row.

sizing handles Small boxes surrounding a selected control that are used to size the control.

Show box   A box in the Show row of the design grid that, when checked, indicates that the field will be displayed in the query result.

Sort   To temporarily reorder table records in the datasheet.

source file   The document in which a linked object is created.

tab order   The order in which Access moves through a form or table when the [Tab ⇆] key is pressed.

table   Consists of vertical columns and horizontal rows of information about a particular category of things.

tabular form   A form layout in row-and-column format with records in rows and fields in columns.

task pane   A separate scrollable pane displaying shortcuts to frequently used features.

unbound control   A control that is not connected to a field in an underlying table.

unbound object   A graphic object that is associated with the table as a whole, not with a specific record, and does not change when you move from record to record.

Undo   A feature used to cancel your last action.

validation rule   An expression that defines the acceptable values in a validity check.

validation text   Text that is displayed when a validation rule is violated.

validity check   Process of checking to see whether data meets certain criteria.

views   One of several windows or formats that Access provides for working with and looking at data.

value   A part of an expression that is a number, date, or character string.

workspace   The large area of the screen where different Access windows are displayed as you are using the program.

PowerPoint Glossary of Key Terms

alignment   Settings that allow you to change the horizontal placement of an entry in a placeholder or a table cell.

animation   Effect that adds action to text and graphics so they move around on the screen.

animation scheme   A preset visual effect that can be added to slide text.

AutoContent Wizard   A guided approach that helps you determine the content and organization of your presentation through a series of questions.

AutoCorrect   Feature that makes certain types of corrections automatically as you enter text.

AutoShape   A ready-made drawing project supplied with PowerPoint.

build   An effect that progressively displays bulleted items as the presentation proceeds.

cell   The intersection of a row and column in a table.

character formatting   Formatting features that affect the selected characters only.

clip art   Professionally drawn images.

Clips   Media files such as art, sound, animation and movies.

custom dictionary   A dictionary you can create to hold words you commonly use but that are not included in the dictionary that is supplied with the program.

default   Initial program settings.

demote   To move a topic down one level in the outline hierarchy.

design template   Professionally created slide design that can be applied to your presentation.

destination file   The document receiving the linked or embedded object.

drawing object   An object consisting of shapes such as lines and boxes that can be created using the Drawing toolbar.

Drawing toolbar   A toolbar that is used to add objects such as lines, circles, and boxes.

embedded object   An object that is inserted into another application and becomes part of the document. It can be edited from within the document using the source program.

font   A set of characters with a specific design.

font size   The height and width of a character, commonly measured in points.

footer   Text or graphics that appear on the bottom of each slide.

format   To enhance the appearance of a slide to make it more readable or attractive.

Formatting toolbar   A toolbar that contains buttons used to modify text.

graphics   A non-text element, such as a chart, drawing, picture, or scanned photograph, in a slide.

landscape   Orientation of the printed output across the length of the paper.

layout   A predefined slide organization that is used to control the placement of elements on a slide.

linked object   An object that is created in a source file and linked to a destination file. Edits made to the source file are automatically reflected in the destination file.

live link   A link that automatically updates the linked object whenever changes are made to it in the source file.

main dictionary   Dictionary that comes with the Ofice XP programs.

master A special slide on which the formatting of all slides in a presentation is defined.

move handle Used to move menu bars and toolbars to a new location.

notes page Printed output that shows a miniature of the slide and provides an area for speaker notes.

object An item on a slide that can be selected and modified.

Office Assistant Used to get help on features specific to the Office application you are using.

Outlining toolbar Displayed in Outline view, it is used to modify the presentation outline.

pane In Normal view, the separate divisions of the window that allow you to work on all aspects of your presentation in one place.

paragraph formatting Formatting features that affect entire paragraphs.

picture An image such as a graphic illustration or a scanned photograph.

placeholder Box that is designed to contain objects such as the slide title, bulleted text, charts, tables, and pictures.

point A unit of type measurement. One point equals about 1/72 inch.

portrait Orientation of the printed output across the width of the paper.

promote To move a topic up one level in the outline hierarchy.

rotate handle The [747] on the selection rectangle of a selected object that allows you to rotate the object in any direction.

sans serif A font that does not have a flair at the base of each letter, such as Arial or Helvetica.

selection rectangle Hashed border that surrounds a selected placeholder.

serif A font that has a flair at the base of each letter, such as Roman or Times New Roman.

sizing handles Small boxes surrounding selected objects that are used to change the size of the object.

slide An individual page of the presentation.

slide show Used to practice or to present the presentation. It displays each slide in final form.

source file The file from which a linked or embedded object is obtained.

source program The program used to create the linked or embedded object.

stacking order The order in which objects are inserted into layers in the slide.

standard toolbar A toolbar that contains buttons that give quick access to the most frequently used program features.

table An arrangement of horizontal rows and vertical columns.

template A file that includes predefined settings that can be used as a pattern to create many common types of presentations.

text box A container for text or graphics.

thumbnail A miniature view of a slide.

transition An effect that controls how a slide moves off the screen and the next one appears.

typeface A set of characters with a specific design

view A way of looking at the presentation.

workspace The large area containing the slide where your presentations are displayed as you create and edit them.

Word Reference 1

Data File List

Supplied/Used File	Created/Saved As
Lab 1	
	Flyer
wd01_Flyer2	Flyer3
wd01_Elephants (graphic)	
Step-by-Step	
1.	Dress Code
2.	Top Stresses
wd01_Stress (graphic)	
3.	Executive Style
wd01_Executive1 (graphic)	
wd01_Executive2 (graphic)	
4.	B&B Ad
wd01_Sunshine (graphic)	
5. wd01_Making Sushi	Making Sushi2
wd01_sushi (graphic)	
On Your Own	
1.	Career Report
2.	Reunion
3.	Lab Rules
4.	PomPom
5.	Cruise Flyer
On the Web	
1.	Writing Tips
Lab 2	
wd02_Tour Letter	Tour Letter2
wd02_ Flyer4	
Step-By-Step	
1. wd02_Cleaning Checklist	Cleaning Checklist2
2.	Career Fair
3. Making Sushi2 (from Lab 1, PE 5)	Making Sushi3
wd02_Rice	
4. wd02_Thank You Letter	Thank You Letter2
5. wd02_Coffee Flyer	Coffee Flyer2

Supplied/Used File	Created/Saved As
On Your Own	
1.	Internship Letter
2.	Insurance Comparison
3.	To Do List
4.	New Staff Memo
5.	For Sale Flyer
On the Web	
1.	Election Results
Lab 3	
wd03_Tour Research	Tour Research2
	Research Outline
wd03_Lions (graphic)	
wd03_Parrots (graphic)	
Step-By-Step	
1.	Workout
2. wd03_Internet	Internet2
3. wd03_Antique Shops	Antique Shops2
4. wd03_Cafe Flyer	Cafe Flyer2
wd03_coffee (graphic)	
wd03_Computer User (graphic)	
5. wd03_Scenic Drives	Scenic Drives2
wd03_Mountain (graphic)	
6. wd03_Water	Water2
wd03_Swimmer (graphic)	
On Your Own	
1. wd03_Alzheimer	Alzheimer2
2. wd03_Computer	Computer2
3.	Job Search
4.	Research
On the Web	
1.	Computer Virus
Working Together	
wdwt_Tour Flyer	New Tour Presentations
wdwt_Locations	Locations
Step-by-Step	
1. Locations (from WT Lab)	LosAngeles
wdwt1_LosAngeles	
2. Executive Style (from Lab 1, PE 3)	Executive Style
3. B&B Ad (from Lab 1, PE 4)	B&B
On Your Own	
1.	Web Design

Excel Reference 1

Data File List

Supplied/Used file	Created/Saved As
Lab 1	
	Forecast
ex01_Forecast2	Forecast3
ex01_Internet (graphic)	
Step-by-Step	
1. ex01_Improvements	Park Improvements
2. ex01_New Positions	Jobs
3. ex01_Poverty Level	Poverty Level
ex01_Family (graphic)	
4. ex01_IT Salaries	IT Salaries
ex01_Disks (graphic)	
5. ex01_Springs Budget	Springs Projected Budget
On Your Own	
1.	Class Grades
2.	Personal Budget
3.	Weekly Sales
4.	Job Analysis
5.	Membership
On the Web	
1.	Spreadsheet Design
Lab 2	
ex02_Cafe Sales	Cafe Sales Charts
Step-by-Step	
1. ex02_Real Estate Prices	Real Estate Charts
2. ex02_Tiger Data	Tiger Charts
3. ex02_Birds	Bird Observations
4.	Youth Sport Charts
5. ex02_Higher Education	Higher Education Charts

Supplied/Used file	Created/Saved As
On Your Own	
1. ex02_Job Market	Seminar
2.	Grades
3.	Stocks
4.	Statistics
5.	Insurance
Lab 3	
ex03_First Quarter Forecast	Forecast4
ex03_Annual Forecast	Annual Forecast Revised
Step-by-Step	
1. ex03_Sandwich Shop	Sandwich Shop2
2. ex03_West Income Statement	West Income Statement2
3. ex03_Time Sheets	Time Sheets2
4. ex03_Grade Report	Grade Report2
5. ex03_Springs Forecast	Springs Forecast2
6. ex03_African Safari	African Safari2
On Your Own	
1. Personal Budget (from Lab 1)	Personal Budget2
2.	Art Expenses
3.	Stock Analysis
On the Web	
1.	My Business
Working Together	
exwt1_Sales Forecast Memo	Sales Forecast Memo Linked
Cafe Sales Charts (from Lab 2)	Cafe Sales Charts Linked
exwt1_Forecast Memo	Second Quarter Forecast
Annual Forecast Revised (from Lab 3)	
Practice Exercises	
1. exwt1_Rescue Memo	Rescue Memo Linked
exwt1_Contributions	Contributions2
2. exwt1_Tour Status Report	March Status Report
exwt1_Adventure Travel Monthly	Adventure Travel Monthly2
3. exwt1_Hotel Memo	Hotel Memo2
exwt1_Hotel Data	

Access Reference 1

Data File List

Supplied/Used File	Created/Saved As
Lab 1	
	Lifestyle Fitness Employees: Employees (table)
ac01_Friend1 (graphic)	
Step-by-Step	
1.	Beautiful: Clients (table)
2.	Happenings: Advertisers (table)
3.	Supplies: Vendors (table)
4.	Adventure Travel: Travel Packages (table)
5.	Animal Rescue: Tracking (table)
ac01_Whitedog (graphic)	
On Your Own	
1.	Music Collection: CD Catalog (table)
2.	Lewis Personnel: Phone List (table)
3.	Patient Information: Patient Data (table)
4.	JK Enterprises: Expenses (table)
On the Web	
1.	Golden Oldies: Inventory (table)
Lab 2	
ac02_EmployeeRecords	Employee Data Form (form)
Step-by-Step	
1. ac02_Simply Beautiful	Client Info (form)
2. ac02_Happening Ads	Advertiser Information (form)
3. ac02_Cafe Supplies	Vendor Info (table)
4. ac02_Learning	EduSoft Titles (form)
5. ac02_AA	Angel's Animals (form)
On Your Own	
1. Adventure Travel (from Lab 1)	Packages (form)
2. JK Enterprises	JK Expenses (form)
3. Patient Information (from Lab 1)	Administration (form)
4. Lewis Personnel: Phone List	Human Resources (form)

Supplied/Used File	Created/Saved As
On the Web	
1. Golden Oldies (from Lab 1)	Collectibles (form)
Lab 3	
ac03_Personnel Records	Car Pool (query)
	3-year Service Awards (query)
	5-year Service Awards (query)
	Employee Address Report (report)
	Iona to Fort Meyers Car Pool Report (report)
Step-by-Step	
1. ac02_Simply Beautiful	
2. ac02_ Happening Ads	Bimonthly Advertisers (query)
3. ac02_ Cafe Supplies	Low Stock (query)
	Order Items (report)
4. ac02_ Learning	Old Math and Science (query)
	96-97 Math and Science Titles (report)
5. ac03_Angels	Adoptees (query)
	Animal Adoption Report (report)
On Your Own	
1. ac02_Learning	
2. Lewis Personnel (from Lab 2)	Home Address (query)
3. JK Enterprise (from Lab 2)	Pending (query)
	Pending Expenses (report)
4. ac03_Angels	Foster (query)
	Foster Angels (report)
On the Web	
1. Golden Oldies (from Lab 2)	Complete Products (query)
Working Together	
acw1_ServiceAwards	
ac03_Personnel Records	Service Awards Linked (document)
Step-by-Step	
1. ac02_Simply Beautiful	Beautiful 35+ Clients (document)
2. ac02_Cafe Supplies	Special Orders (query)
	Special Orders (document)
3. ac02_Learning	3+ Products (query)
Old Math and Science (query)	EduSoft 3+ (document)

PowerPoint Reference 1

Data File List

Supplied/Used File	Created/Saved As
Lab 1	
	Volunteer
pp01_Volunteer1	Volunteer2
pp01_Puppy (graphic)	
Step-by-Step	
1. pp01_Balance	Balance1
pp01_Time (graphic)	
pp01_Traffic (graphic)	
pp01_QuestionMark (graphic)	
2. pp01_Resume	Resume1
pp01_Goals (graphic)	
pp01_Correspondence (graphic)	
3.	Blowouts
pp01_Tire (graphic)	
pp01_Wheel (graphic)	
pp01_Unprepared (graphic)	
pp01_Repair (graphic)	
4.	Coffee
pp01_CoffeeShop (graphic)	
pp01_CoffeeMug (graphic)	
pp01_Cup (graphic)	
5.	Workplace Issues
pp01_Ergonomics (graphic)	
pp01_PhysicalHealth (graphic)	
pp01_MentalHealth (graphic)	
pp01_Handshake (graphic)	
pp01_Board Meeting (graphic)	

Supplied/Used File	Created/Saved As
On Your Own	
1.	Better Bike Safety
pp01_BikeSafety (data)	
2.	Phone Etiquette
pp01_Memo (data)	
3.	Presentation Aids
pp01_VisualAids (data)	
4.	Placement Services
5.	Web Design
Lab 2	
pp02_Volunteer2	Volunteer3
pp02_QuestionMark (graphic)	
Step-by-Step	
1. Balance1 (from Lab 1)	Balance2
2. pp02_ASU Presentation	ASU Presentation1
pp02_PalmWalk (graphic)	
pp02_StudentServices (graphic)	
pp02_Library (graphic)	
pp02_FineArts (graphic)	
3. Blowouts (from Lab 1)	Blowouts2
4. Coffee (from Lab 1)	Coffee Show
5. Workplace Issues (from Lab 1)	Workplace Issues2
pp02_Arrows (graphic)	
On Your Own	
1.	Interview Techniques
2. Better Bikes Safety (from Lab 1)	Better Bikes Safety2
3.	Travel Italy
4. Web Design (from Lab 1)	Web Design2
5.	Travel Favorites
Working Together	
Volunteer3 (from Lab 2)	Volunteer3 Linked
ppwt1_OrientationMeetings	
ppwt1_RescueData	Rescue Data Linked
Step-by-Step	
1. ppwt1_Blowout Signs	Blowouts3
Blowouts2 (from Lab 2)	
2. ppwt1_CoffeePrices	Coffee Prices Linked
Coffee (from Lab 1)	Coffee Show Linked
3. Workplace Issues2 (from Lab 2)	Workplace Issues2 Linked
ppwt1_EnergyUse	EnergyUse Linked

Word Reference 2

Word Core Certification

Standardized Coding Number	Activity	Lab Exercises			
		Lab	Page	Step-By-Step	On Your Own
W2002-1	**Inserting and Modifying Text**				
W2002-1-1	Insert, modify, and move text and symbols	1	1.2,1.39	1,2,3,4,5	1,2,3,5
		2	2.12,2.14,2.2	1,3,4,5	2,5
W2002-1-2	Apply and modify text formats	1	1.46	1,2,3,4	1,2
		2	2.48	1,2,5	
W2002-1-3	Correct spelling and grammar usage	1	1.18,1.23	1,2,3,4,5	
		2	2.1,2.5	1,4	
W2002-1-4	Apply font and text effects	1	1.50	1,2,3,4,5	2
		2	2.41, 2.42	2,3,5	
W2002-1-5	Enter and format Date and Time	2	2.24	2,3,4	1
W2002-1-6	Apply character styles	3	3.6	1,2,3,4,5	1,2,3,4
W2002-2	**Creating and Modifying Paragraphs**				
W2002-2-1	Modify paragraph formats	1	1.53	1,3,4,5	1,2,4
		2	2.28,2.31	1,2	
W2002-2-2	Set and modify tabs	2	2.35	2,5	2,5
W2002-2-3	Apply bullet, outline, and numbering format to paragraphs	2	2.46	3,4	1,2,4,5
		3	3.6	1	1,2
W2002-2-4	Apply paragraph styles	3	3.6	1,3,4,5	1,3,4
W2002-3	**Formatting Documents**				
W2002-3-1	Create and modify a header and footer	3	3.54	2,3,4,5	1,2,3,4
W2002-3-2	Apply and modify column settings				
W2002-3-3	Modify document layout and Page Setup options	2	2.18,2.28	1,2,3	
		3	3.25	5,6	4,3
W2002-3-4	Create and modify tables	3	3.45,3.51 3.48,3.50	5,6	1,2,3,4
W2002-3-5	Preview and print documents, envelopes, and labels	1	1.61,1.62	1,2,3,4,5	
		2	2.55,2.57	1,2,3,4	
		3	3.65		1,2,3,4
W2002-4	**Managing Documents**				
W2002-4-1	Manage files and folders for documents	3	3.14		
W2002-4-2	Create documents using templates	1	1.7		
W2002-4-3	Save documents using different names and file formats	2	2.28		
		WT	2	2,3	

Standardized Coding Number	Activity	Lab	Page	Lab Exercises	
				Step-By-Step	On Your Own
W2002-5	**Working with Graphics**				
W2002-5-1	Insert images and graphics	1	1.55	2,3,4,5	2,3,4,5
W2002-5-2	Create and modify diagrams and charts				
W2002-6	**Workgroup Collaboration**				
W2002-6-1	Compare and Merge documents				
W2002-6-2	Insert, view and edit comments				
W2002-6-3	Convert documents into Web pages	WT	2,11	2,3	

Excel Reference 2

Excel Core Certification

Standardized Coding Number	Activity	Lab	Page	Step-By-Step	On Your Own
				Lab Exercises	
Ex2002-1	**Working with Cells and Cell Data**				
Ex2002-1-1	Insert, delete, and move cells	1	1.36,1.37,1.53	1,2,3,4,5	1,2,3,4,5
		3	3.14	1,2,3,4,5	1,2,3,4,5
Ex2002-1-2	Enter and edit cell data including text, numbers,and formulas	1	1.15–1.23,1.39, 1.42,1.59	1,2,3,4,5	1,2,3,4,5
Ex2002-1-3	Check spelling	3	3.4	1,5,6	
Ex2002-1-4	Find and replace cell data and formats	3	3.31		
Ex2002-1-5	Use automated tools to filter lists				
Ex2002-2	**Managing Workbooks**				
Ex2002-2-1	Manage workbook files and folders	1	1.28	1,2,3,4,5	1,2,3,4,5
Ex2002-2-2	Create workbooks using templates	1	1.5		
Ex2002-2-3	Save workbooks using different names and file formats	1	1.26	1,2,3,4,5	1,2,3,4,5
Ex2002-3	**Formatting and Printing Worksheets**				
Ex2002-3-1	Apply and modify cell formats	1	1.54–1.60	1,2,3,4,5	1,2,3,4,5
Ex2002-3-2	Modify row and column settings	1	1.48	1,2,3,4,5	
		3	3.5	1,2,3,4,5	
Ex2002-3-3	Modify row and column formats	1	1.24–1.26,1.49	1,2,3,4,5	
Ex2002-3-4	Apply styles	1	1.61	1,2,3,4,5	
Ex2002-3-5	Use automated tools to format worksheets				
Ex2002-3-6	Modify Page Setup options for worksheets	2	2.51	1,2,3,4,5	
		3	3.44,3.47	1,2,3,4,5,6	
Ex2002-3-7	Preview and print worksheets and workbooks	1	1.69	1,2,3,4,5	1,2,3,4
Ex2002-4	**Modifying Workbooks**				
Ex2002-4-1	Insert and delete worksheets	3	3.27	1,3,4,5,6	2,3,4
Ex2002-4-2	Modify worksheet names and positions	3	3.25,3.27	1,3,4,5,6	2,3,4
Ex2002-4-3	Use 3-D references	3	3.24	1	

Standardized Coding Number	Activity	Lab Exercises				
		Lab	Page	Step-By-Step	On Your Own
Ex2002-5	**Creating and Revising Formulas**				
Ex2002-5-1	Create and revise formulas	1	1.39,1.41,1.46		
		3	3.11	1,2,3,4,5,6	1,2,3,4
Ex2002-5-2	Use statistical, date and time, financial, and logical functions in formulas	1	1.42	1,2,3,4,5	1,2,3,4
		3	3.11	1,2,3,4,5,6	1,2,3,4
Ex2002-6	**Creating and Modifying Graphics**				
Ex2002-6-1	Create, modify, position, and print charts	2	2.7–2.22,2.49	1,2,3,4,5	1,2,3,4,5
Ex2002-6-2	Create, modify, and position graphics	1	1.65–1.68	1,2,3,4,5	
Ex2002-7	**Workgroup Collaboration**				
Ex2002-7-1	Convert worksheets into Web pages				
Ex2002-7-2	Create hyperlinks				
Ex2002-7-3	View and edit comments				

Access Reference 2

Access 2002 Core Certification

Standardized Coding Number	Activity	Lab	Page	Lab Exercises Step-By-Step	On Your Own
AC2002-1	**Creating and Using Databases**				
Ac2002-1-1	Create Access databases	1	AC1.8	1,2,3,4,5	1,2,3,4,5
Ac2002-1-2	Open database objects in multiple views	1	AC1.25	2,3,4	
		2	AC2.40	1,2,3,4,5	1,2,3,4,5
		3	AC3.16,AC3.39	3	
Ac2002-1-3	Move among records	1	AC1.36	1,2,3,4,5	1,2,3,4,5
		2	AC2.6	1,2,3,4,5	1,2,3,4
Ac2002-1-4	Format datasheets	2	AC2.30		
Ac2002-2	**Creating and Modifying Tables**				
Ac2002-2-1	Create and modify tables	1	AC1.10,AC1.23	1,2,3,4,5	1,2,3,4,5
		2	AC2.8	1,2,3,4,5	1,2,3,4
Ac2002-2-2	Add a predefined input mask to a field				
Ac2002-2-3	Create Lookup fields				
Ac2002-2-4	Modify field properties	1	AC1.18	1,2,3,4,5	
		2	AC2.8	1,2,3,4,5	
Ac2002-3	**Creating and Modifying Queries**				
Ac2002-3-1	Create and modify select queries	3	AC3.12	2,3,4,5	
Ac2002-3-2	Add calculated fields to select queries				
Ac2002-4	**Creating and Modifying Forms**				
Ac2002-4-1	Create and display forms	2	AC2.32	1,2,3,4,5	1,2,3,4
Ac2002-4-2	Modify form properties				
Ac2002-5	**Viewing and Organizing Information**				
Ac2002-5-1	Enter, edit, and delete records	1	AC1.27,AC1.47	1,2,3,4,5	1,2,3,4,5
		2	AC2.39	1,2,3,4,5	1,2,3,4
Ac2002-5-2	Create queries	3	AC3.11	2,3,4,5	2,3,4
Ac2002-5-3	Sort records	2	AC2.27		
Ac2002-5-4	Filter records	3	AC3.4	1	1

Standardized Coding Number	Activity	Lab Exercises			
		Lab	Page	Step-By-Step	On Your Own
Ac2002-6	**Defining Relationships**				
Ac2002-6-1	Create one-to-many relationships				
Ac2002-6-2	Enforce referential integrity				
Ac2002-7	**Producing Reports**				
Ac2002-7-1	Create and format reports	3	AC3.31	3,4,5	3,4
Ac2002-7-2	Add calculated controls to reports				
Ac2002-7-3	Preview and print reports	3	AC3.45	3,4,5	3,4
Ac2002-8	**Integrating with Other Applications**				
Ac2002-8-1	Import data to Access				
Ac2002-8-2	Export data from Access				
Ac2002-8-3	Create a simple data access page				

PowerPoint Reference 2

$$\boxed{\text{MOUS Skills}}$$

PowerPoint Comprehensive Certification

Standardized Coding Number	Activity	Lab	Page	Step-by-Step	On Your Own
				Lab Exercises	
PP2002-1	**Creating Presentations**				
PP2002-1-1	Create presentations (manually and using automated tools)	1	1.7	1,2,3,4,5	1,2,3,4,5
PP2002-1-2	Add slides to and delete slides from presentations	1 2	1.33,1.35 2.8,2.37	1,2,3,4,5 1,2,4,5	1,2,3,4,5
PP2002-1-3	Modify headers and footers in the slide master	2	2.31	1,3,4	
PP2002-2	**Inserting and Modifying Text**				
PP2002-2-1	Import text from Word				
PP2002-2-2	Insert, format, and modify text	1 2	1.14–1.25, 1.30,1.41–1.44 2.5,2.9	1,2,3,4,5 1,2,3,4,5	1,2,3,4,5 1,2,3,4,5
PP2002-3	**Inserting and Modifying Visual Elements**				
PP2002-3-1	Add tables, charts, clip art, and bitmap images to slides	1 2	1.45–1.50, 1.67,1.73 2.8	1,2,3,4,5 1,2,4,5	3 5
PP2002-3-2	Customize slide backgrounds				
PP2002-3-3	Add OfficeArt elements to slides	2	2.19,2.38	5	1,2,4
PP2002-3-4	Apply custom formats to tables	2	2.10–2.17	1,4	
PP2002-4	**Modifying Presentation Formats**				
PP2002-4-1	Apply formats to presentations	2	2.25,2.30, 2.33	1,2,3,4,5	1,2,3,4,5
PP2002-4-2	Apply animation schemes	2	2.42,2.46		
PP2002-4-3	Apply slide transitions	2	2.44	2,5	5

Standardized Coding Number	Activity	Lab Exercises			
		Lab	Page	Step-by-Step	On Your Own
PP2002-4-4	Customize slide formats	2	2.26	4,5	1,2,3,4,5
PP2002-4-5	Customize slide templates	2	2.24	4,5	
PP2002-4-6	Manage a slide master				
PP2002-4-7	Rehearse timing				
PP2002-4-8	Rearrange slides	1	1.34	2	
		2	2.37	2	
PP2002-4-9	Modify slide layout	2	2.17	1,2,3,4,5	1,2,3,4,5
PP2002-4-10	Add links to a presentation				
PP2002-5	**Printing Presentations**				
PP2002-5-1	Preview and print slides, outlines, handouts, and speaker notes	1	1.52	1,2,3,4,5	1,2,3,4,5
		2	2.60	1,2,3,4,5	
		WT	14	1,2,3	
PP2002-6	**Working with Data from Other Sources**				
PP2002-6-1	Import Excel charts to slides	WT	8	3	
PP2002-6-2	Add sound and video to slides	2	2.43		
PP2002-6-3	Insert Word tables on slides	WT	4	1,2	
PP2002-6-4	Export a presentation as an outline				
PP2002-7	**Managing and Delivering Presentations**				
PP2002-7-1	Set up slide shows				
PP2002-7-2	Deliver presentations	1	1.39		
		2	2.47		
PP2002-7-3	Manage files and folders for presentations				
PP2002-7-4	Work with embedded fonts				
PP2002-7-5	Publish presentations to the Web				
PP2002-7-6	Use Pack and Go				
PP2002-8	**Workgroup Collaboration**				
PP2002-8-1	Set up a review cycle				
PP2002-8-2	Review presentation comments				
PP2002-8-3	Schedule and deliver presentation broadcasts				
PP2002-8-4	Publish presentations to the Web				

Index